THE POLITICS

OF

UNITED STATES

FOREIGN POLICY

Second Edition

Jerel A. Rosati

University of South Carolina

Harcourt Brace College Publishers

Fort Worth   Philadelphia   San Diego   New York   Orlando   Austin   San Antonio
Toronto   Montreal   London   Sydney   Tokyo

Publisher	Earl McPeek
Acquisitions Editor	David Tatom
Market Strategist	Steve Drummond
Developmental Editor	Stacey Sims
Art Director	Vicki Whistler
Production Manager	Linda McMillan
Project Editor	Michael E. Norris

ISBN: 0–03–018063–5

Library of Congress Catalog Card Number: 98–71719

Address for Orders
Harcourt Brace College Publishers, 6277 Sea Harbor Drive, Orlando, FL 32887–6777
1–800–782–4479

Address for Editorial Correspondence
Harcourt Brace College Publishers, 301 Commerce Street, Suite 3700, Fort Worth, TX 76102

Web Site Address
http://www.hbcollege.com

Printed in the United States of America

8 9 0 1 2 3 4 5 6 7   039   9 8 7 6 5 4 3 2 1

To my three children, Kristen, David, and Lauren,
and to all students who strive to learn

PREFACE TO THE SECOND EDITION

The politics of U.S. foreign policy is complex. Within the past thirty years numerous developments have occurred throughout the world and within American society that have made the politics of U.S. foreign policy even more complicated. The Vietnam War, the collapse of the gold standard, Watergate, détente, the oil embargo, the Iran hostage crisis, the Iran-Contra affair, large federal deficits, the collapse of the Soviet Union and communism in Eastern Europe, and the Persian Gulf conflict are just some of the developments that suggest the need for a new look at how U.S. foreign policy is made. This book provides fresh insight into the complex politics of U.S. foreign policy in light of recent history. In this respect, *The Politics of United States Foreign Policy* has been written with four general goals in mind: to be comprehensive in topical coverage, to address central themes in U.S. foreign policy, to provide a strong sense of the actual workings of politics, and to be accessible and interesting to the reader.

The first goal of the book is *to be comprehensive in topical coverage* from three perspectives. This book provides a broad discussion of the government, the society, and the global environment, explaining how they interact and affect the foreign policy process of the United States. Beyond some familiarity with the president and Congress, many undergraduate (and graduate) students know little about the basic institutions within the foreign policy bureaucracy, such as the National Security Council, the State Department, and the intelligence community. Hence, these institutions are discussed fully. *The Politics of United States Foreign Policy* also discusses other important institutions that are often ignored, such as the military establishment, the foreign economic and cultural bureaucracy, the courts, state and local government, and the political culture of the Washington, D.C., community. Because students may similarly lack extensive knowledge of

American society and America's role within the global environment, these two perspectives merit extended coverage as well. Most textbooks downplay the significance of public opinion, political culture and ideology, electoral and group politics, the exercise of civil liberties, and the impact of media on the foreign policy process. They also ignore ways in which the global environment and changes in America's role within it affect domestic and governmental politics. Only by integrating all three perspectives—government, society, and the environment—can one have the basis for developing a comprehensive understanding of the politics of U.S. foreign policy.

The second goal of the book is *to address three themes that are central* to the politics of U.S. foreign policy. Many textbooks provide detailed information yet do not address large questions that allow the student to make sense of the material. This book synthesizes what has been learned about how U.S. foreign policy is made in order to maximize knowledge and understanding. It does this by posing three questions that have been particularly significant in attracting the interest of scholars:

1. What have been the dominant patterns of *continuity and change* in the foreign policy process over time?
2. To what extent has the *president been able to govern* foreign policy?
3. How has the constant *tension between democracy and national security* evolved?

While a historical perspective is provided, the emphasis is on the key patterns that have prevailed since World War II. Students should learn that while continuity has been the norm in the short term, the foreign policy process has undergone considerable change over time, as experienced during the late 1940s and early 1950s with World War II and the rise of the cold war and then again during the late 1960s and early 1970s following the Vietnam War and Watergate. Compared to the cold war years, for instance, the president currently finds it much more difficult to govern foreign policy, as the tension between national security and democracy has increased since Vietnam. Such patterns may be open to further change with the end of the cold war as the United States approaches the twenty-first century.

The third goal of the book is to *provide a strong sense of the politics involved* in the making of U.S. foreign policy. Few textbooks capture the "real world" and dynamic nature of politics. In this respect, it is important to acquire not only a basic knowledge of important institutions and the policy-making process but also an appreciation of the ways in which they actually operate within the foreign policy environment. To understand the practice of U.S. foreign policy, students need to have a feeling for and a comprehension of the politics involved—both within government and throughout society. They need to learn who the players are and how they operate, interact, conflict, win, compromise, and lose. Students must come to understand the beliefs and the personalities that prevail in American politics as well as the language of politics. In this way they can better understand the use of power and symbols, which, in a country like the United States with more than 250 million people, is a very political, complex, and messy process.

The final goal of *The Politics of United States Foreign Policy* is to *provide information and knowledge that is both accessible and interesting* to students. Many introductory textbooks are plagued by an encyclopedic scope. From a learning perspective, this can be counterproductive, and this book addresses the problem by emphasizing the most pertinent information and significant patterns in the politics of U.S. foreign policy as opposed to giving "equal time" to all potentially relevant information. Such information and knowledge are consistently linked to the three central themes of the book to maximize understanding. Student interest and learning are also furthered by the book's broad topical coverage and description of the actual dynamics of American politics in accessible prose.

PEDAGOGICAL FEATURES

In order to further these goals and provide a strong understanding of the politics of U.S. foreign policy, this book relies on five pedagogical features. First, *examples and historical context* are used to help students understand the nature of the institutions involved, the dynamics of the process, and the larger themes addressed. Discussions about the Vietnam War and the Iran-Contra affair, for instance, help to illuminate the central themes of continuity and change, the president's ability to govern, and the tension between national security and democracy. Historical background also is provided to supply perspective over time, something many students lack.

Second, *concepts and theoretical approaches are introduced* at various points in the book to help integrate and make sense of the material covered as well as to emphasize the importance of conceptual thinking to further understanding. This is crucial to avoid the problem of presenting an excess of information without providing the necessary analytical tools that allow students to absorb and comprehend the material. Thus, description, history, and theory are woven together throughout the book in order to provide a strong understanding of the politics of U.S. foreign policy.

The third device for promoting interest and learning is the *use of essays*—short narratives that shed additional light on the main topic under discussion. The boxed features provide examples of how foreign policy operates in the "real world" by presenting key policy issues, controversies, challenges, and trends and examining the contributions of major figures impacting foreign policy institutions and processes. This unique feature of the book allows for more in-depth exploration of subjects related to the chapter, thus provoking greater interest without detracting from the presentation of the core material.

The fourth feature is the *inclusion of brief bibliographic essays* at the end of each chapter. More comprehensive than a list of recommended readings, each bibliographic essay highlights and comments on the best sources for additional information on the topic. The bibliographic essays serve as valuable tools that assist students in sorting through the hundreds of relevant books and articles that are available on a given topic. The works cited in the bibliographic essays (and in the chapter notes) draw on a variety of different sources that I relied upon in writing the book: scholarly and policy-oriented books and articles, newspapers and journalistic accounts, and government documents.

Finally, the *sequence of topics* is organized in a way that maximizes understanding of the foreign policy process. Beginning with the presidency—the center of the foreign policymaking process and a topic with which students have greatest familiarity—the book moves outward through the foreign policy bureaucracy, on to Congress and the rest of government, then to the larger society and domestic politics, and finally to the global environment. Although each chapter stands on its own (and, thus, instructors can use chapters in any order), the book is organized so that the topics discussed in each chapter build on those covered in previous chapters.

CHANGES IN THE SECOND EDITION
. . . .

I have been extremely pleased with the response to the first edition of *The Politics of United States Foreign Policy*. It has been used at more than 200 colleges and universities throughout North America, in more than a dozen countries, and has been translated into Chinese. This has greatly exceeded my expectations and hopes. Because so many have found the textbook of value, its basic integrity has been maintained in the second edition, although a number of changes have been made, which I believe have resulted in an even better and stronger textbook. They include:

- A reorganization of the three basic parts so that the book begins, rather than ends, with the historical and global context;
- New chapters on the "History of United States Foreign Relations," "Presidential Leadership," and a concluding chapter on "Into the Twenty-First Century";

- More coverage of international economics and foreign economic policymaking;
- Coverage of new issues such as immigration, gender and the role of women, the war on drugs, campaign financing, the Internet and Web sites;
- Greater integration and discussion of theory, such as decision making, the psychological role of personality and cognition, models of state-societal relations, and foreign policy change.

I also discuss the substance and practice of foreign policy in more detail in this edition, and, of course, topics throughout have been updated to reflect post–cold war trends and important developments during the Clinton administration. The new edition includes a number of new tables, figures, and essays and more extensive use of boldfacing and italicizing to help the reader identify and review key points more readily. Finally, I have updated the bibliographic essays and expanded the author and subject indices.

A FINAL NOTE
. . . .

Let me close by offering a few thoughts about textbooks in general. The academic profession has increasingly come to regard the writing of textbooks as an unimportant and unscholarly effort of little value beyond the classroom. I find this to be a very disturbing and provincial view. A good textbook—Thomas Kuhn makes a distinction between an elementary and advanced textbook in *The Structure of Scientific Revolutions*—provides critical information and knowledge about a given area of study. It engenders learning and interest and may even inspire further inquiry and learning. It reflects and may even help to define the field. But most importantly, a good textbook provides a synthesis of the accumulated knowledge of a subject at a time when specialization and the overabundance of information and published material make the need for synthesis greater than it ever has been.

This need is a widely recognized within the study of international relations and U.S. foreign policy. In their statement of editorial philosophy for the recent

International Studies Review, Margaret Hermann and Robert Woyach point out that "the isolation of the different specialties in international studies limits the cross-fertilization that could lead to more integrative and synthetic perspectives." Bernard Cohen, one of the classic students of the field, noted the problem as early as 1956 in *The Political Process and Foreign Policy* when he wrote, "while there may be widespread recognition of the desirability of knowing more about how foreign policy is made, it is a far from simple task actually to build up a useful body of relevant knowledge about overall processes."

This textbook attempts to do just that. As I stated in the preface to the first edition, "I hope that this book not only serves as a worthwhile pedagogical tool but that it also contributes to a scholarly synthesis and understanding of the politics of U.S. foreign policy." I have been inspired to that task by the example of the classic texts I used as a student myself, whose breadth and depth of knowledge and rich and coherent understanding provide the foundation for my own.

ACKNOWLEDGMENTS

. . . .

I am indebted to a number of people who took the time and effort to directly assist and support me in the writing of this book. I remain especially grateful to the colleagues and students who assisted in the preparation of the first edition. For their constructive comments and suggestions for the second edition, I would like to thank Dave Cohen, Tina Morgan, Bret Traw, Jennifer Willand, and, in particular, Dwayne Fulmer, as well as the reviewers for Harcourt Brace, who include Douglas A. Borer, Virginia Polytechnic Institute and State University; Joseph Lepgold, Georgetown University; J. Patrice McSherry, SUNY—New Paltz; David W. Thornton, Campbell University; and Walter F. Weiker, Rutgers University.

For editorial, production, and marketing work at Harcourt Brace, I thank also David Tatom, Chris Nelson, Stacey Sims, Mike Norris, Linda McMillan, Laura Brennan, and Steve Drummond. As always, crucial psychological support was provided by my family.

As I consider the next edition down the road, I welcome hearing from you about what you have learned from the book and about how I might further strengthen it. My E-mail address is rosati@ garnet.cla.sc.edu.

Jerel A. Rosati
University of South Carolina
1998

CONTENTS

ESSAYS

FIGURES

TABLES

PART
ONE

. . . .

INTRODUCTION

Chapter 1 introduces the concept of foreign policy and the underlying analytical framework used throughout the book for studying and understanding the complex politics of U.S. foreign policy.

CHAPTER 1

....

THE POLITICS OF U.S. FOREIGN POLICY

The foreign policy of the United States has experienced important changes over time. Following World War II and with the rise of the cold war, United States foreign policy during the fifties and sixties revolved around the containment of Soviet and communist expansion throughout the world. The cold war years were also a time when the power of the presidency was preeminent in the making of U.S. foreign policy. Yet, over the last thirty years numerous developments have occurred throughout the world and American society that have affected the conduct of U.S. foreign policy. Events such as the Vietnam War and Watergate challenged America's postwar containment policy and the power of the presidency. More recently, the end of the cold war, brought about by the collapse of the Soviet Union and communism in Eastern Europe, has opened up new opportunities and constraints for U.S. foreign policy.

Why did the United States pursue a policy of global containment following World War II and why did it prevail throughout the fifties and sixties?

What impact did events such as the Vietnam War and Watergate have on U.S. foreign policy during the seventies and eighties? What impact does the end of the cold war have on foreign policy as the United States enters the twenty-first century? Answers to these crucial questions can be found only upon examining the politics of U.S. foreign policy.

UNDERSTANDING FOREIGN POLICY, COMPLEXITY, AND POLITICS

....

Examining the politics of U.S. foreign policy not only provides an understanding of the foreign policy process of the United States, it also provides a foundation for understanding the kinds of foreign policies that the United States has pursued over time. At this point, it may be helpful to pause for a moment and ask the question, what is meant by foreign policy? This term is used all the time and we probably know foreign policy when we see it. But this concept is rarely, if ever, defined, and the lack of clarity concerning what is meant by it contributes to ambiguity, confusion, and unnecessary disagreement. Very simply, **foreign policy,** or foreign relations, in this book refers to the scope of involvement abroad and the collection of goals, strategies, and instruments that are selected by governmental policymakers.[1]

In order to understand the foreign policy of a country, one needs to recognize who decides and acts. To say that the "United States intervened" is part of our everyday language. But what do people mean when they use this phrase? In reality, countries do not act, people act. What is usually meant is that certain governmental officials, representing the state—that is, the United States—acted. A **state** is a legal concept that refers to the governmental institutions through which policymakers act in the name of the people of a given territory. The **foreign policy process,** therefore, refers to how governmental decisions and policies are formulated and implemented. The focus in this book then is on examining the foreign policy process of the United States and how decisions and policies are made. The substance of policy, nevertheless, will be woven throughout in order to better understand the politics of U.S. foreign policy.

With this in mind, *two very important points must be understood about the nature of the foreign policy process* within the United States: that it is a very complex process and that it is a very political process. First, the U.S. foreign policy process is very "complex" and extremely messy. Many Americans tend to initially operate with a rather simple and straightforward view of the foreign policy process: that U.S. foreign policy is made and defined basically at the top of the political hierarchy, especially by the president. According to Roger Hilsman, former assistant secretary of state for Far Eastern Affairs in the Kennedy administration, "As Americans, we think it only reasonable that the procedures for making national decisions should be orderly, with clear lines of responsibility and authority." We expect decisions to be made by "the proper, official, and authorized persons, and to know that the really

big decisions will be made at the top . . . with each of the participants having roles and powers so well and precisely defined that they can be held accountable for their actions by their superiors and eventually by the electorate."[2]

Clearly, the president and his beliefs play a crucial role in the making of U.S. foreign policy. However, the president does not make U.S. foreign policy alone. According to Charles Maechling, "In propagating the delusion of a master hand and only one tiller, both the executive branch and the news media have collaborated as if in a silent conspiracy—the executive branch in order to enhance the prestige and image of its political leadership, and the news media to simplify the task of reporting and enlarge their audience by dramatizing a few personalities."[3]

The reality is that many other individuals and institutions are involved within the government and throughout the society in the foreign policy process: presidential advisers, high-level officials within the executive branch, the foreign policy bureaucracies, Congress, the courts, state and local governments, the public, political parties, interest groups and social movements, the media, and international actors. It is in this sense that the making of U.S. foreign policy is a complex process. It is also a messy process, for the variety of individuals and institutions that affect U.S. foreign policy do not stand still, but constantly interact with and have an impact on one another. In other words, the policymaking process is not static, but, as the word "process" implies, dynamic. If the process initially sounds confusing, don't be dismayed; given its overall complexity, the foreign policy process can easily be confusing.

Second, the foreign policy process within the United States is also very much a "political" process. We need to examine politics for it is the essence of the foreign policy process. What is politics? In the minds of many Americans, politics is a dirty word that implies unsavory behavior in the political arena. Given such a negative connotation, there appears to be a widespread set of expectations and hopes that American politics should result in a rational process that is somehow above politics. Turning to Roger Hilsman once again, "As Americans, with our flair for the mechanical and love of efficiency combined with a moralistic Puritan heritage, we would like to think not only that policymaking is a conscious and deliberate act, one of analyzing problems and systematically examining grand alternatives in all their implications, but also that the alternative chosen is aimed at achieving overarching ends that serve a high moral purpose. . . . And we feel that the entire decision-making process ought to be a dignified, even majestic [process]."[4] This, unfortunately, is a rather simple and unrealistic view of the nature of politics.

One common definition of **politics** is "who gets what, when, and how."[5] This definition emphasizes that politics is, as Hedrick Smith says in *The Power Game,* a "serious game with high stakes, one in which the winners and losers affect many lives—yours, mine, those of the people down the street, and of people all over the world."[6] Another definition of politics is the "competition for power and shared meaning." This simple but meaningful definition emphasizes the importance that ideas and symbolism play in the policy process. A final definition describes politics as "competition between different individuals and groups for control of the government, and support of the public and influence throughout society, in order to promote certain ends." This is the broadest of the three definitions, emphasizing the role of different goal-oriented individuals and groups and the various arenas in which the political process takes place.

The three definitions are complementary and contribute to an understanding of what politics is all about. Together, they illustrate that the politics of U.S. foreign policy involves competition among differently motivated individuals and groups, that politics involves the flow of power and symbolism throughout government and society, and that it involves winners and losers. Such politics defines **the national interest**—a concept that is supposed to represent what is best for the country. However, it is a very subjective concept, for different people will define what is best for the country differently. Not surprisingly, the term *national interest* is often invoked behind a particular policy view to garner support throughout government and society.[7] Ultimately, U.S. foreign policy (and the so-called na-

tional interest) tends to reflect the goals and priorities of those individuals and groups who are the most successful in influencing the political process within government and throughout society. Such a foreign policy process may be more or less moral depending on the type of value judgment that is made.

Clearly, the making of U.S. foreign policy is a complex and political process inseparable from politics. This has been a dominant theme that most of the early theorists—such as Gabriel Almond, Paul Hammond, Roger Hilsman, Stanley Hoffmann, Charles Lindblom, Richard Neustadt, Warner Schilling, Glenn Snyder, and Richard Snyder—emphasized throughout their work on the U.S. foreign policymaking process during the "high cold war" period of the fifties and sixties when the world seemed simpler—a time when presidential power and the cold war consensus were at their apex.[8]

Since the Vietnam War, the complexity and political nature of the policy process has become more intense and increasingly visible. As we will see, it has become very difficult for a president to govern successfully and lead the country in foreign policy. In the words of I. M. Destler, Leslie H. Gelb, and Anthony Lake, in *Our Own Worst Enemy: The Unmaking of American Foreign Policy,* "The making of American foreign policy had entered a new and far more ideological and political phase."[9] Or as Hedrick Smith likewise observed in the eighties, "Presidents now have much greater difficulty marshaling governing coalitions" for "it is a much looser power game now, more wide open, harder to manage and manipulate than it was a quarter of a century ago when I came to town."[10] The complex politics of United States foreign policy, if anything, has been heightened with the collapse of the cold war.

THE STUDY OF U.S. FOREIGN POLICY

The purpose of this book is to provide a strong understanding of the complex politics inherent in United States foreign policy. Clearly, most Americans, as indicated above, tend to have a rather simple and often naive view of American politics and the making of U.S. foreign policy. But such a simple view shared by most Americans is not theirs alone. Most non-Americans and observers of the American scene from abroad tend to simplify the American political process as well—often equating "the president" with "United States foreign policy." Even the most educated and successful Americans within the United States often fail to fully appreciate the complexity and political essence of the policy process. As Hedrick Smith found, "Some of the most sophisticated people around the country often fail to understand the rules of the Washington power game.[11]

How does one study and understand the complex politics of U.S. foreign policy? *Three different approaches to the study of U.S. foreign policy* have predominated over the years: the policy approach, the historical approach, and the social science approach. Although these approaches are not mutually exclusive, Alexander George has highlighted over the years that different approaches to the study of U.S. foreign policy has produced different cultures, or communities of individuals who have been "socialized in quite different professional and intellectual worlds."[12] This has created a gap in communication and understanding not only between academic scholars and practitioners, but also among academic scholars who take different approaches to the study of U.S. foreign policy as well.[13]

The **policy approach** predominates among practitioners and those involved in politics and the policy world. Policy analysts tend to concern themselves primarily with contemporary affairs, emphasize the present and the near future, make policy recommendations, and write for policymakers and a broad, general audience. Policy analysts may use the tools of the historian or the social scientist. The **historical approach** to U.S. foreign policy comes out of the scholarly tradition of history and the humanities within academia. It tends to emphasize a historical understanding of U.S. foreign policy, attempts to recapture the specifics of the times, recognizes a wealth of factors influencing foreign policy, relies heavily on primary source documentation, and results in well-written narratives for a scholarly and more general audience.[14] Finally, the **social science approach** to U.S. foreign policy reflects the rise of science within academia, as can be found in the disciplines of anthropology, economics, psychology, sociology, and, in particular, political science. Social scientists tend to be concerned with explaining more limited facets of foreign policy in order to identify basic patterns; they attempt to understand these patterns through the use of concepts and the development of theory, employ more systematic research tools for collecting and analyzing information, and communicate their conclusions predominantly to fellow social scientists.

Each approach or orientation has something important to contribute to an understanding of U.S. foreign policy. Yet, each approach cannot stand alone in furnishing a comprehensive understanding of the politics of U.S. foreign policy; *complementation and synthesis* of the three approaches is the key to acquiring breadth and depth of knowledge and understanding. In this respect, this work is sensitive to broad patterns and specific information about the politics of U.S. foreign policy, contemporary politics and past politics, a theoretical and historical understanding, competing policy recommendations, and a reliance on a variety of sources of information and studies from all three approaches. In other words, my orientation to the study of foreign policy is that of a social scientist who is sensitive to the importance of history and practice, thereby achieving a full understanding of the politics of U.S. foreign policy.

THE ANALYTICAL FRAMEWORK

How will we make sense of the complex politics of U.S. foreign policy? First, we will examine the policy process from three different perspectives or levels: (1) the historical and global context, (2) the government, and (3) the role of society and domestic politics. Second, we will address three themes that have been integral to the study of U.S. foreign policy since World War II: (1) continuity and change, (2) presidential governance, and (3) the tension between national security and democracy. These two strategies will not only make us aware of the complexity and politics of the foreign policy process, but they will allow us to make sense of the process and understand how American foreign policy is made.

THE THREE PERSPECTIVES

To make the complex politics of U.S. foreign policy fully understandable, *this book is organized into three basic parts,* each reflecting a particular perspective or level of analysis:

1. Part II discusses the historical and global context.
2. Part III focuses on the government and the policymaking process.
3. Part IV concentrates on society and domestic politics.

Each part examines the key actors and forces involved and how they interact and impact on the politics of U.S. foreign policy. As Burton Sapin argued in his classic work, *The Making of United States Foreign Policy,* "while the characteristics of the contemporary international scene are of fundamental importance in shaping the contours of American foreign policy, they are not completely determining. . . . An important part of the explanation for American foreign policy actions lies in the nature of American society and the functioning of its political system and its national governmental machinery."[15] It is only by examining all three elements—the context, the government, and society—that one can arrive at a comprehensive understanding of how American foreign policy is made (see **figure 1.1**).[16]

Historical and Global Context. We begin in Part II with the historical and global context; that is, the

FIGURE 1.1
EXPLAINING FOREIGN POLICY

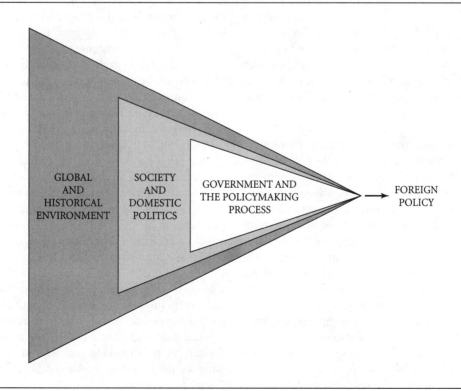

GLOBAL AND HISTORICAL ENVIRONMENT

SOCIETY AND DOMESTIC POLITICS

GOVERNMENT AND THE POLICYMAKING PROCESS

FOREIGN POLICY

environment or setting in which the politics of U.S. foreign policy operates. The historical and global context tend to be the most "indirect" sources of influence on the policy process and, hence, the most difficult to see, although the immediate situation can directly impact the political process as well. The historical and global context set the stage and provide the foundation for the politics of U.S. foreign policy throughout government and society. Chapter 2 provides the historical context, where a brief overview of the major patterns in the history of U.S. foreign policy, from its beginning to the present, is presented. Clearly, the present flows out of and is impacted by the past. Chapter 3 describes the global context. Since the end of World War II, the world has experienced considerable change, such as the rise and end of the cold war. Such changes in the global environment affect the nature of American power and the political process throughout society and the government, thus influencing U.S. foreign policy. In sum, both the historical and global context affect America's role in the world and impact the policymaking process within the United States. In fact, not only is a discussion of the historical and the global environment vital for understanding the contemporary nature of the foreign policy process, the context—such as the end of the cold war—has significant implications for the future politics of U.S. foreign policy as well.

Government and the Policymaking Process. In Part III we delve into the center of the policymaking process with the government—beginning with the president, who has the most immediate and direct impact on policy, and then move outward. Chapters 4 and 5 examine presidential power and the president's ability to direct U.S. foreign policy. In many ways, chapters 4 and 5 provide an overview of the politics of U.S. foreign policy for the rest of the book. Chapter 6 discusses how the president attempts to manage foreign policy and makes use of the National Security Council within the executive branch. This sets the stage for examination of the major institutions of the foreign policy bureaucracy and their input in the policy process: the State Department in chapter 7, the military establishment in

chapter 8, the intelligence community in chapter 9, the foreign economic bureaucracy and the rest of the foreign policy bureaucracy in chapter 10. Chapter 11 employs different decision-making models to discuss the interaction of these institutions and explain the dynamics of the policymaking process within the executive branch, and their impact on presidential power. Following coverage of the executive branch, chapter 12 examines the role of Congress in foreign policy and the nature of legislative-executive relations. Chapter 13 then briefly discusses the remaining governmental bodies involved in foreign policymaking: the judiciary, state and local governments, and the unique political culture of the Washington, D.C., community. Much of the book focuses on the government because an understanding of the foreign policy process requires considerable knowledge of the major governmental institutions and players involved in U.S. foreign policy.

Society and Domestic Politics. Part IV examines how the larger society and domestic politics affect the government and the policymaking process; this knowledge is absolutely essential to a complete understanding of the making of foreign policy. We begin in chapter 14 with the role of the public and its beliefs: public opinion, political ideology, and political culture. This leads to a discussion of the impact of political participation on U.S. foreign policy, examining the input of party politics and the electoral process in chapter 15 and the role of interest groups and social movements in chapter 16. Chapter 17 examines the relationship between national security and the exercise of civil liberties in order to better understand the history and future of political participation in American politics. The effect of the media and the role of communications on the policy process is examined in chapter 18.

The book concludes in chapters 19 and 20 with a synthesis of how global, governmental, and societal factors interact, employing different conceptual models to provide varying interpretations of the dynamic nature of domestic politics and its impact on the foreign policymaking process and its implications for the future as the United States enters the twenty-first century.

THE THREE THEMES

The information and knowledge that is presented in the following chapters is integrated around three themes. These themes are interrelated and address *three significant questions* that have been particularly significant in attracting the interest of scholars and are integral to understanding the foreign policy process, especially since World War II:

1. What have been the dominant patterns of continuity and change in the foreign policy process over time?
2. To what extent has the president been able to manage and govern foreign policy?
3. How have the tensions between democracy and national security evolved?

Continuity and Change. It is important to identify major patterns of continuity and change in the foreign policy process over time in order to better understand U.S. foreign policy in the present and into the future. To identify major patterns of continuity and change, especially since World War II, a number of questions are addressed: What changes in the U.S. foreign policy process occurred following World War II? What elements of the policy process have remained the same since the 1950s? What elements have changed, especially during the post-Vietnam years? What are the current and future implications for the making of U.S. foreign policy since the end of the cold war? Answers to these questions allow us to come to grips with the key patterns that have prevailed in the foreign policy process within the United States.

Whereas some analysts emphasize the prevalence of continuity—that is, little or incremental change over time—in the foreign policy process since World War II, other analysts emphasize change. In fact, three major patterns involving both continuity and change have predominated since the Second World War. First, World War II and the rise of the cold war resulted in a revolutionary change in the making of U.S. foreign policy, such as the dominance of American power throughout the world, an increase in presidential power, the establishment of a national security bureaucracy, and the rise of an anticommunist consensus throughout government and society. These foreign policy developments continued to affect foreign policymaking throughout the fifties and sixties until America's failure in Vietnam resulted in a second pattern of new changes that persist to this day, such as the decline of presidential power, the rise of the foreign economic bureaucracy, the collapse of the anticommunist consensus, and the decline of American power abroad. Not all has changed since the fifties, however, and this is reflected in a third pattern: the continuation, for example, of a large and significant national security bureaucracy within government tied closely to society since World War II. What will be the impact of the end of the cold war? This will be explored throughout the book. Ultimately, these patterns of continuity and change allow us to make sense of the policy process and understand the evolution of U.S. policy into the twenty-first century.

Presidential Governance of Foreign Policy. The second theme involves the president's ability to manage and govern U.S. foreign policy. When most Americans think about who makes foreign policy, they immediately think of the president as the commander in chief. The story, in fact, is much more complex than this, as discussed in chapter 4. In brief, prior to World War II the continuous struggle for power between the president and Congress in making U.S. foreign policy usually resulted in Congress dominating in times of peace and the president dominating in times of war. It was only with American involvement in World War II and, subsequently, when the cold war began that power seemed to shift permanently to the president in foreign affairs, laying the basis for this popular perception.

Two patterns have, in fact, prevailed since World War II with regard to the president's role in foreign policy. During the cold war years from Harry Truman to Lyndon Johnson, the president and the executive branch dominated the making of U.S. foreign policy. However, in the post-Vietnam War years, the president's power has declined within government and throughout society, making it more difficult for the president to manage and govern foreign policy successfully. In other words, presidents are no longer as powerful as they once were in leading the country in U.S. foreign policy. It appears that this post-Vietnam trend has continued with the end of the cold war, where presidents face considerable opportunities as well as risks, as Presidents George Bush and Bill Clinton have found, as the United States enters the twenty-first century.

Tensions Between Democracy and National Security. Another major theme that has confronted Americans, especially since World War II, is the constant tension between the demand for democracy and the demand for national security. The democratic foundation of the United States, especially the Declaration of Independence and the Bill of Rights, is premised on individual rights and the need to protect individual freedom and civil liberties from the central government. However, World War II and the cold war resulted in a massive expansion of the national security apparatus within the United States government. This has resulted in a classic contradiction. Democracy demands an informed and active citizenry, individual access to information, an open dialogue about the ends and means of society, and governmental accountability—often a cumbersome process. The demands of national security traditionally are quite the opposite: secrecy, distrust of enemies from without and within, unquestioning mass support, and an efficient process allowing quick responses to events abroad. Therefore, democracy and national security are in constant tension with each other.

Two patterns have prevailed in the tension between national security and democracy since World War II. First, during the cold war years when most Americans perceived a major threat posed by Soviet communism, national security gained undisputed priority over democratic practice in the politics of U.S. foreign policy. Second, during the post-Vietnam years, democratic considerations have grown in importance due to changes in the foreign policy process in the wake of the Vietnam War. Since Vietnam, the tension between democracy and national security has grown because both orientations lack sufficient political support throughout government and society to be ascendant. The Iran-Contra affair

is symptomatic of the difficulty of balancing these contradictory demands. This is a dilemma which, in all likelihood, will continue to confront Americans in the foreseeable future despite the collapse of the cold war.

POLITICS INTO THE TWENTY-FIRST CENTURY
. . . .

This book is organized in terms of the three perspectives discussed above, while the three themes will be discussed throughout the book. Together, the analytical framework provides a meaningful way to make sense of the complexity and politics of U.S. foreign policy. The net result, hopefully, will be the acquisition of a powerful understanding of United States foreign policy.

This is a particularly interesting time to examine the complex politics of United States foreign policy for not only has the cold war come to an end, the United States will soon be entering the twenty-first century. The implications may be limited or quite profound for the future of the policy process and United States foreign policy, as we will explore throughout the book. But in order to fully grasp the present and to be able to look into the future, we must be grounded in the past. Therefore, we turn to Part II to examine the historical and global context of the politics of United States foreign policy. Although the focus of this volume is on the time period since the Second World War, historical background is constantly woven in along the way, beginning with chapter 2.

BIBLIOGRAPHIC ESSAY
. . . .

The concept of "foreign policy" has received very little attention and inadequate treatment for the most part. The most helpful work that clarifies the meaning of foreign policy, the difference between process and policy, and its determinants is provided by James N. Rosenau, "The Study of Foreign Policy," in James N. Rosenau, Gavin Boyd, and Kenneth W. Thompson, eds., *World Politics* (New York: Free Press, 1976), pp. 15–35. A strong sense of the complexity and politics of U.S. foreign policy is provided by Roger Hilsman, *To Move a Nation: The Politics of Foreign Policy in the Administration of John F. Kennedy* (New York: Delta, 1964), especially chapters 1 and 35; Stanley Hoffmann, *Gulliver's Troubles or the Setting of American Foreign Policy* (New York: McGraw-Hill, 1968), especially part III; and Hedrick Smith, *The Power Game: How Washington Works* (New York: Ballantine, 1988).

Two classic statements about analyzing foreign policy from a "levels of analysis" perspective are Kenneth N. Waltz, *Man, the State, and War* (New York: Columbia University Press, 1959), and J. David Singer, "The Level-of-Analysis Problem in International Relations," in Klaus Knorr and Sidney Verba, *The International System: Theoretical Essays* (Princeton: Princeton University Press, 1961), pp. 77–92. The classic work that synthesized different levels into a dynamic foreign policy framework is Richard C. Snyder, H. W. Bruck, and Burton Sapin, "Decision-Making as an Approach to the Study of International Politics," in Richard C. Snyder, H. W. Bruck, and Burton Sapin, eds., *Foreign Policy Decision-Making* (Glencoe, Ill.: Free Press, 1962), pp. 14–185. For a more contemporary treatment, with a focus on the analysis of American foreign economic policy, see G. John Ikenberry, David A. Lake, and Michael Mastanduno, eds., "The State and American Foreign Economic Policy," *International Organization* 42 (Winter 1988): 1–14.

ENDNOTES

1. On the concept of foreign policy, see Chuck F. Hermann, "Foreign Policy Behavior: That Which Is to be Explained," in Maurice A. East, Stephen A. Salmore, and Charles F. Hermann, eds., *Why Nations Act* (Beverly Hills: Sage, 1978), pp. 25–47, and James N. Rosenau, "The Study of Foreign Policy," in James N. Rosenau, Gavin Boyd, and Kenneth W. Thompson, eds., *World Politics* (New York: Free Press, 1976), pp. 15–35. Although the concept of foreign policy is defined in reference to governments and, in particular, the United States in this book, it can also be argued that non-state and nongovernmental actors can be said to have foreign policies as well (such as individuals or groups, as will be discussed in chapter 15).

2. Roger Hilsman, *To Move a Nation: The Politics of Foreign Policy in the Administration of John F. Kennedy* (New York: Delta, 1964), p. 5.

3. Charles Maechling, Jr., "Foreign Policy-Makers: The Weakest Link?" *The Virginia Quarterly Review* 52 (Winter 1976): 1.

4. Hilsman, *To Move a Nation*, pp. 4, 5.

5. This definition is from Harold D. Lasswell, *Politics: Who Gets What, When, and How* (New York: McGraw-Hill, 1938). The next two definitions that follow were developed by the author.

6. Hedrick Smith, *The Power Game: How Washington Works* (New York: Ballantine, 1988), p. xvi.

7. See Charles A. Beard, *The Idea of National Interest: An Analytical Study in American Foreign Policy* (New York: Macmillan, 1934); Donald E. Nuechterlein, "The Concept of "National Interest": A Time for New Approaches," *Orbis* (Spring 1979): 73–92; and James N. Rosenau, "The National Interest," in *The Scientific Study of Foreign Policy* (London: Frances Pinter, 1980), pp. 283–93.

8. See Gabriel A. Almond, *The American People and Foreign Policy* (New York: Harcourt Brace, 1950; Praeger, 1960); Roger Hilsman, "Congressional-Executive Relations and the Foreign Policy Consensus," *American Political Science Review* (September 1958): 725–44, "The Foreign Policy Consensus: An Interim Report," *Journal of Conflict Resolution* (December 1959): 361–82, and *To Move a Nation*; Stanley Hoffmann, *Gulliver's Troubles or the Setting of American Foreign Policy* (New York: McGraw-Hill, 1968); Samuel P. Huntington, *The Common Defense: Strategic Programs in National Politics* (New York: Columbia University Press, 1961); Charles E. Lindblom, "The Science of 'Muddling' Through," *Public Administration Review* 19 (Spring 1959), *The Intelligence of Democracy: Decision Making Through Mutual Adjustment* (New York: Free Press, 1965), and with David Braybrooke, *A Strategy of Decision* (Glencoe, Ill.: 1963); Richard A. Neusdadt, *Presidential Power: The Politics of Leadership* (New York: John Wiley, 1960); Warner R. Schilling, Paul T. Hammond, and Glenn H. Snyder, *Strategy, Politics and Defense Budgets* (New York: Columbia University Press, 1962); and Richard C. Snyder, "A Decision-Making Approach to the Study of Political Phenomena," in R. Young, editor, *Approaches to the Study of Politics* (Evanston, Ill.: Northwestern University Press, 1958), pp. 3–37. On this first wave of policymaking theorists, see Graham Allison, *Essence of Decision: Explaining the Cuban Missile Crisis* (Boston:

Little, Brown, 1971), chapter 5, and Robert Art, "Bureaucratic Politics and American Foreign Policy: A Critique," *Policy Sciences* 4 (1973): 467–90.

9. I. M. Destler, Leslie H. Gelb, and Anthony Lake, in *Our Own Worst Enemy: The Unmaking of American Foreign Policy* (New York: Simon and Schuster, 1984), p. 20

10. Smith, *The Power Game*, p. xvi.

11. Smith, *The Power Game*, p. xx.

12. Alexander L. George, *Bridging the Gap: Theory and Practice in Foreign Policy* (Washington, D.C., United States Institute of Peace, 1993), p. 3.

13. For some historical perspective, see Stanley Hoffmann, "An American Social Science: International Relations," *Daedalus* 106 (1977): 41–60.

14. Typical examples of primary source documentation include government documents, memoirs, and private papers of individuals.

15. Burton M. Sapin, *The Making of United States Foreign Policy* (New York: Praeger, 1966), p. 1.

16. The conceptual framework revolving around the three perspectives is similar to the "frame of reference" originally suggested by Richard Snyder in his path-breaking work on decision makers and the decision-making process operating in an organizational context and affected by various elements of the internal and external setting. Richard C. Snyder, H. W. Bruck, and Burton Sapin, "Decision-Making as an Approach to the Study of International Politics," in Richard C. Snyder, H. W. Bruck, and Burton Sapin, eds., *Foreign Policy Decision-Making* (Glencoe, Ill.: Free Press, 1962), pp. 14–185. For a similar but more contemporary framework based on systemic-centered explanations, society-centered explanations, and state-centered explanations of contemporary U.S. foreign economic policy, see G. John Ikenberry, David A. Lake, and Michael Mastanduno, eds., "The State and American Foreign Economic Policy," *International Organization* 42 (Winter 1988), special issue, and G. John Ikenberry, *Reasons of State: Oil Politics and The Capacities of American Government* (Ithaca, N.Y.: Cornell University Press, 1988). Two of the classic statements about different "levels of analysis" are Kenneth N. Waltz, *Man, the State, and War* (New York: Columbia University Press, 1959) and J. David Singer, "The Level-of-Analysis Problem in International Relations," in Klaus Knorr and Sidney Verba, *The International System: Theoretical Essays* (Princeton: Princeton University Press, 1961), pp. 77–92. For a more contemporary approach to bridging the micro-macro problem, see Walter Carlsnaes, "The Agency-Structure Problem in Foreign Policy Analysis," *International Studies Quarterly* 36 (1992): 245–70

PART TWO

. . . .

HISTORICAL AND GLOBAL CONTEXT

Part II provides the historical and global context; that is, the environment or milieu in which the politics of U.S. foreign policy operates. Chapter 2 provides an overview of the major patterns in the history of U.S. foreign policy, from its roots to the present. Chapter 3 discusses the evolution of world politics and American power, especially since the Second World War, and their implications for the politics of U.S. foreign policy in the past, present, and future.

CHAPTER 2

HISTORY OF UNITED STATES FOREIGN RELATIONS

*I*t is important to realize that arriving at an understanding of the foreign policy process provides the foundation for understanding the evolution of the substance of U.S. foreign policy. It provides the foundation for understanding why, for example, the United States fought a cold war and pursued a policy of containment around the world; why the United States intervened and Americanized the war in Vietnam which ultimately became a national tragedy; to what extent the United States might continue to intervene and lead the world in a post-cold war environment as it enters the twenty-first century.

Familiarity with the evolution of the substance of U.S. foreign policy, likewise, should be valuable for better understanding the patterns of continuity and change that have occurred in the making of U.S. foreign policy over time. The history of U.S. foreign policy, in other words, influences the policymaking process over time. Clearly, both elements—policy and process—are closely linked, interact, and are crucial for arriving at a full understanding of U.S. foreign policy. Therefore, a brief overview of the major patterns in the history of U.S. foreign relations is provided. Such historical context will help set the stage for better understanding the politics of U.S. foreign policy in the past, the present, and into the future.

MAJOR HISTORICAL PATTERNS

Many Americans have the perception that U.S. foreign policy was isolationist until World War II and internationalist thereafter. However, as any U.S. diplomatic historian knows, this simple breakdown of U.S. foreign policy over time distorts much more than it enlightens.

THE MYTH OF ISOLATIONISM

If one defines **isolationism** to mean "uninvolvement abroad," clearly the United States has never been isolationist during its history. If one defines isolationism more loosely to mean uninvolvement in European political affairs, as some people do, it would still be stretching reality to conclude that U.S. foreign policy was isolationist. The European powers, regardless of their geographic distance from the United States, were active in North America and throughout the Western Hemisphere after U.S. independence. Furthermore, the United States has never been able to avoid involvement in any of the major European wars since the rise of Napoleon in the early nineteenth century. No matter, one cannot speak of U.S. foreign policy solely in terms of "U.S.-European relations" for it does not capture the full scope of its involvement abroad.

As recently stated by A. J. Bacevich, "Only by the loosest conceivable definition of the term, however, could "isolation" be said to represent the reality of United States policy during the first century-and-a-half of American independence. A nation that by 1900 had quadrupled its land mass at the expense of other claimants, engaged in multiple wars of conquest, vigorously pursued access to markets in every quarter of the globe, and acquired by force an overseas empire could hardly be said to have been "isolated" in any meaningful sense."[1] In fact, as early as 1940 historian Albert Weinberg observed that isolationism "was the coinage, not of advocates of reserve, but of opponents seeking to discredit them by exaggeration."[2]

A study by the United States Congress, in fact, makes clear the long *history of the use of U.S. armed force throughout the world since 1798* (see **table 2.1**). Before World War II, U.S. armed forces were used abroad 163 times. Before the Spanish-American War of 1898 there were 98 uses of U.S. armed forces abroad. Overall, the frequency of American armed intervention has remained pretty much the same over time—an average of about "one armed intervention per year" for over 140 years.

The extent of the use of armed force throughout the world by the U.S. government since the begin-ning of independence may come as a surprise to many Americans. Nevertheless, it serves to demonstrate the U.S.'s internationalist orientation from the beginning. Although the scope of armed intervention tended to be concentrated throughout the Western Hemisphere and Asia, it clearly intervened all over the world as well.[3] Not only is it indicative that the United States was quite active internationally and behaved similarly to other European powers abroad, such interventionist behavior inevitably made the United States a part of the evolving international political economy that was dominated by European states. It is important to point out that this congressional study "excludes" the use of U.S. armed forces against Native American people as the United States expanded westward throughout the nineteenth century. Clearly, the United States has been anything but isolationist in its foreign policy throughout its history.

EUROPEAN AND ENGLISH COLONIAL ROOTS

In fact, it is important to remember that *the original thirteen colonies were created as a result of European expansion throughout the world.* During the fifteenth and sixteenth centuries, Europe was emerging out of its feudal age and becoming the most dynamic global force. This was the beginning of an age of European "discovery" and "expansion" that would last into the twentieth century. The rise of Europe, and so-called European great powers, would forever change the map of the world: initially by the rise of Spain and Portugal, followed by the Dutch, and then the English and the French. By the seventeenth century, following Christopher Columbus's historic voyage, most of present-day South America, Central America, and the Caribbean was colonized by Spain and Portugal. By this time, though, the power of Spain and Portugal were in decline, while that of England and France, in particular, were on the rise.

England and France were actively expanding and colonizing throughout the world in search of power and wealth, including the "new world" of present-day North America. The founding of Jamestown (in

TABLE 2.1
U.S. MILITARY INTERVENTIONS BEFORE WORLD WAR II

1798-1800—Undeclared naval war with France	1844—Mexico	1882—Egypt	1912-41—China
1801-05—Tripoli	1846-48—Mexico	1885—Panama	1913—Mexico
1806—Mexico	1849—Smyrna	1888—Korea	1914—Haiti
1806-10—Gulf of Mexico	1851—Turkey	1888—Haiti	1914—Dominican Republic
1810—West Florida (Spanish Territory)	1851—Johanna Island	1888-89—Samoa	1914-17—Mexico
1812—East Florida (Spanish Territory)	1852-53—Argentina	1889—Hawaiian Islands	1915-34—Haiti
1812-15—Great Britain	1853—Nicaragua	1890—Argentina	1916—China
1813—West Florida (Spain)	1853-54—Japan	1891—Haiti	1916-24—Dominican Republic
1813-15—Marquesas Islands	1853-54—Ryukyu and Bonin Islands	1891—Bering Sea	1917—China
1814—Spanish Florida	1854—China	1891—Chile	1917-18—World War I
1814-25—Caribbean	1854—Nicaragua	1893—Hawaii	1917-22—Cuba
1815—Algiers	1855—China	1894—Brazil	1918-19—Mexico
1815—Tripoli	18555—Fiji Islands	1894—Nicaragua	1918-20—Panama
1816—Spanish Florida	1855—Uruguay	1894-95—China	1918-20—Soviet Russia
1816-18—Spanish Florida (First Seminole War)	1856—Panama	1894-96—Korea	1919—Dalmatia
1817—Amelia Island (Spanish Territory)	1856—China	1895—Colombia	1919—Turkey
1818—Oregon	1857—Nicaragua	1896—Nicaragua	1919—Honduras
1820-23—Africa	1858—Uruguay	1898—Spain	1920—China
1822—Cuba	1858—Fiji Islands	1898-99—China	1920—Guatemala
1823—Cuba	1858-59—Turkey	1899—Nicaragua	1920-22—Russia
1824—Cuba	1859—Paraguay	1899—Samoa	1921—Panama-Costa Rica
1824—Puerto Rico (Spanish Territory)	1859—Mexico	1899-1901—Philippines	1922—Turkey
1825—Cuba	1859—China	1900—China	1922-23—China
1827—Greece	1860—Angola, Portuguese West Africa	1901—Colombia	1924—Honduras
1831-32—Falkland Islands	1860—Colombia	1902—Colombia	1924—China
1832—Sumatra	1863—Japan	1903—Honduras	1925—Honduras
1833—Argentina	1864—Japan	1903—Dominican Republic	1925—Panama
1835-36—Peru	1864—Japan	1903—Syria	1926—China
1836—Mexico	1865—Panama	1903-04—Abyssinia	1926-33—Nicaragua
1838-39—Sumatra	1866—Mexico	1903-14—Panama	1927—China
1840—Fiji Islands	1866—China	1904—Dominican Republic	1932—China
1841—Drummond Islands	1867—Nicaragua	1904—Tangier, Morocco	1933—Cuba
1841—Samoa	1868—Japan	1904—Panama	1934—China
1842—Mexico	1868—Uruguay	1904-05—Korea	1940—Newfoundland, Bermuda, St. Lucia, Bahamas, Jamaica, Antigua, Trinidad, and British Guiana
1843—China	1868—Colombia	1906-09—Cuba	1941—Greenland
1843—Africa	1870—Mexico	1907—Honduras	1941—Dutch Guiana
	1870—Hawaiian Islands	1910—Nicaragua	1941—Iceland
	1871—Korea	1911—Honduras	1941—Germany
	1873—Colombia	1911—China	1941-45—World War II
	1873—Mexico	1912—Honduras	
	1874—Hawaiian Islands	1912—Panama	
	1876—Mexico	1912—Cuba	
		1912—China	
		1912—Turkey	

SOURCE: U.S. Congress, House, Committee on Foreign Relations, *Background Information on the Use of U.S. Armed Forces in Foreign Countries, 1975 Revision,* Committee Print (94th Cong., 1st Sess., 1975).

present-day Virginia) in 1607 and Plymouth (in present-day Massachusetts) in 1620 represented the beginnings of what was to become the thirteen "English" colonies. As stated by Gregory Nobles,

> Europeans did not come to North America just to explore, convert, and trade, of course; they came to stay. From their first footholds they extended their reach into the interior and planted permanent settlements. As they did so, the eastern half of North America became a patchwork of power bases, with European enclaves interspersed among traditional tribal territories.[4]

From a global and European perspective, such settlements resulted in the extension of the British empire into the eastern seaboard of North America and intensified European rivalry, especially between the French and British, for imperial control of the continent. Hence, the historical roots of the United States can be found in European expansion and rivalry that was proceeding throughout the world.[5]

By the latter part of the eighteenth century, what eventually resulted in **the American revolution** involved Englishmen fighting Englishmen for the future destiny of the Eastern seaboard and, with hindsight, much of the continent of North America. Once loyal British subjects, the issues that over time incited the American revolutionaries involved the nature of the imperial relationship with the "mother" country. From the perspective of the British crown, the thirteen colonies were an integral part of the British colonial and mercantile empire that increasingly spanned the globe. Therefore, the colonists rightfully were "subjects" of British imperial rule. From the perspective of the colonists, who increasingly saw themselves as Englishmen who should have the "rights" of Englishmen, the British increasingly were abusing their power as they fought representation, taxed the colonies, and controlled trade with the rest of the world.

Eventually the political and economic conflicts escalated to the point of a formal "Declaration of Independence" in 1776. The document, after describing certain "truths" and natural rights and listing the "history of repeated injuries and usurpations" by the

King of Great Britain, ended by declaring "that these United Colonies are, and of right ought to be, FREE AND INDEPENDENT STATES; that they are absolved from all allegiance to the British Crown, and that all political connection between them and the state of Great Britain is, and ought to be, totally dissolved; and that, as free and independent states, they have full power to levy war, conclude peace, contract alliances, establish commerce, and do all other acts and things which independent states may of right do."[6]

The British, unsuccessfully, attempted to put down the "rebellion" and a "war of independence" was fought by the colonialists for five long years. The outcome was far from preordained. American independence was finally won when British General Cornwallis surrendered at Yorktown in 1781 and the United States was officially recognized with the signing of the Treaty of Paris of 1783 (by England, France, Spain, and the United States). Ironically, the Treaty of Paris "gave the new American nation what England had fought for over a century to obtain: the vast interior region that reached westward to the Mississippi and ran from the upper Great Lakes almost to the Gulf of Mexico (Spain obtained all of Florida, which included the coastal region as far west as the Mississippi)."[7]

It is important to recall, despite the hard-fought effort of American troops under General George Washington (and American colonialists who supported the independence effort), that *other European powers were heavily involved* in the war given its implications for the European balance of power system and for the world. Therefore, German (Hessian) troops fought alongside British troops. And the Americans (through the Continental Congress—the governing institution at the time) entered into a formal "alliance" with France, who supplied badly needed money and supplies (including arms), and a French fleet which was able to penetrate the British blockade and prevent General Cornwallis's escape. Furthermore, American merchants and traders actively traded for guns and other essential items with other Europeans, especially the Dutch. As compellingly depicted by Barbara Tuchman in *The First Salute: A View of the American Revolution,* such European support and commerce, although typically underplayed in American history books, were absolutely essential to the success of the American war effort.[8]

The creation of the United States, hence, was a function of European power politics and expansion. And the importance of Europe and the larger global environment would continue to play an integral role in United States foreign policy after independence. Therefore, one way to think about the history of U.S. foreign policy is to divide it into *three major periods or eras since independence:*

1. The Continental Era, 1776–1860s;
2. The Regional Era, 1860s–1940s; and
3. The Global Era, 1940s–present.

U.S. foreign policy, in other words, represented both continuity and change over time. On the one hand, it grew in power and expanded steadily throughout North America and the world. On the other hand, the United States experienced major changes in its foreign policy goals and the scope of its involvement abroad over time as well. Although dividing U.S. foreign policy into three periods runs the risk of simplifying the complex history of U.S. foreign relations, it should help the reader better understand the general patterns of continuity and change that have evolved throughout the history of U.S. foreign policy (see **essay 2.1** on the historiography and differing interpretations of U.S. foreign relations,).[9]

THE CONTINENTAL ERA

. . . .

The United States was never isolationist; from its earliest days as an independent state, the United States had an active foreign policy. In his famous "Farewell Address," George Washington, the first president of the United States, argued not in favor of isolationism, but in favor of a foreign policy of "nonalignment"—that the United States should avoid permanent alliances and permanent entanglements. U.S. governmental officials followed his advice throughout this era, although most U.S. actions

focused on the surrounding North American continent until the latter half of the nineteenth century. During this time, *two general goals preoccupied most American leaders:* nation building and continental expansion.

The United States was a new and relatively weak country at the turn of the nineteenth century. It had won its national independence from the global superpower of its time, England, but it faced many of the problems that any new country with a colonial history faces upon gaining independence. Although far from Europe, the former thirteen colonies were surrounded by territory that England, France, Spain, and Russia coveted and fought over. As stated by Walter LaFeber, "From the beginning of their history, Americans lived not in any splendid isolation, far from the turmoil and corruption of Europe many had hoped to escape. They instead had to live in settlements that were surrounded by great and ambitious European powers."[10]

The U.S. economy also had been dependent on the English economy throughout the colonial era. The new country, in addition, was attempting to implement the first democratic experiment in the modern world. Given this environment, a priority for most Americans was **nation building**: to build an independent country safe from its neighbors, to construct a strong national economy, and to establish a stable democratic polity. Therefore, much of the focus was on strengthening the internal situation in the United States.

The second goal, **continental expansion**, was closely linked to nation building. What better way to protect oneself from potentially hostile neighbors than to expand one's territory and push the British, French, Spanish, and Russians (as well as the Mexicans and Native Americans) farther and farther away from the eastern seaboard, preferably off the North American continent and out of the Western Hemisphere? What better way to build a strong economy than through the acquisition of more land that could be put to work? And strengthening national security and the national economy contributed to political stability. But this meant that "Americans—whether they liked it or not—were part of European power politics even as they moved

ESSAY 2.1
HISTORIOGRAPHY AND DIFFERING INTERPRETATIONS OF U.S. FOREIGN RELATIONS

The study of the conduct of United States foreign policy has always been characterized by disagreement and differing interpretations, or schools of thought. Usually, one interpretation tends to dominate or prevail among scholars of U.S. foreign policy—usually referred to as the "traditional" or **orthodox** interpretation. With time and new sources, other interpretations—**revisionist** schools—emerge that revise and challenge this orthodoxy. Sometimes a melding of orthodox and revisionist interpretations eventually occurs, producing a **post-revisionist** synthesis. Such is the nature of historiography.

As reflected in the overview of *American Diplomatic History* by Jerald Combs, there has been two centuries of changing interpretations of American diplomatic history. Given this penchant for interpretation and reevaluation, an understanding of the historiography and the differing interpretations produced over time becomes important for a full understanding of the evolution of United States foreign relations.

By the 1950s and the height of the cold war years, it was popular for diplomatic historians to depict the Spanish-American War of 1898 as "the" break point in United States foreign policy, where the United States was characterized as more isolationist before war and then emerged as a world power with the war. This interpretation about "discontinuity" in U.S. foreign policy became the orthodox interpretation among American diplomatic historians, as represented by Dexter Perkins in *The American Approach to Foreign Policy*. But despite the use of a language of "isolationism" and the description of the growth of isolationist sentiment among the mass public toward European wars, U.S. foreign policy was still depicted as quite active abroad although limited in geographic scope. Nevertheless, such an interpretation helped to propagate in the minds of the general public that U.S. foreign policy was "isolationist" throughout much of its history, including after World War I—that is, until the cataclysmic events of World War II forced U.S. international involvement.

Eventually throughout the sixties and seventies, revisionist interpretations grew in popularity and importance among diplomatic historians, challenging the conventional understanding and its isolationist implications for U.S. foreign policy. Revisionists rejected the isolationist thesis and tended to depict the history of U.S. foreign policy as being much more "continuous" and expansive over its history. Such a perspective is reflected in such classic works as William Appleman Williams' *The Tragedy of American Diplomacy* and Richard Van Alstyne's *The Rising American Empire.*

As Thomas Bailey, one of America's preeminent diplomatic historians, basically confessed, "The embarrassing truth is that for eighteen years I further misled the youth of this land [about U.S. isolationism]. . . . By the time I became a graduate student I should have realized that cataclysmic changes, especially in the power position of a nation, seldom or never occur overnight. I should also have known that the very first obligation of the scholar is to examine critically all basic assumptions—the more basic the more critically."

The interpretation presented in this chapter represents more of a post-revisionist synthesis. Although U.S. foreign policy was never isolationist, it did experience both continuity and change over time. On the one hand, the United States steadily grew in power and steadily expanded throughout North America and the world. On the other hand, the United States experienced changes in its foreign policy, most importantly the scope of its involvement abroad grew over time. Therefore, United States foreign policy can be said to have evolved through three major historical eras which reflected its steady rise over two hundred years to become the world power of its time.

SOURCES: Thomas A. Bailey, "America's Emergence as a World Power: The Myth and the Verity," *Pacific Historical Review* 30 (February 1961); Jerald A. Combs, *American Diplomatic History: Two Centuries of Changing Interpretations* (Berkeley: University of California Press, 1983); Dexter Perkins, *The American Approach to Foreign Policy* (New York: Atheneum, 1968); Richard W. Van Alstyne, *The Rising American Empire*, (Chicago: Quadrangle Books, 1965); William Appleman Williams, *The Tragedy of American Diplomacy* (New York: Norton, 1959).

into the forests and fertile lands beyond the Appalachian Mountains. They could not separate their destiny from the destiny of those they had left behind in Europe."[11]

Up to and including the acquisition of Alaska from Russia in 1867, U.S. foreign policy was responsible for acquiring increasing amounts of territory throughout the North American continent, which was eventually annexed into the United States of America. *Territory that was inhabited predominantly by Native Americans and claimed by European states was acquired by the United States:* from England in the north and northwest, such as northern Maine and the Oregon territories; from France in the Louisiana territories to the west; from Spain in the Florida territories to the south; from Mexico in the southwest, such as Texas and the southwest territories (including California); and from Russia in the farthest reaches of the northwest with Alaska (see **figure 2.1**).

Contrary to popular folklore, American continental expansion generated considerable involvement, diplomacy, and conflict with European states, Mexico, and Native Americans. Nevertheless, in the words of Gregory Nobles in *American Frontiers: Cultural Encounters and Continental Conquest,*

> Often these stories are oversimplified and stereotypical, offering one-sided views that implicitly separate the world into "good guys" and "bad guys." Yet that simplicity is the source of their power: repeated over and over, the images and stories that permeate popular culture come together to form a more enduring American myth, what some historians call a "master narrative," which provides both an explanation for the past and a justification for the present.[12]

Much of the land, in fact, was sold to the United States as the weaker country in response to European power struggles going on at the time or was literally taken by force. Americans, for example, during colonial times and after independence attacked Canada, a dominion of the British empire, repeatedly in attempting to expand northward.

Shortly after independence, in fact, the U.S. government devised a plan that outlined a process for annexing new territory into the United States—

thereby allowing new states into the Union. *The Northwest Ordinance of 1787,* originally devised by a committee of the Continental Congress chaired by Thomas Jefferson, called for dividing territory into a gridwork of townships. "Once the land had been surveyed, it could be sold to land companies or individuals, thus creating not just a source of revenue for the government but also a pattern of orderly settlement in the territory." Eventually, when the population reached sixty thousand, the territory could enter the Union "on an equal footing with the original states in all respects whatsoever."[13]

Native American peoples, naturally, suffered the most from Western expansion. According to Walter LaFeber, "a central theme of American diplomatic history must be the clash between the European settlers and the Native Americans"—a population estimated to be between 8 million to 10 million inhabitants throughout North America by the time Christopher Columbus first arrived.[14] Clashes were constant with Indians as Americans expanded westward. Despite coexistence and the signing of treaties, the same pattern was repeated as Americans expanded farther and farther. "As usual with Indian treaties, this land was granted to them 'as long as the waters shall run and the grass shall grow.' And as usual, whites began to violate their own treaty."[15] Ultimately, the fate of the Indians was sealed given the growing power and technological superiority of the United States.[16]

The U.S. government "adopted a variety of distinct, sometimes seemingly contradictory strategies in dealing with the Indians who inhabited the interior. Soldiers and social reformers argued over appropriate policies for pacifying native people, and the government pursued two or more policies at once, making war or peace as best suited the situation." And like earlier European imperial powers, the U.S. government played "one Indian group against the other in military or diplomatic or economic alliances. But in the end United States Indian policy pointed in only one direction: toward the reservation."[17]

It is important to point out that the *"agents" of U.S. continental expansion* were not only the government, especially the army, but also thousands of private and entrepreneurial Americans spilling

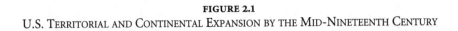

FIGURE 2.1
U.S. TERRITORIAL AND CONTINENTAL EXPANSION BY THE MID-NINETEENTH CENTURY

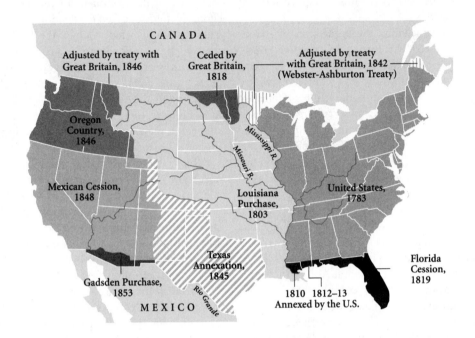

SOURCE: Walter LaFeber, *The American Age: United States Foreign Policy at Home and Abroad,* 2nd ed. (New York: Norton, 1994), p. 132.

westward in search of land, gold, profit, and freedom.[18] The net result was that by the 1860s, the United States had grown from the thirteen original colonies on the eastern seaboard to a country that spanned the continent to the Pacific Ocean.

Richard Van Alstyne has referred to the United States as *The Rising American Empire.* "The early colonies were no sooner established in the seventeenth century than expansionist impulses began to register in each of them. Imperial patterns took shape, and before the middle of the eighteenth century the concept of an empire that would take in the whole continent was fully formed."[19] Or in the words of diplomatic historian Thomas Bailey, "The point is often missed that during the nineteenth century the United States practiced internal colonialism and imperialism on a continental scale."[20] Given its

strategic location in the new world, facing relatively weak indigenous peoples and European forces far from the center of Europe, it could also be said that "from its birth the United States has been incomparably the luckiest of all the great nations—so far."[21]

The United States was a creature of the British tradition and conceived in terms of empire—*an imperial republic*—by American leaders. Thomas Jefferson, author of the Declaration of Independence and the third president of the United States—who dramatically increased the size of the United States with the purchase of the Louisiana territories in 1803 and sponsored the Lewis and Clark expedition to discover the west and search for a northwest passage to the Pacific (and the Orient)—communicated his expansive vision of an "empire of liberty" to James Monroe in 1801:

However our present interests may restrain us within our limits, it is impossible not to look forward to distant times, when our rapid multiplication will expand it beyond those limits, and cover the whole northern if not the southern continent, with people speaking the same language, governed in similar forms, and by similar laws.[22]

Although Van Alstyne understood that his use of the *language of "empire"* was controversial, he argued nevertheless that "its evolution from a group of small, disunited English colonies strung out on a long coastline to a world power with commitments on every sea and in every continent, has been a characteristically imperial type of growth." In other words, the United States, was not different, but quite similar to other European states in growing in power and expanding its influence abroad.

The U.S. was **active beyond the continent** as well, but this activity was more sporadic in nature. *American commerce* and merchants were active in all areas of the globe, especially Europe, the West Indies (i.e., the Caribbean), the Orient, and the slave trade of Africa. As stated by Van Alstyne,

As a coastal country of the eighteenth century, the United States looked seaward as well as landward, and the paths of its growing empire in the nineteenth century stretched out to sea as well as across the continent. The United States was a commercial and seafaring state, as well as an agrarian state; and its mercantile and seafaring population was busily active in extending and developing long-distance sea routes even while the physical handicaps to transcontinental migration remained unsolved.[23]

In the tradition of European expansion and the search for wealth abroad, "China was the magnet which accounted for the path of empire into the Pacific broken by Yankee shipping in the 1780s. . . . From Portsmouth, New Hampshire, to Charleston, South Carolina, there was hardly a port on the Atlantic seaboard that did not have its China merchants." As explained by Van Alstyne,

Sealskins from the Falkland Islands, seaotter pelts from the Pacific northwest, natural sandalwood from the Sandwich Islands [the Hawaiian Islands of today], ginseng from the Pacific southwest, opium from Turkey and India, kegs of Spanish silver dollars, and finally cotton-piece goods from the new New England mill towns furnished the bulk of the cargoes with which the American China merchants maintained a balance of payments for their purchases [of such commodities as spices, silk, porcelain, and tea] in China.[24]

"During the eighteenth and nineteenth centuries," according to Alfred Eckes, "the founders of U.S. foreign policy pressed to open markets and attacked mercantilistic barriers abroad in order to bolster the domestic economy and secure independence."[25] Interruption of American commerce by the British during the Napoleonic War, for example, was a major cause of the War of 1812 between the United States and England.

Despite the "spirit of commerce" since colonial times, American merchants were unable to open up the mercantilist regulation of trade by the European powers and increasingly adopted a policy of economic nationalism and the use of tariffs to encourage (and protect) the growth of domestic manufactures. Increasingly, tariff policy became trade policy in the nineteenth century. As Eckes found, "In practice the high-tariff position generally carried the day. Over a forty-year period from 1821 to 1861, the ratio of duties to total imports ranged from a low of 14.21 percent in 1861 to over 57 percent in 1832 under the Tariff of Abominations."[26]

The U.S. government, especially through the navy, was also *politically and militarily active* beyond the continent (review table 2.1 again). As early as 1821 "the navy began operating a squadron off the west coast of South America; and by 1835 intercourse with China and the East Indies reached the point where it justified the establishment of a separate East India squadron."[27]

In Latin America, in 1823 the "Monroe Doctrine" was declared, stating that the new world in the Western Hemisphere was not open to colonization by Europeans. The United States negotiated as early as 1850 the Clayton-Bulwer Treaty for rights to build an interoceanic canal. And attempts also were made to annex Cuba and Santo Domingo (now known as the Dominican Republic) into the U.S. republic. In Asia, the United States, led by Daniel Webster, negotiated the Treaty of Wangxia giving Americans "most-favored-nation" status (like other European countries) in trade and extraterritorial rights with China; Americans, led by Commodore Matthew C. Perry, forced Japan to open itself up to foreigners and commerce in 1854; and the Hawaiian and Midway Islands were occupied as a transit point for American commerce with the Orient.

Unlike the thrust over the North American continent, these policies beyond the continent were much more sporadic, lacking any consistent pattern over time. Thus, it is more helpful to view this era as a period of continentalism in U.S. foreign policy.

THE REGIONAL ERA

. . . .

By the latter half of the nineteenth century, the United States had been quite successful in building an independent and transcontinental country that was growing more powerful. With steady continental expansion and the end of the Civil War, the United States no longer faced any immediate threats from its neighbors. The Civil War also settled the divisions between the North and the South, allowing political stability to be achieved at the national level. Also, the national economy was vibrant and growing, and the transcontinental railroad was completed in 1869. In the words of Van Alstyne, "By all tests of pragmatism the United States emerged from that war more than ever an imperial state. It entered its period of consolidation and centralization, it began developing its internal economy intensively, and abroad it soon joined in the international scramble for material wealth and power."[28]

As the United States reached its limits of continental expansion, more and more Americans during the latter half of the nineteenth century were beginning to speak of the future of the United States in terms of a *manifest destiny*.[29] Such a nationalistic and expansive vision was clearly articulated in the language of the times by William H. Seward, a Senator from New York and later a prominent Secretary of State under Presidents Lincoln, Johnson, and Grant, as early as 1850:

> The world contains no seat of empire so magnificent as this, which, while it embraces all the varying climates of the temperate zone, and is traversed by the wide-expanding lakes and long branching rivers, offers supplies on the Atlantic shores to the over-crowded nations of Europe, while on the Pacific coast it intercepts the commerce of the Indies. The nation thus situated, and enjoying forest, mineral, and agricultural resources unequalled ... must command the empire of the seas, which alone is real empire.... The Atlantic States, through their commercial, social, and political affinities and sympathies, are steadily renovating the Governments and social constitutions of Europe and Africa; the Pacific States must necessarily perform the same sublime and beneficent functions in Asia. If, then, the American people shall remain an undivided nation, the ripening civilization of the West, after a separation growing wider and wider for four thousand years, will in its circuit of the world, meet again, and mingle with the declining civilization of the East on our own free soil, and a new and more perfect civilization will arise to bless the earth, under the sway of our own cherished and beneficent democratic institutions.[30]

Following the Civil War, in fact, *U.S. foreign policy actively promoted political stability and economic expansion abroad, especially in two regions of the world:* Latin America and Asia. United States foreign policy became increasingly a presence on the global stage best symbolized by the Spanish-American War fought in 1898. "The Spanish-American

War was an expression of two powerful historic drives: the pull to the south, and the pull across the Pacific toward Asia."[31]

The U.S. government and American business dramatically increased their presence **in Latin America**, especially throughout Central America and the Caribbean. The presence of American business intensified with the rapid expansion of American trade, loans, and foreign investment throughout the region. The U.S. government was also active in promoting friendly political regimes in the region which would be unresponsive to European involvement, open to American trade and investment, and stable enough to pay back their American bank loans.

Involvement of the U.S. government and American business in Latin America—a region which was experiencing decolonization, nation building efforts by independent states, and considerable political instability—resulted in constant American military intervention and occupation, especially after the turn of the century. As proclaimed by Secretary of State Richard Olney in 1895, "the United States is practically sovereign on this continent, and its fiat is law upon the subjects to which it confines its interposition." The Olney Proclamation reinforced the original purpose of the Monroe Doctrine, that the United States had the right, and now the power, to intervene and dominate its "own backyard"—foreshadowing what was to come with and following the Spanish-American War.

From President Teddy Roosevelt's "Big Stick" policies to William Howard Taft's "Dollar Diplomacy" and Woodrow Wilson's "New Freedom," through the Warren Harding, Calvin Coolidge, and Herbert Hoover administrations, the United States regularly sent the Marines to crush local rebellions, prop up old or new regimes, and restore political stability in virtually every major state in Central America and the Caribbean, often only to return again and again. Military intervention usually meant that the local "customs houses" were subsequently run by U.S. government officials to guarantee that revenues from tariffs and duties were collected to repay American loans. Financial supervision, for example, lasted 13 years in Nicaragua (1911–1924), 25

years in Haiti (1916–1941), and 36 years in the Dominican Republic (1905–1941). American leaders so badly wanted a canal to connect the Atlantic and Pacific oceans, that in 1903 President Roosevelt actively supported and instigated Panamanian independence from Colombia. He then immediately recognized the new country and signed a treaty giving Panama $10 million plus $250,000 a year for rights "in perpetuity" for a ten-mile-wide strip—which became the Panama Canal Zone—that cut the new country literally in half.

Clearly, American involvement and power had carved out a regional "sphere of influence." This was the period during which the United States acquired—primarily as a result of its diplomatic demands over Cuba that triggered the so-called "splendid little war" with Spain (referring to the ease of the victory)—its earliest colonial possessions (and "protectorates") in the area: including Cuba, Puerto Rico, and the Virgin Islands. It wasn't until the 1920s with Herbert Hoover and then Franklin Roosevelt's "Good Neighbor" policy that direct intervention of American troops into the domestic affairs of its neighbors was temporarily abandoned.

American foreign policy was in search of political stability and U.S. economic expansion **in Asia** as well, with China being the major prize. "Merchants, missionaries, adventurers, sea captains, naval officers, and consular officers crowded into the Pacific during the nineteenth century and spun a web whose strands extended to every part of the ocean."[32] Unlike Latin America, which was Christianized by the Spanish, there was a large American "missionary" presence in Asia, particularly in Japan and China. And with the crisis with Spain over Cuba and just before the Spanish-American War broke out, the U.S. navy attacked the remnants of the Spanish empire, producing American Samoa, Guam, Wake Island, and, most importantly, the Philippines as Asian colonies of the United States.[33]

American involvement, however, resulted in a much more limited use of force (unlike Latin America) given the region's distance from American shores and the strong military presence of England, France, Russia, and Japan. U.S. foreign policy in China, for example, emphasized an "Open Door" approach to maximize American involvement and trade.[34] Therefore, America's military and commercial involvement resulted in fewer costs as well as fewer gains. The United States, nevertheless, sent more than 120,000 American troops from 1899–1902 to fight its first counterinsurgency war and defeat a national independence movement in the Philippines to preserve its new colonial control.

Even though U.S. foreign policy was oriented toward the regions to its immediate south and west, it became *increasingly active in European affairs and on the world scene* in general. While officially neutral during the early part of World War I, the United States eventually became a major participant in impacting the outcome of the war. Woodrow Wilson was, in fact, highly instrumental in influencing the Treaty of Versailles, which officially ended the war and attempted to create a new liberal world order through the League of Nations. During 1918–1919, the United States even sent 14,000 military troops, along with the British, Canadians, French, Czechs, and Japanese, to occupy part of the newly declared Soviet Union in an effort to aid the anti-Bolsheviks and try to reestablish a Russian front against Germany.

The "twenties and thirties" are popularly thought of as the height of isolationism in U.S. foreign policy. There is some truth to this, evidenced by the U.S. rejection of American participation in the League of Nations, the rise of isolationist sentiment among the American public and a strong peace movement, and its reluctance to become actively involved in European conflicts (especially following the Great Depression and during the early years of World War II). Nevertheless, as stated by William Cohen, "Rejection of the Treaty of Versailles and lack of membership in the League had little impact, however, on American involvement in world affairs in the decade that followed. In the 1920s the United States was more profoundly engaged in international matters than in any peacetime era in its history."[35]

Not only was U.S. foreign policy active in Latin America and Asia, but the United States also took a number of *important diplomatic initiatives* with the Europeans and Japanese. From November 1921 to February 1922, the United States hosted and actively promoted a major naval disarmament conference in Washington, D.C., that resulted in the "first" major arms control treaty in modern times (in addition, the same conference produced a Four-Power Treaty and a Nine-Power Treaty involving Pacific island possessions and the rivalry in China, signed by the United States). It was "an extraordinary event, symbolic of America's new role in world affairs."[36] In 1928 the United States and France also jointly sponsored the Kellogg-Briand Pact in an effort to outlaw war. The United States also began to play an active although "unofficial" role relative to League activities.

It is important to point out that despite U.S. rejection of formal participation in the League of Nations, the United States became *increasingly important to the international political economy* following the First World War, which was still dominated by the Europeans. As a result of the debts and damage incurred by the war, European economies became increasingly dependent on the United States government and on American business as a source of trade and finance. "Demand for American capital was intense throughout the decade despite high interest rates. Europeans needed dollars to purchase American goods needed for reconstruction, and they borrowed regardless of cost. The rest of the world, which traditionally turned to European bankers, had no alternative in the 1920s but to queue up in Wall Street."[37]

This foreshadowed the global leadership role that the United States would not yet fully occupy until Europe once again rebuilt and launched into the Second World War. As stated by Cohen, "Clearly, the impact of American trade, investments, and tourism on the world economy in the 1920s was enormous. No other nation even approximated the United States in economic importance. The British, who kept first place among importing nations, lost their preeminent investment role in Latin America and Canada, and were being challenged throughout Europe and the rest of the world, including their colonies, by American capitalists."[38]

By the 1920s, in the judgment of diplomatic historian William Cohen the United States had become a great power and acquired a "formal" and "informal" empire. As he stated in *Empire Without Tears:*

> It controlled an empire that included not only the Caribbean basin, but stretched across the Pacific, north and south, through Hawaii and Alaska, Midway, Wake, Guam, Samoa, and the Aleutians, to East Asia and the Philippines. Manufacturers nurtured markets and sired multinational corporations in Europe, while mining and lumber interests scoured North and South America. American entrepreneurs and missionaries wandered across the Middle East, South Asia, and Africa. It was the dawning of what Henry Luce would later call the "American century."[39]

Clearly, the United States was growing into a formidable power on the world stage, while at the same time trying to maintain considerable "independence" of action. Nevertheless, outside of Latin America and Asia, U.S. foreign policy, especially in the security area, lacked coherence and consistent involvement. Therefore, this era of U.S. foreign policy is best remembered as predominantly regionalist in orientation.

THE GLOBAL ERA

· · · · · · · · · · · · · ·

The Japanese attack on Pearl Harbor on December 7, 1941, abruptly ended the regional era in U.S. foreign policy. The next four years saw the beginning of a new era of global involvement in which the United States, along with the Soviets, British, Chinese, French, and other allies, fought the Axis powers of Germany and Japan over the destiny of the globe. And with the end of World War II, the United States became an active global power throughout the world scene and developed foreign policies of global consequence. It also reflected the time when the President was able to govern the making of foreign policy and lead the country.

WORLD WAR II AND IMMEDIATE POSTWAR FOREIGN POLICY

Consistent with U.S. foreign policy throughout its history, *the Roosevelt administration's postwar aims revolved around the two key issues of:*

1. economics, and
2. national security

But now the United States took an active leadership role in world affairs.

The first goal involved the need "to restore economic stability and prosperity" in the United States, as well as in Western Europe and throughout the world. This was deemed essential because the U.S. economy was heavily intertwined with the larger global capitalist economy, particularly the Western European economies—once the core of the global economy and shattered by the Great Depression and World War II. Many Americans also feared that the end of the war would produce a massive recession within the U.S. economy.

The original strategy, arrived at in Bretton Woods, New Hampshire, in 1944, was to promote "multilateral" efforts with American allies to restore and manage an increasingly liberal, global market economy, based on a new system of fixed exchange rates and open, free trade. What came to be called **the Bretton Woods system** would provide necessary assistance and rules for economic transactions principally through the creation of three multilateral international organizations: the International Bank for Reconstruction and Development (IBRD, known as the World Bank) for loans for economic recovery and development, the International Monetary Fund (IMF) to support the stability of national currencies based on gold, and the General Agreement on Tariffs and Trade (GATT) to promote and govern open trade.[40] Success on the economic front in promoting a liberal capitalist world order was thought to be crucial for ensuring peace and minimizing threats to national security, as occurred when the Great Depression led to the rise of Adolf Hitler.

The second goal involved U.S. attempts to "construct a new international political order" that was stable and promoted the national security of the United States and its wartime allies, thereby preventing the outbreak of further wars. U.S. postwar involvement was deemed vital because of the collapse of Europe, which had dominated world politics for over two hundred years until the impact of the two world wars. In an effort to protect national security, President Franklin Roosevelt relied on a "strategy of multilateral cooperation" based on a **spheres-of-influence approach** and the creation of a new international organization to replace the League of Nations—**the United Nations**.

Roosevelt's strategy depended on global cooperation among members of the "Grand Alliance" during the war: the United States, Soviet Union, Great Britain, France, and China. The instrument for maintaining cooperation among the "big five" and preventing a challenge to the status quo, which could have led to the outbreak of a new war, was the creation of the United Nations, and especially the operation of the United Nations Security Council (a body in which each of the big five held veto power). Roosevelt also assumed that each of the five powers would exercise power over its regional spheres-of-influence: the United States in Latin America, the Soviet Union in Eastern Europe, Great Britain and France in Europe and their colonial possessions, and China in East Asia. This multilateral strategy of promoting global peace complemented the strategy of promoting global economic recovery and prosperity.

It should be pointed out that there is "little scholarly consensus" on the particular nature of the Roosevelt administration's postwar goals and strategy. Some scholars highlight President Roosevelt's idealism and commitment to democracy, human rights, and social welfare, emphasizing the role of the United Nations and other international organizations. Other scholars see President Roosevelt as much more pragmatic and concerned with restoring political and economic stability, concentrating on the role of power and spheres-of-influence. President Roosevelt, and the foreign policy that emanated from his administration, was very complex

and, at times, contradictory. In fact, it could be argued that he was both hopeful and pragmatic.[41]

Whatever the particular case, Roosevelt's overall strategy for restoring economic prosperity and national security quickly unraveled during the latter part of the 1940s. Before the war even came to an end, Roosevelt died and was succeeded as president by Harry Truman, who was unfamiliar with Roosevelt's postwar plans and lacked Roosevelt's considerable experience. The European economies were in much worse shape than most people had thought and were in need of assistance beyond that which the multilateral international organizations were capable of providing. Finally, any hope for lasting cooperation among members of the Grand Alliance in the area of national security quickly eroded as distrust, fear, and conflict between the United States and the Soviet Union escalated.

With the collapse of Roosevelt's grand strategy, U.S. foreign policy took a new course and can be seen as going through three periods or eras since the Second World War:

1. The Cold War Era, late 1940s–1960s;
2. The Post–Vietnam War Era, late 1960s–1980s;
3. The Post–Cold War Era, 1990s–present.

Familiarity with the dominant patterns in U.S. foreign policy that have prevailed since World War II is particularly important for giving the reader the historical context for better understanding how the politics of U.S. foreign policy has evolved over these same years.[42]

THE COLD WAR ERA

For roughly twenty years, *from the administrations of President Truman through President Johnson, U.S. foreign policy experienced considerable continuity based upon the twin goals of national security and economic prosperity* that had remained unresolved following the war: first, the quest for global security and stability from the "threat" of Soviet communist expansionism and, second, the promotion of an international market economy based upon the principles of free "open" trade and fixed exchange rates. This era also represented the height of the president's power to lead the country in the cold war.

Following the war, for the first time since independence and the period of continentalism Americans began to *perceive an external threat* to their national security: the advance of Soviet communism. Because the fear of Soviet communism became the key problem for most Americans, national security concerns drove U.S. foreign policy during the cold war. U.S. national security was defined in terms of global security and stability, for the threat was perceived to be global in nature and American leaders believed that, with the collapse of the British and French empires, only the United States had the power to respond. Therefore, under American leadership a **strategy of containment** was developed that aimed to deter by the threat of coercion the spread of Soviet communism, first in Europe, then Asia, and eventually throughout the world (see **essay 2.2** on George Kennan, father and critic of containment).[43]

The containment strategy was initially embodied in **the "Truman Doctrine"** announced in 1947, directed at containing Soviet expansion in the eastern Mediterranean countries of Greece and Turkey. In the words of one analyst, its future implications for U.S. foreign policy were to be global and quite profound:

The Truman Doctrine contained the seeds of American aid, economic or military, to more than one hundred countries; of mutual defense treaties with more than forty of them; of the great regional pacts, alliances, and unilateral commitments: to NATO, to the Middle East, to the Western Hemisphere, and to Southeast Asia. It justified fleets of carriers patrolling the Mediterranean and the South China sea, nuclear submarines under the polar icecap, air bases in the Thai jungle, and police advisers in Uruguay and Bolivia. In support of it, an average of a million soldiers were deployed for twenty-five years in some four thousand bases in thirty countries. It contained the seeds of a habit of intervention: clandestine in Iran, Guatemala, Cuba, the Philippines, Chile, and the CIA alone knows where else; overt in Korea, Lebanon,

the Dominican Republic, Laos, Cambodia and Vietnam.[44]

The U.S. global strategy that developed during the late forties and fifties was to surround the Soviet Union and its allies in Eastern Europe and mainland Asia with American allies, alliances, and military forces in order to deter the Soviet Union from initiating a military strike and possibly triggering World War III. Containment of the Soviet Union and the People's Republic of China throughout the Eurasian continent was to be accomplished through the threat and use of conventional and, especially, nuclear military forces. In the Third World, where the U.S.-Soviet confrontation tended to be fought more indirectly over the "hearts and minds" of local elites and peoples, the United States relied on foreign assistance, counterinsurgency, and the use of covert paramilitary operations to promote friendly regimes. Containment of the Soviet Union was also pursued through the use of broad economic sanctions by the United States against it and its allies (such as in Eastern Europe and Cuba). Diplomacy and other noncoercive instruments of policy were pushed to the side by the United States in East-West relations and superseded by the threat and use of coercion in responding to what American leaders saw as major challenges to American national security commitments and national interests.[45]

Given the inability of Western European economies to recover from the depression and the war, the United States also took the lead in unilaterally sustaining the Bretton Woods system—this was really **Bretton Woods II**—to promote a stable and prosperous international market economy. The original Bretton Woods system was to be based on a "multilateral" effort by the Europeans and Americans. However, the war-torn European economies were in need of recovery which prevented the Bretton Woods system from operating as originally agreed. Instead, the strength of the American economy allowed the United States to "unilaterally" support the Bretton Woods system and European economic recovery—hence Bretton Woods II.

The revival of the European economies was to be accomplished by providing massive capital

---

ESSAY 2.2
GEORGE KENNAN, FATHER AND CRITIC OF CONTAINMENT

George Kennan has been one of the more influential individuals in the foreign policymaking community since World War II. An iconoclast throughout his foreign service and public career, he initially was the father of containment and then became one of its leading critics.

George Kennan, born into a middle-class Wisconsin family, became a traditionalist and a romantic in the aristocratic tradition. In foreign affairs, he was both a Russophile, strongly anticommunist and fond of the Czarist past, and a believer in realpolitik. After joining the Foreign Service in the late 1920s, Kennan remained a relatively obscure European and Soviet specialist for the next two decades, especially once diplomatic relations between the U.S. and the Soviet Union were restored and the two countries became wartime allies.

With the end of World War II, however, and the increasing tension between the United States and the Soviet Union, Kennan suddenly rose to prominence in 1946 as a result of writing a "Long Telegram" from the American embassy in Moscow to the State Department. In this communiqué, he described the Soviet Union as a weak, cautious, insecure, yet ideological, dogmatic, and expansionist state that needed to be contained. A subsequent famous *Foreign Affairs* article published in 1947 and entitled "Sources of Soviet Conduct," authored by George Kennan under the pseudonym "Mr. X," was an expanded version of this telegram. In it he argued that "the main element of any United States policy toward the Soviet Union must be that of a long-term, patient but firm and vigi-

lant containment of Russian expansive tendencies." This meant "the adroit and vigilant application of counter-force at a series of constantly shifting geographical and political points, corresponding to the shifts and maneuvers of Soviet policy." Clearly, Kennan was an early and powerful advocate for a strong American response to Soviet communist expansion, as well as the need to rebuild Western Europe (such as through the Marshall Plan).

Although Kennan is considered the "father" of containment, he also soon became an "early critic" of the U.S. practice of containment. As the policy became increasingly globalized and militarized, his influence within the State Department and the U.S. government quickly eroded. Kennan resigned in 1953 and became a historian at Princeton University where he went public with his criticism. He maintained that U.S. policymakers had turned his recommendations into a rigid doctrine much too reliant on the use of force and applied too indiscriminately abroad.

In the 1970s and 1980s, Kennan, while always the realist, became a major proponent of a semi-isolationist position. Given developments in the global and domestic environment, he argued for a major reduction in America's military establishment, reliance on nuclear weapons, and military presence abroad. In essence, he believed—as he had always argued—that U.S. foreign policy should revolve around its most vital interests: the geostrategic areas of North America, Western Europe, and Japan.

SOURCES: John Lewis Gaddis, *Strategies of Containment* (Oxford: Oxford University Press, 1982); George F. Kennan, *Around the Cragged Hill: A Personal and Political Philosophy* (New York: Norton, 1993); George F. Kennan, *At a Century's Ending: Reflections, 1982–1995* (New York: Norton, 1996); George F. Kennan, *Memoirs: 1925–1950* (Boston: Atlantic Monthly Press, 1967); George F. Kennan, *Sketches From a Life* (New York: Pantheon, 1989); David Mayers, *George Kennan and the Dilemmas of U.S. Foreign Policy* (New York: Oxford University Press, 1989); Anders Stephanson, *Kennan and the Art of Foreign Policy* (Boston: Harvard University Press, 1989); and Daniel Yergin, *Shattered Peace* (Boston: Houghton Mifflin, 1978); U.S., Department of State, George F. Kennan's "Long Telegram" (February 22, 1946); Mr. X, "The Sources of Soviet Conduct," *Foreign Affairs* (July 1947).

outlays in the form of American assistance (such as the Marshall Plan), private investment and loans by United States multinational corporations, and trade based on opening the U.S. domestic market to foreign imports. Therefore, the Bretton Woods international economic system based on free trade and fixed exchange rates became dependent on the United States acting as the world's banker. Although primarily European-oriented, and later also Japanese-oriented, U.S. foreign economic policy was also active in promoting a market system in the Third World through its support for private investment and development abroad.[46]

With European economic recovery under way and America's growing prosperity during the fifties, national security policy became the predominant concern of most American leaders. Foreign economic policy often came to be referred to as **low policy** while national security policy was usually referred to as **high policy**—an indication of their level of significance for those engaged in making U.S. foreign policy during the cold war years.[47]

For twenty years American leaders, preoccupied with promoting national security throughout the globe, relied on a strategy of global containment and deterrence, trying to prevent Soviet communism from expanding its empire. American policymakers believed that protecting other countries from the Soviet threat indirectly protected the United States and enhanced its national security. Hence, lines were drawn, countries were labeled friend or foe, and national commitments to friendly regimes were made. And when foreign threats were perceived, the United States responded. This policy of global containment inevitably led to American interventionism abroad and its tragic involvement in the Vietnam War.

THE POST–VIETNAM WAR ERA

The Vietnam War was the first major war in the history of the United States that it lost. Simply put, after investing as much as $30 billion a year and over 500,000 troops during the height of American involvement in a war that lasted at least fifteen years,

the United States' containment strategy was unsuccessful in keeping South Vietnam an independent, noncommunist country. As a result of America's failure in Vietnam, the policy of global containment of Soviet communism, which had prevailed since World War II, was challenged by competing foreign policy perspectives in American politics. U.S. foreign economic policy also changed in 1971 when President Richard Nixon discarded the convertibility of the U.S. dollar to gold and placed a 10 percent surcharge on Japanese imports, violating the principles of fixed exchange rates and free trade, which contributed to a situation in which the Bretton Woods system was no longer sustainable. This was a time when challenges to American power and the future of U.S. foreign policy were increasingly heard (see **essay 2.3** on Senator J. William Fulbright and the evolution of liberal internationalism).

The failure in Vietnam and the breakdown of the Bretton Woods system represented international and domestic changes that have resulted in *three new patterns in U.S. foreign policy during the post–Vietnam War years.* First, with the growth of economic problems at home and abroad, foreign economic policy has become "high" policy again, becoming a major agenda item facing all presidents. Although most American leaders continue to see the need for a stable and liberal international market economy, they often are unsure over the particular strategy and means to promote economic stability. Second, with each new administration there has been a modification in the direction of U.S. national security policy. Although a policy of containment continued to have its share of advocates, other policy orientations gained legitimacy and influenced the policymaking process. Third, in contrast to the cold war years, since the Vietnam War it has become very difficult for any president or administration to devise a foreign policy that has been successful in responding to changes in the global environment and in obtaining substantial domestic support over time. This has forced every president to change or modify their foreign policies during their terms of office, usually towards the political center. The result of these three patterns is that the continuity in foreign policy

ESSAY 2.3
SENATOR J. WILLIAM FULBRIGHT AND THE EVOLUTION
OF LIBERAL INTERNATIONALISM

Senator J. William Fulbright traveled a well-worn political path familiar to major political figures during the cold war and post–Vietnam War years. During the 1940s, Fulbright became an ardent liberal internationalist who was opposed to U.S. isolationism in world affairs; during the 1950s, he became a cold warrior in support of administration policy; and beginning in the mid-1960s, he became a critic of U.S. global containment, arguing in favor of a new liberal internationalism. As a member and then chairman of the Senate Foreign Relations Committee from 1944 to 1974, Senator Fulbright also played a leading role in the evolution of U.S. foreign policy. A brief examination of Fulbright's career should enhance an understanding of the evolution of the liberal internationalist orientation which has been so powerful in U.S. foreign policy over time.

J. William Fulbright was born in 1905. The son of a wealthy businessman, he was raised in Fayetteville, the site of the University of Arkansas. After quarterbacking the Razorback football team, he went to Oxford University as a Rhodes scholar in 1925. He became an admirer of **Woodrow Wilson and liberal internationalism**, who envisioned a peaceful and cooperative world order based on the spread of democracy and capitalism. After completing his studies at Oxford, he returned to Arkansas to teach constitutional law at the University of Arkansas. By 1939, at 34, he had become the youngest university president in the nation. Fulbright was elected to Congress in 1942 and gained a seat in the Senate two years later.

From the beginning of his political career, foreign affairs was his passion. As a freshman congressman, he authored the resolution that cleared the way for U.S. participation in the United Nations. This achievement gave him national prominence as an internationalist in a climate still dominated by isolationists. In 1946, as a member of the Senate Foreign Relations Committee, he steered a program through Congress that embodied his Wilsonian idealism—

the Fulbright Scholar international exchange program. He championed American liberal internationalism and was a believer in the "American century," that is, that America had the will and the power to make the world freer, more prosperous, and more just.

In the late 1940s and 1950s, Fulbright began to reflect the more conservative political climate in the United States concerning foreign affairs. During the cold war, he became an ardent supporter of interventionist policies designed to contain the threat of communism. He backed all the major cold war initiatives, such as the Truman Doctrine and American intervention in the Korean War. And, in 1954, his concern over Chinese expansionism prompted him to urge American intervention in Indochina in the event of a communist victory over the French.

In 1959, Fulbright became chairman of the Senate Foreign Relations Committee. In this powerful position, he remained highly supportive of America's global containment policies during the John Kennedy and Lyndon Johnson years. His 1963 book, *Prospects for the West,* rejoiced in the preeminence of American "world power and responsibility." In 1964, he not only voted for the Gulf of Tonkin resolution, but introduced the resolution into the Senate for President Johnson and expedited its passage as a demonstration of support for the president and his policies in Vietnam.

Although a cold warrior, Fulbright occasionally strayed from the governmental line. He tended to see "imperialist Russia," rather than "communism," as America's principal enemy. Although Fulbright believed that the United States should contain Soviet and Chinese expansionism, he did not believe that ideological differences created an unbridgeable gap between the United States and the communist nations. Instead, he foresaw a gradual adjustment between West and East through negotiations. In *Old Myths and New Realities* in 1964, Fulbright argued that the Cuban missile crisis and the U.S.-Soviet negotiation of the test-ban treaty demonstrated that the cold war could be resolved. Toward this end, he called for recognition of China and further negotiations with the Soviet Union. Furthermore, he did not fear all global change, drawing a distinction between Third World nationalism and communism. This complex and optimistic view, which lay submerged in Fulbright's thought during the 1950s, became the foundation of his dissent in the 1960s.

Fulbright's first major break with Lyndon Johnson came when the president deployed Marines in the Dominican Republic in 1965. Fulbright publicly criticized the Dominican intervention as being counterproductive to American interests, which consisted of promoting stability and peace in the region. He believed that by stifling change and supporting the status quo, American policy actually promoted radicalism and revolution as the only means of change in Latin America. Fulbright continued to believe in the progress and hope that the United States represented; however, he now dissented from the "methods" used to affect foreign policy and argued that the United States should support, rather than oppose, third-world nationalism.

His dissent over Vietnam finally led him to question the "ends" of U.S. cold war policy as well. Fulbright refused to see the Vietnam War as part of a monolithic Communist offensive. He suggested that a unified Vietnam under the nationalist rule of Ho Chi Minh and Vietnamese communism was compatible with American national interests, for it would restrain Chinese expansionism in Southeast Asia. He believed that U.S. refusal to recognize the new regime in China in 1949 was a fateful mistake. In January 1966, Fulbright began a series of hearings that placed him outside administration policy by using the Senate Foreign Relations Committee to educate the American public about Vietnam and U.S. foreign policy.

In *The Arrogance of Power* in 1966, Fulbright took the argument a step further and entirely abandoned the cold war framework of analysis. He argued that there were two Americas: one was generous, humane, and judicious; the other narrowly egotistical and self-righteous. For Fulbright, cold war policies and U.S. interventionism abroad indicated that an aggressive and self-righteous America was prevailing in U.S. foreign policy.

For the most part America has made good use of her blessings, especially in her internal life but also in her foreign relations. Having done so much and succeeded so well, America is now at that historical point at which a great nation is in danger of losing its perspective on what exactly is within the realm of its power and what is beyond it. Other great nations, reaching this critical juncture, have aspired to do too much, and by overextension of effort have declined and fallen.[A]

The United States, in other words, was beginning to suffer the fate of Rome, Britain, and other past imperial powers, where "power tends to confuse itself with virtue and a great nation is peculiarly susceptible to the idea that its power is a sign of God's favor, conferring upon it a special responsibility for other nations—to make them richer and happier and wise, to remake them, that is, in its own shining image."[B] Thus, U.S. foreign policy, especially as it was being executed in Vietnam, demonstrated an "arrogance of power" by acting as the world's policeman. "In so doing we are not living up to our capacity and promise as a civilized example for the world."[C]

The arrogance of U.S. foreign policy was a topic he continued to pursue in *The Crippled Giant* in 1972, discussing also its detrimental domestic consequences. Fulbright concluded that "Having begun the postwar period with the idealism of the United Nations Charter, we retreated in disillusion to the cold war, to the Truman Doctrine and its consummation in Vietnam, easing the transition by telling ourselves that we were not really abandoning the old values at all but simply applying them in more practical ways. Now, having failed most shockingly and dismally [in Vietnam], we are beginning to cast about for a new set of values."[D] Fulbright's

---

A. J. William Fulbright, *The Arrogance of Power* (New York: Vintage, 1966), p. 3.
B. Ibid.
C. Ibid., p. 22.
D. J. William Fulbright, *The Crippled Giant: American Foreign Policy and Its Domestic Consequences* (New York: Vintage, 1972), p. 177.

recommendation: "perhaps we will settle for an old idealism—the one we conceived and commended to the world but have never tried"—the liberal internationalism of the 1940s.[E]

Fulbright was severely criticized by conservatives and cold warriors. However, to liberals and members of the growing antiwar movement, Fulbright became something of a hero; he was the most prominent American leader to publicly criticize the administration's Vietnam policy and the containment policies that dominated the cold war. Fulbright helped to legitimize public dissent and promote a more open dialogue concerning the ends and means of U.S. foreign policy. Fulbright was ultimately defeated for reelection in 1974. Yet, his liberal internationalist perspective on world affairs and U.S. foreign policy remains a powerful force in motivating Americans during the post–Vietnam War and post–cold war years.

E. Ibid., p. 173.

SOURCES: J. William Fulbright, *Prospects for the West* (Cambridge, Mass.: Harvard University Press, 1963); J. William Fulbright, *Old Myths and New Realities* (New York: Random House, 1964); J. William Fulbright, *The Arrogance of Power* (New York: Vintage, 1966); J. William Fulbright, *The Crippled Giant: American Foreign Policy and Its Domestic Consequences* (New York: Vintage, 1972); and J. William Fulbright with Seth P. Tillman, *The Price of Empire* (New York: Pantheon, 1989).

---

experienced during the cold war years has been replaced by much less consistency and much more incoherence in U.S. foreign policy since Vietnam.[48]

Although U.S. *foreign economic policy* became "high" policy, with the breakdown of the Bretton Woods system in 1971, it has lacked much coherence over time. This is because of the increasing necessity for the government to address complex and intractable economic issues—such as inflation, unemployment, energy needs, deficits, and environmental concerns—in both the domestic and international arena. Presidents Nixon, Gerald Ford, and Jimmy Carter each have relied on different strategies at home and ad hoc approaches abroad to handle economic problems as they developed. Each attempted to maintain the stability of the international market economy by getting the multilateral support of the major allies—Western Europe, Canada, and Japan—for stopgap measures. In other words, U.S. foreign economic policy has lacked design and been defensive and reactive to domestic and international economic problems as they have arisen. The Reagan administration took a different approach, relying on a laissez-faire philosophy of minimal state intervention in the international political economy and emphasizing domestic economic growth as the key to expanding the global economy.

In some ways incoherence and inconsistency in U.S. foreign policy is even more visible in the *national security area*. The *Nixon and Ford administrations* represented the first real change in the global containment orientation of U.S. cold war policy. National security policy changed from the cold war emphasis on containment of Soviet communism to ensure global security to a "realpolitik" emphasis on counterbalancing the Soviet Union as a traditional great power to promote global stability and order. For Henry Kissinger, who for a time was both the national security adviser and the secretary of state under Presidents Nixon and Ford, the major threat was not communist expansion and Soviet hegemony but global instability, which Soviet interventionism could only exacerbate. Therefore, the key was not just to contain the Soviet threat through force, but also to encourage the Soviet Union to change from a revolutionary, expansionist global actor into a legitimate, status quo actor. This was to be done through a policy of **détente** based on the concept of "linkage": accommodation (such as the provision of prestige through summit meetings and economic assistance through trade, technology, and financing) when the Soviet Union was acting in accord with American desires; the threat and use of force when the Soviets were perceived as attempting to upset the existing balance of power.

There is disagreement over the extent to which
U.S. foreign policy changed during the Nixon and
Ford administrations. One school argues that the
Kissinger years were a period of continuity with earlier cold war policies because attempts were still
being made to contain the Soviet Union, although
not only through the use of force. Another school
argues that this was a time of discontinuity in U.S.
foreign policy because Kissinger downplayed the
threat of communism, emphasizing traditional great
power politics. Both schools shed light on the question, but tend to be incomplete. In fact, the
Kissinger years represented a time of both continuity and change in U.S. foreign policy—a period of
transition between the cold war policies of the past
and the post–cold war policies of Jimmy Carter.[49]

Although U.S. foreign policy during the Nixon
and Ford years of détente represented a change from
the cold war policies of global containment, the real
break in the cold war came in 1977 when the *Carter
administration* rejected containment as the basis of
its foreign policy. The people who initially staffed
the Carter administration no longer saw a bipolar
international system that pitted communism against
the free world in a global cold war, or a traditional
great power struggle between the Soviet Union and
the United States. This cold war perception of international relations was replaced by the first truly
post–cold war orientation in U.S. foreign policy
since the end of World War II. The Carter administration saw a world of complex interdependence in
which the United States would take the lead in the
building of a cooperative global community. They
downplayed the role of great powers, such as the Soviet Union, the utility of force, and preoccupations
with traditional security issues. Instead, Carter pursued a foreign policy of adjustment to international
change based on moral leadership and preventive
diplomacy, emphasizing human rights and negotiations instead of the use of force.

Although there was much disagreement during
the early 1980s as to the nature of the Carter administration's foreign policy, a broad consensus has recently emerged that the Carter administration entered office with an optimistic vision of global

change and liberal internationalist orientation. Disagreement exists, however, concerning to what extent the Carter administration's early foreign policy
abandoned the containment strategy.[50]

With the coming of the *Reagan administration*
in 1981, U.S. foreign policy returned to an emphasis
on global containment of Soviet communism
through the threat and use of force reminiscent of
the cold war era of the 1950s and 1960s, while re-
treating from multilateralism as well. The foreign
policy emphasis was with a large military buildup
and the restoration of cold war policies in order to
deter and challenge the Soviet Union in world politics. The Iran-Contra affair demonstrated the extent
to which the Reagan administration was dedicated
to fighting the cold war and "rolling back" Soviet-
supported communism.[51]

Comparing the goals and strategies under Presidents Nixon and Ford, Carter, and Reagan demonstrates that, unlike the cold war years, the post–
Vietnam War period has witnessed the initiation of
different foreign policy orientations by each new
administration. Given existing international and
domestic constraints, each administration has also
been forced to *moderate its initial policies with time.*
In the area of foreign economics, it was easy for the
Nixon, Ford, and Carter administrations to modify
their policies since they had never actually devised a
coherent strategy. However, the Reagan administration quickly found out that its unilateral supply-side
and free market approach did not sit well among allies abroad or many Americans at home, and was
forced to modify many of its policies during the latter part of the administration.

It is in national security policy, however, where
changes in policy over time within the same administration were most obvious. For example, by the
end of the Ford administration, the policy of détente was on the defensive. It was attacked by members of the Democratic party who were angry at
American intervention in Angola and by members
of Ford's own Republican party who perceived it as
appeasement of the Soviet Union. President Carter
came into office rejecting containment as the basis
of his foreign policy, only to reinstate it by the last

year of his administration following the Iran hostage crisis and the intervention of Soviet troops in Afghanistan. And although President Reagan came into office as a cold-warrior "hawk" ready to do battle with the "evil empire," he left office as an arms-control "dove," meeting four times with Mikhail Gorbachev, the general secretary of the Soviet Communist party, and signing the Intermediate Nuclear Forces Treaty.

Thus, the global era in U.S. foreign policy that began with American involvement in World War II has resulted in two global-oriented foreign policy periods separated by the Vietnam War. World War II and the rise of the cold war reflected international and domestic changes that produced twenty years of continuity in U.S. foreign policy. During this time, American national security policy was devoted to containing the threat of Soviet communism throughout the globe, supported by a foreign economic policy based on American leadership of the international political economy. The Vietnam War and the breakdown of the Bretton Woods system represented international and domestic changes that put in question the viability of the United States to promote a global containment policy and to maintain economic prosperity at home. During the post–Vietnam War period, unlike the cold war years, foreign economic policy has been restored to a significant place on the foreign policy agenda, different foreign policy initiatives have been taken by different administrations, and each administration has eventually been forced by circumstances outside its control to moderate its initial policies.

THE POST–COLD WAR ERA?

. . . .

With the collapse of communism in Eastern Europe and the collapse of the Soviet Union, the United States appears to have entered a new era in foreign policy—a post–cold war era beginning in the 1990s. U.S. foreign policy may have entered a time span where the contradictions between the legacy of America's expansive and cold war past, the implications of the tremendous changes that have enveloped the Soviet Union and Eastern Europe, and the uncertainty of domestic support need to be addressed and reconciled. In this respect, the end of the cold war has provided current and future administrations with new opportunities and constraints in its conduct of foreign policy.

Although the *Bush administration* has been accused of lacking global vision, Bush's foreign policy in fact appeared to be heavily influenced by a realpolitik and power politics approach to world politics, leading to a strategy that remained heavily conditioned by the cold war legacy of containment. Its inclination, states political scientist Charles Kegley, was "to look to the future with a vision inspired by the past, and to postpone the awesome task of developing a comprehensive policy response to the profound changes that have recently transpired."[52] Not surprisingly, no dominant and consistent foreign policy pattern prevailed during the Bush administration. Instead, the Bush administration displayed a "mixture of competence and drift, of tactical mastery set in a larger pattern of strategic indirection."[53]

These contradictory patterns were best epitomized by its foreign policy toward the end of the cold war issues and the Persian Gulf conflict. On the one hand, the Bush administration was very cautious and tentative in responding to global issues that were beyond the cold war. For example, the Bush administration elected to let Western European countries take the foreign policy initiative relative to the collapse of communism in Eastern Europe, the changes confronting the Soviet Union, the reunification of Germany, and the formal integration of the European Community. On the other hand, the Bush administration took the foreign policy initiative relative to international security issues more reminiscent of the past. For instance, the Bush administration's support for the People's Republic of China following Tiananmen Square, the American invasion of Panama, and the policy of brinksmanship and war in the Persian Gulf can best be understood from a power politics perspective in which American strategy remained heavily influenced by a reliance on the threat and use of force. In other words, the Bush administration's foreign policy appeared to be caught between the strong legacy of the cold war past and the great uncertainty of a post–cold war future.[54]

Since its coming to office in 1993, the *Clinton administration* has been accused of considerable vacillation and hesitancy in the conduct of U.S. foreign policy. However, the administration from the beginning has attempted to promote American leadership and a liberal international orientation abroad. The enlargement of democracy and the enlargement of the international market economy have been consistent themes throughout the administration.[55]

Nevertheless, efforts to promote a more "multilateral-oriented" foreign policy faced early setbacks, especially in Somalia. At the same time, President Clinton did manage to initiate several significant foreign policy actions in Haiti, Mexico, Bosnia, and the Middle East. So far major foreign policy failures have been avoided while the administration has chosen to highlight domestic policy and international economics. Most prominent in this regard were passage of NAFTA—the North American Free Trade Agreement—and the Uruguay round of the GATT agreement producing a World Trade Organization.

Despite its liberal internationalist orientation, the Clinton administration, very much like the Bush administration, has tended to become increasingly "reactive"—as opposed to "proactive"—abroad and, hence, U.S. foreign policy has been somewhat incoherent and inconsistent. There is little doubt that the United States will continue to have a major impact throughout the world and have a global-oriented foreign policy. But in the complexity and uncertainty of the post–cold war, presidents clearly have found it difficult to lead U.S. foreign policy for a sustained period of time, regardless of its internationalist orientation. It may simply be that the cold war era has been superseded by an increasingly complex and domestic environment in which the days of grand design have given way, despite the enormous power of the United States, to a more pragmatic time of muddling through.[56]

INTO THE TWENTY-FIRST CENTURY

· · · · · · · · · · · · · · ·

What explains the dominant patterns and policies in the history of U.S. foreign relations? Why does the United States have a long history of international involvement and expansion despite the rise of isolationist sentiment? Why did cold war policies prevail for twenty years following World War II? In what ways did the cold war patterns in U.S. foreign policy change in the post–Vietnam War era and why? How will the end of the cold war and the Persian Gulf War affect the future of U.S. foreign policy? Will the scope of U.S. involvement remain global? To what extent will the United States' national security and economic goals abroad change or remain the same? To what extent will the United States intervene and use force? To address these questions, one must understand the politics of U.S. foreign policy.

But before we jump into the center of the policymaking process, it is important to look at the larger setting and global context in which the foreign policy process takes place. Changes in the global milieu often set the stage for changes in government and society. Therefore, the next chapter examines the impact that the evolution of American resources, the global context, and the U.S. role throughout the world have on domestic politics and governmental policymaking. The impact of the end of the cold war and the war in the Persian Gulf is also discussed. This will provide us with a better understanding of the history, and the possible future, of the complex politics of U.S. foreign policy.

BIBLIOGRAPHIC ESSAY

· · · · · · · · · · · · · · ·

There is a massive amount of literature on the history of U.S. foreign policy. Valuable historical overviews are provided by Walter LaFeber, *The American Age: United States Foreign Policy at Home and Abroad Since 1750* (New York: W.W. Norton, 1989) and Richard W. Van Alstyne, *The Rising American Empire*

(Chicago: Quadrangle Books, 1965). Gregory Nobles provides an excellent overview of American continental expansion in *American Frontiers: Cultural Encounters and Continental Conquest* (New York: Hill and Wang, 1997). A valuable general reference source is *The Encyclopedia of U.S. Foreign Relations,* edited by Bruce W. Jentleson and Thomas G. Paterson (New York: Oxford University Press, 1997). More generally, James MacGregor Burns has produced a three-volume modern classic on the history of America: *The Vineyard of Liberty* (New York: Alfred A. Knopf, 1982), *The Workshop of Democracy* (New York: Alfred A. Knopf, 1985), and *The Crosswinds of Freedom* (New York: Alfred A. Knopf, 1989).

A good overview of America's growing internationalism following World War I can be found in William Cohen, *Empire Without Tears: America's Foreign Relations, 1921–1933* (New York: Alfred A. Knopf, 1987). Excellent discussions of the postwar aims of the Roosevelt administration and the origins of the cold war can be found in John Lewis Gaddis, *The United States and the Origins of the Cold War, 1941–1947* (New York: Columbia University Press, 1972), Daniel Yergin, *Shattered Peace: The Origins of the Cold War and the National Security State* (Boston: Houghton Mifflin, 1983), and Melvyn P. Leffler, *A Preponderance of Power: National Security, the Truman Administration, and the Cold War* (Stanford, Calif.: Stanford University Press, 1992). Richard A. Melanson, *Writing History and Making Policy: The Cold War, Vietnam, and Revisionism* (Lanham, Md.: University Press of America, 1983) provides an excellent overview of competing interpretations of the origins of the cold war. Informative descriptions and assessments of U.S. foreign policy since World War II can be found in Richard J. Barnet, *The Alliance: America-Europe-Japan, Makers of the Postwar World* (New York: Simon and Schuster, 1983), Seyom Brown, *The Faces of Power: Constancy and Change in Foreign Policy from Truman to Clinton* (New York: Columbia University Press, 1994), and Walter LaFeber, *America, Russia, and the Cold War 1948–1992* (New York: McGraw-Hill, 1993).

ENDNOTES

1. A.J. Bacevich, "Charles Beard, Properly Understood," *National Interest* (Spring 1994), p. 75.

2. Albert K. Weinberg, "The Historical Meaning of the American Doctrine of Isolation," *American Political Science Review* 34 (June 1940), p. 539.

3. Although many of the cases might be considered "minor" incidents, especially from a contemporary-day perspective, they all involved the "official" use of United States armed forces, involved conflictual situations with other states, and reflected an expression of American interests throughout the world.

4. Gregory H. Nobles, *American Frontiers: Cultural Encounters and Continental Conquest* (New York: Hill and Wang, 1997), p. 54.

5. See also Ian K. Steele, *Warpaths: Invasions of North America* (New York: Oxford University Press, 1994). For a more global perspective, see Geoffrey Barraclough, *An Introduction to Contemporary History* (London: Penguin, 1964); Torbjorn L. Knutsen, *A History of International Relations Theory* (Manchester: Manchester University Press, 1992); Hugh Thomas, *A History of the World* (New York: Harper, 1979); Eric Wolfe, *Europe and the People Without History* (Berkeley: University of California Press, 1982).

6. U.S., Declaration of Independence (July 4, 1776).

7. Nobles, *American Frontiers*, p. 91. See also Alan Brinkley, *The Unfinished Nation: A Concise History of the American People* (New York: McGraw-Hill, 1993); James MacGregor Burns, *The Vineyard of Liberty* (New York: Alfred A. Knopf, 1982); Walter LaFeber, *The American Age: U.S. Foreign Policy at Home and Abroad Since 1750* (New York: W.W. Norton, 1989).

8. Barbara W. Tuchman, *The First Salute: A View of the American Revolution* (New York: Ballantine, 1988).

9. For a standard, orthodox overview of U.S. Diplomatic history, see Thomas A. Bailey, *A Diplomatic History of the American People* (Englewood Cliffs, N.J.: Prentice Hall, 1980), and Samuel Flagg Bemis, *A Diplomatic History of the United States* (New York: Holt, Rinehart and Winston, 1965). For more critical, revisionist accounts, see Charles A. Beard, *The Idea of National Interest: An Analytical Study in American Foreign Policy* (Chicago: Quadrangle, 1934), LaFeber, *The American Age*, and Thomas G. Paterson, J. Garry Clifford, and Kenneth J. Hagan, *American Foreign Policy, A History* (Lexington, MA: D.C. Heath, 1983). Richard W. Van Alstyne, in *The Rising American Empire* (Chicago: Quadrangle Books, 1965), emphasizes the important role of nationalism and expansionism in the history of U.S. foreign policy. See also Walter A. McDougall, *Promised Land, Crusader State: The American En-*

counter with the World Since 1776 (Boston: Houghton Mifflin, 1997), and Paul A. Varg, *America, From Client State to World Power: Six Major Transitions in United States Foreign Relations* (Norman, Okla.: University of Oklahoma Press, 1990). Carl N. Degler, *Out of Our Past: The Forces That Shaped Modern America* (New York: Harper and Row, 1984) provides a valuable overview of U.S. foreign policy while, at the same time, placing it in the context of economic and social change in U.S. history. James MacGregor Burns has produced a three-volume modern classic on America's history: *The Vineyard of Liberty, The Workshop of Democracy* (New York: Alfred A. Knopf, 1985), and *The Crosswinds of Freedom* (New York: Alfred A. Knopf, 1989). An annotated bibliography to the literature is provided by Richard Dean Burns, ed., *Guide to American Foreign Relations Since 1700* (Santa Barbara, Calif.: ABC-Clio, 1983). See also Gerald K. Haines and J. Samuel Walker, editors, *American Foreign Relations: A Historiographical Review* (Westport, Conn.: Greenwood Press, 1981).

10. LaFeber, *The American Age*, pp. 11–12.
11. LaFeber, *The American Age*, p. 12.
12. Nobles, *American Frontiers*, pp. x–xi.
13. Nobles, *American Frontiers*, pp. 93, 94.
14. LaFeber, *The American Age*, p. 10.
15. James M. McPherson, "Bib Little Big Horn," *The New Republic* (July 29, 1996), p. 40.
16. But as pointed out by Nobles, developments were rather complex. "Euro-Americans [such as the English, the French, and later Americans] fought among themselves for control of the continent, and they often enlisted Indian allies to help them defeat fellow Europeans. . . . By the same token, the natives the Europeans lumped together as Indians were in reality a remarkably diverse people encompassing many different cultural and tribal groups. They had different belief systems, different ways of life, and different relationships with Europeans. Like Europeans, they could be honorable allies or vicious enemies, equally capable of creating beauty and committing atrocity." Nobles, *American Frontiers*, pp. 12–13.
17. Nobles, *American Frontiers*, p. 242. As he states on p. 120, "Government policy did not call for the extermination of Indians, only their cultural transformation. That is, in order to live peaceably in the United States, Indians would be pressured to give up their language, their way of life, and much of their land. In the minds of Jefferson and other leaders, such a policy was in the

Indians' best interests, offering them incorporation into 'civilized' society. Yet, as the government extended this open hand of philanthropy, it kept in the background the closed fist of force."

18. As stated by Nobles, "To be sure, the relationship between settlers and the state was often a troubled, even tumultuous one, and the desires of independent-minded people often clashed with the designs of government officials for 'orderly' settlement. Still, whatever the underlying uneasiness, common people and policymakers ultimately became allies in a process of conquest." Nobles, *American Frontiers*, p. 15.
19. Richard W. Van Alstyne, *The Rising American Empire* (Norton, 1974), p. v.
20. Bailey, "America's Emergence as a World Power," p. 9.
21. Ibid, p. 3.
22. Van Alstyne, *The Rising American Empire*, p. 87.
23. Van Alstyne, *The Rising American Empire*, p. 100.
24. Ibid, p. 170.
25. Alfred E. Eckes, Jr., *Opening America's Market: U.S. Foreign Trade Policy Since 1776* (Chapel Hill, N.C.: University of North Carolina, 1995), p. 1.
26. Ibid, p. 23. For a historical overview, see also Charles P. Kindleberger, "U.S. Foreign Economic Policy, 1776–1976," *Foreign Affairs* (January 1977), pp. 395–417.
27. Van Alstyne, *The Rising American Empire*, p. 126.
28. Richard W. Alstyne, *The American Empire: Its Historical Pattern and Evolution* (London: Historical Association, General Series Number 43 Pamphlet, 1960), p. 10.
29. See, e.g., Anders Stephanson, *Manifest Destiny: American Expansion and the Empire of Right* (New York: Hill and Wang, 1995).
30. Van Alstyne, *The Rising American Empire*, p. 146.
31. Van Alstyne, *The Rising American Empire*, p. 166.
32. Van Alstyne, *The Rising American Empire*, p. 125. See also Emily S. Rosenberg, *Spreading the American Dream: American Economic and Cultural Expansion, 1890–1945* (New York: Hill and Wang, 1982).
33. According to Van Alstyne, "There has never been a satisfactory explanation as to why this attack took place. The direct order to attack was given, February 25, 1898, by Theodore Roosevelt, who was temporarily occupying the Secretary of the Navy's chair in Washington. This was ten days after the mysterious sinking of the battleship *Maine* in Havana harbour, but nearly two months before the start of hostilities." Van Alstyne, *The Rising American Empire*, p. 185. See

also J. Rogers Hollingsworth, editor, *American Expansion in the Late Nineteenth Century: Colonialist or Anticolonialist?* (New York: Holt, Rinehart and Winston, 1968).

34. See, for example, William Appleman Williams, *The Tragedy of American Diplomacy* (New York: Norton, 1988).

35. William I. Cohen, *Empire Without Tears: America's Foreign Relations, 1921–1933* (New York: Alfred A. Knopf, 1987), p. xii.

36. Cohen, *Empire Without Tears*, p. 54.

37. Cohen, *Empire Without Tears*, p. 28.

38. Cohen, *Empire Without Tears*, p. 41. See also David A. Lake, "International Economic Structures and American Foreign Economic Policy, 1887–1934," *World Politics* 35 (July 1983), pp. 517-543.

39. Cohen, *Empire Without Tears*, xii.

40. The original agreement at Bretton Woods called for the creation of an International Trade Organization (ITO). But due to the opposition of the U.S. Congress, the GATT was subsequently created in its place. See Richard N. Gardner, *Sterling-Dollar Diplomacy in Current Perspective: The Origins and the Prospects of Our International Economic Order* (New York: Columbia University Press, 1980), and G. John Ikenberry, "A World Economy Restored: Expert Consensus and the Anglo-American Post War Settlement," *International Organization* 46 (Winter 1992), pp. 289–321.

41. A good overview of the literature is provided by Mark A. Stoler, "World War II Diplomacy in Historical Writing: Prelude to Cold War," in Gerald K. Haines and J. Samuel Walker, eds., *American Foreign Relations: A Historiographical Review* (Westport, Conn.: Greenwood Press, 1981), pp. 187–206. See also Robert Dallek, *Franklin Roosevelt and American Foreign Policy, 1932–1945* (Oxford: Oxford University Press, 1979), and John Lewis Gaddis, *The United States and the Origins of the Cold War, 1941–1947,* (New York: Columbia University Press, 1972).

42. For standard orthodox accounts of the development of U.S. foreign policy since World War II, see Stephen E. Ambrose, *Rise to Globalism* (Middlesex, England: Penguin Books, 1983); Seyom Brown, *The Faces of Power: Constancy and Change in United State Foreign Policy from Truman to Reagan* (New York: Columbia University Press, 1983); John Lewis Gaddis, *Strategies of Containment: A Critical Appraisal of Postwar American National Security Policy* (Oxford: Oxford University Press, 1982); and John Spanier and Steven W.

Hook, *American Foreign Policy Since World War II* (Washington: Congressional Quarterly Press, 1995). For more critical and revisionist accounts, which often integrate economic motives, see Richard J. Barnet, *The Alliance: America-Europe-Japan, Makers of the Postwar World* (New York: Simon and Schuster, 1983); Walter LaFeber, *America, Russia, and the Cold War 1948–1990* (New York: McGraw-Hill, 1991); and James A. Nathan and James K. Oliver, *United States Foreign Policy and World Order* (Glenview, Ill.: Scott, Foresman, 1989).

43. The origins and development of the cold war is a topic of unending interest to scholars. Richard A. Melanson, *Writing History and Making Policy: The Cold War, Vietnam, and Revisionism* (Lanham, Md.: University Press of America, 1983), and J. Samuel Walker, "Historians and Cold War Origins: The New Consensus," in Gerald K. Haines and J. Samuel Walker, eds., *American Foreign Relations: A Historiographical Review* (Westport, Conn.: Greenwood Press, 1981), pp. 207–236, provide excellent literature reviews of the origins of the cold war. They cover the orthodox interpretation that the Soviets caused the cold war, revisionist accounts emphasizing the U.S. role in contributing to the cold war, and postrevisionism, an increasingly popular interpretation that combines orthodox and, especially, revisionist explanations. Daniel Yergin, a postrevisionist, has written an excellent book, *Shattered Peace: The Origins of the Cold War and the National Security State* (Boston: Houghton Mifflin, 1983), explaining the rise of American cold war beliefs and the national security state in terms of the bureaucratic and domestic politics that dominated the times. See also Melvyn P. Leffler, *A Preponderance of Power: National Security, the Truman Administration, and the Cold War* (Stanford, Calif.: Stanford University Press, 1992).

44. Godfrey Hodgson, *America in Our Time* (New York: Vintage, 1976), p. 32.

45. On the assumptions behind deterrence theory and the global strategy of containment, see Gaddis, *Strategies of Containment*; Alexander L. George and Richard Smoke, *Deterrence in American Foreign Policy: Theory and Practice* (New York: Columbia University Press, 1974); and Bruce W. Jentleson, "American Commitments in the Third World: Theory vs. Practice," *International Organization* 41 (Autumn 1987), pp. 667–704. See also Michael Mastanduno, "Strategies of Economic Containment: U.S. Trade Relations with

the Soviet Union," *World Politics* 37 (July 1985), pp. 503–31.

46. See, for example, Joan Edelman Spero, *The Politics of International Economic Relations* (New York: St. Martin's Press, 1997).

47. See, e.g., Alfred E. Eckes, "Trading American Interests," *Foreign Affairs* (Fall 1992), pp. 135–154, and Yergin, Shattered Peace, especially chapter 12. It is interesting to note that one of the consequences of the distinction between high and low policy is that most scholars of U.S. foreign policy and world politics since World War II, including those cited above, tend to emphasize American national security policy. This has begun to change recently as foreign and international economics have become more prominent. Clearly, it is necessary to integrate both national security and foreign economic policy in order to arrive at a more comprehensive understanding of U.S. foreign policy. This book attempts to integrate both aspects and will discuss both areas of the foreign policy process, although I too am guilty of spending more time on national security issues.

48. Many scholars tend to see continuity in U.S. foreign policy since World War II. Most orthodox scholars tend to emphasize the permanence of containment as the basis of U.S. foreign policy since World War II; many revisionist scholars tend to emphasize the constant role of American economic expansion and management of the international political economy since the war. However, an increasing number of scholars and analysts have begun to conclude that the Vietnam War represented an important break in U.S. foreign policy in the post–World War II period. For those who emphasize continuity during the cold war years and change since the Vietnam War, see Godfrey Hodgson, *America in Our Time* (New York: Vintage Books, 1976); Richard A. Melanson, *American Foreign Policy Since the Vietnam War: The Search for Consensus from Nixon to Clinton* (Armonk, N.Y.: M.E. Sharpe, 1996); Nathan and Oliver, *United States Foreign Policy and World Order*; Kenneth A. Oye, Robert L. Lieber, and Donald Rothchild, eds., *Eagle Resurgent? The Reagan Era in American Foreign Policy* (Boston: Little Brown and Co., 1987); Jerry W. Sanders, *Peddlers of Crisis: The Committee on the Present Danger and the Politics of Containment* (Boston: South End Press, 1983); and John W. Spanier and Steven W. Hook, *American Foreign Policy Since World War II.*

49. See Seymour Hersh, *The Price of Power: Kissinger in the Nixon White House* (New York: Summit Books, 1983); Stanley Hoffmann, *Primacy or World Order: American Foreign Policy Since the Cold War* (New York: McGraw-Hill, 1978); Harvey Starr, *Henry Kissinger: Perceptions of International Politics* (Lexington, Ky.: University of Kentucky Press, 1980); and Stephen G. Walker, "The Interface Between Beliefs and Behavior: Henry Kissinger's Operational Code and the Vietnam War." *Journal of Conflict Resolution* 21 (1977), pp. 129–68.

50. See Jerel A. Rosati, "Jimmy Carter, A Man Before His Time? The Emergence and Collapse of the First Post–Cold War Presidency." *Presidential Studies Quarterly* 23 (Summer 1993), pp. 459–76; Jerel A. Rosati, *The Carter Administration's Quest for Global Community: Beliefs and Their Impact on Behavior,* (Columbia, S.C.: University of South Carolina Press, 1987); and Gaddis Smith, *Morality, Reason, and Power: American Diplomacy in the Carter Years,* (New York: Hill and Wang, 1986).

51. Although memoirs, biographies, and articles have been written, few major works have been produced on the Reagan administration's foreign policy. For an insightful analysis of Reagan's foreign policy in the context of the post–Vietnam War years, see Terry L. Deibel, "Reagan's Mixed Legacy," *Foreign Policy* 75 (Summer 1989), pp. 34–55; Kenneth Oye, "Constrained Confidence and the Evolution of Reagan's Foreign Policy" in Oye, Lieber, and Rothchild, *Eagle Resurgent?*, pp. 3–39; James M. Scott, *Deciding to Intervene: The Reagan Doctrine and American Foreign Policy* (Durham, N.C.: Duke University Press, 1996); Robert W. Tucker, "Reagan's Foreign Policy," *Foreign Affairs* (American and the World 1988/89), pp. 1–27; and Fareed Zakaria, "The Reagan Strategy of Containment," *Political Science Quarterly* 105 (Fall 1990), pp. 373–96.

52. Charles W. Kegley, Jr., "The Bush Administration and the Future of American Foreign Policy: Pragmatism, or Procrastination?" *Presidential Studies Quarterly* 19 (Fall 1989), p. 730. See also Michael Mandelbaum, "The Bush Foreign Policy," *Foreign Affairs* 70 (America and the World, 1990/91), pp. 5–22.

53. Terry L. Deibel, "Bush's Foreign Policy: Mastery and Inaction," *Foreign Policy* 84 (Fall 1991), p. 3.

54. This is reminiscent of the Truman administration following World War II trying to cope with a postwar future of great uncertainty and conflict.

55. For an overview of the Clinton administration's initial foreign policy orientation, see, for example, Anthony Lake, "From Containment to Enlargement," *U.S. Department of State Dispatch* 4:39 (September 27, 1993), pp. 658–64; Owen Harries, "My So-called Foreign Policy," *The New Republic* (October 10, 1994); and *A National Security Strategy of Engagement and Enlargement* (Washington, D.C.: U.S. Government Printing Office, July 1994).

56. See Mark Danner, "Marooned in the Cold War: America, the Alliance, and the Quest for a Vanished World," *World Policy Journal* (Fall 1997), pp. 1–23; Christopher Layne, "From Preponderance to Offshore Balancing: America's Future Grand Strategy," *International Security* 22 (Summer 1997), pp. 86–124; Jerel Rosati, "United States Leadership Into the Next Millennium: A Question of Politics," *International Journal* (Spring 1997), pp. 297–315; Benjamin Schwarz, "The Vision Thing: Sustaining the Unsustainable," *World Policy Journal* (Winter 1994/95), pp. 101–121.

CHAPTER 3

....

THE GLOBAL CONTEXT AND
AMERICAN POWER

*O*ur understanding of the complex politics of U.S. foreign policy would be incomplete if it were limited to the two perspectives that will be the focus of this book: the government and policymaking process, and the society and domestic politics. It is the interaction of the government, the society, and the larger context in which foreign policy is made that allows one to fully understand the complex politics of U.S. foreign policy. Consequently, it is necessary to examine the role of the global environment and American power in which domestic politics and the government policymaking process take place.

Changes in the global environment and American power throughout the twentieth century set the stage for continuity and change in the politics of U.S. foreign policy throughout society and government, affecting the president's ability to govern and the demands of national security versus democracy.

Thus, the historical and global context play a crucial role in affecting the complex politics of U.S. foreign policy and will continue to do so in the future.

INFLUENCE ON GOVERNMENT
AND SOCIETY

....

The **global context**—or setting or environment or milieu—refers to phenomena beyond or external to the institutions, beliefs, and processes of human interaction within government and throughout society. The context, therefore, includes such elements as a country's resources, its level of technology, and the larger global arena of which the United States is but a part. Clearly, developments in the global environment and American power both directly and indirectly affect the political process throughout society and the government in the making of U.S. foreign policy.

Although frequently obscure in the causal chain of events and hence difficult to ascertain, *the environment plays a significant role in the politics of U.S. foreign policy in two principal ways.* First, global patterns set the "underlying" conditions or parameters of likely U.S. foreign policy. For example, the general patterns that prevail throughout the globe affect American power and the international role of the United States, thus setting the context in which the politics of U.S. foreign policy operates in society and government.[1] Second, particular events and relationships occurring throughout the world often have an "immediate" impact on domestic politics and the policymaking process within the United States. **International crises**, for example, often play an influential role in the politics of U.S. foreign policy.[2] It should be pointed out that specific events and relationships tend to be symptomatic of larger, general patterns in world politics. Therefore, both general patterns and immediate events in the American context affect one another and are often mutually reinforcing.

The underlying and immediate impact of the global context on politics occurs in two ways: through the perceptions that people have of the world and by directly affecting the performance and outcome of foreign policy behavior. This distinction has been referred to by Harold and Margaret Sprout in *The Ecological Perspective on Human Affairs* as the difference between the **"psychological environment"** and the **"objective environment."** As they explain it, "So far as we can determine, environmental factors (both nonhuman and social) can affect human activities in only two ways: such factors can be perceived, reacted to, and taken into account by the human individual or individuals under consideration. In this way, and in this way only . . . environmental factors can be said to 'influence,' or to 'condition,' or otherwise to 'affect' human values and preferences, moods, and attitudes, choices and decision." On the other hand, environmental factors limit the execution of human undertakings. "Such limitations on performance, accomplishment, outcome, or operational result may not—often do

not—derive from or depend upon the individual's perception or other psychological behavior."[3]

The global context or environment, in other words, sets the parameters of opportunities and constraints that shape the perceptions of Americans in government and throughout society concerning the world, affecting probable courses of U.S. foreign policy action. The nature of the global environment and American power also determines the likelihood that the pursuit of U.S. foreign policy will be successful abroad. Under both circumstances, the context heavily circumscribes the politics of U.S. foreign policy.

Together, the interaction of the global context, government, and society are responsible for the politics of U.S. foreign policy. In this respect, the evolution of American power and the global environment set the stage or setting for the patterns in the politics of U.S. foreign policy that we are to discuss throughout this book. One cannot, therefore, fully understand continuity and change, the president's ability to govern, and the evolving tension between national security and democracy in the making of U.S. foreign policy, especially since World War II, without understanding the key patterns that have transpired in the evolution of American power and the global environment.

Although there are numerous ways to organize these larger contextual patterns, it is useful to speak in terms of *three sets of developments, or major stages, in the evolution of the global environment and American power that have been dominant throughout the twentieth century:*

1. The rise of the cold war era in world politics;
2. The rise of greater global complexity; and
3. The rise of a post–cold war era in world politics.

These historical developments in the global environment and American power have set the stage for continuity and change in the politics of U.S. foreign policy. The rise of a cold war in world politics was instrumental in affecting the development of the foreign policy process following the Second World War. The subsequent rise of global complexity was consequential in stimulating the foreign policy changes that have occurred since Vietnam. The collapse of the cold war, likewise, has set the context for the future politics of foreign policy as the United States enters the twenty-first century.

THE COLD WAR ERA IN WORLD POLITICS

· · · · · · · · · · · · · · ·

A number of significant developments in the global context and American power have played an important role in the politics of U.S. foreign policy during the postwar years. Of these, *two major global developments stand out:*

1. The rise of the East-West conflict;
2. The rise of American power.

These developments precipitated a number of events and relationships throughout the globe that played a prominent role in the politics of U.S. foreign policy during the late 1940s and the 1950s. Together, the interaction of these global developments, along with domestic developments within American society and government in the postwar years, produced what is often referred to as the "cold war" era in world politics.

THE RISE OF THE EAST-WEST CONFLICT

The rise of the East-West conflict occurred following World War II with the increasing domination of the United States and the Soviet Union in world politics. This development coincided with *the demise of the European empires*, whose roots lay deep in the past.[4]

With the rise of technology and industrialization in Europe since the fifteenth century, European countries—such as Spain, Portugal, the Netherlands, France, and Great Britain—grew in power and came to dominate world politics. These countries were responsible for what has been called within Western civilization the "age of discovery and colonization." They extended their power throughout the planet, colonizing people and territory to form vast European empires (including throughout North America). Hence, European power rivalries and wars had profound consequences for world politics.

World War I and World War II represented the twentieth-century struggle for European and global hegemony. Entering the twentieth century, France and, especially, Great Britain were the two global powers who dominated the global status quo. At the same time, Japan and Germany rapidly grew in power and challenged Great Britain, France, and the status quo to acquire their "place in the sun." The result was war on a global scale. Ironically, rather than creating a new German and Japanese hegemony or restoring the old European hegemony, the two world wars contributed to the demise of Europe as the center of world politics.

With the decline of Europe, the Soviet Union and the United States filled the political vacuum. Actually, *the Soviet Union and the United States grew in power throughout the nineteenth and twentieth centuries.* As we briefly discussed in chapter 2, the United States began as a new, liberal nation (gaining independence from the British empire), expanded westward to become a continental power by the mid-nineteenth century, attained regional power status by the turn of the century, and ultimately emerged as a global power by mid-twentieth century. As the United States expanded westward and industrialized, a very similar process occurred in Russia (and the Soviet Union): it became a Eurasian power by expanding eastward and industrializing (at a less dynamic pace than the United States) under both the czars and then Bolshevism. Therefore, the decline of European power was accompanied by the rise of the Soviet Union and the United States in world affairs.

The ascendance of the Soviet Union and the United States in the face of the European collapse *made an American-Soviet conflict of some type virtually inevitable for a variety of reasons.* In response to the rise of Adolf Hitler, the Soviet Union and the United States were cautious partners during World War II who found themselves in an "alliance of convenience"—an alliance that would have great difficulty surviving the postwar peace. For one thing, the war played out differently for each country: the

United States focused its initial efforts in the Pacific and prospered tremendously from the war; in contrast the Soviet Union bore the brunt of the European fighting and saw its country ravaged by the conflict. In addition, the fate of Europe—the world's industrial heartland over the previous centuries, whose economies were destroyed and social fabric was torn apart by the war—was determined by American and Soviet power. This set the stage for territorial disputes when American-led allied forces prevailed in Western Europe while Soviet-led forces occupied Eastern Europe with Germany split in two (as was the case with Korea in Asia). Finally, American and Soviet leaders came from societies with different histories, different value systems, and different postwar goals. U.S.-led efforts, for instance, to promote an international political economic order reflecting its liberal ideology were in contradiction to Soviet postwar goals that emphasized spheres-of-influence, the imposition of so-called friendly communist neighboring regimes, and domestic reconstruction. With the end of war, therefore, near-perfect conditions existed for the development of mutual suspicion and hostility, centered in Europe, between the Soviet Union and the United States.

Specific international events and crises reflecting these World War II and postwar developments impacted domestic politics and the government policymaking process in such a way that they spurred the rise of the cold war. Within the United States, for example, disputes over postwar economic reconstruction, the German question, the rise of communism in Eastern Europe, the Soviet-American conflict over Iran, Greece, and Turkey, the fall of Chiang Kai-shek and the Nationalist government in China, the North Korean attack on South Korea, and the Soviet explosion of an atomic bomb all contributed to the growing cold war environment both abroad and at home. With these events, the debate over American foreign policy that emerged following the war was soon dominated by a view that no longer saw the Soviet Union as an ally, but an evil enemy attempting to achieve world empire.[5]

Therefore, in response to these international developments and events, U.S. foreign policy be-

came global in scope and increasingly became oriented toward the perceived need to contain the threat posed by the Soviet Union and communism throughout the globe. These events and policies were accompanied by the governmental and societal patterns that will be discussed throughout the book, such as the rise of McCarthyism, the development of the anticommunist consensus, the rise of the national security bureaucracy and ethos, and the growth of presidential power.

These developments in global context, government, and domestic society were mutually reinforcing in the politics of U.S. foreign policy during the cold war years. Events during the 1950s and early 1960s—such as the Hungarian uprising, the rise of Third World nationalism and nonalignment, the rise of Fidel Castro in Cuba, the launching of the Soviet satellite *Sputnik*, the Cuban missile crisis, and the war in Indochina—fed American fears, influenced American politics, and promoted continuity in the cold war politics of U.S. foreign policy. Americans throughout government and society saw a "free world," led by the United States, pitted against the "totalitarian world," led by the Soviet Union, in a global cold war throughout the 1950s and early 1960s. Hence, the rise of the East-West conflict gave rise to presidential preeminence in the making of U.S. foreign policy, allowing the demands of national security to prevail over the demands of democracy.

THE RISE OF AMERICAN POWER

The politics of U.S. foreign policy also were affected heavily by the rise of American power throughout the world. As discussed in chapter 2, the United States had steadily grown more powerful since its independence, increasing the scope of its foreign policy involvement from a continental to a regional orientation. By the twentieth century, the United States clearly had become one of the world's "great powers." Yet, it was not until the events of World War II that the United States fully entered the global era in its foreign policy.

Following the Second World War the United States was able to pursue a policy of global containment because it was clearly the most powerful country in the world—possibly in the history of the world. While Europe, the Soviet Union, and Japan lost millions of people and saw their economies devastated by war, the United States suffered much less loss of human life. More importantly, however, the war effort lifted the American economy out of the Great Depression of the 1930s and catapulted it into unprecedented prosperity. Clearly, the United States was the global power or "superpower" of its time, setting the context for the politics of U.S. foreign policy that would prevail during the cold war era.

While the late 1940s and 1950s were the height of American power throughout the world, the power of the Soviet Union was much more limited throughout the globe. The Soviet Union both benefited and suffered from the war. Although the Soviet empire expanded throughout much of Eastern Europe, the Soviet Union had to recover from the devastation of the war—twenty million people died during the conflict and the economy was destroyed. The Soviet Union developed a formidable military as a result of World War II, but it was predominantly a land army, limited to the continents of Europe and Asia. It has been argued that the Soviet Union's greatest asset was the ideological appeal of communism, which was potentially global in nature. Ultimately, however, the economic, military, and political capabilities of the Soviet Union made it a Eurasian power throughout the cold war years, especially during the period immediately following the war.[6]

United States economic, military, and political power, on the other hand, was immense and far-reaching following the war and expanded throughout the 1950s. In the immediate postwar years, *the American economy* was the most powerful in the history of the world. American economic production was the key to allied success in the war and was responsible for producing almost half of the world's gross national product (GNP) following the conflict. As stated by Godfrey Hodgson:

In 1945, the United States was bulging with an abundance of every resource that held the key to power in the modern world: with land, food, raw materials, industrial plant, monetary reserves, scientific talent, and trained manpower. It was in the war years that the United States shot ahead of all its rivals economically. In four years, national income, national wealth, and industrial production all doubled or more than doubled. In the same period, . . . every other industrial nation came out of the war poorer and weaker than when it went in.[7]

Globally, American multinational corporations and financial investment, which had been expanding since the turn of the century, came to dominate the postwar international marketplace.[8]

This allowed the United States to develop a large military and intelligence capability whose scope of activities was worldwide. Over half of an expanded federal budget, in fact, was devoted to the national security bureaucracy during the 1950s. Furthermore, a large portion of the American economy was placed on a war-footing with the development of a military-industrial-scientific infrastructure in support of the demands of national security. These developments eventually provided the president and the executive branch with the capability to pursue and implement a global policy based on the strategy of containment.

The importance of the global context on the politics of U.S. foreign policy and American power can also be seen in areas traditionally considered of a domestic nature. Major investments by the U.S. government, for example, were also made—in the name of national security—in transportation and education to strengthen American capabilities in support of an activist foreign policy. The United States experienced considerable *transportation* bottlenecks during World War II due to its dependence on an aging railroad system. Therefore, one of the major purposes behind the creation of the interstate highway system in the 1950s, with 90 percent of the funding provided by the federal government, was to create the means to efficiently and reliably transport military troops and equipment across the country in times of national emergency and war.

Similarly, much of the expansion that took place in *higher education* during the 1960s was fueled by the *Sputnik*-stimulated fear that the United States was falling behind the Soviet Union in science and technology. In response, a major effort was made by the U.S. government to support higher education. For example, the U.S. government initiated a financial aid system to increase college enrollments which began with the offering of National Defense Student Loans (NDSLs), as they were first called.

United States *military and political clout* following the war was considerably strengthened throughout the world and affected its foreign policy. The United States government and American multinational corporations dominated the international political economy of the so-called free world. As the French and British empires collapsed, American power usually filled the vacuum and replaced European power, as occurred in Turkey, Iran, and Vietnam. The U.S. government, in fact, began to negotiate what became an extensive system of alliances and military bases to permanently deploy American troops overseas in noncolonized areas.

The development of international law and organizations was heavily influenced by the United States in the postwar world as well, symbolized by the creation of the United Nations (and Bretton Woods) system, including the Security Council, General Assembly, International Bank for Reconstruction and Development (the World Bank), International Monetary Fund (IMF), and the General Agreement on Trade and Tariffs (GATT). America's moral appeal as the victorious country promoting a liberal world order was also widespread following the war, especially in Western Europe.

The United States was so powerful following the war that it has been referred to not only as a great power or a superpower, but as the **hegemonic power** of its time.[9] In the *more common language* used by American leaders and the general public, the United States was considered the "world's policeman" and the "world's banker." American power was seen as so immense during the 1950s that the twentieth century was often referred to as the "American century." The consequence of all these developments meant that the rise of American power provided the means and supported the perception that the United States could intervene throughout the world to contain Soviet communist aggression, could defeat threats to the status quo arising from political instability and insurgency, and could promote "nation-building" in Third World countries in accordance with the American liberal model of political and economic development.

The immensity of American power, symbolized by its nuclear capability and its widespread military presence abroad, created incredibly high expectations of foreign policy success. Consequently, policy failure, which did occur—such as with the Korean War—produced much political frustration, contributing to such developments as the rise of McCarthyism in American politics. For as powerful and hegemonic as the United States became during the postwar years, it, nevertheless, did not become so powerful and omnipotent that the U.S. could fully control its destiny and the destiny of others in world affairs.[10]

The world, despite the rise of a cold war as the overarching issue and the flowering of American power, remained vast and complex in many ways. Differences existed among American allies, nationalism was increasing throughout the world, international organizations gained a life of their own, the opposition of adversaries was often formidable, the complex politics of U.S. foreign policy compromised or constrained strategy and programs abroad, and there was always the uncertain role of chance or fortune in world politics. Therefore, United States foreign policy was pursued in the complex environment of world politics with no guarantees of success. But clearly, the 1950s represented the height of American power in both cold war politics at home and cold war policies abroad; and although far from omnipotent, the United States was at the apex of its global power and was overwhelmingly the single most powerful actor on the global stage.

In sum, the major environmental developments during the cold war era in world politics discussed above set the underlying and immediate stage for the politics of U.S. foreign policy. The expansion of American power, coupled with the rise of the East-West conflict, contributed to the growth of presidential power and the prevalence of the demands of national security in American politics that became the foundation of a global policy of containment during the Truman, Eisenhower, Kennedy, and Johnson administrations. At the same time, developments in government and throughout society in the politics of U.S. foreign policy contributed to the rise of the East-West conflict and the exercise of American power abroad. Therefore, a symbiotic process took place between government, society, and the global context that interacted to produce the complex politics of U.S. foreign policy that came to dominate the cold war era.

THE RISE OF GREATER GLOBAL COMPLEXITY
. . . .

During the 1960s, certain trends in the global environment and American power became increasingly consequential for the politics of U.S. foreign policy. *Two general global developments stand out in world politics:*

1. The rise of global pluralism and interdependence, and
2. The relative decline of American power.

These developments resulted in greater global complexity, deeply affecting domestic politics and the governmental policymaking process. A more pluralistic and interdependent world, combined with the decline of American power, made it increasingly difficult for the United States to successfully pursue its cold war policies abroad—best illustrated by the American failure in the Vietnam War and the ending of the Bretton Woods economic system based on fixed currency rates and the gold standard. Thus, the rise of global complexity contributed to foreign policy failures and changes in the politics of U.S. foreign policy that came about since the Vietnam War.

The Vietnam War represented both the height of the cold war era and existence of much greater global complexity. From the late 1940s to the mid-1960s, the American effort to contain communism in Vietnam and Americanize the war was symptomatic of the rise of the East-West conflict and American power. By the late 1960s, however, it was also

becoming increasingly clear that U.S. failure to win the war reflected the rise of a more complex world and the decline of American power. The American failure in Vietnam, along with other events of the 1960s and 1970s, triggered the rise of a more pluralistic foreign policy process within the United States. This has made it difficult for presidents to successfully govern foreign policy as experienced by Richard Nixon, Gerald Ford, Jimmy Carter, and Ronald Reagan, as we will discuss in chapter 4, and contributed to changes in the conduct of U.S. foreign policy, between and within administrations, as discussed in chapter 2. Together, the rise of complexity abroad and pluralism at home have reinforced the dominant patterns in the politics of U.S. foreign policy that have prevailed since Vietnam.

THE RISE OF GLOBAL PLURALISM AND INTERDEPENDENCE

Since the end of World War II, the world also has grown in complexity. Among the most important global developments have been the economic recovery and rise of Western Europe and Japan, the rise of the Organization of Petroleum Exporting Countries (OPEC), new industrializing nations and other actors in the international political economy, the growth of Third World independence and nationalism, and the diffusion of technology and armaments worldwide. As a consequence of these global developments, it has become more difficult for great powers to successfully exercise influence abroad, especially through the use of force, and economic issues have climbed to the top of the global agenda alongside national security issues—both impacting on U.S. foreign policy. Therefore, the East-West conflict between the United States and the Soviet Union that once dominated world politics during the 1950s was joined by the rise of global pluralism and interdependence. *These global developments did not occur overnight, but evolved over time and have historical roots.*[11]

The rise of global pluralism and interdependence was heavily a function of the resurgence of

Europe and Japan in world affairs. Although the European and Japanese economies were destroyed by the war, it was only a matter of time before economic recovery took place, given their technological know-how and previous level of economic development. Economic recovery was fostered by American assistance provided through the Marshall Plan, the opening of the American economy to foreign imports, and the U.S. bearing a disproportionate share of the defense burden, including the stationing of American troops abroad. By the 1960s Europe—especially West Germany—and Japan had become prominent forces in the international political economy. In fact, the European and Japanese economies became so strong relative to the American economy that the Bretton Woods system—the international economic system that had developed following World War II, based on fixed exchange rates and free trade—no longer became sustainable by the early 1970s.

In addition, other developments contributed to the rise of pluralism and interdependence in the international political economy. Newly industrializing countries, such as South Korea, Taiwan, Singapore, and Brazil, were becoming more competitive in international economics. With oil as the basic source of energy in industrialized societies, OPEC also became more consequential politically and financially due to its ability to periodically impact oil prices. Third World countries, in general, were becoming increasingly important to industrialized economies as a source of raw materials, as export markets for finished goods, and as borrowers of capital, resulting in large foreign debts. Also, with the rise of détente, the Soviet Union, Eastern Europe, and the People's Republic of China became more intertwined within the global capitalist economy. Furthermore, multinational corporations spread and expanded their influence throughout the globe, gaining greater independence from government control. Finally, the breakdown of the Bretton Woods system increased the political and economic importance of international governmental organizations such as the IMF, the World Bank, and the GATT on the workings of the international political economy.

The growth of economic pluralism and interdependence made it more difficult for the United States to successfully pursue its foreign economic policy abroad and promote economic prosperity at home. In other words, *the U.S. economy became increasingly dependent upon and affected by forces beyond its borders*—similar to before World War II and as other governments have been all too aware. The net result was that the American and international political economies were becoming increasingly difficult to influence and control. Not surprisingly, the experience of economic problems at home and abroad grew after the early 1960s and contributed to the metamorphosis of foreign economic policy from "low" to "high" priority in the politics of U.S. foreign policy.

Changes in the context of the United States became more consequential for the American economy. For example, the cyclical nature of oil prices after the 1973 OPEC embargo and the demographic changes within the United States contributed to both recession and growth in the American economy. During the late 1970s, the American economy suffered from double-digit inflation and unemployment, much of which was fueled by the doubling of oil prices following the Iran-Iraq war and a bulge in the labor force as the baby boomers of the 1950s flooded the job market. During the early 1980s, these same environmental factors acted in reverse—oil prices and new entrants into the labor force declined dramatically, generating a decline in inflation and an economic expansion.

Clearly, the American economy was far beyond the control of the government and the president. As described by one journalist at the time, "Carter was battered by the same fundamental forces that bolstered Ronald Reagan. Yet neither had any real control over these forces. Nothing the White House has done, whether in style or in substance, has significantly affected the ebb and flow of our national economy in the past decade."[12] Although overstated, there is much truth to the general implication that America's ability to control its own economy and destiny was becoming increasingly problematic in a world of greater complexity.

With the rise of global pluralism and interdependence, the United States by the 1960s experienced *similar constraints in exerting influence and control in national security affairs.* Europe, for example, not only recovered economically but began exercising greater political independence in world politics. France acted increasingly independent of U.S. foreign policy and withdrew from NATO, while West Germany initiated the "Ostpolitik" policy of building bridges with communist governments in Eastern Europe, thus stimulating the beginnings of détente. The development of nuclear weapons and the military competition between the United States and the Soviet Union produced a "balance of terror." In addition, the Soviet Union became a global "military" power during the late 1960s and 1970s, while simultaneously playing a more active political role through its involvement in the détente process. Furthermore, nuclear weapons capabilities spread to France, Great Britain, and the People's Republic of China. To complicate matters further, most countries in the world had won their political independence by the 1960s, making Third World nationalism a growing force. Technology was diffusing throughout the world, especially sophisticated armaments, as a result of American, Soviet, and European exports. Conflicts proliferated and intensified throughout the world, most of which were civil conflicts and unconventional in nature. Together, these developments throughout the global environment made it much more difficult for even a great power, such as the United States or the Soviet Union, to successfully exercise political and military influence abroad—as each experienced in Vietnam and Afghanistan.

The rise of global pluralism and interdependence made the world more complex, messier, and increasingly consequential in affecting and constraining the foreign policies and domestic situations of all countries. The global environment had often acted to constrain the foreign policies of small countries, but the growth in global complexity also constrained the foreign policy of the larger and more powerful countries as well, including the United States.[13] In other words, the rise of global pluralism and interdependence meant a corresponding decline in American power throughout the world.

THE RELATIVE DECLINE OF AMERICAN POWER

As the world became noticeably more pluralistic and interdependent by the 1960s, the economic and military ability of the United States to influence the world declined. It was not that the United States was declining"absolutely," that is, in real terms, but that American power was in decline "relative" to changes that were occurring throughout the global environment. This relative decline of American power contributed to the U.S. defeat in Vietnam and the changes experienced by the Bretton Woods system. Ultimately, these dramatic events played an important role in the decline of presidential power in the making of U.S. foreign policy and the crisis of governance that has plagued American politics during the post–Vietnam War years.

In some respects, the decline of American power was "inevitable." The immensity of American power during the late 1940s and early 1950s was clearly "extraordinary," and temporary, given the devastation wrought by the war throughout most of the world. As Europe, Japan, and the Soviet Union recovered from the war, American power could only decline in comparison. Many of these changes were a function of the success of the United States in promoting a liberal international economic order, reinforced further by the general growth in global pluralism and interdependence. Overall, these environmental changes resulting in the rise of global complexity contributed to American relative decline. This has led to a significant paradox in U.S. foreign policy that might be called the **paradox of American power;** that is, the United States continued to be the most powerful country in the world, but it no longer was able to exercise the kind of economic, political, and military influence that it enjoyed at its height during the late 1940s and 1950s.

Although the United States remained the preeminent economic power, its economic influence nonetheless had declined quite dramatically during the 1970s and 1980s from its post–World War II peak—the time period that provided the foundation for American global interventionism and the rise of presidential power in foreign policy. *A comparison of*

America's economic role in the world between 1950 and 1976 highlights the relative decline:

1. The percentage of world GNP produced within the United States declined from almost 50 percent to 24 percent;
2. The American share of world crude steel production fell from 45 percent to 17 percent;
3. American iron ore production shrank from 42 percent to 10 percent of the world total;
4. Crude petroleum production declined from 53 percent to 14 percent; the percentage of international financial reserves decreased from 49 percent to 7 percent; American exports fell from 18 percent to 11 percent of world trade; and,
5. Even American wheat production as a percentage of global production declined from 17 percent to 14 percent.[14]

Very simply, economic production in Europe, Japan, and throughout the world had increased more rapidly than in the United States. In some cases, such as with oil, there had actually been an absolute decline in American production.

The relative decline of the American economy was not simply "quantitative," but "qualitative" as well. In numerous areas, American companies lost the technological lead to foreign competitors, especially the Japanese. Where during the cold war years "Made in the U.S.A." was considered the mark of excellence, during the 1970s and 1980s American products were no longer held in such high esteem either abroad or at home. Likewise, where "Made in Japan" was once an indication of cheap and unreliable goods as recently as the 1960s, it became the symbol of the highest quality available for manufactured and technological goods.

The relative decline of the American economy, especially in the manufacturing sector, can also be attributed to significant contextual developments at home. Since the 1960s, inflation and federal deficits increased dramatically, hurting the American economy. American management styles became top-heavy in personnel, produced bloated salaries, and emphasized a short-term profit outlook. Moreover, rising affluence and mass consumption were accompanied by declining worker productivity. Also, the industrial, union, transportation, and educational infrastructures were aging and became difficult and costly to revitalize. All of these factors and more contributed to the overall economic decline of the United States both at home and abroad during the 1970s and 1980s.[15]

A similar pattern occurred with respect to *U.S. ability to threaten and use force successfully abroad* in the post–Vietnam War years. The U.S. government found it increasingly difficult to promote political stability and to successfully exercise overt and covert military force. In Iran, for example, the United States was able to covertly overthrow the Iranian government with relative ease, imposing the Shah in 1953. Twenty-five years later, however, the United States could not stop the Iranian revolution and the rise of the Ayatollah Khomeini, triggering the Iran hostage crisis in American politics. Even in Central America, the traditional region of American hegemony, the United States faced new obstacles to the exercise of foreign policy influence. Small military or covert operations by the United States had determined the fate of Central American countries throughout most of the twentieth century; by the 1980s, however, the Reagan administration's covert war against Nicaragua involving over 10,000 *contras* was unable to defeat militarily the Sandinistas. Clearly, quick and easy military victories, such as in Grenada and Panama, were still possible, but they were becoming more costly politically and becoming the exception to the rule with the rise of global complexity.

The Vietnam War was symptomatic of the increased resistance that the United States was likely to find when attempting to exercise political and military force abroad. First, strong multilateral support for American military intervention abroad became less certain. Over fifteen allied countries had supplied combat troops in the Korean War; fewer than five did so in the Vietnam War. Europe not only failed to provide troops, but criticized American involvement throughout the war. Second, beleaguered governments dependent on American support became more difficult to influence. As Lawrence Grinter demonstrated in "Bargaining Between Saigon and Washington," the governments of South Vietnam and the United States continually worked at cross-purposes with each other.[16] The South Vietnamese leadership aspired to maintain power and attract American assistance during the war, while the American leadership was preoccupied with containing communism and protecting American prestige. The net result was that the South Vietnamese government was not simply a "puppet on a string," but was able to resist and manipulate United States policy. A third difficulty that the United States faced was that nationalism was a force with which to be reckoned. Vietnamese nationalism was the major asset of the Vietnamese communists in defeating the United States and the South Vietnamese. John Mueller demonstrated in "The Search for the 'Breaking Point' in Vietnam" that the Vietnamese communists were a most formidable enemy: over the centuries they had resisted and defeated the Chinese, Japanese, French, and finally the Americans.[17] The Soviet Union faced a similar problem in Afghanistan in the 1980s. Finally, the adversary was able to find sources of vital goods and supplies in order to carry out the war. The Vietnamese communists were able to take advantage of the East-West rivalry and the growing Sino-Soviet split to get Chinese and Soviet support.

The Vietnam War was indicative that the "good ole days" of simple power politics—in which great powers could easily dominate lesser powers through the threat of war, use of force, and covert paramilitary action with minimal political costs—had disappeared. As Richard Feinberg wrote in the 1980s,

> Compared to the situation that the colonial powers found in the heyday of imperialism, when a small flotilla of gunboats could manhandle an ancient civilization or conquer disorganized territories, many of today's Third World states wield much more formidable degrees of organized power. . . . While most Third World states may not yet be powerful enough to guarantee their own sovereignty, it has certainly become more problematical for foreign powers arbitrarily to impose their will upon them.[18]

In other words, the rise of global complexity weakened the likelihood of the successful application of military force. The American failure in Vietnam, most importantly, acted as a catalyst for the collapse of the anticommunist consensus, reassertion of Congress, and the more pluralistic domestic environment that have multiplied the constraints on the president's ability to exercise force abroad, especially on a large scale over a prolonged period of time.

Overall, during the 1970s and 1980s the United States was no longer the world's banker and found it increasingly difficult to act unilaterally as the world's policeman. The exercise of American power throughout the world "remained formidable" in comparison to any other single actor, but it was not what it once was. American power throughout the global arena, in other words, experienced relative decline since its height following World War II. This has raised key questions. Will the United States continue to decline? Can American power be renewed? These questions have been openly debated in American politics since the 1970s and are examined in **essay 3.1** on **American decline or revival?** Whatever the future of American power, however, its evolution will continue to play an integral role in the future politics of U.S. foreign policy.

In summary, the growth of global complexity has played a major role in the politics of U.S. foreign policy. The rise of global pluralism and interdependence have been accompanied by the decline of American power. These developments made it much more difficult for the United States to successfully pursue the foreign policies of the cold war years. The American failure in Vietnam and the changes in the Bretton Woods system were symptoms of these changes in American power and the global environment. These failures triggered political instability and a crisis of governance in American politics during the late 1960s and 1970s, resulting in important changes in the politics of U.S. foreign policy. As a result of the dynamic interaction of the government, the society, and the larger global environment, presidents have found it more difficult to govern foreign policy while the contradictions between national security and democracy have grown since the Vietnam War years.

ESSAY 3.1
AMERICAN DECLINE OR REVIVAL?

Most scholars and analysts of world politics and U.S. foreign policy agree that the relative power of the United States has declined from its post–World War II peak. Following the devastation of the war, the United States found itself in an extraordinary period of world history that could not last forever. However, there is considerable disagreement over the extent of the U.S. decline and whether American power will continue to decline or is likely to be renewed. This is not merely an academic debate, for the evolution of American power has serious implications for the future of U.S. foreign policy and the standard of living of Americans.

"Declinists" tend to emphasize that the United States has experienced economic and military decline in global affairs, that this trend is continuing, and that its reversal is unlikely over time. This position gained notoriety with the publication of *The Rise and Fall of the Great Powers* in 1987 by Paul Kennedy and has been the focal point of the debate ever since. Kennedy's book is "about national and international power in the modern—that is, post-Renaissance—period. It seeks to trace and to explain how the various Great Powers have risen and fallen, relative to each other, over the five centuries since the formation of the new monarchies of Western Europe and the beginnings of the transoceanic, global system of states."[A]

Like William Fulbright in essay 2.3, Kennedy believes that the power of all societies throughout history has been dynamic—that great powers pass through "cycles of rise and decline." "The relative strengths of the leading nations in world affairs never remain constant, principally because of the uneven rate of growth among different societies and of the technological and organizational breakthroughs which bring a greater advantage to one society than to another."[B] These are the sources of a country's economic and military power and determine its relative rise and decline in world affairs. Furthermore, "wealth," states Kennedy, "is usually needed to underpin military power, and military power is usually needed to acquire and protect wealth." However, if "too large a proportion of the state's resources is diverted from wealth creation and allocated instead to military purposes, then that is likely to lead to a weakening of national power over the long term." Furthermore, "if a state overextends itself strategically—by, say, the conquest of extensive territories or the waging of costly wars—it runs the risk that the potential benefits from external expansion may be outweighed by the great expense of it all—a dilemma which becomes acute if the nation concerned has entered a period of relative economic decline."[C]

Thus, great powers which have risen to global prominence as a result of gains in economic and military power eventually experience decline in world affairs when their economies weaken and they engage in "imperial overstretch." In other words, decline occurs if the gap increases between the ends and means of a state—that is, between the foreign policy goals of a great power and its ability to carry them out. This means that a country must either expand its economic capabilities to slow and avoid decline, limit its foreign policy goals and curtail its national security commitments in order to adjust to decline, or experience further decline.

Kennedy found that the great powers of modern western history—Spain, the Netherlands, France, and Great Britain—usually failed to recognize decline and responded with too little, too late. "Like all other civilizations at the top of the wheel of fortune," states Kennedy, "the British could believe that their position was both natural and destined to continue. And just like all those other civilizations, they were in for a rude shock."[D] Kennedy believes that the United

---

A. Paul Kennedy, *The Rise and Fall of the Great Powers: Economic Change and Military Conflict from 1500 to 2000* (New York: Random House, 1987), p. xv.
B. Ibid., pp. xv–xvi.

C. Ibid., p. xvi.
D. Ibid., p.158.

States currently is in a similar situation that Great Britain and previous great powers once faced.

For Kennedy, the United States confronts the "two key tests" of being "number one" in a situation of relative decline. First, "whether, in the military/strategical realm, it can preserve a reasonable balance between the nation's perceived defense requirements and the means it possesses to maintain those commitments."[E] Second, whether "it can preserve the technological and economic bases of its power from relative erosion in the face of the ever-shifting patterns of global production."[F] Overall, Kennedy is pessimistic concerning the ability of the United States to reverse its downward course, given changes in the global environment beyond American control and the political obstacles posed to internal change within American government and society.

"What we are witnessing at the moment is the early decades of the ebbing" of America's extraordinary economic power following World War II to its more natural state. "That decline is being masked by the country's enormous military capabilities at present, and also by its success in internationalizing American capitalism and culture." Kennedy points out, however, that even when the United States "declines to occupy its natural share of the world's wealth and power, a long time into the future, the United States will still be a very significant power in a multipolar world, simply because of its size."[G] Therefore, the task facing American political leaders into the twenty-first century "is to recognize that broad trends are under way, and that there is a need to manage affairs so that the relative erosion of the United States' position takes place slowly and smoothly, and is not accelerated by policies which bring merely short-term advantage but longer-term disadvantage."[H]

"Revivalists" tend to argue that the United States has not declined as rapidly as the declinists claim and that the revival of American power in the future is likely. Samuel Huntington, in "The U.S.—Decline or Renewal," is among the most optimistic proponents of revivalism. He argues that claims about American decline are widely exaggerated, that they have occurred frequently in the past, and that there is a "self-renewing genius" to American society (although, with the collapse of the cold war, he has become more pessimistic about America's future given the coming "Clash of Civilizations"). In *Bound to Lead*, Joseph Nye acknowledges that the United States has experienced decline, but emphasizes that the United States was not as powerful following World War II as declinists often suggest, has not declined as precipitously as the declinists argue, and faces no rival that can replace the United States as the global power in world affairs in the near future. Furthermore, the United States continues to enjoy certain advantages, such as the power of ideas, financial flows, and mass communications, which will allow the United States to exercise global leadership in the future.

Henry Nau, in *The Myth of America's Decline*, emphasizes the increasing convergence toward democracy and freer markets among the industrial countries since World War II. From this perspective, a decline in relative American power may actually translate into an overall increase in America's position throughout the world community if America's economy is strengthened. Richard Rosecrance, in *America's Economic Resurgence*, discusses the preconditions necessary for making the United States into a "trading state," allowing for the revival of American power, such as the need to reduce the federal deficit, improve the quality of education, increase savings and investment in research and development, cut bureaucracy, curb the preoccupation of American business and finance with short-term profits at the cost of long-term market shares, and divert resources from external military requirements to internal needs. Although optimistic, Rosecrance recognizes that these necessary changes are likely to be forced upon the United States as it becomes more fully integrated within the international political economy and faces international crises.

In assessing this debate, *a number of important points must be kept in mind*. First, the United States remains the most powerful single actor on the global stage; even in decline, it is the only complete

---

E. Ibid., p. 514.
F. Ibid., pp. 514–15.
G. Ibid., pp. 533–34.
H. Ibid., p. 5

superpower. Second, while the economic and military power of the United States has declined since World War II, the power of American culture—American ideas, science and technology, the English language, and popular culture—has actually grown throughout the world, providing the United States government with new opportunities in world affairs. Third, the chief strength of a market-oriented political economic system is the "dynamism" of capitalism. Hence, it is possible that change sufficient to slow, or possibly even reverse, American decline, could be generated within the American political economy. Finally, the United States has been a major beneficiary of the collapse of the Soviet empire and any threat it may have posed. The decline of its major adversary increases American power, allowing policymakers to exercise leadership and exert more force abroad for a period of time. More importantly, it buys time for the United States to adjust to developments abroad and promote renewal at home.

For even more powerful reasons, however, it is likely that the United States will find it very difficult to adjust, let alone reverse, its slowly declining position in global affairs. First, most of the key global developments contributing to the relative decline of the United States are simply beyond American control. Second, as will be discussed throughout this book, continuity tends to prevail over change in the complex politics of the United States. Established groups and institutions throughout society and the government tend to be status quo oriented and have the power to resist change; and peoples' beliefs are usually more a function of lessons derived from the past than a response to the needs of the future. Third, the collapse of communism and the Soviet Union may produce a false sense of optimism concerning the future, prompting deferment of needed changes within soci-

ety and government—reinforced by the successful military outcome in the Persian Gulf conflict. Fourth, governments and societies tend to be "reactive" in nature, requiring crises to produce change. "Long-term planning," for example, plays little role in American government or throughout the private sector. Finally, if changes do occur in American society and government, there is little guarantee that they will be successful in addressing, let alone arresting, decline. Change can take many forms and have different consequences; the most likely development prevailing within the American political economy is a "Band-Aid" approach to the problem—responding to the immediate symptoms, rather than the underlying causes, of decline.

In sum, people within the United States have the opportunity to arrest decline and move in new directions, but it will have great difficulty in doing so. This means that it is likely that the United States will remain the most powerful country in the world while slowly, but inevitably, experiencing greater decline in the future. This will continue to affect the politics of U.S. foreign policy as well as impact the standard of living and quality of life experienced by Americans throughout society. One likely consequence of decline, for example, is increasing inequality and stratification within society over time.

American decline, however, will probably be unlike that experienced by any other great previous power. Throughout history, great powers in decline have traditionally faced a great power war which accelerated their fall—a most unlikely future scenario for the United States given its nuclear arsenal and the collapse of the Soviet Union. Therefore, the United States is in somewhat of a "fortunate" situation, allowing the society and government to muddle through the twenty-first century as a declining, yet formidable, global power.

SOURCES: Lincoln Bloomfield, "Planning Foreign Policy: Can it be Done?," *Political Science Quarterly* 93 (Fall 1978): 369–92; David P. Calleo, *Beyond American Hegemony: The Future of the Western Alliance* (New York: Basic Books, 1987); Charles H. Ferguson, "America's High-Tech Decline," *Foreign Policy* 74 (Spring 1989): 123–44; Samuel P. Huntington, "The U.S.—Decline or Renewal?," *Foreign Affairs* (Winter 1988/89): 76–96; Samuel P. Huntington, *The Clash of Civilizations and the Remaking of World Order* (New York: Simon and Schuster, 1996); Paul Kennedy, *The Rise and Fall of the Great Powers: Economic Change and Military Conflict from 1500 to 2000* (New York: Random House, 1987); Walter Russell Mead, *Mortal Splendor: The American Empire in Transition* (Boston: Houghton Mifflin, 1987); Henry R. Nau, *The Myth of America's Decline: Leading the World Economy into the 1990s* (New York: Oxford University Press, 1990); Joseph S. Nye, Jr., *Bound to Lead: The Changing Nature of American Power* (New York: Basic Books, 1990); Richard Rosecrance, *America's Economic Resurgence: A Bold New Strategy* (New York: Harper and Row, 1990); and Bruce Russett, "The Mysterious Case of Vanishing Hegemony; or, Is Mark Twain Really Dead?," *International Organization* 39 (Spring 1985): 207–32.

THE POST–COLD WAR ERA IN WORLD POLITICS

· · · · · · · · · · · · · ·

The collapse of the cold war appears to have made the world an even more complex place, with contradictory implications for United States foreign policy. Some global developments seem to have reinforced continuity while others appear to have promoted change. Thus far, *two countervailing trends appear to be most important for the future politics of U.S. foreign policy:*[19]

1. The collapse of communism and other profound global changes, and
2. The Persian Gulf conflict and other global conflicts.

The most significant long-term development in the global environment is the collapse of communism, which appears to have reinforced and intensified the changes that have occurred in the politics of U.S. foreign policy since the Vietnam War. The collapse of the Soviet empire is a momentous event in the twentieth century and world history, for it means the end of the cold war and a world of greater complexity.

The collapse of communism and the Soviet Union is consequential for the future politics of U.S. foreign policy for a very simple, but fundamental, reason. The rise of Soviet communism and the cold war following World War II was the principal justification for development of the institutions and beliefs throughout American society and government that we will examine, which led to the policy of global containment and intervention and the preeminence of presidential power in the making of U.S. foreign policy. Therefore, the collapse of communism and the Soviet Union should further reduce the demands of national security and presidential power.

At the same time, the collapse of the cold war allows for the possibility that American resources might be redirected toward revitalizing its economy. After all, the end of the Soviet communist threat reinforces the increasing importance of the "high politics" of American foreign economic policy and America's role within the international political economy. The international economic crises of the late 1990s, such as the collapse of the Mexican peso and the collapse of the Asian tiger economies, highlights the extent to which the United States is heavily interwoven into the fabric of the larger global economic system. (See **essay 3.2** on Treasury Secretary Robert Rubin and his explanation of "why" the United States must actively and aggressively intervene and lead an international effort to stabilize the Asian economies). Such a world of global complexity and interdependence is only likely to grow, and thus becomes increasingly important for United States foreign policy and for Americans as the U.S. enters the twenty-first century.

On the other hand, the end of the cold war does not signal the end of conflict throughout the world, nor does it mean "peace is at hand." In fact, the end of the cold war may produce more conflict in a world of greater complexity where global issues proliferate and power is diffused. Although not on the scale of a U.S.-Soviet conflict, such conflicts have the potential to trigger American intervention in the world.

The most significant short-term development in this regard has been the Persian Gulf conflict, which has reinforced concern with national security and the elements supporting strong presidential power in the foreign policy process. As the war made clear, the United States is the lone superpower in the world, which increases the opportunities for the United States to exercise force abroad. The immediate result of the Persian Gulf War, hence, has been to counteract the effect that the collapse of the Soviet Union and the communist threat to America had in prompting changes within American government and society as it adapts to the future of a post–cold war world.

Clearly, the end of the cold war and the evolving post–cold war global environment have contradictory implications for the future politics of U.S. foreign policy. The end of the cold war has created increasing global complexity, posing both greater opportunities and constraints for the evolution and exercise of American power. And whatever the consequences, it is also quite clear that the United States

ESSAY 3.2
THE ASIAN "ECONOMIC" FLU AND AMERICAN/IMF MULTILATERAL INTERVENTION WITHIN THE INTERNATIONAL POLITICAL ECONOMY

In the summer of 1997, the economy of Thailand began to go into a tailspin. Throughout the fall and then the winter of 1998, other Asian economies—such as Indonesia, Malaysia, the Philippines, South Korea, Taiwan—experienced a similar economic situation. These countries were referred to as the Asian "tigers" throughout the 1980s and 1990s because of their incredibly high rates of economic growth. But virtually overnight, their economies collapsed and investments fled the country to other economies, creating huge devaluations in their currencies (where the value dropped by as much as 80 percent) and, hence, triggered an international economic crisis.

The United States, along with Western European countries and Japan and the International Monetary Fund, was quick to intervene to try to stabilize the international situation. Robert Rubin, the treasury secretary (and previously President Clinton's national economic adviser and head of the newly created National Economic Council in 1993), addressed the Asian financial situation in a major public speech. In the speech, Rubin explained why the United States had intervened in the international economy to play such an active role, how it affected the American economy and the lives of Americans, and why it must work "multilaterally" with other countries and international organizations, such as the International Monetary Fund (IMF).

Much of what Rubin says may go against the grain of how many Americans understand the nature of the so-called "free market." He describes a very complex, and confusing, international political economy. Nevertheless, it should shed light on why the United States—with the world's largest and strongest economy—has played such a vital role and intervened in the past, such as with Russia's emerging market after the collapse of communism or when the Mexican economy and peso collapsed precipitously in 1995. It should also shed light on the views held by many American leaders of the international political economy and why the United States is likely to intervene in the future as the world enters the twenty-first century. What follows is an abridged version of the speech on January 21, 1998, by Treasury Secretary Robert E. Rubin.

Today I would like to discuss the financial crisis in Asia; why the United States must protect its vital economic and national security interests by working to help restore financial stability and economic growth to that troubled region; and why acting promptly and effectively to do so protects the economic interests of every American.

To begin, I think it is important to place the recent events in Asia in the context of the emergence of the global financial system. Over the last several years, we have entered a new era for global financial markets and the global economy—an era of interdependence, complexity and opportunity. Expanding economic ties through greatly increased trade and vastly increased capital flows has brought tremendous benefits to the American people through greater exports, more high-paying jobs, and higher standards of living and through lower inflation than would have been expected with the strong growth we've had. And countries in the developing world and emerging markets have also benefited enormously from this environment, which has allowed them to attract previously unimaginable flows of private capital for investment. That investment has helped foster growth and lift millions out of poverty.

Yet just as this era brings great opportunities for the United States and the rest of the world, so does it present new risks. In recent months, these risks have been brought home as financial instability in Asia has shaken the region and affected markets around the world. Just a few years ago, it would have been unimaginable for the fluctuations of the Thai baht, or the fortunes of the Korean stock market to impact U.S. markets to be printed on the front page of newspapers every day.

In the face of this challenge, our first job is clear: to help stabilize the immediate crisis. Yet, to make the most of the opportunities and limit the risks of the new global financial system and to have a viable situation for the years ahead, we must also modernize the architecture of the international financial markets that we helped create and that has served us so well for the last fifty years. This will be a long and complex process—which we actually began several years ago—involving great intellectual effort and extensive international coordination, yet it is imperative for the strength of our economy and the prosperity of our citizens as we enter a new century.

The United States has enormously important economic and national security interests at stake in promoting restoration of financial stability in Asia. When we act to resolve the Asian crisis, we act to protect and benefit the American people.

The countries in Asia are our customers, our competitors and our security partners. Financial instability, economic distress, and depreciating currencies all have direct effects on the pace of our exports, the competitiveness of our companies, the growth of our economy and, ultimately, the well-being of American workers. Thirty percent of U.S. exports go to Asia, supporting millions of U.S. jobs, and we export more to Asia than Europe. In states like California, Oregon, and Washington, exports to Asia account for more than half of each state's total exports.

Thus far, the effects on our economy, though real, are relatively moderate and the most likely scenario for the next year is continued solid growth and low inflation. However, the risks in this crisis are not just confined to the Asia countries now most directly involved. Roughly forty percent of our exports have been going to emerging markets around the globe. If the crisis were to spread more broadly to other emerging markets, then the impact on American workers and businesses could be much greater. Simply put, we cannot afford to stand back and gamble that the crisis will resolve itself.

The United States also has critical national security interests in seeing a restoration of financial stability in the region. We have 100,000 troops based in Asia, 37,000 on the Korean peninsula alone, where we have spent forty-five years keeping the peace, and where North and South Korea have only just begun negotiating a possible end to their conflict. History has shown that economic distress and financial instability can threaten political stability and security. A stable and prosperous Asia is more likely to be a peaceful Asia. . . .

While economies usually adjust in a relatively orderly fashion to market swings, in this case the combination of factors proved combustible. When these crises began, foreign investors started to withdraw capital, local companies sought to hedge currency exposures, exporters stopped bringing their export earnings home, and citizens moved their savings abroad. . . . This process brought stock prices and land values down sharply across the region, imposed severe strains on Asian banks and companies, and led to acute depreciations of exchange rates and greatly reduced economic growth.

From the very beginning of this crisis, we at Treasury, in close cooperation with Chairman Greenspan and the staff of the Federal Reserve Board, have been deeply involved in crafting an international response involving the countries of the region, the G-7 (the Group of 7, which includes Canada, France, Great Britain, Germany, Italy, and Japan along with the U.S.), the World Bank, and the Asian Development Bank—all working with the International Monetary Fund. The president's national security team including Secretary (of State) Albright, Secretary (of Defense) Cohen, and National Security Advisor Berger, have been integrally and critically involved in this effort.

The program we have supported has focused on four key elements: supporting reform programs in individual nations; providing temporary financial assistance when needed; encouraging strong action by Japan and the other major economic powers to promote global growth; and fostering policies in other developing and emerging economies to reduce the risk of contagion. . . .

The central provider of this financial assistance (involving the equivalent of billions of dollars) is the International Monetary Fund, with additional support from the World Bank and the Asian Development Bank. In addition, the United States has joined other industrial countries in indicating its willingness to provide supplementary financial resources in some situations if a country fully adheres to the reform program and further resources become necessary. Up to this point, we have not actually disbursed any of this money, and those disbursements—to the extent they occur—will be in the form of short term loans whose payment is guaranteed by the borrowing government. . . .

The IMF is the right institution to be at the center of these support programs. This institution, which was established at the initiative of the United States fifty years ago, has long benefited Americans. The core mission of the IMF has always remained the same—to promote financial stability, trade and economic growth.

The United States has worked forcefully to help the IMF meet the new challenges of the modern financial system, and there is simply no other institution capable of performing its mission. With tremendous expertise and technical resources, the IMF has the ability to shape effective reform programs. As a multinational organization, it is able to require an economically distressed country to accept conditions that no contributing nation could require on its own. Finally—and critically important—the IMF internationalizes the burden during a global financial crisis by using its pool of capital instead of the United States having to bear that burden alone.

The American people should also know this: over the past fifty years our contribution to the IMF has not cost the taxpayer one dime. When the IMF draws on our commitments, we receive a liquid, interest bearing offsetting claim on the IMF. There are no budgetary outlays. Our contribution does not increase the deficit, or divert resources from other spending priorities.

Support for our periodic pledge to the IMF, and support for a new emergency fund, the New Arrangements to Borrow, which supplements the IMF's resources to deal with crises such as this one, is critical. . . . Moreover, failure to provide funding could reduce our leverage in the IMF, and could shake confidence in American leadership in the global economy at a time when confidence is so important in re-establishing stability in Asia. . . .

A number of concerns have been raised with respect to these programs. Let me try to respond to them.

First, some have said that it's not in our interest to help countries that are seen as our competitors, especially when falling currencies make their products cheaper. The exact opposite is the case. Without support, it is highly likely that these countries will have much deeper recessions and much weaker currencies, hurting U.S. exports and our competitiveness with far greater damage to American businesses and workers. With support, these countries have the best chance to restore growth, restore the capacity to buy more of our goods, and restore currency values.

A second criticism has been that these programs do not require nations to take specific steps to promote the environment, protect core labor standards and ensure human rights. Let me be clear: these issues are critically important to the United States, and we are pursuing them actively through other initiatives and in other fora. And there is no question that financial stability, growth and prosperity provide an environment most conducive to advancing these objectives, while instability and economic duress are inimicable to these objectives. Moreover, designing and obtaining sustained adherence to programs to restore financial stability is extremely difficult. To add these three objectives—however important—would vastly complicate this effort and greatly reduce its chance of success. Also, if these objectives were added others would clearly seek to add still more objectives, and the whole undertaking would become impossible.

Third, some have said that providing financial assistance to these countries shields investors and countries from the consequences of bad decisions and sows the seeds of future crises. This problem—often called the problem of moral hazard—has two dimensions: the impact on the behavior of countries, and the impact of the behavior of investors and lenders. For the countries, it should be obvious that they are not shielded from the effects of their bad decisions. They may receive temporary financial assistance, but they also inevitably go through a very difficult economic period before recovery takes hold. No county would opt to go through what Mexico went through, or what various Asian countries are going through now.

As to investors and lenders, the problem is more complicated. Let me just say that I would not give one nickel to help any creditor or investor. And, in fact vast numbers of investors and creditors have taken large losses in Asia. Foreign banks and other creditors to corporate and other borrowers throughout the region now have many troubled or bad loans, real estate investors have almost universally sustained large asset depreciations, and investors have suffered the consequences of stock markets that are down more than fifty percent from their highs. Just today three major U.S. banks—J. P. Morgan, Chase, and Citibank—have reported that developments in Asia have

had a substantial negative impact on their profits. The crisis in Asia has clearly taken its toll on American investors and creditors.

To those who argue that we must ensure that all creditors take a loss, my answer is this: The reality of the situation is much more complex. A byproduct of programs designed to restore stability and growth may be that some creditors will be protected from the full consequences of their actions. But any action to force investors and creditors involuntarily to take losses, however appropriate that might seem, would risk serious adverse consequences. It could cause banks to pull their money out of the country involved. It could reduce that nation's ability to access new sources of private capital, and, perhaps most tellingly, it could cause banks to pull back from other emerging markets. . . .

Fourth, some say that doing nothing would be best, because markets would ultimately solve the problem on their own. Let me say as someone who spent twenty-six years on Wall Street and who has an enormous belief in markets, there are problems that markets alone cannot solve. In this country, we recognized that long ago, with measures such as the Federal Reserve System, the Securities and Exchange Commission, and deposit insurance. Laws and institutions support healthy free market activity by dealing with issues beyond the ability of unfettered markets to handle. There is simply too much risk that markets alone will not resolve these problems of financial instability, and therefore given our stakes in Asia we must try to help get these countries back on track. . . .

The approach I have described today is the best and most likely the only viable way to succeed. . . .

The United States has enormous economic and national security interests in a strong and vibrant Asia. Financial instability in Asia is a threat not only to the region, but to economies all over the world, and even ourselves. We cannot ignore these risks. We must act to best protect and promote our interests.

As I said at the beginning, we are at the frontier of a new era. When America has entered new eras in the past it has done so with vigor and determination. Our leadership is critical to guiding the global economy into the twenty-first century, and to protecting the in-terests of the American people. This is no time to turn our back. We must confront the crisis today, and build for tomorrow. The actions we take now are critical to our economic well-being today, and for the future. Thank you very much.

SOURCE: U.S., Treasury, Office of Public Affairs, "Treasury Secretary Robert E. Rubin Address on the Asian Financial Situation to Georgetown University," (Washington, D.C., January 21, 1998).

will continue to be a global power, with interests throughout the world and which pursues a global-oriented foreign policy for the foreseeable future.

In sum, contemporary patterns in the global environment and the evolution of American power have played a significant role in the politics of U.S. foreign policy throughout the 1990s and will continue to do so into the twenty-first century. Ultimately, it is the dynamic interaction between the government, the society, and the global context that will determine the complexity and direction of the future politics of U.S. foreign policy, which will be explored at greater length throughout the book and in the concluding chapter. Yet, it is to the government and the policymaking process that we now turn, beginning at the center of the policy process by addressing presidential power and the president's ability to govern U.S. foreign policy.

BIBLIOGRAPHIC ESSAY

. . . .

Much has been written about recent international developments and the evolution of world politics. Geoffrey Barraclough, in *An Introduction to Contemporary History* (Middlesex, England: Penguin, 1964), provides a classic statement of the decline of Europe and the rise of the Soviet Union and the United States in world politics, as does Eric Hobsbawm in his more contemporary *The Age of Extremes: A History of the World, 1914–1991* (New York: Vintage, 1994). The evolution of the international political economy since World War II, and the role of the United States within it, are described by Joan Edelman Spero in *The Politics of International Economic Relations* (New York: St. Martin's, 1997), and in Daniel Yergin and Joseph Stanislaw, *The Commanding Heights: The Battle Between Government and the Marketplace That Is Remaking the Modern World* (New York: Simon and Schuster, 1998). General theoretical implications of these global changes, emphasizing the rise of pluralism and interdependence, for the making of foreign policy are discussed in Edward L. Morse, *Foreign Policy in Gaullist France* (Princeton, N.J.: Princeton University Press, 1973).

A proliferation of work has been published that focuses on the rise and decline of American power in world affairs. The classic statement on American decline remains Paul Kennedy's *The Rise and Fall of the Great Powers: Economic Change and Military Conflict from 1500 to 2000* (New York: Random House, 1987). See also Charles H. Ferguson, "America's High-Tech Decline," *Foreign Policy* 74 (Spring 1989): 123–44, and Walter Russell Mead, *Mortal Splendor: The American Empire in Transition* (Boston: Houghton Mifflin, 1987). A more optimistic picture of America's future can be found in Joseph S. Nye, Jr., *Bound to Lead: The Changing Nature of American Power* (New York: Basic Books, 1990), and Bruce Russett, "The Mysterious Case of Vanishing Hegemony; or, Is Mark Twain Really Dead?", *International Organization* 39 (Spring 1985): 207–32.

Occasionally, efforts are made down the uncertain and treacherous path of predicting broad future trends in world politics and their implications for the future of U.S. foreign policy. Some of the more interesting and provocative efforts are by Daniel Bell, "The Future World Disorder," *Foreign Policy* 27 (Summer 1977): 109–35; Seyom Brown, in *New Forces, Old Forces, and the Future of World Politics* (Glenview, Ill.: Scott, Foreman, 1988), Zbigniew Brzezinski, *Global Turmoil on the Eve of the 21st Century* (New York: Charles Scribner, 1992), Paul Kennedy, *Preparing for* the *Twenty-First Century* (New York: Random House, 1993), Nicholas X. Rizopoulos, ed., *Sea-Changes: American Foreign Policy in a World Transformed* (New York: Council on Foreign Relations Press, 1990), and Richard Rosecrance, "The Rise of the Virtual State," *Foreign Affairs* (July/August 1996): 45–61. A broad discussion of the evolving international political economy and its implications for the future of the American economy and how it will impact Americans is made by Robert Kuttner in *The End of Laissez-Faire: National Purpose and the Global Economy After the Cold War* (New York: Alfred A. Knopf, 1991).

ENDNOTES

1. For a general discussion of the underlying impact of the global environment on foreign policy, see Peter Gourevitch, "The Second Image Reversed: The International Sources of Domestic Politics," *International Organization* 32 (Autumn 1978): 881–912; Robert Gilpin, *War and Change in World Politics* (Cambridge, Mass.: Cambridge University Press, 1981); David A. Lake, *Power, Protection, and Free Trade: International Sources of U.S. Commercial Strategy, 1887–1939* (Ithaca, N.Y.: Cornell University Press, 1988); Edward L. Morse, *Foreign Policy and Interdependence in Gaullist France* (Princeton, N.J.: Princeton University Press, 1973); Robert C. North and Nazli Choucri, "Population, Technology, and Resources in the Future International System," *Journal of International Affairs* 25 (1971): 224–37; Immanuel Wallerstein, *The Capitalist World-Economy* (London: Cambridge University Press, 1979); and Kenneth N. Waltz, *Man, the State, and War: A Theoretical Analysis* (New York: Columbia University Press, 1954).

2. For a general discussion of the immediate impact of international phenomena on foreign policy, see Charles F. Hermann, "International Crises as a Situational Variable," in James N. Rosenau, ed., *International Politics and Foreign Policy* (New York: Free Press, 1969): 409–21; Richard Ned Lebow, *Between Peace and War: The Nature of International Crisis* (Baltimore: John Hopkins University Press, 1981); Arthur A. Stein and Bruce M. Russett, "Evaluating War: Outcomes and Consequences," in Ted R. Gurr, ed., *Handbook of Political Conflict: Theory and Research* (New York: Free Press, 1980): 399–422; John A. Vasquez, "Domestic Contention on Critical Foreign Policy Is-

sues: The Case of the United States," *International Organization* 39 (Autumn 1985): 643–66; and John A. Vasquez and Richard W. Mansbach, "The Issue Cycle: Conceptualizing Long-Term Global Political Change," *International Organization* 37 (1983): 257–79.

3. Harold and Margaret Sprout, *The Ecological Perspective on Human Affairs* (Princeton, N.J.: Princeton University Press, 1965), p. 11.

4. For an overview of the evolution of Europe, the Soviet Union, and the United States in world politics, see Geoffrey Barraclough, *An Introduction to Contemporary History* (Middlesex, England: Penguin, 1964); John Lewis Gaddis, *Russia, The Soviet Union, and the United States: An Interpretive History* (New York: Alfred A. Knopf, 1978); Eric Hobsbawm, *The Age of Extremes: A History of the World, 1914–1991* (New York: Vintage, 1994), Paul Kennedy, *The Rise and Fall of the Great Powers: Economic Change and Military Conflict from 1500 to 2000* (New York: Random House, 1987); Hugh Thomas, *A History of the World* (New York: Harper, 1979); Eric R. Wolfe, *Europe and the People Without History* (Berkeley: University of California Press, 1982).

5. See chapter 2 for sources on the origins of the cold war.

6. See, e.g., R. Harrison Wagner, "What Was Bipolarity?" *International Organization* 47 (Winter 1993): 77–106.

7. Godfrey Hodgson, *America in Our Time* (New York: Vintage, 1976), p. 19.

8. See, e.g., Simon Bromley, *American Hegemony and World Oil: The Industry, the State System, and the World Economy* (University Park, Pa.: Pennsylvania State University Press, 1991), and Daniel Yergin, *The Prize: The Epic Quest for Oil, Money, and Power* (New York: Simon and Schuster, 1991).

9. For a discussion of American hegemony, see Gilpin, *War and Change in World Politics;* Kennedy, *The Rise and Fall of Great Powers;* and George Modelski, "The Long Cycle of Global Politics," *Comparative Studies in Society and History* 20 (April 1978). pp. 214–35. To place this in a broader context, see Donald J. Puchala, "The History of the Future of International Relations," *Ethics & International Affairs* 8 (1994): 177–202, and "International Encounters of Another Kind," *Global Society* 11 (1997): 5–29.

10. See, for example, G. John Ikenberry, "Rethinking the Origins of American Hegemony," *Political Science Quarterly* 104 (Fall 1989): 375–400. See also Stephen Gill, *American Hegemony and the Trilateral Commission* (Cambridge: Cambridge University Press, 1990).

11. For an overview of the rise of global pluralism and interdependence, see Seyom Brown, *New Forces, Old Forces, and the Future of World Politics* (Glenview, Ill.: Scott, Foresman, 1988); Robert O. Keohane and Joseph S. Nye, *Power and Interdependence: World Politics in Transition* (Glenview, Ill.: Scott, Foresman, 1989); Lynn H. Miller, *Global Order: Values and Power in International Politics* (Boulder, Colo.: Westview Press, 1985); Kenneth A. Oye, "Beyond Postwar Order and New World Order: American Foreign Policy in Transition," in *Eagle in a New World: American Grand Strategy in the Post–Cold War Era* (New York: Harper Collins, 1993), edited by Kenneth A. Oye, Robert J. Lieber, and Donald Rothchild, pp. 3–33, and Joan Edelman Spero, *The Politics of International Economic Relations* (New York: St. Martin's Press, 1997).

12. David Morris, "Circumstances Shine on Reagan," *St. Paul Pioneer Press and Dispatch* (July 18, 1988). p. 13A.

13. See, for example, Morse, *Foreign Policy and Interdependence in Gaullist France*.

14. Stephen D. Krasner, "American Policy and Global Economic Stability," in William P. Avery and Rapkin, eds., *America in a Changing World Political Economy* (New York: Longman, 1982), p. 38.

15. See, for example, Robert Kuttner, *The End of Laissez-Faire: National Purpose and the Global Economy After the Cold War* (New York: Alfred A. Knopf, 1991), and Robert B. Reich, *The Work of Nations: Preparing Ourselves for 21st Century Capitalism* (New York: Alfred A. Knopf, 1991).

16. Lawrence E. Grinter, "Bargaining Between Saigon and Washington: Dilemmas of Linkage Politics During War," *Orbis* (Fall 1974): 837–65.

17. John E. Mueller, "The Search for the 'Breaking Point' in Vietnam: The Statistics of a Deadly Quarrel," *International Studies Quarterly* 24 (December 1980): 497–519.

18. Richard E. Feinberg, *The Intemperate Zone: The Third World Challenge to U.S. Foreign Policy* (New York: W.W. Norton, 1983), p. 34.

19. For an overview of future global prospects and its implications for U.S. foreign policy, see Daniel Bell, "The Future World Disorder," *Foreign Policy* 27 (Summer 1977): 109–35; Seyom Brown, *New Forces, Old Forces and the Future of World Politics* (Glenview, Ill.: Scott, Foresman, 1988); James M. Goldgeier and Michael McFaul, "A Tale of Two Worlds: Core and Periphery in the Post–Cold War Era," *International Organization* 46 (Spring 1992): 467–91; Paul Kennedy, *Preparing for the Twenty-first Century* (New York: Random House, 1993); Robert Kuttner, *The End of Laissez-Faire: National Purpose and the Global Economy After the Cold War* (New York: Alfred A. Knopf, 1991); Michael Howard, "Cold War, Chill Peace," *World Policy Journal* (Winter 1993/94): 27–34; William Pfaff, "Redefining World Power," *Foreign Affairs* 70 (America and the World 1990/91): 34–48; John J. Mearsheimer, "Why We Will Soon Miss the Cold War," *The Atlantic Monthly* (August 1990): 35–50; John Mueller, *Retreat from Doomsday: The Obsolescence of Major War* (New York: Basic Books, 1989); Nicholas X. Rizopoulos, ed., *Sea-Changes: American Foreign Policy in a World Transformed* (New York: Council on Foreign Relations Press, 1990), Richard Rosecrance, "The Rise of the Virtual State," *Foreign Affairs* (July/August 1996): 45–61.

PART THREE

GOVERNMENT AND THE POLICYMAKING PROCESS

Part III examines the center of the policymaking process beginning with the president and moving outward. Chapters 4 and 5 discuss the paradox of presidential power and the importance of presidential leadership in governing foreign policy. Chapter 6 discusses presidential management of the bureaucracy and the National Security Council process. Chapters 7, 8, and 9 discuss the bureaucratic role of the State Department, the military establishment, and the intelligence community. Chapter 10 focuses on the foreign economic bureaucracy. Chapter 11 provides a summary of decision-making theory and the nature of policymaking throughout the executive branch. Chapter 12 discusses the judiciary, state and local governments, and the Washington political community.

CHAPTER 4

THE PARADOX OF PRESIDENTIAL POWER

*M*ost Americans are raised to believe that the president is the most powerful figure in the United States. In fact, many of us acquire an image of an omnipotent president. At a very young age, we are taught that the president is a very benevolent father figure who controls the government and represents the American people.[1] As Stanley Hoffmann observed thirty years ago, "The American system of government seems unable to prevent a kind of hand-wringing, starry-eyed, and slightly embarrassing deification of the man in the White House, a doleful celebration of his solitude and his burdens." Naturally, Hoffmann added parenthetically, "When things go badly, there is, of course, a tendency to besmirch the fallen idol."[2]

In this chapter, we examine the extent to which this popular image of a near omnipotent president is accurate. How much power does the president really have? What implications does this have for presidential governance, especially in the area of foreign affairs? As we will see, it is very difficult for a president to govern successfully and lead the country in

foreign policy, especially since the Vietnam and Watergate years. The end of the cold war has created new opportunities for U.S. foreign policy, but it has also exacerbated the difficulties that a president faces in exercising power. Ultimately, the ability that a president demonstrates in leading the country and managing the executive branch is consequential in affecting the future conduct of U.S. foreign policy.

THE ELEMENTS OF PRESIDENTIAL POWER

The president is the most powerful political actor in the United States. He occupies many constitutional roles and has many capabilities that contribute to his power. However, the president also faces many constraints and uncertainties that limit his power. Therefore, the president, although powerful, is not nearly as powerful as the popular stereotype held by many Americans.

CONSTITUTIONAL ROLES AND STRENGTHS

The president occupies many different roles, or wears many different hats, that provide him with the capability to exercise considerable power. Among the *roles that are most important in contributing to presidential power* are the following:[3]

1. Commander in chief;
2. Chief diplomat;
3. Chief administrator;
4. Chief of state;
5. Chief legislator;
6. Voice of the people; and
7. Chief judicial officer.

These roles have their origins in Article II of the Constitution and have evolved throughout the history of the United States.

Commander in Chief. The president is the commander in chief, which means that he has ultimate authority over the military. According to the U.S. Constitution, the military is under the authority of the elected civilian leadership. In theory, then, the president controls the U.S. military. This means that when the president gives an order, members of the military and the Department of Defense comply. By virtue of his position as president, he is to be treated as a six-star general. This gives the president considerable power because, as commander in chief, he dictates the use of American armed forces abroad.

Since World War II, the president has exercised his powers as commander in chief very broadly. It was President Harry Truman who decided to send American troops to Korea in 1950 to fight in America's first war since World War II. American escalation and use of armed force in Vietnam throughout the 1950s, 1960s, and 1970s was a result of decisions made by Presidents Dwight Eisenhower, John Kennedy, Lyndon Johnson, and Richard Nixon. The decision to secretly support the contras in their effort to overthrow the Sandinistas in Nicaragua was made by President Ronald Reagan. President George Bush invaded Panama and had over 500,000 American troops fight a war in the Persian Gulf. Each of these examples represents a major commitment in U.S. foreign policy. They also represent presidential decisions in which there was little, if any, involvement by the Congress of the United States. Although only Congress has the constitutional right to declare war, these were presidential initiatives and presidential wars.

Chief Diplomat. The president is also often referred to as the chief diplomat or the chief negotiator representing the United States. This role originates with the president's constitutional duty to nominate the secretary of state and ambassadors to countries abroad, as well as receive foreign ambassadors. Although the secretary of state and ambassadors have traditionally been responsible for the day-to-day practice of diplomacy abroad, the appointive power helps to ensure that their actions represent presidential wishes and presidential decisions. Presidents also have the right to provide, or withdraw, official U.S. diplomatic relations with foreign governments. For example, with regard to U.S. foreign policy in East Asia, President Carter in 1979 granted official American recognition to the government of the People's Republic of China in Beijing for the first time in thirty years and withdrew official recognition from the nationalist Chinese government in Taiwan.

More recently, the president has begun to exercise his right to act as an actual negotiator himself by heading American diplomatic delegations, something which has increased in frequency over the last two decades with the rise of **summitry**. President Nixon led the American delegation to Moscow in 1972 to complete the first Strategic Arms Limitation Talks (SALT) with the Soviet Union. President Ford met with Leonid Brezhnev, general secretary of the Communist party of the Soviet Union, in Vladivostok in 1974 to lay the foundation for SALT II. President Carter spent thirteen days negotiating with President Anwar Sadat of Egypt and Prime Minister Menachim Begin of Israel in 1978 to produce the Camp David Accords. President Reagan had more major summits than any previous president since Franklin Roosevelt—four with Soviet leader Mikhail Gorbachev between 1985 and 1989, emphasizing arms control and the Strategic Arms Reduction Talks (START). And every year U.S. presidents participate with leaders from the major industrialized democracies in a summit to discuss measures to contribute to the stability and growth of the international political economy.

Chief Administrator. The president is also the chief administrator, which means he has authority over the executive branch. So, in theory, all the governmental agencies within the executive branch, all the cabinet secretaries and all the bureaucrats, respond to presidential wishes and decisions. One of the major ways the president exercises this administrative power is through appointments. The president selects his personal staff, nominates cabinet secretaries, and appoints most of the high-level officials in each of the departments and agencies that make up the executive branch. This important aspect of presidential power reinforces his roles as commander in chief and chief diplomat. In foreign policy, this means that the president has authority and considerable power over the foreign policy apparatus within the executive branch. Thus, he relies on the National Security Council, State Department, Department of Defense, the intelligence community, and other bureaucratic agencies to assist him in formulating and implementing U.S. foreign policy decisions.

Chief of State. The president is not only the chief administrator, or official head of the government, but is also the chief of state. This means that the president, through the office of the presidency, represents the state of the United States of America and, thus, is the symbolic political leader of the United States. In many countries throughout the world, the person at the head of the government is not the same person who is the chief of state. For example, in Great Britain and Japan, governments are headed by prime ministers while the chief of state is a monarch or emperor. In the United States, these two roles are combined in the single office of the presidency.

The role of the chief of state is primarily a symbolic role which, nonetheless, is another ingredient of presidential power. The importance of symbolism should not be downplayed for the outcomes of politics are heavily a function of the successful use of symbolism. To use Great Britain and the United States as an example once again, when a foreign head of state arrives in Great Britain the first "official" visit, according to the diplomatic protocols of international behavior, is with the queen, for she represents the state. In contrast, the same foreign leader coming to the United States will pay official respects first to the president. This indicates the additional status that the president has in his role as head of state, which translates into another important element of his power.

Chief Legislator. Although the president is not a member of Congress, he does occupy the role of "de facto" chief legislator. In the modern relationship between the legislative branch and the executive branch, much of the legislation before Congress originates in the executive branch and is submitted by the president. For example, the president submits the budget of the U.S. government to Congress, as well as his programs for defense spending and foreign assistance. Therefore, Congress often responds to the president's agenda, thereby giving him a political advantage for gaining acceptance of his programs when dealing with Congress.

The other technique that contributes to the president's legislative powers is his constitutional right to veto legislation. Not only does he initiate much legislation, he can prevent legislation from becoming law if he so chooses. Congress may override a presidential veto with a two-thirds affirmative vote for the legislation in the House of Representatives and the Senate, but this happens infrequently. Therefore, the president can stop legislation he does not like or, by threatening a veto, force members of Congress to modify legislation to conform with his desires—an important exercise of presidential power in the legislative area.

Voice of the People. The president is often referred to as the "voice of the people" because he (as well as the vice president) is the only public official who is elected by the entire American populace. A member of Congress represents a district of roughly a half-million people. A senator represents a state, which may represent only a few million Nevadans or as many as thirty million Californians. But, only the president can argue that he has a "national electoral mandate" and represents all of the American people, reinforcing his role as chief of state.

Each candidate who has been successful in gaining the presidency has claimed the possession of an electoral mandate because his majority vote demonstrates that his goals represent the wishes of the American people. Therefore, most presidents act as if they have a mandate to promote and implement those policies that were promised and discussed during the presidential campaign. President Nixon claimed that he represented the "silent majority" of the late 1960s and early 1970s. President Carter claimed to represent a new, more enlightened majority following the years of the Vietnam War and Watergate. President Reagan claimed that he represented a new conservative majority to restore a more traditional America. President Bush argued that the country supported a "kinder and gentler" set of policies consistent with his predecessor. President Clinton claimed support to strengthen the political economy and improve America's economic competitiveness abroad. Each president, in other words, tends to argue that he had obtained a public consensus behind him and his vision of America. Claiming an election mandate, that his goals and policies are representative of the vast majority of the American people, is another important symbolic way to exercise presidential power.[4]

Chief Judicial Officer. The president also enjoys important judicial powers in two areas. First, the president has the authority to pardon any individual guilty of a crime. For example, President Ford pardoned former President Nixon before he was indicted for breaking the law in the Watergate affair. Second, all of the judges who serve on federal district courts, the federal court of appeals, and the United States Supreme Court are nominated by the president. This can be a very important source of presidential power since federal judges, unlike state and local judges, are appointed for life and are the final arbiters of the law of the land. As presidents appoint new judges to the courts, judicial decisions may change over time, thus effecting public policy. For example, the Supreme Court under Chief Justice Earl Warren was considered a liberal court during the 1950s and 1960s. However, with four appointments by President Nixon, one by President Ford, three by President Reagan, and two by President Bush since the 1970s, the Supreme Court changed and adopted a much more conservative orientation under Chief Justice William Rehnquist. President Clinton is the first Democratic president in over 20 years to make appointments to the Supreme Court. The nomination of federal judges, however, may be the power of least significance to the president in exercising control over foreign policy for, as we will see in chapter 13, the judiciary typically tends to play a passive role in the making of U.S. foreign policy.

LIMITS AND CONSTRAINTS

The president occupies a number of important roles that allow him to exercise considerable power. At the same time, it is important not to overestimate his power, which often occurs given the popular conception expressed by most Americans. The president faces a *number of limitations and constraints* in exercising power, including:

1. Time;
2. Information;
3. The bureaucracy;
4. Congress;
5. State and local governments;
6. Political parties; and
7. Interest groups and social movements.

These limitations and constraints mean that on many occasions the president finds that, regardless of his wishes, he has great difficulty in successfully getting his way. The limits and constraints on presidential power tend to be strongest when it comes to domestic policy, but they exist for foreign policy as well.

Time. The president's first major problem is insufficient time to complete all of the tasks that are necessary to govern successfully. The president has one of the most demanding jobs imaginable: he is trying to govern a very complex society of over two hundred and fifty million people and he is responsible for representing the United States abroad in all of its international interactions. This means that the president is responsible for dealing with hundreds of individuals and issues every day. And more people and issues are trying to get his attention all the time. The president is also generally interested in implementing a program in accordance with his own vision of America and the world.

The president, however, like any human being, has only so much time to devote to people and issues. Beyond eating and sleeping and attending to a few other personal needs, the presidency is a full-time occupation seven days a week. The job of president is actually much more complicated than the simple picture portrayed. Much of his day is occupied with staff meetings and performing ceremonial duties, such as entertaining foreign dignitaries, publicly signing new pieces of legislation, or responding to national issues and disasters. Although each president has his own style, the job demands a great deal of time and energy, especially if the president wants to govern successfully. (See **essay 4.1** for more on the president's schedule.)

The president's time is limited not only from a daily perspective, but in terms of his time in office as well. The president may have as little as four years and certainly no more than eight years (according to the Twenty-second Amendment to the Constitution) to accomplish all that he has set his sights on—not much time given the demands of the job. Therefore, given the limited amount of time available, presidents are forced to be selective as to how they will occupy their time. For those issues on which the president is extremely attentive, he may exercise considerable power. However, for the remaining issues on which he lacks interest or time, the president may find that he is the president in name only.

Information. Another limitation on presidential power involves information problems. Most presidents are politicians who possess, at best, only general knowledge of the world around them. Much of

their knowledge is acquired through on-the-job training as a result of their previous positions. Unfortunately, there is no existing occupation which can adequately prepare one for becoming president of the United States. Many presidents were previously governors or members of Congress, which is certainly helpful for learning about different policies and how the policy process operates. Nevertheless, presidents undergo a considerable amount of on-the-job learning, using up valuable time and requiring much staff support for information and advice.

The president faces two problems in terms of information: scarcity and overabundance. A president may find that he does not have enough information. This is quite common, especially in the area of foreign policy. Presidents often have great difficulty getting sufficient information about international events, particularly during crises when time becomes so limited and important. Unfortunately, even without adequate information, a president may have no choice but to make decisions. The other problem is that the president often gets too much information in dealing with an issue. The problem here is that, given his pressing schedule, he doesn't have enough time to digest all the available information, or he may be provided with contradictory information. Nevertheless, decisions must be made. Take the example of a summit meeting between an American president and a foreign leader. The president is typically briefed before a visit about the leader's views and priorities, and the major issues that are included on the summit agenda. The president will also be given a large amount of information—that is, "homework"—which he is supposed to review in preparation for the meeting. However, other pressing duties may beckon him. Having too little or too much information makes it that much harder for the president to successfully exercise power.

The Bureaucracy. The third major constraint is the bureaucracy. As we discussed above, the president is the chief administrator and, in theory, the bureaucracy responds to his desires. This description has much truth to it. The president's personal staff and advisers are crucial to his exercise of power. However,

ESSAY 4.1
TIME CONSTRAINTS AND THE PRESIDENT'S DAILY SCHEDULE

The president is a busy person. Given the size of the U.S. government and its high level of international involvement, the presidency may be the most demanding job in the world. He must be on constant call, and he is heavily dependent on his staff to assist him in arranging his schedule and getting him through the many items and issues he must attend to during a day. Some presidents tend to be more active and involved than other presidents such as Jimmy Carter. Nevertheless, the **time constraints and workload** for all presidents are quite demanding.

The schedule below illustrates *the life of a president for a typical day*, in this case for President Carter on Friday, November 16, 1979.

5:00 A.M.	President received a wake up call from White House operator.
5:29	The president went to the Oval Office.
7:15–7:25	The president met with his assistant for National Security Affairs, Zbigniew Brzezinski.
7:30	The president went to Cabinet Room to participate in a breakfast meeting to discuss foreign policy issues with Walter F. Mondale, vice president; Cyrus R. Vance, secretary of state; Harold Brown, secretary of defense; Lloyd N. Cutler, counsel; Hedley W. Donovan, senior adviser; Hamilton Jordan, chief of staff.
8:22	The president returned to the Oval Office, accompanied by and met with Vice President Mondale, Secretary of State Vance, and National Security Adviser Brzezinski.
8:55–9:12	The president met with Secretary of Defense Brown.
9:27	The president went to the South Grounds.
9:28	The president motored from the south grounds to the Washington Hilton Hotel where he participated in the White House Conference on Libraries and Information Services.
9:31	The president was greeted by Charles Benton, chairman, and Marilyn K. Gell, director of the White House Conference on Libraries and Information Services.
9:35	The president went to the off-stage announcement area, then to the podium in the International Ballroom and was introduced by Mr. Benton.
9:39–9:52	The president addressed approximately 1,200 guests attending the conference, with members of the press present.
9:55	The president returned to his motorcade and returned to the south grounds of the White House.
10:02	The president returned to the Oval Office.
10:06–10:08	The president placed a call to Senator Howard W. Cannon (D-Nevada).
10:30–11:00	The president met with Vice President Mondale; Hamilton Jordan, staff aide; Joseph L. "Jody" Powell, press secretary; Alonzo L. McDonald, Jr., White House staff director; Frank B. Moore, assistant for Congressional Liaison; Ray Jenkins, special assistant, Press Office; Stuart E. Eizenstat, assistant for Domestic Affairs and Policy; Counsel Cutler; and National Security Adviser Brzezinski.
11:30	The president met with Neil Hartigan, lt. governor (D-Illinois) and Robert S. Strauss, ambassador at large designate.
11:35–12:10	The president met with Hedley Donovan, senior presidential adviser.
11:35	The president received a call by Representative Eligio "Kika" de la Garza (D-Texas).

11:46–11:51   The president received a call from Representative James Wright (D-Texas).

12:16   The president participated in a photo opportunity with Charles Richard Stanton, mayor (D-Manchester, New Hampshire); John Hoben, coordinator of Resources and Development, Manchester, New Hampshire; and Bruce Kirschenbaum, associate for Intergovernmental Affairs.

12:19   The president participated in a photo opportunity with James Whitmore, actor; Mrs. James (Mary) Whitmore; and Alan G. Raymond, staff assistant, Office of Communications.

12:20–12:23   The president participated in a farewell photo opportunity with Doris Brenner, departing administrative assistant, Office of Congressional Liaison, and Danny C. Tate, deputy assistant for Congressional Liaison.

12:27   The president returned to the second floor residence.

12:30   The president and the first lady had lunch.

12:47   The president returned to the Oval Office.

1:03   The president participated in a briefing for state governors to discuss the Iranian situation and the energy supply, with members of the press present.

1:39   The president returned to the Oval Office.

1:45–1:50   The president met with his speechwriter, Achsah P. Nesmith.

2:22   The president met with Timothy E. Kraft, campaign manager, Carter-Mondale Presidential Committee, Inc.

2:25   The president met with Press Secretary Powell.

2:31   The president met with Ed Kelly, commissioner of Parks and Recreation for the city of Chicago, Illinois, and Campaign Manager Kraft.

2:40–2:50   The president met with Secretary of State Vance and National Security Adviser Brzezinski.

2:52–5:00   The president returned to the Cabinet Room and participated in a meeting to discuss defense appropriations for the 1981 U.S. budget with James McIntyre, director of the Office of Management and Budget, and other officials.

3:06–3:13   The president received a call from Senator Robert C. Byrd (D-West Virginia), Majority Leader of the Senate.

4:31   The president received a call from Robert Krueger, ambassador at large and coordinator for Mexican Affairs.

5:00   The president returned to the Oval Office.

5:05   The president met with Jack Watson, Jr., assistant for Intergovernmental Affairs and Cabinet secretary.

5:07–5:22   The president met with Luther H. Hodges, Jr., under secretary of Commerce.

5:45   The president and the first lady hosted a reception for members of the National Council of Negro Women on the State Floor.

6:07–6:30   The president addressed approximately 485 guests attending the reception, with members of the press present.

6:30   The president returned to the second floor residence.

7:01–7:14   The president received a call from Benjamin R. Civiletti, attorney general.

7:08–7:11   The president placed a call to Counsel Cutler.

7:10   The president had dinner with the first lady; Amy Carter; Joanne and Paloma Kressman of Portsmouth, New Hampshire. Paloma Kressman was an elementary school student who asked a question at the president's town meeting in Portsmouth.

7:49   The presidential party went to the family theater where they watched the movie, If I Had a Million.

8:57	The president returned to the second floor residence.	10:28	The president returned to the second floor residence.
10:09	The president went to the south grounds and went jogging.	11:45 P.M.	The president retired.

SOURCES: U.S., President, Jimmy Carter, *The Daily Diary of President Jimmy Carter* (November 16, 1979); U.S., White House, *The President's Schedule* (November 16, 1979); and U.S., White House, *The President's Schedule,* Revised (November 16, 1979).

the bureaucracy has also become so large and entrenched that it is often unresponsive to the president. Therefore, the development of a large bureaucracy has had contradictory consequences for presidential power: it can be of great value for the president in his roles as commander in chief, chief diplomat, chief administrator or chief legislator, yet it can also be extremely unresponsive to presidential requests or commands.

A major constraint a new president faces when he enters office is the set of policies and programs administered by the bureaucracy already in place. Each bureaucratic organization tends to develop its own goals and subculture over time which may be at odds with the policies preferred by the president. *Bureaucratic organizations have a number of advantages* that allow them to remain autonomous and free of presidential control.

First, the president is heavily dependent on the bureaucracy for information. The bureaucracy not only determines the quantity of information available to the president, but also its quality: its level of comprehensiveness, the interpretation of reality embedded in the language, and the range of viable options for presidential consideration. Such information is not politically neutral and bureaucrats are adept at providing information and analyses which protect and improve the political position of their organization (or the position of individual bureaucrats).

Another advantage that members of the bureaucracy have is time. The president and his personal staff are there for only four or eight years. However, many bureaucrats occupy positions of importance for ten, twenty, or thirty years—they can always outlast a president who they feel wants to change too much too quickly. And there is very little that the president can do about bureaucratic opposition. As government employees, bureaucrats are members of **the civil service** and have tenure or other rights that make it very difficult for presidents to fire them—even for incompetence.[5]

Another advantage that bureaucrats have in affecting presidential power is their close relationship with Congress. The approval of programs and funding for organizations within the executive branch is heavily influenced by the Congress. Therefore, it is not unusual for networks to develop between executive branch employees and members of Congress around different issues, with each group dependent on the other. For example, a mutually reinforcing relationship has existed for a long time between members of the military and members of Congress on the House and Senate Armed Services Committees. These networks are very difficult for the president to break, and if he does attempt to do so members of the bureaucratic organization being challenged can always turn to their well-placed friends in Congress for support.

The final advantage that bureaucratic organizations enjoy is official independence from presidential authority. Most of the organizations and agencies within the executive branch, such as those involved in national security, like the State Department, Department of Defense, and Central Intelligence Agency, are under presidential authority. However, many organizations, such as the Federal Reserve Board, are independent of presidential authority, at least in daily operations. This situation has arisen because of congressional decisions in the creation of these organizations, granting them legal autonomy to ensure that they would be more responsive to Congress than the president. These officially autonomous organizations can not only resist the president's exercise of power by taking advantage of their information and close relationships with members of Congress, but also have the legal right to ignore presidential requests. Therefore, the president, although the chief administrator, faces considerable bureaucratic constraints on the exercise of his power.

Congress. The president and Congress share power. Therefore, while the president initiates and can veto legislation, Congress is often a major constraint on the exercise of presidential power. When the president first enters office, he usually enjoys a honeymoon with Congress. This means that members of Congress usually are extraordinarily responsive to presidential requests in light of the president's recent victory, indicating that a majority of the American people support him and his policies. However, the honeymoon rarely lasts more than a few months and then it's back to business as usual in presidential-congressional relations. Given the constitutional foundations of congressional power and the contemporary dynamics of the two chambers, to be discussed in chapter 12, the president quickly finds that Congress is often extremely unresponsive to his requests and can be quite obstructionist at times.

Traditionally, members of Congress actively influence domestic policies, much to the president's chagrin. Although more responsive and less obstructionist in the area of foreign policy since World War II, the Vietnam War and Watergate have led to a much more independent and assertive Congress in this area as well. After the honeymoon, a president quickly finds that many members of Congress do not share his vision of America and the world, and are unsympathetic to many of his policies. Many congressmen also have agendas of their own that may be incompatible with the president's agenda. Furthermore, since the Vietnam War years, the U.S. government has usually been divided (with a Republican president and a Democratic-run Congress, or vice versa) making it that much more difficult for the president to be effective. In sum, the fact that the legislature is an independent branch with independent power means that Congress and the president will be involved in a constant struggle for power.

State and Local Governments. Another constraint on the president's ability to exercise power is the role of state and local governments. The president may be the commander in chief, the chief of state, and the chief administrator; however, he has no legal authority over state and local governments. State governments have their own power base within the United States, symbolized by the fifty state constitutions. The founding fathers created a federal system of government in which two sets of governments, each with its own sovereignty and authority, were established: a central government, usually referred to as the federal government by Americans, and state governments. Although state and local governments are most active in the domestic area, chapter 13 reviews how the role of state and local governments has grown in foreign affairs, most notably their influence on foreign economic policy.

Political Parties. The president is the head of his party. However, in the United States, being party leader does not translate into great political influence. Unlike the situation in most other countries, parties are weak in the United States. Hence, the Democratic and Republican parties are weak tools of presidential power. For example, presidents cannot force members of their own party to support them in Congress, for congressional members have independent power bases. Nor can the president dictate his heir for the presidential nomination to the party or even prevent a challenge to his own renomination, as President Ford experienced in 1976 with the Reagan challenge. Therefore, the weakness of American parties, in comparison to the strengths of parties abroad, makes it that much more difficult for the president to exercise power successfully.

Interest Groups and Social Movements. A final impediment to the exercise of presidential power is the impact of interest groups and social movements on domestic politics and the governmental process. The United States contains thousands and thousands of groups organized to promote their own goals and interests, regardless of what the president believes or wants. These groups utilize all avenues available to them in making their views known and promoting their interests, including influencing Congress, members of the executive branch bureaucracy, the media, and the American public.

Presidents who attempt to change aspects of public policy find not only resistance within the federal bureaucracy and Congress, but throughout society from groups which are quite comfortable with the status quo. At the same time, many social movements and groups demand changes in governmental policy which, if opposed by the president, may result in the creation of political antagonists or enemies. Interest groups and social movements tend to be more visible when it comes to domestic policies concerning issues such as abortion or taxation. However, as discussed in chapter 16, they have grown in importance in the area of foreign policy as well, thus complicating the lives of presidents even further.

UNCERTAIN ELEMENTS

In addition to the strengths presidents possess and the limitations they face in the exercise of power, a number of uncertain elements that a president cannot control affect his ability to govern. Sometimes these elements may work for him, making him more powerful. Other times they work against him, acting as another constraint on presidential power. These *uncertain elements in the makeup of presidential power* include:

1. The courts;
2. Public opinion;
3. The media; and
4. The environment.

The Courts. Although the president nominates all federal judges and the Senate tends to approve, with an occasional exception, virtually all of these nominations, this does not guarantee that judges' rulings will support presidential policies. The classic example of an appointment run amok, at least from the

president's perspective, was President Eisenhower's appointment of Earl Warren as chief justice to the Supreme Court. Eisenhower thought he was appointing a political moderate, but Earl Warren led the Supreme Court in a liberal direction over the course of the next two decades. The uncertainty of predicting the political views of judicial appointees is reinforced by the fact that most judicial rulings are made by federal judges who were appointed by previous presidents. Therefore, while the courts generally tend to play a passive role in the area of foreign policy, the impact of judicial rulings on presidential power varies.

Public Opinion. The public is an important source of presidential power. Yet, public opinion can also turn against a sitting president, as Johnson, Nixon, Ford, Carter, and Bush discovered. Public opinion tends to be most supportive of the president when he enters office, declining over time. Initially, there is a honeymoon period in which the public thinks highly of the new president and gives him the benefit of the doubt. During times of crisis the public also tends to rally around the president. However, public approval of the president and his policies tends to diminish the longer he stays in office. Therefore, public opinion strengthens a president's power early in office, but increasingly constrains presidential power throughout his tenure.

The Media. The media is another source of great uncertainty in the exercise of presidential power. In order to better understand media coverage and its impact, which will be discussed in chapter 18, it is important to remember that different individuals and groups, within the government and throughout society, try to influence the media and the power they have over the communications process to gain control of the government and influence domestic politics. Presidents, in particular, are heavily dependent on the media and attempt to promote a positive image. Overall, there is a cyclical pattern in the media's impact on presidential power. The media is a crucial source of presidential power early on for gaining the presidential nomination, winning the election, and exercising power in a new administration. However, the media is also a source of much of the difficulty that presidents face later in office, regardless of who is in office or the individual's party affiliation, which contributes to the negative impact of the other constraints and uncertainties on presidential power discussed above.

The Global Context. The final element that has an inconsistent impact on presidential power is the global context, as already discussed in chapter 3. Although presidents make decisions that impact the global environment, presidents often react to events and developments as they occur abroad. President Nixon, for example, was forced to respond to the dramatic rise in oil prices precipitated by the Arab oil embargo of 1973. President Ford had little time to pull out the remaining Americans from the chaos of South Vietnam after the collapse of the South Vietnamese military in 1975. President Carter had no choice but to deal with the fall of the shah in Iran and the taking of American hostages in 1979. President Reagan had to respond to Mikhail Gorbachev, a new Soviet leader in 1985, who proposed numerous initiatives toward further arms control and disarmament. President Bush faced an environment where, on the one hand, the cold war had ended with the collapse of communism in Eastern Europe and the Soviet Union and, on the other hand, Iraq invaded Kuwait. President Clinton came into office at a time when the state of Yugoslavia broke up, resulting in new states and the outbreak of violent conflicts. Sometimes international events and developments strengthen the president's exercise of power; sometimes they create problems.

Not only are presidents unable to control the particular international situation with which they are faced, they have little control over America's global position, which reflects a set of underlying, long-term trends within the international system. Truman, Eisenhower, Kennedy, and Johnson each had the good fortune to be president during a period in which the United States was clearly the global superpower in every dimension. However, subsequent presidents, beginning with Nixon, came to office during a time when the United States was experiencing a relative decline of national power, which was reflected in the military challenge of the Soviet Union and the economic challenges posed by Europe, Japan, and the Pacific rim countries. Although the end of the cold war has provided new opportunities, Presidents Bush and Clinton have the disadvantage of exercising power, especially in foreign policy, at a time when United States influence throughout the world is not what it once was in the cold war past.

THE PARADOX OF PRESIDENTIAL POWER

· · · · · · · · · · · · · ·

How do we make sense of the nature of presidential power given all of the elements discussed above? The president has important constitutional roles and strengths that make him a powerful player in the political arena. At the same time the president faces limits and constraints on his ability to exercise power. The successful exercise of presidential power becomes even more problematic when one considers uncertain elements that impact on the president with little regularity, sometimes strengthening his hand and other times weakening it. When all is said and done, presidents face a **paradox of presidential power:** on the one hand, the president is a powerful actor; on the other hand—relative to the rest of government, the society, and the context—he faces many constraints in successfully exercising power.[6]

The president is not nearly as powerful as most Americans believe. While at times he is able to successfully influence the policy process, at other times he has very little impact on the policy process, regardless of his best efforts to exercise power. As President John F. Kennedy understood, the president "is rightly described as a man of extraordinary powers. Yet it is also true that he must wield those powers under extraordinary limitations."[7] One of Harry Truman's more famous remarks was in reference to presidential power after meeting his successor, General Eisenhower: "He'll sit right here and he'll say, 'Do this. Do that!' And nothing will happen. Poor Ike—it won't be a bit like the army. He'll find it very frustrating."[8]

The notion of a paradox provides us with a general understanding of the nature of presidential power. Much more, however, must be said about when and where the president is most able, and least able, to exercise power. To be more specific about this, we need a better understanding of the concept of power and how it is exercised. We must also be aware of different domains or areas in which it is possible to exercise power.

Power, very simply, is the ability to influence the surrounding environment in ways that one prefers. *The exercise of power can be accomplished in one of two ways.* First, there is the "positive" exercise of power; that is, the ability to initiate, to implement, to make something happen. This is what most people think of when it comes to the exercise of power: making others do something that they are reluctant or opposed to doing. A second way to exercise power, which may be called "negative" power, is the ability to negate, to prevent others from doing something against your wishes. The use of negative power is typically ignored, yet is important in the overall exercise of power.[9]

Does a president generally have the upper hand in exercising positive or negative power? To initiate and implement policy, he usually needs the support of others—a demanding task given the constraints and uncertainties he faces. He needs to build political coalitions to support his initiatives and, at a minimum, convince others not to oppose his policies. The exercise of negative power, on the other hand, is less demanding. It is easier for a president to stifle or negate something. This does not require building and maintaining extensive political coalitions in support of policy initiatives as they evolve over time. Rather, negation is more a question of preventing an initiative from surfacing on the political agenda or stopping it after it has surfaced—a much simpler task. The president, for example, has the unique ability to stifle virtually any piece of legislation he chooses through his use of the veto, which is rarely overridden. Although there is no guarantee that the president will be successful in exercising negative power, the odds are much higher than in his efforts to exercise positive power.

To have a clearer understanding of presidential power, we also need to discuss the domain or **issue-area** in which power is exercised. For some issues, the president is likely to be a powerful political figure. However, on other issues, the president may lack power. But which issues? Issues may be classified in a variety of ways, but a *breakdown into two traditional issue-areas is helpful:* domestic policy and foreign policy. Although distinctions between policies that are primarily domestically oriented or globally oriented are increasingly difficult to make, this traditional division serves the purpose of clarifying the paradox of presidential power.[10]

The president has greater strengths and fewer weaknesses in the exercise of power in foreign policy as opposed to domestic policy. Three of the constitutional roles contributing to presidential power really involve only foreign affairs: commander in chief, chief diplomat, and chief of state. These roles allow the president to exercise much more power, both positive and negative, in the foreign policy area, especially during crises. Furthermore, many of the constraints that he faces tend to be weaker in the area of foreign policy. The bureaucracy, Congress, the courts, state and local governments, the public, political parties, the media, and interest groups all play an independent role in the making of U.S. foreign policy. However, they tend to be more active and influential concerning domestic policies. When it comes to formulating policies to cope with domestic economic issues, for instance, everyone gets into the act and attempts to obtain a piece of the pie.

By combining the two ways power can be exercised with the two types of issue-areas, we can develop a simple, yet valuable, two-by-two classification scheme for making better sense of the paradox of presidential power (see **figure 4.1**). What we find is that the president is most powerful in influencing U.S. foreign policy, especially if he is opposed to an initiative or decides to do nothing, that is, not to act. The president still enjoys considerable power in initiating foreign policies, but he has had to face more constraints since Vietnam. His greatest influence on domestic policy lies in his ability to oppose policy initiatives taken by others. He is least powerful when he attempts to influence domestic policy positively,

FIGURE 4.1
CATEGORIZING PRESIDENTIAL POWER

The Exercise of Power

	Positive	Negative
Foreign policy	Moderate	High
Domestic policy	Low	Moderate

Issue Area

especially if he is attempting to initiate policy, whether it involves the budget, welfare, or the economy.

In sum, the question of presidential power does not allow for a simple black or white answer. Instead, there exists a paradox of presidential power. A variety of factors influence presidential power and the net result is that the president is both the most powerful political figure in the United States and, at the same time, extremely constrained. He is most powerful in areas of foreign policy and least powerful in the domestic policy arena. He is most successful in exercising power when he opposes the initiatives of others, but requires more skill and luck to promote successfully policies of his own. These are the patterns or trends that make up the paradox of presidential power, making it difficult for a president to govern successfully and, consequently, fulfill the high expectations that most Americans have of him.

THE PROBLEM OF PRESIDENTIAL GOVERNANCE

· · · · · · · · · · · · · · ·

The paradox of presidential power makes it extremely difficult for a president to govern success-

fully today. *Two patterns seem to prevail when it comes to the president's ability to govern and lead the country:*

1. A president tends to go through a presidential life cycle in which presidents are strongest when they enter office and their power tends to decline over time;
2. A crisis of governance seems to exist in American politics in which no individual or organization, including the presidency, is able to lead the government and country.

These patterns have become increasingly visible since the Vietnam War and have important consequences for the policymaking process in foreign policy.[11]

THE PRESIDENTIAL LIFE CYCLE

The paradox of presidential power has important consequences for the way in which the political process works and for the president's ability to influence that process over time. Most presidents find that their ability to exercise power tends to go through a cyclical process over the course of their term of office: they enter office near the peak of their power and by the end of their term they are considerably weaker. To explain this **presidential life cycle,** one must understand how the paradox of presidential power impacts on the president's ability to govern over time.

A president enters office with all of his constitutional roles fully available to him, constraints at their weakest, and with most of the uncertain elements working in his favor. Newly elected presidents, as discussed above, proclaim an **electoral mandate** behind them, and their policies. During the first few months in office, the president not only enjoys a **honeymoon** with the Congress, but with the media and the public as well.[12] This begins with the inauguration of the president, celebrated as a triumph of American democracy in action. People tend to be hopeful and interested in the new president, his first lady, their personal characteristics, and style of governing, and the president enters a relatively hospitable political environment in which he is provided the leeway to initiate new policies. This makes it a most inopportune time for individuals and groups to be critical of the new leader of the United States.

Within a short period of time, however, the honeymoon with Congress and the media is over. Congress begins to act independently of presidential wishes, especially if the majority party is different from the president's party—a common occurrence since Vietnam. Members of the media soon spend more time addressing the issues and critically analyzing presidential policies. Interest groups and social movements make concerted efforts to influence the policymaking process. Under such conditions a president quickly finds he is no longer operating with a clean slate in an optimistic political environment. In fact, the longer the president is in office, the more likely that critical judgments will be made by individuals and groups throughout government and society concerning how well the president is doing and who benefits from his policies. As the political environment becomes more critical and uncontrollable, the president finds that his public approval rating also tends to decline.

Lyndon Baines Johnson, a former majority leader in the U.S. Senate and a shrewd observer of American politics, once gave the following portrayal of the presidential life cycle after a landslide victory:

When you win big you can have anything you want for a time. You come home with that big landslide and there isn't a one of them [in Congress] who'll stand in your way. No, they'll be glad to be aboard and to have their photograph taken with you and be part of all that victory. They'll come along and they'll give you almost everything you want for a while and then they'll turn on you. They always do. They'll lay in waiting, waiting for you to make a slip and you will. They'll give you almost everything and then they'll make you pay for it. They'll get tired of all those columnists writing how smart you are and how weak they are and then the pendulum will swing back.[13]

The president's ability to exercise power successfully usually declines significantly within a few years. During this period, a president's strengths have diminished, his constraints have intensified, and the uncertain elements tend to work, more often then not, against him. The decline of public support does not consist of a linear pattern, but of a bumpy road, with peaks and valleys, that tends to move downward. The major exception to this pattern is during times of national emergency and crisis, when the constraints on presidential power are temporarily reduced as the public turns to the president for leadership and resolution of the crisis. These spurts of public approval are reinforced by congressional deference to the president during times of crisis, especially in foreign policy, and his tendency to dominate communications and the media. However, once the crisis subsides, normal politics resurfaces and the downward pattern tends to continue. Eventually, the constraints multiply to the point where the president has considerable difficulty exercising power over most issues. By the end of his term of office, he may be so weak that he is referred to as a **lame-duck** president.

Figure 4.2 demonstrates the overall decline in public approval that every contemporary president has faced throughout the life cycle of their presidencies.[14] Lyndon Johnson had an instinctive feel for the rhythm of the presidency, especially in terms of the

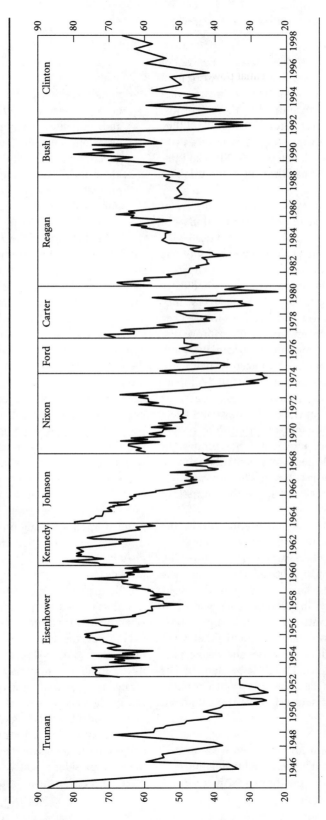

FIGURE 4.2
PUBLIC APPROVAL OF PRESIDENTIAL PERFORMANCE, 1945–1988

SOURCE: The Gallup Opinion Index; The Gallup Report.

president's relationship with Congress. "You've got to give it all you can, that first year," Johnson told Harry McPherson, a top aide. "Doesn't matter what kind of majority you come in with. You've got just one year when they treat you right and before they start worrying about themselves. The third year, you lose votes. . . . The fourth's all politics. You can't put anything through when half the Congress is thinking how to beat you."[15]

This cyclical pattern is largely a function of **presidential promises and public expectations**—in the minds of political leaders, the politically involved and active, and especially members of the general public.[16] During the presidential nomination and general election campaigns, all candidates promise the American people that, if elected, they will improve the quality of voters' lives. They promise to clean the environment, improve the quality of education, prevent American men and women from dying abroad, and keep America free and strong. These promises are particularly important when it comes to bread-and-butter issues, for they tend to interest Americans the most and affect them most directly. Candidates promise to restore or maintain economic prosperity; they promise to reduce inflation and unemployment; they promise to improve the economy so that all Americans will have a better chance of attaining the "American Dream."

These promises, certainly a normal part of any election process, create expectations among the public that presidents are simply unable to fulfill. Regardless of how many issues are actually addressed by presidents, however, most of the problems do not go away. In fact, many get worse and new ones arise constantly. Why? Very simply, presidents are not powerful enough, nor do they serve long enough, to fulfill the promises and high expectations they have created. David Halberstam, in *The Best and the Brightest,* described the problem of high expectations that President Kennedy encountered this way:

As President, Kennedy was faced with the great gap of any modern politician, but perhaps greatest in contemporary America:

the gap between the new unbelievable velocity of modern life which can send information and images hurtling through the air onto the television screen, exciting desires and appetites, changing mores almost overnight, and the slowness of traditional governmental institutions produced by ideas and laws of another era, bound in normal bureaucratic red tape and traditional seniority.[17]

Take the **issue of the national economy** where candidates typically promise that under their administration there will be higher growth, lower inflation, and lower unemployment. How can the president fulfill these promises? The two major strategies open to the government to manipulate the economy are beyond presidential control: "monetary" policy and "fiscal" policy. The government's ability to control interest rates and the money supply is determined by the Federal Reserve Board, an independent agency within the executive branch that has no legal obligation to respond to presidential requests and often does not. Fiscal policy, the ability to affect taxation and government spending, is primarily a function of the legislative process, which the president does not dictate. So, candidates make economic promises to a very interested American electorate which cannot be easily fulfilled upon attaining office. The process of promoting expectations that are likely to remain unfulfilled reinforces the vicious life cycle of presidential power.

By the end of his term in office, therefore, it is not unusual that the president is much weaker than when he first took the oath of office. The presidential life cycle makes it very difficult for him to implement successfully his preferred policies. The inability to fulfill the optimism and high expectations created early on also means that much of the American public will grow disenchanted with the incumbent president, preferring to see a new individual as president of the United States. This sets the stage for a repeat performance of the presidential life cycle for the new president—early optimism eventually replaced by pessimism and frustration.

AMERICAN POLITICS AND THE CRISIS OF GOVERNANCE

The paradox and life cycle of presidential power have led to a **crisis of governance** in American politics that has heightened since the Vietnam years and the end of the cold war. Presidents are elected to govern and lead the country, but they are unable to do so for political power is dispersed throughout government and society and the president faces major limitations and constraints in the exercise of his power. This means that even when the problems facing the country are growing in their severity, presidents are not only unable to govern and lead, their administrations are often seen as failures in the public eye. The crisis of governance actually has intensified over the years as a result of the rise of "divided government" in which the president and Congress are led by people of opposing political parties.[18]

The endemic U.S. governmental **debt problem** illustrates the crisis of governance facing the country. Ronald Reagan promised that as president he would reduce the growing federal deficit and balance the budget. Yet, during the Reagan administration's term of office, the total national debt of the U.S. government almost tripled, from $908 billion in 1980 to $2.6 trillion in 1988. As the size of the debt has increased, the interest that the government has had to pay to finance the debt has also grown, from 8.9 percent of the federal budget in 1980 to 14 percent by 1988.[19] With the debt problem perceived as a growing crisis, governmental efforts have been made periodically since the mid-eighties to control and reduce the deficit. In fact, there has been much talk of a balanced budget under President Clinton and the Republican-controlled Congress in the 1990s. Yet total governmental debt continues to mount. No one individual or institution has the ability to impose its will on the budget process. The trend is more of the same—increasing debt. Even when it comes to a crucial issue such as this, where most people agree that large federal deficits sap the strength of the U.S. government and the country, a crisis of governance and leadership exists. Therefore, the budget deficit continues to eat away at the fabric of America's economic strength. That is, until a crisis results which

compels political action to be taken, and gives the president the opportunity to take the lead.

Yet, given the popular image of presidential power, presidents are given credit when things are perceived as going well and they are blamed when things go badly. Unfortunately, American politics and the policy process, such as with the budget deficit, are incredibly complex and beyond considerable presidential control. With so many complex problems to address—the debt problem, the economy, energy, welfare, education, the environment, foreign policy—it is a very demanding time to be president. As long as presidential promises and public expectations remain high, the president's job becomes virtually an impossible task.

Should success occur, given the lack of presidential power, it is probably not by the president's own design. Nonetheless, the president—the person perceived to be the leader of the country—will be rewarded in terms of public prestige, greater power, and reelection (for him or his successor). On the other hand, if the president is perceived as unsuccessful—a failure—this results not only in a weakened president, but one that the public wants replaced. This produces the opportunity to challenge an incumbent president or his heir as presidential nominee. It also reinforces the notion that the new president, from whichever party, will want to distance himself from many of the policies of his predecessor. This contributes to change, as opposed to continuity, in the types of public policies pursued by presidents, making it very difficult for the U.S. government to form a coherent long-term program for governing and leading the country into the twenty-first century.

PRESIDENTIAL POWER AND THE CONDUCT OF FOREIGN POLICY

· · · · · · · · · · · · · ·

To what extent does the paradox of presidential power and the presidential life cycle affect the president's ability to govern U.S. foreign policy? To what extent does a crisis of governance exist in the foreign policy-making process? Although not nearly as powerful as the popular stereotype held by many, the president has greater strengths and fewer weaknesses in the exercise of power in foreign, as opposed to domestic, policy. In fact, it was during the cold war years that presidential power in the making of foreign policy reached its height. Since the Vietnam War, however, the president's ability to govern and lead foreign policy has declined and become much more complex. Such a state of presidential power has intensified with the collapse of the cold war as the United States approaches the twenty-first century.

SOME HISTORICAL CONTEXT

The president has not consistently dominated the foreign policy process throughout American history. As will be discussed in greater depth in chapter 12, the Constitution of the United States produced a central government with "separate institutions sharing powers," resulting in an "invitation to struggle" between the executive and legislative branches.[20] In fact, executive-legislative relations in foreign policy have been fluid and dynamic, and have fluctuated with changes in the political environment.

As described by Arthur Schlesinger, Jr., in *The Imperial Presidency*, executive-legislative relations have been characterized by a kind of "pendulum or cyclical effect."[21] In times of national emergency, particularly war, power tends to flow toward the president and the executive branch. During times of peace—that is, when conflict has subsided—power tends to flow back to Congress. Yet, while Congress tends to reassert its constitutional authority and power following war, increases in presidential power during periods of conflict tend to be so extensive that it seldom returns to prewar levels. Thus, the cyclical ebb and flow in executive-legislative relations in foreign policy has enabled a president to accumulate greater power over time.

PRESIDENTIAL SUPREMACY DURING THE COLD WAR YEARS

As a result of World War II and with the rise of the cold war, the president became supreme in the making of foreign policy. Aaron Wildavsky wrote an influential article three decades ago in favor of the **two presidencies thesis.**[22] He argued that there were really two presidencies: a powerful presidency in foreign policy and a weak presidency in domestic policy. Examining the legislative-executive relationship during the fifties and sixties, he found that presidents were much more successful in influencing foreign policy legislation than they were in affecting the outcome of domestic legislation. According to the two presidencies thesis, the paradox and life cycle of presidential power were operative only in the realm of domestic policy, but the president was able to govern and lead the country when it came to foreign policy.

This was a powerful analysis and gained much popularity. In the fifties and sixties—the high cold war era—presidents were extremely powerful political actors in the making of U.S. foreign policy. Constraints were relatively weak and the uncertain elements tended to be supportive of presidential efforts to contain the threat of communism. The foreign policy bureaucracy, for example, expanded and became an important tool for implementing the president's containment policies. Congress largely was acquiescent and supportive of most presidential initiatives during the cold war years of globalism in U.S. foreign policy. A strong anticommunist consensus developed among the American citizenry and foreign policy elite, resulting in strong public, media, and interest group support of a policy of containment and presidential actions abroad. This was also a period in which political party differences were minimal and state and local governments and the courts were inactive in foreign policy. This supportive domestic climate also existed at a time when the United States was the preeminent power in all the world. The preference for a strong presidency, especially in foreign policy, was strong not only throughout the country, but particularly in liberal, academic, and intellectual circles.[23]

It is important to recall that before World War II "few" institutions within the government were oriented toward foreign affairs and national security. The policymaking elite was extremely small and centered within the State Department. World War II "changed" this dramatically. Overnight, the U.S. government was redirected to devote itself to fighting a global war: the military expanded enormously and civilian agencies grew to assist the president in fighting the war. The governmental war effort, in turn, put the economy and society on a war-footing to provide the necessary personnel, equipment and services to achieve U.S. victory. However, unlike previous wars in American history, the United States demobilized only for a short time following victory. With the rise of anti-communism, the United States quickly remobilized and expanded its resources in order to fight a global cold war. The power of the presidency and the foreign policy bureaucracy, thus, continued to grow during the cold war years, becoming a permanent part of the American landscape.[24]

The 1950s and 1960s were perceived to be a time when communism directly threatened the security of the United States. During such times of perceived national emergency, the president could exert considerable powers as commander in chief, head of state, chief diplomat, and chief administrator, with Congress increasingly acquiescent to presidential initiatives. In fact, by the mid-fifties a bipartisan consensus developed between Democrats and Republicans in support of the president and U.S. foreign policy.

The cold war years of American globalism were, thus, a time of extraordinary presidential power in foreign affairs. This is not to say that the president faced no opposition or that he controlled all foreign policy issues. Nonetheless, the president was clearly the dominant political figure and exercised a disproportionate amount of influence over U.S. foreign policy. Presidents had the ability to formulate and implement policies in accordance with their cold war beliefs.[25]

THE DECLINE OF PRESIDENTIAL POWER SINCE VIETNAM AND THE END OF THE COLD WAR

The tragedies of Vietnam and Watergate symbolized the end of the dominance of global containment as the basis of U.S. foreign policy and signified the end of the extraordinary power that presidents enjoyed in making foreign policy. The president retains the ability to exercise considerable power in foreign affairs; however, the constraints and uncertainties facing him have increased during the post-Vietnam years, making it much more difficult for the president to successfully dominate foreign policy. With the end of the cold war, the constraints and uncertainties facing presidents in the making of foreign policy have continued to multiply.

The anticommunist consensus that existed throughout government and society could not survive the Vietnam War. Its collapse produced a reassertive Congress, new and varied interest groups and social movements, a more critical media, and a cynical public. The post-Vietnam years also symbolized and accelerated the weakening of American power relative to other world actors in the international political economy. Foreign economics, and other so-called "low policy" and "intermestic" issues, likewise, rose in significance and increasingly became a part of the foreign policy agenda.[26] Therefore, a president entered office facing constraints and uncertainties that hampered his ability to utilize the sources of presidential power described above. In fact, all presidents since Vietnam have experienced considerable problems in governing and leading the country in foreign policy.

In the past, given the rise of anticommunism and the national security state, the president could lead the country, but only in the direction of fervent anticommunism, containment, and interventionism. Since Vietnam, with the collapse of the anticommunist consensus and the rise of pluralist politics, the president—and in reality, the political system—has a difficult time generating leadership in any direction for a sustained period of time. Every post-Vietnam president has failed to generate a new consensus or sustain sufficient support behind their policies for any length of time.

Whereas a president's positive and negative power in foreign affairs was quite high during the cold war years, his power today has diminished, especially his ability to exercise positive power in foreign policy. During the cold war years the paradox and life cycle of presidential power did not seem to affect presidents much in the area of foreign policy; however, in the wake of Vietnam and Watergate, presidents must now contend with these patterns. The era of two presidencies and extraordinary presidential power in foreign policy is over. Presidents are still the most powerful individual actors, but they no longer automatically govern and dominate the making of U.S. foreign policy.[27]

GOVERNANCE PROBLEMS IN THE POST–VIETNAM WAR ERA

. . . .

Although the crisis of governance is greater in the area of domestic policy, it has also become a problem for presidents in foreign policy during the post–Vietnam War years. The issues facing the country are of greater complexity and scope than ever before, contributing to the perception of failed presidents since the Vietnam War. Presidents Nixon, Ford, and Carter all experienced crises of governance in foreign policy and were perceived as failures. Only President Reagan was able to buck the trend, yet even he was politically damaged and considered a lame duck at the close of his term.[28]

The Johnson Presidency. The first contemporary president suffering political damage as a result of frustrated attempts to govern U.S. foreign policy was Lyndon Baines Johnson. Johnson became president after the assassination of President John F. Kennedy in 1963. In 1964, he was elected president for four additional years in a landslide over the Republican challenger, Barry Goldwater. One of the campaign promises Johnson made during the election was that American troops would not die abroad in a war in Indochina. However, shortly after his election, President Johnson and his closest advisers decided that the **situation in Vietnam** was badly deteriorating and that the South Vietnamese government would only be able to maintain its independence from North Vietnam with greater American involvement. Operating with cold war beliefs emphasizing the necessity of containing communist aggression, presi-

dential decisions were made that resulted in the escalation of American intervention in Vietnam, which increased from 18,000 American troops under President Kennedy in 1963 to over 500,000 troops by 1966 under President Johnson. The Vietnam War had, thus, become Americanized.

While the American role escalated and the war continued, President Johnson and other military and administrative leaders told the American people that it was only a matter of time until the Vietnam War would be won; that is, the American policy of containment would allow the South Vietnamese to maintain their independence. On many occasions, the administration issued upbeat claims of a "light at the end of the tunnel." Then in February of 1968, during the Vietnamese holiday of Tet, the North Vietnamese army and Vietcong guerrillas launched a major offensive in which most of the country, including cities throughout the south and the U.S. Embassy in Saigon, came under enemy occupation or siege.

Although the offensive was repulsed by American and South Vietnamese forces, the damage was done. **The Tet offensive** indicated that the Johnson administration's public optimism was unjustified. President Johnson's credibility with the American people was destroyed. The president, the American war effort in Vietnam, and the cold war beliefs on which the containment strategy was founded, were increasingly challenged both within the government and throughout the domestic arena by a growing antiwar movement and public disenchantment. The president's power was dealt such a severe blow and Johnson was so deeply affected that he declined to seek the Democratic presidential nomination for the 1968 election. Johnson was the first presidential casualty of a failed U.S. foreign policy initiative.

The Nixon Presidency. The 1968 election pitted Hubert Humphrey, President Johnson's vice president, against the Republican challenger, Richard Nixon. Even though Nixon barely won the election, major foreign policy changes were initiated under his administration. President Richard Nixon attempted to promote a more stable global order through a realpolitik policy based on a new relationship of détente with the Soviet Union, negotiating the SALT I (Strategic Arms Limitation Talks) arms control treaty, and normalizing relations with the People's Republic of China. In an effort to respond to a weakening economy, he took the U.S. dollar off the gold standard, placed a 10 percent surcharge on Japanese imports, and installed wage and price controls. The early 1970s seemed to be a time of great success, for his policies were well-received and President Nixon was overwhelmingly reelected in 1972 with one of the largest popular vote totals in American history—63 percent.

The key to understanding the fate of President Nixon, however, was his policy toward the war in Vietnam. He had told the American public that his **"secret plan" to end the Vietnam War** would restore peace while maintaining American honor. The secret plan consisted of a strategy involving simultaneous de-escalation, escalation, and negotiations. De-escalation meant that U.S. troops were slowly phased out through a process of "Vietnamization."[29] Escalation entailed stepped-up American bombing of Indochina, as well as invading guerrilla sanctuaries in Cambodia and Laos. De-escalation and escalation, reinforced by détente initiatives with the Soviet Union and the People's Republic of China, were intended to elicit a negotiated agreement with the North Vietnamese, producing "peace with honor" and buying South Vietnam a "decent interval" for survival.

However, with the escalation, the antiwar movement reached its height. Antiwar activists called for the immediate withdrawal of all U.S. forces from Indochina and challenged American interventionism abroad. Nixon, a scrappy fighter from his earliest political days, responded by attacking the domestic opposition as if it were the enemy. This led to a number of illegal and unconstitutional activities by the Nixon White House. Revelations about Nixon's abuse of presidential power, known as **Watergate,** led to his downfall. First, a Senate committee held hearings, followed by House Judiciary Committee hearings which voted three counts of impeachment. This led President Nixon to resign in 1974, fearing a House of Representatives vote in favor of impeachment and conviction in the Senate.

Therefore, soon after his triumphant reelection, Nixon was forced to leave office in disgrace.

The impact of the Vietnam War and Watergate on the Nixon administration illustrates the incredible tension that can develop between the demands of national security and democracy. Many of the difficulties President Nixon faced were of his own making, for he had failed to understand the limitations and constraints on the exercise of presidential power generated by events such as the Vietnam War. Watergate resulted from President Nixon's efforts, in the name of national security, to implement his secret plan to provide peace with honor in Vietnam and win reelection while simultaneously using his office to thwart the rise of a legitimate political opposition. President Nixon, acting as if he had the ultimate authority over foreign policy, was unwilling to accept democratic challenges to his exercise of power. Very simply, Richard Nixon's downfall was a result of his abuse of presidential power. He was only the second president faced with impeachment for "high crimes and misdemeanors" in American history.[30] Hence, Nixon was the second presidential casualty of U.S. foreign policy in Vietnam. (For an overview, see **essay 4.2** on what Watergate was all about.)

The Ford Presidency. President Ford was unable to overcome the stigma of Watergate and his "pardon" of President Nixon. He continued to pursue many of the policies emphasized during the Nixon administration, reflected by retaining Henry Kissinger as secretary of state. However, many of these policies were now under attack. American intervention in Angola was cut off by liberal advocates who feared another Vietnam. Détente with the Soviet Union and efforts to normalize relations with the People's Republic of China were attacked for being too "soft" by conservative anticommunists within his own party. In fact, Ford barely survived a challenge by Ronald Reagan for the presidential nomination of the Republican party. The situation got so bad that Ford and Kissinger no longer used the word "détente" when discussing U.S. foreign policy. It was not surprising, then, that he was voted out of office in 1976 after having been president only three years—another failed president.

ESSAY 4.2
A CRISIS OF GOVERNANCE FACES THE PRESIDENCY: WHAT WATERGATE WAS ALL ABOUT

The "origins" of Watergate began with President Nixon's Vietnam policy. During 1969, the president decided to order the U.S. military to secretly bomb enemy forces along the Ho Chi Minh trail in Cambodia, a country which was officially a neutral party in the Vietnam War. On September 6, the story broke on the front page of the *New York Times*, triggering massive antiwar demonstrations throughout the country. Nixon and Kissinger were furious, to say the least. At Kissinger's request, President Nixon agreed to allow the Federal Bureau of Investigation (FBI) to "wiretap," illegally, members of Kissinger's National Security Council staff and a number of journalists in an effort to determine who was leaking information to the media. As the leaks continued, President Nixon turned to members of the White House staff—such as H. R. Haldeman, John Erlichman, Charles Colson, and G. Gordon Liddy, who came to be known as **the "plumbers"**—to plug White House leaks (all were later criminally indicted, found guilty, and sentenced to prison).

Throughout 1970, in response to intensified American bombing in Indochina and the invasion of Cambodia, the antiwar movement grew larger and louder, threatening Nixon's Vietnam policy. The response of the White House was to treat the antiwar movement as the enemy and devise a campaign to damage its credibility and destroy Nixon's critics, which included students, academics, journalists, and, members of what Nixon often referred to as the liberal establishment.

The **"enemies project"** resulted in a wide range of illegal activities such as the surveillance of activist groups and sabotage of demonstrations, use of the Federal Communications Commission to coerce the news media into providing less negative coverage of the administration, and threatening individuals with tax audits by the Internal Revenue Service. The most infamous exploit of the plumbers involved the burglary of Daniel Ellsberg's

psychiatrist's office in an effort to find scandalous information which would discredit Ellsberg, who had been responsible for leaking the explosive Pentagon Papers (which had exposed the government's Vietnam policy process throughout the 1960s) to the media.

By 1971, President Nixon had begun to worry about the outcome of the 1972 presidential election. The economy was overheating, the policy of détente had yet to produce any great accomplishments, the North Vietnamese were completely unresponsive at the negotiating table, and domestic opposition was increasingly vocal. Nixon's reelection fears turned the attention of the White House to the upcoming presidential campaign. The Nixon White House came up with a number of dirty tricks and illegal activities designed to **ensure the president's reelection**. This included illegally spying on the leading Democratic contenders, especially Senator Edward Kennedy. Millions of dollars were also covertly solicited from wealthy individuals and large corporations by the Committee to Reelect the President (CREEP), directed by Attorney General John Mitchell—a direct violation of a new 1972 federal campaign law requiring public disclosure.

Taking no chances, the Nixon White House also attempted to "sabotage" the campaigns of the political opposition. Its most notorious effort involved the manufacture of a fictitious letter slandering Senator Edmund Muskie's wife. Printed in the *Manchester Union Leader* just prior to the New Hampshire primary, the episode ruined Muskie's hopes for gaining the Democratic nomination. It was this type of activity that led to the "burglary" of the Democratic party headquarters in the Watergate Hotel in Washington, D.C., which eventually gave the scandal its name and publicly exposed the wide-ranging illegalities and subsequent cover-up by President Nixon.

From wiretapping, to the "enemies project," to efforts to ensure the reelection of the president, and finally to the "cover up," the legacy of these illegal and unconstitutional activities was a destroyed president and the long-term diminution of presidential power.

SOURCES: Carl Bernstein and Bob Woodward, *All the President's Men* (New York: Warner, 1974); John Dean, *Blind Ambition* (New York: Pocket Books, 1977); J. Anthony Lukas, *Nightmare: The Underside of the Nixon Years* (New York: Penguin, 1973); Jonathan Schell, *The Time of Illusion* (New York: Vintage, 1975); and Theodore H. White, *Breach of Faith: The Fall of Richard Nixon* (New York: Dell, 1975).

The Carter Presidency. Jimmy Carter attempted to put the tragic episodes of Vietnam and Watergate behind the country by instilling a new spirit of honesty and idealism, represented by his commitment to human rights and peace. He tried to promote human rights and a global community in response to a complex world by emphasizing preventive diplomacy across a variety of issues. Considerable optimism surrounded the beginning of his presidency. He was initially successful and popular, symbolized by his human rights campaign and his ability to bring peace to Egypt and Israel with the Camp David Accords. By the end of his administration, however, the economy went into a tailspin with double-digit inflation and unemployment. Moreover, the public's perception of his mishandling of U.S. foreign policy abroad haunted him as it had his predecessors.

After years of U.S. support since the 1950s, the shah of Iran fell from power in 1979. Ayatollah Khomeini, a prominent religious figure, became Iran's new leader and in the political turmoil 52 American diplomatic personnel were taken hostage in Teheran. For 444 days, **the "hostage crisis"** was the lead story throughout American politics. This initially resulted in a rise in public support for the president, but Carter's inability to free the American hostages destroyed the earlier optimism that had surrounded his presidency. Americans became frustrated with the impotence of the Carter administration's efforts to free the hostages. This frustration was intensified when the Soviet Union invaded neighboring Afghanistan to prop up their allied regime in Kabul. The events in Iran and Afghanistan were the equivalent of a one-two knockout punch, for President Carter was never able to recover politically. Carter was another victim of the crisis of governance, written off by most of the public as a failure.

The Reagan Presidency. Ronald Reagan has been the only president during the post–Vietnam War years able to overcome the crisis of governance created by the paradox and life cycle of presidential power. He is the only recent president who has occupied the office for a full two terms and been perceived as a popular and successful president. But even Reagan experienced a major crisis of governance during his administration—the **Iran-Contra** affair. This political crisis was a result of foreign policy initiatives he undertook toward Iran and in support of the Nicaraguan contras. After months of great uncertainty, he was able to overcome the crisis, although his public approval and his ability to govern were damaged considerably. In fact, during the height of the crisis in 1987, it was unclear whether President Reagan would survive politically.

President Reagan assumed office prepared to initiate a new conservative agenda: to strengthen American defense forces and resolve overseas while "unleashing" the market to restore economic prosperity at home and abroad. He pledged to renew and strengthen America's efforts to combat terrorism and communism abroad. The Reagan administration dramatized the threat of terrorism to Americans and U.S. national security. President Reagan promised that he would never negotiate with terrorists because the only thing they understood was force. The administration emphasized the Middle East as the region of the world where the threat of terrorism was greatest because of the support given to terrorists by Colonel Moammar Gadhafi of Libya and the Ayatollah Khomeini of Iran. American policy was to make a strong show of force and, in fact, the U.S. military engaged the Libyans in two short conflicts in 1986. Nevertheless, a handful of Americans were taken hostage by Middle Eastern terrorists who, it was argued, responded to the direction of the Ayatollah Khomeini.

The other high priority of the Reagan administration was to defeat and contain the communist threat directed by the Soviet Union. The area of the world most endangered in the eyes of President Reagan and his advisers was Central America. The goal of U.S. foreign policy was to defeat the Marxist-Leninist-led guerrillas in El Salvador and to overthrow the Sandinista revolutionary regime in Nicaragua through the threat and use of force. The United States government provided financial and military support to friendly regimes in the region, such as El Salvador, Guatemala, and Honduras, to help them in their fight. The U.S. military also began to conduct exercises regularly near Nicaragua to demonstrate that the United States meant business. Covertly, the Central Intelligence Agency (CIA) became responsible for creating, arming, and supporting a counterrevolutionary group to overthrow the Sandinistas, known as the contras.

To finance his Central American policy, President Reagan requested large amounts of assistance, over $200 million a year, from Congress. In support of these policies, President Reagan and members of his administration tried to raise public consciousness about the gravity of the situation and the necessity of a United States response. However, the threat of communism in Central America never became a high-priority issue among the majority of the public. In fact, there was much public criticism of Reagan's Central American policy, activating the political opposition of many groups and social movements. Consequently, Congress became a major obstacle to President Reagan's efforts to control Central American policy. Members of Congress only granted the Reagan administration a portion of the assistance it wanted during the first few years, with the biggest political battles fought over covert assistance to the contras. The issue became so politicized that Congress prohibited the U.S. government from providing any support or assistance to the contras at all during 1985 and 1986. This set the stage for the Iran-Contra affair.

President Reagan faced two potentially explosive issues. What should be done about the half-dozen American hostages remaining in Lebanon, presumably under Iranian control? What should be done about the cutoff of aid to the contras? Regardless of the congressional ban, he decided that the threat of communism and the future of Nicaragua required that the administration continue to support the contras. United States support for the contras was to be supervised and conducted by the National Security Council staff, where Colonel Oliver North was to be a key operative (a discussion of covert operations in support of the contras is contained in chapter 9, which examines the intelligence community). The other decision taken by President Reagan was that he was willing to sell arms to Iran in exchange for American hostages.

It was not long before White House operations in support of the contras leaked to the press. The revelation, however, which really came to haunt the Reagan presidency involved the story that the U.S. was trading arms for hostages with Iran. After being told by Reagan that he would never negotiate secretly with terrorists and that they only understood force, most Americans could not believe that the president had agreed to negotiate with the so-called leading terrorist of them all, the Ayatollah Khomeini. President Reagan's denials only made the political situation much worse for him and his administration. Then the public learned that some of the money the administration had received from the Iranian arms deal had been illegally diverted from the U.S. Treasury to the contras.

As with Watergate, a "congressional investigation" proceeded to determine the level of presidential abuse of power, and members of his administration were indicted. For almost a year, President Reagan and his administration were badly shaken and on the defensive about Iran-Contra. Ultimately, President Reagan was able to survive the crisis and complete his term, although he was considerably diminished in power and public prestige. (See **essay 4.3** on the stress presidents face in office and the toll it takes on them.)

ESSAY 4.3
THE STRESS AND TOLL OF THE OFFICE

Modern presidents have experienced considerable problems in governing and leading the country. Presidents Johnson, Nixon, Carter, and Reagan all experienced a crisis of governance in foreign policy that gave rise to a domestic political crisis. In fact, the crises became so severe that each president became "overwhelmed" by them. They found little time and energy to respond to other issues and presidential responsibilities, which were either put on hold or carried out by subordinates with little presidential supervision. Clearly, the stress and toll of the office is immense in which many presidents noticeably "age" during their presidencies.

President Johnson was constantly preoccupied by the Vietnam quagmire during the last three years of his administration. During this time it was difficult for his advisers and staff to get his attention on other matters. The same situation was true for Richard Nixon. As President Nixon's cover-up of Watergate unraveled, he devoted himself to "damage control." As Congress came closer to impeaching him, his moods would swing from tenacious defense of his office to incredible despair and hopelessness. Little else but his future as president occupied his thoughts. This meant, for example, that Henry Kissinger, who now enjoyed the two roles of national security adviser and secretary of state, was literally in charge of U.S. foreign policy. Jimmy Carter, with the Iran hostage crisis, experienced political and emotional suffering similar to his predecessors. Because he was so preoccupied with the release of the hostages, other issues of importance did not receive the attention they deserved by the president and his staff.

In some ways, Ronald Reagan may have been affected the most by his political crisis. Reagan was completely "shocked" by the political damage that the Iran-Contra revelations produced. Here was an individual who had beat the odds all his life—first as an actor in Hollywood, then in the California governorship, and finally with the U.S. presidency. Even though he was heavily criticized throughout his administra-tion, President Reagan was extremely popular with the American people and was very successful in exercising power, getting much of his political agenda (such as tax cuts and more defense spending) through Congress. And he had won a landslide reelection in 1984.

Then, all of a sudden, the world had turned upside down. When Americans learned that President Reagan had given arms to Iran they couldn't believe it, for most Americans saw the Ayatollah Khomeini as the lunatic responsible for the hostage crisis. When Reagan denied any involvement, his credibility was questioned for the first time, and the so-called **"Teflon" presidency** had come to an end. When it was learned that some of the money received in the arms-for hostages deals had gone to the contras, in direct opposition to a congressional ban on all contra aid, congressional investigations were triggered to examine Iran-Contra and determine whether the president had abused the powers of his office.

President Reagan, who had appeared to be at the height of his power, was now on the defensive, trying to minimize the political damage. Reagan, never one to be too heavily involved in the day-to-day details of governing, was so badly shaken that for a time he became virtually paralyzed as president. It was reported that the situation became so bad at one point that his advisers began to discuss seriously whether they should invoke the "Twenty-fifth Amendment," which allows the vice president to temporarily act as president if the sitting president becomes physically or emotionally disabled.

While it was found that "the common ingredients of the Iran and Contra policies were secrecy, deception, and disdain for the law," Congress concluded, unlike the Watergate hearings, that President Reagan was guilty primarily of bad judgment and losing touch with activities taken by subordinates in the name of the president. Although badly shaken and damaged politically, Reagan politically survived and recovered to some extent to complete his term of office.

SOURCES: Jane Mayer and Doyle McManus, *Landslide: The Unmaking of the President, 1984–1988* (Boston: Houghton Mifflin, 1988), prologue.

POST–COLD WAR OPPORTUNITIES AND RISKS

. . . .

Due to changes in the domestic environment since Vietnam and the end of the cold war, a crisis of leadership for the presidency and the country exists. The president, the only person capable of providing sustained national leadership, has a very difficult time leading the country. The fragmented nature of American beliefs, as well as competing domestic interests and institutions, has constrained presidential action. Regardless of what the president promises in either domestic or foreign policy, he has been unable to fulfill expectations for long. The complexity of the domestic environment, reinforced by the complexity of the global system, simply no longer allows much latitude for presidential success.

Presidents find it very difficult to lead and manage foreign policy for a sustained period of time, whether in an internationalist direction or not. The net result of this crisis of leadership has been that with each new administration, as well as over the course of the same administration, U.S. foreign policy has tended to become **increasingly reactive—as opposed to proactive**—and, hence, incoherent and inconsistent over time. This is likely to continue into the twenty-first century, making it very difficult for the United States to exercise the kind of sustained global leadership that so many seem to hope for, or fear.[31]

The collapse of the cold war has produced an interesting paradox for presidential leadership relative to the future of U.S. foreign policy: it gives a President great opportunities but also creates great risks. Unlike the 1950s, presidents are no longer driven to pursue only an anticommunist containment policy. Presidents now have more flexibility to pursue a wider range of foreign policy options abroad. Yet, at the same time, it is unclear how far a president may go in pursuing any policy before losing public and governmental support.

As Destler, Gelb, and Lake argue, "The making of American foreign policy has been growing far more political—or more precisely, far more partisan and ideological."[32] Hence, according to Alexander George, "the necessity for ad hoc day-to-day building of consensus under these circumstances makes it virtually impossible for the President to conduct long-range foreign policy in a coherent, effective manner."[33] This has meant that each administration since the end of Vietnam has been forced to modify its initial policies abroad, usually towards the ideological center, in response to domestic political challenges. This helps to account for why U.S. foreign policy often appears to lack coherence and consistency since Vietnam, and why this is likely to continue in the post–cold war era.

The Bush Presidency. George Bush became president at a time when the world would soon witness the collapse of the Soviet Union and communism throughout Eastern Europe. These momentous events have, if anything, intensified the rise of diversity and pluralist politics in the making of U.S. foreign policy that began with the Vietnam War, complicating the president's ability to govern. Bush, who was widely considered to be a strong president in the realm of foreign policy, was unable to take advantage of the post–cold war environment and a tremendously successful and popular war in the Persian Gulf to win reelection in 1992. He was undone predominantly by domestic economic difficulties that he could not control and for which he was publicly viewed for not paying sufficient attention.

The Clinton Presidency. President Clinton has experienced considerable difficulty in governing throughout his tenure both at home and abroad. According to one analysis, "No president since World War II has faced such relentless and vitriolic criticism in the beginning of his term."[34]

He suffered early political defeats, such as with appointments and, in particular, over his effort to legitimize "gays in the military"—which really hurt his public prestige and professional reputation. During his first two years he wasn't even able to get major parts of his legislative program (such as his first budget and his major initiative to reform health care) through a Congress controlled by his own party. And then in 1994 the Democratic party suffered a huge electoral defeat where the Republican party gained control of both the Senate and the House of Representatives—the first time since 1954—producing divided government once again.

Clinton was commonly perceived of trying to do "too much too quickly," to the point where it was difficult for people to acquire a positive image of the man and the direction he wanted to take the country. He was also handicapped early on by a very tough Democratic primary race and by questions of personal and financial infidelity that have continued to surround him and his aides. All this has been reinforced by the "Hillary factor" of having a very strong and capable woman as First Lady who is a lawyer and accustomed to being active throughout her professional life—which has resonated well with some people but not with others.

President Clinton also has been accused of considerable vacillation and hesitancy in the conduct of U.S. foreign policy. Efforts to promote a more "multilateral-oriented" foreign policy faced early setbacks, especially in Somalia. At the same time, President Clinton did manage to initiate several significant foreign policy actions in Haiti, Mexico, and Bosnia in spite of public and congressional opposition. So far major foreign policy failures have been avoided while the administration has chosen to emphasize domestic policy and international economics. Most prominent in this regard were passage of NAFTA—the North American Free Trade Agreement—and the Uruguay round of the GATT agreement producing a World Trade Organization.

Although Bill Clinton has not been held in particularly high regard as a political leader, he was able to rebound politically when he won a major showdown with the Republican-led Congress in late 1995 and early 1996 over the budget—which included two government shutdowns. In fact, he is the first president elected to serve "two terms" in the post–cold war era (and the first Democratic president to do so since Franklin Delano Roosevelt). Overall, he has managed to escape the presidential life cycle, won reelection against a weak Republican candidate, and has begun his second term of office with more popularity than he enjoyed when he started his first term. Nevertheless, President Clin-

ton has experienced considerable difficulty in governing throughout his tenure both at home and abroad.

SUMMARY

. . . .

This is an important chapter because it *provides an overview of the politics of U.S. foreign policy.* We began by introducing the major elements within government, society, and the environment that make an impact on presidential power. We found that while most Americans have high expectations of presidential power, in reality, these elements produce a paradox of presidential power. Although presidents possess significant constitutional roles and strengths, they also face important constraints and uncertainties. Presidents usually go through a presidential life cycle in which they leave office much weaker than they were when they entered. Together, the paradox of presidential power and the presidential life cycle have created a crisis of governance, making it difficult for any president to govern successfully and lead the country in a direction consistent with his beliefs. Although these patterns of presidential power are strongest in the area of domestic policy, they have impacted foreign policy in the years since the Vietnam War and the end of the cold war.

The discussion of presidential power and governance provides an initial *overview of the three foreign policymaking themes*—continuity and change, the president's ability to govern, and the tension between democracy and national security—addressed throughout this book. First, the foreign policy process has become more complex because of the changes that have occurred in the wake of the Vietnam War and Watergate. Presidents now face more constraints and opposition throughout government, society, and the environment in the conduct of foreign policy. Second, presidents have had a difficult time governing and leading the nation since Vietnam, even in the area of foreign policy. Given the extraordinary powers suggested by the two presidencies thesis, the president was able to govern foreign policy with minimal difficulty during the cold war years. Since the mid-sixties, however, the paradox of presidential power and the presidential life cycle has made presidential governance of foreign policy much more problematic. Third, when presidents have exerted prerogative government and pressed assertive foreign policies since Vietnam, tensions between democracy and national security have produced political crises for both the president and the political system. The tension between democracy and national security peaked during Watergate, destroying President Nixon and damaging the presidency. The tension rose again during the Iran-Contra affair, but President Reagan and his presidency survived.

The events of Watergate and Iran-Contra illustrate the changes that have occurred in the foreign policymaking process since the cold war years and the difficulty that presidents now have in governing foreign policy in the post–cold war era. They also demonstrate that the foreign policy process has become increasingly democratic and that presidents are now commonly challenged in their conduct of foreign policy. In sum, presidents must realize that they can no longer exercise power and prerogative government in the name of national security, as commonly occurred during the cold war years, without risking considerable political backlash and possible overshoot and collapse. Not even Ronald Reagan, with his tremendous symbolic skills and prestige with the American people, was able to rise above the paradox of presidential power. And if Reagan was unable to avoid a crisis of governance and the presidential life cycle, what is the omen for presidents with lesser leadership skills? It is to the significance of presidential leadership and presidential management that we turn in chapters 5 and 6.

BIBLIOGRAPHIC ESSAY

. . . .

The classic statement on presidential power is Richard E. Neustadt's, *Presidential Power: The Politics of Leadership* (New York: John Wiley, 1960). Three fine works addressing the paradox of presidential power and its consequences for governance are James MacGregor Burns, *The Power to Lead: The Crisis of the American Presidency* (New York: Simon and Schuster, 1984); Godfrey Hodgson, *All Things to All Men: The False Promise of the Modern American Presidency* (New York: Touchstone, 1980); and Richard M. Pious, *The American Presidency* (New York: Basic Books, 1996). Hedrick Smith, in *The Power Game: How Washington Really Works* (New York: Ballantine, 1988), provides an excellent discussion and feel for the realities of presidential power and American politics through use of the Reagan years. A strong general reference source on the office of the presidency and on individual presidents in the context of American politics is the *Encyclopedia of the American Presidency*, edited by Leonard W. Levy and Louis Fisher (New York: Simon and Schuster, 1994), volumes 1–4.

Arthur M. Schlesinger, Jr., in *The Imperial Presidency* (New York: Houghton Mifflin, 1989), provides an excellent history of the evolution of executive-legislative relations in foreign affairs by describing the growth of presidential power leading up to Watergate. For a general assessment of the two presidencies thesis during the post–World War II era, see Steven A. Shull, ed., *The Two Presidencies: A Quarter Century Assessment* (Chicago: Nelson-Hall, 1991). Godfrey Hodgson, in *America in Our Time* (New York: Vintage, 1976), describes the rise of academic, liberal, and public support during the 1950s and 1960s behind a strong, activist presidency as well as the challenges to presidential power that arose out of the events of the 1960s.

The changes affecting presidential power and governance in foreign policy since Vietnam are impressively captured by Thomas E. Mann in "Making Foreign Policy: President and Congress," Thomas E. Mann, ed., *A Question of Balance: The President, The Congress and Foreign Policy* (Washington, D.C.: Brookings, 1990), pp. 1–34, and I. M. Destler, Leslie H. Gelb, and Anthony Lake in *Our Own Worst Enemy: The Unmaking of American Foreign Policy* (New York: Simon and Schuster, 1984). Jerel Rosati addresses the future implications of the end of the cold war on presidential power and U.S. leadership abroad in "United States Leadership Into the Next Millennium: A Question of Politics," *International Journal* (Spring 1997): 297–315.

ENDNOTES

1. See, for example, Harold M. Barger, "Suspending Disbelief: The President in Pre-College Textbooks," *Presidential Studies Quarterly* (Winter 1990): 55–70.

2. Stanley Hoffmann, *Gulliver's Troubles or the Setting of American Foreign Policy* (New York: McGraw-Hill, 1968), p. 289.

3. The classic statement on this is Clinton Rossiter, *The American Presidency* (New York: Harcourt, Brace, Jovanovich, 1960).

4. See Robert A. Dahl, "Myth of the Presidential Mandate," *Political Science Quarterly* 105 (Fall 1990): 355–372.

5. The civil service was originally created during the 1890s to protect governmental employees from presidential abuse through firing and hiring in order to provide political patronage to presidential supporters—a very common practice at the time.

6. For a general discussion of the paradox of presidential power, see Thomas E. Cronin, *The State of the Presidency* (Boston: Little, Brown, 1975); Godfrey Hodgson, *All Things to All Men: The False Promise of the Modern American Presidency* (New York: Touchstone, 1980); Richard E. Neustadt, *Presidential Power: The Politics of Leadership* (New York: John Wiley, 1960); Richard Pious, *The American Presidency* (New York: Basic Books, 1979); and Hedrick Smith, *The Power Game* (New York: Ballantine, 1988).

7. John F. Kennedy, foreword to Theodore C. Sorensen, *Decision-Making in the White House: The Olive Branch or the Arrows* (New York: Columbia University Press, 1963), p. xii.

8. Harry Truman, in Hedrick Smith, *The Power Game* (New York: Ballantine, 1988) p. 14.

9. See Dorothy Buckton James, *The Contemporary Presidency* (New York: Pegasus, 1974), chapter 1.

10. On the issue area concept in foreign policy, see Matthew Evangelista, "Issue-Area and Foreign Policy Revisited," *International Organization* 43 (Winter 1989): 147–171, and William C. Potter "Issue Area and Foreign Policy Analysis," *International Organization* 34 (Summer 1980).

11. For a general discussion of the presidential life cycle and the crisis of governance, see James MacGregor Burns, *The Power to Lead: The Crisis of the American Presidency* (New York: Simon and Schuster, 1984); John E. Chubb and Paul E. Peterson, eds., *Can the Government Govern?* (Washington, D.C.: Brookings, 1989); Stephen D. Hess, *Organizing the Presidency* (Washington, D.C.: Brookings, 1976); Hodgson, *All Things to All Men*; Samuel P. Huntington, *American Politics: The Promise of Disharmony* (Cambridge, Mass.: Harvard University Press, 1981); Theodore J. Lowi, *The Personal President: Power Invested, Promise Unfulfilled* (Ithaca, N.Y.: Cornell University Press, 1985); Pious, *The American Presidency*; Smith, *The Power Game*; and James L Sundquist, "The Crisis of Competence in Our National Government," *Political Science Quarterly* 95 (Summer 1980): 183–208.

12. Why the term "honeymoon"? With the election of a new president, as well as a House of Representatives and a Senate composed of new members, it is as if the president and Congress have become married in their joint effort to govern. So, as with any honeymooners, the president and members of Congress go out of their way to be nice to each other, usually resulting in a great deal of early legislative success for the president.

13. Halberstam, *The Best and Brightest*, pp. 424–425.

14. See, for example, Paul Brzce, "The Structure of Presidential Approval: Constraints within and Across Presidencies," *Journal of Politics* 53 (November 1991): 993–1017; Robine F. Marra, Charles W. Ostrom, Jr., and Dennis M. Simon, "Foreign Policy and Presidential Popularity: Creating Windows of Opportunity in the Perpetual Election," *Journal of Conflict Resolution* 34 (December 1990): 588–623; and John E. Mueller, "Presidential Popularity from Truman to Johnson," *American Political Science Review* 64 (1970): 18–34.

15. Lyndon B. Johnson, in Smith, *The Power Game*, p. 333.

16. See, for example, Richard A. Brody, *Assessing the President: The Media, Elite Opinion, and Public Support* (Stanford: Stanford University Press, 1991).

17. David Halberstam, *The Best and the Brightest* (New York: Random House, 1969), pp. 64–65.

18. For a conceptual discussion of the domestic and international sources of the modern crisis of governance, see Michel Crozier, Samuel P. Huntington, and Joji Watanuki, *The Crisis of Democracy* (New York: New York University Press, 1975); Edward L. Morse, *Foreign Policy and Interdependence in Gaullist France* (Princeton, N.J.: Princeton University Press, 1973); and Harold and Margaret Sprout, "The Dilemma of Rising Demands and Insufficient Resources," *World Politics* 20 (1968): 660–93. The paradox of presidential power and the crisis of governance are not unique to the present time, but have been a staple of American history. See James MacGregor Burns, *The Deadlock of Democracy: Four-Party Politics in America* (Englewood Cliffs, N.J.: Prentice-Hall, 1963); Huntington, *American Politics*; and Arthur Schlesinger, Jr., *The Imperial Presidency* (New York, Houghton Mifflin, 1989). On divided government, see Michael Laver and Kenneth A. Shepsle, "Divided Government: America Is Not 'Exceptional,' " *Governance* 4 (July 1991): 250–69.

19. United States Congress, Joint Economic Committee, *Economic Indicators*, December 1990 (101st Cong. 2nd sess., 1990).

20. The classic statement on this is Edward S. Corwin, *The President: Office and Powers, 1787–1957* (New York: New York University Press, 1957). See also Cecil V. Crabb, Jr., and Pat M. Holt, *Invitation to Struggle: Congress, the President, and Foreign Policy* (Washington, D.C.: Congressional Quarterly Press, 1992).

21. Arthur Schlesinger, Jr., *The Imperial Presidency* (New York: Houghton Mifflin, 1989).

22. Aaron Wildavsky, "The Two Presidencies Thesis," *Transaction* 4 (1966): 7–14. For a general assessment, see Steven A. Shull, ed., *The Two Presidencies: A Quarter Century Assessment* (Chicago: Nelson-Hall, 1991).

23 See, for example, Godfrey Hodgson, *America in Our Time* (New York: Vintage, 1976), chapter 5, and J. Richard Piper, "Situational Constitutionalism and Presidential Power: The Rise and Fall of the Liberal Model of Presidential Government." *Presidential Studies Quarterly* 24 (1994): 577–94.

24. See, for example, Hodgson, *America in Our Time*; Ernst R. May, "The U.S. Government, a Legacy of the Cold War," *Diplomatic History* 16 (Spring 1992): 269–277; James Q. Wilson, *The Bureaucracy* (New York: Basic Books, 1989); and Daniel Yergin, *Shattered Peace: The Origins of the Cold War and the National Security State* (Boston: Houghton Mifflin, 1983).

25. For a superb discussion of the impediments on presidential power in foreign policy during the cold war years, see Roger Hilsman, *To Move a Nation: The Politics of Foreign Policy in the Administration of John F. Kennedy* (New York: Delta, 1964), and Hoffmann, *Gulliver's Troubles*.

26. See Bayless Manning, "The Congress, The Executive, and Intermestic Affairs: Three Proposals," *Foreign Affairs* 55 (1977): 306–22.

27. See Duane M. Oldfield and Aaron Wildavsky, "Reconsidering the Two Presidencies," *Society* (July/August 1989): 54–59. See also Shull, *The Two Presidencies*. For a general discussion of the paradox of presidential power operating in foreign affairs, see I. M. Destler, Leslie H. Gelb, and Anthony Lake, *Our Own Worst Enemy: The Unmaking of American Foreign Policy* (New York: Simon and Schuster, 1984); Hodgson, *America in Our Time*; and Thomas E. Mann, " Making Foreign Policy: President and Congress," in Thomas E. Mann, ed., *A Question of Balance: The President,* *The Congress and Foreign Policy* (Washington, D.C.: Brookings, 1990): 1–34.

28. The problem of governance is not unique to the United States, but is faced by governments in other modern, industrial democracies as well. For example, Carter and the Democratic party were not the only people in power voted out of office around 1980. In 1979, liberals or social democrats were voted out in Great Britain and West Germany, while conservatives lost power in France, Spain, Australia, Greece, and Italy. The only things that all these leaders shared in common was incumbency and a problem of governance.

29. Vietnamization was the American strategy of withdrawing American ground forces from Vietnam while training, equipping, and supporting the South Vietnamese army to carry the burden of fighting the war as it did under the Eisenhower administration.

30. The House Judiciary Committee voted three counts of impeachment against President Nixon. The Senate never noted whether to convict Nixon on any of the impeachment counts for which he resigned from office.

31. See Jerel A. Rosati, "The Domestic Environment," in Peter A. Schraeder, ed., *Intervention into the 1990s: United States Foreign Policy in the Third World* (Boulder, Colo.: Lynne Rienner Publishers, 1992), pp. 175–91; and Jerel A. Rosati, "United States Leadership Into the Next Millennium: A Question of Politics," *International Journal* (Spring 1997): 297–315.

32. Destler, Lake, and Gelb, *Our Own Worst Enemy*, p. 13.

33. Alexander L. George, "Domestic Constraints on Regime Change in U.S. Foreign Policy: The Need for Policy Legitimacy," in Ole R. Holsti, Randolph Siverson, and Alexander L. George, eds., *Change in the International System* (Boulder, Colo.: Westview Press, 1980), p. 236.

34. Jack Nelson and Robert J. Donovan, *The State* (August 1, 1993), 1D.

35. For an overview of the Clinton administration's initial foreign policy orientation, see, for example, Anthony Lake, "From Containment to Enlargement," *U.S. Department of State Dispatch* 4:39 (September 27, 1993): 658–64; Owen Harries, "My So-called Foreign Policy," *The New Republic* (October 10, 1994); and *A National Security Strategy of Engagement and Enlargement* (Washington, D.C.: U.S. Government Printing Office, July 1994).

CHAPTER
5

. . . .

PRESIDENTIAL LEADERSHIP

ow do presidents maximize their power and success? How can they overcome or minimize the crisis of governance embedded in American politics? How can they increase their ability to govern foreign policy? The key is presidential **leadership**.[1] Strong leaders are able to maximize their strengths and capabilities, minimize the constraints they face, and force the uncertain elements to work better and longer in their favor. Strong presidents are more able to exercise power and govern. Weak leaders, on the other hand, have great difficulty exercising power and governing for they operate in a world dominated by insurmountable obstacles and constraints. Although this is particularly the case in domestic policy, presidential leadership is also important for presidential power and governance in foreign policy.

THE POWER TO PERSUADE AND ACT

. . . .

The classic statement on presidential leadership is *Presidential Power: The Politics of Leadership* by Richard Neustadt.[2] His basic argument is that the key to presidential power is the **power to persuade,** which is a function of political leadership. Presidents who enter office and expect to "command" are quickly disappointed and frustrated. Barking orders may get results for military leaders, but it does not work within the government. Because of the paradox of presidential power and the existence of the presidential life cycle, presidents cannot command. In fact, as Neustadt points out, efforts at exerting presidential power through command are an indication of presidential weakness, for presidents should rely on their legal and formal authority only as a last resort. The command model of governing may be consistent with the way most Americans are raised to think of presidential power, but the key for presidential governance is to persuade others that it is in their best interest to do what the president prefers.

Neustadt understood the problem of presidential governance in the American system. The only way to overcome the constraints and uncertainties that a president faces is through the power of persuasion. This ability depends on the qualities of political leadership that the individual brings to office and develops as president. Neustadt identified *three crucial elements of political leadership and presidential power:* professional reputation, public prestige, and presidential choices.

Professional reputation refers to how other political actors in Washington, D.C., and beyond judge the president's ability to get things accomplished. Presidents with a reputation for being very skillful in exercising power, for having to be reckoned with when opposed, are most persuasive. **Public prestige** refers to how other political actors—whether in the bureaucracy, Congress, interest groups, or the media—perceive the level of public support for the president. Presidents with a positive public image are more powerful, for high credibility and popular support throughout the country are important political assets in Washington. Strong presidents who are able to persuade successfully are those with high levels of professional reputation and public prestige.

Discussion of professional reputation and prestige underscores the importance of perceptions and images. A president exercises leadership and political power by influencing the image others have of him. Leadership involves the ability to create the illusion of being powerful. According to Hedrick Smith in *The Power Game,* "Presidents—past, present, and future—have less power than the country imagines, but the successful ones convey the impression of power and get reputations as strong presidents by playing down their problems and trumpeting their few clear victories."[3]

Perceptions and images have always been important in politics, but with the rise of the electronic media, the importance of **symbolism and symbolic politics** has grown. People and groups interact politically based on the images they hold of each other and the images they have of what is possible, whether or not those images closely correspond to reality. Thus, the power to persuade depends on how a president and his administration are perceived by others.

Much of a president's professional reputation and public prestige are a function of his **personality**—his particular way of operating and presenting himself in different social situations.[4] The impact of a president's personality varies, contributing to or hindering his professional reputation and public prestige, depending upon how his personal characteristics affect his leadership style. It is important to remember that an individual, or president, cannot easily alter his personal characteristics and habits, for they have been learned since childhood. Nevertheless, since images and symbolism are so crucial to professional reputation and public prestige, a president can try to mold a more positive image of himself. Presidents who want to exercise power successfully and govern need to be aware of these aspects of leadership long before they decide to run for the office.

The third important element of presidential leadership is **presidential choices**. A president's ability to lead and persuade is a function of the choices that he makes, for which only he is responsible. The choices that are made by a president affect his professional reputation and public prestige. Presidential choices may allow a president to take advantage of opportunities as they arise, exercising power when little opportunity seems available given existing constraints. Ultimately, this requires that *the President, and his staff, need to be skillful:*

1. in managing the executive branch and the decision-making process,
2. in building coalitions and politically interacting with other players in Washington D.C., and beyond, and
3. in symbolically communicating his priorities and preferences throughout society and the world.

These are political requirements involving important choices for successful presidential leadership.

According to Neustadt, "passive" presidents tend to be little more than clerks who merely occupy the office. To lead and govern, presidents must be "active"—actively involved in becoming informed, making decisions, and supervising their implementation. They must know who they can and cannot rely on throughout the government and beyond. They must be aware of the political implications of what they say and do. In other words, a president's choices are the means by which he exercises leadership and power in the complex politics of U.S. foreign policy.

Richard Pious, in *The American Presidency*, has added important insights concerning the impact of presidential choice and activism on presidential leadership. He argues that the paradox of presidential power has become so constraining that a president must exercise **prerogative government** if he wants to govern and lead the country. By prerogative government, Pious means that presidents must be very active and arrive at decisions that push the Constitution to its limits in exercising presidential power. "The president justifies his decisions on constitutional grounds, on powers enumerated, or on those claimed. . . . When his expansive interpretation is challenged, he appeals to the public for support by defining his actions in terms of 'national security' or 'the national interest.' "[5]

Those presidents who have a more expansive view of presidential power tend to be the most successful in governing and go down in history as the best presidents. However, activist presidents who exercise prerogative government also run the political risk of abusing their power, which can damage or destroy them. This is because the Constitution is an ambiguous document, and it is often unclear whether a president is exercising power legitimately or abusing power. Presidents have the greatest opportunity to exercise prerogative government during times of crises and national emergencies. However, the final determinant of the legitimate exercise of presidential power is politics.

Pious finds that, throughout American history, *three political outcomes have occurred when presidents have exercised prerogative government.* First, presidents are most successful in exercising prerogative government in the area of foreign affairs during a time of national emergency, such as war. During such times, the president is able to exercise legitimately extraordinary powers because of the urgency of the situation. This is what happened under Presidents Abraham Lincoln and Franklin Roosevelt as they exercised prerogative government in the face of the greatest of all national emergencies, a civil war and a world war. The worst that presidents can expect under such circumstances is what Pious calls "frontlash" after the emergency has subsided. That is, presidents can expect Congress and domestic politics to reassert themselves during times of normalcy, again constraining presidential power.

Second, presidents may experience political "backlash" if they exercise prerogative government over domestic policy, even during a national emergency. In domestic policy, unlike foreign policy, presidents are not given much leeway or flexibility to respond to crises. Bureaucrats, congressmen, and other political players are very protective of their positions and involvement in the domestic policymaking process. Such was the case with President Harry Truman's seizure of steel mills in 1951, in the name of national security, in response to a strike during the Korean War. The political response was very critical of Truman for his exercise of emergency national security powers involving a labor-management dispute—clearly a domestic issue. Presidents with an expansive view of the Constitution during domestic emergencies will eventually be perceived as abusing power and may expect to suffer severe political setbacks.

Presidents also run the risk of "overshoot and collapse" when exercising prerogative government, which results in a president's fall from power. This is most likely to occur in situations in which there is no perception of emergency throughout the society, and is especially acute if domestic affairs are involved. A president exercising prerogative government under these conditions will be widely perceived as abusing his power and oath of office. The domestic political resistance is likely to be so severe that the president may have to fight for his political life. President Reagan faced this possibility with Iran-Contra and survived, however, President

Nixon suffered from overshoot and collapse as a result of the events surrounding Watergate.

PATTERNS IN PRESIDENTIAL LEADERSHIP AND GOVERNANCE
. . . .

The concepts of professional reputation, public prestige, and prerogative government are helpful for understanding the president's ability to lead and govern in general and in foreign affairs. These three elements of presidential leadership explain why Franklin Roosevelt was the most successful president in modern times, why Presidents Truman, Eisenhower, and Kennedy were able to dominate foreign policy during the cold war years, why the situation began to change under President Johnson, and why it has been so difficult for presidents to govern in foreign affairs since Vietnam and the end of the cold war.

THE ROOSEVELT PRESIDENCY

Regardless of whether one liked the direction in which he led the country, Franklin Delano Roosevelt was one of America's greatest presidents if measured in terms of his ability to govern and lead. He was elected president an unprecedented four times and occupied the office for thirteen years. Why? Because he was a politician with tremendous leadership skills and he became president at a unique time in American history.

Roosevelt entered office in 1933 when the United States was experiencing the full force of the Great Depression, the greatest national emergency to face the United States since the Civil War. As a newly elected Democratic president, replacing Republican Herbert Hoover, he represented a change and hope for the future—two things for which people were looking, given the severity of the economic collapse. As an activist president, he took advantage of the extraordinary situation to pass his New Deal legislation through Congress as he presided over the most active 100 days in the history of legislative-executive relations. Roosevelt was also a consummate

politician, who personally ran the White House and restored the faith of the American people through his famous "fireside" chats over the radio. Moreover, the Japanese attack on Pearl Harbor in 1941 presented the president and the country with another national emergency, which gave Roosevelt extraordinary powers to wage war as commander in chief.

Roosevelt was an extremely powerful president and successful political leader—to students of the presidency he is often considered **the model presidential leader** in modern American politics. Not surprisingly, it has been virtually impossible for subsequent presidents to match his feat, for not only did Roosevelt enjoy high professional reputation and public prestige, he operated during times of domestic and international emergency allowing him to exercise prerogative government.[6]

THE COLD WAR YEARS

U.S. involvement in World War II took the country out of the depression, but it did not produce lasting peace after the war. Instead, escalation of mutual suspicion and fear between the United States and the Soviet Union led to the rise of the cold war—another time of national emergency in the minds of most Americans. This sense of national emergency gave presidents during the 1950s and 1960s extraordinary powers over national security and foreign policy, accounting for the "two presidencies thesis" formulated by Aaron Wildavsky.

It is not that these presidents had great leadership skills stemming from professional reputation and public prestige—that situation varied from president to president. The consequential factor was public perception that the cold war represented a war that the United States and the free world could not afford to lose. It was fought through the strategy of containment, which emphasized the threat and use of force. These cold war beliefs and policies required a strong president who was able to combat the enemy quickly and secretly with public support and little opposition. To respond to the threat of communism, therefore, the demands of national security took precedence.

This national security ethos was so widely accepted throughout the country that presidents were able to exercise prerogative government in foreign policy as the norm for twenty years. During the cold war years, presidents were virtually undisputed on questions of war and peace, as demonstrated by the long history of presidential decisions taken by Truman, Eisenhower, Kennedy, and finally Johnson, resulting in the Americanization of the war in Vietnam.

THE TRANSITION YEARS

Ironically, the Vietnam War represented not only the height of presidential power, but also the beginning of the end of the extraordinary exercise of prerogative and presidential power in foreign affairs. Because of Vietnam, presidents were challenged about their conduct of foreign policy for the first time in over twenty years. What had been accepted as a legitimate exercise of presidential power in the political climate of the cold war years became increasingly considered presidential abuse of power in the political climate of the post-Vietnam years. The uncertainties and constraints on presidential power, either silent or supportive of the president during the cold war years, resurfaced.

President Lyndon Johnson represented both the height and decline of what became referred to as **the imperial presidency.**[7] He was the first victim of the changed political environment facing the president. Since his days as Senate majority leader, he had been known for his ability to wheel and deal in Washington's corridors of power. His very high professional reputation was a result of his overall aggressiveness and strong style of personal interaction. However, Johnson was very uncomfortable before the general public. He lacked charisma and was unable to display a sense of confidence in public appearances, such as on national television. Therefore, his public prestige, although quite high following the 1964 electoral landslide, lacked a strong bedrock of public support and declined severely as his administration's handling of the Vietnam War was increasingly challenged. Although Johnson was, in many ways, a master of the political smoke-filled room, his weak

skills at promoting his public prestige made it impossible for him to overcome the crisis of governance that he experienced over the Vietnam War. Rather than fight the political changes that were taking place around him, Johnson withdrew his name from the presidential race in 1968.

THE POST–VIETNAM WAR YEARS

By the late 1960s, presidents attempted to govern and lead in a new political environment that was no longer automatically hospitable to the exercise of presidential power in foreign affairs. Consequently, presidential governance in foreign affairs became "increasingly" dependent on the presidential leadership skills that involved professional reputation, public prestige, and presidential choices.

If we examine recent presidents, we see that it is very rare to find a president who enjoyed high levels of both professional reputation and public prestige throughout his administration. *Strong and durable political leadership is not a common commodity.* Neither Johnson, Nixon, Ford or Carter had strong leadership skills overall. Consequently, these presidents have been perceived as failures by the end of their term of office. During the post–Vietnam War years, only President Reagan seemed to have maintained high levels of professional reputation and public prestige in support of presidential initiatives, which may explain why he has been the most successful of contemporary presidents, even while suffering from the Iran-Contra affair.

President Nixon, like Johnson before him, was also known for exercising power better within Washington than amongst the general public. Unlike that of his predecessor, Nixon's professional reputation was neither as strong nor his public prestige as weak as Johnson's. President Nixon was able to build a strong staff that centralized and exercised power in the White House. Although not a strong orator, he was better able to communicate to what he called the "silent majority" and, given all his years in public life, he had strong support among more conservative segments of the public.

Nixon's downfall came because he did not fully "understand" (or accept) the extent to which the domestic political environment was changing. As his predecessors had, Nixon tried to govern foreign policy with a free hand, while more and more Americans doubted the validity of communism as the major threat to the United States and questioned the basis of twenty years of containment policies and of presidential prerogative government in foreign affairs. From Nixon's perspective, the traditional authority of presidential power in national security affairs was being challenged. His reaction was to set in motion activities to fight the domestic political opposition, leading to Watergate and abuse of presidential power.

The overshoot and collapse of the Nixon presidency came not only from changes in the political environment which had new negative consequences for presidential exercise of prerogative government, but also from the fragility of Nixon's public prestige. Nixon was "not particularly admired or well-liked" by either his political peers or the general public. He had been in the public limelight since the late forties, usually attacking others politically, as with the Alger Hiss affair, or defending his record, as he had done as vice president under Eisenhower and following his unsuccessful race for the presidency in 1960. He created political enemies along the way and developed a reputation among much of the public as a mean-spirited politician (symbolized by the popular expression "Tricky Dick"). The weak foundation of Nixon's public prestige, therefore, made him politically vulnerable during Watergate.

Ford was a "relatively passive president" who had low levels of professional reputation and public prestige. Gerald Ford was a likable person but never would have become president on his own. Nixon had picked him as vice president to replace Spiro T. Agnew, who had been forced to resign on charges of corruption. Not only was Ford catapulted overnight into the presidency after having been minority leader in the House of Representatives, he also possessed no election mandate. These circumstances were reinforced by his passivity in managing the government and the general public perception that he was not a particularly "presidential" individual.

In fact, by his final year in office his level of competence was openly questioned and he had become the butt of public jokes. Given his low levels of professional reputation and public prestige, it is hardly surprising that his administration was popularly perceived as having accomplished very little, contributing to his inability to win election in 1976.

Of all the contemporary presidents, Jimmy Carter may well be remembered by the public as the weakest. Ironically, he entered office an activist president with relatively high public prestige and very low professional reputation. Carter was the first person to gain the presidency by running against Washington, pledging that he would clean up governmental corruption and discard the politics-as-usual approach, which was epitomized by the Vietnam War and Watergate. Carter was also the first president who was a true "outsider" to national politics. His political experience had been as governor of Georgia, not in Washington, D.C. He entered office resistant to the politics of Washington and with few political friends. Nevertheless, although not a great orator, his public presence instilled hope and high public expectations about the future, especially among the more liberal segments of the population.

Although an extremely intelligent individual, President Carter was "naive" about the importance of presidential leadership and the difficulties of exercising political power. Early on, he antagonized members of Congress and the bureaucracy, thus destroying his honeymoon and further damaging his professional reputation. By his last year in office, with the economy gone sour and Americans faced with an ongoing hostage crisis, the hopes and expectations that Carter had built up among the public were also destroyed.

Since he left office, popular approval and admiration have "grown" for Jimmy Carter. Unlike most former presidents, Jimmy Carter has not disappeared into retirement and private life. Instead, Carter has chosen to remain involved in world affairs through his activities with the Carter Center in Atlanta. He has committed himself to the pursuit of "good works" such as promoting human rights, overseeing foreign democratic elections, negotiating regional conflicts, and assisting human development abroad and at home. All of this is quite unique among post-presidents.[8]

As the only contemporary president who has enjoyed high levels of both public prestige and professional reputation, Ronald Reagan was able to overcome the constraints and uncertainties that a president faces throughout his term of office. A lot of debate exists over exactly what made Reagan tick and how this affected his ability to govern and lead, for he clearly had leadership skills that made him a political force that Washington had not witnessed for some time before or since.

Reagan actually entered politics with low levels of both public prestige and professional reputation. When Reagan assumed the governorship of California, he had been written off as a conservative ideologue and two-bit actor. He proved the political pundits wrong then and would do so again. It may be that these initially "low expectations" about a Reagan presidency worked to his advantage.

Reagan was, in fact, a "complex man of many contradictions." While he rarely immersed himself in the issues, he entered office with a very active agenda. Though he was relatively uninvolved in the daily operations of presidential governance, he recruited a strong presidential staff that was capable of pursuing his policies. This played to his greatest strength: his ability to communicate to the general public.

Reagan, as an individual, became well "liked" by the American people. He had the ability to speak to them and gain their support by using language and symbols that most Americans understood and to which they responded. It was as if the more the American people became familiar with Reagan, the more they liked him. For example, Reagan was widely acclaimed for the way in which he had handled himself during his assassination attempt only seventy days after being sworn in as president. Not only was Reagan good at being the "great communicator," he actually was most comfortable when in the public limelight. It was his rise in public prestige, reinforced by his growing professional reputation, that was the key to his ability to govern and lead. (See **essay 5.1** on who was the real Ronald Reagan?"

Iran-Contra demonstrates that Reagan was also a president willing to exercise prerogative government in support of foreign policy goals that he deemed vital. Like Nixon before him, he acted as if the political environment had not changed since the 1950s. He felt that the president, as commander in chief, possessed the same rights as presidents before him during the cold war—to conduct U.S. foreign policy as he saw fit. As long as the operations involving Nicaragua and Iran remained covert or were kept off the public agenda, Reagan was a formidable president. However, once the stories broke, Reagan experienced a crisis of governance that damaged both his professional reputation and public prestige. Unlike Nixon, Reagan's presidential abuse of power was not considered as severe, limited to the conduct of foreign policy, and his high level of public prestige allowed him to weather the political storm. Also, unlike his immediate predecessors, Ronald Reagan has been the only president during the post–Vietnam War period to have occupied the presidency for two full terms, and left office with a general reputation as a successful president.

THE POST–COLD WAR YEARS

It would appear that these same presidential leadership skills, including the occasional resort to prerogative government, are still necessary for presidents to successfully govern in the post–cold war era. If anything, strong and judicious presidential leadership has become increasingly important for the conduct of U.S. foreign policy. No sense of national emergency exists or appears on the horizon to rival the cold war, which was so crucial for presidential power.[9]

To be able to govern in foreign policy, therefore, not only must presidents exercise prerogative government while avoiding being perceived as abusing power, they must also make the kind of presidential choices that maximizes political support—throughout the country and inside the beltway in Washington, D.C.—behind their policies and results in electoral success. Unfortunately, most individuals elected as president of the United States have not been viewed as particularly strong and successful leaders—such leadership skills may be quite uncommon.

ESSAY 5.1
PRESIDENTIAL PERSONALITY AND LEADERSHIP TRAITS:
WHO WAS THE REAL RONALD REAGAN?

Who was the real Ronald Reagan? How was he able to maintain an image as a strong leader, especially his high public prestige, for such a long time? Was Reagan an ideologue who attempted to promote a conservative agenda, or was he a pragmatic politician who was willing to compromise? Was he involved or uninvolved in the day-to-day operations of his administration? Did Reagan arrive at his own decisions or was he easily swayed by the recommendations of his closest advisers? Reagan seemed to be all of these things and more. Scholars of the Reagan presidency and American history will be trying to answer these questions for years to come.

One place where initial answers can be found are in **memoirs** written by former members of the Reagan administration. The production of memoirs is quite common. But to have so many of them come out so soon, even while President Reagan was still in office, is unique in modern American history, especially given many of the criticisms of President Reagan and his administration. These "kiss and tell" books discuss different facets of the man, and while they provide a common view, they also present different pieces of information that may be used to solve the puzzle of the real Ronald Reagan.

The *general portrait* given by these accounts is of a man who had certain predispositions, but was complex and characterized by contradictions. Reagan tended to be deeply committed to certain ideological values and programs, yet he was receptive to compromise if the political obstacles were great and the nature of the compromise appeared to be consistent with the original values promoted. Reagan's natural inclination was to provide the vision and remain distant from the policy process. He was normally open to advice and preferred to delegate authority to his subordinates to devise specific policies and strategies. However, he did become attached and committed to a few issues, such as the need for tax cuts, larger defense spending, the Strategic Defense Initiative (SDI), support for the contras, and

the fate of American hostages in the Middle East. By nature, Reagan was an optimist, loved to be around people, disliked confrontations, and quickly became bored with the substance of policy. This was a person who enjoyed being president, loved the public limelight, and liked to communicate his general vision of America to large audiences, no matter how staged the event.

A number of interesting episodes discussed in the memoirs reveal some of the idiosyncrasies of the man. Larry Speakes, President Reagan's White House spokesman, describes how the president wanted to respond to the constant questioning of reporters but often misspoke in spontaneous situations. Thus, Speakes frequently had to correct the record in the name of the president, sometimes not even clearing these statements with Reagan. Donald Regan, Reagan's secretary of treasury and then chief of staff, discusses what he calls the "Guesswork Presidency": how as treasury secretary he never received any guidance on policy and yet the president accepted most of his advice. Instead, Reagan preferred to exercise the symbolic powers of his office, even though his public appearances were closely scripted and choreographed by his aides, down to the opening and closing phrases he would utter. What irked Regan most as chief of staff is what he saw as constant meddling by the president's wife, Nancy Reagan. She became preoccupied with "Ronnie's" safety following the assassination attempt and consulted an astrologer in determining the president's public schedule.

David Stockman, President Reagan's young director of Management and Budget, describes in great detail how the 1981 economic program of large tax cuts and increased defense spending, combined with difficulties in cutting domestic programs, set in motion the massive budget deficits still facing the country. Reagan emerges from this account as a good-hearted conservative president who was committed to tax cuts and the theory of supply-side economics, although oblivious to the fine points of economic management and tax policy. William Niskanen, a member of the President's Council of Economic Advisers, summed up the overall consensus view: "Ronald Reagan has been the most transparent person in American public life. . . . He is at peace with himself, comfortable with his convictions, intuitive rather than analytical, youthful in spirit, infectiously optimistic, and gracious in his personal relations."[A]

Nancy Reagan, miffed by much of the material disclosed in the memoirs of President Reagan's former associates, especially the attack by Donald Regan on her meddling in White House affairs, took

---

A. William Niskanen, *Reaganomics: An Insider's Account of the Policies and the People* (New York: Oxford University Press, 1988), p. 284.

the opportunity to respond in her own memoir titled *My Turn.* Ironically, even though she attempted to defend her role and clarify the real "Ronnie," her discussion ends up confirming accounts of her husband's leadership style, as well as the conventional wisdom about her behind-the-scenes role.

All of these accounts, and others not discussed here, provide a close look at Ronald Reagan the man and the workings of his presidency—the good, the bad, and the ugly. However, memoirs must be read with a critical eye for it is important to consider the motives of the people who write memoirs: money, fame, and the chance to provide their view of history and events. Given the success and controversy of the Reagan presidency, we can be sure of one thing— more memoirs and other accounts will be written in the unending effort to determine who is the real Ronald Reagan.

SOURCES: Fred I. Greenstein, "Ronald Reagan—Another Hidden-Hand Ike?" *Political Science* 23 (March 1990): 7–13; William Niskanen, *Reaganomics: An Insider's Account of the Policies and the People* (New York: Oxford University Press, 1988); Nancy Reagan, *My Turn: The Memoirs of Nancy Reagan* (New York: Random House, 1989); Donald Regan, *For the*

Record: From Wall Street to Washington (San Diego: Harcourt, Brace, Jovanovich, 1988); Larry Speakes, with Robert Pack, *Speaking Out: Inside the Reagan White House* (New York: Charles Scribner's Sons, 1988); and David Stockman, *The Triumph of Politics: Why the Reagan Revolution Failed* (New York: Harper & Row, 1986).

President Bush.   Bush entered office pledging to use his considerable governmental experience to continue most of the policies of his predecessor, but with a "kinder and gentler" style. Bush's leadership style was quite different from Reagan's: more informal and low-keyed, more active and hands-on, less ideological, and more politically sensitive. The most common criticisms of President Bush was that he attempted to govern without a vision or an agenda, that his presidency was too reactive and cautious, and that he was too sensitive to public relations and politics. Yet, early on, Bush's leadership style paid off. His public approval ratings into his third year were over 70 percent, an all-time high for post–World War II presidents.

However, as we have learned, to begin office strong is not unusual. Although his public approval was high, unlike Reagan and many of his predecessors, Bush lacked truly strong political support.

Also, he was not a particularly good public speaker. Furthermore, President Bush did not develop an active domestic agenda and faced an economic recession. Nor did he inspire confidence in a foreign policy based on a realpolitik vision of the world in which his administration was highly reactive to events and initiatives taken by others, such as those taken by Soviet leader Mikhail Gorbachev or Iraq's Saddam Hussein.

There is no doubt that George Bush was shocked to discover that, despite his great victory in the Persian Gulf War and public approval ratings approaching 90 percent, he was soon voted out of office, largely due to perceptions that he did little to address the domestic ills of the United States. President Bush clearly made the crucial mistake of underestimating the "softness" of presidential support and the volatility of the domestic political environment since Vietnam.

President Clinton. Despite relatively low public prestige, President Clinton has managed to escape the presidential life cycle, won reelection against a weak Republican candidate, and began his second term of office with more popularity than he enjoyed when he started his first term. In fact, he is the first president to serve an entire term in the post–cold war era and the first Democratic president to be reelected since FDR over fifty years ago.

Bill Clinton's political success may be, in part, due to the fact that most Americans may have "lower expectations," at least relative to him and his presidency. He was elected with only 43 percent of the vote after all, as a result of a three-way race in 1992. And while most Americans do not seem to particularly admire the man, especially concerning his personal character and charges of womanizing, they appear to see him as more acceptable then any of the viable alternatives. Most importantly, Bill Clinton has been the beneficiary of an economy that has not only avoided going into recession but has actually been growing throughout his presidency.[10]

Bill Clinton has demonstrated throughout his political career that he is a political "survivor." Back in the 1992 presidential campaign, he was often referred to as "Slick Willy" because he was able to rebound when he appeared close to defeat and he has the uncanny ability to occupy the political center. Somewhat like Ronald Reagan's "Teflon presidency," but for very different reasons, nothing seems to politically damage Clinton all that much or for too long.

Bill Clinton appears to be a very complex man who seems to have *contradictory leadership styles.* On the one hand, he has a strong interest and concern for both policy and politics. His verbal facility and intelligence is formidable and he has brought energy and optimism to the White House. In the words of Jack Watson, a former White House chief of staff, he is "exuberant, informal, interactive, non-hierarchical, and indefatigable."[11] On the other hand, Clinton often gets himself into trouble by lacking self-discipline and not focusing on a set of specific goals. He is amiable to the point of being ingratiating with friends as well as foes. He is very articulate, but his ability to communicate in public is hurt by his tendency to be too long-winded and mired in detailed lists.

As Fred Greenstein has stated, "I have been particularly struck by the diversity of the qualities Clinton brings to his leadership, the extent to which they seem at times to be warring with one another, and the novelty of their combination in a single individual."[12] Sometimes these traits come together to make him a relatively strong leader, but much of the time they come together to hinder his ability to lead and govern. (See **essay 5.2** on the sources of Clinton's personality and leadership style.

Bill Clinton's interest in policy and politics for the most part has been directed towards the domestic arena and economics (including international economics). Nevertheless, he has taken some major foreign policy initiatives—Haiti, Mexico, and Bosnia—which may be considered an exercise of prerogative government. In each case the administration was faced with considerable public and congressional opposition to the initiative in question, and proceeded nonetheless. In each case there were many in Congress who argued that the president did not have the authority to act alone, and yet he acted alone. Furthermore, each of these instances of prerogative government occurred in the absence of any semblance of national emergency. And yet in none of the cases did the Clinton administration suffer from "backlash" or "overshoot and collapse." Perhaps political backlash was avoided in each case because the policies, thus far, were successful—or at least they weren't seen as failures—and seemed distant from the vital concerns of most Americans.

The political risks taken by the Clinton administration for each of these initiatives seem to have paid off to the extent that Haiti, Bosnia, and Mexico all ceased being potentially damaging foreign policy problems for Clinton. Hence, the continued importance of prerogative government to presidential leadership and power, although Clinton's second term may help clarify whether the risks associated with prerogative government and the need for strong presidential leadership have somehow changed in the post–cold war era.

ESSAY 5.2
SOURCES OF PERSONALITY AND LEADERSHIP STYLE:
WILLIAM JEFFERSON CLINTON'S UPBRINGING AND EXPERIENCES

Much of Bill Clinton's contradictory characteristics and styles of operating reflect his personality. Who is the real Bill Clinton and what makes him tick? These are very difficult questions that we need to ask of all political and prominent figures if we are to better understand them and the role they play in the political process. It must be kept in mind that "psychological profiles" are difficult to develop with any degree of certainty. Nevertheless, the "sources" of a person's personality and style of operating tend to be found in one's upbringing and formative experiences.

Some of the "pieces" to the puzzle to better understand Clinton's personality and leadership styles include the following: born on August 19, 1946 as William Jefferson Blythe III; raised in the small town of Hope, Arkansas; mother was a smoker and drinker, and a hard worker who eventually became a nurse anesthetist; biological father died in a car crash months before Clinton's birth; upon the mother's remarriage, became the son of an alcoholic and abusive stepfather; grandmother was a strict disciplinarian and strict timewise; very bright, good-looking, glib, and social; active in the church; easily made friends, impressed adults, and stood out in a crowd; small town student leader who was active in the local community; went to Boys Nation, a "camp" of sorts for academic overachievers and future leaders, where he shook hands with President John Kennedy, his idol; a Rhodes Scholar, a graduate of Georgetown University and Yale Law School; worked on national political campaigns and the staff of Arkansas Senator J. William Fulbright; married Hilary Rodham, a midwestern woman who graduated from Wellesley College and Yale Law School, who was a liberal with strong career aspirations of her own; returned to Arkansas in 1981 as a young governor in a conservative state dominated in business and politics by a small network of wealthy individuals; reflected the new wave of moderate southern Democrats; failed to be reelected, but then won the governorship again four years later; successfully gained the Democratic nomination for president and won the presidential election of 1992.

Exactly how all these experiences add up is speculative, but clearly it produced a "natural born politician"—a man composed of great complexity and extraordinary contradictions that has served him well and, at the same time, hindered him in the political world throughout his career.

SOURCES: John Brummett, *Highwire: From the Backroads to the Beltway: The Education of Bill Clinton* (Hyperion, 1994); Elizabeth Drew, *On the Edge: The Clinton Presidency* (New York: Simon and Schuster, 1994); David Maranis, *First in His Class: A Biography of Bill Clinton* (New York: Simon and Schuster, 1995); R. Emmett Tyrell, Jr., *Boy Clinton: The Political Biography* (Washington, D.C.: Regnery, 1996).

THE CHALLENGES OF THE POST–COLD WAR WORLD

· · · · · · · · · · · · · ·

The collapse of communism and the Soviet Union provide unique opportunities for more foreign policy change in a direction away from cold war policies of the past, but it has also further weakened the president's ability to govern foreign policy into the future. It was the sense of national emergency associated with the cold war during the fifties and sixties, after all, that was the ultimate source of presidential power and American global leadership following World War II.

Clearly, such a sense of national emergency no longer exists in the post–cold war era—the perception of a "cold war" has been replaced with the perception of a time of "relative peace" abroad in the minds of most Americans. This means that the fragmented and pluralist political environment that has prevailed since Vietnam will likely continue in the post–cold war future, posing greater foreign policy opportunities and political risks for presidents and American leadership abroad. But much will depend on the image that Americans have of a president's policies and of their relative success, at home and abroad—a function of the fate of events and the strength of presidential leadership.

The post–cold war era will present U.S. presidents with new types of constraints on their power, but also with new types of opportunities. As the American public focuses its concern more and more on "intermestic"—especially economic—issues, both at home and abroad, presidents who are perceived as dealing "successfully" with those issues are likely to enjoy an increase in their popularity and ability to govern in foreign policy and in general. This seems to have been the case for both Presidents Bush and Clinton thus far, although only time will tell whether or not this will be a larger post–cold war trend.

Ultimately, the president's ability to govern into the future is clearly impacted by the dynamic interaction between global developments and the domestic environment that determines the politics of United States foreign policy. This makes it difficult to envision a strong, proactive global leadership role for the United States across different administrations navigating the challenges of the twenty-first century over a sustained period of time. It may simply be that the cold war era has been superseded by an increasingly complex global and domestic environment where the days of presidential supremacy and grand design in foreign policy have given way to a time when U.S. foreign policy is more likely to be reactive—a time of muddling through. This may not be what most people mean by American leadership in the world. But this appears to be the case thus far under George Bush and Bill Clinton—the first two post–cold war presidents.

The best way for a president to exercise power and govern is through strong political leadership. The exercise of presidential power is much dependent on the president's professional reputation, public prestige, and level of activism in arriving at presidential decisions. Presidents must do what they can to maximize each of these elements in order to govern, realizing at the same time that there are no guarantees of success in the complex politics of U.S. foreign policy. Clearly, the quality of leadership remains consequential with respect to the president's ability to govern since the end of the cold war. We now turn to one of the most significant sources that a president has to exercise leadership and power—his efforts to manage the executive branch and the foreign policy bureaucracy.

BIBLIOGRAPHIC ESSAY
· · · · · · · · · · · · · ·

The classic statement on presidential leadership is Richard E. Neustadt's, *Presidential Power: The Politics of Leadership* (New York: John Wiley, 1960). Another excellent work is Richard M. Pious's, *The American Presidency* (New York: Basic Books, 1996), especially his discussion of the exercise of prerogative government. For a general overview of the significance and basis of leadership in political affairs, see James MacGregor Burns, *Leadership* (New York: Harper Torchbooks, 1978).

The following sources provide strong discussions of different administrations and presidential leadership styles. Doris Kearns's, *Lyndon Johnson and the American Dream* (New York: New American Library, 1976) does a fascinating job of explaining Johnson's life and presidency in terms of his personality, his role in American politics, and his place in America's political culture. Gary Wills, in *Nixon Agonistes,* has written a very interesting political biography of Richard Nixon in the context of American history. Two revealing insights into Jimmy Carter and his presidency are the memoirs by Hamilton Jordan, *Crisis: The Last Year of the Carter Presidency* (New York: G.P. Putnam's Sons, 1982), and the psychobiography by Betty Glad, *Jimmy Carter* (New York: Norton, 1980). An excellent account of the Reagan presidency can be found in Lou Cannon, *President Reagan: The Role of a Lifetime* (New York: Simon and Schuster), while Gary Wills has written a powerful analysis of the life of Ronald Reagan and his place in American history entitled *Reagan's America* (New York: Penguin,

1988). Fred Greenstein provides thoughtful insights into President Clinton's personality and leadership styles in "The Two Leadership Styles of William Jefferson Clinton," *Political Psychology* 15 (June 1994): 351–62, as does David Maranis in *First in His Class: A Biography of Bill Cllinton* (New York: Simon and Schuster, 1995). For a general assessment of the Clinton presidency, see Colin Campbell and Bert Rockman, editors, *The Clinton Presidency: First Appraisals* (Chatham, N.J.: Chatham House, 1996).

ENDNOTES

1. For a discussion of the importance of presidential leadership, see James MacGregor Burns, *Presidential Government: The Crucible of Leadership* (New York: Avon, 1965); Erwin Hargrove, *Jimmy Carter as President: Leadership and the Politics of the Public Good* (Baton Rouge: Louisiana State University Press, 1988); Barbara Kellerman, *The Political Presidency: Practice of Leadership* (New York: Oxford University Press, 1984); Theodore J. Lowi, *The Personal President: Power Invested, Promise Unfulfilled* (Ithaca, N.Y.: Cornell University Press, 1985); Stephen Skowronek, *The Politics Presidents Make: Leadership from John Adams to George Bush* (Cambridge, Mass.: Harvard University Press, 1993). For a general overview of the significance and basis of leadership in political affairs, see James MacGregor Burns, *Leadership* (New York: Harper Torchbooks, 1978).

2. Richard E. Neustadt's, *Presidential Power: The Politics of Leadership* (New York: John Wiley, 1960). Since its initial publication in 1960, it has been periodically revised with additional reflections on more current presidents.

3. Hedrick Smith, *The Power Game: How Washington Really Works* (New York: Ballantine, 1988), p. 56.

4. See, for example, James David Barber, *The Presidential Character: Predicting Performance in the White House* (Englewood Cliffs, N.J.: Prentice-Hall, 1972); Erwin C. Hargrove, *The Power of the Modern Presidency* (New York: Alfred A. Knopf, 1974), chapter 2; and Doris Kearns, *Lyndon Johnson and the American Dream* (New York: New American Library, 1976).

5. Richard M. Pious, *The American Presidency* (New York: Basic Books, 1979), p. 47. See also Daniel P. Franklin, *Extraordinary Measures: The Exercise of Prerogative Powers in the United States* (Pittsburgh: University of Pittsburgh Press, 1991).

6. See, for example, James MacGregor Burns, *The Crosswinds of Freedom* (New York: Vintage, 1989), and William E. Leuchtenburg, *In the Shadow of FDR: From Harry Truman to Ronald Reagan* (Ithaca, N.Y.: Cornell University Press, 1985).

7. See Arthur Schlesinger, Jr., *The Imperial Presidency*, and George E. Reedy, *The Twilight of the Presidency* (New York: New American Library, 1970).

8. See Mark J. Rozell, "Carter Rehabilitated," *Presidential Studies Quarterly* 5 (Spring 1993): 317–30.

9. See Glenn P. Hastedt and Anthony J. Eksterowicz, "Presidential Leadership in the Post Cold War Era," *Presidential Studies Quarterly*; Jerel A. Rosati, "United States Leadership Into the Next Millennium: A Question of Politics," *International Journal* (Spring 1997): 297–315.

10. For an overview, see Colin Campbell and Bert A. Rockman, eds., *The Clinton Presidency: First Appraisals* (Chatham, N.J.: Chatham House, 1996).

11. Jack H. Watson, Jr., "The Clinton White House," *Presidential Studies Quarterly* (1993): 431.

12. Fred I. Greenstein, "The Presidential Leadership Style of Bill Clinton: An Early Appraisal," *Political Science Quarterly* 108 (Winter 1993-94): 592. See also Fred I. Greenstein, "The Two Leadership Styles of William Jefferson Clinton," *Political Psychology* 15 (June 1994): 351–62.

CHAPTER 6

PRESIDENTIAL MANAGEMENT AND THE NSC

he president's beliefs about the nature of the world and America's role within it are a very important guide to the type of foreign policy that will be pursued under his administration. Setting the general direction and tone of an administration, however, does not guarantee that a president's vision and priorities will prevail. Although two previous chapters have emphasized the powers and actions of the president, he does not and cannot operate alone. Much of the government's foreign policy is made and carried out by the bureaucracy. Presidential governance, therefore, requires that presidents not only be strong political leaders, but strong managers as well.

The president's ability to govern is heavily dependent on the foreign policy bureaucracy, yet the bureaucracy is so large and complex that it is very difficult to control. A president's success in managing the bureaucracy is very much a function of his choices concerning his personal agenda and level of involvement, the personnel that will staff his administration, and how he organizes the foreign policy-

making process. These choices are particularly important when it comes to the operations of the White House and the National Security Council (NSC) apparatus. The more successful he is in this management task the more he will be able to exercise presidential power in accordance with his roles as commander in chief, chief diplomat, chief administrator, and chief legislator. In other words, presidential management of the foreign policy bureaucracy is a key determinant of the extent to which the president will be able to govern U.S. foreign policy.

THE FOREIGN POLICY BUREAUCRACY

The president is the chief administrator, but much of the bureaucracy is beyond presidential control. *The bureaucracy is both a source of presidential power and a constraint on presidential power.* The more successful a president is in managing the bureaucracy, the fewer the bureaucratic constraints and the greater his ability to exercise power. Strong presidential management indicates strong leadership skills for it provides an important indication of a president's professional reputation and his ability to make important presidential choices.

Presidential management has been significant throughout the cold war years and has become of greater importance since the decline of presidential power following the Vietnam War and the end of the cold war. If the president is to exercise much power in his efforts to govern, in foreign policy as well as in domestic policy, he must attempt to manage and control the federal bureaucracy.

Yet, presidential management of the executive branch is not an easy task. There are *three major complications to the task of presidential management and administration of the bureaucracy:*

1. The size of the bureaucracy;
2. The complexity of the bureaucracy; and
3. The development of the bureaucracy.[1]

Bureaucratic Size. The United States executive branch bureaucracy is "huge." The president presides over five million personnel, located in thirteen major departments and hundreds of other organizations and agencies, who spend well over one trillion dollars a year on thousands of programs and policies throughout the United States and the world. The executive branch involves so many people, agencies, funds, and programs that the president's job as chief administrator is simply an impossible task. However, he has no choice but to try to manage and control as many areas as possible if he is to exercise any power over the bureaucracy.

The foreign policy bureaucracy itself is quite large. The Department of Defense (DOD) is the largest of all executive branch organizations; it employs over three million civilian and military personnel (including reserves) throughout the world and spends over $300 billion a year. In addition, many other agencies, such as the Department of State, the Central Intelligence Agency (CIA), the United States Information Agency (USIA), and the Agency for International Development (AID), are

devoted to foreign affairs. It would not be an exaggeration to say that virtually every department and agency in the executive branch contains an international component. The international side of the U.S. government's "war on drugs," for example, not only involves traditional foreign affairs agencies such as the State Department, DOD, and the CIA; it also involves agencies more commonly associated with domestic program priorities, such as the Department of Justice's Drug Enforcement Administration (DEA) and the Federal Bureau of Investigation (FBI). The scope of government with which a president must deal in his effort to manage the foreign policy bureaucracy is staggering.

Bureaucratic Complexity. Not only is the bureaucracy immense, it is also "incredibly complex." Some organizations like the Department of Defense are quite large; others are tiny, like the Peace Corps. Each organization has its own set of goals and missions. Some organizations, like DOD, have multiple goals and missions; others, like the Peace Corps, have very few functions. Many times the functions of different organizations overlap. For instance, the intelligence community, as will be discussed in chapter 9, is made up of many organizations throughout the executive branch that contribute information and analyses to high-level policymakers, thereby performing functions that often force them to compete with each other.

Another component of bureaucratic complexity is the degree to which various organizations have different "levels of autonomy" from presidential authority. The president's legal authority within the executive branch exists over those organizations located in the Executive Office of the Presidency (for example, the White House Office, the National Security Council), classified as cabinet departments (for example, DOD), or presidential agencies (for example, the CIA). Most of the executive branch organizations that are classified as regulatory commissions (such as the Federal Reserve Board), foundations and institutes (such as the National Institutes of Health, the Rand Corporation), and government corporations (such as the Export-Import Bank) are independent of presidential authority. Fortunately, from a presidential perspective, most, but by no means all, of the traditional foreign affairs organizations are legally under the president's authority.

Adding to the complexity of the foreign policy bureaucracy is the "fading distinction between foreign and domestic policy" bureaucracies. Traditional national security bureaucracies were easy to identify, such as the State Department, the military, and the intelligence community. With the collapse of the foreign policy consensus behind containment during the 1960s and the growth of global interdependence, these distinctions have lost much of their meaning. Foreign policy is now more than just national security policy; foreign economic, immigration, environmental, and drug policies are all important parts of overall U.S. foreign policy. Many of the agencies responsible for these areas of policy were generally considered domestic-oriented in the past. Today these agencies have an important international dimension—an indication of the increasing complexity and "internationalization" of the bureaucracy in general.[2]

Bureaucratic Development. Two hundred years ago, the United States government was a microcosm of what it is today; it was composed of the president, the vice president, a small personal staff, and four small departments: State, Treasury, War, and Justice. Although the federal bureaucracy has expanded in the last two centuries, most of the growth in the size and complexity of the bureaucracy has occurred during the twentieth century.

Bureaucratic growth has taken place in three successive waves. The first major expansion of the federal bureaucracy resulted from the New Deal legislation of the 1930s under President Franklin Roosevelt. The second expansion of the bureaucracy took place in national security and foreign affairs during World War II and the cold war under Presidents Roosevelt, Harry Truman, and Dwight Eisenhower. The last major expansion of the federal bureaucracy occurred with President Lyndon Johnson's Great Society programs of the 1960s.

The expansion of the bureaucracy came from government's attempts to respond to the urgency of events and the times. Government did not grow by design; it grew in response to situations that were perceived to be so dire and widespread that only the federal government, as opposed to state and local governments (or private initiatives), had the capability to address them. New bureaucratic agencies with new organizational goals and missions were created to respond to new problems. Governmental bureaucracy and programs grew during the 1930s to respond to the economic woes of the Great Depression; the bureaucracy increased during the 1940s and 1950s in response to the national security challenges posed by international fascism and communism; and it grew again during the 1960s to address the problems of poverty and inequality raised by social movements and events of that decade.[3]

A primary reason for lack of foresight and design in bureaucratic growth is that such growth can only occur if approved by Congress. Members of Congress were aware that creating new executive agencies would bolster presidential power in executive-legislative relations. Because of congressional reluctance to place new agencies under presidential authority, many of these agencies were created through political compromise as a means to retain congressional influence within the executive branch. Furthermore, although the political will can be found to create a new agency and new jobs, it has rarely surfaced to eliminate an old, outdated agency and superfluous jobs. These political actions help to explain how bureaucratic growth occurs. Adding one bureaucratic layer on top of another, with differing degrees of autonomy given to different agencies, has created the bureaucratic complexity that makes it so difficult for presidents to act as chief executives.[4]

With respect to the conduct of U.S. foreign policy, the foreign affairs bureaucracy was relatively small in the years before World War II.

> Before World War II, the foreign policy decision apparatus—to the extent that it existed at all—consisted of the president and secretary of state; a handful of administration appointees in the Department of State and major embassies; the senior diplomats of a tiny but adequate Foreign Service; a

few military and naval officers serving in important commands or as attaches; and a constellation of influential lawyers and bankers, involved in the Council of Foreign Relations and largely residing on the East Coast.[5]

The tremendous expansion of the bureaucracy in foreign policy took place over two decades in response to two major conflicts: World War II and the cold war. The key law that was the basis for the permanent expansion of the foreign policy bureaucracy was the **National Security Act of 1947.** It was one of the most important bureaucratic acts ever passed by Congress and signed by the president because it laid the foundation for the modern foreign policy bureaucracy. The act *restructured the national security process in three major areas:*

1. The military, by creating the National Military Establishment (forerunner to the Department of Defense) consisting of the Secretary of Defense and the Departments of Army, Navy, and Air Force;
2. Intelligence, by creating the Central Intelligence Agency; and
3. National security advice to the president, by creating the National Security Council.

The genesis of this restructuring was "the British War Cabinet and chiefs of staff committee system, later modified to conform to American notions of command responsibility and staff function."[6] The major intent behind the restructuring was to produce a more efficient national security process that would be more valuable to the president in his conduct of foreign policy. At first, the foreign policy bureaucracy was a major source of additional presidential power during the early cold war years, for the president was chiefly responsible for influencing the early goals and missions of the new bureaucratic organizations in support of his foreign policies. However, the foreign policy bureaucracy soon became so large, so complex, and so entrenched that presidents have had to be actively concerned with management of the bureaucracy in

order to maximize their ability to govern foreign policy.

PRESIDENTIAL MANAGEMENT
. . . .

Given that the bureaucracy has become so large and complex, how can a president manage the bureaucracy and make it work for him? *Three sets of presidential choices are vital* in determining the president's ability to manage the foreign policy bureaucracy. They involve:

1. The president's foreign policy orientation, agenda, and level of involvement;
2. The appointment of executive branch personnel; and
3. The organization of the foreign policymaking process.

These choices must be made early and will be among the most important decisions the president makes. They are so important that the candidate who has been newly elected in November will have made many of these decisions even before he officially assumes office in January.

The three-month transition for the president-elect is spent determining the president's agenda, the personnel he will appoint to work for him, and how the various foreign policymakers and organizations throughout the executive branch will interact. These decisions must be made "early" if a president wants to enter office ready to exercise power and govern, thereby taking advantage of the honeymoon period and early optimism that surrounds the start of a new administration.[7]

THE PRESIDENT'S ORIENTATION, AGENDA, AND LEVEL OF INVOLVEMENT

The president's beliefs and worldview set the general direction and **foreign policy orientation** for the administration. Different presidents have different foreign policy orientations and, consequently, establish different **policy agendas** as to what issues and policies should receive priority and attention. The foreign policy orientations and agendas of successive presidents, especially since World War II, have been briefly described in chapter 2 (on the history of U.S. foreign relations) and chapter 4 (on presidential governance in foreign policy).

Presidents try to set goals and promote policies that reflect their foreign policy orientation and agenda. And as already discussed, the stronger the presidential leadership the greater the likelihood that a president will gain political support for his initiatives and policies. However, such broad support does not automatically translate into bureaucratic responsiveness to him throughout the executive branch as well. He is chief administrator in name only. And the role of the bureaucracy is too important to be left to chance; a president must be attentive and actively involved in the operations of the bureaucracy to ensure that U.S. foreign policy during his administration is in accordance with his preferences. The more a president is attentive and involved concerning what goes on throughout the executive branch, the more likely he will influence and manage the bureaucracy in accordance with a foreign policy orientation and agenda of his choosing.

Because the bureaucracy is so large and complex, a president must be "selective" as to the issues most important to him, given the time and information constraints he faces. He must understand that while he can never gain complete mastery over the entire bureaucracy, the bureaucracy will be most responsive to those issues that he most prizes and is most active in promoting. General policy reviews, especially at the beginning of a new administration, involvement in the policymaking process, and the delivery of presidential speeches offer unique opportunities for the president to gain control over the bureaucracy and foreign policy.

But, ultimately, the president must rely on others to assist him in governing, in exercising presidential leadership, and in managing the bureaucracy. Hence, the role of presidential staff and advisers, and the nature of the policymaking process, are absolutely critical in affecting the extent to which the bureaucracy responds to the president's wishes and agenda.

APPOINTMENT OF STAFF AND ADVISERS

To this point we have emphasized what the president can do as an "individual" through his use of presidential power and governance, presidential leadership, and presidential management of the bureaucracy. However, the president is not alone and is dependent on others in efforts to manage the bureaucracy and govern. This is why the term **presidency** has been used throughout to refer to the "institution" or "office of the presidency," composed of the president and other individuals and organizations who represent, work for, and act in the president's name.

In deciding who will serve in his administration, the president must make *three general sets of appointments:*

1. Personal White House staff;
2. Major policy advisers; and
3. High-level officials responsible for other cabinet departments and executive agencies.

The president must rely on these people to manage the bureaucracy and exercise presidential leadership and power. Their performance affects his ability to govern foreign policy. It also means that with each new president, there will be considerable change in top-level personnel, most of which come from outside the executive branch, which is a uniquely American system of governmental management.

Franklin Roosevelt was the first modern president to expand his personal staff by creating the **Executive Office of the Presidency** (EOP) as a means to manage and cope with a bureaucracy that was rapidly growing in size and complexity. Today, the Executive Office of the Presidency contains the people and organizations that a president tends to rely on most in managing the bureaucracy and governing: the White House Office, Office of Management and Budget, National Security

Council, and National Economic Council (see **figure 6.1**).

The president's **personal staff** works directly for him in such places as the **White House Office**. These are the people who act as the eyes and ears of the president, and who are preoccupied with protecting and promoting his professional reputation, public prestige, and presidential choices. They are responsible for the president's daily schedule and help him to prepare for public appearances.

The **chief of staff** is the most significant of the president's personal staff and interacts with the president more frequently than anyone else. The chief of staff is responsible for the president's daily schedule and oversees the rest of the White House staff. This is a very consequential position because the chief of staff usually acts as the intermediary between the president and all staff and advisers who interact with him.

Some of the other important White House staff would include positions such as communications director, press secretary, chief political strategist, legislative affairs, and White House counsel. Another position which has become increasingly valuable to presidents of late has been the vice president (see **essay 6.1** on transforming the vice presidency and the role of Al Gore). It is quite common that the chief of staff, and maybe one or two others on the White House staff, are the president's close personal friends and, consequently, may also act as trusted policy advisers as well.

During President Reagan's first term, he relied heavily on a "triumvirate" of three members of his personal staff to assist him in day-to-day presidential governance: James Baker, the chief of staff; Michael Deaver, the deputy chief of staff; and Edwin Meese, the policy counselor. Under these three men, the White House staff enabled President Reagan to be effective in exercising presidential power. Reagan was very comfortable with this setup, especially in his interactions with Deaver and Meese who had been with him since his days as governor. After winning reelection in 1984, however, major changes occurred in **Reagan's White House staff**. Deaver left

FIGURE 6.1
THE EXECUTIVE BRANCH

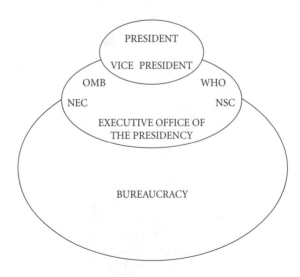

ESSAY 6.1
TRANSFORMING THE VICE PRESIDENCY AND THE ROLE OF AL GORE

The office of the vice president has been in transition over the last two decades. Throughout much of American history, **the vice president** has been a relatively insignificant player in the policymaking process, unless the president died (which was responsible for Harry Truman, Lyndon Johnson, and Gerald Ford becoming president since World War II). The vice presidency, likewise, has been an important "stepping stone" for eventually gaining the party's nomination to run for president (after the president's term of office ended). Nevertheless, people were chosen as vice president predominantly for political purposes, such as to "balance" the ticket within the party for the upcoming presidential election (to win over voters of certain geographical areas or ideological orientations). Not being trusted adviser or friend, the vice president was usually relegated to symbolic and unimportant activities (such as to preside over the Senate as stipulated in the Constitution).

Thomas Marshall, vice president under Woodrow Wilson, described the job by saying: "The only business of the vice president is to ring the White House bell every morning and ask what is the state of health of the president." This began to change in the 1980s under President Jimmy Carter who turned increasingly to Vice President Walter Mondale for counsel and political support. The importance of the role of the vice president continued, although more selectively, with George Bush under President Ronald Reagan and Dan Quayle under President Bush. However, with the election of Bill Clinton as president and Al Gore as vice president, the office of the vice president has acquired a much enhanced position of power and respect.

Born March 31, 1948, in Carthage, Tennessee, Albert Gore, Jr., was the son of a U.S. Senator. A member of the "baby boomer" generation, **Al Gore** graduated from Harvard in 1969, served in the army during the Vietnam War as a journalist, and

was eventually elected Senator from the state of Tennessee, following in his father's footsteps. He, unlike vice presidents chosen in the past, wasn't asked to be the vice presidential candidate in 1992 by Clinton merely for the sake of party balance. Gore, who is in the same age group and born in the same geographic region as Clinton, was chosen more because he made a reputation for himself as a deep thinker committed to several issues and as a politically savvy individual who seemed to be "above politics."

Within Clinton's White House, Gore has become an active participant and trusted adviser. Perhaps Gore's most defining issue is his commitment to the environment. He also has pushed to "reinvent government" by lessening red tape and making governmental bodies more efficient. Gore has been one of the first vice presidents to effectively promote "high-profile national issue(s)" and, as a "serious player," has been considered "more presidential than the president."

Gore's reputation has also become more pronounced. How he acts affects more than just domestic public opinion; Gore's high-profile responsibilities makes him the most prominent figure for the Democratic presidential nomination in the year 2000. It has been suggested that with time, Gore will start to diverge away from some of Clinton's ideas and build a political reputation more of his own. Even then, however, he may not be able to escape his time as Clinton's heir apparent: Gore is closely associated with the Clinton administration and has been linked to Clinton's fund-raising scandals.

The future of Al Gore and the vice presidency remains unclear. Gore's "squeaky clean" image has been challenged for the first time, but probably not for the last time as the presidential election approaches—from Republicans as well as by Democrats eyeing the presidential nomination. As Clinton and Gore wade through the accusations and political waters, Gore will likely come under more and more intense scrutiny. To what extent he will maintain a positive image may not only affect his future, but may impact the future of the office of vice president as well.

SOURCES: R. W. Apple, Jr., "Gore Is Crossing Starting Line for Year 2000," *New York Times* (January 19, 1997), sec. 1, p. 20; Howard Fineman, "Collision Course: Al Gore and Fred Thompson Get Ready to Do Battle Over the 'Asia Connection,'" *Newsweek* (March 3, 1997): 5–51; Howard Fineman, "Gore's World," *Newsweek* (December 23, 1996): 22–25; Paul C. Light, *Vice Presidential Power: Advice and Influence in the White House* (Baltimore: The Johns Hopkins University Press, 1984); Elaine Sciolino and Todd S. Purdum, "Al Gore, One Vice President Who Is Eluding the Shadows," *New York Times* (February 19, 1995): 1, 32; Evan Thomas, "Friends for Now," *Newsweek* (January 27, 1997): 40–41.

the White House to become a political consultant, Meese was appointed attorney general, and James Baker switched positions with Donald Regan to become secretary of the treasury. President Reagan approved these major changes nonchalantly, yet this presidential choice may not have served the president well during a difficult and trying second term. With hindsight, this may have been one of the most fateful personnel decisions made by President Reagan, for the old team of Baker, Deaver, and Meese may have been much more protective of the president and critical of the activities that produced the Iran-Contra affair.

The president must also decide who will occupy key policy positions in the U.S. government and act as his **policy advisers**. Of the many appointments a president makes, *six key foreign policy appointments stand out:*

1. Special assistant to the president for National Security Affairs (better known as the national security adviser or NSC adviser);
2. Secretary of state;
3. Secretary of defense;
4. Director of central intelligence;
5. Special assistant to the president for Economic Affairs (called the national economic adviser or NEC adviser); and
6. Secretary of the treasury.

These officials are responsible for the most important foreign policy organizations within the executive branch: the National Security Council, the Department of State, the Department of Defense, the Central Intelligence Agency, the National Economic Council, and the Department of Treasury. Together, they are the people with whom the president will interact most on a daily basis in making foreign policy, with the national economic adviser and secretary of treasury most instrumental for foreign economic policy and the other officials more consequential in the national security area.

The president also appoints hundreds of **other high-level officials** to fill positions throughout the executive branch. *For most agencies, he appoints the head or director and the positions at the next three or four hierarchical levels* within the agency. In the State Department, the president has the authority to make appointments at the five highest hierarchical levels: the secretary of state, deputy secretary of state, undersecretaries of state, assistant secretaries of state, and deputy assistant secretaries of state. These appointments do not guarantee presidential control, as will be discussed in greater depth in the next few chapters, for the bureaucracy has a life of its own and often "captures" appointees to reflect bureaucratic interests. Yet, these appointments are one of the key means available for a president to manage and control as much of the bureaucracy as possible in support of his agenda and worldview.

Essay 6.2 discusses the criteria that presidents consider in making their appointments and the background of most officials—a topic of great importance. "Time" affects these decisions, for many are made by the president-elect during the brief

ESSAY 6.2
SELECTION AND BACKGROUND OF MAJOR STAFF AND ADVISERS: THE CASE OF CLINTON

The American system of governmental management is unique among modern industrialized societies. With each new president there is considerable change in top-level personnel throughout the executive branch. And there is usually turnover in major staff and advisers during a president's term of office, especially after reelection. On the one hand, this gives the president the opportunity to better control and manage the executive branch. On the other hand, the lack of stability and expertise at the top can also be a major disadvantage as well, especially in the conduct of foreign policy.

As Bill Quandt has found when it comes to U.S. foreign policy, especially towards the Middle East, the last seven presidents—from Johnson to Clinton—who have occupied the Oval Office have:

> appointed 10 Secretaries of State, 9 Directors of Central Intelligence, 11 Secretaries of Defense, and 12 national security advisers. During this same period 9 different Assistant Secretaries for Near Eastern and South Asian Affairs have served, as have 9 directors of the Middle East office of the National Security Council. On average, then, the top personnel in charge of Middle East policy changes about every three or four years.[A]

Clearly, it is important to understand how a president selects his staff and advisers, and where they tend to come from.

The people the president appoints as his major staff and advisers are usually chosen based on a number of **selection criteria**. Presidents try to appoint people who are knowledgeable and who share their ideological outlook and world-view. They also try to select people with whom they are comfortable and whom they believe to be loyal.

The appointments of personal staff usually involve individuals who have supported the president over the years. Most members of the White House staff, for example, usually consist of people with whom the president has grown familiar and comfortable, often recruited from his campaign team. It is quite common that the chief of staff, and maybe one or two others on the White House staff, are the president's close personal friends and, consequently, may also act as trusted policy advisers as well. The people during the campaign who acted as his advisers (for both domestic and foreign policy), who briefed him and wrote his foreign policy speeches, often are appointed to key positions and become major policy advisers.

Unlike the White House staff and a few major policy advisers, people selected to fill other major policy roles and official positions may not be close to the president and tend to have broader **backgrounds**. For these positions, the president must rely on his personal staff for information and recommendations concerning the candidates for appointment. Most major appointments tend to consist of white males (although no longer exclusively the case), who are highly educated and *come from prominent institutions throughout the country, especially the following professions:*

1. law;
2. business;
3. politics and government; and
4. academia and research institutes.

President Clinton's major staff and advisers—probably the most diverse in American history—are listed nearby, along with their backgrounds (see

A. William B. Quandt, *Peace Process, American Diplomacy and the Arab-Israeli Conflict Since 1967* (Berkeley: University of California Press, 1996).

TABLE 6.1
PRESIDENT CLINTON'S STAFF AND ADVISERS

POSITION	NAME	BACKGROUND
CHIEF OF STAFF	Thomas "Mack" McLarty	Business
	Leon Panetta	Law and Congress
	Erskine Bowles	Business
DEPUTY CHIEF OF STAFF	Philip Lader	Law, Business, Academia, Government
	Harold Ickes	Law and Politics
SENIOR POLICY ADVISER	George Stephanopoulos	Government
	Rahm Emmanuel	Politics
PRESS SECRETARY	DeeDee Myers	Politics
	Mike McCurry	Government and Politics
WHITE HOUSE COUNSEL	Bernard Nussbaum	Law
WHITE HOUSE PERSONNEL DIRECTOR	Bruce Lindsey	Law
NATIONAL SECURITY ADVISER	Anthony Lake	Government/Academia
	Sandy Berger	Law and Government
NATIONAL ECONOMIC ADVISER	Robert Rubin	Law and Wall Street
	Laura D'Andrea Tyson	Academia
	Gene Sperling	Law and Government
SECRETARY OF STATE	Warren Christopher	Law and Government
	Madeline Albright	Academia and Government
SECRETARY OF DEFENSE	Les Aspin	Academia and Congress
	William Perry	Academia and Business
	William Cohen	Law and Congress
DIRECTOR OF CENTRAL INTELLIGENCE	R. James Woolsey	Law and Government
	John Deutsch	Academia and Government
	George Teret	Government
SECRETARY OF THE TREASURY	Lloyd Benson	Law and Congress
	Robert Rubin	Law and Wall Street

table 6.1). The White House staff is drawn primarily from Arkansas and the campaign team. The vast majority of his major advisers and officials have law degrees or doctorates, many from Harvard, Yale or Georgetown—the schools attended by Clinton and Vice President Gore. There are at least fifteen Rhodes scholars, like Clinton, in the administration.

As stated by one analyst, "It is education, more than birth, wealth, or previous experience in government, that defines the people Mr. Clinton has chosen to serve with him."[B] But education, experience, and connections that have crossed the career path of Bill Clinton also figure, for "they all seem to know each other. . . . Friendships formed at elite colleges and law

schools have been sustained through an archipelago of think tanks, foundations, councils and associations."[C] Overall, they appear to represent a collection of the "best and the brightest" in the tradition of Clinton's idol, John F. Kennedy.

B. Jack H. Watson, Jr. "The Clinton White House," *Presidential Studies Quarterly* 23 (1993): 433.

C. David Ignatius, "The Curse of the Merit Class," *Washington Post* (February 27, 1994): C1.

SOURCES: Richard Barnet, *Roots of War: Men and Institutions Behind U.S. Foreign Policy* (New York: Penguin, 1972); David Ignatius, "The Curse of the Merit Class," *Washington Post* (February 27, 1994); Charles Maechling, Jr., "Foreign Policy-Makers: The Weakest Link?" *The Virginia Quarterly Review* 52 (Winter 1976): 1–23; William B. Quandt, *Peace Process, American Diplomacy and the Arab-Israeli Conflict Since 1967* (Berkeley: University of California Press, 1996); and Jack H. Watson, Jr., "The Clinton White House," *Presidential Studies Quarterly* 23 (1993): 429–35.

three-month transition period. And there is no guarantee that people will accept when asked—President Clinton has repeatedly struggled to find a Director of Central Intelligence. All of these factors affect how well the president will select competent bureaucratic managers to carry out his agenda.

Presidential management in the Bush administration, for example, was hindered by the slow rate of presidential appointments. Sixteen weeks after President Bush took office, 80 percent of the senior positions in government departments and agencies remained unfilled—half the rate that occurred under President Reagan, who had filled positions slower than his predecessors. Of forty-four senior appointments in the Department of Defense, only nine people had been nominated by the president and two confirmed by the Senate. This meant that five months into the Bush administration, most of the bureaucracy was still being run and managed by President Reagan's appointees. President Clinton's rate of appointments has been even slower than that of his predecessors.[8]

Another important issue is senatorial approval. The people appointed to staff agencies within the Executive Office of the Presidency, such as the White House Office and the National Security Council, do not require Senate approval. From a constitutional perspective, these personnel and

agencies are considered the personal staff of the president. Most other high-level appointments in the executive branch require the **advice and consent** of the Senate. A president tries to nominate people who will gain Senate approval as soon as possible, thereby getting his people in position to help him manage the bureaucracy.

When a president does nominate a person to a governmental position, there is usually little difficulty in gaining Senate approval. However, every now and then a presidential appointment can become controversial, as when President Bush nominated John Tower, a former senator from Texas, to be his secretary of defense. Questions were raised about Tower's close connections with the defense industry, as former chair of the Senate Armed Services Committee and subsequently as a political consultant, and his personal habits, which had aroused accusations about his drinking and promiscuity. President Bush refused to withdraw the Tower nomination and the Senate refused to approve, resulting in a major defeat early in Bush's administration. President Clinton also suffered politically early on from some ill-fated appointments, such as Zoe Baird's nomination for head of the Justice Department. And following his successful reelection in 1996, President Clinton nominated his national security adviser, Anthony Lake, to be Director of Central Intelligence only to find the senatorial hearings becoming controversial and politicized, leading to Lake's withdrawal.

ORGANIZING THE POLICYMAKING PROCESS

The president not only must decide who he will appoint to staff his administration, but how they will interact so that he is kept informed, able to arrive at decisions, and have decisions implemented in accordance with his wishes. The president cannot assume when he takes office that the policymaking system in place will automatically do these things for him, allowing him to manage the bureaucracy. On the contrary, if a president wants to manage the bureaucracy, as opposed to responding to bureaucratic momentum, he must initiate a policy process that responds to his demands.

Among the more *important questions about how to organize the policymaking process* that a president must address are:

1. Should the process be White House centered, State Department centered, or mixed/ad hoc?
2. Should the process be centralized or decentralized?
3. Should the process be open or closed to staff and advisers?

The president must decide whether to rely on a lead agency to be responsible for coordinating the foreign policy process and, if so, whether it should be the State Department or the White House using the National Security Council. He must also decide whether he prefers to have only a few individuals who are allowed to act in the president's name responsible for the overall conduct of foreign policy or whether power should be more decentralized throughout the foreign policy bureaucracy. He must also determine the level of access different policymaking officials will have in the process, especially at the presidential level.

Decisions about these issues determine how the foreign policymaking process will operate. These are decisions that presidents-elect must make before they enter office. If a president, or his personal staff, are reluctant to be involved in influencing the policymaking process, answers will soon develop by *fait accompli* without presidential input, thereby weakening the president's ability to manage the foreign policy bureaucracy. As Richard Neustadt in *Presidential Power* would say, unless the president is willing and able to make hard choices, he is more likely to act as a clerk than a leader. These are crucial decisions, for how the policy process operates determines the extent to which information and policy alternatives flow to the president, whether the bureaucracy is responsive to the president's agenda, and whether policies are implemented in accordance with his decisions.

It is not unusual for presidents to enter office claiming that they will rely on **cabinet government** as their principal means of managing the bureaucracy. This means that the president plans to rely heavily on his cabinet secretaries and cabinet departments for information and advice. Under cabinet government, the president meets periodically with all thirteen members of his cabinet to discuss various issues and arrive at policy decisions. Such a policymaking process tends to be highly decentralized and open, often allowing the State Department to act as the lead agency responsible for coordinating the conduct of U.S. foreign policy. In this scenario, the secretary of state would be the principal spokesperson for U.S. foreign policy, acting as the major adviser to the president, and the State Department would be responsible for coordinating the policy process within the rest of the foreign policy bureaucracy.

Cabinet government and a **State Department-centered** foreign policy process constitute the popular perception of presidential power and executive branch operation: the president meets with all of his major advisers around a big table and arrives at policy decisions. Unfortunately, a president who attempts to operate this way quickly discovers that the bureaucracy, including the cabinet departments and many of the cabinet secretaries that he appointed himself, are not very responsive to him. Presidents cannot afford to assume that simply because they occupy the Oval Office the bureaucracy will be responsive to them—it is too big, complex, and set in its ways.

Despite early optimism about cabinet government, a strong State Department, and a decentralized and open policy process, presidents quickly learn that this is not the way to manage effectively the foreign policy bureaucracy and maximize presidential power. In fact, *three general patterns have prevailed in the foreign policy process* for most presidents since World War II:

1. Presidents tend to rely on a White House-centered system;
2. The policymaking process tends to become more centralized with time;
3. The level of participation in the process tends to narrow and close over time.

Though presidents may initiate a decentralized and open policy process, one that may be State Department-centered, they quickly turn to rely on those they trust most, which tend to be the White House staff and agencies within the Executive Office of the Presidency. Within a short time, the president usually begins to rely on a small number of advisers. This occurs because of time constraints on the president and increasing familiarity among the president and his advisers. Hence, the predominance of a **White House-centered system**.

At first, the president does not know his appointees well. Then, as the president begins to interact with his advisers, he begins to learn more about their policy views, personalities, and operating styles and makes judgments about the value of their advice, trust, and friendship. With time the president tends to become more selective as to whom he interacts with and relies on for advice. This often tends to "close" the policymaking process and narrow the range of information and opinions that come before the president because the presidency is such an "awesome office . . . where no one really stands up to the president, where there is no equality, where no one tells the president he is wrong." In other words, inevitably "it tends by its nature to inhibit dissent and opposition."[9]

In managing the foreign policymaking process, presidents have increasingly relied on the national security adviser and the National Security Council. Unlike much of the established and entrenched bureaucracy, including the Department of State and the Department of Defense, members of the White House Office and the National Security Council are most responsive to the president. They lack an independent base of power, working only for him and under his complete authority. Bureaucratic autonomy also tends to promote a more centralized process that limits presidential access to those policymakers in whom the president has greatest confidence and with whom he is most comfortable.

To sum up, the key to presidential management of the foreign policy bureaucracy involves the choices the president makes concerning his foreign policy orientation, personal agenda and his level of involvement, his executive-level appointments, and the dynamics of the policymaking process. These presidential choices determine the extent to which the president will manage the bureaucracy and make it responsive to him. However, what works for one president may not work for others. *These presidential choices are very much a function of a president's personal characteristics:* his beliefs, personality, and operating style.[10]

Over the years there have been numerous commissions created and studies conducted which have called for **governmental reform** and a restructuring of the foreign policy process. Some scholars used to maintain that a State Department-centered foreign policy system was preferable.[11] However, it has become increasingly understood that what counts is what the president prefers and finds most comfortable given his orientation and personality. Therefore, it is not surprising that presidential management of foreign policy tends to revolve around a White House-centered system that becomes more centralized and closed over time, for it is most responsive to presidents and their personal characteristics. To better understand presidential management of the foreign policy bureaucracy and the operations of a White House-centered system, especially in the area of national security, we must examine the National Security Council and the process by which it operates.

THE NATIONAL SECURITY COUNCIL

. . . .

The **National Security Council (NSC)**, within the Executive Office of the Presidency, is the key organization which the president has relied on since World War II to manage the foreign policy bureaucracy. The **national security adviser** usually is the single most important appointment the president makes. He is often the most important policy adviser to the president and is responsible for coordinating the foreign policymaking process within the executive branch. Therefore, one cannot really understand how the president manages American foreign policy unless one understands the operations of the National Security Council, especially its origins, evolution, and process.[12]

Origins. The National Security Council came into existence in 1947 with the passage of the National Security Act which restructured the policy process in the areas of defense, intelligence, and national security advice to the president. The NSC was created to serve three principal **functions:**

1. Advise the president;
2. Act as a vehicle for long-range planning; and
3. Promote the coordination and integration of the national security process.

The NSC was originally intended to be the major group to provide foreign policy advice to the president.

The **structure** of the National Security Council consisted of two elements:

1. A formal decision-making council composed of high-level foreign policy officials;
2. A small support staff.

The "original statutory members" of the National Security Council included the president, secretary of state, secretary of defense, secretary of the army, secretary of the navy, secretary of the air force, and the chairman of the National Security Resources Board (responsible for emergency planning and civil defense). A small staff, headed by a civilian executive secretary, provided support for the formal council advisory meetings, helped coordinate the policy process, and conducted long-range planning.

The purpose of the National Security Council Act was to rationalize the national security process and force the president to be more responsive to formal lines of authority throughout the foreign policy bureaucracy, especially within the military. The formulation and passage of the National Security Act was a response to what many people thought was a chaotic national security policymaking process during World War II. Within months, the United States was transformed from an officially neutral country with a tiny foreign policy bureaucracy to a participant in the war with a rapidly growing national security bureaucracy. The expansion of U.S. armed forces, and the bureaucracy to support and implement the use of troops in both theaters of war, was so massive and so rapid that the policy process within the military became chaotic.

Not only did frustration exist with the U.S. government's difficulty in administering a large wartime bureaucracy, but many people were unhappy with President **Roosevelt's management style.** Roosevelt was not one to rely on formal channels of communication; instead, he relied on an informal, ad hoc managerial style. He oversaw the bureaucracy and made policy by relying on a variety of individuals of different ranks located throughout the bureaucracy. This managerial style served Roosevelt well as president, but displeased many high-level officials, especially within the military, whom Roosevelt bypassed in the formal chain of command. This concern with a chaotic process and informal managerial style was reinforced by the rise to the presidency of Harry Truman, a man who lacked considerable knowledge and experience in foreign policy.

These perceptions provided the original incentive behind the National Security Act of 1947. The desire to provide the U.S. government with a policymaking apparatus that would promote greater efficiency and preparedness in the national security process accounts for the advice, long-term planning, and coordination functions of the NSC. At the same time, to force the president to comply with a more formal process and adhere to the chain of command, the membership of the NSC was set by law and composed largely of members of the newly created National Military Establishment (forerunner to the Department of Defense). Modeled after the British War Cabinet, it was a means of imposing a cabinet government on the president when national security decisions were involved. The only legal flexibility that a president was given to determine the composition of the NSC was the ability to invite additional officials to National Security Council meetings.[13]

Changing Patterns in the NSC. Presidents have found the NSC, as originally designed, to be both a potentially useful tool and a frustrating means of managing foreign policy. It should not be surprising to learn that presidents have used those aspects of the NSC they have found useful while ignoring or circumventing those aspects they have found constraining. Presidents have made valuable use of the National Security Council in ways that were unintended by those who drafted and supported the National Security Act of 1947. *Two major changes to the original NSC under postwar presidents are evident:*

1. Providing policy advice and coordinating the policy process for the president have become the two major functions of the NSC, while long-term planning has become unimportant;
2. The NSC staff has become more significant over time, while the National Security Council as a decision-making body has declined in importance.

Advising the president and coordinating the foreign policy machinery remain the two major functions of the National Security Council. However, the third function, **long-term planning**, has almost never been implemented. The one possible exception involved the Truman administration and the development of **NSC-68.** National Security Council memorandum No. 68 was a staff document approved by the president in 1950. It represented a concerted effort by members of the NSC staff to predict U.S.-Soviet relations into the 1950s and recommend U.S. foreign policy alternatives for presidential consideration. NSC-68 provided the official justification of the policy of global containment of Soviet communism and, through the institutionalization of this policy due to the Korean War, influenced the foreign policies of subsequent administrations during the cold war years.

The National Security Council has not developed any important long-term planning since NSC-68. This may not serve the country's best interests for, as the United States enters the twenty-first century, the lack of a long-term strategy may hamper the conduct of U.S. foreign policy. On the other hand, the absence of long-term planning is not unique to the NSC nor is it difficult to understand. The NSC staff is small compared to other governmental organizations and incredibly overworked. The staff responds to the needs of the national security adviser and the president, who are primarily preoccupied with responding to immediate events and day-to-day governing. Consequently, there is little time, interest, or reward involved in long-term planning. Although long-term planning makes a lot of sense and can be of great value to the president and the future conduct of foreign policy, the NSC staff is simply too busy responding to the short-time demands of its superiors.

Although the National Security Council has grown in significance for the president, the National Security Act of 1947 legally defined whom the president must accept as his major foreign advisers. Clearly, this is not acceptable to most presidents. If a president wants to exercise power, as opposed to being a clerk, he must be allowed to determine whom he will rely on for foreign policy advice. Changes in the law have been made reflecting this concern—the current statutory members of the council are the president, vice president, national security adviser, secretary of state, secretary of defense, and chair of the joint chiefs of staff. The president can invite other individuals to participate as he sees fit. Very simply, presidents will interact with those policymakers they trust the most and will avoid officials with whom they have policy disagreements or personality conflicts. The president is the key figure in affecting the dynamics of the policy process, at least at the presidential level, and he will manage the bureaucracy in ways that are consistent with his operating style. A particular foreign policy process cannot be superimposed on a president by law.

Each president has used the NSC as it has suited him. This has ultimately resulted in the decline of the council's significance as a formal decision-making body while the national security adviser and staff have grown in importance. Therefore, the foreign policy process has gradually become White House centered as the president increasingly relies on the national security adviser and the NSC staff to manage the process and provide him with an independent source of information and advice (see **table 6.2** for a list of national security advisers and their backgrounds).[14]

TABLE 6.2
NATIONAL SECURITY ADVISERS

NAME	YEAR APPOINTED	BACKGROUND
Sydney W. Souers	1947	Business and Navy
James S. Lay, Jr.	1950	Business and Army
Robert Cutler	1953	Law and Army
Dillon Anderson	1955	Law and Army
William Jackson	1956	Law, Business, and Army
Robert Cutler	1957	Law and Army
Gordon Gray	1958	Law, Army, and Journalism
McGeorge Bundy	1961	Academia
Walt W. Rostow	1966	Academia and Government
Henry A. Kissinger	1969	Academia
Brent Scowcroft	1975	Army and Academia
Zbigniew Brzezinski	1977	Academia
Richard V. Allen	1981	Academia and Government
William P. Clark	1982	Law
Robert C. McFarlane	1983	Army and Government
John M. Poindexter	1985	Navy
Frank C. Carlucci	1987	Business and Government
Colin L. Powell	1987	Army
Brent Scowcroft	1989	Army and Academia
Anthony Lake	1993	Academia and Government
Samuel "Sandy" Berger	1997	Law and Government

PRESIDENTIAL MANAGEMENT STYLES AND THE ROLE OF THE NSC

. . . .

Presidential management styles have differed with each president and have evolved over time. According to I. M. Destler, Leslie H. Gelb, and Anthony Lake, in *Our Own Worst Enemy: The Unmaking of American Foreign Policy,* there have been *three major stages in the evolution of the National Security Council* and the foreign policy process at the presidential level:[15]

1. Presidents Truman and Eisenhower used the NSC Council as an advisory body with a staff to support their reliance on cabinet secretaries and departments;
2. Under Presidents Kennedy and Johnson, the NSC Council was eclipsed and the traditional role of the cabinet, especially the State Department, was challenged by the rise of the national security adviser and staff;
3. Beginning with President Nixon, the national security adviser and staff became ascendant in the policymaking process.

THE EARLY NSC AS ADVISORY BODY

During the 1950s, the National Security Council was used as an advisory body to assist the president in making foreign policy. This worked well with the management styles of Presidents Truman and Eisenhower, who relied on strong cabinet officers, such as the secretary of state, for information and advice. Even though the NSC operated to provide information and advice to the president, the secretary of state remained the chief foreign policy spokesperson and adviser to the president, and the State Department often acted as the lead organization in formulating and implementing foreign policy.

Truman's Management Style. Harry Truman was president during the difficult time between the end

of World War II and the escalation of the cold war. Truman lacked the international experience and expertise requisite to deal with the unfolding transition in America's global role. As president, he relied on the secretary of state, Dean Acheson, and the secretary of defense, General George C. Marshall, for counsel and to carry out presidential policy. Along with his White House presidential counselor, Clark Clifford, an informal advisory process developed between President Truman and these officials.

Truman initially was hesitant to compromise his independence by relying on the NSC, but following the North Korean attack on South Korea in 1950 it became a regular forum for discussion. The NSC staff was kept very small, consisting of roughly twenty people under an executive director who organized and provided support for the council meetings. As the National Security Council grew in use as an advisory body, President Truman came to rely on two major channels for information and advice: the formal NSC advisory process through use of the council and an informal process of personal interaction between the president and his closest advisers.

Eisenhower's Management Style. Under President Eisenhower, the U.S. policy of global containment became institutionalized through the expanded national security bureaucracy. In managing the bureaucracy and the policy process, Eisenhower was more comfortable utilizing the NSC. He was accustomed to such formal mechanisms in the military and it fit well with his particular style. The National Security Council was relied upon heavily as an advisory body to President Eisenhower. And the position of **special assistant to the president for National Security Affairs** (referred to as the national security adviser) was created to supervise the staff.

In eight years, the NSC held 346 meetings, roughly one each week, compared to 128 meetings in over five years under President Truman. Most of the meetings lasted two-and-a-half hours with President Eisenhower usually presiding.[16] Two interagency committees were created to assist in preparation for the formal meetings and to oversee policy implementation, both managed by the national security adviser. The NSC staff tripled in size and became the major vehicle for coordinating the information and advice provided to the president by the national security departments and agencies.

President Eisenhower did not rely solely on the formal NSC process for information and advice. John Foster Dulles, the secretary of state, was the major foreign policy spokesperson throughout the administration and acted as a major adviser to the president. Furthermore, because the National Security Council process tended to be slow and cumbersome, President Eisenhower also relied on more "informal channels" of interaction. When it came to fast-moving developments and crises, President Eisenhower, as had President Truman before him and presidents after him, arrived at policy decisions after informally consulting the most trusted members of his administration. (See **essay 6.3** for a closer examination of President Eisenhower's management style and relationship with his secretary of state.)

THE RISE OF THE NSC ADVISER AND STAFF

Changes during the Eisenhower administration set the stage for the decline of the NSC as a formal advisory body and the rise of the national security adviser and staff as independent sources of information and advice for the president. It was not, however, until the Kennedy administration that the national security adviser and staff occupied these new roles, eclipsing the role of the National Security Council and challenging traditional cabinet organizations such as the State Department. By the early 1960s, the modern NSC process was in place and *three contemporary characteristics have become commonplace for presidential management:*

1. The formal National Security Council as advisory body was replaced by interagency groups whose membership was determined by the president;
2. The NSC staff became the personal staff to the president for foreign policy; and
3. The national security adviser became the key official responsible for managing the interagency groups and coordinating the policy process, as well as for providing information and advice to the president.

Presidential management of the foreign policy decision-making process, in other words, has come to rely increasingly on a White House-centered system that emphasized the use of the national security adviser and staff.

JFK's Management Style. John Kennedy entered office as an activist president who was ready to get the country moving and lead the free world. However, he had no clear strategy for managing the foreign policy process. His personal management style tended to be very informal and akin to the ad hoc style used by Franklin Roosevelt. He was uncomfortable relying on a large advisory body such as the National Security Council and quickly scrapped Eisenhower's formal foreign policy apparatus. With this decision, the National Security Council—as a formal advisory body whose membership is stipulated by law—ceased to be influential. However, Kennedy offered no alternative decision-making structure. The initial policymaking process under Kennedy resulted in ad hoc interaction among his foreign policy advisers, the creation of informal interagency groups whose membership was decided by the president, and considerable leeway for departments and agencies. This **ad hoc management style** lasted only a few months—until the **Bay of Pigs fiasco**.

The covert effort to train a Cuban military force and overthrow Castro by invading Cuba, which began under President Eisenhower, failed miserably when Kennedy allowed it to go forward in April 1961. Much of the blame was attributed to the decentralized and chaotic nature of the decision-making process that had first developed under Kennedy. To address the problem, the decision-making process became more centralized through the national security adviser who ensured that all information and advice reached the president. The informal interagency groups were now managed by National Security Adviser McGeorge Bundy. In this climate, the national security adviser increasingly came to act as a personal adviser to the president, as well as a manager. This advisory role was reinforced by the

ESSAY 6.3
PRESIDENTIAL MANAGEMENT IN ACTION: REASSESSING EISENHOWER'S ROLE

Dwight D. Eisenhower has typically been portrayed as a passive president whose management style involved delegation of authority to others while he remained largely uninvolved in day-to-day governing. In the area of foreign policy, the common perception was that President Eisenhower was dependent on the formal National Security Council process he instituted and that Secretary of State **John Foster Dulles**, not the president, was the major source of the administration's foreign policy.

It was not uncommon to hear political jokes about how Eisenhower was more interested in playing golf than governing or that the president seemed unknowledgeable about his own administration's policies given the way he abused the English language during press conferences. By the end of Eisenhower's term of office, his administration was critically attacked by both conservatives and liberals, within his own Republican party and the Democratic party, for "losing" the cold war and lacking the initiative and dynamism to respond to international events. Symbolic of this criticism was the establishment of the Senate Government Operations Subcommittee on National Security Machinery to provide a "nonpartisan study of how well our government is now organized to develop, coordinate, and execute foreign and defense policy."[A]

Since the mid-seventies, a "reassessment" of Eisenhower's role as president has developed. This **revisionist perspective**, popularized by scholars such as Fred Greenstein in *The Hidden-Hand Presidency,* argues that the portrait of Eisenhower as passive and uninvolved is a caricature of his real role. This view portrays Eisenhower as a much more complex man than commonly thought, involved and exercising considerable influence throughout the policy process, and claims that Secretary of State Dulles was highly responsive to Eisenhower in the conduct of U.S. foreign policy.

According to this view, few people were aware of Eisenhower's real management style because he preferred to work behind the scenes and take a low profile in public. This management style was also smart politics, for Eisenhower was able to maintain high public prestige and public approval as an individual, even while criticism for his administration's policies was increasing. The major weakness of this hidden-hand presidential style was that Eisenhower was unable to explain publicly how his administration operated and stem the attacks on his management style. The belief that his management was inefficient was best symbolized by changes in the foreign policy process instituted by the Kennedy administration.

Two important points arise from this brief review of Eisenhower's foreign policy management style. First, differing interpretations of the same phenomena tend to develop, with popular perceptions often changing over time. The view of Eisenhower as aloof and responsive to others, accepted for roughly twenty years, is now being seriously challenged by a revisionist interpretation that is growing in popularity, at least among scholars and historians. Second, the initial orthodox interpretation of Eisenhower's management style is very similar to the popular portrayal of President Reagan's management style. As discussed in essay 5.1, it will be interesting to see the extent to which new interpretations, suggesting a more complex Reagan presidency, develop and grow in popularity.

A. U.S. Senate, Committee on Government Operations, Subcommittee on National Policy Machinery, *Organizing for National Security,* Vol. I (Washington, D.C.: U.S. Government Printing Office, 1961), p. iii.

SOURCES: Stephen E. Ambrose, *Eisenhower: The President and the Elder Statesman* (New York: Simon and Schuster, 1984); Fred I. Greenstein, *The Hidden-Hand Presidency: Eisenhower as Leader* (New York: Basic Books, 1982); and Robert W. Kagan, "Why Like Ike?" *National Interest* (Summer 1986): 88–94.

substantial growth in foreign policy expertise and specialization in the NSC staff, providing the president with an independent source of information and advice. An indication of the growing status and influence of the national security adviser and staff was the **location of the offices**. They moved from the basement of the Executive Office Building (across from the White House) to the basement of the White House—much closer to the president.

Given popular notions about the significance of the National Security Council as a decision-making body, presidents feel compelled to act symbolically as if they rely on the NSC in order to comply with the law and maintain legitimacy with segments of the public who think that the NSC is important. For example, even though President Kennedy was the first to scrap use of the NSC, the deliberating body he relied upon during the Cuban Missile Crisis was called **Excomm**, which stood for the Executive Committee to the National Security Council. Under Kennedy, a **situation room** for crisis management was also set up in the basement of the White House enabling the president to receive and transmit international communications.

Such White House activism was reinforced by President Kennedy's low regard for the competence of the State Department and his appointment of Dean Rusk as secretary of state. A practice evolved whereby the NSC staff worked with people in the bureaucracy that they found responsive to Kennedy's agenda and style, for example, people within Secretary Robert McNamara's Department of Defense and within the State Department at the undersecretary or assistant secretary level.

LBJ's Management Style. This pattern of growing White House management continued under President Johnson, although Johnson's particular management style was quite different from his predecessor's. With the assassination of John Kennedy in November 1963, Lyndon Johnson was thrust into office. Johnson initially decided to work with Kennedy's appointees to maintain continuity and promote legitimacy for his presidency. However, as vice president he had never been comfortable and felt like an outsider with Kennedy's people.

The relationship between Johnson and Robert Kennedy, John Kennedy's younger brother and attorney general, was quite hostile. While Kennedy had preferred to work with the "best and the brightest," drawn from such elite universities as Harvard, and he actively engaged such individuals for information and advice, Johnson preferred men who were loyal and supportive, especially after he had arrived at a decision. With time, President Johnson came to rely on his own group of advisers and replaced many of Kennedy's appointees, such as McGeorge Bundy who was replaced as national security adviser by Walt Rostow in March 1966.

Johnson was neither knowledgeable about nor interested in foreign policy. He was much more interested and involved in domestic policy. As a Texas politician and former majority leader in the U.S. Senate, he loved to be "in the know" and "wheel and deal" in politics. He also became president just prior to the 1964 presidential elections, so he was preoccupied quite early with winning election and acquiring a mandate for his Great Society agenda. Johnson's management style in foreign policy reflected all of these factors.

For most foreign policy issues, Johnson remained uninvolved, except when he had to respond to a crisis such as the revolution in the Dominican Republic in 1965 or, increasingly, the Vietnam War. He preferred to "delegate" authority to people with whom he was impressed and could trust, such as Robert McNamara at the Department of Defense and Dean Rusk at the State Department. When he wanted additional advice, he did not turn to his young staff as Kennedy had, but rather to those senior political figures he knew well, such as former advisers Dean Acheson and Clark Clifford.

Although interagency groups did operate, key presidential decisions were made in informal sessions with his closest advisers. Many of his most important decisions involving Vietnam, for instance, were made during his **Tuesday Lunch group** composed of senior advisers Clifford, McNamara, Rostow, and Rusk. When he did get highly involved, he tended to dominate the policy process. Therefore, Johnson's tendency was either to delegate authority and let the bureaucracy develop a consensus position or to be highly involved in promoting consensus behind him.

The NSC Adviser and Staff Ascendant

Beginning with President Nixon, the national security adviser and staff became ascendant over the cabinet officers and departments for information, advice, and management of the policy process for the president. As presidents began to rely more on their national security advisers, the position gained prominence and power. The national security adviser also began to act as a spokesperson for the president and became active in the actual operations and conduct of U.S. foreign policy. The national security adviser became first among equals relative to other key foreign policy officials. To assist the national security adviser, the staff grew in size and influence as well.

The "height" of White House centralization of the policymaking process was reached under President Nixon with Henry Kissinger as national security adviser. In contrast to earlier administrations, in which the national security adviser and staff coordinated and managed the foreign policy bureaucracy, Nixon and Kissinger attempted to control the bureaucracy by using it or circumventing it. Under the Nixon-Kissinger system, the secretary of state and the State Department, in particular, suffered a great loss of prestige and power to influence U.S. foreign policy.

The level of centralization was modified under President Ford and more so under President Carter. In contrast to the Nixon administration, other cabinet officers and departments were able to play a greater role. Nevertheless, the policy process remained White House centered with the national security adviser and NSC staff responsible for managing the system and operating as the president's personal foreign policy staff. President Reagan, a believer in delegation and cabinet government, attempted to reverse these trends but had little success.

The *policymaking process at the presidential level has tended to operate at two overlapping levels:*

1. An informal process among the president's closest advisers; and
2. A formal NSC interagency process through use of the national security adviser and the NSC staff.

The informal process usually involves the president meeting with his closest advisers in person or speaking with them over the phone. Ultimately, as described by Charles Maechling, Jr.:

> No important decision in the area of national security or foreign policy is made by a president ... without in some degree being shaped and formulated by an interdepartmental decision process. Even the information and advice on which a decision is based filters through to the highest authority in a form that consciously or unconsciously reflects the assumptions and viewpoints of key subordinates and second-level decision-makers.[17]

Both post–cold war administrations have continued to rely on an informal advisory process and a formal NSC interagency process. In this respect, not much has changed with the end of the cold war. Presidents Bush and Clinton have continued along the lines of Presidents Ford and Carter of having strong cabinet officials operating within a White House-centered foreign policy system. To better understand how contemporary presidents have managed the executive branch, a more detailed look at the actual operation of the foreign policymaking process is needed.

The Nixon-Kissinger System. Nixon came to the presidency with a strong interest in foreign affairs. He also came into office with a great distrust of the bureaucracy, which he felt tended to limit information and options available to the president. President Nixon's management strategy was to use the White House as the major instrument in foreign policymaking. This resulted in a very centralized decision-making structure that relied, not on the

National Security Council as an advisory body, but the national security adviser, Henry Kissinger.[18]

The NSC system that Nixon and Kissinger set up attempted to use the bureaucracy to provide a broad array of information and options to the president on those issues he considered important. This was to be done through the creation of numerous interagency committees, whose membership was decided by the president and Kissinger. Although some of the committees met more frequently than others, all were chaired by Kissinger. President Nixon, always the loner, rarely attended, preferring to consider the products of the committees by himself and personally consult with his closest advisers, who increasingly became Henry Kissinger for foreign policy. (See **figure 6.2** for an overview of the Nixon-Kissinger policy process.)

Nixon and Kissinger activated the bureaucracy by issuing a **National Security Study Memorandum** **(NSSM)**, which laid out the issue to be addressed, the agencies involved, and presented deadlines for agency submission of policy recommendations. Once the studies and recommendations were complete, interagency meetings chaired by Kissinger would be convened to consider policy options and make recommendations for transmittal to the president. Once the president decided on a particular course of action, often in consultation with Kissinger, a **National Security Decision Memorandum (NSDM)** would be issued describing the president's decision and instructing the bureaucracy on implementation of the policy. Henry Kissinger's staff oversaw this complex policy process, serving as an independent source of information and options for Kissinger and the president.

Initially, this policy process worked by forcing the bureaucracy to provide information and advice to the president and allowing him to arrive at deci-

FIGURE 6.2
THE NIXON-KISSINGER SYSTEM

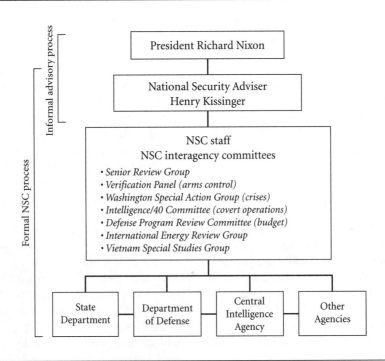

sions that would be communicated to the bureaucracy for implementation. By the second year in office, however, President Nixon had a stronger sense of the foreign policy goals and strategy he wanted to pursue and formed a special relationship with Henry Kissinger. Thus, Nixon and Kissinger were no longer as interested in information and advice, but concentrated on policy initiatives and implementation. The result was that Kissinger and the NSC system were increasingly used as a means to control and circumvent the bureaucracy.

Kissinger became the president's manager, major adviser, spokesman, and, in some cases, implementer of foreign policy. Kissinger's power was symbolized by his movement from the basement of the White House to a prestigious office on the main floor of the west wing, down the hall from the Oval Office of the president. Kissinger came to act as Nixon's alter ego in foreign policy, especially once Watergate began to break. The policy process became so centralized in the hands of Kissinger that the ability of many traditional foreign policy agencies and officials to influence the process dwindled.

Nowhere was this truer than in the State Department, where William Rogers was the secretary of state in name only. This process also resulted in some major political battles over defense policy between Kissinger and Melvin Laird, the secretary of defense. Although Kissinger often bypassed the involvement of other foreign policy officials, usually with Nixon's blessing, he and his staff did develop important contacts and networks with trusted lower-level officials throughout the bureaucracy. Given Kissinger's crucial role, the size of the NSC staff reached its height of over one hundred staffers during this period.

Nixon and Kissinger did not trust the bureaucracy to implement major policy initiatives; it was perceived as too resistant, cumbersome, and leaky. The principal method used by President Nixon for controlling the implementation process was **the back channel**. During negotiations over the SALT I arms control treaty, for example, while the official American and Soviet delegations met formally—"the front channel"—Henry Kissinger often met with the Soviet ambassador to the United States in

secret. In this way, President Nixon was able to communicate his position more directly to the Soviet leaders, and the bureaucracy was often circumvented and uninformed concerning presidential policy. This also occurred when the Nixon White House announced that Kissinger was in Peking negotiating the normalization of relations with the People's Republic of China, altering thirty years of U.S. foreign policy and shocking most foreign policy officials. During the Nixon administration, the national security adviser, rather than the secretary of state, came to act as the chief negotiator in the name of the president.

Henry Kissinger, and thus the office of national security adviser, reached a "pinnacle" of power under President Nixon that no single policymaker had experienced before or since. When William Rogers eventually resigned in 1973, Nixon appointed Kissinger as the secretary of state as well, and one man held the two most important foreign policy positions in the U.S. government. Such a centralized policy process was responsive to Nixon and Kissinger for those issues in which the president was most interested. However, few policy alternatives tended to be considered and there was considerable internal dissent throughout the executive branch. The major weakness of the system was that Kissinger was a single individual who was only able to accomplish so much. Consequently, the Nixon-Kissinger system was unable to gain control or heavily influence dozens of other foreign policy issues in which the U.S. government remained constantly involved. (See **essay 6.4** for more discussion about the unique role of Kissinger within the foreign policy-making process.)

This White House-centered system under Henry Kissinger continued to operate under **President Ford and his management style**, although with some modifications. New appointments made by Ford opened up the policy process to other officials, such as Donald Rumsfeld as secretary of defense. In 1975, Lieutenant General Brent Scowcroft, Kissinger's deputy national security assistant since 1973, became the national security adviser and managed the day-to-day NSC process. Nonetheless, Gerald Ford, who had minimal exposure to foreign

ESSAY 6.4
HENRY KISSINGER: SCHOLAR, STATESMAN, REALPOLITICIAN, MANIPULATOR, SPOKESPERSON, CELEBRITY

Henry Kissinger, who was born in Germany but became a naturalized U.S. citizen, achieved the pinnacle of power within his profession. Following World War II, he became a professor of Government at Harvard University and was a well-respected scholar and author on international politics, U.S. foreign policy, and political-military strategy. During the cold war years, he also became a member of the prestigious Council on Foreign Relations, which was composed of prominent experts in the area of foreign affairs and was often referred to as the "foreign policy establishment." Before his appointment as national security adviser by Richard Nixon, Kissinger had been in and out of government and had acted as a close adviser to presidential hopeful, and Nixon rival, Nelson Rockefeller. He stands out because he embodied the realpolitik tradition in foreign policy and made the national security adviser ascendant in the making of U.S. foreign policy.

Kissinger is often remembered as a policymaker because of his distinctive worldview, which heavily influenced the Nixon administration's foreign policy. Kissinger, unlike many other American policymakers, came from the **realpolitik tradition** of understanding world politics. He was not really interested in morality or reforming the world, more in the "Wilsonian" tradition. Instead of fighting an "ideological" cold war between the free world and communist totalitarianism, Kissinger believed in the overriding importance of maintaining "stability" between the two great powers, the United States and the Soviet Union, through the exercise of "power" and force abroad. Thus, he was a key force in initiating détente with the Soviet Union and normalizing relations with the People's Republic of China.

What is less well known about Kissinger was his ability to "acquire and maintain power" within the policymaking process. Kissinger dominated the NSC process and drove the staff members relentlessly. They worked for him, not the president. He was extremely demanding and when staff work did not meet his standards, it was not unusual for him to explode and berate staffers for their shoddy work. Kissinger came to rely on a staff-within-a-staff, those he found to be most capable and trustworthy. But he was suspicious of much of his staff. For example, when word leaked out to the press about America's secret bombing of Cambodia in 1969, Kissinger was furious and requested that Nixon wiretap members of the NSC staff—the earliest beginnings of Watergate. His autocratic style resulted in much discontent among his staff, many of whom resigned (later to appear as advisers to Democratic presidential hopefuls, such as Jimmy Carter). He operated the same way as secretary of state in that he didn't utilize the State Department as an institution but acted as a "lone ranger" with the support of a small, loyal staff.

Kissinger was a master at maximizing his position and influence within the Nixon and Ford administrations. Like Nixon, he deeply distrusted the bureaucracy and had a passion for secrecy and manipulation. His rise to power and special status with presidents came at the expense of others. This was most blatant with **Secretary of State William Rogers**, a personal friend and confidant of Richard Nixon, who was publicly and repeatedly humiliated by Kissinger. Yet, President Nixon rarely objected to Kissinger's maneuvers because he often saw his cabinet officers as lightweights, like Rogers, or bureaucratic impediments to conducting foreign policy.

Kissinger eventually became the major foreign policy "spokesman" for the president. Initially, this was done behind the scenes in **background briefings** to journalists who attributed their information to a "senior official." Kissinger was truly a master at feeding (and leaking) information to the media to promote the president's policies. He worked the media like no foreign policy official before him or since. By 1973, Kissinger came out in the open as the public spokesman for foreign policy. Over the next two years he became a media star and celebrity. This caused conflict with Nixon's personal White House staff, because they feared that Kissinger's publicity was detracting from the president's public prestige. However, with President Nixon soon fighting for his political life over Watergate, Kissinger was perceived as one of the few shining lights within the administration.

Kissinger had a very large and, at the same time, fragile "ego." His unfinished two-volume memoirs, already over 2000 pages, is indicative of this. Kissinger loved to exercise power; yet he was extremely jealous and protective of his policy views. When his position was challenged or he did not come out on top in the policy process, it was not unusual for him to become extremely upset. Kissinger submitted his resignation numerous times, yet it was never accepted. Instead, he was soothed and, in the end, often got his way.

Although Kissinger has not had an official governmental position since President Ford left office, he has continued to enjoy great stature and influence within the Washington political community. Kissinger has remained visible in the national media, has built a prestigious consulting firm, Kissinger Associates, and two of his closest associates, Brent Scowcroft and Lawrence Eagleberger, were appointed national security adviser and secretary of state by President George Bush.

SOURCES: Seymour H. Hersh, *The Price of Power: Kissinger in the Nixon White House* (New York: Summit Books, 1983); Marvin Kalb and Bernard Kalb, *Kissinger* (New York: Dell, 1974); Roger Morris, *Uncertain Greatness: Henry Kissinger and American Foreign Policy* (New York: Harper and Row, 1977); John Newhouse, *Cold Dawn: The Story of SALT* (New York: Holt, Rinehart and Winston, 1973); and Bob Woodward and Carl Bernstein, *The Final Days* (New York: Avon, 1986).

---

affairs, developed a close working relationship with Henry Kissinger, and remained dependent on his secretary of state throughout his term of office.

Carter's Management Style. Jimmy Carter entered the presidency committed to a new and optimistic foreign policy agenda intended to respond to a changing international environment. Although Carter's worldview was very different from Nixon's, the Carter administration's foreign policymaking apparatus was very similar to that which existed early in the Nixon administration. While the Carter foreign policy system was centralized within the White House, it was still relatively open to input by cabinet officials and departments. President Carter managed U.S. foreign policy by relying upon a formal NSC process and an informal advisory process dependent on his national security adviser and secretary of state.[19]

Though the National Security Council was again intended to be used as the main decision-making body, it fell into disuse relatively early in the Carter administration. Two formal interagency groups within the NSC system became primarily responsible for the working operations of the foreign policy process: the Policy Review Committee and the Special Coordinating Committee. The **Policy Review Committee (PRC)** was established to develop policy at the secretarial level on issues in which one department had been designated as the lead agency by the president. Secretary of Defense Harold Brown was usually the designated chairman for military issues (such as those questions that regarded the provision of arms to Middle Eastern countries) while Secretary of State Cyrus Vance chaired the PRC when more political-military issues were involved (such as the Panama Canal negotiations and improving relations with the People's Republic of China). The **Special Coordinating Committee (SCC)**, chaired by National Security Adviser Zbigniew Brzezinski, was established to deal with crosscutting issues, such as arms control and crisis management. At the lowest level of the NSC system were two groups at the assistant secretary level which did much of the legwork for the PRC and SCC and were also responsible for issues of lesser significance: interdepartmental groups (geographically oriented) and ad hoc groups.

As with the Nixon administration, the foreign policy process was activated when the president issued a **presidential review memorandum (PRM)** identifying the issue and requiring policy research by the appropriate committees and agencies. Once the study was completed and transmitted to the president, he would decide on a particular course of action. At this point, a **presidential directive (PD)** was issued describing the president's decision and instructing the bureaucracy on the procedures for implementation. Obviously, the process was much more confusing and cumbersome than this simplistic portrayal. The president had to decide or agree on the issues to be reviewed, the agencies and individuals involved, and the individual responsible for chairing the Policy Review Committee (or a given interdepartmental or ad hoc group). Papers had to

be prepared and revised and meetings scheduled to discuss and debate the issue, all of which consumed a considerable amount of time and effort. The paperwork was then organized and synthesized and the completed report then sent to the president, usually with a brief summary and a one- or two-page memorandum. The president had to review the material, consult with his advisers, and arrive at a decision; then the wheels of implementation, if required, had to turn. (See **figure 6.3** for an overview of the process as it existed in the Carter administration.)

President Carter relied principally upon two individuals he respected and admired, **Zbigniew Brzezinski and Cyrus Vance**, in making the foreign policy process viable and effective. Brzezinski, as

FIGURE 6.3
CARTER'S FOREIGN POLICY SYSTEM

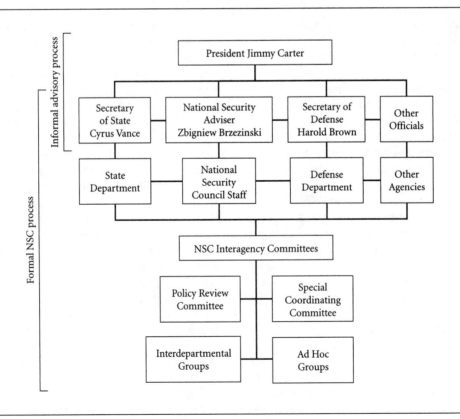

national security adviser and head of the NSC staff, was primarily responsible for coordinating the interagency operations of the NSC system, while Secretary of State Vance was the chief negotiator and major spokesperson for the president. Both individuals were key advisers to the president in foreign affairs, staying in close contact with the president and each other throughout the course of the day. Brzezinski usually briefed the president in the morning concerning major world developments and their effect on U.S. foreign policy. In the evening, Vance often sent a report directly to the president summarizing his views for the day. Important issues were discussed during President Carter's weekly "foreign policy breakfasts" on Fridays with Brzezinski, Vance, and other presidential advisers such as Secretary of Defense Brown, Vice President Walter Mondale, and Chief of Staff Hamilton Jordan. Brzezinski also presided over a "weekly luncheon" with Vance and Brown. The informal advisory process did not end there, however, for President Carter was usually available in the Oval Office to see his advisers or discuss policy with them over the phone.

The foreign policy system worked fairly well during the first two years. It was White House-centered, yet open and flexible, providing the president with a wide array of information and advice. Carter lacked considerable experience and knowledge of foreign affairs, but he was very active in learning about world politics and was involved in daily decision making. Carter, Brzezinski, and Vance got along together and shared a sense of optimism about the future of U.S. foreign policy. The main problem that President Carter experienced during this period was that he pressed too many initiatives too quickly: promoting human rights, negotiating SALT II with the Soviet Union, attempting to limit arms sales and curb nuclear proliferation, reducing the number of American troops in Korea, normalizing relations with the People's Republic of China and Vietnam, concluding a treaty on the Panama Canal, and promoting a comprehensive settlement to the conflict in the Middle East. President Carter was ahead of his advisers sometimes and of the foreign policy bureaucracy most of the time.

By the third year the foreign policy process began to break down. Initial deterioration was due to Brzezinski's growing "hard-line" views concerning the need to contain Soviet interventionism abroad, reinforced by the president's growing indecisiveness regarding the utility of force in dealing with situations such as the shah's unstable regime in Iran. Not only did Brzezinski and Vance increasingly differ over proper policy, but their personal styles of action exacerbated the situation. Vance had risen through the ranks of the foreign policy establishment during the cold war years in which one operated in a gentlemanly, nonpartisan, and quiet fashion; Brzezinski represented the new type of ambitious, partisan, and activist foreign policy professional. The growing conflict over policy and personal style resulted in considerable bureaucratic infighting, especially between the Brzezinski and Vance staffs.

With the taking of American hostages in Iran and the Soviet intervention in Afghanistan in late 1979, President Carter supported Brzezinski over Vance, reinstating the containment strategy as the cornerstone of U.S. foreign policy. President Carter also decided to attempt a military rescue of the hostages, a decision arrived at while Vance, the lone dissenter, was vacationing in Florida. With Vance no longer enjoying the confidence of the president and his policy views increasingly isolated within the administration, he resigned, thus becoming the first secretary of state to resign voluntarily on a matter of principle in over sixty years.[20] Consequently, Zbigniew Brzezinski and his NSC staff had clearly become ascendant within the foreign policy process by the end of Carter's term of office.

Reagan's Management Style. President Reagan entered office committed to reversing the Carter trend toward a strong national security adviser and NSC staff. Reagan preferred to rely on his foreign policy officials and their agencies for information and advice. It was much more of a cabinet-style government which, nonetheless, remained White House-centered because of the dominant role played by Reagan's White House staff. As with previous presidents, a two-tiered system developed: a formal NSC process and a more important informal advisory process. However, unlike other recent presidents, Reagan's national security adviser and staff were supposed to act as little more than custodians responsible for coordinating the process, reminiscent of their role during the early NSC days.[21]

Three major interagency committees, referred to as **senior interdepartmental groups (SIGs)**, were created within the NSC as the means to generate information and advice to the president. One SIG covered intelligence matters and was chaired by the director of central intelligence, another involved defense policy and was chaired by the secretary of defense, the third major SIG was chaired by the secretary of state and

dealt with more traditional foreign policy matters. As under President Carter, the interagency process was triggered by the issue of a presidential review memorandum (PRM) which ultimately led to a presidential decision (PD). Eventually, a **crisis management group** was also created, chaired by Vice President George Bush. Each of these committees reported to the president through his White House staff. (See **figure 6.4** for an overview of the process.)

Unlike the Nixon administration, in which Kissinger chaired all the interagency committees, or the Carter administration, where Brzezinski chaired some of the interagency committees, Reagan's national security adviser did not chair any committees.

FIGURE 6.4
REAGAN'S EARLY FOREIGN POLICY SYSTEM

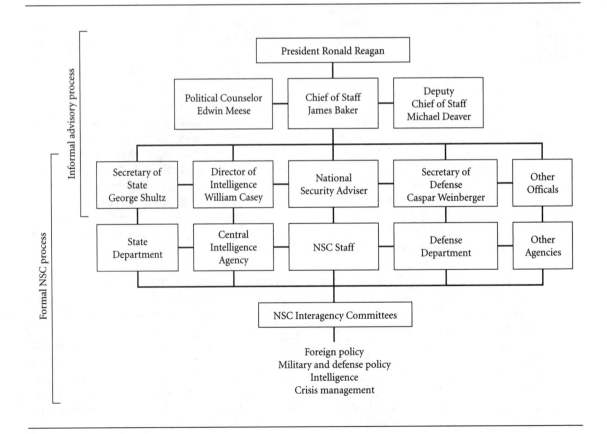

The national security adviser's job was to supervise the staff and provide support for the formal NSC process described above. Nor did Reagan's first appointee as national security adviser, Richard Allen, act as a major adviser or spokesperson for the president. Under President Reagan, unlike his predecessors, he reported to the president through the White House staff. As an indication of the decline in the national security adviser's stature and influence within the Reagan administration, his office was moved away from the president into the basement of the White House.

President Reagan relied on a much larger informal advisory process than his predecessors. Reagan preferred to delegate authority, tended to remain uninvolved in daily operations, and lacked considerable experience and knowledge of foreign affairs. The principal foreign policy officials on which Reagan depended for information and advice were Secretary of State Alexander Haig (later George Shultz), Secretary of Defense Caspar Weinberger, and Director of Central Intelligence William Casey. Unlike his immediate predecessors, however, Reagan also relied heavily upon his White House staff—James Baker, Michael Deaver, and Edwin Meese during his first term and Donald Regan, then Howard Baker during his second term. They were not only among his closest confidants, but also acted as intermediary links between the president and the formal NSC system.

From the beginning, the foreign policymaking process "failed" to function smoothly. The first major problem involved "the secretary of state's role" within the system. **Alexander Haig** thought that he was going to be responsible for developing a State Department-centered system for the president. Haig had the greatest amount of governmental experience in foreign affairs, previously acting as Kissinger's deputy national security adviser, Nixon's chief of staff, and supreme commander of Allied Forces in Europe under Ford. He also had a strong and assertive personality. He believed that he was to be the key foreign policy spokesperson, major foreign policy adviser, and foreign policy manager—the *vicar* of the Reagan administration's foreign policy.

Haig could not understand that even though Reagan had de-emphasized the role of the national security adviser and staff, he preferred a White House-centered system, which relied on his personal staff. President Reagan, who preferred a collegial atmosphere of interaction with his advisers, was uncomfortable with Haig's strong and intense personality. Haig did not help himself politically when he stated on national television that "I am in control," after the attempted assassination of the president. The result was constant political infighting between Haig and the White House staff.[22] Divisions over the proper way to manage the foreign policy process were so severe, reinforced by policy differences, that Haig threatened to resign numerous times. Haig was flabbergasted when President Reagan finally accepted his resignation in 1982 in a dispute over the president's opposition to the European construction of a pipeline for Soviet natural gas.

The second major problem involved "frequent turnover of key personnel" under President Reagan. Reagan had six national security advisers; each one lasted little more than a year. Even though the role of the national security adviser was downplayed, the national security adviser still had an important position to play in coordinating the policy process; and, given the size and complexity of the foreign policy bureaucracy, it took time to master the workings of the executive branch and devise a proper strategy for managing the bureaucracy. National security advisers, like presidents, had to learn on the job. They had to mold a close working relationship with the president and other foreign policy officials. The problem under President Reagan was that after months of learning, adjusting, and tinkering with the policymaking process, the national security adviser was replaced by a different individual. Richard Allen was replaced by William Clark, then by Robert McFarlane, John Poindexter, Frank Carlucci, and finally Colin Powell.

These constant changes of crucial personnel created havoc within the foreign policy process. They reduced the national security adviser's clout within the executive branch even further than originally intended by the president; the major exception was William Clark who, although he knew little about foreign policy, was personally close to the president.[23] Consequently, the national security adviser was often unable, through insufficient influence or lack of experience, to manage the process. Power moved to other officials in the policy process, such as Baker, Meese, George Shultz (who replaced Haig as secretary of state), and Weinberger.

The "political infighting" among Reagan's principal advisers became legendary. The national security adviser was unable to either stop it or channel it in more productive directions and President Reagan had great difficulty facing such confrontations and disciplining his subordinates. Major political battles regularly were fought over who became the next national security adviser.[24] The disarray in the policymaking process only got worse when Reagan's personal aides—Baker, Deaver, and Meese—left the White House.

There was so little management of the policy process by the middle years of the Reagan administration that informal coalitions between officials and groups developed over different issues. For example, a consensus arose within the administration in support of contras and their effort to overthrow the Sandinistas in Nicaragua, even after American assistance was banned by Congress. Therefore, most of the major officials and foreign policy bureaucracy was involved in continuing to support the contras. But there was considerable disagreement among Reagan's advisers over exchanging arms for hostages with Iran—Shultz and Weinberger fought the initiative. President Reagan, however, was committed to the Iran venture and, consequently, the circle of participants within the policy process narrowed: the White House, the National Security Council, and the CIA remained involved, while the secretary of state and the secretary of defense were eliminated or circumvented. The actual implementation of both of these initiatives was taken by the NSC staff. Thus, the **operational NSC staff**, begun under Kissinger, reached its height under the Reagan administration and contributed to the NSC's ascendance within Reagan's second term.

For a number of reasons, success in managing the bureaucracy in the name of the president was greater by the "latter part" of the administration. First, Frank Carlucci, and then Colin Powell was brought in as national security adviser. These were two able men with considerable foreign policy experience who restored the stature of the national security adviser and staff and increased their influence over the policy process. Two of the dominant personalities and foreign policy officials within the Reagan administration also departed: Secretary of Defense Weinberger returned to private life and Director of Central Intelligence Casey died in office. Finally, former Senator Howard Baker replaced Donald Regan as chief of staff, helping to make the policy process work more efficiently for the president. Hence, President Reagan left office with a White House-centered system under the able management of a strengthened national security adviser and staff.

Bush's Management Style. The initial foreign policy process in the Bush administration was similar to what transpired under President Ford, the early Carter years, and late in the Reagan administration—a White House-centered system revolving around an NSC process where cabinet officials and departments play a prominent role. President Bush was comfortable with such a White House-centered policymaking process because of the foreign policy expertise and policymaking experience he acquired during the Nixon, Ford, and Reagan years, especially given his roles as director of central intelligence, U.S. ambassador to the United Nations, and vice president.[25]

President Bush relied on a "formal interagency policy process" dependent on the NSC staff and the coordination of National Security Adviser Brent Scowcroft, a position he held under President Ford. Interagency groups operated at different levels: the interaction of senior governmental officials for more significant and general issues and, for lesser issues, the involvement of groups of lower-level officials representing the foreign policy bureaucracy organized along more specific geographical and functional lines.

Bush personally relied most on a "small informal advisory process" that usually included National

Security Adviser Scowcroft, the White House chief of staff (initially John Sununu, then Samuel Skinner), Secretary of State James Baker, Secretary of Defense Richard Cheney, and Chairman of the Joint Chiefs of Staff Colin Powell. Emphasis was with loyalty and quiet teamwork, "in marked contrast to the public feuds over policy and bureaucratic turf in previous administrations—the Shultz-Weinberger, Vance-Brzezinski, or Rogers-Kissinger battles."[26] President Bush, for example, relied heavily on this small group of officials for information and advice in formulating the decisions following Iraq's August 2, 1990, invasion of Kuwait to respond forcefully in defense of Saudi Arabia, to pursue a policy of brinksmanship to compel Iraq to withdraw from Kuwait, and then, when that failed, to go to war (see **figure 6.5** for an overview of the process).

CLINTON'S MANAGEMENT STYLE AND NSC
. . . .

Like his predecessor, President Clinton supplements a formal NSC interagency process with a heavy reliance upon informal meetings among his principal foreign policy advisers.[27] However, Clinton, as a politician and former governor, is a "relative newcomer" to the world of foreign, especially national security, affairs. Domestic policy and (domestic and international) economics are never far from his mind. Consequently, much of his time, especially early on, has been spent on foreign policy cramming and learning to get up to speed. Clinton's preference has been to set broad guidelines and pay spasmodic

FIGURE 6.5
BUSH'S FOREIGN POLICY SYSTEM

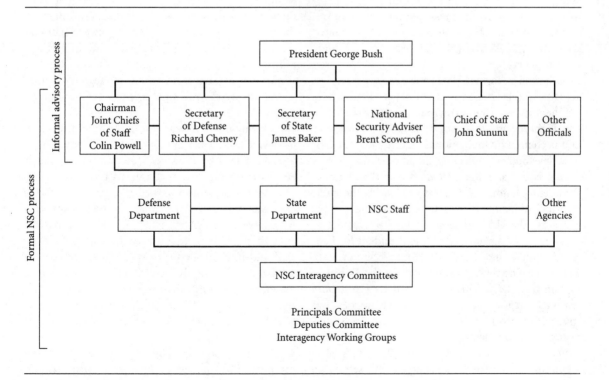

attention to different issues as they arise. As Secretary of State Warren Christopher delicately put it, President Clinton lays down "the broad guidelines of foreign policy, expecting his State Department and national security advisers to implement them as a team, working together, and holding them accountable if they don't carry it out in a fairly straightforward way."[28]

In his first term Clinton showed a strong preference for informal meetings with his closest advisers, especially Secretary of State Warren Christopher, National Security Adviser Anthony Lake and Defense Secretary Les Aspin and later Aspin's successor William Perry. He often meets or talks privately with one, or more, of his foreign policy principals. "Three informal settings" have become particularly important: the president's early morning foreign policy briefing by the national security adviser; discussions with top aides after meetings with foreign leaders; and the weekly Wednesday lunch among Clinton's foreign policy principals in the West Wing. In fact, early on in the administration Clinton's apparent unwillingness to establish more frequent formal meetings on foreign policy created concern among advisers like Secretary of State Christopher.

Clinton's "formal NSC interagency process" is actually closely modeled on the Bush NSC system. At the top was the **Principals Committee (PC)**, which serves as the senior interagency committee and is chaired by the national security adviser. One new development reflecting the importance of economic issues and the post–cold war world under President Clinton was that he broadened the circle of principal members to include the Secretary of the Treasury, the U.S. Ambassador to the United Nations, the Special Assistant to the President for Economic Policy; and the White House Chief of Staff. Below the Principals Committee was the **Deputies Committee (DC)**, which is chaired by the deputy national security adviser and which carries out much of the work of the interagency process, supervising policy implementation, and reviewing issue papers to be used by the NSC Principals. The Deputies Committee is also charged with setting up and supervising a series of **Interagency Working Groups (IWGs)** at the assistant secretary level to help prepare policy studies and to help facilitate implementation of decisions within bureaucratic agencies (see **figure 6.6** for an overview of the process).

The Clinton administration did bring some reorganization to the NSC staff, dividing up the European Affairs office into an office for Western Europe and an office for Russia, Ukraine, and Eurasian Affairs, and creating offices for Non-Proliferation Policy, Environmental Affairs, and Democracy Affairs to reflect new post–cold war policy concerns. At the same time the size of the NSC staff was cut from approximately 180 in the Bush administration to 150 people (of which 90 are detailees from other executive branch agencies).[29]

The person responsible for coordination of the national security machinery, **National Security Adviser Anthony Lake**, very much like National Security Adviser Brent Scowcroft under President Bush, entered office determined to keep a lower public profile. Lake believed that keeping a lower profile would not only enhance his role as coordinator of the policy process, but would also prevent much of the bitter infighting that occurred between national security advisers and secretaries of state in past administrations. Indeed, observers of the Clinton White House have reported a high degree of collegiality among the principal members of the foreign policy team.[30]

During the first two years of the administration, however, both Lake and his deputy Sandy Berger were criticized by observers for putting too much emphasis on presenting consensus positions to the president, which both slowed the advisory process and watered down the final product. Lake and Berger were also criticized for not being proactive enough in the important tasks of managing the NSC staff and interagency process. Observers of the administration generally agree that the above mentioned shortcomings were largely worked out during the second half of the president's term with the result being a much more efficient and effective process.

With a now experienced **Sandy Berger** being promoted to national security adviser for the second term, the process may likely continue to improve in

FIGURE 6.6
CLINTON'S FOREIGN POLICY SYSTEM

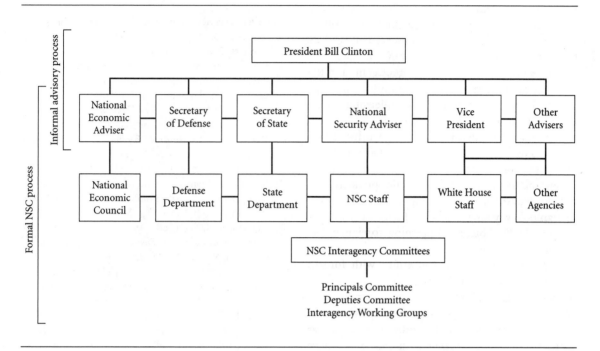

efficiency and effectiveness. Among other personnel changes, the most significant for foreign policy and the informal advisory process that President Clinton depends on is that Warren Christopher stepped down as secretary of state and was replaced by Madeline Albright, former ambassador to the United Nations; and William Cohen is the new secretary of defense, a former senator from Maine and only major Clinton appointee from the Republican party.

Unlike traditional national security policy, Clinton from the very beginning has taken an active interest, and is extremely knowledgeable, about **domestic and international economics**—a relatively unique phenomena among modern presidents. Given its importance to him, and in order to better coordinate and centralize the administration's economic policy—both domestic and foreign, President Clinton created the National Economic Council,

modeled on the NSC. The role of the foreign economic policymaking process in general, and the NEC and the national economic adviser under Bill Clinton, will be discussed at much greater length in chapter 10.

THE NSC PROCESS IN PERSPECTIVE

. . . .

All post–World War II presidents have had mixed success in managing the foreign policy bureaucracy. Presidential management depends on the important choices a president makes about his foreign policy orientation, political agenda and level of involvement, presidential appointments, and the organization of the decision-making process. As the bureaucracy has grown in size and complexity, the National

Security Council has come to be the major institution involved in managing the foreign policy bureaucracy, although not as originally intended. The president has come to rely increasingly on a White House-centered foreign policy process managed by the national security adviser and staff.

These developments do not guarantee that the formal NSC process will run smoothly or that the informal advisory process will be collegial as presidents would like. In fact, many observers of U.S. foreign policy believe that the national security adviser has become too prominent as a foreign policy adviser and spokesman, to the detriment of his more important role as coordinator of the policymaking process. Nevertheless, successful management of the foreign policymaking process will depend largely on the president's choices and particular style of interaction.

The National Security Council was created and evolved around national security issues. As will be shown in chapter 10, the NSC process has not been all that helpful to the president in areas that once were considered "low" policy during the cold war years. Issues such as foreign economic policy have grown in importance for American society and U.S. foreign policy over the last few decades. The national security adviser and the NSC staff, however, tend to lack interest and expertise in these "nontraditional" areas and generally interact more with the national security bureaucracy. Thus, issues that do not easily come under the purview of the national security bureaucracy have been very problematic in presidential management of foreign policy.

The National Security Council process is best equipped for assisting the president in managing the bureaucracy on more traditional issues of national security, such as the use of force or diplomacy in support of foreign policy. For these issues the State Department, the military, and the intelligence community have a history and a bureaucratic life of their own that has complicated the president's management task. Therefore, as we will see in the next three chapters, the national security bureaucracy has evolved to be both an important tool and constraint on the exercise of presidential power in foreign policy.

BIBLIOGRAPHIC ESSAY

. . . .

An excellent overview of the federal bureaucracy is provided by James Q. Wilson, *Bureaucracy: What Government Agencies Do and Why They Do It* (New York: Basic Books, 1989). For excellent overviews of the rise of the foreign policy bureaucracy and foreign policy managers, see Charles Maechling, Jr., "Foreign Policy-Makers: The Weakest Link?" *The Virginia Quarterly Review* 52 (Winter 1976): 1–23 and Richard Barnet, *Roots of War: Men and Institutions Behind U.S. Foreign Policy* (New York: Penguin, 1972), part I. On developments and implications of the post–cold war era, see Randall B. Ripley and James M. Lindsay, eds., *U.S. Foreign Policy After the Cold War: Processes, Structures, and Decisions* (Pittsburgh: University of Pittsburgh Press, 1997); and James M. Scott, ed., *After the End: Making U.S. Foreign Policy in the Post–Cold War Environment* (Durham, N.C.: Duke University Press, 1998).

An extensive literature has developed on presidential management of the policymaking process and the role of the National Security Council. I. M. Destler, Leslie H. Gelb, and Anthony Lake, in *Our Own Worst Enemy: The Unmaking of American Foreign Policy* (New York: Simon and Schuster, 1984), provide an excellent overview of the evolution of the policy process and the NSC. *Decisions of the Highest Order: Perspectives on the National Security Council,* Karl F. Inderfurth and Loch K. Johnson, eds., (Pacific Grove, Calif.: Brooks/Cole, 1988), and U.S., Congress, Senate, Committee on Foreign Relations, *The National Security Adviser: Role and Accountability,* Hearings (96th Cong., 2nd sess., April 17, 1980) also provide a good historical overview of the NSC.

Alexander L. George, in *Presidential Decisionmaking: The Effective Use of Information and Advice* (Boulder, Colo.: Westview Press, 1980), provides not only a good overview of presidential management styles and models, but an excellent discussion of the major impediments to a rational policy process and means to improve presidential management based on the major findings of social science. For a helpful typology of the national security advisory system, see Kevin V. Mulcahy and Harold F. Kendrick, "The National Security Adviser: A Presidential Perspective," in *Executive Leadership in Anglo-American Systems,* edited by Colin Campbell and Margaret Jane Wyszomirsky (Pittsburgh: University of Pittsburgh Press, 1991), pp. 259–79.

ENDNOTES

1. For a general overview of the federal bureaucracy, see Hugh Heclo, *A Government of Strangers: Executive Politics in Washington* (Washington, D.C.: Brookings, 1977); Harold Seidman, *Politics, Position and Power: The Dynamics of Federal Organization* (New York: Oxford University Press, 1980); and James Q. Wilson, *Bureaucracy: What Government Agencies Do and Why They Do It* (New York: Basic Books, 1989).

2. See, for example, Raymond F. Hopkins, "Global Management Networks: The Internationalization of Domestic Bureaucracies," *International Social Science Journal* (30 (1978): 31–44.

3. For a general discussion of the growth of American bureaucracy and how it developed in comparison to bureaucratic growth throughout Europe, see G. John Ikenberry, *Reasons of State: Oil Politics and the Capacities of American Government* (Ithaca, N.Y.: Cornell University Press, 1988), chapter 3.

4. See, for example, Randall B. Ripley and Grace A. Franklin, *Congress, the Bureaucracy, and Public Policy* (Homewood, Ill.: Dorsey Press, 1980).

5. Charles Maechling, Jr., "Foreign Policy-Makers: The Weakest Link?" *The Virginia Quarterly Review* 52 (Winter 1976): 6.

6. Maechling, "Foreign Policy-Makers," p. 2.

7. For an overview of presidential management of the executive branch, see, for example, George C. Edwards III and Stephen J. Wayne, *Presidential Leadership: Politics and Policy Making* (New York: St. Martin's Press, 1990), and Richard M. Pious, *The American Presidency* (New York: Basic Books, 1996). For a focus on the making of U.S. foreign policy, especially in the post–cold war era, see Randall B. Ripley and James M. Lindsay, eds., *U.S. Foreign Policy After the Cold War* (Pittsburgh: University of Pittsburgh Press, 1997); and James M. Scott, editor, *Ater the End: Making U.S. Foreign Policy in the Post–Cold War Environment* (Durham, N.C.: Duke University Press, 1998).

8. Douglas Jehl, "High-Level Grumbing Over Pace of Appointments," *New York Times* (February 25, 1993): A8; David E. Rosenbaum, "80% of Senior Positions Under Bush Still Empty," *New York Times* (May 13, 1989): 9.

9. David Halberstam, *The Best and the Brightest* (New York: Random House, 1969), p. 456.

10. See, for example, Alexander L. George, *Presidential Decisionmaking in Foreign Policy: The Effective Use of Information and Advice* (Boulder, Colo.: Westview Press, 1980).

11. See, for example, I.M. Destler, *Presidents, Bureaucrats, and Foreign Policy* (Princeton, N.J.: Princeton University Press, 1972).

12. For an overview of the National Security Council, see Zbigniew Brzezinski, "NSC's Mdilife Crisis," *Foreign Policy* 69 (Winter 1987-88): 80–99; I. M. Destler, "National Security Advice to U.S. Presidents: Some Lessons from Thirty Years," *World Politics* (January 1977): 143–76; Karl F. Inderfurth and Lock K. Johnson, eds., *Decisions of the Highest Order: Perspectives on the National Security Council* (Pacific Grove, Calif.: Brooks/Cole, 1988); Mark M. Lowenthal, *The National Security Council: Organizational History*, Congressional Research Service (June 27, 1978); Kevin V. Mulcahy and Harold F. Kendrick, "The National Security Adviser: A Presidential Perspective," in *Executive Leadership in Anglo-American Systems*, edited by Colin Campbell and Margaret Jane Wyszomirsky (Pittsburgh: University of Pittsburgh Press, 1991): 259–79; and U.S., Congress, Senate, Committee on Foreign Relations, *The National Security Adviser: Role and Accountability*, Hearings (96th Cong., 2nd sess., April 17, 1980).

13. Actually, according to the original National Security Act of 1947, the president also could designate the secretaries of the executive departments, the chairman of the munitions board, and the chairman of the research and development board to participate "from time to time." Other individuals could not be designated by the president to particpate in the National Security Council "until the advice and consent of the Senate has been given." U.S., *The National Security Act of 1947*, Public Law 253 (80th Cong. 1st sess., July 26, 1947).

14. See, for example, Bert A. Rockman, "America's Departments of State: Irregular and Regular Syndromes of Policy Making," *American Political Science Review* 75 (December 1981): 911–27.

15. I.M. Destler, Leslie H. Gelb, and Anthony Lake, *Our Own Worst Enemy: The Unmaking of American Foreign Policy* (New York: Simon and Schuster, 1984). See also William P. Bundy, "The National Security Process: Plus Ca Change?" *International Security* (Winter 1982/1983): 94–109; Destler, *Presidents, Bureaucrats, and Foreign Policy*; I.M. Destler, "The Rise of the National Security Assistant, 1961–1981," in Charles W. Kegley, Jr., and Eugene R. Wittkopf, eds., *Perspectives on American Foreign Polciy: Selected Readings* (New York: St. Martin's Press, 1983), pp. 260–81.

16. Destler, Gelb, and Leak, *Our Own Worst Enemy*, p. 172.

17. Maechling, "Foreign Policy-Makers," p. 3.

18. For an overview of the foreign policy process under Presidents Nixon and Ford, see Seymour H. Hersh, *The Price of Power: Kissinger in the Nixon White House* (New York: Summit Books, 1983); Marvin and Bernard Kalb, *Kissinger* (New York: Dell, 1974); Henry Kissinger, *White House Years* (Boston: Little, Brown, 1979); Roger Morris, *Uncertain Greatness: Henry Kissinger and American Foreign Poilcy* (New York: Harper and Row, 1977); and John Newhouse, *Cold Dawn: The Story of SALT* (New York: Holt, Rinehart and Winston, 1973).

19. For an overview of the Carter administration's foreign policy process, see Zbigniew Brzezinski, *Power and Principle: Memoirs of the National Security Adviser, 1977–1981* (New York: Farrar, Straus, Giroux, 1983); Hamilton Jordan, *Crisis: The Last Year of the Carter Presidency* (New York: G.P. Putnam's Sons, 1982); Alexander Moens, *Foreign Policy Under Carter: Testing Multiple Advocacy Decision Making* (Boulder, Colo.: Westview Press, 1990); Jerel A. Rosati, *The Carter Administration's Quest for Global Community: Beliefs and Their Impact on Behavior* (Columbia, S.C.: University of South Carolina Press, 1987); and Cyrus Vance, *Hard Choices: Critical Years in America's Foreign Policy* (New York: Simon and Schuster, 1983).

20. Resignations based on principle have become quite rare in U.S. government service. The last principled resignation by a secretary of state occurred under Woodrow Wilson. William Jennings Bryan resigned over the administration's response to the sinking of the Lusitania, and Robert Lansing, Bryan's replacement, resigned because of policy differences with Wilson over the Versailles Treaty. It was reported that Vance also nearly resigned in 1979 over the appointment of Robert Strauss as Middle East ambassador. See R. Ajemian, "Vance Nearly Quit Over Strauss," *Washington Star* (August 27, 1979): 1.

21. For an overview of the foreign policy process under President Reagan, see Alexander Haig, *Caveat: Realism, Reagan, and Foreign Policy* (New York: Macmillan, 1984); Hedrick Smith, *The Power Game: How Washington Works* (New York: Ballantine, 1988); and Tower Commission (Prsident's Special Review Board), *The Tower Commission Report* (New York: Bantam, 1987).

22. There was infighting, for example, over who sould chair the crisis management group. Vice President George Bush was selected to chair the group as a compromise, for he was perceived as less a threat to the influence and positions of other officials.

23. Clark, first appointed deputy secretary of state and then national security adviser, had virtually no knowledge about foreign policy and world affairs but was a close friend and long-time confidant of Ronald Reagan. During the Senate confirmation hearings, for example, Clark was unable to recognize the names of many important foreign leaders.

24. With William Clark's resignation as national security adviser and appointment as secretary of the interior in 1983, Chief of Staff James Baker attempted to have President Reagan select him as national security adviser, with Michael Deaver becoming the chief of staff. The Baker-Deaver plan was vehemently opposed by Clark and Secretary of Defense Weinberger, who preferred United Nations Ambassador Jeane Kirkpatrick for the NSC job, and set off a political storm in the Reagan administration. Eventually, Robert McFarlane, Clark's more moderate deputy, became the compromise choice for the position of national security adviser. See Smith, *The Power Game*, pp. 317–21.

25. For an overview of the foreign policy process in the Bush administration, see Maureen Dowd, "The Longest Week: How President Decided to Draw the Line," *New York Times* (August 9, 1990): 17A; David Hoffman, "President Scales Back National Security Council," *Washington Post* (February 3, 1989): A8; Kevin V. Mulcahy, "The Bush Administration and National Security Policy-Making: A Preliminary Assessment," *Governance* (April 1991): 207–20; Andrew Rosenthal, "Scowcroft and Gates: A Team Rivals Baker," *New York Times* (February 21, 1991): A6; Charlotte Saikowski, "Brent Scowcraft: Quiet Adviser," *Christian Science Monitor* (February 14, 1989): 8; and Bernard Weinraub, "Bush Backs Plan to Enhance Role of Security Staff," *New York Times* (February 2 1989): A1, A7.

26. Terry L. Deibel, "Bush's Foreign Policy: Mastery and Inaction," *Foreign Policy* 84 (Fall 1991): 5.

27. For an overview, see Terry Atlas, "Clinton Foreign Policy Team Charts Collegial Path," *Chicago Tribune* (July 25, 1993): 1; Vincent A. Auger, "The National Security Council System After the Cold War," in Randall B. Ripley and James M. Lindsay, eds., *U.S. Foreign Policy After the Cold War* (Pittsburgh: University of Pittsburgh Press, 1996), pp. 42–73; Michael Elliott, "Damned Yankees," *Newsweek* (October 25, 1993): 21–24; Thomas L. Friedman, "Clinton's Foreign Policy: Top Advisor Speaks Up," *New York Times* (October 31, 1993): 8; Thomas Friedman and Elaine Sciolino, "Clinton and Foreign Issues"; Jacob Heilibrunn,

"Lake Inferior," *The New Republic* (September 20, and 27, 1993): 29–35; Gwen Ifill, "Security Official Guides U.S. Aims at Conference," *New York Times* (July 5, 1993): A-5; Elaine Sciolino, "Christopher and Lake Vying for Control of Foreign Policy," *New York Times* (September 23, 1994): A1, A5; Elaine Sciolino, "Three Players Seek a Director for Foreign Policy Story," *New York Times* (Novermber 8, 1993): A-1.

28. Thomas Friedman and Elaine Sciolino, "Clinton and Foreign Issues; Spasms of Attention," *New York Times* (March 22, 1993): A3.

29. See also Vincent Auger, "The National Security Council System After the Cold War," in Randall B. Ripley and James M. Lindsay, eds., *Change in U.S. Foreign Policy After the Cold War: Processes, Structures, and Decisions*, (Pittsburgh: University of Pittsburgh Press 1997).

30. See also Jason DeParle, "The Man Inside Bill Clinton's Foreign Policy," *New York Times Magazine* (August 20, 1995); Thomas L. Friedman, "Clinton's Foreign Policy: Top Advisor Speaks Up," *New York Times* (October 31, 1993): 8; Jacob Heilbrunn, "Lake Inferior," *The New Republic* (September 20 & 27, 1993): 29–35; and Elaine Sciolino, "Christopher and Lake Vying for Control of Foreign Policy," *New York Times* (September 23, 1994): A1, A5.

CHAPTER 7

. . . .

THE STATE DEPARTMENT
AT HOME AND ABROAD

he Department of State is one of the most important organizations involved in the making of U.S. foreign policy within the executive branch. The State Department was one of four original cabinet departments created as part of the new government of the United States in 1789. Throughout most of American history, the State Department was the lead organization responsible for the conduct of U.S. foreign policy. However, with the rise of the cold war, the containment strategy, and the president's effort to manage foreign policy, the influence of the State Department has declined. Although the policymaking process is no longer State Department centered, the State Department remains an important bureaucratic institution involved in foreign policy.

In this chapter, the decline and current role of the Department of State in U.S. foreign policy will be discussed. The Department of State also is the first of a number of bureaucratic organizations which we will examine that play a critical role in the making of U.S. foreign policy. Therefore, this chapter also introduces **a framework, or approach**, for analyzing and better understanding the workings and nature of bureaucracy. *Four basic elements or characteristics need to be examined* to better comprehend any bureaucratic organization:

1. The historical context,
2. The functions (or mission or tasks),
3. The structure (or organization), and
4. The subculture.[1]

By examining its broad historical context, purpose, bureaucratic organization, and subculture, we will gain a better understanding of the evolution and role of the Department of State in the making of U.S. foreign policy (see **figure 7.1**).

FIGURE 7.1
EXPLAINING BUREAUCRATIC ORGANIZATIONS

Historical Context

Functions (or mission or tasks)

Subculture   } Bureaucracy

Structure (or organization)

THE CONTEXT BEHIND THE DECLINE OF STATE'S HISTORIC ROLE

. . . .

For more than one hundred and fifty years, until World War II, the State Department was **the lead organization** responsible for foreign affairs. U.S. foreign policy was made within the State Department, managed by members of the department, and carried out by ambassadors and other members of the department abroad. Other organizations within the government, such as the Treasury Department and especially the military, were involved in the conduct of U.S. foreign policy, but the State Department was the dominant foreign policy agency. During the twentieth century, however, power in the conduct of U.S. foreign policy began to flow to other agencies in the governmental bureaucracy and to the White House. Thus, the State Department has experienced a real decline in its overall influence in the conduct of U.S. foreign policy.

Four global and historical patterns account for the decline of the central importance of the State Department in the making of U.S. foreign policy:

1. The growing importance of international affairs for the United States;
2. The growing power of the United States in the world;
3. The communications revolution throughout the world;

4. The rise in the use of force in U.S. foreign policy.

These broad patterns of change throughout the world and within the United States set the stage for the rise of the presidency and other foreign policy agencies at the expense of the State Department.

Increasing Importance of International Affairs. Within this century, international affairs have become increasingly important for the United States. From its inception and throughout the nineteenth century, the United States government had the good fortune to be surrounded by two oceans and weak neighbors, which has allowed the government to concentrate on internal development and expansion across the North American continent with minimal opposition. However, with World War I, the global depression of the 1930s, the global war of the 1940s, the cold war of the 1950s and 1960s, and the increasing interdependence of the international political economy, events far beyond American borders greatly affect the United States. The U.S. government, including the president, can no longer afford to concentrate solely on domestic affairs and be unresponsive to the international scene. As discussed in the previous chapter, the governmental bureaucracy has grown in size and complexity to respond to these international changes and events. With the creation and expansion of the National Security Council, Department of Defense, intelligence community, Department of Treasury, and other foreign affairs agencies, the State Department was no longer the only organization within the executive branch with major responsibilities for the conduct of foreign affairs.

Rise of American Power. The United States also became more powerful throughout this period. A regional power at the turn of the century, by World War II the United States had become the most powerful country in the history of the world. Therefore, not only was the United States increasingly impacted by the international system, but U.S. foreign policy was also increasingly affecting the workings of the international system. America's growing global role during World War II and the cold war increased presidential power in the making of foreign policy. The United States was now so powerful, and the implications of its actions abroad were seen as so important, that the conduct of foreign policy could no longer be left to the State Department. Instead, presidents now attempted to directly govern foreign policy and manage the growing foreign policy bureaucracy. With the growth in presidential interest and involvement, therefore, presidential management of the foreign policy system increasingly revolved around a White House-centered system using the National Security Council adviser and staff.

The Global Communications Revolution. The third major reason for the decline in the influence of the State Department was the communications revolution. Before the existence of the airplane and telephone, it took months for American officials to travel or communicate with each other throughout the world. The president was dependent on the State Department and its members located abroad to officially represent the U.S. government. American ambassadors and other State Department employees consequently had wide latitude in influencing negotiating positions or other important aspects of U.S. foreign policy. The development of instant communications has allowed the president to become less dependent on the State Department in his day-to-day management of foreign policy.

Increasing Reliance on Force. The final reason for the State Department's fall from its leading position

in the policymaking process has been the reliance on force as a major instrument in U.S. foreign policy. With the rise of the cold war, U.S. foreign policy focused on the need to contain the threat of Soviet communism throughout the globe. The basis of the containment strategy—that is, the effort to confine the Soviet empire to Eastern Europe and China— was to deter a Soviet challenge to the international status quo through the threat of force and, if this failed, to use force to roll back Soviet gains. The containment policy resulted in the expansion of America's military capabilities through the development of nuclear weapons, a large standing conventional military force, counterinsurgency forces, and covert operations. This meant not only the growth of the military and the Central Intelligence Agency (CIA) as bureaucratic organizations, but the president's increasing use of these organizations as the means of conducting U.S. foreign policy. Diplomacy, the strength of the State Department, was superseded by the threat and use of force during the cold war years. Hence, the rise of force as the major instrument in U.S. policy reinforced the decline of the State Department relative to other parts of the foreign policy bureaucracy.

STATE'S FUNCTIONS OVER TIME

Although the State Department has declined in its overall importance, it remains oriented to fulfilling the *five major purposes or missions* for which it was originally created:[2]

1. To represent the government overseas;
2. To present the views of foreigners to the U.S. government;
3. To engage in diplomacy and negotiations;
4. To analyze and report on events abroad;
5. To provide policy advice.

One of the most important purposes of the State Department is to represent the U.S. government overseas, usually to foreign governments. Members of the State Department, known as

foreign service officers (FSOs), serve abroad in embassies in the capital cities of foreign countries, in consulates in major cities of foreign countries, in other missions abroad, and in international governmental organizations such as the United Nations. In this role, the U.S. ambassador and the foreign service officer act in the name of the United States government and communicate the "official" foreign policy of the U.S. to people abroad. Given the primitive nature of transportation and communications fifty years ago, this was a crucial role because the foreign service officer was the principal channel through which governments communicated. Today, with more and more organizations of the U.S. government employing official representatives overseas, this unique role of the foreign service officer has declined in importance. Also, with the technological revolution in transportation and instant communications, the U.S. president and foreign leaders no longer are dependent on foreign service officers to communicate official governmental policy.

A second major purpose is to represent the views of foreigners, usually foreign governments, to the U.S. government. More than 120 foreign governments maintain embassies in Washington, D.C., staffed principally by members of their foreign ministries (equivalents of the State Department). An important job of the foreign service is to interact with foreign government officials in the United States and abroad, learn their official positions on international issues, and communicate their views within the U.S. government. The fact that the State Department represents the views of a certain constituency is not unique within the bureaucracy. It is quite common, for example, that the Department of Labor tends to represent the views of unions, the Department of Commerce represents business, the Department of Agriculture represents farmers, and so on. However, the fact that the State Department represents the views of foreign governments, as opposed to organized domestic interests, is unique within the bureaucracy, possibly making it more difficult for foreign service officers to understand domestic politics and influence the policymaking process. Also, with the rise of other bureaucratic agencies and the mass media, contemporary presidents are no longer as dependent on the State Department for learning the foreign policies of other governments.

The third major purpose of the State Department is to be responsible for **diplomacy and negotiations** abroad. In the past, if the president wanted to conclude a treaty or come to some common understanding with an adversary or friend, he had to rely on ambassadors and foreign service officers to negotiate in the name of the U.S. government. Before the existence of the airplane and the telephone, it took months for communications from the president or the secretary of state to reach American embassies abroad and for messages to return home. Communications were so slow that the president had little choice but to entrust considerable authority to his ambassadors and subordinates abroad. Not only were they the primary international representatives of the U.S. government, they also were the major negotiators and diplomats. This is no longer the case. The speed of communications now gives presidents the ability to control negotiations on those issues they deem most important. President Richard Nixon felt that opening relations with the People's Republic of China and concluding a SALT treaty with the Soviet Union were too important to entrust to the bureaucracy, so he relied instead on the personal diplomacy of National Security Adviser Henry Kissinger. Nor is it unusual for the president to appoint a special envoy to represent the U.S. government in his name for a particular foreign policy issue or for the president, or his closest advisers, to pick up the phone and communicate directly with international leaders. President George Bush regularly used the phone to interact with political leaders throughout the world in pursuit of his foreign policy objectives.[3]

The fourth major purpose of the State Department is to analyze and report on foreign events. Most foreign service officers located abroad spend the bulk of their time analyzing events and transmitting these analyses through "cables" back to the State Department in Washington, D.C. Most of the FSOs in Washington spend much of their time reading the cables, using them as the principal source of information for communicating with their superiors—ultimately the secretary of state—and fulfilling their foreign policy functions. Decisions and directions for implementing and representing U.S. foreign policy abroad are subsequently communicated via cable to the embassies, consulates, and missions in the field. In some ways, the **cable traffic** remains the heart and soul of the contemporary State Department—today consisting of over 2.5 million cables and 25 million e-mail messages a year. It is the means by which members of the State Department communicate and interact with each other all over the world.[4] Yet, where past presidents may have relied to a considerable extent on reports and analysis of foreign events provided by the State Department, they now tend to rely on their own staff through the national security adviser, have a large bureaucracy at their disposal (such as the intelligence community), and pay attention to the mass media for keeping informed about world politics.

The final major function of the State Department is to provide policy advice to the president. The foreign policy process tended to be State Department centered before World War II, but has become increasingly White House centered since the 1940s. Beginning with the National Security Act of 1947 the president has come to rely increasingly on the NSC adviser and staff for the information and policy advice essential to day-to-day management of foreign policy. In other words, the president has come to rely less on the State Department in managing and making foreign policy. Whatever information and advice does seep up to the White House from the State Department must work its way through the formal NSC process used by the president for managing U.S. foreign policy. The president also tends to rely on a small informal circle of major advisers, one of which may be the secretary of state. Thus, the overall policy influence of State depends on the working relationship between the president and the secretary of state.

Overall, the State Department continues to play an important role in U.S. foreign policy—this is important to understand—but the State Department as an institution within the executive branch has suffered a decline of influence from its once leading role in the foreign policy process. The expansion of the bureaucracy since the 1940s has made the State Department one of a number of important institutions in foreign policy and has made the president less dependent on it. Although no longer dominant, the State Department continues to perform its primary functions and continues to play a major role in the politics of U.S. foreign policy.

BUREAUCRATIC ORGANIZATION AND STRUCTURE

. . . .

The State Department began in 1789 with a staff of six, a budget of $7,961, and two diplomatic missions. During the 1990s, the State Department employed more than 24,000 people, had a budget of almost $6 billion, and operated more than 250 diplomatic missions overseas.[5] Of its 24,000 employees, only about 3,500 are foreign service officers. Other employees are basically support personnel: doctors, security officers, secretaries, drivers, and other occupations that provide assistance to the FSOs, who have primary responsibility for fulfilling the State Department's major functions. Of the total Department of State employees, roughly two-thirds are located in its home office in **Foggy Bottom** in Washington, D.C., and one-third are located abroad. For foreign service officers within the department, the reverse is true; roughly one-third of all FSOs are located in Washington, D.C., while two-thirds are located at missions abroad.

In comparison to most bureaucracies within the U.S. government, the **State Department is actually very small**. If one considers the State Department as an organization consisting of 3,500 people with a large support staff for a total of over 24,000 employees, it is among the smaller organizations in the U.S. government. At the same time, the State Department is a very complex organization because it is a global bureaucracy and most of its foreign service officers are located abroad. In fact, because of its geographic scope and the foreign service subculture (to be discussed later), the State Department has come to operate as if it were a very large bureaucratic organization.

Examining the State Department in some detail will not only allow us to learn more about how the department operates in particular, but also will enhance our understanding of how bureaucracies operate in general and their implications for presidential governance of U.S. foreign policy. It is important for students of U.S. foreign policy to understand how a **bureaucracy** works; otherwise institutions like the State Department, the Department of Defense, and the intelligence community will remain so distant that their particular role in the policy process will not be fully appreciated. It is with this in mind that we take a brief but very close look at the bureaucratic organization of the Department of State at home and abroad.

At Home

The State Department shares the *common elements found in any government or private sector bureaucracy:*

1. Hierarchy (of authority and status),
2. Specialization,
3. Routinization.[6]

Bureaucratic organizations are hierarchically structured with divisions of authority and labor specified throughout. Hierarchy involves a top-down division of authority in which every official occupies a particular authority role. People in positions near the top of the organization not only enjoy more authority, they also require more general knowledge and skills since they deal with large questions and the "bigger picture." As one moves down into the bureaucracy, positions become increasingly specialized and routinized with less and less authority to act independently of superiors. Individuals may be employed in positions responsible for repeatedly performing the same task that involves a tiny facet of the operation of the organization. To use an example from the private sector, the chief executive officer (CEO) of General Motors is a generalist who is responsible for governing and managing all of its car divisions (such as Chevrolet, Pontiac, and Cadillac). However, at the bottom of the hierarchy, assembly line workers are responsible for very specific and repetitive tasks, such as attaching a single bolt onto the doors of new cars that are produced in a single plant in Detroit.

Figure 7.2 shows that there are *five major hierarchical levels* within the State Department: the secretary of state, deputy secretary of state, under secretaries of state, assistant secretaries of state, and deputy assistant secretaries of state. The top three levels of officials are referred to as the "seventh floor principals," because their offices are on the top floor—the seventh floor—of the State Department building in Washington, D.C. The **secretary of state** is the chief officer responsible for governing and managing the State Department for the president. The **deputy secretary of state** runs the State Department when the secretary is absent, for example on a foreign trip, and often acts as the secretary's alter ego. The secretary and deputy secretary have the support of four **under secretaries**, each with a support staff, responsible for supervising a broad area: political affairs, economic affairs, science and technology, and management (including budget and personnel). The counselor and the Policy Planning Council also may be of value to the secretary of state; both were created after World War II to assist the secretary in providing a broader long-term perspective. However, the counselor, director of policy planning, and the policy planning staff have been used in various ways by the secretary, depending largely on the personalities involved.

The seventh-floor principals are the highest-ranking officials within the State Department, tend to be generalists, and are responsible for the overall conduct of the department. Most of the specialized work of the department, however, occurs at **the bureau level**. The State Department, like other bureaucracies involved in foreign policy, is organized into geographic and issue-oriented bureaus. There are six geographic bureaus: African Affairs, East Asian and Pacific Affairs, European and Canadian Affairs (this includes Russia), Inter-American Affairs, Near Eastern Affairs, and South Asian Affairs (including the Arabic countries of northern Africa). The bureaus are run by **assistant secretaries** and **deputy assistant secretaries** (or directors and deputy directors)—referred to as "bureau principals"—the fourth and fifth hierarchical levels within the State Department.

FIGURE 7.2
OVERVIEW OF STATE DEPARTMENT ORGANIZATION

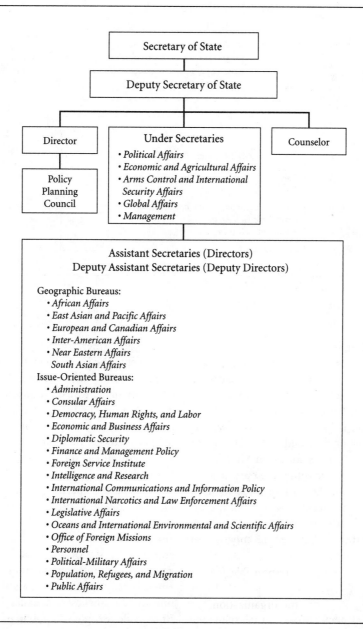

SOURCE:. U.S. Department of State, *Atlas of United States Foreign Relations. United States Government Manual.*

Within a bureau, such as the one depicted in **figure 7.3**, we see that the assistant secretary of Near Eastern and South Asian Affairs has six deputies, while the regional focus of a geographic bureau is further divided into single countries or small groupings of countries. These country subdivisions are managed by a **country director** who reports to one of the deputy assistant secretaries responsible for

FIGURE 7.3
ORGANIZATION OF NEAR EASTERN AFFAIRS BUREAU

SOURCE: U.S. Congress, *Congressional Directory*.

that part of the region, who in turn reports to the assistant secretary. Thus, the assistant secretary and the deputy assistant secretaries develop expertise and have responsibilities at the regional level. The assistant secretary for Near Eastern and South Asian Affairs, for example, is likely to be a principal adviser to the secretary of state and one of the major officials within the U.S. government on Middle East issues. The country director within the bureau is the specialist, the expert on the current situation in a particular country and the key link in all of the information and decisions communicated—through the so-called cable traffic—between his superiors at home and those in the field.

ABROAD

In the State Department abroad, more than 280 diplomatic missions are operated internationally. About 170 of these are **embassy missions** in countries with which the United States maintains official diplomatic relations. The remaining hundred or so missions are **consular posts** that provide various services for Americans and issue visas to foreigners for travel to the United States, support the main embassy in larger metropolitan areas, and maintain other permanent missions, such as to international organizations like the United Nations or Organization of American States. The United States has no official missions or diplomatic relations with only a few countries, such as Iran, North Korea, and Vietnam.[7]

The State Department employs over 8,000 people in its missions abroad, and roughly two-thirds of its foreign service officers, about 2,300 members, are also stationed abroad. The size and complexity of embassies vary enormously, although they are all organized in a similar bureaucratic fashion. The largest embassy is in London with a staff approaching 300; one of the smallest embassies is, for example, in Brazzaville, People's Republic of the Congo, with a staff of only a few people.[8]

Figure 7.4 gives a brief idea of how an overseas mission, such as an embassy, is organized. The common bureaucratic elements are evident: hierarchy, specialization, and routinization. The **ambassador** is

FIGURE 7.4

A. U.S. MISSION IN A FOREIGN COUNTRY—VENEZUELA

Chief of Mission
Ambassador
Personal Representative of the President

Deputy Chief of Mission
Minister–Counselor

---------- COUNTRY TEAM ----------

Mission Unit	Agricultural Trade Office	Agricultural Counselor	Public Affairs Counselor	Commercial Counselor	Political Counselor	Economic Counselor	Administrative Counselor	Consul General	Defense Attaché	Head Military Group (advisory)	Other Agencies Present: Drug Enforcement Agency Federal Aviation Administration Inter-American Geodetic Survey Internal Revenue Service	U.S. Consulate in Maracaibo, U.S. staff: 3 State 1 USIA
Home Agency	Agriculture	Agriculture	USIA	Commerce	Department of State				Defense	Defense		

SOURCE: U.S. Department of State, *Atlas of United States Foreign Relations* (December 1985), p. 9.

the chief of mission, the highest representative of the United States stationed abroad, with responsibility over those individuals employed by the embassy. He has the assistance of a deputy chief of mission and a country team, composed of foreign service officers from the Department of State and other governmental agencies with more specific areas of responsibility.[9]

An interesting aspect of figure 7.4 is the **overseas presence of personnel of other agencies** than the State Department. Until World War II, most officials stationed abroad as representatives of the U.S. government were from the State Department. This is no longer the case, symbolizing the decline of the State Department's role in the overall conduct of U.S. foreign policy. The U.S. government has at least 30,000 employees abroad (not counting American troops in military bases or CIA personnel). Of these, State Department personnel comprise roughly 25 percent of the total, a sizable segment but not as dominant as in the past. In addition to the State Department, most government personnel abroad work for the Agency for International Development (about 20 percent), Department of Defense (about 25 percent, excluding troops), Peace Corps (about 20 percent), and the United States Information Service (about 5 percent). The presence of some of these agencies is so large that they may have their own facilities separate from the main embassy, although the ambassador remains the senior U.S. governmental official within the country. As discussed in the previous chapter, almost every department and agency within the executive branch is internationally involved in some way and has representatives overseas.

One agency that is not depicted in figure 7.4 is the Central Intelligence Agency. It does have a major presence abroad but is officially kept secret. The **CIA station chief**, for instance, is likely to have an official position attached to the embassy, to provide "cover" and diplomatic immunity. Other CIA personnel and operatives will either be attached to the embassy or occupy private roles within the country (such as working for a multinational corporation). Examining the government's official presence abroad rein-

forces the conclusions drawn above concerning changes in the foreign policy bureaucracy over time; while the State Department's influence has declined, the influence of other agencies, such as the Department of Defense and the CIA, has increased tremendously.

BUREAUCRATIC PATTERNS

Three patterns concerning bureaucratic structure within the State Department must be kept in mind:

1. It is a hierarchical organization.
2. The policy process is complex and issue dependent.
3. The presidential appointment process has produced controversy.

These patterns are not unique to the State Department, but apply to other organizations within the foreign policy bureaucracy as well.

First, the State Department is hierarchically organized and structured. Not only is there a top-to-bottom hierarchy of authority and labor, but a **pecking order** also exists within each level. For example, at the under secretary level, management is considered the least significant and prestigious of the four positions, while the under secretary for political affairs is considered the most significant and prestigious by members of the foreign service because it is a policy position involving the essence of State Department activity. A similar pecking order exists at the bureau level and abroad. The geographic bureaus are considered more important and prestigious than those that involve cross-cutting issues, with the European Bureau traditionally the most prestigious (given its focus on Western Europe, Eastern Europe, and now Russia) and the African Bureau the least prestigious (rarely an important area in U.S. foreign policy). The issue-oriented bureaus that are involved in political matters, such as the Political-Military Bureau, also are considered more important. Abroad, large embassies in industrialized countries, as in London, England, are more desirable and prestigious than small embassies in Third World countries, as in Brazzaville, Congo.

Likewise, the "political" counselor position is preferable abroad. These patterns of hierarchy and prestige tend to hold generally, but the rise of "hot" issues will temporarily enhance one bureau or position over another: as when the Vietnam War increased the importance of the East Asian and Pacific Bureau and the Southeast Asia embassies during the 1960s and the conflict in Central America increased the importance of the Inter-American Bureau and the regional embassies during the 1980s.

Second, the nature of the policy process within the State Department is heavily dependent on the **importance of the foreign policy issue** involved. To understand this process, it is helpful to see the department as a complex bureaucracy addressing numerous issues that determine who will be involved and at what level. The secretary of state, like the president, is most influential for those issues in which he is most interested and involved. Yet, most issues are routine (involving visas, a report, or a local incident abroad) and can be handled by a few people in the appropriate bureau at home and in the field abroad. In these cases, a bureaucratic process exists in which information and decisions routinely flow up and down within the department at home as well as between Washington, D.C., and the field offices through **regularized channels**.

Those issues perceived to be more significant for U.S. foreign policy involve a much larger process, including higher-level officials within and beyond the State Department. For example, while the United States would neither officially recognize nor talk with the Palestine Liberation Organization (PLO) for twenty years, a new and controversial policy of engaging in an **official dialogue with the PLO** began during the latter part of the Ronald Reagan administration, in an effort to further a comprehensive settlement of the Arab-Israeli conflict. This issue fell within the jurisdiction of the Bureau for Near Eastern and South Asian Affairs (they have subsequently been split into two bureaus) and, since the talks took place in Tunis, the country director of Tunisia had primary responsibility within the State Department while the ambassador to Tunisia had primary responsibility in the field. But the impor-

tance of the issue increased the scope of the participants. The Near Eastern Affairs bureau principals and many of the seventh floor principals, possibly including the secretary of state, were likely to be involved and kept abreast of matters. At the time, the talks also had important implications for other country directors within the bureau—Israel, Jordan, Egypt, Syria, and Lebanon—and for other bureaus—European Affairs (given their dependency on Arab oil), Political-Military Affairs (since it involves a major conflict), Human Rights and Humanitarian Affairs (given the Palestinian refugee status and violence in the West Bank and Gaza Strip), Legal Affairs (for questions involving international law), Congressional Relations (given the interest of certain members and committees), and Public Affairs (given the interest of the media and the public). Nor was this issue restricted to the State Department; the president and other elements of the foreign policy bureaucracy were likely to be involved. Therefore, the more an issue is perceived as significant, the more likely a variety of bureaus will be involved, the higher up the issue will go within the department, and the more likely other elements of the foreign policy bureaucracy will also be involved, resulting in a larger, more complex policy process.[10]

The third important point concerns the controversy over **the appointment process and personnel**. The president technically appoints all ambassadors and major officials within the State Department down to the deputy assistant secretarial level. Since the president is not likely to have much foreign policy expertise, he relies on his personal staff and the secretary of state for selecting appropriate people. Remaining policy positions, such as country directors at home or members of the embassies abroad, are staffed by foreign service officers who are placed through a long-standing personnel system administered by the director general of the foreign service under the under secretary for management. As with the civil service and the military service, the president has very little, if any, influence over personnel decisions within **the foreign service**.

Controversy has always existed concerning presidential appointments. Members of the foreign service tend to believe that foreign service officers should be appointed as ambassador and to high-level positions below the secretary of state for they have the greatest expertise and understand the workings of the State Department. Some presidents have appointed more FSOs to important policy positions than others, but non-FSOs have been increasingly appointed at the assistant secretary and deputy assistant secretary levels as well as ambassadors. FSOs have been getting fewer significant appointments at home and often become ambassadors to smaller, less important countries.[11] Outside appointees tend to be from business, academia and research institutes, or government and they may be knowledgeable about foreign affairs, although they may know little about the foreign service or the operations of the department. This pattern is bothersome to the foreign service, and particularly irksome are presidential "political" appointments as ambassadors, many of whom are rewarded for their political contributions to a president's campaign and have no knowledge about the country for which they are destined. (See **essay 7.1** on the tradition of political ambassadors.)

The bureaucratic patterns found in the State Department are common to bureaucracies in general, including other foreign policy agencies within the executive branch. Bureaucracies, like the State Department, are complex institutions of hierarchy, specialization, and routinization in which the policymaking process is affected by the nature of the issue. This often produces political tension between bureaucratic **insiders**—members of the permanent bureaucracy—and bureaucratic outsiders—presidential appointees who are often referred to as **in-outers** since they tend to go back and forth between the government and private sectors and from one government position to another. Insiders, such as the foreign service within the State Department, tend to be part of a particular subculture and loyal to the institution where they have worked for years. In-outers tend to have little understanding or allegiance to the particular bureaucracy for which they work. How this tension between insiders and in-outers plays itself out has important ramifications

for the role of the State Department and the foreign service within the foreign policy process.[12]

THE FOREIGN SERVICE SUBCULTURE

To fully understand the behavior of a bureaucracy such as the State Department, it is vital that we examine its **organizational subculture** in addition to its organizational structure. Every organization or bureaucracy eventually develops a subculture, or a number of subcultures. A subculture refers to the common set of goals and norms acquired by individuals within a group or organization, such as the State Department's foreign service. These beliefs and norms result in certain incentives, and disincentives, which influence the behavior of individuals within the organization.[13] The subculture, according to James Q. Wilson in *Bureaucracy,* produces "a persistent, patterned way of thinking about the central tasks of and human relationships within an organization. Culture is to an organization what personality is to an individual. Like human culture generally, it is passed on from one generation to the next. It changes slowly, if at all."[14]

New members of a group or organization quickly discover they are expected to learn and absorb the rules and norms that pervade the organization. These rules and norms are formally or officially communicated and enforced (for example, by disseminating departmental guidelines on appropriate "professional" behavior or by affecting career advancement through the personnel evaluation and promotion system) and informally enforced (such as through peer interaction). People quickly learn how to play by the rules of the game if they want to be accepted by their peers and be professionally successful within the organization. This produces conformity in the behavior of most individuals, thereby reinforcing and promoting the organizational subculture. The subculture of the foreign service is particularly strong because of its small size—only 3,500 foreign service officers—relative to other bureau-

ESSAY 7.1
THE TRADITION OF "POLITICAL" AMBASSADORS

Ambassadors representing the United States government often are presidential appointees from outside the foreign service. Many of these **political appointees** have interest and knowledge of international affairs, including the specific country for which they will be responsible. However, many of the individuals nominated as ambassadors are unqualified for the job—they are friends or, more often, major contributors to the president's campaign who possess little foreign policy interest or knowledge. In these cases, the prestige of being appointed as ambassador, a title that reverts to the individual for life, is thought to be a personal "thank you" for friendship and political support, not a request for commitment and hard work.

George Bush as president continued a tradition that extended back to President Andrew Jackson and the early nineteenth century. While roughly one-third of the ambassadors have been non-foreign service career appointees, more than 50 percent of the ambassadorships have gone to outsiders under President Bush. Some examples provide the flavor of the more controversial ambassadorial appointments by the president:

Peter Secchia, a multimillionaire lumber tycoon who was crucial in Bush's Michigan Republican party caucus victory over presidential challenger Pat Robertson, was appointed ambassador to Italy.

J. Giffen Weinmann, president of Waverly Oil Corporation and a member of Bush's 1988 presidential fund-raising committee, was appointed ambassador to Finland.

Joseph Zappala, a Florida land developer and cochair of Bush's 1988 presidential fund-raising committee, was appointed ambassador to Spain.

Melvin Sembler, a Florida shopping-center developer and Republican party contributor to the tune of $100,000, was appointed ambassador to Australia.

Not only do these political appointees have little interest and expertise in foreign affairs, they can sometimes cause controversy and diplomatic *faux pas* abroad. For example, Ambassador Secchia created controversy in Italy by his tendency to use profanity and make sexist remarks in public. Nevertheless, there are often some positive benefits. Appointees may often breathe fresh air into an embassy abroad. The personal connections the appointee has with the president and the presence of a capable foreign service officer as the deputy chief of mission can make a strong team abroad. Regardless of the merits and objections from the foreign service and elsewhere, the tradition of political ambassadors has continued under President Clinton and is bound to continue into the future (with the blessing of the U.S. Senate, which usually approves presidential appointments with little or no dissent).

SOURCES: Steven Greenhouse, "Clinton Is Faulted on Political Choices for Envoy Posts," *New York Times* (April 13, 1994): A15; "Notorious Ambassadors," *Newsweek* (June 5, 1989): 25–26; Thomas Omestad, "Green With Envoy," *New Republic* (August 8, 1994): 20–22; Elaine Sciolino, "Friends as Ambassadors: How Many Is Too Many?" *New York Times* (November 7, 1989): 1, 6; Laurence H. Silberman, "Toward Presidential Control of the State Department," *Foreign Affairs* (Spring 1979): 872–93; and U.S., Congress, Senate, Committee on Foreign Relations, *The Ambassador in U.S. Foreign Policy: Changing Patterns in Roles, Selection, and Designations* (97th Cong., 1st sess., July 1981).

cratic organizations. Together, the structure and subculture of the State Department bureaucracy determine how well the department fulfills its primary functions and influences the overall policymaking process.

What are the characteristics common to the subculture of the foreign service? Identifying and describing a subculture is not a simple feat. Discussing the major beliefs and norms that prevail in a group or organization necessarily results in broad generalizations that oversimplify the complexity of the organization and are unlikely to apply to any single individual. Despite these complications, much work has been done on the subculture of the foreign service and a consensus does exist on its major attributes.[15] It is commonly argued that *five key characteristics* comprise the subculture of the foreign service officer:

1. A tendency to be elitist or exclusivist;
2. A preference for overseas experience and to identify with foreign viewpoints;
3. An emphasis on the policy instruments of diplomacy and negotiation;
4. A tendency to be generalists;
5. A tendency to be loyal and cautious.

The foreign service is commonly considered an elitist or exclusivist group. This takes two forms. First, the foreign service is elitist in the sense that it is difficult to become a foreign service officer and FSOs consider themselves to be the "crème de la crème" of the government in foreign policy expertise. There is much truth to this, for the demand to join the foreign service is extraordinarily high and the job openings are few. The Foreign Service Exam also is extremely demanding. Few applicants do well and those that score high have no guarantee that a position will be found for them.

The foreign service is also considered elitist in another sense. Throughout most of its history, membership in the foreign service consisted of men who were white, Anglo-Saxon Protestants (WASPs) from wealthy, urbane families who often attended Ivy League educational institutions. In other words, the foreign service consisted of a very exclusive **old boy network**. Entrance into the foreign service was anything but meritorious. Instead, the key was an individual's "pedigree"—family, background, education—and his connections. This exclusiveness resulted in an air of superiority among foreign service officers relative to other government employees, especially as other foreign policy bureaucracies expanded with World War II and the cold war.[16]

Much has changed within the State Department, especially over the last twenty years. The old boy system has opened up to new entrees. Connec-

tions and pedigrees have been replaced by a more demanding merit system based upon the Foreign Service Exam. Women, minorities, and individuals who are not from the Northeast, nor Protestant, nor upper- or upper-middle class, have become part of the foreign service. Nonetheless, the process of change has been a slow one and the foreign service continues to be dominated by white men from affluent segments of society. (See **essay 7.2** on discrimination in hiring and the personnel system.)

A second characteristic of the foreign service subculture is that FSOs usually prefer to be stationed abroad and tend to identify with foreign viewpoints. For a foreign service officer, to be abroad, as opposed to being in Washington, D.C., is to be where the action and excitement is—in the field. It is also the way to see and experience the world, often a key motivating factor among foreign service applicants. This is reinforced by a foreign service officer's lifestyle abroad, which tends to be quite privileged, as with many American officials overseas. The preference is not only for overseas experience, but also to be stationed abroad in choice assignments, such as London, Paris, or Rome. This orientation toward overseas experience and identifying with foreign countries is reinforced by **the foreign service personnel system** in which career advancement is based on service abroad. To be posted in Washington, D.C., too often or too long hurts career opportunities. In fact, the ultimate career goal of a foreign service officer is to become an ambassador, not a secretary of state or other major policymaking official close to the president.

This emphasis on overseas experience and identifying with foreign viewpoints often is detrimental to the ability of FSOs to operate successfully in the foreign policy maze at home. Because foreign service officers are more interested and knowledgeable about what is happening abroad than at home, they may not be motivated or equipped to influence the policymaking process outside the State Department. Since they are perceived as identifying with foreign viewpoints, they often are accused of going "native" and other officials in the policymaking process may not take FSO policy positions seriously.[17] Although the foreign service has produced some top policy-

ESSAY 7.2
DISCRIMINATION IN HIRING AND THE PERSONNEL SYSTEM

Considerable controversy exists over the present composition of the foreign service. Even though personnel selection and promotion is currently based on a merit system, most foreign service officers are white men from more privileged backgrounds. More women and minorities have gained entry to the foreign service, but they remain completely underrepresented in comparison to their numbers in society. This pattern becomes even more noticeable as one moves up the career ladder to more senior positions within the foreign service.

In a 1989 class action suit, the U.S. Court of Appeals found the State Department guilty of **sex discrimination** against women in its hiring and promotion practices and ordered that such promotion practices were to be remedied and the Foreign Service Exam was to be revised. Yet, some people remain frustrated with the gradual nature of the changing composition; they emphasize the need to make the foreign service more democratic and more representative and argue that diversity can be a source of strength to the department's international efforts in a world of great heterogeneity. Other people tend to emphasize the importance of tradition or competence as the supreme goals of the service.

This controversy is not unique to the foreign service. Unrepresentative personnel patterns have dominated governmental, and private, organizations throughout most of American history. Nor has the exclusivist bias been the exclusive monopoly of the State Department. It also existed in the Office of Strategic Services (OSS), for example, during World War II. But since that time, most government organizations have experienced a "leveling" process as they have expanded in size and as American society has become more open. Yet some organizations, like the Federal Bureau of Investigation under the domineering leadership of J. Edgar Hoover and subsequent directors, have resisted to the present day. The State Department falls somewhere between these two extremes.

Although slow to change, the State Department's personnel system is becoming more merit oriented. Yet, because the Foreign Service Exam is so demanding, those from more advantaged backgrounds are likely to perform better on the exam. Also, because of the small size of the foreign service, job openings are few and the rate of turnover is slow. New personnel problems are also arising. Where once the spouse (and children) accompanied the foreign service officer from post to post and played the important role of "host," the rise of professional careers for both the husband and the wife has generated much frustration with the rotation tradition of "worldwide availability." As always, controversies over personnel are likely to plague the State Department, and other governmental organizations into the future.

SOURCES: Judith Havemann, "State Department Acknowledges Sex Bias," *Washington Post* (April 20, 1989): A1, A20; Philip Shenon, "F.B.I. Orders 11 Hispanic Agents To Be Promoted After Bias Suit," *New York Times* (September 20, 1990): A11; Philip Shenon, "F.B.I. Settles Suit by Black Workers on Discrimination," *New York Times* (January 12, 1990): 1, 12; U.S., Congress, General Accounting Office, *State Department: Minorities and Women are Underrepresented in the Foreign Service* (June 1989); James Workman, "Gender Norming," *New Republic* (July 1, 1991): 16–17.

makers, such as Lawrence Eagleberger who was secretary of state under President Bush, governmental politics tends to be an FSO's weakest suit. These subcultural traits make it difficult for the State Department as an organization to influence strongly the foreign policymaking process.

The third major characteristic of the foreign service is its emphasis on diplomacy as the principal tool of U.S. foreign policy. Foreign service officers see themselves as diplomats—a long-honored profession in the history of world politics. And the ability to engage in diplomacy and conduct negotiations is seen as an art. Diplomacy is not something one learns in a book, but is something acquired through field experience overseas (or in earlier times, the art of diplomacy was part of an elitist subculture into which one was born). The problem with the foreign service's focus on diplomacy is that, with the rise of the cold war, the U.S. de-emphasized the role of diplomacy as an instrument of its foreign policy. It was superseded by increased reliance on the military, economic, and cultural instruments of foreign policy: force, covert operations, assistance, trade, sanctions, cultural programs, and international broadcasting. Despite the collapse of the cold war, as the instruments to support America's global policy have multiplied, the foreign service emphasis on the role of diplomacy has contributed to the decline of the State Department.

Fourth, foreign service officers tend to be generalists. Although the foreign service prides itself on its foreign policy expertise, most FSOs are not specialists. This is a function of the personnel system within the foreign service. Not only is there an emphasis on overseas service, but a rotation system operates based on three-year tours. This means that every three years an FSO is stationed in a new post abroad (although every third or fourth tour may be at home), often in a new region of the world. It is not unusual, for example, to find a new foreign service officer with a degree in East Asian studies posted first in Haiti, then maybe in Somalia, then in Washington, D.C., in the Inter-American bureau, abroad again in Cameroon, and so on, maybe never getting the opportunity to use his or her original East Asian training. The little specialized training that does take place is within the State Department (no bureaucratic incentives exist to obtain, for example, graduate degrees).[18] The emphasis, rather, is to produce well-rounded experts with wide-ranging experience and intuitive understanding able to fulfill any foreign policy position. Those individuals who prefer to stay within a region and specialize do so at the risk of career advancement. The major exception to this pattern is when an FSO begins to gain considerable seniority; at that point an area of specialization may be carved out. But the ideal goal for most

FSOs remains to be stationed in Europe and to achieve an ambassadorship.

This emphasis on the creation of well-rounded diplomats who are generalists runs counter to the expansion of bureaucracy, which emphasizes the development of specialists. On the one hand, the development of personnel with general knowledge and a broader perspective allows for the integration of context and history in policy analysis, something which has eroded with the growth of specialization on top of specialization. On the other hand, FSOs are often at a disadvantage with their counterparts from other bureaucracies because they may lack detailed knowledge vital to an issue making its way through the policy process. This also produces problems of competency abroad. The rotation system provides little incentive for learning the local language and culture, for each posting tends to be a way station toward career advancement. In those few cases when an FSO has begun to learn about Somalia and speak Somali, for example, he or she is sent to a new post.[19]

The fifth characteristic common to FSOs is their tendency to be **loyal and cautious**. Foreign service officers are loyal to the foreign service and identify closely with the State Department as an institution. Such loyalty is easy to understand, for most FSOs spend their adult careers within the foreign service and the State Department. Given the limited number of foreign service officers, an FSO ends up working and interacting with familiar colleagues through the course of fifteen or twenty years. Informal networks of relationships that build up with time are reinforced by the formal personnel process in which one's immediate superiors regularly evaluate his or her performance. These factors help to explain why the foreign service subculture is so pervasive and institutional loyalty so strong.

FSOs are also known for being cautious. They not only are cautious about bucking the dominant beliefs and norms of the foreign service, but they often provide "low-risk" advice and are hesitant to take individual policy initiatives. As discussed above, even though the State Department is a small bureaucracy, it operates as a very large bureaucratic structure. Before a request or decision is cabled abroad, for instance, the desk officer with primary jurisdiction must make sure it has been cleared—that is, approved—by all other officials interested in the issue. If an issue triggers the participation of officials from seven or eight bureaus, no matter how distant their involvement, all the participants are kept appraised of the process and sign off on any decisions, even if they are quite minor and routine. These overlapping jurisdictions result in a cautious, cumbersome process built around compromise and consensus among the parties involved.

Why so loyal and cautious? These traits can be found in the history of the State Department from the beginning, but they intensified during the late 1940s and 1950s. The end of World War II and the coming of the cold war brought in the rise of anti-communism and "McCarthyism" in the country and the government, especially in Congress. It seemed to many Americans as if their great victory in war was being lost in peace as Eastern Europe became communist, the People's Republic of China was proclaimed, and North Korea invaded South Korea. The explanation in which many Americans found comfort was that there were spies and traitors throughout American society and in government who were aiding and abetting the communist effort, directed by Stalin, to conquer the world. Joseph McCarthy, a Republican senator from Wisconsin, popularized this explanation during the early 1950s and gave this ultraconservative movement its name, although McCarthyism as a political movement existed before and after his personal rise and fall.

McCarthyism resulted in political charges of un-Americanism and communism against individuals and institutions throughout American society and government. One of the major institutions attacked for "losing the cold war and selling out America to communism" was the State Department. **Alger Hiss**, a high-level State Department official, was accused in 1948 of being a traitor for his activities during the war and was convicted of perjury (resulting in the rise of Congressman Richard Nixon, who led the political attack against Hiss). With **the "fall" of China** in 1949, senior officials of the Far

Eastern bureau who predicted that the Chinese Nationalists, given their corruption and brutal authoritarian behavior, would lose the civil war to the Chinese Communists became scapegoats and were forced out of the department and their careers destroyed. By the early 1950s, McCarthyism became so powerful and reckless that high-level officials within the Harry Truman administration were attacked for being "appeasers" and "fellow travelers" of communism. The secretary of state and the department were, for example, referred to as the "Dean Acheson College for Cowardly Containment of Communism" by Congressman Richard Nixon. With the attacks continuing under President Harry Truman and after the election of President Dwight Eisenhower as a Republican president, loyalty oaths and loyalty programs were instituted throughout the government and the practice developed of expanding the scope of classified information, making it unavailable to the public in the name of national security.

With this political climate, many officials were purged within the State Department for not having correct and sufficiently "hard-line" anticommunist views. Journalist David Halberstam described the situation among the East Asian specialists as, "the best had been destroyed and the new experts were different, lesser men who had learned their lessons, and who were first and foremost good anti-communists."[20] Survivors of the political attacks and purges within the State Department—such as **Dean Rusk**, who was in the Far Eastern bureau at the time and later became secretary of state under Presidents Kennedy and Johnson—drew the obvious lesson that to take the initiative and stand out from the pack in foreign policy was a major risk to one's career. Those who attempted to operate as policy entrepreneurs and buck the status quo, such as former State Department official **George Kennan**, who was actively involved in initiating the Marshall Plan and the containment strategy, were pushed to peripheral positions, if they remained in the foreign service at all. Thus, cautiousness and secrecy increased within the foreign service and an extensive clearance procedure developed within the State Department, to ensure that an individual was not alone in approving decisions which could become politically controversial.[21]

This portrait of the foreign service subculture is not particularly complimentary. Many FSOs are likely to disagree with what they might consider to be a caricature of the foreign service. However, this is the consensus position within the foreign policy literature and this perspective also tends to be shared by other members of the foreign policy bureaucracy, including members of the White House staffs. Therefore, even if these perceptions are overly simplistic, they are the images upon which other policymakers tend to operate. As we will discuss in the next section, if the president and other policymakers in the foreign policy bureaucracy perceive the State Department and the foreign service in this way, it is treated as reality and has important implications for State's role in the policymaking process.

CONSEQUENCES FOR PRESIDENTIAL RELIANCE ON STATE

Presidents, and their closest advisers, have generally had a negative perception of the performance of the State Department in the last few decades. John Kennedy, for example, referred to the State Department as a "bowl of jelly." Lyndon Johnson considered members of the foreign service to be "sissies, snobs, and lightweights who sacrificed too little and thought themselves better than their country." Richard Nixon declared in the 1968 campaign that "I want a secretary of state who will join me in cleaning house in the State Department."[22] The State Department's bureaucratic structure and subculture have contributed to this negative perception throughout the foreign policy bureaucracy. These negative images and experiences in working with the State Department have contributed to presidents having relied on a White House-centered policymaking process.

From a presidential perspective, *six complaints are often voiced* about the State Department's performance:[23]

1. Inefficient and slow;
2. Poor staff work;
3. Unresponsive;
4. Resistant to change;
5. Incapable of putting its house in order;
6. Unable to lead.

It is often argued that the State Department is inefficient and slow. As discussed above, the State Department operates as a very large, cumbersome bureaucracy with an extended clearance procedure that involves numerous officials and bureaus for any issue. The president and other major foreign policy officials have often found that the State Department moves too slowly, especially if there is a pressing issue at hand. When the State Department does respond, another complaint is that the staff work is often poor. National Security Adviser Kissinger, upon the issuance of a National Security Study Memorandum directing the bureaucracy to provide information, analyses, and policy alternatives, was often frustrated with the work produced by the State Department, and forced them to prepare new studies.

Another complaint is that the State Department is unresponsive to the president. Not only is it said that staff work is slow and inadequate, but it is argued that they are unable to follow orders well. The State Department is perceived as being unresponsive since foreign service officers are permanent members of the bureaucracy who will outlive the short political life of any president. Furthermore, given the particular subculture of the foreign service, they often seem to act as if they know what is best for U.S. foreign policy. A closely related complaint often heard is that the State Department resists change. Bureaucratic resistance to change is not unique to the State Department; all bureaucracies develop patterns and policies over time, making them resistant to changes the president may want to initiate.

The fifth common complaint is that the State Department is incapable of putting its own house in order. In other words, the State Department has not been successful in reforming its structure and sub-culture so that it operates more efficiently, produces higher quality staff work, and is more responsive to presidential orders and initiatives. Endless studies of the operations of the State Department have been conducted, and a number of efforts at reorganiza-tion have occurred since World War II. The net re-sult has been superficial change in the formal orga-nization chart while the foreign service subculture and day-to-day bureaucratic operations of the State Department remain intact.[24] The difficulty in chang-ing a bureaucratic organization, from without or within, is not limited to the State Department. The subculture of any organization tends to produce bu-reaucrats—foreign service officers in the case of the State Department—who believe that they are per-forming their jobs properly, helping to fulfill the functions of the organization, and making a contri-bution to the public policy of the United States government.

Considering these complaints, it is not surpris-ing that presidents have found the State Depart-ment unable to lead U.S. foreign policy—the final complaint commonly heard. No matter how much a president may want to rely on the State Depart-ment for the conduct of U.S. foreign policy, he soon finds that State is unable to lead, for it has resisted change in the internal workings of the department and the foreign service. This is why the roles of the national security adviser and staff have grown tremendously over time to the detriment of the State Department.

Officials within State. Despite the decline of the State Department "as an institution," individual State Department officials have played influential roles in the making of U.S. foreign policy for the president and within the policymaking process. The **distinction between the State Department as an in-stitution and individuals within the State Depart-ment** is very important to understand. Secretaries of state often act as major spokespersons for the ad-ministration in foreign policy and major advisers to the president, as was discussed in the previous chap-ter about presidential management of the foreign policy process. And lower level State Department of-ficials may also play important roles depending on the people involved and the issue.

Table 7.1 details the secretaries of state since the Roosevelt years. Many of the people who have served as secretary of state have been consequential in the making of U.S. foreign policy (see, for exam-ple, essay 6.3 on President Eisenhower and Secre-tary of State John Foster Dulles). Henry Kissinger, Cyrus Vance, George Shultz, James Baker, Warren Christopher, and Madeline Albright are all examples of strong and powerful secretaries of state in U.S. foreign policy who have had good relationships with the president since the ascendancy of a White House-centered system.

Strong and powerful secretaries of state, in turn, rely heavily on many officials within the State Department (some of which are in-outers) for the information and advice in formulating their policy positions. Hence, the decline of the State Depart-ment as an institution in the formal policymaking process has not foreclosed key State Department officials from exercising influence in the foreign policymaking process. The case of **Madeline Al-bright** under President Clinton is particularly in-teresting since she is the first woman to become secretary of state in the history of the United States (see **essay 7.3**).

THE FUTURE?

With the end of the cold war, the State Department as an institution may play a more prominent role in the making of U.S. foreign policy. The functions of the State Department would appear to be in greater demand in a post–cold war environment. Yet, it must be pointed out that the negative perceptions of the competency of the State Department shared by political leaders and the likelihood of global conflict, such as the Persian Gulf War, suggest that the de-partment's status is not likely to change dramati-cally.[25]

According to a management task force commis-sioned by the U.S. Department of State to examine its role and needs into the future, entitled *State 2000:*

TABLE 7.1
SECRETARIES OF STATE

NAME	YEAR APPOINTED	BACKGROUND
Edward R. Stettinius	1944	Business and Government
James F. Byrnes	1945	Law, Congress, and Supreme Court
George C. Marshall	1947	Army
Dean Acheson	1949	Law and Government
John Foster Dulles	1953	Law and Government
Christian A. Herter	1959	Congress and Government
Dean Rusk	1961	Foundation and Government
William P. Rogers	1969	Law and Government
Henry A. Kissinger	1973	Academia and Government
Cyrus R. Vance	1976	Law and Government
Edmund S. Muskie	1980	Law, Congress, and Government
Alexander M. Haig	1981	Army and Government
George P. Shultz	1982	Academia, Business, and Government
James A. Baker, III	1989	Law and Government
Lawrence S. Eagleburger	1992	Government
Warren M. Christopher	1993	Law and Government
Madeline K. Albright	1997	Academia and Government

A New Model for Managing Foreign Affairs, they concluded that "This report puts a particular premium on leadership of the Department of State that is open to new ideas and that promotes a new culture in the institution. It is time to forge a new mindset." They also acknowledged that it will be "a difficult adaptation for an institution bound in tradition" and "there are, of course, limits to what the leadership of the Department can do about the culture of the institution." Nonetheless, as the report concluded, "The Cold War is over. . . . If we cannot change now—as a nation, as a government and as an institution—when can we?"[26]

Although the State Department will remain a key agency in the foreign policy bureaucracy and individual officials within the department will continue to play significant roles, the president has turned to other agencies within the government for information, advice, and management of the national security process, in particular, the Department of Defense and the intelligence community in addition to the National Security Council. Yet, as we will see in the next two chapters, the president has had problems in managing these bureaucratic organizations as well.

BIBLIOGRAPHIC ESSAY
. . . .

The State Department and the foreign service have not received the kind of popular attention that other elements of the national security bureaucracy such as the NSC, the military establishment, and the CIA have received. Nevertheless, for a good history and overview of the State Department in U.S. foreign policy, see Barry Rubin, *Secrets of State: The State De-*

ESSAY 7.3
MADELINE ALBRIGHT: THE FIRST WOMAN AT THE TOP OF FOGGY BOTTOM

Madeline K. Albright secured her place in history as the **first woman as Secretary of State** in February 1997. Throughout American history, the making of U.S. **foreign policy has been fundamentally a male affair**. However, since the 1960s and the Vietnam War, more and more women have become involved in international affairs and have begun to occupy more foreign policy positions and more prominent roles. Jeane Kirkpatrick became the first American ambassador to the United Nations under President Reagan. Laura Tyson was President Clinton's national economic adviser. But the appointment of Albright is the most significant because of the secretary of state's special, prominent role in U.S. foreign policy.

Her rise is a great success story for an immigrant and a woman. Born in Czechoslovakia in 1937, Albright had to flee from her home country when it was taken over by communists in 1948. She and her family eventually immigrated to the United States where she was educated at Wellesley, a women's college. She got involved in politics during her college years as a volunteer for Adlai Stevenson. Her marriage from 1959 to 1982 with Joseph Albright saw her through the raising of three daughters, a Ph.D. in political science, and a budding political career with the Democratic party. Strangely, it wasn't until the time that she was appointed secretary of state that she publicly acknowledged that she had just become aware—60 years after her birth—of her Jewish heritage.

Her appointment as United States ambassador to the United Nations secured her a prominent position in the arena of foreign policy. From 1993 to 1996, Albright firmly asserted President Clinton's wishes for tough rhetoric on issues ranging from Bosnia to Haiti. In her early years at the U.N., she promoted the practice of "assertive multilateralism." When Secretary of State Warren Christopher made it clear to President Clinton that he wanted to leave government service, Albright finally got the call she had been longing for—although as with most major

presidential appointments the choice was far from unanimous among Clinton's inner circle.

An advocate of American activism and assertiveness, Secretary Albright is not likely to sit on her hands and wait for crises to arise. She prefers a proactive approach to foreign policy, and so far she appears to have been successful in getting the support of the president and Congress. A staunch Democrat, Albright has secured favor with many leading Republicans, including Senator Jesse Helms, who chairs the Senate Foreign Relations Committee. She's known as a strong advocate within the policy-making process and one who likes the limelight. With American foreign policy becoming increasingly an extension of trade policy, Secretary Albright must be able to shift gears between strategic military and international economic issues, and focus some of her attention on Asia where much American foreign policy attention will be directed in the coming century. Like her predecessor, Warren Christopher, many argue that she does not think strategically or broadly. Some skeptics question Albright's ability to play these roles, but Albright herself is confident in her abilities to navigate and negotiate where necessary.

Albright has proven a strong foreign policy voice. Unlike Warren Christopher, Albright is a master of the press conference. One of her goals is to make foreign policy "less foreign" to the American public. She takes her messages directly to the American public in the hope of securing support. Her direct dealings with Congress have also been beneficial for the passage of key policies such as the ratification of the Chemical Weapons Convention. Albright has been quoted as saying, "We live in an image society. Speeches are not what anybody cares about; what they care about is the picture." She projects an image of strength complemented with enough femininity to win her the respect of top foreign leaders.

In a society where women are highly underrepresented throughout government, particularly at the higher levels, even the image of breaking into top positions offers encouragement to the ranks of women and minorities hoping to garner employment in foreign policy. Fittingly, one journalist has written of Albright's appointment as secretary of state, "The image of a woman leading American

diplomacy makes a statement that no slogan can." Albright's assertiveness, loyalty, and visibility come together to represent a new type of American foreign policy leader.

SOURCES: Matthew Cooper, "The Lady Is a Hawk," *Newsweek* (December 16, 1996): 24–28; Matthew Cooper and Melinda Liu, "Bright Light," *Newsweek* (February 10, 1997): 22–29; Michael Dobbs, "Plain-English Foreign Policy," *Washington Post National Weekly Edition* (June 23, 1997): 6–7; Nancy Gibbs, "The Many Lives of Madeline," *Time* (February 17, 1997): 52–61; Jacob Heilbrunn, "Albright's Mission," *New Republic* (August 22 & 29, 1994): 19–25; Melinda Liu and Russell Watson, "Measuring Madeline," *Newsweek* (August 11, 1997): 34–36; Johanna McGeary, "Blunt But Flexible," *Time* (February 17, 1997): 56–57.

partment and the Struggle Over U.S. Foreign Policy* (New York: Oxford University Press, 1985). A strong analysis of the tension between insiders and in-outers and its impact on the State Department and the NSC in the policymaking process is given by Bert A. Rockman in "America's Department of State: Irregular and Regular Syndromes of Policy Making," *American Political Science Review* (December 1981): 911–27. Anthony Lake, director of policy planning under President Carter, provides an informative illustration of the dynamics of the State Department's policymaking process toward Nicaragua in *Somoza Falling* (Boston: Houghton Mifflin, 1989).

An excellent discussion of the foreign service subculture and its impact on the State Department's role in the policy process is supplied by Duncan Clarke, "Why State Can't Lead," *Foreign Policy* (Spring 1987): 128–42. Although dated, Charlton Ogburn, Jr., provides a realistic description of the typical day-to-day bureaucratic flow of activity and cable traffic within the Department of State in "The Flow of Policy Making in the Department of State," in H. Field Haviland, Jr., and Associates, *The Formulation and Administration of United States Foreign Policy, a Report for the Committee on Foreign Relations of the United States Senate* (Washington, D.C.: Brookings Institution, 1960): 172–77. For a look inside the workings of an embassy abroad, see Robert Hopkins Miller, *Inside an Embassy: The Political Role of Diplomats Abroad* (Washington, D.C.: Congressional Quarterly, 1992).

The opportunities and challenges that the end of the cold war have posed for the State Department as an institution are discussed by John Owens, "The U.S. Foreign Service: An Institution in Crisis," *Mediterranean Quarterly* (Summer 1991): 27–50; and U.S., Department of State, *State 2000: A New Model for Managing Foreign Affairs* (December 1992).

ENDNOTES

1. For a general overview of bureaucracy, see Morton H. Halperin, *Bureaucratic Politics and Foreign Policy* (Washington, D.C.: Brookings Institution, 1974); Hugh Heclo, *A Government of Strangers: Executive Politics in Washington* (Washington, D.C.: Brookings, 1977); Harold Seidman, *Politics, Position and Power: The Dynamics of Federal Organization* (New York: Oxford University Press, 1980); and James Q. Wilson, *Bureaucracy: What Government Agencies Do and Why They Do It* (New York: Basic Books, 1989).

2. For an overview of the State Department, see John Franklin Campbell, *The Foreign Affairs Fudge Factory* (New York: Basic Books, 1971); Anthony Lake, *Somoza Falling* (Boston: Houghton Mifflin, 1989); Barry Rubin, *Secrets of State: The State Department and the Struggle Over U.S. Foreign Policy* (New York: Oxford University Press, 1985); and Burton M. Sapin, *The Making of United States Foreign Policy* (New York: Praeger, 1966).

3. See Gerald F. Seib, "Personal Touch: Bush Shapes His Policy by Often Telephoning Other World Leaders," *Wall Street Journal* (November 30, 1989): A1, A9.

4. Tim Zimmerman, "Twilight of the Diplomats," *U.S. News & World Report* (January 27, 1997): 48–50.

5. U.S., Department of State, "Department Commemorates 200th Anniversary," *Update* (September-October 1989); U.S., *Statistics* 28 (Washington, D.C.: U.S. Government Printing Office, 1997).

6. For a general overview of bureaucracy, see note 1.

7. U.S., Department of State, Bureau of Public Affairs, *Atlas of United States Foreign Relations* (Washington, D.C.: Government Printing Office, 1990); *United States Government Manual* (1996).

8. Ibid., p. 9.

9. For an overview, see Robert Hopkins Miller, *Inside an Embassy: The Political Role of Diplomats Abroad*

(Washington, D.C.: Congressional Quarterly, 1992); and U.S., Congress, General Accounting Office, *State Department: Survey of Administrative Issues Affecting Embassies* (July 1993).

10. For an illustration of the dynamics of the policymaking process relative to U.S. foreign policy toward Nicaragua during the Carter years, see Lake, *Somoza Falling*.

11. David Corn, "At the Foggy Bottom of the Barrel, Political Hacks," *Washington Post* (January 10, 1993).

12. See, for example, Halperin, *Bureaucratic Politics and Foreign Policy*; Hugh Heclo, "The In-and-Outer System," *Political Science Quarterly* (Spring 1988): 37–56; and Bert A. Rockman, "America's Department of State: Irregular and Regular Syndromes of Policy Making," *American Political Science Review* (December 1981): 911–27.

13. See, for example, Andrew M. Scott, in "The Department of State: Formal Organization and Informal Culture," *International Studies Quarterly* (March 1969): 1–18. For a general discussion of the significance of organizational subculture, see the classic by William Whyte, *The Organization Man* (New York: Simon and Schuster, 1956).

14. Wilson, *Bureaucracy*, p. 91.

15. See Duncan Clarke, "Why State Can't Lead," *Foreign Policy* (Spring 1987): 128–42; I. M. Destler, *Presidents, Bureaucrats, and Foreign Policy* (Princeton, N.J.: Princeton University Press, 1972); Robert Pringle, "Creeping Irrelevance at Foggy Bottom," *Foreign Policy* 29 (Fall 1977): 128–39; Rockman, "America's Department of State"; Rubin, *Secrets of State*; Scott, "The Department of State"; and U.S., Department of State, *Diplomacy for the 70's: A Program of Management Reform for the Department of State* (December 1970). For a recent informal perspective from a junior officer in the foreign service, see Harry Crosby (a pseudonym), "Too At Home Abroad: Swilling Beer, Licking Boots, and Ignoring the Natives with One of Jim Baker's Finest," *The Washington Monthly* (September 1991): 16–20.

16. For a more in-depth discussion, see Martin Weil, *A Pretty Good Club* (New York: W.W. Norton, 1978).

17. See, for example, Robert D. Kaplan, *The Arabists: The Romance of an American Elite* (New York: Free Press, 1994).

18. See, for example, B. Drummond Ayres, Jr., "A New Breed of Diplomat," *New York Times Magazine* (September 11, 1983): 66–67, 70–73, 105, and William I. Bacchus, *Staffing for Foreign Affairs: Personnel Systems for the 1980's and 1990's* (Princeton, N.J.: Princeton University Pres, 1983).

19. The example of Somalia was drawn from the author's personal experience. I was there as part of a United States Information Agency (USIA) grant, which funded a University of South Carolina-Somali National University Linkage Program intended to develop an international studies curriculum and program within Somalia. The American governmental presence consisted of over 100 official personnel, primarily from the Agency for International Development, but also from Department of Defense, the State Department, and USIA (and the covert CIA). Only one American spoke Somali—the everyday language of the people. A young female foreign service information officer with USIA became fluent in Somali and developed a special relationship with many of the Somali people. Near the end of her three-year tour, she requested to stay in Somalia so she could put her language and Somali expertise to use. The State Department and USIA (an autonomous agency located within the State Department, which operates as part of the foreign service) declined her request and posted her to the highly prestigious London embassy. See also John W. Tuthill, "What Can Be Done at Foggy Bottom: Operation Topsy," *Foreign Policy* 8 (Fall 1972): 62–85.

20. David Halberstam, *The Best and the Brightest* (New York: Random House, 1969), p. 390.

21. See Halberstam, *The Best and the Brightest*; E. J. Kahn, Jr.'s, *The China Hands: America's Foreign Service Officers and What Befell Them* (New York: Viking Press, 1972); Robert P. Newman, *Owen Lattimore and the "Loss" of China* (Berkeley: University of California, 1992). McCarthyism as a political movement and force in the politics of U.S. foreign policy will be discussed at greater length in chapter 12 on Congress and chapter 17 on the impact of national security on the exercise of civil liberties.

22. In Destler, *Presidents, Bureaucrats, and Foreign Policy*, p. 154, and David Halberstam, *The Best and the Brightest* (New York: Random House, 1969), p. 299.

23. For an overview of this perspective, see note 15.

24. See, for example, Destler, *Presidents, Bureaucrats, and Foreign Policy*.

25. John Owens, "The U.S. Foreign Service: An Institution in Crisis," *Mediterranean Quarterly* (Summer 1991): 27–50.

26. U.S., Department of State, *State 2000: A New Model for Managing Foreign Affairs* (December 1992): 79–80.

CHAPTER
8

....

THE MILITARY ESTABLISHMENT

*T*he U.S. military is a governmental institution that has experienced tremendous growth in the twentieth century. Throughout most of its history, the United States had a modestly sized military that is distant from much of American society. But with World War II and the rise of the cold war, the military grew to be the largest bureaucratic institution in the United States and a major force in American foreign policy. This chapter will examine the historical evolution, purpose, organizational structure, and subcultures of the military establishment—relying on the same framework described in the previous chapter for examining the bureaucracy—and discuss their effects upon the policymaking process and conduct of U.S. foreign policy.

HISTORICAL TRENDS

....

Two very different militaries have existed since the beginning of the United States of America: a small

professional military throughout most of American history and an immense military establishment since World War II.[1]

THE OLD U.S. MILITARY

Three characteristics prevailed throughout much of American military history to World War II. First, the United States generally maintained only a small, career military; a large, permanent, professional standing army was established only after the Second World War. During times of conflict—such as the War of 1812, the Mexican-American War, the Civil War, and World War I—the United States government recruited a **citizen militia**, forming a large military to fight the war, which was quickly demobilized when hostilities ceased. Much of this can be explained by the limited threats to the U.S. government and its citizens, given its fortunate geographic location and the relative weakness of its two neighbors. This policy was reinforced by a popular feeling of distrust of the large professional military establishments that had existed in the "old world" of Europe.

The second characteristic of the military was that it was extremely fragmented and decentralized. The United States government did not maintain a unified military with different services responsible for different missions. Instead, the United States maintained two separate military departments: a **Department of the Navy** (including the Marines) and a **War Department** (consisting of the army and later an army air corps—the embryo of today's separate air force). These were two of the four original departments included in the executive branch and they were separate and autonomous. Overall direction and coordination were not the responsibility of the military, but of a civilian commander in chief, the president of the United States.

The third important characteristic of the military was that it was an important source of **political recruitment** through much of American history. Many of America's major political leaders were once generals in the U.S. Army. For example, Presidents George Washington, Andrew Jackson, Ulysses Grant, and Dwight Eisenhower, to name a few, were prominent generals in the army. It was their prowess as warriors that was responsible for their later political recruitment and success. The role of military experience and a "war record" in political recruitment and success has not been restricted to the presidency, but has been apparent at all levels of America's political system throughout its history. With America's trying experience in the Vietnam War, the issue of military experience lost much of its value in the recruitment of candidates and political campaigning. But it did become an important political issue during the 1988 presidential campaign, when it was revealed that vice-presidential candidate Dan Quayle supported America's effort in the Vietnam War although he avoided the draft by joining the Indiana National Guard, and in the 1992 presidential campaign, when the question of Bill Clinton's avoidance of the draft also became an issue.

Although the professional U.S. military has been small, structurally fragmented, and a source of political recruitment throughout much of its history, one should not conclude that it has not been an active force in U.S. foreign policy. In addition to protecting the territorial integrity of the United States before World War II, the U.S. military was actively used to support westward expansion (for example, to defeat and control the Native Americans), as well as American commerce and interests abroad. As discussed in chapter 2, from 1798 to *before* the beginning of World War II there were 162 instances of the use of United States armed forces abroad (review **table 2.1**).[2] This figure excludes the use of U.S. armed forces against Native Americans. Thus, the military has played an active part in the history of United States foreign policy as it evolved from a continental power to a regional power. With World War II and the cold war, however, the United States became a global power and the military was greatly transformed.

THE MODERN MILITARY ESTABLISHMENT

America's entry into World War II and its efforts to contain the threat of Soviet communism during the subsequent cold war resulted in a set of major changes in the U.S. military. *Three modern patterns have prevailed:*

1. Efforts were made to promote greater centralization.
2. There was the rise of a large, permanent professional military.
3. The military experienced tremendous expansion in bureaucratic size and scope.

With these changes, the military of the past was transformed into a modern military establishment, which has had a major impact on American society and the conduct of U.S. foreign policy.

Efforts at Greater Centralization. The experience of World War II created concern for the need to centralize the military, symbolized by the passage of the National Security Act of 1947. Not only was there concern over the nature of the policymaking process at the presidential level during World War

II, prompting the creation of the National Security Council, there was also concern about the fragmentation, lack of coordination, and infighting among the different services in support of the war effort. Nowhere was this more noticeable than in the **Pacific theater of World War II**, where the United States military lacked an overall commander of American armed forces. Jurisdiction was divided between the army and the navy: General Douglas MacArthur was in charge of American forces in the Southeastern Asian theater (with General Joseph W. Stilwell in charge of the China-Burma-India theater), while Admiral Chester Nimitz was responsible for military operations throughout the northern and central Pacific. This division of authority resulted in two major, and not always complementary, military strategies being implemented by the United States in the Pacific.

The war experience of a fragmented and decentralized military triggered efforts to address this problem. A major debate ensued within the military and the political environment. The army favored a highly integrated military system, but the navy was strongly opposed. The National Security Act reflected a compromise: the old War and Navy Departments were replaced by a single **Department of Defense (DOD)** (after the initial creation of the National Military Establishment) composed of a loose confederation of four services: the army, navy, air force, and marines. Coordination of service activities was to be accomplished by the Joint Chiefs of Staff, and the Office of the Secretary of Defense was created to make the military more responsive to the president as the commander in chief. However, as will be discussed further below, while the military may be less organizationally fragmented than it once was, it remains among the most decentralized bureaucracies within the U.S. government.

Large, Permanent Military. The second major change was the development of a large, permanent military. No longer was the U.S. military a small career force that temporarily grew in size during times of war. Although the U.S. military did begin to demobilize after the end of World War II, the rise of the cold war resulted in a reinstitution of **the draft**

in 1947 in order to maintain a large military force that received extensive training even during a time of peace (that is, when a major "hot war" did not exist).

This revolutionary transformation in the American military did not come easily, and was bitterly fought within Congress during the late 1940s until the Korean War resulted in American military intervention. This change occurred because, for the first time in their history, Americans feared for the security of their country as Eastern Europe came under communist rule and Western Europe was on the verge of economic collapse after World War II. Most Americans eventually became convinced that the threat of communism required the development of a large, permanent, professional military to keep the peace.

Expansion in Size and Scope. Following World War II, the Department of Defense became the **largest bureaucracy in the U.S. government** and American society. In 1989—the year the Berlin Wall came down—the DOD spent almost $300 billion per year and employed over four million people: about two million full-time soldiers, one million troops in the reserves and the National Guard, and one million civilians. Military spending represented roughly 30 percent of all expenditures by the U.S. government combined (this percentage was much higher during the 1950s and 1960s); DOD also employed roughly 60 percent of all U.S. government full-time employees (this excluded members of the National Guard) and one-third of all federal civil servants.

Not only was this the largest American bureaucracy in numbers, it was also vast because of the geographic scope of its **deployment at home and abroad.** DOD personnel were located on over 900 military bases and other military properties in every state of the Union (representing more than twenty-four million acres, equivalent to the territories of Connecticut, Massachusetts, New Hampshire, Rhode Island, Vermont, and two Delawares). Some 500,000 troops were permanently stationed throughout the world in over 3000 installations, including over 330 military bases in twenty-one countries and twenty-five U.S.

overseas territories (such as the Panama Canal territory), predominantly in Europe, Asia, and the Pacific.[3] With military personnel in over 130 countries, "the United States provides military training, in one form or another, to 75 percent of the world's armed forces."[4] To operate and fulfill its functions, the Department of Defense had developed a massive, global bureaucracy.

Since, the collapse of the Soviet Union, the Department of Defense has experienced some **downsizing.** Military spending has declined since the late eighties, but is still over $250 billion per year. The biggest cuts, around 40 percent since the eighties, have been made in personnel. There are about 2.3 million personnel within DOD: about one million full-time soldiers; 700,000 in the reserves and the National Guard; and about 600,000 civilians. The number of military bases within the United States and abroad has also been reduced, with almost 300,000 active duty personnel stationed abroad.[5] Although smaller, the Department of Defense remains huge in size and scope, and the largest bureaucracy.

The military consists of a **society within American society.** The military has its own system of laws, courts, and military police (MPs). Each military base is a completely self-sufficient urban complex that maintains barracks and residential facilities for families, medical (for example, hospitals) and educational facilities (from kindergarten to adult extension college classes), commissaries and PXs (military supermarkets and department stores), and recreational facilities (bowling alleys, movie theaters, and country clubs). The military has made an effort, at taxpayer expense, to provide its personnel at home and abroad with every amenity of modern life, at least in terms of material comfort.[6]

In addition to the three Army, Navy, and Air Force academies, the military operates its own system of graduate colleges and universities for preparing its middle officers for senior staff and command positions, including the Army War College, Naval War College, Air University, Armed Forces Staff College, Defense Systems Management School, and the National Defense University which consists of the National War College and Industrial College of the Armed Forces. The military services, individually

and jointly, also maintain a number of colleges and research institutes in the health sciences as well as a **Reserve Officer Training Corps (ROTC) program** located in almost every public college and university in the country. DOD also owns more than 70 industrial plants and facilities, many dating back to World War II.

The Department of Defense and the military services expanded so much in the 1940s and 1950s and in so many areas of everyday life that they have become the major "socialist"—that is, government-supported—sector in American society. Given both its tremendous size and scope, it may be that the Department of Defense has become the single largest bureaucracy in the world. Furthermore, the military is considerably more than the Department of Defense. For example, the Department of Transportation includes the **Coast Guard**, which has important military functions. The **Department of Veterans Affairs (VA)** was created to assist wounded war veterans and maintains an extensive system of VA hospitals throughout the country. The **Arms Control and Disarmament Agency (ACDA)** is a small civilian-based agency involved in military and political issues of arms control. The space program within the **National Aeronautics and Space Administration (NASA)**, originally a civilian-run organization to promote a nonmilitary space mission, supports more military than civilian missions today.[7] The **Department of Energy** is responsible for the research and development of nuclear weapons. (See **essay 8.1** for an overview of the nuclear weapons acquisitions process.) In sum, the modern military has developed into such an immense bureaucracy in comparison to the military of the past that it is more accurate and helpful to speak of the **military establishment.**

The rise of the cold war permanently transformed the American military. Since the early 1950s, the military has become less fragmented, has developed into a large, permanent, professional force during times of peace, and has grown enormously in size and scope. What has not changed are the **functions** or purposes that the military continues to serve. The primary purpose of the military is to defend and protect the government and the state. A second function of the military is to fight and de-

ESSAY 8.1
The Department of Energy, the Nuclear Weapons Productions Process, and the Environmental Threat

The Department of Energy has responsibility for the design, manufacture, testing, and retirement of nuclear weapons for the U.S. government. This practice originated with the **Manhattan Project**, which developed the atomic bomb during World War II. The rise of the cold war necessitated increasing production of nuclear bombs and warheads, providing America with a military arsenal to contain the threat of Soviet communism. During the 1940s and 1950s, an extensive network of government-owned plants was built to produce nuclear weapons and, later, fuel for nuclear submarines. These were operated by private industry and universities under contract and supervised by the **Atomic Energy Commission**, which became subsumed under the Department of Energy in the 1970s.

The nuclear weapons production process demonstrates the role of the permanent military establishment and its presence in American society following World War II. For over forty years, this large governmental industrial infrastructure existed to produce nuclear weapons for the U.S. military, thereby contributing to the formation of a close relationship among the military, civilians within the government (as within the Department of Defense and Department of Energy), private industry, the scientific community, and local communities in the defense process. The government's production system for nuclear weapons included the following *major facilities and activities:*

Los Alamos Scientific Laboratory, Los Alamos, New Mexico (operated by University of California). Home of the first atomic bombs; designs nuclear weapons.

Lawrence Livermore Laboratory, Livermore, California (operated by University of California). Designs nuclear weapons.

Sandia National Laboratories, Albuquerque, New Mexico (operated by Sandia Corporation). Conducts research, development, and engineering of nuclear weapons systems.

Argonne National Laboratory, Argonne, Illinois (operated by University of Chicago). Conducts research and development on nuclear fuel cycle systems.

Oak Ridge Reservation, Oak Ridge, Tennessee (operated by Martin Marietta Energy Systems). Enriches uranium.

Paducah Gaseous Diffusion Plant, Paducah, Kentucky (operated by Martin Marietta Energy Systems). Enriches uranium.

Portsmouth Gaseous Diffusion Plant, Piketon, Ohio (operated by Goodyear Corporation). Enriches uranium.

Feed Materials Production Center, Fernald, Ohio (operated by Westinghouse Materials Company). Processes uranium for use in nuclear warheads.

Ashtabula Extrusion Plant, Ashtabula, Ohio (owned and operated by Reactive Metals). Processes uranium for use in nuclear warheads.

Hanford Production Operations, Richland, Washington (operated by Westinghouse Electric and other corporations). Conducts nuclear research and development; makes plutonium from uranium; stores high-level radioactive waste.

Savannah River Plant, Aiken, South Carolina (operated by DuPont Corporation). Makes plutonium and tritium from uranium; stores high-level radioactive waste.

Rocky Flats Plant, Golden, Colorado (operated by Rockwell International). Processes plutonium for use in nuclear warheads.

Kansas City Plant, Kansas City, Missouri (operated by Allied Corporation). Produces non-nuclear components for nuclear warheads.

Mound Facility, Miamisburg, Ohio (operated by Monsanto Chemical Corporation). Makes detonators and timers for nuclear warheads.

Pinellas Plant, St. Petersburg, Florida (operated by General Electric Company). Produces components for nuclear warheads and measuring devices for nuclear weapons testing.

Pantex Plant, Amarillo, Texas (operated by Mason and Hanger-Silas Mason Company). Final nuclear warhead assembly point for new nuclear warheads; disassembly for old nuclear warheads.

Nevada Test Site, about 65 miles northwest of Las Vegas, Nevada (operated by consortium of corporations). Tests nuclear warheads underground.

Tonopah Test Range, Tonopah, Nevada (operated by Sandia National Laboratories). Tests the ballistics of nuclear weapons above ground.

These government-owned facilities covered 3900 square miles and employ some 90,000 people. Since much of the work is subcontracted out by the Department of Energy, the overall production of nuclear weapons—at its height during the eighties—involved over 140,000 workers in over 120 (public and private) facilities scattered across 23 states. The complicated route from nuclear weapons conception to governmental approval and then to actual testing and production takes five to ten years. The stockpile life of a completed nuclear warhead is roughly fifteen to twenty years, for which the Department of Energy is also responsible.

With the growing pursuit of arms control (such as the Test Ban Treaty), the end of the cold war, and the collapse of the Soviet Union, much of the nuclear production facilities, although still owned by the U.S. government, have been mothballed. Much of the nuclear material that has been produced is, in fact, reusable in nuclear weaponry. However, questions have now been raised as to what to do with these facilities and, most importantly, how to address the vast environmental problems and negligence that have accumulated over the years. Vast resources also are needed to dispose of 2,700 tons of spent fuel, 10,500 hazardous substances, and 100 million gallons of high-level waste over 2.3 million acres of land, involving 120 million square feet of buildings on 120 sites. Some of the deadly radioactive waste must be stored for thousands of years. Estimates of environmental "clean-up" range anywhere from $175 billion to $500 billion, and would probably involve decades.

SOURCES: James Brooke, "Plutonium Stockpile Fosters Fears of 'a Disaster Waiting to Happen,'" *New York Times* (December 11, 1996): A16; Thomas B. Cochran, William M. Arkin, Robert S. Norris, and Milton M. Hoenig, *Nuclear Weapons Databook: Volume II, U.S. Nuclear Warhead Production,* and *Volume III, U.S. Nuclear Warhead Facility Profiles* (Cambridge, Mass.: Ballinger, 1987); "Los Alamos Takes Step Back to Its Roots," *Science* (March 8, 1996): 1355–56; "Nuclear Danger and Deceit," *Newsweek* (October 31, 1988): 28–30; Walter Pincus, "U.S. Launches Major A-Arms Program," *Washington Post* (December 10, 1978): A1, A14–A15; Walter Pincus, "2 Labs Battle To Be No. 1," *Washington Post* (December 12, 1978): A1, A10; Klaus B. Stadie, "The Nuclear Weapons Legacy," *Environment* (January/February 1996): 3–5; U.S. Congress, Congressional Budget Office, *Cleaning Up the Department of Energy's Nuclear Weapons Complex* (May 1994).

stroy (and be willing to give up one's life) in support of one's country. This is the soldier's ultimate mission and is such a unique function, in comparison to any other organization's within the government or society, that it requires unique training methods to resocialize individuals to accept and engage in mass killing. The third function of the American military is to respond to civilian leadership as stipulated in the Constitution of the United States.

Even though these functions have remained the same throughout American history, the military has been transformed into a modern military establishment. The threat and use of military force became the basis for the U.S. policy of containment during the cold war years. American troops have been sent abroad in conflict situations during the Korean War, in Lebanon in 1958, the Dominican Republic in 1965, and the Vietnam War. Barry Blechman and Stephen Kaplan, in *Force Without War: U.S. Armed Forces as a Political Instrument,* found that in the thirty-year period between 1946 and 1975 American policymakers have used the **armed forces as a political instrument** to influence the actions of other countries 215 times.[8] The threat and use of military force has continued since the Vietnam War, most visibly in Grenada, Panama, the Persian Gulf, and Bosnia. Knowledge of the bureaucratic organization and subcultures of the Department of Defense is needed to better understand the role of the military establishment in the making and conduct of U.S. foreign policy.

DOD'S BUREAUCRATIC STRUCTURE AND PROCESS

. . . .

The Department of Defense has expanded into an enormous national and global bureaucracy. As with any bureaucracy, DOD is based on hierarchy, specialization, and routinization. In order to better understand the dynamics of the defense process, one has to compare the formal organizational model to political reality.

THE FORMAL IDEAL

According to the formal organization chart and the ideal bureaucratic model, the Department of Defense operates very rationally within *a pyramid-type structure composed of three levels:* the individual services implement and carry out the plans and policies

of their superiors: the Joint Chiefs of Staff, who consist of the senior military officers, and the Office of the Secretary of Defense, which represents the president and the civilian control dictated by the Constitution (see **figure 8.1**).

The **services** are the implementers of United States defense policy. The army, navy, air force, and the marines each have specialized responsibilities in preparing for and engaging in war. Each service operates bases throughout the country and the world where the troops are stationed and weapons kept. Of the roughly 1.5 million active and reserve military personnel, about 500,000 are in the army, about 400,000 are in the navy, almost 200,000 are in the marine corps, and about 400,000 are in the air force. **Strategic nuclear forces** (that is, long-range nuclear strike forces) are operated by the air force (such as the Minuteman and MX intercontinental ballistic missiles; the B-52, FB-111, B-1 and B-2 bombers) and the navy (the Poseidon and Trident submarine-launched ballistic missiles). All four services (and the guard and reserve components of each) are also a part of the military's **general purpose forces**—the classic combat forces trained and equipped for

FIGURE 8.1
DEPARTMENT OF DEFENSE POLICY PROCESSES

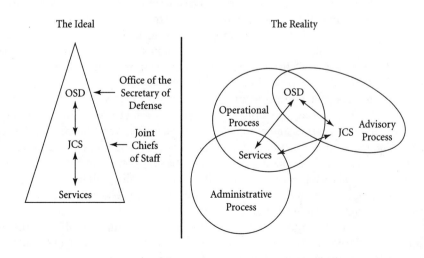

conventional war. The **army** is primarily responsible for land warfare and is reliant on weaponry such as tanks, artillery, and helicopters in support of the basic infantry soldier. The **navy** maintains over 500 ships, including 12 aircraft carriers with hundreds of aircraft, for sea and coastal warfare. The **air force** operates over 2000 aircraft in support of its air warfare mission. The **marine corps** mission is as an assault force, maintaining its own air and landing craft.[9] Day-to-day military operations are based on clearly defined divisions of labor (between and within services) and rank (from general down to private in the army).

The **Joint Chiefs of Staff (JCS)** is responsible for formulating overall military strategy and advising the secretary of defense and the president. The JCS consists of the six highest military officers: the chairman, the vice-chairman, the chief of staff of the army, the chief of naval operations, the chief of staff of the air force, and commandant of the marine corps.[10] The chairman of the JCS is appointed by the president for up to four years, while the other positions are a function of the personnel systems within the individual services. A joint staff, no larger than 400 military officers on loan from the individual services for a limited term by law (to preclude the creation of a de facto "general staff" on the Prussian model), exists to support the work and mission of the JCS. The JCS, located in the Pentagon headquarters of the Department of Defense, was created to coordinate military strategy among the services and represent the entire military in advising its civilian superiors.

The **Office of the Secretary of Defense** (OSD) was created to provide better civilian control of the military and to advise the president. OSD is the predominantly civilian side of the Department of Defense and is bureaucratically organized similar to the State Department. The major hierarchy of administrative officers are the secretary of defense, a deputy secretary, under secretaries, assistant secretaries, and deputy assistant secretaries, all nominated by the president. Most of the routine day-to-day activity within OSD takes place in organizational units or bureaus that specialize in certain defense subjects and issues. The structure of the Department of Defense allows for the military through the Office of the Secretary of Defense to be responsive to the president in accordance with his constitutional role as commander in chief.

THE POLITICAL REALITY

Unfortunately, the political reality of the policymaking process within the Department of Defense is far removed from the ideal and the formal organizational charts that depict a simple decision-making process in which the military services respond to the JCS and civilian control of the military is exercised at the top through OSD. The process and workings of the Department of Defense are among the most complex of any governmental bureaucracy. *Three major reasons explain the complexity of the military establishment:*

1. The bureaucracy is huge,
2. The department is decentralized, and
3. Additional bureaucratic complexities exist.

The result has been the development of military services that possess their own missions, standard operating procedures, and subcultures over which the president has been able to exercise only limited control.

Bureaucratic Size. As discussed above, the military establishment is a huge bureaucracy. Despite the downsizing, the military is so enormous that it is literally impossible for the president to oversee, even with the support of the Office of the Secretary of Defense. Once a program or activity is in place, like the production of a weapons system or the establishment of a military base with building facilities and employees, it is very difficult to change because of the economic and political costs involved. If a president has no complaints concerning the services as they are, he will be pleased with their performance. However, if a president wants to fine-tune the military, or a particular operation, or wants to reform the overall structure, he will find the military to be unresponsive to the commander in chief, as will be discussed below.

Departmental Decentralization. In addition to its immense size, the Department of Defense remains extremely decentralized. Although the National Security Act of 1947 reduced some of the fragmentation, very little progress has been made in promoting centralization under civilian and presidential control.

The Joint Chiefs of Staff has actually been a weak body for much of its history, unable to enforce a coherent military policy and coordinate the individual services. The chairman of the JCS, the only presidential appointment representing the entire military, had only one vote and, until recently, no power to force the other members to support him. Each of the other four members represents the interests of their individual services. Decisions over issues tend to produce competing interests that are resolved through compromise and consensus among the JCS, and each service tends to get most, but not all, of its demands met. In this way, the JCS was able to symbolically present a unified military position

that the civilians in the Office of the Secretary of Defense and the president find difficult to combat.[11]

In 1987, **the Goldwater-Nichols Act** was passed to address some of these problems within the JCS. The act increased the power of the chairman of the JCS (CJCS), by providing him with a vice chairman and a joint staff that is now responsive to him, making him the preeminent adviser to the president on military affairs. The appointment of **General Colin Powell** in 1989 also increased the power of the chairman of the JCS because of his considerable political skills in operating within the military and as a presidential adviser. This has made the presidential appointment of the chairman of the JCS even more important and "politicized," where a certain amount of interservice rivalry has always existed (see **table 8.1** for the chairmen of the Joint Chiefs of Staff).

Some analysts fear that the chairman of the JCS and military leaders have grown too powerful, especially relative to the civilian leadership. Others believe that many of the problems within the military

TABLE 8.1
CHAIRMEN OF THE JOINT CHIEFS OF STAFF

NAME	YEAR APPOINTED	BACKGROUND
Omar N. Bradley	1949	Army
Arthur W. Radford	1953	Navy
Nathan F. Twining	1957	Air Force
Lyman L. Lemnitzer	1960	Army
Maxwell D. Taylor	1962	Army
Earle G. Wheeler	1964	Army
Thomas H. Moorer	1970	Navy
George S. Brown	1974	Air Force
David C. Jones	1978	Air Force
John W. Vessey	1982	Army
William J. Crowe, Jr.	1985	Navy
Colin L. Powell	1989	Army
John M. Shalikashvili	1993	Army
Henry Shelton	1997	Army

and the JCS remain, as discussed above, but now there is the potential for the chairman of the JCS, in consultation with civilian leaders, to bring some centralization and order to the process.[12]

The Office of the Secretary of Defense has little legal authority to influence the operations of the JCS or the individual services. To illustrate the fragmentation within the Department of Defense and the independent autonomy of the individual services, official U.S. governmental publications, such as *The United States Government Manual* and the *Congressional Directory,* list the army, navy, and air force (the Marine Corps is an autonomous part of the navy) as separate "departments" within the executive branch even though they are officially a part of the Department of Defense. Robert McNamara, the secretary of defense under Presidents John Kennedy and Lyndon Johnson, probably had the most success in influencing the bureaucratic operations of the military.[13] Nevertheless, as even McNamara experienced, the individual services tend to have almost autonomous power within the Department of Defense, making it virtually impossible for the president to formulate a comprehensive and coherent military policy. Much depends on the working relationships that develop between the secretary of defense and the president, and their advisers, and the chairman and members of the JCS (see **table 8.2** for the secretaries of defense since DOD was created).

TABLE 8.2
SECRETARIES OF DEFENSE

NAME	YEAR APPOINTED	BACKGROUND
James V. Forrestal	1947	Wall Street and Government
Louis A. Johnson	1949	Law and Government
George C. Marshall	1950	Army
Robert A. Lovett	1951	Wall Street and Government
Charles E. Wilson	1953	Business
Neil H. McElroy	1957	Business
Thomas S. Gates, Jr.	1959	Business and Government
Robert S. McNamara	1961	Academia and Business
Clark M. Clifford	1968	Law and Government
Melvin R. Laird	1969	Congress
Elliot L. Richardson	1973	Law and Government
James R. Schlesinger	1973	Academia and Government
Donald Rumsfeld	1975	Congress and Government
Harold Brown	1977	Academia and Government
Caspar W. Weinberger	1981	Law and Government
Frank C. Carlucci	1987	Business and Government
Richard B. Cheney	1989	Congress and Government
Les Aspin, Jr.	1993	Academia and Congress
William J. Perry	1994	Academia and Business
William Cohen	1997	Law and Congress

The key to understanding the decentralized process of the Department of Defense is to examine who controls the **budget and personnel systems,** for they determine how any organization actually operates.[14] Decisions about the military budget (how to spend the money available) and military personnel (tours of duty and promotions) are made within each of the services. Furthermore, the budgetary and personnel practices within each service have become institutionalized and standardized, making them very resistant to change. As General David C. Jones, former chairman of the JCS, has stated, "He who controls dollars, promotions and assignments controls the organization—and the services so control, especially with regard to personnel actions."[15]

Decisions over which weapons to build, where they should be deployed, and how they will be used in combat are typically made within an individual service, validated by the JCS, and usually approved within OSD—all within the "constraints" of the overall military budget. The president and the secretary of defense might exercise influence on those issues in which they are most interested and attentive. Otherwise, the Joint Chiefs of Staff, the Office of the Secretary of Defense, and the president have limited impact on the actual operations of the services—the heart and soul of the military.

Additional Bureaucratic Complexities. The service bureaucracies have become difficult to influence or change for several additional reasons. One reason is that there is a tremendous **surplus of military officers.** The ratio of officers to enlisted personnel has grown dramatically since World War II. Initially, it was argued before Congress that an officer surplus would allow the military to expand greatly in the event of a World War III mobilization, but eventually it became a way of life that led to fragmentation of duties and a diminution of responsibilities. This was accomplished by bureaucratic expansion within each of the services of new positions, more specialization, and additional programs (all requiring more funding).[16] Such bureaucratic growth of programs, personnel, and money is not unique to the military, but a characteristic common to all bureaucracies. However, the military bureaucracy is so enormous that additional bureaucratic

growth makes the military services that much more complex and difficult for an outsider, such as the president, to contend with. The downsizing of the military since the end of the cold war has not really addressed or remedied this problem.

One more complexity deserves mention. In addition to the military services, the JCS, and the OSD, a fourth bureaucratic element exists within the Department of Defense. Each of the three major services is officially under an **Office of the Secretary of the Army, Navy, and Air Force** to provide additional civilian control of the military. Each of these offices encompasses a full-scale bureaucracy (like the Office of the Secretary of Defense) for administering each of the services under the authority of the secretary of defense and the president. The reality, however, is that the secretaries of the army, navy, and the air force tend to be civilian spokespersons and promoters of the individual services. Therefore, these offices do not truly promote civilian control of the military so much as they "water down" the secretary of defense's role. This additional bureaucratic layer has further complicated the president's constitutional role of commander in chief.

In sum, the Department of Defense has become such an enormous, complex, and confusing enterprise that probably no human being really understands how the entire process operates. Nevertheless, it is possible to identify general patterns of behavior that take place within DOD. Rather than a simple top-down centralized, civilian-controlled process, the workings of the Department of Defense can be better understood if seen as *three different but overlapping systems* (return to figure 8.1 for an illustration):

1. An advisory process;
2. An operational process;
3. An administrative process.

This simplifies the complex policy process within the department, yet provides a means for making sense of the basic operating patterns and for understanding the implications for presidential governance of foreign policy.

In the *advisory process* concerning decisions of war and peace, the Office of the Secretary of Defense and the Joint Chiefs of Staff—especially the chairman—are the most important organizational elements within the Department of Defense. The president is the commander in chief and determines when and where to use armed force abroad. Most presidents rely on their most trusted foreign policy advisers, including the secretary of defense, when it comes to such important decisions. The advisory role of the JCS depends on the particular president's relationship with his senior military officers. Usually, the chairman of the JCS has the greatest credibility with the president because he is the only member not representing the interests of a particular service.

The *operational process* refers to the military strategy and tactics employed by the armed forces and involves both the individual services, the Office of the Secretary of Defense, and with the Goldwater-Nichols Act, the chairman of the Joint Chiefs of Staff. The secretary of defense and OSD clearly have their greatest independent impact, when they have any impact at all, at the strategic level. A president may be able to affect war preparations and national military strategy, but this will largely be a function of past strategy and current service policies. Civilians have influenced the development of nuclear deterrence doctrine during the 1950s, the size and scope of conventional forces abroad, and the Strategic Defense Initiative during the 1980s. They may also influence overall force structure, such as the building of a 600-ship navy, as well as the development of one of the larger weapons programs, such as the MX missile.

Much of OSD's strategic influence naturally will be a function of politics, depending on the level of interest and attention displayed by the president, the secretary of defense, and the secretary's immediate subordinates (as well as their working relationship with the JCS, especially the chairman). Even then, OSD has to contend with a military strategy and infrastructure that is already in place (for the most part, since the 1940s and 1950s) and service requests for more resources, such as weaponry and money, to promote their mission as they see it. The services, which actually administer the armed forces and en-

gage in combat, are a powerful bureaucratic force in support of more weapons and resources to maintain the strategic status quo.

At the tactical level, the services dominate military operations through the **Unified Commands**. Unified commands contain forces from two or more services (the Navy and Marine Corps are considered within the same department) and are regional or functional in orientation. It is the unified Commander in Chief (CINC), usually the regional CINC, who is responsible for employing the forces of the different services. The Commander in Chief of each regional or functional command traditionally comes from the same service; each CINC has subordinate component commanders who represent each service under his control (see **table 8.3** for an overview of the unified commands).

Once a presidential decision is made to go to war or to intervene militarily, the president has little control over the existing command structure and bureaucratic set of standard operating procedures for implementing the presidential decision within each of the services. A president, through the secretary of defense and OSD and the advice of the chairman of the JCS, may be able to fine-tune specific military tactics. During the Vietnam War, President Johnson made certain operations off limits, such as attacking Cambodia, Laos, or North Vietnam, for fear of triggering the People's Republic of China's military intervention in the war (as occurred during the Korean War when American troops pushed up the Korean Peninsula approaching the Chinese border). Although certain political restrictions have always been imposed by civilian leadership during time of war, actual military operations are conducted by the unified commands and the services. Thus, the basic tactical strategy of "search and destroy" was selected by General William Westmoreland, the Commander in Chief of American forces in Vietnam.[17]

The final major process within the Department of Defense is the *administrative process*. This involves day-to-day management within the military and is controlled by the individual services. Personnel decisions, about recruiting, training, tours, and pro-

TABLE 8.3
THE MILITARY'S UNIFIED COMMAND STRUCTURE

COMMANDS	AREA OF RESPONSIBILITY	TRADITIONAL COMMANDER IN CHIEF (CINC)
REGIONAL		
European Command (EUCOM)	Europe, Sub-Saharan Africa, and Israel	Army or Air Force General
Pacific Command (PACOM)	The Pacific, Asia, and the Indian Ocean	Navy Admiral
Central Command (CENTCOM)	Mideast and North Africa	Army or Marine General
Southern Command (SOUTHCOM)	Central and South America	Army General
Atlantic Command (LANTCOM)	North America, the Atlantic, and the Caribbean	Marine General or Navy Admiral
FUNCTIONAL		
Strategic Command (STRATCOM)	Nuclear Forces	Air Force General
Transportation Command (TRANSCOM)	Movement of forces and material	Air Force General
Space Command (SPACECOM)	Space operations and satellites	Air Force General
Special Operations Command (SOCOM)	Special Purpose Forces of all services	Army General

motion, are individual service affairs. The routines and activities each day within the military concerning health, schooling, provisions, recreation, security, and so on also are determined within the individual services.

In sum, decisions to use American armed forces are dominated by the civilian leadership. However, decisions concerning basic operations and administration of the armed forces are made within the individual services. With the tremendous expansion of the military since World War II, a system has evolved in which the president determines when and where to use armed force, but the military services determine the actual conduct of the war. In other words, presidents can begin and end wars, but the military fights them. On the one hand, this relationship in **civil-military relations** has prevailed throughout American history; on the other hand, as presidents have attempted to exercise more power during the nuclear age, the military has become increasingly bureaucratic and political—hence, more

difficult to influence. This is the kind of division of labor that is preferred by most within the military, but often frustrates presidents who want to control and govern U.S. foreign policy.[18]

THE MILITARY SUBCULTURE

To fully understand the workings of the military and civil-military relations within the Department of Defense, one has to examine its organizational subculture in addition to its bureaucratic structure. It would be a mistake to speak of a single subculture for the entire department. Not only is DOD an enormous bureaucracy, it is also a diverse bureaucracy composed of many different elements. DOD contains both civilian and military personnel, with the military component organized into four different services. Additional distinctions also exist within the military, as between officers and enlisted personnel.

Thus, one should speak of multiple subcultures. The point is that the Department of Defense is a large and diverse bureaucracy whose subcultural patterns are quite complex.

Diversity notwithstanding, there has been a growing consensus among scholars and analysts of the U.S. military that a number of general characteristics have pervaded the military over the years.[19] Most *members of the military, especially career officers, tend to share five characteristics:*

1. Prevalence of a managerial style;
2. Pursuit of procurement and high technology;
3. Preoccupation with careerism;
4. Promotion of attrition warfare strategies;
5. Belief in the separation of politics and military combat.

Many of these characteristics are shared by the permanent civilian bureaucracy within the military establishment as well, but the focus here is on the military subculture.

It is commonly argued that the military no longer produces warriors, but a **managerial class** of military leaders. The primary purpose of the military is to prepare and engage in war and, historically, carrying out this function required the development of a warrior class within society. In the United States, the military has been the institution where this warrior tradition was fostered. However, the "manager" has become ascendant over the warrior since modern bureaucratic warfare demands the ability of officers to become "managers of violence."

Given the enormous expansion of the military bureaucracy in size, scope, and complexity, this is a natural development. The warrior is most appropriate for command positions in the field, not for administering a large bureaucracy. The skills that have increasingly been in demand as the bureaucracy has grown in size have been administrative. This natural bureaucratic development has been reinforced by the civilian leadership of the Department of Defense, especially beginning with Secretary of Defense **Robert McNamara**. McNamara entered office with a commitment to seize control of the Department of Defense and make it more efficient and responsive

to the president. McNamara's background was in the corporate world. He had gained a reputation as an excellent manager while chief executive officer of the Ford Corporation. In the tradition of the Kennedy administration, McNamara appointed numerous "whiz" kids to positions in the Office of the Secretary of Defense to restructure the department. Major efforts were made to streamline and improve the flow of information and the budgetary process. Although the basic military missions of the services continued, McNamara was successful in having his managerial approach penetrate throughout the military.

Over time, a managerial class has come to replace the warrior class of military officers. Military officers with administrative skills are the individuals most successful in the military today. Symptomatic of this change is the type of post-graduate degrees and curriculum pursued by senior officers. Where once upon a time degrees and courses in history and military strategy were the norm, today the emphasis is on business administration, public administration, and engineering. Even at U.S. military colleges, knowledge of military history, international conflict, and military strategy is no longer dominant (except at the Army War College, Naval War College, Air University, and National War College for senior officers). The emphasis is not on the art of war, but on learning how to administer a large bureaucracy.[20] Symptomatic of this administrative trend is the rise of **bureaucratese within the military**—the development of a "technical" language among a select group of professionals and bureaucrats (including academics). Acronyms and jargon such as MAD, MIA, and "collateral damage"—which stand for Mutual Assured Destruction, Missing in Action, and civilian injuries and property damage—have proliferated, distancing the military and civilian managers from the brutality of war.[21]

The rise of "managerialism" has been reinforced by a second characteristic of the military subculture, the **quest for more procurement and high technology**. A strong norm has developed that a modern military requires expensive "hardware" (weaponry and support facilities). This means not only a large quantity of hardware, but the best and most technologically sophisticated hardware available. For years there has been tremendous pressure within the air force, for example, to replace the aging B-52 with the B-1 and the B-2 Stealth bombers. This pursuit of high technology is not unique to the military, but shared by most civilians within the Department of Defense as well. Much of American society has an abiding faith in the promise of technology. The goal is not only to deter and win wars, but to gain the symbolic and prestige value conferred by weapons that represent the state of the art. This pursuit of high technology has intensified with cuts in personnel that the military has experienced over the past decade.

This "materialist" bias for more weapons, particularly those that are the "state of the art," reinforces a decline in the importance of the soldier-warrior, requires more expert personnel to maintain and administer the hardware, and de-emphasizes the importance of intangibles—such as leadership and will—during time of conflict. It also has led the upper echelons of the military to take a much more active political role in civil-military relations: influencing the president, lobbying Congress (along with civilian cohorts in defense industry), using the media, and campaigning before the public in support of more procurement and high technology (and obviously challenging those who oppose military requests or want defense cuts). Thus, the military, and its supporters, has become a potent political force in the politics of national defense, reducing military accountability to civilian leadership and exacerbating the difficulties the president faces as commander in chief.

A third characteristic of the military subculture is the rise of **careerism**. Many junior officers deplore the paper pushing, the high-tech syndrome, and the politicking as not contributing to mission readiness, but they are understandably reluctant to buck the power of bureaucracy. A personnel system has developed within each of the services that promotes individual conformity to the dominant norms and status quo and places a premium on individual preoccupation with career advancement. There is an "up or out" expectation that either an officer is regularly promoted within the service or his career will

suffer. In order for an officer to be successfully promoted, however, he must have very high evaluations from his superiors with "zero defects" (that is, no negative criticism). Furthermore, officers are expected to **punch their tickets**, that is, serve in a variety of positions and roles throughout their service. This must include a combat record, which is absolutely crucial to high career advancement. As many observers have pointed out, the military career ladder is now little different from the career ladder in government or the corporate world, typical of large bureaucracy in general. Its effect is also quite similar: to develop an "organization man or woman." In each of the services, the end product is a military officer who learns organizational norms and is able to contribute to the performance of the missions of the individual services as they currently exist.

One of the beliefs that is socialized or conditioned into military personnel is the overriding importance of **attrition warfare**, the fourth characteristic of the military subculture, as the basic military approach to war. The U.S. military is organized, equipped, and trained for attrition warfare. The strategy of attrition is the effort to deter, weaken, exhaust, and ultimately defeat the enemy through the concentration and delivery of massive firepower. Given the different responsibilities and missions of each service, this emphasis has resulted in the development of three different strategies of attrition. The army emphasizes a landpower strategy, which calls for control of land through the destruction of the enemy's army and occupation of his territory; the navy emphasizes a maritime strategy of control of the sea by decisive defeat of the enemy's fleet; and the air force relies on an air strategy, which asserts the primacy of airpower over every other form of combat for defeating the enemy.[22]

Since World War II, strategies of attrition warfare have been oriented toward the Soviet Union, portrayed as a militarist and expansionist enemy. Hence, the development of large general-purpose forces, many of which are stationed on military bases in allied countries, intended to prevent the Soviet Union from militarily expanding beyond the Eurasian continent. This conventional military force was reinforced by the development of large nuclear forces to deter a Soviet attack by the threat of total destruction. Implementing these strategies of attrition by the services reinforces the need for high-technology military administered by a large bureaucratic apparatus. This also has had implications, as will soon be discussed, for the military's battlefield performance. With the collapse of the Soviet empire, the military has had to redirect the strategy of attrition toward new adversaries and areas of the world.

The final characteristic of the military's subculture is a belief in the **separation of politics and military combat**. Given the nature of the American Constitution, the military perspective is that the civilian leadership, symbolized by the president and the Congress, decide when and where to go to war; but once the decision has been made, it is time for the politicians and civilians to stand aside and let the military do what it does best: fight wars. Some within the military also have concluded, therefore, that the services should control the administrative and operational process during times of peace as well as war, since peace is a time in which to prepare for war. Presidents and other civilians see the nature of civil-military relations quite differently. They believe that the president is the commander in chief before a war, during a war, and after a war, and as stipulated in the U.S. Constitution, the military should be responsive to civilian leadership and presidential orders.

Given the opposing interpretations, the military and civilian leadership often have found themselves in political battles during times of peace and war. For example, during the Korean War President Harry Truman relieved **General Douglas MacArthur** from his command of the United Nations forces for insubordination, triggering a national controversy over the conduct of the war and the containment policy. The American failure in the Vietnam War fueled a similar debate, for many attributed the loss of the war to civilian interference with the military's ability to perform its mission, while others pointed the finger at the military's inability to succeed within the appropriately described limitations set by the civilian leadership as the major cause of defeat.[23]

PATTERNS IN DOD's MILITARY BEHAVIOR

. . . .

What are the implications of DOD's bureaucratic structure and the military's subculture for the foreign policymaking process and American military conduct? A *number of patterns have developed* in the military's behavior, affecting both its performance and U.S. foreign policy:

1. Lack of military coordination;
2. Information problems;
3. Duplication and overlapping activities;
4. Waste and inefficiency;
5. Decline in leadership and morale;
6. Rise of all-volunteer military;
7. Military advice ignored by civilians.

These are common problems found in complex bureaucracies in general. However, with regard to the military they have remained distant from most Americans given the unquestioning patriotism toward the armed forces, the popular folklore about American military prowess, and the Pentagon's public relations campaign to promote the military, for example, through commercials on television. Overall, the U.S. military "war machine" is big and powerful, yet a close examination demonstrates that it is not nearly as effective a fighting force or as fine-tuned during times of war and peace as many Americans commonly believe.[24]

Lack of Coordination. Within the military establishment there is a general consensus on goals and "official" national military strategy. However, because coordination has been problematic among the services, this has made it difficult to develop a truly unified and mutually reinforcing military orientation that coheres overall. Each service tends to pursue its own mission and tactical orientation largely independent of the others. Thus, the United States maintains a "patchwork" military strategy representing the different missions and orientations of the various services, which together may or may not promote the overriding goals of U.S. foreign policy.

Why is coordination within the military so difficult? First, as discussed above, the tremendous size and decentralization of the bureaucracy allows minimal civilian control, and that is exacerbated by the strength of the military subcultures. Second, in addition to minimal civilian control, **interservice rivalry** pervades the military. Not only is the Department of Defense decentralized, this decentralization is reinforced by the strong, competitive subcultures within each of the services. The army, navy, air force, and marines all compete with each other for resources, control, and preeminence. Even though the military has enjoyed substantial financial support by the president, Congress, and the public at large throughout most of the post–World War II period, competition has been severe among the services on how to divide the pie—the ultimate indicator of success and the main tool for building a modern force. Leaders of the services typically have dealt with this problem by agreeing to roughly equal shares, with the air force usually the most favored (given its responsibility for nuclear strategic forces and technologically sophisticated warplanes) and the army least favored (given its reliance on manpower). This has allowed the services to staple together their individual requests for resources and present a unified position to the president, the Congress, and the country, thereby maximizing their political chances of success.[25]

The same lack of real coordination exists in military operations. Once American forces are engaged in combat abroad, every service wants to be involved. In the Vietnam War not only were the army, navy, air force, and marines all involved, but the U.S. Coast Guard patrolled the inland waterways along the Mekong Delta. The **Iran hostage rescue mission** in 1980 involved a mixed military team from the different services trained to fly special army helicopters equipped for the desert. Yet, at the request of the navy, a last-minute military decision was made to include navy helicopters, which were the helicopters that failed. An unspoken rule is that all of the services are expected to get a piece of the action, if for no other reason than to keep the peace between them. The need to involve all of the services and the lack of coordination among them has made

it more difficult for the military to perform successfully.

In addition to the strong interservice rivalry (between services), much **intraservice rivalry** (within a service) exists as well. Within the air force, for example, the Strategic Air Command (responsible for nuclear forces), Tactical Air Command (conventional bomber and fighter forces), and Military Airlift Command (movers of military personnel and equipment) have been responsible for different but mutually supporting missions.[26] However, each command sees the others as rivals for limited resources available within the air force. This is reinforced by the particular subcultures within each of the commands, with which individual soldiers tend to identify strongly. Also, as with the State Department, **a pecking order of prestige** exists within the services as well. For example, because the aircraft carrier is considered the mainstay of the U.S. Navy, aviators are more revered than surface sailors and submariners.[27]

This intraservice rivalry has important implications for America's ability to conduct warfare successfully. During the early stages of the Vietnam War under President John F. Kennedy, for example, most of the 18,000 troops sent were **U.S. Army Special Forces, or Green Berets**. During the early 1960s, Green Berets were specially trained to perform counterinsurgency operations. These operations required certain political, economic, and cultural skills (such as language training), in addition to military skills, to help the population defend itself.[28] However, once the war became Americanized, more and more conventionally trained soldiers became involved, pushing counterinsurgency into the background. This was reinforced by the subculture that dominated the army. Although Green Berets are held in high regard for their prowess, they are also considered the service's deviants or "ugly ducklings." Green Berets are not trained to do things the conventional army way; their mission is not to mass concentrations of firepower through reliance on the latest technological weapons. Although they are part of the army, they are not trained to think or act as typical army soldiers. Therefore, as the war became Americanized, army leaders operating within the dominant subculture pushed the Green Berets to more peripheral roles, such as helping local Indochinese who were off the beaten path in mountain or border regions. The conventional army, instead, came to rely on the helicopter and the air cavalry, who quickly were able to move personnel and equipment in support of "search and destroy" operations.[29]

The rivalry between, and within, the services continues. But there also appears to be a new military emphasis on **"jointness,"** in part because the military must operate in a world of diminishing resources. This may be especially the case at the operational level with stronger unified commands and a stronger Chairman of the JCS providing military advice. The military subculture also may be incorporating more of a joint orientation, especially at the more senior levels. All senior officers are now expected to complete at least two years of "joint duty"; those who get the opportunity to go to the war colleges (and rise to the top) often attend a war college of another service; and the "joint staff" of the JCS is now considered a significant duty and an important stepping stone to career advancement.

Problems of Information. Beyond the difficulty of communicating within such an enormous bureaucracy, other information problems plague the military. The rise of bureaucracy and preoccupations with managerialism, maximizing control and procurement, and careerism have combined to produce *two information patterns* within the military since the cold war. The first is a heavy reliance on obtaining measurable indicators of military capabilities and operations, de-emphasizing the more intangible or human dimensions of warfare. Second is a tendency to inflate or deflate the information in accordance with service interests. Two examples will illustrate these points.

Every year the president requests funds for **the military budget** from Congress. The president and the military must justify their regular request for last year's amount and any annual percentage increase (which represents billions of dollars). This was traditionally done by having high-level military officers testify before Congress with charts and figures that

Soviet forces were growing larger and more threatening relative to American forces. The military undertook this ritual each year to gain political support, appealing as much to the emotions of Americans (in terms of patriotism and fear of communism) as to their intellect.[30] It is important to point out that this tendency to rely on quantitative data and to inflate threats to national security often involves the civilian leadership too, including the president of the United States. In fact, since World War II, the military has learned from its civilian counterparts, becoming more politically astute in protecting and promoting its perceived interests.

During the height of the cold war the military had little trouble in securing domestic support for its requests. However, with the Vietnam War and, especially, with the collapse of the Soviet Union, large and growing military budgets were threatened for the first time since the 1950s. Some downsizing and American cuts have taken place. However, the military success of the Persian Gulf War appears to have undercut some of the political momentum behind those advocating more substantial cuts and military reform in a post–cold war global environment.

Another example of difficulties with information comes from the American experience in Vietnam. Under General Westmoreland and Secretary of Defense McNamara, **body counts** became the ultimate "objective" indicator of how well or poorly the United States was performing in the war. Thus, if enemy body counts went up, this was used as an indication to the Department of Defense and the country that the United States was winning. This ignored other relevant information and failed to analyze it in terms of the larger context or environment. Nonetheless, the military and civilian leadership wanted body counts, and body counts they got. After a firefight it was expected that the American soldier on the ground would seek out those who were killed and then report the body count up the chain of command. From the soldiers' perspective, estimates from a distance were much safer than risking ambush to get specific body counts. Officers learned to err on the side of higher body counts to please their superiors and advance their careers. All of this resulted in the overreporting of enemy killed-in-action figures.

While incentives were built into the military's reporting system to inflate enemy body counts, there were also incentives to deflate the number of North Vietnamese Army (NVA) troops coming down the Ho Chi Minh trail into South Vietnam. Political battles were fought between the Central Intelligence Agency (CIA) and the military over the **order of battle**—that is, the size of enemy forces in South Vietnam. CIA estimates were much higher than the military's throughout 1967; the CIA also argued that NVA forces were growing while the military argued that troop infiltration from the north had stabilized. The military won the political fight in Washington, but historical hindsight supports the CIA position.

Fifteen years later, the television program "60 Minutes" charged **General Westmoreland** and the military leadership of the Military Assistance Command in Vietnam (MACV) with knowingly deflating and covering up evidence of larger North Vietnamese troop infiltration southward. Westmoreland sued CBS, and after a prolonged legal process and trial the parties settled out of court. The information disclosed during the trial revealed that CBS's cover-up charge was correct but they had unjustly accused Westmoreland as the highest superior responsible. In fact, the evidence demonstrated that, in addition to Westmoreland, the Joint Chiefs of Staff and the civilian leadership, including President Johnson, were aware of the accuracy of the larger enemy numbers.[31] They simply found the conservative estimates more politically appealing for boosting public optimism and combating the antiwar demonstrations that were increasing on the home front. Thus, the reporting system from the ground to the military and civilian leadership in Washington reinforced overreporting of enemy body counts and underreporting of enemy forces, suggesting a false optimism to the American people that there was "light at the end of the tunnel."

Duplication and Overlapping Activities. Given the size, autonomy, and competition between the services, considerable duplication and overlap of activities have resulted. Most Americans believe that the U.S. military has one air force. It is true that there is one military service referred to as the air force. But, in fact, the U.S. military has at least four air forces: the air force itself; the army air force which maintains more aircraft than the air force, consisting primarily of helicopters to support its land mission; the naval air arm, involving a large carrier air force to defend the navy fleet and undertake air strikes; and the marine air force to support its own mission. In Vietnam, each of the services flew its own sorties (air missions) against the enemy, often with little coordination between the services.

Why does each service have its own air force and fly its own missions? The bureaucratic structure and service subcultures prevent a well-coordinated and unified military that works together, despite the existence of the unified commands. The absence of dependable support from the other services, such as the air force in the case of air support, has forced each service to fend for itself, promoting duplication. Some duplication may be helpful to ensure the success of a mission, but the military services are so decentralized and autonomous that excessive duplication is the norm.

The **air war in Vietnam**, for example, was more complex than this, because President Johnson and his foreign policy advisers controlled the air war over North Vietnam while the services ran their own air wars in the South. Furthermore, the CIA maintained its own air force in support of its covert missions. Thus, the United States not only controlled the skies over Indochina, but fought numerous air wars at the same time. In fact, the best way to understand the Americanization of the war in Vietnam is not as a unified military effort under a single commander, but as a number of different wars fought by different components of the U.S. government.

Another example of duplication is America's strategic nuclear forces, where a **nuclear triad** is maintained. The United States has had three ways to deliver nuclear warheads on Soviet territory since the 1960s: intercontinental ballistic missiles (ICBMs), from land to land; submarine-launched ballistic missiles (SLBMs), from sea to land; and bombers, from air to land. Although Secretary of Defense McNamara concluded during the 1960s that it would take only roughly 200 one-megaton warheads to destroy the Soviet Union as a functioning society, the U.S. military has maintained thousands of nuclear warheads for over thirty years, long before the Soviet nuclear buildup achieved rough parity with the United States in the late 1960s.

Why? A number of reasons have been offered: developing enough forces to retaliate after a Soviet attack, overcoming possible faulty intelligence on the Soviet military, and overselling the threat of Soviet nuclear forces. But part of the explanation is also bureaucratic and organizational. Once the civilian leadership became committed during the 1950s to developing nuclear forces to deter Soviet expansion, each service attempted to carve out a nuclear role for itself. Thus, by the 1960s, the air force became responsible for strategic bombers and ICBMs while the navy was responsible for SLBMs. The army's nuclear role was limited to theater nuclear weapons and efforts to develop an antiballistic missile (ABM) force—which eventually became a vital component of the **Strategic Defense Initiative (SDI)** program begun by President Ronald Reagan. Each service attempted to gain as much control of the strategic nuclear mission as possible and each constantly pushed for increases in the size and technological sophistication of their strategic forces (such as improvements in warhead accuracy and multiple independently targeted reentry vehicles, known as MIRVs). This bureaucratic drive for control and procurement among the services contributed to the development of the triad and the tremendous growth of destructive power in America's nuclear arsenal, intensifying rather than stabilizing the nuclear arms competition between the United States and the Soviet Union.

Waste and Inefficiency. Most Americans are raised to be distrustful of large bureaucracies, which they believe are wasteful and inefficient. There is enough truth in this claim to nourish this unfavorable stereotype of large bureaucracies. The largest American bureaucracy is the military establishment. Thus, it is not surprising to find a large amount of waste and inefficiency within the military.

Nowhere is waste more visible than in the **weapons procurement process**. The Department of Defense contracts with private industry to produce the weapons and equipment agreed to by the Congress and the president in the budget. The defense contract process is supervised by the Office of the Secretary of Defense and the civilian offices of the individual services to ensure that private competition, quality production, and fair prices are maintained. However, the weapons acquisition process has rarely, if ever, operated according to this ideal. Instead, during the 1950s and 1960s, a time of tremendous expansion of the military's bureaucracy and budget, a network of relationships developed among the military, civilians within DOD, members of Congress, and private industry (supported by much of the scientific community). In fact, a revolving door situation has developed among these institutions in which, for example, retired military officers are hired by defense industry, and defense industry executives or Armed Services Committee staffers are appointed to positions within the Office of the Secretary of Defense. Everybody benefits: the services receive money from Congress to procure the weapons they want; members of Congress see military spending and defense industry money create jobs for their constituents back home; corporate executives expand their business activities and make nice profits in defense production; and civilians in DOD wield power over the policy of containment (and deterrence) by overseeing the largest peacetime buildup in American history.[32] Although there was never enough money to please everybody involved, it was always plentiful because the military was the favored institution within the U.S. government. During the 1950s, over half of the budget of the government of the United States went to one department—the Department of Defense.

For over forty years, military growth and production in the name of national security and American patriotism has been a major emphasis within the government and society. Consequently, little incentive has been given to produce an efficient and cost-effective budgetary and weapons acquisition process. **High prices** and **cost overruns** have become the norm. Prices and cost overruns have escalated since the 1950s as DOD has become increasingly dependent on a small core of private corporations engaged predominantly in defense production, inflation has increased, and weapons have become more technologically sophisticated. Private industry bids are rarely competitive (often involving only one or two companies) and are often artificially low in estimated cost to the government to maximize the chances of securing contracts. The military has contributed to the situation through "goldplating," demanding that every type of technological gadgetry be added to its weapons systems. The net result is that unless the government cancels a project, an unlikely prospect, costs are commonly at least 50 percent higher than the original projection.

These cost-plus factors are most noticeable in "big-ticket" military items, such as bombers, fighters, missiles, aircraft carriers and other large surface ships, submarines, and tanks. For example, an F-15 fighter aircraft costs over $50 million and an Aegis guided-missile cruiser runs $1.25 billion apiece. Incredibly high costs involve not only big-ticket items, but almost all military purchases. Simple spare parts, for example, have been sold by the defense industry, and purchased by the military, for absurdly high prices. Hammers that could be purchased at a local hardware store for $18 were sold to the military for $450 each; standard 39-cent washers were purchased for $387 apiece; 13-cent washers were purchased for as high as $2,043 each. Also, the military doesn't buy a few items at a time, but hundreds, thousands, and millions. Probably the most notorious of all the military costs were coffeemakers for warplanes that the military purchased for $3,046 each. In an effort to defend its exorbitant cost, the company spokesman insisted that "what you have here is a very complicated device. . . . There are some people who would rather go down to the supermarket and buy these items for an airplane. But I wouldn't particularly want to be on that airplane."[33]

These high costs and constant overruns are not simply a function of economics and politics, but **corruption** as well. This has been pervasive in the military procurement establishment for decades and

well known to insiders. Yet, the general public has been kept in the dark because few insiders speak up publicly, and those who become "whistleblowers" are harshly treated by the individuals and organizations involved with the military establishment (usually, careers are destroyed and their legitimacy as individuals lost).[34] Besides, for twenty years there was an anticommunist consensus throughout the country, and it was considered unpatriotic to question the American military. In recent years, however, the media and the public have become more receptive to reports and studies detailing waste and corruption within the military at the taxpayers' expense. The U.S. Justice Department, in fact, has finally taken legal action against military fraud and corruption (see **essay 8.2**).

Considerable **waste** pervades the military establishment. Estimates of waste and corruption within the military and its procurement process range from a low of $50 billion per year to over $100 billion a year. Robert Costello, an under secretary of defense for acquisition in the Reagan administration, publicly stated that up to 30 percent of the $150 billion spent yearly by the Pentagon on procurement is squandered.[35] Although such information about Pentagon spending can be pieced together from the public record, the costs of many of its most expensive weapons, such as the B-2 Stealth bomber, remain hidden from public view in the Department of Defense's "black budget" that was originally designed to secretly fund the covert activities of the intelligence community.[36]

Unfortunately, it is not only a question of incredible waste, but of **military readiness and performance**. Weapons have become so expensive that fewer items, such as tanks or fighters, can be afforded by the military. Not only have the numbers of many important weapons declined over time, they have become so technologically sophisticated that they require much more expertise to use, tend to be less reliable, especially in combat, and require more time and skill to repair. As weapons become more sophisticated, the likelihood of flaws in design and production increases. Therefore, becoming dependent on fewer and

ESSAY 8.2
THE PENTAGON PROCUREMENT SCANDAL

During the late 1980s, the U.S. Department of Justice investigated hundreds of procurement fraud and bribery cases in which members of the defense industry had paid Pentagon insiders for documents, information, and competitive bidding advantages. Offices of the country's largest defense contractors and high-ranking former employees of the Department of Defense have been raided by the Federal Bureau of Investigation. Indictments have been handed down and dozens of individuals and over twenty-five companies—including Boeing Company, GTE Corporation, General Electric, General Motors, Northrup Corporation, and Raytheon—have pleaded guilty. For example, Unisys Corporation, the country's third-largest computer manufacturer, agreed in 1991 to pay $190 million to settle charges ranging from bribery and false claims to illegal campaign contributions and fraud. These cases represent the government's greatest effort thus far to crack down on fraud and corruption in the defense procurement process. Unfortunately, fraud and corruption have been endemic in defense procurement since the initial growth of the modern military establishment during the 1940s and 1950s.

The **procurement of military airlift transport** during the 1980s typifies this practice. The competition between the Boeing and Lockheed Corporations, to the extent that competition is evident, demonstrates the mutually supportive relationships that develop between defense participants regardless of ethics or the law. In this case, the General Accounting Office (GAO), the investigative arm of the U.S. Congress, found that "an extensive and cooperative effort was made by officials of the air force, the Office of the Secretary of Defense, the Lockheed Corporation, and several other defense contractors and subcontractors during the period May 14, 1982, through July 22, 1982, to influence members of the House of Representatives, and later the House and Senate conferees, on the proposed $10 billion procurement of the C-5B aircraft."[A]

The GAO described a massive **lobbying** campaign that included over 500 congressional visits "by air force, army, and marine officials, other congressmen, Lockheed Corporation officials, and representatives of other companies that had an interest in the C-5B program or did business with Lockheed or the Department of Defense."[B] The purpose of the campaign was to overturn an earlier Senate decision to purchase civilian 747s from Boeing (after a Boeing lobbying campaign led by Senator "Scoop" Jackson from Washington had successfully reversed an earlier decision to purchase McDonnell Douglas C-17s). The Lockheed lobbying campaign in the Senate was led by Senator Sam Nunn from Georgia. A computerized "action plan" was maintained by Lockheed, listing, for example, businesses in 260 of the 435 House districts that would lose money and jobs if Boeing, rather than Lockheed, was awarded the contract.

High-level officials within the Department of Defense acknowledged that actions to promote the C-5B program were similar to those taken for other large weapons programs. One senior air force official, in fact, commented that the lobbying effort was "democracy in action."[C] The problem is that this type of corrupt behavior is not unusual because most of it remains hidden, the laws are lax, investigations rarely produce indictments, and penalties are extremely light upon conviction. Therefore, few incentives exist to change the defense procurement process, especially if it stays off the public agenda.

In the case of the C-5B aircraft procurement program, private industry lobbying was legal. It was the "air force and OSD officials [who] violated Federal anti-lobbying laws by expending appropriated funds in the aiding and supporting of contractors to perform lobbying activities."[D] Yet, the maximum penalty is a fine of not more than $500 or imprisonment for not more than one year, or both, and re-

---

A. U.S. Congress, General Accounting Office, *Improper Lobbying Activities by the Department of Defense on the Proposed Procurement of the C-5B Aircraft* (September 29, 1982), p. 1.

B. Ibid., p. 10.
C. Ibid., p. 17.
D. Ibid., p. 23.

moval from office after notice and a hearing. According to the General Accounting Office, "no one has ever been successfully prosecuted under this statute."[E] Furthermore, federal contract law allowed Lockheed Corporation to be reimbursed by the U.S. government, and the American taxpayer, for its legitimate lobbying costs—in this case over $496,000 (Boeing was reimbursed for lobbying costs of $22,000).

Consider the severity of the penalties in the Justice Department cases. GTE Corporation agreed to plead guilty to one felony count involving the illegal use of Pentagon planning documents. In return, GTE had to undergo a 14-item plan of internal improvements to avoid suspension from U.S. government contracts and pay the government $580,000 for the cost of the inquiry. Boeing Company, with more than $3 billion in military contracts, pleaded guilty to two felony counts and agreed to pay a fine of $5 million—an amount that the federal judge overseeing the case questioned as being too light for a "very serious breach of security." Northrup Corporation, the manufacturer of the B-2 Stealth

bomber, pleaded guilty to 34 counts involving failing to test parts for the air force's cruise missile and the marine corps' Harrier jet and was fined the maximum of $500,000 for each count for a total fine of $17 million. In return the Justice Department agreed to drop 141 other counts against Northrup and drop charges against two Northrup executives. Typically, however, the Department of Defense voluntarily pays the fines for the defense industry as well. And although members of Congress were involved, they were beyond investigation and prosecution because of "political" immunity.

Fraud and corruption in defense procurement demonstrates the difficulty of reconciling democratic practice and accountability with the existence of a large military establishment. However, these types of incestuous and corrupt governmental-private relationships are not unique to the military and the defense procurement process. A number of other scandals came to the public's attention since the early 1980s concerning the government and the private market. Corruption and scandal may be found wherever money, power, and prestige are highly valued, and these are certainly important attributes for the people and organizations involved in the military establishment and the U.S. defense process.

E. Ibid., p. 19.

SOURCES: James Coates and Michael Kilian, *Heavy Losses: The Dangerous Decline of American Defense* (New York: Penguin, 1985), chapter 7; Steven Engelberg, "Boeing Expected to Plead Guilty in Pentagon Case," *New York Times* (November 7, 1989): 1, 30; Molly Moore and Robert P. Howe, "Boeing Co. Is Guilty in Defense Case," *The Washington Post* (November 14, 1987): A1, A4; "Payoffs at the Pentagon," *Newsweek* (June 27, 1988): 20–22; Eric Schmitt, "Guilty Plea By Unisys Is Expected," *New York Times* (September 6, 1991): C1, C4; Richard W. Stevenson, "Northrup Inquiries Ended After Guilty Plea," *New York Times* (March 1, 1990): C2; Richard W. Stevenson, "Many Caught but Few Punished for U.S. Military Contract Fraud," *New York Times* (November 12, 1990): A1, A13; and U.S., Congress, General Accounting Office, *Improper Lobbying Activities by the Department of Defense on the Proposed Procurement of the C-5B Aircraft* (September 29, 1982).

---

more technologically sophisticated weapons, although ones with greater potential to deliver firepower, has, in some ways, reduced the military's overall combat readiness and effectiveness.[37]

Weapons are developed and deployed with great fanfare by the military and defense industry, but they often promise much more than the weapon can deliver. The F-16 and F-18 are promoted as fighters that can travel faster than Mach 2 (1200 miles per hour), but they quickly run out of gas at

such speeds so that capability is of little consequence in most combat situations. Problems produced by a technologically sophisticated weapon, some of which threaten lives beyond the normal risks of war, are well known to the soldier in the field. The antitank TOW missile has great accuracy, but requires the soldier to remain immobile until the missile hits the tank hundreds of yards away. The Bradley Fighting Vehicle was developed for the army to rapidly move infantry around the battlefield while providing protection from enemy fire, but initial tests demonstrated it easily exploded on contact, killing everyone inside.[38]

Critics say some of these weapons should never have been built or should have been redesigned according to realistic performance and reliability standards, and with the safety of the soldier in mind. Supporters emphasize the genuine technical difficulties of weapons development. However, once a decision is made, usually years before a weapon is actually produced for deployment by the military, the tendency is to turn a blind eye to any and all criticism and proceed full speed ahead. In the case of the Bradley Fighting Vehicle, civilian and military personnel within the Department of Defense, along with the defense contractor, went so far as to rig the tests to cover up fatal design flaws—which caused a public furor once it was exposed and led to the development of an improved "A2 Bradley model."[39]

When weapons systems do not perform as promised and American soldiers die in the process, the *official military position is always human error*—that individuals screwed up. For example, in 1987 in the Persian Gulf, the USS *Stark's* radar was unable to see an incoming Iraqi missile that struck the *Stark,* killing 37 people. A year later, the USS *Vincennes,* with the most sophisticated Aegis air-defense system available, shot down an Iranian civilian jetliner which it mistook for an F-14 warplane, killing 290 innocent people. In both cases, the official navy report cited human error as the culprit. However, the USS *Stark* was badly designed and its sophisticated electronic surveillance equipment failed to see the Iraqi missile approaching. (It was finally spotted by a sailor on board just before it hit.) The sophisticated command and communications center of the USS *Vincennes* not only was unable to distinguish between a civilian jetliner and a fighter, but also was extremely complex and difficult to operate, contributing to the likelihood of human error during a time of great stress, such as combat.[40] However, if the military takes an official position other than "human error," both the military and the defense industry are potentially subject to criticism and libel, threatening the cozy network of relationships that have developed in the military procurement process.

At the same time, the American public needs to have a more realistic understanding that wars are—by definition—times of great danger, when there is much confusion and people suffer—what the great Prussian military strategist Carl Von Clausewitz referred to as "the fog of war."[41]

Decline in Leadership and Morale. As the military has become increasingly bureaucratic and managerial, strong leadership, especially on the field of battle, and the morale of the combat soldier declined. It wasn't until the **military's experience with the Vietnam War** that the problem of leadership and morale truly hit home. During the early phases of American military intervention, from the early 1960s to 1968, morale was quite high. The common assumption among the troops and officers, as well as the civilian leadership and most Americans, was that a strong military response would successfully keep South Vietnam an independent noncommunist ally of the United States. This optimism and high morale were shattered as the American public lost confidence following the Tet Offensive of 1968.

When it became clear that the United States was not winning the war, morale and leadership within the military suffered, especially among foot soldiers. Failure to succeed was the major cause for declining morale, but the bureaucratic structure and procedures of the military reinforced this trend. For example, within the U.S. Army, the combat **tours of duty** for officers were six months, but one year for enlisted personnel. This created many problems in the field. To grasp this, it is important to understand that the American soldier, trained for conventional war, was transported within days from the States into an alien world where the war was unconventional and the people were from a different culture. A soldier who became a "grunt" on the ground quickly learned that the army handbook had not prepared him for Vietnam. Hence, new recruits "in country" had to learn what Vietnam was all about, adapt, and acquire new skills while on the march. Within a few months, they became hardened soldiers who had learned how to fight the enemy and stay alive. Unfortunately, the hardened soldier in the field was often commanded by officers who were completely new to Vietnam and tried to command by the book.

From a bureaucratic perspective, the six-month command tour allowed most of the officer corps to "punch their ticket" and acquire combat experience to promote their careers before serving out their one-year tour in a staff position. To a youthful, largely draftee army, increasingly with new, inexperienced officers and fated to spend a full year in the bush unless wounded or killed, the practice often produced internal conflict among the troops. This situation spread in the late 1960s as the resistance to the war built at home and American troops were slowly withdrawn from the war as part of the "Vietnamization" process. Where those officers proved inept or uncaring, dissatisfaction spread and some soldiers engaged in minor mutinies and "fragging" incidents—assassination attempts against the officer in command.

Much of the bitterness that developed among combat soldiers was reinforced by the fact that less than half of American troops in Vietnam were involved in combat—the vast majority of military personnel were in support roles (logistics and administration). Of the half million troops stationed in Vietnam at the height of the war, no more than 200,000 were actually engaged in combat.[42] This was a function of the military's administrative orientation and its effort to Americanize the war by building military bases, supporting the latest technological weapons, and providing American personnel with the best shelter, food, clothing, and rest and recreation available. Much can be said for efforts to make overseas combat situations as endurable as possible, but this goal requires large numbers of personnel to support the soldier in the field.

The problems of leadership and morale were reinforced by events at home. With the installation of the draft and availability of deferments to college students, enlisted personnel in the army became disproportionately working class and minority. The unrepresentative nature of the military, especially for the infantryman in the field, could be embittering. Black soldiers, in particular, had a hard time reconciling fighting for the "white man's country" abroad, while their brothers were fighting for black civil rights at home. Not surprisingly, the military experienced much racial strife. Morale sank so low that drug use among American personnel became common, especially the use of marijuana and heroin which were readily available in the "Golden Triangle" of Indochina (where Burma, Laos, and Thailand meet). Efforts by the military to control drug use often added to the conflicts over authority.

To add insult to injury, American soldiers returned from Vietnam in the late 1960s and early 1970s to find their country in domestic turmoil. After their tour of duty, they immediately were flown back to the States. Unfortunately, after experiencing the reality of war, many were poorly prepared and received little guidance from the military for coping with **reentry into American society** and civilian life given their stressful combat roles. Their "homecoming" was often quite a shock, for they tended to receive two responses from their fellow citizens: the antiwar movement demonstrated against them (for they represented the military), and they were ignored by the mass public, who preferred to forget about a war that America was losing. There were no homecoming parades in that war. Uniforms quickly were discarded, and the **Vietnam veterans** had to deal on their own with the war and personal problems they might have developed. Little support for the Vietnam veteran was forthcoming from society (even among existing veterans' organizations, whose membership was overwhelmingly composed of World War II and Korean War veterans) or the government (including the military and the Veterans Administration).[43]

The negative legacy of Vietnam still lingers for the U.S. military. It required a decade for Americans to begin to cope with the experience of Vietnam. Yet, the completion of the **Vietnam War Memorial** in Washington, D.C., helped to heal some of the wounds of war, especially for the Vietnam veteran. President Reagan's commitment to a large defense and praise for the American military rebuilt morale within the military, reinforced by the successful military outcomes in Grenada and Panama. Most importantly, the military triumph in the Persian Gulf War and the "welcome home" to the troops contributed to the restoration of morale within the military and throughout American society.

Rise of a Volunteer and Diverse Military. Not only has the military become "civilianized" by bureaucratic development over time, it has also become an all-volunteer and much more diverse military with time. The peacetime draft was abolished in 1973 in reaction to the Vietnam War, and polls indicate that most Americans remain strongly opposed to a draft. However, the all-volunteer force presents new problems for the U.S. military and its foreign policy.

The military, particularly the army, has had difficulty recruiting sufficient numbers of skilled individuals. **Recruitment** tends to be less a problem when unemployment increases, for the military becomes a more attractive option for the unemployed. The military has made a concerted effort to attract recruits through a major marketing campaign, especially concentrating on television advertising. However, the recruitment emphasis since Vietnam has not marketed the warrior aspect of military service (with the possible exception of the marines), but has concentrated on the excitement of visiting exotic lands and acquiring technical skills that will be helpful in obtaining jobs in the civilian economy.

The rise of a volunteer, civilianized military has resulted in a debate over the quality of the armed services, especially in the army. Some observers argue that the caliber of the military soldier is, on the whole, higher today than ever before. They point to overall higher levels of education to illustrate their position. However, other observers argue that the skill potential of new recruits has increased little, an especially troubling situation in an era of increasingly sophisticated weaponry. Furthermore, retention rates (that is, reenlistments) have declined, providing little continuity in weapons systems skills. Consequently, the military's readiness and performance has been hindered as the sophistication of weaponry has increased over time.

Another issue which has been raised is the overall **diversity** and **representativeness** of the U.S. military in a democratic society. With the all-volunteer military, fewer whites and fewer people from the middle and upper classes are serving in the military.

In many ways the military has become a vehicle for promoting opportunity to individuals from more disadvantaged backgrounds. However, the fairness of a situation in which the least advantaged should bear the burden of defending all Americans has raised debate about the value of a national draft of young Americans and national service (military and civilian) for their country. Other important questions also have been raised about the proper role of women, the situation that families faced in the Persian Gulf conflict, and about gays in the military (see **essay 8.3**).

This also raises a related issue: the decline of a knowledgeable public when it comes to the military and use of force. The military increasingly relies on Americans least likely to participate politically, while those who tend to participate in politics come from segments of society with little experience in the military.[44] In other words, important public policy decisions over defense spending and military force are increasingly made and influenced by people with little experience and knowledge of the military or war. There are no easy answers to these issues, but having a universal service requirement versus an all-volunteer military clearly has implications for the composition of the military, its conduct on the field, and the future of U.S. foreign policy.

Value of Military Advice. The final pattern in DOD's military behavior is, more often than not, that the civilian leadership, including the secretary of defense and the president, are skeptical of military advice. They realize that the military leadership, including the Joint Chiefs of Staff, identify and speak for the interests of their individual services. The Chairman of the JCS tends to have the greatest credibility, for he is the only high-ranking military officer who does not represent individual service interests. In the final analysis, the value of military advice will depend on personalities and working relationships. While President Nixon tended to be skeptical of military advice, for example, Presidents Reagan and Bush tended to be receptive.[45]

The credibility of military advice appears to have improved since Goldwater-Nichols and the prominence of the Chairman of the JCS as military

ESSAY 8.3
THE NEW FACE OF THE AMERICAN MILITARY:
MINORITIES, WOMEN, FAMILIES, AND GAYS

The last few decades has witnessed a considerable change in the make-up of the American military. According to Martin Binkin, "Once peopled mostly by young, unmarried, white males, today's armed forces are composed of unprecedented proportions of minorities, women, married couples, and single parents and are dependent more than ever before on part-time reservists." Such changes parallel other changes in the public sector of society, but special problems may exist given the military subculture and the unique function of the military to engage in war.

Minorities, especially **African Americans**, have succeeded in joining all areas of the American armed forces since the 1970s. It wasn't until the 1940s under President Truman that the military became integrated. The debates were rancorous, such as the impact on military cohesion and combat effectiveness, and the transition was difficult over the years, but for the most part blacks have become accepted members of the American military. In fact, African-Americans currently comprise about 20 percent of the U.S. military—with over 30 percent in the army—and represented 25 percent of the troops who served in the Gulf War. In addition, African-Americans are more likely than whites to make a life-long career out of the military. Moreover, advancement opportunities are opening up for African-American men in the military, as seen with the rise of General Colin Powell to Chairman of the Joint Chiefs of Staff. Nevertheless, a number of sensitive issues have been raised about "economic" conscription, the likelihood of a disproportionate amount of black casualties in a future war, and inter-racial strife within the military—all of which were evident during the Vietnam War, but were avoided by the overwhelming speed and triumph of the Persian Gulf war.

Women now make up 14 percent of the armed forces—over 200,000 soldiers (as opposed to 2 percent in the early 1970s). According to Binkin, "The transition, however, has been anything but smooth. The armed services, traditionally *one of the most male-dominated institutions in American society*, has had great difficulty adapting to the wider role of women." Major debates have surfaced over the role of women within the military, including basic training, accommodations, and involvement in combat. When the U.S. military first opened its doors to women on active duty, women were limited to "non-combat" positions. However, women have increasingly been allowed in combat positions, as the definition of what is combat has become blurred, and in combat environments, as occurred in the Persian Gulf War.

Another major issue of increasing concern involves the question of **sexual harassment**. Incidents, like the 1991 Tailhook scandal involving a convention of naval aviators where women were often abused and in some cases raped, have become increasingly evident and public over the years. What Gregory Vistica, in *Fall from Glory,* says about the Navy is true about the military in general: "Sexual abuse is difficult to root out because it is now so embedded in the Navy's day-to-day culture. Over the last 30 years, an attitude of contempt toward women has become routine not only below decks but also in the officers' quarters." And with more issues of sexual harassment becoming public, advancement within the military has been hampered and careers have been ruined—for both men and women. This has become a huge and very difficult issue to address, where even the "top brass" are increasingly concerned about the repercussions of sexual harassment.

Gays in the military also has become a prominent issue. Homosexuals (including lesbians) have always been a part of the military throughout history. But only recently has the issue of gays and lesbians become public. And given the "male, macho, and homophobic" orientation of the prevailing subculture within the military, this issue has been as controversial and emotional as the issue of the proper role of women in the military—maybe even more so. President Clinton's effort to legitimize the role of gays in the military shortly after he took office created a huge furor within the military and throughout American society, which severely damaged his public prestige and destroyed his "honeymoon" early on in his administration, making it much more difficult for him to govern.

One issue that has not received much attention given the changing nature of the military, is the issue of the **family** within the military. Over 100,000 members of the military are "single parents" (including about 40,000 men) and "dual service parents" (where both the father and mother are in military active or reserve units). This has been a growing trend, with over 50 percent of its enlisted members married (in 1971 only 20% were married). This has produced inevitable problems about assignment and deployment, as well as who'll take care of the kids during a time of emergency or war?

Clearly, the changing nature of the military, of "combat," and of American society, have produced a transformation in the face of the American armed forces. Issues about minorities, women, gays, families, and more are here to stay and may never be that resolvable. Many of them go to the heart of the military as an institution and to its unique function about preparing people to fight and possibly die. Nevertheless, as Binkin concludes,

> With the quick end to Operation Desert Storm, these issues failed to develop into real problems. Understandably, the inclination now is to ignore them. But left unattended, they will return to haunt future military conflicts. Their unpredictable, but potentially damaging, military, political, and social implications argue strongly that they be resolved now, while memories are still fresh and while a fundamental rethinking of the post–cold war U.S. military establishment is already under way.

SOURCES: Martin Binkin, "The New Face of the American Military," *The Brookings Review* (Summer 1991): 7–13; John Boswell, "Battle-Worn: Gays in the Military, 300 B.C.," *New Republic* (May 10, 1993): 15–18; Carol Burke, "Dames at Sea," *New Republic* (August 17 and 24, 1992): 16–20; "Gays and the Military," *Newsweek* (February 1, 1993): 52–58; Gerald J. Garvey and John J. DiIulio, Jr., "Only Connect? Cohesion vs. Combat Effectiveness," *New Republic* (April 26, 193): 18–21; Stephanie Gutmann, "Sex and the Soldier," *New Republic* (February 24, 1997): 18–22; Charles C. Moskos and John Sibley Butler, *All That We Can Be: Black Leadership and Racial Integration the Army Way* (New York: Basic Books, 1996); "Our Women in the Desert," *Newsweek* (September 10, 1990): 22–25; Randy Shilts, *Conduct Unbecoming: Lesbians and Gays in the U.S. Military,* (New York: St. Martin's Press, 1993); Gregory Vistica, *Fall from Glory* (New York: Simon and Schuster, 1995).

adviser to the last three presidents. President Clinton, despite (maybe because of) his non-military credentials and early controversy involving gays in the military, actually has had a close working relationship with the military, especially through the Chairman of the JCS.

The common stereotype portrays the military as always **recommending the use of force** to deal with international crises. In fact, studies of military advice during crises suggest that the military tends to be reluctant to initiate the use of force. In *Soldiers, Statesmen, and Cold War Crises,* Richard Betts found the army to be the most cautious in recommending force (since it takes the brunt of the casualties), while the air force tends to be most optimistic about

force, especially the use of air power.[46] He also found that the military has its greatest impact on civilian leadership when military advice opposes the use of force (since this is the unexpected position), while it is least credible when it recommends force. The military may be eager to expand its capabilities through more sophisticated weaponry and more personnel, but it tends to be reluctant to put them at risk. However, once a decision to use force has been made, the military forcefully argues that civilians should stand aside and allow the military to do whatever is necessary to succeed, which may require escalation.

Through most of the cold war years, in fact, the *civilians were more hard-line* and quicker to recommend force and take a hard-line stance to impress military leaders, as occurred during the Vietnam War.[47] This trend has continued to the present and was evident during the Reagan administration, in which major internal battles ensued over the use of force. With regard to terrorism abroad, for example, Secretary of State George Shultz was the major advocate of a military response while Secretary of Defense Caspar Weinberger, representing the military, was reluctant to use force unless it had the full support of the American public. Concerning U.S. foreign policy toward Central America, Secretary of State Alexander Haig and later Assistant Secretary of State for Inter-American Affairs Elliott Abrams were vocal proponents of the threat and use of force, as opposed to the more skeptical position of Chairman of the JCS Admiral William Crowe.[48] Likewise in the Bush administration, Bob Woodward in *The Commanders* reports that President Bush and National Security Adviser Brent Scowcroft were the most vehement in support of a major military response to the Iraqi invasion of Kuwait and the need to take Saddam Hussein to the brink of war to compel his withdrawal, while Secretary of State James Baker and the Joint Chiefs of Staff, particularly Chairman Colin Powell, were much more cautious and supportive of the use of economic sanctions over the use of force.[49] Clearly, one of the major lessons learned by the military from the Vietnam War, especially within the army, is to avoid the use of troops unless there is strong and visible public backing.

This is not an overall flattering portrait of the U.S. military in operation. In no way does this description mean to suggest that members of the U.S. military are incapable and uncaring human beings. To the contrary, the evidence suggests that the military is made up of competent and able people. The military officers, for instance, that have studied in my graduate courses consistently have been among the most highly motivated and capable students. However, as these same officers have been the first to point out, the problems lie not with the individual but with the military institutions in which the individual lives and performs.[50] In other words, the bureaucratic structure and subcultures of the military often promote the kind of behavior that has hindered the military's ability to perform on the field of battle.

THE AMERICAN WAY OF WAR: MILITARY STRATEGY AND PERFORMANCE

. . . .

The result of the Department of Defense structure, the orientation of the military subculture, and the behavioral patterns discussed above, produces *a tremendous paradox:* the U.S. military has become a most powerful force over time, yet it is limited in what it is able to perform. The military primarily is organized and trained to fight nuclear and conventional wars—the American way of war—with only limited elements devoted to subconventional or "low-intensity" warfare. As discussed above, a general strategy of attrition reigns supreme. If one examines the military's record in warfare since the 1950s, the quality of its performance has been unimpressive, except for those few occasions involving a conventional war.

Throughout its history, the U.S. military has been organized and trained for classical **conventional warfare.** The great military strategists and wars that have influenced the U.S. military historically have come from Europe, the British military being the model for emulation. World War I and World War II, the greatest conventional military clashes in world history, demonstrated the need to organize and train for massive, general, conventional war and concentrated on a strategy of attrition to defeat the enemy. This was reinforced by **the Korean War,** where the U.S. militarily stopped the North Korean invasion of South Korea after the peninsula was divided following World War II. Although limited, it was the only traditional conventional war the United States has fought since World War II until the war in the Persian Gulf.

The atomic bombing of Hiroshima and Nagasaki did not change this strategy initially; nuclear weapons merely became a part of the general arsenal in support of the conventional strategy of attrition.

The development of nuclear deterrence theory, the increasing destructiveness of nuclear weapons, and advances in missile technology during the 1950s resulted in the military also being organized and trained for a new form of war, nuclear war. Since World War II, therefore, *the U.S. military has been prepared to fight two types of wars:* most importantly, a conventional war as well as a nuclear war.

For forty years, U.S. military plans have focused on conventional and nuclear war with the Soviet Union. This preparation was the foundation of the containment and the **deterrence strategy**, to stop Soviet expansionism through the threat and use of military force. They have presupposed a conventional war most likely occurring in central Europe and then in the Korean Peninsula in Asia. They have planned for a nuclear battle to be predominantly fought on the territories of the United States and the Soviet Union. Refinements have been made to these general strategies, such as a concern with limited nuclear war, limited conventional war, and the creation of a Rapid Deployment Force, not all directed solely at the Soviet Union. Nevertheless, the bulk of America's military has been organized, equipped, trained, and deployed to fight in a general conventional war, first and foremost, and then a nuclear war.

Historically, reliance on a conventionally trained military did not pose a problem for dealing with uprisings or guerrilla war. Such conflicts were not widespread and were easily subdued by sending American marines to restore stability in places like Nicaragua, as was often done during the early part of this century. However, beginning with World War II, in addition to the rise of the United States and the Soviet Union after the destruction of the European empires, there has been an explosion of nationalism, an increase in new states and nonstate actors, and a proliferation of weaponry throughout the globe. This has had two implications for warfare. First, third-world states have become better able to resist militarily the projection of great power military force abroad. Second, most of the actual conflicts throughout the world, such as civil wars, guerrilla wars, and terrorism, do not directly involve the great powers as the term **low-intensity conflict** implies

(the military refers to these military operations as "Military Operations Other Than War"—which clearly communicates their low priority nature). This has meant that use of conventional force has become less appropriate with time and has had greater difficulty succeeding. During the 1980s, for example, a 15,000-strong contra force supported by the United States was unable to dislodge militarily the Sandinista government in Nicaragua. This situation is not unique to the United States, but confronts all conventional military forces, as illustrated by the Soviet experience in Afghanistan.

The United States first faced this new environment in the Vietnam War. Most American leaders, and the public, operated under the assumption that the projection of American military force into Vietnam would quickly contain the enemy and stabilize the situation. Yet, the United States and the American military were poorly prepared for a war in which there were no front lines, where one couldn't distinguish between friend or foe, where a peasant by day could be a Viet Cong guerrilla by night, and where the enemy's will to resist was greater than the American will to win. Thus, a conventionally trained military was thrown into a most unconventional war. The military attempted to adapt its conventional strategy as the situation evolved, but even a half-million troops and $35 billion a year were not enough to defeat the enemy and obtain the objectives of the political leadership. Instead, the military and the United States suffered its first major defeat in war.

The **military lessons of Vietnam** have been hotly debated. Some have emphasized that, should war occur again, the U.S. military must emphasize the ability to deliver massive conventional force more quickly with greater freedom of action from the political leadership. Others have emphasized the need for military reform in order to have a more efficient and flexible military that can adapt to changing war environments and respond to the goals of the president of the United States.

On Strategy by Harry Summers, a retired colonel in the U.S. Army, was the first major analysis of American's military experience in Vietnam to be well received within the military.[51] Summers argued that the U.S. military mistakenly tried to adapt its strategy and tactics to fight a counterinsurgency war, when in fact the enemy was engaging predominantly in conventional combat by the mid-1960s. He argued the United States should have allowed the Army of the Republic of Vietnam (ARVN) to pursue counterinsurgency in South Vietnam while the U.S. military formed a conventional front along the demilitarized zone between North and South Vietnam (the DMZ) and, by invading Laos, extend it across Laos to the Thai border to prevent North Vietnamese infiltration into South Vietnam.

Beyond the difficulty of training the South Vietnamese Army in counterinsurgency warfare, for which the American military was ill-equipped, Summers' analysis has been severely criticized as misconstruing the nature of the Vietnam War. According to Major Andrew Krepinevich, in *The Army and Vietnam,* the enemy relied on an unconventional strategy until the latter years of the war. Despite tactical modifications, the U.S. military was ill-equipped and ill-trained for the war throughout both the "advisory" and intervention periods that lasted from 1954 to 1973. One quote is particularly telling:

> General Williams agreed that "if you really want to be cost-effective, you have to fight the war the way the VC [Vietcong] fought it. You have to fight it down in the muck and in the mud and at night, and on a day-to-day basis." Yet, the general told the correspondent, "that's not the American way, and you are not going to get the American soldier to fight that way."[52]

In *The Limits of Air Power,* Mark Clodfelter, an air force major, found that, although the United States dropped more bombs in Indochina than were dropped by all the allies during World War II, the conventional use of air power failed to deter the enemy.[53] From this perspective, the lesson of Vietnam is that unless the U.S. military acquires a real counterinsurgency and low-intensity military capability, it will continue to experience major problems when conflicts do not fit the conventional mold.

The Vietnam War, for the most part, has reinforced the bureaucratic structure and subculture of the military in support of a strategy of attrition—to overwhelm the enemy with a quick delivery of massive firepower—along with a new interest in force mobility. Hence, very little money, resources, and personnel have been used by the military to prepare for low-intensity conflicts given its low priority. The Kennedy administration tried to reorient the army to counterinsurgency warfare, but failed. The contemporary military does have some forces for counterinsurgency and low-intensity warfare: the Green Berets and the Delta Force in the army and the SEALS in the navy. However, they are few in number and usually play a support role to larger conventional missions. Symptomatic of this is that the U.S. military has trained the El Salvadoran Army during the 1980s to conduct the same kind of strategies and tactics for fighting their civil war that the ARVN was taught in Vietnam. This lack of low-intensity warfare capability has been quickly demonstrated when the military has been called upon to perform in unconventional military situations.

The U.S. military also has had difficulty performing well in more conventional conflicts. As General David Jones, former chairman of the Joint Chiefs of Staff, explained, the U.S. military always has been slow to get on track and perform well. Most Americans remember **World War II** to be a great military victory, and it was. But as General Jones points out, the key to American success was time and industrial production: time to get industry mobilized for war production and time to get the equipment and troops to the field. It took two years for the military to be organized and equipped to really damage and wear down the enemy.[54]

Although American society and government have been constantly mobilized for war since World War II, military performance, especially since the Vietnam War, has been often found lacking. As military strategist Edward Luttwak concluded in *The Pentagon and the Art of War:*

> Irrefutable facts overwhelm the patriotic impulse to overlook our failures in war—from Vietnam in its most varied and prolonged entirety; to the clumsy Mayaguez raid of 1975, in which forty-one died to save forty; to the Iran rescue attempt in

1980, which ended in bitter humiliation, with eight dead and none rescued; to the avoidable tragedy of Beirut, which took the lives of 241 Marines and other servicemen in October 1983; to the Grenada operation of the same month, in which the high heroism of the troops had to redeem gross failure of planning and command; to the Lebanon bombing raid of December 4, 1983, in which the Navy lost two costly aircraft, where others bombed day after day losing no aircraft at all.[55]

American military incompetence since the Vietnam War reached its peak during **the Grenada invasion** as described in **essay 8.4**, prompting military reforms such as the Goldwater-Nichols Act.

Knowledge of the actual performance of the U.S. military, however, largely has remained hidden from the American public. One of the factors that has contributed to this is the Pentagon's effort to control the information communicated through the media when American troops are engaged abroad in order to strengthen public support—the major lesson it learned from the Vietnam War (discussed in chapter 18 on the media and the communications process). A policy of **media censorship** by the government, in fact, has prevailed in war beginning with the Grenada invasion when President Reagan proclaimed it a great triumph regardless of the poor (and hidden) military performance on the ground. America's military performance, although often found wanting, recently has found greater success in the Panama invasion and the Persian Gulf War.

The December 1989 **invasion of Panama** was successful in overthrowing General Manuel Noriega—an inevitable outcome. Nevertheless, many problems existed with the invasion and Panama may have been an exceptional case. The United States military enjoyed extremely close proximity, with 12,000 troops stationed throughout the Panama Canal Zone, and began to plan for the operation as early as October. Furthermore, the military's Southern Command for the region was based in Panama City, the capital of Panama, and Americans were highly familiar with the country. Even with these ad-

vantages, the invasion force was so large—24,000 troops—that it failed to surprise the poorly trained 12,000-man Panamanian Defense Forces, intelligence on the whereabouts of Noriega and the level of armed resistance was faulty, the military did not attempt to control or destroy the government's communications center for almost a full day (allowing Noriega to broadcast nationally), and widespread looting was allowed to occur. Much of this was due to the fact that, as stated in the *New York Times,* "the main part of the Panama attack was a virtual replay of a World War II battle, with paratroops dropping from the sky and tanks blasting through a city to overwhelm the opposition."[56] Ultimately, the United States was successful in overthrowing Noriega and imposing a new government on Panama within a short period of time, fulfilling domestic political expectations within the United States. Yet, the victory came at the cost of twenty-five American soldiers killed and hundreds wounded (many due to friendly fire), thousands of Panamanian civilian casualties (and displaced persons) through indiscriminate bombing and shelling, the maintenance of a large American military occupation force, the provision of millions of dollars in reconstruction aid to the new government, and widespread global condemnation for American gunboat diplomacy, especially given its twelve previous invasions of Panama.[57]

The strategy of attrition was applied to **the Persian Gulf conflict** with much greater success. Clearly, the movement of over 500,000 American troops to the Persian Gulf following Iraq's invasion of Kuwait on August 2, 1990, was an impressive feat. No country other than the United States has the capability to move and maintain such a massive force so far and for so long. This was followed by quick military success in war led by the air campaign in response to President Bush's decision to strike followed by a quick land campaign. In fact, one major military innovation, in the wake of the Vietnam War in particular, was the army's adoption of the **AirLand battle doctrine**. As opposed to the more conventional technique of directing massive firepower at the heart of the enemy, the AirLand battle orientation emphasizes "mobility" and "flexibility" in the concentration and application of firepower on the

ESSAY 8.4
THE GRENADA VICTORY AS MILITARY FIASCO

Many Americans celebrated the American invasion of Grenada as a great victory. Much of the excitement created by the Grenada invasion was due to the fact that it occurred immediately after the killing of over two hundred American soldiers in Beirut and, more importantly, it represented America's first military victory since the loss in Vietnam. On closer inspection, however, the Grenada Invasion was not as spectacular a victory as the Reagan administration attempted to make it appear. It could not have been lost by the U.S. military despite the fact that the military operations were often incredibly inept from beginning to end.

The U.S. military performed miserably in Grenada. What should have been a quick advance and mopping-up exercise became an incredibly slow, cumbersome, and inefficient military operation. Consider the mission: to defeat a token force of 679 Cubans, most of whom were construction workers, and a few Grenadians on an island that was only 133 square miles (twice the size of the District of Columbia). Yet, "Operation Urgent Fury" required three days and over 7000 marines, rangers, paratroopers, and independent commando teams from all the services, backed up by the aircraft carrier Independence's task force, to subdue the enemy and occupy the island.

The problems were endless. First, the intelligence was poor. The intelligence community did not know the number of enemy troops or how well they were equipped. When the military operations bogged down after the first day, estimates escalated as high as several thousand Cuban troops. The military did not have maps of the island, requiring many of the invading troops to rely on tourist maps from Exxon during the three-day operation. And the invading troops were never briefed about a second medical school campus with American students.

Second, the command structure was inappropriate for the task. Although this was a land operation, the military strategy was planned and commanded by naval officers for the simple reason that

Grenada is geographically located within the boundaries of the navy-dominated Atlantic Command in Norfolk, Virginia. Thus, the operational commander was a vice-admiral on the aircraft carrier Independence. Furthermore, there was never any agreement concerning the existence of a single commander for the ground forces and every service naturally had to play a role in the invasion.

Third, the military operations were slow and inefficient. Army rangers (the army's elite conventional troops) invaded from the north, while the marines invaded from the south. Yet, advances were repeatedly stalled by sporadic enemy fire and over-inflated reports of enemy strength. The rangers and marines had to be reinforced by paratroopers from the army's 82nd Airborne Division on the second and third days. A team of the navy's elite troops (the SEALs) was dispatched to rescue the governor-general of Grenada, but became trapped with the governor and his family in the Governor's residence. A secret Delta force of elite army commandos failed in its mission to rescue political prisoners. Both the SEALs and the Delta force eventually were rescued by the marines.

Fourth, the communication between the different U.S. troops was poor. Units from various services had difficulty communicating with one another. In one case, it was reported that a ranger unit was unable to call in an air strike to the navy command. To overcome this obstacle an ingenious soldier slipped into a nearby phone booth and used his AT&T-long-distance card to reach Fort Bragg, North Carolina, which relayed the request through the Pentagon to the Independence for the air strike.

In the end, U.S. forces suffered 18 killed (and 116 wounded) as opposed to 25 Cubans killed. Accidents also occurred: 21 Grenadian civilians were killed by a bombing error, 14 American soldiers were wounded by an errant air strike, several rangers were killed when two helicopters collided, and 4 Navy SEALs drowned in an overturned boat. The operation was so slow in rescuing the American students that 224 of them may have been placed at greater risk by the operation itself since they were completely at the mercy of the Cubans and Grenadians. However sloppy the military operation, it was ultimately successful and was claimed a great military victory by the Reagan administration. The military response was to issue over 1600 medals for meritorious service and heroism, even though only 7000 American troops set foot on the island and a much smaller number were actually involved in combat.

The U.S. government was able to convince most Americans that Grenada was a great military success because the press was completely "censored" from covering the invasion. This was the major lesson of Vietnam learned by the military— that the press contributed to the military's failure and needed to be controlled. Thus, the media received and communicated the "official" version of what happened in Grenada from the Pentagon and the Reagan White House. By the time the press learned and reported the real story of the "great military triumph," most Americans were no longer paying attention.

SOURCES: Major Mark Adkin, *Urgent Fury: The Battle for Grenada* (Lexington, Mass.: Lexington Books, 1989); Drummond Ayres, Jr., "Grenada Invasion: A Series of Surprises," *New York Times* (November 14, 1983): A1, A6; James Coates and Michael Kilian, *Heavy Losses: The Dangerous Decline of American Defense* (New York: Penguin, 1985); Edward N. Luttwak, *The Pentagon and the Art of War;* and Stuart Taylor, Jr., "In Wake of Invasion, Much Official Misinformation by U.S. Comes to Light," *New York Times* (November 6, 1983): A20.

---

ground with the support of the other services in the air to attack the enemy where they might be most vulnerable. The famous "left hook" ground attack by American and allied forces was tremendously successful against the Iraqi forces, and there was considerable air support by the Air Force and Navy.

Because of the stunning success in light of past performances, this raises the question: Why did the U.S. military perform so successfully in the Persian Gulf War? Principally, because this was the kind of conventional war that the American military is best trained and equipped to fight. The U.S. military, and its allies, was able to control the skies and deliver massive firepower in Kuwait and Iraq to damage and wear down a predominantly conventionally trained and equipped land army with low morale away from home. In addition, according to military strategist Eliot Cohen, "The United States fought in a theater ideally suited to our military strengths, an empty desert. . . . We had half a year to mass and train troops, and to prepare elaborate plans to attack. . . . We also had the luxury of one of the best port, road, and air base networks in the world, including military facilities built by our engineers, and the support of a wealthy and cooperative host nation." Also, with Iraq facing economic sanctions and isolated

from the world, "we could bring to bear the weight of our cold war-rich armed forces without fear of Soviet opposition in the theater or aggression elsewhere."[58] The Persian Gulf War, in other words, represented a classic conventional confrontation involving the U.S. military not seen since the Korean War in which the conditions were optimal for a compelling American military victory in war.

As successful as the military operation was, it should be pointed out that Iraq was not an easy military target like Grenada or Panama. The military defeat of Iraq, a country with a gross national product (GNP) of only $40 billion, was a costly venture that required over a half-million American and allied troops in a massive and prolonged military campaign resulting in mass destruction and thousands of casualties. Such a large American military force has fought in war only two times previously since World War II—the Korean War and the Vietnam War. Although the military campaign was a great success, significant problems also were encountered. For all the success of the air war, the most advanced and costly strategic bombers—the B-1 and B-2 Stealth bombers—were not used in combat given flaws in design and problems experienced in staying in flight. The air force, instead, relied on the aging B-52 and the F-111 bombers. Nevertheless, the tremendous success of the air war was so overwhelming that the army and marines, given the shortness of the ground war and the rout of the Iraqi army, were never really tested. Yet, equipment and training problems affected the ground campaign. Secretary of Defense Richard Cheney, for example, criticized the National Guard for its lack of short-term readiness—it was activated, but only the noncombat units were deployed.[59] And questions persist about strange illnesses to many of the veterans referred to as "Gulf War syndrome." The Persian Gulf War, therefore, was an American military triumph, but one which must be placed in perspective.

Overall, *the president is faced with serious limitations in his choices with respect to the use of force.* First, the president has few viable military options from which to choose: principally some type of nuclear strike or some type of conventional strike in a world where nuclear war has been avoided and conventional battles are rare. As Eliot Cohen has concluded, "The most substantial constraints on America's ability to conduct small wars result from the resistance of the American defense establishment to the very notion of engaging in such conflicts, and from the unsuitability of that establishment for fighting such wars."[60] Second, changes in the international environment, such as nationalism and the proliferation of weaponry, make it increasingly costly and difficult for a great power to exercise force successfully abroad. Third, when the military has exercised force abroad, its performance, especially for low-intensity conflict, has been quite poor. Finally, the Vietnam War shattered the anticommunist consensus that had pervaded American society and guaranteed public support when the president called for the use of force.

Today, presidents have to be much more cautious than during the cold war past because of the breakdown of consensus and the fact that Americans have high expectations for quick success. It is important to remember that President Bush took a divided country to war in the Persian Gulf on January 17, 1991. Thus, presidents face difficult and politically risky decisions concerning the use of force. Furthermore, there are no simple solutions concern-

ing appropriate military strategy in a post–cold war environment of great complexity. Some critics argue that if U.S. foreign policy is to continue to rely on the threat and use of force, the military must be reformed to improve its conventional performance and gain a real capability in low-intensity warfare. Others argue that the U.S. government and military should continue to rely on its principal nuclear and conventional missions. These are important issues with important trade-offs that will affect the American military into the future.

REFORM AND THE FUTURE OF THE MILITARY

Many of the characteristics that have been attributed to the U.S. military pertain to other large institutions also. The U.S. military is not alone in being large, bureaucratic, possessing a particular organizational subculture, and promising more than it can deliver. These characteristics hold true for private industry, as indicated by the bankruptcy of the Chrysler Corporation during the 1970s and the drastic drop of General Motors' American market share from 66 percent during the 1960s to 30 percent today. These characteristics can be applied to American adversaries as well; for example, the Soviet military suffered from many of the same problems throughout the post–World War II period.

In actuality, the U.S. military is relatively efficient in pursuing the missions and norms that have prevailed within the individual services, especially given the fact that the military establishment is a "huge, institutional, bureaucratic, juggernaut." However, the key question remains: How relevant are the missions and norms of the military establishment for confronting the problems facing U.S. foreign policy and national security in the post–cold war era and into the next millennium?

Many of the bureaucratic problems discussed are inevitable functions of the size of modern society. Large populations require large bureaucracies, which do not easily adapt to changes in the environment. But this does not mean that changes cannot be made within a bureaucracy such as the American military, or that the organization cannot be improved. However, **institutional change and reform** are not easy. Real reform requires change in the organizational structure and subculture. In the case of the military, these structural and subcultural patterns have been in place, producing certain habits of behavior, for a long time. This leads to political resistance to change among those individuals and organizations with a vested interest in maintaining the military establishment as it now stands.[61]

The Department of Defense, nevertheless, has undergone some changes over the years, especially since the Vietnam War and the collapse of the cold war. The U.S. Army has moved towards a form of "AirLand" maneuver warfare; Congress passed the Goldwater-Nichols bill giving the chairman of the Joint Chiefs of Staff somewhat more power; President Reagan appointed a presidential commission that began a process of phasing out numerous military bases; and the military has been experiencing some downsizing in the past decade.[62] But are these changes sufficient as the United States moves into the twenty-first century?

Many argue that the military remains so large and complex that these have not fundamentally changed the basic orientation of the military. The disaster of the Vietnam War and other faulty military performances simply have not led to much reform within the military establishment. For forty years, the United States military has expanded and been oriented toward fighting the Soviet Union throughout the world. With the collapse of the Soviet Union and much of communism, Americans have much less to fear. In such a global environment, not only is the United States finding it difficult to project successful force abroad in a complex world, but it may also find that there is less need to do so.

The post–cold war environment may be a unique opportunity to achieve real reform within the military establishment for the world of the twenty-first century. Yet, the U.S. military is an institution that remains very much the same and is still essentially organized to fight large conventional wars.[63] In fact, the assumption of the possibility of

two major regional conflicts (such as in the Persian Gulf War and the Korean Peninsula) drives the "official" post–cold war national military strategy, justifying the force requirements for each of the services as well as to promote the U.S. government's ability to maintain global military primacy and prevent the rise of any new, major adversaries.[64]

It should not come as a surprise that many of the individuals and organizations that comprise the military establishment, with their allies throughout government and society, will resist challenges for major change and reform.[65] At the same time, the decline of communism and the Soviet empire have triggered the search for **new military missions** away from Europe and toward low-intensity conflicts in the third world where the use of force is more likely—such as with the "drug war," "anti-terrorism," "peacekeeping," and "humanitarian intervention"—to help justify maintaining a huge military establishment.

Such "Military Operations Other Than War" are increasingly the norm in a post–cold war world. Such operations, nevertheless, do not reflect the core mission and essence of the American military. The American triumph in the Persian Gulf War, furthermore, has bolstered those resisting change to the basic orientation of the military establishment. Therefore, the end of the cold war and the success in the Persian Gulf War have contradictory implications for the future of the military establishment. In the final analysis, the extent to which change and real reform within the military will occur, if at all, depends on the politics of U.S. foreign policy.

BIBLIOGRAPHIC ESSAY

. . . .

A wealth of material has been written in the last decade on the military, most of which has taken a critical perspective. The more critical analyses throughout the post–World War II years came from the liberal and left political perspectives. Today, however, the military establishment is commonly critiqued from all sides. Excellent overviews and analyses of the military, for example, have been provided by James Fallows, a liberal journalist, in *National Defense* (New

York: Vintage, 1981); James Coates and Michael Kilian, conservative journalists, in *Heavy Losses: The Dangerous Decline of American Defense* (New York: Penguin, 1985); Edward N. Luttwak, a military strategist, in *The Pentagon and the Art of War* (New York: Touchstone, 1985); and General David C. Jones, former chairman of the JCS, in "What's Wrong with Our Defense Establishment," *New York Times Magazine* (November 7, 1982): 38–42, 70–83. An excellent contemporary overview is provided by Peter L. Hays, Brenda J. Vallance, and Alan R. Van Tassel, *American Defense Policy* (Baltimore: Johns Hopkins University Press, 1997).

Andrew F. Krepinevich, Jr., in *The Army and Vietnam* (Baltimore: Johns Hopkins University Press, 1986), provides a good discussion of the Army's conventional strategy of attrition and how this affected the military conduct of the Vietnam War. Neil Sheehan tells a powerful story of the history of American participation in the Vietnam War in *A Bright Shining Lie: John Paul Vann and America in Vietnam* (New York: Vintage, 1988), while David Halberstam provides an excellent portrayal of the policymaking process responsible for the Americanization of the war in *The Best and the Brightest* (New York: Random House, 1969). Three books providing a strong sense of war as it took place in Vietnam are a novel by Tim O'Brien, *Going After Cacciato* (New York: Dell, 1975); *Dispatches* (New York: Avon, 1968) by journalist Michael Herr; and *The Real War* (New York: Pantheon, 1987) by journalist Jonathan Schell. Myra MacPherson illuminates the effect of the Vietnam War on the generation asked to fight it in *Long Time Passing: Vietnam and the Haunted Generation* (New York: New American Library, 1984).

Two excellent case studies of the nature of the weapons procurement process are Nick Kotz's *Wild Blue Yonder and the B-1 Bomber* (Princeton, N.J.: Princeton University Press, 1988) and Patrick Tyler's *Running Critical: The Silent War, Rickover, and General Dynamics* (New York: Harper & Row, 1986). An informative account of civil-military relations and military advice on the use of force can be found in Richard K. Betts, *Soldiers, Statesmen, and Cold War Crises* (Cambridge, Mass.: Harvard University Press, 1977). Eliot A. Cohen provides a good overview in the "Constraints on America's Conduct of Small Wars," *International Security* 9 (Fall 1984): 151–81, and an assessment of the Persian Gulf War in "After the Battle," *New Republic* (April 1, 1991), 19–26.

Lawrence J. Korb provides an assessment of the military's budget and strategy in a post–cold war environment in "Our Overstuffed Armed Forces," *Foreign Affairs* (November/December 1995): 22–34. A wide-ranging discussion of the theory and use of force throughout modern American history is conducted by Bernard Brodie, one of the original modern civilian strategists, in *War and Politics* (New York: Macmillan, 1973).

Finally, on the important issue about the changing composition of the military, including the controversies over women and gays, see Martin Binkin, "The New Face of the American Military," *The Brookings Review* (Summer 1991): 7–13; Gerald J. Garvey and John J. DiIulio, Jr., "Only Connect? Cohesion vs. Combat Effectiveness," *New Republic* (April 26, 1993): 18–21; Stephanie Gutmann, "Sex and the Soldier," *New Republic* (February 24, 1997): 18–22; Randy Shilts, *Conduct Unbecoming: Lesbians and Gays in the U.S. Military,* (New York: St. Martin's Press, 1993); and Gregory Vistica, *Fall from Glory* (New York: Simon and Schuster, 1995).

ENDNOTES

1. For a good historical overview, see Allan R. Millett and Peter Maslowski, *For the Common Defense: A Military History of the United States of America* (New York: Free Press, 1985). See also Geoffrey Perret, *A Country Made by War: From the Revolution to Vietnam—The Story of America's Rise to Power* (New York: Vintage, 1990).

2. U.S. House of Representatives, Committee on International Relations, *Background Information on the Use of U.S. Armed Forces in Foreign Countries*, Committee Print (94th Cong., 1st sess., 1975): 58–66.

3. See James Coates and Michael Kilian, *Heavy Losses: The Dangerous Decline of American Defense* (New York: Penguin, 1985), chapter 2; Edward N. Luttwak, *The Pentagon and the Art of War* (New York: Simon and Schuster, 1985), pp. 68–92; and U.S. Senate Committee on Foreign Relations, *United States Foreign Policy Objectives and Overseas Military Installations*, Committee Print (96th Cong. 1st sess., 1979).

4. Carl E. Vuono, "Desert Storm and the Future of Conventional Forces," *Foreign Affairs* (Spring 1991): 55.

5. *Statistics* V.28 (Washington, D.C.: U.S. Government Printing Office, 1996); U.S. Office of Assistant Secretary of Defense, *Military Strength Figures* (March 31, 1997).

6. See, for example, U.S. Congress, Congressional Budget Office, *The Costs and Benefits of Retail Activities at Military Bases* (October 1997).

7. See, for example, U.S., Congress, General Accounting Office, *Implications of Joint NASA/DOD Participation in Space Shuttle Operations* (November 7, 1983).

8. Barry M. Blecham and Stephen S. Kaplan, *Force Without War: U.S. Armed Forces as a Political Instrument* (Washington, D.C.: The Brookings Institution, 1978).

9. See U.S., Department of Defense, *Annual Report to the Congress, Fiscal Year 1990.; Statistics V.28* (Washington, D.C.: U.S. Government Printing Office, 1996).

10. The commandant of the Marine Corps was not added to the JCS until 1958 when the National Security Act was amended; the vice chairman was added in 1987 with the Goldwaters-Nichols Act.

11. See, for example, Mark Perry, *Four Stars* (Boston: Houghton Mifflin, 1989).

12. See, for example, Edward N. Luttwak, "Washington's Biggest Scandal," *Commentary* (May 1994): 29–33.

13. See, for example, Geoffrey Piller, "DOD's Office of International Security Affairs," *Political Science Quarterly* 98 (Spring 1983): 59–78.

14. See, for example, Lawrence J. Korb, "The Budget Process in the Department of Defense, 1947–1977: The Strengths and Weaknesses of Three Systems," *Public Administration Review* (July/August 1977): 334–46.

15. David C. Jones, "What's Wrong with Our Defense Establishment," *New York Times Magazine* (November 7, 1982), p. 79.

16. See, for example, Luttwak, *The Pentagon and the Art of War*, chapter 6.

17. See Douglas Kinnard, *The War Managers* (Hanover, N.H.: University Press of New England, 1977).

18. See, for example, Samuel P. Huntington, *The Soldier and the State: The Theory and Politics of Civil-Military Relations* (Cambridge, Mass.: Harvard University Press, 1957).

19. See, for example, Carl Kenneth Allard, Jr., *Command, Control and the Common Defense* (New Haven, Conn.: Yale University Press, 1990); Richard K. Betts, *Soldiers, Statesmen, and Cold War Crises* (Cambridge, Mass.: Harvard University Press, 1977); Coates and Kilian, *Heavy Losses*; James Fallows, *National Defense* (New York: Vintage, 1981); Arthur T. Hadley, *The Straw Giant, Triumph and Failure: America's Armed Forces* (New York: Random House, 1986); Jones, "What's Wrong with Our Defense Establishment"; Luttwak, *The Pentagon and the Art of War*; Clark R. Mollenhoff, *The Pentagon* (New York: Pinnacle Books, 1967); and Adam Yarmolinsky, *The Military Establishment: Its Impacts on American Society* (New York: Harper & Row, 1971).

20. See, for example, Howard Graves, "The U.S. Army War College: Gearing Up for the 21st Century," *Parameters* 18 (December 1988): 2–12; U.S. Congress, General Accounting Office, *Department of Defense: Professional Military Education at the Four Intermediate Service Schools* (June 1991); U.S. Congress, General Accounting Office, *Department of Defense: Professional Military Education at the Three Senior Service Schools* (June 1991); U.S. Congress, General Accounting Office, *Military Education: Curriculum Changes at the Armed Forces Staff College* (September 1991).

21. For a good overview of the role of technology and the rise of military managers throughout western history, see Martin van Creveld, *Technology and War: From 2000 BC to the Present* (New York: Macmillan, 1989).

22. See Allard, *Command, Control and the Common Defense*; Vincent Davis, *The Admiral Lobby* (Chapel Hill, N.C.: University of North Carolina Press, 1967); and J.C. Wylie, *Military Strategy: A General Theory of Power Control* (New Brunswick, N.J.: Rutgers University Press, 1966).

23. See, for example, Richard H. Kohn, "Out of Control: The Crisis in Civil-Military Relations," *National Interest* (Spring 1994): 3–17.

24. See note 14 for the general sources relied upon in this section.

25. For the modern origins of the different functions of the services and interservice rivalry, see Morton H. Halperin and David Halperin, "The Key West Key," *Foreign Policy* 53 (Winter 1983–84): 114–30.

26. The functional commands were restructured in the last decade (see table 8.3).

27. And officers with flight backgrounds are more likely to reach top command positions in the Navy.

28. They were originally trained during the late 1950s to conduct behind-the-lines training of partisan forces against U.S. cold war enemies, particularly in Eastern Europe.

29. See Betts, *Soldiers, Statesmen, and Cold War Crises*, pp. 128–34.

30. See, for example, Less Aspin, "Games the Pentagon Plays," *Foreign Policy* 11 (Summer 1973): 80–92.

31. See also, Larry Berman, *Lyndon Johnson's War: The Road to Stalemate in Vietnam* (New York: W.W. Norton, 1989).

32. For an overview of the weapons acquisition process, see Jacob Goodwin, *Brotherhood of Arms: General Dynamics and the Business of Defending America* (New York: Times Books, 1985); William H. Gregory, *The Defense Procurement Mess* (Lexington, Mass.: Lexington Books, 1989); Nick Kotz, *Wild Blue Yonder and the B-1 Bomber* (Princeton, N.J.: Princeton University Press, 1988); Patrick Tyler, *Running Critical: The Silent War, Rickover, and General Dynamics* (New York: Harper & Row, 1986); and U.S. Congress, General Accounting Office, *DOD Revolving Door* (September 1989). The network of relationships that have developed in the defense process will be discussed at greater length in chapter 16 when we examine the extent to which a military-industrial complex exists in the United States.

33. "Producers Defend Costs of Military Parts," *The State*, Columbia, S.C. (September 26, 1984): 2A.

34. See, for example, A. Ernest Fitzgerald, *The Pentagonists: An Insider's View of Waste, Mismanagement, and Fraud in Defense Spending* (Boston: Houghton Mifflin, 1989), and Dina Rasor, *The Pentagon Underground* (New York: Times Books, 1985).

35. "Pentagon Efficiency Stressed," *The State*, Columbia, S.C. (February 11, 1988): 2A. See also, for example, U.S. Congress, General Accounting Office, *Financial Audit: Air Force Does Not Effectively Account for Billions of Dollars of Resources* (February 1990).

36. Tim Weiner estimates that in 1989 at least $36 billion of DOD spending was kept secret. Tim Weiner, *Blank Check: The Pentagon's Black Budget* (New York: Warner Books, 1990).

37. See Chris C. Demchak, *Military Organizations, Complex Machines: Modernization in the U.S. Armed Services* (Ithaca, N.Y.: Cornell University Press, 1991).

38. See, for example, "The Winds of Reform: Runaway Weapons Costs Prompt a New Look at Military Planning," *Time* (March 7, 1983): 12–16, 23, 26–30, and U.S. Congress, General Accounting Office, *Weapon Performance: Operational Test and Evaluation Can Contribute More to Decisionmaking* (December 1986).

39. See U.S. General Accounting Office, *Operation Desert Storm: Early Performance Assessment of Bradley and Abrams* (January 1992).

40. See, for example, "A Case of Human Error," *Newsweek* (August 15, 1988): 18–20; John Barry and Roger Charles, "Sea of Lies," *Newsweek* (July 13, 1992): 29–39; and Wayne Biddle, "Testing Charade," *The Nation* (August 27/September 2, 1988): 153.

41. Carl Von Clausewitz, *On War* (London: Penguin, 1832). See also Eliot A. Cohen, "The Mystique of U.S. Air Power," *Foreign Affairs* (January/February 1994): 109–124.

42. The percentage of troops involved in a combat role varies from a low of 15 to 20 percent to a high of about 40 percent, depending upon the time period discussed and the source. Luttwak, in *The Pentagon and the Art of War* (p. 32) for example, concludes that roughly one-third of the troops were involved in combat during the height of America's involvement. Clearly, it is difficult to come up with definitive figures. Nevertheless, a consensus exists among scholars and analysts of the Vietnam War that once American military involvement escalated, most of the troops occupied support roles.

43. See Myra MacPherson, *Long Time Passing: Vietnam and the Haunted Generation* (New York: New American Library, 1984). Richard Severo and Lewis Milford, in *The Wages of War: When America's Soldiers Came Home—From Valley Forge to Vietnam* (New York: Simon and Schuster, 1989), demonstrate that the warm welcome and generous government benefits awarded to World War II veterans were "the exception" to the rule. In this respect, although the general climate may have been more divisive, Vietnam War veterans were treated as most veterans have been treated throughout American history.

44. In fact, people in uniform are almost politically silent. They can vote, but are prohibited from many of the partisan political activities other Americans take part in. In addition, because they move frequently, they are either unable to establish the residency requirements needed to register, or they vote by absentee ballots (which usually aren't consequential and are counted late).

45. Richard Halloran, "Reagan as Military Commander," *New York Times Magazine* (January 15, 1984): 25, 56–62, 68.

46. Betts, *Soldiers, Statesman, and Cold War Crises.*

47. See, for example, Paul M. Kattenburg, *The Vietnam Trauma in American Foreign Policy*, 1945–75 (New Brunswick, N.J.: Transaction Books, 1980), pp. 73–75, for his discussion of the "machismo factor" in U.S. foreign policy.

48. See, for example, Leslie H. Gelb, "Shultz, Pushing a Hard Line, Becomes Key Voice in Crises," *New York Times* (November 7, 1983): 1, 15; and Elaine Sciolino, "Crowe vs. Abrams: Bitterness and Reagan Policies," *Washington Post* (October 23, 1989), p. 7.

49. Bob Woodward, *The Commanders* (New York: Simon and Schuster, 1991).

50. Hedrick Smith discusses the dissent that exists within the military among the rank and file against the top brass in *The Power Game: How Washington Works* (New York: Ballantine, 1988), chapter 8.

51. Harry G. Summers, Jr., *On Strategy: A Critical Analysis of the Vietnam War* (Novato, Calif: Presidio, 1982).

52. Andrew F. Krepinevich, Jr., *The Army and Vietnam* (Baltimore: Johns Hopkins University Press, 1986), p. 171. See also D. Michael Shafer, *Deadly Paradigms: The Failure of U.S. Counterinsurgency Policy* (Princeton, N.J.: Princeton University Press, 1988).

53. Mark Clodfelter, *The Limits of Air Power: The American Bombing of North Vietnam* (New York: Free Press, 1989).

54. Jones, "What's Wrong With Our Defense Establishment."

55. Luttwak, *The Pentagon and the Art of War*, p. 17.

56. Bernard E. Trainor, "Flaws in Panama Attack," *New York Times* (December 31, 1989): 1, 6.

57. See "An Accident-Prone Army," *Newsweek* (November 5, 1990), p. 7, and Douglas Jehl and Bob Secter, "U.S., Noriega Both Found Invasion Surprises," *Los Angeles Times* (December 27, 1989): A1, A6, A10.

58. Eliot A. Cohen, "After the Battle," *New Republic* (April 1, 1991): 22. See also Stephen Biddle, "Victory Misunderstood: What the Gulf War Tells Us About the Future of Conflict," *International Security* (Fall 1996): 139–79; Gregg Easterbrook, "Operation Desert Shill," *New Republic* (September 30, 1991): 32–42; U.S. Congress, House, Committee on Armed Services, *Defense for a New Era: Lessons of the Persian Gulf War* (Washington, D.C.: U.S. Government Printing Office, 1992).

59. See Barton Gellman, "Cheney Says Guard Units May Need Reorganizing," *Washington Post* (March 15, 1991): 34; Michael R. Gordon with Eric Schmitt, "Radios and Such: U.S. War Problem," *New York Times* (March 28, 1991): A8, "Panel Says B-1 Cannot Cope with Ice and Radar," *New York Times* (March 4, 1991): A11; Patrick E. Tyler, "Did Patriot Missiles Work? Not So Well, Scientists Say," *New York Times* (April 17, 1991): A6; U.S. Congress, General Accounting Office, *National Guard: Peacetime Training Did Not Adequately Prepare Combat Brigades for Gulf War* (September 1991); U.S., Congress, General Accounting Office, *Operation Desert Shield: Problems Encountered by Activated Reservists* (September 1991).

60. See, for example, Eliot A. Cohen, "Constraints on America's Conduct of Small Wars," *International Security* 9 (Fall 1984): 165.

61. For a general discussion of the importance of size and history in creating governmental institutions that are highly resistant to change in foreign policy, see Richard Holbrooke, "The Machine That Fails," *Foreign Policy* (Winter 1970–71): 65–77.

62. In addition to what was cited above, see U.S. Congress, Congressional Research Service, *Defense Department Reorganization*, Issue Brief Number IB77028 (September 7, 1979); U.S. Congress, General Accounting Office, *Defense Reorganization: Progress and Concerns at JCS and Combatant Commands* (March 1989); and U.S. Congress, General Accounting Office, *Military Bases: An Analysis of the Commission's Realignment and Closure Recommendations* (November 1989).

63. See Lawrence J. Korb, "Peace Without Dividend: Why We Can't Seem to Cut the Defense Budget, " *Washington Post* (July 9, 1995); Lawrence J. Korb, "Our Overstuffed Armed Forces," *Foreign Affairs* (November/December 1995): 22–34.

64. See Robert L. Borosage, "Inventing the Threat: Clinton's Defense Budget," *World Policy Journal* (Winter 1993/94): 7–15; Eliot A. Cohen, "Down the Hatch," *New Republic* (March 7, 1994): 14–19; Patrick E. Tyler, "U.S. Strategy Plan Calls for Insuring No Rivals Develop," *New York Times* (March 7, 1987): A1, A14. The official policy can be found in Colin L. Powell, "U.S. Forces: Challenges Ahead," *Foreign Affairs* (Winter 1992/93): 32–45; and William S. Cohen, Secretary of Defense, *Report of the Quadrennial Defense Review* (May 1997).

65. For a somewhat contrary view, see Stephen Peter Rosen, *Winning the Next War: Innovation and the Modern Military* (Ithaca, N.Y.: Cornell University Press, 1991).

CHAPTER
9

. . . .

THE INTELLIGENCE COMMUNITY

An important development affecting U.S. foreign policy in the post–World War II period has been the rise of an extensive intelligence community within the executive branch. As with the presidency and the military, the United States intelligence community had only a limited capability before the war. With the onset of the cold war and the U.S. policy of containment, however, a number of bureaucratic organizations developed with responsibilities in the area of intelligence. This chapter discusses the nature of the intelligence community and its impact on U.S. foreign policy. It also reviews the tensions that have developed between the demands of national security and the demands of democracy since the rise of the intelligence community and a national security ethos throughout the government.

PURPOSE AND ACTIVITIES OF INTELLIGENCE

. . . .

The meaning of the term **intelligence** has become quite elastic over the years.[1] During the early part of the twentieth century, intelligence simply referred to information or news. By the 1940s, the word meant information that had been evaluated. Since the 1950s, however, *intelligence has referred to three sets of activities* performed by certain organizations within the U.S. government:

1. Data collection and analysis;
2. Counterintelligence;
3. Political and paramilitary intervention.

The primary purpose of the intelligence community is to provide information to policymakers. Most intelligence organizations are engaged in collecting and analyzing information for military and civilian policymakers in the executive branch. As discussed in earlier chapters, the president requires information to make decisions and govern U.S. foreign policy. Thus, information is both an important source and constraint on the exercise of presidential power.

Another important role of intelligence is "counterintelligence," that is, protecting intelligence information, personnel, and national security organizations from eavesdroppers, spies, and double agents. For forty years, American counterintelligence has focused on protecting the national security bureaucracy from penetration by its major adversary, the Soviet Union, and its allies. The need to insulate the intelligence community and national security bureaucracy has resulted in the development of an extensive security and secrecy system throughout the government.

In addition to the two traditional intelligence functions discussed above, American intelligence agencies also have often been tasked to perform covert political and paramilitary operations in support of U.S. foreign policy. These involve governmental acts, such as propaganda campaigns, psychological warfare, secret financial assistance, destabilization campaigns, partisan resistance movements, assassinations, and coups d'etat. The Central Intelligence Agency (CIA) is most involved in this area and has developed a certain notoriety for its covert operations over the years.

THE MAJOR INTELLIGENCE ORGANIZATIONS
. . . .

The **historical development** of intelligence in the modern sense of the term began at the beginning of the twentieth century in Great Britain. During the 1920s and 1930s, intelligence functions developed in most European states. In comparison, modern intelligence developed more slowly within the United States. A common attitude towards intelligence held by many policymakers up to World War II was symbolized by Secretary of State Henry Stimson during a 1929 discussion of the need for intelligence when he proclaimed that "Gentlemen do not read each other's mail."[2] This attitude was consistent with the political culture of the American public. U.S. citizens believed that the United States represented democratic ideals and principles, as opposed to the warlike attitudes and balance of power politics that prevailed in Europe, which held that individual freedom and rights were something to uphold while big government spying abroad and at home was something to fear.

In the United States, the demand for intelligence grew slowly in the first half of the twentieth century, became a high priority during World War II and, with the passage of the National Security Act of 1947, expanded into its modern form during the cold war years. Not only did the National Security Act restructure policy advice to the president, by creating the National Security Council and reorganizing the military under the newly created Department of Defense, it also provided the president with a permanent intelligence capability under the direction of a new organization, the Central Intelligence Agency.

Much of the public equates governmental intelligence activity with the Central Intelligence Agency or CIA; however, the intelligence community is much more than just the CIA. Since the 1940s, **a large and complex intelligence community** has developed within the executive branch of the U.S. government. Most intelligence organizations, in fact, are officially a part of the Department of Defense. *Several major bureaucratic organizations are involved in intelligence:*[3]

1. The National Security Agency;
2. Army, Navy, and Air Force Intelligence;
3. The National Reconnaissance Office;
4. The Defense Intelligence Agency;
5. The State Department's Intelligence and Research Bureau;
6. The Federal Bureau of Investigation;
7. The Central Intelligence Agency.

The National Security Agency. The National Security Agency (NSA) was created in 1952 within the Department of Defense, although its origins go back to World War I and the army's Signal Corps. It has grown to become the largest and, along with the CIA, most important intelligence agency. Unlike the CIA, the NSA has been successful in keeping its existence and operations hidden from the public.

The major function of the National Security Agency is the collection and analysis of communication and electronic data. NSA maintains "listening posts" around the world, equipped with sophisticated electronics for intercepting communications messages, for example, via telephone or microwave. Most of these listening posts are located in U.S. governmental facilities abroad, including U.S. embassies and particularly American military bases. The intercepted messages are relayed to NSA's Fort Meade, Maryland, headquarters, where an extensive and sophisticated array of computers process the information for further evaluation by intelligence analysts.

NSA also has special responsibility in **cryptology,** the study of making and breaking codes. Because everyone in the intelligence business is conditioned to be extremely security conscious and aware of eavesdropping efforts by other governments, many of the messages communicated between governmental officials are sent in code to protect their contents if intercepted. The National Security Agency devises the codes for the U.S. government, performing an important counterintelligence function. Since much of the information that NSA intercepts is in code, efforts are made to break the codes of other countries and decipher the messages, unbeknownst to the original source. More and more people have come to realize the importance of breaking enemy codes, especially in times of war. During World War II, much of the allies' early success against the axis powers was a result of British and American efforts to break German and Japanese codes. In fact, the crucial Battle of Midway for naval control of the Pacific was an American triumph largely because of knowledge of the Japanese fleet's general destination, gained as a result of the Japanese code being broken.

Army, Navy, and Air Force Intelligence. Each of the military services maintains its own intelligence capability. American military intelligence consists primarily of service efforts to collect and analyze tactical military information, including the force structures, tactics employed, and operational capabilities of other military forces—especially those of the Soviet Union since World War II. **Army intelligence (G-2)** is one of the oldest of the nation's intelligence operations. In addition to its focus on military tactical intelligence, G-2 has a counterintelligence function and has an extensive history of involvement in preventing treason, espionage, sabotage, gambling, prostitution, and black marketeering at home and abroad.

Many of the personnel who work for military intelligence also work for the National Security Agency. Most of NSA's listening posts for intercepting communications are located on U.S. military bases and facilities operated by military intelligence personnel. In 1968, for example, the U.S. government was involved in a conflict with the North Korean government over the "*Pueblo* incident." According to the U.S. government, the *Pueblo* was a private American ship that was in international waters off the coast of North Korea. It was seized and held by the North Korean government for nine months before the boat and the crew were released. It was later revealed that the *Pueblo* was, in fact, loaded with electronics equipment operated by the U.S. military, thus enabling the NSA to eavesdrop on North Korea. With over 2000 military installations throughout the world and American forces on constant patrol, it should be clear that NSA has a tremendous capacity for intercepting global communications.

The National Reconnaissance Office. The National Reconnaissance Office (NRO) is another important intelligence organization within the Department of Defense that has not had much visibility over the years. The National Reconnaissance Office is responsible for the development and supervision of high-altitude surveillance mechanisms. Information provided by **aerial surveillance** has played an important role in the conduct of U.S. foreign policy since the late 1950s, especially in defense policy and arms control.

In the 1950s, U.S. governmental knowledge of the Soviet Union was very sparse. Yet important national security decisions had to be made. "Sovietology" was a new field within the United States and the Soviet Union remained a closed society. NSA's capabilities in communications intelligence were primitive during this time and the CIA had difficulty penetrating the Soviet system through espionage. This lack of information existed at a time when a very intense anticommunist climate permeated American society. Americans initially came to fear a "bomber gap," and then later a "missile gap" when the Soviet Union successfully launched **Sputnik** in 1958—the first satellite placed in global orbit. In this environment, the U.S. government made important national security decisions to expand its military capabilities and nuclear strategic forces in accordance with its containment policy based on a "worst case scenario" of the military threat and capabilities posed by the Soviet Union.

In the late 1950s, a major technological development occurred that helped to address this information problem. The United States developed the **U-2** spy plane, a fast high-altitude plane designed to fly long distances over the Soviet Union and equipped with photographic equipment for taking detailed ground pictures. The U-2 became an important source of early information on Soviet military forces and demonstrated, among other things, that the bomber and missile gaps were in favor of the United States. U-2 flights by the CIA and air force intelligence also helped to verify the existence of Soviet intermediate-range missiles in Cuba during the early days of the Cuban Missile Crisis in 1962.[4]

The public first became aware of the super secret spy plane when pilot Gary Powers and his U-2 were shot down and captured by the Soviet Union in 1960. In response to this event, and to better coordinate aerial reconnaissance, the National Reconnaissance Office was created in 1960. During the Cuban Missile Crisis, a U-2 was actually shot down over Cuba. As the U-2 became increasingly vulnerable to surface-to-air missiles, the National Reconnaissance Office began to rely on a new spy plane—the SR-71—and the use of satellites to obtain military information about the Soviet Union. Over the years, major advances have been made in the capabilities of satellites to see tremendous detail on the ground. Beginning with the SALT I treaty negotiated under President Richard Nixon in 1972, **satellite reconnaissance** has become the major means available to the U.S. government for verifying Soviet compliance to arms control treaties.

The Defense Intelligence Agency. The Defense Intelligence Agency (DIA) was created in 1961 in response to the Bay of Pigs fiasco, where the Central Intelligence Agency trained Cuban expatriates to invade Cuba and overthrow Fidel Castro—an operation that failed miserably and led to the condemnation of the United States throughout the globe. The purpose of the DIA was to better coordinate the many intelligence activities undertaken by the Department of Defense in the hope of giving the military a single and more influential voice in the government's intelligence process.

Although it made sense to create a new organization to coordinate and centralize the military intelligence process, it has not worked so smoothly in practice. Many of the problems that afflict the military establishment also plague the Defense Intelligence Agency. Staff consists of military and civilian analysts drawn from the individual services and the Office of the Secretary of Defense. Given the different subcultures and divided loyalties within the organization, DIA operates very similar to the system within the Joint Chiefs of Staff where compromised intelligence assessments tend to be the order of the day.

The Bureau of Intelligence and Research. The State Department is also involved in intelligence work, predominantly in analysis through its Bureau of Intelligence and Research (INR). INR analyzes the department's cable traffic from abroad and information from other agencies within the intelligence community. It is actively involved in the process that produces community-wide intelligence estimates and provides advice to the secretary of state and State Department personnel on intelligence matters.

The FBI. The Federal Bureau of Investigation (FBI) is a part of the Department of Justice. It began as the Bureau of Investigation in 1908 and is the oldest governmental organization developed solely for the purpose of intelligence. Although the FBI is now the intelligence organization with primary responsibility for domestic counterintelligence and internal security within the United States, it had a more varied life in its earlier days.

During World War II and before the creation of the CIA, the FBI was active throughout Latin America—a region of the world where the United States was the major financial and military power, particularly throughout the Caribbean and Central America. As the United States government became involved in World War II, President Franklin Roosevelt instructed the FBI to develop an intelligence capability for collecting information, counterintelligence, and political action in the region.

Since the creation of the Central Intelligence Agency, the FBI's **legal jurisdiction** has been limited to activities within the United States. Not only is the FBI unique in terms of its geographic focus on the United States, it performs both domestic-oriented and foreign policy functions: federal law enforcement, foreign counterintelligence, and internal security against threats to the U.S. government. From 1924 to 1972 the FBI was run by one man—**J. Edgar Hoover**. The FBI's structure, subculture, and actions were heavily influenced by Hoover and continue to reflect his reign, although to a lesser extent, today. (See **essay 9.1** on Hoover and the FBI's pursuit of security.)[5]

The CIA. Created by the National Security Act of 1947, the Central Intelligence Agency soon became the "single most important agency responsible for intelligence abroad." The CIA has played an important role in the collection and analysis of data, is the primary intelligence organization responsible for foreign counterintelligence beyond the United States, and has become the major intelligence organization engaged in political and paramilitary action

abroad. In addition to these three intelligence functions, the director of central intelligence is responsible for coordinating the entire intelligence community for the president of the United States. Further analysis of the CIA's intelligence activity and its role in U.S. foreign policy is provided below.

PATTERNS IN THE INTELLIGENCE PROCESS
. . . .

The **size of the intelligence community** has grown enormously over time. "Although most Americans believe the United States did not become deeply involved in intelligence operations until the creation of the Office of Strategic Services (OSS) during World War II," Nathan Miller demonstrates in *Spying for America: The Hidden History of U.S. Intelligence* that the U.S. government has "participated in such activities—with varying degrees of success—since the Revolution."[6] The U.S. government had a very limited intelligence capability during the nineteenth century, relying on the Secret Service, military intelligence, and the State Department. American intelligence became more professional and grew during the first half of the twentieth century within the military, with the creation of the FBI, and, during World War II, with the establishment of the Office of Strategic Services (OSS), the precursor of the CIA. However, it was not until the National Security Act of 1947 and the cold war years that a large, complex, modern intelligence community developed. Each major intelligence organization (except the State Department's INR) has evolved into a large bureaucracy. Although the information is classified, it has been estimated that during the 1980s the American intelligence community employed over 150,000 people and spent as much as $15 billion annually to implement its intelligence missions.[7] Since the collapse of the Soviet Union, it is believed that the intelligence budget and staff have experienced some downsizing.

Not only has the size of the intelligence community grown throughout the twentieth century, especially since the Second World War, it has also

ESSAY 9.1
J. EDGAR HOOVER AND THE PURSUIT OF SECURITY

J. Edgar Hoover was one of the most powerful figures in the United Sates government through much of the twentieth century. He served in the Department of Justice under nineteen attorneys general, including forty-eight years as director of the Federal Bureau of Investigation (FBI). In the minds of most Americans, his name and agency were synonymous with the defense of American security against threats to law and order. With Hoover's death, however, new information has appeared which documents a much more sordid history. Recent works, such as *Secrecy and Power: The Life of J. Edgar Hoover* by Richard Powers, demonstrate that Hoover ran the national police force with an iron grip. He regularly violated people's civil liberties and rights in order to destroy perceived threats to national security. Examining the life of Hoover allows one to better understand the rise of the FBI as an important intelligence organization, the history of American anticommunism, and the contradictions that have developed between democratic practice and the pursuit of national security.

Hoover was born in Washington, D.C., in 1895, the fourth child in the family. He never married and resided in his parents' house near the Capitol until his mother died in 1938. He never joined a political party nor voted. Yet, according to Powers, Hoover developed very strong political and moral beliefs that were shaped by his upbringing during turn-of-the-century Washington and his formative experience in the Justice Department during the World War I years.

During the early years of the twentieth century Washington, D.C., was very much a small southern company town. Hoover was raised in a family, neighborhood, and city that was overwhelmingly middle class, white, Christian, and Protestant. Between 1900 and 1920, the District systematically institutionalized "Jim Crow" laws segregating the races. In this environment, J. Edgar Hoover acquired a "turn-of-the-century vision of America as a small community of like-minded neighbors, proud of their achievements, resentful of criticism, fiercely opposed to change."[A]

During the late nineteenth century and early twentieth century, the United States was undergoing massive and rapid change as a result of industrialization and immigration. **Nativist sentiments**—that is, anti-foreign attitudes—grew in response to changes symbolized by alien ideas and habits that threatened their way of life. Hoover shared these concerns and devoted his life to eradicating these threats to America, rising to prominence in the process. "As twentieth century standards of the mass society swept over traditional America, subverting old values, disrupting old customs, and dislodging old leaders," states Powers, "Americans who were frightened by the loss of their community saw in Hoover a man who understood their concerns and shared their anger, a powerful defender who would guard their America of memory against a world of alien forces, strange people, and dangerous ideas."[B]

Hoover was literally born into the federal government, for most of his family and relatives worked for the government. He went to work for the Library of Congress in 1913, received a law degree from George Washington University, and joined the Justice Department as a clerk in 1917. He won quick promotion to "attorney," and helped to administer the department's supervision of German aliens in the **Alien Enemy Bureau** during World War I. This is where Hoover first witnessed the country's growing hysteria over German spies, traitors, and saboteurs and the government's campaign to destroy political dissent.

Near the end of the war, a new hysteria developed over bolshevism with the Bolshevik Revolu-

A. Richard Gid Powers, *Secrecy and Power: The Life of J. Edgar Hoover* (New York: Free Press, 1987), p. 3.
B. Ibid., pp. 3–4.

tion in 1917 and the rise of business-labor disputes at home. The Justice Department, under Attorney General A. Mitchell Palmer, dealt with **the "Red Scare"** by conducting mass roundups and deportations of alien radicals. Hoover was promoted to special assistant to the attorney general in charge of the Radical Division's campaign against communism. Although Palmer and Hoover did not succeed in using the Red Scare raids to pass a peacetime sedition law to set strict legal limits on political dissent, they severely damaged the communist, socialist, and labor movements. As part of the antiradical campaign, Hoover relied on the assistance of private anticommunist organizations and devised a public relations campaign to promote anticommunism throughout the media and the public.

The antiradical campaign ended when excesses against innocent victims and violations of civil liberties and rights were exposed. Nevertheless, the campaign gave Hoover "and his Bureau a claim to be the government's official authority on anything involving communist activities. Hoover's 1919 studies of communism were, with little exaggeration, fundamental texts in the evolution of the anticommunism that was American orthodoxy for the next fifty years."[C] And starting in 1924 as director of the Bureau of Investigation (which became the FBI in 1934), Hoover used the same strategy and methods to destroy threats to national security that he had utilized during the World War I antisedition and Red Scare years.

In the 1920s and 1930s Hoover reformed the FBI into a modern and professional bureaucracy under his control. Through Hoover's authoritarian rule, he molded the FBI to represent the legal and moral guardian of the nation. Much of this period was spent improving the FBI's criminal intelligence capabilities and fighting a war on gangsters and crime, symbolized by the triumphs (often fictionalized) and celebrity of Hoover and his **G-men**—that is, the government men in the FBI.

World War II and the cold war fed new fears and hysteria concerning what Hoover had always believed to be the greatest threat to national security: subversion and communism. During the late 1930s, under the direction of President Franklin Roosevelt, "the Bureau was once again creating indexes of dangerous citizens and aliens, infiltrating political groups to gather general intelligence, and tapping phones, but by then Hoover had become such a reassuring symbol of security and stability to Americans that any protests were drowned out in the applause for Public Hero Number One."[D]

World War II and the cold war eliminated all restraints from Hoover's surveillance and involvement in America's political scene. For the next thirty years, Hoover and the FBI targeted political dissenters in a renewed antiradical campaign against communism. During the late 1940s and early 1950s, Hoover fed the growing anticommunist hysteria and the McCarthy movement. According to Powers, "throughout the fifties, despite the total collapse of American communism, Hoover never slackened in his efforts to persuade the president and the public that, all appearances to the contrary, the threat from communism was greater than ever."[E] In fact, in 1956 **Operation Cointelpro** was instigated to employ illegal and unconstitutional means to sabotage and destroy communists, communist-sympathizers, and fellow travelers. This paranoia with subversion and treason led him to extend Operation Cointelpro to the civil rights, black nationalism, and antiwar movements during the 1960s, for Hoover saw them as vulnerable to communism and a threat to American security. His nemesis became Martin Luther King, Jr., who Hoover believed was a communist and a personal threat to the small-town traditional values that Hoover was determined to uphold.

J. Edgar Hoover became so powerful that no president dared to replace him, even after retirement age. He died in office in 1972 at the age of 77 as a controversial figure who had directed the Bureau of

C. Ibid., p. 97.

D. Ibid., p. 227.
E. Ibid., p. 337.

Investigation for 48 years. Hoover's legacy left a profound impact on the FBI, the U.S. government's quest for national security, and American politics. In the end, as Powers concludes, "he achieved his life's goal by destroying American communism, and was a powerful supporter for traditional values; however, those values supported racial and other injustices, and his covert attacks on personal and public enemies violated principles of constitutional limits on governmental power."[F]

F. Ibid., p. 492.

SOURCES: William Keller, *The Liberals and J. Edgar Hoover: Rise and Fall of a Domestic Intelligence State* (Princeton, N.J.: Princeton University Press, 1989); Kenneth O'Reilly, *Hoover and the Un-Americans: The FBI, HUAC, and the Red Menace* (Philadel-phia: Temple University Press, 1983); and Richard Gid Powers, *Secrecy and Power: The Life of J. Edgar Hoover* (New York: Free Press, 1987).

---

become much more complex over time. At least seven major bureaucratic organizations are involved in intelligence in the traditional security area (nine if you count each of the service intelligence units separately). And many other executive agencies have intelligence roles in foreign policy as well, each with a unique intelligence purpose and mission—which may grow in a post–cold war environment, especially in non-traditional areas such as economics.[8] This complexity has been reinforced by the development of different subcultures since these intelligence organizations were created at different times, evolved under different conditions and leadership, and performed different intelligence functions.

The rise of a large and complex intelligence community has affected both the intelligence product and process.[9] *Three patterns have developed that have affected the collection, analysis, and use of intelligence:*

1. Difficulties in achieving coordination;
2. Producer-consumer problems;
3. Variations in intelligence success.

COORDINATION PROBLEMS

The intelligence community has become so large and complex that coordinating the organizations to work together in support of the president's foreign policy is very difficult. This is a recurring theme within the executive branch, as was noted concerning presidential management of foreign policy in chapter 6 and the military establishment in chapter 8.

The **director of central intelligence (DCI)** is charged to coordinate the intelligence process and act as the principal intelligence officer and adviser to the president. However, beyond managing the CIA and targeting certain intelligence priorities, the DCI has limited authority and power to govern the larger intelligence community. The NSA, army, navy and air force intelligence, the NRO, and the DIA are part of the Department of Defense and most of the personnel operate within the military chain of command. The Intelligence and Research Bureau is responsive to the structure and norms of the State Department. And the FBI is a semiautonomous agency within the Department of Justice (see **table 9.1** for directors of central intelligence).

The decentralized bureaucratic nature of the intelligence community means that considerable independent action is performed by the various intelligence agencies and, when they do interact, the policymaking process experiences infighting and compromise. During the **Cuban missile crisis**, for example, when the president was trying to verify whether intermediate-range strategic missiles capable of delivering nuclear warheads on the United States were stationed in Cuba, the National Reconnaissance Office and the CIA were feuding over which bureaucracy had responsibility for the U-2 flights. U-2 flights were deferred for two days, until the NRO and the CIA agreed that they would each be responsible for alternate flights. Thus crucial information was delayed during a period when the United States and the Soviet Union faced their greatest crisis.[10]

TABLE 9.1
DIRECTORS OF CENTRAL INTELLIGENCE

NAME	YEAR APPOINTED	BACKGROUND
Sidney W. Souers	1946	Business and Navy
Hoyt S. Vandenberg	1946	Air Force
Roscoe H. Hillenkoetter	1947	Navy
Walter Bedell Smith	1950	Army and Diplomat
Allen Welsh Dulles	1953	Law and Government
John A. McCone	1961	Business and Government
Willaim F. Raborn, Jr.	1965	Nay and Business
Richard M. Helms	1966	Journalism and Government
James R. Schlesinger	1972	Academia and Government
William E. Colby	1973	Law and Government
George H.W. Bush	1975	Business, Congress and Government
Stansfield Turner	1977	Navy
William J. Casey	1981	Law and Business
William H. Webster	1987	Law and Government
Robert M. Gates	1991	Government
R. James Woolsey	1993	Law and Government
John M. Deutsch	1995	Academia and Government
George J. Tenet	1997	Government

PRODUCER-CONSUMER PROBLEMS

Problems have developed between the "producers" of intelligence—analysts within the intelligence community—and the "consumers" of intelligence—the policymakers, especially the president and other high-level officials, who use this information to make decisions and justify their policies. The problem is that the producers and consumers often don't see eye to eye. The president often finds that the intelligence community does not provide him with useful information, while members of the intelligence community often get ambiguous and contradictory guidelines from their superiors and the president.

The president, as well as other policymakers, and members of the intelligence bureaucracy occupy different roles and different motivations influence their behavior. Consequently, it should not be too surprising that a producer-consumer problem has arisen and become a common part of the intelligence process. Presidents are always sensitive to the domestic political implications of their policies as they try to gain control of the bureaucracy, govern in the area of foreign policy, and lead the country. When they have not already made up their minds or when they are not strongly leaning in a particular direction, presidents often want relevant information and honest intelligence appraisals to better understand the issue and arrive at an optimal decision. However, when a course of action has been already decided or if a president is ideologically predisposed, he is likely to want information that reinforces his views. Under either of these circumstances, a president may become frustrated with the intelligence product that comes across his desk, especially if it is a result of infighting and compromise.

In the bureaucratic and political environment in which the intelligence community operates, it is easy to see how analysts can also become frustrated with the intelligence process. The ideal mission of intelligence officers involved in data collection and analysis is to provide a comprehensive and honest assessment of available information. Yet, they operate within a bureaucratic setting and must be cognizant of how their work affects their careers. Furthermore, they have to be very attuned to the policy inclinations and personal perspectives of higher-level officials, such as the president and his political appointees.

The producer-consumer problem affected **intelligence estimates in Vietnam**. According to John Huizenga, chief of intelligence estimates for Soviet affairs during the Lyndon Johnson administration, "In doing estimates about Vietnam, the problem was that if you believed that the policy being pursued was going to be a flat failure, and you said so, you were going to be out of business."[11] Beliefs about anticommunism and the invincibility of American power were so firmly embedded in the minds of American officials that it only allowed for certain narrow interpretations of the data that were in conformity with governmental policy. Ironically, as described by Daniel Ellsberg, a former Department of Defense official and eventual critic of the war, "There has never been an official of Deputy Assistant Secretary rank or higher (including myself) who could have passed in office a midterm freshman exam in modern Vietnamese history, if such a course existed in this country."[12]

The same pattern of the **politicization of intelligence** plagued the process in the Reagan administration. Reagan officials ignored National Security Agency information indicating that the Soviet generals who ordered the destruction of a South Korean jetliner in 1983 had genuinely believed that it was a spy plane, pressured the CIA to produce studies

concluding that El Salvadoran guerrillas and the Nicaraguan government posed a threat to U.S. security, and compelled the CIA to bring its estimates of Soviet military expenditures and production into accordance with the more pessimistic assessments made by military intelligence.[13] In other words, the intense anticommunism of President Reagan and other administration high-level officials, such as Director of Central Intelligence William Casey, was said to have slanted and tainted the honesty of the process responsible for intelligence information and assessments. One of the few times such producer-consumer problems, as took place under Director Casey, were aired before the public occurred in the fall of 1991 during the **nomination hearings of Robert Gates** to be President George Bush's director of central intelligence. Gates previously had been Casey's deputy director of intelligence.[14] Clearly, members of the intelligence community often must respond to cross-cutting pressures, and this affects the intelligence process and often contributes to producer-consumer problems.

VARIATION IN INTELLIGENCE SUCCESS

In an ideal setting, the intelligence community is engaged in a very precarious business. Even without problems in the producer-consumer relationship and coordination difficulties due to the large size, bureaucratic nature, and complexity of the intelligence community, the success of intelligence is not guaranteed. The world is simply too big, too complex, and constantly evolving. Information will always be incomplete and inadequate, while predictions about future behavior and trends can never be more than probabilities. For example, the incredible changes that have taken place in the Soviet Union and throughout Eastern Europe during the late 1980s and early 1990s understandably surprised and shocked the Western intelligence community. Thus, intelligence failures are inevitable.[15]

When one combines the patterns of size and complexity of the intelligence community, difficulties in coordination, and producer-consumer problems, a considerable amount of **intelligence failure**

is inevitable in actual practice. The ambiguity of the phenomena to be explained and predicted, the bureaucratic structures of the intelligence community, and the personality and beliefs held by major policymakers together determine the nature of the intelligence process and the value of the end-product. Along with intelligence successes, such as the Cuban Missile Crisis, there must be intelligence failures.

During the Vietnam War key questions involved the strength of the enemy's forces and the ability of the U.S. military to destroy enemy personnel and supplies getting into South Vietnam, thus weakening the will of the enemy. Yet, uncertainty is always the norm in war, especially a war fought in an unconventional way and far from home. Nevertheless, as noted in the previous chapter, the military and the CIA constantly fought over these intelligence estimates during the mid-1960s, while President Johnson and his closest military and civilian advisers supported the more optimistic military assessments. Therefore, the **Tet Offensive** represented a critical intelligence failure that led to the fall of President Johnson and the defeat of the United States in Vietnam.

The size and scope of the **Iranian revolution** against the Shah of Iran in 1979, as well as the failure of the Shah to repress it, was a surprise to members of the U.S. government. Although it is impossible to predict the time and intensity of any domestic instability, one of the reasons why developments in Iran came as such a surprise to the U.S. government was because the intelligence information relied upon by American policymakers had come from sources close to the Shah's regime. The American intelligence community did not have access to Iranians who were critical of the Shah. Since the beginning of the close relationship between the United States and Iranian governments in 1953, the American intelligence community relied increasingly on official Iranian sources and on "Savak", Iran's intelligence agency, for information about Iran's domestic situation. The information provided portrayed a stable and vibrant Shah regime, even though the domestic opposition was slowly building over the years.

Once the domestic uprising began, questions arose as to whether the Shah could survive the up-heaval and what U.S. policy should be. Traditional sources of intelligence, still close to the Shah's regime, argued that the Shah could survive if he repressed the opposition through military force and, once the Shah fell, argued that order could be restored through a military coup—the policy favored by National Security Adviser Zbigniew Brzezinski. Other policy analysts in the administration argued that the Shah's days were numbered, and promoted a more moderate solution designed to support a national coalition government—the position taken by Secretary of State Cyrus Vance. While the administration debated the nature of future developments in Iranian and American policy, events passed it by. During the year, the Shah fell, two moderate civilian governments arose and fell, and the revolutionary change was completed with the rise of the Ayatollah Khomeini to power. The intelligence failures in assessing the stability of the Shah and the nature of the new political situation resulting from the upheaval were complete.[16]

Iraq's attack of Kuwait on August 2, 1990, represented both intelligence failure and success. First, the U.S. intelligence community and policymakers showed little foresight concerning any threat that Iraq posed to American interests. On the contrary, after the rise of Ayatollah Khomeini in Iran, the Reagan and Bush administrations supported and sided with President Saddam Hussein throughout the 1980s. Second, although there was little intelligence foresight, as Saddam Hussein's threats against Kuwait increased and he began to mass Iraqi troops along the Kuwaiti border in July of 1990, the CIA warned administration policymakers of a possible invasion and predicted that one was imminent twenty-four to forty-eight hours before it occurred. Third, though an intelligence warning of the attack was made, President Bush and his close advisers chose to discount and ignore the warning as unlikely—a classic example of the producer-consumer problem over intelligence estimates. Hence, when the Iraqi invasion occurred on August 2, President Bush and his advisers were initially shocked and caught by surprise. It has been reported that the national intelligence officer responsible for the warnings about the impending

Iraqi attack was subsequently demoted.[17] It has also been reported that President Bush's decision to double the American military presence in the Persian Gulf to over 500,000 troops for a possible offensive may have been based on intelligence reports that overestimated the Iraqi military in and around Kuwait by as much as 300,000 troops.[18]

On August 18, 1991, President Bush, and other high-level officials of his administration, were shocked to find out about the **overthrow of Mikhail Gorbachev**, the president of the Soviet Union. Yet, "for nearly a year the CIA and the Pentagon's DIA had peppered the Bush administration with a series of increasingly dire warnings that Mikhail Gorbachev's days were numbered. The problem was getting anyone to pay attention."[19] In fact, on August 17, the day before the coup, "the CIA's National Intelligence Daily (NID), which circulates among top administration officials, said Kremlin conservatives were prepared to move against the Soviet president." Nevertheless, "until tanks rolled in the streets of Moscow, the White House and the State Department insisted that Gorbachev could weather any challenge."[20] One of the problems was that the State Department's Bureau of Intelligence and Research maintained that Gorbachev's future was safe. More importantly, however, it appears that President Bush's, and his senior advisers', commitment and reliance on Gorbachev in American-Soviet relations colored his optimism. Thus, what could have been a great intelligence success ended being an intelligence failure.[21]

Intelligence estimates are both a vital part of the policymaking process and a very difficult process for maximizing the success of U.S. foreign policy. Yet, the patterns of coordination problems, consumer-producer problems, and variations in intelligence success are not well known or understood among the general public. Americans are brought up with such great faith in science, learning, technological know-how and American ingenuity that they do not appreciate the global complexity, uncertainty, and unpredictability that presidents and governments must cope with in formulating and implementing policy. Intelligence failures are inevitable and future events are often unpredictable and uncontrollable.[22] The collapse of communism in Eastern Europe sym-

bolized by the **fall of the Berlin Wall** and the collapse of the Soviet Union in the late eighties and early nineties is the ultimate illustration of this, for it came as a shock and a surprise to virtually everyone within the intelligence community and throughout the world.[23] Nevertheless, the politics of U.S. foreign policy are such that presidents are heavily judged on how they respond to such unpredictable events and, most importantly, on their outcomes, thus impacting on their future ability to govern.

THE CENTRAL INTELLIGENCE AGENCY

"Of all the organizations that miss having the Soviet Union as an enemy, the CIA has undoubtedly been hit the hardest." In the words of Theodore Draper, "The reason is that the CIA was specifically established in 1947 to struggle with the Soviet enemy. . . . But now the enemy has vanished. Its most dedicated American antagonist has been deprived of its mission." Now, "the CIA wanders about in a wilderness of self-doubt and recrimination."[24]

The **origins of the CIA** lie with the operations of the **Office of Strategic Services (OSS)**, which was originally created on June 13, 1942, under the Chiefs of Staff of the armed services in support of U.S. efforts in World War II. Although the OSS is often remembered for some daring (and usually unsuccessful) covert operations behind enemy lines under Director "Wild Bill" Donovan, the OSS was also engaged in analyzing the enemy using bright, young minds of all ages and diverse backgrounds. The OSS utilized civilians and members of all branches of the armed forces in gathering and evaluating information from the major theaters of operations as well as from underground groups in enemy-occupied territory. The OSS was disbanded following the war in which many of its intelligence activities and personnel resided temporarily with the Central Intelligence Group until the passage of the National Security Act of 1947 created the CIA.

The National Security Act that created the Central Intelligence Agency as the major agency responsible for intelligence abroad was the product of political compromise. Many believed that there was a need for a foreign intelligence capability during peacetime and supported an agency that could centralize the intelligence process. However, others argued against the rise of a super spy agency reminiscent of the German Gestapo and some saw the power of centralization as a threat to those agencies already involved in intelligence. Therefore, a new intelligence agency was created, but placed under civilian **leadership**. At least one of the two leadership positions, the director of Central Intelligence or the deputy director, had to be occupied by a civilian. Both positions had to be confirmed by the Senate and the DCI reported directly to the president. While the DCI was given authority to coordinate the intelligence process throughout the government and to act as the major adviser to the president on intelligence matters, the other intelligence agencies kept their autonomy. The act also attempted to clarify jurisdictional boundaries and disputes, restricting the FBI to domestic activities and limiting the CIA's legal role to outside U.S. borders.

When most people think of the CIA, they think of covert operations and "dirty tricks." As essay 9.1 on Hoover and the FBI shows, the CIA is not the only intelligence agency involved in covert operations. Although the CIA is the intelligence organization primarily engaged in political and paramilitary covert operations abroad, these are not the only **functions** and activities performed by the agency. The CIA is heavily involved in all three basic intelligence functions and bears the additional responsibility of coordinating the intelligence community, making it a unique intelligence agency.[25]

Since its beginnings, the CIA has developed into *a large bureaucratic organization composed of four general divisions:* intelligence, science and technology, administration, and operations. Most current CIA personnel are involved in the basic intelligence functions of data collection and analysis. The intelligence division is responsible for producing the CIA's own **intelligence assessments (IAs)** for the policymaking community and coordinating the **national intelligence estimates (NIEs)** which are a product of the entire intelligence community. The science and

technology division is responsible for developing mechanisms and gadgets used in the type of intelligence activities made most famous in the 007 James Bond movies (although they were always more science fiction than reality). The science and technology division, for instance, developed the U-2 and SR-71 spy planes. The administration division engages in personnel decisions and manages the paperwork throughout the CIA bureaucracy. The personnel within intelligence, science and technology, and administration occupy traditional professional roles; only those within the operations division are involved in covert operations.

The **operations division** is responsible for the CIA's most renowned activities—covert operations. *Operations actually involve two types of activities:* espionage and political/paramilitary intervention. **Espionage** involves "human intelligence" and counterintelligence, such as running spies and double agents abroad in order to access information and prevent foreign intelligence agencies from penetrating the CIA. Political and paramilitary action involve the covert operations area where so-called dirty tricks are most commonly practiced.

The CIA, in other words, operates as a large bureaucracy with a significant division of labor. Given its size and complexity, the CIA is **composed of different subcultures**. The intelligence and the science and technology divisions tend to employ analysts and scientists who often hold Ph.D.s and are research and scholarly oriented, paralleling what one might find in a research institute or university. Operations, on the other hand, is composed of two different subcultures because espionage and political/paramilitary intervention are two different activities and require different kinds of skills. Espionage agents act as spies and tend to be secretive, cautious, and loyal. Their style of operation is most realistically depicted in the novels by John le Carré, such as *The Spy Who Came in From the Cold.* CIA operatives involved in political and paramilitary activities tend to be much more action-oriented, adventuristic, bold, and often flamboyant. In fact, the upper echelon in operations and throughout the CIA, going back to the days of the OSS, have been charged with elitism since they predominantly come from the most prominent universities and socioeconomic backgrounds.[26]

EVOLUTION OF THE CIA AND COVERT OPERATIONS

. . . .

The CIA is much more than a group of covert operatives who spy abroad and manipulate others in the name of U.S. national security. It is *important to understand the evolution of the CIA and its covert operations for two reasons,* especially as it pertains to political and paramilitary action. First, operations and action-types—often referred to as "cowboys"—have dominated CIA leadership throughout most of its history. Directors of central intelligence, for example, have tended to come from the operations side of intelligence within the government and the military as indicated in table 9.1 (many of the earlier DCIs were originally with the OSS). Second, American policymakers have relied upon CIA covert operations as a major U.S. foreign policy instrument since World War II. While the U.S. government attempted to deter Soviet expansion through the threat of nuclear and conventional war, it relied on political and paramilitary intervention to fight communism covertly throughout the globe during the cold war. Theodore Shackley, a senior covert operations specialist who spent twenty-eight years with the CIA, has referred to political and paramilitary action as *The Third Option,* superior to diplomacy and war.[27]

In order to fully understand the intelligence community and U.S. foreign policy since World War II, it is crucial to go beyond the government's overt behavior and examine its covert action as well. The CIA is the major organization within the government responsible for **covert foreign policy behavior.** Most Americans, however, do not understand the individuals, alliances, and activities that pervade the global underworld. They underestimate the important role that the secret world of covert operations has played in the U.S. government's effort to fight the cold war for over forty years. Given its secrecy and preoccupation with manipulation, we can never know everything about covert operations and must remain skeptical of new information as it arises. Nonetheless, beginning in the 1970s a growing body of information has painted a consistent picture of CIA covert operations in pursuit of American national security.[28] *Since its creation, the CIA and its covert operations have evolved through three stages until the collapse of the Soviet Union:*

1. The "Good Ole" Days, 1947 through early 1970s;
2. The "Fall" and Reform, early 1970s through 1979;
3. The Resurgence, 1980s.

THE "GOOD OLE" DAYS

As with most of the national security bureaucracy, the late 1940s and 1950s represented a time when the **CIA quickly grew in budget, personnel, and missions.** The bureaucratic divisions and functions of the CIA expanded, but none more than the operations division. Estimates are that the vast majority of the CIA's budget and personnel throughout the cold war years were devoted to operations. The president used the CIA to perform certain covert political and paramilitary actions that no other agency performed and that were officially denied in public. CIA covert operations became the "hidden hand" of U.S. foreign policy.

The CIA was allowed **considerable independence** in running its covert operations under presidential supervision. New presidents often retained the previous DCI and, when new appointments were made, chose an individual who had risen within the CIA and the operations division. This maximized the continuity and power of the CIA over the years. The heyday of covert operations occurred under DCI **Allen Dulles** from 1952–1961, a time when his brother, John Foster Dulles, also served as secretary of state.[29] Even though the president often remained distant from the details of an operation, the DCI responded to presidential initiative and choice. Also, no real oversight existed outside the executive branch. The CIA had considerable leeway in its covert operations because the cold war period was a time when the president and the executive branch were dominant in national security policy and an anticommunist consensus existed throughout the government and society. Members of Congress basically supported presidential foreign policies, preferring to remain uninvolved and, for the most part, uninformed about the CIA's covert activities. This perspective was reflected among the public and the media as well.

Such a permissive attitude toward the CIA did not exist at its creation. According to the **CIA's charter** in the National Security Act of 1947, no political and paramilitary role was envisioned. The CIA was created to provide the president with an intelligence capability to engage in data collection and analysis as well as coordinate the larger intelligence community existing at the time. In fact, "in spite of the anticommunist tenor of the Truman Doctrine, and in spite of the presence of anticommunists in Congress, nobody mentioned the Soviet Union or its clandestine services in the congressional debate on the CIA provision of the National Security Act. Congressmen were introspectively concerned with gestapo-like tendencies at home."[30] However, one clause of the CIA charter allowed it to "perform such other functions and duties related to intelligence affecting the national security as the National Security Council may from time to time direct," and this provided the later legal justification for involving the CIA in "cloak and dagger" operations.[31] Thus, the CIA soon became the major governmental organization responsible for covert actions abroad in support of the policy of containment.

One can better understand the vital role that political and paramilitary intervention was to play in U.S. foreign policy if one imagines the post–World War II world that most American leaders saw. It was a world perceived to be divided between the forces of good and evil—the free world represented by the United States, democracy, freedom, and Christianity against the communist bloc represented by the Soviet Union, communism, totalitarianism, and atheism. It was a world of great power rivalry where the Soviet Union was seen as aggressive, expanding its territorial control, and directly threatening American interests and the status quo. American policy-

makers were preoccupied with rearming and creating alliances to deter Soviet expansionism and, if deterrence failed, to fighting a "hot" war. At the same time, American policymakers increasingly came to rely on covert operations to fight the "cold war." Reliance on covert operations intensified as American public opinion turned sour towards America's military stalemate in the Korean War, where no end was in sight, and American troops increasingly came home injured and dead.

The CIA became an important tool of U.S. foreign policy during the Harry Truman administration immediately after its creation in 1947. One of its earliest actions involved the effort to manipulate the **1948 Italian elections** through a propaganda campaign. World War II had destroyed the economies of the European states and created political instability throughout Europe. Legal Communist parties were flourishing in France and Italy. American policymakers feared that a victory by the Italian Communist party in the 1948 elections would result in the fall of Italian democracy and provide an important strategic ally to the Soviet bloc. The CIA intervened to fund and support the Christian Democratic party. Intervention included efforts to discredit the Italian Communist party election campaign by distributing propaganda and disinformation through a network of Italian media "assets" (paid agents) employed throughout the print and electronic media: newspaper, magazine, and radio reporters and editors. The Christian Democrats won the election, although it remains unclear whether the CIA played a decisive role. The irony of the covert Italian campaign was that U.S. foreign policy manipulated a democratic election abroad while publicly committed to the promotion of democratic practice. The success of the Italian covert campaign set the stage for future CIA intervention in democratic politics in Italy, Europe, and wherever a threat to American interests was perceived.

In the late 1940s and 1950s, the CIA also supported **partisan resistance movements** in communist countries to promote internal instability and domestic uprisings. The CIA trained emigres and secretly transported them into Albania, Poland, Yugoslavia, the Baltic states, Soviet Georgia and the

Ukraine. After the nationalist supporters of Chiang Kai-shek were driven out of mainland China and established a new Taiwan government on the island of Formosa, the CIA set up a partisan movement in Burma where many of the nationalist forces had fled. These partisan resistance efforts made very little headway; in fact, in most cases they were quick and complete failures.

Under President Dwight Eisenhower, the CIA became involved in its **first successful overthrow of a foreign government—the Iranian coup of 1953**. Historically, Iran had been ruled by the Pahlavi dynasty, with the Shah as King, in a region of the world traditionally dominated by Great Britain. The Second World War, however, unleashed third-world nationalism which gained strength in Iran until the Shah and the Pahlavi dynasty collapsed in 1953. The leader of the Iranian nationalists, Mohammed Mossadegh, proclaimed an independent and neutralist state in the growing cold war and demanded that Great Britain renegotiate its most favorable contract for Iranian oil. The British, whose empire was in eclipse at this time, asked for U.S. assistance to oust the new nationalist regime. U.S. policymakers feared that Mossadegh was playing into the hands of the communists and the Soviet Union. Thus, the CIA and the British MI6 (its CIA equivalent) staged a military coup in which Mossadegh was overthrown and the Shah's regime was restored. The Shah subsequently awarded Gulf, Standard of New Jersey, Texaco, and Socony-Mobil a 40 percent share of Iranian oil rights.[32]

The **1954 coup in Guatemala** is one of the more important actions taken by the CIA; it became the model for many of its subsequent actions. Guatemala had a history of dictatorial rule. In 1950, Guatemala experienced its first taste of democracy with the election of Jacabo Arbenz Guzmán as president. However, relations between Guatemala and the United States faltered when Arbenz promoted agrarian reform to improve the situation of the impoverished masses. These reforms alienated the oligarchy that dominated the Guatemalan economy and American policymaker preferences for U.S. foreign investment and reliance on the market as the path to economic development. The situation deteriorated further when Arbenz expropriated 234,000 acres of uncultivated land owned by the United Fruit Company, an American company which owned over 40 percent of Guatemalan territory. By late summer of 1953, American policymakers, such as President Eisenhower and Secretary of State Dulles, concluded that the Arbenz regime was becoming increasingly communist and posed a threat to American national security. A shipment of Soviet bloc (Czechoslovakian) arms to the Guatemalan military in May 1954, in response to American governmental cuts in ties, served to confirm and justify the need for a covert overthrow of the Arbenz government. Unlike the Iranian case, this was a CIA "controlled" operation from beginning to end, for Central America was a region that the United States traditionally dominated. The CIA trained several hundred Guatemalans on a United Fruit Company plantation in neighboring Honduras and chose Colonel Carlos Castillo Armas to lead the attack. On June 18, the small military force led by Colonel Armas crossed into Guatemala toward Guatemala City, the capital. Actually, President Arbenz could have easily defeated the small invading army. However, the invasion force appeared much larger and closer in part due to the CIA's psychological warfare campaign. Psychological covert operations were reinforced when several small planes piloted by CIA operatives bombed Guatemala City and other key towns. Arbenz lost his nerve, fled the country and Castillo Armas became the new military dictator. Democracy in Guatemala, thus, was overthrown by the CIA and Guatemala would not experience another move towards constitutional democracy until the 1980s.[33]

The most unsavory type of CIA covert operation was **foreign assassinations**. During the 1960 independence crisis in the Congo (later known as Zaire), it is alleged that the CIA attempted to assassinate the first prime minister and nationalist African leader, **Patrice Lumumba**, who was perceived as being too independent of American interests and open to communist subversion. The CIA was supposedly unsuccessful in its assassination attempts. However, Lumumba was assassinated eventually, although it remains unclear who was the culprit. With

Lumumba and others out of the way, the CIA and the U.S. government backed the rise to power of Mobutu Sese Seko, general of the army, who ruled a corrupt regime for thirty years and impoverished the country.[34]

In addition to destabilizing, overthrowing, and eliminating so-called unfriendly regimes and leaders, the CIA was active in **supporting the stability of foreign governments** allied to the United States and supporting the status quo. Such support often included participating in an allied government's violent repression of its own people. As George Kennan, in a report to Secretary of State Dean Acheson, stated as early as 1950:

> We cannot be too dogmatic about the methods by which local communists can be dealt with. . . . Where the concepts and the traditions of popular government are too weak to absorb successfully the intensity of communist attack, then we must concede that harsh governmental measures of repression may be the only answer; that these measures may have to proceed from regimes whose origins and methods would not stand the test of American concepts of democratic procedure; and that such regimes and such methods may be preferable alternatives, and indeed the only alternatives, to further communist successes.[35]

In **Indonesia**, for example, the U.S. government and the CIA, beginning in 1958, actively tried to destabilize President Sukarno, a prominent leader of the third-world non-aligned movement (like many Indonesians, he had only one name). After his overthrow in 1965, American intelligence assisted the new government of General Suharto in eliminating Indonesian Communist Party (PKI) members and repressing all internal dissent, which included providing the Indonesian army with lists of people to be arrested and killed. As one former U.S. embassy official put it, "It was a big help to the army. They probably killed a lot of people, and I probably have a lot of blood on my hands, but that's not all bad. There's a time when you have to strike hard at the decisive moment." Estimates of the number of Indonesians

killed in the ruthless campaign range from 300,000 to one million, with hundreds of thousands jailed without trial. Within the agency the Indonesian experience was considered another model for future operations.[36] U.S. governmental support for brutal dictatorial regimes throughout the world, in fact, was common, including the Mobutu government in Zaire, the Shah of Iran, and the Somoza government in Nicaragua.

Not only was the CIA active in supporting allied governments, foreign leaders were often on the CIA payroll and the CIA frequently engaged in **training of foreign intelligence personnel**, including those engaged in covert operations. The armed forces and the national police of many governments allied to the United States also were trained by U.S. military and government personnel. Thus, the U.S. government was heavily engaged in providing overt and covert support with billions of dollars of foreign assistance to friendly governments to ensure their security as part of America's larger campaign to combat the cold war. In what CIA officers at the time considered to be one of their "greatest coups," a tip from a "deep cover" CIA agent in South Africa led to the August 5, 1962, **arrest of Nelson Mandela**, the underground leader of the African National Congress (ANC), which was the major force opposing the Afrikaner government and the system of apartheid.[37] Nelson Mandela was not released from prison by the South African government until February 1990 and after the transition to black majority rule became the first president of South Africa.

Covert operations were used in the U.S. government's effort to be rid of **Fidel Castro** in Cuba, which began under the Eisenhower administration. The operation was designed and implemented very much like the 1954 Guatemalan operation. Hundreds of Cubans who had left Cuba and were living in Miami were recruited and trained by the CIA in Honduras as an invasion force. In 1961, President John Kennedy supported the **Bay of Pigs operation** and the Cubans invaded, with limited air cover provided by the CIA. Unlike the Guatemalan operation, however, the Bay of Pigs invasion was a complete failure. The actual invasion strategy was flawed to begin with and Castro did not flee, but used the

Cuban military to destroy and capture the invading force. The Bay of Pigs fiasco was the first major CIA covert operation that became public, embarrassing the U.S. government and President Kennedy.[38]

From that point on President John Kennedy and his brother, Attorney General Robert Kennedy, mounted a vendetta against Fidel Castro. They gave the CIA authority to use all means available to destabilize and assassinate Castro. The CIA went so far as to turn to the Mafia for assistance, for the Mafia maintained connections in Cuba, forged in the days when they ran gambling casinos before Castro took power. Yet, the covert plans to assassinate Castro failed. Most were harebrained schemes that only James Bond could have pulled off, such as attempts to slip Castro the hallucinogen LSD via a cigar, to give him a pen with a poison tip, to explode clamshells while he dove in the Caribbean, and to sprinkle his shoes with an agent to make his beard fall out and with it, according to the psychological warfare experts, his Latin machismo.[39] Many people think that all the intrigue and activities involving the CIA, the Cubans, the Mafia, and the intelligence underworld had something to do with the events surrounding the assassination of President John F. Kennedy.

Failures did not deter the CIA's involvement in covert operations, nor the president from relying on such operations as a major instrument of U.S. foreign policy. The early successes of the Italian elections and the Iranian and Guatemalan coups reinforced an optimism that pervaded the world of covert operations. Thus the United States' Americanization of the war in Vietnam not only led to a major overt military effort to keep South Vietnam independent of North Vietnamese communism, but included major **covert efforts in Vietnam** as well. The U.S. government, with the use of the CIA, supported President Ngo Dinh Diem beginning in 1954. As Diem became less effective and lost credibility as an independent leader of South Vietnam, the U.S. government backed a military coup against Diem in 1963. From that point on, South Vietnam experienced a revolving-door government, as one military general after another became the president, with U.S. government support crucial for each leader's

rise and fall. The CIA was also active in training members of the Meo and Hmong tribes to conduct military operations in support of the American war effort, including a secret war in Laos. The Vietnam era program for which the CIA was most notorious was the **Phoenix program**, which resulted in the development of a massive internal security apparatus for identifying and "neutralizing" thousands of suspected Vietcong and communist supporters. Not only were many innocent individuals jailed, but torture, terrorism, and political assassination were also used as part of the Phoenix operation.

Beginning with the Bay of Pigs fiasco and through the 1960s, the CIA started to decline. CIA intelligence estimates were losing credibility in the White House, especially under Presidents Johnson and Nixon. Operations were less successful than in the 1950s and were being exposed in the media, creating embarrassment and controversy for the United States government and the American people at home and abroad. Nonetheless, even though the political fortunes of the CIA declined, the president felt that he had little choice but to rely on the CIA and its covert operations to support U.S. global commitments and a containment strategy designed to eradicate threats to American national security.

The last major covert operation during the socalled "Good Ole" Days occurred in **Chile** during the Nixon administration. Chile had been operating as a democracy since the early 1960s. However, the popularity of the Christian Democratic leader, Eduardo Frei, was declining by the late 1960s. The major challenger in the 1970 national elections was Salvador Allende, an avowed Marxist who believed in socialist democracy. Although the CIA intervened heavily in the elections, Allende received a plurality and became the president of Chile. Allende's economic policies angered American multinational companies, such as ITT and the copper industry, and the U.S. government imposed economic sanctions on the new government. Covertly, the CIA under President Nixon led a campaign to destabilize the Chilean economy and persuaded the Chilean military to stage a coup. The military coup came in 1973, and installed Augusto Pinochet as the dictator of Chile for the next 16 years.

The cases discussed above highlight but a few of the *important covert activities abroad involving:* support for friendly governments, counterinsurgency operations, propaganda campaigns and psychological warfare, partisan resistance movements, sabotage and destabilization campaigns, invasions and coups d'etat, and assassinations conducted by the CIA. It has been reported that by 1953 the CIA had major covert operations in progress in forty-eight countries, while three-fourths of the agency's budget and two-thirds of its employees were devoted to espionage and political intervention.[40] A U.S. Senate special select committee investigating foreign and military intelligence in 1975 found that the CIA had "conducted some 900 major or sensitive covert action projects plus several thousand smaller projects since 1961."[41] In other words, the CIA, in its heyday, was engaged in covert operations all over the world, with as much as one-third of its interventions taking place in "pro-Western" democracies.[42] **Table 9.2** highlights some of the major covert operations that have come to light during the "Good Ole" Days. The nature of covert operations and the secrecy involved means much CIA covert activity remains unknown.

The **CIA was also active at home**, although CIA domestic covert activity was in violation of the law as stipulated in the National Security Act of 1947. The CIA spent millions of dollars funding hundreds of private individuals and groups active in business, labor, journalism, education, philanthropy, religion, and the arts as a means to promote the anticommunist message and stifle dissent to the U.S. policy of containment. Within academia, hundreds of academics located in over 100 American colleges and universities contributed to CIA-funded projects while the National Students Association, the largest student organization in the country, was funded primarily by the CIA from 1952 to 1967. Although those who were directly supported agreed to work and front for the CIA, thousands of others unknowingly and indirectly aided the CIA bidding by joining CIA-sponsored organizations.[43]

With the growing movement against the Vietnam War in the middle 1960s, the CIA under Presidents Johnson and Nixon conducted **Operation Chaos** "to find out [the] extent to which Soviets, Chicoms [Chinese Communists] and Cubans are exploiting our domestic problems in terms of espionage and subversion."[44] This resulted in CIA attempts to infiltrate the antiwar movement and undermine its credibility and impact. No evidence was ever found that the mounting unrest was anything other than indigenous and democratic. Yet, a computerized list was developed, naming over three hundred thousand citizens and organizations that the CIA deemed to be potential security threats.[45] Not only did the president and the CIA violate the intelligence legal charter, Operation Chaos violated the constitutional right of American citizens freely to voice their opinions and participate in the democratic practice of politics (this will be discussed at greater length in chapter 17 on civil liberties).

THE "FALL" AND REFORM

The Americanization of the war in Vietnam and the failure of the U.S. military to succeed politicized segments of American society contributed in leading to the collapse of the anticommunist consensus. The domestic political environment became even more critical when the revelations of Watergate uncovered abuses of presidential power. These abuses included the use of current and former CIA operatives such as E. Howard Hunt and a number of Cubans from Miami who were a part of the original Bay of Pigs operation, in illegal and unconstitutional activities. In this new political climate, charges were made that the president had become too powerful and abused his office in the name of national security. The CIA was a special focus of attention and was accused of activities which were immoral, illegal, and counterproductive to the long-term interests of the American people.

President Gerald Ford appointed the **Rockefeller Commission** in 1975 to investigate the intelligence community and recommend reforms. But, as with many presidential commissions, the Rockefeller Commission had little credibility. It was seen as a means for removing the issue of covert operations from the national spotlight and minimizing the demands for reform. From the president's perspective, covert operations were a useful instrument

TABLE 9.2
Major CIA Covert Operations During the "Good Ole" Days

1947–48	Propaganda campaign during the 1948 Italian national elections
1947–48	Propaganda campaign during the 1948 French national elections
1948–52	Partisan resistance movements in Eastern Europe and Soviet Union
1949	Anglo-American effort to overthrow the Albanian government
1950–70s	Propaganda campaigns through Radio Liberty and Radio Free Europe
1952–60	KMT Chinese partisan resistance movement on Sino-Burmese border
1953	Anglo-American overthrow of Prime Minister Mohammed Mossadegh of Iran
1953–54	Campaign to support Ramon Magsaysay's presidential candidacy and counter Huk insurgency in Philippines
1954	Overthrow of President Jacobo Arbenz of Guatemala
1950s–70s	Subsidization of domestic and foreign groups and publications
1953–70s	Drug testing and mind control program
1954–70s	Effort to overthrow leader Ho Chi Minh and the North Vietnamese goverment
1955	Effort to destablize President José Figueres's government of Costa Rica
1958	Support of Tibetan partisan resistance movement in China
1958–65	Effort to destablize President Sukarno of Indonesia
1960	Alleged effort to assassinate General Abdul Kassem, leader of Iraq
1960	Alleged effort to assassinate President Abdul Nasser of Egypt
1960	Alleged effort to assassinate political leader Patrice Lumumba of Congo
1961	Effort to overthrow Fidel Castro, leader of Cuba
1961	Effort to assassinate Rafael Trujillo, leader of Dominican Republic
1961	Effort to destablize President Kwame Nkrumah of Ghana
1960s	Effort to assassinate Fidel Castro of Cuba
1960s	Fought secret war in Laos
1962–63	Destablized the Ecuadorean governments of Ibarra and Arosemena
1963	Destablized Prime Minister Cheddi Jagan's government of British Guiana
1963	Supported overthrow of President Ngo Dinh Diem of South Vietnam
1960s	Conducted pacification and Phoenix programs in Vietnam
1964	Campaign in support of President Eduardo Frei in 1964 Chilean elections
1964	Supported military coup against President Joao Goulart of Brazil
1967	Supported military coup in Greece
1967–70s	Domestic campaign against antiwar movement and political dissent
1970–73	Destablized President Salvador Allende of Chile

SOURCES: Rhodri Jeffreys-Jones, *CIA and American Democracy* (New Haven, CT: Yale University Press, 1989); Jonathan Kwitny, *Endless Enemies* ((New York: Penguin, 1984); Thomas Powers, *The Man Who Kept the Secrets* (New York: Pocket Books, 1979); John Prados, *President's Secret Wars* (New York: William Morrow, 1986); John Ranelagh, *The Agency* (New York: Simon and Schuster, 1986); David Wise and Thomas B. Ross, *The Invisible Government* (New York: Vintage, 1974); U.S., Congress, Senate, *Alleged Assassination Plots Involving Foreign Leaders*, Congressional Report (94th Cong., 1st sess., November 18, 1975); and U.S. Congress, Senate, *Final Report of the Select Committee to Study Governmental Operations with Respect to Intelligence Activities*, Books 1–6, Congressional Report (94th Cong., 2nd sess., April 14, 1976).

of foreign policy. In fact, while the Rockefeller Commission was operating, President Ford and Secretary of State Henry Kissinger were supervising a **major CIA covert operation in Angola**. This involved funding, training, and equipping two independence forces who were battling for control of Angola with a Soviet-backed independence force following the end of Portuguese colonialism. Ford and Kissinger tried to keep the operation secret from Congress at a time when members of Congress were reasserting their authority in foreign affairs. When word of the Angolan operation leaked, Congress voted to abort it and began its own investigation of intelligence.[46]

The House and Senate each conducted major investigations of the intelligence community and covert operations. The **congressional investigations** led to the first public knowledge of the scale of covert operations conducted by the CIA. To put it mildly, most Americans were shocked to discover the degree to which their government was in the business of overthrowing democracies, conducting coups d'etat, and performing political assassinations. The exposés were responsible for the negative image that most Americans now hold of the CIA as the super secret "cloak-and-dagger" arm of the U.S. government. The exposés also led to the fall of the CIA and the **call for intelligence reform**.

In this political climate, the intelligence community, especially the CIA and covert operations, experienced a major decline. Under President Ford, and to a greater extent under President Jimmy Carter, the CIA budget and personnel were cut, while greater emphasis was placed on the intelligence side of the agency and its technological capabilities. During this time, DCIs such as George Bush under President Ford and Admiral Stansfield Turner under President Carter, were recruited from outside the intelligence community. Nowhere were the cuts greater than in the operations division, for both espionage and political action. During this time over 1,800 covert operatives were fired or forced to take early retirement and most covert operations were cut, including major political and paramilitary programs. Presidential executive orders were issued that limited the kinds of covert operations the CIA could conduct. This included forbidding U.S. governmen-

tal personnel from becoming involved in political assassinations.

In addition to greater limitations and oversight of intelligence activities within the executive branch, Congress became actively involved in overseeing covert operations by the **creation of intelligence committees** in both chambers. The **Freedom of Information Act**, passed in 1967, was strengthened to allow public access to classified information. Members of Congress also attempted to produce a new intelligence charter, allowing further control of the intelligence community. Yet they could not reach a compromise on a final product. Nevertheless, the use of covert operations as a tool of U.S. foreign policy, and morale among covert operatives, reached its nadir by the end of the 1970s.

THE RESURGENCE

Beginning in 1980, the CIA and covert operations got a new lease on life. The resurgence of the CIA began during the last year of the Carter administration, reflecting the rise of political conservatism and growing concern with the threat of the Soviet Union. The Iran hostage crisis that President Carter faced and the Soviet invasion of Afghanistan in December 1979 resulted in the reinstatement of containment at the forefront of U.S. foreign policy. As part of the commitment to contain the Soviet Union within the Persian Gulf area, President Carter approved a major covert operation to send money and arms to the Afghan resistance forces through U.S.-controlled sources and agents in Pakistan. It was under the Reagan administration, however, that the CIA and the use of covert operations became a major force in U.S. foreign policy reminiscent of the cold war days. **William Casey**, a personal friend of President Reagan, a self-made businessman and millionaire, a strident anticommunist, and a former member of the OSS during World War II days, was selected as the director of central intelligence. Under Casey, the CIA rejuvenated its operations division and rehired many former covert operatives. Although the CIA's budget remained secret, experts believe that the budget of the CIA may have grown over 20 percent a year—a faster rate of growth than experienced by the military in its buildup and at a time when efforts were made to impose domestic spending cuts.[47]

U.S. foreign policy again became preoccupied with the threat of Soviet communism. The Reagan administration greatly expanded the U.S. government's military and intelligence capabilities to deter and fight the enemy. It also tried to recreate a cold war climate in which the demands of national security would be supreme. The CIA under Casey immediately became active in combating communism abroad. The CIA launched over a dozen "major" covert operations (defined by the congressional intelligence committees as an operation costing over five million dollars or designed to overthrow a foreign government) in places such as Central America, Afghanistan, Angola, Iran, Libya, Ethiopia, Mauritius, and Cambodia.[48]

With the exception of the defense buildup, President Reagan was unable to convince most Americans of the critical and immediate nature of the communist threat, even in nearby Central America. Given the political environment and its commitment to defeat communism, Reagan administration policymakers felt that they had no choice but to rely on covert operations and mislead the public about its Central American policies. The most important of these operations involved creating the contra resistance force in an attempt to destabilize and overthrow the new Nicaraguan Sandinista regime—the most significant covert operation during the Reagan administration.

The **contra covert war** was eventually outlawed by Congress in 1985 and 1986. Nevertheless, the Reagan administration circumvented the law by pursuing the contra operation through the NSC staff and relying on private operatives and groups. President Reagan chose to exercise "prerogative government" at a time when most Americans were not convinced that the threat of communism constituted a national emergency. In the post–Vietnam War environment, however, it is extremely difficult to keep covert operations covert for long. Therefore, the lack of political support in the country for a return to the cold war guaranteed a crisis of governance for the Reagan presidency when the true na-

ture of the contra covert operations became exposed. (See **essay 9.2** for an overview of the secret contra war.)

Colonel **Moammar Gadhafi**, the leader of Libya, also was the target of efforts to destabilize and overthrow his regime. Just as the Soviet Union represented the source of all evil in the world in the mind of President Reagan, Gadhafi was perceived as the major instigator of world terrorism. Although most of the CIA plots either were not carried out or failed, the stage was set for military conflict between the United States and Libya, and brought the U.S. military attack in 1986. One of the purposes of the American attack, which included bombing locations where Gadhafi was known to have slept, was to assassinate him, according to writer Seymour Hersh. It was revealed that the White House also attempted to destabilize the Libyan government in October of 1986 through the use of disinformation in the Western and American media.[49]

One plot that has received virtually no attention was the CIA plan to destabilize the Marxist regime in **Grenada** as early as summer of 1981. The American invasion of Grenada was justified to the American public as a humanitarian effort to save Americans whose lives were endangered. Yet the story is much more complex than portrayed by the Reagan administration. The tiny West Indies island of Grenada had a Marxist government, led by Prime Minister Maurice Bishop, which was receiving assistance from Cuba. Soon after President Reagan took office, the CIA presented to the congressional intelligence committees a covert plan to destabilize the economy and the Bishop government. The reception by members of the intelligence committees was negative and the plans were shelved. In 1983, however, a power struggle ensued within the ruling Marxist leadership and Prime Minister Bishop was deposed by his more radical adversary. The bloody coup gave the Reagan administration the justification for doing overtly what it had originally wanted to do covertly. The U.S. military was called upon to invade and occupy the island to overthrow the Marxist government, send a signal to the Sandinistas and Fidel Castro (the longtime American adversary who was supporting the Nicaraguan government)

ESSAY 9.2
THE SECRET CONTRA WAR

The highest priority of President Reagan's foreign policy team when he entered office was to deter and combat the threat of communism abroad. Nowhere was the threat perceived to be greater than in Central America, especially in Nicaragua, where the administration attempted to destabilize the country and overthrow the government. The Reagan administration's scheme to defeat communism in Nicaragua was quite complex. The U.S. "rollback" policy consisted of overt action and covert war. The U.S. government imposed economic sanctions and cut off trade to damage the Nicaraguan economy (historically dependent on American trade). The U.S. military threatened the use of force against Nicaragua by regularly conducting military exercises off the Nicaraguan coasts and in Honduras near the northern border of Nicaragua (where American military bases and airstrips were built). The ultimate means employed by the Reagan administration to overthrow the Sandinistas, however, was reliance on covert war. Under DCI William Casey, a major covert operation was devised by the CIA to develop, train, and equip a counterrevolutionary force of Nicaraguans, known as the contras. By the mid-1980s, the contras had been molded into a 10,000- to 15,000-strong military force and were conducting military operations in Nicaragua.

The Reagan administration needed congressional approval for its policies and attempted to persuade the American people that communism in Central America was a real and immediate threat to American security. The government public relations campaign included the use of political propaganda and disinformation to maximize support and minimize dissent. Nevertheless, most of the public was unresponsive. Consequently, Congress never gave President Reagan all that he wanted and often imposed restrictions on the conduct of policy. In fact, domestic opposition grew to the point that Congress passed the **Boland Amendments** beginning in 1982, prohibiting U.S. attempts to overthrow the Nicaraguan government, and in 1985 and 1986,

making it illegal for the U.S. government to directly or indirectly assist the contras.

In the minds of most Reagan administration officials, however, the urgency of the communist threat outweighed congressional restrictions imposed by law under the Constitution. President Reagan decided in the name of national security to pursue the contra war as originally intended, and attempted to keep it secret from Congress and the American public. The covert contra war not only became a major part of the Iran-Contra scandal for President Reagan, it also led to considerable CIA excesses reminiscent of the "good ole" days.

Beginning in 1981, virtually all high-level foreign policy officials within the Reagan administration—including President Reagan, Vice President Bush, Director Casey, and Secretary of State George Shultz—were involved in a broad variety of covert activities in support of the contras, implemented through the intelligence community and the national security bureaucracy, thus circumventing the law long before congressional passage of the Boland Amendment cut off assistance to the contras. These activities included CIA—rather than contra—attacks on Nicaraguan oil installations and mining of Nicaraguan harbors; the secret channeling of military equipment to the contras from the Pentagon or cooperative third countries (such as Honduras and Panama); CIA advocacy of terrorist strategies, including assassination, in a training manual it produced for the contras; and efforts to pressure Costa Rica (which was officially neutral) to support the creation of a "southern front" for the contras (such as the CIA staging phony Sandinista raids on the Costa Rican border).

The Reagan administration tried to disassociate the CIA and the government officially from its covert contra war. In the early years, efforts were made to create new intelligence units within DOD for conducting covert political and paramilitary operations. More importantly, White House operatives created a secret network of private individuals and groups, including former intelligence and covert operators (such as General Richard Secord and numerous Cubans from the Bay of Pigs days) and staunch anticommunists (such as General John Singlaub and Carl "Spitz" Channel), to assist the contras in Central America and to raise money and equipment. These private efforts intensified after the Boland Amendments were passed, cutting off assistance. Supervision of the covert operations was transferred to the NSC (under National Security Advisers Robert McFarlane and John Poindexter, and NSC staffer Colonel Oliver North) in an effort to avoid the letter of the law. However, the Reagan administration remained actively involved: the CIA continued to employ agents on the ground in Central America (such as Felix Rodriguez); and administration officials, including President Reagan, Assistant Secretary of State for Inter-American Affairs Elliott Abrams, and Colonel Oliver North, personally solicited millions of dollars from private Americans and foreign countries (such as Saudi Arabia, Brunei, Israel, South Africa, South Korea, and Taiwan).

As news of these activities leaked out, the administration tried to cover them up. Administration officials, including McFarlane, Casey, and Abrams, misled and lied to Congress. Attorney General Edwin Meese obstructed FBI investigations in Miami that involved gun-running operations to the contras (Miami was the major transit point for the contras in the United States). When the diversion of money to the contras from the Iranian arms-for-hostages swap was revealed, Colonel North was busy shredding official governmental documents while Department of Justice officials were sitting outside his office.

The Reagan preoccupation with eradicating communism at all costs resulted in other unconstitutional and antidemocratic excesses. In 1983, an administration proposal was developed, originating in the NSC under Colonel North, to devise a plan to declare "martial law" and suspend the Constitution if domestic dissent occurred after U.S. military intervention in a foreign conflict. The FBI, under Director William Webster (who became the DCI after Casey's death), conducted a surveillance and harassment campaign against domestic dissenters to Reagan's Central American policies. In another action, money that was raised by Channel and North for the contras was diverted to support pro-contra Republican candidates in 1986 congressional races against Democratic candidates critical of the administration's policies.

The anticommunist, "ends-justify-the-means" mindset that prevailed throughout the intelligence community, especially within the CIA and its covert operatives, allowed other excesses, such as personal corruption and profiteering from the contra operation. General Secord and his financial associate, Albert Hakim, charged exorbitant prices for the guns they transported, accumulating millions of dollars in Swiss bank accounts (some of which went to Colonel North). Many of the contras, as well as covert operatives recruited by the CIA to support them, were selling weapons and supplies on the black market, laundering money, and smuggling drugs into the United States. Although CIA and NSC officials were aware of this behavior, they chose to ignore it for the larger goal of overthrowing the Sandinistas and rolling back communism.

Clearly, the secret contra war raises significant questions about acting above the law and the Constitution, highlighting the contradictions between the demands of national security and democracy. It also helps to provide an understanding why, when many of these activities were publicly exposed, they triggered a constitutional crisis for the country and the presidency of Ronald Reagan.

SOURCES: Leslie Cockburn, *Out of Control: The Story of the Reagan Administration's Secret War in Nicaragua, the Illegal Arms Pipeline, and the Contra Drug Connection* (New York: Atlantic Monthly Press, 1987); Theodore Draper, *A Very Thin Line: The Iran-Contra Affairs* (New York: Hill and Wang, 1991); Steven Emerson, *Secret Warriors: Inside the Covert Military Operations of the Reagan Era* (New York: G.P. Putnam's Sons, 1988); Jane Hunter, Jonathan Marshall, and Peter Dale Scott, *The Iran-Contra Connection: Secret Teams and Covert Operations in the Reagan Era* (Boston: South End Press, 1987); Robert Parry and Peter Kornbluh, "Iran-Contra's Untold Story," *Foreign Policy* (Fall 1988): 3–30; U.S. Congress, *Report of the Congressional Committees Investigating the Iran-Contra Affairs: With Supplemental, Minority, and Additional Views* (Washington, D.C.: U.S. Government Printing Office, 1987); and Bob Woodward, *Veil: The Secret War of the CIA* (New York: Simon and Schuster, 1987).

that the United States meant business, and rescue American medical students, who were never threatened by the coup in the first place. The Grenadian invasion was a part of the administration's overall effort to eradicate communism throughout Central America, although this aspect of the invasion was de-emphasized for public consumption.[50]

Not only did the CIA become more active in political and paramilitary operations, but President Reagan and DCI Casey **waived or ignored many of the restrictions** imposed on such operations by Presidents Ford and Carter. Surveillance by the intelligence community of Americans abroad, restricted during the 1970s, was again allowed. Intelligence agencies could also open U.S. mail with the approval of the attorney general—a court order had been necessary under Presidents Ford and Carter. President Reagan also eased restrictions on the conduct of intelligence operations within the United States. These changes occurred because members of the Reagan administration were prone to see communist threats at home and abroad.[51]

President Reagan also **tightened the security and secrecy system** that had developed throughout the intelligence community and the government. It became much more difficult for the public to gain access to information under the Freedom of Information Act. President Reagan not only tried to institute a lie detector program for members of the intelligence community, but for all civilian employees of the U.S. government. These actions created a political ruckus, within and beyond the administration. The president had to tone down most of these efforts in response to the dissent and opposition it created (his own secretary of state, George Shultz, threatened to resign over it), but the intelligence community and the government became much more security conscious during the Reagan administration. Ironically, American intelligence suffered more breaches of security and treasonous behavior during the 1980s than ever before, symbolized by the Walker family—John, Arthur, and Michael— spy scandals. In most cases, members of American intelligence did not give classified information to the Soviet Union for ideological reasons, but simply for money and personal greed.

To pursue its covert operations, the Reagan administration resisted and circumvented congressional oversight of the intelligence community. Administration officials regularly misled and lied to members of Congress. Director Casey, for example, was extremely reluctant to share information with the two congressional intelligence committees; he was notorious for evading questions and mumbling answers. Yet, administration officials were not reluctant to "leak" and manipulate classified information for political ends.

One of the most controversial areas in which the Reagan administration attempted to change policy was American involvement with "political assassinations." This became a major issue during the CIA's contra operation. One of the training manuals prepared by the CIA for the contras recommended that they engage in terrorism and "neutralization"— the operative word for assassinations—even against civilians. When word of this leaked to the press, such a political furor erupted that President Reagan publicly stated that no changes in the restrictions involving assassinations had been made.

Under President Bush the growth in the CIA budget slowed, but covert operations have continued to play an active role. The **case of Panama** illustrates this. President Bush ordered the invasion of Panama with 24,000 troops in December 1989 to topple General Manuel Noriega, who was said to pose a threat to the Panama Canal and American lives. To maximize public support for the operation, following Noriega's capture, the Bush administration portrayed Noriega as a petty dictator, common criminal, and drug addict who was also involved in the practice of voodoo. Although there is much truth to this, the story is more complex and has a longer history than most Americans are aware.

President Bush seems to have had a fixation on the need to overthrow **General Manuel Noriega** since the closing days of his vice-presidency. Bush perceived Noriega as a constant thorn in his side— similar to the way the Kennedys felt about Castro or President Reagan perceived Gadhafi. Before the American invasion, near the end of the Reagan administration, five covert plans were implemented to overthrow Noriega. When the failure of the October

1989 coup attempt—the fourth such attempt—became public, political accusations of incompetence and failure of nerve were leveled against President Bush. The Bush administration's response was that the restrictions on political assassination prevented the president from becoming involved in the coup. The failed effort to overthrow Noriega produced a political battle over the restrictions and the need to loosen them in future covert operations.

The story is even more complex than this, for Noriega also had a long history of involvement with American intelligence operatives, including George Bush. Noriega became a CIA asset as early as 1960 when he was first recruited by American intelligence as an officer in training at Peru's military academy. He was also trained by the American military in the School of the Americas in Panama, where he excelled in three courses on espionage. He continued on the CIA payroll during his rise as Panama's intelligence chief and president of Panama. While George Bush was director of Central Intelligence in 1976, Noriega is reported to have received more than $100,000 a year for his cooperation and intelligence information. DCI Stansfield Turner, under President Carter, cut the relationship between Noriega and the CIA (although he was still used as a liaison for U.S. agencies). However, it was renewed in 1981 to the reported tune of $200,000 per year when William Casey became the new DCI under President Reagan. In 1984, although Noriega rigged the Panamanian presidential election against the popular opposition candidate, he continued to receive the support of the U.S. government.

If Noriega understood anything, he understood wealth and power. Not only was he employed by the CIA, he was also working for Fidel Castro, the Colombian Medellin drug cartel, and the Sandinistas, and making a great deal of money in the process. The CIA was aware of Noriega's duplicity and double-dealings, including his involvement with the drug trade since 1971. However, the CIA chose to protect Noriega, for he had occasionally provided information which enabled the Drug Enforcement Administration to intercept drug traffickers (although he protected the major drug players in the trade). Most importantly, Noriega was helping the Reagan administration and CIA to support the contras with guns, money, and training in its covert war against the Sandinistas.

Noriega's relationship with the Reagan administration eventually turned sour. In 1986, when he was approached by Reagan administration officials, including Colonel Oliver North and National Security Adviser John Poindexter, to pressure Costa Rica to provide assistance for a southern front against the Sandinistas, Noriega refused. Panama under Noriega also became one of four key Latin American states to push the Contadora process, which promoted peace in Central America through diplomacy. Noriega was also becoming an embarrassment for the U.S. government as his longtime connection to American intelligence and involvement in the drug trade began to leak out in the American press. It appears that it was the reversal of Noriega's Nicaraguan policy, reinforced by the potential security risk and public embarrassment that he now posed, which led the Reagan and Bush administrations to seek to topple him through economic sanctions, covert overthrow efforts, and, finally, the American invasion of Panama.[52]

THE TENSIONS BETWEEN NATIONAL SECURITY AND DEMOCRACY

· · · · · · · · · · · · · ·

The American cold war preoccupation with threats to American national security, and the development of a large and complex intelligence community, has resulted in the **existence of an extensive security and secrecy system throughout the government.** This development has created a dilemma for the United States and its citizens, for the demands of national security and the demands of democracy are often incompatible. *Tensions between national security and democracy are particularly significant in three areas*:

1. Independence versus accountability;
2. Secrecy versus availability of information;
3. The legitimacy of covert operations.

"Democracy" requires that governmental agencies be held accountable to elected leaders and the public. "Accountability" requires a public that is informed, watchful, and politically active. Such a democratic process is often slow and cumbersome. The practice of democracy at home, and its emphasis on civil liberties and human rights, also tends to lead citizens to question the legitimacy of unsavory and ruthless covert operations such as manipulating elections, promoting coups, and engaging in political assassinations in the name of freedom and democracy abroad.

The "demands of national security," on the other hand, often require a quick and efficient foreign policy response. A premium is placed on the independence and secrecy of governmental operations to keep the enemy at bay. The use of all means available to protect and further national security is considered a necessity in a world where morality is seen to have little relevance. Consequently, the interests of national security require that the public be supportive of the government's foreign policy.

As we have seen, tensions between the requirements of national security and democracy have fluctuated over time. According to Harry Howe Ransom, **American threat perceptions** are a crucial factor in explaining the changing tensions between national security and democracy and the evolution of intelligence and covert operations. When perceptions of enemy threat are high, the demands of national security tend to prevail and result in the rise of intelligence activities, particularly covert operations. When threat perceptions decline, democratic considerations tend to rise and the legitimacy of intelligence functions, especially covert operations, is often questioned.[53] This explains *the major patterns that have prevailed since the end of World War II:*

1. During the cold war years the demands of national security prevailed over democracy;
2. Since the Vietnam War democratic norms have grown in importance while the demands of national security have lost much of their legitimacy outside the government, although the national security ethos continues to prevail within government.

The Prevalence of a National Security Ethos. The cold war period represented a time when most Americans felt that the security of the United States was greatly threatened by the Soviet Union and communism. This was the political environment in which a large and complex intelligence community developed. There was minimal democratic accountability and maximal independence, most information was classified and secrecy became the norm, and an "anything goes" attitude toward covert operations developed. Thus, power moved to the president, and the CIA's covert operations became a major foreign policy tool. These practices resulted in the **rise of a national security ethos** in which the values of power politics, independence, and secrecy permeated the minds and subcultures of the individuals and organizations who were part of the national security community. Such an orientation emphasizes a preoccupation with great power rivalry, the maintenance of stability and order, and the exercise of force and power independent of domestic and democratic politics in the name of national security.[54]

The overwhelming preoccupation with national security and power politics during the cold war years and the "Good Ole" Days of the CIA led to considerable excesses. No real oversight, for example, of the intelligence community and CIA operations ever took place. The so-called "independent" oversight boards within the executive branch were active only infrequently and staffed by kindred spirits who shared the national security ethos. Intelligence spending was hidden in the Department of Defense budget. With the prevailing anticommunist consensus and the president's commitment to containment, the CIA had wide leeway in acting abroad. For the most part, the Congress, judiciary, media, and public went along with what they were told in the name of national security.

The national security ethos first developed out of concern with protecting American security from foreign enemies, but soon resulted in a preoccupation with secrecy and a growing distrust of the American public. Although a **secrecy and classification system** did not formally exist within the government until 1951, the norm quickly became to label virtually all government documents and information that involved national security as classified.[55] This created a conflict between those who were "in the know" and everyone else. Restriction of information also allowed the president and members of the national security bureaucracy to monopolize information and control the foreign policy process. The public was kept uninformed and forced to accept official policies at face value, creating contempt among public officials about the ignorance and fickleness of the American people.

The national security ethos' preoccupation with secrecy legitimized the right of officials in their minds to mislead and lie to the public. Incredibly, the government not only officially denied its involvement in covert operations, it actually denied the existence of the CIA for a while. Such half-truths or lies were always justified in terms of the ultimate goal of national security. As explained by Assistant Secretary of Defense Arthur Sylvester in 1963, "when the nation's security is at stake, the government has the right, indeed the duty, to lie if necessary to mislead an enemy and protect the people it represents."[56] Therefore, presidential directives, such as NSC 5412/I on March 12, 1955, called for covert operations "so planned and executed that any U.S. Government responsibility for them is not evident to unauthorized persons and that if uncovered the U.S. Government can plausibly disclaim any responsibility for them."[57]

The secrecy system allowed the president and the national security bureaucracy to use classified information to hide incompetence and garner political support throughout American society. Furthermore, secrecy and deception protected officials from the political and public backlash that they feared might result if some of the information was made public, for intelligence activities were often inconsistent with public rhetoric about democracy, human rights, and freedom. For example, immediately following World War II, **Nazi (including Gestapo and SS) intelligence officers were recruited** by American intelligence. Even though some were known to have committed war crimes and crimes against humanity, their knowledge of the Soviet military, Eastern Europe, and access to anticommunist spy networks, was considered invaluable for U.S. cold war covert operations. The army's Counter Intelligence Corps was the U.S. military's primary group for finding, arresting, and recruiting Nazis. Klaus Barbie, the "butcher of Lyon," was recruited by the army's Counter Intelligence Corps, which protected him from extradition to France where he was wanted for war crimes and helped him to escape to South America in 1951.[58]

In covert operations, no effort was made to discriminate between types of undercover activities. Morality, higher principles, and international law were not allowed to get in the way of power politics and fighting a "cold" war where the security of the United States was perceived to be at stake. As NSC 5412/I stipulated, everything and anything was allowed:

> Propaganda, political action; economic warfare; escape and evasion and evacuation measures; subversion against hostile states or groups including assistance to underground movements, guerrillas and refugee liberation groups; support of indigenous and anticommunist elements in threatened countries of the free world; deception plans and operations; and all activities compatible with this directive necessary to accomplish the foregoing.[59]

This 1955 mandate often resulted in the support of ruthless dictatorships, the manipulation of democratic elections and, if need be, the overthrow of democracy, political assassinations, and murder.

Such measures were justified in terms of an anticommunist philosophy and power politics "ends-justifies-the-means" strategy that became the basis of the national security ethos. As explained by the top secret report of the General James Doolittle Committee to the 1954 Hoover Commission on government organization:

> It is now clear that we are facing an implacable enemy whose avowed objective is world domination by whatever means at whatever cost. There are no rules in such a game. Hitherto acceptable norms of human conduct do not apply. If the U.S. is to survive, long-standing American con-

cepts of "fair play" must be reconsidered. We must develop effective espionage and counterespionage services. We must learn to subvert, sabotage and destroy our enemies by more clever, more sophisticated and more effective methods than those used against us. It may become necessary that the American people will be made acquainted with, understand and support this fundamentally repugnant philosophy.[60]

Many of these covert operations were so incompatible with the American political culture of liberal democracy that secrecy was of the essence. Often, the goal was not really to maintain secrets from enemies abroad; the existence of an operation was often exposed, sometimes deliberately, on the assumption that knowledge of a CIA operation invoked sufficient fear to promote its success. Instead, it was imperative to maintain secrecy at home for fear that leaks would trigger domestic opposition which would place the future of covert operations at risk. The exercise of power to combat communism preoccupied U.S. officials above all else, to the extent that they were willing to interact with anybody—including Nazis and the criminal underworld—in the name of national security.

A preoccupation with national security and secrecy also **bred distrust of democracy and constitutional rights at home**. The fear of communism was so great that the president and the intelligence agencies saw any domestic dissent as an internal threat and acted to repress it. Domestic covert operations included the CIA's Operation Chaos, the FBI's Operation Cointelpro, and large spying operations by NSA and army intelligence. The CIA opened the mail of American citizens, kept over 1.5 million names on file, and infiltrated religious, media, and academic organizations; the FBI carried out more than five hundred thousand investigations of so-called subversives without a single court conviction and created files on over one million Americans; the National Security Agency monitored all cables sent overseas or received by Americans from 1947 to 1975; army intelligence investigated over one hundred thousand American citizens during the Vietnam War era; and the Internal

Revenue Service allowed tax information to be misused by intelligence agencies for political purposes.[61]

In other words, a wide-ranging set of domestic covert operations were performed that broke the law and violated the civil rights and liberties of American citizens in the name of the protection of American democracy. National security and politics became completely interwoven and democratic practice suffered the consequences. The president and the intelligence community took the law and the Constitution into their own hands to silence and destroy those individuals and organizations who were challenging their political goals and interests. Recalling the argument of Richard Pious, discussed in chapter 5, the 1950s and 1960s represented a time when the president exercised prerogative government over the conduct of foreign policy.

The national security and power politics mindset was such that virtually any kind of activity, no matter how bizarre, was deemed necessary to fight the cold war regardless of the law, ethics, or the rights and safety of human beings. Paranoia about threats to security in the late 1950s was so great that **Project MKULTRA** was created. Its purpose was to acquire "brainwashing" techniques that the U.S. intelligence community was convinced were used by the Chinese, North Korean, and Eastern European governments. Project MKULTRA consisted of "Frankenstein" projects that involved mind-control experiments on human beings. One CIA-funded project involved work by a Canadian psychiatrist designed to wipe the human mind clean through extensive electroshocks, LSD injections, and weeks of drug-induced suspended animation. Following this process of "depatterning," the patient was exposed to a series of positive messages designed to replace the negative ones supposedly destroyed. Over 100 Canadians were used as guinea pigs in this project and suffered severely. Nine of the Canadians sued the U.S. government after eventually learning of these activities, and the U.S. government subsequently paid them $750,000 in an out-of-court settlement. Yet, the U.S. government did not admit any fault or wrongdoing. From 1953 to 1963 the CIA was responsible under Project MKULTRA for funding over two hundred mind-control projects on Americans and Canadians in universities and institutions throughout the United States and Canada.[62]

The excesses of the national security ethos, as demonstrated by CIA covert operations, **damaged the reputation of the U.S. government** and its foreign policy. The independence and secrecy required by the CIA was supposed to help defeat communism while promoting security and democracy for America and its allies. Instead, American excesses played into the hands of U.S. critics and made the U.S. government and the CIA the personification of evil to many abroad. In Iran, for example, the U.S. government overthrew a nationalist leader, installed the Shah of Iran on the throne, and backed his ruthless and brutal dictatorship for over twenty-five years. This knowledge should allow Americans to better understand the hatred that so many Iranians felt toward the U.S. government and why the U.S. was portrayed as the "Great Satan" under Ayatollah Khomeini. It has also bred mistrust among U.S. allies, whose secrets have been compromised and whose involvement risks considerable political embarrassment. It has made it difficult for the CIA to recruit quality personnel and produce credible intelligence estimates. Finally, it has bred distrust among the American public, who have felt deceived and do not know what to believe about their government.[63]

The Rise of Democratic Norms. The American failure in Vietnam, the normalization of relations with the People's Republic of China, and the détente policies of the early and mid-1970s resulted in a political climate where many Americans no longer saw the Soviet Union or international communism as a threat to U.S. national security. Other problems competed for attention, such as the strength of the American economy at home and abroad. In this political environment, presidential and covert foreign policy activities typical of the cold war were now seen as unnecessary, immoral, and illegal. In the post–Vietnam War era, covert activities were judged by more democratic norms of behavior, resulting in Watergate, the fall of the CIA, and efforts at intelligence reform.

Excesses were experienced in this period as well, as the political pendulum swung from one extreme to another. Revelations concerning the CIA and its covert operations produced such a domestic political uproar that an intelligent debate about the purpose and need for intelligence never resulted. Instead, political leaders, especially in Congress, rushed to find blame and castigate the intelligence community in response to the new political climate. Not only did the CIA's covert operations suffer, but the credibility of its intelligence estimates were questioned as well.

Changes were made concerning intelligence information and activities, but **little real reform was accomplished**. The president and Congress were unable to agree on an intelligence charter that set legal guidelines on the intelligence community in a way that balanced the demands of national security and democracy. Rather, the CIA and, in particular, the operations division suffered from severe cuts, personnel changes, and a decline in morale. Yet, although the CIA experienced decline and limitations, its organizational structure and subcultures remained in place, and a national security ethos continued to prevail throughout much of the government.

The Uneasy Coexistence of National Security and Democracy. The presidency of Ronald Reagan increased the tension between the quest for national security and democracy. This tension was symbolized by the Iran-Contra affair, which represented the old cold war policies of the past operating in a post–cold war political environment. The lack of real, permanent intelligence reform during the 1970s and the Iran-Contra affair of the 1980s indicate that the national security ethos pervading the government and intelligence operations has not diminished over the years. And although Iran-Contra produced a political and constitutional crisis, it resulted in no new reforms. Unlike the 1975 congressional revelations about CIA activities, the **Tower Commission and the joint congressional committee reports** treated the covert and questionable activities associated with Iran-Contra as an aberration due to faulty leadership, as opposed to a long-standing institutional and historical pattern in U.S. national security policy.[64]

The national security bureaucracy continued to be large and extensive throughout the 1980s. What altered was the domestic political environment, which became much more receptive to democratic standards during the post–Vietnam War era. Thus, a national security ethos continued to prevail throughout the executive branch at a time when many Americans increasingly questioned the intelligence community's unaccountability, secrecy, and covert operations. As journalist Tim Weiner revealed, government spending for covert intelligence activities remained buried and hidden in the Department of Defense's "black budget," which grew to over $36 billion by 1989, making such activities difficult if not impossible to hold accountable in accordance with democratic practice.[65]

The existence of a national security bureaucracy and ethos operating in a post–cold war domestic environment have produced a political situation open to excess, abuse, and scandal.[66] Covert operatives, for example, continued to be heavily involved in an underworld where criminals abound and are called upon to support covert activities in the name of national security. For example, the CIA's connections with the Mafia, General Noriega, and the contras illustrate that it relied upon individuals and organizations who were **involved in the illegal narcotics trade**. According to a report by the U.S. Senate Subcommittee on Terrorism, Narcotics and International Operations of the Committee on Foreign Relations, "Instances in which foreign policy considerations took precedence over the war on drugs included . . . law enforcement investigations into illegal activities associated with the contras on the Southern Front, a narcotics sting operation directed at a high Bahamian government official, the intervention of U.S. officials on behalf of the Honduran General convicted in a narco-terrorism plot, and the handling of Panama's General Manuel Antonio Noriega."[67] Such covert operations were in direct contradiction to the U.S. government's overt rhetoric concerning the "war on drugs."[68]

The potential for abuse is not limited to the CIA, but continues to exist throughout the intelligence community and national security bureaucracy. For example, following the failed Iran hostage rescue attempt in 1980, and the frustration over interservice rivalry and CIA ineptitude, the Joint Chiefs of Staff created a number of supersecret military intelligence units (secret even to most members of the intelligence community). With capabilities similar to the CIA, the task of these units was to conduct counterterrorist missions and carry out covert operations throughout the world. As information about these supersecret operations began to leak throughout the national security bureaucracy, bureaucratic rivalry and charges of improprieties led to a series of secret military court-martials during the mid-1980s in which the units were disbanded.[69] DCI William Casey used these secret intelligence units to support the contras and circumvent the Congress.

Recent activities by the FBI demonstrate that the legacy of Hoover also continued to live on. During the 1980s, agents from 52 of the FBI's 59 national offices conducted investigations of over 2,300 individuals and 1,300 groups opposed to President Reagan's Central American policies, including such organizations as the National Council of Churches, the Maryknoll Sisters, the United Automobile Workers, and the National Education Association. Although no criminal activity was ever uncovered, only six FBI agents were disciplined, and the director of the FBI during that time, William Webster, was later selected as director of central intelligence by President Ronald Reagan.[70] Another illustration is the controversy that arose during the late 1980s over the FBI's "Library Awareness Program" designed to get librarians to help the bureau identify Soviet spies—four years after the rise of Soviet leader Mikhail Gorbachev and just months before the initial collapse of communism in Eastern Europe. Librarians who resisted and criticized the program were placed under surveillance by the FBI, according to a February 6, 1989, memo to Director William S. Sessions, "to determine whether a Soviet active-measures campaign had been initiated to discredit the Library Awareness Program."[71] These illustrations indicate that old habits die hard while the unresolved contradictions between national security and democracy continue to intensify.

The CIA in particular has been wracked by problems and scandal over the decade.[72] With the collapse of the Soviet Union, it has become an organization in search of a mission. Its budget and staff have undergone major cuts. Leadership has experienced continuous turnover with presidents having great difficulty in finding people willing to serve. Morale within the agency appears to be extremely low. Nowhere have the problems of the CIA been more evident than in the area of counterintelligence where the agency has had a sordid history and has recently been struck by scandal after scandal where American spies have turned traitor (see **essay 9.3** on spies gone bad.)

A POST–COLD WAR ERA OF UNCERTAINTY?

· · · · · · · · · · · · · ·

The collapse of the Soviet Union and the end of the cold war represent a historic opportunity for some serious rethinking about the role of intelligence within American society and U.S. foreign policy. For example, what is the proper relationship between the demands of national security and democracy? How large and what kind of intelligence community is required as the United States enters the twenty-first century? How much accountability and independence should intelligence agencies possess? How much information should be made available to the public and how much secrecy does the government need? What types of covert operations are illegitimate, given the United States' commitment to democracy at home and abroad? Americans need to give these crucial questions much thought. Americans must also consider their country's proper role in the world since it is the foreign policy of global containment which has exacerbated the tremendous tensions between national security and democracy. Unfortunately, there are no easy and simple answers.

In the post–World War II years, when the rise of the intelligence community fully developed, an-

swers to these questions were overwhelmingly in favor of the demands of national security. Today, there is little agreement in the political system. The demands for national security and for greater concern with democracy both are heard. Yet, despite the end of the cold war, few efforts have been made to address these contradictory demands. Hence, there is much uncertainty about the future of intelligence.

One of the many legacies of the cold war covert operations, for example, is **the "disposal" problem**: that is, what to do about the hundreds of covert operators who were let go by the agency during the 1970s and the 1990s, but whose livelihood and activities continue in the subterranean world of intelligence and paramilitary action. It was to many of these covert operators, and their operation networks, that the Reagan administration and the CIA turned to support the contra war. According to Colonel Oliver North's testimony during the congressional investigations of Iran-Contra, Casey envisioned a completely "privatized" nongovernmental, secret, self-financing global intelligence service. Such an intelligence service, resembling "the enterprise" run by General Richard Secord and financed by Albert Hakim, was a means to evade the legal controls instituted since the mid-1970s in reaction to earlier CIA excesses.

The most obvious threat—and some might say opportunity—to the future of the intelligence community and the national security ethos is the end of the cold war. According to Stansfield Turner, director of Central Intelligence from 1977 to 1981, "It is difficult to exaggerate how thoroughly the gathering of information on the Soviet Union, and especially its military power, has dominated U.S. intelligence operations since the Cold War began. Today, in light of the diminished Soviet military threat to Western Europe, the sharp decline in the Soviet economy and the centrifugal forces pulling the Soviet Union apart, . . . it is difficult to see how anyone could argue that a substantial adjustment by the intelligence community is not in order."[73]

Turner suggests a shift toward economic intelligence, political intelligence on third-world countries, and intelligence toward growing global problems such as terrorism, drug trafficking, and the

ESSAY 9.3
SPIES GONE BAD: COUNTERINTELLIGENCE, JAMES ANGLETON, AND ALDRICH AMES

Within the field of U.S. intelligence, there lies the insular and secretive world of counterintelligence. Those assigned to this area are responsible for the protection of secrets from the prying eyes and ears of foreign intelligence agencies, both at home and abroad. The duties of the men and women of **counterintelligence (CI)** range widely and include the prevention and investigation of espionage, subversion, and sabotage against American targets. In order to perform these tasks, CI agents utilize skills in surveillance, investigation, interviewing and interrogation. The functions performed by CI are of the highest priority, for they are intended to protect American secrets from those who would use such information to harm the United States. Counterintelligence also provides for the self-inspection and self-regulation of the intelligence community. It is in this last area that the field of counterintelligence has recently come under particular scrutiny and criticism. Revelations of "moles" within the U.S. intelligence community, especially within the CIA, have brought about much talk about the need for intelligence reform and major restructuring.

World War I provided an environment ripe for the emergence of what could be called America's first counterintelligence organ. Due to the widespread hysteria spreading throughout the country over pro-German spies, traitors, and saboteurs, the fledgling Federal Bureau of Investigation was assigned the task of supervising German aliens in the United States, in which J. Edgar Hoover was soon to rise to prominence, as discussed in essay 9.1. Until World War II, and the wartime creation of the OSS, the FBI had the corner on the CI market. But with the passage of the National Security Act of 1947, the CIA was born and became responsible for counterintelligence abroad, with the FBI their domestic counterpart.

Counterintelligence within the CIA was dominated throughout much of the cold war era by one man, the legendary **James J. Angleton**. In 1943, after graduating from Yale University and completing more than a year at Harvard Law School, Angleton enlisted in the army as a private. He served with the OSS counterintelligence arm (X-2) in London, eventually managing the Italian desk. After the war Angleton served briefly as personal assistant to DCI Admiral Roscoe Hillenkoetter, then was promoted into the Directorate of Operations (DO), where he became the chief of the CI staff from 1954 until 1974.

Throughout his reign, Angleton was obsessed with ferreting out **"moles"**—members of the American intelligence community who were acting as "double agents" and betraying their country; and ensuring that "defectors" from foreign intelligence services, such as the Soviet KGB, were authentic (and not deceptive so as to penetrate and manipulate American intelligence). At the time it was thought that if an American citizen was to betray his or her country, it would be for reasons of ideology—the turncoat would have secret sympathies for the Soviet Union and communism.

Angleton's tenure as head of CI was marked by paranoia and an obsessive preoccupation with giant conspiracies and elaborate schemes of deceptions. Angleton was in constant search of a master mole—a senior American official secretly controlled by the Kremlin, burrowed deep inside the inner sanctum of the CIA. This led to countless mole hunts, most of which were fruitless—ruining the careers of a number of his loyal colleagues (especially within the CIA's important Soviet division) and treating Soviet defectors as if they were all deceptive. Much of Angleton's paranoia may have been a function of his friendship with Kim Philby in the early fifties, a British agent, who actually was a Soviet mole who later escaped to Moscow in 1963. Whatever the explanation, Angleton not only was feared, but his excessive paranoia and molehunts damaged the agency and led to an oppressive, overly suspicious atmosphere at Langley. In fact, according to Joseph Finder, Angleton was "an extreme manifestation of the collective psychosis that gripped the intelligence community during the fevered years of the cold war.

He was the purest distillation of cold war theology, or pathology."

Eventually Angleton's paranoia and witchhunts for American traitors led to his downfall given the public revelations about the CIA in the wake of the Vietnam War and the congressional, especially Church committee, investigations of the CIA in 1974. In Angleton's absence and with the general breakdown of governmental trust common in the post-Vietnam era, a less vigilant counterintelligence environment prevailed at the CIA. Ironically, beginning in the 1980s, American intelligence suffered numerous breaches of security and treasonous behavior that it had never experienced before, symbolized by the Walker family, Pollard, and Ames spy scandals. In all of these spy cases, ideology was not the culprit, but predominantly money and personal greed.

The recent **Ames spy scandal** was particularly egregious. Rick Ames joined the CIA in 1962 and was engaged in espionage activity throughout his CIA career. But something seemed to happen to his life and his work in the early 1980s when he was stationed in Mexico City, where he was recruiting defectors and running double agents as part of the cold war with the Soviet Union. In 1985 Ames began to meet secretly with Soviet officials and provide them with secret information. At one point he became chief of the Soviet counterintelligence branch of the Soviet/East Europe Division of the CIA. For nearly ten years he sold Moscow nearly every secret about American espionage activities in Russia. In return, Ames was paid considerable money, somewhere between $1 million to $3 million. In fact, in 1989 Ames paid $540,000 in cash for a home in a suburb of Washington, D.C.

Even though Ames had a history of heavy drinking, had worked in the CIA's Soviet division, and began to spend far more money than his salary allowed, it took the CIA eight years to identify him as a mole. Counterintelligence within the CIA had become careless, and it was almost as if the CIA as an institution did not want to face the possibility that it had been penetrated by one of their own agents.

James Angleton's search for the "master spy" finally ended in 1995. Although Ames was convicted and sentenced to life imprisonment, it was an intelligence disaster for the United States, especially for the CIA. Ames betrayed dozens of Soviets whom the CIA had recruited and revealed hundreds of American intelligence operations to the Soviet KGB. Within the CIA, no one was dismissed or demoted—eleven officers were reprimanded—despite the systematic failure to weed out Ames. Finally, the Ames case also serves as a reminder that although the cold war is over, the intelligence business and the spy war goes on.

SOURCES: Brian Duffy, "The Cold War's Last Spy," *U.S. News & World Report* (March 6, 1995): 48–57; Joseph Finder, "The Life and Strange Career of a Mole Hunter," *New York Times Book Review* (June 30, 1991): 11–12; Tom Mangold, *Cold Warrior: James Angleton: The CIA's Master Spy Hunter* (New York: Simon and Schuster, 1991); Tim Weiner, David Johnston, and Neil A. Lewis, *Betrayal: The Story of Aldrich Ames, an American Spy* (New York: Random House, 1995); Robin W. Winks, *Cloak & Gown: Scholars in the Secret War* (New York: William Morrow, 1987); David Wise, *Molehunt: The Secret Search for Traitors That Shattered the CIA* (New York: Random House, 1995).

---

environment. Yet, as Turner acknowledges, "Any reduction in effort against the Soviet Union will be resisted strongly in the CIA, where the Cold War ethos runs very deep" and "will be opposed by the various military intelligence agencies when, after all, that threat is their raison d'etre."[74]

Despite regular calls and reports for intelligence reform, the reality thus far is that while the intelligence community has undergone some change, little real reform is evident. Despite cutbacks in the intelligence budget to $28 billion (over $3 billion for the CIA; over $13 billion for the major Pentagon intelligence agencies; and over $10 billion for Army, Navy, and Air Force intelligence), the community is a creature of the past, and old habits tend to prevail.[75] A preoccupation with secrecy continues to drive the national security bureaucracy and policymakers. According to *Secrecy: A Report of the Commission on Protecting and Reducing Government Secrecy,* chaired by Senators Daniel Patrick Moynihan and Larry Combest, as recently as 1995 there were an estimated 3.6 million classification actions, of which about 400,000 were "Top Secret." Some two million civilian and military federal officials (along with another one million people in industry) can classify information.[76] Such practice is indicative of an intelligence community which remains heavily influenced by powerful bureaucratic functions, structures, and subcultures that have developed over time as it attempts to adapt and seek new missions now that the cold war is over. If anything, competition for diminishing resources is likely to escalate within this new domestic and international environment, with the CIA, in particular, most politically vulnerable.[77]

There is much uncertainty, but a demand for intelligence collection and analysis to help policymakers steer the ship of state in the future will likely continue. The Persian Gulf victory has strengthened those forces resisting major change and intelligence reform. In the final analysis, until the proper role of intelligence and, in particular, paramilitary action within a democracy in a post–cold war era are publicly aired and debated, the tension between national security and democracy is likely to pose a basic dilemma for the United States into the foreseeable future. How these contradictory forces will affect the future of the intelligence community, and the tension between national security and democracy, ultimately will depend on the interplay of international developments and the complex politics of U.S. foreign policy.

BIBLIOGRAPHIC ESSAY

· · · · · · · · · · · · · ·

The 1960s marked the beginning of a growing body of literature on intelligence, especially with regard to the CIA and its covert operations. Many of the earlier books were written by insiders who were either promotive and apologists for the agency or extremely critical. However, the last decade has produced a spate of books that have a more analytical and schol-

arly orientation. Nathan Miller, in *Spying for America: The Hidden History of U.S. Intelligence* (New York: Paragon House, 1989), provides a very informative history of the evolution of American intelligence, its professionalization and bureaucratization, since the founding of the republic. Loch Johnson, in *America's Secret Power: The CIA in a Democratic Society* (New York: Oxford University Press, 1989), provides an excellent overview of the modern intelligence community, the intelligence process, and the CIA. Richard K. Betts explains the likelihood of intelligence failures from a more theoretical perspective, in "Analysis, War, and Decision: Why Intelligence Failures Are Inevitable," *World Politics* 31 (October 1978): 61–90.

The Man Who Kept the Secrets: Richard Helms and the CIA (New York: Pocket Books, 1979) by Thomas Powers, *Gentleman Spy: The Life of Allen Dulles* (Houghton Mifflin, 1995) by Peter Grose, and *The Agency: The Rise and Decline of the CIA* (New York: Simon and Schuster, 1986) by John Ranelagh provide excellent overviews of the history of the CIA. A good analytical treatment, emphasizing the impact of politics on the evolution of the CIA can be found in Rhodri Jeffreys-Jones, in *The CIA and American Democracy* (New Haven, Conn.: Yale University Press, 1989). An excellent discussion of the policymaking process involving covert action, the growth of democratic accountability, and the potential for abuse is provided by Loch Johnson in "Covert Action and Accountability: Decision-Making for America's Secret Foreign Policy," *International Studies Quarterly* 33 (March 1989): 81–109. Theodore Draper, in *A Very Thin Line: The Iran-Contra Affairs* (New York: Hill and Wang, 1991), provides the best, although somewhat incomplete, overview of Iran-Contra.

One of the best biographies of Hoover and discussions of the FBI is *Secrecy and Power: The Life of J. Edgar Hoover* (New York: Free Press, 1987) by Richard Powers. The rest of the intelligence community has not received the attention it deserves. For example, little was known or written about the National Security Agency until *The Puzzle Palace: A Report on America's Most Secret Agency* (New York: Penguin, 1982) was published by James Bamford.

In addition to those cited above, for a disturbing, but fascinating, look into the rise of the national security ethos within intelligence and the U.S. government, and its contrariness to the demands of democracy, see Christopher Simpson, *Blowback: America's*

Recruitment of Nazis and Its Effects on the Cold War (New York: Macmillan, 1988). The implications of the end of the cold war for the future of intelligence and the CIA is addressed by Loch K. Johnson, *Secret Agencies: U.S. Intelligence in a Hostile World* (New Haven: Yale University Press, 1996) and Tim Weiner, "The CIA's Most Important Mission: Itself," *New York Times Magazine* (December 10, 1995): 62–76, 80–82, 104–105.

ENDNOTES

1. See Rhodri Jeffreys-Jones, *The CIA and American Democracy* (New Haven, Conn.: Yale University Press, 1989), p. 257.

2. John Ranelagh, *The Agency: The Rise and Decline of the CIA* (New York: Simon and Schuster, 1986), p. 27.

3. For an overview of the intelligence community, see Jeffreys-Jones, *CIA and American Democracy*; Loch Johnson, *America's Secret Power: The CIA in a Democratic Society* (New York: Oxford University Press, 1989); and Jeffrey Richelson, *The U.S. Intelligence Community* (Cambridge, Mass.: Ballinger, 1985). For an overview of the literature, see John Ferris, "Coming in from the Cold War: The Historiography of American Intelligence, 1945–1960," *Diplomatic History* (Winter 1995): 87–115.

4. See Graham T. Allison, *Essence of Decision: Explaining the Cuban Missile Crisis* (Boston: Little, Brown, 1971) and Jerome H. Kahan, *Security in the Nuclear Age: Developing U.S. Strategic Arms Policy* (Washington, D.C.: The Brookings Institution, 1975).

5. See Ronald Kessler, *The FBI: Inside the World's Most Powerful Law Enforcement Agency* (New York: Pocket Books, 1994).

6. Nathan Miller, *Spying for America: The Hidden History of U.S. Intelligence* (New York: Paragon House, 1989). See also Charles D. Ameringer, *U.S. Foreign Intelligence: The Secret Side of American History* (Lexington, Mass.: Lexington books, 1990).

7. See, for example, Johnson, *America's Secret Power*, p. 38, and David Wise and Thomas B. Ross, *The Invisible Government* (New York: Vintage, 1974), p. 4.

8. See Richelson, *U.S. Intelligence Community*.

9. See Bruce D. Berkowitz and Allan E. Goodman, *Strategic Intelligence for American National Security* (Princeton, N.J.: Princeton University Press, 1989); Stephen J. Flanagan, "Managing the Intelligence Community," *International Security* 10 (Summer 1985): 58–95;

Robert M. Gates, "The CIA and American Foreign Policy," *Foreign Affairs* (Winter 1987/88); 215–30; and Johnson, *America's Secret Power*.

10. See Allison, *Essence of Decision*.

11. Ranelagh, *The Agency*, p. 455.

12. Daniel Ellsberg, *Papers on the War* (New York: Simon and Schuster, 1972), p. 28.

13. Jeffreys-Jones, *CIA and American Democracy*, 238–45.

14. See, for example, Elaine Sciolino, "Gates Almost a Side Issue in Hearings," *New York Times* (October 1, 1991): A11; Elaine Sciolino "Starkly Different Gates Portraits Emerge as Secrets Are Laid Bare," *New York Times* (October 2, 1991): A1, A13; and Elaijne Sciolino, "Senate Panel's Democrats Voice Skepticism on Choice for CIA," *New York Times* (October 3, 1991): A1, A13.

15. See, for example, Richard K. Betts, "Analysis, War, and Decision: Why Intelligence Failures Are Inevitable," *World Politics* 31 (October 1978): 61–90.

16. See Gary Sick, *All Fall Down: America's Tragic Encounter with Iran* (New York: Penguin, 1985).

17. See Michael Wines, "C.I.A. Sidelines Its Gulf Cassandra," *New York Times* (January 24, 1991): A13, and Michael Wines, "U.S. Says Bush Was Surprised by the Iraqi Strike," *New York Times* (August 5, 1990): 8.

18. Bob Woodward, *The Commanders* (New York: Simon and Schuster, 1991).

19. "The CIA Called It—But Nobody Listened," *Newsweek* (September 2, 1991): 44.

20. Ibid.

21. See also Fred Barnes, "White House Watch: Gate Crasher," *The New Republic* (September 16 and 23, 1991): 10–12.

22. See Willis C. Armstrong, William Leonhart, William McCaffrey, and Herbert C. Rothenberg, "The Hazards of Single-Outcome Forecasting," in H. Bradford Westerfield, ed., *Inside the CIA's Private World* (New Haven: Yale University Press, 1995).

23. See Bruce D. Berkowitz and Jeffrey T. Richelson, "The CIA Vindicated," *National Interest* (Fall 1995): 36–47 for a different perspective.

24. Theodore Draper, "Is the CIA Necessary?" *New York Times Review of Books* (August 14, 1997): 18.

25. For an overview of the origins and organization of the CIA, see Jeffreys-Jones, *CIA and American Democracy*; Johnson, *America's Secret Power*; Thomas Powers, *The Man Who Kept the Secrets: Richard Helms and the CIA* (New York: Pocket Books, 1979); Ranelagh, *The Agency*; and Wise and Ross, *Invisible Government*.

26. See Burton Hersh, *The Old Boys: The American Elite and the Origins of the CIA* (Charles Scribner's Sons, 1992).

27. Theodore Shackley, *The Third Option: An American View of Counterinsurgency Operations* (New York: Dell, 1981).

28. See Jeffreys-Jones, *CIA and American Democracy*; Loch K. Johnson, "Covert Action and Accountability: Decision-Making for America's Secret Foreign Policy," *International Studies Quarterly* 33 (March 1989): 81–109; Johnson, *America's Secret Power*; Jonathan Kwitny, *Endless Enemies: The Making of an Unfriendly World* (New York: Penguin, 1984); Powers, *Man Who Kept the Secrets*; John Prados, *President's Secret Wars: CIA and Pentagon Operations Since World War II* (New York: William Morrow, 1986); Ranelagh, *The Agency*; Wise and Ross, *The Invisible Government*; U.S. Senate, *Alleged Assassination Plots Involving Foreign Leaders*, Congressional Report (94th Cong., 1st sess., November 18, 1975); and U.S. Congress, Senate, *Final Report of the Select Committee to Study Governmental Operations with Respect to Intelligence Activities, Books 1–6*, Congressional Report (94th Cong., 2nd sess., April 14, 1976).

29. See Peter Grose, *Gentleman Spy: The Life of Allen Dulles* (Houghton Mifflin, 1995); Jacob Heilbrunn, "The Old Boy at War," *The New Republic* (March 27, 1995): 32–37.

30. Jeffreys-Jones, *CIA and American Democracy*, p. 41.

31. In interpreting the meaning of the act's phrase, the CIA's first general counsel, Lawrence Houston, concluded that "taken out of context and without knowledge of [the act's] history, these Sections could bear almost unlimited interpretation. In our opinion, however, either [progaganda or commando type] activity would be an unwarranted extension of the functions authorized" by the act. "We do not believe that there was any thought in the minds of Congress that the Central Intelligence Agency under this authority would take positive action for subversion and sabotage." Any such missions would necessitate going to Congress "for authority and funds." Such authority eventually was provided by passage of the Central Intelligence Act of 1949. Jay Peterzell, "Legal and Constitutional Authority for Covert Operation," *First Principles* 10 (Spring 1985): 1–3. See also Jeffreys-Jones, *CIA and American Democracy*, chapter 3.

32. See James A. Bill, *The Eagle and the Lion: The Tragedy of American-Iranian Relations* (New Haven, Conn.: Yale University Press, 1988), and Jonathan Kwitny, *Endless Enemies: The Making of an Unfriendly World* (New York: Penguin, 1984).

33. See Richard H. Immerman, *The CIA in Guatemala: The Foreign Policy of Intervention* (Austin: University of Texas Press, 1982), and Stephen Schlesinger and Stephen Kinzer, *Bitter Fruit: The Untold Story of the American Coup in Guatemala* (New York: Doubleday, 1982).

34. See Madelaine G. Kalb, *The Congo Cables: The Cold War in Africa from Eisenhower to Kennedy* (New York: Macmillan, 1981).

35. U.S. Department of State, *Foreign Relations of the United States, 1950*, v.2, p. 607.

36. Joel Bleifuss, "The First Stone," *In These Times* (July 4–17, 1990): 4. See also Peter Dale Scott, "The United States and the Overthrow of Sukarno, 1965–1967," *Pacific Affairs* and Joseph B. Smith, *Portrait of a Cold Warrior* (New York: Ballantine Books, 1976).

37. Joseph Albright and Marcia Kunstel, "CIA Tip Led to '62 Arrest of Mandela: Ex-Official Tells of U.S. 'Coup' to Aid S. Africa," *Atlanta Constitution* (June 10, 1990): A14.

38. See Peter Wyden, *Bay of Pigs: The Untold Story* (London, Jonathan Cape, 1979).

39. Jeffreys-Jones, *CIA and American Democracy*, p. 132.

40. Kornbluh, "The Iran-Contra Scandal," p. 139, and Harry Howe Ransom, "Strategic Intelligence and Intermestic Politics," in Charles W. Kegley, Jr., and Eugene R. Wittkopf, eds., *Perspectives on American Foreign Policy: Selected Readings* (New York: St. Martin's, 1983), p. 303.

41. U.S. Congress, Senate, *Final Report of the Select Committee to Study Governmental Operations with Respect to Intelligence Activities, Foreign and Military Intelligence, Book I*, Congressional Report (94th Cong., 2nd sess., April 14, 1976), p. 445.

42. Jeffreys-Jones, *CIA and American Democracy*, p. 51.

43. U.S. Congress, Senate, *Final Report, Book 1, Foreign and Military Intelligence*, Congressional Report (94th Cong., 2nd sess., April 14, 1976): 179–204. See also, for example, Robin W. Winks, *Cloak & Gown: Scholars in the Secret War* (New York: William Morrow, 1987).

44. Jeffreys-Jones, *CIA and American Democracy*, p. 167.

45. Ibid., p. 203.

46. See John Stockwell, *In Search of Enemies: A CIA Story* (New York: W.W. Norton, 1978). During this time, the CIA may have politically intervened in Australian politics leading to the fall of E. Gough Whitlam in 1975, the Labor Prime Minister. See Denis Freney *The CIA's Australian Connection* (Sydney: Denis Freney,

1977), and James A. Nathan, "Dateline Australia: America's Foreign Watergate," *Foreign Policy* 49 (Winter 1982–83): 168–85.

47. Philip Taubman, "Casey and His CIA on the Rebound," *New York Times Magazine* (January 16, 1983): 21.

48. Jeffreys-Jones, *CIA and American Democracy*, p. 235.

49. See Seymour Hersh, "Target Qaddafi," *New York Times Magazine* (February 22, 1987): 16–26, 48, and Bob Woodward, *Veil: The Secret Wars of the CIA 1981–1987* (New York: Simon and Schuster, 1987).

50. Patrick E. Tyler, "U.S. Tracks Cuban Aid to Grenada," *Washington Post* (February 27, 1983): A1, A11.

51. See, for example, Duncan L. Clarke and Edward L. Neveleff, "Secrecy, Foreign Intelligence, and Civil Liberties: Has the Pendulum Swung Too Far?" *Political Science Quarterly* 99 (Fall 1984): 493–513, and Stansfield Turner and George Thibault, "Intelligence: The Right Rules." *Foreign Policy* 48 (Fall 1982): 122–38.

52. See "Anatomy of a Fiasco," *Newsweek* (June 6, 1988): 36–39; John Dinges, *Our Man In Panama: How General Noriega Used the United States and Made Millions in Drugs and Arms* (New York: Random House, 1990); "Drugs, Politics, and the Noriega Connection," *Frontline*, a PBS TV show (January 30, 1990); Stephen Engelberg with Susan F. Rasky, "White House, Noriega, and Battle in Congress," *New York Times* (October 25, 1989): 4; "Noriega's Surrender," *Newsweek* (January 15, 1990): 14–18; "20-plus Years of Service," *In These Times* (January 10–16, 1990): 4–5; and Michael Wines, "U.S. Plans New Effort to Oust Noriega," *New York Times* (November 17, 1989): 3.

53. Ransom, "Strategic Intelligence and Intermestic Politics," pp. 299–319.

54. I thank my colleague, Paul Kattenburg, from whom I borrowed the term *ethos*. See Daniel Yergin, *Shattered Peace: The Origins of the Cold War and the National Security State* (Boston: Houghton Mifflin, 1976), especially chapter 8.

55. Actually, the army was the first to classify on an organized basis during World War I. Then in March 1940, President Franklin Roosevelt issued an executive order for a military classification system. It was not, however, until September 1951 that the secrecy system was extended to civilian departments as a result of an executive order by President Harry Truman. See, U.S. Congress, Committee on Foreign Relations, *Security Classification as a Problem in the Congressional Role in Foreign Policy* (92nd Cong., 1st sess., December 1971), and David Wise, *The Politics of Lying: Government De-*

ception, Secrecy, and Power (New York: Vintage, 1973), pp. 89–91.

56. U.S. Congress, Senate, 69th Cong., 1st sess., *Congressional Record* (June 24, 1963), p. 859.

57. Jeffreys-Jones, *CIA and American Democracy*, p. 83.

58. See Christopher Simpson, *Blowback: America's Recruitment of Nazis and Its Effects on the Cold War* (New York: Weidenfeld & Nicolson, 1988), and U.S. Congress, General Accounting Office, *Nazis and Axis Collaborators Were Used to Further U.S. Anti-Communist Objectives in Europe—Some Immigrated to the United States* (June 28, 1985). See also John Gimbel, "Project Paperclip: German Scientists, American Policy, and the Cold War," *Diplomatic History* 14 (Summer 1990): 343–65.

59. Jeffreys-Jones, *CIA and American Democracy*, p. 83.

60. U.S. Congress, Senate, *Final Report* (94th Cong., 2nd sess.), p. 9.

61. See Frank J. Donner, *The Age of Surveillance* (New York: Vintage Books, 1981); Robert J. Goldstein, *Political Repression in Modern America: From 1870 to the Present* (Cambridge, Mass.: Schenkman, 1977); Morton H. Halperin, Jerry J. Berman, Robert L. Borosage, and Christine M. Marvick, *The Lawless State: The Crimes of the U.S. Intelligence Agencies* (New York: Penguin, 1976); Joan M. Jensen, *Army Surveillance in America, 1775–1980* (New Haven, Conn.: Yale University Press, 1992); Richard E. Morgan, *Domestic Intelligence: Monitoring Dissent in America* (Austin: University of Texas Press, 1980); Athan Theoharis, *Spying on Americans: Political Surveillance from Hoover to the Huston Plan* (Philadelphia: Temple University Press, 1978); U.S. Congress, Senate, *Final Report*, (94th Cong., 2nd sess.); and Wiese, *The Politics of Lying*.

62. See Ann Colins, *In the Sleep Room: The Story of the CIA Brainwashing Experiments in Canada* (Toronto: Lester & Orpen Dennys, 1990); Harvey Weinstein, *A Father, A Son and the CIA* (Toronto: James Lorimer, 1990); and U.S. Congress, *Final Report*, chapter 17.

63. See Anthony Lake, "Lying Around Washington," *Foreign Policy* 2 (Spring 1971): 91–113.

64. See, for example, Theodore Draper, *A Very Thin Line: The Iran-Contra Affairs* (New York: Hill and Wang, 1991), and Kenneth E. Sharpe, "The Real Cause of Irangate," *Foreign Policy* 68 (Fall 1987): 19–41.

65. Tim Weiner, *Blank Check: The Pentagon's Black Budget* (New York: Basic Books, 1990), pp. 5–6.

66. See, for example, Richard O. Curry, *Freedom at Risk: Secrecy, Censorship, and Repression in the 1980s* (Philadelphia: Temple University Press, 1988).

67. With respect to the contras, the committee report concluded that there was "substantial evidence of drug smuggling through the war zones on the part of individual contras, pilots who flew supplies, mercenaries who worked for the Contras, and Contra supporters throughout the region. There is also evidence on the record that U.S. officials involved in assisting the Contras knew that drug smugglers were exploiting the clandestine infrastructure established to support the war and that Contras were receiving assistance derived from drug traffickers." U.S. Congress, Senate, Subcommittee on Terrorism, Narcotics and International Operations of the Committee on Foreign Relations, *Drugs, Law Enforcement and Foreign Policy*, Committee Print (100th Cong., 2nd sess., December 1989): 120, 136.

68. See also Jonathan Kwitny, *Crimes of Patriots: A True Tale of Dope, Dirty Money, and the CIA* (New York: W.W. Norton, 1987); Alfred W. McCoy, *The Politics of Heroin in Southeast Asia* (New York: Harper & Row, 1991); Peter Dale Scott and Jonathan Marshall, *Cocaine Politics: Drugs, Armies, and the CIA in Central America* (Berkeley: University of California Press, 1991); and Jacqueline Sharkey, "The Contra-Drug Trade Off," *Common Cause Magazine* (September/October 1988): 23–33.

69. Steven Emerson, *Secret Warriors: Inside the Covert Military Operations of the Reagan Era* (New York: G.P. Putnam's Sons, 1988).

70. "Going After Dissidents," *Newsweek* (February 8, 1988): 29 "FBI Will Purge Files on Protester," *New York Times* (November 5, 1989): 17; and U.S. Congress, General Accounting Office, *FBI Investigates Domestic Activities to Identify Terrorists* (September 1990).

71. David Johnston, "Documents Disclose FBI Investigations of Some Librarians," *New York Times* (November 7, 1989): 1, and Michael Wines, "Director of FBI Defends Checks into Backgrounds of Librarians," *New York Times* (November 8, 1989): 12.

72. See, for example, Draper, "Is the CIA Necessary?" Tim Weiner, "The CIA's Most Important Mission: Itself," *New York Times Magazine* (December 10, 1995): 62–76, 80–82,104–105.

73. Stansfield Turner, "Intelligence for a New World Order," *Foreign Affairs* (Fall 1991): 150. See also Bruce D. Berkowitz, "Reform of the Intelligence Community," *Orbis* (Fall 1996): 653–63; David L. Boren "The Intelligence Community: How Crucial?" *Foreign Affairs* (Summer 1992): 52–62; John Canham-Clyne, "Business as Usual: Iran-Contra and the National Security State," *World Policy Journal* (Fall/Winter 1992): 617–37; Dave McCurdy, "Glasnost for the CIA," *Foreign Affairs* (January/February 1994): 125–32; Roger Hilsman, "Does the CIA Still Have a Role?" *Foreign Affairs* (September/October 1995): 104–16; Loch K. Johnson, *Secret Agencies: U.S. Intelligence in a Hostile World* (New Haven, Conn.: Yale University Press, 1996); Abram N. Skulsky and Gary J. Schmitt, "The Future of Intelligence," *National Interest* (Winter 1994/95): 63–73.

74. Ibid.

75. The official intelligence figures, normally hidden in the military budget, were accidentally published by Congress. See Hilsman, "Does the CIA Still Have a Role?" p. 105.

76. *Secrecy: Report of the Commission on Protecting and Reducing Government Secrecy* (Washington, D.C.: Government Printing Office, 1997). See also George Lardner, Jr., "A Cutback in Classified Information?" *Washington Post* (April 10, 1990): A21.

77. Robert Dreyfuss, "Spy vs. No-Spy," *The New Republic* (December 2, 1996): 9–10; Joseph Finder, "Spy vs. Spy," *The New Republic* (April 6, 1996): 16–21.

CHAPTER
10

. . . .

FOREIGN ECONOMICS
AND THE REST OF THE BUREAUCRACY

revious chapters have reviewed the president and executive branch agencies which are most important in the making of American "national security policy." The foreign policy bureaucracy, however, includes numerous less visible agencies that play a vital role in the making of U.S. foreign policy. This chapter provides an overview of the rest of the foreign policy bureaucracy, focusing on the foreign economic bureaucracy given its growing importance. It is only by understanding the complexity and scope of the foreign policy bureaucracy in its entirety that one can begin to fully comprehend the role of the executive branch in the making and conduct of U.S. foreign policy.

as a result of a number of factors such as: the rise of industrialization and American economic expansion abroad, the onset of the Great Depression, American global economic ascendance with World War II and the cold war, and the relative decline of America's economy and its role in the international political economy in the post–Vietnam War era. In order to better understand the contemporary significance of the federal economic bureaucracy, the key institutions involved, their culture, and their policymaking impact on the making of U.S. foreign policy, some historical background is necessary.

THE FOREIGN ECONOMIC
BUREAUCRACY

. . . .

The foreign economic bureaucracy has expanded in size and importance throughout the twentieth century

U.S. FOREIGN ECONOMIC
POLICY IN HISTORICAL
CONTEXT

The United States has always had an active foreign economic policy. Throughout most of its history, the emphasis has been on internal economic development throughout the continent, the protection of domestic industry from foreign competition and investment, and the expansion of American commerce abroad, especially in Latin America and Asia. This pattern in U.S. foreign economic policy was deeply affected by the collapse of the international economy symbolized by the Great Depression and the onset of World War II. This eventually resulted in the United States becoming economically ascendant throughout the world and actively involved in efforts to restore a new stability and prosperity to the international political economy. As briefly discussed in chapter 2, these efforts led to the creation of the Bretton Woods international economic system founded on the principles of free trade, fixed exchange rates based on the gold standard, reconstruction and development aid, and the development of international economic organizations (such as the General Agreement on Tariffs and Trade, the International Monetary Fund, and the World Bank).[1] These developments reinforced the great importance of foreign economics in U.S. foreign policy and contributed to the expansion of the foreign economic bureaucracy.

With the preeminence of the American economy in the international political economy *during the cold war years, the president was able to subordinate foreign economic policy to the pursuit of national security* and the containment of Soviet communism. Throughout the 1950s and 1960s the American economy had recovered from the Great Depression and prospered; American business expanded its multinational presence throughout the world; European economies recovered and the international economy grew with the United States occupying the role of global banker and consumer; and economic sanctions were imposed on the Soviet Union and its close allies in support of the containment strategy. Thus, foreign economic policy was typically considered "low" policy, requiring little attention and expertise by most policymakers involved in the "high" policy of national security affairs. Responsibility, therefore, for the conduct of U.S. foreign economic policy resided with the foreign economic bureaucracy throughout the cold war era.

Foreign economic policy is no longer low policy in the contemporary era. Beginning in the 1960s the international economic system experienced increasing instability while the strength of the American economy declined. As an indicator of a weakening of the American economy, in 1968 exports of American cars abroad were surpassed for the first time by imports of foreign cars into the United States. By 1971 the Bretton Woods system no longer could be sustained: President Nixon removed a weakened dollar from the gold standard and allowed its value to float relative to other major currencies; a surcharge was placed on Japanese imports to offset growing deficits in the balance of payments and the rise of protectionist sentiment at home; and wage and price controls were imposed on the American economy to arrest the rise of domestic inflation. Beginning in 1973, America's energy costs also began to escalate with the rise of the ability of the Organization of Petroleum Exporting Countries (OPEC) to influence the supply of oil. These changes in the international economic environment have intensified many of the problems, involving inflation, unemployment, and deficits experienced by the economy and Americans at all levels—national, state, and local. Such conditions have forced international economic issues onto the government and public agendas, making foreign economic policy and the foreign economic bureaucracy part of the high politics of U.S. foreign policy.[2] The signing and passage of NAFTA (the North American Free Trade Agreement) as well as the creation and American participation in the International Trade Organization (ITO) under Presidents Bush and Clinton are indicative of the high politics of U.S. foreign economic policy.

CONTEMPORARY U.S. GLOBAL ECONOMIC INVOLVEMENT AND INTERDEPENDENCE

American ascendance in the international political economy has experienced relative decline since its height during the 1950s, as discussed in chapter 3. Today, the United States economy has become more intertwined with the workings of the international economy. American economic transactions have proliferated abroad and continue to have considerable impact on the evolution of the international political economy. At the same time, economic transactions emanating from abroad have increasingly penetrated and impacted the workings of the American economy. Thus, the American economy has become more heavily a part of, and dependent upon, the international political economy, thereby increasing the importance of foreign economic policy and policymaking. As the patterns in trade, energy, and investment discussed below indicate, these trends are likely to continue in the future. This profoundly affects employment, wage, and other economic patterns that impact American society and the standard of living, and quality of life, of Americans.

United States international trade has both increased and deteriorated over the years. American exports of merchandise goods were worth $15.5 billion in 1955, rose to $49 billion in 1972, exploded to $320 billion by 1988, and by the late nineties climbed to more then $600 billion. Likewise for foreign imports: $11.6 billion in 1955, $55.3 billion in 1972, $441 billion in 1988, and more than $800 billion in the late nineties.[3] Most U.S. trade is with Japan, Canada, and Western Europe, although over $200 billion worth of exports and imports in 1988 involved countries of the developing world. Where the United States typically ran small merchandise trade surpluses throughout the 1950s and 1960s (exporting more then importing), annual trade deficits began in 1971 and have been the norm since. The trade deficits have grown quite large since the 1980s, running anywhere from $100 billion to $200 billion respectively. Thus, the American economy and the standard of living of Americans has become increasingly affected by the flows of international trade.

Beginning in the 1970s, the American economy could no longer rely on the reliable flow of cheap oil. American production had declined at home while American and Western multinational oil companies increasingly lost control of production abroad ever since 1973 with the OPEC Arab embargo of oil exports following the outbreak of the Arab-Israeli Yom Kippur War. Steps were taken to slow the rate of **energy consumption**. Nevertheless, while the United States represents 5 percent of the world's population, it consumes roughly one-fourth of the world's energy. Thus, the United States remains highly dependent on the foreign importation of oil—the key source of energy in industrialized societies—for roughly 50 percent of its oil consumption.[4] American energy dependence on foreign oil played an important role in making the Middle East region of great strategic importance, as demonstrated in the Persian Gulf War of 1991.

American **international investment** has also proliferated dramatically, while the American economy has become more heavily affected by foreign investment. American (governmental and private) investment assets abroad, once $85.6 billion in 1960, totaled $1.25 trillion in 1988, and is approaching $3 trillion in the late nineties.[5] Total foreign investment assets within the United States also exploded from $40.9 billion in 1960 to $1.79 trillion in 1988, and is approaching $4 trillion in the late nineties. Much of these foreign assets are investments in securities and other liabilities to finance U.S. corporate and government deficits that have ballooned since the 1980s. Most of the American investment abroad—as much as 90 percent—represents private assets. Direct foreign investment by American companies abroad was $327 billion in 1988, a year in which it was surpassed for the first time since World War II by direct investment of foreign companies in the United States totaling $329 billion. It has since surpassed $700 billion by the late 1990s. Although three quarters of direct American investment abroad is made within developed countries, over $150 billion was made in developing countries, especially in Latin America and Asia.

This brief overview of American foreign economic transactions should illuminate the increasing importance of the international political economy for the American economy. It should also help to explain the rise of economic issues to the realm of high politics in U.S. foreign policy as well as the need to review the relevant governmental institutions involved in the foreign economic policymaking process.

RELEVANT GOVERNMENTAL INSTITUTIONS

The government's involvement in the politics of U.S. foreign economic policy has expanded, resulting in an expanded bureaucratic structure. Since the 1950s, small departmental advisory staffs with international responsibilities have turned into full-fledged bureaus while agencies within the Executive Office of the presidency have become more active in international economic matters. Furthermore, the jurisdictional lines between those governmental institutions that have primary responsibility for domestic economic policy, as opposed to foreign economic policy, have become blurred, for domestic and international economics have become much more intertwined.

Therefore, *numerous governmental institutions play a role, some large, some small, in the making of U.S. foreign economic policy.*[6] Among those most directly involved are the

1. Treasury Department;
2. Department of State;
3. Department of Agriculture;
4. Department of Commerce;
5. Department of Energy;
6. Federal Reserve Board;
7. Department of Labor;
8. International Trade Commission;
9. Export-Import Bank;
10. Overseas Private Investment Corporation;
11. Trade and Development Agency;
12. Council of Economic Advisers;
13. Agency for International Development (and the Peace Corps);
14. Office of Management and Budget; and
15. Office of United States Trade Representative.

The **Treasury Department** is probably the most important agency in areas of international economics, such as trade and monetary issues, and it has increasingly taken the lead on questions of foreign economic policy in general. The secretary of the treasury acts as a major policy adviser to the president with responsibilities involving domestic and international financial, economic, and tax policy. The *treasury secretary also officially represents the U.S. government in international economic organizations* such as the International Monetary Fund (IMF), the World Bank, the Inter-American Development Bank, and the African Development Bank (see **table 10.1** for a listing of the secretaries of the treasury and their background since the Roosevelt administration).

The secretary heads a large, complex bureaucratic department of which the under secretary for International Affairs and the **Office of the Assistant Secretary for International Affairs** has primary departmental responsibility over international monetary, financial, commercial, energy, and trade policies and programs. The office plays an important role in diplomatic negotiations concerning international economic matters and oversees U.S. participation in the multilateral development banks, such as the World Bank, to which the U.S. government provided $9.3 billion in grants and credits in 1987.[7] The Treasury Department also houses the U.S. Customs Service which oversees imports into the United States.

The **Department of State** also plays a prominent role in all areas of U.S. foreign economic policy. Although the State Department has had a long history of managing U.S. external relations, it has declined relative to the Department of Treasury in its influence over U.S. international economic policy. At the senior official level, the **under secretary for Economic and Agricultural Affairs** acts as principal adviser to the secretary concerning international trade, agriculture, energy, finance, transportation, and relations with developing countries.

At the lower bureaucratic level, the **Bureau for Economic and Business Affairs** has primary day-to-day departmental responsibility for formulating and implementing policy with regard to foreign economic matters. Other bureaus share some major responsibilities in international economic issues as well, such as the Bureau of International Organization Affairs and the Bureau of Oceans and International Environmental and Scientific Affairs. The Department of State and, increasingly, the Department of Treasury are the two major bureaucratic institu-

TABLE 10.1
SECRETARIES OF THE TREASURY

NAME	YEAR APPOINTED	BACKGROUND
Henry Morganthau, Jr.	1934	Law, Agriculture, and Government
Fred M. Vinson	1945	Law, Business, and Government
John W. Snyder	1946	Banking and Government
George M. Humphrey	1953	Law and Business
Robert B. Anderson	1957	Law, Education, and Government
C. Douglas Dillon	1961	Business and Government
Henry H. Fowler	1965	Law and Government
Joseph W. Barr	1968	Law, Business, and Government
David M. Kennedy	1969	Law, Business, and Government
John B. Connally	1971	Law and Government
George P. Shultz	1972	Academia, Business, and Government
William E. Simon	1974	Business and Government
W. Michael Blumenthal	1977	Academia, Business, and Government
G. William Miller	1979	Law, Business, and Government
Donald T. Regan	1981	Wall Street
James A. Baker III	1985	Law and Government
Nicholas F. Brady	1988	Business and Government
Lloyd Bentson	1993	Law and Congress
Robert Rubin	1995	Law and Wall Street

tions involved in all aspects of foreign economic policymaking.

The **Department of Agriculture** plays a major role in the area of agricultural trade. The **Office of International Cooperation and Development** works with international food and agricultural organizations and provides technical assistance and training in agriculture to other countries, particularly in the developing world. In 1953 a **Foreign Agricultural Service** was created to stimulate overseas markets for U.S. agricultural products, principally through its network of agricultural counselors, attaches, and trade officers stationed overseas and reinforced by a support staff abroad and at home.

The Foreign Agricultural Service, like the State Department's Foreign Service, has its own organi-

zational structure and subculture. It maintains a worldwide agricultural intelligence and reporting system and plays an active role in U.S. governmental trade policy and trade negotiations. The Foreign Agricultural Service also supervises and participates in the **Food for Peace Program** (Public Law 480 Program) and the **Commodity Credit Corporation**, which provides grants and credits to foreign governments and purchasers as economic assistance and to encourage the development and expansion of overseas markets for U.S. agricultural commodities.

The **Department of Commerce** has important international responsibilities in the area of trade. The department's **International Trade Administration** has the primary responsibility for the importation of foreign products, international economic policy, and trade promotion, especially of a nonagricultural nature. A **Foreign Commercial Service** is stationed overseas to provide services to the U.S. exporting and international business community. A major effort to more aggressively promote American exports abroad has been made under the Clinton administration, especially when Ron Brown was the Secretary of Commerce.[8]

The United States **Travel and Tourism Administration** is the bureaucratic agency within the Commerce Department that attempts to promote foreign tourism in the United States. Foreign visitors to the United States has steadily grown from over 10 million in 1970, to over 20 million by 1980, and almost 40 million by 1990. Foreign visitors are approaching 50 million by the end of the nineties who will spend over $80 billion.[9] The **Bureau of Export Administration** directs the government's export control policy, which includes processing license applications and enforcing U.S. export control laws.

Export controls have been used heavily for national security purposes since World War II. Throughout the cold war, the United States, in coordination with U.S. western allies through **CoCom** (the Coordinating Committee for Export Controls), restricted exports to the Soviet Union and its allies—engaging in **economic containment** as part of the larger containment strategy. The U.S. advocated a strict and wide embargo, with its allies preferring a more narrow strategic embargo. Although controls for national security purposes have loosened considerably, especially following the détente years and the profound changes in Eastern Europe and the Soviet Union (with the major exception of the continued economic embargo directed at Cuba), certain U.S. export controls continue for such goods as high-technology items.[10]

The **Department of Energy** has the major responsibility for energy policies, plans, and programs. The **Office of Assistant Secretary for International Affairs and Energy Emergencies** manages programs and activities relating to the international aspects of overall energy policy. These activities include energy preparedness and plans in case of national emergency, involvement in international energy nego-tiations, and coordination of international energy programs with foreign governments and international organizations such as the International Energy Agency and the International Atomic Energy Agency.

Similar to other agencies with specialized missions, the involvement of the **Federal Reserve Board** (**the FED**, referred to as one word) in the international economic sphere flows from its mission of monetary management within the domestic economy. The FED is an independent agency that determines and executes the general monetary, credit, and operating principles for the Federal Reserve System throughout the country, serving as the government's central bank. It is headed up by a Board of Governors that makes the key financial decisions and oversees the FED system as a whole, including the twelve federal reserve banks and their twenty-five branches and other facilities located throughout the country.

By influencing the lending and investing activities of American commercial banks, such as the cost and availability of money and credit, the Federal Reserve Board not only affects the state of the American economy but the country's international balance of payments position and the government's foreign economic policy as well. FED policies not only impact the American and international political economy by directly influencing the American banking system, but their policies influence the activities of other major banking systems as well, such as in Europe and Japan.[11]

The president appoints the seven members of the Board of Governors of the FED, with the advice and consent of the Senate, and designates the chair. But as an independent agency, and unlike the cabinet departments or agencies discussed above, the FED and, in particular, its chair are not "officially" under presidential control. **Alan Greenspan** has been head of the FED for over 10 years—the longest reign of any chair of the FED in its history. The FED through Alan Greenspan has become very prominent in affecting U.S. economic policy at home and abroad under Presidents Bush and Clinton.

Other agencies are involved with more narrow responsibilities that affect U.S. foreign economic policy. The **Department of Labor** handles questions concerning domestic and international labor. The department's **Bureau of International Labor Affairs** assists in formulating international economic and trade policies that affect American workers, represents the United States in international bodies such as the International Labor Organization, and engages in technical assistance abroad and trade union exchange programs.

The United States **International Trade Commission** (ITC) is an independent agency with broad powers of investigation relating to customs laws, export and import trade, and foreign competition. For example, the commission often adjudicates disputes between American industry and international corporations within the United States over charges of unfair trading practices. The ITC is made up of six commissioners appointed by the president with the advice and consent of the Senate for nine-year terms.

The **Export-Import Bank (Eximbank)** is a government corporation that subsidizes American company exports abroad. Although established in 1934 to promote trade with the Soviet Union, it has not been employed for that purpose throughout most of its history. Instead, it provides grants and credits to aid the export financing of U.S. goods and services, but is prohibited from competing with private financing. Outstanding credits of the Export-Import Bank authorized in 1995 were $12 billion and not to exceed $75 billion in total.[12] It also guarantees the Foreign Credit Insurance Association, an association of U.S. insurance companies organized by Eximbank in 1961, to ensure export transactions against risk of default. Supporters maintain that Eximbank assistance is an important tool for generating employment and income in the domestic economy and strengthening U.S. foreign trade. Opposition has ranged from charges that government participation in export financing is inequitable and an unnecessary intrusion into the private sector to complaints about Eximbank's emphasis on nuclear power and commercial aircraft exports.[13]

The **Overseas Private Investment Corporation** (OPIC) is an independent agency that stimulates foreign investment, predominantly in developing countries. It offers U.S. exporters assistance in finding investment opportunities, insurance to protect their investments, and loans and loan guaranties to help finance their projects. OPIC insures American companies against the political risks of foreign investment, such as expropriation and damage from war, revolution, insurrection, or civil strife. With the collapse of Stalinist regimes throughout Europe, OPIC has begun to become active in supporting American investment in the economies of Eastern Europe.[14]

The **Trade and Development Agency** is another governmental agency, becoming independent in 1992, designed to assist in the creation of jobs for Americans by helping U.S. companies export and pursue other overseas business opportunities. It tries to work closely with middle-income and developing countries abroad.

The **Agency for International Development** (AID) is the governmental agency with the principal responsibility to administer economic assistance and supervise economic development policy abroad. Although associated with the Department of State, it is basically an autonomous and independent agency. AID's mission has been part of a larger governmental effort to provide foreign assistance abroad, in part to engage in third-world nation building and, in part, so as to contain the expansion of the Soviet Union and communism throughout the cold war (see **essay 10.1** for an overview.)

Agencies within the Executive Office of the Presidency also have become more active in the making of U.S. foreign economic policy. The **Council of Economic Advisers** (CEA), with three members and a small staff, was created in 1946 to assess the state of the American economy and advise the president on economic matters. One of the three members of the CEA is assigned international responsibilities and participates in official delegations to the Organization for Economic Cooperation and Development (OECD) countries—Western Europe, Canada, and Japan.

Finally, the Office of Management and Budget and the Office of United States Trade Representative, located within the Executive Office of the Presidency

ESSAY 10.1
FOREIGN ASSISTANCE, NATION BUILDING, AND AID

Following World War II, the U.S. government began to engage in the practice of **foreign assistance**. Most of this assistance in the post-war years went to Western Europe in the form of **the Marshall Plan** to help them reconstruct their economies and to stabilize their political systems. As Western Europe recovered from the war and with the rise of the cold war, more and more of American foreign assistance was directed to other areas of the world as part of the U.S.'s larger strategy to contain the Soviet Union and communism.

Foreign assistance involves a variety of assistance programs and government agencies. **Security-related assistance**—that is, programs that are targeted to stabilize foreign governments and strengthen police and military forces—is provided covertly by the Central Intelligence Agency (CIA) and, principally, by the Department of Defense. **Economic-developmental assistance**—that is, programs to promote human welfare, economic development, and political stability in other societies—is provided by the Department of Agriculture (Food for Peace Program), the Department of the Treasury (through multilateral assistance to international governmental organizations such as the World Bank, African Development Bank, Asian Development Bank, Inter-American Development Bank, and other United Nations agencies), the **Peace Corps** (created by President John Kennedy to send so-called "volunteers" abroad to help people of developing countries—over 6,000 volunteers today in more than seventy countries—to meet basic needs for health, food, shelter, and education), and, most importantly, the Agency for International Development. During the 1990s, U.S. foreign assistance has been fluctuating around $15 billion a year, with security-related and developmental aid to other countries around $9 billion and $6 billion respectively. The largest recipients over the past decade have been Egypt and, in particular, Israel who together receive over one-third of American assistance since the signing of the Camp David Accords brought peace between the two countries.

The Agency for International Development (**AID**) was established in 1961 by President John F. Kennedy (along with the Peace Corps) to help third world countries develop and to counter the expansion of Soviet influence around the world. AID provides loans, grants, and technical assistance to developing countries to spur economic and political development. AID administers its bilateral assistance programs through a central headquarters and overseas offices, with a workforce composed of direct hires and the contracting of personal services (both U.S. and foreign national personnel). As discussed in chapter 7 on the State Department, AID maintains large missions abroad to support its assistance programs, often having a larger overseas presence than the foreign service in a developing country.

Much of the economic assistance has been directed to support countries of special political or security interest to the United States—that is, allied governments. For example, large amounts of developmental assistance went to Vietnam during the 1960s and to El Salvador during the 1980s—countries perceived to be directly threatened by communist movements internally and communist powers externally. The goal of developmental assistance, especially during the cold war, was to help states develop mature market economies and stable, effective governments so as to resist these threats. In other words, the U.S. government and AID in particular have been engaged in the very difficult and controversial task of **nation building** and modernizing societies abroad in the promotion of U.S. foreign policy. Recent interventions in Panama, Somalia, and Haiti suggest that the American effort to build stable and modernizing nations, even in a post–cold war environment, continues to be problematic at best.

Beginning with the rise of East-West détente of the 1970s, but especially with the collapse of the Soviet Union, AID's policies have been redirected increasingly away from security concerns. The agency's officially stated objectives today include:

1. advancing democracy,
2. promoting economic growth,
3. protecting public health and family planning,
4. providing humanitarian assistance, and
5. protecting the environment.

In the 1990s, AID has had a budget of about $7 billion and been active in over 100 countries, with personnel in over 90 countries. AID's methods include providing technical assistance and financial support for various in-country projects. Much of the money has been used to provide economic support for the balance of payments deficits that most third world countries have to finance. Furthermore, many of the foreign assistance laws require donor countries to purchase American products.

In the cold war era, foreign aid was partly justified as a way to counter Soviet influence. However, in today's political environment foreign aid is a particularly difficult sell. Members of Congress, who heavily influence foreign assistance legislation and budgets, do not believe that foreign aid is a salient issue with voters, and public opinion on foreign aid often gives policymakers contradictory signals: Americans believe in helping those in need, but are much more concerned with the needs of American

society at home than of societies abroad. Most Americans also tend to greatly overestimate the amount of foreign assistance spent by the United States. Americans would be surprised to know that the foreign assistance budget is less then one-fourth of one percent of the total federal budget and that it has not grown in constant dollars in over a decade (thus actually declining quite a bit in "real" dollars). Americans also see foreign assistance as "charity," not as a vital part of U.S. foreign policy since World War II.

Even AID's small piece of the budget pie has been shrinking. AID has responded by embarking on an ambitious reform plan and found ways to cut over 1800 staff and dozens of organization units. The agency has attempted to shed programs that aren't clearly related to development and has reevaluated the countries and programs receiving aid. In addition to organizational reform, AID has had to reform a scandal-ridden procurement process (to purchase technical and material support) and respond to criticisms that its policies were helping American business locate overseas at the expense of American jobs. These may have saved the agency from further budget cuts and threats to AID's organizational existence. If so, AID will continue to play a vital role in foreign assistance and U.S. foreign policy around the world.

SOURCES: Dick Kirschten, "Rescuing AID," *National Journal* (October 2, 1993): 2369–72; Robert A. Packenham, *Liberal America and the Third World: Political Development Ideas in Foreign Aid and Social Science* (Princeton, N.J.: Princeton University Press, 1973); Vernon W. Ruttan, *United States Development Assistance Policy: The Domestic Politics of Foreign Economic Aid* (Baltimore: Johns Hopkins University Press, 1996); U.S., Congress, Congressional Budget Office, *Enhancing U.S. Security Through Foreign Aid* (April 1994); U.S., Congress, Congressional Budget Office, *The Role of Foreign Aid in Development* (May 1997); U.S., Congress, Congressional Research Service, *Foreign Assistance: A Profile of the Agency for International Development* (April 1992); U.S., Agency for International Development, *USAID's Strategies for Sustainable Development* (August 2, 1997).

---

and which are discussed in greater detail below, have major responsibilities concerning budgetary and trade matters and play important roles with respect to the president's effort to coordinate and manage U.S. foreign policy as it affects economic policy.

COORDINATION PROBLEMS FROM ABOVE

So many agencies are involved in U.S. foreign economic policy that a major **problem of governmental coordination** has arisen within the executive branch.[15] Historically, the State Department was the lead agency responsible for coordinating U.S. foreign economic policy (except during times of war when the White House usually became more prominent). But the foreign economic bureaucracy was much smaller, and less complex and bureaucratic, throughout much of American history.

This really begins to change during the twentieth century, especially during the post–World War II years and since the 1960s. The foreign economic bureaucracy has expanded in size and complexity, and it has become more important for overall U.S. foreign policy. However, the State Department's role as lead agency has declined in foreign economic policy as well as in national security affairs (as discussed in chapter 7). The Treasury Department, on the other hand, has grown in prominence, but not to the point of being powerful enough or able to coordinate foreign economic policy—it's a department that is more like "a first among equals." Power, therefore, is extremely decentralized within the foreign economic bureaucracy and this has made it very difficult for the president to manage economic aspects of foreign policy.

Presidents have used different strategies to coordinate the foreign economic policymaking process. In addition to reliance on the State Department, an early effort at coordination involved **the government's budgetary process**. The Bureau of the Budget was created in 1921 and placed within the Executive Office of the Presidency by President Franklin Roosevelt in 1939 in order to coordinate and streamline the budgetary process of an expanding government. The Bureau of the Budget was the precursor of the **Office of Management and Budget (OMB),** created in 1970 to coordinate and supervise the budget and fiscal program of the government for the president. The formulation of the budget of the U.S. government is of great importance because if affects the activities of all bureaucratic agencies and represents the fiscal and spending policies of the federal government to the tune of almost $2 trillion per year, heavily influencing the American economy and foreign economic policy. As one analyst has stated, "Although the politics of the budget is often consid-

ered an internal concern, no external issue is as critical to foreign and national security strategy."[16]

According to journalist Hedrick Smith, during the Reagan years the apparatus of OMB was "the second most powerful staff in Washington, almost rivaling the top White House staff. . . . Its staff of six hundred included some of the very best career professionals in government, experts on every field."[17] Although the president's ability to coordinate and manage the government's budget and fiscal policies has improved with the assistance of OMB, this has not allowed the president to develop a coherent governmental policy with respect to issues involving international monetary matters, trade, investment, energy, and assistance.

In response to the breakdown of the Bretton Woods System in 1971, the president's need to centralize and coordinate the foreign economic policymaking process gained new urgency. Most presidents have come to rely on the **creation of interagency committees** at the cabinet and subcabinet levels to promote interaction and coordination of foreign economic policy; these agencies are chaired by the lead agency, most often the Treasury Department. These efforts have had mixed success and none of the interagency groups has gained the kind of permanence and prestige that the National Security Council (NSC) system has come to enjoy in national security policy.[18] Yet the NSC system, as discussed in chapter 3, has rarely played more than a peripheral role in foreign economic policy, being more oriented toward political and military affairs. As journalist John Leacacos put it, "The Achilles' heel of the NSC system has been international economics."[19]

Beyond continued reliance on different interagency groups, the late 1970s witnessed the growing prominence of the **Office of the United States Trade Representative** (USTR) as a coordinator of U.S. trade policy. Created by Congress in 1962 as part of the Executive Office of the Presidency, the **United States trade representative**, a cabinet-level official with the rank of ambassador, acts as a major presidential adviser, public spokesperson, and often the chief representative of the U.S. government on trade matters. Overall, despite the importance of USTR, it has had limited success in directing and managing U.S. trade policy for the president, much of which has depended on the strength of the individual special trade representative, his or her relationship with the president, and the quality of the USTR staff.

Part of the problem in coordinating the foreign economic bureaucracy involved the **lack of presidential attention and knowledge** with respect to international economic affairs. Most presidents, and their closest foreign policy advisers, have been more knowledgeable and comfortable dealing with traditional political and military issues associated with national security policy since World War II. Paul Volcker, former chair of the Federal Reserve Board, has commented that American presidents "have not in my experience wanted to spend much time on the complexities of international finance."[20]

Most presidents and foreign policy advisers have not been well versed in the complexities of international economics. This occurred primarily because during the cold war era foreign economics was not considered "high" policy and, hence, did not require much presidential attention. Much of this was a function not only of the importance of national security policy and the need to contain the Soviet Union, but also because of America's unique position within the international political economy following World War II for at least two decades—while other industrial societies were trying to rebuild their destroyed economies from the war the U.S. economy prospered and dominated global trade and finance. In other words, as the United States became the central market and banker to the world, presidents, and their advisers, didn't have to pay much attention to international economic affairs. This produced few individuals, whether in academia or among practitioners in or out of government, who were well-rounded in both national security and foreign economic policy, reinforcing what would increasingly become a problem for U.S. foreign policy with time.

Not surprisingly, the low politics of international economics during the cold war has left a strong legacy in the making of U.S. foreign policy: a foreign economic bureaucracy expanding in size and power but which maintained considerable freedom of independence from presidential supervision and control. As I. M. Destler puts it, the net result has been a divided governmental policymaking process with a relatively centralized "security complex" and a decentralized "economic complex."[21] The overall result for the making of foreign economic policy, according to Harald Malmgren, a former deputy special representative for trade negotiations for the president, is that "widespread confusion exists as to who is responsible for what. Both policy and daily decisions seem to be aimed in several different directions simultaneously."[22] As explained by Destler, "Decentralization is inevitable, not only of operational responsibility but of leadership and coordination responsibility as well."[23]

For certain policy areas, appropriate lead agencies are readily identifiable: the Department of Treasury for monetary matters, USTR for most trade issues, the Department of Agriculture for food, the Department of Energy for issues within its sphere, and the Department of State for matters concerning assistance and many third-world issues. "But it is much harder, of course, to assure that they will keep their parochialism in check. And no single department or cabinet member can exercise effective oversight of overall foreign economic policy."

In order to promote greater policy coordination and coherence, a number of reforms and reorganization of the foreign economic policymaking process has been recommended. Stephen Cohen, for example, in *The Making of United States International Economic Policy,* proposed the establishment of a Department of International Trade (or its equivalent), the creation of a permanent assistant to the president for International Economic Affairs with a small staff, and the creation of a cabinet-level Committee for International Economic Policy on a permanent basis with the president as chair.[24] Little had come of this and other recommendations to better coordinate and centralize the making of U.S. foreign economic policy under the president, until the arrival of Bill Clinton as president and the creation of the National Economic

Council. Nevertheless, a free market ethos did develop following World War II throughout American society and impacted the workings of the foreign economic bureaucracy.

ECONOMIC CULTURE AND THE FREE MARKET ETHOS

Even though a vast decentralized structure of competing interests permeate throughout the foreign economic bureaucracy, an underlying consensus in "**economic culture**" and shared values provides a certain degree of coherence and common direction in U.S. foreign economic policy.[25] A **strong free market ethos based upon a liberal economic paradigm** prevails throughout much of the foreign economic bureaucracy and American society. The free market ethos refers to the faith and belief in the power of the private market to promote growth and prosperity with minimal governmental intervention.[26]

Throughout American history, a strong faith in the free market ethos about the evolution of capitalism and the workings of the domestic economy has grown. However, given America's economic nationalist and protectionist past, only since World War II has the free market ethos provided the basis for thinking about U.S. foreign economic policy—a time when the United States became the world's economic superpower. Today, these beliefs have become so firmly embedded in American culture that the free market ethos provides the common understanding by which most Americans believe in the benefits of "free trade" and the proper path of "economic development." As Herbert McClosky and John Zaller found in their study of *The American Ethos,* alongside a strong belief in democracy a faith in capitalism and the free market was the foundation of American cultural identity.[27]

The free market ethos is a conception **held by most policymakers**. Officials throughout the foreign economic bureaucracy, such as former Assistant Secretary of International Affairs Gerald L. Parsky in the Department of Treasury, consistently proclaimed the free market ethos as the basis of policy: "It is our firm conviction that the market mechanism is on the whole the most efficient method of assuring that supply and demand of commodities are kept in balance in a dynamic world. Although markets do not always operate efficiently, the appropriate remedy is to strengthen their functioning, not intervene, or further impede market operations."[28] Although presidents and other high-level officials may lack knowledge and confidence in matters of international economics in comparison to specialists, their understanding of the world and their policy inclinations have tended to be heavily informed from a free market perspective as well.

The free market ethos that permeates government doesn't eliminate the political and bureaucratic infighting that runs rampant, but the common outlook toward capitalism and free trade does allow for compromise and provides a relatively consistent general orientation to U.S. foreign economic policy. **Differences in policy orientations** between administrations and within administrations over international economics have grown over the years, but they still tend to be more a matter of degree, involving priorities and the tactics of policy as opposed to basic goals. Some American officials emphasize the need for minimal cooperation and intervention by governments in the international political economy to allow the magic of the marketplace to work, while others advocate greater multilateral management to minimize instability and maximize economic growth in a global economy of growing interdependence. But both positions are market oriented and reside within the free market ethos.[29]

As illustrated by analyst Stephen Cohen, "No agency has openly argued in the post–World War II period for a permanent shift in the essentially **open-door policy** for U.S. companies wishing to invest overseas or for foreign companies wishing to invest in the United States. There has been a general agreement in the executive branch that the burden of proof is on the advocates of utilizing governmental restrictions or subsidies to affect the global flow of goods, services, and capital."[30] Therefore, although the principles and institutions in support of free trade have come under criticism, scholar Judith Goldstein finds that "liberalism still holds a social position not unlike a 'sacred cow' in the policymaking community."[31] This common free market ethos in American government and society may help to account for why presidents have not felt the same urgency to coordinate and centralize the foreign economic policy machinery within the White House as they have attempted to do in the national security area—that is, until Bill Clinton and the National Economic Council.

THE NATIONAL ECONOMIC COUNCIL

A significant change in the making of U.S. foreign economic policy has been made under President Clinton. He created the **National Economic Council (NEC)** shortly after becoming president in 1993 in an attempt to coordinate and integrate economic policy—both domestic and foreign. The *functions of the new organization* were:

1. to coordinate the economic policymaking process with respect to domestic and international economic issues;
2. to coordinate economic policy advice to the president;
3. to ensure that economic policy decisions and programs are consistent with the president's stated goals, and to ensure that those goals are being effectively pursued; and
4. to monitor implementation of the president's economic policy agenda.[32]

Although Bill Clinton has been accused of being a neophyte in the area of foreign policy, this is actually a simplification of reality. There is no doubt that President Clinton is a relative novice in the area of national security affairs and, like many presidents, was forced to experience a lot of on-the-job training and learning. But Bill Clinton, unlike previous presidents, is deeply interested and knowledgeable about issues of economics, both domestic and international. This meant that Bill Clinton's attention, knowledge, and involvement in economic policy placed a premium on the need to better organize and coordinate the (foreign) economic bureaucracy. Hence, a new unit within the Executive Office of the

Presidency—the National Economic Council—was born.

The NEC, like the National Security Council after which it was modeled, is a formal mechanism that is led by a special assistant to the president for economic affairs—**the national economic adviser**—and a small staff (of two or three dozen personnel). It is designed to function as an honest policy broker, coordinating the making and implementation of policy among the major policymakers and the variety of executive agencies involved in economic policy. It has been described as a "low-profile but powerful institutional mechanism created to coordinate the Administration's Cabinet-level economic policy making. The goal was to do for economic policy what the National Security Council (NSC) has done for national security policy."[33]

Into his second term of office, Bill Clinton has, thus far, relied on three national economic advisers to help him manage the bureaucracy and make economic policy at home and abroad (see **table 10.2**). Along with the secretary of the treasury, the OMB director, the chair of the Council of Economic Advisers, and the secretary of commerce, the new national economic adviser clearly has become one of the president's most prominent policymakers in the making of U.S. economic policy (review table 6.1).

Robert Rubin, the first national economic adviser who subsequently has become the treasury secretary, was consequential in defining the initial role of the position and the council operations. He "conceived his role as honest broker, organizing options for the president, but he has not been hesitant about articulating his own views" as well.[34] Rubin molded the NEC into the center of White House economic policymaking. This was a major challenge because "other institutions had important process leadership roles too: the NSC, the Office of the US Special Trade Representative (USTR), the OMB, and most important of all for economic issues, the Department of Treasury. The NEC would have to negotiate a role for itself—and jurisdictional boundaries with each of them—or else fight with them."[35] Thus far the national economics adviser and the NEC has been able to minimize conflict that its creation has engendered with the economic bureaucracy while

TABLE 10.2
NATIONAL ECONOMIC ADVISERS

NAME	YEAR APPOINTED	BACKGROUND
Robert Rubin	1993	Law and Wall Street
Laura D'Andrea Tyson	1995	Academia
Gene Sperling	1997	Law and Government

promoting a relatively open and collegial process, reflecting the teamwork and interaction that President Clinton prefers.[36]

The NEC is structured in a very similar fashion as the NSC, with the major exception that the NEC's staff is considerably smaller—a few dozen staff within the NEC versus well over 100 staff within the NSC. The National Economic Adviser "serves as Clinton's senior economic adviser—chairing senior staff meetings and conferring with the president privately."[37] A "core group" of senior officials, or principals, meets for the most prominent issues usually led by the national economic adviser, with other interagency "working groups" made of deputies, chaired by key NEC aides.

"The early National Economic Council made its mark through immersion in front-burner action issues: the budget, the North American Free Trade Agreement (NAFTA), the Uruguay Round, Japan."[38] Because the national economic adviser and the NEC became a significant force as a result of its role in coordinating myriad bureaucratic agencies and officials involved in economics and providing policy advice for the president, the scope of its activities has expanded. "The NEC is playing a growing role in shaping the president's political messages, working with the White House's communications and political advisers on events and speeches designed to highlight Clinton's economic views and plans."[39]

As I. M. Destler has pointed out, the NEC system has not been without problems. "Interagency coordination is extraordinarily difficult, particularly on economic issues, and particularly with a president who engages in a freewheeling and not always predictable manner."[40] Nevertheless,

President Clinton's National Economic Council started off strong, with Robert Rubin's exceptional adroitness joined to the president's priority agenda. The NEC recognized the primacy of informal relationships; it set out to show all the important players the benefits of working with and through its staff and its procedures. To a substantial degree, it made itself the central institution within its designated policy sphere. To a lesser but significant degree, it was an effective manager of policy.

At the same time, "even in its glory days, however, there were signs of trouble ahead. There were limits in substantive reach and difficulties in focusing very far ahead. . . . There was the sense of informality run rampant, particularly at the deputies level: meetings leading mainly to more meetings, without decisions taken or choices clarified or follow-up work assigned.[41]

Overall, Destler found that the NEC system was a relative success in helping the president manage the making of U.S. economic policy. *The NEC tended to work well, especially when four criteria were met:*

1. the issue was important to the president and the administration,
2. the issue was clearly within NEC jurisdiction,
3. the NEC had firm deadlines and action-forcing events that required central decisions, and
4. there was a natural lead operating agency.[42]

It is important to point out that these are the formative years of what might very well be a significant institutionalized presence of a powerful NEC in the making of foreign policy. Much ultimately will depend on presidential interest in international economics and the future use of the NEC following Bill Clinton. But clearly, the creation and development of the NEC symbolizes the continued trend toward White House-centered policymaking in response to presidential efforts to better manage and govern foreign policy.

THE CULTURAL AND COMMUNICATIONS BUREAUCRACY

. . . .

The U.S. government, especially since World War II, also has been involved in disseminating information about the United States and in promoting U.S. cultural activities abroad. The globalization of U.S. foreign policy and the anticommunist foundation of the containment policy have resulted in the presence of a small yet important bureaucracy involved in communications and cultural foreign policy.[43]

The **United States Information Agency (USIA)**, which is referred to as United States Information Service (USIS) abroad, is the major cultural and communications agency of the U.S. government. It is engaged in a variety of informational, educational and cultural activities in more than 200 overseas posts in more than 120 countries. These activities include international broadcasting, press releases; the publication of magazines; the development and release of film, television, and videotape programs; the maintenance of libraries and book programs; lectures and cultural presentations; and English instruction.

USIA also administers a number of **international exchange programs**, such as the Fulbright program, involving over 20,000 students, scholars, and practitioners from America and abroad (this is actually one large part of over seventy international exchange and training programs administered in more then fifteen federal departments and agencies involving over 60,000 people).[44] These programs and activities are most visible in the developing countries of the world. The purpose behind USIA's activities is to promote cross-cultural knowledge and understanding which, it is argued, will promote a more supportive environment for U.S. foreign policy.

A major emphasis by the U.S. government has been its involvement in international broadcasting and communication. **International broadcasting** represents a major element by the U.S. government to communicate information and propaganda about America and the world so as to support U.S. foreign policy. The major broadcasting arm and official voice of the U.S. government is **Voice of America (VOA)**, which operated under the auspices of the United States Information Agency. Begun during World War II as part of the war effort, VOA broadcasts a mixture of general news, public affairs programs, music, and entertainment throughout the world in over forty languages (through a global network of short-wave and medium wave "AM band" transmitters) to an estimated audience of over 100 million people. It maintains a staff of over 2000, the vast majority of whom work in the United States. The broadcasts originate in Washington, D.C., and are transmitted overseas via relay stations and commercial satellite circuits.

Since its creation, the nature of VOA's broadcast format and content has been debated. Some advocate that VOA should serve purely as a propaganda outlet in which the United States is portrayed in a positive light while American adversaries are portrayed negatively. Others feel that it should operate more subtly, reflecting some of the norms of the journalistic profession and the American national media.

Given this debate, the nature of Voice of America's programming has fluctuated under different administrations. During the Reagan administration, for example, VOA became much more propaganda oriented as seen through the development of **Radio Martí** and **Television Martí** to propagandize the virtues of the American way of life to the people of Cuba. Since the collapse of the Soviet Union and communism in Eastern Europe, VOA has been having difficulties adjusting to a post–cold war world and modernizing its facilities.[45]

In cooperation with the West German government, the United States Information Agency also funds **Radio in the American Sector (RIAS)**. This radio service was originally established in 1946 to broadcast to Germans in the American sector of Berlin, but was heard throughout the two Germanys. The Department of Defense also maintains the U.S. Armed Forces Radio and Television Service, which broadcasts to U.S. military bases and ships around the world.

Two other important agencies involved in international broadcasting are **Radio Free Europe** (RFE) and **Radio Liberty** (RL). They were created in 1950 and 1953, respectively, by the U.S. government to broadcast anticommunist propaganda to the peoples of Eastern Europe and the Soviet Union. RFE and RL were set up to appear as private entities, staffed by emigrés from Eastern Europe and the Soviet Union, while covertly funded by the CIA. Broadcasts attempted to foment domestic unrest and instability based on the assumption that people in mass society are vulnerable to simple and aggressive "persuasive communications."[46]

After the CIA's covert role became public in the early 1970s, RFE and RL became independent of the CIA and were supervised by an independent **Board for International Broadcasting.** Nevertheless, their bureaucratic structures and subcultures have not fundamentally altered, and they continued to broadcast propaganda to create unrest within the Soviet Union and Eastern Europe.[47] As a response to the Soviet invasion of Afghanistan in 1979, Radio Liberty began to operate **Radio Free Afghanistan.** During the 1980s, Radio Free Europe and Radio Liberty broadcasted throughout the day in six languages to Eastern Europe and in fifteen languages to the Soviet Union, employed over 1,700 people, and spent an annual budget of more than $100 million.[48]

The collapse of the Stalinist regimes in the Soviet Union and Eastern Europe has deeply affected Radio Liberty and Radio Free Europe. Until recently, information for their propaganda broadcasts was heavily dependent on third-party sources due to their limited access to the Soviet Union and Eastern Europe. Today, the content of the broadcasts is much more positive about internal developments. The stations' editors and reporters have access to the countries to which they broadcast and increasingly rely on their own reporting. As of the early nineties, Radio Free Europe and Radio Liberty operated bureaus throughout Eastern Europe and the former Soviet Union.

The dramatic changes throughout Europe raise questions concerning the future and ultimate purpose of Radio Liberty and Radio Free Europe. They have moved their operations from Munich, Germany, to Prague in the Czech Republic, while experiencing considerable downsizing in staff and budget. Some people have argued that Radio Liberty and Radio Free Europe can be abandoned completely now that communism has collapsed in Eastern Europe and the Soviet Union has declined as a threat. Others have argued that Radio Liberty and Radio Free Europe should serve a new mission to provide an alternative domestic medium of communications that promotes democracy in the region. Clearly, they are seeking a new role in the twenty-first century.[49]

In 1983, the Reagan administration created the **National Endowment for Democracy** (NED). It is an independent quasi-governmental organization intended to support free and democratic institutions throughout the world. The NED, which is funded by USIA, provides grants for international activities carried out by American labor, business, and the Democratic and Republican parties.

The National Endowment for Democracy has been controversial from its inception because many people argue that it represents a narrow, conservative segment of American society.[50] Under President Reagan, most of the funding by the endowment went to two private organizations with strong anticommunist credentials: the American Federation of Labor—Congress of Industrial Organizations (AFL-CIO) and the U.S. Chamber of Commerce. During the Nicaraguan election of 1990, for example, the NED spent over $6 million to promote Nicaraguan democracy, much of which went to the political coalition led by Violeta Chamarro, who eventually emerged victorious.[51]

Supporters tend to argue that such activities help to promote democracy abroad. Critics, on the other hand, tend to emphasize that the agency is mismanaged and that many of its measures represent efforts to intervene and manipulate democracy in the name of national security. As some studies have concluded, the overall record of the National Endowment for Democracy and its impact abroad is mixed and remains somewhat unclear.[52]

Unlike the national security and foreign economic bureaucracy, the communications and cultural bureaucracy is quite small. Furthermore, it remains a low priority in the eyes of most policymakers for communications and cultural policies are considered peripheral instruments of U.S. foreign policy. A simple illustration of this is that the total operating budget of USIA represents less than .25 of a percent of total military spending.[53] This has resulted in a continuous debate about the importance of the role of culture and communications in U.S. foreign policy as well as how to use the limited resources available. In this respect, the collapse of communism in Eastern Europe and the decline of the Soviet Union represents an opportune time to rethink the priority and purpose of U.S. cultural and communications policy.

Many people argue that cultural and communications policy is a powerful instrument and should play a more vital role in U.S. foreign policy. But they often disagree over priorities and the form it should take. Some have advocated, as within the Reagan administration, greater reliance on the power of international broadcasting and propaganda to support U.S. foreign policy. Others have supported a greater commitment to educational and cultural programs to promote mutual understanding and friendship as an important basis of U.S. foreign policy. Nevertheless, most policymakers give cultural and communications policy little notice. Therefore, with little effort by the president and his major advisers to centralize and bring coherence to cultural and communications policy, the bureaucratic agencies involved are permitted to act with relative autonomy with what resources they have in this area.

OTHER ELEMENTS OF THE FOREIGN POLICY BUREAUCRACY

. . . .

Clearly, the foreign policy bureaucracy is huge, complex, and of recent development. Governmental agencies involved in foreign policy, in fact, are not limited to national security policy, foreign economic policy, and communications and cultural policy. **Other issues**, such as technology, transportation, immigration, the environment, and narcotics, also have become important parts of overall U.S. foreign policy and have spawned bureaucratic elements.[54] As explained by Professor Edward Morse, in *Foreign Policy and Interdependence,* the spread of technology, modernization, and global interdependence has led to the breakdown in the separation between foreign and domestic policy as well as between high and low politics.[55] Therefore, many of the agencies traditionally considered to be domestic oriented have important international dimensions as well. (See **table 10.3** for a contemporary listing of the more active agencies involved in foreign affairs.)

Within the Office of the White House, the **Office of Science and Technology Policy** advises the president of scientific and technological considerations involving national concern, including national security and foreign relations. The **Office of National Drug Control Policy** was established under President Reagan to try to coordinate and add some coherence to the myriad of executive branch agencies which have become involved in the "war on drugs."

Other cabinet departments have units which have selective, but important international roles. The **Department of Transportation**, in addition to housing the U.S. Coast Guard, is responsible for the government's policy on international aviation and maritime issues through the Office of the Assistant Secretary for Aviation and International Affairs, the Federal Aviation Administration, and the Maritime Administration. In addition to the FBI, the Department of Justice contains the **Drug Enforcement Agency**, the lead agency in actually fighting the drug

TABLE 10.3
THE FOREIGN POLICY BUREAUCRACY

	INTERNATIONALLY ORIENTED AGENCIES	DOMESTICALLY ORIENTED AGENCIES
Executive Office of the President	National Security Council	White House Office
	National Economic Council	Office of Management and Budget
	Office of the U.S. Trade Representative	Office of Science and Technology Policy
		Office of National Drug Control Policy
Presidential Departments and Agencies	Department of State	Department of Treasury
	Department of Defense	Department of Agriculture
	Department of Energy	Department of Commerce
	Central Intelligence Agency	Department of Labor
	Agency for International Development	Department of Justice
	U.S. Information Agency	Department of Veterans Affairs
	Arms Control and Disarmament Agency	Department of Transportation
	Peace Corps	
Independent Agencies	International Trade Commission	Federal Reserve Board
	Export-Import Bank	National Aeronautics and Space Administration
	Overseas Protection Investment Corporation	Environmental Protection Agency
	Trade and Development Agency	Federal Maritime Commission
	Board for International Broadcasting	
	National Endowment for Democracy	
	African Development Foundation	
	Inter-American Foundation	
	Panama Canal Commission	
	U.S. Institute for Peace	

SOURCE: *United States Government Manual.*

war with offices in over 50 countries. Also within the Justice Department, the **Immigration and Naturalization Service** is very important when it comes to immigration policy (see **essay 10.2** for an overview).

A number of independent agencies and governmental corporations are also heavily involved in the international political economy. The **Environmental Protection Agency** is heavily responsible

ESSAY 10.2
DEMOGRAPHICS, IMMIGRATION, AND THE INS

The United States has been heavily affected by demographic changes and migration patterns throughout the world. Not only have people immigrated to the U.S. throughout its history, but immigrants have changed in composition. Earlier immigrants were overwhelmingly of European descent. Throughout this century, however, more immigrants from all over the world have entered American borders, especially from Asia and Latin America. Recently, immigrants also have increasingly entered illegally (especially from Mexico, El Salvador, Guatemala, and Canada).

The Immigration and Naturalization Service (**INS**), within the Department of Justice, is the lead agency when it comes to immigration policy. It has a variety of missions including: overseeing alien entry, supervision of over 200 ports of entry, patrolling the borders, preventing illegal entries, adjudicating citizenship claims, and investigating criminal immigrant activities. The INS maintains three regional offices, thirty-three district offices, and twenty-one border patrol sectors throughout the United States, while maintaining three offices abroad in Bangkok, Mexico City, and Rome.

Two key legislative acts prompted recent reform in U.S. immigration policy—attempting to reconcile the need for a more flexible system of legal immigration while attempting to prevent illegal immigration—and affected the INS: the Immigration Reform and Control Act of 1986 and the Immigration Act of 1990. The 1986 act dealt with tightening employer sanctions, legalization, agricultural workers, state legislation, and alien verification. The 1990 act capped legal immigration, increased overall admissions, increased family-based immigration, and aimed to reduce illegal immigration.

During the nineties, anywhere from 800,000 to 1.5 million immigrants are now "legally" admitted into the United States each year, of which 10 percent to 20 percent are from Europe. And almost 2 million people a year apply for American citizenship, with a backlog of over 1 million people. In response to the acts, the volume of people involved, and the climate of opinion, the INS has tightened its rules and administration of the immigration process—some argue maybe too much. This is because the INS is the agency which ultimately determines whether a person can legally enter and reside in the United States (and eventually become a U.S. citizen), or whether an immigrant has to leave or be deported. And recent changes in immigration laws have made things even more complicated for thousands of people affected and the INS.

The issue of **illegal immigration** has become increasingly controversial in the United States. In the late 1990s, there were an estimated 5 million illegal immigrants in the United States. President Clinton has made various efforts to tighten security on illegal entry into the United States, with some marginal success. For example, the number of immigrants deported in 1996 increased by almost 20,000 from the previous year. California accounts for 40 percent of the nation's illegal immigrants, or over 2 million illegal immigrants, most of whom illegally cross the border from Mexico, followed by Texas, New York, and Florida. Many of the illegal immigrants are eagerly employed by American businesses in low-paying, low-skilled jobs in urban and rural areas, such as migrant farm workers. It is estimated that almost half of those entering the United States illegally have expired tourist or working visas.

Immigrants have generated considerable controversy throughout American history, especially in the twentieth century with an increasing influx of non-Europeans and during downturns in the American economy. Issues involving humanitarian assistance to refugees, jobs and opportunity, welfare and educational benefits, the role of English and other languages (especially Spanish), the racial composition of American society, and more have been raised due to both legal and illegal immigration. These are important and often emotional issues which get to the core of American identity and culture.

Another important issue has been a rising concern with terrorism in the United States. Terrorist activities have recently spurred the INS to crack down on fraudulent documents. This has raised all sorts of concerns about the civil rights and liberties of both American citizens and immigrants. Arab-Americans are particularly offended at some of the heightened security measures because many Arab-Americans fear that Middle Eastern immigrants are specifically targeted for inspection.

The Immigration and Naturalization Service has been experiencing high volumes of activity coupled with an increasing need to tighten security measures without abusing people's civil rights and liberties. These are difficult roles and responsibilities to reconcile. Some have argued for more INS officers and a larger INS budget, but this is unlikely to solve the problems. As a federal advisory commission on the country's immigration system recently concluded, it may very well be that the volume and complexity of immigration are just too taxing for an agency not designed for such a broad, and often contradictory, range of responsibilities today.

SOURCES: Frank D. Bean and Michael Fox, "The Significance of Recent Immigration Policy Reforms in the United States," in Gary P. Freeman and James Jupp, eds., *Nations of Immigrants: Australia, the United States, and International Migration* (Oxford: Oxford University Press, 1992); Nadine Cohodas, "Immigration Law, Terrorism Make for Tough Times at INS," *Congressional Quarterly Weekly* (February 14, 1987): 288–90; Mirta Ojito, "Immigration Law Changes Force Many to Make Tough Choices," *New York Times* (September 25, 1997); Eric Schmitt, "Breakup of Immigration Service Urged by Advisory Panel," *New York Times* (August 5, 1997); Eric Schmitt, "Under Fire, Immigration Agency Changes Its Fingerprinting," *New York Times* (September 18, 1997).

for international environmental issues within the executive branch. The **Federal Maritime Commission** is an independent agency that regulates the waterborne domestic and foreign offshore commerce of the United States. The **African Development Foundation** and the **Inter-American Foundation** are nonprofit, government corporations that provide grants and loans to local private groups within the region that promote development. The **Panama Canal Commission** is an independent agency that operates and maintains the Panama Canal and surrounding territory until December 31, 1999, when the Republic of Panama will assume full authority. The **United States Institute for Peace** is an independent, federal, nonprofit corporation whose purpose is to develop and disseminate knowledge about the peaceful resolution of international conflict.

In fact, it is fair to say that virtually every executive branch department and agency is involved in international affairs in some way. For example, the **Department of the Interior's** Office of Insular Affairs coordinates and oversees federal policy toward the territories of American Samoa, Guam, the U.S. Virgin Islands, the Commonwealth of the Northern Mariana Islands, the Republic of the Marshall Islands, the Federal States of Micronesia, and the Republic of Palau—all part of the U.S.'s colonial acquisitions from earlier days. The Center for International Education is part of the **Department of Education**, while the **Department of Health and Human Services** is involved in issues of international health through its Office of International and Refugee Health. The **Federal Communications Commission** regulates foreign communications by Americans while the **Federal Emergency Management Agency (FEMA)** develops and coordinates national programs to respond to any national security emergency. Even the **Department of Housing and Urban Development** has an assistant to the secretary for International Affairs.

Numerous **governmental boards, committees, and commissions** also have been created whose activities, usually symbolic, involve international affairs. Among these would be included the Committee on Foreign Investment in the United States, the Japan-United States Friendship Commission, the President's Foreign Intelligence Advisory Board, the Textile Trade Policy Group, and the Trade Policy Committee.

The breadth of governmental involvement in international affairs indicates the increasing complexity and internationalization of the foreign policy bureaucracy over time. Raymond Hopkins was one of the earliest scholars to highlight the **internationalization of domestic bureaucracies** and the development of global networks of bureaucratic interaction, especially in such "principal areas of food, energy, finance, communication, environment, economic growth, and the spread of technology."[56] This has contributed to the relative independence and autonomy of much of the bureaucracy from presidential authority.

As Edward Morse pointed out in the early 1970s, "Most of the departments and ministries of modern governments associated with predominantly domestic areas have some kind of international bureau. The proliferation of these international bureaus severely undercuts the ability of one foreign ministry or department to control the external policies of its government, thus severely restricting the coordination of foreign policies."[57] The consequences of such complexity, internationalization, and independence of the governmental bureaucracy has been that the president's management task has become increasingly complicated and impossible.

MAJOR FOREIGN POLICY PATTERNS REVISITED
. . . .

In order to place the foreign policy process within the executive branch in proper perspective, it is important to *review the major post–World War II foreign policy patterns that have been discussed so far.* Seven key patterns stand out:

First, World War II and the cold war resulted in the globalization of U.S. foreign policy.

Second, following World War II the United States became the preeminent global actor in which American power reached its zenith during the cold war years.

Third, the World War II and cold war years resulted in the rise of presidential power in foreign policy. However, the Vietnam War, the breakdown of the Bretton Woods economic system, and Watergate all helped to restrict presidential power and were symptomatic of greater global and domestic complexity.

Fourth, the National Security Council system has become increasingly powerful, gradually replacing the State Department as the tool for presidential management of national security policy.

Fifth, there has been a rise in the national security bureaucracy, increasing the foreign policy role of elements such as the military establishment and the intelligence community.

Sixth, bureaucratic agencies not devoted to traditional national security issues, especially the foreign economic bureaucracy, have become more visible and important in U.S. foreign policy during the post-Vietnam era.

Finally, all of these patterns together—especially the tremendous expansion in the size, scope and complexity of the foreign policy bureaucracy—have complicated greatly presidential efforts to manage and control foreign policy within the executive branch.

These patterns have produced some contradictory outcomes. On the one hand, the president has grown more powerful in foreign policy. On the other hand, the president has found it more difficult to manage the foreign policy bureaucracy. The NSC adviser and staff have become more significant in presidential management; yet contemporary U.S. foreign policy involves much more than traditional national security policy. These patterns also have intensified the tensions between the demands of democracy and those of national security within American society and U.S. foreign policy. How these patterns and contradictions affect the policymaking process within the executive branch and the foreign policy of the United States will be discussed in the next chapter.

BIBLIOGRAPHIC ESSAY

. . . .

Most studies of the politics of U.S. foreign policy focus on the national security bureaucracy. Little attention has been directed toward the foreign economic bureaucracy, until recently. An informative overview of the history of U.S. foreign economic policy can be found in Joan Edelman Spero, *The Politics of International Economic Relations* (New York: St. Martin's Press, 1997). An overview of the foreign economic bureaucracy and policymaking process is provided by Stephen D. Cohen, *The Making of United States International Economic Policy: Principles, Problems, and Proposals for Reform* (New York: Praeger, 1988). Karen Mingst provides a good discussion of the free market ethos in "Process and Policy in U.S. Commodities: The Impact of the Liberal Economic Paradigm," in William P. Avery and David Rapkin, eds., *America in a Changing World Political Economy* (New York: Longman, 1982), pp. 191–206. I. M. Destler discusses the development of the NEC in *The National Economic Council: A Work in Progress* (Washington, D.C.: Institute for International Economics, 1996).

Much has been written on the U.S. bureaucracy and foreign policy in the cultural and communications area. A good overview of USIA can be found in Richard N. Gardner, "Selling America in the Marketplace of Ideas," *New York Times Magazine* (March 20, 1983): 44, 58–61, and Allen C. Hansen, *U.S. Information Agency: Public Diplomacy in the Computer Age* (New York: Praeger, 1984). Informative and interesting discussions of U.S. international broadcasting are provided by Kim Andrew Elliott, "Too Many Voices of America," *Foreign Policy* 77 (Winter 1989–90): 113–31; Sig Mickelson, *America's Other Voice: The Story of Radio Free Europe and Radio Liberty* (New York: Praeger, 1983); and John Spicer Nichols, "Wasting the Propaganda Dollar," *Foreign Policy* 56 (Fall 1984): 129–40. The origins and background of the psychological warfare of international broadcasting can be found in Christopher Simpson, *Science of Coercion: Communication Research and Psychological Warfare, 1945–1960* (New York: Oxford University Press, 1994). A good overview of the National Endowment for Democracy is provided by Thomas Carothers, "The NED at 10," *Foreign Policy* (Summer 1994): 123–38.

For a brief and official overview of the entire bureaucracy, see the *United States Government Manual* (Washington, D.C.: U.S. Government Printing Office). Raymond F. Hopkins provides valuable insights about recent bureaucratic developments in "Global Management Networks: The Internationalization of Domestic Bureaucracies," *International Social Science Journal* 30 (1978): 31–45.

ENDNOTES

1. For an overview of U.S. foreign economic policy, see Alfred E. Eckes, Jr., *Opening America's Market: U.S. Foreign Trade Since 1776* (Chapel Hill: University of North Carolina Press, 1995); Charles P. Kindleberger, "U.S. Foreign Economic Policy 1776–1976," *Foreign Affairs* (January 1977): 395–417; David A. Lake, *Power, Protection, and Free Trade: International Sources of U.S. Commercial Strategy, 1887–1939* (Ithaca: N.Y.: Cornell University Press, 1988); Stefanie Ann Lenway, *The Politics of U.S. International Trade: Protection, Expansion and Escape* (Boston: Pittman, 1985); Emily S. Rosenberg, *Spreading the American Dream: American Economic and Cultural Expansion, 1890–1945* (New York: Hill and Wang, 1982); and Joan Edelman Spero, *The Politics of International Economic Relations* (New York: St. Martin's Press, 1997).

2. To understand the dissolution of the distinction between high and low politics in an increasingly interdependent age, see Edward L. Morse, *Foreign Policy and Interdependence in Gaullist France* (Princeton, N.J.: Princeton University Press, 1973).

3. All trade statistics come, or are derived, from United Nations, *International Trade Statistics Yearbook* (1995), and United States, *Statistical Abstracts of the United States* (1996).

4. Energy statistics can be found in United States, *Statistical Abstracts.*

5. Statistics on investment are based on *Europa World Yearbook* (1995), and United States, *Statistical Abstracts.*

6. For an overview, see Chester Roe Goddard, *The Politics of Market Maintenance: U.S. Foreign Economic Policy and the Latin American Debt Issue, 1982–1985* (University of South Carolina, dissertation, 1990); Stephen D. Cohen, *The Making of United States Inter-*

national Economic Policy: Principles, Problems, and Proposals for Reform (New York: Praeger, 1988); and United States, The United States Government Manual (1989/1990).

7. United States, Statistical Abstracts, p. 799.

8. Keith Brahsher, "Administration Plans New Export Initiative," New York Times (September 27, 1993): C1–C2.

9. Europa World Yearbook (1989), p. 2806.

10. See William J. Long, U.S. Export Control Policy: Executive Autonomy vs. Congressional Reform (New York: Columbia University Press, 1989); Michael Mastanduno, Economic Containment: CoCom and the Politics of East-West Trade (Ithaca, N.Y.: Cornell University Press, 1992) and "Strategies of Economic Containment: U.S. Trade Relations with the Soviet Union," World Politics 37 (July 1985): 503–31; U.S., Congress, General Accounting Office, Export Controls: Multilateral Efforts to Improve Enforcement (May 1992).

11. See, for example, William Greider, Secrets of the Temple: How the Federal Reserve Runs the Country (New York: Simon and Schuster, 1987); I. M. Destler, Dollar Politics: Exchange Rate Policymaking in the United States (Washington, D.C.: Institute for International Economics, 1989).

12. United States, Statistical Abstracts.

13. See, for example, James J. Emery and Michael C. Oppenheimer, The U.S. Export-Import Bank (Boulder, Colo.: Westview Press, 1983).

14. See, for example, Clyde H. Farnsworth, "A Spotlight on Obscure Agency," New York Times (February 19, 1990): C1, C3.

15. See Cohen, Making of United States International Economic Policy; I. M. Destler, American Trade Politics (Washington, D.C.: Brookings, 1995); and Harald B. Malmgren, "Managing Foreign Economic Policy," Foreign Policy 6 (Spring 1972): 42–63.

16. Terry L. Deibel, "Bush's Foreign Policy: Mastery and Inaction," Foreign Policy 84 (Fall 1991): 15.

17. Hedrick Smith, The Power Game: How Washington Works (New York: Ballantine, 1988), p. 350.

18. See, for example, U.S. Congress, General Accounting Office, Export Promotion: Federal Programs Lack Organizational and Funding Cohesiveness (January 1992).

19. John P. Leacacos, "The Nixon NSC: Kissinger's Apparat," Foreign Policy 5 (Winter 1971–1972): 18.

20. Goddard, Politics of Market Maintenance, p. 176.

21. I. M. Destler, "A Government Divided: The Security Complex and the Economic Complex," in David A. Deese, ed., The New Politics of American Foreign Policy, (New York: St. Martin's Press, 1994), pp. 132–47.

22. Malmgren, "Managing Foreign Economic Policy," p. 42.

23. I. M. Destler, Making Foreign Economic Policy (Washington, D.C.: Brooking, 1983), p. 215.

24. Cohen, Making of United States International Economic Policy, chapter 12. See also Bruce Stokes, "Organizing to Trade," Foreign Policy (Winter 1992–93): 36–52.

25. On the concept of economic culture, see Paul Egon Rohrlich, "Economic Culture and Foreign Policy: The Cognitive Analysis of Economic Policy Making," International Organization 41 (Winter 1987): 61–92.

26. See Goddard, The Politics of Market Maintenance, chapter 4; Lake, Power, Protection, and Free Trade; Judith Goldstein, "Ideas, Institutions, and American Trade Policy," International Organization 42 (Winter 1988): 179–217; Karen Mingst, "Process and Policy in U.S. Commodities: The Impact of the Liberal Economic Paradigm," in William P. Avery and David Rapkin, eds., America in a Changing World Political Economy (New York: Longman, 1982), pp. 191–206; John S. Odell, U.S. International Monetary Policy: Markets, Power, and Ideas as Sources of Change (Princeton, N.J.: Princeton University Press, 1982); and Robert Pastor, Congress and the Politics of U.S. Foreign Economic Policy: 1929–1976 (Berkeley: University of California Press, 1980).

27. Herbert McClosky and John Zaller, The American Ethos: Public Attitudes Toward Capitalism and Democracy (Cambridge, Mass.: Harvard University Press, 1984).

28. In Mingst, "Process and Policy in U.S. Commodities," p. 193.

29. See, for example, M. Leann Brown and Jerel A. Rosati, "The Reagan Administration and Economic Interdependence: Turbulent Relations with the EC," International Journal 42 (Summer 1987): 438–72.

30. Cohen, The Making of United States International Economic Policy, p. 159. For the roots of the open-door policy, see William Appleman Williams, The Tragedy of American Diplomacy (New York: Delta, 1959).

31. Goldstein, "Ideas, Institution, and American Trade Policy," p. 187.

32. I. M. Destler, The National Economic Council: A Work in Progress (Washington, D.C.: Institute for International Economics, 1996), p.1.

33. Ben Wildavsky, "Under the Gun," National Journal (June 29, 1996): 1417.

34. John B. Judis, "Old Master," The New Republic (December 13, 1993): 21.

35. Destler, The National Economic Council, p. 10.

36. Fred Barnes, "Cabinet Losers," *The New Republic* (February 28, 1994): 22–29.

37. Judis, "Old Master," p. 25.

38. Destler, *The National Economic Council*, p. 29.

39. Ibid., p. 1418.

40. Ibid., p. 40.

41. Ibid., p. 61.

42. Idid., p. 36.

43. For an overview, see Kim Andrew Elliott, "Too Many Voices of America," *Foreign Policy* 77 (Winter 1989–90): 113–31; Richard N. Gardner, "Selling America in the Marketplace of Ideas," *New York Times Magazine* (March 20, 1983): 44, 58–61; Allen C. Hansen, *U.S. Information Agency: Public Diplomacy in the Computer Age* (New York: Praeger, 1984); Sig Mickelson, *America's Other Voice: The Story of Radio Free Europe and Radio Liberty* (New York: Praeger, 1983); and John Spicer Nichols, "Wasting the Propaganda Dollar," *Foreign Policy* 56 (Fall 1984): 129–40.

44. U.S., Congress, General Accounting Office, *Exchange Progams: Inventory of International Educational, Cultural, and Training Programs* (June 1993); U.S., United States Information Agency, *U.S. Government International Exchange and Training Activities* (1990).

45. U.S., Congress, General Accounting Office, *TV Martí: Costs and Compliance with Broadcast Standards and International Agreements* (May 1992); U.S., Congress, General Accounting Office, *Voice of America: Management Actions Needed to Adjust to a Changing Environment* (July 1992).

46. See Nichols, "Wasting the Propaganda Dollar"; Christopher Simpson, *Science of Coercion: Communication Research and Psychological Warfare, 1945–1960* (New York: Oxford University Press, 1994).

47. See Lars-Erick Nelson, "Dateline Washington: Anti-Semitism and the Airwaves," *Foreign Policy* 61 (Winter 1985–1986): 180–96, and U.S., Congress, General Accounting Office, *Improved Oversight Can Reduce Broadcast Violations at Radio Free Europe/Radio Liberty* (June 24, 1985).

48. Mickelson, *America's Other Voice*, pp. 3–4.

49. See Henry Kamm, " 'Free' Europe Embraces That Radio and Its Mate," *New York Times* (May 6, 1990): 8; U.S., Congress, General Accounting Office, *International Broadcasting: Downsizing and Relocating Radio Free Europe/Radio Liberty* (April 1995).

50. Thomas Carothers, "The NED at 10," *Foreign Policy* (Summer 1994): 123–38; U.S., Congress, General Accounting Office, *Events Leading to the Establishment of the National Endowment for Democracy* (July 6, 1984).

51. See Jacqueline Sharkey, "Anatomy of an Election: How U.S. Money Affected the Outcome in Nicaragua," *Common Cause Magazine* (May/June 1990): 20-29.

52. See Carothers, "The NED at 10"; Larry Diamond, "Promoting Democracy," *Foreign Policy* (Summer 1992): 25–46; and U.S., Congress, General Accounting Office, *Promoting Democracy: The National Endowment for Democracy's Management of Grants Needs Improvement* (March 1991).

53. Gardner, "Selling America," p. 44.

54. See United States, *United States Government Manual.*

55. Morse, *Foreign Policy and Interdependence*, chaps. 1–2.

56. Raymond F. Hopkins, "Global Management Networks: The Internationalization of Domestic Bureaucracies," *International Social Science Journal* 30 (1978): 31–45. See also the special issue of *International Organization* (winter 1992) for a related discussion of international networks in terms of the existence of "epistemic communities."

57. Morse, *Foreign Policy and Interdependence*, p. 37.

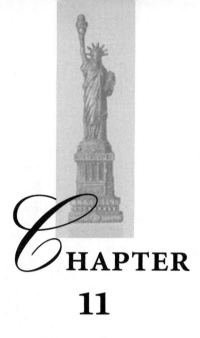

CHAPTER 11

. . . .

DECISION-MAKING THEORY
AND EXECUTIVE BRANCH POLICYMAKING

$\mathcal{H}$aving examined the role of the president, the National Security Council, the State Department, the military establishment, the intelligence community, foreign economics and the rest of the foreign policy bureaucracy, it is important to fully understand the dynamic process by which foreign policymakers and agencies interact to produce U.S. foreign policy. In order to do this we turn to **decision-making theory**—a body of knowledge developed by scholars to better understand the policymaking process within the executive branch.

Many people tend to assume that foreign policy is made by the president and is based on some type of grand design. Yet, as many of the previous chapters have indicated, far less purpose and grand design goes on inside the White House and the executive branch than most people assume. In the words of Fred Dutton, former White House adviser to President John Kennedy, "Washington isn't all that thought out. So much of it is improvisation. Too much rationality and planning can be attributed to it. Much of it is trying something, taking a pratfall, and then looking either bad or good when you do."[1] Usually, in fact, as stated by Charles Maechling, Jr., "the making and implementation of foreign policy is a collective process involving half a dozen agencies and hundreds of anonymous officials. In propagating the delusion of a master hand and only one tiller, both the executive branch and the news media have collaborated as if in a silent conspiracy."[2]

This chapter provides the necessary analytical perspective for understanding the complexity and dominant patterns that prevail in the policymaking process within the executive branch. This is done by discussing different stages of policymaking, describing four basic models of decision-making, and highlighting major policymaking patterns and tendencies within the executive branch in order to better understand the complex politics of U.S. foreign policy.

POLICYMAKING STAGES

. . . .

Policymaking is a complex process that involves a number of different stages. Although any number of stages can be delineated, most scholars of foreign policy emphasize the involvement of at least *three general stages in the policymaking or decision-making process:*[3]

1. Agenda-setting;
2. Policy formulation;
3. Policy implementation.

The initial stage of policymaking is **agenda-setting**. An issue must get the attention of governmental officials and organizations if policy is eventually to be produced. The second stage, **policy formulation**, is what most people think of when it comes to policymaking—the interaction of policymakers in arriving at some type of decision. Finally, in the **policy implementation** stage the decision is carried out by members of the government.

The distinction between agenda-setting, policy formulation, and policy implementation is not as clear cut as described, for policymaking is usually a complex, political, and messy process. For example, once an issue is on the governmental agenda, its level of importance may change due to events at home and abroad. Issues and policies are not formulated solely at one point in time, but often involve a series of decisions over time. Furthermore, the implementation of policy does not necessarily end the policymaking process for any one issue, for its success or failure often affects its future agenda status, which may produce changes in policy. In other words, the agenda-setting, policy formulation, and policy implementation stages affect each other and overlap throughout the entire policymaking process. Nevertheless, the three stages serve as useful analytical tools for making sense of the nature of policymaking within the executive branch.

DECISION-MAKING MODELS

. . . .

Scholars of U.S. foreign policy have developed *four theoretical models of how the policymaking process operates within the executive branch:*

1. Rational actor;
2. Groupthink;
3. Governmental politics;
4. Organizational process.

These models provide four alternative understandings of presidential power, the nature of the policymaking process within the executive branch, and the politics of U.S. foreign policy.

The rational actor model involves the "ideal type" of process that most people assume takes place when they think of foreign policymaking. Under the rational actor model, the president is in full control of U.S. foreign policy and arrives at decisions through a very rational process. Groupthink, governmental politics, and organizational process describe a less rational and more political process in which the beliefs, personalities, and roles of officials are consequential in effecting the outcomes. Whereas groupthink portrays a centralized policymaking process under presidential control, governmental politics and organizational process portray a decentralized policymaking process with little control exercised by the president (**table 11.1** provides an overview of each of the models).

THE RATIONAL ACTOR IDEAL

On Tuesday, October 16, 1962, President John Kennedy was informed by the intelligence community that the Soviet Union was in the process of transporting and deploying medium-range and intermediate-range ballistic missiles with nuclear warheads in Cuba, which had the potential of striking substantial parts of the continental United States. This triggered what has become known as **the Cuban Missile Crisis** and the president assembled his most trusted advisers to consider the American

TABLE 11.1
DECISION-MAKING MODELS

THE MODEL	DECISION STRUCTURE AND PROCESS	KEY EXPLANATORY CONCEPTS
RATONAL ACTOR	Centralized	Presidential goals and beliefs
	Rational	
GROUPTHINK	Centralized	Beliefs of leader(s)
	Irrational	Personality of leader(s)
		Group norms and dynamics
GOVERNMENTAL POLITICS	Pluralistic	Policymaker beliefs and personality
	Political	Policymaker roles and power
ORGANIZATIONAL PROCESS	Decentralized	Organizational missions/functions
	Relative autonomous bureaucratic dynamics	Organizational structures and roles
		Organizational subcultures
		Organizational programs and routines

response. They included Attorney General Robert Kennedy, Secretary of State Dean Rusk, Secretary of Defense Robert McNamara, Director of Central Intelligence John McCone, Secretary of the Treasury Douglas Dillon, Special Assistant for National Security Affairs McGeorge Bundy, Special Counsel Theodore Sorensen, Under Secretary of State George Ball, Deputy Under Secretary of State U. Alexis Johnson, Assistant Secretary of State Edwin Martin, Soviet expert Llewellyn Thompson, Deputy Secretary of Defense Roswell Gilpatric, Assistant Secretary of Defense Paul Nitze, and Chairman of the Joint Chiefs of Staff Maxwell Taylor. For five days they met secretly and virtually around-the-clock, discussing and debating the foreign policy goals involved, the information available, and the possible policy options. Then on Saturday, October 20, President Kennedy decided to publicly blockade Cuba and privately offered Nikita Khrushchev, chairman of the Communist Party of the Soviet Union, a political solution (withdrawal of Soviet missiles in Cuba for withdrawal of American missiles in Turkey and a U.S. pledge not to invade Cuba). By the following Sunday, October 28, the Soviet leader had agreed and the Cuban Missile Crisis was history.[4]

As Graham Allison demonstrated in the *Essence of Decision: Explaining the Cuban Missile Crisis*, most people assume that the policymaking process operates according to what scholars have referred to as the **rational actor model**.[5] Most scholars have, in fact, concluded that the policymaking process that led to President Kennedy's decision closely approximated a rational process under presidential control, contributing to the prompt resolution of the crisis.[6] This is the **"ideal type or model"** that is consistent with the formal organization charts that portray the government as extremely hierarchical.

According to this conception, the executive branch operates according to a pyramid of authority. The president is on top and exercises power over foreign policy, using his staff within the Executive Office of the Presidency, such as the National Security Council (NSC) and his cabinet appointees for managing and coordinating the vast bureaucracy. Thus, the president governs foreign policy and the bureaucracy serves and responds to presidential interests—consistent with the popular image of policymaking.

This perspective not only assumes that the president is ultimately in charge, but that the nature of the policymaking process tends to proceed in accordance with a **"rational process"** responsive to presidential beliefs and wishes. That is, once an issue gets on the governmental agenda, the president determines the foreign policy goals that he wants to achieve, acquires lots of information from the bureaucracy and by consulting his advisers, considers a wide assortment of policy options, and selects the policy alternative that promises to fulfill successfully his foreign policy goals. The president typically does not come to such a rational decision in isolation. He relies on formal policymaking channels (such as the cabinet or the NSC process) for information and advice, and informally consults governmental policymakers whom he has come to trust. The rational actor model also assumes that once the president makes a decision, the bureaucracy faithfully implements the policy in accordance with his wishes.

The rational actor model depicts an executive branch policymaking process that is rational and responsive to the president. This is consistent with the everyday language of foreign policy in which the public, journalists, and scholars typically use phrases such as the "United States government" did this or the "president" did that.[7] The rational actor model is not only applied to explain U.S. foreign policy but is also regularly applied to explain the foreign policies of other countries. For example, although considerable disagreement remains concerning why the Soviet Union invaded Afghanistan in 1979, popular agreement was that the decision was made within the Politburo by Leonid Brezhnev, general secretary of the Community Party, and that it was a function of rational design.

Therefore, the rational actor model sees foreign policy as a result of a policymaking process that is both "centralized" and "rational," thereby giving the model its name. The policymaking process may, in fact, operate in a way that approximates the rational actor model. It is possible for the president to dominate the policymaking process for those issues in which he has expressed the greatest interest. The policymaking process may also approximate a rational process in which a variety of information and policy alternatives are considered by the president, but much depends on the president's beliefs and

personality. As discussed in the chapters on presidential leadership and management, the dynamics of the policymaking process are heavily a function of the choices a president makes concerning his agenda, level of active involvement concerning issues and policymaking, executive-level appointments of staff and advisers, and organization of the policymaking process.

Presidential control and management may result from direct personal intervention by the president or, indirectly, through the involvement of his closest personal advisers, such as his chief of staff or the NSC adviser. A rational process may be imposed on the bureaucracy by the president as occurred through Henry Kissinger and the NSC early in the Richard Nixon administration. In contrast, a rational process may occur because the president and his major foreign policy advisers enjoy a collegial relationship or considerable consensus in foreign policy views—conditions that characterized the early Jimmy Carter administration years. Furthermore, presidential decisions may be implemented through established bureaucratic procedures or, as occurred under President Nixon, by having trusted advisers, such as Henry Kissinger and the NSC staff, take an operational role.

In sum, diplomatic history and foreign policymaking is often explained in terms of a rational actor model. At times the policymaking process within the executive branch does in fact approximate a rational actor model, such as occurred during the Cuban Missile Crisis. Nevertheless, the policymaking process often diverges from the centralized and rational process portrayed by the rational actor model.

GROUPTHINK

From 1964 to 1968, President Lyndon Johnson and a small group of advisers agreed to a number of decisions that were responsible for **escalating American involvement in the Vietnam War**. Once the initial decision was taken to rely on the use of force to defeat North Vietnamese aggression, there was no looking back. At each stage of the Vietnam War policymaking process, decisions centered on force levels and how much force should be used to maintain an independent South Vietnam. Information and policy alternatives that diverged from, or contradicted, the escalatory path were ignored or poorly received within the policymaking group. This was primarily because President Johnson was accustomed to getting his way once he had made a decision. Through his strong personality, he dominated the policymaking process on Vietnam. Administration policymakers quickly learned that Johnson was committed to avoiding a loss of South Vietnam to communism. He did not want doubt or open discussion, but loyalty and support for his Vietnam policy. Only the shock of the Tet Offensive and the collapse of the cold war consensus within government and throughout society forced Johnson to reconsider his policies.[8]

The Vietnam War policymaking process under President Johnson did not reflect the rational actor model. It reflected **groupthink,** a concept developed by Irving Janis as a result of his work in social psychology.[9] Janis found that the adage, "two minds are better than one," often is not borne out by the dynamics of small group behavior. Instead, high cohesiveness and esprit de corps often develops among members of a group. This is true especially when members have similar backgrounds and beliefs, a strong leader emerges within the group, and the group faces a stressful situation. Under these circumstances, the group develops a strong concurrence-seeking tendency and members tend to conform to group norms or decisions.

Groupthink describes a different policymaking process than is found in the rational actor model. On the one hand, the rational actor model and groupthink share a "centralized" policymaking structure under presidential control.[10] However, while the rational actor model depicts an open and rational process, a groupthink process is anything but rational. Instead of searching for information, considering alternatives, and selecting the policy option that maximizes goals, groupthink often results in an "irrational" process. *Symptoms of groupthink include* an overestimation of the competency and inherent morality of the group; a tendency to stereotype out-groups and rationalize decisions; and the

tendency to pressure members toward uniformity (usually through self-censorship), providing the illusion of unanimity. Groupthink—that is, having members of the group think alike—is often promoted and maintained because of a strong domineering leader within the group.

Janis predicts that the more a policymaking process takes the form of groupthink, the lower the probability that the decisions will have a successful outcome. Failure results because the policymaking group is not open to new information and resists considering alternative policy options. These deficiencies prevent adjustments in policy to maximize the chances of success, as prescribed by the rational actor model. Under groupthink, the group is committed to a particular policy regardless of changes or developments. Groupthink characteristics help to explain the rigidity and ultimate failure of LBJ's Vietnam policy.

A similar situation occurred with **the Reagan administration's Iranian initiative**. Throughout 1985 and 1986, a number of decisions were made by President Ronald Reagan that led to efforts to sell arms to Iran in exchange for the release of American hostages held in the Middle East. Once it became public, the Iranian initiative led to an outcry against President Reagan and triggered the Iran-Contra affair. The failure of the Iranian initiative, much more so then the contra initiative, appears to have been heavily a function of the groupthink process. While Reagan administration foreign policy officials fully supported and actively engaged in efforts to support the contras and overthrow the Nicaraguan Sandinistas, a major policy split developed within the administration over the Iranian initiative. During the initial policymaking meetings, Secretary of State George Shultz and Secretary of Defense Caspar Weinberger were strongly opposed to the Iranian initiative on both moral and practical grounds. In fact, on two different occasions Shultz and Weinberger believed they had convinced President Reagan to abandon the policy. However, President Reagan was personally interested in the fate of the hostages, and the NSC adviser (first Robert McFarlane and then John Poindexter) and Director of Central Intelligence William Casey were strong advocates of the initiative. With President Reagan committed to the Iranian initiative, the policymaking circle narrowed to include only those who supported the initiative. Thus, dissenters within the administration were circumvented and a small group of likeminded individuals implemented U.S. foreign policy who were committed to the release of the hostages. Groupthink processes also explain the NSC's operational role in actually carrying out the Iranian initiative, keeping most of the government in the dark.[11]

The information on the Bush administration suggests that **the policymaking process during the Persian Gulf crisis** may have fallen victim to groupthink, led by George Bush who was determined to respond strongly to Iraq's invasion of Kuwait. After the initial surprise, uncertainty, and undecidedness of President Bush and his advisers following the invasion on Thursday, August 2, 1990, a mere forty-eight hours later the president decided to make a major American commitment that resulted in sending over 100,000 American troops to Saudi Arabia and the Persian Gulf. The president apparently made the crucial decision on Saturday, August 4, at Camp David while consulting with a small circle of his closest advisers in which there was little debate or discussion about alternative policies once the president's strong views were expressed. Instead, the meeting was devoted almost entirely to military options and how to get Saudi Arabia to approve. It was actively led by National Security Adviser Brent Scowcroft and, most vehemently, by President Bush. Hence, American underreaction before August 2 may have bred the president's initial surprise and subsequent strong stance. The same situation prevailed when the president decided in late October to double American forces and abandon economic sanctions in favor of an offensive strategy, which was announced after the November elections. As Bob Woodward in *The Commanders* makes clear, the Joint Chiefs of Staff and, in particular, Chairman Colin Powell thought that such early reliance on the use of force and subsequent turn to a policy of brinksmanship were ill-advised, yet were hesitant to challenge the civilian leadership.[12]

If, in fact, the decisions to respond forcefully following the invasion and then to pursue a brinksmanship strategy to force Iraqi withdrawal were heavily conditioned by groupthink, it demonstrates that a groupthink process does not necessarily produce policies that lead to fiascoes, as Janis had predicted and many Americans had feared at the time.[13] Although President Bush failed to compel Iraq to withdraw from Kuwait, the resulting war ended in a military rout by the American and coalition forces.

GOVERNMENTAL POLITICS

In a speech before the United Nations on May 20, 1968, the Russians signaled that they were interested in responding to the Johnson administration's overtures to reach an agreement on arms limitations. This was the beginning of the Strategic Arms Limitations Talks—known as **SALT I**. Although President Johnson wanted a U.S. SALT position ready by late summer, he refused to involve the White House in the policymaking process. Instead, he wanted to present the U.S.S.R. with a consensus SALT position that reflected bureaucratic concerns. "Neither Johnson nor his staff would take part in bureaucracy's epic struggle to produce not just a simple, clear proposal, but one that would actually make a serious matter of SALT. In Johnson's day there was no Henry Kissinger to hold the bureaucracy in line and to force up presidential options, as distinct from the preferences of the various parts of the government. Unlike Nixon, Johnson—as everyone in government knew—wanted agreement, not options. This meant that the Joint Chiefs had to be on board."[14] Accordingly, the national security bureaucracy—the Defense Department, State Department, Arms Control and Disarmament Agency, and the Central Intelligence Agency—was left on its own to interact, bargain, and agree on a consensus SALT position.[15]

The formulation of the U.S. government's first SALT position resulted from a policymaking process that did not reflect rational actor or groupthink models. It reflected a policymaking process that

Graham Allison, in *Essence of Decision*, has called **governmental politics.**[16] Governmental politics describes a policymaking process which is neither centralized under the president nor rational. Rather, governmental politics is based on a pluralistic policymaking environment where power is diffused and the process revolves around political competition and compromise among the policymakers. This conception of politics is a common one in the field of political science.

Under governmental politics, an issue is likely to trigger involvement of individuals from a variety of bureaucratic organizations, each differing in goals and objectives. However, no policymaker or organization is preponderant; the president (or the White House), if involved, is merely one participant, although his influence may be the most powerful. In this "pluralistic structure" within the policymaking process, different policymakers tend to provide information and advocate different policy alternatives. Given the competition and advocacy among the participants, none of which can dominate the process, decisions emerge from "political bargaining, coalition building, and compromise." Nor does the policymaking process necessarily cease once a decision is made. Policymakers and bureaucratic organizations least satisfied by the decision may continue to "politic," that is, try to reverse or modify the decision and its implementation. Therefore, policymaking is a pluralistic and political process where policymakers attempt to advance their personal, organizational, and national interests.

A governmental politics process is likely to prevail for agenda issues that are important enough to trigger the involvement of a number of policymakers and bureaucratic organizations, but not important enough to engage the dominant interest and involvement of the president (or a personal adviser acting in the name of the president). It is *particularly useful for understanding "the interagency process" for a number of reasons.* First, the president and his closest advisers must be selective as to which issues to emphasize, leaving governmental politics to prevail for most other issues. President Johnson and his closest advisers were overwhelmed by the Vietnam War by 1968, and thus the bureaucracy dominated the SALT policymaking process.

Second, the president's management style may be such that it tends to reinforce the practice of governmental politics. President Reagan, for instance, downplayed the role of the NSC adviser and staff, preferring to delegate authority and remain removed from most foreign policy issues as discussed in chapter 5. This management style intensified the political infighting among policymakers that tends to naturally occur in the foreign policy bureaucracy. As described by Hedrick Smith in *The Power Game*, "The factional strife that plagued the making of Reagan's foreign policy will outlive Reagan—just as it preceded his presidency—because it lies deeply imbedded in our governmental system. . . . They fit a pattern of bureaucratic tribal warfare—institutional conflict fired by the pride, interests, loyalties, and jealousies of large bureaucratic clans, protecting their policy turf and using guile as well as argument to prevail in the battle over policy."[17]

Finally, even when the president, or his closest adviser, becomes heavily involved he may be unable to dominate policymaking. Failure may occur because some of the participants may be quite formidable and the president remains uncommitted to any policy option. Such a situation characterized the Carter administration in its third year during the Iranian revolution. While President Carter appeared to be uncertain as to what was in the best interests of the United States, NSC Adviser Zbigniew Brzezinski became a major advocate of using force in Iran and lobbied against the more moderate policy recommendations of Secretary of State Cyrus Vance.

In sum, governmental politics describes policymaking that is extremely "political." Unlike the rational actor model or groupthink, the president does not ultimately control the policymaking process. Instead, policymaking is more pluralistic and a variety of policymakers and bureaucratic organizations are involved, each exercising some political clout. The actual decision-making process is neither as rational as the rational actor model describes nor as conformist as groupthink. When no one actor is able to dominate the policymaking process, competitive politics usually prevail and decisions become a function of bargaining, infighting, pulling and hauling, coalition building, and compromise.

ORGANIZATIONAL PROCESS

On January 28, 1986, the military's ability to place reconnaissance satellites in orbit and the National Aeronautics and Space Administration's (NASA) space program came to an abrupt halt when **the *Challenger* space shuttle** exploded shortly after liftoff. Americans were shocked by the tragedy and tried to understand who was to blame for what went wrong. Governmental investigations were launched. Efforts to locate the responsible parties were based on the assumption that the government operated according to the rational actor model and that particular individuals were in charge. But this is not how the policymaking process for the space shuttle program operated. Nor do the policymaking models of groupthink or governmental politics enlighten us in this case.

To really understand what happened to the *Challenger* and why, one has to look at the organizational routines within the bureaucracies involved, principally the National Aeronautics and Space Administration, the Department of Defense, and their corporate suppliers. NASA's major mission by the 1980s had become the space shuttle. Following repeated delays in the expected launch of the *Challenger*, NASA's mission and standard operating procedures resulted in a tendency to de-emphasize equipment deficiencies and overlook safety precautions to expedite the launch. The Department of Defense was under pressure to replace aging military reconnaissance satellites with newer, more sophisticated versions. The major mission of Morton Thiokol, Inc., the manufacturer of the rocket boosters, was to make money and maintain its production schedule without damaging the overall reliability of the equipment (such as the O-rings) vital for the space shuttle launchings. Therefore, the power of the different bureaucratic missions and routines resulted in each of the organizational hierarchies, especially within NASA, ignoring warnings about equipment defects and deficiencies. This situation

prevailed because all of the organizations involved had played their respective roles for years and enjoyed a string of successful shuttle launches. However, on the day the shuttle exploded, the flaws produced by the organizational routines and standard operating procedures came together, surpassing a critical threshold that resulted in tragedy.[18]

Who was to blame? No particular individual or set of individuals was to blame. Fault actually lay with a bureaucratic system of numerous organizations and with the structures and subcultures which prevailed within those organizations. U.S. space policy and the *Challenger* tragedy were a function of the different behaviors produced by the organizations involved in the shuttle program. In *Essence of Decision,* Graham Allison describes this situation as the **organizational process** model of policymaking.[19] The source of this model lies in the study of bureaucracy and organizational behavior that has prevailed within the fields of economics and public administration.

The organizational process model depicts a "decentralized government" in which the key actors are bureaucratic organizations, rather than the president or a group of policymakers. Policymaking tends to be feudal, with most bureaucratic organizations relatively autonomous from the political leadership and each other. In this process, U.S. foreign policy consists of the sum of the various foreign policies produced by the organizations comprising the foreign policy bureaucracy. In other words, the bureaucracy has become so large and complex that it is an independent driving force behind policy and the president, more often than not, is only the symbolic leader. As discussed in chapter 8, the United States does not have a single military under the centralized control of civilian leadership. Rather, it has four militaries, reflected by each of the individual services and the overall decentralization of the Department of Defense.

A policymaking process dominated by the bureaucracy may not only prevent foreign policy coherence, it may produce contradictory policies. To use an example from the domestic policy arena, the Department of Health and Human Services spends millions of dollars a year to convince Americans that smoking is dangerous while, simultaneously, the Department of Agriculture spends millions of dollars a year to subsidize tobacco growers and, indirectly, the tobacco industry. In the area of foreign policy, this helps to explain why the Central Intelligence Agency's covert national security operations often involve individuals and groups within the criminal underworld, including those involved in the drug trade, even though the government has been fighting a long-standing war on drugs. These contradictions are one of the by-products of the president's limited ability to control the immense bureaucracy and promote a rational policymaking process throughout the executive branch.

Each bureaucracy develops its own "organizational missions, occupational roles, and standard operating procedures." As discussed in chapter 6 and subsequent chapters, each bureaucracy is based on hierarchy, specialization, and routinization. These characteristics are reflected in the bureaucratic structures and subcultures that develop over time. Hence, organizational behavior tends to be "incremental" in nature, where members of organizations act very similarly from one day to the next. In other words, much of contemporary policymaking and U.S. foreign policy reflects bureaucratic momentum which has accumulated over the years.

An organizational process model is most helpful in understanding policy formulation for agenda issues which are not important enough to gain presidential attention. Much of the day-to-day policy set by the executive branch involves minor issues which are the domain of bureaucratic organizations. These issues do not move up the bureaucratic hierarchy, or they are routinely rubber stamped by superiors. Such issues turn bureaucrats into policymakers by allowing them to make and implement policies usually in accordance with their organization's norms and routines.

For those issues that do gain the attention of high-level officials, policymakers are still dependent on the bureaucracy for information, policy alternatives, and policy implementation. These organizational programs and routines often constrain what policymakers can do in the future and determine how their decisions actually will be carried out. In-

telligence assessments and military requirements of Iraq, for example, heavily influenced President Bush's decisions concerning troop levels and strategy that led to war following Iraq's invasion of Kuwait in the following ways: once the president had decided to send troops to Saudi Arabia, the military pushed for a large force of at least 100,000 troops to ensure they could repel an Iraqi attack should one occur; the lack of contingency plans for such an emergency forced the military to rely on its all-purpose general deployment plans and resulted in a swelling of the forces sent to the Persian Gulf to over 200,000; deployment of such a large force required mobilizing the reserves; the military routine of a six-month rotation threatened the maintenance of such a large force abroad and its abandonment threatened troop morale. All these bureaucratic imperatives forced and contributed to a presidential decision to abandon economic sanctions to compel a withdrawal, which would have required months to cripple Iraq, in favor of a strategy of brinksmanship based on the threat of war. In fact, military bureaucratic imperatives were such that the presidential decisions to commence war with a large-scale bombing campaign in mid-January followed by a ground campaign late in February were set in motion as early as late October. Ironically, at the time, General "Stormin' " Norman Schwarzkopf initially presented a traditional military plan for a direct frontal assault into the Iraqi forces in Kuwait (which was likely to produce thousands of American and allied casualties). He had to be prodded by his superiors to come up with the "left hook" offensive strategy that became so famous for overwhelming the Iraqi military.[20]

It is the implementation stage of the policymaking process that the organizational process model describes most powerfully. For example, although President Reagan made the decision to invade Grenada in 1983, the military bureaucracy was responsible for the bungled operation that eventually succeeded in occupying the island. Likewise, that same military bureaucracy was responsible for the tremendous success of Operation Desert Storm once President Bush officially decided to go to war with Iraq in January 1991.

To use another example, recently presidents have highlighted the importance of "fighting a war on drugs." However, **the war on drugs** is being fought and implemented by the governmental bureaucracy. The point here is that the bureaucracy employs the programs, routines, and standard operating procedures for implementing presidential decisions (see **essay 11.1** on the American bureaucratic war on drugs.]

Although the policymaking process in "the Cuban Missile Crisis" has been held up as a model of presidential control and rationality, it should be pointed out that a number of difficulties were experienced in the policymaking process due to problems involving bureaucratic programs and standard operating procedures.[21] In the early phases of the policy formulation process, President Kennedy and some of his advisers were leaning in favor of a "surgical air strike" to knock out the Soviet missiles in Cuba before they became operational. However, they were soon informed that the air force's operational plans for an air strike involved a massive bombing campaign throughout Cuba to complement a full-scale invasion. No matter how surgical the strike, Russian soldiers operating the missiles would die in the process. This knowledge was crucial in the decision by Kennedy and his advisers to rule out the air strike and opt for the blockade.

Once President Kennedy decided to offer Chairman Nikita Khrushchev a political solution while blockading Cuba as a demonstration of force, the navy bureaucracy was responsible for "implementing the blockade." The navy set up a blockade of warships around the island roughly 500 miles from shore. At one point, a Soviet warship approached the blockade while President Kennedy was still waiting for a response from Khrushchev. To avoid a military confrontation and give Khrushchev more time to respond, Kennedy ordered the navy to pull the blockade closer to Cuba. Yet, the navy never moved the blockade. At another point Secretary of Defense Robert McNamara, concerned with the delicate nature of the operations, confronted Admiral George Anderson, chief of naval operations. McNamara asked Anderson what he would do if he boarded a Soviet ship and the Soviet captain refused to answer questions about his cargo. Anderson, irritated at being interrogated, picked up the Manual of Naval Regulations and, waving it in McNamara's face, shouted "It's all in there." To which McNamara replied, "I don't give a damn what John Paul Jones would have done. I want to know what you are going to do now." The face-off ended with Anderson commenting, "Now, Mr. Secretary, if you and your deputy will go back to your office, the Navy will run the blockade."[22]

To summarize briefly, four ways of making sense of the policymaking process have been presented. *Each model reaches a different conclusion about the decision-making structure and process:*

The rational actor model sees a rational process under the centralized control of the president.

Groupthink depicts a centralized structure in which the process is irrational.

Governmental politics portrays a pluralistic structure in which the process consists of bargaining and compromise.

The organizational process model emphasizes an extremely decentralized structure in which the process consists of organizational routines.[23]

All four models also highlight different concepts to explain the policymaking process in U.S. foreign policy: the rational actor model emphasizes the "beliefs" of the president (and his closest advisers); groupthink focuses on the "beliefs and personality" of the leaders within the group and the "norms" that prevail for the group; governmental politics emphasizes the "varying beliefs, personalities, roles, and positions of power" that policymakers occupy; and the organizational process model emphasizes "organizational missions, bureaucratic structures and subcultures, roles, and standard operating procedures."

The *four models have different implications for* **government learning** and for the possibilities of continuity and change in U.S. foreign policy.[24] The rational actor model suggests that presidents and government officials are receptive to new informa-

ESSAY 11.1
THE U.S. BUREAUCRATIC "WAR ON DRUGS"

Under President Ronald Reagan, a "war on drugs" was declared and became a relatively high priority within the U.S. government. It is a war fought abroad and at home, focusing on the "control of supply" of narcotics at three levels of the global drug trade. According to Eva Bertram, Morris Blachman, Kenneth Sharpe, and Peter Andreas, in *Drug War Politics,* "First, U.S. antidrug agencies target drugs at the source by pressuring foreign governments to eliminate coca, poppy, and marijuana production (with eradication or crop-substitution programs) and to attack the refining facilities that convert the crops into heroin or cocaine." Second, "antidrug agencies target drugs at or en route to U.S. borders, using planes, boats, border patrols, and customs officers to interdict drug shipments." Finally, "drug-enforcement agents and local police go after drugs within the United States by trying to locate, arrest, and prosecute drug dealers and to seize drug supplies."

The drug war has created a rather **extensive drug-enforcement bureaucracy**. Actually, "today's drug-enforcement bureaucracy began in 1914 as a small bureau in the Treasury Department (what became the current Bureau of Alcohol and Narcotics Control), charged with ensuring that only doctors and pharmacists sold cocaine and heroin-based drugs"—the first effort to limit the use of such drugs and narcotics. With the increasing "illegalization" of such drugs, the drug-enforcement bureaucracy increased. But as late as the 1960s the federal drug-control bureaucracy was a relatively small operation, with only a few hundred agents.

It was President Nixon who began to transform that operation into a sprawling "**narco-enforcement complex**." By the 1980s, President Ronald Reagan requested over $30 million a year from Congress to control the production and transport of heroin, cocaine, and marijuana throughout Latin America, Southeast Asia, and Southwest Asia. Under President George Bush, the war on drugs at home and

abroad gained greater urgency and more resources have been committed to international narcotics control efforts. By the late 1990s, under President Clinton, the total budget for domestic and international counternarcotic programs has grown to almost $15 billion a year.

A variety of agencies within the executive branch has become involved in narcotics control in what has become an extensive bureaucratic complex to fight the drug war. Traditional national security agencies and more domestically oriented agencies are involved in the drug war since it crosses domestic and foreign policy. Agencies in the Departments of Justice, Treasury, and Defense are the most active and command the largest share of the nation's drug enforcement budget.

The Drug Enforcement Administration (DEA), within the Department of Justice, is the lead agency in the drug war, with a budget over $1 billion and more then 3000 special agents and over 6000 employees in more than 170 offices throughout the United States and in 48 foreign countries. Nevertheless, "at the Justice Department the DEA was by 1993 only one of fifteen agencies or programs involved in drug enforcement. . . . The FBI conducted investigations into organized trafficking groups. The Immigration and Naturalization Service detected and apprehended drug smugglers and illegal aliens at or near the border. The U.S. Marshals Service received funds for judicial security, prisoner transportation and detention, fugitive apprehension, and seized-assets management. The Bureau of Prisons provided custodial care for federal drug offenders and other inmates nationwide and constructed and maintain prison facilities.

At least seven agencies in the Department of Treasury are involved in drug enforcement. The U.S. Customs Service, for example, was charged with interdicting and disrupting the illegal flow of drugs by air, sea, and land. Even the IRS is involved: its role is "to identify and impede the transfer of drug-generated funds and to disrupt and dismantle—through select investigation, prosecution and asset forfeiture—the country's major narcotics and narcotics money-laundering organizations."

The Department of Defense receives the next highest share of the drug budget. "To carry out its drug war mission, the Pentagon created three new joint task forces. Fifty percent of the time of the North American Aerospace Defense Command, a command originally created to track incoming Soviet bombers and missiles, was redirected to targeting drug smugglers. The U.S. Southern Command (SOUTHCOM) in Panama was reorganized to fight the drug war in Latin America; its responsibilities included training local security forces for counternarcotics operations." The National Guard is also "involved in interdiction and eradication campaigns in all fifty-four U.S. states and territories; guardsmen searched cargo, patrolled borders, flew aerial surveillance, eradicated marijuana crops, and lent expertise and equipment to law-enforcement agencies."

"The reach of the narco-enforcement complex extends far beyond the Justice, Treasury, and Defense Departments." The State Department's Bureau of International Narcotics and Law Enforcement Affairs funds international law enforcement assistance and interdiction activities. The Agency for International Development provides assistance for crop-substitution programs. Within the Department of Transportation, the Coast Guard attempts to seize and disrupt drug smuggling on maritime routes, while the Federal Aviation Administration helps to identify "airborne drug smugglers by using radar, posting aircraft lookouts, and tracking the movement of suspected aircraft."

At the Department of the Interior, the Bureau of Land Management is involved in the eradication of illegal drugs grown on the approximately 270 million acres of public land under its control. The National Park Service and the Fish and Wildlife Service are also involved with fighting drug production and smuggling on the vast lands they control. At the Department of Agriculture, the Forest Service is engaged in the drug war with the 156 national forests and lands under its control—some 191 million acres. And the Agricultural Research Service develops herbicides to eradicate illegal drug crops, especially coca. And "beyond the executive branch bureaucracy, the vast system of federal, state, and local courts adds a further dimension to the complex."

Presidential efforts have been made over the years to coordinate and manage the war on drugs and the drug-enforcement bureaucracy. A variety of interagency groups have been established at different times under different presidents. In 1988 the Office of National Drug Control Policy was established to try to coordinate and add some coherence to the myriad of bureaucratic agencies—at last count, involving about 50 U.S. departments, agencies, and bureaus—which have become a part of the war on drugs. The Office is headed by the Director of National Drug Control Policy—the so-called "drug czar," appointed by the president with the advice and consent of the Senate, to oversee international and domestic drug programs.

The reality, nevertheless, is that the essentially decentralized nature of the bureaucratic war on drugs continues to prevail. And the bureaucracy implements policy by developing programs in accordance with its organizational missions, structures, and subcultures. Therefore, although presidents have been successful in making the drug war an increasingly important agenda item for the government and American society, the war is being fought from below by an extensive bureaucratic complex which is likely to expand with no end in sight.

SOURCES: Eva Bertram, Morris Blachman, Kenneth Sharpe, and Peter Andreas, in *Drug War Politics: The Price of Denial* (Berkeley: University of California Press, 1996; U.S., Congress, General Accounting Office, *Drug Control: Coordination of Intelligence Activities* (April 1993); U.S., Congress, General Accounting Office, *Drug Control: Status Report on DOD Support to Counternarcotics Activities* (June 1991); U.S., Congress, General Accounting Office, *Drugs: International Efforts to Attack a Global Problem* (June 1993); U.S., Congress, General Accounting Office, *War on Drugs: Federal Assistance to State and Local Drug Enforcement* (April 1993); U.S., *U.S. Government Manual* (Washington, D.C.: U.S. Government Printing Office, 1997).

tion and readily adapt to changes in the environment in order to maximize the opportunity to promote appropriate and successful policies. In other words, such rationality provides optimism about the ability of governments to "learn" and change their foreign policy. This explains why the rational actor model is considered the ideal type and preferable way to arrive at decisions.[25]

The implications of groupthink, governmental politics, and organizational process, on the other hand, are much more pessimistic about the government's ability to learn and change its foreign policy. These three models suggest that there are considerable psychological, social, political, and bureaucratic obstacles to government learning and that continuity and incrementalism are likely to prevail in U.S. foreign policy over time until crises and failure occur. With these competing conceptions of the policymaking process within the executive branch, we turn to the policymaking patterns that are most likely to occur in the actual "practice" of U.S. foreign policy.[27]

POLICYMAKING PATTERNS

. . . .

During the late 1960s and 1970s, the groupthink, governmental politics, and organizational process models gained popularity relative to the rational actor model as alternative and superior ways of understanding the policymaking process. Yet the groupthink, governmental politics, and organizational process models were also criticized on a number of grounds. Analysts and scholars felt that it was not clear "when" these models actually explained policymaking; discussions of the models were often too rigid, for they specified a particular policymaking structure and process, thereby precluding the variety and complexity of political possibilities; and the models were treated in isolation from one another when, in fact, they overlapped and more than one model was often involved for any particular policymaking process. In other words, it was argued that these models oversimplified the political messi-

ness and complexity of the policymaking process in U.S. foreign policy.[26]

The four models provide valuable insights concerning some of the key patterns that prevail in policymaking, but as the critics suggest, the models tend to oversimplify the politics and complexity of the policymaking process. In order to maximize the strengths of the four models and incorporate the criticisms discussed above, it is useful to think in terms of *two general types or patterns for understanding the nature of policymaking within the executive branch:*

1. Presidential politics;
2. Bureaucratic politics.

PRESIDENTIAL AND BUREAUCRATIC POLITICS

Presidential politics operates when the president becomes interested and active in an issue, through direct personal involvement or indirectly when his staff and advisers act in his name. As discussed in chapter 6, presidents rely both on informal channels of communication with close advisers and a more formal process, usually under the supervision of the NSC adviser and staff. When an issue is of sufficient importance to gain the attention and interest of the president (or his surrogates), the policymaking process is also likely to involve other high-level policymakers from executive branch bureaucratic organizations and agencies. Such was the case, for example, during the Cuban Missile Crisis, decisions leading to the escalation of the war in Vietnam, the Iran hostage crisis, and the Persian Gulf crisis of 1990–1991. Thus, presidential politics refers to **high-level policymaking** within the executive branch.

The notion of presidential politics makes it clear that the president's involvement is crucial. Presidential politics also tells us that the policymaking process is very political, without precluding any possibilities about the particular dynamics of the process. A relatively "open" policymaking process may occur in which there is a broad search for information, where policy views and alternatives are aired as suggested by the rational actor model. However, presidential politics may result in a relatively "closed" process more akin to groupthink. Other patterns may operate as well, creating situations in which participants may be dissatisfied with presidential decisions and attempt to get them reversed or modified. In all cases, policymaking and politics are inseparable, for prominent individuals are involved, the issues affect the future of U.S. foreign policy, and the stakes are high. In the final analysis, how the politics of the policymaking process actually proceeds depends on the beliefs, personalities, and roles of the participants and the nature of their interaction.[28]

Bureaucratic politics prevails when the president and his closest advisers remain relatively uninvolved or are unable to dominate the policymaking process. Under these circumstances, other policymakers and bureaucratic organizations become the key determinants of policymaking and the interagency process. This perspective is powerfully described by Charles Maechling:

> The principal actors represent giant departments and agencies, each with its own constellation of vested interests and statutory responsibilities. Nearly all the actors are transients in space and time—whether plucked out of private life or promoted from the bureaucracy, they are usually newcomers to the immediate subject matter and prisoners of their position papers. Their latitude of action is always circumscribed by statutory restrictions, policy guidelines and prior decisions. Behind the confidant facade that each actor presents to his colleagues and to the outside world lurks a morbid compulsion to protect himself from the unexpected, to make the weight of one's agency count and to appear effective in the eyes of superiors—but with the gnawing realization that the options available are limited and the course of events uncontrollable.[29]

American foreign policy towards Japan, for example, often is dominated by competing bureaucratic interests. According to Robert Pear in "Confusion Is Operative Word in U.S. Policy toward Japan," "the State Department, the Pentagon, and the National Security Council emphasize Japan's value as a geopolitical and strategic asset and are seen by officials in other agencies as overly protective of Japan." The Department of Commerce and the Office of United States Trade Representative "worry about the health of the American economy and favor a tougher attitude." The Department of the Treasury, the Office of Management and Budget, and the Council of Economic Advisers "adhere to free market principles and have generally opposed any government intervention to help American businesses compete with the Japanese."[30] Not surprisingly, the United States government is not able to pursue a coherent policy toward Japan because of the series of "turf wars" among federal agencies in which there is little communication and coordination. This illustration also demonstrates the difficulty of making foreign policy when national security and foreign economic interests intersect.

Such bureaucratic politics may reflect the bargaining, coalition building, and compromise described by the governmental politics model; or, officials may pursue independent policies based on organizational routines as suggested by the organizational process model.[31] Other possibilities, however, cannot be ruled out. For example, bureaucratic and personal infighting could be so intense that compromise among the participants is not possible—instead, political winners and losers result. Regardless of the particular policymaking process, bureaucratic politics always involves a political process reflecting the interactions between the officials, organizations, and the political environment prevailing at the time. The beliefs, personalities, and roles of the individuals involved, often reflecting the bureaucratic structures and subcultures of their respective organizations, determine the nature of bureaucratic policymaking.

Since the president and his closest advisers are involved for only selective issues, bureaucratic politics tends to prevail for most issues in U.S. foreign policy. As discussed by Charles Maechling, Jr., "For every publicized decision he [the president] makes, this second echelon of decision-makers makes a hundred equally important ones. And it is this steady stream of less conspicuous decisions, building on and interlocking with their predecessors, that fixes the direction and contours of foreign policy, just as effectively as the few spectacular decisions that are the result of conscious deliberation at the top."[32]

The **important role of personality and beliefs** needs to be highlighted in order to fully understand both presidential and bureaucratic politics.[33] Reference to the importance of personality and beliefs to the politics of U.S. foreign policy has been made repeatedly throughout the book. Presidential politics are heavily a function of the personality and beliefs of the president, and his closest advisers, for most of the other policymakers involved take their cues from him and, ultimately, the president makes the decision (see **essay 11.2** on the impact of Lyndon Johnson's personality and beliefs on the foreign policymaking process).

Bureaucratic politics are also heavily influenced by the personalities and beliefs of the individuals involved. The behavior of career officials, for instance, is heavily influenced and socialized by the subcultures that dominate their bureaucracies. It is also important to point out that the beliefs of government officials tend to reflect the beliefs that prevail throughout society, as we will see later. As discussed in the chapters above, anticommunism, a national security ethos, and a free market ethos have been the foundation for the beliefs held by most officials in government since World War II.

POLICYMAKING TENDENCIES

We have seen that two general policymaking patterns are likely to prevail within the executive branch: presidential politics or bureaucratic politics. However, much remains ambiguous. When is each pattern likely to occur? What is the likely nature of the actual policy formulation and implementation process? The following are *broad generalizations about policymaking tendencies* that provide some initial answers to these questions, based on knowledge of foreign policy decision making.[34] Detailed information of what happened in a particular case is nec-

essary for fully understanding the policymaking process (a difficult requirement to fulfill). These generalizations, therefore, provide a starting point for explaining and predicting how U.S. foreign policy tends to be made within the executive branch.

Agenda-setting Patterns. Attention to agenda-setting in the making of U.S. foreign policy has not received the attention that it deserves.[35] Nevertheless, *two generalizations involving the relationship between the importance of an issue and the policymaking process* seem to hold:[36]

1. The greater the perceived importance of an issue, the more likely that it will attract presidential interest and involvement, resulting in presidential politics.
2. Conversely, the more insignificant and routine an issue is perceived to be, the greater the likelihood that the president will remain uninvolved, resulting in bureaucratic politics.

It is the nature of the issue which triggers the policymaking process and determines which officials and organizations become involved.

Issues become part of the government's agenda in a variety of ways. First, issues get on the agenda as a result of initiatives taken by officials, including the president. Hedrick Smith points out in *The Power Game* the importance of defining and manipulating issues to affect the "power loop"—that is, to affect which participants are involved and the circulation of information in order to control the policymaking process. "Those who are in control of policy, whether the President and his top advisers or bureaucrats buried in the bowels of government, will try desperately to keep the information loop small, no matter what the issue; those who are on the losing side internally will try to widen the circle."[37] The Strategic Defense Initiative, for example, was placed on government and public agendas by President Reagan during a speech to the nation so he could circumvent a skeptical and obstructionist foreign policy bureaucracy.

Second, issues that the government has considered important in the past tend to remain on the

ESSAY 11.2
THE IMPACT OF LBJ'S PERSONALITY AND BELIEFS ON POLICYMAKING

The case of Lyndon Johnson, while not unique, demonstrates the impact of an individual's personality and beliefs on the foreign policymaking process and U.S. foreign policy. It demonstrates how prominent individuals are often driven and influenced by basic emotional needs—such as the need for love, for power and control, and to do good. According to Doris Kearns Goodwin, in *Lyndon Johnson and the American Dream,* one must delve into Johnson's childhood and personal development in the context of the times to understand the private man behind the public figure.

Lyndon Johnson, the eldest of five children, was born in Stonewall, Blanco County, Texas, a small rural community, in 1908. His mother came from a family who had money, position, and respectability—her father was a lawyer, educator, and lay Baptist preacher. His father came from the other side of the tracks—a small-time farmer, heavily involved in local Democratic politics, crude and vulgar, and a hard drinker. According to Goodwin, "the picture of Johnson's early life suggests a childhood torn between the irreconcilable demands of his mother—who hoped to find in his intellectual and cultural achievement a recompense of her dead father, unhappy marriage, and thwarted ambition—and those of his father—who considered intellect and culture unmanly pursuits."[A] In this environment, Lyndon did not feel loved for who he was and seemed unable to please his parents. The only time Lyndon felt comfortable and secure was with his grandfather, who would reminisce and romanticize about the glory days of the intrepid cowboy and the reformism of the Populist Party. The situation worsened as Lyndon grew older, for when his grandfather died he drew closer to his father, to the disapproval of his mother.

In order to overcome his terrible fear of rejection that resulted from his upbringing, Goodwin argues that Johnson developed a desperate and insatiable need to be loved. His tremendous **drive to acquire power and achieve good works** was an attempt to fulfill this need. Given his background, his boundless energy was directed into politics, initially as a staff aide to a congressman, then as a participant in Franklin Roosevelt's New Deal, later as a member of the House of Representatives, then as a senator (becoming the youngest majority leader in history), and finally in the White House, first as vice-president and then president. Johnson was the consummate political animal, who lived and breathed politics, and bargained and compromised to make deals and policy. Yet, given his family and his rural, Texan roots during the first half of the twentieth century, he also strived to achieve "great works," to help people as he understood them. This is best embodied in his commitment to eliminate poverty through his Great Society programs, which Goodwin argues acted as a vehicle to attract the admiration and love of Americans, fellow Texans, and, ultimately, his parents.

His personality helps to explain **his particular management style** as president. Johnson could not bear to be alone and always had to be in control. He was constantly in motion, on the phone, with the radio or television always on around him. The Johnson White House revolved around his need for people to love, support, and be loyal to him. He often challenged his aides in acts of manhood in order for them to display this loyalty. Once Johnson made up his mind, he wanted consensus and support behind his position. As Johnson himself could so graphically state, "I don't want loyalty. I want *loyalty.* I want him to kiss my ass in Macy's window at high noon and tell me it smells like roses. I want his pecker in my pocket."[B]

Johnson was very "thin-skinned," overly defensive, and sensitive to any criticism. Those who were

A. Doris Kearns Goodwin, *Lyndon Johnson and the American Dream* (New York: New American Library, 1976), p. 385.

B. David Halberstam, *The Best and the Brightest* (New York: Random House, 1969), p. 434.

skeptical or didn't go along received the famous **Johnson treatment**—the use of friendship, intimacy, bargaining, horsetrading, gifts, and anything else it might take to get them on board. Continued criticism or disagreement represented disloyalty and those involved would eventually be completely frozen out of the power loop and Johnson's life. He was so sensitive to what was said about him, for example, that it was not unusual for him to watch the evening news on all three networks at the same time, all the while paying attention to how they reported "his" presidency.

Johnson was primarily interested and comfortable in dealing with domestic issues and politics. Yet, as president he was also responsible for U.S. foreign policy. "In dealing with foreign policy, however, he was insecure, fearful, his touch unsure. . . . As a result, his greatest anxiety—unlike his attitude toward domestic affairs—was to avoid making a serious error rather than to achieve great things."[C] Johnson tended to be heavily dependent on his advisers for information and understanding about world politics. His foreign policy beliefs reflected the cold war consensus in U.S. foreign policy that prevailed during the 1950s and 1960s.

The **experience of World War II and Korea**—the need to avoid appeasement at all costs—made a far-reaching and decisive impression on Johnson as it did for many of the cold war leadership generation. According to Goodwin, Johnson believed that "the way to prevent conflict was to stop aggressors at the start—the **lesson of Munich**. In every war, Johnson believed, the enemy is an alien force that 'invades' the allies' house. . . . America alone, our attitudes and behavior, were the key to war and peace. Nor was this mode of thought unique to Lyndon Johnson. On the contrary, it was deeply rooted in the American experience."[D] These beliefs were the foundation for the global policy of containment that, in failing to discriminate between different situations at different times, led Johnson to Americanize the war in Vietnam.

"The very qualities and experiences that had led to his political and legislative success," Goodwin argues, "were precisely those that now operated to destroy him."[E] Where Johnson was sophisticated and pragmatic in domestic affairs, he operated as much more the **idealist and ideologue in foreign affairs and for Vietnam**. "In domestic affairs, particularly in the passage of legislation, he was used to grasping practical realities first and then adapting his goals to those realities. But his lack of intimate knowledge about foreign policy and Vietnam led him to rely, instead, on the goals and principles themselves, losing sight of the question of available means. . . . Faced with a situation he could not control and an adversary who was unwilling to bargain, Johnson would force him to bargain."[F]

Although Johnson delegated much authority in foreign policy, he was a **domineering leader** on those issues in which he was interested. With regard to the deteriorating situation in Vietnam, once the decision to escalate U.S. involvement was made early in his administration, the decision process was then closed. Future decisions never involved a serious consideration of de-escalation or withdrawal—the choices were always between more or less and different types of escalation as a means of finding light at the end of the tunnel. As discussed by David Halberstam, "the Presidency is an awesome office, even with a mild inhabitant. It tends by its nature to inhibit dissent and opposition, and with a man like Johnson it was simply too much, too powerful an office occupied by too forceful a man."[G]

The **advisers he came to rely on**, Walt Rostow and Dean Rusk, shared his anticommunist philosophy and belief in the "utility of force." When one of his advisers, Robert McNamara, came to reconsider and question the policies in Vietnam, he was shunned and eventually forced to resign. "The President's will, once expressed, was not challenged," states Goodwin. "Advisers began to anticipate his reactions before they said or did anything; self-deceptions multiplied in this hall of distorting

---

C. Goodwin, *Lyndon Johnson and the American Dream*, p. 268.
D. Ibid., pp. 100–101.

E. Ibid., p. 416.
F. Ibid., p. 415.
G. Halberstam, *The Best and the Brightest*, p. 456.

mirrors. The more Johnson's energies turned to his critics, the more obsessed he became with the need to discredit his opponents, the less anyone tried to stop him."[H]

As the consensus behind Vietnam within his administration and the country began to break, a type of **siege mentality developed** and he began to insulate himself, finding comfort in his small group of loyal advisers. As the situation abroad and at home deteriorated, Johnson's moods increasingly oscil-

H. Goodwin, *Lyndon Johnson and the American Dream,* p. 418.

SOURCES: James David Barber, *The Presidential Character* (Englewood Cliffs, N.J.: Prentice-Hall, 1972); Larry Berman, *Planning a Tragedy: The Americanization of the War in Vietnam* (New York: Norton, 1982); Robert Dallek, *Lone Star Rising: Lyndon Johnson and His Times, 1908–1960* (New York: Oxford University Press, 1991); David Halberstam, *The Best and the Brightest* (New York: Random House, 1969); Townsend Hoopes, *The Limits of Intervention: An Inside Account of How the Johnson Policy of Esca-*lation in Vietnam was Reversed (New York: David McKay, 1973); Doris Kearns Goodwin, *Lyndon Johnson and the American Dream* (New York: New American Library, 1976); Herbert Y. Schandler, *The Unmaking of the President: Lyndon Johnson and Vietnam* (Princeton, N.J.: Princeton University Press, 1977); James C. Thomson, Jr., "How Could Vietnam Happen? An Autopsy," *Atlantic Monthly;* and Tom Wicker, *JFK and LBJ: The Influence of Personality Upon Politics* (Baltimore: Penguin, 1968).

lated and critics were perceived as enemies. As Doris Kearns Goodwin explains it, only when many of his advisers and much of the country turned against the American war in Vietnam was Johnson able to realize the tragedy he faced. The Tet Offensive and the growing challenges by Eugene McCarthy and his arch rival Robert Kennedy in the presidential primaries, were clear indicators that Johnson had lost control of his presidency and the country. Although he had risen to the top, the love and admiration he so needed to receive from the American people had been denied him and he withdrew from public life.

agenda. Continuing agenda status explains much governmental behavior, for the hundreds of issues that the bureaucracy considers daily are usually of this type. This also accounts for why presidents have such a difficult time managing the bureaucracy; so much of what the government does involves refining and implementing policies that were devised in the past. Many of these policies become so institutionalized and routinized that it allows careerists "to control policy by keeping the power loop small."[38]

Finally, issues are placed on the agenda as a result of domestic and international events. This is a common agenda-setting path. For example, crises such as the 1979 Soviet invasion of Afghanistan or the Iraqi invasion of Kuwait in 1990 usually go immediately to the top of the agenda and force policymakers to respond. The media often plays a consequential role in agenda-setting during such times. They are the vehicle by which most members of the executive branch are informed about developments throughout the world, within the domestic arena, and in government. The role of the media, discussed extensively in chapter 18, highlights the crucial importance of perceptions formed by people outside and inside the government, for this affects which issues acquire agenda status and the nature of the policymaking process within the executive branch.

Policy Formulation Patterns. For issues that are considered extremely important by the president, presidential politics is likely to prevail in the formulation of U.S. foreign policy. But, what form is the policymaking process likely to take? *Two generalizations about presidential politics, based on the beliefs and personality of the president and his closest advisers, are warranted:*

1. The more strongly a president with a domineering personality holds beliefs about an issue, the more likely there will be a closed policymaking process.
2. Conversely, the more a president is uncommitted about an issue and lacks a domineering personality, the more likely an open policymaking process will result.

The beliefs and personality of the president, and the people who speak on his behalf, are major determinants of the actual nature of the policymaking process at the presidential level. Jimmy Carter, for example, usually was relatively open to information and advice, which often led to a more open policy-making process. As we have seen, Lyndon Johnson's strong domineering personality and anticommunist beliefs, on the other hand, made him a rigid decision maker who promoted groupthink in the policymaking process.

The **intensity of an issue** may also affect the dynamics of presidential politics. Different issues affect the government's agenda in different ways at different times—the relative importance of any single issue may fall anywhere between a range from extremely significant to of minor significance. Usually, only a few issues are able to dominate the government's agenda and presidential attention. "Crises" are times that catapult an issue on the agenda and trigger intense presidential politics. Times of crisis, in fact, tend to produce considerable emotional and psychological stress on policymakers which often inhibit an open and rational decision-making process. (See **essay 11.3** for a discussion of the impact of crisis and stress on decision making.)

The above generalizations suggest that *considerable variation may exist in the policymaking process.* Presidential politics rarely involves either a purely open or closed process in accordance with the rational actor model and groupthink. Instead, presidential politics usually contains elements that are both open and closed. Furthermore, for any particular issue, sometimes the policymaking process is more rational, sometimes it is less rational—the dynamics change with time. Ultimately, the nature of policymaking within presidential politics is a function of the beliefs, personalities, roles, and group dynamics of the policymakers involved in response to changes in the domestic and international environment.

Attempting to generalize about the nature of the policymaking process in a bureaucratic politics situation is very difficult given the possibilities. However, *two generalizations about bureaucratic politics* can be made concerning the relationship between the complexity of the process and the importance of an issue:

1. The less significant and more routine an issue, the fewer officials and organizations involved.
2. Conversely, in the absence of presidential interest and involvement, the more significant and less routine an issue, the more officials and organizations involved.

A minor issue is likely to attract the attention of only a small number of participants. Minor issues do not cross over many organizational jurisdictions and the stakes are not high enough to concern many officials. Barnett Rubin's case study on the 1971 Janata Vimukti Peramuna (JVP) insurgency in Sri Lanka provides an excellent example of a **"localized" policymaking process.**[39] "Although it took place at a time when the Nixon-Kissinger National Security Council (NSC) system dominated American foreign policy, the emergency was mainly handled within the State Department, where the regional bureau staff had the action." No agency opposed the leadership of the Bureau for Near East and South Asia Affairs (NEA). As a result, U.S. policy was formulated within NEA, at the country director level.[40] Other officials and agencies within the government did not perceive the issue to be of sufficient consequence to warrant participation. Much of the day-to-day policy routines made within the executive branch involves only a few persons from one or two organizations, involving such issues as the military deployment decisions within the Department of Defense, the issuing of visas and passports within the Department of State, or the granting of food assistance within the Department of Agriculture. Thus, the missions, structures and subcultures, and routines and standard operating procedures of the organizations involved are likely to prevail in accordance with the organizational process model for the more minor issues.

More important issues will attract the attention of many more officials and bureaucratic organizations. This, for instance, occurred with regard to the formulation of a governmental policy for the Strategic Arms Limitation Talks under President Lyndon Johnson as discussed previously. It is impossible, however, to predict which particular pattern will

---

ESSAY 11.3
CRISIS, STRESS, AND DECISION MAKING

Emphasis has been placed on the importance of the beliefs, personalities, and roles of policymakers, the role of group dynamics and interaction, and the role of bureaucratic norms and routines for understanding the policymaking process. Scholars have also found that **the decision-making context**—that is, the environment in which decisions are made has an important influence on individual behavior and the policymaking process. Ole Holsti has reviewed the literature on the relationship between crisis, stress, and decision-making. He found that situations perceived to be crises produced individual stress and affected the nature of decision-making for individuals and policymaking groups.

Times of **stress** influences individual decision-making. *Two patterns, based on experimental work in psychology, were found.* On the one hand, Holsti found that low and moderate levels of stress were often conducive to rational decision-making, for individuals became more attentive and motivated to find a solution to the problem at hand. In some cases, high levels of stress may increase performance for elementary tasks over limited periods of time. On the other hand, prolonged periods of high stress tend to result in defective decision-making, especially for tasks which are complex, ambiguous, and involve uncertainty. **Foreign policy crises** (those involving surprise, a threat to values, and little time to respond), Holsti's major concern, involve periods of high stress and decisions concerning such complex and ambiguous issues. During such crises, "lack of rest and diversion, combined with excessively long working hours, are likely to magnify the stresses in the situation."[A]

Holsti found that the preponderance of evidence from psychological experiments, psychological field research (for example, studies of individual behavior during natural disasters and combat), and historical studies of international crises indicated "that intense and protracted stress erodes rather than enhances the ability of individuals to cope with complex problems."[B] He found *a number of patterns associated with high stress and its impact on individual and group decision-making.* Specifically, high stress tends to:

1. Heighten the salience of time by distorting judgment and usually leading to a significant over-estimation of how fast time is passing;
2. Reduce the size of the policymaking group;
3. Reduce tolerance for ambiguity and increase the likelihood to stereotype and rationalize;
4. Increase cognitive rigidity, reliance on familiar decision rules, and use of basic beliefs and metaphorical thinking;
5. Encourage random and selective search for information;
6. Produce concern for the present and immediate future;
7. Minimize communication with potential adversaries;
8. Increase use of ad hoc communication channels;
9. Limit the search and assessment of alternatives, often to one approach;
10. Increase the likelihood of a polarized choice, favoring positions of over-cautiousness or greater risk taking;
11. Disrupt complex learning and the reexamination of decisions.

The stress produced by foreign policy crises, in other words, often contributes to poor policymaking performance and maladaptive behavior. Each of the eleven patterns mentioned above, with the exception of number eight, tends to contribute to a more closed decision-making process. Crises, therefore, may help trigger a groupthink policymaking process, especially if a strong domineering leader is present in the group.

A. Ole R. Hosti, "Crisis Management," in Betty Glad, ed., *Psychological Dimensions of War* (Newberry Park, Calif.: Sage, 1990), p. 124.

B. Ibid.

It is important, however, to emphasize that stress does not guarantee defective decision-making; it only makes it more likely that rational decision making will be constrained or inhibited. This is because "individuals appear to differ rather widely in the ability to tolerate stress, the threshold at which it begins to impair performance, and strategies for coping with various types of stress."[C] Ultimately, the policymaking process will be heavily affected by individual personality and perceptions (and misperceptions)—which are usually heightened during periods of crisis and high stress.

Although international crises usually inhibit rational decision-making, Holsti recognizes that "not all crises spin out of control owing to misperceptions, miscalculations, or other cognitive malfunc-

tions."[D] Therefore, "just as we cannot assume that 'good' processes will ensure high-quality decisions, we cannot assume that erratic processes will always result in low-quality decisions" or end up in fiascoes.[E] Nevertheless, theories of deterrence and compellence, which have been so central to great power politics and U.S. foreign policy, "presuppose rational and predictable decision processes" and "scholars and policymakers tend to be sanguine about the ability of policymakers to be creative when the situation requires it."[F] Therefore, it is important to understand that periods of intense crisis and stress may inhibit and overwhelm rationality during times when it is most needed.

C. Ibid., p. 127.

D. Ibid., p. 131.
E. Ibid., p. 127.
F. Ibid., p. 117.

SOURCES: Ole R. Hosti, "Crisis Management," in Betty Glad, ed., *Psychological Dimensions of War* (Newberry Park, Calif.: Sage, 1990), pp. 116–42; Ole R. Holsti, "Crisis, Stress and Decision-Making," *International Social Science Journal* 23 (1971), pp. 53–67; Irving L. Janis and Leon Mann, *Decision Making: A Psychological Analysis of Conflict, Choice, and Commitment* (New York: Free Press, 1977);

Richard Ned Lebow, *Between Peace and War: The Nature of International Crisis* (Baltimore: Johns Hopkins University Press, 1981); John R. O'Neal, "The Rationality of Decision Making During International Crises," *Polity* 20 (Summer 1988), pp. 598–622; and Jack L. Snyder, "Rationality at the Brink: The Role of Cognitive Processes in Failures of Deterrence," *World Politics* (April 1978), pp. 344–65.

prevail in the policymaking process. The policymaking process could resemble Allison's governmental politics model, but it could also take many other forms. Since no policymaker (or organization) dominates the entire process, the beliefs, personalities, and roles of the participants, which ultimately determine the actual policymaking process, may produce endless combinations.

Policy Implementation Patterns. The implementation of policy presents the most *clear and consistent patterns since the bureaucracy implements most governmental policy:*

1. Policy implementation tends to result in bureaucratic politics where particular organizations dominate the implementation process.
2. Presidents are most likely to be in control when they decide to take "no" action,

thereby circumventing the need for bureaucratic implementation altogether.

Not only does bureaucratic politics tend to prevail, but the implementation process reflects the bureaucratic structures and subcultures of the organizations involved, thus resembling the organizational process model. Presidential politics may intrude occasionally, as with President Kennedy's efforts to influence policy implementation during the Cuban Missile Crisis. In some instances, presidential politics may be consequential, as was the case with Kissinger's use of back channels to the People's Republic of China and the Soviet Union under President Nixon. However, most presidential decisions that require implementation are dependent on the bureaucracy.

As Morton Halperin puts it in *Bureaucratic Politics and Foreign Policy*, "At one extreme, if an action is a simple one capable of being carried out by a single individual in Washington without detailed technical expertise or training, presidential influence is likely to be overwhelming. To the degree that an action is a complicated one, requiring the cooperation of large numbers of people, many of them stationed outside of Washington, presidential influence on implementation fades."[41] Therefore, the most effective way a president can control the policy implementation stage is to decide against any action, thereby circumventing the need for bureaucratic implementation altogether.

THE COMPLEX REALITY OF POLICYMAKING

. . . .

We have examined the complexity of how policymaking operates within the executive branch. We have seen that policymaking involves three stages: agenda-setting, policy formulation, and policy implementation. We reviewed four policymaking models and highlighted two general policymaking patterns: presidential politics and bureaucratic politics. Finally, generalizations were proposed suggesting situations in which presidential politics and bureaucratic politics were likely to occur and the nature of the policymaking process that was likely to result with each of these patterns. The reader should now have a fuller understanding of the president's power over the policymaking process, including the power of the bureaucracy and the difficulties he encounters in managing the executive branch.

The picture provided actually oversimplifies policymaking within the executive branch. First, the government does not consider one issue at a time, but hundreds of foreign policy issues simultaneously. In other words, numerous policymaking processes operate within the executive branch at the same time. Presidential politics prevails for the more important issues, while bureaucratic politics guides the process for the remainder. Nor are agenda-setting, policy formation, and policy implementation processes clearly separated—they often overlap and impact on one another. Ultimately, policymaking efforts to address the dozens of issues involves the input of the beliefs, personalities, and bureaucratic roles of hundreds of individuals from numerous organizations throughout the executive branch. In other words, the president, his closest advisers, and bureaucratic officials and organizations throughout the executive branch are constantly initiating and responding to issues, participating in and influencing decisions, and implementing policies. These interactions and dynamic processes represent the complex politics of U.S. foreign policy as it takes place within the executive branch.

At the same time, it is important to point out that policymakers do not operate in a political vacuum, but in a large governmental, societal, and global context. This was a dominant theme that most of the early theorists of the U.S. policymaking process emphasized throughout their work; theorists such as Paul Hammond, Roger Hilsman, Richard Neustadt, Warner Schilling, Glenn Snyder, and Richard Snyder.[42] As Samuel Huntington made clear in his study of the national security process from 1945 to 1960, *The Common Defense,* "If this book has any distinctive message, it is that military policy can only be understood as the responses of the government to conflicting pressures from its foreign and domestic environments. . . . Military policy cannot be separated from foreign policy, fiscal policy, and domestic policy. It is part of the warp and woof of American politics."[43] Reflecting this concern throughout this book, we now turn to the remainder of the government, beginning with the role of Congress, before integrating the role of society and domestic politics in the complex politics of U.S. foreign policy.

BIBLIOGRAPHIC ESSAY

. . . .

The nature of policymaking within the executive branch has received considerable attention, with an emphasis on national security affairs. Graham T. Allison's *Essence of Decision: Explaining the Cuban Missile Crisis* (Boston: Little, Brown, 1973) provides a classic comparative analysis of the rational actor, governmental politics, and organizational process models of decision making. Less conceptual with greater emphasis on the reality of the bureaucratic political process is Morton H. Halperin's *Bureaucratic Politics and Foreign Policy* (Washington, D.C.: Brookings, 1974); Richard Holbrooke, "The Machine That Fails," *Foreign Policy* (Winter 1970–71), pp. 65–77; and Charles Maechling, Jr., "Foreign Policy-Makers: The Weakest Link?" *The Virginia Quarterly Review* 52 (Winter 1976), pp. 1–23. Irving L. Janis describes the groupthink process in *Groupthink* (New York: Houghton Mifflin, 1982). Valuable critiques of the policymaking models and generalizations discussed above are offered by Stephen D. Krasner, "Are Bureaucracies Important? (Or Allison's Wonderland)," *Foreign Policy* 7 (Summer 1972), pp. 159–79; Jerel A. Rosati, "Developing a Systematic Decision-Making Framework: Bureaucratic Politics in Perspective" *World Politics* 33 (January 1981), pp. 234–52; and John R. O'Neal, "The Rationality of Decision Making During International Crises," *Polity* 20 (Summer 1988), pp. 598–622.

Excellent overviews of the general role of personality, beliefs, and interpersonal relations on the policymaking process can be found in Joseph H. deRivera, *The Psychological Dimension of Foreign Policy* (Columbus, Ohio: Charles E. Merrill, 1968); Alexander L. George, *Presidential Decisionmaking in Foreign Policy: The Effective Use of Information and Advice* (Boulder, Colo.: Westview Press, 1980); Robert Jervis, *Perception and Misperception in International Politics* (Princeton, N.J.: Princeton University Press, 1976); Richard Ned Lebow, *Between Peace and War: The Nature of International Crisis* (Baltimore: Johns Hopkins University Press, 1981), and Jerel A. Rosati, "A Cognitive Approach to the Study of Foreign Policy," in *Foreign Policy Analysis: Continuity and Change in its Second Generation*, edited by Laura Neack, Patrick J. Haney, and Jeanne A. K. Hey (Englewood Cliffs, N.J.: Prentice-Hall, 1995), pp. 49–70.

More specifically, Doris Kearns Goodwin provides a fascinating psychological portrait of President Johnson and his impact on U.S. foreign policy in *Lyndon Johnson and the American Dream* (New York: Signet, 1976). Yuen Foong Khong highlights the importance of the beliefs of American leaders and the historical analogies used during the Vietnam War in *Analogies at War: Korea, Munich, Dien Bien Phu, and the Vietnam Decision of 1965* (Princeton, N.J.: Princeton University Press, 1992). Jerel A. Rosati takes a broad psychological approach to explain presidential poli-

tics in the Jimmy Carter administration: examining the president's early foreign policy optimism and idealism, the disagreements that arose between Secretary of State Cyrus Vance and National Security Adviser Zbigniew Brzezinski, and the reinstatement of the past containment policies of the cold war during Carter's final year in office in *The Carter Administration's Quest for Global Community: Beliefs and Their Impact on Behavior* (Columbia, S.C.: University of South Carolina Press, 1987).

ENDNOTES

1. Hedrick Smith, *The Power Game: How Washington Works* (New York: Ballantine, 1988), p. 56.
2. Charles Maechling, Jr., "Foreign Policy-Makers: The Weakest Link?" *The Virginia Quarterly Review* 52 (Winter 1976): 1–23.
3. See James A. Robinson and R. Roger Majak, "The Theory of Decision-Making," in James C. Charlesworth, ed., *Contemporary Political Analysis* (New York: Free Press, 1967), pp. 175–88; and James A. Robinson and Richard C. Snyder, "Decision-Making in International Politics," in Herbert C. Kelman, ed., *International Behavior: A Social-Psychological Analysis* (New York: Holt, Rinehart and Winston, 1965), pp. 433–63.
4. See, for example, Graham T. Allison, *Essence of Decision: Explaining the Cuban Missile Crisis* (Boston: Little, Brown, 1973). Much has been written on the events of the Cuban Missile Crisis subsequently, incorporating additional sources and perspectives. For a more comprehensie historical description involving all the major parties, see Bruce J. Allyn, James G. Blight, and David A. Welch, "Essence of Revision: Moscow, Havana, and the Cuban Missile Crisis," *International Security* 14 (Winter 1989–1990): 136–72; James G. Blight and David A. Welch, *On the Brink: Americans and Soviets Reexamine the Cuban Missile Crisis* (New York: Hill and Wang, 1989); Philip Brenner, "Cuba and the Missile Crisis," *Journal of Latin American Studies* 22 (February 1990): 115–42; Laurence Chang, ed., *Chronology of the Cuban Missile Crisis* (Washington, D.C.: Chadwyck-Healey, 1989); Raymond L. Garthoff, "Cuban Missile Crisis: The Soviet Story," *Foreign Policy* 72 (Fall 1988): 61–80; and Raymond L. Garthoff, *Reflections on the Cuban Missile Crisis* (Washington, D.C.: Brookings, 1989).

5. Allison, *Essence of Decision*. See also John D. Steinbruner, *The Cybernetic Theory of Decision* (Princeton, N.J.: Princeton University Press, 1974).

6. Questions have been raised as to the extent to which President John Kennedy acted rationally. See Richard Ned Lebow, *Between Peace and War: The Nature of International Crisis* (Baltimore: Johns Hopkins University Press, 1981), chapter 8; James A. Nathan, "The Missile Crisis: His Finest Hour Now," *World Politics* (January 1975): 256–81; and Jack L. Snyder, "Rationality at the Brink: The Role of Cognitive Processes in Failures of Deterrence," *World Politics* (April 1978): 344–65.

7. To save time and avoid complicating things, such shorthand phrases are necessary. These phrases, however, may be more than figures of speech, reflecting a set of assumptions about how people come to understand the world around them.

8. Irving L. Janis, *Groupthink* (New York: Houghton Mifflin, 1982). See also the sources listed in essay 11.1.

9. Janis, *Groupthink*. See also Dean A. Minix, *Small Groups and Foreign Policy Decision-Making* (Lanham, Md.: University Press of America, 1978). David M. Barrett disagrees with the consensus position that Johnson's policymaking process reflected groupthink, resulting in the escalation of the war in Vietnam, in "The Mythology Surrounding Lyndon Johnson, His Advisers, and the 1965 Decision to Escalate the Vietnam War," *Political Science Quarterly* (Winter 1988–1989): 637–64.

10. It should be pointed out that it is possible for either rational actor or groupthink policymaking processes to occur below the presidential level, although this is not how the models are typically discussed.

11. See Smith, *The Power Game*; Tower Commission (President's Special Review Board), *The Tower Commission Report* (New York: Bantam, 1987); and Bob Woodward, *Veil: The Secret Wars of the CIA 1981–1987* (New York: Simon and Schuster, 1987).

12. Bob Woodward, *The Commanders* (New York: Simon and Schuster, 1991). See also Maureen Dowd, "The Longest Week: How President Decided to Draw the Line," *New York Times* (August 9, 1990): 17A; Elizabeth Drew, "Letter From Washington," *New Yorker* (September 14, 1990; February 4, 1991): 103–112, 82–90; Thomas L. Friedman and Patrick E. Tyler, "From the First, U.S. Resolve to Fight," *New York Times* (March 3, 1991): 1, 12; and "To the Brink of War" *Frontline* PBS (January 15, 1991); William H. Kincade, "On the Brink in the Gulf, Part I: Onset of

the 'Classic' 1990 Crisis," *Security Studies* (Winter 1992): 163–200, and "On the Brink in the Gulf, Part II: The Route to War," *Security Studies* (Winter 1993–94): 295–329; Don Oberdorfer, "Missed Signals in the Middle East," *Washington Post Magazine* (March 17, 1991): 19–23, 36–41; Jean Edward Smith, *George Bush's War* (Henry Holt, 1992).

13. See, for example, Gregory M. Herek, Irving L. Janis, and Paul Huth, "Decision Making During International Crises: Is Quality of Process Related to Outcome?" *Journal of Conflict Resolution* 31 (June 1987): 203–26.

14. John Newhouse, *Cold Dawn: The Story of SALT* (New York: Holt, Rinehart and Winston, 1973), p. 108.

15. See Newhouse, *Cold Dawn*, and Jerel A. Rosati, "Developing a Systematic Decision-Making Framework: Bureaucratic Politics in Perspective," *World Politics* 33 (January 1981): 234–52.

16. Allison, *Essence of Decision*. See also Morton H. Halperin, *Bureaucratic Politics and Foreign Policy* (Washington, D.C.: Brookings, 1974), and Morton H. Halperin and Arnold Kanter, eds., *Readings in American Foreign Policy: A Bureaucratic Perspective* (Boston: Little, Brown, 1973).

17. Smith, *The Power Game*, p. 561.

18. See, for example, "A Fatal Error of Judgement," *Newsweek* (March 3, 1986): 14–19.

19. See also Steinbruner, *The Cybernetic Theory of Decision*.

20. Friedman and Tyler, "From the First," p. 12; Michael Massing, "The Way to War," *New York Review of Books* (March 28, 1991): 17–20, 22; and Woodward, *The Commanders*.

21. For sources, see notes 3 and 5.

22. Allison, *Essence of Decision*, pp. 131—32.

23. It should be pointed out that the models of governmental politics and organization process assume that individuals act rationally, although this is not likely to translate into a rational process at the national policymaking level.

24. For a general discussion of the concept of government learning, see Lloyd S. Etheredge, *Can Governments Learn? American Foreign Policy and Central American Revolutions* (New York: Pergamon Press, 1985), and Jack S. Levy, "Learning and Foreign Policy: Sweeping a Conceptual Minefield," *International Organization* (Spring 1994): 279–312.

25. Alexander L. George argues for a "multiple advocacy" approach in order to promote rational decision-making, in "The Case for Multiple Advocacy in Making

Foreign Policy," *American Political Science Review* 66 (1972): 751–85. James Nathan, in "The Cuban Missile Crisis," makes a compelling case that lessons from the Cuban missile crisis were overdrawn and overlearned by Kennedy administration officials and American policymakers. Furthermore, not everyone accepts that a purely rational process is the optimal way to arrive at decisions. Miriam Steiner in a very interesting article argues in favor of a decision-making process that comprises both rationalistic and nonrationalistic dimensions, in "The Search for Order in a Disorderly World: Worldviews and Prescriptive Decision Paradigms," *International Organization* 37 (Summer 1983): 373–413.

26. See Robert Art, "Bureaucratic Politics and American Foreign Policy: A Critique," *Policy Sciences* 4 (1973): 467–90; Stephen D. Krasner, "Are Bureaucracies Important? (Or Allison Wonderland)," *Foreign Policy* 7 (Summer 1972): 159–79; Jeanne Longley and Dean G. Pruitt, "Groupthink: A Critique of Janis's Theory," Review of *Personality and Social Psychology* 1 (1980): 74–93; Developing a Systematic Decision-Making Framework"; Snyder, "Rationality at the Brink"; and Steinbruner, *Cybernetic Theory of Decision.*

27. See Margaret G. Hermann and Charles F. Hermann, "Who Makes Foreign Policy Decisions and How: An Empirical Inquiry," *International Studies Quarterly* 33 (December 1989): 361–88; Rosati, "Developing a Systematic Decision-Making Framework"; and, in particular, Peter J. Schraeder, *Speaking With Many Voices: Incrementalism, Crisis, and Change in U.S. Intervention in Africa* (Ph.D. dissertation, University of South Carolina, 1991).

28. See, for example, Fred I. Greenstein and John P. Burke, "The Dynamics of Presidential Reality Testing: Evidence From Two Vietnam Decisions," *Political Science Quarterly* 104 (Winter 1980–1990): 557–80; and *How Presidents Test Reality: Decisions on Vietnam, 1954 and 1965* (New York: Russell Sage Foundation, 1989).

29. Maechling, "Foreign Policy-Makers," p. 18.

30. Robert Pear, "Confusion Is Operative Word in U.S. Policy Toward Japan," *New York Times* (March 20, 1989): 1. See also, Stephen W. Twing, *The FSX Affair: Putting Bureaucratic Politics into Context* (Master's Thesis, University of South Carolina, 1990).

31. At times, Allison has referred to a bureaucratic politics model, which is a fusion of the governmental politics and organizational process models. See, in particular, Graham T. Allison and Morton H. Halperin, "Bureaucratic Politics: A Paradigm and some Policy Implications," *World Politics* 24 (Spring 1972): 40–79.

32. Maechling, "Foreign Policy-Makers," p. 3.

33. For a general discussion of the role of personality and beliefs on the foreign policymaking process, see Joseph H. deRivera, *The Psychological Dimension of Foreign Policy* (Columbus, Ohio: Charles E. Merrill, 1968); Lloyd S. Etheredge, "Personality Effects on American Foreign Policy, 1899–1968: A Test of Interpersonal Generalization Theory," *American Political Science Review* 72 (June 1978): 434–51; Alexander L. George, *Presidential Decisionmaking in Foreign Policy: The Effective Use of Information and Advice* (Boulder, Colo: Westview Press, 1980); Robert Jervis, *Perception and Misperception in International Politics* (Princeton, N.J.: Princeton University Press, 1976); Yuen Foong Khong, *Analogies at War: Korea, Munich, Dien Bien Phu, and the Vietnam Decision of 1965* (Princeton, N.J.: Princeton University Press, 1992); Deborah Welch Larson, *Origins of Containment: A Psychological Explanation* (Princeton, N.J.: Princeton University Press, 1985); Michael W. Link and Betty Glad, "Exploring the Psychopolitical Dynamics of Advisory Relations: The Carter Administration's 'Crisis of Confidence,' " *Political Psychology* 15 (September 1994): 461–80; Jerel A. Rosati, "Continuity and Change in the Foreign Policy Beliefs of Political Leaders: Addressing the Controversy Over the Carter Administration," *Political Psychology* 9 (September 1988): 471–505; Jerel A. Rosati, *The Carter Administration's Quest for Global Community: Beliefs and Their Impact on Behavior* (Columbia, S.C.: University of South Carolina Press, 1987); Jerel A. Rosati, "A Cognitive Approach to the Study of Foreign Policy," in *Foreign Policy Analysis; Continuity and Change in Its Second Generation*, edited by Laura Neack, Patrick J. Haney, and Jeanne A.K. Hey (Englewood Cliffs, N.J.: Prentice-Hall, 1995), pp. 49–70; and Stephen G. Walker, "The Interface Between Beliefs and Behavior: Henry Kissinger's Operational Code and the Vietnam War," *Journal of Conflict Resolution* 21 (March 1977): 129–68.

34. These generalizations are derived from much of the literature already cited, but especially the following: Allison, *Essence of Decision*; Art, "Bureaucratic Politics and American Foreign Policy"; deRivera, *The Psychological Dimension of Foreign Policy*; Etheredge, *Can Governments Learn?*; George, *Presidential Decisionmaking in Foreign Policy*; Halperin, *Bureaucratic Politics and Foreign Policy*; Charles F. Hermann, "Decision Structure and Process: Influences on Foreign Policy," in Maurice A. East, Stephen A. Salmore, and Charles F. Hermann, eds., *Why Nations Act* (Beverly Hills:

Sage, 1978), pp. 49–68; Janis, *Groupthink*; Irving L. Janis and Leon Mann, *Decision Making: A Psychological Analysis of Conflict, Choice, and Commitment* (New York: Free Press, 1977); Jervis, *Perception and Misperception in International Politics*; Lebow, *Between Peace and War*; Rosati, "Developing a Decision-Making Framework"; and Steinbruner, *Cybernetic Theory of Decision.*

35. See Jerel Rosati, Ken Rogerson, and Richard Haeuber, "Agenda-Setting, World Affairs Organizations, and the Making of U.S. Foreign Policy," (manuscript, 1997). For an overview of the importance and impact of agenda-setting, see John W. Kingdon, *Agendas, Alternatives, and Public Policies* (Boston: Little, Brown, 1984), and David A. Rochefort and Roger W. Cobb, "Problem Definition, Agenda Access, and Policy Choice," *Policy Studies Journal* 21 (1993): 56–71.

36. See, for example, Charles F. Hermann, "International Crisis as a Situational Variable," in James N. Rosenau, ed., *International Politics and Foreign Policy* (New York: Free Press, 1969), pp. 409–21.

37. Smith, *The Power Game*, p. 83. On the general impact of the scope of conflict for political outcomes, see E.E. Schattschneider, *The Semisovereign People: A Realist's View of Democracy in America* (Hinsdale, Ill.: Dryden Press, 1960), chapter 1.

38. Ibid., p. 80.

39. See Rosati, "Developing a Systematic Decision-Making Framework," for a discussion of "localized" decision-making.

40. Barnett Rubin, "The U.S. Response to the JVP Insurgency in Sri Lanka," *Commission on the Organization of the Government for the Conduct of Foreign Policy*, VII, Appendices (Washington, D.C.: U.S. Government Printing Office), p. 179.

41. Halperin, *Bureaucratic Politics and Foreign Policy*, p. 290.

42. Roger Hilsman, *To Move a Nation: The Politics of Foreign Policy in the Administration of John F. Kennedy* (New York: Delta, 1964): Richard E. Neustadt, *Presidential Power: The Politics of Leadership* (New York: John Wiley, 1960); Warner R. Schilling, Paul T. Hammond, and Glenn H. Snyder, *Strategy, Politics and Defense Budgets* (New York: Columbia University Press, 1962); and Richard C. Snyder, H.W. Bruck, and Burton Sapin, *Foreign Policy Decision-Making: An Approach to the Study of International Politics* (New York: Free Press of Glencoe, 1962). On this first wave of policymaking theorists, see Art, "Bureaucratic Politics and American Foreign Policy." Although Art criticized the so-called second wave of policymaking theorists, such as Graham Allison and Morton Halperin, for their narrow conceptualization of the policymaking process limited to the executive branch, it needs to be pointed out that they recognized the important role that domestic politics had on policymaking. See, for example, Halperin, *Bureaucratic Politics and Foreign Policy.*

43. Samuel P. Huntington, *The Common Defense: Strategic Programs in National Politics* (New York: Columbia University Press, 1961), pp. x, xi.

CHAPTER 12

......

CONGRESS
AND LEGISLATIVE-EXECUTIVE RELATIONS

Congress plays a key and often controversial role in the making of U.S. foreign policy. This chapter will examine the history of legislative-executive relations and efforts by members of Congress to reassert their authority in U.S. foreign policy since the Vietnam War. The discussion of Congress will provide insight into the themes of continuity and change in the policymaking process over time, the constraints that presidents face in governing U.S. foreign policy, and the tensions between the demands of national security and democracy.

THE HISTORY
OF LEGISLATIVE-EXECUTIVE
RELATIONS

......

The role of Congress in U.S. foreign policy has been frequently misunderstood. It has often been portrayed from the perspective of a **partisan debate**, where ideology and party play prominent roles. Since the Vietnam War, "conservatives," often found within the Republican party, tend to criticize congressional involvement in foreign policy, favoring greater exercise of presidential power in foreign policymaking. They typically argue that the president has been supreme in the making of U.S. foreign policy throughout history and that this is consistent with the original intent of the Constitution. On the other hand, "liberals," usually within the Democratic party, tend to argue that the Constitution resulted in a sharing of foreign policy power between Congress and the president and, therefore, both institutions have major roles to play.

Such partisan perceptions of the constitutional foundation of U.S. foreign policy have shaped the competing interpretations of important foreign policy issues, such as the Iran-Contra affair. Conservatives and Republicans have been most likely to see the Iran-Contra affair as no more than the exercise of poor judgment by the president and his adminis-tration. Liberals and Democrats, on the other hand, have been more likely to see Iran-Contra as a con-certed presidential effort to circumvent the law and the constitutional role of Congress in foreign policy.[1] Similar partisan debates about congressional and presidential roles in the making of U.S. foreign policy became visible during the Persian Gulf crisis.

A particularly fascinating aspect of this debate is the reversal of these positions during the cold war years. Thirty years ago, liberal Democrats argued that the president was supreme in foreign policy, as intended by the Constitution. In contrast, conserva-tives argued that the Constitution required a vital and independent role for Congress in the foreign policymaking process. What could explain this "re-versal of views" within thirty years?

The change in positions should not come as a surprise if one sees each view as a function of politi-cal partisanship, rather than a function of constitu-tional philosophy. Liberal Democrats have champi-oned the presidency since World War II, a time when they were more successful in influencing poli-cymaking within the executive branch—beginning with the election of Franklin Roosevelt and continu-ing with Harry Truman, John F. Kennedy, and Lyn-don Johnson to the presidency. On the other hand, conservative influence was more likely to emanate within the institution of Congress. Conservative in-fluence in the executive branch, however, has grown since Vietnam under the presidencies of Richard Nixon, Gerald Ford, Ronald Reagan, and George Bush, while liberal influence has been much more relegated to Congress. Therefore, conservatives and Republicans have been more likely to prefer a strong presidency. On the other hand, liberals and Democ-rats tend to look more favorably toward the role of Congress, the institution with which they have ex-ercised greatest influence since the Vietnam War.[2] The election and reelection of Bill Clinton as presi-dent has naturally affected the partisan debate accordingly.

Because of its overtly partisan and political na-ture, this debate sheds little light on the nature of legislative-executive relations in the making of U.S. foreign policy. What is required, instead, is *an exam-ination and appraisal of the role of Congress in foreign policy in two areas:*

1. The constitutional foundation of the distrib-ution of power within the national govern-ment;
2. The history of legislative-executive relations.

Examination of these two areas will provide the background for understanding the contemporary role of Congress in the making of U.S. foreign policy.

THE CONSTITUTION AND FOREIGN POLICY

What does the Constitution say about the distribu-tion of power between the executive and legislative branches of government in the making of foreign policy? Before fully addressing this question, a num-ber of points must be kept in mind. First, the docu-ment Americans refer to as **the Constitution** is actu-ally the second constitution of the United States of America. The first constitution, **the Articles of Con-federation**, lasted only from 1781 to 1787. It created a weak central government, in which most of the governmental powers resided with the states. Sec-ond, the Constitution is a short and ambiguous doc-ument. It is no more than a few pages long—one of the shortest written constitutions in the world. This means that the document consists of sweeping state-ments and generalizations, making it difficult to pinpoint the specific distribution of power through-out the government. Third, the Constitution is over two hundred years old. It was written for the eigh-teenth century, not for the twentieth or twenty-first centuries, although it has been remarkably adaptable to changing circumstances. Lastly, the final language of the Constitution, which became the law of the land, was largely a function of political compromise. The fifty-five so-called "founding fathers" that de-vised the Constitution at the Philadelphia Conven-tion had very different interests in mind. They seri-ously debated the document's purpose, contents and language; in fact, three founding fathers refused to sign the final document.

Because the Constitution is a short, ambiguous, and old document arrived at by negotiation and compromise, it is difficult to be definitive about the **founding fathers' intent**. It may be neither fair nor relevant to talk about the "founders' intent," given the two hundred years that have passed since ratification. Still, the Constitution broadly defines the distribution of power in the government and provides the initial foundation for understanding legislative-executive relations in the making of foreign policy.

As initially discussed in chapter 4, *Article II of the Constitution enumerates the powers of the president.* With regard to foreign policy, the president is the "Commander in Chief of the Army and Navy of the United States, and of the Militia of the several States, when called into the actual Service of the United States." Furthermore, "He shall have Power, by and with the Advice and Consent of the Senate, to make Treaties, provided two thirds of the Senators present concur; and he shall nominate, and by and with the Advice and Consent of the Senate, shall appoint Ambassadors, other public ministers and Consuls." The president "shall receive Ambassadors and other public Ministers; he shall take Care that the Laws be faithfully executed, and shall Commission all the Officers of the United States." Finally, the president has the power to veto legislation. In sum, the Constitution gives the president formidable powers in foreign policy, especially in the areas of treaties, appointments, and his role as commander in chief.

Article I of the Constitution enumerates the powers of the legislative branch. In comparison to Article II, Article I is three times as long. Among the important congressional powers stipulated in the Constitution, especially with respect to foreign policy, are that Congress shall "provide for the common Defense and general Welfare of the United States"; "regulate Commerce with foreign Nations, and among the several States, and with the Indian Tribes"; "define and punish Piracies and Felonies committed on the high Seas, and Offenses against the Law of Nations"; "declare War, grant Letters of Marque and Reprisal, and make Rules concerning Captures on Land and Water"; "raise and support Armies"; "provide and maintain a Navy"; "make

Rules for the Government and Regulation of the land and naval Forces"; and "provide for calling forth the Militia to execute the Laws of the Union, suppress Insurrections and repel Invasions." Finally, in addition to the Senate's advice and consent power, Congress shall have the power "to make all Laws which shall be necessary and proper for carrying into Execution the foregoing Powers, and all other Powers vested by this Constitution in the Government of the United States, or in any Department or Officer thereof."

The Constitution clearly gives the Congress formidable powers in the area of foreign policy. Unlike most legislatures throughout the world, as in parliamentary systems of government, the U.S. Congress is an independent and powerful branch of government. In fact, most scholars of the Constitution have concluded that the founding fathers intended and expected that the Constitution would create a legislature that would be the preeminent branch within the government. Nonetheless, the Constitution did not give power in the area of foreign policy solely to the Congress or the president—power was distributed between the two branches of government.[3]

Americans have been raised to understand the distribution of power between Congress and the president as a **separation of powers.** But this concept does not accurately represent reality, for the Constitution did not create separate institutions with separate powers. Instead, the Constitution created separate institutions that share power—which is what is meant by the existence of "checks and balances." While the Congress provides military funding and declares war, the president is the commander in chief. Congress may pass bills, but the president may veto them and Congress may then override the veto. The president is able to make treaties and appointments, but the Senate must provide its advice and consent. In this way, the Constitution has produced a central government with "separate institutions sharing powers." As students of the Constitution have indicated, the result was an **"invitation to struggle,"** which has fostered recurring conflicts between Congress and the president in the making of foreign policy throughout American history.

AN OVERVIEW OF LEGISLATIVE-EXECUTIVE RELATIONS

Given the sharing of power by separate institutions and the basic ambiguity of the Constitution, the distribution of foreign policymaking power between Congress and the president has fluctuated politically over time. There has not been a single pattern in foreign policymaking throughout American history. Neither Congress nor the president has always predominated in foreign policy. Legislative-executive relations in foreign policy have been fluid and dynamic, and have fluctuated with changes in the political environment. Therefore, the key to understanding the history of legislative-executive relations is to see it in terms of the political interaction of these two branches of government over time.

As described by Arthur Schlesinger, Jr., in *The Imperial Presidency,* the politics of legislative-executive relations in foreign policy has been characterized by a kind of **"pendulum or cyclical effect"** throughout American history.[4] In times of national emergency, particularly war, power tends to flow toward the president and the executive branch. During times of peace—that is, when conflict has subsided—power tends to flow back to Congress. Yet, while Congress tends to reassert its constitutional authority and power following war, increases in presidential power during periods of conflict tend to be so extensive that it seldom returns to prewar levels. Thus, the cyclical ebb and flow in legislative-executive relations in foreign policy has enabled the president to accumulate greater power over time.

The growth in power that the president and executive branch experience during periods of war was evident in the War of 1812, Mexican-American War, Civil War, Spanish-American War, and the first and second World Wars. Two major factors account for this expansion of presidential power. First, in times of conflict the president's roles of commander in chief and chief executive give him control over the conduct of war. This fact is reinforced by the tendency of Congress to delegate extensive emergency powers to the president during wartime.[5] Second, periods of perceived national emergency are also

times when most Americans throughout the government and society turn to the president and rally behind him as the key authority for addressing the gravity of the situation. Referring back to our discussion of Richard Pious's work in chapter 2, periods of war and national emergency are times when the president can exercise prerogative government. That is, the president can push the constitution to its extreme in the exercise of presidential power, with the likelihood of only minimal political backlash. This is exactly what occurred, for example, under the administrations of Abraham Lincoln, Woodrow Wilson, and Franklin Roosevelt.

With the end of war and national emergency, the conditions that gave rise to the expansion of presidential power disappear. Periods of normalcy or relative stability result in congressional reassertion of power. Hence, the president experiences greater constraints on his ability to exercise power in foreign policy. Such cutbacks occurred after all of the major wars, but most noticeably following World War I. The Senate rejected the Treaty of Versailles that President Wilson negotiated in Paris and that included his grand design for a League of Nations. Also, during the interwar years, Congress passed legislation that increasingly affected the conduct of U.S. foreign policy and constrained presidential power, culminating in the neutrality legislation that tied the hands of President Franklin Roosevelt as World War II approached.

Even though postwar years of peace and relative stability increase congressional strength in legislative-executive foreign policy relations, the president's power nonetheless tends to experience net growth in comparison to prewar years. Thus, although the neutrality legislation certainly constrained Roosevelt's efforts to support Great Britain and the allies as World War II approached and during the initial years of the war, President Roosevelt had the U.S. military participate in an "undeclared naval war" in the mid-Atlantic in support of the British about six months before the Japanese attack on Pearl Harbor legitimized full-scale American intervention in the war. Congressional reassertion also did not prevent presidents from pursuing an active foreign policy in areas deemed particularly important for U.S. national interests, such as Asia and Latin America. The interwar years, for example, were a time when American presidents routinely intervened militarily throughout the Caribbean and Central America, frequently relying on the use of American armed forces to exercise influence in the region.

The historical pattern is one in which presidents have accumulated more and more power in foreign policy over time as a result of war and national emergencies; at the same time, Congress has attempted, with only moderate success, to reassert its constitutional authority in foreign policy during times of peace. As a result, Congress has become increasingly unable to exercise preeminence in the making of foreign policy. Thus, times of war and national emergency are likely to be times of presidential preeminence, while times of peace are likely to result not in congressional ascendance but in political struggles in legislative-executive relations over foreign policy. This cyclical pattern and the politics of legislative-executive relations was played out following World War II.

World War II and the Postwar Years

. . . .

American intervention in World War II in 1941 resulted in a major expansion of the national security bureaucracy and of presidential power in foreign policy. With the war's end in 1945, the U.S. government demobilized its military forces and global presence. At the same time, Congress began to reassert its authority in foreign policy. However, the jubilation of victory in World War II and peacetime hopes were quickly replaced by new fears and a new enemy—Soviet communism. Consequently, **the post–World War II years** never became a "time of peace;" the late 1940s, 1950s, and early 1960s were a time when most Americans perceived a major threat to their national security. For the first time in its history, the United States remobilized and remilitarized on a permanent peacetime basis to deter and contain what was believed to be the rise of a communist threat abroad. This period of perceived national emergency resulted in renewed expansion of the national security bureaucracy and enhanced presidential power in foreign policy.

Although the United States and the Soviet Union never engaged in a "hot war" (that is, a direct military clash), the United States prepared for a direct military confrontation with the Soviet Union and engaged in a global cold war. The cold war climate produced a major expansion of presidential power, restoring the president's preeminence in the making of U.S. foreign policy. The threat to national security was felt so intensely that a cold war consensus developed throughout America in support of the president's effort to fight the cold war. With the president receiving such widespread support, congressional reassertion over foreign policy was deferred during the cold war years and reappeared only during the late 1960s with the growing dispute over the Vietnam War. Thus, *legislative-executive relations have gone through two general phases during the post–World War II years:*

1. Presidential preeminence and congressional acquiescence from the late 1940s to the mid-1960s, when the cold war dominated U.S. foreign policy;
2. Congressional reassertion in foreign policy, which has occurred since the height of the Vietnam War in the late 1960s.

Presidential Preeminence in the Cold War Era

. . . .

The president and the executive branch dominated the legislative branch in the making of foreign policy during the cold war years. At the same time, American politics and legislative-executive relations were much more complex than this simple generalization implies. Presidential preeminence neither occurred overnight nor dominated the entire history of the cold war years. *The congressional role in legislative-executive relations evolved through four phases or periods during the cold war years:*[6]

1. Accommodation, from 1944 to 1950;
2. Antagonism, from 1951 to 1955;
3. Acquiescence, from 1955 to 1965;
4. Ambiguity, from 1966 to 1969.

Congressional Accommodation, 1944 to 1950. What began as congressional assertion quickly became **congressional accommodation** in legislative-executive relations in the immediate postwar years. Tension between members of Congress and the president initially surfaced over the future of U.S. foreign policy. In response to the devastation suffered by Europe in the war, President Truman proposed **the Marshall Plan** to provide American assistance for European economic reconstruction. However, isolationist sentiment was still very strong among members of Congress, especially within the Republican party. Truman overcame congressional resistance to such an active American role abroad only by working closely with members of Congress and convincing them, and the American people, of the grave political instability that most European states faced from their economic situation and from the growing threat of Soviet communism. The Marshall Plan was eventually approved by Congress with considerable bipartisan support and symbolized an accommodationist relationship between the legislative and the executive branches.

During the immediate post–World War II years, most key decisions behind U.S. cold war and containment policies were a result of **joint participation** by the president and members of Congress. This was a period in which the evolving legislative-executive partnership approved of American participation in the United Nations, the International Bank for Reconstruction and Development (World Bank), the International Monetary Fund (IMF), and the General Agreement on Tariffs and Trade (GATT). It was also a time when the National Security Act of 1947 became law, foreign assistance to Greece and Turkey was approved in support of the Truman Doctrine, and the military was remobilized. Joint legislative-executive action supported a strong American global role, culminating in the **Senate approval of NATO** (North Atlantic Treaty Organization) and the permanent stationing of American troops in Europe—an unprecedented American military commitment in a time of peace.

Congressional Antagonism, 1951 to 1955. Although members of Congress and President Truman, followed by President Dwight Eisenhower, espoused a bipartisan approach to foreign policy, a growing segment of Congress was increasingly dissatisfied with U.S. foreign policy and global developments. Much of this frustration was experienced by more conservative members of Congress, especially within the Republican party. They saw a world in which the United States had won the war, but was losing the peace. According to this view events such as Soviet communist consolidation of power in Eastern Europe, the "fall" of Chiang Kai-shek and the Nationalists in China, and the North Korean attack on South Korea demonstrated that U.S. foreign policy was a failure and too weak to respond to the ever-growing communist threat.

How could this happen? How could the United States win the war and emerge as the strongest country in the world, yet fail to contain the expansion of communism? The answer was simple in the minds of many people—treason must be afoot. In other words, Americans were losing the war to communism abroad because communists, "fellow travelers," and liberal-leftists had penetrated the major institutions of American society, including the executive branch, and were aiding and abetting the enemy. Thus, it was not enough to just contain communism abroad; one had to "roll it back" both abroad and at home.

This extremely pessimistic view had played a role in the politics of U.S. foreign policy since the end of World War II. However, it became much more prominent when the Republican party gained control of both chambers of Congress, first after the 1946 congressional elections and, especially, after the 1952 elections. **Republican ascendance** resulted in sweeping congressional investigations of communist threats at home, as well as growing political attacks against the Truman administration and the Democratic party.

"Republicans began referring to their congressional adversaries as members of 'the party of treason'—a slur that [Democratic leader Sam] Rayburn attributed to Nixon, and never forgave," according to William Manchester, in *The Glory and the Dream.* "Congressman Karl Mundt of South Dakota demanded that the President 'ferret out' those on the federal payroll 'whose Soviet leanings have contributed so greatly to the deplorable mess in our foreign policy.' Congressman Harold Velde of Illinois announced that Soviet spies were 'infesting the entire country,' like gypsy moths; Congressman Robert Rich of Pennsylvania charged that [Secretary of State] Dean Acheson was on Joseph Stalin's payroll." Manchester's narrative history provides a feel for the language and the nature of the times. "To [Senator William] Jenner of Indiana, every American whose advice to Chiang Kai-shek had failed to staunch the Red tide was, almost by definition, a criminal. Jenner called General [George] Marshall 'a front man for traitors,' a 'living lie' who had joined hands 'with this criminal crowd of traitors and Communist appeasers who, under the continuing influence of Mr. Truman and Mr. Acheson, are still selling America down the river.' "[7] It was in this political climate that Senator Joseph McCarthy of Wisconsin thrived and gave the conservative movement its name— **McCarthyism**. (See **essay 12.1** for more on Joseph McCarthy and McCarthyism.)

With the growing power of the Republican party and the rise of McCarthyism, U.S. foreign policy became an increasingly partisan political battleground, symbolized by the **"Truman-MacArthur controversy"** of 1951. President Truman fired General Douglas MacArthur as commander of the allied forces in Korea, charging him with insubordination and carelessly escalating the Korean conflict by triggering the military involvement of communist China (the People's Republic of China). President Truman represented a more moderate position and supported the containment goal of restoring the original status quo of a divided yet peaceful Korean Peninsula. General MacArthur, a hero of the conservative right, represented the quest for victory, the rollback of communism in North Korea, and Korean reunification. This controversy eventually died down, but the Korean War had become the Democrats' and "Truman's War," and foreign policy issues

played a prominent role in the 1952 presidential election campaign between Democratic candidate Adlai Stevenson and Republican candidate Dwight Eisenhower.

With the election of Eisenhower as president, political attacks from the right did not stop. The administration's rhetoric, particularly from Secretary of State John Foster Dulles, emphasized the need to roll back communism and liberate people from totalitarianism. Yet, President Eisenhower basically continued the foreign policy of containment initiated by President Truman. Truman had started the effort to contain Soviet communism in Europe and, with the Korean War, extended it to Asia. Under Eisenhower, the containment policy was extended throughout the world and further institutionalized within the U.S. government. Yet in the minds of the more conservative members of Congress, nothing had really changed and the cold war was still being lost.

The **peak of antagonism** in legislative-executive relations came with the dispute over an attempt by Republican Senator John W. Bricker to amend the Constitution in 1953. **The Bricker amendment** would have provided Congress with the responsibility and authority to approve all international agreements (in addition to treaties) entered into by the president; in effect, conservative (and isolationist) elements in Congress did not trust the president to act in the name of the U.S. government and the American people. After a year of intense debate, the Bricker amendment failed by a single vote (60–31) to achieve the necessary two-thirds majority. "The Bricker Amendment both symbolized and brought to an end this period of antagonism in legislative-executive relations."[8]

Congressional Acquiescence, 1955 to 1965. With the decline of McCarthyism, the cold war consensus behind U.S. foreign policy and the containment strategy solidified. This period constituted the height of **bipartisanship**—mutual support behind the president, regardless of party affiliation, in the making of U.S. foreign policy.[9] The cold war consensus provided the basis for presidential support within Congress and throughout American society.

ESSAY 12.1
JOSEPH MCCARTHY AND MCCARTHYISM

Journalist Richard H. Rovere begins his biography, *Senator Joe McCarthy,* by writing that "the late Joseph R. McCarthy, a United States Senator from Wisconsin, was in many ways the most gifted demagogue ever bred on these shores. No bolder seditionist ever moved among us—not any politician with a surer, swifter access to the dark places of the American mind."[A] McCarthy's political prominence was brief. His rise to power began in 1950, four years after he won a seat in the Senate. Within weeks, he became a major political figure known, loved, hated, and feared throughout the country and the world. By 1954, his career ended when the Senate passed a resolution of censure against him. He died a drunk three years later at age forty-eight. Yet, the impact of Joseph McCarthy and McCarthyism was immense.

Joseph McCarthy both reflected and promoted the anticommunist climate of the times. He embodied a political force—McCarthyism—that dominated American politics during the early 1950s and was instrumental in pushing the country and U.S. foreign policy to the political right. Joseph McCarthy and McCarthyism led to "the purge of thousands of government employees, educators, labor leaders, journalists, scientists, writers, and entertainers and, perhaps more important, the intimidation of hundreds of thousands more."[B]

Joseph McCarthy started out as a Democrat and made his first run for office in 1939 as a supporter of Franklin D. Roosevelt. He became a Republican and won election to the Senate in 1946 as "Tail Gunner Joe"—a war hero who never actually fought in the war. During his early years in the Senate, McCarthy was "known as a cheap politician of vulgar, flamboyant ways and a casual approach to the public interest."[C] One night in January 1950 in a small restaurant in Washington, D.C., while talking with three dinner companions about his Senate reelection possibilities, he discovered communism as an issue—not out of real concern for American national security, but as an issue that would win him reelection.

He tested the issue in a speech he gave on February 9, 1950, in Wheeling, West Virginia, in which he claimed that the Department of State was full of communists and that he and the secretary of state knew their names. To this day, nobody is sure whether he stated that there were 205, 81, 57, or "a lot" of communists; more important was the charge that communists "known to the secretary of state" were "still working and making policy." Although McCarthy was one of many politicians voicing the anticommunist theme, he gained the public spotlight like no other.

Following his Wheeling speech, he accused the Democratic administration of conniving with communists: "The Democratic label is now the property of men and women who have . . . bent to the whispered pleas from the lips of traitors . . . men and women who wear the political label stitched with the idiocy of a Truman, rotted by the deceit of a [Secretary of State Dean] Acheson, corrupted by the red slime of a [Director of the International Monetary Fund Harry Dexter] White."[D] He claimed that the Democratic years had been "twenty years of treason." The timing of the charges was impeccable. On January 21, Alger Hiss, a State Department official accused of being a communist, was convicted of perjury and in June the communist government of North Korea invaded South Korea, vindicating and feeding the anticommunist hysteria that McCarthy represented.

Over the course of the next four years, four different congressional committees conducted **five major congressional investigations** into the threat of communism and alleged treasonous behavior at home. Although congressional investigations of communism in different walks of American life had

---

A. Richard H. Rovere, *Senator Joe McCarthy* (New York: World Publishing, 1959), p. 3.
B. Robert Griffith, *The Politics of Fear: Joseph R. McCarthy and the Senate* (New York: Hayden, 1987), p. xix.
C. Rovere, *Senator Joe McCarthy,* p. 6.

D. Ibid., p. 11.

begun as early as 1938 with the creation of the House Committee on Un-American Activities, it was not until after World War II that such investigations began to gather momentum. The rise of McCarthy intensified this process and gave it renewed prominence in American politics. He used these committees as his bully pulpits for investigating the government and leveling accusations of communist infiltration in America.

McCarthy was a **master of publicity and use of the media** to give him power over his senatorial colleagues and throughout American politics. "He would say anything that came into his head and worry later, if at all, about defending what he had said."[E] For four years, he was the master of what Rovere called the "Multiple Untruth." The accusations got bolder and wilder with time. He let scarcely a day pass without demanding the resignation of Dean Acheson or the impeachment of Harry Truman. He relied on a secret network of extremely conservative individuals and groups, in government and throughout society, especially his ally J. Edgar Hoover and the FBI (review essay 9.1) to feed him information for his accusations and investigations. In Rovere's words, McCarthy walked "with a heavy tread over large parts of the Constitution of the United States, and he cloaked his own gross figure in the sovereignty it asserts and the power it distributes. He usurped executive and judicial authority whenever the fancy struck him. It struck him often."[F]

McCarthy's popularity represented and intensified the **rise of conservatism** that was national in force. McCarthyism represented a diverse "coalition of the aggrieved," opposed to a variety of trends of the previous few decades: the growth of the left, including communism, liberalism, the New Deal, and the welfare state; American internationalism and Atlanticism; and Franklin Roosevelt and the Democratic party. "Into it came large numbers of regular Republicans who had coolly decided that there was no longer any respectable way of unhorsing the Democrats and that only McCarthy's wild and conscience-

less politics could do the job."[G] At his height, polls indicated that a majority of the American people had a "favorable opinion" of McCarthy and felt he was serving the country in useful ways. "It was a melancholy time," Rovere has observed, "and the Chief Justice of the United States was probably right when he said at the time that if the Bill of Rights was put to a vote, it would lose."[H]

Nothing was immune from attack by Joseph McCarthy. The United Nations, State Department, federal government, Truman administration, Democratic party, Eisenhower administration, academia, and more were all charged with being infested with communists and traitors who were selling the country down the river. The truth demanded congressional investigations, often led by McCarthy and his staff. "He was a great sophisticate in human relationships, as every demagogue must be. He knew a good deal about people's fears and anxieties, and he was a superb juggler of them. But he was himself numb to the sensations he produced in others. He could not comprehend true outrage, true indignation, true anything."[I]

In 1954, he finally went too far—he attacked and investigated the United States Army for being subversive. The investigation was initiated in order to prevent one of his staffers, David Schine, from being inducted into the army. However, it quickly ballooned out of control. McCarthy was not crushed; instead, it was as if Americans finally began to tire of his outrageous and unscrupulous behavior. This turn of events gave his Senate colleagues the courage to vote to **censure** him. His quick political decline led to more drinking, charges of personal corruption, and death within three years.

There was great irony in the rise and decline of Joseph McCarthy. He was a pragmatist and cynic, a great believer in the promotion of Joseph McCarthy, "a political speculator, a prospector who drilled Communism and saw it come up a gusher."[J] Nevertheless, Joseph McCarthy and McCarthyism made

---

E. Ibid., p. 46.
F. Ibid., p. 5.

G. Ibid., p. 21.
H. Ibid., p. 23.
I. Ibid., p. 60.
J. Ibid., p. 72.

their political mark on American history. According to Rovere, they "had enormous impact on American foreign policy at a time when that policy bore heavily on the course of world history, and American diplomacy might bear a different aspect today if McCarthy had never lived."[K]

K. Ibid., p. 5.

SOURCES: Daniel Bell, ed., *The Radical Right* (New York: Anchor, 1963); Eric F. Goldman, *The Crucial Decade—and After: America, 1945–1960* (New York: Vintage, 1960); Richard M. Fried, *Nightmare in Red: The McCarthy Era in Perspective* (New York: Oxford University Press, 1990); Robert Griffith, *The Politics of Fear: Joseph R. McCarthy and the Senate* (New York: Hayden, 1987); Godfrey Hodgson, *America in Our Time* (New York: Vintage, 1976); William Manchester, *The Glory and the Dream: A Narrative History of America, 1932–1972* (New York: Bantam, 1973); and Richard H. Rovere, *Senator Joe McCarthy* (New York: World Publishing, 1959).

Criticism of U.S. foreign policy tended to come from the political Right, even though that political challenge had been largely defeated. Challenges to the U.S. containment policy that might have issued from liberals and the Left were overwhelmed and silenced by the rise of McCarthyism, and this legacy of McCarthyism lived on during the 1950s and 1960s. Therefore, this period was the heyday of presidential power and the president's ability to exercise prerogative government in order to fight the cold war in the name of national security.

The president's foreign policies were rarely, if ever, seriously challenged during this time of congressional acquiescence. Congress rarely gave the president all that he wanted in important areas, such as defense and foreign assistance; but except for fine-tuning of presidential requests, the president usually proposed and Congress approved. During the cold war years, members of Congress acquiesced and supported the growing independence and preeminence of the executive branch and the president in the making of U.S. foreign policy. In fact, most members of Congress preferred to remain uninformed, such as when it came to various intelligence activities conducted in the name of national security. Thus, the demands of national security took precedence over all other concerns and Congress virtually abdicated its constitutional role in foreign policy. According to Frank Bax, "the chief function of Congress became the legitimizing of presidential decisions."[10]

David Halberstam explained the increasing acquiescence of the Congress in terms of "the fear of a democracy's vulnerability to a totalitarian aggressor, a belief that the speed of war had outstripped a democracy's capacity to debate it, an abiding guilt about what the Senate in a previous era had done to the League of Nations, a fear of taking on the President and looking soft on communism, and a belief that the President had genuine experts in foreign policy, that he had *all* the information. That, and a trust of the President as an extension of the nation."[11] Given this environment, the leadership promoted congressional acquiescence, such as in Halberstam's depiction of Sam Rayburn, Speaker of the House of Representatives during the latter fifties:

> He had, on most crucial issues, turned the House into an extension of the executive branch, making it an offering to the President. This was not a happenstance thing, it was very deliberate on his part. He talked often in great privacy about the limits of his own knowledge, the limits of the knowledge—indeed, the ignorance—of his colleagues. Their backgrounds were terribly narrow and he was appalled by the idea of getting involved in areas of national security.[12]

The cold war consensus and bipartisanship were so supportive of the president that, in many cases, foreign policy decisions were made without consulting Congress or getting its formal approval; at best, congressional leaders might be informed after the fact. As chapter 9 on intelligence states, a large foreign policy bureaucracy, permeated with a strong national security ethos, was in place by the late 1950s and responded to the president's bidding in fighting the cold war. Thus, the president no longer needed to work closely with members of Congress in the pursuit of foreign policy, especially with regard to the "high" policy of national security affairs. This unilateral tendency reached its height under Presidents Kennedy and Johnson.[13]

This background helps to account for **the increasing American commitment and involvement in the Vietnam War.** U.S. involvement began as a small assistance program to help the French maintain their colonial control of Indochina in order to prevent Vietnamese independence under Ho Chi Minh and Vietnamese communism. With the Korean War, the U.S. commitment escalated to the point that by 1954 (the year of the battle of Dien Bien Phu and the Geneva Accords, which forced the French out of Vietnam), the United States government was paying for 85 percent of the French war effort. Under President Eisenhower, the U.S. assumed primary responsibility for supporting and maintaining the independence of South Vietnam. This policy led to increases in the number of "advisers" to the point that 18,000 American troops were in Vietnam by the time President John Kennedy was assassinated.

The steady and increasing American commitment to South Vietnam was never seriously challenged within the executive branch or by members of Congress. American policymakers, in both the executive branch and Congress, were operating within the cold war consensus. South Vietnam was seen as an independent state threatened by communist aggression from North Vietnam. For U.S. cold warriors, this represented the expansionist designs of a communist monolith which the United States could not afford to appease anywhere in the world for fear that this would feed the appetite of the aggressor. Therefore, it was believed to be vital for the United States to contain the communist threat in South Vietnam in order to prevent other Southeast Asian countries from falling to communism in accordance with **the "domino theory."** The cold war consensus prevented questions from being asked by American policymakers about whether the United States should or should not commit itself to defend South Vietnam from communism—this commitment was automatically assumed to be in the national interest. Rather, the questions always revolved only around how much American involvement it would take to contain communist aggression and prevent the downfall of an ally.

The high-water mark of the president's power to govern foreign policy was reached under Lyndon Johnson. Under his presidency the fateful decisions to fully Americanize the Vietnam War were made. These vital decisions of war and peace were made with virtually no input from Congress. From the president's perspective, the years of presidential preeminence in foreign policy since the 1940s and the strength of the cold war consensus made congressional input appear unnecessary. Consider congressional action following the Gulf of Tonkin incidents in August 1964. Rather than seriously debating the pros and cons of the resolution submitted by President Johnson to gain support for his actions, members of Congress rushed **the Tonkin Gulf resolution** through—the vote was unanimous, 416–0, in the House of Representatives and 88–2 in the Senate. In effect, President Johnson was given what he considered to be a blank check for containing communism in Southeast Asia.

Ambiguity, 1966 to 1969. By 1966, members of Congress had become somewhat uneasy about U.S. foreign policy in Vietnam. More and more troops were pouring into Vietnam, but there still seemed to be no "light at the end of the tunnel." As a result, some members of Congress began to criticize the administration's overemphasis on the use of force in Vietnam; others became critical of the lack of restraint in the use of military force. Such criticism led to a **series of congressional investigations of American policy in Vietnam**, best symbolized by the hearings convened by the Senate Foreign Relations Committee under the chairmanship of J. William Fulbright.

Even with increasing congressional interest and concern expressed over the policy in Vietnam, nearly all members of Congress continued to support the president. By 1967, presidential decisions arrived at without any congressional input had resulted in over 550,000 American troops being committed to war in Vietnam. Yet Congress not only refused to oppose the war, but continued to appropriate the necessary funds. The popular argument in support of U.S. foreign policy in Vietnam no longer stressed only the need to contain the threat of communism. Now that a major commitment of American troops was involved, the policy proponents stressed that continuing the war was essential to maintain U.S. prestige and credibility throughout the world and to support "American boys" who were risking their lives for their country.

The late 1960s thus represented a time of increasing ambiguity in legislative-executive relations. Given the incredible amount of American human and material resources committed to the conflict, members of Congress became uncomfortable with the lack of progress in the war effort in Vietnam. More and more members of Congress felt that they should be consulted by the president on crucial questions of war and peace. In June 1969, a National Commitments Resolution was passed by the Senate by a 76 to 19 vote, which increasingly symbolized this congressional concern. Yet, most members of Congress continued to support the war effort in Vietnam. This increasing congressional ambiguity set the stage for the congressional reassertion in legislative-executive relations that has dominated the post–Vietnam War years.

CONGRESSIONAL REASSERTION IN THE POST–VIETNAM WAR ERA

. . . .

In the late 1960s, Congress began to reassert its constitutional authority in the making of U.S. foreign policy. The congressional role increasingly shifted from acquiescence to reassertion because the political environment abroad and at home was undergoing change. Congressional behavior often reflects the times for its members are among the most politically sensitive of elected officials. *The reassertion of congressional authority in foreign policy occurred for a number of complementary reasons, most of which had to do with the Vietnam War.*

First, the war was not going well. Over half a million American troops and $30 billion a year were not producing the light at the end of the tunnel that President Johnson and General Westmoreland were proclaiming. In fact, North Vietnam launched what became known as the **"Tet" Offensive** in early 1968. Although finally beaten back by the U.S. military, the North Vietnamese still successfully contested most of South Vietnam for a short time, including occupying major cities and even the American embassy in Saigon. Second, the lack of success in Vietnam, especially after the Tet Offensive, caused growing segments of the American public to question LBJ's handling of the war. Some Americans favored more escalation to win the war, but increasing numbers of Americans preferred withdrawal. This change was reinforced by a third factor: international pressures. U.S. policy in Vietnam was increasingly criticized by other countries, including the British, French and other American allies in Europe. U.S. policymakers and Americans were finding the world increasingly hostile towards its containment policy.

A fourth reason was that the **election of 1968** resulted in "divided government" in legislative-executive relations. The Republican candidate, Richard Nixon, defeated Hubert Humphrey, the Democratic candidate and Johnson's vice-president, in an election in which dispute over the Vietnam War played a large role. Democratic defeat gave the Republicans control of the presidency while the Democrats controlled the Congress. This event added a more partisan dimension to legislative-executive relations by escalating the influence of party politics. The impact of party politics was exacerbated by the fact that, unlike Eisenhower, Nixon was perceived as being extremely partisan throughout his political career. Finally, and of great importance, a **"secret plan" to end the war** advocated by Henry Kissinger, President Nixon's national security adviser, included not only withdrawing American troops but escalating the levels of military conflict to achieve "peace with honor" before the troops left. Military escalation served to intensify all of the factors discussed above and accelerated and intensified congressional reassertion.

With the growing conflict over Vietnam during the late 1960s and early 1970s, the cold war consensus that had existed throughout the U.S. government and American society came unglued. The cold war consensus had been the key to the rise of a large national security bureaucracy, to the enormous increases in presidential foreign policy power, to the cold war policies pursued by administrations from Truman to Johnson, and to congressional acquiescence in legislative-executive relations throughout the cold war years. With the consensus breaking apart over Vietnam, congressional acquiescence evolved increasingly into congressional reassertion.

Although Nixon and Kissinger were aware of this problem, they remained committed to many elements of previous cold war policies, particularly a belief in the utility of force. Thus, they **pursued a two-track policy in Vietnam**, withdrawing American troops while escalating the level of American military involvement in an attempt to force a negotiated solution on North and South Vietnam that would allow the U.S. to walk away from the conflict. This strategy, particularly the Vietnamization program involving withdrawal of American troops, found public support, but the military escalation triggered more domestic political opposition that was reflected in Congress. The secret bombing of Cambodia (which was leaked to the press), the 1970 invasion of Cambodia, the 1971 invasion of Laos, the 1972 mining of the harbor of Haiphong in North Vietnam, and the stepped-up bombing of North Vietnam all intensified growing antiwar sentiment throughout the country and in Congress.

A classic struggle between the legislative and the executive branches ensued. Members of Congress, increasingly reflecting the change in views as experienced by Senator J. William Fulbright discussed earlier (review essay 2.3), became more active in the making of U.S. foreign policy, demanding from the president and the executive branch more information, consultation, and participation in policymaking. In fact, by 1973 Congress cut off all funding of

direct American military involvement in the Vietnam War; and with the end of the war, congressional reassertion intensified. In 1973 the War Powers Act was passed over President Nixon's veto, shortly followed by the Budget and Impoundment Control Act of 1974—both symbolic of congressional reassertion.

President Nixon, however, resisted congressional reassertion every step of the way. He was still operating from cold war assumptions of presidential preeminence in legislative-executive relations. As Nixon and his supporters saw it, both congressional and societal oppositional forces were obstructing the president's constitutional authority to conduct foreign policy and the war in Vietnam. Given this view, it didn't take much for the president and his men to see the antiwar movement and other opposition forces, including the Democratic party, as the enemy and as subversive—not as American citizens who were exercising their constitutional rights. Given Nixon's presidential actions and the changing political environment, more and more people decided that an **imperial presidency** had arisen, and that President Nixon had stepped well beyond the boundaries of the Constitution. It was President Nixon's inability, as discussed in chapter 4, to adjust to changing times that led to the Constitutional crisis of Watergate and his forced resignation in 1974 (review essay 4.2).

The end of the Vietnam War and the Watergate affair released a flood of congressional involvement in foreign policy. Members of Congress not only demanded a greater role in the policymaking process, but became increasingly involved in the details of foreign policymaking in a wide variety of areas. Since 1974, all presidents have had to face a more powerful Congress and have had greater difficulty in governing foreign policy. In fact, every president has faced major foreign policy setbacks as a result of **congressional reassertion**. This factor has contributed to the general perception of "failed" presidents since the Johnson presidency: Nixon experienced Watergate; the Nixon-Ford détente policies toward the Soviet Union were thwarted by congressional concern about Jewish immigration from the

Soviet Union and a covert war in Angola; Carter could not get Senate approval of SALT II; and Reagan suffered from the Iran-Contra affairs.

The history of legislative-executive relations demonstrates that *the greater the congressional success in reasserting its constitutional authority, the more constrained are presidents in governing foreign policy.* Presidential preeminence in foreign policy, the norm during World War II and most of the cold war, has become the exception rather than the rule in the post–Vietnam War years. Changes in the post–Vietnam War political environment have resulted in the relative decline of presidential power in the making of foreign policy and this is reflected by greater congressional involvement.[14]

In sum, two major patterns have evolved in legislative-executive relations since World War II. Presidential preeminence and congressional acquiescence have prevailed during times of national emergency and war—that is, for the twenty-five-year period encompassing World War II and most of the cold war years. This has been followed by congressional reassertion during a period of peace—the post–Vietnam War years. Presidents like Nixon and Reagan, who have attempted to exercise power in foreign policy as if the cold war political environment still existed, have triggered constitutional crises. At the same time, presidents who do not attempt to exercise any prerogative government are likely to be highly constrained in their efforts to govern foreign policy. Clearly, then, the post–Vietnam War years represent a frustrating time to be president; yet, they are also an exciting period in legislative-executive relations that impact U.S. foreign policy.

CONTEMPORARY INSTITUTIONAL CHANGES

. . . .

How is it that Congress as an institution has been able to reassert its authority during the post–Vietnam War years? Very simply, Congress has changed as an institution. The contemporary House of Representatives and Senate are different legislative bodies from those in the past. Although bureaucracies tend to be resistant to change, Congress is a **relatively dynamic American political institution**. This is not to say that Congress easily undergoes change, but that Congress is more open to change than most bureaucratic institutions.

Historically, Congress has experienced long periods of continuity. On occasion, it has also experienced short periods of rapid change. This pattern exists because Congress is composed of a relatively small number of people, and its composition and interactions tend to be heavily affected by changes in the domestic political environment. The most obvious influence is that the 435 representatives and 100 senators are elected by the public. Very simply, the events of the 1960s and early 1970s involving the civil rights movement, Vietnam War, and Watergate affected the political environment in such a dramatic way that major institutional changes occurred in Congress.

Numerous congressional reforms and changes took place in three key areas during, and since, the 1970s:

1. Membership;
2. Institutional structure and process;
3. Support.

The trend has created a more diverse, representative, decentralized, open, informed, and independent body.[15] These changes have been instrumental in promoting and maintaining congressional reassertion in the making of U.S. foreign policy.

Membership. Congress experienced a major turnover in its membership during the 1970s. *Changes occurred in region, party, and ideology.* Throughout the cold war years of the 1950s and 1960s, both the House and Senate were dominated by southerners, members of the Democratic party, and political conservatives. This was because key positions within Congress were awarded on the basis of **"seniority"** and **southern Democrats** usually had the greatest seniority. Since the Civil War, the South was a one-party region dominated by the Democratic party. Consequently, incumbent representatives or senators from the South never faced serious Republican challengers and were rarely challenged within the Democratic party. Because this was not the case in other regions of the country, southern Democrats acquired a disproportionate amount of seniority and influence in Congress.

The situation changed during the early 1970s. By this time, many of the more powerful southern Democrats had gotten so old that they either died in office or retired. They were replaced by younger members of Congress who still tended to be Democrats, but were less conservative. This situation resulted in a **new Democratic leadership** that was much more liberal and much less southern. The rise of the new leadership was reinforced by the 1974 post–Vietnam War and post-Watergate congressional elections where Republicans faced major losses, resulting in a large influx of new liberal Democrats into Congress.[16]

The new Democratic leadership, in coalition with the new members of Congress, took a more activist congressional role in U.S. foreign policy. The new leaders and members were much more critical of cold war policies. The Senate, for instance, moved from a pro- to anti-involvement stance concerning the Vietnam War primarily because war supporters had been replaced by their opponents.[17] The liberal congressional leadership and membership were also critical of congressional passivity in foreign policy, which they felt had contributed to growth of the imperial presidency. Consequently, they promoted a number of structural and procedural changes affecting the way in which Congress conducted its business.

Another change in congressional membership occurred during the late 1970s and early 1980s. Beginning in 1978, Republicans and conservative members of Congress became more influential, reflecting the rise of conservatism in the domestic environment. The 1980 election was particularly important in this respect. Not only did it result in the election of Ronald Reagan as president, but Republicans picked up seats in the House and gained control of the Senate for the first time since 1954. **The 1994 election** reinforced and intensified this trend when the Republican party became the majority party within both houses of Congress for the first

time since 1932—producing a **new Republican leadership** represented by Newt Gingrich (chapter 15 will discuss the importance of electoral politics in greater depth). The overall result of these changes has been a more diverse, representative and politicized Congress that contained very active liberal and conservative members, and much greater party competitiveness between the Republicans and the Democrats for congressional control.

Congressional Structure and Process. Throughout the 1950s and 1960s, a small group of senior members of Congress, many of whom were southern Democrats, controlled the workings of Congress. Congress did most of its work within a **committee system**, where each committee had jurisdiction over certain policy issues and membership consisted of no more than two dozen members of the House or Senate from both parties (the ratio of Democratic to Republican committee members reflected the ratio of Democrats to Republicans in the entire chamber). The most influential members of Congress chaired the most important committees. Due to seniority, powerful committees were frequently dominated by older, more conservative members who tended to be southern Democrats.

A small group of **congressional "barons"** thus enjoyed the real power within Congress. Most of the old House and Senate leaders were staunch cold warriors and were part of the cold war consensus that had pervaded American government and society, which accounted for the bipartisanship that prevailed in foreign policy. Such a situation also helps to explain why no civil rights legislation was passed by Congress until after the landslide Democratic victory in 1964. This election infused Congress with new blood, which was reinforced by the backing of a very strong legislative president—Lyndon Johnson.

The change in congressional membership during the 1970s also produced changes in the distribution and exercise of power within Congress. The new Democratic liberal leadership *changed the congressional committee rules of the game.* Power was stripped from committees and, in particular, from committee chairs. Every committee was now required to have multiple subcommittees, subdividing

TABLE 12.1
HOUSE COMMITTEES WITH JURISDICTION IN FOREIGN POLICY,
105TH CONGRESS, 1997–98

COMMITTEE (SUBCOMMITTEE) RELEVANT SUBCOMMITTEES	MEMBERS (REPS/DEMS)
Agriculture (5)	27/23
Dept. Operations, Nutrition, & Foreign Agriculture	7/5
Appropriations (13)	34/26
Commerce, Justice, State, and Judiciary	6/3
Foreign Operations, Export Financing, & Related Programs	8/5
Military Construction	8/5
National Security	9/6
Banking and Financial Services (5)	31/26/1
Domestic and International Monetary Policy	14/10
Budget (0)	24/10
Commerce (5)	28/23
Energy and Power	15/12
Telecommunications, Trade, & Consumer Protection	15/12
Government Reform and Oversight (7)	24/19/1
National Security, International Affairs, & Criminal Justice	10/8
Intelligence, Permanent (2)	8/7
Human Intelligence, Analysis, & Counterintelligence	6/4
Technical and Tactical Intelligence	6/4
International Relations (5)	26/22
Africa	6/4
Asia and the Pacific	10/8
International Economic Policy, & Trade	10/8
International Operations & Human Rights	9/7
The Western Hemisphere	9/7
Judiciary (6)	20/15
Immigration and Claims	7/5
National Security (5)	31/26
Military Installations and Facilities	10/8
Military Personnel	9/7
Military Procurement	15/12
Military Readiness	12/10
Military Research and Development	15/12
Resources (5)	27/23
Energy and Mineral Resources	8/6
Science (4)	25/21
Energy and Environment	10/8
Space and Aeronautics	13/10
Small Business (4)	19/16
Tax, Finance, and Exports	6/5
Transportation and Infrastructure (6)	40/33
Aviation	18/14
Coast Guard and Maritime Transportation	4/3
Veterans Affairs (3)	17/13
Ways and Means (5)	23/16
Trade	9/6

SOURCE: U.S., Congress, House, *Committees Telephone Directory* (http://clerkweb.house.gov, Oct. 13, 1997).

both issues and committee membership. Also, sub-committee chairmanships were required to be awarded to different individuals, further dispersing the distribution of power. Thus, power has moved from committees and committee chairs to subcommittees and subcommittee chairs. The dynamics of each committee and subcommittee naturally is heavily dependent not only on its historical context, functions, structure, and subculture, but also the personalities and styles of its members, especially the chair (and to a lesser extent, the ranking minority member).

More committees (and subcommittees) also have gained jurisdiction over foreign policy issues. For example, new committees covering intelligence and the budget were created. Furthermore, where the Armed Services, Foreign Relations, and Intelligence committees of both chambers are actively involved in national security affairs, many other committees have become more active in foreign policy. This has been especially the case for other types of international issues, such as trade, finance, energy, transportation, communications, tourism, technology and space, immigration, and the environment—all of which have grown in importance in foreign policy. These changes have resulted in greater committee and congressional involvement in the making of U.S. foreign policy (see **tables 12.1 and 12.2** for a listing of relevant committees and subcommittees).

Congressional procedures were also changed. Throughout the cold war years, congressional barons generally exercised power behind the scenes. Thus, committee hearings and votes were often held behind closed doors. Congressional reforms during the 1970s resulted in a much more open and democratic process. Most formal committee activity is now open to the media and the public. Furthermore, changes have taken place in floor voting, which involves all members of Congress in each chamber. Voice votes (the option to vote as a group and thus remain unaccountable) have been mostly replaced by roll-call votes, in which each member must take an independent public stand on the issue.

The greater openness of congressional procedures does not mean that informal interaction and bargaining does not occur behind the scenes. It con-tinues to occur for it has always been an essential element of politics. In fact, committee hearings and activities concerning issues which members of the executive branch define as grave matters of national security, such as intelligence issues, continue to be closed to the public. Nevertheless, congressional procedures are more open today than in the past (as reflected in **C-Span television coverage** of House and Senate hearings and proceedings in the two chambers).

Decentralization of power and more public procedures also have affected *the norms governing congressional operations.* It could be argued that a strong congressional subculture existed under the centralized "old boy" leadership of the past. Structural and procedural changes have altered the norms of "specialization" and "apprenticeship" promoted by the old boy network, particularly in the Senate. Nevertheless, norms continue to prevail which affect congressional behavior, despite the increase in partisanship and politicization. These include the importance of "reciprocity," "public collegiality," and "constituent casework" for representatives and senators.[18]

Overall, these changes in structure, procedures and behavioral norms provided the foundation for members of Congress to become more active in the making of foreign policy. Although many analysts argue that these changes provide the possibility for a more informed public and greater democratic accountability, other observers also argue that they have had detrimental effects as well, such as reinforcing congressional preoccupation with reelection and political posturing.

Congressional Support. Throughout the cold war years, members of Congress tended to have very small support staffs, giving the executive branch a decisive advantage in foreign policymaking. The executive branch enjoyed a virtual monopoly of information on which Congress was totally dependent. It is commonly argued that this was reinforced by the fact that most members of Congress preferred to place their faith in the president and support his conduct of foreign policy. In either case, the lack of congressional support staff and information

TABLE 12.2
SENATE COMMITTEES WITH JURISDICTION IN FOREIGN POLICY,
105TH CONGRESS, 1997–98

COMMITTEE (SUBCOMMITTEES) RELEVANT SUBCOMMITTEES	MEMBERS (REPS/DEMS)
Agriculture, Nutrition, and Forestry (5)	10/8
Marketing, Inspection, and Product Promotion	4/3
Appropriations (13)	15/13
Commerce, Justice, State, and the Judiciary	6/6
Defense	9/8
Foreign Operations	7/7
Military Construction	5/4
Armed Services (6)	10/8
Acquisition and Technology	5/4
Airland Forces	7/6
Personnel	5/4
Readiness	5/4
Seapower	6/5
Banking, Housing, and Urban Affairs (5)	10/8
International Finance	5/4
Budget (0)	12/10
Commerce, Science, and Transportation (7)	11/9
Communications	9/8
Consumer Affairs, Foreign Commerce, & Terrorism	5/3
Manufacturing and Competitiveness	5/4
Oceans and Fisheries	4/3
Science, Technology, and Space	5/4
Energy and Natural Resources (4)	11/9
Environment and Public Works (4)	10/8
Finance (5)	11/9
International Trade	9/8
Foreign Relations (7)	10/8
African Affairs	4/3
East Asian and Pacific Affairs	6/5
European Affairs	6/4
International Economic Policy, Export & Trade Protection	5/8
International Operations	4/4
Near Eastern and South Asian Affairs	5/5
Western Hemisphere, Peace Corps, Narcotics, & Terrorism	4/4
Governmental Affairs (3)	9/7
International Security, Proliferation, & Federal Services	7/6
Immigration	4/3
Technology, Terrorism, & Governmental Information	4/3
Intelligence	10/9
Veterans Affairs	7/5

SOURCE: U.S., Congress, Senate, *Senate Committees* (http:/www.senate.gov, Oct. 13, 1997).

contributed to congressional acquiescence throughout the 1950s and 1960s.

An important source of power is **control of information**. Congressional reformers during the 1970s realized that this deficiency had to be addressed if Congress were seriously to reassert its authority in foreign policy. Consequently, *congressional staffs expanded tremendously during the post–Vietnam War years*. Individual representatives and senators began to enjoy the presence of large "personal staffs," consisting of up to a few dozen individuals. "**Committee staffs**" of both the majority and minority parties, such as for the Senate Committee on Foreign Relations, also expanded tremendously in size. With the increase in staffing, members of Congress were no longer as dependent on the executive branch for information about foreign policy and world affairs.

Congress also increased the size of its **support agencies** and began using them consistently.[19] The General Accounting Office, Congressional Research Service, Office of Technology Assessment, and Congressional Budget Office are nonpartisan research agencies intended to support the role of Congress. The **General Accounting Office (GAO)** is the investigative arm of Congress and the largest support agency, employing almost 20,000 people. The **Congressional Research Service (CRS)**, with almost 15,000 people, provides research and analyses on issues of importance to congressional committees and individual members of Congress. Created in 1972, the **Office of Technology Assessment (OTA)** is the smallest support agency and the source of specialized knowledge concerning technology questions (which was disbanded in the 1990s). Finally, the **Congressional Budget Office (CBO)**, which was created in 1974 to provide financial and budgetary information and assessments, gives Congress an alternative to reliance on the executive's Office of Management and Budget.

Clearly, members of Congress now have independent sources of information and are no longer as dependent on the executive branch. The personal, committee, and support agency staffs in Congress have expanded so quickly and have become so large

that we can now speak of the existence of a congressional bureaucracy that employs over 50,000 people. Although adding to more bureaucracy, staff increases have contributed to congressional reassertion in foreign policy. These changes in congressional membership, structure, procedural, and support systems have produced a more independent, active, and influential body in the making of U.S. foreign policy.

CONTEMPORARY LEGISLATIVE-EXECUTIVE RELATIONS

To what extent is Congress a force to be reckoned with in the making of contemporary U.S. foreign policy? There is no consensus answer to this question. *Three schools of thought have evolved concerning the contemporary legislative-executive foreign policy relationship.*[20] One school of thought still perceives **presidential dominance**—that the president remains the dominant actor. The fact that Congress has asserted greater authority in foreign policy is recognized; yet it is argued that congressional reassertion has constrained the president only minimally and that he has maintained his role as the major actor in foreign affairs.[21] A second school of thought believes that the contemporary legislative-executive relationship is one of "**codetermination**." The argument is that Congress has successfully asserted its authority and has become a formidable force in the realm of foreign affairs—an equal actor with the executive branch.[22] The third school of thought argues that the pendulum has swung in favor of Congress in foreign affairs—that **congressional dominance** now prevails. Proponents emphasize that congressional constraints on the president have become so great that his ability to formulate and implement the nation's foreign policy has diminished considerably.[23] Conservatives are most likely to criticize congressional initiatives, describing it as the rise of an "imperial Congress."[24]

All three schools of thought—presidential dominance, codetermination and congressional dominance—paint an overly simplistic picture of the complex politics of legislative-executive relations. *No simple answer or single relationship prevails today between the legislative and executive branches in the making of U.S. foreign policy. Rather, four important patterns exist, which suggest a much more complex reality in legislative-executive relations* during the post–Vietnam War era.

First, the "**type of issue**" affects legislative-executive relations. The more an issue involves questions of war and peace, the more likely it is that the president will continue to enjoy disproportionate influence in the making of policy for that issue. For example, Congress has attempted to reassert its authority over the war power, but has had only limited success. This is not to say that the president is as preeminent in the use of troops abroad as he was during the cold war years; the times have changed and the president faces more domestic constraints. However, he continues to exercise considerable power concerning the use of force abroad. On the other hand, the more an issue becomes divorced from the use of force, the more likely it is that Congress will play an active and influential role in the policymaking process. Thus, the type of issue on the political agenda is very important in determining the nature of legislative-executive relations.[25]

The second pattern to consider is that Congress tends to be a "**reactive**" body. The president usually takes most of the policy initiatives, and the executive branch actually implements foreign policy. When Congress becomes involved in foreign policy, it tends to be in reaction to presidential initiatives and policies pursued by the executive branch. There are times and issues when Congress takes the initiative, but they are rare. Congress is reactive in another way as well. Not only is congressional action usually in response to executive action, but *congressional involvement in policy tends to be of a focused, specialized, and legalistic nature.* The president tends to set the policy agenda and frame the issues which Congress addresses, while Congress is more competent in influencing the specific features of a policy.[26] Many scholars have long argued that Congress

should focus on large policy questions and guidelines while leaving the details of policy to the executive branch. However, for better or worse, Congress is best equipped for manipulating policy details (it should be noted that, in terms of background, most members of Congress are "lawyers" and from the law profession).

The third pattern to consider is that Congress is **the ultimate "political" body** within the U.S. government. Members of Congress are "political animals" who are preoccupied with their institutional status and power, their electoral security, and how they are perceived within and beyond the Washington beltway. They tend to be obsessed with reelection and are constantly soliciting funds from private contributors for reelection campaigns. A *preoccupation with reelection* also makes them overly sensitive to public perceptions, political support, political trends, and their public image.[27] If the public and their constituents are interested in an issue and have staked out a position, members of Congress tend to reflect the dominant public mood. If the public is uninterested, members of Congress have more freedom of action; yet, they are constantly pressured by the president, executive agencies, special interest groups, and congressional colleagues.

No matter how politically conscious members of Congress may be, they must attempt to present a public image which indicates that they are above politics and motivated only by constituent and national interests. This is reinforced by the fact that the president is also extremely image conscious and politically oriented. Therefore, the particular nature of executive-legislative relations is often difficult to anticipate and congressional behavior is influenced by political considerations, domestic political trends, and symbolic politics. The rise of **Newt Gingrich** as Speaker of the House in 1995 clearly demonstrates the role of politics and symbolism, ambition and power, and how quickly they can ebb and flow in the contemporary era (see **essay 12.2**).

Finally, **divided government** appears to have become endemic in American politics since the 1968 election. "Divided government" refers to a time when each branch of government and the presidency is "not" controlled by the same political party,

ESSAY 12.2
NEWT GINGRICH, AMBITION, AND THE RISE AND DECLINE OF POWER

As a result of the election of 1994, Newt Gingrich became the first "Republican" Speaker of the House of Representatives in over forty years. After four decades of Democratic rule and being in the political wilderness for so long, the Republican party finally had the opportunity to exercise major political influence—to implement "the Contract with America" and to govern. And for Newt, he had finally achieved what he had been striving for throughout much of his life. He was on top of the "political world" in January of 1995. But within two years, Newt Gingrich had fallen from political grace. He lost so much public support so quickly that he had become a political "pariah."

What happened to the so-called Republican revolution? As Garry Wills stated, "the villain in the piece was, as is usual in such cases, also the hero. Gingrich was undone by his own devices. He had the genius to invent the "congressional mandate," and the gullibility to believe in his own invention. A master of destructive techniques, he did not suspect that mere destruction destroys itself. "Much of this had to do with Gingrich's **personal ambition**, with his unrelenting **quest for power and glory** in the world of politics.

"Washington lies at the epicenter of power. All force collides here. In Washington resides the power to take money and spend money, the power to decide what people can do and what people cannot do, the power to make a nation strong or weak, the power to wage war or make peace." This is the political world of Washington, D.C. as described by journalist John Barry in *The Ambition and the Power*. It is not uncommon that individuals strive to be on top of such a world, although it is very difficult to achieve as well as to maintain.

As explained by Barry, "By rising he exposed himself, made himself a target, and exposed his weaknesses. Now those weaknesses would be explored, probed, stressed, tested, to see if they could withstand the pressure. Perhaps his biggest weakness was ambition itself, an ambition dangerously close

to hubris." In fact, "it was hubris, and the admixture of arrogance and innocence in him, to demand that others see the world his way," and to believe "that rules did not apply to him." Barry actually was describing the rise and fall of Jim Wright, the Democratic Speaker of the House during the eighties. Newt Gingrich was instrumental in bringing Wright down, leading to his eventual rise as Speaker of the House. But what Barry described about politics in Washington and about Jim Wright, also pertained to Newt Gingrich as well.

When Gingrich took the podium for the first time as Speaker of the House, Republicans chanted, "Newt. Newt. Newt." He had a forceful presence, constantly offering new ideas for the future of the country. With the landslide electoral victory producing a huge Republican triumph behind "the Contract with America," he was opposed to the president's and Democrats' agenda. He seemed to enjoy being confrontational. He encouraged partisan politics, while readily espousing his knowledge and thoughts. He loved the limelight and all the attention he was getting. For a while, he was so much in the spotlight that he declared himself more important then President Clinton.

But Gingrich's ambition and hubris—his exaggerated self-confidence to the point of arrogance—quickly got him into trouble and made him increasingly vulnerable, politically. He was offered and agreed to a $4.5 million advance to write *The Contract with America* while Speaker of the House—a similar situation that triggered the eventual fall of Jim Wright—thus creating a political controversy that eventually forced him to give up the advance. In fact, after serving as the driving force to get Jim Wright to resign as Speaker because of violation of ethics charges, Gingrich started to understand the proverb, "What goes around, comes around." A two-year investigation by a panel of two Republicans and two Democrats found that Gingrich used tax-exempt charitable contributions to fund a televised college course that was deemed as a "recruiting vehicle." Gingrich was fined $300,000, and in a move some characterized as unethical, accepted a loan from former presidential candidate Robert Dole with provisions more favorable than a bank loan. In addition, his confrontation with President Clinton peaked in the winter of 1996 in the fight over the budget, in which Gingrich and the Republicans forced the government to shut down for several days—a tactic that backfired with the public.

By this time, Gingrich's personality, leadership tactics, and behavior was increasingly self-destructive for him and for the Republicans. He was too much in the spotlight and "overexposed," turning off a lot of people. The public, as well as members of his own party, began to sour on Newt Gingrich. As stated by Gary Wills, Gingrich became "the most unpopular politician on the national scene. Even those who disliked Gingrich had, heretofore, credited him with political shrewdness. Now they were wondering about that." The Republican's ability to dominate the agenda and influence politics that the 1994 election provided was being lost.

Gingrich's public approval declined so dramatically that members of his own party actually tried to overthrow him as Speaker. Although reelected as Speaker of the House in 1997, nine Republicans voted against him and many other Republicans openly admitted that they voted for him only out of party loyalty (and because no better candidate was available). Within two years, Newt Gingrich had seen his ambition, power and glory run aground. His loss of political clout and public appeal made him a kind of "lame duck" Speaker.

Actually, the patterns of great victory and defeat have accompanied Gingrich throughout much of his political life. Gingrich has demonstrated little reluctance, and remorse, to do what is necessary to gain prominence and power until he pushes too hard and takes a fall. Once a member of the House without much influence, he fastened tightly when an opportunity came. He would come out hard and fast, relenting to no one—not even the president. Later after political blunders, he would vanish and disappear, only to return with a newly waxed halo. After regaining his confidence and with a new strategy, he would offer an "olive branch" to his enemies and those he bruised along the way, only to shortly turn around and engage in "**hard-ball politics**" once again. Such a pattern has served him well, but in the incredibly visible arena of national politics it may be more difficult for people to forget, and maybe to forgive. Unlike Ronald Reagan and even Bill Clinton, who are seen as more personable and likable, Newt Gingrich's image is much more one of arrogance.

The personal ambition, and quest for power and glory, is not unique to Newt Gingrich. It is very much a part of the world of politics and striving to get to the top. Naturally, much of what transpires depends on the man and the times. And ultimately, what John Barry said of Jim Wright clearly applies to Newt Gringrich as well: He "had a brief, shining moment in the sun. He was alone, soaring above his colleagues, above the Congress, above the White House, his will his wings. He soared above the moment. For a moment."

SOURCES: John M. Barry, *The Ambition and the Power* New York: Penguin, 19879); Adam Clymer, "G.O.P Narrowly Reelects Gingrich as House Speaker, Despite Ethics Accusations," *New York Times* (January 8, 1977): 1; Lloyd Etheredge, "Hardball Politics: A Model," *Political Psychology* (Spring 1979): 3–26; Newt Gingrich, *To Renew America* (New York: HarperCollins, 1995);

Joan Didion, "The Teachings of Speaker Gingrich," *New York Review of Books* (August 10, 1995): 10–13; Garry Wills, "What Happened to the Revolution," *New York Review of Books* (June 6, 1996): 11–16; Hanna Rosin, "Newest Newt," *The New Republic* (December 16, 1996): 12–16; Howard Fineman, "Gingrich Goes on the Dole," *Newsweek* (April 28, 1997): 38–39.

increasing the likelihood for interbranch disagreement and conflict. Such divided government has grown over time: from 1901 to 1944, divided government prevailed for only 14 percent of the time (for six years); from 1945 to 1968, it prevailed for 33 percent of the time (for eight years); and from 1969 to 1998, divided government has increased dramatically to 80 percent of the time—for twenty-four years of the past thirty years (see **table 12.3** on party control of the presidency and Congress in the twentieth century). As James Sundquist recognized over a decade ago, "the country passed from a long era of

TABLE 12.3

PARTY CONTROL OF THE PRESIDENCY AND CONGRESS IN THE TWENTIETH CENTURY

				SENATE			HOUSE		
CONGRESS	YEARS	PRESIDENT	PARTY	D	R	OTHER	D	R	OTHER
57th	1901–03	McKinley	R	29	56	3	153	198	5
		T. Roosevelt	R						
58th	1903–05	T. Roosevelt	R	32	58	—	178	207	—
59th	1905–07	T. Roosevelt	R	32	58	—	136	250	—
60th	1907–09	T. Roosevelt	R	29	61	—	164	222	—
61st	1909–11	Taft	R	32	59	—	172	219	—
62d	1911–13	Taft	R	42	49	—	228‡	162	1
63d	1913–15	Wilson	D	51	44	1	290	127	18
64th	1915–17	Wilson	D	56	39	1	230	193	8
65th	1917–19	Wilson	D	53	42	1	200	216	9
66th	1919–21	Wilson	D	48	49‡	1	191	237‡	7
67th	1921–23	Harding	R	37	59	—	132	300	1
68th	1923–25	Coolidge	R	43	51	2	207	225	3
69th	1925–27	Coolidge	R	40	54	1	183	247	5
70th	1927–29	Coolidge	R	47	48	1	195	237	3
71st	1929–31	Hoover	R	39	56	1	163	267	1
72d	1931–33	Hoover	R	47	48	1	220‡	218	1
73d	1933–35	F. Roosevelt	D	59	36	1	313	117	5
74th	1935–37	F. Roosevelt	D	69	25	2	322	103	10
75th	1937–39	F. Roosevelt	D	75	17	4	333	89	13
76th	1939–41	F. Roosevelt	D	69	23	4	262	169	4
77th	1941–43	F. Roosevelt	D	66	28	2	267	162	6
78th	1943–45	F. Roosevelt	D	57	38	1	222	209	4
79th	1945–47	Truman	D	57	38	1	243	190	2
80th	1947–49	Truman	D	45	51‡	—	188	246‡	1
81st	1949–51	Truman	D	54	42	—	263	171	1
82d	1951–53	Truman	D	48	47	1	234	199	2
83d	1953–55	Eisenhower	R	47	48	1	213	221	1
84th	1955–57	Eisenhower	R	48‡	47	1	232‡	203	—
85th	1957–59	Eisenhower	R	49‡	47	—	234‡	201	—
86th	1959–61	Eisenhower	R	64‡	34	—	283‡	154	—
87th	1961–63	Kennedy	D	64	36	—	263	174	—
88th	1963–65	Kennedy	D	67	33	—	258	176	—
		Johnson	D						
89th	1965–67	Johnson	D	68	32	—	295	140	—
90th	1967–69	Johnson	D	64	36	—	248	187	—
91st	1969–71	Nixon	R	58‡	42	—	243‡	192	—
92d	1971–73	Nixon	R	55‡	45	—	255‡	180	—
93d	1973–75	Nixon	R	57‡	43	—	243‡	192	—
		Ford	R						
94th	1975–77	Ford	R	61‡	38	—	291‡	144	—
95th	1977–79	Carter	D	62	38	—	292	143	—
96th	1979–81	Carter	D	59	41	—	277	158	—
97th	1981–83	Reagan	R	47	53	—	243‡	192	—
98th	1983–85	Reagan	R	46	54	—	269‡	166	—
99th	1985–87	Reagan	R	47	53	—	253‡	182	—
100th	1987–89	Reagan	R	55‡	45	—	258‡	177	—
101st	1989–91	Bush	R	55‡	45	—	260‡	175	—
102d	1991–93	Bush	R	56‡	44	—	267‡	167	1
103d	1993–95	Clinton	D	57	43	—	258	176	1
104th	1995–97	Clinton	D	46	54‡	—	202	232‡	1
105th	1997–99	Clinton	D	45	55‡	—	206	228‡	1

‡Chamber controlled by party other than that of the president.

D=Democrat   R=Republican

party government, when either the Republican or the Democratic Party controlled both the presidency and the Congress almost all of the time, to an era when the government was divided between the parties most of the time."[28]

The existence of divided government is consequential because members of the "opposition" party of the president can exercise greater control within Congress, as a result of their majority status. This gives the opposition party the ability to dominate *the organization of Congress:* in "leadership positions" (such as Speaker of the House and Senate Majority Leader), as "chairs" of committees and subcommittees, and with "majority representation" on each and every committee and subcommittee (review tables 12.1 and 12.2 for the distribution of Republican and Democratic members). Hence, President Bill Clinton, a Democrat, must deal with a Congress which organizationally is dominated by Republicans. Clearly, this has reinforced and intensified congressional reassertion within interbranch relations. And unlike the fifties and sixties, which were times of bipartisanship and a cold war consensus—minimizing the impact of divided government in the making of foreign policy—divided government since Vietnam is much more prone to promote conflict with the collapse of bipartisanship and the anticommunist consensus.[29]

In sum, the president tended to be predominant in the making of U.S. foreign policy during the cold war years. However, there is no simple trend in legislative-executive relations during the post–Vietnam War years. Political scientist Bruce Jentleson found *during the Reagan years that " 'Pennsylvania Avenue diplomatic relations' on major issues of U.S. international diplomacy were characterized by four distinct patterns."*[30] First, on a number of regional issues— Nicaragua, South Africa, arms sales to Saudi Arabia and other Arab states—there was outright "confrontation." Second, there was generalized "institutional competition" over much of the day-to-day conduct of diplomacy, such as foreign assistance. Third, on military aid to El Salvador and the leadership crisis in the Philippines, "constructive compromise" was eventually worked out. Finally, for a number of issues, such as the use of force in Afghanistan and the Persian Gulf (to reflag Kuwaiti tankers), and relations with the Soviet Union and the People's Republic of China—especially late in the administration—"bipartisan cooperation" prevailed. Therefore, U.S. foreign policy is increasingly a function of diverse patterns in the complex politics of legislative-executive interaction.

To better understand congressional influence and legislative-executive relations in U.S. foreign policy, we will examine four general areas:

1. The war power;
2. Advice and consent;
3. The power of the purse and to make laws;
4. The power of oversight and investigation.

These are not mutually exclusive categories. The Iran-Contra affairs, for example, involved Congress in all areas, with the exception of advice and consent. A brief examination of each of these areas should help to clarify questions concerning congressional influence and the president's ability to govern foreign policy.

THE WAR POWER

The use of American armed forces abroad has been the factor most responsible for the growth of presidential power and the straining of relations between Congress and the president. Only Congress has the constitutional authority to declare war. As Louis Henkin has summarized the constitutional foundation of the power to make war in his *Foreign Affairs and the Constitution,* "There is no evidence that the framers contemplated any significant independent role—or authority—for the President as the Commander in chief when there was no war."[31] Yet Congress has declared war just five times in American history while presidents have committed military forces abroad in over two hundred instances. Therefore, as discussed above on the history of legislative-executive relations, the president's power over questions of war and peace has grown remarkably over time, particularly during times of conflict.[32]

Presidential power in the use of force reached its peak during World War II and continued during the cold war years. For example, President Truman committed American troops to the Korean Peninsula in 1950 to defend against the North Korean invasion. Yet, **the Korean War** was never officially declared by Congress. It was a presidential war; American involvement was initiated, formulated, approved, and implemented within the executive branch. Congress stayed in the background, remaining acquiescent and providing support. Throughout the cold war, the president directed American forces in a very similar vein, intervening overtly and covertly around the globe.

Only after the bitter experience with the Vietnam War did Congress attempt to redress the imbalance. With the collapse of the cold war consensus, President Nixon's escalatory actions in Vietnam resulted in numerous antiwar proposals in Congress. Members were at first unable to obtain enough support to pass the resolutions. However, in the spring of 1973, they finally cut off all funding for direct American military intervention in Indochina, foreshadowing a major congressional attempt to regain control of its lost war power.

Members of Congress had become frustrated with their ineffectual influence on American military involvement in Indochina and on the scope of U.S. foreign military commitments abroad throughout the cold war years. Consequently, members of Congress overrode a veto by President Nixon and enacted a bill designed to limit the president's power to commit American armed forces abroad without congressional approval. The purpose of **the War Powers Act** was "to fulfill the intent of the framers of the Constitution of the United States and insure that the collective judgment of both the Congress and the President will apply to the introduction of United States Armed Forces" into conflict situations abroad.[33]

The War Powers Act (WPA) attempted to redress the historical growth of presidential war-making power in three ways, by requiring "presidential consultation" before troops are committed abroad; "presidential reporting" after troops are committed; and "congressional action" if American troops abroad become involved in a "situation of hostilities." In the latter situation, three outcomes were envisioned as possible: by doing nothing Congress would force the president to withdraw the troops after ninety days; Congress could terminate the military intervention before ninety days; or it could extend the ninety-day deadline. (See **essay 12.3** for a more specific discussion of the requirements of the War Powers Act.) The WPA represented a major symbolic effort at congressional reassertion and complicates the president's ability to use force abroad, yet it has not fundamentally altered the president's preeminent position over the war power.[34]

How effective has the War Powers Act been in restoring joint legislative-executive possession of the war power? It appears that early pronouncements proclaiming a major redistribution of power in legislative-executive relations were exaggerated. Since 1973, there have been over twenty cases in which the president has used U.S. armed forces abroad in situations involving the War Powers Act. These have included numerous military efforts to evacuate Americans abroad, the Mayaguez incident in Indochina, the Iran hostage rescue attempt, the placement of peace-keeping forces in Lebanon, military encounters with Libya, the reflagging of Kuwaiti tankers in the Persian Gulf, the invasions of Grenada and Panama, the deployment of over 500,000 American troops to the Persian Gulf who eventually engaged in war, the use of military troops in Somalia, Haiti, and Bosnia. In each case, the president initiated, formulated, and approved the use of military troops without congressional participation. The congressional role remained limited even after the commitment of troops, with Lebanon being the major exception and representing the height of congressional involvement under the War Powers Act. Thus, the record suggests that the War Powers Act has had little impact on presidential preeminence over policy formulation and only limited influence on policy implementation involving the actual use of force abroad.

In reality, the War Powers Act has given the president great leeway to initiate, formulate, and approve the use of American armed force overseas. This is because the act does not actually require prior presidential consultation; rather it requires

ESSAY 12.3
REQUIREMENTS OF THE WAR POWERS ACT

The first requirement of the War Powers Act (WPA) is **presidential consultation**. During the cold war years, the president usually circumvented Congress entirely and informed members only after the decision to use force had been made. According to the War Powers Act, "the President in every possible instance shall consult with Congress before introducing United States Armed Forces" into situations of conflict abroad and "after such introduction shall consult regularly with the Congress until" they have been removed from such situations.[A] Congress intended that the president consult with them *before* a final decision was made.

The second requirement is **presidential reporting**. According to subsection 4(a) of the WPA, the president shall submit a report to Congress within forty-eight hours if, in the absence of a declaration of war, U.S. armed forces are introduced abroad *under the following three situations:*

1. "into hostilities or into situations where imminent involvement in hostilities is clearly indicated by the circumstances;"
2. "into the territory, airspace or waters of a foreign nation, while equipped for combat, except for deployments which relate solely to supply, replacement, repair, or training of such forces;"
3. "in numbers which substantially enlarge United States Armed Forces equipped for combat already located in a foreign nation."[B]

A report is required to describe the circumstances, the president's constitutional and legislative authority, and the estimated scope and duration of involvement. If U.S. armed forces remain in a situation of hostilities in accordance with subsection 4(a)(1), the president must continue to report to Congress at least every six months. The reporting requirement was intended to force the president to keep Congress informed *after* the decision to use troops abroad was taken.

The final requirement is **congressional action**. If U.S. armed forces are introduced into a situation of hostilities, as stipulated in subsection 4(a)(1), the president must terminate their involvement within sixty days unless Congress extends the deadline. The president actually can extend the deadline for an additional thirty days, if deemed necessary for the safe withdrawal of American troops. This gives the president a total of ninety days before he must terminate the military commitment.[C] In this situation, three options are available to Congress. Congress may pass a "concurrent resolution" to terminate the military intervention earlier; this requires a simple majority in both chambers and is not subject to presidential veto. Second, Congress may pass a "joint resolution," signed by the president, to extend the deadline. Finally, Congress may do nothing, allowing the time limitation to take effect. Provisions for the time limitation and congressional involvement under subsection 4(a)(1) of the War Powers Act were the ultimate manifestation of congressional reassertion involving the war power.

A. U.S., Congress, House, Committee on International Relations, *The War Powers Resolution: Relevant Documents, Correspondence, Reports,* Committee Print (94th Cong., 2nd sess., 1975), p. 1.
B. Ibid.

C. Actually, the president potentially has two additional days of leeway because the sixty-day period does not commence until the report is "submitted or required to be submitted." Therefore, this allows the president up to ninety-two days before the commitment must be terminated or before Congress must approve the activity.

SOURCE: U.S., Congress, House, Committee on International Relations, *The War Powers Resolution: Relevant Documents, Correspondence, Reports,* Committee Print (94th Cong., 2nd sess., 1975).

only that it should occur "in every possible instance." Not surprisingly, the president has never consulted Congress before arriving at a decision. In a few instances, a president has talked to members of Congress, informally and privately, about the use of force. However, the norm has been to avoid official consultation and for the president to inform members of Congress only after a decision (or the actual introduction of troops) has taken place.

At the same time, the War Powers Act does give Congress the potential to influence the president's decision to use troops abroad through the reporting requirement and its ability to terminate, modify, or approve military action if U.S. troops are committed. In this respect, the president must be cautious in deciding when, where, and how U.S. troops are to be committed. However, in situations since 1973 where American troops have been committed abroad, especially for short periods of time, the congressional tendency has been to give the president a free hand.

Three factors account for presidential freedom when military action is taken. First is the role of politics. The typical response to hostilities by most members of Congress and the public is to "rally around the flag" in support of the president. This was the case when American force was used in places like Grenada, Libya, Panama, and Somalia. Political support during the Persian Gulf crisis, as with Haiti and Bosnia was more complex: rally around the flag occurred with the initial deployment of American troops to the Persian Gulf following the Iraq invasion of Kuwait in August; by November domestic support dwindled and became divided; and the public once again rallied behind the flag with President Bush's decision to go to war in January 1991. This rally-around-the-flag pattern is unlikely to change in the future. Therefore, it appears doubtful that Congress would be willing to thwart such a major presidential initiative in its early phases—time is needed to demonstrate whether the military intervention is unsuccessful and counterproductive—bringing into play countervailing political forces critical of the president's policy.

Second, the lack of congressional will, reinforced by ambiguity in the language of the War Powers Act, has allowed the president to minimize the reporting requirements and avoid triggering congressional action. In many instances, the president has failed to submit any report at all, ignoring the War Powers Act altogether. In those cases when the president has submitted a report to Congress, he has avoided acknowledging that U.S. armed forces are involved in "a situation of hostilities," which would trigger the time limitation and congressional action (according to subsection 4(a)(1)).[35] For example, the so-called "peacekeeping" military forces in Haiti and Bosnia (like the "humanitarian" forces in Somalia) are not officially considered to be involved in "a situation of hostilities." This political strategy has been successful because most members of Congress are reluctant to force the president's hand and since Vietnam the hostilities have tended to be short in duration.

The final reason the War Powers Act has had minimal impact on the president's use of force can be found in the **role of the judiciary**. In 1983, the Supreme Court ruled in *Immigration and Naturalization Service v. Chadha* that the "congressional veto," involving an immigration case, was unconstitutional because it violated the separation of powers. Although this was not a direct ruling on the congressional veto in the War Powers Act, the Supreme Court ruling, nevertheless, means that it may be unconstitutional for Congress to pass a concurrent resolution without the president's signature, preventing Congress from forcing the president to terminate the use of force abroad before the ninety-day deadline allowed in the War Powers Act.[36]

The War Powers Act has its greatest potential significance for congressional involvement when a president commits American troops abroad into a situation of hostilities for an extended period of time when the time limitation and the direct participation of Congress come into play. This has only occurred with Lebanon in 1983, the Persian Gulf in 1990, and the Somalia intervention in the early 1990s (and potentially in Bosnia under President Clinton). Yet, where Lebanon represented a partial victory for Congress and the War Powers Act, the WPA played virtually no role whatsoever during the

Persian Gulf crisis and war, as well as in Somalia and in the Bosnian conflict.

The first major test of the role of congressional action within the confines of the War Powers Act occurred when President Reagan deployed 1,500 American troops in Beirut from September 1982 to March 1984 to promote stability in **Lebanon**. When President Reagan sent U.S. troops (along with British, French, and Italian troops) to Beirut, "he reported to Congress in accordance with the WPA. However, he also stated that there is no intention or expectation that U.S. Armed Forces will become involved in hostilities," thereby circumventing the time limitation and the further participation of Congress.[37] As the conflict in Beirut escalated and American troops were fired upon, a major debate ensued between members of Congress and the president over what constituted a "situation of hostilities." The debate intensified and appeared to be leading toward a constitutional crisis over the war power. But a legislative-executive compromise was negotiated in which Congress agreed to activate subsection 4(a)(1) indicating a situation of hostilities by the passage of a joint resolution that the president would acknowledge by signing; in return the president received congressional support to use military troops in Lebanon for up to eighteen months.

The Lebanese case appeared to be the first real victory for Congress in reasserting its authority and participation in the policymaking process through the use of the WPA. However, the situation is more ambiguous than it appears because the statement that accompanied the presidential signing of the congressional resolution did not acknowledge the legitimacy of the War Powers Act. The statement first discussed a number of disagreements with Congress's findings involving application of the War Powers Act to Lebanon. President Reagan then proclaimed that "In signing this resolution . . . I do not and cannot cede any of the authority vested in me under the Constitution as President and as Commander in Chief of United States armed forces. Nor should my signing be viewed as any acknowledgment that the President's constitutional authority can be impermissibly infringed by statutes."[38] What happened was that the president made an expedient political agreement with Congress over the use of troops in Lebanon, yet continued to deny the legitimacy of the War Powers Act. President Reagan, nevertheless, was forced to bring the troops home after 256 soldiers died in their barracks in a bomb explosion, triggering a political outcry of growing political domestic and congressional dissent.

From the president's perspective, it is unwise to acknowledge either the existence of a situation of hostilities or even the legitimacy of the WPA for it will limit his freedom of action and legitimize the constitutionality of the War Powers Act. At the same time, presidents are hesitant to ignore the War Powers Act altogether for frustration among members of Congress might grow to the point where they become even more obstructionist in foreign policy. Congress might pass new amendments to the War Powers Act, strengthening its legislative role. It is important to keep in mind that politics is extremely consequential in influencing the nature of the legislative-executive relationship and, in this case, the significance of the War Powers Act.

Unlike Lebanon, the War Powers Act played virtually no role during **the Persian Gulf crisis**, even though over 500,000 American troops were committed to the region over a period of months and participated in war. President Bush did report the troop commitment in accordance with the War Powers Act and Congress did become actively involved in the policymaking process, eventually authorizing presidential use of force. But congressional involvement came late in the crisis and, rather than relying on the War Powers Act, turned to its power of investigation and legislation as the source of its activity and authorization. Hence, the president's commitment of over half a million troops abroad and Congress's eventual endorsement of the president's brinksmanship strategy leading to war has weakened the legitimacy and strength of the War Powers Act as a tool of congressional involvement in the making of U.S. foreign policy.[39]

In **Somalia**, like Lebanon and the Persian Gulf crisis, Presidents Bush and Clinton attempted to downplay and circumvent the War Powers Act, that is until it became a prominent and controversial item on the national agenda after American troops were shot at and killed as the civil war intensified—forcing Clinton to bring the troops back home sooner then intended. The signing of the Dayton Accords among the relevant parties has allowed President Clinton to send over 20,000 American troops to **Bosnia** as part of a multilateral "peacekeeping" force while minimizing the role of the War Powers Act. As long as the mission appears to be succeeding and the conflict situation on the ground in Bosnia remains relatively calm, presidential policy will likely prevail. However, should the Bosnian conflict escalate and intensify, with American troops taking fire and casualties, the situation is likely to become politicized and Congress, possibly through the War Powers Act, will likely take a more active and critical role.

The War Powers Act also has limited teeth to constrain the president's ability to use force due to *what is not mentioned in the act*. The WPA applies only to the use of U.S. "armed forces" in a "situation of hostilities" or "in the territory of a foreign nation, while equipped for combat." These cases do not include the use of U.S. military troops as "advisers" abroad in noncombatant situations, "reconnaissance missions" over foreign territory involving military personnel if they are not equipped for combat, or U.S. "military training maneuvers" intended for political purposes. Most importantly, the War Powers Act does not apply to Americans engaged in "covert paramilitary action," for they are not officially U.S. armed forces. All of these activities were regularly used as part of the Reagan administration's Central American foreign policy to support the government of El Salvador and overthrow the government of Nicaragua.

In sum, the War Powers Act has given Congress the potential to play a more active role in the use of force abroad. However, members of Congress have been extremely cautious in challenging presidential initiatives in so vital a matter. The War Powers Act has been of major symbolic importance in promoting congressional reassertion in foreign policy and has served as a model for other legislation. The War Powers Act is indicative of a more reassertive Congress and a transformed political environment since Vietnam. While the president continues to be stronger than Congress with respect to the war power, he is nonetheless much more constrained and must be much more cautious today than in the cold war years.

In fact, even though Congress has been unable to exert great influence through the War Powers Act, it has constrained the president's ability to use military force by other means: the power of legislation and investigations. As Presidents Nixon and Reagan learned, even without a strong War Powers Act, presidents are open to political challenge for abusing their power, especially their power to make war abroad. In this respect, one should recall that while President Bush was successful in pursuing a brinksmanship strategy in the Persian Gulf crisis and leading the country to war against Iraq, it was preceded by a very close and divided vote in the Congress.

ADVICE AND CONSENT

The Senate has the constitutional authority to advise and consent to presidential appointments and treaties. These are two areas in which senators possess power in foreign policy matters that members of the House of Representatives do not share, helping to account for the **greater Senate prestige and power** within the Congress. Since World War II, however, members of the Senate have tended to be hesitant to exercise this power and challenge presidential foreign policy initiatives.[40]

With regard to **presidential appointments**, the nature of legislative-executive relations has not changed substantially in the post–Vietnam War period. *Three patterns have prevailed.* First, the Senate has tended to "rubber stamp" ambassadorships and presidential appointments to the executive branch. The Senate—particularly the Committee on Foreign Relations—holds hearings to examine the nominee's qualifications and views before deciding whether to approve the appointment. Appointments are considered first in committee, then by the entire Senate. These usually have been brief affairs, with the Senate merely going through the motions of providing advice and consent.

A second pattern has evolved into one in which some appointments result in political and partisan struggles. It is not unusual for at least one major presidential appointment to draw a great deal of attention and political controversy during a president's term of office. For example, President Jimmy Carter's initial appointment as director of central intelligence was Theodore Sorenson. A White House aide and speechwriter for President Kennedy, Sorenson was heavily criticized by the political right and conservative members of Congress. When Sorenson was unable to gain majority support in the Committee on Foreign Relations, President Carter withdrew the nomination. President Bush suffered a similar fate when his nomination of John Tower as secretary of defense was denied by a Senate vote. The nomination of Robert Gates as director of central intelligence by Presidents Reagan and Bush also encountered obstacles over Iran-Contra.

Congressional impact can occur at different, and sometimes less visible, levels. Republican Senator **Jesse Helms**, for example, of North Carolina has been particularly active in the appointment process. As a member of the Committee on Foreign Relations, he has held up and criticized many appointments made by Presidents Reagan and Bush, especially to the State Department, for holding insufficiently conservative views. With the 1994 Republican electoral triumph in Congress, Helms, who became chair of the Foreign Relations Committee, has become much more powerful and obstructionist, often successfully resisting President Clinton's appointments.[41]

The third pattern involves the Senate's reluctance to provide advice and consent for a growing number of prominent positions within the White House and the Executive Office of the President. Individuals within these positions have been treated as the president's "personal staff" and not as "officers." Such important positions as the national security adviser, national economic adviser, and director of the Office of Management and Budget have not required Senate approval. This reinforces the historical trend toward presidential autonomy in appointing personnel, with occasional appointments becoming controversial.

With regard to the Senate's **treaty power**, the president continues to possess the dominant voice.

A large number of overseas commitments have been made by the United States since the end of World War II through the use of international agreements. In fact, the United States government became party to over 7,000 agreements with other states between 1946 and 1974. Of these agreements, approximately 6 percent were formal "treaties" requiring Senate confirmation, while 87 percent were pursuant to congressional legislation. Roughly 7 percent were so-called **executive agreements** consummated by the executive branch without congressional involvement. Together, these international agreements involved a wide range of cultural, technical, economic, diplomatic, and military issues. Most importantly, if an agreement entailed a significant military commitment, it was likely to take the form of an executive agreement.[42]

As with the war power, the treaty powers of Congress had become dormant during the cold war years. The growth of executive agreements alarmed many members of Congress. They felt that agreements often represented significant policy decisions that were being made without congressional consultation. In response, *Congress has tried four techniques in attempting to restore its advice and consent role in the agreement-making process.*[43] First, Congress has passed laws forcing the president to provide it with basic information when agreements are signed. Such legislation was considered a prerequisite for strengthening the congressional advice and consent role. Second, members of Congress have tried to force the president to submit executive agreements to the Senate as treaties. While, for example, the Senate forced President Nixon to submit the agreement to return Okinawa to Japan to the Senate as a treaty, this strategy has met with little overall success. Third, Congress has used the power of the purse in some cases, withholding funds necessary to implement executive agreements. This is a way for members of the House to become involved in the treaty power, as they did over the implementation of the Panama Canal treaties. Finally, Congress has tried to subject executive agreements to veto or approval, with limited success and the likelihood that such requirements may be unconstitutional.

Congress has made an effort to redress imbalances in the making of executive agreements, but its overall effect has been minimal. Nevertheless, these efforts are symbolic of increased congressional efforts to reassert its authority in the post–Vietnam War environment. The president must be sensitive to congressional concerns in negotiating executive agreements for he wants to avoid creating political controversies that might precipitate greater efforts by Congress to strengthen its role. This political caution is reinforced by the fact that international agreements in the form of treaties are subject to formal ratification by the Senate, with a two-thirds vote required for approval.

The Senate's role has been much more pronounced when it involves **formal treaties**. Part of the reason is that treaties require more then a simple majority, which is not easy to acquire. This was clearly evident in the ratification process over the **Panama Canal Treaties**. Senate skepticism and involvement, for example, were significant in extending the long-drawn-out negotiation process that began during the early 1960s. In order to gain approval for the final treaties in 1978 that would return the canal to Panamanian control at the end of the century (or as opponents put it, "to give up our canal"), President Carter was forced to accept two controversial amendments that emphasized American security concerns to protect the canal. Treaty passage was so controversial that it contributed to the weakening of president Carter's ability to gain future political support on "the Hill"—somewhat reminiscent of Woodrow Wilson's defeats to get Senate approval for the Treaty of Versailles following World War I, which included American involvement in the League of Nations. Another way Senate opposition can be exercised is simply by keeping treaties from ever coming to the floor for a final vote, which has been done repeatedly with international human rights covenants.[44]

Throughout the 1970s and 1980s, the **Strategic Arms Limitation Talks (SALT)** negotiations were the most prominent example of congressional participation and influence in the treaty-making process. The congressional debate over the Anti-Ballistic Missile System (ABM), for example, was consequential in reducing the size of the program, which contributed to the success of SALT I under President Nixon and its approval by Congress. Congress also played a crucial role in the treaty-making process for SALT II. Initially, members of the Senate were influential in getting the executive branch to push for U.S. and Soviet strategic forces that were "essentially equivalent." Even with this guidance, the climate of opinion on SALT II following the Soviet invasion of Afghanistan in 1979 became so conservative and negative that President Carter withdrew the treaty from Senate consideration for fear of defeat in the final vote. This was a major political defeat for Carter, although American presidents continued to abide by the SALT II treaty subsequently (with the possible exception of President Reagan's Strategic Defense Initiative).[45]

The Senate has been very active in the area of foreign economics and trade policy, often through its treaty powers. The trilateral countries—the industrialized democracies in North America, Europe, and Asia (and increasingly over time other countries of the world) have gone through periodic negotiations since the creation of the original Bretton Woods system during World War II in an effort to arrive at common "rules of the game" for engaging in economic transactions as the world has changed and gotten more complex, especially involving trade. The most recent "Uruguay round" of negotiations that began in the late seventies resulted in an international treaty that produced a more international liberal trading regime and the creation of the World Trade Organization (WTO) to replace the GATT (review chapter 2). Another set of negotiations between Canada, Mexico, and the United States since the eighties produced **the North American Free Trade Agreement (NAFTA)**.

In both cases, the Senate agreed to provide the executive branch and the president with what is referred to as a **"fast track" authority** to negotiate such international economic agreements. Realizing that foreign economics inevitably is about domestic economics and, hence, would result in the Congress and the Senate micro-managing the negotiations and endlessly amending the final negotiated treaties (as it commonly does with domestic legislation), fast track legislation is a pragmatic effort to give the president a certain amount of freedom and leeway to negotiate for the United States, while giving the Senate the final choice to vote the "entire" final treaty package "up" or "down."[46] Despite being very controversial—raising concerns and passions about free trade and economic growth, the future of American jobs, labor and working conditions, environmental consequences—the WTO and NAFTA were ultimately passed by Congress under President Clinton.

President Clinton, like presidents before him, has been attempting to get congressional support for additional fast track legislation for future international economic and trade agreements. Congress, for its part, will continue to reflect a diversity of interests—free trade, fair trade, strategic trade, and protectionism—and will remain heavily involved, in one way or another, in the making of U.S. foreign trade policy.[47]

In sum, the Senate tends to approve most presidential appointments with little difficulty, although some are controversial and can become a political liability for presidents. Also, while Congress lacks influence in the making of executive agreements, the Senate must approve all treaties. Therefore, even though the president is preeminent much of the time, there are plenty of times when Congress does play an influential advice and consent role. This is indicative of a Congress that has become more active and involved in reasserting its role in foreign policy. And given the paradox of presidential power which has developed since Vietnam, it does not take many political controversies and failures to weaken the president's ability to govern, even in foreign policy.

THE POWER OF THE PURSE AND TO MAKE LAWS

Although Congress has only been somewhat successful in increasing either its war power and its advice and consent role relative to the president, it is still a force to be reckoned with, especially given its control of the purse and its ability to make laws. This has always been the greatest strength of the legislative branch, guaranteeing it a role in the policy-making process for most foreign policy issues. The tendency has been for the president and executive branch to develop legislation and submit it to Congress, which then approves, modifies, or rejects it. In this respect, Congress reacts to the president's political agenda. Yet, the legislative process requires Congress to ultimately decide on the final laws and the appropriation of money. Congressional attempts to control policy by this means have intensified since the Vietnam War.[48]

Consider the example of congressional **involvement in foreign assistance**. As discussed in essay 10.1 the U.S. government provides roughly $15 billion annually of foreign assistance to countries around the world, the two largest recipients being Israel and Egypt. Since the beginning of the foreign assistance program following World War II, congressional involvement and influence has always been considerable. As described by political scientist Barbara Hinckley in 1975, "its general policy has been less aid, for less time, tied to more restraints, and more loans and fewer grants, with loans repayable in American dollars."[49] Congress's influence over foreign assistance has become even more pervasive during the last two decades.

Congressional involvement in foreign assistance policy has often been used by members of Congress to influence U.S. foreign policy generally. For example, despite congressional failure to regain its claimed constitutional authority through the War Powers Act or the treaty-making process, Congress has been able to use its influence over foreign assistance to make occasional inroads over the war power. The first major effort along these lines involved the Vietnam War, in which Congress ended all U.S. military assistance to South Vietnam and Cambodia in February 1975, thereby accelerating the ending of the war in April of that year.

Congress also has taken two other major actions intended to deter the president's ability to exercise war abroad. The first major effort occurred in **the Angolan civil war**. In the mid-1970s, President Ford and Secretary of State Henry Kissinger were attempting to establish a new, stable relationship with the Soviet Union through a policy of détente. Détente involved efforts to entice the Soviet Union to accept the global status quo by providing it with status, trade, and technology, while at the same time containing Soviet expansionism through the threat of force. To American policymakers, the Soviet Union acted in an expansionist manner when it intervened in a civil war in Angola in 1975 following the abrupt departure of the Portuguese colonial presence. This Soviet action was seen as a threat to Kissinger's detonate strategy. In response, the Ford administration increased its CIA-funneled covert military assistance to two pro-Western groups in Angola. The Soviet Union countered by increasing its support to a third Angolan group. However, American involvement soon became public. With fresh memories of the Vietnam War and CIA covert operations in mind, Congress refused an executive request for additional funding and barred all U.S. assistance for any activities directly or indirectly involving Angola.[50] This marked a major triumph for congressional foreign policy action, for it thwarted an important presidential foreign policy initiative involving the use of force.

The other major policy action by Congress involved U.S. **foreign policy toward Central America**. Congressional action in this area was intended to affect the Reagan administration's efforts to conduct a covert war and overthrow the Nicaraguan government. It was through foreign assistance laws that Congress influenced Central American policy. During the early 1980s, Congress approved considerably less foreign assistance for El Salvador and the Nicaraguan contras than the administration requested. Eventually, **the Boland amendments** were passed in 1984 and 1985 cutting off all American "direct and indirect" assistance to the contras during 1985 and 1986. President Reagan responded by circumventing congressional action and covertly supporting the contras.[51] When the public discovered this and the arms for hostages exchanges, the Iran-Contra affair broke. The Iran-Contra scandal constituted a major political crisis for President Reagan and the U.S. government because it involved constitutional questions concerning legislative versus executive authority to make foreign policy and war.

At times, Congress has taken the initiative through its power of the purse in setting the public agenda and steering foreign policy. For example, U.S. government concern with **human rights** is commonly attributed to the initiative taken by President Jimmy Carter, who was a major advocate of international human rights. However, U.S. support for human rights actually was initiated within Congress following Watergate, manifested primarily through U.S. foreign assistance policy. Foreign assistance legislation was amended to prohibit security and developmental assistance to any country engaging in a consistent pattern of gross violations of internationally recognized human rights. These restrictions played an important role in influencing U.S. foreign policy in Central America and contributed to passage of the Boland amendments. Likewise, Congress's threatened passage of the anti-apartheid bill over President Reagan's veto forced him to issue an executive order imposing sanctions on South Africa.

The same patterns that have evolved with congressional involvement in foreign assistance also operate in other areas of foreign policy, such as national defense, trade, energy, immigration, and environmental policy. First, members of Congress have taken a renewed interest in foreign policy issues during the post–Vietnam War period. Second, while the president usually initiates policy and proposes legislation, the Congress shapes it. Sometimes, major presidential initiatives are rejected outright; more often they are modified or fine-tuned by Congress. Third, Congress occasionally takes the initiative or replaces a presidential initiative with one of its own. Fourth, the more an issue involves "low" policy—that is, an issue divorced from national security affairs or the use of force—the greater the congressional attention, involvement, and influence. Where the legacy of presidential power over "high" national security policy during the cold war years remains strong, congressional activity in so-called "low" foreign policy issues is reinforced by the fact that they resemble domestic policy issues for members of Congress—which is why they have been referred to as "**intermestic issues**".[52] Congressional constituents, such as the public and interest groups, are often interested in issues such as trade, energy, immigration, and the environment because of the direct impact of these areas on their lives.

The Legislative Process and Congressional Politics.
How is it that members of Congress are able to exert the power of the purse and make laws that affect U.S. foreign policy? Very simply, through the legislative process and the nature of congressional politics. **The legislative process** is extremely complex and can be quite confusing. Although most Americans have been schooled on "how a bill becomes a law," this grossly simplifies the complexity and the politics of the legislative process. It is so complex that not even people who work on "the hill" or study Congress can comprehend all the intricacies involved in the passage of legislation. Yet, it is the complexity of the overall legislative process that allows individual members of Congress to play a vital role in the making of public policy. (See **essay 12.4** for a discussion of the complex reality of the legislative process.)

The legislative process is not only an incredibly complex process, it is also a very "political" process. Given the diffusion of power throughout Congress, congressional politics revolve around bargaining, **coalition-building**, and compromise. Majority coalitions need to be constructed and maintained for every stage of the process if a bill is to survive and become law. Coalitions are formed through policy agreement, ideological affinity, personal relationships, persuasion, bargaining, "horse-trading," coercion, or any tactic that is necessary, depending upon the perceived importance of the issue. Ultimately, compromise is the key to legislative success, for a majority of representatives and senators must reach an agreement in an institution where power is quite decentralized. The political nature of the process is not unique to Congress, for as we saw in chapter 11 executive branch policymaking is also very political—this is the essence of politics, as we discussed in the very first chapter.

Congressional politics involves members who are motivated for different private and public reasons. As discussed above, members of Congress are "political animals" who are preoccupied with their institutional status and power as well as their electoral security, fundraising, and winning reelection. Senators and representatives also tend to be quite sensitive to the way in which power is exercised within Congress (and the beltway) and how their activities are perceived in public. Furthermore, it not only involves representatives and senators interacting, but also includes efforts by the president, members of different executive departments and agencies as well as social movements and interest groups (or special interests) to influence the legislative process. Thus, alliances and coalitions are made between representatives and senators within Congress and by members of Congress with other individuals and groups throughout the executive branch and society. At the same time, given the importance of their constituents and the public, members of Congress are preoccupied with how their actions will "play in Peoria" and affect their reelection efforts. Much of the time this political process takes place with little public visibility, although sometimes it occurs under the media spotlight. Such is the nature of politics.[53]

It is the intricacies and complexity of the legislative process and congressional politics that allows Congress as an institution to wield power in the making of U.S. foreign policy. Presidents have commonly complained that they have to deal with 535 politicized people who act as if they are all secretaries of state. Regardless of whether one is satisfied with the legislative process and the nature of congressional politics, these are the ingredients that constrain presidential power and affect legislative-executive relations.

THE POWER OF OVERSIGHT AND INVESTIGATIONS

Congress also has the power to oversee and investigate public policy matters. This includes Congress's constitutional right to ensure that the president "take Care that the Laws be faithfully executed." **Congressional oversight** to ensure that the president and executive branch implement policies in accordance with the letter and intent of legislation can act as a powerful restraint on presidential power and the foreign policy bureaucracy. This right represents, in fact, the ultimate means by which Congress may exercise its constitutional role. Because of

ESSAY 12.4
THE COMPLEX REALITY OF THE LEGISLATIVE PROCESS

Most Americans are schooled from an early age on how a bill becomes a law. After a bill is introduced in the House or the Senate, it is then introduced in the other house. It goes to the relevant committee with jurisdiction within each chamber; each committee holds hearings, amends, and votes on the bill. If the legislation survives the committees, it goes to the floor of the House and Senate for debate, more amendments, and a vote. After the floor vote, the legislation goes to a joint conference committee of senators and representatives to resolve the differences between the separate bills. Once the differences are ironed out, the bills go back to each chamber for a final vote, and then on to the president's desk for his signature or veto. A two-thirds vote in both the House and Senate is required to override a veto. This does provide a crude overview, but it does not communicate the complexity of the legislative process that really accounts for the way Congress is able to exercise power through its ability to make laws and control the purse.

Once introduced in Congress, legislation is "farmed out" to committees. **Committee jurisdiction** is rarely clear-cut, and it is common that two or more committees within each chamber will consider the same legislation (in some cases, each committee involved will consider the entire bill or, in other cases, only a part of the bill). For example, the 1988 trade bill was considered by ten committees in the Senate and twelve committees in the House (which explains the need for fast-track presidential authority). Committee hearings, "mark-up" sessions, and voting on the bill do take place; yet, before this occurs the bill usually is divided into parts and sent to subcommittees for hearings and mark-up. The entire package is then reassembled and considered by the full committee. For instance, the annual foreign assistance bill is always considered by the **Senate Committee on Foreign Relations**, although it is initially submitted to seven subcommittees for consideration: International Economic Policy; Arms Control, Oceans, International Operations and Environment; African Affairs; European Affairs; East Asian and Pacific Affairs; Near Eastern and South Asian Affairs; and Western Hemispheric Affairs.

If a bill gains majority approval within committee, it is passed on to the full House or Senate for consideration. The House of Representatives (the larger body) has strict **procedures** for considering a bill, while the Senate operates in much less rigid fashion. For example, the House Rules Committee determines when the bill will be considered and under what conditions. In the Senate, on the other hand, bills automatically proceed to the floor. However, they can be "filibustered"; that is, a senator can take the floor and hold all other Senate bills hostage in an effort to have the targeted bill withdrawn from Senate consideration. A filibuster can only be overcome by a "cloture" vote of sixty senators. Another indication of the different operating styles of the two chambers is that in the House only "germane" amendments can be attached to bills. In contrast, any amendments can be attached to a Senate bill with a majority vote.

Given the complex process and "hoops and ladders" that a bill must go through before final passage, one should be able to better understand why only a small percentage of the few thousand bills introduced are ever passed. Moreover, those few dozen bills that are successful in becoming law look quite different from their initial form by the end of the process. In other words, it is easy to introduce legislation, but difficult to pass laws. This is due to the numerous stages in the process in both chambers of Congress where the legislation can be amended or killed. This accounts for the fact that presidents are easily frustrated by Congress and must exercise strong leadership skills if they are to govern.

The legislative process is actually much more complex than portrayed above. Laws that require the expenditure of money by the government necessitate that a money bill also be passed. In effect, many governmental policies require two legislative processes in which bills become law: **an authorization process and an appropriation process**. In other words, separate bills must be passed that "authorize" a governmental program and "appropriate" money for its implementation. This is in accordance with the constitutional provision in Article I that "No Money shall be drawn from the Treasury, but in Consequence of Appropriations made by Law." Only the appropriations committees within the House and Senate appropriate money; all other congressional committees are authorization committees. This explains why the "appropriations committees" are considered the most powerful committees in each chamber.

For example, the Senate Committee on Foreign Relations and the House Committee on Foreign Affairs authorize the president to provide foreign assistance to certain countries, stipulating certain "ceiling" amounts of money that can be spent in each country. However, they do not appropriate these funds. The president must also submit an appropriations bill to Congress. This separate legislation is considered by the two committees on appropriations and must proceed through another entire legislative process before the money is actually provided to the authorized program. Therefore, opponents of foreign assistance can derail presidential requests either in the authorization or appropriations process. The president, on the other hand, must be successful in both processes. Congress recently passed a law giving the President the **line item veto**—that is, the ability to veto particular spending items within an appropriations bill, in addition to vetoing the entire bill (although its constitutionality is likely to be tested). To further complicate things, the authorization and appropriations processes tend to occur almost simultaneously for the same issue, and Congress typically considers dozens of issues each year. While this may not be the most efficient way to conduct business, this is how Congress operates.

An additional factor complicates and confuses the legislative process even more. The U.S. government budget operates under a **fiscal year** that begins on October 1 and ends the last day of September. In other words, the 1999 fiscal year budget starts in October of 1998 and ends in September of 1999. This means that Congress has only nine months from convening in January 1998 to pass the "thirteen" appropriations bills that fund the government's entire budget for the next fiscal year. Congress rarely passes all thirteen appropriations bills by October and, thus, must pass a "continuing resolution" allowing the government to expend funds and continue operating (usually at the previous year's funding level).

To place congressional appropriations in perspective, those bills are only one part and one year of a three-part and three-year **budgetary process** for the entire government. The executive branch prepares the 1999 budget during 1997 and the president submits it to Congress at the beginning of 1998. The budget then proceeds through the legislative process as thirteen appropriations bills throughout the year, and is eventually spent by the government in 1999. Another way to look at it is that in 1998 the executive branch prepares the budget for the year 2000, fights for the 1999 budget before Congress, and spends the 1998 budget already approved by Congress. This is truly an immense undertaking; not only is it a three-year, overlapping process, but the U.S. government's annual budget is more than one and one-half trillion dollars. Although Congress only plays one part in the overall budgetary process, it is a very consequential part.[A]

It is easy to be confused by the intricacies of the legislative and budgetary process. As David Stockman, former Director of the Office of Management and Budget under President Reagan, once said, "None of us really understands what's going on."

A. Congress attempted to streamline its operations by passing the Budget and Impoundment Control Act in 1974, which added a budget committee in each chamber and the Congressional Budget Office. Congress is now better informed, strengthening its legislative involvement. However, it has also complicated things further by adding a toothless third layer—the budget resolution process—on top of the authorization and appropriation processes.

Yet, one does not need to comprehend all the specifics of the process, but only to identify the key patterns that prevail. In sum, Congress exerts considerable influence through its power to make laws and appropriate funds. This is done through an elaborate and complex political process involving the passage of legislation, authorization of specific programs, and appropriation of money for budgets operating in fiscal years.

SOURCES: Lewis A. Froman, Jr., *The Congressional Process: Strategies, Rules, and Procedures* (Boston: Little, Brown, 1967); Eric Redman, *The Dance of Legislation* (New York: Simon and Schuster, 1973); Hedrick Smith, *The Power Game: How Washington Works* (New York: Ballantine, 1988); David Stockman, *The Triumph of Politics: How the Reagan Revolution Failed* (New York: Harper & Row, 1986); and U.S., Congress, House of Representatives, *How Our Laws Are Made* (95th Cong., 1st sess., 1978).

the delicacy and uncertainty involved in legislative-executive confrontations where outcomes could have major political ramifications, Congress has been particularly reluctant to challenge the president by using its oversight power. For if sufficient abuse of power is determined by Congress, the president ultimately may be "removed from Office on Impeachment for, and Conviction of, Treason, Bribery, or other high Crimes and Misdemeanors."

Impeachment proceedings have only occurred twice in American history. However, the power to investigate and engage in oversight has been a potent tool that Congress has exercised. *Since World War II, the use of congressional oversight and investigations in an effort to influence U.S. foreign policy has gone through three phases, sometimes challenging and, at other times, legitimizing presidential power in U.S. foreign policy.*[54]

The first phase occurred during the late 1940s and early 1950s. Extremely conservative members of Congress became increasingly active in conducting congressional investigations to eradicate a supposed threat of communism in the United States. As discussed in essay 12.1, a number of congressional committees—such as the House Committee on Un-American Activities and the Senate Committee on Internal Security—were active in investigating communist influence in government, academia and education, the media, Hollywood, and other walks of American life. The frequency of separate *congressional investigations about the internal threat posed by communism and subversion* is nothing less than staggering: four investigations during the 79th Congress (1945–1947); twenty-two during the Republican 80th Congress (1947–1949); twenty-four during the 81st Congress (1949–1951); thirty-four during the 82nd Congress (1951–1953); and fifty-one, an all-time high, during the Republican 83rd Congress (1953–1955).[55] Although the gap was immense between the alleged communist threat at home and the small number of communists (usually ex-communists) that were found, the large number of well-publicized investigations led to the destruction and silencing of the American Left. Likewise, liberals, the Truman administration, and Democrats were challenged, placed on the political defensive and given notice that an anticommunist political assault could raise its head again in the future. The rise of McCarthyism, led by congressional investigations, pushed public opinion to the right and cemented the anticommunist consensus that drove U.S. foreign policy during the cold war years.

The second phase of congressional oversight came at the height of the cold war, when Congress became relatively inactive in overseeing the president and the executive branch. This was a time of cold war consensus and bipartisanship in the making of U.S. foreign policy. The norm was congressional acquiescence in legislative-executive relations. The general attitude toward oversight of the national security bureaucracy at the time was expressed by Senator Leverett Saltonstall, the ranking Republican on the Armed Services Committee: "It is not a question of reluctance on the part of the CIA officials to speak to us. Instead, it is a question of our reluctance, if you will, to seek information and knowledge on subjects which I personally, as a member of Congress and as a citizen, would rather not have."[56] The few congressional hearings and investigations that did occur during the height of the cold war in the area of foreign policy were brief, intended more to legitimize than to investigate presidential foreign policy.

The third investigative phase began at the height of the Vietnam War and continues to operate in the post-Vietnam years. Congressional reassertion began with the investigation of the Vietnam War by the Senate Foreign Relations Committee—**the Fulbright hearings**. They helped trigger other congressional hearings and investigations into the exercise of presidential power and U.S. foreign policy. This has led to congressional efforts to reassert foreign policymaking power, such as passage of the War Powers Act, and has been an important means of acquiring information from the executive branch. Heightened congressional involvement has resulted in a proliferation of executive branch activity on the Hill as depicted by Bruce Jentleson, "The number of times the Secretary of State and top officials must come to Capitol Hill to testify, the number of reports that have to be written, the number of negotiating sessions that have to be held, the amount of congressional staff time invested, the days of floor debate taken up—all these come out of a finite stock of time and energy."[57]

The ultimate manifestation of renewed congressional power came with **the Watergate hearings**—the congressional investigation of Nixon's presidential conduct. The issue arose over President Nixon's ability to engage in war at a time when the political environment that had legitimized and supported an imperial presidency was breaking down. What began as an effort by members of Congress to reassert their constitutional authority in foreign policy eventually turned into a political challenge against a sitting president who was perceived as abusing the powers of his office. In effect, President Nixon's effort to fight the Vietnam War abroad and at home in a post–cold war political environment produced a full-blown constitutional crisis (review essay 2.2 on Watergate). The Watergate investigation by Congress eventually produced three impeachment counts by the House Judiciary Committee and forced President Nixon's resignation. The reassertion of congressional powers in legislative-executive relations was established.

The Watergate episode reinforced congressional involvement in the making of U.S. foreign policy. Two detailed House and Senate investigations of the intelligence community and their role in U.S. foreign policy were undertaken by the Pike and Church committees in 1975. These investigations, more than any others, shocked most Americans about U.S. foreign policy. They revealed that the president and the executive branch were systematically involved in a variety of cloak-and-dagger operations, including foreign assassinations and blatant violations of American constitutional rights at home. As discussed in chapter 9, these investigations stimulated the **creation of intelligence oversight committees** within each chamber and triggered efforts at intelligence reform.

The mid-1970s, especially from 1973 to 1975, may have represented the height of congressional reassertion of its foreign policy power. Congressional investigations in this period involved getting the facts and achieving an understanding of what happened and why. However, they also represented "partisan and political" struggles between Democrats and Republicans, liberals and conservatives, members of the legislative and the executive, supporters of the president and his opponents. Different people within Congress, the executive branch, and beyond government were involved for different reasons; yet, they acted before the public spotlight as if they were above it all. Congressional reassertion and presidential resistance represented "hardball" politics of the highest order, for the stakes involved President Nixon's political future, the future of presidential power and legislative-executive relations in foreign policy, and, in some respects, the future direction of American politics.

This was also the case with **congressional involvement in the Iran-Contra affair**, which represented the second major legislative-executive struggle since Vietnam over foreign policy. The Reagan administration's efforts to covertly exchange arms for hostages with Iran and to fight a secret war to overthrow the Sandinista Nicaraguan government, in violation of the Boland amendments passed by Congress prohibiting all "direct and indirect" governmental assistance to the contras, triggered a political crisis for President Reagan when it eventually became public. When his initial denials failed to quash the story, President Reagan appointed a presidential commission, whose members were chosen by him, to investigate matters. **The Tower Commission**—consisting of John Tower, Brent Scowcroft, and Edmund Muskie—constituted another effort at political "damage control" as it was intended to buy time and soften criticism when the commission's report was released. Although the Tower Commission report concluded that the Iran-Contra affair reflected flawed, not illegal, policy and resulted due to poor management style in the White House, the political storm grew nonetheless, triggering the congressional investigations.

In accordance with intelligence community preferences, the initial congressional investigations were performed by the intelligence committees, which were not known for their aggressive oversight role.[58] Intelligence committee investigations were held behind closed doors, respecting presidential claims that secrecy was necessary to preserve national security—a continuing legacy of the cold war era. However, when knowledge of the diversion of Iran arms sales funds to support the contras became public, a joint House and Senate congressional investigation could no longer be avoided.

For many Americans, **the Iran-Contra hearings** by a joint congressional committee were interesting and entertaining. This was one of the few times that average citizens became actively interested in national politics, and figures like Oliver North became household names. While it was predominantly entertaining and of momentary interest for the public, Iran-Contra involved a major constitutional crisis and political struggle.[59]

Once again, it was primarily the result of a president's efforts to exercise extraordinary power in order to conduct a war abroad in the name of national security in a post–cold war environment. As former Assistant Secretary of State for Inter-American Affairs under President Reagan, Elliot Abrams, described the conflict between Congress and the executive over U.S. foreign policy: "We were at war, we and the Democrats in Congress, or so we

thought and they thought.... So when I was asked for information [on Central America] that might help them, might give them yet more ammunition, I tried to deny it to them. I tried to figure out how I could give them the least information possible (review essay 9.2 on the secret Contra war)."[60]

As with Watergate, the constitutional and political crisis that peaked during the Iran-Contra hearings involved a major partisan and political struggle that affected the future of a president, his party, and the nature of legislative-executive relations in foreign policy. President Reagan and most of his staff understood that they were fighting for their political lives, which accounts for their efforts to minimize the negative political consequences through damage control. Members of Congress were quite aware of the seriousness of the situation and many chose sides accordingly, with most Republicans supporting the president and the Tower Commission view. In contrast, most Democrats were in the opposition camp, although they operated very cautiously since they were challenging a sitting president who was immensely popular. All those involved in this epic struggle remained sensitive to the need to play to the media and, ultimately, the public.

Considerable amounts of damaging information surfaced during the congressional inquiry concerning presidential abuse of power, particularly the circumvention of Congress and the public in pursuit of the covert contra war in Nicaragua. *The Report of the Congressional Committee Investigating the Iran-Contra Affair* ultimately found that "The common ingredients of the Iran and Contra policies were secrecy, deception, and disdain for the law. A small group of senior officials believed that they alone knew what was right.[61] Within the Reagan administration, the demands of national security had prevailed over the demands of democracy. Yet, unlike Watergate, the Iran-Contra hearings did not result in impeachment proceedings and President Reagan managed to survive the political storm. Also unlike after Watergate and the CIA revelations, the congressional investigation treated Iran-Contra as an aberration that did not result in any major efforts to strengthen the congressional role or reform the covert aspects of U.S. foreign policy.[62]

According to Senators William Cohen and George Mitchell, the congressional committee wanted to avoid confronting the larger constitutional issues and the possibility of impeachment because of the difficulty of challenging such a popular sitting president and the fear of creating governmental paralysis in the making of foreign policy at a time when serious arms control negotiations with the Soviet Union were possible with the rise of Mikhail Gorbachev.[63] Therefore, according to Seymour Hersh in "The Iran-Contra Committees," the investigation was flawed from the beginning in a number of ways: in terms of the composition of the committee, the imposition of an unrealistic deadline for ending it, permitting the White House to review all internal documents for relevance before releasing them, not requesting other government sources of information, avoiding certain topics of investigation altogether, not calling forth relevant witnesses before private and public sessions, granting immunity prematurely to key witnesses, and finally by committee members being intimidated in response to the political environment surrounding the testimony of Oliver North and Admiral John Poindexter.[64]

Despite considerable weaknesses and limitations in the congressional investigation of Iran-Contra, the fact that the inquiry was held nonetheless is indicative of the reassertion of Congress in the post–Vietnam War era. Therefore, while President Reagan avoided "overshoot and collapse" (to use Richard Pious's term discussed in chapter 4), he did suffer considerable political "backlash" that damaged his professional reputation and public prestige. As a result, presidential power eroded and President Reagan became a lame duck near the end of his administration.

Both Watergate and Iran-Contra entailed foreign policy and constitutional struggles over the war power illustrating the contradiction between the demands of national security and the demands of democracy. This tension produced a political struggle between the legacy of the cold war—where the President was preeminent over war and peace—and the political changes that have occurred in the post–Vietnam War era, which were manifested by the reassertion of congressional power. Both crises resulted in the curtailment of presidential power by the power of congressional oversight and investigations.

Will other political and constitutional crises result from future legislative-executive conflicts over foreign policy? Certainly, an institutional structure remains in place that allows for such an occurrence. An immense and powerful national security bureaucracy continues to exist alongside a reassertive Congress. The contradictions between the demands of national security and the demands of democracy have not been resolved. Much will depend on each president, the nature of his administration and his foreign policy, for the catalyst in both crises has involved major presidential commitments in the use of force. It is likely that the collapse of the Soviet Union and of communism in Eastern Europe and promise of the cold war's end may diminish the appeal of anticommunism as a justification for American military intervention abroad, and may minimize the chances for a new legislative-executive crisis. On the other hand, the Persian Gulf War demonstrates that force remains a key instrument of presidential policy and Congress's role remains an uncertain one depending on the outcome of the conflict.

It is important to point out that the power of oversight and investigations allowed Congress to play an important role during the events preceding the Persian Gulf War. **Congressional involvement in the Persian Gulf crisis** went from initial passivity and support early on, to greater involvement and criticism as the crisis lengthened, and then rallied around the flag when the war began. On the one hand, congressional passivity and support demonstrates the president's ability to dominate foreign policy during times of crisis involving the use of force. On the other hand, the period of congressional activism and criticism also demonstrates that the president faces a much more uncertain and inhospitable environment in the post–Vietnam War era, even during a time of crisis involving the use of American troops abroad.

In response to Iraq's invasion of Kuwait on August 2, 1990, President Bush, after consulting with his closest advisers, decided to deploy over 100,000

American troops to defend Saudi Arabia from further Iraqi expansion. Although Congress remained uninvolved, these significant early decisions by the Bush administration were met with initial support by most members of Congress and the general population—the country rallied around the flag during a time of crisis. However, this supportive domestic environment changed once President Bush announced—following November congressional elections—that he was doubling American troop strength to over 400,000 and moving from a defensive military strategy reliant on economic sanctions to an offensive strategy to force Iraq to withdraw from Kuwait.

As the crisis became prolonged and the threat of a bloody war appeared on the horizon, members of Congress and people throughout American society became increasingly uncertain and critical as to whether Bush's resort to brinksmanship was the most sensible way to proceed. Relying on its power to investigate, Congress became active in the Persian Gulf crisis and increasingly critical of the president's policy to threaten the use of military force to get Iraq to withdraw without war. The **Senate Armed Services Committee held hearings under Chairman Sam Nunn**, one of the most respected members of Congress on questions of defense, in late November and December on the president's Gulf policy. Of the numerous individuals who testified, including former secretaries of defense, chairmen of the Joint Chiefs of Staff, and other prominent officials, most expressed opposition to the Bush administration's change in policy away from reliance on economic sanctions to military force. Congress, thus, was acting as a forum by which presidential use of military force was being challenged during a foreign policy crisis in a way not seen since World War II. With divisions growing in Congress and throughout the country, along with President Bush's issuance of a January 15 ultimatum for Iraq to withdraw, the House and Senate debated and voted. It was a historic debate, and the "final vote" authorizing presidential use of force against Iraq, reflecting a divided country on the eve of war, was very close: 52 to 47 in favor in the Senate; 250 to 183 in favor in the House of Representatives.

Once President Bush took the country to war with Iraq on January 16, 1991, the Congress and the country again rallied behind the flag. Uncertainty and questions remained in the minds of many Americans and members of Congress about the costs of the war. But as the air war proceeded with little loss of American lives, followed by a ground war that fully routed the Iraqi military, most doubts were forgotten. Thus, the quick and decisive military victory squelched the doubts and criticisms of the Bush administration's handling of foreign policy in the Gulf and strengthened the president's ability to dominate policymaking during crisis over the war power.

The rapidity with which the country and the Congress became divided over the Persian Gulf policy, nevertheless, indicates that presidents do not automatically dominate crises and war making as they once did during the cold war years. While the Fulbright hearings occurred in 1966 during the height of the Vietnam War "after" American troops had been fighting for some time, the Nunn hearings occurred "before" the war in the Persian Gulf began. Also, unlike the Tonkin Gulf resolution which was "unanimously" approved in 1964 with only two votes in opposition, the resolution authorizing presidential use of military force in the Persian Gulf in 1991 was a "divided" and close vote. Watergate, Iran-Contra, and the Persian Gulf War are testaments to the reassertion of congressional power and the greater uncertainty that presidents face since Vietnam in attempting to govern foreign policy.

President Clinton has experienced a number of congressional investigations during his term of office, although in a somewhat different fashion than what has been discussed above. Committee investigations in both the House and the Senate have been conducted into such matters as Whitewater, Clinton and Gore's 1996 presidential campaign and fundraising efforts, and the foreign policy impact of political contributions from the People's Republic of China to the Clinton-Gore campaign. Although most of the investigations have not been oriented on foreign policy per se, and regardless of the significance and the truth of these matters, they do impact the president's overall ability to govern and lead, including in the area of foreign policy. Like investigations of the past, as discussed above, they are heavily partisan as a result of "divided government"—led by Republican members of Congress after the 1994 elections to damage a sitting Democrat in the White House.

Despite the investigations and the demands for the attorney general to appoint special prosecutors to further investigate, President Clinton, and his administration, has attempted to defend himself and minimize the negative impact on his ability to govern. Vice President Al Gore also has been quite concerned about damage control because this is the first time that his "squeaky clean" image has been tainted as he keeps his eye on the presidential elections in the year 2000. Whatever the outcome, such is the nature of legislative-excecutive relations as the United States approaches the twenty-first century.

PROSPECTS

. . . .

Clearly, the post-Vietnam years have produced a legislative branch more attentive and active in the making of U.S. foreign policy. Although Congress has been unsuccessful in fundamentally restricting presidential power and fully reasserting its own foreign policy power, the president nonetheless faces considerably greater congressional constraints than during the cold war. From the president's perspective, Congress is basically an obstructionist institution that prevents the country from achieving a coherent foreign policy that efficiently responds to the demands of national security. From the perspective of many members of Congress—depending on who is the president and his party identification—Congress is fulfilling its constitutional duties and acting as a check on presidential abuse of power. The argument is that a U.S. foreign policy that appears a little messy and inconsistent reflects the nature of American democracy.[65]

Regardless of one's sympathies in the continuing debate over the demands of American national security and the demands of American democracy, this is the nature of legislative-executive relations in

the post–Vietnam War years. This raises two important questions. First, what are the possibilities for reform in legislative-executive relations? Second, how might the complex politics of legislative-executive relations evolve in the future?

Legislative-Executive Reform? The reassertion of congressional power within legislative-executive relations has led to calls for efforts to rationalize the process. The reforms tend to revolve around the need to promote a more cooperative and efficient working relationship between the legislative and the executive branches to overcome the divided government that appears to have become endemic in American politics. Some of the reforms emphasize the need to increase the presidential power and the president's ability to govern, such as recommendations to limit the president to a single six-year term and to synchronize the terms of national office so that elections would be held for representatives every four years and senators every eight years when presidential elections were held. Other reforms represent efforts to make members of Congress less responsive to special interests and more responsive to the general public, as reflected in the recent call for "term limits" for members of Congress.[66] Reformers believe that changes such as these will strengthen the president's governing coalitions and allow more freedom of action. However, these recommendations do have problems. Constitutional amendments must be passed before they can become law—not an easy task. More importantly, a single presidential term of office eliminates the presidential accountability inherent in maintaining a reelection posture, a major strike against democracy in the name of greater efficiency.[67] And term limits do not guarantee that individual members will be more responsive to most of their constituents and the so-called general welfare.

Most of the reforms that have been proposed represent efforts to "fine-tune" the workings of legislative-executive relations and address the "crisis of leadership" discussed in chapter 4. Strong leadership under a dynamic president can minimize the paradox of presidential power and get government to work more efficiently; yet, presidential leadership that strong is a rarity. For example, even the powerful popularity of President Reagan was insufficient to persuade Congress and the public to support Reagan's Central American policy. This produced a situation that the president had to either accept or ignore, both at great political cost. Consequently, many recommendations to reform legislative-executive relations have attempted to make it easier for the president to lead and govern foreign policy.[68]

Other reformers are more pessimistic about the stalemate in legislative-executive relations. They see the problem to be less a crisis of leadership—although leadership is important—and much more a "**crisis of governance**." They argue that the paradox of presidential power is so severe today that a president can no longer "form a government." This problem is most visible in the constant struggles and divisions in legislative-executive relations. This governmental gridlock represents larger patterns in society as well, such as weak political parties and strong interest groups. More pessimistic reformers advocate a radical restructuring of the Constitution, such as towards a more parliamentary system of government along the lines of the English system.[69] They argue that this centralizes power under a strong chief executive while simultaneously maintaining strong democratic accountability. Regardless of one's view of such proposals, the obvious problem with it is the unlikelihood that the American public will choose to abandon a presidential system for a parliamentary one after two hundred years.

The Future? Aside from possibilities of reform, many observers question the ability of Congress to maintain a prolonged influence over foreign policy. They argue that Congress has excessive constraints that hamper its role as an effective and significant policy force. They point to the cyclical nature of legislative-executive foreign policy relations throughout American history. On these grounds, congressional reassertion is said to have peaked—a temporary phenomenon to be overwhelmed by the stronger pattern of presidential and executive dominance.[70] The reassertion of congressional authority that has accompanied the post–Vietnam War years, however, is unlikely to disappear in the foreseeable future.

Three principal elements support the continuation of an active, although sporadic, congressional role in the foreign policymaking process. First, Congress has experienced institutional changes that were instrumental in allowing congressional reassertion in foreign policy. These changes are not temporary, but have been institutionalized in a more bureaucratic environment. Furthermore, major membership turnover—which has the potential to alter Congress as an institution—is difficult to achieve in a short period of time given the high reelection rates of incumbents and the large number of "safe seats."

Second, changes in the domestic environment since the cold war years have prompted and reinforced congressional activism in foreign affairs. The cold war consensus that fueled bipartisanship and the imperial presidency has collapsed, replaced by competing policy perspectives and greater diversity in domestic politics, which constrains presidential power while strengthening Congress's role in foreign policy. The importance of the domestic political setting in examining the role of the president, the foreign policy bureaucracy, and legislative-executive relations in the making of U.S. foreign policy will be examined in part III.

Finally, changes in the international environment have affected the foreign policy agenda in ways that should ensure congressional involvement. The international system has become more complex in comparison to the simple worldview that prevailed during the 1950s, when most Americans saw the world divided between two superpowers and opposing forces. A more complex international environment has provided the setting for America's failure in Vietnam and the shattering of the cold war consensus in domestic politics. Furthermore, it has elevated what were once considered "low" policy issues, such as international economics, to the top of the contemporary foreign policy agenda—intermestic issues that members of Congress traditionally influence. This has been reinforced by the demise of the Soviet empire and the changes taking place in Eastern Europe.

Although institutional changes in Congress, changes in the domestic environment, and changes in the international environment and foreign policy agenda combine to ensure a prominent role for Congress in the future conduct of U.S. foreign policy, *a strong presidential role in foreign policy also will continue for the following reasons.* First, Congress has great difficulty coordinating its efforts, and this frequently makes its involvement ineffective and counterproductive for U.S. foreign policy. Until Congress improves its collective leadership, which is unlikely, it will remain an institution that largely reacts to presidential initiatives. Second, congressional involvement in foreign policy has been reinforced by the existence of relatively weak presidents. Nixon became consumed with Watergate, Ford was a passive president, and Carter's naiveté quickly led to the alienation of Congress. Bush and Clinton have not been particularly strong and successful post–cold war presidents. Nevertheless, the powers of the president remain formidable and can be revived under strong leadership, as Ronald Reagan demonstrated. Third, times of crisis tend to be moments of presidential dominance. The country tends to turn to the president during national emergencies, especially if they involve the use of American troops abroad as was the case with the Persian Gulf War. Finally, the growing complexity and demands of international politics upon American society and the governmental system will continue to require a strong presidency. The end of the cold war may result in the decline of the size of the national security bureaucracy and the use of military force abroad, but U.S. involvement and leadership in world affairs will, for better or worse, continue.

Ultimately, the president is the primary political figure capable of leading the government and the country in foreign policy. Yet, the days of presidential supremacy in most areas of foreign policy are a thing of the past; for a president to behave as if executive dominance prevails is to risk the type of political and constitutional crises that Nixon and Reagan experienced. Unless a global calamity occurs that creates the perception of a chronic state of national emergency for the United States, ushering in a new period of legislative-executive relations, considerable congressional involvement and influence will continue for the foreseeable future.

BIBLIOGRAPHIC ESSAY

An abundance of literature on Congress and foreign policy is available. Arthur M. Schlesinger, Jr., in *The Imperial Presidency* (Boston: Houghton Mifflin, 1989), provides an excellent historical overview of legislative-executive relations and the rise of presidential power from the constitutional foundations to Watergate, with a perspective on Iran-Contra. An excellent analysis of the rise and impact of McCarthy and McCarthyism in Congress and U.S. foreign policy is provided by Robert Griffith, in *The Politics of Fear: Joseph R. McCarthy and the Senate* (Amherst, Mass.: University of Massachusetts Press, 1987). Louis Henkin provides a good summary assessment of the constitutional basis for the sharing of power in foreign affairs and its continued relevance for understanding contemporary legislative-executive relations in U.S. foreign policy in "Foreign Affairs and the Constitution," *Foreign Affairs* 66 (Winter 1987/88): 284–310.

An extremely informative overview and discussion of the role of Congress in foreign policy since Vietnam is provided by Thomas M. Franck and Edward Weisband in *Foreign Policy by Congress* (New York: Oxford University Press, 1979), James M. Lindsay, *Congress and the Politics of U.S. Foreign Policy* (Baltimore: Johns Hopkins University Press, 1994), and Randall B. Ripley and James M Lindsay, eds., in *Congress Resurgent: Foreign and Defense Policy on Capitol Hill* (Ann Arbor, Mich.: University of Michigan Press, 1993). Thomas E. Mann provides an excellent overview of the contemporary legislative-executive relationship in foreign policy in "Making Foreign Policy: President and Congress," in Thomas E. Mann, ed., *A Question of Balance: The President, the Congress and Foreign Policy* (Washington, D.C.: Brookings Institution, 1990): 1–34. James L. Sundquist presents an excellent overview of the idea of party government and a theory of divided government in "The New Era of Coalition Government in the United States," *Political Science Quarterly* (1988): 613–35.

Good overviews of how Congress operates as an institution are provided by Randall B. Ripley, in *Congress: Process and Policy* (New York: W.W. Norton, 1983), and Lawrence C. Dodd and Bruce I. Oppenheimer, eds., in *Congress Reconsidered* (Washington, D.C.: Congressional Quarterly Press, 1997). An excellent and informative discussion of the actual workings of the legislative process and congressional politics can be found in John M. Barry, *The Ambition and the Power* (New York: Viking Penguin, 1989), and Hedrick Smith, *The Power Game: How Washington Works* (New York: Ballantine, 1988). Eric Alterman provides a fascinating portrayal of the institutional norms and expectations that exist throughout Congress in order for individuals to become effective by describing the evolution of Ron Dellums from radical outsider to "Ron Dellums: Radical Insider," in *World Policy Journal* (Winter 1993/94): 35–46.

ENDNOTES

1. See U.S., Congress, *Report of the Congressional Committees Investigating the Iran-Contra Affair, with Supplemental, Minority, and Additional Views* (100th Cong., 1st sess., November 1987), and *The Tower Commission Report* (New York: Bantam, 1987). The Minority Report of the Committee and the Tower Commission Report reflect the more conservative view; the Majority Report of the Committee reflects the more liberal view.

2. See, for example, Godfrey Hodgson, *America in Our Time* (New York: Vintage, 1976), chapter 5; Samuel P. Huntington, "Congressional Responses to the Twentieth Century," in David B. Truman, ed., *The Congress and America's Future* (New York: Columbia University Press, 1965); Richard J. Piper, "Presidential-Congressional Power Prescriptions in Conservative Political Thought Since 1933," *Presidential Studies Quarterly* (Winter 1991): 35–54; and George Szamuely, "The Imperial Congress," *Commentary* (September 1987): 27–32.

3. The classic statement on this is Edward S. Corwin, *The President: Office and Powers, 1878–1957* (New York: New York University Press, 1957). See also Cecil V. Crabb, Jr., and Pat M. Holt, *Invitation to Struggle: Congress, the President and Foreign Policy* (Washington, D.C.: Congressional Quarterly Press, 1992); Michael J. Glennon, *Constitutional Diplomacy* (Princeton, N.J.: Princeton University Press, 1991); Louis Henkin, "Foreign Affairs and the Constitution," *Foreign Affairs* 66 (Winter 1987/88): 284–310; Louis Henkin, *Constitutionalism, Democracy, and Foreign Affairs* (New York: Columbia University Press, 1990); and Arthur Schlesinger, Jr., *The Imperial Presidency* (New York: Houghton Mifflin, 1989).

4. Schlesinger, *The Imperial Presidency.*

5. For an overview, see U.S., Congress, Senate, Special Committee on National Emergencies and Delegated Emergency Powers, *A Brief History of Emergency Powers in the United States* (93d Cong., 2nd sess., July 1974). This study concluded that "especially since the days of the 1933 economic emergency, it has been Congress' habit to delegate extensive emergency authority—which continues even when the emergency has passed—and not to set a terminating date" (p. v). By the early seventies, the president could make use of over 470 emergency power statutes in exercising power—most of which continue to exist to the present day.

6. Frank R. Bax, "The Legislative-Executive Relationship in Foreign Policy: New Partnership or New Competition," *Orbis* 20 (Winter 1977): 881–904. See also James A. Robinson, *Congress and Foreign Policy-Making* (Homewood, Ill.: Dorsey Press, 1967); John Rourke, *Congress and the Presidency in U.S. Foreign Policymaking: A Study of Interaction and Influence, 1945–1982* (Boulder, Colo.: Westview Press, 1983); and Aaron Wildavsky, "The Two Presidencies," *Transaction* 4 (1966): 175–86.

7. William Manchester, *The Glory and the Dream: A Narrative History of America, 1932–1972.* (New York: Bantam, 1975), pp. 491–92.

8. Bax, "Legislative-Executive Relationship," p. 886. See also Natalie Hevener Kaufman and David Whiteman, "Opposition to Human Rights Treaties in the United States Senate: The Legacy of the Bricker Amendment," *Human Rights Quarterly* 10 (1988): 309–37, Cathal J. Nolan, "The Last Hurrah of Conservative Isolationism: Eisenhower, Congress, and the Bricker Amendment," *Presidential Studies Quarterly* (Spring 1992): 337–49; and Duane Tananbaum, *The Bricker Amendment Controversy: A Test of Eisenhower's Political Leadership* (Ithaca, N.Y.: Cornell University Press, 1988).

9. See, for example, James M. McCormick and Eugene R. Wittkopf, "Bipartisanship, Partisanship, and Ideology in Congressional-Executive Foreign Policy Relations, 1947–1988," *Journal of Politics* 52 (November 1990): 1077–1100; and James Meernik, "Presidential Support in Congress: Conflict and Consensus on Foreign and Defense Policy," *Journal of Politics* (August 1993): 569–87.

10. Bax, "Legislative-Executive Relationship," p. 887. See also Alton Frye, *A Responsible Congress: The Politics of National Security* (New York: McGraw-Hill, 1975).

11. David Halberstam, *The Powers That Be* (New York: Alfred A. Knopf, 1979), pp. 496–97.

12. Halberstam, *The Powers That Be*, p. 248.

13. President Dwight Eisenhower and Secretary of State John Foster Dulles were much more concerned and active in interacting with Congress in order to promote and maintain bipartisanship. See Anna Kasten Nelson, "John Foster Dulles and the Bipartisan Congress," *Political Science Quarterly* 102 (Spring 1987): 43–64.

14. An overview of congressional reassertion since Vietnam is provided by Barry M. Blechman, *The Politics of National Security: Congress and U.S. Defense Policy* (New York: Oxford University Press, 1990); Crabb and Holt, *Invitation to Struggle*; Thomas M. Franck and Edward Weisband, *Foreign Policy by Congress* (New York: Oxford University Press, 1979); Richard Haass, "Congressional Power: Implications for American Security Policy," *Adelphi Papers*, No. 153 (London: International Institute for Strategic Studies, 1979); Thomas E. Mann, ed., *A Question of Balance: The President, the Congress and Foreign Policy* (Washington, D.C.: Brookings Institution, 1990); and John Spanier and Joseph Nogee, eds., *Congress, The Presidency and American Foreign Policy* (New York: Pergamon Press, 1981).

15. For an overview of these changes and their consequences, see Crabb and Holt, *Invitation to Struggle*; Lawrence C. Dodd and Bruce I. Oppenheimer, eds., *Congress Reconsidered* (Washington, D.C.: Congressional Quarterly Press, 1997); Franck and Weisband, *Foreign Policy by Congress*; William J. Keefe, *Congress and the American People* (Englewood Cliffs, N.J.: Prentice-Hall, 1980); James M. Lindsay, *Congress and the Politics of U.S. Foreign Policy* (Baltimore: Johns Hopkins University Press, 1994); Randall B. Ripley, *Congress: Process and Policy* (New York: W.W. Norton, 1983); Randall B. Ripley and James M. Lindsay, eds., *Congress Resurgent: Foreign and Defense Policy on Capitol Hill* (Ann Arbor, Mich.: University of Michigan Press, 1993); Jerel A. Rosati, "Congressional Influence in American Foreign Policy: Addressing the Controversy," *Journal of Political and Military Sociology* 12 (Fall 1984): 311–33; Hedrick Smith, *The Power Game: How Washington Works* (New York: Ballantine, 1988); and Charles W. Whalen, Jr., *The House and Foreign Policy: The Irony of Congressional Reform* (Chapel HIll, N.C.: University of North Carolina Press, 1982).

16. For an excellent discussion of the Democratic class of 1974 and its political orientation, see William Schneider, "JFK's Children: The Class of '74," *The Atlantic Monthly* (March 1989): 35–58.

17. See, for example, Paul Berstein and William Freudenberg, "Ending the Vietnam War: Components of Change in Senate Voting on Vietnam War Bills," *American Journal of Sociology* 82 (1977): 991–1006, and Jerold E. Schneider, *Ideological Coalitions in Congress* (Westport, Conn.: Greenwood Press, 1979).

18. See, e.g., Eric Alterman "Ron Dellums: Radical Insider," *World Policy Journal* (Winter 1993/94): 35–46.

19. See, for example, U.S., Congress, House, Committee on Foreign Affairs, *Executive-Legislative Consultation on Foreign Policy: Strengthening Foreign Policy Information Sources for Congress*, Congress and Foreign Policy Series No. 4 (Washington, D.C.: U.S. Government Printing Office, February 1982).

20. See Franck and Weisband, *Foreign Policy by Congress*; Robert A. Pastor, *Congress and the Politics of U.S. Foreign Economic Policy, 1929–1976* (Berkeley: University of California Press, 1980); Rosati, "Congressional Influence in American Foreign Policy."

21. See Morton Berkowitz, P.G. Bock, and Vincent J. Fuccillo, *The Politics of American Foreign Policy: The Social Context of Decisions* (Englewood Cliffs, N.J.: Prentice-Hall, 1977); Charles W. Kegley, Jr., and Eugene R. Wittkopf, *American Foreign Policy: Pattern and Process* (New York: St. Martin's Press, 1987); Paul E. Peterson, "The President's Dominance in Foreign Policy Making," *Political Science Quarterly* (Summer 1994): 215–34; and John Spanier and Eric M. Uslaner, *How American Foreign Policy Is Made* (New York: Holt, Rinehart and Winston, 1978).

22. See Crabb and Holt, *Invitation to Struggle*; Franck and Weisband, *Foreign Policy by Congress*; Haass, "Congressional Power"; and Lee H. Hamilton and Michael H. Van Dusen, "Making the Separation of Powers Work," *Foreign Affair* 57 (1978): 17–39.

23. See Lloyd N. Cutler, "To Form a Government," *Foreign Affairs* 59 (1980): 126–43, and William D. Rogers, "Who's in Charge of Foreign Policy?" *New York Times Magazine* (September 9, 1979).

24. See, for example, Szamuely, "The Imperial Congress."

25. See Rosati, "Congressional Influence in American Foreign Policy."

26. See, for example, James A. Robinson, *Congress and Foreign Policy-Making: A Study in Legislative Influence and Initiative* (Homewood, Ill.: Dorsey Press, 1967).

27. See Richard F. Fenno, Jr., *Home Style: House Members in Their Districts* (Boston: Little, Brown, 1978); Morris P. Fiorina, *Congress: Keystone of the Washington Establishment* (New Haven, Conn.: Yale University Press, 1977); David R. Mayhew, *Congress: The Electoral Con-*

nection (New York: Yale University Press, 1974); Warren E. Miller and Donald E. Stokes, "Constituency Influence in Congress, *American Political Science Review* 57 (1963): 45–56; and Smith, *The Power Game*.

28. James L. Sundquist, "Needed: A Political Theory for the New Era of Coalition Government in the United States," *Political Science Quarterly* (1988): 614.

29. See also Morris P. Fiorina, *Divided Government* (Boston: Allyn and Bacon, 1996); David R. Mayhew, *Divided We Govern* (New Haven, Conn.: Yale University Press, 1991); James A. Thurber, ed., *Divided Democracy: Cooperation and Conflict Between the President and Congress* (Washington, D.C.: Congressional Quarterly Press, 1991).

30. Bruce W. Jentleson, "American Diplomacy: Around the World and Along Pennsylvania Avenue," in Thomas E. Mann, ed., *A Question of Balance: The President, the Congress and Foreign Policy* (Washington, D.C.: Brookings Institution, 1990), p. 146. See also Robert A. Pastor, *Congress and the Politics of U.S. Foreign Policy, 1929–1976* (Berkeley, Calif.: University of California Press, 1980), and Rosati, "Congressional Influence in American Foreign Policy."

31. Henkin, *Foreign Affairs and the Constitution*, p. 290. See also David Gray Adler, "The Constitution and Presidential Warmaking: The Enduring Debate," *Political Science Quarterly* 103 (Spring 1988): 1–36, and Abraham D. Sofaer, *War, Foreign Affairs and Constitutional Power: The Origins* (Cambridge, Mass.: Ballinger, 1976).

32. For a historical overview, see Franck and Weisband, *Foreign Policy by Congress*, chapter 3, and Schlesinger, *The Imperial Presidency*.

33. U.S., Congress, House, Committee on International Relations, *The War Powers Resolution: Relevant Documents, Correspondence, Reports*, Committee Print (94th Cong., 2nd sess., 1975), p.1.

34. An overview of the legislative history that led to the passage of the War Powers Act and the act's impact through the early 1980s can be found in U.S., Congress, Committee on Foreign Affairs, *The War Powers Resolution*, Committee Print (Washington, D.C.: U.S. Government Printing Office, 1982).

35. Rarely has the president specifically cited subsection 4(a)(1) involving a situation of hostilities, such as in the Mayaguez rescue attempt, but the report was submitted after the forty-eight hours required by the WPA had elapsed and the military incident was over.

36. U.S., Supreme Court, *Immigration and Naturalization Service v. Chadha* 77 L Ed 2d 317 (June 23, 1983). It has also been pointed out that the Supreme Court decision may ironically be detrimental to the president in the long run, for it will likely force Congress to pass less flexible legislation and become more involved in the details of policy. See, for example, I.M. Destler, "Dateline Washington: Life After the Veto," *Foreign Policy* 52 (Fall 1983): 181–86.

37. U.S., House, Committee on Foreign Affairs, *Use of U.S. Armed Forces in Lebanon, Communication from the President of the U.S.* (97th Cong., 2nd sess., 1982).

38. "Statement by Reagan on Resolution," *New York Times* (October 13, 1983): A7.

39. James Nathan, "Salvaging the War Powers Resolution," *Presidential Studies Quarterly* (Spring 1993): 235–68.

40. For an overview, see Franck and Weisband, *Foreign Policy by Congress*, chapter 6; Loch K. Johnson, *The Making of International Agreements; Congress Confronts the Executive* (New York: New York University Press, 1985); and U.S., Congress, Senate, Committee on Foreign Relations, *The Senate Role in Foreign Affairs Appointments*, Committee Print (97th Cong., 2nd sess., July 1982).

41. See, for example, Smith, *The Power Game*, pp. 63–69.

42. Loch Johnson and James M. McCormick, "Foreign Policy by Executive Fiat," *Foreign Policy* 38 (1977): 117–38. See also Johnson, *The Making of International Agreements*, and C.J. Stevens, "The Use and Control of Executive Agreements: Recent Congressional Initiatives," *Orbis* 20 (1977): 205–21.

43. See Rosati, "Congressional Influence in American Foreign Policy."

44. See Natalie Hevener Kaufman, *Human Rights Treaties and the Senate: A History of Opposition* (Chapel Hill, N.C.: University of North Carolina Press, 1990).

45. See, for example, Frye, *A Responsible Congress*, chapters 2, 3, and 4.

46. I. M. Destler, "Delegating Trade Policy," in *The President, The Congress, and The Making of Foreign Policy* (Norman, Okla.: University of Oklahoma Press, 1994), pp. 228–45.

47. See Stanley D. Nollen and Dennis P. Quinn, "Free Trade, Fair Trade, Strategic Trade, and Protectionism in the U.S. Congress, 1987-88," *International Organization* (Summer 1994): 491–525.

48. For an overview, see Franck and Weisband, *Foreign Policy by Congress*.

49. Barbara Hinckley, *Stability and Change in Congress* (New York: W.W. Norton, 1975), p. 75. Hinckley has since done some rethinking in *Less Than Meets the Eye:*

Foreign Policy Making and the Myth of the Assertive Congress (Chicago: University of Chicago Press, 1994).

50. See, for example, Franck and Weisband, *Foreign Policy by Congress,* chapter 2, and N.C. Livingstone and M. von Nordheim, "The United States Congress and the Angola Crisis," *Strategic Review* 5 (1977): 34–44.

51. See, for example, Cynthia J. Arnson, *Crossroads: Congress, the Reagan Administration, and Central America* (New York: Pantheon, 1989).

52. See Bayless Manning, "The Congress, The Executive, and Intermestic Affairs: Three Proposals," *Foreign Affairs* 55 (1977): 306–32.

53. See John M. Barry, *The Ambition and the Power: The Fall of Jim Wright: A True Story of Washington* (New York: Viking Penguin, 1989); Ikwo Kabashima and Hideo Sato, "Local Context and Congressional Politics: Interest-Group Theory and Foreign-Policy Implications," *International Studies Quarterly* 30 (September 1986): 295–314; and Smith, *The Power Game.*

54. For an overview, see Joel D. Aberbach, *Keeping a Watchful Eye: The Politics of Congressional Oversight* (Washington, D.C.: Brookings, 1990); Timothy M. Cole, "Congressional Investigation of American Foreign Policy: Iran-Contra in Perspective," *Congress and the Presidency* (Spring 1994): 29–48; and Franck and Weisband, *Foreign Policy by Congress.*

55. Robert Griffith, "American Politics and the Origins of 'McCarthyism,'" in William H. Chafe and Harvard Sitkoff, ed., *A History of Our Time: Readings on Postwar America* (New York: Oxford University Press, 1991), p. 70.

56. Gregory F. Treverton, "Intelligence: Welcome to the American Government," in Thomas E. Mann, ed., *A Question of Balance: The President, the Congress and Foreign Policy* (Washington, D.C.: Brookings Institution, 1990), p. 74.

57. Jentleson, "American Diplomacy," p. 171.

58. See Loch K. Johnson, "Covert Action and Accountability: Decision-Making for America's Secret Foreign Policy," *International Studies Quarterly* 33 (March 1989); 81–109.

59. See, for example, Harold Hongju Koh, *The National Security Constitution: Sharing Power After the Iran-Contra Affair* (New Haven, Conn.: Yale University Press, 1990).

60. Elliott Abrams, *Undue Process: A Story of How Political Differences Are Turned into Crimes* (New York: Free Press, 1993), p. 223.

61. U.S., Congress, *Report of the Congressional Committees Investigating the Iran-Contra Affair,* p. 11. The minority report of the committee came to a similar conclusion as the Tower Commission report.

62. See, for example, Koh, *The National Security Constitution,* and Peter Kornbluh, "The Iran-Contra Scandal: A Postmortem," *World Policy Journal* 5 (Winter 1987–88): 129–50.

63. William S. Cohen and George J. Mitchell, *Men of Zeal* (New York: Viking, 1988).

64. Seymour M. Hersh, "The Iran-Contra Committees: Did They Protect Reagan?" *New York Times Magazine* (April 29, 1990): 46–47, 61, 64, 67,70, 77–78. See also Peter Kornbluh, "The Iran-Contra Scandal: A Postmortem," *World Policy Journal* (Winter 1987–88): 129–150.

65. For an overview of the different political cultures within Congress and the executive branch and how they affect foreign policy relations between the two branches, see Stanley J. Heginbotham, "Dateline Washington: The Rules of the Game," *Foreign Policy* 53 (Winter 1983–1984): 157–72.

66. See, e.g., George F. Will, *Restoration: Congress, Term Limits and the Recovery of Deliberative Democracy* (New York: Free Press, 1992).

67. This is true with a second presidential term today since passage of the Twenty-second Amendment in 1951, which has resulted in no electoral accountability during the second four years.

68. See, for example, Smith, *The Power Game,* chapter 20.

69. See, for example, Lloyd N. Cutler, "To Form a Government," *Foreign Affairs* 59 (Fall 1980): 126–43.

70. See, for example, Lawrence C. Dodd, "Congress and the Quest for Power," in Dodd and Oppenheimer, *Congress Reconsidered,* pp. 269–207, and Harvey G. Zeidenstein, "The Reassertion of Presidential Power: New Curbs on the President," *Political Science Quarterly* 93 (1978); 393–410.

CHAPTER 13

. . . .

THE REST OF GOVERNMENT

When discussing the government and foreign policymaking process, most observers focus on the role of the president, the bureaucracy, and Congress. These are the three key actors or sets of institutions directly involved in making foreign policy. To achieve a comprehensive understanding of governmental politics, however, it is also important to be aware of the remainder of the government and its place in foreign policy. This chapter discusses the role of the judiciary, state and local governments, and the Washington political community to provide a more thorough understanding of the complex politics of U.S. foreign policy.

THE JUDICIARY

. . . .

The role of the judiciary has been ignored in the study of U.S. foreign policy. Most scholars assume that **judicial restraint** has prevailed in foreign af-

fairs. It is commonly assumed that the judiciary rarely decides a case which directly involves foreign policy and that when the judiciary does arrive at a decision concerning foreign policy, it usually reaffirms the status quo. This assumption of judicial restraint simplifies the complex reality of American history.[1]

HISTORICAL OVERVIEW

The judiciary has played a role in influencing U.S. foreign policy since the beginning of the country. The Constitution of the United States is quite explicit about judicial power in foreign affairs as prescribed in Article III, section 2:

> The judicial Power shall extend to all Cases, in Law and Equity, arising under this Constitution, the Laws of the United States, and Treaties made, or which shall be made, under their Authority;—to all Cases affecting

Ambassadors, other public Ministers and Consuls; . . . to Controversies . . . between a State, or the Citizens thereof, and foreign States, Citizens or Subjects.

In all Cases affecting Ambassadors, other public Ministers and Consuls, and those in which a State shall be Party, the supreme Court shall have original Jurisdiction. In all the other Cases before mentioned, the supreme Court shall have appellate Jurisdiction, both as to Law and Fact, with such Exceptions, and under such Regulations as the Congress shall make.

Yet, as discussed in the previous chapter, the Constitution was ambiguous in specifying the powers of governmental institutions and the workings of the political system in the United States. Consequently, the judiciary has been crucial in deciding the parameters or boundaries of legitimate behavior for different actors within the political process. *The judiciary has been a significant force in interpreting the Constitution in two fundamental areas affecting foreign policy:* determining the legitimate relationship between the state governments and the national government, and the distribution of power within the national government.

The first major constitutional issue to confront the country concerned the question of federalism, that is, **state versus national supremacy**. The early power of the state governments clouded the nature of the powers of the national government. Because the Constitution had little to say about the distribution of power between the state governments and the national government, the judiciary helped fill an important void. Basing its decisions upon the Constitution and the concept of nation-state sovereignty, the Supreme Court usually ruled that the national government was supreme, especially concerning questions of war and peace. Beginning under the first chief justice, **John Marshall**, the Supreme Court has rendered significant decisions concerning the nature of federalism that have had a major impact on foreign as well as domestic policy.

The second major constitutional issue involved **the distribution of power within the national government**. As discussed in chapter 12, a governmental arrangement of different institutions sharing power created major disputes between the legislature and the executive. As explained by Louis Henkin in *Foreign Affairs and the Constitution*, although "there is virtually nothing related to foreign affairs that is beyond the constitutional powers of the federal government . . . we are not told how the undifferentiated bundle of powers inherent in sovereignty is distributed among the federal branches."[2] The judiciary helped to fill the void. In foreign policy, the Supreme Court has tended to rule that the office of the president predominates, especially involving the use of force abroad.

By the twentieth century, major constitutional contention over federalism and the distribution of legislative-executive power gave way to a growing consensus that the national government was supreme and that the president was preeminent in foreign affairs. This perception was reinforced by America's participation in the First and Second World Wars. With these controversial questions apparently settled, the judiciary's activity and influence in foreign policy diminished. Hence, what most Americans take for granted today—that the national government and the president are supreme in foreign affairs, especially over questions of war and peace—was the product of long historical development in which the judiciary played a vital role, especially in the nineteenth century.

The mid-twentieth century probably represented the height of judicial restraint because of the rise of the cold war. Perceptions of a national emergency due to the cold war consensus propelled the president to the forefront of the foreign policymaking process, supported by the actions of Congress. As with other public and private institutions in American society, the cold war was a time when the judiciary was hesitant to become involved in major issues of foreign policy. Moreover, when it did decide a relevant case, the judiciary usually reaffirmed the political status quo. Judicial restraint and occasional involvement, in other words, served to legitimize the extraordinary powers of the president and the executive branch.[3]

THE CONTEMPORARY ERA

The height of the cold war is the period from which many Americans have based their view of the foreign policymaking process. It was an extraordinary time during which presidential supremacy and judicial restraint were the norm. Thus, the Supreme Court and the judiciary could be ignored, particularly if one was interested in understanding the sources of U.S. national security policy. The post–Vietnam War era, however, represents a movement away from the extraordinary years of the cold war. The breakdown of the cold war consensus not only resulted in the relative decline of presidential power and the reassertion of congressional authority in foreign policy, it also allowed other government actors such as the judiciary to play a more active role.

Numerous contemporary cases suggest that the judiciary has become more active and influential in the area of foreign policy. In a 1983 decision, for example, the Supreme Court ruled in *Immigration and Naturalization Service v. Chadha* that the "legislative veto," involving an immigration case, was unconstitutional because it violated the separation of powers. The veto was one of the major procedural techniques used by Congress to assert its influence over executive branch decisions in a number of areas including foreign policy. The decision called into question Congress's ability to veto presidential decisions—that is, to pass a concurrent resolution without the president's signature—concerning the use of force abroad under the War Powers Act, sales of major weapons systems to foreign governments under the International Security Assistance and Arms Export Control Act, and the export of nuclear fuel and facilities to foreign countries under the Nonproliferation Act.[4]

In the same month, the Supreme Court ruled in *Capital Industries-EMI, Inc. v. Bennett* that the state of California may base its taxation on a corporation's worldwide income rather than on income earned solely within the state. This decision to allow a "unitary" system of taxation had important impli-

cations for the location of corporate headquarters and subsidiaries, thereby influencing America's international economic policy.[5]

Contemporary judicial decisions have affected U.S. foreign policy in a wide variety of cases. These have included labor stoppages involving foreign trade, trade issues in violation of U.S. law, job discrimination in foreign multinational corporations located within the United States, the rights of refugees and immigrants, foreign debt payments to private U.S. banks, nuclear proliferation and waste disposal, libel suits against the press, and the release of classified government information.[6] Such cases are symbolic of a judiciary which has become more active and important in foreign policy.

As suggested by Louis Henkin nearly thirty years ago:

> Common preoccupation with the Supreme Court in its role as the arbiter of the power of the political branches tends to conceal its other powers relevant to foreign policy. . . . They have not been wholly content to sit outside the growing field of foreign relations. The "infallibility" that comes from having final say on the meaning of the Constitution allows the courts to determine also what they may and will do in the exercise of their own judicial power, and they have been asserting it to play small parts—some old, some new— in regard to foreign relations.[7]

And in the post–Vietnam War era, the judiciary has asserted its role to play a larger part with regard to foreign relations.

This is not to say that the judiciary is as consequential as the legislature or the executive in influencing foreign policy. Rather, the point is that the judiciary is more active and more influential in the post–Vietnam War era than it was during the cold war years. Judicial decisions no longer simply reaffirm the status quo, but have become increasingly independent and act as additional constraints on the president's ability to govern foreign policy.

The judiciary is most likely to play a significant role in **issues divorced from political-military**

affairs, in what traditionally has been referred to as "low" foreign policy. The judiciary, particularly the Supreme Court, has been reluctant to decide controversial **"political questions"** with direct political-military implications, usually preferring that the political system resolve these matters on its own. Nevertheless, the judiciary's power to resolve disputes involving the nature of the Constitution and the political process allows it to affect issues of foreign policy and play a growing role.[8]

Judicial activity in foreign policy tends to involve the resolution of disputes in three areas of the political process: between the national government and the state governments, the Congress and the presidency, and, recently, the government and individuals. The first two areas have involved questions of traditional judicial involvement. In addition, the Supreme Court under **Chief Justice Warren** in the 1960s extended and intensified the protection of the Bill of Rights to individuals (civil liberties and rights in the making of foreign policy will be examined in chapter 17). This action provided a foundation for greater judicial involvement and activism. Adjudication of these three types of disputes has resulted in increased direct judicial involvement in the policymaking process and, indirectly, in growing influence of the judiciary over policy areas such as international economics and immigration.

Although the judiciary may be most active and influential in issues traditionally considered "low" policy, such issues have become more important in the post–Vietnam War era, and they do impact on more traditional national security issues. The courts, for example, were used to prosecute members of the president's staff and administration for violating laws resulting from presidential abuse of power in the Watergate and Iran-Contra affairs. With respect to Watergate, not only was President Richard Nixon forced to resign, but many of his advisers and members of the White House staff were found guilty and served prison terms (while over twenty business executives were convicted of giving illegal campaign contributions).

With respect to criminal prosecution in Iran-Contra, four patterns predominated. First, a number

of individuals carrying out the policies of the Reagan administration pleaded guilty or were convicted of violating laws related to the Iran-Contra scandal. They include National Security Adviser Robert McFarlane, National Security Adviser John Poindexter, National Security Council staffer Oliver North, Assistant Secretary of State Elliott Abrams, courier Robert Owen, private fundraiser Carl Channel, private fundraiser Richard Miller, arms merchant Richard Secord, financier Albert Hakim, and former officials of the Central Intelligence Agency (CIA) Thomas Clines, Alan Fiers, and Clair George. Second, most of the sentences were relatively light, involving probation, modest fines, and community service. In fact, President Bush pardoned six people on Christmas Eve of 1992: McFarlane, Abrams, Fiers, George, Duanne Clarridge, former senior CIA official (indicted but not yet tried), and Caspar Weinberger, Secretary of Defense under President Reagan (who was indicted but not yet tried). However, the lives of the individuals involved were completely disrupted by the congressional investigations and the public trials. Robert McFarlane became so distraught that at one point he tried to take his life.[9]

Third, the trials demonstrated that **the courts are not "above politics"** or the role of ideology. For example, Colonel Oliver North appealed his four convictions in Federal District Court to the Court of Appeals. The Court of Appeals ruled, in a 2 to 1 decision, to overturn one conviction and to send the other three convictions back to the Federal District Court to have the presiding judge determine if the trial proceedings were tainted by previous information disclosed during the congressional investigation of Iran-Contra. The two Court of Appeals judges in favor of the decision were appointed by President Ronald Reagan, while the judge opposed was appointed by President Jimmy Carter. Furthermore, it was reported that one of the Reagan-appointed federal judges, Laurence H. Silberman, previously had been a longtime CIA agent who also was involved in the Iran-Contra affair early on, thus resulting in a classic case of conflict of interest.[10] Ultimately, the charges and convictions against Oliver North (and John Poindexter) were dismissed over the legal technicality that the judicial proceedings involved information that was derived from North's earlier "immune" testimony before Congress.

Finally, the Iran-Contra trials also demonstrated the continuing tension between the demands of national security and democracy. A strong case by the government Special Prosecutor Lawrence Walsh and the right to a fair trial for the defendants required "access to classified information," while the national security ethos required the primacy of government secrecy. "Thus we have here a strange judicial proceeding brought in the name of the government but hamstrung by the same government."[11] Compromises were reached, such as President Reagan agreeing to testify, but the special prosecutor had to drop the most serious charges in most cases because of the secret classification of the evidence.[12] In other cases, such as that of Felix Rodriguez, former CIA station chief in Costa Rica, all charges were dismissed because the U.S. Justice Department blocked the release of classified information.[13]

Special Prosecutor Lawrence Walsh was furious with governmental blockage of information in the name of national security. In a report he sent to the House and Senate intelligence committees he stated:

> The Attorney General and the CIA not only frustrated the public development of this proof but did so in a manner that exasperated the district court and dragged out the resolution of this issue in unproductive litigation. . . . The administration's actions in *United States vs. Fernandez* and in the other Iran-Contra prosecutions underscore the need for objective standards to govern the release of classified information in criminal prosecutions. . . . This lack of objective standards can lead to the frustration of law enforcement.[14]

Walsh's preoccupation with legality and objective standards ignored the crucial role politics played throughout the Iran-Contra episode, including the judicial proceedings. As Theodore Draper concluded in "Revelations of the North Trial":

> So long as a few officials in the government can withhold documents, justice cannot be served. Once the defense demands the appearance in court of classified documents and the government decides to withhold them, the government—an interested party in these proceedings—has the power to determine the very nature of the trial.[15]

The role of the judiciary ultimately is heavily a function of Supreme Court actions. **The Supreme Court** is the most influential judicial body for its behavior is fundamental in establishing legitimacy for judicial activism in all areas of public policy—both for lower federal courts (Courts of Appeals and District Courts) and for all state courts.[16] Supreme Court rulings represent the "law of the land"; their significance lies in the authority of the Supreme Court to undertake **judicial review** and to determine the constitutionality of a law. Not only is the Supreme Court the ultimate arbiter of the Constitution and domestic law, it is also the major interpreter of international law for the United States, and its decisions occasionally result in additions to the body of international law.[17]

The future role of the judiciary—its level of involvement and the nature of its decisions—is heavily affected by the **presidential appointments** to the Supreme Court. When an opening on the court appears, the president usually nominates someone who reflects his political beliefs, with the advice and consent of the Senate. Therefore, presidential appointments affect the court's ideological orientation as replacements on the court occur and as the political landscape evolves—a slow process involving long time lags, for federal justices can remain on the bench for life.

Such a change in the ideological orientation is exactly what has happened over the past twenty-five years to the Supreme Court as a result of the Republican party dominance of the presidency that allowed Presidents Reagan and Bush to make a majority of appointments to the high court. Under **Chief Justice William Rehnquist** in the 1980s and 1990s, the Supreme Court has increasingly reflected a more conservative orientation.[18]

The **Clarence Thomas confirmation hearings** demonstrated the political importance and political nature of the appointment and confirmation process. The testimony revolving around the charges of sexual harassment also was one of the few times that the significance of individual contacts and networking in Washington, D.C., was made painfully visible to the general public. During the administration of Bill Clinton—unlike the previous Democratic president, Jimmy Carter—the opportunity arose to appoint two individuals more liberal in orientation and affect the ideological dynamics of the Supreme Court (see **table 13.1** on Supreme Court Justices).

It is not exactly clear how these developments will affect Supreme Court and judicial decisions in the area of foreign policy. On the one hand, a more conservative court may be more likely to exercise judicial restraint concerning so-called political questions and, when cases are reviewed, may be more likely to decide them in deference to the president over questions of war and peace. On the other hand, much uncertainty remains in the post–Vietnam War era, for many questions that bear on foreign policy that come before the court will involve nontraditional foreign policy issues, such as civil rights, economics, and immigration—areas where ideology may not provide simple and straightforward answers (See **essay 13.1** for a discussion of the two major competing judicial interpretations and their impact on the foreign policymaking process.).

At a minimum, the post–Vietnam War era has seen less judicial restraint and more judicial involvement in cases that affect U.S. foreign policy. Judicial involvement is most likely to influence the policymaking process for issues that are more divorced from traditional national security concerns. As Henkin has concluded in his revised edition of *Foreign Affairs and the Constitution*:

> The role of the courts in foreign relations appears likely to remain modest, even more modest than its constitutional role generally. But it may yet become less modest if President and Congress are again tempted—as they were during the Cold War—to tread on important individual rights in the name of national security. Overall, the contribution of the courts to foreign policy and their impact on foreign

TABLE 13.1
SUPREME COURT JUSTICES [IN ORDER OF SENIORITY]

NAME	YEAR OF BIRTH	PRIOR EXPERIENCE	APPOINTED BY	YEAR OF APPOINTMENT
William H. Rehnquist *Chief Justice*	1924	Assistant Attorney General	Nixon*	1972
John Paul Stevens	1920	Federal Judge	Ford	1975
Sandra Day O'Connor	1930	State Judge	Reagan	1981
Antonin Scalia	1936	Law Professor, Federal Judge	Reagan	1986
Anthony Kennedy	1936	Federal Judge	Reagan	1988
David Souter	1939	Federal Judge	Bush	1990
Clarence Thomas	1948	Federal Judge	Bush	1991
Ruth Bader Ginsburg	1933	Federal Judge	Clinton	1993
Stephen Breyer	1938	Federal Judge	Clinton	1994

*Appointed chief justice by Reagan in 1986.

ESSAY 13.1
CURTISS-WRIGHT VS. THE YOUNGSTOWN STEEL SEIZURE CASE

Although the Constitution is ambiguous, *two major judicial interpretations of the distribution of power between the executive, legislative, and judicial branches in foreign policy have prevailed since World War II.* The *Curtiss-Wright* case in 1936 concluded that the president was supreme in foreign policymaking, and served to legitimize the extraordinary rise of presidential power during the cold war years. The steel seizure case in 1952 concluded that foreign policy was produced by different governmental institutions that shared power, and has come to serve as an accurate barometer of the policymaking process that has evolved since the Vietnam War.

United States v. Curtiss-Wright Export Corp. has been cited by the president, and those who support presidential preeminence in foreign policy, as a major source of presidential power since World War II. The Supreme Court not only upheld a congressional grant of authority to the president to prevent the sale of arms to belligerents (which the Curtiss-Wright Corporation had violated in a war involving Bolivia and Paraguay), it ruled generally in favor of national governmental and presidential supremacy in foreign policy. The famous **majority opinion written by Justice George Sutherland** in 1936 legitimized in the most sweeping terms the president's implied constitutional authority to conduct foreign affairs, claiming that the president's "very delicate, plenary and exclusive power . . . as the sole organ of the federal government in the field of international relations . . . does not require as a basis for its exercise an act of Congress."[A]

In *Youngstown Sheet & Tube Co. v. Sawyer,* the Supreme Court in 1952 invalidated President Harry Truman's attempt to invoke national security "emergency powers" during the Korean War to seize domestic steel mills that were under nationwide strike. The Supreme Court found that the president's steel seizure was not authorized by Congress.

Thus, the president had violated Congress' lawmaking authority. The famous **concurring opinion by Justice Robert Jackson** described a more flexible relationship, in which separate institutions shared power: "Presidential powers are not fixed but fluctuate, depending on their disjunction or conjunction with those of Congress."[B]

Justice Jackson's opinion established a three-tiered hierarchy of legitimate presidential actions in terms of legislative-executive relations. First, "when the President acts pursuant to an express or implied authorization of Congress, his authority is at its maximum, for it includes all that he possesses in his own right plus all that Congress can delegate." Second, "when the President acts in absence of either a congressional grant or denial of authority, he can only rely upon his own independent powers, but there is a zone of twilight in which he and Congress may have concurrent authority, or in which its distribution is uncertain." The third level occurs "when the President takes measures incompatible with the express or implied will of Congress, his power is at its lowest ebb, for then he can rely only upon his own constitutional powers minus any constitutional powers of Congress over the matter."[C]

Thus, two very different perspectives, represented by these two important Supreme Court rulings, have developed as to the distribution of power over foreign policy. The *Curtiss-Wright* interpretation that the president is "the sole organ of the federal government" in the making of U.S. foreign policy legitimized the growth of presidential and executive branch power, congressional acquiescence, and judicial restraint during the cold war years. Its legacy influenced presidential actions under Richard Nixon and Ronald Reagan, thereby triggering constitutional crises during the post–Vietnam War era.

A. U.S., Supreme Court, *United States v. Curtiss Wright Export Corporation,* 299 U.S. 305 (1936).

B. U.S., Supreme Court, *Youngstown Sheet & Tube Co. v. Sawyer* (Steel Seizure case), 343 U.S. 579 (1952).
C. Ibid.

The steel seizure case, on the other hand, is a more accurate reflector of the nature of legislative-executive relations in foreign policy since the Vietnam War. Congressional reassertion has constrained the president's ability to govern foreign policy and the legislative-executive relationship has varied, depending on the issue and other factors. The president is preeminent in some cases—reflecting Justice Jackson's first constitutional level in which presidential authority is at its maximum. Yet, many foreign policy issues are a function of joint participation—Justice Jackson's twilight zone of shared powers. As Louis Henkin has observed, "Important foreign affairs powers lie in that twilight zone. Indeed, in few other respects is our constitutional system as troubled by uncertainty in principle and by conflict in practice between Congress and the President. The effect is to raise intractable issues of constitutional jurisprudence and constitutional politics."[D]

Therefore, Jackson's third level of interaction is particularly instructive: "when the President takes measures *incompatible with the express or implied will of Congress, his power is at its lowest ebb*" (my emphasis). This is the position in which both Presidents Nixon and Reagan found themselves with regard to Vietnam and Nicaragua. Rather than abstaining from acting or modifying their policy initiatives in accordance with congressional action,

they circumvented Congress and triggered the Watergate and Iran-Contra scandals.

The Jackson opinion in the steel seizure case also expressly rejected judicial restraint in foreign policy and national security affairs. Rather, Justice Jackson defined a pivotal role for the courts as arbiters of the nature of the legislative-executive relationship. Jackson argued that when challenges were made to the president's sweeping claims of exclusive control over foreign affairs, the courts should not abstain but "must . . . scrutinize [those claims] with caution, for what is at stake is the equilibrium established by our constitutional system."[E] The contemporary era, in fact, has seen an increase in judicial involvement and influence in foreign policy, although the future remains unclear.

It is interesting to note that the height of the influence of the *Curtiss-Wright* case was twenty years after the decision was rendered in 1936—a time when the president was far from the "sole organ" in foreign policy. Likewise, the philosophy of the steel seizure case reflects the policymaking process in the post-Vietnam era, roughly forty years after the original decision in 1952 at a time when the president's power was almost supreme in foreign affairs. Thus, it may be only a matter of time before a new perspective arises, reflecting a different judicial ruling and offering a new interpretation of the role of the executive, the legislature, and the judiciary in the making of foreign policy.

D. Louis Henkin, "Foreign Affairs and the Constitution," *Foreign Affairs* 66 (Winter 1987/88), p. 285.

E. Ibid., p. 1285.

SOURCES: Louis Henkin, *Foreign Affairs and the Constitution* (Mineola, N.Y.: Foundation Press, 1972); Harold Hongju Koh, "Why the President (Almost) Always Wins in Foreign Affairs: Lessons of the Iran-Contra Affair," *Yale Law Journal* 97 (June 1988): 1281–1342; Harold Hongju Koh, *The National Security Constitution: Sharing Power After the Iran-Contra Affair* (New Haven, Conn.: Yale University Press, 1990); Gordon Silverstein, "Constitutional Interpretation and American Foreign Policy: What Congress and the Executive Can Learn from the Courts," in *The President, the Congress, and the Making of Foreign Policy* (Norman, Okla.: University of Oklahoma Press, 1994).

relations are significant but not large. The Supreme Court in particular intervenes only infrequently and its foreign affairs cases are few and haphazard. The Court does not build and refine steadily case by case, it develops no expertise or experts; the Justices have no matured or clear philosophies; the precedents are flimsy and often reflect the spirit of another day. But though the courts have only a supporting part, it is indispensable and inevitable.[19]

Although the judiciary remains a peripheral institution in the making of U.S. foreign policy compared to the executive and legislative branches, its involvement does complicate the policymaking process, especially for the president and his efforts to govern foreign policy. In the final analysis, the degree to which a more active judicial role is forthcoming depends on the direction taken by the Supreme Court and the judicial interpretation that guides its actions.

STATE AND LOCAL GOVERNMENTS
. . . .

The role of state and local governments has received little attention in the study of U.S. foreign policy. However, due to the decline of the foreign policy consensus of the cold war years, state and local governments are playing a more active and visible role in U.S. foreign policy in the post–Vietnam War era. As with the judiciary, state and local governments play a peripheral role and are most active on issues that are removed from national security affairs. Nonetheless, state and local governments have become increasingly involved in the complex politics of U.S. foreign policy.

State and local governments have become a part of the foreign policy political process for three principal reasons. First, the United States Constitution created a federal form of government. **Federalism** involves the "sharing of sovereignty"—the supreme authority to govern—between two sets of governments. Most countries have a "unitary" system of government in which sovereignty resides with the national government alone. In the United States, however, sovereignty is shared between the central government—commonly referred to as the federal government by Americans—and the state governments. The creation of a federal governmental system is a function of America's early history, in which thirteen separate colonies with strong state governments coexisted under the Articles of Confederation. Within a federal system, the state governments have certain rights and powers which the central government cannot restrict. This explains the existence of fifty-one constitutions in the United States—one for the

central government and one for each of the fifty state governments. Although the Supreme Court has tended to rule in favor of the national government over state governments in disputes, state governments remain independent and retain significant sources of power, allowing them to carve out areas of influence that impinge upon U.S. foreign policy.[20]

The second reason why state and local governments have impacted foreign policy is that *the United States has "tons" of state and local government.* The United States has over 80,000 different governmental bodies: one central government, fifty state governments, and a multitude of local governments that take the form of cities, townships, counties, school districts, and special districts (for fire protection, water service, and so on). Of the sixteen million governmental bureaucrats in the United States, 80 percent are employees of state and local governments. State and local governments spend over half a trillion dollars—one-third of all governmental expenditures combined. Clearly, the United States has much government below the central governmental level. There is a certain irony in the immense size of state and local government: Americans are very individualistic and cynical of large government, especially the federal government; yet most of the government is located at the local level and was created by the states. The sheer size and existence of state and local government throughout the United States has made it a part of the complex politics of U.S. foreign policy.

Finally, state and local governments play a more active role in U.S. foreign policy due to the growth of interdependence throughout the world. American society, including state and local communities, have become increasingly affected by international developments. Over two decades ago, Professor Chadwick Alger documented the wide-ranging networks of interdependence that existed between Columbus, Ohio, and the rest of the world.[21] As Alger has found throughout his work, "There is no doubt that the global context of cities is changing and that the self-conscious and organized responsiveness of people to these changes is growing."[22] John Hamilton has described the growing connections between the smallest communities throughout the United States and the rest of the world in *Mainstreet America and the Third World.*[23]

The growth in the foreign policy activity of state and local government has impacted the making of U.S. foreign policy in two general ways. First, state and local government predominantly impacts "low" policy issue areas, the most obvious being in **trade and business investment**. In the last few decades, state governments have become increasingly involved in foreign trade and investment, with state trade missions to foreign countries now routine affairs. As discussed in chapter 10, foreign imports of merchandise goods into the United States has exploded from $11.6 billion in 1955, to $55.3 billion in 1972, to $441 billion in 1988, to more than $800 billion in the late nineties. Likewise, American exports have risen from $15.5 billion in 1955, to $49 billion in 1972, to $320 billion in 1988, and climbed to more then $600 billion by the late nineties. Such a large and growing volume of international trade has major consequences for the economies of states and localities. **Table 13.2** lists the top 25 metropolitan areas throughout the United States engaged in exports and heavily impacted by international trade.

Not surprisingly, state and city governments have gotten increasingly involved in matters of international economics. The competition between different locales throughout the country for foreign investment, such as for a Toyota or Sony plant, has become quite intense. This activity not only affects local economies, but state and local governments have increasingly played a direct role in international economics and indirectly affected U.S. foreign economic policy (see **essay 13.2** on foreign investment and the role of state and local government.).[24]

Immigration is another intermestic issue of great importance to the United States and for many states. As discussed in essay 10.2, anywhere from 800,000 to 1.5 million immigrants are "legally" admitted into the United States each year. More controversial has been the larger flow of "illegal" people into the United States. California, Texas, Florida, and New York have been most affected by large numbers of illegal immigrants. Over the last decade

Florida has had to face huge waves of so-called "boat people" fleeing Cuba and Haiti—in the tens of thousands—in an effort to become refugees and enter the United States. The governor of Florida in response to the crises, and domestic concerns and politics, has been forced to declare "states of emergency" and become actively involved in U.S. immigration policy. Clearly, immigration flows and demographic changes have profound effects on the economies and governments of states and locales.

Second, state and local governments also play a role in directly affecting U.S. national security policy as well. With the rise of McCarthyism during the cold war era, for instance, state government actions **reinforced the politics of anticommunism** that was prevailing in national politics. Over thirty states passed legislation, mirroring laws at the federal level, requiring public employees to take loyalty oaths and barring public employment to individuals engaged in subversive practices or involved in organizations on the attorney general's subversive list. Among those most affected were public school teachers—from elementary schools to universities—who were also prohibited from engaging in "seditious" classroom instruction. "Anti-radical legislation was not, of course, new to most states," according to historian Robert Griffith. "Yet what was remarkable about the great outpouring of the late forties was that so many legislatures acted at the same time and in the same way."[25] Municipalities likewise, among them Detroit and New York City, passed similar ordinances.[26] Clearly, cold war-era politics were pervasive at the national, state, and local levels, thus reinforcing and heightening the anticommunism of the times.

With the collapse of the anticommunist consensus, state and local governmental activity has affected U.S. national security policy in more diverse ways in the post–Vietnam War years. During the early 1970s, for example, the port authority of New York—a local government—created a furor in U.S., French, and British relations when it denied landing clearance for **the French- and British-made Super Sonic Transport (SST)** at Kennedy Airport because it violated local noise regulations. The French and the British could not understand why the president

TABLE 13.2
Top 25 Metropolitan Exporters

Cities	Exports [in billions of $]
1. Detroit, MI	27.3
2. New York, NY	27.1
3. San Jose, CA	26.8
4. Los Angeles–Long Beach, CA*	24.7
5. Chicago, IL	21.1
6. Seattle–Bellevue–Everett, WA	17.8
7. Houston, TX	16.2
8. Minneapolis–St. Paul, MN–WI	11.1
9. Miami, FL	10.2
10. Portland–Vancouver, OR–WA	8.9
11. Washington, DC–MD–WA–WV	8.4
12. San Francisco, CA	8.1
13. Orange County, CA*	8.0
14. Boston, MA–NH	7.9
15. Philadelphia, PA–NJ	7.9
16. Dallas, TX	6.9
17. Phoenix–Mesa, AZ	6.8
18. Oakland, CA	6.4
19. San Diego, CA	5.9
20. Atlanta, GA	5.8
21. Newark, NJ	5.6
22. Richmond–Petersburg, VA	5.4
23. Stamford–Norwalk, CT	4.9
24. Bergen–Passaic, NJ	4.8
25. Cleveland–Lorain–Elyria, OH	4.7

SOURCE: U.S., Dept. of Commerce, 1995.

*Orange County is actually part of metropolitan L.A.

or the central government was unable to overrule the port authority of New York. In the 1980s, state and local governments became important arenas for making **the nuclear freeze and anti-South Africa apartheid issues** of national concern. Grassroots efforts by local groups were successful in passing nuclear freeze resolutions by local governments and in promoting divestment of government funds from American companies doing business with South Africa.[27] These efforts at the state and local level catalyzed social movements that influenced governmental politics at the national level. Thus,

ESSAY 13.2
FOREIGN INVESTMENT, STATE AND LOCAL GOVERNMENTS, AND THE COMPETITIVE SPIRIT

When foreign companies look to invest in America, states become aggressive in competing with each other through different development strategies and incentives packages. Foreign investment brings local jobs and an influx in the economy. Not surprisingly, state and local governments have become increasingly active in attempting to attract new foreign investment (from abroad as well as from outside the state), while trying to keep traditional businesses alive and in the state (as opposed to leaving the state and investing beyond). Such is not only the case for large states, like California and New York, but also for small states as well. In South Carolina, for example, foreign companies have had a stronghold in the economy since the 1960s. Clearly, the implications for local economies and politics, as well as the politics of U.S. foreign policy, loom large.

Foreign investment has grown enormously within the United States. Direct foreign investment in property, plant, and equipment in the U.S. approached $1 trillion by the mid-nineties and employed over 5 million people. States offer big money to win foreign investment, and the trend has been to offer more and more incentives with time. For example, in the 1980s, Honda Corporation got a $16 million grant from the state of Ohio for a plant in Marysville. Kentucky had to agree to more than $125 million in perks for a Toyota Motor Corporation plant in Georgetown—it's estimated, in fact, that state and local governments will have paid as much as $350 million in incentives when all of the numbers are finalized.

Competition between states and locales have become, if anything, more and more fierce. The state of Tennessee had to offer the investors of a Japanese auto-parts plant highway improvements, new sewer lines, tax abatements, discounted utility rates, English language lessons, and driving lessons to win the plant. And the trend with most companies, especially Japanese-owned ones, is to know what the last investor got and use that as a starting point for negotiations. Some states have even attempted to get airlines to offer direct flights to Japan.

Similar incentives were given to BMW to build a plant in South Carolina—to invest a total of $800 million by 1998 and create over 2,200 jobs. The tax incentives alone provided by the state of South Carolina and by local governments totaled over $200 million. The incentive package included $70 million for state and local tax breaks, $62 million for airport improvements, $37 million for land, $23 million for site improvements, and $10 million for training costs. A $100 million widening of the interstate highway was also to occur, most of it funded by the federal government. As the headline of Columbia's *The State* newspaper put it, "S.C.'s Incentive Deal for BMW Equals $100,000 per Job."

South Carolina is a good illustration of the importance of these international economic activities for state and local governments. Within the state one of the most important governmental agencies is the Department of Commerce, which actively attempts to attract foreign investment into South Carolina (and promote exports abroad). Although the value of foreign investment is not particularly large in comparison to other states—South Carolina has only 3 million people—it has a larger percentage of employees working for foreign-owned companies than virtually any other state. In fact, South Carolina has been ranked No. 1 in the Southeast for foreign investment in the nineties.

Since 1960, more than $15 billion of foreign corporate investment in manufacturing, distribution, and administrative headquarters have entered the state, producing more then 80,000 jobs. And foreign investment has steadily grown as **table 13.3** demonstrates.

In 1996 alone, 202 international firms invested over $2 billion in South Carolina, a 25 percent increase over 1995 and 114 percent higher than 1994. International companies created about 5,000 new jobs in 1996, 22 percent more than in 1994. "New" international firms to the state created 1,396 new jobs during 1996. In 1995 and 1996 combined, 356 international firms invested over $4 billion in South Carolina, creating over 11,000 new jobs. New interna-

TABLE 13.3
INTERNATIONAL CAPITAL INVESTMENT ACTIVITY
SOUTH CAROLINA HISTORICAL TRENDS
1960–1996

YEAR	EMPLOYMENT	INVESTMENT [$000]
1996	4,981	$2,254,888
1995	6,307	$1,832,930
1994	4,089	$1,049,859
1993	3,376	$670,210
1992	5,085	$1,397,302
1991	2,043	$830,089
1990	2,424	$912,607
1989	3,503	$1,114,258
1988	3,162	$710,255
1987	5,226	$618,511
1986	1,819	$153,909
1985	2,228	$188,259
1984	1,225	$136,379
1983	1,164	$130,695
1982	965	$450,460
1981	2,716	$492,816
1980	1,347	$348,908
1979	3,988	$392,535
1978	2,719	$208,205
1977	3,825	$408,162
1976	2,260	$186,005
1975	275	$58,800
1974	3,005	$313,053
1973	3,713	$340,660
1972	705	$61,900
1971	290	$4,635
1970	940	$72,300
1969	610	$48,400
1968	2,525	$184,500
1967	350	$17,750
1966	2,582	$152,800
1965	2,200	$79,250
1964	510	$29,506
1963	825	$40,182
1962	50	$485
1961	0	$500
1960	500	$32,083
Prior 1960	970	$79,560
Totals	**78,195**	**$14,090,716**

SOURCE: South Carolina, Department of Commerce, *1996 Annual Report.*

tional companies often tend to have a "ripple effect" on the activities of other local companies. BMW, for example, engaged in subcontracting with at least fifteen other companies for supplies and parts.

South Carolina has attracted foreign investment from fifteen countries thus far. Of this, the bulk of the foreign investment comes from Germany, Japan, France, Sweden, the United Kingdom, and Canada. **Table 13.4** breaks down foreign investment within South Carolina in 1996.

South Carolina has become increasingly attractive to a widening range of high-tech, high value-added companies, especially in the areas of textile products, chemicals, rubber and plastics, metals and equipment, transportation equipment, distribution, and research and development. Although international companies have invested in plant and equipment throughout the state, most of the activity has

been located near the three major metropolitan areas of Charleston, Columbia, and, especially, Greenville-Spartarburg, as detailed by **figure 13.1**.

Clearly, for South Carolina as with many states, foreign investment is a major state and local strategy for promoting economic development. South Carolina has also been active in its trade promotion abroad. In 1996, South Carolina firms exported $6.7 billion of made-in-South Carolina products, up 24 percent from 1994. The Department of Commerce established a trade office in Frankfurt for promoting markets in Europe, Africa, and the Middle East. They also increased participation in international trade missions and trade shows, scheduling eighteen trade events, up from just two the previous year. Locations included Israel, South Africa, Austria, Australia, South America, the Philippines, Poland, Japan, Germany, the Czech Republic, and the Slovak Republic.

TABLE 13.4

INTERNATIONAL CAPITAL INVESTMENT ACTIVITY IN SOUTH CAROLINA
BY INVESTMENT LEVEL
1996

COUNTRY	FIRMS	%	JOBS	%	INVESTMENT	%
GERMANY	59	29.6%	1,554	31.5%	$950,529,345	42.3%
JAPAN	27	13.6%	919	18.6%	$531,598,372	23.6%
FRANCE	16	7.9%	361	7.2%	$290,895,000	12.9%
SWEDEN	7	3.5%	686	13.8%	$152,375,000	6.8%
UNITED KINGDOM	38	19.1%	480	9.7%	$102,308,000	4.6%
CANADA	13	6.5%	409	8.3%	$59,163,292	2.6%
BELGIUM	5	2.5%	102	2.1%	$47,825,000	2.1%
SWITZERLAND	11	5.5%	69	1.4%	$30,075,000	1.3%
ITALY	10	5.0%	262	5.3%	$29,247,400	1.3%
NETHERLANDS	5	2.5%	39	0.8%	$26,116,027	1.2%
DENMARK	4	2.0%	C	C	$12,906,000	0.6%
AUSTRALIA	3	1.5%	C	C	$10,250,000	0.5%
IRELAND	2	1.0%	C	C	$6,150,000	0.3%
AUSTRIA	1	0.5%	26	0.5%	C	C
SINGAPORE	1	0.5%	3	0.1%	C	C
Totals	202		4,981		$2,254,888,436	

C indicates *confidential information* withheld at the request of the company.

SOURCE: South Carolina, Department of Commerce, *1996 Annual Report.*

FIGURE 13.1
INTERNATIONAL FIRMS CAPITAL INVESTMENT 1996
THROUGHOUT SOUTH CAROLINA

COUNTRY	FIRMS
Germany	59
United Kingdom	38
Japan	27
France	16
Canada	13
Switzerland	11
Italy	10
Sweden	7
Belgium	5
Netherlands	5
Denmark	4
Australia	3
Ireland	2
Austria	1
Singapore	1

NOTE: Symbols are not precise location of facilities nor exact replicas of national flags.

SOURCE: South Carolina, Department of Commerce, *1996 Annual Report.*

Because of all the economic implications of foreign trade and investment, there is much room for political gain and controversy. Increased jobs and growing economies, whatever their source, tend to play well in state and local politics. On the other hand, the closing of plants and jobs—especially if they move abroad—can destroy a local community and produce popular resentment. For example, in South Carolina, where international companies are newly investing, older businesses, such as textiles, have been closing their doors. Such is the complex politics of international trade and investment at the national, state, and local levels as the United States enters the twenty-first century.

SOURCES: Chris Burritt, "BMW Eases Boom and Bust of Textiles," *Atlanta Constitution* (April 14, 1996), Sec. H, p. 9; Allen R. Myerson, "Prosperity with an Asterisk," *New York Times* (Jan. 2, 1996), Sec. C, p. 12; Bill Powell, "War Between the States," *Newsweek* (May 30, 1988) pp. 44–45; Gerald F. Seib and John Harwood, "Foreign Competition Batters State's Textiles, but Fuji and BMW Provide Jobs," *Wall Street Journal* (Feb. 28, 1996), Sec. A, p. 1; South Carolina, Department of Commerce, *1996 Annual Report;* Betsy Teter, "S.C.'s Incentive Deal for BMW Equals $100,00 per Job," *The State* (September 27, 1992), 1A, 11A; Wendy Warren, "S.C. Leads Southeast States in 1992 Foreign Investment," *The State* (Sept. 27, 1993), Sec. C, p. 7;

grassroots efforts helped produce political controversy for the Reagan administration's arms-control policies and forced U.S. government economic sanctions against South Africa. The SST case illustrates how so-called low foreign policy issues have a great impact on foreign policy relations in general, while the nuclear freeze and anti-apartheid movements dealt with matters of great national security concern.

Michael Shuman, in "Dateline Main Street: Local Foreign Policies," points out that the *foreign policy actions by state and local governments fall into three rough categories:* consciousness-raising measures, unilateral measures, and bilateral measures.[28] "Most local governments, whether they realize it or not, are involved in raising public consciousness on foreign affairs through education, research, and lobbying." According to Shuman, "virtually every municipality has international affairs-related curricula in its public schools, its adult education courses, and its museums and cultural centers."[29] Lobbying campaigns also have been used by local governments to promote the visibility of issues. Resolutions, as discussed above, were passed at the local level to promote the nuclear freeze and anti-apartheid issues.

State and local foreign governments have also taken unilateral initiatives, such as the use of policing, zoning, contracting, and investing powers. These activities range from the creation of "nuclear free zones," to giving sanctuary to Central American refugees, to various measures to divest and restrict relations with South Africa and with companies doing business in South Africa. In fact, the impact of state and local governments continued after President George Bush lifted economic sanctions in September 1991 against South Africa following some progress in the dismantling of the legal policy of apartheid. Over twenty-five states, twenty counties, and eighty cities (plus many other public and private institutions), including big city governments such as Los Angeles, New York, and San Francisco, continued to impose sanctions until apartheid was completely abolished, thus contributing to very low levels of U.S.-South African trade.[30]

In a proactive initiative due to the large influx of people from the Caribbean and Central America, the state of Florida created **the "Florida International Volunteer Corps"**—a type of state-level "Peace Corps" to promote economic and political development throughout the region. The intent is for volunteers in a wide variety of professions and fields to provide short-term, small-scale, self-help, overseas technical assistance and training in health, agriculture, social services, education, the environment, and more. The Florida International Volunteer Corps acts in partnership with its Caribbean neighbors, as well as the U.S. government (such as the Agency for International Development) and various international developmental organizations, on the assumption that Florida's future is interwoven with its Caribbean neighbors.[31]

Finally, state and local governments have negotiated thousands of bilateral agreements with foreign governments. For example, over 1,280 **"sister" city arrangements** between over 780 American and 1,150 foreign cities exist, ranging across all fifty states and over eighty-five foreign countries.[32] Sister city relationships began to spread following World War II as a means to provide American humanitarian and cultural assistance; they have proliferated in the last two decades and are likely to involve economic trade now as well. State governments, as discussed above, have been most active in establishing bilateral economic relationships abroad.

Whether the role of state and local governments will become more influential remains to be seen. Judicial decisions have ruled in favor of national supremacy, limiting foreign policy actions by state and local governments.[33] Nevertheless, the post–Vietnam War political environment has given state and local governments greater flexibility for action. This is likely to be reinforced by changes in East-West relations with the end of the cold war, the increasing interdependence between America and the world, and the continuing revolution in global communications. Although state and local governments remain peripheral foreign policy players for the most part, their involvement makes the politics of U.S. foreign policy an even messier and more complex process.

THE WASHINGTON
POLITICAL COMMUNITY
. . . .

The final governmental source of influence on the policymaking process that needs noting is the Washington political community. The **annual Gridiron dinner** exemplifies this side of life in the nation's capital. "The annual spring dinner of the Gridiron Club, an elitist social club of sixty print journalists, is one of the high tribal rites of Washington insiders. It is a gathering of political celebrities that combines snob appeal with Hollywood glitter."[34] The Gridiron dinner brings together six hundred of the most powerful, best-known people in America at the Capitol Hilton hotel; every president since Benjamin Harrison has participated at least once. The Gridiron dinner is "Hollywood stars rubbing elbows with the captains of industry, the anchors of television, the publishers and other princes of the print press, the deans of the diplomatic corps, the elders of the Supreme Court, the movers and shakers of Congress, and the ranking echelons of the current administration."[35]

It's an evening of making fun of and roasting the nation's leaders. "For some politicians, the Gridiron has been a priceless forum for reshaping their images and reputations by showing a human side, an ability to laugh at themselves, which is the principal formula of success at the dinner."[36] The beauty of it all is that there is no television coverage of the Gridiron dinner and virtually no press coverage—it's basically a private affair of the rich, powerful, and famous.

Nancy Reagan used the Gridiron dinner in 1982 to improve her embittered image among the powerful guests whose opinions are so consequential in shaping the opinions of others. By the end of 1981, Nancy Reagan was receiving "bad press" about her wardrobe and lavish spending habits, such as the $209,000 she spent on new china for the White House. She was increasingly depicted as an uncaring, self-absorbed socialite—all of which was detracting from the president's program and popularity. Members of Nancy Reagan's and President Reagan's staffs sought ways to improve her public image and to show that she was a caring human being. One strategy was to get her involved in antidrug work; another was to have her perform a vaudeville skit at the Gridiron dinner in which Nancy mocked herself.

On March 27, 1982, most guests at the annual Gridiron dinner were unaware of what was to transpire; even Ronald Reagan was in the dark. Late in the evening, Nancy Reagan excused herself from the table. Moments later she burst onto the stage dancing and singing to the old tune "Secondhand Rose" recast as "Secondhand Clothes." "She was clad in an outlandish getup, an aqua skirt with red and yellow flowers held together by safety pins, a floppy feathered hat, and a feathered boa."[37] There was a moment of shock and deafening silence in the hall, but soon people jumped to their feet and applauded Nancy who was "unbelievably" mocking herself and her lavish style. For an exit, she tried to shatter a china plate on the stage and the cheering crowd brought her back for an encore. "The affair remained unreported. Only the inner core of the Washington community had seen this side of Mrs. Reagan. But that community included most of the important journalists and politicians, and among this crucial audience, Mrs. Reagan's image had been remade in a few short minutes";[38] that is, until her involvement with astrology and her bitter relationship with Chief of Staff Donald Regan became public during President Reagan's second term of office.

The annual Gridiron dinner and the Nancy Reagan episode are indicative of what Hedrick Smith, in *The Power Game: How Washington Works,* calls "Life Inside the Beltway: The Folkways of Washington."[39] A subculture and set of norms pervades Washington, D.C., and the national political community. President Jimmy Carter referred to Washington and "Washingtonians" as an island isolated from the rest of America. On the one hand, Washington, D.C., is a large and complex metropolitan area that includes northern Virginia and part of Maryland. Consisting of almost four million people, most of whom are Americans from all different walks of life, it is no different from many other urban areas in America. On the other hand, Washington is the seat of national government and attracts a large number of people in and out of government who become absorbed with politics.

The **Washington political community** refers to the "one hundred thousand or so whose life revolves around government, especially the few thousand at the peak who live and breathe politics."[40] It was the Washington political community and its particular subculture to which Jimmy Carter referred above. *At least eight characteristics pervade the Washington political community:*[41]

1. Preoccupation with politics;
2. Quest for power, status, and visibility;
3. Importance of networking;
4. Prominence of pragmatism;
5. Prevalence of workaholism;
6. Use of jargon;
7. Prevalence of a lonely existence;
8. Domination by men.

Many of these characteristics that pervade the political world of Washington have been mentioned in previous chapters and essays (such as essay 12.3 on Newt Gingrich, personal ambition, and the quest for power and glory). For understanding these norms and folkways helps to develop a strong understanding of how the complex politics of U.S. foreign policy are played out at the nation's capital and in the higher echelons of power of American society.

First is the **preoccupation with politics**. For all its size, complexity, and cosmopolitan flavor, Washington is very much a "company town." Washington is dominated by a single employer, the federal government. The existence and growth of the federal government is the reason why Washington has grown and prospered as an urban area. It explains why it has also attracted a large private sector filled with lawyers, lobbyists, policy analysts, and consultants. Governmental and national politics dominate the lives of the Washington political community and trickle down to affect local residents as well. It is a town where cab drivers regularly talk politics and where local television news shows begin their programs with national and international news. Politics is an all-day-and-night affair for the most politically active, and after-work hours are filled with cocktail parties and social functions that revolve around politics.

A second characteristic of the Washington political community is the **quest for power, status and visibility**. "Power, of course, is the aphrodisiac—the special brand of federal power that is Washington's monopoly."[42] The town attracts and rewards those who are the most ambitious and have the most powerful egos. People are wrapped up in their own self-importance, and attempt to acquire and exercise power to demonstrate their importance to "relevant others." Those who are new, young, and ambitious quickly learn the significance of position, status, and influence. Many catch "Potomac Fever"—the "incurable addiction of wielding power or feeling at the political center."[43]

Established figures are particularly preoccupied with placing themselves on public display and maintaining and promoting their status and influence. In the words of Elliot Richardson, who has held four cabinet positions in the Nixon and Ford administrations, "Washington is really, when you come right down to it, a city of cocker spaniels. . . . It's a city of people who are more interested in being petted and admired than in rendering the exercise of power."[44] Politicians, in particular, "love to be noticed, and they take their notices very seriously, assuming their own importance and grasping for daily confirmation in the attention of the press and television." Regardless of one's place within the Washington political community, "it is a self-selected group, ambitious and aggressive, marked by collective immodesty."[45]

For all its preoccupation with power, status and visibility, the Washington political community actually is quite "porous." Newcomers to Washington with prominent positions are readily accepted. "Indeed, Washington regularly takes in newcomers, absorbs them and makes them its own."[46] Young, ambitious types "wet behind the ears" can rise in position and influence if they are extremely "résumé" conscious and are ready to make new inroads within the Washington political community. Where forty years ago the Washington political community was smaller and much more closed to outsiders, today it is larger and more permeable than ever.

The third characteristic of the Washington political community is the crucial **importance of "networking."** One quickly learns that the key to individual upward mobility is to extend one's network: to get to know other people, to become visible to others, and to be informed about what's going on. No matter how powerful and close to the center of things one gets, power is so diffused throughout the government and dispersed among so many groups and individuals, that maintaining and extending one's networks is the key to exercising power and influence. According to Hedrick Smith, "political alliances are vital not only for survival but to promote policies, to lobby former colleagues, or to play the more personal game of 'careers,' advancement up the ladder for the in-and-outers who ride the ebb and flow of partisan politics upward with each generation."[47]

Interacting and building coalitions with others is a crucial and necessary aspect of politics. Much of the interaction and the development of networks occurs informally and behind the scenes. Nothing is sinister about this activity; for the most part it reflects normal human interaction. Informal occasions, such as a cocktail party, a round of golf, or a beer at a local hangout, are likely to be when new ties are made and important business is conducted. Indicative of the preoccupation with networking in Washington is that upon leaving a social function with a spouse or friend, the first question is never, "Did you have a good time?" but "Who did you meet? What did you hear?"

Politicians and members of the Washington political community also have a **tendency to be pragmatic**, which is consistent with the three first characteristics. To gain power and prestige, one must work with others. As the old adage says, "to get along one must go along." Few individuals can afford to make many enemies if they want to be politically successful and exercise influence. Some individuals and groups in Washington operate more ideologically. However, most Washingtonians quickly learn the value of political moderation, the need to compromise with adversaries, and the importance of not holding a grudge if they want to survive and prosper.

"Newcomers arrive full of idealism and energy only to discover what a tiny fragment of power they retain."[48] This fact reinforces the need to network

and be pragmatic. The common problem is that pragmatism, and the other characteristics of the Washington community, push idealism and principles aside in the long run. In this respect, ideology and principle—at least **the appearance of being principled** and above politics—tend to be saved especially for the public and the folks back home. Nowhere is the gap between daily behavior and public pronouncements greater than among members of Congress. Thus, it should not be surprising that Washington can be a town of strange bedfellows, where "personal relationships often cut across party and ideological lines, so that conservative and liberal leopards who roar at each other in congressional debates play tennis on the weekends or joke together in the Capitol cloakrooms."[49]

A fifth characteristic is that Washington is a community of **workaholics**. "People coming into government from private life are shocked at the compulsive intensity and workaholic ethic of Washington."[50] Sixty- and seventy-hour, six- and seven-day work weeks are common in and out of government; and, this does not include the socializing after work that goes on where politicking and business continues. To "make it" and play an influential role, a degree of workaholism is required because of the increasing demands of the job, the incredible size of the government, the ever-expanding size of the Washington political community, and the faster pace of modern lifestyles. Yet, this is also the case because the more ambitious "overachievers" who get drawn to the top are people who have little difficulty working long hours. While some get "burnt out" and leave Washington altogether, others thrive in this environment. Among those who gain prominence "most stay in Washington and become lawyers, lobbyists, or consultants, because they've grown accustomed to Washington's ways and to thinking of themselves as movers and shakers, and no other place has quite the same excitement and allure."[51]

Washingtonians also communicate and interact in a language which is extremely jargonistic, a sixth characteristic. Much of the language is dry and formal because of the legal training of so many people and because of the bureaucratic nature of government that operates in terms of laws, statutes, and regulations written in "legalese" and "bureaucratese." This is combined with a Washingtonian fondness for acronyms and other shorthand phrases. For example, the National Security Council is referred to as the "NSC," whereas the State Department goes by "State" or "Foggy Bottom." Where information is a source of power, **language** is often a sign of status, for it allows a Washingtonian quickly to know whether one is an outsider or an insider, and how much he or she is "in the know."

A seventh characteristic is that members of Washington's political community, especially those who have risen to the height of political power and prestige, live a **rather lonely existence**. The networks that one develops may be quite extensive, but most of the people are, at best, acquaintances. Everybody is perceived as being on the political make, interacting for a particular political purpose. "The competitiveness of the power game inhibits people from revealing the kind of personal vulnerability and doubts about life that are vital to forming close and sincere friendships. . . . The risk of inner self-revelation, which genuine intimacy requires, is too dangerous for most politicians and public officials."[52] Therefore, friendships are difficult to make and sustain.

Finally, Washington remains a "man's town" to this day. Women have progressed a great deal within Washington. Inroads have been made by women into the Washington political community, many reaching highly visible and prominent positions; but most women in Washington fill secretarial and service positions. Although much has changed as discussed in the chapters above, the more one examines positions of power, prestige, and visibility, the more likely it is that one will find that the players are men.

The Washington political community has always been around, yet it has experienced some change over time. Forty years ago, Washington was a smaller, sleepy, southern town with much less government, and politics was dominated by a small **"good ole boy network."** This has changed. Power has dispersed and the Washington community has grown in size. "Washington used to be cozy," observed Barbara Bamarekian, who worked in the Kennedy White House and later became a *New York Times* reporter. "You could go to a party, a reception of a hundred people, and look around and say, 'Well, everybody's here—everybody who counts.' You can't do that anymore. The city has grown big and amorphous. There are so many social circles: the administration people, the corporate crowd, members of Congress, patrons of the arts, the old Kennedy-Johnson crowd, the Reagan Republicans, the Nixon-Ford Republicans. These circles bump up against each other now but it's not one cozy network anymore."[53]

The development of a dominant subculture among a select community of individuals is *not unique to Washington*. Such is the norm in all walks of life: whether for national government in Washington or local government elsewhere, in business and on Wall Street, within academia, in the entertainment world of Hollywood, or on Main Street U.S.A. The top of all professions and spheres of life tends to be dominated by a relatively small group of more active and involved individuals who operate according to a certain unwritten set of subcultural rules and norms. Yet, the subculture pervading the Washington political community remains "one of the great mysteries of American politics."

Bits and pieces of information about the Washington political community may be gleaned from the media. Yet, most Americans are unaware of this subculture. When they visit Washington, they see the shining facades of the government buildings, the memorials, and the nice speeches that are part of the grand tours. More surprisingly, many academics, including political scientists, are unaware of the workings of the Washington political community or ignore its political importance. Whatever the case, *to ignore the Washington political community is to ignore an important ingredient* in understanding the complex politics of U.S. foreign policy.

The Washington political community describes the immediate political environment in which governmental policymaking in the executive branch and the Congress operates. As we will discuss in part III, it is the same political environment where, for example, interest groups throughout society and the media also operate. Thus, the Washington political community is where much of domestic politics and governmental policymaking intersect, affecting agenda-setting, policy formulation, and the implementation of policy.

Comprehending the nature of the Washington political community allows for a better understanding of how issues get on the political agenda, are dealt with, and disappear. While most of the hundreds of issues that the government deals with daily attract little attention, a few issues gain great national visibility, but rarely for more than a brief period. As Hedrick Smith notes, "Washington is a city mercurial in its moods, short in its attention span, and given to fetishes. Events flash and disappear like episodes in a soap opera, intensely important for a brief period and then quickly forgotten."[54] Subcultural rules and norms also explain why networking, coalition-building, persuading, bargaining, and compromise are an integral part of politics within government and throughout the political community in the formulation and implementation of public policy.

The prevalence and power of life within the Washington political community account for the reason politics "inside the beltway" is different from politics as seen by the public outside the beltway. It **helps to explain why the politics of symbolism prevails** when political issues are before the media spotlight and the public. Under these conditions, most involved in the privileged Washington community present a public persona that is more principled, more idealistic, and more in accord with dominant American values than exists in reality. This has helped to create a gap between public expectations and political performance.

It also helps to explain why a president's professional reputation and public prestige, as discussed in chapter 5, are crucial ingredients in exercising leadership and governing. Presidents who have poorly understood the nature of the Washington political community, such as Jimmy Carter and his staff, have had great difficulty exercising power. Those who have understood the game better, such as Ronald Reagan and his staff, have been able to govern more successfully. In this respect, understanding the subculture of the Washington political community is one key to understanding the complex politics of U.S. foreign policy.

Governmental Politics in Perspective

We have now completed our overview of the government and the policymaking process as it affects U.S. foreign policy. Presidential power, the foreign policy bureaucracy, Congress and the rest of government, including the Washington political community, have all been examined. Together, they provide a picture of the three foreign policy themes addressed throughout: continuity and change, the president's ability to govern, and the tension between national security and democracy. Therefore, one should now have a better grasp of the complexity and the politics of the foreign policy process.

To fully understand how U.S. foreign policy is made, however, one must place governmental politics in perspective, for it is derived from and influences the larger domestic political environment. Thus, the next part of this book focuses on society and the role of domestic politics in influencing the government and the policymaking process. More specifically, we examine the public and its beliefs, electoral and group politics, and the media and the communications process in an effort to more fully understand the complex politics of U.S. foreign policy.

Bibliographic Essay

The role of the Constitution and the judiciary in foreign affairs was once a popular scholarly topic, but the rise of presidential power during the cold war years diminished most interest, except among constitutional and legal scholars. Also, the changes of the post–Vietnam War years as well as the constitutional crises of

Watergate and Iran-Contra have not rekindled much interest in the judicial role in foreign affairs. Nevertheless, a few important works on the Constitution and the judiciary are available. *Foreign Affairs and the Constitution* (Mineola, N.Y.: Foundation Press, first edition in 1972, revised in 1996) by Louis Henkin remains the definitive constitutional study of the distribution of power in the national government, federalism, and individual rights relative to foreign policy, including the role of the courts. Henkin also has published a more current series of thoughtful essays in *Constitutionalism, Democracy, and Foreign Affairs* (New York: Columbia University Press, 1990). A nice overview from a legal perspective is provided by Thomas M. Franck and Michael J. Glennon, in *Foreign Relations and National Security Law: Cases, Materials and Simulations* (St. Paul, Minn.: West, 1987). Harold Hongju Koh assesses the constitutional interpretations and judicial developments that contributed to the Iran-Contra affair, in *The National Security Constitution: Sharing Power After the Iran-Contra Affair* (New Haven, Conn.: Yale University Press, 1990).

While the role of state and local governments in foreign policy has historically attracted little attention, some scholarship has been generated over the last decade. Chadwick F. Alger discusses the changing global context of cities and its general impact on foreign policy in "The World Relations of Cities: Closing the Gap Between Social Science Paradigms and Everyday Human Experience," *International Studies Quarterly* 34 (December 1990): 493–518. Journalist John Maxwell Hamilton describes myriad connections between local American communities and the world in *Mainstreet America and the Third World* (Cabin John, Md.: Seven Locks Press, 1986). Michael H. Shuman provides an informative overview of the foreign policies of local governments in "Dateline Main Street: Local Foreign Policies," *Foreign Policy* 65 (Winter 1986–1987): 154–74.

The nature and importance of the Washington political community has been almost completely ignored, especially by political scientists. Beyond the feel of the Washington subculture that one can derive from reading memoirs of political figures, Hedrick Smith provides an excellent portrayal of "Life Inside the Beltway: The Folkways of Washington" in *The Power Game* (New York: Ballantine, 1988), pp. 89–118, as does John M. Barry in *The Ambition and the Power: The Fall of Jim Wright, A True Story of Washington* (New York: Penguin, 1989).

ENDNOTES

1. See Thomas M. Franck and Michael J. Glennon, *Foreign Relations and National Security Law: Cases, Materials and Simulations* (St. Paul, Minn.: West Publishing, 1987); Michael J. Glennon, *Constitutional Diplomacy* (Princeton, N.J.: Princeton University Press, 1991); Louis Henkin, *Foreign Affairs and the Constitution* (Mineola, N.Y.: Foundation Press, 1972 and 1996); Jerel A. Rosati, "A Neglected Actor in American Foreign Policy: The Role of the Judiciary," *International Studies Notes* 12 (Fall 1985): 10–15; and Jean E. Smith, *The Constitution and American Foreign Policy* (St. Paul, Minn.: West Publishing, 1989).

2. Henkin, *Foreign Affairs and the Constitution*, p. 27.

3. See also Edward S. Corwin, *The President: Office and Powers* (New York: New York University Press, 1957); Clinton Rossiter with Richard P. Longaker, *The Supreme Court and the Commander in Chief* (Ithaca, N.Y.: Cornell University Press, 1976).

4. *Immigration and Naturalization Service v. Chadha*, 77 U.S. 317 (1983). See also U.S., Congress, Congressional Research Service, *Foreign Policy: Effect of the Supreme Court's Legislative Veto Decision*, Issue Brief IB83123 (September 6, 1983). These are only a few of the acts affecting foreign policy that contain a legislative veto; see U.S., Department of Justice, Office of Legal Counsel, *Compilation of Currently Effective Statutes that Contain Legislative Veto Provisions* (July 15, 1983).

5. *Capital Industries-EMI, Inc. v. Bennet*, 82 U.S. 688 (1983) See Linda Greenhouse, "Justices Get Corporate Tax Dispute," *New York Times* (November 2, 1993).

6. Rosati, "Neglected Actor in America," pp. 11–12.

7. Louis Henkin, "Constitutional Issues in Foreign Policy," *Journal of International Affairs* 23 (1969): 221.

8. See A.D. D'Amato and Robert M. O'Neil, *The Judiciary and Vietnam* (New York: St. Martin's Press, 1972); Louis Henkin, "Is There a 'Political Question' Doctrine?" *Yale Law Journal* 85 (April 1976): 597–695; and Howard E. Shuman and Walter R. Thomas, eds., *The Constitution and National Security* (Washington, D.C.: National Defense University Press, 1990).

9. See Bob Cohn, "Anatomy of a Pardon: Why Weinberger Walked," *Newsweek* (January 11, 1993); 22–23; David Johnston, "Ex-CIA Agent Is Guilty of Tax Charges in Iran-Contra Affair," *New York Times* (September 19, 1990): A14; David Johnston, "Poindexter Is Found Guilty of All 5 Criminal Charges for Iran-Contra Cover-up," *New York Times* (April 8, 1990): 1,

16; and George Lardner, Jr. and Walter Pincus, "Ex-CIA Aide Admits Iran-Contra Role," *Washington Post* (July 10, 1991).

10. Aaron Epstein, "Federal Appeals Panel Sets Aside North's Convictions," *The State*, Columbia, S.C. (July 12, 1990): 1A, 4A, and Joel Bleifuss, "Decade of Deceit," *In These Times* (November 7–13, 1990): 4–5. For similar argument about the role of politics, but from a completely different perspective, see Elliot Abrams, *Undue Process: A Story of How Political Differences Are Turned Into Crimes* (New York: Free Press, 1993) and Gideon Rose, "When Presidents Break the Law," *The National Interest* (Fall 1987): 50–63.

11. Theodore Draper, "Revelations of the North Trial," *New York Review of Books* (August 17, 1989): 55.

12. Ronald Reagan agreed to a taped interview while in office as president for the Oliver North trial and testified in person out of office in the trial of John Poindexter.

13. David Johnston, "Case Dismissed in Contra Affair, Clearing Agent," *New York Times* (November 25, 1989): 1, 10 and Doe Pichirallo, "Thornburgh Blocks Release of Secrets in Iran-Contra Trial," *Washington Post* (November 23, 1989): A1, A12.

14. Joel Bleifuss, "Decade of Deceit," *In These Times* (November, 7–13, 1990): 4.

15. Draper, "Revelations of the North Trial," p. 59. The National Security Agency traditionally has been the most secretive bureaucracy within the intelligence community and was the most obstructionist in opposing the release of any classified information, even where it already existed in the public record. See George Lardner, Jr., "Uncompromising NSA Frustrated Prosecutors in Iran-Contra Case," *Washington Post* (March 19, 1990) A1, A4.

16. In addition, at the federal level there are the Territorial Courts, the United States Court of International Trade, the United States Court of Federal Claims, the United States Court of Appeals for the Armed Forces, and the United States Court of Veterans Appeals, which are described in the *U.S. Government Manual*.

17. For an overview of the Supreme Court and the judicial system, see Henry J. Abraham, *The Judiciary: The Supreme Court in the Governmental Process* (Boston: Allyna and Bacon, 1983), and Lawrence Baum, *The Supreme Court* (Washington, D.C.: Congressional Quarterly Press, 1981).

18. See, for example, David G. Savage, *Turning Right: The Making of the Rehnquist Supreme Court* (New York: Wiley, 1992).

19. Henkin, *Foreign Affairs and the Constitution* (1996), pp. 148–49.

20. For some background, see Samuel H. Beer, *To Make a Nation: The Rediscovery of American Federalism* (Cambridge: Harvard University Press, 1993).

21. Chadwick F. Alger, "Columbus in the World: The World in Columbus," *International Associations* (1974): 393–405.

22. Chadwick F. Alger, "The World Relations of Cities: Closing the Gap Between Social Science Paradigms and Everyday Human Experience," *International Studies Quarterly* 34 (December 1990): 493–518. See also Chadwick F. Alger, " 'Foreign' Policies of U.S. Publics," *International Studies Quarterly* 21 (June 1977): 277–318.

23. John Maxwell Hamilton, *Mainstreet America and the Third World* (Cabin John, Md.: Seven Locks Press, 1986).

24. See Douglas M. Brown and Earl H. Fry, eds., *States and Provinces in the International Economy* (Berkeley, Calif.: Institute of Governmental Studies Press, 1993); John M. Kline, *State Government Influence in U.S. International Economic Policy* (Lexington, Mass.: Lexington Books. 1983); Hugh O'Neill, "The Role of States in Trade Development," in Frank J. Macchiarola, ed., *International Trade: The Changing Role of the United States* (New York: The Academy of Political Science, 1990): 181–89.

25. Robert Griffith, "American Politics and the Origins of 'McCarthyism,' " in William H. Chafe and Harvard Sitkoff, eds., *A History of Our Time: Readings on Postwar America* (New York: Oxford University Press, 1991), p. 71.

26. See also David Caute, *The Great Fear: The Anti-Communist Purge Under Truman and Eisenhower* (New York: Simon and Schuster, 1978).

27. See Janice Love, *The U.S. Anti-Apartheid Movement: Local Activism in Global Politics* (New York: Praeger, 1986).

28. Michael H. Shuman, "Dateline Main Street: Local Foreign Policies," *Foreign Policy* 65 (Winter 1986–1987): 154–74. See also James O. Goldsborough, "California's Foreign Policy," *Foreign Affairs* (Spring 1993): 88–96; Heidi H. Hobbs, *City Hall Goes Abroad: The Foreign Policy of Local Politics* (Thousand Oaks, Calif.: Sage, 1994); John M. Kline, "A New Federalism for United States Foreign Policy," *International Journal* (Summer 1986): 507–38; Paul L. Knox and Peter J. Taylor, eds., *World Cities in a World System* (New York: Cambridge University Press, 1995). There is

even a national journal published on *Municipal Foreign Policies.*

29. Shuman, "Dateline Main Street," pp. 159–60.

30. See, for example, "A Farewell to Sanctions," *Newsweek* (July 22, 1991): 20.

31. U.S., State of Florida, *Florida International Volunteer Corps*, brochure (1997).

32. See, for example, Jeffrey Pasley, "Twisted Sisters," *New Republic* (June 22, 1987); 14–18.

33. See, for example, Michael H. Shuman, "Dateline Main Street: Courts v. Local Foreign Policies," *Foreign Policy* (Spring 1992): 158–77.

34. Hedirck Smith, *The Power Game: How Washington Works* (New York: Ballantine, 1988), p. 388.

35. Ibid.

36. Ibid.

37. Ibid., p. 391.

38. Ibid., p. 292.

39. Ibid., chapter 6.

40. Ibid., p. 92.

41. For an overview, see the special issue on Washington, D.C., in *The New Republic* (July 9 and 16, 1977); John M. Barry, *The Ambition and the Power: The Fall of Jim Wright, A True Story of Washington* (New York: Penguin, 1989); Nelson W. Polsby, "The Washington Community," in Thomas E. Mann and Norman J. Ornstein, eds., *The New Congress* (Washington: American Enterprise Institute for Public Policy Research, 1981); and Smith, *The Power Game*, chapter 6. Many of the observations that follow were also derived from having lived and worked in Washington from 1978 to 1982.

42. Smith, *The Power Game*, p. 91.

43. Ibid., p. 91.

44. Ibid., pp. 94–95.

45. Ibid., p. 94.

46. Ibid., p. 90.

47. Ibid., p. 99.

48. Ibid., p. 90.

49. Ibid., p. 91.

50. Ibid., p. 107.

51. Ibid., p. 91.

52. Ibid., p. 111.

53. Ibid., p. 28.

54. Ibid., p. 96.

PART FOUR

·············

THE SOCIETY AND DOMESTIC POLITICS

Part IV examines how the larger society and domestic politics affect the government and the policymaking process. Chapter 14 discusses the role of the public and citizens' beliefs in foreign policy. Chapters 15 and 16 discuss the role of electoral and group politics. Chapter 17 discusses the impact of national security on political participation and the exercise of civil liberties. Chapter 18 discusses the role of the media and the communications process.

CHAPTER 14

. . . .

THE PUBLIC AND ITS BELIEFS

The role of the public in the foreign policy process is a most misunderstood, difficult, and important topic in the complex politics of U.S. foreign policy. It is misunderstood because observers tend to make sweeping generalizations, particularly asserting the insignificance of the public and its beliefs in foreign policy. It is difficult because it is a complex topic involving different types of publics holding different kinds of beliefs which indirectly, as well as directly, affect the policymaking process. Finally, it may be the most important topic because the public—what the American people believe and how they behave—sets the social context and domestic political boundaries within which the government and the policymaking process must operate.

This chapter discusses the public's beliefs about the world and its influence on foreign policy, while chapters 15, 16, and 17 concentrate on the public's direct participation in the political process. Examination of the public and its beliefs provides a foundation for understanding continuity and change, presidential governance, and the tensions between national security and democracy in the making of U.S. foreign policy.

THE TRADITIONAL WISDOM

. . . .

The common view held by most observers of American politics, as well as most Americans, is that the public plays a relatively insignificant role in the making of U.S. foreign policy. They posit that it does not matter what the public thinks about foreign policy issues, for it has little impact on the government and the policymaking process. Moreover, they say public indifference allows political leaders, especially the president, a great degree of freedom of action in foreign policymaking. Therefore, most observers of U.S. foreign policy focus on government policymakers and institutions in explaining how U.S. foreign policy is made, while ignoring the public and much of society.[1]

Why is the public portrayed as being relatively unimportant in the making of U.S. foreign policy?

The traditional wisdom sees the public as uninterested and uninformed regarding foreign policy issues, "fickle" in its opinions, typically fluctuating day-by-day if not hour-by-hour, and responsive to political leadership, especially during times of crises. A more cynical, critical perspective perceives a public that is easily manipulated by political elites. Regardless of the language or the political perspective, many observers of U.S. foreign policy hold the opinion, shared by much of the general public, that the impact of the public is fleeting and usually unimportant in influencing policymakers.

This traditional view leads to a harsh conclusion about American democracy, and for the tension between the demands of national security and democratic practice. Americans pride themselves on having developed a democratic society based on a republican system of government in which political leaders are selected by the people and are responsive and accountable to the electorate. Yet, if the public role is minimal, and the public is extremely responsive to and easily manipulated by political leaders, then U.S. foreign policymaking is not as democratic as it may seem. Many observers and policymakers throughout American history, in fact, have held an **"elitist" view of the public and foreign policymaking**, arguing that policymakers should be distanced from the public. Those who hold this view tend to fear that the public is an ignorant, emotional "mob" that, when mobilized, often counteracts the cold, rational calculations of national interest that national security demands.[2]

As with any stereotype, this traditional picture of the public holds much truth. The majority of the public is uninformed, fickle, and responsive to established leaders. These characteristics often have given the president great flexibility in governing foreign policy and have allowed the demands of national security to prevail over the demands of democracy. However, the American public and its beliefs are more complex than this simple picture suggests. While the traditional wisdom concerning the insignificance of public opinion may help explain some of the politics of foreign policy during the cold war era, this view obscures a full understanding of the politics of U.S. foreign policy, especially during the post–Vietnam War years.

A MORE COMPLEX AND CONSEQUENTIAL PUBLIC

Contrary to the traditional wisdom, in order to fully understand United States foreign policy during the cold war period and post–Vietnam War era, one must carefully examine the public and its role in domestic politics. "There is an American myth that politics stops at the water's edge, that the normal play of partisan competition and dissent gives way to unity in matters of foreign policy. This myth is unfounded but nevertheless potent." So states Leslie Gelb in *The Irony of Vietnam: The System Worked,* arguing that when it came to U.S. foreign policy in Vietnam "practical political imperatives against losing, as well as the shared foreign policy beliefs against losing, were very much on every President's mind"; in this sense the political system and democratic politics worked as intended.[3]

At the same time, continues Gelb, "academicians and public-opinion experts have helped to perpetuate the myth in their own way by 'demonstrating' that foreign policy simply is not a salient issue to the voter and that whatever the president says and does goes," while "official silence on the subject prevails." But, states Gelb, presidents have "known better. Citizens may not single out national security affairs as the basis for their votes—although war and peace issues often are so mentioned—but the security area inevitably plays an important part in determining their overall impression of how the President is doing his job. Moreover, communication leaders and 'elites' judge the President's performance with regard to national security, and the mood which they convey to the public affects public appraisals of the man in the White House."[4] Hence for Gelb, "American public opinion was the essential domino" affecting U.S. foreign policy in Vietnam.[5]

A growing number of observers of U.S. foreign policy, like Leslie Gelb, have challenged the simple traditional view that the role of the American public is inconsequential to the making of public policy, especially foreign policy.[6] Over thirty years ago, when the traditional view of the American public was in vogue, V. O. Key referred to the public in terms of *A Responsible Electorate.*[7] Since the Vietnam War, a more positive portrayal and consequential interpretation has grown, as represented by Benjamin Page and Robert Shapiro's study of *The Rational Public,* Samuel Popkin's *The Reasoning Voter,* and Bruce Jentleson's "The Pretty Prudent Public."[8]

Unraveling the role of the public and its beliefs in the making of U.S. foreign policy is not a simple task for as V. O. Key, Jr., found in *Public Opinion and American Democracy,* "the exploration of public attitudes is a pursuit of endless fascination—and frustration."[9] Nevertheless, *three major points indicate that the traditional view is simplistic and incomplete.* First, different types of publics exist: elite and mass publics. Second, members of the public hold different types of beliefs: opinions, ideological beliefs, and cultural values. Finally, the public exercises influence through a number of different behaviors: directly through polls, through participation in electoral and group politics, and, most indirectly, through **political socialization** (the informal process of human interaction by which Americans acquire their political beliefs from parents, schools, peers, etc.). The traditional wisdom tends to focus predominantly on "public opinion," that is, the level of influence that the opinions of the mass public have directly on policymakers, predominantly through the impact of polls. Yet, it ignores the role of the elite public, political ideology and culture, and the other ways in which the public influences domestic politics and the governmental policymaking process.[10]

The public's overall role in U.S. foreign policy can only be understood in terms of the interaction of the different types of publics, beliefs, and behaviors. Chapters 15 and 16 focus on the public's participation in electoral and group politics and its implications for foreign policy, followed by a discussion of the relationship between national security and the exercise of civil liberties in chapter 17 and the role of the media in chapter 18. This chapter emphasizes the beliefs that are held by members of the public and, in doing so, discusses the role of different types of publics and the various ways they influence U.S. foreign policy.[11]

Whereas the traditional view limits itself to the study of public opinion, it is vital to examine American political ideology and political culture to understand fully the role of the public in the complex politics of U.S. foreign policy. American political culture sets the broad context within which the politics of U.S. foreign policy operates. The ideological beliefs of Americans further narrow what is possible and probable within domestic politics and the policy-making process. Finally, public opinion affects the foreign policy process as it fluctuates within the confines of American political culture and ideology. An examination of public opinion, political ideology, and political culture allows for a more comprehensive understanding of the role of the public in U.S. foreign policy. It demonstrates that the beliefs of the public have experienced both continuity and change over time, and that this is quite significant for understanding the president's ability to govern foreign policy and the tension between national security and democracy that has evolved during the cold war and post–Vietnam War years.

PUBLIC OPINION

Public opinion does play a role in the making of U.S. foreign policy. However, to assess its role one must be clear concerning the type of public most involved, the type of beliefs that opinions represent, and the type of influence most likely to be expressed. We begin with a discussion of the difference between elite and mass publics.

ELITE AND MASS PUBLICS

Typically, when people discuss the public they are referring to the mass of all Americans. It is easy to dismiss the public as an inconsequential actor in foreign policy at this level. The traditional wisdom, however, is misleading when it treats the **"public"** as a single, homogeneous entity. The United States is a complex and diverse society of over 250 million people. Certainly, not all Americans are inconsequential in American politics and the making of U.S. foreign policy. Therefore to better understand the role of the public, *it is important to recognize at least two basic types of publics:*[12]

1. The elite public;
2. The mass public.

The **elite public** *may be distilled further into two general groupings:* opinion leaders and the attentive public. **Opinion leaders** are "all members of the society who occupy positions which enable them regularly to transmit, either locally or nationally, opinions about any issue to unknown persons outside of their occupational field or about more than one class of issues to unknown professional colleagues."[13] National opinion leaders consist of people in various leadership positions throughout the country, such as major governmental and business leaders, well-known journalists, established professors and professionals, and other prominent individuals from different walks of life. Opinion leaders obviously constitute a very small percentage of people within American society, fluctuating depending upon each issue.

Opinion leaders generally are the people who are most informed about national and international affairs and whose ideas and views tend to be communicated broadly. This is not to say that the information and views they hold are correct; rather, it is that their understanding of the world tends to be more readily communicated to other members of society. In other words, opinion leaders tend to have great visibility throughout American society, and their views usually are considered more credible and legitimate by other members of society. This is what makes them opinion leaders, for their information and views carry weight and influence what other people in society and government believe about the world.

The **attentive public** refers to people who are also relatively attentive and informed about national and international affairs, but whose views are not as widely disseminated as those of opinion leaders. The size of the attentive public varies from issue to issue.

For the most visible issues, the attentive public may be as large as one-fourth of the entire public. For most issues that do not receive wide media coverage, the attentive public may represent less then ten percent of the population. As with opinion leaders, this represents a minority of the larger public; but it is an important minority. Members of the attentive public tend to be invisible at the national and community levels, but among their peers they may act as opinion leaders. Thus, it is often said that the attentive public acts as local mediators between opinion leaders and the mass public.

Most Americans are not members of the elite public, but of the mass public. The **mass public** is the segment of the American population emphasized by the traditional wisdom. Although the number varies, at least two-thirds to three-fourths of Americans are the mass public for most issues. Members of the mass public tend to have little interest in national and international affairs. Only those issues that make it to the front page of the newspaper and receive considerable media play gain the attention of the mass public, and then usually only briefly. Therefore, the mass public tends to be poorly informed about national and international affairs.

Because the mass public includes most Americans, there is obviously tremendous variation in the level of interest and information within this segment of the population. Some Americans, as many as 20 percent, have virtually no interest in public affairs or limited access to information, and have been labeled "chronic know-nothings." Other members of the mass public may be more attentive and better informed about foreign policy issues. Within this broad range are most Americans who generally demonstrate little interest, but acquire some information about national and international affairs through upbringing, education, and watching the news.[14]

What accounts for the differing levels of interest and information about national and international affairs between the elite and the mass publics? Two key characteristics stand out: level of **education** and socioeconomic class.[15] The more educated an individual, the more likely that he or she will be interested in, and informed about, national and international affairs. There is no simple educational threshold beyond which a member of the mass public becomes a member of the elite public, for membership of these publics varies with the times and the individual. Sixty years ago a high school education (as well as experience in life) was likely to provide a stronger base of information than an undergraduate degree from college today. Nowadays members of the elite public are likely to have acquired a graduate university degree or have been among the better undergraduate students, particularly if they attended a higher-quality educational institution and majored in the humanities, social sciences, or the arts.

The second important factor in differentiating among types of publics is **socioeconomic class**. Although Americans commonly think they are all members of one large middle-class, definite differences exist within American society in wealth, occupation, and status. Individuals raised in upper-middle-class or upper-class families and environments are the people most likely to become interested and informed about national and international affairs. Clearly, level of socioeconomic class and education are closely related. The higher the class background, the more likely one will go to college and pursue a graduate degree; moreover, the higher the level of education achieved, the more likely one will acquire more wealth, a professional occupation, and higher status within society. High levels of socioeconomic status and education not only reinforce each other and produce individuals with high levels of interest and information about national and international affairs, they are also consequential in providing the analytical and communication skills that tend to separate the elite public from the mass public.

MAJOR PATTERNS IN PUBLIC OPINION

Public opinion refers to the attitudes held by Americans generally toward specific issues and topics, expressed primarily through polls and, periodically, through voting. Hence, we are concerned predominantly with the role of the mass public. Public opinion includes views held by the elite public as well, but they represent no more than a small minority of

Americans. *Three major patterns characterize American public opinion.* Generally, public opinion tends to be:

1. Inattentive;
2. Uninformed;
3. Volatile.

These traits support the traditional understanding of the nature of public opinion. However, this fact does not foreclose public opinion from influencing domestic politics and the policymaking process.[16]

First, public opinion represents views expressed by Americans who, for the most part, are **inattentive**—that is, they have little interest in national and international affairs. Most Americans are exposed to a great deal of information about national and international affairs through the mass media; and, if they go beyond the mass media and visit a local library or bookstore, they would find that an incredible amount of information is readily available. However, few Americans take advantage of the available information because they are uninterested. This is illustrated simply if one examines the circulation of the leading magazines in the country (see **table 14.1**). Only three of the fifty best-selling magazines—*Time, Newsweek,* and *U.S. News & World Report*—emphasize national and/or international affairs. Clearly, most Americans who try to acquire information beyond television, radio, and the local newspaper by subscribing to magazines are interested in things other than politics: entertainment, travel, household, fashion, sex, sports and recreation, mechanics, family matters, and more.

This slight interest in national and international affairs produces and reinforces the second major pattern: most Americans are relatively **uninformed** about national and international affairs. The mass public acquires little information about the political world and much of the information it does acquire tends to be simplistic and often inaccurate. For example, a poll was taken in 1964 to determine the level of information that Americans had about major events in Asia during a time when the United States had roughly 20,000 troops in Vietnam and the Vietnam War was beginning to receive considerable media coverage. The poll revealed that:

TABLE 14.1
CIRCULATION OF FIFTY LEADING U.S. MAGAZINES

MAGAZINE	CIRCULATION	MAGAZINE	CIRCULATION
1. Reader's Digest	15,103,830	26. Smithsonian	2,151,172
2. TV Guide	13,175,549	27. Glamour	2,141,752
3. National Geographic Magazine	8,988,444	28. Field & Stream	2,001,875
4. Better Homes and Gardens	7,603,207	29. Ebony	1,927,675
5. Good Housekeeping	5,372,786	30. Money	1,922,737
6. Ladies' Home Journal	5,045,644	31. Parents	1,848,008
7. Family Circle	5,007,542	32. Country Living	1,838,808
8. Woman's Day	4,707,330	33. Popular Science	1,805,525
9. McCall's	4,520,186	34. American Rifleman	1,666,398
10. Car & Travel Magazine	4,150,352	35. Popular Mechanics	1,586,137
11. **Time**	4,083,105	36. Life	1,556,189
12. People Weekly	3,321,198	37. Golf Digest	1,501,525
13. Playboy	3,283,272	38. Sunset	1,451,846
14. Prevention	3,252,115	39. Martha Stewart Living	1,449,744
15. Redbook	3,173,313	40. Soap Opera Digest	1,372,316
16. Sports Illustrated	3,157,303	41. Woman's World	1,363,240
17. **Newsweek**	3,155,155	42. 'Teen	1,360,411
18. National Enquirer	2,613,647	43. Outdoor Life	1,358,647
19. Cosmopolitan	2,569,186	44. Discover	1,320,701
20. Southern Living	2,471,170	45. Men's Health	1,314,802
21. Star	2,406,150	46. The American Hunter	1,303,067
22. Motorland	2,334,938	47. Golf Magazine	1,283,925
23. **U.S. News & World Report**	**2,220,327**	48. Mademoiselle	1,280,169
24. Seventeen	2,172,923	49. New Woman	1,262,003
25. YM	2,165,079	50. Consumers Digest	1,254,879

NOTE: Magazines that emphasize national and international news are boldfaced.

SOURCE: 1997 The World Almanac and Book of Facts.

25 percent of all Americans had never heard of the war in Vietnam;

28 percent did not know that mainland China was communist;

29 percent were unaware that another Chinese government existed on the island of Taiwan; and

54 percent had never heard of Mao Tse-tung, chairman of the Communist Party of the People's Republic of China.

During the height of the cold war between the United States and the Soviet Union in the early 1960s, barely more than half of Americans polled could describe the meaning of the "cold war" in a reasonably correct fashion. Surveys of American "geographical" knowledge at the time demonstrated that only 65 percent of people could point out England on a map of Europe and only 60 percent could show Brazil's position in South America, while most other countries were located correctly by less than one-third of the respondents.[17]

As the U.S. approaches the twenty-first century, little appears to have changed in terms of public information about international affairs. A survey in 1988 found that with regard to U.S. foreign policy in Central America—a salient national security issue in which the Reagan administration's secret contra war was exposed during the Iran-Contra episode— only half of all Americans knew that the Sandinistas and contras had been fighting. Furthermore, a majority of Americans incorrectly believed that the U.S. government was supporting the guerrillas in El Salvador and the government in Nicaragua. During the same year, one in three Americans could not name a single member of NATO, whereas—it's hard to believe—16 percent thought the Soviet Union was a member of the Western alliance. Americans had difficulty identifying countries and regions on a world map, as was shown when 75 percent of "adult" Americans polled were unable to locate the Persian Gulf, 50 percent could not identify Japan and South Africa (and were unaware that apartheid was the official government policy), and 14 percent could not even correctly locate the United States.[18]

The low levels of attention, information, and understanding about national and international affairs among the American public are *relatively normal and quite understandable for most people.* In most countries, the mass public exhibits characteristics similar to Americans. One may argue whether Americans are more or less interested and informed than other people in industrialized countries (recent surveys have placed Americans near the middle of the rankings, with the 18- to 24-year-old Americans usually dead last).[19] Nevertheless, the pattern remains the same—the mass public, whether in the United States or abroad, is minimally interested and poorly informed, especially in comparison to members of the elite public.

Low levels of political interest and information are also quite understandable if one examines **"everyday life."** Most Americans, like people everywhere, face numerous daily demands and responsibilities that appear to have little to do with politics. While their lives are impacted by politics, it is at a distance removed from the individual. The lives of most individuals revolve around work, family, household, and friends. With the increase of divorce and two-income families, adults lead ever busier and more demanding lives. Most want to relax and enjoy life during their leisure time, which is rarely spent reading, talking, or thinking about national and international affairs. Instead, American pastimes emphasize activities other than politics, such as sports or shopping.[20]

It would be a mistake, therefore, to conclude that the ignorance of most Americans is a function of stupidity—a view often held by the more traditional and elitist perspective of the mass public. Rather, it is primarily a function of the various pursuits and demands of everyday life, which are reinforced by the existence of few incentives within American society for people to become politically informed and active. As many observers have pointed out, a lack of knowledge and understanding about national and international affairs does not preclude the existence of intuition and common sense.[21]

It is also important to *place the low levels of interest and information in historical context, in which three trends appear to have evolved.* First, the level of interest and attention accorded to politics by most Americans has probably declined over the past decades. One hundred years ago politics and election campaigns were one of the few major forms of entertainment for many Americans; today, so many things compete with politics for people's attention—such as television, rock 'n' roll, professional and college sports, Hollywood and movies, the shopping mall and mass consumerism—that a low level of political interest is only natural. Second, although the mass public tends to be poorly informed overall, Americans today are exposed to more information and are likely to have less simplistic images of the United States and the world than they held during periods such as the cold war. Much of this is due to rising enrollments in higher education over the last three decades and improved news coverage in the mass media.[22] The final trend is that the size of the elite public has grown over time as a result of increases in higher education since the 1960s.

Low levels of attention and information produce a third pattern in public opinion—a **tendency to be volatile and to fluctuate** over time. Since most Americans are uninterested and ill-informed, their opinions about national and international issues tend to be very "soft" and open to change. Most Americans give little thought to most issues and are not committed to particular positions. Still, they have opinions and readily offer them when solicited by a public opinion poll. Secretary of State Dean Acheson once observed that most Americans do not feel it necessary to become informed before expressing an opinion. Not surprisingly, as an issue gets more media coverage, public attention increases for a while, members of the mass public acquire more information, and individual opinions change. Hence, opinion is volatile and fluctuates over time; and a **public opinion poll** is no more than a general "snapshot" of what the mass public may think at that brief moment of time.

Such dramatic fluctuations in public opinion can be readily observed for most major events, such as the 1988 presidential elections. During the Democratic primaries, the public opinion polls taken in January placed Gary Hart, one of the few candidates with great visibility, far ahead of other contenders for the Democratic nomination for president. However, once the story of Hart's marital infidelity broke, this high level of attention and information resulted in a decline in Hart's public opinion ratings and ended any hope he had of becoming president. A similar shift in public opinion occurred during the 1988 presidential election. By the end of summer, polls indicated that Michael Dukakis, the Democratic party nominee, had much greater public support for president than George Bush, the Republican candidate. During the next three months, however, public opinion changed dramatically to favor Bush. This change was a function of the Bush campaign's ability, in comparison to the Dukakis campaign, to

present persuasively its images and views of the candidates to the American public. Thus, as Americans acquired new information and new images of Bush and Dukakis, their opinions changed greatly in a very brief time. Ultimately, the public's opinion of the candidates throughout the election process, however erratic, was instrumental in determining who became president of the United States. This is fairly typical of American politics and public opinion.

CONSEQUENCES FOR DOMESTIC POLITICS AND POLICYMAKING

These three public opinion patterns—inattentiveness, low levels of information, and the constancy of change—present **problems for American democracy** as discussed above. Democratic theorists have argued that democracy requires an informed and involved citizenry. However, most Americans are poorly informed about political affairs and do not participate politically, in electoral or group politics. These patterns mean that the general public not only is open to being educated, but is vulnerable to manipulation by individuals and groups, especially through use of communications and the media, throughout society and the government. Overall, limited information and involvement, along with the potential for manipulation, has major implications for determining both the type of democracy the United States will have and the extent to which it exists. This will all be discussed to greater extent in this and subsequent chapters.

How does public opinion influence domestic politics and the policymaking process? In terms of **"immediate and direct" impact** on policymakers within the government, there are two contradictory consequences.[23] The most obvious is that *inattentive, uninformed, and erratic public opinion gives policymakers great leeway in acting on most issues, for three reasons.* First, the content of public opinion serves as a poor guide for policymakers, especially given its fluctuating nature. Second, political leaders are often able to "lead" public opinion—that is educate and manipulate the public—to support and follow their policies. Finally, during crisis periods, such as when troops are deployed abroad, the public tends to **"rally around the flag"** by supporting the president and his policies.

As the traditional wisdom argues, public opinion rarely influences the government and the policymaking process in a direct and immediate way. In fact, public opinion often reinforces and strengthens presidential power because the president is the most visible and legitimate political figure in the United States, especially with respect to foreign policy. This is because the president and members of his administration are often successful in setting the agenda; that is, determining which issues are before the public and how they are discussed.

A second consequence, usually ignored by those who hold to the traditional wisdom, is that *for some issues, especially those that are most salient, public opinion may act as an immediate and direct constraint on political officials in the policymaking process for a number of reasons.*[24] First, "elected officials" are particularly sensitive to public opinion. No matter how inattentive, uninformed, and erratic public opinion is, the public votes political leaders "in" and "out" of office. As discussed in chapter 13, members of Congress are extremely sensitive to public opinion—at least within their own districts—because of their preoccupation with reelection. The same situation holds for the president. Within the White House, it is not uncommon to hear people say that "compared with analysts, Presidents and potential Presidents themselves see a close link between stands in foreign policy and the outcomes of presidential elections."[25] As we observed in our chapter 5 discussion on presidential leadership, public prestige—that is, the perception of the president held by the general public—is an important element in exercising power. Whether a president tries to lead the public, to respond to public opinion, or to ignore public opinion—whatever the particular situation—he is likely to be greatly concerned with his overall level of public approval.

Second, if "public feeling becomes intense" concerning an issue, it severely constrains the choices available within the policymaking process. During the late 1940s and early 1950s following World War II, for example, most Americans had to be convinced that the U.S. government should play an active internationalist role. Once the public was educated and led on the issue of anticommunism, however, American leaders began to feel constrained by public opinion, as cold war lessons—for instance, that the U.S. should never appease aggressors—were internalized by Americans. The result was that American policymakers had much leeway to deal with the Soviet Union and its allies during the cold war years, but only if their policies took a "hardline" approach. Policymakers, hence, were reluctant to appear soft toward communist governments. They could not recognize the People's Republic of China—the largest country in the world—throughout the 1950s and 1960s for fear that strong anticommunist sentiments among the public might be aroused. The last remnant of this anticommunist legacy in the present era is the constraints that it continues to place on policymakers' abilities to make foreign policy changes toward Fidel Castro and Cuba, even though the cold war has ended.

Third, public support for a policy may turn rapidly into public disapproval. Although the public tends to rally around the flag and the president during a crisis such as war, *public support for presidential policies tends to dwindle over time.* Studies, such as John Mueller's *War, Presidents, and Public Opinion,* demonstrate that the longer a war lasts, the more public support will erode.[26] Lengthier wars produce greater numbers of American casualties and indicate that the war is going badly. Such events politicize the issue throughout American society and increase public disapproval of presidential policy. In other words, public support for the use of troops abroad has a limited threshold: quick and successful operations, as in Grenada, Panama, and the Persian Gulf, maximize support; lengthy and unsuccessful conflicts, as in Korea, Vietnam, and Lebanon, bring public disapproval. The Iran-hostage crisis in 1979 quickly rallied support behind President Jimmy Carter, but his inability to resolve the crisis throughout 1980 produced strong public disapproval. Such public disapproval not only constrains presidential power, but can lead to failed presidencies.

Bruce Jentleson also found that public opinion "varies according to the *principal policy objective* for which force is used."[27] The tendency is for greater public support for the use of force in order to "contain" and "restrain" an aggressor state—such as in the Persian Gulf War; as opposed to the use of U.S. force to "initiate" and "impose" internal political change within another state—such as within Nicaragua, Somalia, or Haiti. Obviously, many cases are likely to be, or be perceived to be, somewhat mixed. Nevertheless, Jentleson concludes that

> "The American public is less gun shy than during the Vietnam trauma period of the 1970s, but more cautious than during the Cold War consensus of the 1950s and 1960s. . . . Presidents who contemplate getting militarily involved in internal political conflicts—of which there may well be even more in the post–Cold War world than when bipolarity had its constraining effects—had better get in and out quickly and successfully. Otherwise, the public is strongly disposed to oppose the policy."[28]

Thus, the public tends to discriminate over the use of force more then commonly thought and be "pretty prudent."[29]

Finally, the collapse of the cold war consensus has made public opinion "less responsive to the president" (the rise and decline of the cold war consensus is examined in the next section on political ideology). During the 1950s, most American leaders and members of the elite public shared a similar cold war view of the world that the mass public tended to "follow." Since the Vietnam War, however, differing views of the world and U.S. foreign policy have arisen leading to greater diversity and volatility in public opinion. As political scientist Thomas Mann points out, "There is little doubt that changes in public opinion about foreign policy were the root cause of the weakening of the President's leadership position and of the chronic conflict between the executive and legislative branches that began in the late 1960s."[30] The continued prominence of the president gives him a distinct advantage in influencing public opinion, but the lack of a public consensus in support of presidential policies has made it much more difficult to shape foreign policy.

On the one hand, the president has the potential for more leeway because the split in opinion allows him to promote either a cold war or post–cold war foreign policy; on the other hand, disagreement over foreign policy makes it more difficult for the president to rally and maintain public support for particular policies. Opinion leaders with different foreign policy views now compete with each other for public support. This helps to explain why President Reagan was unsuccessful in persuading no more than 40 percent of Americans to support his anticommunist policies in Central America.[31]

In sum, the influence of public opinion on the foreign policy process is more complex than the traditional wisdom suggests. For many issues, public opinion has little, if any, immediate and direct impact on the policymaking process. However, for other issues high in salience, public opinion has an immediate and direct effect on policymakers within the government, including the president and members of Congress. The common denominator in these two contradictory patterns is: 1) the **level of salience** and the politicization of issues and 2) **the level of success or failure perceived** among a public that tends to be very pragmatic and impatient.[32]

When the public feels things are going well in their lives and for the country, and few issues are salient and controversial, they tend to support the status quo and approve the president's performance. However, if the public perceives problems, such as a foreign policy fiasco or an economic recession, most people will want changes and the president's approval rating will drop. Public perception and satisfaction levels help to explain whether public opinion supports or constrains the president's ability to govern foreign policy. These contradictory public opinion patterns for foreign policy operated during the Persian Gulf crisis, affecting President Bush and the making of U.S. foreign policy. (See **essay 14.1** on public opinion and the Persian Gulf crisis.)

The discussion above should help clarify the more **"indirect and longer-term" influence** of public opinion in domestic politics and on the policymaking process, which is *significant in three basic ways.* First, the public elects major governmental officials. It matters little how interested or informed

ESSAY 14.1
PUBLIC OPINION AND THE PERSIAN GULF CRISIS

Public opinion fluctuated dramatically throughout the Persian Gulf crisis, illustrating the contradictory implications for American politics and presidential power in the making of U.S. foreign policy (see **figure 14.1**). *Three stages evolved:* public opinion was supportive during August and September, strengthening presidential power; it became divided from October to early January, thus constraining presidential power; after the war began it became supportive and reinforced presidential power once again.

Most Americans had little information about U.S. foreign policy toward Iraq and the Persian Gulf before August 2, 1990. Nevertheless, following President George Bush's decision to impose economic sanctions, send over 100,000 American troops to the region, and promote international support through the United Nations in response to Iraq's invasion of Kuwait, the public rallied around the flag. By late August and September, President Bush's public approval ratings towered to historic levels of between 70 percent and 80 percent. Thus, before and immediately after the Iraqi invasion, public opinion had little impact on the policymaking process and, if anything, strengthened presidential power over foreign policy in the Persian Gulf.

FIGURE 14.1
PRESIDENT BUSH'S PUBLIC APPROVAL DURING THE PERSIAN GULF CRISIS

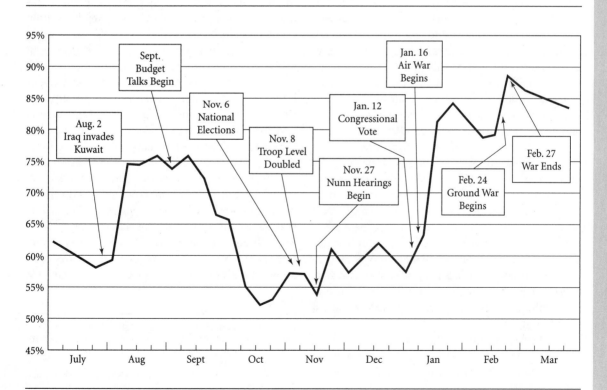

SOURCE: The Gallop Organization.

Beginning in October, however, President Bush's approval ratings plummeted more than twenty points, bottoming around 50 percent, due to the disastrous budget negotiations between the president and the Congress to reduce the growing federal deficits, the 1990 congressional and state elections, and President Bush's subsequent announcement that he was doubling the American military presence in the Persian Gulf to over 400,000 troops, reflecting a change from a defensive strategy to an offensive one to force Iraq to withdraw from Kuwait by taking it to the "brink" of war. What appeared to be solid public support for presidential policy in the Gulf quickly evaporated; public opinion was clearly divided by December over Bush's strategy and the consequences of an increasingly likely war. It was the rise of a divided public and the drop in approval for the president's policies that acted as a catalyst for major congressional involvement—unprecedented in the heat of an international crisis—which resulted in hearings critical of presidential policy and a divided congressional vote authorizing the president to use force. Although Bush was ultimately successful in getting majority congressional support for his policy of brinksmanship, his ability to govern foreign policy was heavily challenged and badly constrained during this time as more and more members of the public criticized and questioned foreign policy developments.

Finally, after President Bush ordered American and allied troops into battle, American public opinion again rallied behind the flag and this sentiment strengthened as the Iraqi military was overwhelmed with minimal loss of American life. Not surprisingly, the quickness and ease of the American allied military victory resulted in public approval ratings reaching new heights of over 80 percent for President Bush. Such public approval gave President Bush a new lease on life to govern foreign policy, so long as public opinion remained highly supportive.

A *fourth stage* in public opinion would have evolved if the Persian Gulf War had been prolonged and not gone well, resulting in thousands of American casualties as many Americans feared. Under these conditions, public dissent and opposition would have increased, weakening presidential power and possibly producing another failed presidency. This did not happen during the Persian Gulf crisis; but in the post–Vietnam War era it remains a distinct possibility in a future crisis as so many other presidents have experienced.

It is important to point out that the three stages occurred during a foreign policy crisis involving the use of American troops, a time when presidents historically dominate the political process until things go sour. This is indicative of the volatility of public opinion in the post–Vietnam War era and the contradictory impact it has on the president's ability to govern foreign policy, even during a time of international crisis. As explained by Thomas Mann, "An administration that sails against the tide of public opinion invites a more active congressional role; a President who succeeds in bringing foreign policy and public opinion into closer conformance—either by adjusting his policy or by reshaping public opinion—will be more successful in diffusing opposition on Capitol Hill."[A]

It appears that President Bush, and his closest advisers, were very sensitive to public opinion throughout the crisis. At one point, for example, political journalist Bob Woodward reported that Chairman of the Joint Chiefs of Staff Colin Powell urged President Bush to hold off on waging war and to rely instead on the international economic sanctions against Iraq, taking pains to explain that the sanctions option "has merit" and "will work" in time. The sanctions option, however, was dismissed by the president with the response, "I don't think that there's time politically for that strategy."[B] Likewise, Elizabeth Drew, in her "Letter from Washington" of January 25, 1991, reported that "It became known here not long ago that John Sununu, the

A. Thomas E. Mann, "Making Foreign Policy: President and Congress," in Thomas E. Mann, ed., *A Question of Balance: The President, the Congress, and Foreign Policy* (Washington, D.C.: Brookings Institution, 1990), p. 11.

B. Bob Woodward, *The Commanders* (New York: Simon and Schuster, 1991), p. 42.

president's chief of staff, was telling people that a short, successful war would be pure political gold for the president—would guarantee his reelection."[C]

C. Elizabeth Drew, "Letter from Washington," *The New Yorker* (January 25, 1991): 83.

SOURCES: Larry Elowitz and John W. Spanier, "Korea and Vietnam: Limited War and the American Political System," *Orbis* (Summer 1974): 510–34; Bruce W. Jentleson, "The Pretty Prudent Public: Post Post-Vietnam American Opinion on the Use of Military Force," *International Studies Quarterly* (1992): 49–74; John Mueller, *Policy and Opinion in the Gulf War* (Chicago: University of Chicago Press, 1994); John E. Mueller, *War, Presidents, and Public Opinion* (New York: Wiley, 1973).

Clearly, presidents take public opinion very seriously. Although the public tends to be uninterested, uninformed, and volatile concerning international affairs, public opinion nevertheless impacts the politics of U.S. foreign policy, posing considerable opportunities and risks for the president's ability to govern.

---

most Americans are concerning foreign policy or whether their vote has anything to do with foreign policy issues. The fact remains that the public, especially the mass public, makes the final decision as to who becomes president and who runs Congress; it "chooses the political leadership" responsible for making U.S. foreign policy. Furthermore, with the collapse of a foreign policy consensus since the Vietnam War, the public's indirect impact on foreign policy through elections has increased, as different elected officials are now more likely to support different foreign policies. Second, the ability of political leaders to influence the policymaking process during their tenure is heavily a function of their public prestige. As figure 4.2 in chapter 4 clearly illustrated, not only does "public approval" of presidential performance fluctuate dramatically with time, public approval also tends to move downward over time for each president. This accounts for the presidential life cycle where the president tends to enter office with high approval in public opinion only to see it diminish with time weakening his ability to govern. Finally, public opinion often sets *the boundaries of legitimate political discourse and domestic politics,* limiting the kinds of issues on the political agenda and decisions considered by policymakers. Although public opinion is erratic, it tends to fluctuate within a certain range of ideological and cultural beliefs that prevail throughout American society. It is to these more indirect and longer-term influences of the public to which we now turn by examining the

role of, first, political ideology and, then, political culture.

POLITICAL IDEOLOGY AND FOREIGN POLICY ORIENTATIONS

A key to understanding how the public affects American politics and U.S. foreign policy is to examine the evolution of the ideological views of Americans. **Political ideology** refers to beliefs about the preferred ends and means of a society (for example, liberty, equality, representative government). In this respect, we are also interested in the **foreign policy orientations** permeating American society— that is, how Americans see the world and the preferred role the U.S. should play in international relations. The ideological and foreign policy orientations prevailing in American society set the broad boundaries of legitimate political discourse and agenda-making within which public opinion operates to influence domestic politics and the policymaking process.

In reviewing the ideological and foreign policy orientations of Americans, *three points need to be kept in mind with respect to the types of publics involved, the nature of public beliefs, and their influence on the politics of U.S. foreign policy.* First, a discussion of ideological and foreign policy views must focus on the elite public and the extent to which it is supported by the mass public, because the elite public tends to have stronger, less moderate, and more influential ideological and foreign policy beliefs than the mass public. This is consistent with an important distinction that Godfrey Hodgson makes in *America in Our Time* between the elite public as the **"moral minority"** and the mass public as the **"pragmatic majority."**[33] During the cold war years, for example, it was popular to conclude that most Americans were not ideological, that it was a time of the "end of ideology."[34] Clearly, if ideology refers to a set of values about the ends and means of a society, all people have ideological beliefs. As political scientist Robert Dahl pointed out over twenty years ago, "Americans are a highly ideological people. It is only that one does not ordinarily notice their ideology because they are, to an astonishing extent, all agreed on the same ideology."[35] What observers of American politics correctly pointed out is that the ideological beliefs of the mass public do not tend to be very sophisticated or consistent in comparison to the elite public; furthermore, most Americans correctly sense that they tend to be very pragmatic, reflecting more moderate and centrist ideological orientations. In other words, the mass public acts as a pragmatic majority while the elite public often operates as the moral minority.[36]

Second, the ideological and foreign policy orientations of Americans tend to be "quite stable" compared to their expressions of public opinion. Ideological beliefs do not readily fluctuate; they tend to resist change. This is especially true among members of the elite public. Their ideological beliefs and foreign policy orientations are formed early in life through the process of political socialization and are based on considerable attention to national and international affairs. Therefore, opinion leaders and members of the attentive public tend to have more knowledge and greater emotional commitment to their views. The pragmatic majority, on the other hand, tends to occupy more centrist positions, while remaining more open and responsive to the ideological and foreign policy appeals of the elite public.

Third, ideology and foreign policy views are consequential in influencing the complex politics of U.S. foreign policy. *The ideological and foreign policy orientations in American society influence the foreign policy process in four ways:* they affect public opinion, influence the electoral process and voters' choices, affect the activity of groups and social movements in domestic politics, and are passed on to newer generations of Americans through the socialization process. In other words, the ideological and foreign policy views of Americans set the broad boundaries within which the complex politics of U.S. foreign policy operate.

A focus on ideology and foreign policy orientations enables one to understand how the national interest is defined throughout American society and government. Government leaders in power always argue that their policies promote the national interests of the United States. However, the **national interest** is clearly a subjective concept, for different people define the national interest differently. Therefore, the national interest varies over time and its character at any one point depends on which ideological beliefs and foreign policy views are prevalent within society and government.

The national interest and the making of U.S. foreign policy, in other words, are influenced heavily by the power of ideas—that is, the power of the ideological and foreign policy orientations held by the elite and mass publics. This has been a major theme running throughout part III of this book in explaining continuity and change, presidential governance, and the tension between national security and democracy within the government and the policymaking process; and it sets the stage from which domestic politics impacts the making of U.S. foreign policy as well. Thus, understanding the evolution of the ideological and foreign policy orientations of Americans throughout history is crucial for understanding how U.S. foreign policy is made.

The ideological and foreign policy orientations of Americans have gone through two major phases since the end of World War II. As Ole Holsti and James Rosenau make clear in *American Leadership in World Affairs,* the cold war years represented a time period of foreign policy consensus throughout America, which was replaced by diverse and competing foreign policy views in the post–Vietnam War years. Likewise, according to Godfrey Hodgson in *America in Our Time,* the cold war years were also a time of ideological consensus throughout America, which was replaced by ideological fragmentation in the post–Vietnam War years.[37] In short, *two stages have characterized the ideological and foreign policy orientations of American in the post–World War II era:*

1. An ideological and foreign policy consensus prevailed during the cold war years;
2. An increase in ideological and foreign policy diversity has occurred since Vietnam.

THE COLD WAR YEARS OF CONSENSUS

The cold war years led to the development of **an ideological and foreign policy consensus** throughout American society and government, an extraordinary time in American history. As explained by Thomas Mann,

> The bipartisan foreign policy consensus that prevailed for almost two decades after World War II was sustained by a leadership stratum that shared an internationalist and interventionist view of the U.S. role in world affairs, an attentive and educated group of citizens who followed and supported this leadership, and a poorly informed and largely inert mass public that tolerated official policy as long as it appeared to be working.[38]

This consensual view throughout American society fostered the rise of presidential power, the expansion of the foreign policy bureaucracy, the development of an acquiescent Congress, and the rise of a national security ethos and free market ethos throughout government and society. It also set the context for understanding the reinforcing role that public opinion and domestic politics played throughout the cold war years in the making of U.S. foreign policy.

The Rise of Foreign Policy Anticommunism. Holsti and Rosenau argue that most Americans in government and society shared a similar foreign policy orientation during the cold war years, which they call **cold war internationalism.** Cold war internationalists saw a conflict-ridden, bipolar world that pitted the Soviet Union and communism against America and democracy. The Soviet Union was seen as an ambitious, aggressive, expansionist empire, leading a strong and patient group of communist allies toward a revolutionary goal: imposing a Moscow-dominated imperial system throughout the world. The United States, in contrast, was seen as the civilized and benevolent leader of democracy and prosperity throughout the so-called "free world." In a world where victory for one side was seen as defeat for the other, the assumed threat to American national security posed by the Soviet Union and communism became the predominant concern of American policymakers. It was this view of the world that laid the basis for the national security ethos to thrive during the cold war years. Therefore, U.S. foreign policy revolved around a strategy of containment of Soviet expansionism through the development, threat, and use of force around the world.

The anticommunist consensus did not develop overnight, but evolved over three phases over time. First, a great debate took place over the future of U.S. foreign policy during the late 1940s in which the cold war internationalist perspective prevailed. Second, cold war internationalism and the policy of containment were challenged by the rise of McCarthyism and the political right during the early 1950s. Finally, an anticommunist consensus in U.S. foreign policy coalesced by the mid-1950s and reigned until the mid-1960s.[39] These domestic patterns discussed below demonstrate the lead role of the elite public as well as the importance of mass public support, for it is the dynamic interaction between the two publics that determines which beliefs prevail in the making of U.S. foreign policy.

Following the end of World War II, the natural inclination of most Americans was to revert to the "isolationist" sentiment that dominated before the war and support military withdrawal from most of the world. However, isolationist tendencies associated with the prewar period had been firmly discredited, especially within the elite public, with the bombing of Pearl Harbor and U.S. entry into World War II. Most American leaders realized that the United States had become too powerful to minimize its global involvement following the war. Increasingly vocal forces also publicized the potential threat posed by the Soviet Union and communism. Therefore, **a post–World War II "great debate"** took place among American leaders and intellectuals—that is, members of the elite public—about the world around them, the nature of the Soviet Union, and the proper foreign policy of the United States.

Some, like *Henry Wallace,* Franklin Roosevelt's former vice-president and the 1948 presidential candidate on the Progressive party ticket, argued in support of the United Nations and the need to maintain a cooperative relationship with the Soviet Union through policies emphasizing spheres of influence and a type of détente. A few, like *Walter Lippmann,* one of America's most eminent journalists, emphasized a more realpolitik postwar approach toward Europe revolving around traditional spheres of influence and balance-of-power statecraft. Others, like *George Kennan,* a Sovietologist and important policymaker in Harry Truman's administration, asserted that the major threat was Soviet expansion in Europe and that the United States needed to contain the Soviet threat in Europe. Still others, like *Paul Nitze,* another important policymaker in the Truman administration, emphasized that the Soviet Union was a revolutionary state with designs to export communism aggressively worldwide and that the United States had no choice but to contain the Soviets militarily throughout the world.

In the late 1940s, individuals representing the two more pessimistic schools of foreign policy thought—European containment versus global containment—struggled for control of the Truman administration's foreign policy. (Review **essay 2.2** on George Kennan). Truman himself was initially undecided about the nature of the Soviet Union and the appropriate U.S. response. With time he became increasingly skeptical of Soviet intentions. Relations were strained by difficulties over Poland and a divided Germany, the communist coup d'etat in Czechoslovakia, the "fall" of China, and the North

Korean attack on South Korea. These events eventually convinced most members of the Truman administration, including the president, that the Soviet Union was indeed a revolutionary communist state attempting to achieve world domination. Therefore, they felt that they had no choice but to assume leadership of the "free world" and stop—that is, contain—communist aggression.

Not surprisingly, members of Congress and much of the public were reluctant to support such an activist international policy so soon after the country had fought a war (particularly since the Soviet Union had been seen as an ally). Yet there was an underlying anticommunist sentiment in U.S. society that could be traced to the Bolshevik revolution in 1917 (see **essay 9.1** on J. Edgar Hoover and the pursuit of security). Therefore, when the Truman administration responded to the post–World War II environment with proclamations like **the Truman Doctrine**, which committed the United States to assist Greece and Turkey to contain the communist threat, this produced growing public support for an overall policy of containment.[40] The paramount **lesson of World War II**—that the "appeasement" of Adolf Hitler and fascism by England and France at Munich only produced more aggression—was applied to the contemporary situation: the U.S. must not appease Stalin and communism; instead, the United States needed to build up its military and contain communist aggression wherever it occurred.

These events also propelled another segment of U.S. society to the forefront of politics—people who feared that the United States was losing the cold war because it was not doing enough to defeat communism. Not only did they perceive that the United States was losing the cold war abroad, especially in Asia, they believed that the U.S. was threatened by subversion from within. Therefore, they argued that containment was not enough; a more aggressive policy was necessary that would roll back and eradicate communism. People who shared this view were most prominent within the Republican party, which had gained control of the Congress during the late 1940s and early 1950s. They attacked the policy of containment, as well as the Truman administration and its supporters, for losing the cold war (see essay 12.1 on Joseph McCarthy and McCarthyism).

"McCarthyism" was not successful in getting either the Truman or Dwight Eisenhower administrations to reorient their foreign policies beyond containment. However, *the challenge from the right had two lasting effects.* It reinforced perceptions held by U.S. policymakers and the American public that global communism was monolithic, controlled by the Soviet Union, and an ever-present threat. Second, foreign policy views that were critical of the containment policy and argued for a more realistic or cooperative policy (for example, as represented by Henry Wallace) lost all credibility and legitimacy during the cold war years. In short, a consensus had developed within the United States during the 1950s that the world was divided between two hostile forces: communism led by the Soviet Union and democracy led by the United States. Despite disagreements over tactics (How much force? Where should it be applied?), most Americans agreed on the nature of the threat—communism—and the necessity of using force to forestall its expansion throughout the world (see **essay 14.2** on the world of cognition).

The Rise of the Liberal-Conservative Ideological Consensus. The growing anticommunist foreign policy consensus reflected a larger set of ideological patterns which evolved throughout American society. During the cold war years according to Godfrey Hodgson, "a strange hybrid, liberal conservatism, blanketed the scene and muffled debate."[41] *The two major aspects of the liberal-conservative consensus were,* first, belief in a democratic-capitalist political economy based on private enterprise and, second, the fear of communism. Thus, the foreign policy consensus behind containing the threat of Soviet communism abroad was part of a larger ideological consensus in American society.

Hodgson summarizes the basic tenets of **the American liberal-conservative consensus.** First, the American free-enterprise system is democratic, creates abundance, and has a revolutionary potential for social justice. Second, the key to this potential is economic growth based on private industry and

governmental support, which allows the needs of all people to be met. Third, meeting popular needs will produce a more equal society in which conflict between social classes becomes unnecessary and obsolete, where workers become members of the middle class. Fourth, social problems can be solved like industrial problems; the economy can be fine-tuned and the welfare state can eradicate poverty. Fifth, the main threat to this beneficent system is communism; therefore, the United States and its free world allies must fight a prolonged struggle against communism while promoting the American free enterprise system throughout the world.[42] This was the ideological foundation for the national security and free market ethos that pervaded the minds of American policymakers.

By the mid-1950s, most Americans within the mass and elite public were part of this liberal-conservative ideological consensus. This consensus became possible during the 1950s because most conservatives accepted the legitimacy of the limited welfare state created by the New Deal under Franklin Roosevelt, while most liberals adopted the anticommunist stance in vogue following World War II. Therefore, the liberal-conservative consensus represented neither liberalism nor conservatism, but was a hybrid or amalgamation of the two ideologies.

Differences did exist among members of the consensus. Liberals were more favorable toward welfare and government intervention in the economy, while conservatives generally were opposed to such policies. Conservatives were more prone to rely on force to respond to instability in the Third World, while liberals were more sympathetic to the need to promote third-world economic and political development. However, such differences were overshadowed by agreement on the promise of the American private market system and the threat of communism. According to Hodgson, "since the consensus had made converts on the Right as well as on the Left, only a handful of dissidents were excluded from the Big Tent: southern diehards, rural reactionaries, the more . . . paranoid fringes of the radical Right, and the divided remnants of the old, Marxist, Left."[43]

ESSAY 14.2
The World of Cognition and "Enemy" Images

It is relatively well known, especially within the study of psychology, that people construct their world to a considerable extent. This helps to explain why people often disagree and see different realities. Walter Lippmann, one of America's most prominent and insightful journalists, stated in his 1922 classic on *Public Opinion,* "We do not first see, and then define, we define first and then see." In other words, individuals tend to have beliefs that simplify reality and often are relatively close-minded to new information. Such is the nature of human **cognition**, and how people perceive and process the world around them.

As John Steinbruner stated in *The Cybernetic Theory of Decision,* "The mind of man, for all its marvels, is a limited instrument." Given the complexity of the world and the limitations of the mind, the mind "constantly struggles to impose clear, coherent meaning on events." In other words, as stated by Jack Snyder who applied a cognitive approach to the failure of deterrence during the Cuban missile crisis, "Cognitive theory argues that the mind craves certainty and will work to establish it even when it is unwarranted by objective conditions." Therefore, as summarized by Alexander George,

> Every individual acquires during the course of development a set of beliefs and personal constructs about the physical and social environment. These beliefs provide him with a relatively coherent way of organizing and making sense of what would otherwise be a confusing and overwhelming array of signals and cues picked up from the environment from his senses. . . . These beliefs and constructs necessarily simplify and structure the external world.

Human beings and human thought are not simply random and idiosyncratic. Human beings are creatures of habit, and patterns exist in their images and thought processes. Basically, the mind imposes clarity and tries to make sense of reality through re-liance on a few *common cognitive principles.* These include:

The principle of cognitive structures of beliefs (that the human mind tends to consist of a vast assortment of beliefs that are organized and internally structured, especially around more central beliefs),

The principle of selective memory (that people tend to remember certain things better then others, especially the general picture or concept, and be loose with details),

The principle of selective attention and perception (although the mind can perceive stable, significant features of the environment, it does tend to be selective and incomplete in its attention),

The principle of causal inference (that people tend to makes inferences about what happened and why based on their beliefs), and

The principle of cognitive stability (that the mind tends to keep internal belief relationships stable once formed, especially in the core structure of beliefs).

How do images and cognition matter? How do they impact world politics? Through *common patterns of perception (and misperception).* Very simply, the mind has a:

1. Tendency to categorize and stereotype,
2. Tendency to simplify causal inferences,
3. Tendency to use historical analogies.

As Robert Jervis stated in *Perception and Misperception in International Politics,* "perceptions of the world and of other actors diverge from reality in patterns that we can detect and for reasons that we can understand."

The human mind perceives the world and processes information by compartmentalizing and sorting things into categories. This necessarily simplifies and often leads to a certain amount of "stereotyping." One common tendency in world politics, in this respect, is for the mind to form beliefs and schemas of the "other." **The "enemy" image**—where "we" are good and "they are "bad" or "evil"—is about the most simple-minded image of all. Such is the image of the Soviet Union and communism that most Americans acquired throughout the cold war years. Once formed, such an image of the enemy tends to be very rigid and resistant to change.

In fact, it's not uncommon for conflict situations to result in **mirror images**—where each party holds an image that is diametrically "opposite" the other. In other words, each party has a positive and benevolent "self-image" while holding a negative and malevolent image of the enemy. As Ralph White found in *Nobody Wanted War,* an analysis of the two World Wars and the Vietnam War, each party tends to hold a "diabolical enemy-image" and a "virile and moral self-image that becomes the source of mutual selective attention, absence of emphathy (for the other), and insecurity. Such "black-and-white" thinking contributes to misperception, escalation, intervention, and war—or a "cold war" in the case of the United States and the Soviet Union.

It should be relatively easy to see, given the mind's need for certainty and clarity, and the tendency to categorize and stereotype, that there will also be a corresponding tendency to simplify inferences about causality. As Jervis stated, "People want to be able to explain as much as possible of what goes on around them. To admit that a phenomenon cannot be explained, or at least cannot be explained without adding numerous and complex exceptions to our beliefs, is both psychologically uncomfortable and intellectually unsatisfying." *Four causal inferences likely to be simplified are particularly relevant to foreign policy:* 1) a tendency to overestimate or underestimate (internal) dispositional or (external) situational causes of behavior, 2) a tendency to overestimate or underestimate one's importance, 3) a tendency to overestimate the degree to which the behavior of others is planned and centralized, and 4) a tendency to overindulge in pessimistic and wishful thinking.

Such tendencies heavily reinforce people's perceptions, especially if they hold images of the enemy. For example, it was virtually inconceivable in the minds of most Americans that the United States could "lose" the war in Vietnam and, nevertheless, they could not allow South Vietnam to fall to communism given the devastating international and domestic consequences that they feared would result. In fact, American (especially civilian) policymakers constantly fluctuated between optimistic and pessimistic assessments in the early 1960s immediately preceding the fateful decisions to militarily intervene and Americanize the war.

The third perceptual tendency is for people to make **use of historical analogies** in making sense of the present. "Previous international events provide the statesman with a range of imaginable situations and allow him to detect patterns and causal links that can help him understand his world," for "we cannot make sense out of our environment without assuming that, in some sense, the future will resemble the past," states Robert Jervis. But, "a too narrow conception of the past and a failure to appreciate the impact of changed circumstances also result in 'the tyranny of the past upon the imagination.'"

Yuen Foong Khong found in *Analogies at War: Korea, Munich, Dien Bien Phu, and the Vietnam Decisions of 1965* that the lessons policymakers drew from Munich, Dien Bien Phu, and, most importantly, the Korean War had a powerful influence on the decision-making process under President Johnson toward Vietnam. The use of these historical analogies helped to reinforce the enemy image and predispose the United States toward military intervention. It also helps to explain how **the domino theory** became a powerful metaphor in the minds of Americans—that the lessons of the past made clear that anything short of a policy of global containment would result in one country after another falling to communist expansion like dominoes.

The enemy image of the Soviet communism, and the cognitive dynamics behind it, was the basis of the foreign policy consensus in the making of U.S. foreign policy during the cold war years. It laid the foundation for the rise of the president and the national security state, and American intervention (overt and covert) throughout the world. Such an enemy image revolving around Soviet communism would not survive the Vietnam War and the collapse of the Soviet Union. But it was a powerful cognitive force in the making of U.S. foreign policy following World War II and continues to have a powerful legacy, even as the United States approaches the twenty-first century.

SOURCES: Alexander L. George, *Presidential Decisionmaking in Foreign Policy: The Effective Use of Information and Advice* (Boulder, Colo.: Westview Press, 1980); Betty Glad and Charles S. Taber, "Images, Learning, and the Decision to Use Force: The Domino Theory of the United States," in Betty Glad, ed., *Psychological Dimensions of War* (Newbury Park, Calif.: Sage, 1990), pp. 56–81; Robert Jervis, *Perception and Misperception in International Politics* (Princeton, N.J.: Princeton University Press, 1976); Yuen Foong Khong, *Analogies at War: Korea, Munich, Dien Bien Phu, and the Vietnam Decision of 1965* (Princeton, N.J.: Princeton University Press, 1992); Jerel A. Rosati, "A Cognitive Approach to the Study of Foreign Policy," in *Foreign Policy Analysis: Continuity and Change in its Second Generation,* edited by Laura Neack, Patrick J. Haney, and Jeanne A. K. Hey (Englewood Cliffs, N.J.: Prentice-Hall, 1995), pp. 49–70; Jerel Rosati, "The Power of Human Images and Cognition in the Study of Foreign Policy (and World Politics)," *Mershon International Studies Review* (1999); John D. Steinbruner, *The Cybernetic Theory of Decision* (Princeton, N.J.: Princeton University Press, 1974); Jack L. Snyder, "Rationality at the Brink: The Role of Cognitive Processes in Failures of Deterrence," *World Politics* (April 1978): 344–65; Ralph K. White, *Nobody Wanted War: Misperception in Vietnam and Other Wars* (Garden City, N.Y.: Doubleday, 1968).

As with the foreign policy consensus, the liberal-conservative consensus did not develop overnight. *Beginning in the 1930s, American ideology went through three phases* which will be discussed below. First, the 1930s and 1940s witnessed the rise of liberalism and the political Left and a corresponding decline of conservatism. Second, the late 1940s and 1950s resulted in the resurgence of conservatism and the political Right. The more extreme conservative elements, represented by McCarthyism, were a powerful force even though they were ultimately unsuccessful in gaining political ascendance. Third, these two trends resulted in the formation of a liberal-conservative consensus by the mid-1950s that lasted throughout much of the 1960s.[44]

The United States experienced considerable change in ideological views from the 1920s to the 1940s. **The Great Depression** represented a momentous crisis in the lives of most Americans that politicized issues in society like no other event since the Civil War. Liberalism grew in popularity and became ascendant as Franklin Roosevelt passed **New Deal programs** based upon activist government to pull the economy out of the depression and provide welfare for the needy and impoverished. Conservatives, dominant before the depression and representing many Americans afterwards, continued to believe in a "laissez-faire" economy based upon minimal government involvement and the magic of the marketplace. The economic collapse, massive unemployment, and impoverishment produced by the depression also resulted in growing popularity for a third group of Americans advocating greater change, represented by socialists and American communists. Thus, politics became very divisive during the 1930s at the same time that the rise of domestic liberalism and greater government activity in the economy was accompanied by the growth of presidential power and the federal bureaucracy. Many conservatives, especially those with extreme views, accused Franklin Roosevelt of becoming a dictator and imposing socialism on Americans through his New Deal programs. Socialists and the Left complained that New Deal policies were inadequate for addressing the mass poverty and inequality, for all they did was reform the capitalist system which was the fundamental source of the problems.

With the **attack on Pearl Harbor**, America's involvement in World War II temporarily united most of these competing ideological factions under the gauntlet of liberalism against the common enemy of fascism. The isolationism behind U.S. foreign policy during the interwar years was overwhelmed by America's war effort. The decline of isolationism was accompanied by the **growth of liberal internationalism** in foreign policy, whose advocates supported the establishment of a liberal international political economy—that is, a democratic-capitalist international order. A liberal world order would flourish through international cooperation, international law, and international organizations, such as the United Nations. Thus, World War II not only represented a time of fear but also of great hope. In fact, the end of World War II was a triumph for the United States and liberalism, for the allies had won the war abroad and, with the war taking the United States out of the Great Depression, Americans were beginning to prosper at home once again.

With the war over, the middle and late 1940s witnessed the beginning of the cold war and a **resurgence of conservatism** in American society. Conservatives renewed their criticism of the New Deal, arguing that the restoration of economic prosperity no longer required the permanent intrusion of massive government in the economy. In foreign policy, conservatives initially promoted a "fortress America" strategy, emphasizing the need for isolationism abroad and military withdrawal, but this political stance was quickly discredited during the great foreign policy debate of the late 1940s. The issue of communism, however, began to surface and reinforced conservative concerns with the New Deal and perceptions of growing socialism at home. By the late 1940s and early 1950s, fear of communism both at home and abroad became the rallying cry of conservatism. McCarthyism represented the height of conservatism and its most extreme positions during the cold war. Its proponents saw themselves as engaged in a battle for the future of America with its major ideological adversaries: liberalism and the Left, Roosevelt's New Deal and Truman's Fair Deal policies at home, and the Democratic party's so-called appeasement policies of containment abroad.[45]

Although conservatism and the political Right were unsuccessful in gaining political ascendance in government and society, they *were instrumental in pushing society to the Right and providing conditions for the establishment of a liberal-conservative consen-*

sus. First, most liberals became strong advocates of anticommunism and containment during the late 1940s and 1950s. "The lesson that Democrats drew was that never again could they afford to expose their foreign policy to the charge that it was soft on communism."[46] Second, conservatives increasingly accepted the notion of a limited welfare state in the domestic economy, especially during the Eisenhower administration. Finally, liberals and the political Left, who were critical of an aggressive U.S. policy of global containment abroad and believed in greater restructuring of American society at home, lost credibility and were silenced throughout the cold war years.

Ideological anticommunism became the glue that bound the consensus among liberals, moderates, and conservatives, especially within the elite public. In the words of David Halberstam in *The Best and the Brightest,* "It was an ideological and bipartisan movement; it enjoyed the support of the press, of the churches, of Hollywood. There was stunningly little debate or sophistication of the levels of anti-communism. It was totally centrist and politically very safe; anything else was politically dangerous."[47] These ideological and foreign policy beliefs provided the foundation for the rise of the national security and free market ethos that prevailed in the minds of policymakers during the cold war years.

The ideological and foreign policy beliefs defined how Americans saw the world and limited the political choices available in the policymaking process. According to Hodgson, "the effect of McCarthyism has to be measured not only in individual careers destroyed but (more significantly for the nation as a whole) in assumptions unchallenged, in questions unasked, in problems ignored for a decade."[48] Therefore, "until after 1965, when the Vietnam crisis broke in full force, there was no opposition to orthodox anti-communism from the Left in the Democratic Party, or none worth a President's consideration. Opposition from the Right was always a more real concern."[49] This domestic political situation prompted greater U.S. intervention in the Vietnam War and eventually led to a crumbling of the foreign policy and ideological consensus.

THE POST–VIETNAM WAR YEARS AND LACK OF CONSENSUS

Events of the 1960s and early 1970s, such as the civil rights movement, the war on poverty, and Watergate, led many Americans to question the ideological and foreign policy beliefs that were the basis of the consensus during the cold war years. But the Vietnam War had the most traumatic impact on Americans, leading to the collapse of the ideological and foreign policy consensus that prevailed throughout the cold war. These events surrounding the collapse of consensus *triggered two parallel and mutually reinforcing patterns.* First, American society became more ideologically diverse: the 1960s and early 1970s resulted in a resurgence of liberalism and the rise of the new Left, while the late 1970s and 1980s witnessed the rise of conservatism and the political Right. Second, the rise of ideological diversity also led to the development of competing foreign policy views or schools of thought. With the collapse of the cold war, these swings in the ideological and foreign policy orientations of Americans set the stage for the post–Vietnam War developments in domestic politics and governmental policymaking that have continued to the present day.

The Rise of Ideological Diversity. Throughout most of the 1950s and early 1960s, the American public—both elites and masses—tacitly supported increasing U.S. involvement in Southeast Asia. In reality, most Americans were unaware of what was happening in Vietnam, or even where it was located geographically. They were not interested in distant foreign policy ventures. Yet, most Americans did not question the assumptions behind the ideological and foreign policy consensus that led to the nation's increasing involvement in Vietnam. Most Americans shared the belief that cold war policies were necessary to defend U.S. national security in Vietnam and promote democracy, freedom, and justice in the world. Therefore, if the president of the United States, supported by most leaders in government and society, contended that Vietnam was vital to American interests and threatened by commu-

nism, and that the free countries of Southeast Asia would fall if the threat was not contained, the American people stood behind him.[50]

The failure of Vietnam undermined many of these beliefs. Americans seemed to be dying for a lost cause—nearly 58,000 Americans would die in Vietnam, with over 350,000 other Americans wounded. For what? The tragic loss of American lives and the failure in Vietnam led people to raise questions about U.S. foreign policy. Was Vietnam vital to U.S. national security? Was it an international war between the forces of communism and the forces of democratic-capitalism or was it a civil war between Vietnamese factions? Were American goals and conduct of the war realistic? Were they just? Members of the mass public came to critique the Vietnam War and U.S. foreign policy predominantly from a pragmatic perspective—they emphasized the limited importance of Vietnam and questioned U.S. failure to win the war. Members of the elite public, on the other hand, were more likely to debate the goals and the justice of U.S. foreign policy. The result was that American failure in Vietnam shattered the ideological and foreign policy consensus, turning the public increasingly against the war (see essay 2.3 on the evolution of Senator J. William Fulbright's views).

A massive antiwar movement developed during the 1960s, advocating U.S. withdrawal from the war. By the late 1960s, a substantial number of average Americans also had turned against the government and its policies in Vietnam; some wanted out through victory and military escalation, but most wanted out via withdrawal. For a while, the polarization between the antiwar movement and supporters of the war, between critics and supporters of mainstream society, appeared to verge on civil war. By the 1970s, however, *polarization had given way to political fragmentation.* Thus, the ideological beliefs based on a liberal-conservative consensus that prevailed during the cold war years shattered, became "polarized" during the late 1960s and early 1970s, and "fragmented" during the post–Vietnam War years.[51]

The events of the 1960s resulted in the **growth of the political Left** in the United States and an alternative understanding of American society. Anticommunism and McCarthyism had silenced most liberals and leftists by the early 1950s. However, the new Left emerged on the political scene in the late 1950s with the rise of the civil rights movement and grew dramatically as the Vietnam War intensified. Members of the new Left and the counterculture dissented and rebelled against the liberal-conservative ideological and anticommunist consensus of mainstream society, which they held responsible for Vietnam (the new Left will be discussed at greater length in chapter 17).

The rise of the new Left politicized society and pushed it in a more liberal direction. Liberalism once again began to emphasize the values of freedom and equality that had predominated throughout the 1930s and 1940s under Franklin Roosevelt by rejecting the importance of anticommunism abroad and at home. Liberals were more likely to promote active governmental intervention in the economy and in support of needy individuals. Moreover, the Vietnam War and events of the 1960s prompted most liberals to become supportive of greater individualism in American life. Thus, liberalism became quite distinct from conservatism in the post-Vietnam years.

At the same time, many Americans continued to hold a more conservative understanding of America and the world, emphasizing the threat of communism abroad and the importance of the private market at home—the same values that had once been the basis of the ideological consensus during the cold war. In fact, the late 1970s witnessed the **resurgence of conservatism and the Right**, best associated with Ronald Reagan, in reaction to the perceived excesses of liberalism and the Left during the 1960s and 1970s. Conservatives were particularly critical of the insufficient concern with the communist threat abroad and the moral decay they believed prevailed at home. These concerns not only account for the rise of conservatism, but the growth of the ultraconservative and political Right as well, including the religious fundamentalist Right (this will also be discussed more in chapter 17).[52]

Thus, cold war dominance of the liberal-conservative consensus was superseded by greater ideological diversity throughout American society. Liberalism and conservatism became increasingly distinct and competed for influence in American society and within the U.S. government. Furthermore, the growth of liberalism was accompanied by the rise of the new Left, while the resurgence of conservatism was accompanied by the growing strength of the political Right (see **essay 14.3** on American liberalism and conservatism).

The Rise of Foreign Policy Diversity. Increasing ideological diversity paralleled the breakdown of the foreign policy consensus and the development of different foreign policy orientations and views. According to Holsti and Rosenau, *three major competing views in foreign policy have dominated the post–Vietnam War years:* cold war internationalism, post–cold war internationalism, and semi-isolationism.[53] These three views are similar to the ones advanced by political analyst William Schneider, although he uses different labels which indicate their ideological home: conservative internationalism, liberal internationalism, and non-internationalism.[54]

To understand the complex politics of U.S. foreign policy in the post–Vietnam War period, it is important to know the general orientation of these three schools of thought. At the same time, it is important to recognize that important differences or variants exist within each of these foreign policy orientations that reflect the broader ideological spectrum throughout American society. Finally, it is also important to keep in mind that some of the foreign policy beliefs held by Americans may be in a process of undergoing change in light of the end of the cold war.[55]

Many Americans, especially conservatives and those on the political Right, have continued to believe in **conservative internationalism** (or cold war internationalism) since Vietnam, especially throughout the 1970s and 1980s. In other words, they felt that the major global threat to the security of the United States and global order was communism directed by the Soviet Union, requiring a strong American military presence throughout much of the world. Yet, disagreement among conservatives existed concerning the severity of the Soviet threat and the appropriate foreign policy

ESSAY 14.3
AMERICAN LIBERALISM AND CONSERVATISM

Most Americans hold beliefs and values that are consistent with liberalism, conservatism, or some mixture of these two broad political ideologies. Yet, there is considerable confusion, especially throughout the mass public, over what the terms "liberalism" and "conservatism" mean. Confusion is understandable given the common roots of liberalism and conservatism and its evolution throughout American history. Therefore, *in order to understand the similarities and differences between American liberalism and conservatism, at least five major points must be kept in mind.*

First, modern or twentieth-century liberalism and conservatism in the United States share the same historical roots. They are both derived from "**classical liberalism**," which developed in the seventeenth and eighteenth centuries in Europe. Liberalism arose in reaction to the order and inequality that characterized medieval society and feudalism under the aristocracy and the church. Classical liberals emphasized the importance of individual freedom in economic and political affairs through the promotion of democracy and capitalism and the separation of church and state. These classical liberal ideas, evident in the work of English philosopher John Locke, influenced many of the founding fathers and, hence, the "Declaration of Independence" and the two constitutions of the United States of America. As Alexis de Tocqueville recognized during the 1830s in his classic *Democracy in America,* the United States was a most liberal society, especially in comparison to Europe.

Second, classical liberalism has evolved throughout American history into two modern derivatives developed during the twentieth century: liberalism and conservatism. **Modern American liberalism and conservatism** share a belief in individual freedom and a preference for a democratic-capitalistic political economy. However, the historical evolution of the American classical liberal tradition has also produced different interpretations and splits on some issues. The first major dispute in this century concerned the role of the government in the economy. The Great Depression convinced many people—who became known as "liberals"—that the government should take a much more active role in regulating and steering the economy. Moreover, they felt that the government should assist the unemployed and the poor, who were frequently victims of the failures and the flaws of the market economy. On the other hand, many people—who became known as "conservatives"—opposed such New Deal policies and preferred a more traditional "laissez-faire," or minimal, governmental role in the economy, where people would prosper through individual work and private charities would support the underprivileged.

The split over the government's role in the economy was the major difference between modern liberals and conservatives from the 1930s until the 1950s. During the 1950s, the cold war was a period of growing ideological consensus between liberals and conservatives because of a shared anticommunism and acceptance of a limited welfare state. The events of the 1960s shattered the consensus, producing new splits between conservatives and liberals.

Divisions over the political economy renewed, while liberals and conservatives increasingly differed over foreign policy and social policy. Liberals became critical of traditional cold war positions, while conservatives continued to adhere to cold war internationalism. For example, conservatives saw Vietnam as an honorable war lost through a failure of national will; in contrast, liberals tended to see Vietnam as a mistake and viewed the American use of force as counterproductive. Furthermore, while conservatives promoted traditional social norms and were concerned with maintaining social stability and order, liberals tended to favor greater individualism in social lifestyles. Therefore, modern American liberalism and conservatism have become increasingly distinct during the post–Vietnam War years, even though both sprang from the classical liberal democratic-capitalistic tradition.

The third point to keep in mind when discussing American liberalism and conservatism is that each ideological orientation is made up of many "variants." Differences exist among liberals and conservatives. These differences are not easy to identify, for they change over time and vary with the issue; nonetheless, they do exist. Liberalism consists of a broad coalition composed of a diverse set of people: "New Deal liberals" who favor more traditional forms of government intervention to support the economy and individuals; "**neo-liberals**" who prefer a more cooperative relationship between government, business, and labor in order to reinvigorate the economy and increase American competitiveness abroad; "populist liberals" who place greater emphasis on reforming the American economy to respond to the needs of the poor, the disadvantaged, and working Americans; "social liberals" who are more concerned with individual lifestyle issues, as well as protecting the environment and human health; and others. Likewise, conservatism also consists of diverse elements: "market conservatives" who continue to emphasize unrestrained market forces as the key to economic growth and prosperity; "populist conservatives" who want more private involvement to supplement governmental support in responding to the needs of Americans; "**neo-conservatives**"—usually ex-cold war liberals—who tend to emphasize the threat of communism abroad,[A] "social conservatives" who want certain norms and moral standards to prevail in society, such as the need for school prayer and anti-abortion; and "**libertarians**" who emphasize individualism and limited government across all issues.

Fourth, liberal and conservative ideological positions "differ in elite and mass publics." Most members of the elite public tend to be more ideologically oriented—whether liberal or conservative—than members of the mass public. The mass public, on the other hand, tends to be more centrist and moderate, reflecting beliefs and positions from both ideological orientations. This distinction between the elite and mass publics in terms of the nature and intensity of their ideological beliefs is consistent with our earlier discussion of Godfrey Hodgson's distinction in *America in Our Time* between the moral minority and the pragmatic majority.

Fifth, the growth of liberalism has been accompanied by the rise of the "political Left," while the ascendance of conservatism has been accompanied by growing strength of the "political Right." American liberalism and conservatism reflect a rather narrow range of ideological beliefs that have competed for power within American society over the last two centuries, especially when compared to the politics of European societies. For all their differences and variations, American liberalism and conservatism have much in common, although they have been challenged by other ideological traditions. The political Left has a long tradition in the history of the United States and there have been periods when it has grown in popularity and influence: democratic socialism became popular during the pre-World War I years, communism and pacifism grew during the 1920s and the post-Depression years, and the new Left was prominent during the 1960s and 1970s. The political Right, likewise, also has had a long history and has been able to attract support at different times, evident in the rise of McCarthyism during the cold war years and the prominence of the secular and fundamentalist Right during the post–Vietnam War era. Therefore, although small and often invisible to most Americans, the traditions of the Left and Right have played an active and sometimes important role in American politics.

This is a simple overview of the history and content of American liberal and conservative thought; but these five points should provide more clarity and understanding of these ideological positions. For example, it should be clear that the popular distinction that most Americans make between liberals as "pro-big government" and conservatives as "anti-big government" is inaccurate, for this difference depends on the issue and the times. For example, liberals usually prefer greater government involvement in the economy and conservatives less government intervention; however, conservatives usually prefer more government defense spending in support of national security, while liberals prefer

---

A. See, for example, Jay Winik, "The Neoconservative Reconstruction," *Foreign Policy* 73 (Winter 1988–1989): 135–52.

less. Likewise, in the area of social policy, liberals emphasize active government in support of the rights of individuals, such as to prevent child abuse, while conservatives emphasize active government to promote certain moral standards, such as school prayer or the prevention of abortion. Regardless of the particular issue and the differences between liberalism and conservatism, however, most Americans have been part of a long (classical) liberal tradition throughout American history.

SOURCES: Louis Hartz, *The Liberal Tradition in America* (New York: Harcourt Brace and World, 1955); Lawrence J. R. Herson, *The Politics of Ideas: Political Theory and American Public Policy* (Prospect Ill.: Waveland Press, 1984); Godfrey Hodgson, *America in Our Time* (New York: Vintage, 1976); Bernard K. Johnpoll with Lillian Johnpoll, *The Impossible Dream: The Rise and Demise of the American Left* (Westport, Conn.: Greenwood Press, 1981);

William S. Maddox and Stuart A. Lilie, *Beyond Liberal and Conservative: Reassessing the Political Spectrum* (Washington, D.C.: Cato Institute, 1984); George H. Nash, *The Conservative Intellectual Movement in America, Since 1945* (New York: Basic Books, 1976); Alexis de Tocqueville, *Democracy in America* (New York: Vintage, 1945); and Gary Wills, *Nixon Agonistes* (New York: Signet, 1976).

strategy. Three variants of the conservative internationalist perspective prevailed throughout the eighties (see **table 14.2**).

More extreme conservatives (or "global crusaders") tended to see communism as monolithic, favoring massive rearmament at home and a policy of aggressive rollback abroad—reminiscent of the policies advocated by McCarthy and the far right during the 1950s. Most conservatives (or "global containers"), recognizing that communism was no longer monolithic, focused on containing Soviet communism through a defense buildup and a containment strategy—reminiscent of government policy during the cold war years and the Reagan years. Finally, more moderate conservatives (or "selective containers") did not emphasize Soviet communism, but stressed the threat of the Soviet Union as a great power to global stability and argued for a realpolitik or power politics strategy of selective containment—a position promoted, for example, by Henry Kissinger under Presidents Nixon and Ford.

Other Americans, especially liberals and those on the political Left, saw a much more complex and interdependent world in the 1970s and 1980s, composed of many important countries, global actors, and issues—a position that Schneider refers to as **liberal internationalism** (and Holsti and Rosenau refer to as post–cold war internationalism). In contrast to conservatives, liberals believed it was important to address not only the East-West conflict, but West-West issues, involving relations between the U.S. and its allies, and North-South issues, focusing on the relationship between industrialized nations and the third world. Although there was general agreement that the cold war preoccupation with the Soviet threat and the use of force must be downplayed in order to promote global stability, peace, and prosperity, two variants of the liberal internationalist perspective existed (see **table 14.3**).

Most liberals (or "global reformers") tended to focus on promoting stability in U.S.-Soviet relations, advocate arms control and other confidence-building measures, while emphasizing the need for cooperative economic relations between Europe, North America, and Asia to develop a liberal economic world order. They also tended to emphasize the importance of human rights, democracy, and the role of diplomacy in resolving disputes and conflict. More extreme views on the political Left (or "global transformers") advocated greater arms control and global disarmament, supported greater efforts to redress third-world poverty and violence, and were concerned with overcoming international environmental destruction.

Proponents of the third popular orientation of the 1970s and 1980s, spanning the political spectrum, recognized the increasing complexity of the world and the difficulty the United States has in affecting it, advocating a type of **non-internationalism** (or semi-isolationism or "selective engager" ori-

TABLE 14.2
COLD WAR INTERNATIONALIST ORIENTATIONS

	GLOBAL CONTAINERS	GLOBAL CRUSADERS	SELECTIVE CONTAINERS
DEPICTION OF THE INTERNATIONAL SYSTEM	Bipolar	Bipolar but with unipolar tendencies	Bimultipolar
MAJOR ACTORS	U.S.—benevolent, defender of freedom, lacks will, militarily deficient	U.S.—morally superior, currently corrupted, militarily weak	U.S.—strong but militarily deficient, naive at times about world
	U.S.S.R.—imperial, communist, totalitarian, militarily stronger	Communists—imperial, evil, militarily superior	U.S.S.R.—great power, opportunistic, expansionistic
MAJOR ISSUES	Cold war, superpower ideological struggle, terrorism, defense policy	Spread of international communism	Global balance of power, superpower rivalry, alliance politics
HISTORICAL LESSONS	WWII—need to reject appeasement, Vietnam—need to stand resolute	All post-WWII history illustrates U.S. foreign failures	WWI and WWII—need to maintain balance of power
PRESCRIPTION	Promote and protect freedom and democracy, global containment of Soviet communism, unilateral action if necessary	Promote freedom and capitalism, roll back communism, unilateral approach	Maintain order and stability, contain expansionism in vital areas, multilateral approach favored

SOURCE: Jerel Rosati and John Creed, "Extending the Three- and Four-Headed Eagles: The Foreign Policy Orientations of American Elites During the 80s and 90s," *Political Psychology* (1997), pp. 583–623.

entation, review **table 14.3**). Some non-internationalists argued that the United States needed to limit its involvement to those areas of the world where it really has vital interests—primarily Western Europe and Japan. Other non-internationalists believed that the United States should de-escalate its overseas mili-tary commitments and presence—in other words, "strategically disengage"—concentrating on improving its international commercial and economic position. Whatever the particular position, non-internationalists were likely to believe that the highest priority of American society and the U.S. government should be to avoid entanglements abroad and address domestic issues and problems at home. Non-internationalists also tended to be more

supportive of protection of American industry and jobs in the international political economy. Such a non-internationalist perspective was most prevalent among the mass public (in comparison to the elite public), where isolationist sentiment has historically been strong and might very well grow in popularity in a post–cold war world.[56]

What about the impact of the collapse of Soviet communism on the foreign policy orientations of Americans for the 1990s? As Norman Ornstein and Mark Schmitt ask, "How will the U.S. political system operate without anticommunism as its central organizing principle?"[57] The momentous events surrounding the end of the cold war, the collapse of communism in Eastern Europe, and the collapse of

TABLE 14.3
POST–COLD WAR INTERNATIONALISTS AND SEMI-ISOLATIONIST ORIENTATIONS

	GLOBAL REFORMERS	GLOBAL TRANSFORMERS	SEMI-ISOLATIONISTS
DEPICTION OF THE INTERNATIONAL SYSTEM	Multipolar, interdependent	Multipolar, with U.S. prevalent	Generally multipolar, interdependent, chaotic
MAJOR ACTORS	U.S.—great power, in decline	U.S.—hegemonic power, in decline	Multitude of potentially important actors
	U.S.S.R.—strong military power, economically weak, opportunistic	U.S.S.R.—strong military power, largely weak and defensive in nature	U.S.—increasingly overcommitted
	Europe + Japan—growing economic powers	Third world actors—often oppressed but offer hope	
	NICs—growing economic force		
MAJOR ISSUES	Superpower relations and arms race, regional conflicts, global economic stability, third world development	Arms race, global expansionism, regional conflict, self-determination, global inequality	Arms race and other transnational problems, domestic issues
HISTORICAL LESSONS	Vietnam—example of decline in the utility of force	Vietnam—example of U.S. expansionism	Vietnam—U.S. global policy prone to failure
PRESCRIPTION	Maintain global order and stability, infuse justice, multilateralism	Restructure U.S. and international institutions to provide justice and dignity to world's people	Limited U.S. involvement in world affairs, only when vital interests at stake

SOURCE: See Table 14.2.

the Soviet Union have raised the possibility of profound changes in American foreign policy orientations. Indeed, **another "great debate"** in the 1990s has been generated over the nature of the world and the proper role of the United States abroad.

There has been a general recognition that, with the collapse of the Soviet Union and its Eastern European empire, the structure of the international system has changed—that the United States is the sole global power (or superpower) and is in a more advantageous position than before. But there is great debate about what this means. In fact, most American opinion leaders seem to be adapting and absorbing such a change within their prevailing foreign policy beliefs, maintaining much of the basic thrust of each of the foreign policy orientations outlined above.

The end of the cold war has reaffirmed the beliefs of liberal internationalists that U.S. foreign policy needs to move beyond the cold war to "cooperative multilateralism" in order to address the myriad issues in a complex and interdependent world. The same is true for semi-isolationists, that U.S. foreign policy should (and can) pursue strategic disengagement and greater independence in world politics. With the collapse of Soviet communism, one might expect to see some significant changes in conservative internationalist orientations. And while there has been some movement more towards semi-isolationism and selective containment, conservative internationalists, for the most part, continue to emphasize security threats to the U.S. and the stability of the world—but now in and from the third world—and the need for American "primacy."[58]

The differences between conservative internationalists, liberal internationalists, and non-internationalists are particularly noticeable in national security affairs as opposed to foreign economics. With the collapse of the foreign policy consensus over the Vietnam War, Americans differ over the nature of world politics and their prescriptions for a U.S. national security policy. Thus, where conservative internationalism once reigned supreme and provided the basis for the "national security ethos" of independence, secrecy, and realpolitik that prevailed among policymakers during the 1950s and 1960s, as discussed in chapter 9, since Vietnam there have been fewer adherents of a strong national security ethos and they must operate in a domestic political climate that, with the rise of liberal internationalism and semi-internationalism, is less receptive to such views.

"Foreign economic policy orientations and the free market ethos," discussed in chapter 10, were much less affected by the Vietnam War and the collapse of the cold war consensus. Internationalists still tend to sympathize with a free market ethos. Conservative internationalists are the most strong believers and advocates of an unregulated international political economy based on a free market. Liberal internationalists, for the most part, also believe in a market-oriented international political economy, but argue for the need for more international multilateral cooperation, management, and regulation. It is the non-internationalists who are the least receptive to the free market ethos and most willing to advocate **protectionism** for local industry and labor.[59] Therefore, the cold war consensus has collapsed, but the split in foreign policy beliefs is much greater in the area of national security than it is over foreign economics. This may undergo some change as the U.S. enters the twenty-first century and the rise of economic issues to the forefront of U.S. foreign policy.

Together, the three broad foreign policy perspectives, and their variations, set the parameters of foreign policy thought and agenda-setting in the making of U.S. foreign policy. Members of the elite public tend to be more committed to some variant of conservative or liberal internationalism, but they usually are opposed to non-internationalism. Members of the mass public tend to be more moderate and pragmatic in their beliefs, demonstrating both liberal and conservative elements, and are more receptive to the non-internationalist orientation.[60]

This configuration of foreign policy beliefs among different types of publics has led to some major contradictions in public opinion, especially over national security policy. Throughout the 1970s and 1980s, for example, most Americans continued to be fearful and skeptical of international communism; yet they also wanted more cooperative and peaceful relations with communist countries, such as the Soviet Union and the People's Republic of China. Likewise, most continued to believe in a strong defense; however, they remained reluctant to support uses of force that may result in American boys dying abroad. Although these contradictory views are not easily resolved, they demonstrate that the legacies of both the cold war and Vietnam War seem to have been absorbed by most Americans within their foreign policy beliefs as the United States moves beyond the cold war in the 1990s.

THE SEARCH FOR CONSENSUS AND POLICY LEGITIMATION

The changes in ideological and foreign policy beliefs have important political implications for the foreign policy process. What is important to understand is that the movement from cold war consensus to post-Vietnam diversity has *widened the agenda of domestic politics and political discourse* in the making of U.S. foreign policy. Such changes in the ideological and foreign policy beliefs cannot be understated for the collapse of the cold war consensus has led to a post–Vietnam War era where public opinion is more volatile, political participation has become more active and diverse, the media is more likely to act independent of the government, Congress has reasserted its authority, and the president's ability to govern foreign policy has weakened and declined. As Richard Melanson has concluded in *Reconstructing Consensus*, "In sum, a **"fragmentation/swing" model** has replaced that of cold war **"followership" model** as the most accurate depiction of foreign policy attitudes . . . and its emergence has surely complicated the efforts of presidents to win and keep public support for their foreign policies."[61]

The diversity of foreign policy beliefs has led to some major fluctuations in public opinion. Where public opinion only fluctuated within a narrow range consistent with the liberal-conservative and cold war internationalist consensus during the cold war years, public opinion is much more open to greater fluctuation reflecting the breakdown of the cold war consensus. This is because, unlike the opinions of the elite public, which tend to reflect their commitment to a particular ideological and foreign policy view, members of the mass public tend to be more centrist and more non-internationalist in their orientations. Therefore, members of the mass public, since they do not internalize the ideological views of the elite public, are more likely to change their opinion and be open to populist appeals: sometimes they are responsive to a more conservative and cold war internationalist position while at other times they are more receptive to a liberal and post–cold war internationalist position.

The post–Vietnam War years of dissension have produced a much more complex and messy political process where public opinion is much more volatile than during the cold war years of consensus. As William Schneider has pointed out, when a foreign policy issue gets on the political agenda and is framed in terms of security and military "strength," then the conservative internationalist orientation tends to win the political debate. However, if it is framed in terms of "peace," then the liberal internationalist perspective tends to prevail. "Instead of elite consensus and mass followership, what emerged was an unstable system of competing coalitions in which the mass public swings left or right unpredictably in response to its current fears and concerns."[62] There are also times when an issue may

trigger a strong semi-isolationist orientation among the public, such as over issues concerning jobs and the economy. Public opinion, therefore, tends to fluctuate dramatically depending on the political issues of the occasion and the success of different groups and leaders in communicating their positions.

This situation is likely to grow with the end of the cold war. The fear of communism—the glue that held the cold war consensus together and has been the foundation for cold war internationalism—has been erased with its collapse in Eastern Europe and the Soviet Union. This may usher in an era where the foreign policy views of Americans may undergo much more substantial change: for example, the collapse of the threat of communism has produced considerable conflict among conservatives and may diminish cold war internationalism's appeal in comparison to liberal internationalism and non-internationalism. Although there exists the potential for such a political realignment in foreign policy thought, the future of world politics, nevertheless, will continue to encompass conflict where the United States will continue to occupy a major global role, as the Persian Gulf War demonstrated. In this respect, it is important to recognize that liberal and conservative internationalism predate the cold war and will continue in a post–cold war international environment.

The fragmentation of public ideological and foreign policy beliefs gives a president great opportunities but also creates great risks. Unlike the 1950s, presidents are no longer driven to pursue only an anticommunist containment policy. Yet, it is unclear how far a president may go in pursuing any policy before losing public support. Presidents no longer come to office with automatic majorities behind their policies. No matter what the president and his advisers believe, a substantial number of Americans—in the mass public and especially the elite public—disagree, or are open to disagreement, with presidential policy. Hence, the presidential search, and frustration, for consensus and **policy legitimation**.[63]

A "new consensus" appears to be nowhere in the making. Given the limited changes that have occurred thus far despite the collapse of Soviet communism, it is likely that the foreign policy orientations of Americans will continue to adapt to a post–cold war world. Where the end of the cold war appears to be reinforcing the beliefs of liberal internationalists and non-internationalists, conservative internationalists appear to be moving more toward an emphasis on power politics and the need for international order, while others may emphasize more the promotion of democracy and a liberal world order. Whatever the case, foreign policy thought is likely to remain highly diverse, especially among members of the elite public, and competitive, particularly for the support of the mass public.[64]

All post–Vietnam War presidents have discovered that most Americans expect presidential promises to be fulfilled, but the dissension of the post–Vietnam War years makes it much more difficult for presidents to deliver. Presidents have found that, in addition to the reassertion of Congress, they face additional constraints on their ability to govern from electoral politics, group politics, and the media and the communications process as a result of the collapse of the cold war consensus, as we will discuss in the next few chapters. All this is likely to continue in a post–cold war political environment. Therefore, differences in the ideological and foreign policy beliefs among the elite public, coupled with a pragmatic but volatile mass public, have provided a new set of domestic boundaries and possibilities for the making of U.S. foreign policy since the post–Vietnam War years.

POLITICAL CULTURE

. . . .

In addition to the role of public opinion and political ideology, **political culture** plays a subtle but significant role in the making of U.S. foreign policy. Political culture refers to how people see themselves and their country relative to the rest of the world. Although American political culture includes a variety of important values, such as democracy and individualism, the focus in this section is on those cultural assumptions that Americans have about their country's role in the world. Not only does this suggest the existence of an **American "national style,"** but such nationalistic beliefs are particularly evident and powerful forces in the politics of U.S. foreign policy in times of crisis and war.[65]

In considering political culture, a number of things must be kept in mind. First, we are most interested in the cultural and national values prevailing in the population; therefore, what the mass public believes plays a predominant role in determining America's national style. Second, cultural values also tend to be the most shared, "resilient," and consistent set of beliefs held by individuals. Nationalistic views and feelings, in other words, strongly resist change, for they are acquired at a very young age. Finally, political culture and national style do not influence domestic politics and the policymaking process in an immediate or direct way, but by coloring how individuals see their country and its special place in the world. Because cultural and national values are socialized and deeply held, most people—within both the mass and elite publics—have a somewhat ethnocentric view of the world, thus affecting how foreign policy is made.

AMERICAN CULTURE AND NATIONAL STYLE

Throughout most of the 1960s and 1970s, American political culture and national style received little study, in part because of the difficulties involved in determining the key elements of a nation's cultural values or character. By the 1980s, however, numerous works had been produced highlighting the important role that American political culture and national style play in the making of U.S. foreign policy.[66] These works tend to agree that most Americans had acquired a similar cultural outlook and developed a strong sense of nationalism by the twentieth century.

Studies of American political culture typically portray Americans as a confident and optimistic people who have a special sense of destiny about the future of their country and its place in the world. In *Backfire*, for example, Loren Baritz argues that *three key characteristics describe how Americans see themselves* relative to the rest of the world: the notion of a "city on a hill," an idealistic and missionary spirit, and the invincibility of American technology. In other words, most Americans tend to believe inherently in

1. American innocence;
2. American benevolence;
3. American exceptionalism.

Americans are raised to believe that the United States is "innocent" in world affairs as a people and a country. In other words, Americans do not see themselves as manipulative and aggressive, but as a benign and defensive people and country. **American innocence** is consistent with the isolationist sentiments that have played such a dominant role in U.S. foreign policy, especially before the cold war.[67] According to this view, Americans have not been an outward-seeking people. Instead, they have been introspective, concerned with nation-building, and serve as a **"city on a hill"** for other people and countries to emulate. Over the years, other countries and other ideologies have forced the United States to become actively involved in war and world politics. The German disregard of American neutrality forced the United States to fight in World War I, while the Japanese bombing of Pearl Harbor forced American entry into World War II. Thus, Americans tend to see themselves and their country as the innocent victims of the acts of others.

When the United States does become involved abroad, American behavior is perceived as "benevolent." Such **benevolence** means that Americans do not become involved in war, for example, solely to defend themselves; rather, they enter wars in order to rid the world of evil and promote peace and freedom for all. As Americans have been taught at a very young age, World War I represented the "war to end all wars." European realpolitik would be replaced by American idealism, as embodied in President Woodrow Wilson's plan to create a League of Nations. In World War II, the United States and its allies were dedicated to ridding the world of fascism and constructing a world based on a liberal political and economic order as represented by the United Nations. In both wars, the United States saw itself as not only defending its national security but fighting for the principles of democracy, freedom, and justice for all.

Finally, Americans not only see themselves as innocent and benevolent, but also have a strong sense of **exceptionalism** as well. When Americans put their minds to something, they succeed in accomplishing their objectives. American history is perceived as one success story after another, from westward expansion to economic development to the rise of the United States as a global power. Much of this is seen as a function of "yankee ingenuity" and American technological superiority over others. There is also an American sense of **manifest destiny**—a belief in the superiority of American culture and way of life and the need to Christianize and Americanize the world.[68] In other words, American exceptionalism implies that God is on America's side and that America represents progress and the best social model for the future of the world. Thus, Americans have a high sense of optimism, that is, confidence about their ability to accomplish any task and faith in their future, "that Americans can do anything they desire, can build nations or rebuild societies, can speed progress, bring freedom and democracy to the world." In other words, James Oliver Robertson concludes, "America, imperial America, *is* "one giant step for mankind.""[69]

The effects of these cultural and national values emphasizing American innocence, benevolence, and exceptionalism on American perceptions of the cold war are obvious. For most Americans, Soviet aggression forced the United States to take an active global leadership role, build up its military to contain aggression, and intervene throughout the world. Thus, Americans were innocent victims of Soviet aggression and needed to contain the threat. Moreover, the cold war was not just a classical struggle for power between two great powers, but represented a messianic struggle between good and evil—the forces of democracy versus totalitarianism, capitalism versus communism, Christianity versus atheism. Thus, the globe was seen to be divided into two hostile blocs:

the "evil" communist world led by the Soviet Union versus the "free world" led by the United States. In addition, the United States had not only rescued Western Europe through its generosity with the Marshall Plan, but promoted liberal societies in third-world countries and assisted their nation-building efforts based on the American model. Americans, therefore, did not see themselves as imperialistic or even self-interested during the cold war years, but as an innocent society composed of benevolent and exceptional people who symbolized progress and a hopeful future for the world.[70]

Innocence, benevolence, and exceptionalism are **not uniquely American** beliefs but to some degree are common cultural and national values within all societies. Groups and societies often see themselves as a superior and chosen people. This is typical of all great powers in world history. For example, the French empire was justified in terms of *mission civilisatrice* (civilizing mission) and the British empire reflected the "white man's burden" to uplift other people and civilize the world. As Godfrey Hodgson has observed, "All nations live by myths. Any nation is the sum of the consciousness of its people: the chaotic infinitude of the experience and perceptions of millions alive and dead."[71]

Although a strong sense of nationalism is not a uniquely American trait, what may be somewhat unique to the United States is the strong belief in **"freedom" (and "liberty")**—the key value that unifies and defines Americans as Alexis de Tocqueville so aptly described in his masterpiece on *Democracy in America* in 1835.[72] This may help to explain why phrases like "the free world," "democracy," "the free market," and "free trade" seem to be used with great regularity since World War II and resonate throughout the body politic. Furthermore, it is also commonly argued that, given America's short history, the rapid changes experienced with industrialization and modernization, and its ethnic diversity, American nationalism is as powerful a cultural force for most Americans as for any people throughout history. In the words of political analyst Richard Barnet, "All nations preach the ethic of national superiority but the United States has made a religion of it."[73]

FOREIGN POLICY IMPLICATIONS

American culture and national style have important implications for U.S. foreign policy. First, America's national style contributes to the tendency of Americans to oversimplify, with a "naive" and "rose-colored" view, the history of the United States and its role in world affairs. Concepts such as "freedom," "democracy," "the free market," and "free trade" have become sacrosanct in the American mind and interwoven with the "United States of America." **Westward expansion**, for example, is fondly recalled in terms of the frontier spirit, individualism, and ruggedness represented by the farmer and gunslinger, ignoring alternative interpretations that emphasize the ruthlessness of westward expansion and the taking of Native American and Mexican land and lives. In fact, the Mexican-American War was not a defensive war fought by the United States, but a war started by President James Polk in support of territorial expansion. Such unattractive points of fact are commonly glossed over in the upbringing and education of most Americans at home, in school, and throughout society.[74]

Much **popular folklore and "myth"** is accepted by Americans as fact and history. According to James Oliver Robertson, in *American Myth, American Reality:*

> Myths are the patterns—of behavior, of belief, and of perception—which people have in common. Myths are not deliberately, or necessarily consciously, fictitious. They provide good, "workable" ways by which the contradictions in a society, the contrasts and conflicts which normally arise among people, among ideals, among the confusing realities, are somehow reconciled, smoother over, or at least made manageable and tolerable.... And they are passed on from one generation to another by an unconscious, non-rational process

somewhat similar to the process by which language is transmitted.[75]

Myths not only help to unite a people and allow them to work together, they also help to produce simplistic and optimistic images, which makes it easy for Americans to ignore history and politics, thus reinforcing low levels of attention and information in public opinion. This also makes it difficult for Americans to tolerate and accept historical facts or political realities that are inconsistent with their optimistic images. It also contributes to the other consequences discussed below.[76]

Second, America's national style is responsible for the **moralization of U.S. foreign policy.** American leaders have often embodied a nationalist and idealist yearning that has turned much of U.S. foreign policy into the equivalent of a moral crusade. This is probably best associated with the presidency of Woodrow Wilson and the coining of the phrase **"Wilsonianism."** As summed up by Robert Nisbet, "From Wilson's day to ours the embedded purpose—sometimes articulated in words, more often not—of American foreign policy, under Democrats and Republics alike oftentimes, has boiled down to America-on-a-Permanent-Mission; a mission to make the rest of the world a little more like America the Beautiful."[77]

The moralization of foreign policy has been a major pattern throughout the twentieth century: Woodrow Wilson led the United States in World War I to "end all wars" and promote self-determination throughout the world; American cold war policies represented freedom against the forces of tyranny; President Carter's post–cold war foreign policy revolved around the promotion of human rights and democracy; and President Reagan's reinstatement of the cold war was an effort to restore American greatness and battle the "evil empire." Although overstated, Nisbet argues that "the single most powerful cause of the present size and the worldwide deployment of the military establishment is the moralization of foreign policy and military ventures that has been deeply ingrained, especially in the minds of presidents, for a long time."[78]

Furthermore, as Stanley Hoffmann has observed,

There is a parallel here: like the ideological tenets of communism, American principles—those of a deeply Christian, liberal society, a kind of synthesis or smorgasbord of Locke, Paine, and Kant—are universal and equalitarian; all the nations of the world are seen capable of living in peace under law in an association of equals devoted to harmony. This mixture of universalism, legalism, and equalitarianism diverts Americans from any suggestion that their attempt to spread the gospel might be imperialistic or self-serving; what is being sought is the common good, in the best interest of all. But the proselytizing contradicts the stated purpose, the method clashes with the intended outcome.[79]

In the words of Reinhold Niebuhr, "Moral pretensions and political parochialism are the two weaknesses of the life of a messianic nation."[80]

Third, this has resulted in major *contradictions between principle and pragmatism*. Despite its moralization, the actual conduct of U.S. foreign policy often involves the pragmatic pursuit of national interests heavily informed by a national security ethos that existed before, and will continue to exist after, the cold war. This means that policymakers engage in secrecy, bargaining, rewards, threats, force, and all of the other instruments associated with "power politics" in order to successfully promote their national interests as they define them. But such amoral and pragmatic behavior by the "superpower" of its day, as we discussed in chapter 9 on covert operations, is not consistent with notions of American innocence, benevolence, and exceptionalism, to the point that much of U.S. foreign policy has had to remain hidden and disguised from the public.

This contradiction has posed real problems for the leaders and makers of U.S. foreign policy, producing a kind-of **American dualism**, the necessity to speak two different languages: the language of power and the language of peace and harmony. "Of course," states Stanley Hoffmann, "only a symbolic eagle can hold both the arrows and the olive branch easily at the same time."[81] Such contradictions between morality and pragmatism explains why the realpolitik foreign policy promoted by Henry Kissinger under Presidents Nixon and Ford was never well received by Americans—it was too "amoral" in nature. This also helps to explain why the economic and geopolitical explanations that President Bush relied on early in the Persian Gulf crisis had difficulty convincing Americans that the American strategy of taking Iraq to the brink of war to force it out of Kuwait while risking American lives was sensitive (at least until war broke out). The unwillingness by Americans to recognize, and deal with, these contradictions between morality and pragmatism in foreign policy has been a topic of concern for quite some time by such thinkers as George Kennan, Hans Morgenthau, Reinhold Niebuhr, and Stanley Hoffmann.[82]

Fourth, American leaders often have to "oversell" their policies in order to legitimate them with the public by simplifying them and infusing them with moral purpose in the process, further reinforcing American culture and nationalism. It matters little whether political leaders themselves share these same cultural and nationalistic values—most do, some do not (at least in varying degrees). The fact is that the pragmatic majority is generally uninterested and uninformed about world affairs, and so political overstatement and oversell is deemed necessary to attract public attention and support, especially when foreign policy changes or the use of force is involved. This compels leaders to speak in terms of power and peace, and to rely on the "politics of symbolism" to legitimize their policies (as discussed above and which will be discussed to a greater extent in chapter 18 on the media).[83]

To arouse public support, political leaders link issues to moral symbols and values with which most Americans identify. As Senator Arthur Vandenburg told senior officials of the Truman administration, the only way to get Congress and the public to support military assistance to Greece and Turkey in 1947, to overcome post–World War II isolationist

tendencies, was to "scare the hell out of the American people" about the threat of communism to freedom, democracy, and the American way of life. Such was the language of the Truman Doctrine.[84] This helps to explain the power of anticommunism in the making of foreign policy since World War II. This also helps to explain why Americans were told that the Grenadian invasion was for the humanitarian purpose of rescuing American students, and that the Panama invasion was designed to help the Panamanian people by ridding them of the evil Noriega. Realpolitik, "power politics" and political reasons were mentioned only briefly or ignored entirely, for President Reagan was trying to rally public support. This also helps one to understand why President Bush increasingly began to equate Saddam Hussein of Iraq with Adolf Hitler of Nazi Germany as the Persian Gulf crisis escalated—to justify the pursuit and exercise of American power abroad.

Fifth, the moralization and the tendency to oversell foreign policy also often breeds "strong doses" of American nationalism and intolerance abroad and at home. Nationalism is often a positive force, for it helps to promote a strong sense of community among members of society in support of a common effort—an essential quality in times of both war and peace. One of the major problems with a strong sense of nationalism, however, is that patriotism often turns into intolerance and **"superpatriotism."** Such attitudes have the tendency to dehumanize adversaries and repress domestic criticism and dissent in the name of national security. Intolerance is particularly evident during periods of national emergency and war, when people feel threats to their values and to their country's security.

Strong doses of nationalism heighten the contradictions between the demands of national security and democracy at home, a topic that will be discussed in some depth in chapter 17 on the exercise of civil liberties. This also has made it difficult for Americans to accept criticism from abroad, including from the country's closest allies, thus reflecting deep-seated isolationist and unilateralist sentiments. As Hoffmann has argued, American foreign policy easily leads to "an activism that others see as imperialistic: for we expect them to join the consensus, we ignore the boundaries and differences between "them" and "us," we prod them out of conviction that we act for their own good, and we do not take resistance gracefully."[85] Americans have such a strong faith in American virtue and progress that it is difficult for them to understand, let alone accept, the value of alternative paths to economic and political development divorced from the American model.

A final consequence of American culture and nationalism is their tendency to contribute to major swings in **public moods** or sentiments with respect to U.S. foreign policy. It is commonly argued that "twentieth-century exceptionalism has *fueled both interventionism and isolationism.*"[86] Richard Barnet, in fact, has argued that "the 'internationalist' versus 'isolationist' debate is really an argument about little more than military strategy" abroad, in which both competing perspectives ultimately reflect an underlying sense of **unilateralism** among the mass public and in America's national style.[87] Or as Stanley Hoffmann has stated, "Both quietism and activism are compensatory assertions of total independence."[88]

Major swings in public opinion have affected U.S. relations with both allies and enemies. This is easily seen in the **cycles of U.S.-Russian relations**. After the Bolshevik revolution the United States invaded the Soviet Union during World War I and refused to recognize it until 1933; during World War II, the Soviet Union under "Uncle Joe" Stalin became the patriotic ally of freedom against fascism; with the rise of the cold war, the Soviet Union represented a monolithic communist threat abroad and at home; the détente years from Nixon to Carter were a time of hope for a cooperative U.S.-Soviet relationship; under Reagan, cooperation was replaced by a new cold war to contain "the evil empire"; and with the collapse of communism Americans hailed Mikhail Gorbachev and Boris Yeltsin as great leaders in a post–cold war future to be characterized by global peace and prosperity.

These dramatic swings in public moods and U.S. foreign policy have occurred with China, Japan, Germany, and other countries as well, while Ameri-

cans have maintained a positive and moral self-image. Although American leaders initiated such foreign policy changes, public expectations and support were critical to their pursuit over time. This has often led the public mood to swing from one extreme to another due to the extraordinary high levels of hope and fear aroused within American culture and politics. Hence, the high hopes and optimism of the immediate post–World War II years were replaced by disillusionment and fear during the cold war years. Such public mood swings, unfortunately, often do not reflect the complexity and messiness of world politics at the time, yet heavily affect the formulation of U.S. foreign policy.

CONTINUITY, CHANGE, AND THE VIETNAM WAR

Most Americans share a common sense of what it is to be an American and this plays an important role in the politics of U.S. foreign policy. Obviously, there are subcultures within American society in which different cultural and national images prevail—some of which may not be composed of such positive views. Nevertheless, most Americans share a belief in the existence of American innocence, benevolence, and exceptionalism at home and abroad. These cultural beliefs were deeply engrained within most Americans by the turn of the century and the time of Woodrow Wilson, the apostle of freedom, self-determination, and the League of Nations.

The "great exception" in American history was the South, for it was the only region of the country that ever seriously attempted to secede from the Union, losing a devastating civil war fought mostly on its lands and coming under military occupation and control following the war. By the cold war years, however, the differences between the South and the North in thought and in practice had diminished. With this great exception, the cultural assumptions of American innocence, benevolence, and exceptionalism seem to have grown stronger over time.

This sense of shared nationalism is especially noticeable during times of war. Thus, despite American fear and apprehension, World War II and the cold war years were also a time of hope and optimism in America. After saving the world from the threat of fascism, most Americans believed that the United States was innocently thrust onto the world stage to save the world from the tyranny of communism. Not only would the U.S. rearm and contain the national security threat, it would actively serve as a model, helping others to find the peace and prosperity that most Americans have experienced. In the minds of many Americans, especially American leaders, the post–World War II years represented **the American century** and the height of American innocence, benevolence, and, in particular, exceptionalism. Such a mindset helped to justify the pursuit and exercise of American power throughout the world in the name of world responsibility.[89]

As relayed by Godfrey Hodgson, the United States entered the 1960s in an Augustan mood: "united, confident, conscious of a historical mission, and mobilized for the great task of carrying it out." If Americans were anxious about danger from abroad, "it was because they saw their own society as so essentially just and benevolent that danger could come only from elsewhere. If they found international affairs frustrating, it was because they found it infuriating that foreigners could not always believe that their only ambition was a generous desire to share the abundance of American capitalism and the promise of American democracy with those less fortunate than themselves."[90]

Such a mood of American confidence and mission was best symbolized by the presidency of John Fitzgerald **Kennedy and his inaugural address** on January 20, 1961, when he declared:

Let the word go forth from this time and place, to friend and foe alike, that the torch has been passed to a new generation of Americans—born in this country, tempered by war, disciplined by a hard and bitter peace, proud of our ancient heritage— and unwilling to witness or permit the slow undoing of those human rights to which this Nation has always been committed, and to which we are committed today at

home and around the world. Let every nation know, whether it wishes us well or ill, that we shall pay any price, bear any burden, meet any hardship, support any friend, oppose any foe, in order to assure the survival and the success of liberty.

It was this sense of American confidence and exceptionalism that ultimately led to war and tragedy in the jungles of Vietnam.

The Vietnam War produced the "first major assault" on these optimistic assumptions of American political culture and national style. The Great Depression of the 1930s had precipitated extreme criticism of the innocence and benevolence of American business and capitalism. In contrast, the events of the 1960s surrounding civil rights and the Vietnam War led many Americans to question the three assumptions in their entirety. How could the United States be innocent if Vietnam was not vital to American security? How could policies that promoted activities such as the "need to destroy cities in order to save them," carpet bombing and the use of napalm, and the My Lai massacre be justified as acts of American benevolence? How did American failure and withdrawal from the war fit with American exceptionalism? Clearly, Vietnam made clear that Americans were not willing to "pay any price" and "bear any burden." And, along with Watergate, most members of the public came to lose their trust in public officials, the government, and the political process.[91]

The split between supporters and critics of the war was more than an ideological disagreement over U.S. foreign policy; it represented a fragmentation of American cultural and nationalistic beliefs. *The Vietnam War produced different lessons* for different segments of the population. Conservatives and the political Right saw the Vietnam War as a just cause that was consistent with American innocence, benevolence, and exceptionalism—its failure was explained by the lack of will among the liberal establishment. Liberals and the political Left believed that the Vietnam War was an example of the lack of sufficient innocence and benevolence in U.S. foreign policy and that the United States should not and could not impose its will on other people. The mass public emphasized more pragmatic lessons: American troops should be used only for the most vital of interests and for a good cause where the war would be swift and involve minimal loss of American lives. Overall, the Vietnam War challenged the cultural assumptions that Americans held about themselves and their place in the world as no event had done before.

The rise of the so-called **"Vietnam syndrome,"** and the negative images associated in the minds of many Americans with the failure of the Vietnam War, were reinforced by the events of the 1980s. American exceptionalism in particular was open to question and doubt given the sense of humiliation Americans felt concerning the 444-day Iran-hostage crisis during the Carter presidency and the killing of 256 American marines in Lebanon under President Reagan, forcing their withdrawal from the region.

This mass feeling of national impotence on a world stage helps to explain why Americans seemed to express such jubilation with the "great victory" involving the invasion of Grenada in 1983, for it followed immediately on the footsteps of the Lebanon fiasco and represented the first American military success abroad since Vietnam (even though the American military performance on the ground was abysmal; see essay 8.4. This was then followed by the successful invasion of Panama in 1989. But it was the **impact of the Persian Gulf War** that really was instrumental in renewing American faith in its cultural assumptions and national style. Although many questioned the vital interests at stake, most Americans saw the U.S. role in the Persian Gulf crisis as a just cause. Most importantly, Americans were able to restore their inherent faith in their exceptionalism with the triumphant and unexpected military rout of Iraq in the war, accounting for the sense of celebration that Americans felt toward the troops who returned from the Persian Gulf and President Bush's historically high public approval ratings following the war.

The Persian Gulf War, although it has helped to restore many of America's cultural assumptions, has not eliminated the memories and shadows of other crucial historical events that have deeply affected the minds of Americans, such as World War II, the Korean War, and the Vietnam War. Although Americans continue to believe in their innocence, benevolence, and exceptionalism, it is colored by their understanding of the past and their hopes for the future. Conservatives and liberals possess strong nationalist sentiments and continue to believe in America, but in different ways. Conservatives, and the Right, believe that American innocence, benevolence, and exceptionalism have prevailed throughout American history; in contrast, liberals, and the Left, are more prone to see the good, the bad, and the ugly in American history, while still believing in the possibility of building an America where innocence, benevolence, and exceptionalism reign supreme. As Robertson has stated it, "As a New World, many American believe their country to be the last, best hope of the world, a place of youth, of new beginnings, of booming. Even those who believe that America is, in reality, no such place of hope or virtue believe it somehow *ought to be.*"[92]

Most members of the mass public, being more pragmatic and centrist, probably entertain both sets of feelings at different times—what they manifest depends upon the salience of the issues and how they are played out politically at the time. A kind of "pessimistic-optimistic dualism," in other words, operates among members of the mass public, since they share a certain cynicism about American politics while still maintaining an optimistic image of American innocence, benevolence, and exceptionalism. This helps to explain how both liberal and conservative views, as embodied, for example, in President Carter's human rights policies and President Reagan's anticommunism, were initially attractive to most members of the public. It also explains why America's culture and national style will remain an integral part of the complex politics of U.S. foreign policy.

PATTERNS IN BELIEFS AND MAKING FOREIGN POLICY

· · · · · · · · · · · · · ·

In summary, the public's role in U.S. foreign policymaking depends on three sets of beliefs, providing a more complex view of what makes the public consequential relative to the traditional wisdom. American political culture and national style set the broad context within which the politics of U.S. foreign policy transpire. Then, the ideological and foreign policy beliefs of Americans further narrow what is possible and probable within domestic politics and the policymaking process. Finally, public opinion affects the foreign policy process as it fluctuates within the confines of American political culture and ideology. Together, the three sets of beliefs among the elite and mass publics are related and impact on one another, accounting for continuity and change in U.S. foreign policy since World War II.

The rise of a strong sense of American optimism and nationalism, of a foreign policy and ideological consensus, and of a responsive public opinion during the cold war led to increasing presidential power in foreign policy, an expanding national security bureaucracy, the development of a national security and free market ethos, and an acquiescent Congress and domestic environment. In this environment, the president and the executive branch dominated the making of U.S. foreign policy, while the demands of national security took precedence over the demands of democracy.

The challenges of Vietnam and the 1960s led Americans to question the assumptions of American innocence, benevolence, and exceptionalism; produced greater ideological and foreign policy diversity; and contributed to public opinion volatility. These developments led to a reassertive Congress and changes in the domestic environment, such as more diverse electoral politics, new and varied interest groups and social movements, and a more critical media—the topics of the next three chapters. Thus, presidents entering office now face a paradox of presidential power, making it very difficult to successfully govern contemporary foreign policy. Changes in political culture, political ideology, and public opinion since the height of the cold war have meant that the era of extraordinary presidential power in foreign policy has passed and tensions between national security and democracy have increased.

Presidents are still powerful, but they no longer automatically govern and dominate the making of U.S. foreign policy. Since Vietnam, presidents have been unable to promote or take advantage of a majoritarian coalition throughout society in support of their foreign policy because of the diversity of thought and the domestic political competition it has generated. Johnson declined to run for reelection in 1968 over the Vietnam War once he lost the support of the American people. Nixon eventually was forced to resign in 1974 over the constitutional crisis of Watergate. Meanwhile, Nixon's détente policies, which continued under Ford, were attacked by both the Left and Right. Carter attempted to promote a post–cold war internationalist foreign policy but was placed on the political defensive by the Right with the Iran hostage crisis and Soviet invasion of Afghanistan. Reagan entered office as a cold warrior, only to encounter liberal resistance which culminated in the Iran-Contra affair and criticism from the Right as he pursued arms control and a more open relationship with the Soviet Union.

What about the future? It is likely that presidents will continue to experience difficulty in governing foreign policy as long as efforts to establish a new consensus are overwhelmed by diversity of thought in American society. The contemporary domestic political environment is made particularly fluid by the dramatic changes taking place in Russia, Eastern Europe, the Middle East, and elsewhere. Presidents Bush and Clinton have had to navigate carefully through treacherous and unstable environments both at home and abroad. The successful military outcome in the Persian Gulf War temporarily strengthened President Bush's ability to govern, only to lose reelection in 1992. As Clinton knows all too well, in a post–cold war era presidents must operate in a domestic political climate where the diversity and volatility of the public and its beliefs create both considerable opportunities and uncertainties in the politics of U.S. foreign policy.

With regard to "public opinion," prolonged habits of interest, information, and thinking about national and international affairs will not change overnight. Americans, especially members of the mass public, are likely to retain very short attention spans, as well as superficial knowledge and simplistic understandings of national and international affairs.

These characteristics are reinforced by the fact that most Americans do not realize the extent to which national and international affairs directly and indirectly affect their daily lives, trends which are likely to grow as interdependence increases throughout the country and the world. The post–Vietnam War diversity of "ideological and foreign policy beliefs" is also likely to continue and may, in fact, increase in the future. While anticommunism was the foundation of the ideological and foreign policy consensus during the cold war years, the end of the cold war has given rise to a new great debate and may impact new interpretations of events. Whatever the case, one thing that can be predicted with great certainty is that the foreign policy orientations competing for control over the future of U.S. foreign policy will be consistent with the moral foundation of American "political culture" and national style.

BIBLIOGRAPHIC ESSAY

. . . .

Since the 1970s, there has been a proliferation of works studying the role of public opinion, political ideology, and political culture in U.S. foreign policy. Ole Holsti provides an excellent overview of the impact of public opinion on foreign policy, including the traditional wisdom and its critique, in "Public Opinion and Foreign Policy: Challenges to the Almond-Lippmann Consensus," *International Studies Quarterly* (1992): 439–66. James N. Rosenau's *Public Opinion and Foreign Policy* (New York: Random House, 1961) remains a classic in delineating the dynamics of opinion flows and influence among the different publics and for policymaking.

A good historical overview of the relationship between public opinion and U.S. foreign policy in American history is provided by Richard J. Barnet in *The Rockets' Red Glare, When America Goes to War: The Presidents and the People* (New York: Simon and Schuster, 1990). A more systematic analysis of the relationship is provided by Benjamin I. Page and Robert Y. Shapiro, *The Rational Public: Fifty Years of Trends in Americans' Policy Preferences* (Chicago: University of Chicago Press, 1992). An informative study of the impact of public opinion during war can be found in Larry Elowitz and John W. Spanier, "Korea and Viet-

nam: Limited War and the American Political System," *Orbis* (Summer 1974): 510–34, and most recently in Bruce W. Jentleson, "The Pretty Prudent Public: Post Post-Vietnam American Opinion on the Use of Military Force," *International Studies Quarterly* (1992): 49–74.

One of the best overviews of ideology and culture in American society and its relevance for understanding American politics is presented by Godfrey Hodgson in *America in Our Time* (New York: Vintage, 1976). He offers an excellent history and analysis of the rise of the anticommunist and liberal-conservative ideological consensus since World War II and its decline due to the impact of the 1960s and the Vietnam War. A good analysis of the major competing schools of thought that arose since Vietnam is provided by Ole R. Holsti and James N. Rosenau, in *American Leadership in World Affairs: Vietnam and the Breakdown of Consensus* (Boston: Allen & Unwin, 1984), William Schneider, in "Public Opinion," in Joseph S. Nye, Jr., ed., *The Making of America's Soviet Policy* (New Haven, Conn.: Yale University Press, 1984), pp. 11–35, and Jerel Rosati and John Creed, "Extending the Three-Headed and Four-Headed Eagles: The Foreign Policy Orientations of American Elites During the 80s and 90s," *Political Psychology* (18 (1997): 583–623.

An excellent discussion of liberal thought during the cold war era can be found in Richard H. Pells, *The Liberal Mind in a Conservative Age: American Intellectuals in the 1940s & 1950s* (New York: Harper & Row, 1985). Leslie H. Gelb, with Richard K. Betts, demonstrates how the anticommunist consensus affected the foreign policymaking process and led to greater U.S. intervention in Vietnam in *The Irony of Vietnam: The System Worked* (Washington, D.C.: Brookings, 1979). Jerome L. Himmelstein analyzes the rise of conservatism, including the change following World War II from isolationism to interventionism, in *To the Right: The Transformation of American Conservatism* (Berkeley, Calif.: University of California Press, 1989), while George H. Nash describes the evolution of conservative intellectual thought into the post-Vietnam era in *The Conservative Intellectual Movement in America, Since 1945* (New York: Basic Books, 1976).

Tami R. Davis and Sean M. Lynn-Jones give a good overview of American political culture and its implications for U.S. foreign policy in "City Upon a Hill," *Foreign Policy* 66 (Spring 1987): 3–19. Paul Loeb provides a fascinating portrait of the political culture that developed around Hanford, Washington, with the growth of the nuclear weapons production complex, and its implications for everyday life and the politics of U.S. foreign policy, in *Nuclear Culture: Living and Working in the World's Largest Atomic Complex* (Philadelphia: New Society Publishers, 1987).

ENDNOTES

1. See Gabriel Almond, *The American People and Foreign Policy* (New York: Praeger, 1960); Bernard C. Cohen, *The Public's Impact on Foreign Policy* (Boston: Little, Brown, 1973); and Burtin Sapin, *The Making of United States Foreign Policy* (New York: Praeger, 1966).

2. For an overview of the role of this elitist view throughout American history, see Richard J. Barnet, *The Rockets' Red Glare, When America Goes to War: The Presidents and the People* (New York: Simon & Schuster, 1990). For classic statements representing this view, see Walter Lippmann, *Public Opinion* (New York: Harcourt, Brace, 1922), *The Phantom Public* (New York: Macmillan, 1927), and *The Public Philosophy* (Boston: Little, Brown, 1955).

3. Leslie H. Gelb, with Richard K. Betts, *The Irony of Vietnam: The System Worked* (Washington, DC: Brookings, 1979), p. 221.

4. Leslie H. Gelb, "The Essential Domino: American Politics and Vietnam," *Foreign Affairs* 50 (April 1972): 461.

5. Ibid., 459.

6. The works of these authors will be discussed and cited throughout the chapter. An excellent overview of the traditional view and its critique is provided by Ole R. Holsti, "Public Opinion and Foreign Policy: Challenges to the Almond-Lippmann Consensus," *International Studies Quarterly* (1992): 439–66. See also Ole R. Holsti, *Public Opinion and American Foreign Policy* (Ann Arbor, Mich.: University of Michigan Press, 1996), and Miroslav Nincic, *Democracy and Foreign Policy: The Fallacy of Political Realism* (New York: Columbia University Press, 1994).

7. V. O. Key, Jr., *The Responsible Electorate* (New York: Vintage, 1966). See also Robert E. Lane, *Political Ideology: Why the American Common Man Believes What He Does* (New York: Free Press, 1962).

8. Benjamin I. Page and Robert Y. Shapiro, *The Rational Public: Fifty Years of Trends in Americans' Policy Preferences* (Chicago: University of Chicago Press, 1992); Samuel L. Popkin, *The Reasoning Voter: Communication and Persuasion in Presidential Campaigns* (Chicago: University of Chicago Press, 1991); Bruce W. Jentleson, "The Pretty Prudent Public: Post Post-Vietnam American Opinion on the Use of Military Force," *International Studies Quarterly* (1992): 49–74. See also Robert Y. Shapiro and Benjamin I. Page, "Foreign Policy and the Rational Public," *Journal of Conflict Resolution* 32 (June 1988): 211–47.

9. V. O. Key, Jr., *Public Opinion and American Democracy* (New York: Alfred A. Knopf, 1961).

10. For a comparative perspective, see Thomas Risse-Kappen, "Public Opinion, Domestic Structure, and Foreign Policy in Liberal Democracies," *World Politics* 43 (July 1991): 479–12.

11. See, for example, Philip J. Powlick, "The Sources of Public Opinion for American Foreign Policy Officials," *International Studies Quarterly* (December 1995): 427–51.

12. See Almond, *The American People;* Johan Galtung, "Foreign Policy as a Function of Social Position," *Journal of Peace Research* 2 (1965): 206–30; Barry B. Hughes, *The Domestic Context of American Foreign Policy* (San Francisco: W.H. Freeman, 1978); W. Russell Neuman, *The Paradox of Mass Politics: Knowledge and Opinion in the American Electorate* (Cambridge, Mass.: Harvard University Press, 1986); and James N. Rosenau, *Public Opinion and Foreign Policy* (New York: Random House, 1961).

13. Rosenau, *Public Opinion,* p. 45.

14. See Herbert Hyman and Paul B. Sheatsley, "Some Reasons Why Information Campaigns Fail," *Public Opinion Quarterly* 11 (1947): 412–23, and Neuman, *The Paradox of Mass Politics.*

15. See Michael X. Delli Carpini and Scott Keeter, *What Americans Know about Politics and Why It Matters* (New Haven, Conn.: Yale University Press, 1996). Other factors, such as ethnicity, gender, and region of the country, also play a role and must be kept in mind when discussing the American people. See, for example, Alexander DeConde, *Ethnicity, Race, and American Foreign Policy: A History* (Boston: Northeastern University Press, 1994); David Fite, Marc Genest, and Clyde Wilcox, "Gender Differences in Foreign Policy Attitudes: A Longitudinal Analysis," *American Politics Quarterly* 18 (October 1990): 492–513, and Bruce M. Russett and Elizabeth C. Hanson, *Interest and Ideology: The Foreign Policy Beliefs of American Businessmen* (San Francisco: W.H. Freeman, 1975).

16. For an overview of the nature of public opinion, see Barnet, *The Rockets' Red Glare;* W. Lance Bennett, *Public Opinion in American Politics* (New York: Harcourt Brace Jovanovich, 1980); Harry Holloway with John George, *Public Opinion: Coalitions, Elites, and Masses* (New York: St. Martin's Press, 1986); Ralph B. Levering, *The Public and American Foreign Policy, 1918–1978* (New York: William Morrow, 1978); and Neuman, *The Paradox of Mass Politics.*

17. H.G. Erskine, "The Polls: The Informed Public," *Public Opinion Quarterly* 26 (1962): 669–77, and H.G. Erskine, "The Polls: Textbook Knowledge," *Public Opinion Quarterly* 27 (1963): 133–41.

18. See "Lost on Planet Earth," *Newsweek* (August 8, 1988): 31, and "Test Reveals Americans' Knowledge of Geography Going Downhill," *The State,* Columbia, S.C. (November 9, 1989): 5A.

19. "Lost on Planet Earth," p. 31, and "Knowledge of Geography," p. 5A.

20. For a discussion of everyday life and its implications for American politics, see Robert D. Holsworth and J. Harry Wray, *American Politics and Everyday Life* (New York: Macmillan, 1987); Paul Loeb, *Nuclear Culture: Living and Working in the World's Largest Atomic Complex* (Philadelphia: New Society Publishers, 1987); and J. Anthony Lukas, *Common Ground: A Turbulent Decade in the Lives of American Families* (New York: Random House, 1985).

21. See Key, *Public Opinion and American Democracy;* Key, *The Responsible Electorate;* Page and Shapiro, *The Rational Public.*

22. See Michael X. Delli Carpini and Scott Keeter, "Stability and Change in the U.S. Public's Knowledge of Politics," *Public Opinion Quarterly* (Winter 1991): 583–612. The trend toward greater levels of education may be offset by the increase in the high school dropout rate in inner cities, especially among the poor and minorities.

23. See, for example, Douglas C. Foyle, "Public Opinion and Foreign Policy: Elite Beliefs as Mediating Variable," *International Studies Quarterly* (March 1997): 141–69.

24. See Stanley Hoffmann, *Gulliver's Troubles or the Setting of American Foreign Policy* (New York: McGraw-Hill, 1968), part III; Benjamin I. Page and Robert Y. Shapiro, "Effects of Public Opinion on Policy," *American Political Science Review* 77 (March 1983): 175–90; Risse-Kappen, "Public Opinion, Domestic Structure"; and Bruce Russett, *Controlling the Sword: The Democratic Governance of National Security* (Cambridge, Mass.: Harvard University Press, 1990).

25. Morton H. Halperin, *Bureaucratic Politics and Foreign Policy* (Washington, D.C.: Brookings, 1974), p. 67.

26. John E. Mueller, *War, Presidents, and Public Opinion* (New York: Wiley, 1973). See also Larry Elowitz and John W. Spanier, "Korea and Vietnam: Limited War and the American Political System," *Orbis* (Summer 1974): 510–34.

27. Jentleson, "The Pretty Prudent Public."

28. Jentleson, "The Pretty Prudent Public," p. 72.

29. See also John R. Oneal, Brad Lian, and James H. Joyner, Jr., "Are the American People "Pretty Prudent"? Public Responses to U.S. Uses of Force, 1950–1988," *International Studies Quarterly* (June 1996): 261–80.

30. Thomas E. Mann, "Making Foreign Policy: President and Congress," in Thomas E. Mann, ed., *A Question of Balance: The President, the Congress, and Foreign Policy* (Washington, D.C.: Brookings Institution, 1990), p. 11.

31. Bruce W. Jentleson, "American Diplomacy: Around the World and along Pennsylvania Avenue," in Thomas E. Mann, ed., *A Question of Balance: The President, the Congress, and Foreign Policy* (Washington, D.C.: Brookings Institution, 1990), p. 185, and Barry Sussman, "On Central America, Reagan Is Consistently Unpersuasive," *Washington Post National Weekly Edition* (May 14, 1984): 37.

32. See, for example, Richard A. Brody, *Assessing the President: The Media, Elite Opinion, and Public Support* (Stanford: Stanford University Press, 1991).

33. Godfrey Hodgson, *America in Our Time* (New York: Vintage, 1976).

34. Intellectuals emphasized the lack of extreme views and ideological content in the beliefs of most Americans. See Daniel Bell, *The End of Ideology: On the Exhaustion of Political Ideas in the Fifties* (New York: Free Press, 1960), and Arthur Schlesinger, Jr., *The Vital Center: The Politics of Freedom* (Houghton Mifflin, 1949). Social scientists emphasized that most Americans did not hold a consistent and logical set of interconnected beliefs which represented specific views, whether conservative or liberal. See Angus Campbell, Philip E. Converse, Warren E. Miller, and Donald E. Stokes, *The American Voter* (New York: John Wiley, 1964), and Philip E. Converse, "The Nature of Belief Systems in Mass Publics," in David Apter, ed., *Ideology and Discontent* (New York: Free Press, 1964), pp. 206–61. The work by Converse deeply affected the study of political science as Gerald M. Pomper describes in "The Impact of 'The American Voter' on Political Science," *Political*

Science Quarterly 93 (1978–1979): 617–28. Most Americans also believe they are nonideological, meaning that they do not give much thought to politics and tend to take more pragmatic and centrist positions on most issues.

35. Robert A. Dahl, *Pluralist Democracy in the United States: Conflict and Consent* (Chicago: Rand McNally, 1967), p. 357.

36. See also Cecil V. Crabb, Jr., *American Diplomacy and the Pragmatic Tradition* (Baton Rouge, La.: Louisiana State University Press, 1989), and Lane, *Political Ideology*.

37. Ole R. Holsti and James N. Rosenau, *American Leadership in World Affairs: Vietnam and the Breakdown of Consensus* (New York: Allen & Unwin, 1984), and Hodgson, *America in Our Time*.

38. Mann, "Making Foreign Policy," pp. 11–12.

39. See Eric F. Goldman, *The Crucial Decade—and After: America, 1945–1960* (New York: Random House, 1961); Hodgson, *America in Our Time*; Levering, *The Public and American Foreign Policy*; William Manchester, *The Glory and the Dream: A Narrative History of America, 1933–1972* (New York: Wiley, 1972); Robert Endicott Osgood, *Ideals and Self-Interest in America's Foreign Relations: The Great Transformation of the Twentieth Century* (Chicago: University of Chicago Press, 1953); and Daniel Yergin, *Shattered Peace: The Origins of the Cold War and the National Security State* (New York: Houghton Mifflin, 1978).

40. See, for example, George H. Quester, "Origins of the Cold War: Some Clues from Public Opinion," *Political Science Quarterly* 93 (Winter 1978–1979): 647–64.

41. Hodgson, *America in Our Time*, p. 73.

42. Ibid., p. 76.

43. Ibid., p. 73.

44. See James MacGregor Burns, *The Crosswinds of Freedom* (New York: Vintage, 1989); Goldman, *The Crucial Decade*; Hodgson, *America in Our Time*; Manchester, *The Glory and the Dream*; and Richard H. Pells, *The Liberal Mind in a Conservative Age: American Intellectuals in the 1940s & 1950s* (New York: Harper & Row, 1985).

45. See Jerome L. Himmelstein, *To the Right: The Transformation of American Conservatism* (Berkeley, Calif.: University of California Press, 1989).

46. Hodgson, *America in Our Time*, p. 46.

47. David Halberstam, *The Best and the Brightest* (New York: Random House, 1969), p. 108.

48. Hodgson, *America in Our Time*, p. 45.

49. Ibid., p. 47.

50. See Gelb, *The Irony of Vietnam*, and Halberstam, *The Best and the Brightest*.

51. See Burns, *The Crosswinds of Freedom*; Hodgson, *America in Our Time*; and Paul M. Kattenburg, *The Vietnam Trauma in American Foreign Policy, 1945–75* (New Brunswick, N.J.: Transaction Books, 1980).

52. For strong overviews, see Himmelstein, *To the Right*; Godfrey Hodgson, *The World Turned Right Side Up: A History of the Conservative Ascendancy in America* (New York: Houghton Mifflin, 1997), Geoge H. Nash, *The Conservative Intellectual Movement in America, Since 1945* (New York: Basic Books, 1976).

53. Holsti and Rosenau, *American Leadership in World Affairs*.

54. William Schneider, "Conservatism, Not Interventionism: Trends in Foreign Policy Opinion, 1974–1982," in Kenneth A. Oye, Robert J. Lieber, and Donald Rothchild, eds., *Eagle Defiant: United States Foreign Policy in the 1980s* (Boston: Little, Brown, 1983), pp. 33–64; William Schneider, "Public Opinion," in Joseph S. Nye, Jr., *The Making of America's Soviet Policy* (New Haven, Conn.: Yale University Press, 1984), pp. 11–35; and William Schneider, " 'Rambo' and Reality: Having It Both Ways," in Kenneth A. Oye, Robert J. Lieber, and Donald Rothchild, eds., *Eagle Resurgent? The Reagan Era in American Foreign Policy* (Boston: Little, Brown, 1987), pp. 41–72.

55. See Cecil V. Crabb, Jr., *Policy-Makers and Critics: Conflicting Theories of American Foreign Policy* (New York: Praeger, 1976); Barry R. Posen and Andrew L. Ross, "Competing Visions for U.S. Grand Strategy," *International Security* (Winter 1996–97): 5–53; Jerel Rosati and John Creed, "Extending the Three-Headed and Four-Headed Eagles: The Foreign Policy Orientations of American Elites During the 80s and 90s," *Political Psychology* 18 (1997): 583–623; and Jerel Rosati, Michael W. Link, and John Creed, "A New Perspective on the Foreign Policy Views of American Opinion Leaders in the Cold War and Post–Cold War Eras," *Political Research Quarterly* (1998). Holsti and Rosenau have come to recognize that their original threefold schools of thought were not as mutually exclusive as they first thought. See Ole R. Holsti and James N. Rosenau, "The Structure of Foreign Policy Attitudes Among American Leaders," *Journal of Politics* 52 (February 1990): 94–125, and Holsti, *Public Opinion and American Foreign Policy*.

56. For a slightly different take on the meaning of semi-isolationism for the mass public, see Steven Kull, "What the Public Knows that Washington Doesn't,"

Foreign Policy (Winter 1995–96): 102–15. For a discussion of the strength of isolationist sentiment in the mass public, see Almond, *American People and Foreign Policy,* and Richard J. Barnet, *Roots of War: The Men and Institutions Behind U.S. Foreign Policy* (New York: Penguin, 1971), Part III.

57. Norman J. Ornstein, and Mark Schmitt, "Dateline Campaign '92: Post–Cold War Politics," *Foreign Policy* 79 (1990): 169.

58. See Posen and Ross, "Competing Visions," Rosati and Creed, "Extending the Three-Headed and Four-Headed Eagles," and Rosati, Link, and Creed, "A New Perspective on the Foreign Policy Views of American Opinion Leaders."

59. William Schneider makes a distinction between "nonself-interested" issues—often national security issues—where public support has dropped, and "self-regarding" issues–such as economic and other intermestic issues–which have gained public support. William Schneider, "The New Isolationism," in *Eagle Adrift: American Foreign Policy at the End of the Century* (New York: Longman, 1997), pp. 26–38.

60. See, for example, Eugene R. Wittkopf, "On the Foreign Policy Beliefs of the American People: A Critique and Some Evidence," *International Studies Quarterly* 30 (1986): 425–45, and Eugene R. Wittkopf, *Faces of Internationalism: Public Opinion and American Foreign Policy* (Durham, N.C.: Duke University Press, 1990). See also Sidney Blumenthal, "The Return of the Repressed: Anti-Internationalism and the American Right," *World Policy Journal* (Fall 1995): 1–13.

61. Richard A. Melanson, *Reconstructing Consensus: American Foreign Policy Since the Vietnam War* (New York: St. Martin's Press, 1990), p. 17.

62. Schneider, " 'Rambo' and Reality," p. 51. See also James A. Stimson, *Public Opinion in America: Moods, Cycles, and Swings* (Boulder, Colo.: Westview Press, 1991).

63. See I. M. Destler, Leslie H. Gelb, and Anthony Lake in *Our Own Worst Enemy: The Unmaking of American Foreign Policy* (New York: Simon and Schuster, 1984); Alexander L. George, "Domestic Constraints on Regime Change in U.S. Foreign Policy: The Need for Policy Legitimacy," in Ole R. Holsti, Randolph Siverson, and Alexander L. George, editors, *Change in the International System* (Boulder, Colo.: Westview Press, 1980); Miroslav Nincic, "The United States, the Soviet Union, and the Politics of Opposites," *World Politics* 40 (July 1988): 452–75; Jerel A. Rosati, "United States Leadership Into the Next Millennium," *International Affairs* (Spring 1997): 297–315; and Daniel Yankelovich, "Farewell to 'President Knows Best'," *Foreign Affairs* (America and the World, 1978): 670–93.

64. See, for example, John E. Rielly, "Public Opinion: The Pulse of the '90s," *Foreign Policy* 82 (Spring 1991): 79–96. For an extended discussion of the impact of the end of the cold war on opinion leaders in U.S. foreign policy, see Rosati and Creed, "Extending the Three-Headed and Four-Headed Eagles."

65. For a general discussion of political culture and the American ethos, see Gabriel A. Almond and Sidney Verba, *The Civic Culture: Political Attitudes and Democracy in Five Nations* (Princeton, N.J.: Princeton University Press, 1963); Clifford Geertz, *The Interpretation of Cultures: Selected Essays* (New York: Basic Books, 1973); Herbert McClosky and John Zaller, *The American Ethos: Public Attitudes Toward Capitalism and Democracy* (Cambridge, Mass.: Harvard University Press, 1984). Two modern classics on American political culture are Louis Hartz, *The Liberal Tradition in America* (New York: Harcourt, Brace & World, 1955), and Richard Hofstadter, *The Age of Reform* (New York: Vintage, 1955). For an alternative interpretation from the perspective of minorities and women, see Rogers M. Smith, "Beyond Tocqueville, Myrdal, and Hartz: The Multiple Traditions in America" *American Political Science Review* (September 1993): 549–66. For an excellent overview of the study of political culture, see Lucian W. Pye, "Political Culture Revisited," *Political Psychology* (1991): 487–508.

66. See Loren Baritz, *Backfire: A History of How American Culture Led Us into Vietnam and Made Us Fight the Way We Did* (New York: Morrow, 1985); Robert Dallek, *The American Style of Foreign Policy: Cultural Politics and Foreign Affairs* (New York: Alfred A. Knopf, 1983); Jack Citrin, Ernst B. Haas, and Christopher Muste, "Is American Nationalism Changing? Implications for Foreign Policy?", *International Studies Quarterly* (1994): 1–31; T. R. Davis and S. M. Lynn-Jones, "City Upon a Hill," *Foreign Policy* 66 (Spring 1987): 20–38; Hodgson, *America in Our Time;* Michael H. Hunt, *Ideology and U.S. Foreign Policy* (New Haven, Conn.: Yale University Press, 1987); and Richard J. Kerry, *The Star-Spangled Mirror: America's Image of Itself and the World* (Savage, Md.: Rowman & Littlefield, 1990). For an example of earlier works emphasizing the importance of American culture, see Almond, *American People and Foreign Policy,* chapter 3, and Hoffmann, *Gulliver's Troubles.*

67. See, for example, Selig Adler, *The Isolationist Impulse* (New York: Free Press, 1966), Almond, *American People and Foreign Policy*, and Barnet, *Roots of War*.

68. See Reginald Horseman, *Race and Manifest Destiny* (Cambridge, Mass.: Harvard University Press, 1981), and Frederick Merk, *Manifest Destiny and Mission in American History* (New York: Vintage, 1963).

69. James Oliver Robertson, *American Myth, American Reality* (New York: Hill & Wang, 1980), p. 349.

70. For an excellent overview of the literature on the origins of the cold war, including the orthodox interpretation, see Richard A. Melanson, *Writing History and Making Policy: The Cold War, Vietnam, and Revisionism* (Lanham, Md.: University Press of America, 1983).

71. Hodgson, *America in Our Time*, pp. 3–4.

72. Alexis de Tocqueville, *Democracy in America* (New York: Vintage, 1945).

73. Barnet, *Roots of War*, p. 251. See also Michael Kammen, "The Problem of American Exceptionalism: A Reconsideration," *American Quarterly* (March 1993): 1–43; Joseph Lepgold and Timothy McKeown, "Is American Foreign Policy Exceptional? An Empirical Analysis," *Political Science Quarterly* (Fall 1995): 369–84; Byron E. Shafer, ed., *Is America Different: A New Look at American Exceptionalism* (New York: Oxford University Press, 1991).

74. See, for example, Alan Brinkley, "The Western Historians: Don't Fence Them In," *The New York Times Review of Books* (September 20, 1992): 1, 22–27; Patricia Nelson Limerick, *The Legacy of Conquest: The Unbroken Past of the American West* (New York: W.W. Norton, 1987).

75. Robertson, *American Myth, American Reality*, p. xv.

76. See also Francis Fitzgerald, *America Revised: History Schoolbooks in the Twentieth Century* (Boston: Atlantic/Little Brown, 1979); Richard Slotkin, *Gunfighter Nation: The Myth of the Frontier in Twentieth-Century America* (Atheneum, 1992).

77. Robert Nisbet, *The Present Age: Progress and Anarchy in Modern America* (New York: Harper & Row, 1988), p. 32.

78. Nisbet, *The Present Age*, p. 29.

79. Hoffmann, *Gulliver's Troubles*, p. 194.

80. Reinhold Niebuhr and Alan Heimert, *A Nation So Conceived* (New York: Charles Scribner's Sons, 1963), p. 150.

81. Hoffmann, *Gulliver's Troubles*, p. 178. See also Donald W. White, *The American Century: The Rise and Decline of the United States as a World Power* (New Haven, Conn.: Yale University Press, 1996).

82. See George F. Kennan, *American Diplomacy, 1900–1950* (New York: Mentor, 1951); Hans J. Morgenthau, *In Defense of the National Interest: A Critical Examination of American Foreign Policy* (New York: Knopf, 1952); and Reinhold Niebuhr, *The Children of Light and the Children of Darkness* (New York: Scribners, 1944), and *Moral Man and Immoral Society* (New York: Charles Scribner's Sons, 1932).

83. See, for example, Destler, *Our Own Worst Enemy*; George, "Domestic Constraints on Regime Change," B. T. Trout, "Rhetoric Revisited: Political Legitimacy and the Cold War," *International Studies Quarterly* (1975): 251–84.

84. See, for example, Richard M. Freeland, *The Truman Doctrine and the Origins of McCarthyism: Foreign Policy, Domestic Politics, and Internal Security, 1946–1948* (New York: Alfred A. Knopf, 1972).

85. Hoffmann, *Gulliver's Troubles*, p. 195.

86. Davis and Lynn-Jones, "City Upon a Hill," p. 24. For a discussion of public moods and its impact on foreign policy, see Almond, *American People and Foreign Policy*; William R. Caspary, "The 'Mood Theory': A Study of Pulic Opinion and Foreign Policy," *American Political Science Revew* (1970): 536–47; Frank L. Klingberg, "The Historical Alternation of Moods in American Foreign Policy," *World Politics* 4 (1952): 239–73; Michael Roskin, "From Pearl Harbor to Vietnam: Shifting Generational Paradigms and Foreign Policy," *Political Science Quarterly* 89 (Fall 1974): 563–88; and Arthur Schlesinger, Jr., *The Cycles of American History* (Boston: Houghton Mifflin, 1986).

87. Barnet, *Roots of War*, p. 259.

88. Hoffmann, *Gulliver's Troubles*, p. 191.

89. See Ronald Steel, *Walter Lippmann and the American Century* (New York: Vintage, 1981); White, *The American Century*.

90. Hodgson, *America in Our Time*, p. 12.

91. See, for example, Seymour Martin Lipset and William Schneider, "The Decline of Confidence in American Institutions," *Political Science Quarterly* 98 (Fall 1983): 379–402.

92. Robertson, *American Myth, American Reality*, p. 348.

CHAPTER 15

POLITICAL PARTICIPATION AND ELECTORAL POLITICS

The public participates in the political process and influences the making of U.S. foreign policy in two basic ways. The public may participate in electoral politics, which is the focus of this chapter, or in group politics, which is the focus of chapter 16. Both of these forms of political participation influence U.S. foreign policymaking through their general impact on the domestic political environment and immediate impact on the policymaking process. Therefore, a discussion of electoral and group politics complements the previous chapter on public beliefs by demonstrating how active public political participation affects continuity and change, presidential governance, and the tensions between national security and democracy in the making of U.S. foreign policy.

POLITICAL PARTICIPATION

The public affects public policy through *the various ways that people participate in the political process.*

People may vote; respond to a public opinion poll; write to their elected representatives; write letters to newspaper or magazine editors; give money for a cause; join an organization or group involved in politics; work for a political party, candidate, or issue; lobby; petition; demonstrate; and become involved in mass movements. In this chapter and the next, we will address *the two most common and important forms of active political participation,* which usually involve all of these activities:

1. **Electoral politics**—that is, political participation in political parties and voting;
2. **Group politics**—that is, political participation in interest groups and social movements.

It is often argued that most members of the public participate little in the political process, if at all; that Americans are politically apathetic. There is much truth in this. The value of **citizenship and civic duty** is not held in as high regard by most

Americans as it was in the past. The events of the 1960s and 1970s, such as the Vietnam War and Watergate, produced a **declining sense of "political efficacy" and trust** in political officials; that is, a sense of powerlessness to affect change in the political process. Also, the common concerns of everyday life in modern America have pushed politics aside. The net result has been the rise of mass apathy throughout American society, which raises some troubling questions about the nature of American democracy.[1]

This broad generalization about American political participation, nevertheless, oversimplifies as much as it enlightens. *Three patterns actually predominate when discussing political participation in the United States.* First, most Americans participate infrequently in the political process and when they do so, it is predominantly through voting. Many Americans, in fact, have completely opted out of any form of political participation. Second, American participation in voting has declined throughout the twentieth century. Since the 1970s, no more than 50 percent of those eligible to vote have cast ballots in presidential general elections and much smaller percentages have voted in presidential primary elections, congressional elections, and state and local elections. Third, although only a minority of Americans participate in interest groups and mass movements, this form of participation actually has increased over time. The rise of interest group and mass movement participation is particularly noticeable if one compares the post–Vietnam War era to the cold war era. In sum, while most Americans do not participate in politics and fewer vote today than in the past, participation in interest groups and social movements has increased in the post–Vietnam War era.[2]

Who participates? Members of the elite public tend to be more likely to vote, join interest groups, and become politically active than members of the mass public. As discussed in the last chapter, members of the elite public tend to be more interested and better informed about politics; they also tend to have greater resources at their disposal—especially information and money—and a greater sense of political efficacy. Members of the mass public also participate; however, they participate less frequently than segments of the public who come from the higher socioeconomic classes and who have higher levels of education.

People participate both to further their own interests and the interests of their country. Interests fluctuate from person to person and depend on how they see the world, which is predominantly a function of their beliefs—that is, of political culture, political ideology, and public opinion (the topics of the previous chapter). While most people who participate do so through voting and, to a lesser extent, through joining groups and giving money, others are more politically "activist"—they give their time and become personally involved.

The minority of Americans who directly participate in electoral and group politics are consequential in affecting continuity and change in the foreign policy process, the ability of the president to govern foreign policy, and the tensions that exist between the demands of national security and democracy. *Electoral and group politics influence U.S. foreign policymaking through* their general impact on the domestic political environment and their immediate impact on the governmental policymaking process. The electoral and group processes are an inseparable part of American politics and are not easily distinguishable, for they affect each other. Electoral politics determines the political leadership of the government and affects leadership behavior once in office. Interest groups and social movements affect who gets elected and the actions of government policymakers. Electoral and group politics also impact on the beliefs and behavior of the general public, influencing their level of political apathy or participation. In effect, electoral and group politics reflect a dynamic interaction between the elite and mass publics and establish the general context of political behavior and agenda-setting throughout the domestic political environment and the policymaking process.

THE ELECTORAL PROCESS

According to the traditional wisdom concerning the role of the public discussed in the previous chapter, electoral politics can be dismissed in the making of U.S. foreign policy. This is consistent with the notion that "politics stops at the water's edge." But clearly, "foreign policy, like domestic policy, does not take place in a political vacuum."[3] Who gets elected, and the underlying electoral patterns that affect party politics, cannot be divorced from the politics of U.S. foreign policy. Therefore, an examination of the electoral process is required to achieve a comprehensive understanding of the politics of U.S. foreign policy.

The electoral process directly involves political parties, candidates competing for governmental offices, and an electorate—that is, members of the public, choosing between party candidates through voting. The United States historically has had a **two-party system**, with the Democratic and Republican parties competing for political power. Each party represents a broad coalition of leaders, active participants, and regular party voters. These coalitions attempt to attract mass support for their parties by nominating appealing candidates for office and putting forth a program of attractive policy proposals: the "party platform."

Because of the U.S. federal system of government, there are 51 Democratic and 51 Republican parties—one in each state and one at the national level. The national organization is the nominal head of the party, but the overall party structure is decentralized and the strongest party organizations are at the state level. As we focus on foreign policy, we are primarily interested in party and electoral politics at the national level, but activity at the state level does affect national politics as well.[4]

In addition to the two major parties, the United States has a long tradition of **third parties**.[5] Though they tend to be relatively short-lived, third parties have affected electoral politics by presenting alternative programs and choices for the public, and by influencing the leadership and programs of the two major parties. In fact, as Martin Wattenberg suggests, third-party candidates have become more prominent recently—indicative of the party changes and volatility of the public which has taken place since the 1960s:

In the hundred years from 1864 to 1964 there were only three elections in which the presidential candidate of a minor party received more than 5 percent of the vote. Since then this threshold has been exceeded by George Wallace [in 1968], John Anderson [in 1980], and Ross Perot. Recently, for the first time ever, a third-party candidate—Perot—garnered more than five percent in two consecutive elections: 19 percent in 1992 and 8 percent in 1996.[6]

The Democratic and Republican parties, nevertheless, consistently have been the key to gaining political office. Therefore, political leaders such as the president are not only sensitive to electoral politics but attempt to influence it as well. Interest groups and social movements also attempt to influence electoral politics as a means of impacting society and the government.

Electoral politics influences the making of U.S. foreign policy in two major ways. First, and most obviously as discussed in earlier chapters, the outcomes of elections *determine presidents and members of Congress.* Because elected officials are significant policymakers and because they recruit personnel for critical positions within the executive, legislative, and judicial branches of government, elections are an important source of influence. In the words of Robert Strauss, a prominent Democratic party leader over the years, "presidential campaigns are particularly important for foreign policy because of the pre-eminent role the eventual winner plays in guiding the country's fortunes abroad."[7] Once in office, elected officials also tend to remain very sensitive to domestic and electoral politics throughout their tenure, especially as election time approaches. Although foreign policy issues rarely are as prominent as domestic issues in affecting voter participation and choice, foreign policy, nevertheless, is "a prism through which voters judge the basic soundness of a candidate to govern the country."[8]

Second, the outcomes of elections also *establish longer-term electoral cycles* that influence domestic politics in society. Elections determine the relative power of the parties, the ideological predispositions of party leaders and the electorate, and affect the general beliefs of the public, which are consequential for policymaking as discussed in the previous chapter. Both the immediate and longer-term effects of electoral politics impact and reinforce one another. Together, they tend to indirectly affect the governmental policymaking process by affecting the domestic politics of U.S. foreign policy.[9]

ELECTORAL PATTERNS OVER TIME

. . . .

As with legislative-executive relations or public beliefs, the American two-party system has been dynamic, evolving through history. A brief overview of major electoral patterns over time allows for a better understanding of how domestic and electoral politics affect the governmental policymaking process in the making of U.S. foreign policy. *Party politics have progressed through three major stages during the twentieth century.*[10]

1. The 1930s were a time of party realignment in which the Democratic party became the majority party and the party of liberalism.
2. The cold war era was a time of bipartisanship in party politics, especially in foreign policy, where a liberal-conservative consensus prevailed.
3. The post–Vietnam War era has been a time of party dealignment in which no majority party exists, in which the Democratic party tends to represent liberalism and the Republican party tends to represent conservatism, and both parties compete for an increasingly independent and apathetic voter.

THE NEW DEAL REALIGNMENT

From the end of the Civil War until the Roaring Twenties, the Republican party was the majority party in American national politics. At the national level, this meant that a majority of representatives from the Senate and the House of Representatives tended to be Republican and Republican candidates were more successful than Democrats in gaining the presidency. At the state level, the Republican party also prevailed in parts of the country where there were strong two-party systems. Because of the Republican party's association with the abolition of slavery and support for reconstruction, the Democratic party dominated the electoral process and politics only in the South.

The Republican party was in power under President Herbert Hoover when the Great Depression hit, following the 1929 stock market crash. Companies went bankrupt, individuals went broke, and as much as one-third of the workforce became unemployed. It was an economic disaster for the country and a time of great misery for large numbers of Americans. In these deteriorating conditions, the public turned against the Republican administration and its "laissez-faire" approach to the depression. Thus, the **1932 presidential victory of Democratic challenger Franklin Roosevelt** reflected the loss of voter confidence in President Hoover and his policies. The public clearly opposed the status quo and supported the only viable alternative—Roosevelt and the Democratic party.

Unlike his predecessor, President Roosevelt instituted active government involvement in the economy designed to pull the country out of the depression. Roosevelt's first hundred days in office produced the most active legislative agenda in American history. His administration attempted to create a "New Deal" through which most Americans could get back on their feet and take advantage of restored economic prosperity. New Deal policies were an invaluable aid to many Americans; however, they did not completely pull the country out of the depression—World War II accomplished that task. Nevertheless, for many Americans, especially the working class, the unemployed and the poor, Roosevelt was a calm, reassuring, and hopeful voice about the future. Hence, Franklin Roosevelt and the Democratic party were rewarded with "reelection in 1936, 1940, and 1944"—an unprecedented four terms in American history.

In the aftermath of the Great Depression, a political realignment had occurred. **Realignment** refers here to a change in the majority and minority status of political parties.[11] Before the Great Depression, the Democratic party was the minority party. After the depression, however, the Democratic party became the "majority party" under Franklin Roosevelt. Not only did Democrats win the presidency, they also won majority control in both houses of Congress from Republicans.

What happened was that a large number of established voters switched their allegiance or support from the Republican party to the Democratic party, while most new (usually younger) voters identified with the Democratic party. The Democratic party came to be seen as the party of hope and prosperity by most Americans, while the Republican party was seen as the party of the depression. Thus, the **Democratic New Deal coalition** was born. The newfound strength of the Democratic party was reinforced by World War II, a second national emergency in which President Roosevelt successfully led the allies to victory against Japan, Germany, and fascism. Thus, the economic war at home and the war abroad acted as catalysts for strong political leadership under Franklin Roosevelt and strong support for the Democratic party.

The Great Depression created major ideological splits, discussed in chapter 14, that we now associate with current-day liberalism and conservatism. The New Deal and the Democratic party came to symbolize a more active governmental role in avoiding depression, regulating the economy, and assisting the disadvantaged—the liberal position. The Republican party continued to emphasize reliance on the private market and a "laissez-faire" governmental role within the political economy—the more conservative orientation. Thus, the rise of the Democratic party during the realigning era of the 1930s and the early 1940s represented the rise of liberalism throughout American society and the policymaking process.

More importantly, given our concern with foreign policy, the election of Franklin Roosevelt and the ascendance of the Democratic party in national elections resulted in the rise of a liberal internationalist orientation in foreign affairs. Although isolationist sentiments that advocated minimal political

and military involvement in European politics and affairs were historically pervasive throughout the country, Franklin **Roosevelt was an internationalist.** Roosevelt approached world politics from a pragmatic perspective; yet, he also represented the quest for global peace, cooperation, and prosperity symbolized by the principles of the Atlantic Charter and the building of a United Nations.[12]

Hence, American involvement in World War II resulted in the beginning of the end of isolationism and the rise of a liberal internationalist perspective associated with Roosevelt and the Democratic party, while the Republican party remained the bastion of isolationist sentiment. This was a significant juncture in the history of U.S. foreign policy. In this respect, the election of Franklin Roosevelt and the ascendance of the Democratic party—in other words, electoral politics—deeply affected the making of U.S. foreign policy and contributed to the United States pursuing an active internationalist policy following the end of World War II.

THE PERIOD OF BIPARTISANSHIP

The New Deal realignment lasted through the 1950s and 1960s. Most members of the public continued to identify with the Democratic party and, throughout much of this time, Democrats controlled Congress and the presidency (as well as most statehouses and governorships). Following the war, however, a bitter fight erupted between Democratic and Republican leaders for national power and control of the government. The Democratic majority held, though only narrowly, and the conflict soon evolved into a bipartisan relationship between the two parties by the mid-1950s, resulting in the formation of a liberal-conservative ideological consensus during the height of the cold war. As will soon be discussed, even though the Democratic party remained the majority party, Democratic leaders worked closely with the Republican leadership for the party no longer represented liberalism to the extent that it had during the 1930s and early 1940s, particularly in the area of foreign policy. Thus, electoral politics contributed to the rise and durability of the ideological and foreign policy consensus that laid the foundation for the making of U.S. foreign policy during the cold war.

On April 12, 1945, President Franklin **Roosevelt died** of a cerebral hemorrhage. The man who occupied the presidency for thirteen years and guided the United States through the depression and World War II had fallen. Harry Truman, Roosevelt's vice president, was thrust into the presidency at a crucial time when he would be responsible for leading the country during the postwar years. Although Truman was not a part of Roosevelt's inner circle or privy to Roosevelt's postwar intentions, he would make decisions over the next few years that would be consequential in leading the United States into a cold war based on a policy of containment.

Would Roosevelt have taken the same course of action? Many have speculated that Roosevelt's foreign policy experience and liberal internationalism might have minimized the level of hostility that eventually arose between the United States and the Soviet Union. Yet, we will never know, for Roosevelt's untimely death is one of those historic twists of fate. What we do know, however, is that the **selection of Missouri Senator Harry Truman as vice president** was a compromise choice by Franklin Roosevelt to balance the presidential ticket in the 1944 elections. In fact, Harry Truman replaced Henry Wallace, Roosevelt's former vice president, who soon became the champion of liberal internationalism and cooperation with the Soviet Union during the postwar years. In this very subtle and roundabout way, electoral politics was instrumental in having Harry Truman occupy the White House in the critical postwar years.

With the death of Roosevelt, the restoration of economic prosperity, the end of World War II, and growing concern over the Soviet Union, the Democratic coalition became unstable and the party's control of government was vulnerable. A political counterattack was mounted during the **1946 election** by conservatives and the Republican party—the party that was opposed to the New Deal at home and Roosevelt's, and Truman's, postwar internationalist

policies abroad. Republican campaigners had a field day with the slogan, "Had enough?": "Got enough inflation? Got enough debt? Got enough strikes? Got enough communism?" Many of the electoral campaigns during this time took the form of **"red-baiting"**—accusing the opponent of being a communist, a fellow traveler, or just generally being "soft" on communism. A young man in California, for example, named Richard Nixon denounced his Democratic liberal opponent as a "lip service American" who consistently voted the Moscow line in Congress and who "fronted for un-American elements . . . by advocating increased federal control over the lives of people."[13] The outcome of the 1946 elections was that Republicans finally were successful in capturing control of Congress; among the victors were Richard Nixon and Joseph McCarthy.

The **1948 elections** looked like another impending disaster for the Democrats with the party splitting between Truman, the Dixiecrats led by Strom Thurmond, and Henry Wallace leading the progressive forces. Miraculously, Truman shocked the country with his surprise reelection victory over Republican Thomas Dewey, while the Democratic party regained majority control of Congress in 1948. Much of Truman's success in overcoming Henry Wallace and his liberal support was, as revealed in presidential aide Clark Clifford's famous election memo of 1947, "to identify and isolate him [Wallace] in the public mind with the communists."[14] Although successful, Truman's campaign strategy legitimized and intensified the politics of anticommunism that led to a Republican resurgence in 1952.

Red-baiting was most prominent and effective during the **1952 elections**, a banner year for the Republican party. Republicans were successful in gaining a narrow majority in Congress: 48 Republicans to 47 Democrats in the Senate; 221 Republicans to 211 Democrats in the House. But regardless of the size of their majority, it gave Republicans the ability to dominate the organization and workings of Congress. This was accomplished with an electoral change of just 1 seat in the Senate and 12 seats in the House in favor of the Republicans. (Before the election, the Democratic majority was 49 to 47 in the

Senate and 234 to 199 in the House.) Yet, these electoral shifts in 1946 and, in particular, 1952 produced **Republican ascendance in Congress** that was consequential to the rise of the politics of anticommunism and McCarthyism. In this way, electoral politics had a major impact on foreign policy attitudes and behavior in the post–World War II era.

Nineteen fifty-two was also the year in which the Republican party was finally successful in capturing the presidency around the anti-Democratic themes of "Korea, communism, and corruption." Dwight Eisenhower charged the Democratic party and their presidential nominee, Adlai Stevenson, with bartering "away freedom in order to appease the Russian rulers."[15] He also selected Richard Nixon as his vice presidential running mate, to appease the political Right, who constantly attacked the Democratic party and their presidential nominee Adlai Stevenson as the bearer of "more Alger Hisses, more atomic spies, more crises."[16] At the same time, the victory of **Eisenhower**, a moderate conservative, played an important role in the development of a liberal-conservative ideological and foreign policy consensus by the mid-1950s.

The key to the consensus that transpired during the Eisenhower administration was that the political forces of liberalism and McCarthyism both declined as most Democrats became more conservative in their foreign policy views while most Republicans became more liberal in their political and economic views. Whereas McCarthyism was successful in ravaging the Democratic party and Truman administration, its anticommunist attacks increasingly lost credibility with Republican ascendance and a popular World War II hero in the White House. Nevertheless, Democrats and liberals became more conservative because the cold war and the challenge of McCarthyism forced them to become ardent anticommunists. Conversely with prosperity restored by Democratic leadership and New Deal policies, Republicans came to accept more governmental involvement in the economy and a limited welfare state. Hence, the election of Dwight Eisenhower, rather than sharpening Democratic-Republican differences, acted as a catalyst for a liberal-conservative

consensus based on anticommunism and a limited welfare capitalist political economy.[17]

The growing ideological consensus produced considerable **bipartisanship in party politics**—following the intense partisanship between Republicans and Democrats previously. Bipartisanship was especially the case in foreign policy, which further reinforced the cold war consensus in the making of U.S. foreign policy. Thus, where electoral politics were instrumental in the early postwar years in contributing to the rise of global containment, McCarthyism, and the formation of a foreign policy consensus, by the mid-1950s electoral politics acted to reinforce these trends into the late 1960s. Leaders from both parties were strong anticommunists who supported the containment policy and American reliance on the use of force abroad. Not surprisingly, candidates for political office nominated by both parties tended to have strong "anticommunist credentials." This was particularly the case in presidential elections, where the consensus and bipartisan years produced American presidents who were strong cold warriors in one form or another.[18]

The **1960 presidential election** illustrates how the liberal-conservative consensus permeated electoral politics. John F. Kennedy was the Democratic party nominee and Richard M. Nixon was the Republican nominee for president. **Kennedy** was Irish Catholic, born to a wealthy and prominent New England family, and schooled at Harvard College. He was also handsome, polished, charismatic, and charming. **Nixon** was a Californian from a very modest background who became a lawyer and rose to the top of the political world. He was also a scrapper and political infighter, more comfortable with politics played behind closed doors. Yet, these were differences of personality and style, not substance.

The first live television debates revealed that, although Kennedy was more impressive than Nixon, both were **"cold warriors."** Each attempted to demonstrate that he was more anticommunist than the other. On domestic issues Kennedy may have been more liberal, or less conservative, than Nixon; on foreign policy issues, however, it was a choice between two similar variants of anticommunism and cold war policies.[19] In *America in Our Time,* Godfrey Hodgson further elaborates upon the consensus nature of the 1960 race:

> The fact remains that they did share the same basic political assumptions: the primacy of foreign over domestic issues, the paramount importance of containing communism, the reign of consensus in domestic affairs, the need to assert the supremacy of the White House as the command post of a society mobilized to meet external danger. So did their staff and advisers. And so, too, did their running mates and closest rivals: Lyndon Johnson and Henry Cabot Lodge, Hubert Humphrey and Nelson Rockefeller, and everyone else who might conceivably have been nominated as a presidential candidate in that year by either the Democrats or by the Republicans.[20]

Such was the case throughout the 1950s and 1960s. Political campaigning between the candidates and the parties was as intense as ever, but differences between the candidates' beliefs and policies were minimal, especially in the realm of foreign policy. There was much truth to the phrase, although overstated, that there wasn't "a dime's worth of difference" between the Democratic and Republican candidates—such as Adlai Stevenson and Dwight Eisenhower in 1952 and 1956, and Kennedy and Nixon in 1960—particularly in the area of foreign policy. There may have been choices between different personalities and parties, but there was not much difference between worldviews or programs. This ideological consensus and party bipartisanship that developed during the cold war helps to explain the rise of presidential power, an acquiescent Congress, and a compliant public in the making of U.S. foreign policy. Thus, electoral politics contributed to the development of a twenty-year period of foreign policy continuity in which cold war policies prevailed, from Harry Truman to Lyndon Johnson. It was a time in which differences between the parties did not mean much in foreign policy—three of the presidents were Democratic and one was Republican.

Only in the **1964 presidential election** was there much difference; and, *once again, the political challenge came from the Right.* Lyndon Johnson, who became president following the assassination of John F. Kennedy, represented the liberal-conservative consensus, while Republican nominee **Barry Goldwater** represented unabashed conservatism. Goldwater and the conservative Right successfully gained control of the Republican party and argued for a more hard-line approach to contain and roll back communism, including a more aggressive stance in Vietnam. Although Goldwater lost in a landslide election (receiving less than 37 percent of the vote), he was the darling of the political Right. More importantly, in the minds of established leaders within the Johnson administration and the Democratic party, the 1964 election also reinforced the importance of sensitivity to the political threat posed by the political Right, and the comparative unimportance of the political Left.

Lyndon **Johnson**, in particular, seemed forever preoccupied with the political threat posed by the Right. Fear of the rise of the political Right—as occurred after the "fall" of China in 1949—is what motivated so many American political leaders like him to do what was necessary to prevent South Vietnam from falling to communism in the future. "I am not going to lose Vietnam," President Johnson said upon taking office. "I am not going to be the President who saw Southeast Asia go the way China went."[21] As David Halberstam explained how Lyndon Johnson saw it in *The Best and the Brightest:*

> If he seemed weak as a President in dealing with Vietnam, he was sure it would undermine him politically. Hell, Truman and Acheson had lost China, and maybe it wasn't their fault, but they were blamed for it, and when it happened the Republicans in Congress were waiting and jumped on it, and Truman lost the Congress and then the country—it hadn't happened over domestic issues, remember that, he said, and Truman and Acheson were as strong anticommunists as anyone he knew. Well, he did not want the blame for losing Vietnam.[22]

In this way national and electoral politics reaffirmed the cold war consensus among most political leaders and the need for Democrats to avoid the charge of being soft on communism abroad.

THE POST–VIETNAM DEALIGNMENT ERA

The stable party alignment that began in the 1930s and lasted through the 1960s could not withstand the upheavals of the civil rights movement, the Vietnam War, Watergate, and other events of the times. *Three critical developments occurred:*

1. The increase of independent voters created a movement toward party dealignment in which a majority party no longer existed;
2. A regional realignment occurred in the South which rejuvenated the Republican party; and
3. Bipartisanship collapsed and was replaced by greater ideological diversity between the Democratic and Republican parties.

These patterns have increasingly led to changes in party control of the executive and legislative branches over time, and the rise of divided government, contributing to the politics of U.S. foreign policy that have come to predominate during the post–Vietnam War era.[23]

First, there has been a large increase in independent voters producing party **dealignment**—as opposed to a party realignment—in which a majority party no longer exists.[24] During the 1960s, 1970s, and 1980s, voters increasingly abandoned the Democratic party. However, they did not register Republican; instead, most became "independent" of any party and some dropped out of the electoral process entirely. While more people continued to register in the Democratic party than the Republican party, both became minority parties. **Independent voters** predominated and overall voter turnout declined. Hence, the turmoil of the 1960s and early 1970s did not create a party realignment in which a new majority party emerged as occurred during the 1930s; rather, what occurred was a process of party

dealignment, in which party identification weakened and no majority party prevailed.

The second important electoral development is that at the regional level a party **realignment in the South** has taken place. Until the 1960s, the South was dominated by the Democratic party, representing the more conservative wing of the party. With the rise of the civil rights and anti-Vietnam War movements and increasing liberalism of the Democratic party, however, white southerners began to turn their party allegiance and support away from the Democratic party. As described by James MacGregor Burns,

> Behind FDR's leadership the Democracy became much more of an urban, trade union, ethnic, and poor people's party, but . . . it retained its old and solid base in the white South. Truman's bold civil rights stance, Kennedy's Catholicism and growing commitment to civil rights, and LBJ's comprehensive civil rights program accelerated the reconstitution of the party. Blacks forsook their ancient allegiance to the Republican party of Lincoln and flocked to the Democracy; white southern Democrats [moved] first toward third-party ventures and then toward their old partisan adversaries, the Republicans.[25]

This regional realignment over the years has produced two patterns. At the state and local levels, a two-party system was reborn in most parts of the South by the 1980s—the Republican party now became competitive with the Democratic party. A more important development, given our focus on foreign policy, occurred at the national level, where the South became a strong supporter of the Republican party, most visibly in presidential elections.[26]

This southern realignment at the presidential level became noticeable during the Goldwater candidacy in 1964. Although Barry Goldwater was badly beaten by Lyndon Johnson, he received considerable support throughout the South. Since that time, the South has been crucial for every Republican presidential victory from Nixon to Bush. The Republican advantage has been due to greater receptivity in the

South to conservative "valence" issues, such as an emphasis on "anti-big government" at home and national security "strength" abroad.

The critical role of southern realignment in presidential elections is due in part to the existence of the **electoral college**. The presidential candidate with the most votes within a state receives "all" the electors for that state (equal to the state's number of senators and representatives in Congress), and a majority of the electors then "officially" chooses the next president. A strong Republican South means that Republican presidential candidates have a strong hold on over one-fourth of the electors—representing more than half of those necessary for election—and require victories in only a few other states outside the South to win. This is obviously a major handicap for Democratic efforts to win the White House. Not surprisingly, the only Democratic successes in the post–Vietnam War years have been southerners: Jimmy Carter, from Georgia, in 1976 and Bill Clinton (and Al Gore), from Arkansas (and Tennessee—a border state), in 1992 and 1996.

Unlike the presidency, southern realignment took a longer time to impact the composition of Congress because both chambers were overwhelmingly Democratic by the 1970s and most constituents tend to reelect their representatives. This reflects the power of **incumbency**—that members of Congress running for reelection are usually safe from potential challengers.[27] One reason for this is that the fund-raising gap between incumbents and challengers is greater than ever. A Federal Election Commission study found that in the final days of 1990 elections, congressional incumbents had twenty times more money to spend than did their challengers: $120 million to $6 million. Of the 406 House members seeking reelection, 178 were considered "financially unopposed" because their challengers had raised less than $25,000.[28]

Nevertheless, Republican strength has grown in Congress. From 1981 to 1986, with Reagan in the White House, Republicans were the majority party in the Senate while the House remained in Democratic hands. Although they subsequently lost control in 1984, with the 1994 congressional elections Republicans gained ascendancy in both the House and the Senate—despite a sitting Democratic president in the White House. Republicans are now able to benefit disproportionately from incumbency, although party dealignment does not guarantee their control of Congress in the future as was the case with the Democratic party previously.

A third critical development also transpired during this period: the liberal-conservative consensus collapsed, ending the period of bipartisanship and producing "greater ideological differences and partisanship" between the two parties, including over foreign policy. The initial assault on the consensus came from the rise of liberalism and the new Left in the 1960s and early 1970s. The **1968 and 1972 presidential elections** were particularly divisive over foreign policy, contributing to the collapse of the cold war consensus. In 1968 the entry of Eugene McCarthy and Robert Kennedy in the Democratic primaries as the "peace" candidates led to President Lyndon Johnson's withdrawal and a bitter nomination process where Vice President Hubert Humphrey emerged victorious. In 1972 George McGovern captured the Democratic nomination by calling for America's quick withdrawal from Vietnam and the restoration of liberalism abroad and at home.

This was accompanied by the rise of conservatism and the far Right with the election of Richard Nixon in 1968 and, more importantly, the rise of Ronald Reagan in the **1976 and 1980 elections**. The political consequences have been that the Democratic party has come to reflect a more liberal ideology and post–cold war internationalist perspective in foreign policy; in contrast, the Republican party has stood for more conservative policies, including a conservative internationalist approach in foreign policy. As political analyst William Schneider has found, the splits between liberal internationalists and conservative internationalists "have now acquired substantial influence within the major political parties."[29]

These ideological differences have occurred primarily among **party leaders and activists**—members of the elite public—where "the polarization of elites has, to a considerable extent, been institutionalized within the party system."[30] Members of the mass public, on the other hand, tend to reflect more moderate and mixed ideological positions and have become more politically apathetic. Therefore, as discussed in the previous chapter, instead of the elite consensus, party bipartisanship, and mass followership of the cold war years, what has emerged since Vietnam has been considerable party partisanship reflecting "an unstable system of competing coalitions in which the mass public swings left or right unpredictably in response to its current fears and concerns."[31]

Under these conditions, the outcomes of elections and selection of political leaders by the public have grown in importance. Who gets elected into Congress and the White House is more meaningful during a time of ideological diversity and party differences as opposed to a time of consensus and bipartisanship. Therefore, it is with some irony to note that as voter turnout has declined, voter impact on American politics has increased. Electoral politics, in other words, may have become even more instrumental in affecting the making of U.S. foreign policy.

Presently, *the American voter is likely to be confronted with choices* between candidates that range across the liberal and conservative political spectrum. In contrast to the cold war years, in which candidates sharing the same beliefs competed for party nominations and national offices, the ideological and foreign policy views of post–Vietnam War era candidates differ in some meaningful ways, including their foreign policy orientations and programs.

Democratic nominees for president—George McGovern in 1972, Jimmy Carter in 1976 and 1980, Walter Mondale in 1984, Michael Dukakis in 1988, and Bill Clinton in 1992 and 1996—tend to offer more liberal internationalist policies. Republican nominees, on the other hand, tend to hold more conservative internationalist views—Nixon in 1972, Gerald Ford in 1976, Ronald Reagan in 1980 and 1984, George Bush in 1988 and 1992, and Bob Dole in 1996.[32] Thus, who gets elected makes a difference as to the direction the president intends to take the United States in world affairs, even if voter choice is not affected much by foreign policy issues.

Political scientists John Aldrich, John Sullivan, and Eugene Borgida, nevertheless, provide a compelling study which counters the conventional wisdom that the time and effort presidential candidates spend campaigning on foreign and defense issues have negligible impact on voter behavior. In fact, they found that foreign policy issues have been prominent in the minds of voters in virtually all presidential elections since World War II and often are "as important as domestic issues in their impact on voting," especially when they perceive foreign policy differences between the candidates. Therefore, "candidates do not waltz before a blind audience. Ironically, it appears that the only blind audience has been a significant portion of the scholarly community."[33]

Who gets elected as president, and changes in who is president, make a difference for the general direction of U.S. foreign policy and the changes it has experienced over time, especially in comparison to the continuity that prevailed during the cold war years. The election of Republican Richard Nixon in 1968 led to the pursuit of much more of a realpolitik and power politics approach in U.S. foreign policy toward the Soviet Union and the world. President Carter attempted to steer U.S. foreign policy away from the containment-oriented policies of the past and in a world order and human rights direction following his 1976 election into the White House. With the election of Ronald Reagan in 1980 efforts were made to reinstitute the policies of global containment reminiscent of the cold war past. The election of George Bush in 1988 softened much of the hard-line rhetoric and behavior associated with the Reagan administration, while emphasizing a realpolitik approach as U.S. foreign policy moved into a post–cold war era. Bill Clinton's election in 1992 and reelection in 1996 placed international economics and competitiveness on the top of the foreign policy agenda along with a more, although pragmatic, liberal internationalist orientation.[34] As Ole Holsti and James Rosenau noted in *American Leadership in World Affairs,* "perhaps the only constancy in American foreign policy since the Vietnam War has been the conspicuous lack of constancy in its conduct."[35]

Electoral politics have also affected the membership of Congress as already discussed, thereby affecting legislative-executive relations in the making of foreign policy. The **post-Watergate congressional elections of 1974**, for example, resulted in major Democratic gains further strengthening their majority position—60 Democrats to 37 Republicans in the Senate (an increase of 4 seats), 291 Democrats to 144 Republicans in the House (an increase of 52 seats). Furthermore, many of the new Democrats represented strong liberal positions in the wake of the Vietnam War and Watergate. These electoral changes were instrumental in providing the basis for congressional resurgence in the making of U.S. foreign policy during the mid-1970s.[36]

The 1978 and 1980 elections resulted in a weakening of the Democratic majorities and brought an infusion of young, Republican conservatives into Congress. In fact, beginning in 1980 the Republican party gained a narrow majority in the Senate for six years—the first time since 1954—producing important congressional support for President Reagan's early political success. And with the so-called **Republican revolution of 1994**—where every close congressional race was won by a Republican—the House and Senate reverted from Democratic control to Republican control. Where Democrats once had a majority during the 103rd Congress of 1993–1994 (56 to 44 in the Senate and 256 to 178 in the House), the Republicans gained ascendancy beginning in the 104th Congress of 1995 (53 to 47 in the Senate and 230 to 204 in the House).

In sum, the changes in congressional membership since Vietnam as a result of electoral politics have changed congressional membership, party control, and politicized Congress over the years, deeply affecting legislative-executive relations in foreign affairs. In fact, as discussed in chapter 12 on Congress, "divided government" has become increasingly the norm and has made it much more difficult for a president to govern, regardless of whether he is a Democrat or Republican. (Review table 12.3 for party control of the executive and legislature over time, including distribution of seats in the House of Representatives and the Senate.)

In addition to the importance of who gets elected, the rise of ideological diversity and party partisanship have *affected the political agenda and politicized foreign policy issues* in electoral politics. Unlike the cold war years, members of the opposition party, as well as factions within the same party, are more prone to question, criticize and obstruct the president. These activities are more likely to damage the president's professional reputation, public prestige, and, therefore, his ability to govern foreign policy.

Vietnam forced President Johnson to withdraw from the Democratic presidential race and helped to elect Republican Richard Nixon over the Democratic nominee, Vice President Hubert Humphrey. President Nixon's realpolitik policies were critiqued from the Left, for being too Soviet and containment oriented, and from the Right, for not being sufficiently anticommunist. President Gerald Ford, who ascended to the presidency following Nixon's resignation over Watergate and tried to win the presidential nomination in the Republican party in 1976 against Ronald Reagan, faced an attack from the Right that became so severe that the word "détente" was banished from the campaign. President Carter's foreign policy was increasingly attacked by conservatives, especially with the Iran-hostage crisis and the Soviet invasion of Afghanistan, contributing to the election of Ronald Reagan in 1980. Yet, President Reagan was placed on the political defensive by the Left with the nuclear freeze and anti-apartheid movements and the Iran-Contra affair, while his policies were attacked by the Right once he began to pursue détente and arms control with the Soviet Union. In each case, the president was forced to moderate many of his initial policies over time in response to the politics of opposition.[37]

Thus far in the post–cold war world, foreign policy issues have not played as prominent a role in electoral politics. They have neither helped nor hurt presidents much, as in the past. George Bush lost reelection despite his crushing triumph in the Persian Gulf War. And although international economics was important in Bill Clinton's presidential campaign, especially in 1992, questions about the direction and state of the nation, with a domestic (as opposed to intermestic) emphasis, dominated the 1992 and, especially, 1996 elections. Hence, the role of foreign policy issues in electoral politics may be one of particular uncertainty and volatility as the U.S. enters the twenty-first century.

Overall, electoral patterns during the post–Vietnam War years have produced contradictory outcomes. On the one hand, dealignment and greater ideological diversity have created greater party competition and choice for the American electorate at the national level. Although these trends maximize democratic politics, they also contribute to a lack of continuity in U.S. foreign policy as different parties and leaders with competing foreign policy views gain influence within the institutions of government. And dealignment and southern realignment have also increased the likelihood of "divided government." This increases the likelihood of legislative-executive competition, partisanship, and policy conflict, which does not help promote strong presidents or coherent foreign policy over time.[38]

CONTEMPORARY ELECTORAL AND CAMPAIGN POLITICS

· · · · · · · · · · · · · ·

It is unclear which electoral patterns and political outcomes will prevail in the future. The rise of the independent voter, the large number of nonvoters, and the more moderate and pragmatic nature of the mass public allow for the possibility of different electoral outcomes at different times. The decline of anticommunism as an election issue—which had permeated electoral politics since the 1940s—as changes in the former Soviet Union and Eastern Europe continue, adds greater confusion to this picture. "As communism recedes," political analysts Norman Ornstein and Mark Schmitt ask, "American politics faces a strange new dilemma: How will the U.S. political system operate without anticommunism as its central organizing principle?"[39]

To what extent will this damage the appeal of the Republican party, which has relied on anticommunism as a key issue throughout the 1970s and 1980s? What new issues will replace anticommunism with the end of the cold war? Which candi-

dates and parties will benefit? Answers to these questions remain open, but much depends on the contemporary nature of electoral politics.

A number of key points about contemporary electoral politics and campaigning must be kept in mind to better understand possible political outcomes and their impact on the future of U.S. foreign policy.[40] First, party leaders have lost control of **the nomination process** in the post–Vietnam War era. In the Democratic party, for example, Hubert Humphrey was the last presidential candidate selected by party leaders. With state primaries replacing party caucuses, the growing influence of professional political consultants, the need for large sums of money for campaigning, and the growing importance of the mass media, especially television, any individual may declare himself a candidate and have a shot at winning the party nomination. Party outsiders—such as George McGovern in 1972, Jimmy Carter in 1976, Ronald Reagan in 1980, and Michael Dukakis in 1988—were able to capture control of their respective parties, even though they were not the preferred choices of regular party leaders. The decline of party control over the election process has led to a corresponding **rise of candidate-centered politics.**[41]

Second, candidates attempting to gain party nominations and win office must be cognizant of key **voting trends** among the American public. Dealignment has resulted in *three voting participation patterns:* first, most Americans do not vote at all; second, roughly half of the eligible electorate vote in general elections when a presidential race is involved; and, third, considerably fewer people vote in national primary elections and general elections when there is no presidential race. This means that the elite public—the high participators—are extremely consequential in determining the outcome of **primary elections**—that is, who the presidential nominees of the Democratic and Republican parties will be; whereas the mass public becomes more important in determining the outcome of **general elections**—deciding which of the two nominees becomes president. Furthermore, in general elections voters, such as independents, who are least likely to regularly identify with the same party over time are the most consequential in determining which candidate receives majority support.[42]

As V. O. Key made clear in *The Responsible Electorate, the voting electorate consists of three general groups:* "standpatters" or those who regularly vote for the same party; "switchers" who vote for different parties at different times; and "new voters" who have never cast a ballot before or who previously opted out of the electoral process.[43] Key also found that the electorate, especially switchers and new voters, often engage in **"retrospective" voting**, that is, voting for or against a candidate (and party) based on, first, a general evaluation of their performance (especially for the incumbent) rather than their programs for the future, and second, whether the times have been good or bad for them and the country. It was in this sense that Key believed in the existence of a "responsible" electorate.[44]

Third, the weakness of parties and the nature of the electorate affect **general campaign strategies**. Candidates usually make more "ideological appeals" during primary elections to gain the party nomination when voter turnout is dominated by the elite public; in contrast, they make more moderate and popular appeals during the general election to win office when the mass public is more likely to vote. Although each party represents a broad coalition of individuals and groups, Republican standpatters are more conservative in their views and Democratic standpatters are more liberal. Therefore, in primary elections candidates for the Republican nomination usually take more conservative positions to win the support of Republicans in primaries; likewise, candidates for the Democratic nomination take more liberal positions to win the support of Democrats. In the general election, on the other hand, party nominees attempt to attract support from members of their own party, independent voters, and members of the opposition party. To use Key's terms, they attempt to retain the support of standpatters and attract the support of switchers and new voters. Thus, candidates tend to take "more moderate and popular" positions during the general election to maximize broad appeal and minimize opposition.

In the **1996 presidential election**, Bill Clinton, the Democratic incumbent, was much more successful in reflecting more moderate and popular po-

sitions for taking the country into the future, while portraying Bob Dole, the Republican candidate, as a man of the past. **Table 15.1** provides a picture of the electorate. Not surprisingly, Bill Clinton was quite successful in gaining the overwhelming support of those who identified themselves as Democrats and liberals, while Bob Dole obtained strong support from Republicans and conservatives—those most likely to be Key's "standpatters." But Bill Clinton's presidential campaign, in comparison to Dole's, was much more successful in appealing to and gaining the support of those most likely to switch their vote for a party and candidate with time—the independents and moderates. Clinton was also more successful in gaining the support of the younger, and usually the "newer," voters. The breakdown of the public vote in terms of gender, race, education, family income, and religion is also provided in the table. Clearly, more of the public was sufficiently satisfied with Clinton as president in comparison to supporting a challenger and newcomer such as Bob Dole (or Ross Perot) for president.[45]

One analyst places Clinton's 1996 election in perspective in the following way:

> Successful politicians know how to play the cards they are dealt, and Clinton is the most successful Democratic politician of the postwar period. As a national candidate, he has no one in his own party to touch him; and although they may seem like the political equivalent of tomato cans now, the two Republicans he defeated (and defeated handily) were the most prominent and least ideologically compromised figures in their party. Clinton's style, a weird combination of compassion, self-centeredness, uplift, and indecisiveness, is a style that seems to suit a politically fractured, intellectually uninspired time."[46]

Although this may seem overstated, it is important to point out that Clinton is the "first" Democrat to be elected and reelected as president since Franklin Roosevelt. And if he completes his second term, he will be only the third president since Roosevelt to have done so.

TABLE 15.1
THE ELECTORAL VOTE OF 1996

	ALL VOTERS(%)	BILL CLINTON	BOB DOLE	ROSS PEROT
POPULAR VOTE (PERCENTAGE)		45,628,667 (49.2%)	37,869,435 (40.8%)	7,874,283 (8.5%)
ELECTORAL VOTES		379	156	0
PARTY IDENTIFICATION				
Democrat	39%	84%	10%	5%
Republican	29	13	80	6
Independent	16	43	35	17
POLITICAL IDEOLOGY				
Liberal	20%	78%	11%	7%
Moderate	47	57	33	9
Conservative	33	20	71	8
GENDER				
Male	48%	53%	44%	10%
Female	52	54	38	7
RACE				
White	83%	43%	46%	9%
African-American	10	84	12	4
Hispanic	5	72	21	6
Asian	1	43	48	8
Other	1	64	21	9
AGE				
18 to 29	17%	53%	34%	10%
30 to 44	33	48	41	9
45 to 59	26	48	41	9
60 or over	24	48	44	7
EDUCATION				
No high school	6%	59%	28%	11%
High school graduate	24	51	35	13
Some college	27	48	40	10
College graduate	26	44	46	8
Post-graduate	17	52	40	5
FAMILY INCOME				
Less than $15,000	11%	59%	28%	11%
$15,000 to $30,000	23	53	36	9
$40,000 to $59,999	27	48	40	10
$60,000 to $74,999	21	47	45	7
$75,000 to $100,000	9	44	48	7
$100,000 and up	9	38	54	6
RELIGION				
Protestant	38%	41%	50%	8%
Catholic	29	53	37	9
Other Christian	16	45	41	12
Jewish	3	78	16	3
No religion	7	59	23	13

SOURCE: CNN/Time All Politics, 1996.

Fourth, larger and larger amounts of money are required to finance election campaigns—which takes us to the importance of **campaign financing**. As discussed in chapter 12, members of Congress are constantly fundraising and running for reelection. Presidents who run for reelection and prospective presidential candidates start earlier and earlier to run, raise money, and build an organization. Given their positions of power and visibility, incumbents are particularly advantaged in this respect and are able to raise large "war chests" to scare off and defeat challengers. The need for increasing amounts of money to run for office and reelection has been a problem in American politics for a long time and became a controversial issue for President Clinton following the 1996 elections (see **essay 15.1** on money, campaigning, and politics).

Finally, given the nature of the electorate and general campaign strategies, **symbolic and negative campaigning** have been an integral part of electioneering. Most campaigns typically gloss over issues or information and emphasize personalities and symbolism, especially in the general election. Since candidates attempt to maximize their appeal by occupying the ideological center, campaigns often become battlegrounds over personal characteristics, leadership skills, experience, and any issue that happens to be on the political agenda. The key aim, however, is not to inform the electorate, but to "market" the candidate to the electorate through use of the mass media. For example, given the legacies of the cold war and the Vietnam War, foreign policy issues that are identified with "nationalism" and "patriotism" tend to play into the hands of Republicans as opposed to Democrats.[47] Thus, campaigns emphasize symbolic appeals to the public in which the candidate is identified with values consistent with American political culture.[48]

The importance of personalities and symbolism, a topic that will be further examined in chapter 18 on the media, also explains the emphasis on "negative" campaigning—attempts to set the agenda for the opposition and put them on the defensive. Symbolic and negative campaigning are deemed necessary to get the attention of the mass public and motivate them to vote—if not for one's own candidate, then at least against the opposing candidate. For example, in comparison to the inept handling of the Dukakis campaign, the **1988 Bush campaign team** was masterful. Images of "Willie Horton" indicated the law and order theme; "read my lips, no new taxes" was juxtaposed against Democratic spending; patriotism was demonstrated when Bush wrapped himself in the flag; and "Boston Harbor" depicted Dukakis's hypocrisy on environmentalism. These images and "sound-bite politics" did little to inform the electorate about what Bush or Dukakis would or could do as president, but they are the "stuff " of which virtually all present-day political campaigns are made.[49] In the 1996 election, Bob Dole's campaign was poorly run in comparison to the workings of the Bill Clinton campaign.[50]

These campaign strategies make political sense when the goal is attracting mass support and winning elections; however, they also have *political consequences*. First, political campaigning often constrains presidential power by building up promises and expectations among the public that the president, in particular, simply cannot fulfill. While symbolic and negative campaign tactics may bolster a president's public prestige in the short term, in the long term public support is likely to wither, as the chapter 4 discussion of the presidential life cycle demonstrates. Making foreign policy statements and taking foreign policy stances in an effort to win election, furthermore, not only affects public expectations at home, but the expectations and behavior of those abroad.[51]

Second, current political campaigning and electioneering methods are losing the interest of the American public. Many observers attribute the low voter turnouts to such things as difficult registration requirements, the demands of everyday life, and even general satisfaction with public policy. There is some truth to these explanations, but the tremendous drop in public trust of government officials and decline in citizen political efficacy since the 1960s also suggests that there are too many elections, too much politicking and manipulation, and too few concrete results for people's lives.[52] In other words, the public has acquired a high degree of cynicism about the nature of American politics, including party and electoral politics.

If low voter turnout is explained by factors other than public satisfaction, it raises serious

ESSAY 15.1
MONEY, CAMPAIGNING, AND POLITICS

Following the reelection of Bill Clinton as president and Al Gore as vice president, controversy arose about whether the Clinton campaign was involved in illegal campaign contributions and fundraising. Questions were raised about the "overnights" and "coffees" provided to Clinton's friends and donors at the White House; about fundraising calls made by Clinton and Gore "from the White House"; about all the "soft money" raised by the Democratic National Committee; about campaign contributions made by "foreign governments," such as China, with the hope of influencing U.S. foreign policy. Such questions, and charges of illegal and unethical behavior, triggered congressional investigations led by Republicans, given their majority control, in both chambers and an investigation by the Department of Justice. The issue became so politicized that it produced a major partisan struggle between Republicans and Democrats, challenged the reputation of Clinton (which had never been impeccable) and Gore (which had been squeaky clean until then), and produced calls for further campaign financing reform.

Despite the Republican charges against the Democrats and the Clinton administration, money and elections and American politics have always been intertwined and of great importance. People who run for office, especially at the national level, need money, and greater and greater amounts to run viable and successful campaigns. And not only are presidents, and prospective presidential candidates, preoccupied with elections, but so are virtually all members of Congress (as discussed in chapter 12 on Congress). Hedrick Smith in *The Power Game,* in fact, refers to members of Congress as being engaged in a "constant campaign" where "money has been mother's milk to American politics." And campaign costs, especially as a result of expensive television ads, have skyrocketed over the years.

How much **money** was raised in 1996? According to the Federal Election Commission, over $2 billion was "officially" raised (at just the federal level):

over $450 million for the presidential race, over $300 million for Senate races, over $500 million for House races, and over $700 million raised by the Democratic and Republican parties (so-called soft money that could be used for any of the elections). And this excludes the money provided to each major presidential candidate for the general election at public expense (over $62 million each for Clinton and Dole). Not only have the costs of running for president increased dramatically, from the 1970s to the 1990s the average successful House campaign costs went from under $100,000 to almost $1 million, while the average successful Senate campaign went from a few hundred thousand dollars to over $5 million during the same time period.

Most of the money is raised from individuals and organizations—such as special interest groups and **PACs** (political action committees, usually formed by organized interest groups such as labor unions and corporations). Most of the money is spent on advertising, salaries for the campaign staff, mailing and polling, and, not surprising, fundraising (it takes money to get money). And all this despite laws supposedly reforming campaign financing during the early and mid-70s: limiting individual giving to no more then $1000 per candidate per election; limiting PACs to no more then $5000 per candidate per election; making taxpayer financing available for presidential candidates; requiring candidates to disclose their finances. Nevertheless, this just produced more concerted fundraising efforts and new ways to find "loopholes" and overcome the limitations of the **campaign finance laws**—such as so-called "soft money" giving to the national parties.

The need for larger amounts of money and the constant campaign have given **congressional incumbents** enormous advantages. In 1996, an incumbent in the House spent on average over $600,000 while a challenger spent over $200,000; in the Senate an incumbent spent on average over $5 million while a challenger spent over $2 million. This helps to explain why usually around 90 percent of incumbents win reelection. And despite all the controversy over the Clinton campaign and Democratic party fundraising efforts, from 1995 to 1996 the Republican party raised some 60 percent more than the Democratic party—about $550 million to the Democrats $330 million (due to the typically larger amount of corporate PAC money).

There is no doubt that the Clinton campaign was extremely successful in raising large amounts of money to fend off potential challengers (such as Jesse Jackson) and to strengthen their presidential election campaign. But as reporters David Grann and Erika Niedowski point out with a certain amount of irony, "As the White House struggles with daily exposes, Congress has kept its virtuous distance, adopting an air of offended propriety." Yet, although "members of Congress may not offer overnight stays at the White House, they still promise their own mix of perks and politics. These fund-raising methods are usually legal, but they are almost always, and increasingly, unseemly." In fact, most members of Congress, especially the Republicans leading the investigations and charges against Clinton and Gore, have much to fear:

> For starters, they know that a modest examination of congressional fundraising practices would show that, like the allegations against Al Gore, they, too, have solicited contributions from their office, in possible violation of federal law. A more serious inquiry would show that some members have sold legislation to the highest bidder. And even the most

cursory probe would reveal to the wider public what is well-known in politics: that the colossal and ever-mounting costs of campaigns have forced officeholders to hustle for contributions from Election Day to Election Day; that the huge increase in the sums that special interests now pump into the parties' soft-money bank accounts has compromised the ability of even reform-minded members to vote their consciences; . . . that lawmakers often exploit staff for campaign purposes at taxpayer's expense.

Despite public disgust and calls for reform, money appears to be embedded in the electoral and political process—a form of "legal" (and illegal) corruption with little end in sight. As summarized by journalist Edward Roeder, "Forget White House coffees for Chinese arms dealers and convicted embezzlers; forget the vice president's phone solicitation. The real scandal in fund-raising is larger, bipartisan and more obviously illegal. Both the national parties, all presidential candidates and most congressional candidates now routinely flout campaign finance law. And the supposed enforcer of that law, the Federal Election Commission, does nothing about it." In the meanwhile, President Clinton and especially Vice President Gore—given his sights on the presidential election of the year 2000—are the focus of attention and may suffer politically. And although reforms, somehow, may occur and be able to improve the process, ultimately they will not eliminate the "mother's milk" of American politics.

SOURCES: Jill Abramson, "Lott, Champion Money-Raiser, Still Champions Rules of the Game," *New York Times* (October 13, 1997); David Grann and Erika Niedowski, "The Dirty Hill," *New Republic* (April 7, 1997): 21–24; Robert A. Rankin, "Campaign $1996," *The State* (March 6, 1997): D1, D5; Edward Roeder, "Blank Check," *New Republic* (April 14, 1997): 19–21; Hedrick Smith, *The Power Game: How Washington Works* (New York: Ballantine, 1988); "Strange Bedfellows," *Newsweek* (March 10, 1997): 22–28; "With Friends Like These . . . ," *Newsweek* (March 17, 1997): 17–23; R. A. Zaldivar, "Cash Lined Campaign Trail to Congress, White House," *The State* (January 19, 1997): D1, D6.

questions about the democratic nature of a political system in which only a minority of the citizenry participates in electoral politics—a topic to which we will turn to in greater depth in chapter 19. This general perception of the declining relevance of po-

litical parties and low participation in electoral politics also contributes to the growing importance of social movements and interest groups in the politics of U.S. foreign policy, the subject of the next chapter.

BIBLIOGRAPHIC ESSAY

. . . .

The study of political participation, party politics, and electoral politics has received considerable attention by scholars and analysts of American politics, but the impact of these subjects on the politics of U.S. foreign policy generally has been ignored. Although most scholars of U.S. foreign policy traditionally have dismissed the role of electoral politics, over the last few years foreign policy specialists have begun to recognize the importance of electoral politics for fully understanding U.S. foreign policy. I. M. Destler, Leslie H. Gelb, and Anthony Lake, in *Our Own Worst Enemy: The Unmaking of American Foreign Policy* (New York: Simon and Schuster, 1984), particularly in chapter 1, provide a good overview of the impact of domestic politics and elections on U.S. foreign policy, as does Miroslav Nincic in "U.S. Soviet Policy and the Electoral Connection," *World Politics* 42 (April 1990): 370–96. John H. Aldrich, John L. Sullivan, and Eugene Borgida demonstrate that foreign policy issues are often as important as domestic issues in affecting voting in presidential elections in "Foreign Affairs and Issue Voting: Do Presidential Candidates 'Waltz' Before a Blind Audience?" *American Political Science Review* 83 (March 1989): 123–41. Martin P. Wattenberg provides a good overview of political participation and party politics in the electoral process over the last few decades in *The Decline of American Political Parties, 1952–1980* (Cambridge, Mass.: Harvard University Press, 1984). An excellent history and analysis of the rise and decline of the Democratic party since the 1930s can be found in James MacGregor Burns, *The Crosswinds of Freedom* (New York: Vintage, 1989) and Steve Fraser and Gary Gerstle, eds., *The Rise and Fall of the New Deal Order, 1930–1980* (Princeton, N.J.: Princeton University Press, 1989). Earl Black and Merle Black, in *Politics and Society in the South* (Cambridge, Mass.: Harvard University Press, 1987), provide the most comprehensive understanding of political change and party realignment in the South.

The Responsible Electorate: Rationality in Presidential Voting, 1936–1960 (New York: Vintage, 1966) by V. O. Key remains a classic on the electorate, as does Joe McGinniss on campaign strategies in *The Selling of the President, 1968* (New York: Pocket Books, 1969). For an excellent discussion of contemporary electoral and campaign politics, see Hedrick Smith, *The Power Game: How Washington Works* (New York: Ballantine, 1988), especially chapters 18 and 19; the work of William Schneider, such as "The New Shape of American Politics" in *The Atlantic Monthly* (January 1987): 39–54; and Anthony King, "Running Scared," *The Atlantic Monthly* (January 1997): 41–61. Kevin Phillips, the godfather of the Republican realignment strategy in the South, has written a provocative work on the future of electoral and domestic politics, predicting the resurgence of liberalism and the Democratic party before the rise of Bill Clinton, in *The Politics of the Rich and Poor: Wealth and the American Electorate in the Reagan Aftermath* (New York: Random House, 1990).

ENDNOTES

1. See Michael X. Delli Carpini and Scott Keeter, *What Americans Know about Politics and Why It Matters* (New Haven, Conn.: Yale University Press, 1996); E. J. Dionne, Jr. *Why Americans Hate Politics* (New York: Simon and Schuster, 1991); Herbert J. Gans, *Middle American Individualism: Political Participation and Liberal Democracy* (New York: Oxford University Press, 1988); Seymour Martin Lipset and William Schneider, "The Decline of Confidence in American Institutions," *Political Science Quarterly* (Fall 1983): 379–402.

2. For an overview of political participation, see M. Margaret Conway, *Political Participation in the United States* (Washington, D.C.: Congressional Quarterly Press, 1991); W. Russell Neuman, *The Paradox of Mass Politics: Knowledge and Opinion in the American Electorate* (Cambridge, Mass.: Harvard University Press, 1986); Sidney Verba and Norman H. Nie, *Participation in America: Political Democracy and Social Equality* (Chicago: University of Chicago Press, 1972); and James Q. Wilson, *Political Organizations* (New York: Basic Books, 1973).

3. Robert S. Strauss, "What's Right with U.S. Campaigns," *Foreign Policy* 55 (Summer 1984): 4.

4. For an overview of the party system in the United States, see, for example, Fred I. Greenstein, *The American Party System and the American People* (Englewood Cliffs, N.J.: Prentice-Hall, 1963), and Frank J. Souraf, *Party Politics in America* (Boston: Little, Brown, 1984).

5. See J. David Gillespie, *Politics at the Periphery: Third Parties in Two Party America* (Columbia: University of South Carolina Press, 1993).

6. Martin P. Wattenberg, "The Crisis of Electoral Politics," *The Atlantic Monthly* (May 1997): 119. See also Guy Molyneux and William Schneider, "Ross *Is* Boss," *The Atlantic Monthly* (May 1993): 84–96.

7. Strauss, "What's Right with U.S. Campaigns," p. 7.

8. William A. Galston and Christopher J. Makins, "Campaign '88 and Foreign Policy," *Foreign Policy* 71 (Summer 1988): 4.

9. For an overview of the role of electoral politics in U.S. foreign policy, see I. M. Destler, Leslie H. Gelb, and Anthony Lake, in *Our Own Worst Enemy: The Unmaking of American Foreign Policy* (New York: Simon and Schuster, 1984); Galston and Makins, "Campaign '88 and Foreign Policy"; Stephen Hess, "Foreign Policy and Presidential Campaigns," *Foreign Policy* 8 (Fall 1972): 3–22; Ralph B. Levering, *The Public and American Foreign Policy, 1918–1978* (New York: William Morrow, 1978); Miroslav Nincic, "U.S. Soviet Policy and the Electoral Connection," *World Politics* 42 (April 1990): 370–96; and William B. Quandt, "The Electoral Cycle and the Conduct of Foreign Policy," *Political Science Quarterly* (Centennial Year, 1986): 825–37.

10. For a historical overview of major party and electoral patterns, see Walter Dean Burnham, *Critical Elections and the Mainsprings of American Politics* (New York: Norton, 1970); James MacGregor Burns, *The Crosswinds of Freedom* (New York: Vintage, 1989); Steve Fraser and Gary Gerstle, eds., *The Rise and Fall of the New Deal Order, 1930–1980* (Princeton, N.J.: Princeton University Press, 1989); Everett Carll Ladd, *American Political Parties: Social Change and Political Response* (New York: W.W. Norton, 1970); James I. Sundquist, *Dynamics of the Party System: Alignment and Realignment of Political Parties in the U.S.* (Washington, D.C.: Brookings, 1983).

11. For a good overview of the concept of realignment, see David G. Lawrence and Richard Fleisher, "Puzzles and Confusions: Political Realignment in the 1980s," *Political Science Quarterly* (Spring 1987): 79–92.

12. Roosevelt's foreign policy is described in greater depth in chapter 2.

13. William H. Chafe, *The Unfinished Journey: America Since World War II* (New York: Oxford University Press, 1991), p. 98.

14. Ibid., p. 103.

15. Robert A. Devine, *Foreign Policy and US Presidential Elections: 1952–1960* (New York: New Viewpoints, 1974), p. 53.

16. William Manchester, *The Glory and the Dream: A Narrative History of America, 1932–1972* (New York: Bantam, 1973), p. 628.

17. This is the major theme of Eric F. Goldman, *The Crucial Decade–and After: America, 1945–1960* (New York: Random House, 1961).

18. See Devine, *Foreign Policy and US Presidential Elections.*

19. See Theodore H. White, *The Making of the President, 1960* (New York: Atheneum, 1961).

20. Godfrey Hodgson, *America in Our Time* (New York: Vintage, 1976), pp. 73–74.

21. David Halberstam, *The Best and the Brightest* (New York: Random House, 1969), p. 298.

22. Ibid., p. 425.

23. For an overview of these electoral patterns since the 1960s, see Everett Carll Ladd, "The Brittle Mandate: Electoral Dealignment and the 1980 Presidental Election," *Political Science Quarterly* (Spring 1981): 1–25; Everett Carll Ladd, "On Mandates, Realignments, and the 1984 Presidential Election," *Political Science Quarterly* (Spring 1985): 1–25; Everett Carll Ladd, "The 1988 Elections: Continuation of the Post–New Deal System," *Political Science Quarterly* (Spring 1989): 1–18; Everett Carll Ladd, "The 1992 Vote for President Clinton: Another Brittle Mandate?" *Political Science Quarterly* (1993): 1–28; and Norman H. Nie, Sidney Verba, and John R. Petrocik, *The Changing American Voter* (Cambridge, Mass.: Harvard University Press, 1976); Martin P. Wattenberg, *The Decline of American Political Parties, 1952–1980* (Cambridge, Mass.: Harvard University Press, 1984).

24. See Byron E. Shafer, ed., *The End of Realignment? Interpreting American Electoral Eras* (Madison: University of Wisconsin Press, 1991); James L. Sundquist, "Needed: A Political Theory for the New Era of Coalition Government in the United States," *Political Science Quarterly* (1988): 613–35. See also Peter F. Nardulli, "The Concept of a Critical Realignment, Electoral Behavior, and Political Change," *American Political Science Review* (March 1995): 10–22.

25. Burns, *Crosswinds of Freedom*, pp. 656–57.

26. See Earl Black and Merle Black, *Politics and Society in the South* (Cambridge, Mass.: Harvard University Press, 1987), and Kevin P. Phillips, *The Emerging Republican Majority* (New Rochelle, N.Y.: Arlington House, 1969).

27. To appreciate the politics involved behind the power of incumbency, see Hedrick Smith, *The Power Game:*

How Washington Works (New York: Ballantine, 1988), chapter 7.

28. Richard L. Berke, "In Fund-Raising Race, Incumbents Are Ahead," *New York Times* (November 5, 1990): A11.

29. William Schneider, " 'Rambo' and Reality: Having It Both Ways," in Kenneth A. Oye, Robert J. Lieber, and Donald Rothchild, eds., *Eagle Resurgent? The Reagan Era in American Foreign Policy* (Boston: Little, Brown, 1987), p. 46. See also Ole R. Holsti and James N. Rosenau, *American Leadership in World Affairs: Vietnam and the Breakdown of Consensus* (New York: Allen & Unwin, 1984), and James N. Rosenau, "U.S. Leadership in a Shrinking World: The Breakdown of Consensuses and the Emergence of Conflict Belief Systems," *World Politics* 35 (April 1983): 368–92.

30. William Schneider, "Public Opinion," in Joseph S. Nye, Jr., *The Making of America's Soviet Policy* (New Haven, Conn.: Yale University Press, 1984), pp. 13–14.

31. Schneider, " 'Rambo' and Reality," p. 51.

32. See, for example, Theodore H. White, *America in Search of Itself: The Making of the President 1956–1980* (New York: Warner, 1983).

33. John H. Aldrich, John L. Sullivan, and Eugene Borgida, "Foreign Affairs and Issue Voting: Do Presidential Candidates 'Waltz' Before a Blind Audience?" *American Political Science Review* 83 (March 1989): 135. See also Miroslav Nincic and Barbara Hinckley, "Foreign Policy and the Evaluation of Presidential Candidates," *Journal of Conflict Resolution* (June 1991): 333–55; Benjamin I. Page and Robert Y. Shapiro, *The Rational Public: Fifty Years of Trends in Americans' Policy Preferences* (Chicago: University of Chicago Press, 1992), and Robert Y. Shapiro and Benjamin I. Page, "Foreign Policy and the Rational Public," *Journal of Conflict Resolution* 32 (June 1988): 211–47.

34. See Thomas Omestad, "Foreign Policy and Campaign '96," *Foreign Policy* (Winter 1996–97): 37–54.

35. Holsti and Rosenau, *American Leadership in World Affairs*, p. 1. See chapter 2 for greater discussion of continuity and change in U.S. foreign policy since Vietnam.

36. See William Schneider, "JFK's Children: The Class of '74," *The Atlantic Monthly* (March 1989): 35–58.

37. See Miroslav Nincic, "The United States, The Soviet Union, and the Politics of Opposites," *World Politics* 40 (July 1988): 452–75; Jerel A. Rosati, "United States Leadership into the Next Millennium," *International Affairs* (Spring 1997): 297–315;

38. See, for example, Benjamin Ginsberg and Martin Shefter, *Politics by Other Means: The Declining Importance of Elections in America* (New York: Basic Books, 1990), and Smith, *The Power Game*, chapters 17 and 18.

39. Norman J. Ornstein and Mark Schmitt, "Dateline Campaign '92: Post–Cold War Politics," *Foreign Policy* 79 (Summer 1990): 169.

40. For an overview of the contemporary electoral process, particularly in presidential races, see Thomas Byrne Edsall with Mary D. Edsall, *Chain Reaction: The Impact of Race, Rights, and Taxes on American Politics* (New York: W.W. Norton, 1992); Thomas Byrne Edsall, "Willie Horton's Message," *New York Review of Books* (February 13, 1992): 7–11; William Schneider, "The New Shape of American Politics," *The Atlantic Monthly* (January 1987): 39–54; Smith, *The Power Game*, chapters 18 and 19; and Stephen J. Wayne, *The Road to the White House: The Politics of Presidential Elections* (New York: St. Martin's Press, 1992).

41. Martin P. Wattenberg, *The Rise of Candidate-Centered Politics: Presidential Elections of the 1980s* (Cambridge, Mass.: Harvard University Press, 1991).

42. In most "primary elections," only registered party members–not independents–can cast a vote and usually only for a nominee from their party (although there is some variation among states). In "general elections," all those registered–including independents–can vote for any party candidate.

43. V. O. Key, Jr., *The Responsible Electorate: Rationality in Presidential Voting, 1936–1960* (New York: Vintage, 1966).

44. Key, *The Responsible Electorate*. See also Richard A. Brody, *Assessing the President: The Media, Public Opinion, and Public Support* (Stanford: Stanford University Press, 1991); Morris P. Fiorina, *Retrospective Voting in American National Elections* (New Haven, Conn.: Yale University Press, 1981); Arthur H. Miller and Martin P. Wattenberg, "Throwing the Rascals Out: Policy and Performance Evaluations of Presidential Candidates, 1952–1980," *American Political Science Review* 79 (June 1985): 359–72; Samuel L. Popkin, *The Reasoning Voter: Communication and Persuasion in Presidential Campaigns* (Chicago: University of Chicago Press, 1991).

45. For an overview of the election, see Larry J. Sabato, ed. *Toward the Millennium: The Elections of 1996* (Boston: Allyn and Bacon, 1997).

46. Louis Menand, "Inside the Billway," *New York Review of Books* (August 14, 1997): 4.

47. See Stephen Hess and Michael Nelson, "Foreign Policy: Dominance and Decisiveness in Presidential Elections," in Michael Nelson, ed., *The Elections of 1984* (Washington, D.C.: Congressional Quarterly Press, 1985), pp. 141–52.

48. See, for example, Anthony King, "Running Scared," *The Atlantic Monthly* (January 1997): 41–61; Joe McGinniss, *The Selling of the President, 1968* (New York: Pocket Books, 1969).

49. See Kathleen Hall Jamieson, *Dirty Politics: Deception, Distraction, and Democracy* (New York: Oxford University Press, 1992); Peter Goldman, Tom Mathews and the Newsweek Special Election Team, *The Quest for the Presidency 1988* (New York: Touchstone, 1989), and Sidney Blumenthal, *Pledging Allegiance: The Last Campaign of the Cold War* (New York: HarperCollins, 1990).

50. See *Newsweek,* Special Election Issue (November 18, 1996); Bob Woodward, *The Choice* (New York: Simon and Schuster, 1996).

51. Robert Strauss also provides a more optimistic discussion of contemporary elections and its impact on foreign policy in "What's Right with U.S. Campaigns."

52. See Everett Carll Ladd, *Where Have All the Voters Gone? The Fracturing of America's Political Parties* (New York: Norton, 1978); Richard M. Valelly, "Vanishing Voters," *The American Prospect* (Spring 1990): 140–50; and Wattenberg, *The Decline of American Political Parties.*

CHAPTER
16

. . . .

GROUP POLITICS

*G*roup politics involves the role of social movements and interest groups in American politics. Political participation in group politics tends to be narrower than in electoral politics and occurs most frequently among members of the elite public. However, many Americans do participate in social movements and in thousands of widely varying groups, such as business, labor, consumer, environmental, religious, ethnic, civic, veterans, and national security groups. These *groups directly and indirectly affect the foreign policymaking process by:*

> lobbying government,
>
> influencing electoral and domestic politics,
>
> participating in the policymaking process,
>
> providing sources of political recruitment for the government, and
>
> undertaking international activity.

In order to better understand how group politics influences U.S. foreign policy, we begin with a general discussion of the origins and development of

groups in American politics, followed by a broad historical overview of the impact of group politics on U.S. foreign policy since World War II. As we will see, continuity and change in group politics parallel the evolution of electoral politics, thus establishing the boundaries of political discourse and behavior within domestic politics and the policymaking process. In this way, group politics, like electoral politics, deeply affects the president's ability to govern foreign policy and the evolution of the tension between the demands of national security and democracy.

GROUP ORIGINS
AND DEVELOPMENT

. . . .

Interest groups are organizations that possess an overriding concern with the political process and policy outcomes. They do not tend to be created randomly or continuously, but often come in waves.

In other words, large numbers of interest groups tend to form at certain times, usually in reaction to key events. For example, large numbers of interest groups formed during the 1930s in response to the Great Depression, during the 1940s and early 1950s in response to World War II and the cold war, and during the late 1960s and 1970s in response to events such as the Vietnam War. These time periods are often characterized by "negative" events—that is, events that hurt or are perceived to be counterproductive for people's lives. Such events activate people, many of whom previously may have been apathetic and politically passive.

Such periods of political instability and turmoil also usually produce **social movements**—large coalitions of individuals and groups that loosely unite around certain issues, usually in opposition to the status quo. Social movements involve thousands, and sometimes millions, of people. They usually involve a change in the way people think about an issue, and these changes in attitudes usually remain even after the social movement fades. Although many of the people may not be part of any specific organized interest group, they nonetheless are motivated to be part of a social movement in order to influence the political system. Social movements also involve dozens, sometimes hundreds, of interest groups—older groups that have been around for a while and more recent groups that have arisen in reaction to the political climate of the times.[1]

Interest groups and social movements influence the domestic political environment and the governmental policymaking process in a number of ways. First, groups usually "lobby" policymakers involved in the policy process. This is done by providing information and money, as well as mobilizing followers to provide support or cause political trouble. Second, the same techniques are used to influence domestic politics more generally, including the political agenda, public beliefs and behavior, and electoral politics. Third, members of some groups, especially those that are well established and have close relationships with government agencies and personnel, are "consulted" often and actually participate with policymakers in the policy process. Fourth,

well-established groups also tend to serve as important sources of "political recruitment" for official positions within government. As was discussed in chapter 6, major presidential appointees usually come from business, law, and academia. Finally, groups that are extremely active internationally, such as multinational corporations, affect U.S. foreign policy and the policymaking process because of their visibility and "activities abroad."

Social movements tend to go through a **life cycle** and tend to have a relatively short life span. Initially highly visible and potentially influential, they wither away as the issue dies due to either success or failure. Interest groups that survive tend to go through a longer life cycle. Groups in their formative stages tend to be more informally structured and nonbureaucratic. New interest groups, like the social movements of which they are often a part, also tend to be more purposive as group leaders and members are motivated to accomplish certain goals. They also tend to be **"challenging" groups** in the sense that group leaders and followers are usually unhappy with things as they currently exist and are change oriented, challenging some aspect of the status quo. With time, interest groups tend to become more formal and less purposive. The activities of older groups tend to be much more bureaucratic and institutionalized. Members of older, **established groups** also tend to join for "material" and "solidaristic" reasons—for example, in order to get certain services or to socialize with others. Older groups, especially those that are accepted or legitimate within society and have been somewhat successful in fulfilling their original purposive goals, also tend to be content with, and supportive of, the status quo.

In sum, American *group politics tends to go through different phases of political stability and instability*. During "more stable periods," established groups and the status quo tend to dominate. Challenging groups exist, but they are often few in number, small in size and support, and invisible to most Americans. However, "times of greater political instability" produce considerable social movement activity and interest group expansion. During these periods, major political challenges of the status quo occur where efforts are made to change the ideological beliefs and institutions that dominate society and the government. The forces in support of the status quo usually have a great advantage in resisting challenging groups, for the status quo tends to have considerable support throughout the government and much of society, at least initially among the mass public. Nevertheless, it is during these times that political changes have the greatest potential and likelihood of occurring.

Every political system, according to David Truman in *The Governmental Process,* "of course, tends to discriminate in favor of established groups of interests, and it may deny to new groups access to points of decision."[2] Established groups tend to support the status quo and, thus, promote continuity in the policy process. Challenging groups, on the other hand, attempt to change domestic politics and the policymaking process. Therefore, in order to understand continuity and change, it is important to determine how successful new groups are in challenging more established groups and the dominant beliefs that exist throughout society and govern-

ment. For James MacGregor Burns in *The Crosswinds of Freedom,* group politics and electoral politics have been intertwined throughout American history:

> Movements emerged out of economic stress and social tension and erupted in conflict, often violent. After a time they dominated political debate, overshadowed more traditional issues, cut across existing lines of party cleavage, polarized groups and parties. The immediate test of success was whether the movement could force one major party or both of them to embrace its cause. The test of long-run success was whether the movement left the whole party system altered and, even more, left the political landscape transformed.[3]

How successful are challenging groups at surviving, being accepted within society, and gaining their original goals? Sociologist William Gamson performed an in-depth study of over fifty major challenging groups throughout American history. As **figure 16.1** depicts, he found that only half of the

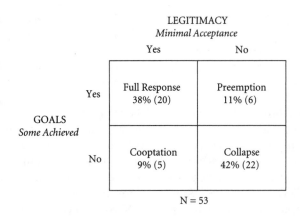

FIGURE 16.1
POLITICAL OUTCOMES FOR CHALLENGING GROUPS

LEGITIMACY
Minimal Acceptance

		Yes	No
	Yes	Full Response 38% (20)	Preemption 11% (6)
GOALS *Some Achieved*	No	Cooptation 9% (5)	Collapse 42% (22)

N = 53

SOURCE: William A. Gamson, *The Strategy of Social Protest* (Homewood, IL: Dorsey Press, 1975), p. 37.

challenging groups were able to survive and gain minimal acceptance within society. Furthermore, only half of the groups were successful in gaining at least some of their goals. Overall, while roughly 40 percent of the challenging groups were successful in both gaining some legitimacy and achieving some of their goals, 40 percent collapsed entirely. As Gamson concludes, "The central difference among political actors is captured by the idea of being inside or outside of the polity. Those who are inside are *members* whose interest is vested—that is, recognized as valid by other members. Those who are outside are challengers. They lack the basic prerogative of members—routine access to decisions that affect them."[4]

Many different factors account for these outcomes. However, one important element involves the **salience of an issue** upon the ability of groups to influence the political agenda. Challenging groups tend to have their greatest impact for those issues that have great salience and visibility in domestic politics. This occurs because issues that become "politicized" attract the attention of the elite and mass public throughout society beyond the confines of government policymakers and established groups. However, for issues of low salience—the normal state of affairs for most issues—challenging groups are usually unable to overcome the lack of public attention and penetrate the web of relations that exists between government policymakers and established groups.

Clearly, group politics is demanding and rough. It tends to pit people from new and challenging social groups and movements against people from more established and status quo-oriented groups. Success for new and challenging groups is an uphill battle, because more established groups tend to enjoy considerable support throughout much of society and the government. However, challenging groups that succeed in gaining legitimacy and promoting their goals are able to affect the public and their beliefs, political participation, domestic politics and the governmental policymaking process. And as we will see, the rise of social movements and the evolution of group politics have deeply influenced the making of U.S. foreign policy during the cold war and post–Vietnam War years.

GROUP POLITICS DURING THE COLD WAR ERA

· · · · · · · · · · · · · ·

Before World War II the group process played a vital role in the domestic politics and policy process of U.S. foreign policymaking, especially with respect to issues of trade and protectionism. For most social movements and interest groups, however, foreign policy was usually secondary to domestic issues. Those few groups that were devoted exclusively to foreign policy rarely had much influence over the policymaking process. This situation permanently changed with American intervention in World War II and the rise of the cold war. *Two patterns evolved with respect to group activity during the 1940s and 1950s.* First, new and established groups throughout American society became heavily involved in the foreign policymaking process. Second, most of these groups were overwhelmingly anticommunist and conservative in their foreign policy orientations. These patterns were promoted and reinforced by the rise of extremely conservative social movements at the time, represented by the forces of McCarthyism. *The results of these developments for group politics and the making of U.S. foreign policy were:*

1. The rise of foreign policy- and cold war-oriented groups;
2. The development of a military-industrial-scientific infrastructure;
3. The rise of a foreign policy establishment.

These patterns in group politics during the cold war years contributed to a domestic context that led to the rise of presidential power, the expansion of the foreign policy bureaucracy, an acquiescent Congress, a supportive public, and bipartisanship in party politics. Thus, a group process evolved during the 1940s and 1950s that became an important part of the anticommunist foreign policy consensus throughout society and enhanced the ability of the U.S. government under the leadership of the president to carry out its national security policies abroad. Groups and movements that challenged containment policies from the political Left did exist during the cold war years. However, they were small in numbers and resources, constantly on the political defensive, and primarily remained outside the realm of mainstream domestic politics.

FOREIGN POLICY AND COLD WAR-ORIENTED GROUPS

The 1940s and 1950s resulted in the *rise of numerous anticommunist groups that became active in the politics of U.S. foreign policy, including:*

1. National security and public policy groups;
2. Veterans and military support groups;
3. Political and civic groups;
4. Business and corporations;
5. Labor unions;
6. Religious groups;
7. Ethnic groups.

These groups directly and indirectly affected the foreign policymaking process by lobbying government, influencing electoral and domestic politics, participating in the policymaking process, providing sources of political recruitment for the government, and undertaking international activity. There were certainly differences in perceptions among leaders and members of these groups concerning the intensity of the Soviet communist threat and the particulars of U.S. national security policy; some were more anticommunist than others. However, all shared a general cold war internationalist orientation that formed the basis of a consensus in the making of U.S. foreign policy.[5]

National security and public policy groups became increasingly active and prominent in the making of U.S. foreign policy during World War II and the cold war. These groups included the Carnegie Endowment for International Peace, Committee on the Present Danger, Council on Foreign Relations, Ford and Rockefeller Foundations, Foreign Policy Research Institute, and the Rand Corporation. Membership and involvement in most of these groups were limited to proponents of American cold war policies, including select government (and ex-

government) officials, business leaders, academics, journalists, and other opinion leaders within American society. The activities of these groups typically consisted of group seminars on important issues, involvement in policy research and proposals, and the publication and communication of members' work. Not only did these activities affect the beliefs of the attentive and mass publics, but many of these groups became extremely important **sources of ideas and personnel** for the government during the cold war years. In this respect, it is important to remember that the foreign policy bureaucracy in government grew tremendously in size during the 1940s and 1950s and many of its policymaking personnel were recruited from such groups.[6] (See **essay 16.1** for a discussion of the significant role the Council on Foreign Relations played in the postwar foreign policymaking process.)

Veterans and military support organizations were staunchly anticommunist supporters of American cold war policies and emphasized a large defense build-up and reliance on force. These organizations included the major veterans organizations, such as the American Legion and the Veterans of Foreign Wars, and military support organizations, such as the Navy League and the American Ordnance Association. Broad-based political and civic organizations also became participants in the foreign policy consensus throughout American politics.[7] Americans for Democratic Action, for example, was launched in the early 1950s by prominent American Democrats and liberals as a means to support the government's cold war policies. Such groups were highly visible, reinforcing the development of an anticommunist consensus throughout society and the government.

Business and labor groups were also part of the consensus supporting U.S. foreign policy. **Business** had long played a prominent role in American politics and government, especially since the rise of industrialization and the development of modern corporations. Much of this was because business leaders were "regularly recruited" into government policymaking positions by political leaders and because of the "increasing scale of activities of American business abroad," especially in Latin America. As

ESSAY 16.1
THE COUNCIL ON FOREIGN RELATIONS

The **Council on Foreign Relations (CFR)** was probably the single most important group involved in the making of U.S. foreign policy during the cold war years. However, it did not exercise influence by immediately affecting the policymaking process, but by providing foreign policy ideas and personnel for government. In this respect, the Council on Foreign Relations served as a forum for bringing policymakers and opinion leaders together and circulating ideas and policy proposals, which often played an important role in the foreign policymaking process.

The Council on Foreign Relations describes itself as "a nonprofit and nonpartisan membership organization dedicated to improved understanding of American foreign policy and international affairs."[A] It was originally established in 1921 in New York City shortly after World War I and the Senate's rejection of the Treaty of Versailles (and U.S. membership in the League of Nations) in order to promote American internationalism and involvement abroad.

The CFR's activities have revolved around *three major areas*. First, the Council on Foreign Relations "strives to bring together experts within the Council membership and distinguished speakers from around the world for a forthright exchange of views that enlightens all participants."[B] These meetings are generally restricted to CFR members and are "off-the-record" (not for public attribution). The second activity is the "Corporate Program" in which corporate executives—from predominantly prominent American companies—participate in discussions with council members and distinguished guests about the state of American business and its relationship to U.S. foreign policy. Finally, the council is very involved in communicating ideas

and foreign policy views. This is done by furnishing policy studies on important contemporary issues to council members, government officials, and relevant policy experts. Most important, the Council on Foreign Relations publishes a quarterly journal, *Foreign Affairs,* which was the most influential policy journal in U.S. foreign policy throughout the 1950s and 1960s, for it was widely read by government officials and opinion leaders (and is still widely read today).

The Council on Foreign Relations caters to a rather narrow and exclusive audience by focusing on national opinion leaders. By its own description, the CFR is "composed of men and women with experience in matters of foreign policy who are leaders in academe, public service, business, and the media."[C] *Membership* is achieved through a very selective process in which individuals are first nominated by a membership committee and then elected by the board of directors. During the cold war years, membership in the Council on Foreign Relations represented the height of prestige and a sure route to participation in the making of U.S. foreign policy. In the political climate of the cold war years, this meant that members tended to be part of the liberal-conservative ideological consensus and, thus, cold warriors in foreign policy.

Given the tremendous prestige of the Council on Foreign Relations, it not only provided a significant forum for generating ideas and policies for opinion leaders and government officials, but it was a significant *source of political recruitment* where many important government positions throughout the foreign policy bureaucracy were often filled by presidential appointment of CFR members, including those at the secretary level and the national security adviser. As Robert Schulzinger concludes in his history of the Council on Foreign Relations entitled *The Wise Men of Foreign Affairs,* its members filled

A. Council on Foreign Relations, *Annual Report, 1985–86* (New York: Council on Foreign Relations, 1986), p. 5.
B. Ibid., p. 8.

C. Ibid., p. 5.

the role of a "professional clergy" for the foreign policy community in and out of government.[D] In

D. Robert D. Schulzinger, *The Wise Men of Foreign Affairs: The History of the Council on Foreign Relations* (New York: Columbia University Press, 1984).

SOURCES: Council on Foreign Relations, *Annual Report, 1985–86* (New York: Council on Foreign Relations, 1986); Council on Foreign Relations, *Annual Report, 1995–96* (New York: Council on Foreign Relations, 1996); Jerel Rosati, Ken Rogerson, and Richard Haeuber, "Agenda-Setting, World Affairs Organizations, and the Making of U.S. Foreign Policy," (unpublished manuscript, 1997); J. Anthony Lukas, "The Council on Foreign Relations: Is It A Club? Seminar? Presidium? 'Invisible Government'?" *New York Times Magazine* (November 21, 1971); and Robert D. Schulzinger, *The Wise Men of Foreign Affairs: The History of the Council on Foreign Relations* (New York: Columbia University Press, 1984).

fact, CFR membership was a clear indication of inclusion in the foreign policy establishment that arose during the cold war years and greatly influenced the making of U.S. foreign policy (discussed in greater detail later in this chapter).

historian William Appleman Williams has argued throughout his work, by the turn of the century U.S. foreign policy became increasingly supportive of an "open door" policy for American business and investment abroad.[8]

Moreover, with World War II and the onset of the cold war, business groups such as the Chamber of Commerce, Committee for Economic Development, and the National Association of Manufacturers became strong supporters of the government's containment policy. Industry involvement in foreign policy was reinforced by the growing role of big business in defense production. As a result, a type of big business and government "partnership" developed in support of U.S. foreign policy during the cold war years. The symbiotic business-government relationship was best expressed by General Motors Chairman Charles Wilson. When asked during his confirmation hearings on January 15, 1953, before the Senate Armed Services Committee whether he could make a decision as secretary of defense that would be adverse to the interests of General Motors, Wilson said, "For years I thought what was good for the country was good for General Motors and vice versa. The difference did not exist."[9]

Anticommunism accompanied the promotion of private enterprise at home and abroad. This was consistent with government efforts to contain communism and promote a liberal political and economic world order. As American banks and companies became increasingly multinationalized following World War II, they located in countries where there was a strong U.S. governmental presence abroad, such as in Latin America and Europe. One can debate whether the American "flag" led the American "dollar" abroad, or vice versa. Regardless, both business and government were driven to promote an open door or "free market" ethos in U.S. foreign policy during the cold war years. The **government-business relationship** was generally interactive and supportive: the increasing global presence of American government and the relocation of American multinational industry abroad led to greater mutual dependency between American business and government abroad. For example, U.S. governmental actions to assist postwar reconstruction of Western Europe through the Marshall Plan also relied on American private investment in the region; in addition, America's military and economy became increasingly dependent on continued access to oil by American petroleum companies, especially in the Middle East. As Michael Stoff concluded in *Oil, War and American National Security,* private corporations, not the government, "became the agents of national policy."[10] In turn, American multinational corporations expected the U.S. government to further American private investment abroad and prevent nationalization by foreign governments.[11]

Organized labor was also a strong supporter of anticommunism at home and abroad. This fact may come as a surprise to many Americans given the popular impression of labor-management conflict and labor's pre–World War II history. Throughout the early part of the twentieth century, efforts by unions to organize, improve working conditions and, among more radical unions, restructure the political economy were vehemently fought by business and government. It was not until after World War I and, in particular, the implementation of 1930s New Deal policies that the government officially recognized the right of workers to form unions. However, factors such as organized labor's growing legitimacy and moderation in goals, the postwar return of economic prosperity, Republican and McCarthyite attacks against New Deal policies and unionization, and the national security demands of World War II and the cold war produced unions that were much more comfortable and supportive of the status quo.

The American Federation of Labor-Congress of Industrial Organizations (**AFL-CIO**), the umbrella organization to which most American unions belonged during the 1950s, strongly supported the government's cold war policies at home and abroad. The AFL-CIO was active in the international labor movement through its International Confederation of Free Trade Unions, in particular in Europe, Asia, and Latin America. The AFL-CIO Institute for Free Labor Development was active, for example, in supporting anticommunist unionization and movements in Latin America (and often worked in conjunction with the CIA). Hence, while many American unions historically were the source of liberalism and the political Left, they too became part of the anticommunist consensus during the cold war years.[12]

Religious and ethnic groups also played prominent anticommunist roles during the cold war years. **Religious movements and groups** have always played a powerful role throughout American history, dating back to the landing of the Pilgrims in Plymouth, Massachusetts. As stated by Garry Wills in *Under God: Religion and American Politics*, "Religion has been at the center of our major political crises, which are always moral crises—the supporting and opposing of wars, of slavery, of corporate power, of civil rights, of sexual codes, of 'the West,'

of American separatism and claims to empire."[13] Domestically, religion has been important because of the periodic occurrences of conservative Protestant revival movements, liberal social gospel movements, and the rise of Catholicism in American society. This has been reinforced by the activities of Protestant **missionaries** abroad who attempted to Christianize foreigners, especially in Asia throughout the nineteenth and early twentieth centuries.[14]

Given this background, religion played a prominent role in the rise of the anticommunist consensus during the post–World War II years. The Catholic church historically was extremely critical of communism and its atheistic views, rallying American Catholics behind the government's cold war policies. The late 1940s and early 1950s also witnessed the rise of Protestant fundamentalism against the secular trends of modern society, which provided support for McCarthyism during the cold war years. Thus, American religion, even given its Christian diversity, reinforced the rise of anticommunism throughout society and the government.[15]

The United States is also a country of great ethnic diversity, and **ethnic groups** have actively influenced the making of U.S. foreign policy. For example, the domination of Eastern Europe by the Soviet Union provoked a strong anticommunist response from ethnic groups with ties to the region. "Polish-Americans," reinforced by their Catholicism, were particularly vocal over the fate of Poland. Furthermore, they also represented a large bloc of potential voters in a number of key industrial states. This domestic political background helps to explain why Stalin's eventual consolidation of power in Poland was one of the important postwar developments during the late 1940s in hardening attitudes within the Truman administration and throughout society around the issue of anticommunism.

The rise of these various cold war-oriented groups laid the foundation for the development of the famed **"China lobby,"** or Taiwan lobby, that gained great prominence during the cold war years. The China lobby consisted primarily of Nationalist Chinese officials and Americans, including government officials, Protestant missionaries, China watchers and journalists, and American business leaders, who were active in China before the 1949 revolution and interested in its future. The China lobby represented a broad coalition of diverse anticommunist groups, such as the American China Policy Association, the Committee to Defend America by Aiding Anti-Communist China, and the Committee for One Million (Against the Admission of Communist China into the United Nations) who shared a common concern over "the fall" of China and identified with the Nationalist Chinese government in Taiwan. Participants within the China lobby tended to emphasize the greater importance of Asia over Europe as a market, for national security reasons, symbolized by the Korean War, and for the future of Christianity. Members of the China lobby attacked the Truman administration for its Eurocentric and inadequate foreign policies, played a prominent role in the rise of McCarthyism, and helped forge an anticommunist consensus throughout society and the government during the cold war years.

The **Committee for One Million**, for example, was officially founded in 1953 by extremely conservative members of Congress and was very prominent and quite successful in lobbying congressional colleagues on China policy. One study conducted by the Congress's Congressional Research Service concluded that "the Committee's legitimation through direct, widespread, and explicit congressional participation in its creation and operation, over several decades, remains a remarkable event in the history of foreign policy lobbying in the Congress."[16] The rise of the China lobby, as embodied in organizations like the Committee for One Million, helps to explain why American presidents and their advisers were always more concerned about the political threat posed by the Right than those on the Left.

In sum, the prevalent social movements and groups during the cold war years together helped to promote and reinforce the development of an anticommunist consensus throughout American society, in electoral and domestic politics, and in the governmental policymaking process. The prominence of these groups contributed to the rise of a powerful president in foreign policy, the expansion of the national security bureaucracy, and the development of an acquiescent and bipartisan Congress—all with strong public support throughout society and the domestic political environment.

Even American **intellectuals,** the traditional dissenters and critics of mainstream society, tended to join the anticommunist bandwagon. For example, the **Congress for Cultural Freedom**—an organization of prominent European and American writers and artists—took a strong anticommunist stand and tended to promote the American way of life in international forums (unbeknownst to most members, it was also heavily funded by the CIA).[17] Clearly, the cold war years were a time in which group politics formed a consensus behind a strong anticommunist foreign policy, and most challenging groups remained on the fringes of American politics.

THE MILITARY-INDUSTRIAL-SCIENTIFIC INFRASTRUCTURE

Before World War II, few institutions within the government or throughout American society were oriented toward foreign affairs and national security. World War II changed this situation dramatically and permanently. Almost overnight, the U.S. government redirected itself to wage a global war in which the military expanded enormously and civilian agencies grew to assist the president in fighting the conflict. This governmental effort, in turn, put the economy and society on a war footing to provide the necessary personnel, equipment, and services to achieve allied victory. Thus, a military-industrial-scientific infrastructure developed throughout society and government to support the war effort.

The national security infrastructure actually had its **origins** long before the 1940s, particularly during World War I when President Woodrow Wilson used the government to mobilize the country for war.[18] However, World War II and the rise of the cold war made this a permanent component of American society. Unlike the aftermath of previous wars in American history, the U.S. military demobilized for only a short time following World War II. With the rise of anticommunism, the United States once more expanded its resources in order to fight a global cold war. This not only resulted in the ascendance of the president in foreign policy and the growth of the foreign policy bureaucracy, but the military-industrial-scientific infrastructure continued to grow during the cold war years and became a permanent part of the American landscape. Thus, the development of the military-industrial-scientific infrastructure played a prominent role in defense politics and the making of U.S. foreign policy during the postwar years.

The **military-industrial complex** is actually a term popularized by President Dwight Eisenhower during his farewell address to the nation. His use of this term did not suggest that there existed a small collection of individuals within the military and private industry who conspired to dominate American national security policy against the wishes of the American people. Rather, Eisenhower understood that the military-industrial complex involved the existence of various segments of society with complementary interests who were mutually dependent on one another and together played a vital role in the politics of U.S. foreign policy. Eisenhower argued that such a complex of private and governmental bureaucratic institutions was an inevitable outcome of a society permanently mobilized for war, embodied in the containment and deterrence policies.

Which organized segments of society comprise the military-industrial complex? *Four major elements exist:*

1. The military establishment within the executive branch;
2. Industry and business;
3. Congress;
4. Academia and the scientific community.

Military-industrial-scientific infrastructure (or national security infrastructure) is a more accurate term than the "military-industrial complex." The latter seems to conjure up simplistic conspiratorial notions and does not capture adequately the important role played by academia and the scientific community.[19]

Each of these organized segments had *complementary interests:* members of the military establishment wanted weaponry and equipment to support containment; industry wanted to expand and make money; members of Congress wanted military bases and defense industry in their districts to provide jobs and votes; and scientists wanted the prestige and prominence that came with large grants and direct involvement in government. These complementary interests supported U.S. foreign policy throughout the 1940s and 1950s. They also developed into a complex web of mutually dependent and cooperative relationships between individuals and groups from these organized segments of society. Ultimately, the general public supported the development of a military-industrial-scientific infrastructure in the name of national security and because it was a key source of employment and prosperity.

As we discussed in chapter 8, "the military establishment" within the executive branch, especially the Department of Defense, grew enormously in size and scope as a result of World War II and the onset of the cold war. Demands for personnel, weaponry, and equipment were equally enormous. The government relied on its own production process, supervised by the Atomic Energy Commission and operated by private industry, for building nuclear weapons (review essay 8.1) "on the nuclear weapons production process). However, the military contracted out to private industry to meet its needs in virtually all other areas from conventional weapons to uniforms to base construction.

Much of American industry became directly involved in equipping the military as a result of the cold war. This transformation began with U.S. entry into World War II, when the production of civilian materials and services changed to military production to defeat Germany and Japan. Large U.S. companies such as General Motors, Chrysler, McDonnell Douglas, and Boeing retooled their assembly lines to produce tanks and bombers rather than cars and commerical airplanes. With the rise of the cold war, these same companies continued working for the government and the Defense Department. By the 1950s, most Fortune 500 companies were **defense contractors** for the U.S. government. Some companies, such as General Dynamics and Rockwell International, became totally dependent on defense production; for other companies, such as General Electric, defense work was only a part of its business. Smaller, local businesses also became involved in defense work through the subcontracting of weapons systems or provision of services at local military bases. Taken together, defense-related industries provided millions of jobs for Americans, gaining the support of organized labor and workers in general. Thus, the permanent cold war economy and a close business-government partnership in defense politics was born.[20]

"Congress" helped to reinforce the networks of relationships that developed in defense politics. Members of Congress had to approve the defense programs and budget for the government. This role gave them considerable power, especially within the Armed Services and Appropriations Committees. In return for political support, members of Congress were able to persuade the Pentagon and defense industry to build military bases and businesses in their states and districts. Not surprisingly, the military came to operate hundreds of bases located in every state, and major weapons systems were typically subcontracted out to dozens of businesses throughout the country. Although many basing and contracting decisions may have been made for sound national security and financial reasons, they also were made in order to win the political support of members of Congress. In this way, members of Congress were able to claim responsibility for economic growth and jobs back home, attracting local constituent support for their reelection.

Although it has typically been de-emphasized in discussions of the military-industrial complex, **academia and the scientific community** represent the final element in the military-industrial-scientific infrastructure. The ties between science and the government date back to the nineteenth century. However, the major drive to bring scientists together to work for the U.S. government began with **the Manhattan Project** effort to develop the atomic bomb during World War II.[21]

Since that time scientists in physics, chemistry, and other "natural sciences" have been employed by government, academia, and research and policy institutes to provide the know-how for designing

weapons and turning ideas into reality. According to Stuart Leslie, "For better and for worse, the Cold War redefined American science. In the decade following the Second World War, the Department of Defense (DOD) became the biggest single patron of American science, predominantly in the physical sciences and engineering but important in many of the natural and social sciences as well."[22] "Social scientists" became heavily involved and provided many of the ideas which became the basis of U.S. national security policy during the cold war years, such as nuclear deterrence theory, the theory of limited war, counterinsurgency warfare, and third-world development strategies for nation building and modernization.[23]

The **militarization of research** was led by the more prominent universities, such as Yale University, Massachusetts Institute of Technology, Stanford University, and the University of California at Berkeley. The University of California, for example, operated the only two facilities responsible for designing nuclear weapons for the U.S. government, Lawrence Livermore Laboratory and Los Alamos Laboratory. Such institutions became heavily involved in conducting military research, received government defense money, and promoted a cold war orientation in their educational curriculum.

Scholarship in international relations proliferated and graduate programs in "international studies" grew to become a key source of recruitment and expertise for U.S. government foreign affairs personnel.[24] The president of the University of Michigan, for example, proudly declared in his annual report for 1958–1959 that "various areas of University teaching have recognized the cold-war struggle and have reflected their concern in our teaching programs." He stressed the importance of new programs emphasizing area studies of third-world regions, such as South Asia and the Middle East. "The Soviet nation has seen with perfect clarity," the president triumphed, that "knowledge through research . . . is the secret of our greatness."[25]

The militarization of research raises serious questions about the purpose and nature of higher education. As Senator J. William Fulbright so forcefully reminded us a generation ago: "When the university turns away from its central purpose and makes itself an appendage to the Government, concerning itself with techniques rather than purposes, with expedients rather than ideas, dispensing conventional orthodoxy rather than new ideas, it is not only failing to meet its responsibilities to its students; it is betraying a public trust."[26] This is a fear that President Eisenhower voiced in his farewell address, as will be discussed below.

In sum, the 1940s and 1950s resulted in the formation of a large military-industrial-scientific infrastructure involving millions of people and the support of most segments of American society. Close and mutually supportive networks of relationships developed between the military establishment, industry, Congress, and the scientific community, particularly among more prominent groups and individuals. These relationships were reinforced by the development of a **revolving door** system through which members of the military were hired by defense industry upon retirement, defense industry leaders were appointed to important positions within the Department of Defense, and so on.[27] The net result of these activities was that each organized segment of society could claim that its activities contributed to strengthening American national security while they were enmeshed in the "politics of national defense":

> The influence of politics on national defense is so pervasive, so deeply embedded at every level, that it becomes difficult even to identify. Virtually every American is involved, directly or indirectly. Selfish political and economic interests in military affairs are often carefully wrapped in the American flag, and defended with the most elegant, sophisticated, and technically complex rationales. . . . Politics influences literally thousands of decisions that constantly must be made to create the treaties, strategies, forces, bases, and weapons that collectively make up our national defense.[28]

The development of a national security infrastructure and the politics of national defense not only contributed to the development of the anti-

communist consensus and a permanent large military establishment in support of the requirements of the containment strategy during the cold war era, but this also contributed to waste, corruption, vested interests, and resistance to any challenges to the status quo (review, for example, the section in chapter 8 on defense waste and inefficiency). This also had a major impact in exacerbating the tensions between the demands of national security and the requirements of democracy. Eisenhower was aware of this possibility and, therefore, in his **farewell address** to the country he warned Americans to be "knowledgeable and alert" concerning the consequences of a military-industrial complex for the functioning of American democracy. (See **essay 16.2** on Eisenhower's farewell address about the military-industrial complex.

THE FOREIGN POLICYMAKING ESTABLISHMENT

The cold war years also saw the rise of a foreign policy establishment. This was not a formal group of individuals per se but consisted of an informal network of like-minded individuals who shared an anticommunist consensus and served in high-level policymaking positions within the executive branch. In other words, the **foreign policy establishment** produced much of the high-level personnel and expertise that provided the basis of U.S. foreign policy throughout the cold war years. Much has been written on the cold war era foreign policymaking establishment in the last three decades. They have been referred to as the "best and the brightest," "national security managers," and "wise men." Godfrey Hodgson, in "The Establishment," argues that *the foreign policy establishment can be defined by a history, policy, aspiration, instinct, and technique.*[29]

The "history" of the foreign policy establishment dates to efforts by a small group of individuals associated with President Woodrow Wilson and his aide Colonel Edward M. House, to combat the rising tide of isolationism following Senate defeat of the League of Nations treaty in 1920. However, the crucial event in the formation of the foreign policy

ESSAY 16.2
EISENHOWER'S FAREWELL ADDRESS ABOUT THE MILITARY-INDUSTRIAL COMPLEX

On January 17, 1961, President Dwight Eisenhower made his farewell address to the American people, imploring them to be alert and knowledgeable citizens to the threats and opportunities that the United States faced both abroad and at home. It is in this speech that the term "military-industrial complex" was first used as Eisenhower warned Americans of the dangers it posed for the workings of democracy. Because he was retiring from public office, Eisenhower's farewell address may have represented a public airing of his most personal thoughts and feelings.

He began by discussing the importance of having a good working relationship between the president and the Congress, and then he turned "to share a few final thoughts" about U.S. foreign policy. Eisenhower pointed out that, although the twentieth century has produced major wars among the great nations, "America is today the strongest, the most influential, and the most productive nation in the world." At the same time, however, "we face a hostile ideology—global in scope, atheistic in character, ruthless in purpose, and insidious in method. Unhappily the danger it poses promises to be of indefinite duration. . . . But threats, new in kind or degree, constantly arise. I mention only two."

First, he *warned of a permanent military-industrial complex.* "A vital element in keeping the peace is our military establishment. Our arms must be mighty, ready for instant action, so that no potential aggressor may be tempted to risk his own destruction." Yet, as Eisenhower pointed out, "our military organization today bears little relation to that known by any of my predecessors in peacetime, or indeed by the fighting men of World War II or Korea. Until the latest of our world conflicts, the United States had no armaments industry. American makers of plowshares could, with time and as required, make swords as well." But, according to Eisenhower, "we can no longer risk emergency improvisation of national defense; we have been compelled to create a permanent armaments industry

of vast proportions. Added to this, three and a half million men and women are directly engaged in the defense establishment. This conjunction of an immense military establishment and a large arms industry is "new" in the American experience. The total influence—economic, political, even spiritual—is felt in every city, every State house, every office of the Federal government." Although Eisenhower recognized "the imperative need for this development," he also believed that Americans "must not fail to comprehend its grave implications. Our toil, resources and livelihood are all involved; so is the very structure of our society."

Eisenhower, therefore, emphasized the *need for vigilance.* "In the councils of government, we must guard against the acquisition of unwarranted influence, whether sought or unsought, by the military-industrial complex. The potential for the disastrous rise of misplaced power exists and will persist." Eisenhower continued, "We must never let the weight of this combination endanger our liberties or democratic processes. We should take nothing for granted. Only an alert and knowledgeable citizenry can compel the proper meshing of the huge industrial and military machinery of defense with our peaceful methods and goals, so that security and liberty may prosper together."

The second new threat that Eisenhower pointed to was the *role of technology, science and academia and the rise of a scientific-technological elite.* "Akin to, and largely responsible for the sweeping changes in our industrial-military posture, has been the technological revolution during the recent decades. In this revolution, research has become central; it also becomes more formalized, complex, and costly. A steadily increasing share is conducted for, by, or at the direction of, the federal government." This technological revolution has changed the nature of academia and the conduct of science. As Eisenhower explained, "Today, the solitary inventor, tinkering in his shop, has been overshadowed by task forces of scientists in laboratories and testing fields. In the same fashion, the free university, historically the fountainhead of free ideas and scientific discovery, has experienced a revolution in the conduct of research." One of the consequences is that "partly because of the huge costs involved, a government contract becomes virtually a substitute for intellectual curiosity." Given these changes, Eisenhower warned that "the prospect of domination of the nation's scholars by federal employment, project allocations, and the power of money is ever present—and is gravely to be regarded. Yet, in holding scientific research and discovery in respect, as we should, we must also be alert to the equal and opposite danger

that public policy could itself become the captive of a scientific-technological elite."

After cautioning Americans to remain knowledgeable and alert to the development of the military-industrial complex and the rise of a scientific-technological elite, Eisenhower ended his farewell address by stressing the need to ultimately overcome war, negotiate and compromise, and find peace among the peoples of the world. Progress in reducing the cold war was crucial in Eisenhower's thinking because the future of American society and democracy was ultimately at stake.

SOURCE: U.S., President Dwight D. Eisenhower, "Farewell Address," (January 17, 1961).

---

establishment was World War II. "It was the war which brought together *the three groups which make up the modern foreign policy establishment:* the internationally-minded lawyers, bankers and executives of international corporations in New York; the government officials in Washington; and the academics."[30] They were initially recruited to staff the ever-expanding national security bureaucracy and meet the war effort in the War Department, the State Department, and the OSS (Office of Strategic Services). It wasn't long before many of these people began to interact with each other and work together, forming working networks of relationships.

With the rise of anticommunism and increasing American global involvement following the war, many of the same people became involved in government efforts to fight the cold war through agencies like the National Security Council, Department of Defense, CIA, and throughout the national security bureaucracy. According to Hodgson, "Each of the great decisions of American policy in the Truman years tied these same ties tighter. Bankers and professors took time off to work in the administration on the Marshall Plan, on NATO, or on rethinking strategic policy. A trickle of academics and lawyers began to go down to Washington as consul-

tants, especially on these international programs."[31] Thus, the foreign policymaking establishment was born.

The foreign policy establishment should not be confused with the upper class, although "it may help you to rise in the establishment if you have inherited wealth, or family connections with powerful men in it, or an Ivy League education."[32] Most individuals who became members of the foreign policymaking establishment actually had upper-middle class backgrounds. The "GI Bill" after World War II was particularly consequential in enabling young men of modest means to attend "Harvard, Yale, or other prestigious universities" where one could study law or international relations—key routes to foreign policy prominence. Nor should the foreign policy establishment be confused with a conspiracy by a small group of individuals to control the government. Rather, the foreign policy establishment consisted of hundreds of individuals of varying degrees of prominence who came to know each other (or of each other) and worked together through governmental service, work outside the government, and through social interaction.

The "policy" emphases of the foreign policy establishment were anti-isolationism and anticommunism. "The American opponents of isolationism, to a man, felt that appeasement had been a disaster, and that the lesson to be drawn from the struggle against Fascism was that there were those in the world who could only be restrained by force."[33] This approach to foreign policy was heavily conditioned by **a realpolitik, or power politics view** of the world where states competed for power, where threats to international stability and order came from unsatisfied and revolutionary great powers, and the threat and use of force was considered the most effective instrument of statecraft.[34]

Individuals of the establishment were particularly concerned with the threat of the Soviet Union and communist expansion, especially in Europe, but had little fear of domestic communism. At the same time, these characteristics distinguished them from the political Right, such as the China lobby and McCarthyism, who were not only preoccupied with communist expansion throughout the world, but at home as well. Nevertheless, such a power politics and anti-Soviet view of the world helps to account for the "national security ethos" that arose within government in the making of U.S. foreign policy.

The "aspiration" of the foreign policy establishment was quite simply the **moral and political leadership of the world**. According to Hodgson, "the American establishment wanted to succeed Britain as the military and economic guarantor and moral leader of an enlightened, liberal, democratic, and capitalist world order."[35] Members of the establishment felt that the postwar years represented "the American century" and they relished exercising the unprecedented economic, military, and political power of the United States throughout the world. As previously discussed about political culture and national style in chapter 14, there was a strong sense of American confidence and exceptionalism that permeated Americans. It's not by accident that America's foreign policymaking elite have been referred to as *The Best and the Brightest* and *The Wise Men*.[36]

This reached its height under President John F. Kennedy and the "New Frontier," and in the competition with the Soviet Union and Premier Nikita Khrushchev for the destiny of the world, in which

the United States was "committed to the cause of the new American empire, in bringing proof that our system was better than theirs." As stated by David Halberstam, "They carried with them an exciting sense of American elitism, a sense that the best men had been summoned forth from the country to harness this dream to a new American nationalism, bringing a new, strong, dynamic spirit to our historic role in world affairs, not necessarily to bring the American dream to reality here at home, but to bring it to reality elsewhere in the world."[37]

Such an attitude exemplified what J. William Fulbright would shortly call *An Arrogance of Power*.[38] Or as theologian Reinhold Neibuhr stated during the 1950s, such an "illusion of American omnipotence is a natural mistake of a commercial community which knows that American hegemony is based upon our technical-economic power but does not understand the vast complexities of ethnic loyalties, of social forces in a decaying agrarian world, of the resentments which a mere display of military power creates among those who are not committed to us."[39]

The establishment's "instinct" was for the political center. "The characteristic men of the establishment—Stimson, McCloy, Acheson, Rusk, Bundy—have always seen themselves as the men of judicious, pragmatic wisdom, avoiding ideology and steering the middle course between the Yahoos of the right and the impractical sentimentality of the left."[40] This reflected a long tradition going back to Teddy Roosevelt, of "an aristocracy come to power, convinced of its own disinterested quality, believing itself above both petty partisan interest and material greed." Hence, they "preferred to view their role as service."[41] And occupying the political Center during the cold war years meant that the establishment represented the anticommunist consensus of the era, while trying to avoid the wrath of the political Right.

The establishment's "technique" was to operate out of public view and within the executive branch, especially the White House. Individuals of the foreign policy establishment were usually appointed by the president to policymaking positions within the foreign policy bureaucracy. They constantly revolved back and forth between government and the private world, continuing to interact informally and through membership in prominent foreign policy groups, most notably the Council on Foreign Relations (review essay 16.1). They virtually never ran for elective office. In fact, they **tended to be distrustful and fearful of mass opinion**, adhering to an elitist view of how U.S. foreign policy should be made as discussed in the chapter on public opinion (for example, recall their opposition against isolationism, which was prevalent among the mass public before and immediately after World War II).

Thus, for Hodgson the foreign policy establishment consisted of "a self-recruiting group of men (virtually no women) who have shared a bipartisan philosophy towards, and have exercised practical influence on, the course of American defense and foreign policy."[42] This is not to assert that the foreign policy establishment was monolithic. "Differences existed" and considerable infighting over U.S. foreign policy took place. However, these were largely tactical differences existing within an overall anticommunist, realpolitik, and interventionist consensus. With regard to American policy toward Vietnam, for example, debates were limited to when and how to intervene: now or later? With advisers or troops? Therefore, "right up to 1965, the year of decision, the overwhelming consensus of the establishment accepted without moral or intellectual doubt that the war would have to be escalated—if the only alternative was losing it."[43]

By the 1950s, therefore, the foreign policy establishment represented an informal network of prominent individuals who shared the assumptions of the anticommunist consensus and exerted a great influence on the making of U.S. foreign policy. By constantly shifting between high-level positions in government and the private world they also provided a critical bridge between the president, the national security bureaucracy, and key groups and institutions throughout American society. Therefore, the rise of national security and cold war-oriented groups, the development of a military-industrial-scientific infrastructure, and the growth of a foreign policy establishment dominated group politics at virtually all levels of society and were critical elements in the politics of U.S. foreign policy during the cold war years.

THE POST–VIETNAM WAR AND POST–COLD WAR YEARS

. . . .

Group politics changed considerably during the post–Vietnam War years. The ideological and foreign policy consensus was challenged initially from the political Left and then from the political Right. In order to understand the collapse of the consensus and its implications for group politics and U.S. foreign policy, one must briefly discuss the rise of liberalism and the new Left during the 1960s and early 1970s, embodied in the civil rights and antiwar movements, and the rise of conservative movements and the Right during the 1970s and 1980s.

THE CIVIL RIGHTS AND ANTIWAR MOVEMENTS

The rise of liberalism and the new Left began in the late 1950s with the rise of the **civil rights movement.** The movement began when groups such as the Southern Christian Leadership Conference (SCLC) under the leadership of Martin Luther King, Jr. and the **Student Nonviolent Coordinating Committee** (SNCC) and thousands of blacks demonstrated for civil rights in the South. Many white liberals, especially students from northern schools and groups such as Students for a Democratic Society (SDS), joined the fight for civil rights during the early 1960s as the movement expanded into the North to address issues of racism and poverty.[44]

The bulk of the civil rights movement represented a "nonviolent" liberal approach to reforming American society. However, the often violent resistance by more extreme segments of the public, established groups, and local governments in the North and the South embittered many of the protesters and radicalized them. This politicization and **radicalizing process** was reinforced by the lack of support for the movement from the Democratic party and the federal government under the leadership of John Kennedy and Lyndon Johnson. Thus, the civil rights movement was accompanied by the "growth of black nationalism and black power," represented by Malcolm X and the Black Panthers.

Although the Civil Rights Act was passed in 1964 and Johnson initiated the War on Poverty, these actions were perceived by many blacks as too little, too late. Black frustration and despair at local resistance, in fact, reached the boiling point, triggering "riots" in Los Angeles, Detroit, and other urban areas throughout the country. Therefore, what began as a liberal hope to bring black Americans into mainstream society ultimately ended with Americans bitterly divided, contributing to the collapse of the liberal-conservative ideological consensus.

A second issue, the Vietnam War, generated the **antiwar movement** during the mid-1960s. The antiwar movement represented a broad coalition of Americans united against escalation and continuation of the war. Many participants in this movement had been involved in, and heavily influenced by, the civil rights movement. The antiwar movement grew from a few dozen disparate groups, during the early 1960s, to represent a loose coalition of well over a thousand groups by the late 1960s. This coalition included a wide variety of groups, such as Quakers, pacifists, students, the old peace movement, Democrats, liberals, and the old Left and new Left. At its height, the antiwar movement was supported by a large segment of society and staged "peaceful" demonstrations involving millions of people throughout the country. Not only did over half a million men refuse to be drafted, but more and more soldiers went AWOL (Absent Without Leave) and service people joined the peace marches as well.[45]

Like the civil rights movement, the antiwar movement represented the rise of challenging movements and groups reflecting the resurgence of liberalism and the ascendance of a new Left. Furthermore, the Johnson administration's continuing escalation of the Vietnam War and the domestic resistance encountered by the antiwar movement embittered and radicalized some of the more active participants and groups. Radicalization led them to question the wisdom of working within the system and relying on nonviolence.[46] Thus, by the late 1960s *opposition to the war took many forms:*

> letters to congressmen and Presidents; advertisements in newspapers; signatures on petitions; vigils in town centers, at government buildings, installations, and other public places; lobbying congressmen; working to elect candidates sympathetic to the cause; tax refusal; draft refusal; desertion from the armed forces; nonviolent civil disobedience resulting in arrest, jailing, and court trials; nonviolent civil disobedience met by tear-gassing and/or violence from police and troops; legal mass marches and rallies of tens and hundreds of thousands of people; strikes on campus or at the workplace; draft board raids to destroy records—burning them or pouring blood on them; illegal, violent acts such as trashing, burning buildings or setting off bombs; suicide.[47]

Things culminated in **1968** as events fed one another: the Tet Offensive in Vietnam; Eugene McCarthy's strong showing in the New Hampshire Democratic primary relative to President Johnson; LBJ's withdrawal from the Democratic presidential nomination; Robert Kennedy's declaration for the Democratic presidential nomination on a platform favoring American de-escalation in Vietnam; the assassination of Martin Luther King, Jr.; urban riots; mass student demonstrations on campuses; and the assassination of Robert Kennedy after his victory in the California primary against Vice President Hubert Humphrey. It seemed like the country was being torn apart at the seams. For the antiwar movement it was a time of considerable hope and fear.

Then came Chicago and the **1968 Democratic National Convention**. While Hubert Humphrey was being nominated by the convention on a ticket supporting LBJ's Vietnam policies, a war was raging in the streets between the Chicago police, the Illinois National Guard, and the FBI against demonstrators opposed to the war and opposed to such Democratic leaders as Mayor Richard Daley and Hubert Humphrey. Events in Chicago further alienated and radicalized members of the antiwar movement, moving them away from the Democratic party and the workings of the political system. It also served to further splinter an unbelieving public who was watching the war at home on television. As a result, much of the public—the so-called "silent majority"—would turn against the demonstrators and toward Richard Nixon, the Republican presidential nominee.

The antiwar movement, the rise of liberalism, and the growth of the new Left actually *peaked in 1972*, with the nomination of George McGovern as the Democratic presidential candidate. As with the rise of conservatism and the Right during the late 1940s and early 1950s, the forces of liberalism and the new Left were unable to fundamentally alter American society or capture control of the government. Nevertheless, the size and intensity of the antiwar movement politicized the issues surrounding the Vietnam War. Pressures by the antiwar movement helped generate majority support in favor of American withdrawal and motivated President Nixon's "Vietnamization" program to bring American soldiers home and placate a war-weary public.[48]

The civil rights and antiwar movements also were responsible for *generating new social movements and politically active groups* in areas such as feminism, native American and Hispanic rights, gay rights, consumer rights (and Ralph Nader), and environmentalism.[49] Many women, for example, were active in the civil rights movement, the antiwar movement, and the new Left. The experiences of these "activist women" were an important element in the mobilization of the modern-women's movement.[50] The movements in favor of pro-choice, nuclear freeze, human rights, anti-apartheid, and sanctuary for Central American refugees that arose in prominence since the 1970s are legacies of the civil rights and antiwar movements.[51] Overall, liberalism and the new Left became an active and influential force in group and domestic politics during the post–Vietnam War years. (See **essay 16.3** for a discussion of the American old and new left.)

THE RESURGENCE OF CONSERVATIVE MOVEMENTS AND THE RIGHT

The events and social movements of the 1960s also contributed to the **resurgence of movements and groups reflecting conservatism and the political Right**. Conservatives and members of the political Right were aghast over the loss of Vietnam to communism, the increasing power of the Soviet Union relative to the United States, the growth of government intervention in the economy and the welfare state represented by President Johnson's Great Society programs, the rise of individualism and sexual promiscuity, and the decline of law and order. Whereas the liberal and new Left social movements prevalent during the 1960s had felt that American society and government policies were inconsistent with the moral and cultural values embodied in the Declaration of Independence and the Constitution, conservatives believed that America was in a state of "moral decline" caused by the rise of liberalism and the Left. Consequently, conservatives began to organize and become politically active. This activity was reinforced by the election of Nixon to the presidency, which enabled many conservatives to become members of the administration. Hence, social movements representing broad coalitions of conservative-oriented groups within society arose in support of anticommunism, private enterprise, and social issues such as school prayer and anti-abortion.[52]

As with the rise of liberalism and the new Left, religious groups and forces played a prominent role in the rise of conservatism and the political Right. **The Christian Right** and religious fundamentalists, such as Jerry Falwell and Pat Robertson and other televangelists, took to the airwaves. They were dedicated to defeating "secular humanism" through the promotion of anticommunism and religious behavior throughout society. As with the growth of liberalism and the Left, the rise of conservatism produced more extremist elements. For example, some religious fundamentalists wanted to change the United States into a theocracy—a religious state; and other groups on the far right attempted to promote change through violence.[53]

ESSAY 16.3
THE OLD AND THE NEW LEFT

The 1960s resulted in the rise of the new Left in American politics. But what is the new Left? How does it differ from the old Left? For most Americans, these political labels are confusing. Nevertheless, it is important to understand these ideological differences in order to comprehend the evolution of American politics and its impact on foreign policy.

The "old Left" involves the period from the late nineteenth century until the 1950s, when American socialist thought and socialist groups dominated the political Left in American politics. During the early twentieth century until the end of World War I, democratic socialism predominated among the political Left. **Democratic socialists** envisioned a fully democratic society in which the economy was responsive to all its citizens. Adherents of democratic socialism were particularly critical of capitalism and big business, which they saw as the key sources of unemployment, poverty, and inequalities of wealth and political influence.

Although never representing more than a minority of Americans, democratic socialism did have a base of support within the mass public and grew in popularity during the 1910s. While business, established groups, and the government fought the rise of socialism, democratic socialists nevertheless had some success in fighting for the rights of workers and in gaining office in American politics. By 1912, in fact, the Socialist Party of America, led by **Eugene Debs**, received nearly a million votes in the presidential election and had elected over 1,200 members to public office throughout the country. However, with American entry in World War I, democratic socialists and others on the political Left declined in popularity as a result of the political conformity and repression imposed by the government and its supporters during and after the war.

With the success of the Bolshevik revolution in 1917, **American communism** grew within the political Left and began to overshadow democratic socialism. During the 1920s, the Soviet Union was often portrayed, especially by American communists, as a worker's paradise where the principles of Marxism were being implemented by the Soviet government and its citizens. This strong sense of identity with the Soviet Union was reinforced by the Great Depression, which devastated the American and European economies and impoverished large masses of people, as predicted by most critics of capitalism. As we have discussed in previous chapters, the mass public turned to more liberal and leftist solutions in pulling the country out of the depression. This period was the height of popularity and influence of the old Left in American politics, for both American communism and noncommunist democratic socialism. American "intellectuals" were particularly attracted to Marxist thought and the American communist movement during the Great Depression years.

With the success of New Deal policies and World War II, growing divisions between different socialist groups, and the rise of the cold war during the 1950s, the old Left declined as a potent political force and fell victim to McCarthyism and the resurgence of conservatism and the political Right. Yet, the growth of the civil rights and anti-Vietnam War movements during the 1960s eventually produced a new Left, which grew in popularity and influence in American politics.

A variety of different sources gave rise to **the new Left.** Many leaders and activists of the new Left were young students who were heavily influenced by their educational experiences, especially in college. While some were the children of socialist parents, known as "red diaper babies," most were the sons and daughters of Roosevelt, Truman, and Kennedy supporters who were instilled with a belief in modern American liberal values. Yet, when they compared their values and life experience to events occurring around them, such as the American war in Vietnam and the prevalence of segregation and racism in America, the contradictions between American ideals and reality politicized and radicalized them.

Whereas the old Left was predominantly socialist in orientation, the "new Left" was predominantly nonsocialist. The new left actually consisted of a variety of different groups and coalitions of individuals, some of whom were politically oriented, while others were more culturally oriented. Those within the new Left who were *more politically oriented*, such as the Students for a Democratic Society (**SDS**), attempted to bring about political change at the local and national level through "participatory democracy" in order to make American society more democratic and just for its inhabitants. The young student activists were both influenced and joined by "religious and secular groups" that were motivated to address issues of civil rights, powerlessness and alienation, inequality, and poverty, thereby embodying a "long historical tradition" within the American political Left. Religious influences, such as Quakers and Jews, were reinforced by the role of pacifist thought and groups, which represented another important historical tradition within the political Left and provided a key element of the antiwar movement and the new Left.

Those within the new Left who were *more culturally oriented* emphasized the need to change American consciousness, beliefs, and ways of life in order to promote individual freedom throughout the country. They were critical of the conformity, rigidity, and "uptightness" of mainstream society and argued instead for greater individualism and emotional spontaneity in thought and lifestyle. They were influenced by the lifestyle of the "beats" during the 1950s and many turned to non-Western sources of thought, such as Buddhism and Hinduism. Not surprisingly, they were referred to as the "**counterculture**" because of their criticism of mainstream societal norms and

lifestyles. Whatever was unacceptable within mainstream society was considered "in" within the counterculture: long hair, informal and flamboyant clothes, premarital sex, illegal drugs, rock music, and so on. Countercultural enclaves were carved out around the country, often near college campuses and in urban areas, such as the Haight-Ashbury district in San Francisco and Telegraph Avenue in Berkeley. The 1960s and 1970s also resulted in an increase of "communal" living, both in cities and in isolated rural areas.

The *growth of the new Left achieved mixed success.* On the one hand, the new Left was unsuccessful in fundamentally changing American society and U.S. foreign policy in accordance with its values. Ultimately, the new Left was too disparate, poorly organized, politically naive, and unappealing—especially symbolically—to the mass public beyond the youth culture. On the other hand, the new Left did contribute to the collapse of the anticommunist and liberal-conservative ideological consensus that dominated the cold war years, precipitating many of the changes in American politics that have occurred in the post–Vietnam War period. Some of the values, lifestyles, and concerns of the new Left (such as environmentalism) have become normal parts of contemporary mainstream society (although often commercialized by the market system). Furthermore, although most members of the new Left have gotten older and live more mainstream lives, many continue to maintain a similar ideological (although much more pragmatic) orientation and they continue to play important political roles through their jobs, as parents, and as citizens—a trend which is reflected in the proliferation of political activism and group activity in support of liberal and new Left causes.

SOURCES: Milton Canton, *The Divided Left: American Radicalism 1900–1975* (New York: Hill & Wang, 1978); Albert Fried, ed., *Socialism in America: From the Shakers to the Third International* (New York: Columbia University Press, 1992); Godfrey Hodgson, *America in Our Time* (New York: Vintage, 1976); Maurice Isserman, *If I Had a Hammer . . . The Death of the Old Left and the Birth of the New Left* (New York: Basic Books, 1987); Kenneth Keniston, *Young Radicals: Notes on Committed Youth* (New York: Harcourt, Brace, and World, 1968); Harvey Klehr, *The Heyday of American Communism: The Depression Decade* (New York: Basic Books, 1984); Lawrence Lader, *Power of the Left: American Radical Movements Since 1946* (New York: W.W. Norton, 1979); Keith Melville, *Communes in the Counterculture: Origins, Theories, Styles of Life* (New York: William Morrow, 1972); and James Miller, *Democracy Is in the Streets: From Port Huron to the Siege of Chicago* (New York: Simon and Schuster, 1987).

The influence of conservative social movements reached its "height in the late 1970s and early 1980s," represented by the election of Ronald Reagan to the presidency. Overall, conservatives and the political Right have become more influential throughout society and within government. The mass public also has tended to become more responsive to the symbolic and nationalist appeals of the Republican party, especially in the South. Conservatives, like the liberals before them, nevertheless have been unable to establish a new consensus behind their ideological view of the world.

CONSEQUENCES
FOR GROUP POLITICS

In sum, the liberal-conservative ideological consensus that dominated the cold war years collapsed during the 1960s and 1970s and was replaced by greater ideological, electoral, and group competition in American politics. Particularly in foreign policy, the social movements that arose from the Left and Right shattered the anticommunist consensus. The breakdown of the foreign policy consensus *affected the post-Vietnam role of group politics in the making of U.S. foreign policy in three ways,* with two of the patterns representing change and one representing continuity:

1. The foreign policy establishment collapsed;
2. There was a proliferation of groups, ideological diversity, and political activism;
3. At the same time, the military-industrial-scientific infrastructure continued to pervade society.

Thus, some cold war patterns continued but were accompanied by new patterns of change. These patters have for the most part continued into the post–cold war years.

As stated by David Truman in *The Governmental Process,* "Any considerable increase in the types of such groups, or any major change in the nature of their interrelationships will be reflected subsequently in the operation of the political system."[54]

These changes in group politics had the contradictory impact during the post–Vietnam War and post–Cold War years of providing the president with greater leeway to influence the direction of U.S. foreign policy, while simultaneously posing greater domestic constraints on his ability to exercise power.

Collapse of the Foreign Policy Establishment. The last time individuals within the foreign policy establishment would operate with a consensus and act in unison was in March of 1968. The war in Vietnam was going badly and the country was being torn apart at home. As he had in the past, President Johnson convened a meeting of his major advisers and a group of senior policy advisers from outside the government, or **"Wise Old Men"** as they came to be called. Johnson met with this collection of prominent individuals, representing members of the foreign policy establishment from as far back as the Truman administration, to decide what to do about U.S. policy in Vietnam. "Dean Acheson was there, and Arthur Dean, George Ball and McGeorge Bundy, Douglas Dillon, Robert Murphy and Cyrus Vance, all down from New York. The President's friend Abe Fortas, then a Supreme Court Justice, was there, and so were two legendary generals from World War II: Omar N. Bradley and Matthew B. Ridgeway." Others were present "by virtue of the office they held in the Administration: Dean Rusk, Clark Clifford, Richard Helms of the CIA, Walt Rostow, Nicholas Katzenbach, Henry Cabot Lodge, Paul Nitze, Averell Harriman, Arthur Goldberg and the older Bundy brother, Bill." In effect, the participants represented a who's who of the foreign policy establishment.[55]

These prominent individuals withdrew their support for further escalation of the war. As described by Godfrey Hodgson, "Deeply discouraged by the way military victory was receding like a mirage into the future; impressed by the passionate opposition to the war they encountered in their children, their law partners, their banking correspondents, and their contacts of every kind across the country; aghast at what might happen to the threatened dollar on the world's exchanges; faithful, finally, to its instinct for the center: the establishment made a characteristic decision not to put good money after bad."[56]

This signified the beginning of the end for the foreign policy establishment. By the early 1970s, the foreign policy establishment was *"bitterly divided" over Vietnam* and the future of U.S. foreign policy. Walt Rostow and Dean Rusk, Johnson's national security adviser and secretary of state, continued to believe that the war was justified and that no major avoidable mistakes had been made in the way it was waged. Others, such as McGeorge Bundy, Kennedy's national security adviser, believed that the war was justified, but that mistakes were made in its conduct. However, some members of the establishment, such as Clark Clifford, adviser to Truman and secretary of defense under Johnson, believed that the Vietnam War was a mistake. Others, like Paul Warnke and George Ball, high-level Johnson officials in the Defense and State Departments, held that the Vietnam War was not only a mistake, but that the pursuit of containment in a non-European context was misguided as well. Finally, people like Daniel Ellsberg, a prominent Defense Department official, believed that containment and U.S. intervention throughout the world was not only inappropriate, but a fundamentally unjust policy as well.

The consensus in foreign policy views of the establishment had collapsed and splintered, contributing to the ideological and foreign policy diversity that would permeate among the elite and mass public.[57] Thus, the foreign policy establishment not only contributed to American escalation in Vietnam, but shattered in the war's aftermath. These prominent individuals within American society would continue to receive attention and exercise influence, but they would no longer do so as a unified force in support of America's cold war policies. Instead, they would compete with each other for influence in the making of U.S. foreign policy by choosing sides in the group politics of the post–Vietnam War era.[58]

Expansion in Group Politics. The rise of social movements of the Left and Right not only led to the collapse of the anticommunist consensus and the foreign policy establishment, it led to the expansion of group politics as well. The events and movements of the 1960s and 1970s, fed by a weakening of American political parties discussed in the previous chapter, resulted in the proliferation of new and old groups in American politics, in increased ideological diversity and competition among groups and in more individual political participation in social movements and group politics.[59]

During the 1970s and 1980s, "liberal and Left-leaning groups" actively supported a U.S. foreign policy that promoted human rights and self-determination, arms control and disarmament, the eradication of third-world hunger and poverty, anti-apartheid and global environmentalism—a more liberal internationalist orientation to world politics. "Conservative and right-wing groups" emphasized expansion of Soviet power and communism, the need for a U.S. defense buildup, and support for third-world allies and market economies abroad—a more conservative internationalist orientation. Hence, the cold war consensus years were replaced by considerable fragmentation and competition in group politics. This fragmentation prompted more Americans to actively attempt to influence American politics and U.S. foreign policy.

Established "foreign policy groups" such as the Carnegie Endowment for International Peace, Council on Foreign Relations, Foreign Policy Research Institute, and Rand Corporation continued to function and were complemented by new groups such as the Trilateral Commission. However, these centrist groups were now joined by more conservative groups, such as the American Enterprise Institute, Heritage Foundation, Hoover Institution, Center for Strategic and International Studies, a new Committee on the Present Danger, the Joseph Coors and John Scaife Foundations, and the Heritage Foundation. In addition, more liberal groups increasingly became prominent and were formed, including the Arms Control Association, Brookings Institution, Center for Defense Information, Institute for Policy Studies, World Policy Institute, and Worldwatch Institute. These institutions also have been joined by those advocating a semi-isolationist orientation, such as the Cato Institute.

By the late 1960s and early 1970s, old think tanks began to grow and new ones were established, and they were increasingly prone to take independent policy initiatives (as opposed to rely on contract work). Overall, of the nearly one hundred or so policy research groups or think tanks in Washington, D.C. (some having fewer than a dozen employees, and others employing up to 250), two-thirds were set up after 1970. "Every year, these institutes conduct thousands of conferences, luncheons, forums, and seminars, while publishing hundreds of books and innumerable pamphlets, reports, newsletters, backgrounders, and occasional essays. In addition, their members write scores of op-ed articles that appear in dozens of newspapers, and their most articulate fellows perform as commentators on radio and television news programs, often coast-to-coast."[60] The net result is that foreign policy expertise and personnel was no longer monopolized by a few old establishment groups, a development which reflected greater ideological diversity, among intellectuals as well, of the post–Vietnam War years (see **table 16.1** for a list of the most prominent groups or **"think tanks"** involved in foreign policy).[61]

Other types of groups involved in the politics of U.S. foreign policy were characterized by similar developments where new groups sprang up and groups representing different ideological positions became active. The older, conservative "veterans associations," for example, were now accompanied by the more liberal Vietnam Veterans Association.

As the anticommunist and free trade consensus shattered in the aftermath of the Vietnam War and the Bretton Woods international economic system no longer functioned as originally intended, *labor and business (and governmental) interests increasingly splintered*. For instance, the AFL-CIO, still very anticommunist, turned increasingly against free trade (such as the contemporary U.S.-Mexico free trade negotiations) in order to protect American jobs as foreign economic competition increased. Within the business community, "domestic-oriented companies" began to push for protectionist measures by the government as large **American multinational corporations (MNCs)** became the champions of free trade. Furthermore, while an international business-government partnership characterized the cold war years, American MNCs began to dissociate themselves from the U.S. government, especially in light of third-world nationalism and the exposure of CIA activities abroad.[62]

Not surprisingly, as business interests have multiplied, their *presence in Washington, D.C.,* also has grown substantially. Before World War II there weren't a dozen trade associations in town; by the 1960s, however, about one hundred corporations and one thousand trade associations maintained offices in Washington; and by 1986 there were over 1,300 corporations and 3,500 trade associations lobbying government and promoting their special interests. In fact, over 80,000 people in Washington worked for trade associations alone.[63] These numbers have, if anything, been increasing into the 1990s. Thus, business interests continue to exert a heavy influence on governmental policies, but in a much more complex and contradictory fashion than prevailed during the cold war years.

"Religious and ethnic groups" continued to play a prominent role in U.S. foreign policy. Conservative groups, such as the Moral Majority and other fundamentalist organizations, became more active. This activity was matched by more liberal groups, such as the National Council of Bishops and the Christic Institute. In the 1970s and 1980s, for instance, Catholic missions and layworkers in Latin America, along with Quakers and such groups as the World Council of Churches, provided a "credible and legitimate voice of opposition" to the Reagan Administration's Central American policies for they were respected on Capitol Hill for the accuracy of their data on human rights abuses. Such activity also contributed to the rise of the sanctuary movement in the United States for refugees fleeing Central America.[64]

Although the old China lobby declined as a force—as evident in the establishment of diplomatic relations with the People's Republic of China in 1978—*new ethnic groups* grew in prominence. "Cuban-American" groups remain very hostile to Fidel Castro and any normalization in American-Cuban relations; "Greek-American" groups promoted the American embargo of Turkey during the

TABLE 16.1
MAJOR FOREIGN POLICY THINK TANKS IN THE 1990s

NAME LOCATION	YEAR BEGAN	ISSUE ORIENTATION	IDEOLOGICAL ORIENTATION
Carnegie Endowment for International Peace Washington, DC	1910	Foreign	Liberal
Foreign Policy Association New York	1918	Foreign	Centrist
Hoover Institution Palo Alto, CA	1919	Domestic & Foreign	Conservative
Council on Foreign Relations New York	1921	Foreign	Centrist
Brookings Institution Washington, DC	1927	Domestic & Foreign	Liberal
American Enterprise Institution Washington, DC	1943	Domestic & Foreign	Conservative
Rand Corporation Santa Monica, CA	1948	Domestic & Foreign	Centrist
Aspen Institute Washington, DC	1951	Foreign	Liberal
Foreign Policy Research Institute Philadelphia	1955	Foreign	Conservative
Hudson Institute Indianapolis	1961	Domestic & Foreign	Conservative
Center for Strategic & International Studies Washington, DC	1962	Foreign	Conservative
Institute for Policy Studies Washington, DC	1963	Domestic & Foreign	Liberal
Center for Defense Information Washington, DC	1972	Foreign	Liberal
Trilateral Commission New York	1973	Domestic & Foreign	Centrist
Heritage Foundation Washington, DC	1974	Domestic & Foreign	Conservative
World Watch Institute Washington, DC	1974	Foreign	Liberal
Cato Institute Washington, DC	1977	Domestic & Foreign	non-Internationalist
Institute for International Economics Washington, DC	1981	Foreign	Liberal
Carter Center Atlanta, GA	1982	Domestic & Foreign	Liberal
World Policy Institute New York	1983	Foreign	Liberal

1970s; and Black American groups played an important role in the anti-apartheid forces leading to U.S. sanctions against South Africa. **The so-called Jewish lobby**, which includes a variety of individuals and groups such as the American Israel Public Affairs Committee (AIPAC), is widely considered the most powerful of all the ethnic groups. This lobby is credited with having gained the backing of members of Congress to provide unwavering support and assistance to the state of Israel. Consistent with interest group patterns in the post–Vietnam War years, however, events in the Middle East during the 1980s have made Jewish-Americans less than a cohesive and homogeneous force, and have seen the development of an Arab lobby as well.[65]

The proliferation of groups and their increasing ideological diversity helps account for **the group politics of Iran-Contra**. For example, in order to circumvent the congressional ban on U.S. governmental assistance to the Central American contras, the Reagan administration turned to various private anticommunist groups for support. These groups included General John Singlaub's American Anti-Communist League, Carl Channel's right-wing fundraising groups, and General Richard Secord's business organizations involved in the arms trade (refer to essay 9.2 on the secret contra war). At the same time, liberal and left-wing groups, as just discussed, were active in criticizing the Reagan administration's Central American policies and raising public awareness of the illegal covert assistance that the Reagan administration was providing to the contras. Groups critical of the Reagan administration's Central American policy were far from completely successful in gaining their goals. However, their activities eventually did contribute to illuminating the Iran-Contra affairs which rocked the Reagan presidency after the 1984 reelection victory.

A similar situation evolved in **the group politics of the Persian Gulf crisis**. After President Bush's announcement in early August that over one hundred thousand American troops were to be dispatched to the Persian Gulf, new and old political activists and peace groups already in place, going back to the Vietnam War and recently engaged in the nuclear freeze and anti-apartheid movements, were activated in opposition to the administration's military response and fear of another major war. Following the November elections, when Bush announced that he was doubling American troops to over four hundred thousand and was abandoning economic sanctions in favor of an offensive policy of brinksmanship to coerce Iraq to withdraw from Kuwait through the threat of war, the country splintered and "the peace movement" grew. New supporters were attracted from all cross-sections of the country, many who before were politically passive, and the peace movement came to represent a sizable segment of the public. The growing crisis and likelihood of war also activated counter-demonstrations and a significant movement in support of the president's policies. Yet unlike the Vietnam War years, the political debate was conducted with much greater civility and the participants were able to separate the politics of the crisis from support for the troops—the true heroes and victims of war. Nevertheless, this "politicized" domestic environment was critical in escalating dissent and triggering congressional action. Ultimately, President Bush was successful in acquiring a majority vote in Congress in support of his policies, but the narrowness of his victory was symbolic of the fluidity of public opinion and group politics that have constrained the president's ability to govern since Vietnam.

The newest form of interest group gaining prominence in U.S. foreign policy has been consulting firms and foreign lobbies. **Consulting firms** representing different clients, in particular corporations, have proliferated since the 1970s. Henry Kissinger, for example, founded the consulting firm **Kissinger Associates** in 1982. For annual fees reported to start at one hundred thousand dollars, clients, which include some of the largest multinational corporations in the world, meet with Kissinger and his associates to get information about world politics and gain access to policymakers around the world. Two of Kissinger's associates, Brent Scowcroft and Lawrence Eagleberger, subsequently became President Bush's national security adviser and deputy secretary of state. As part of Kissinger Associates, Scowcroft received over five hundred thousand dollars a year to represent over seventy companies, including major American defense contractors. Eagleberger received over seven hundred thousand dollars to represent sixteen clients (whose identities were not disclosed) and act as president of Kissinger Associates.[66]

Closely related to the rise of consulting firms is the growth of **foreign lobbies** through which foreign governments (and private interests) attempt to influence American domestic politics and the policymaking process. Foreign lobbies rely heavily on Americans such as consulting firms, law firms, and advertising firms, and operate in a similar fashion as domestic pressure groups. In fact, foreign lobbies have existed throughout American history and often work closely with their domestic counterparts, such as ethnic groups. The Jewish lobby, for example, has always had strong ties with the state of Israel.[67]

Among the most prominent contemporary examples of the foreign lobby are Saudi Arabia and Japan. The Japan lobby is quite multifaceted, ranging from cultural organizations that try to promote favorable American attitudes toward Japan (such as the Japan Foundation) to professional economic organizations (such as the Japanese Economic Institute of America) and direct lobbying activities that represent Japanese business interests. Concerning the latter, according to journalist John Judis, "the Japanese alone have hired about 125 former government officials. These include two of the last three special trade representatives, three of the last four Democratic National Committee chairmen, and the last two Republican chairs."[68] South Africa alone, before the fall of apartheid, had sixteen American firms working for it in the 1980s compared to five a decade prior.[69]

Such "Americans for hire" not only provide information and political access for foreign interests, they also attempt to influence the political agenda and the general political environment. For example, "lobbyists for foreign firms often appear on television or are quoted as objective experts in the press without revealing that they have a vested interest in the opinions they express."[70] Yet, the activities of foreign lobbyists are actually routine practice today. It is estimated that over a thousand American firms

or individuals represent foreign interests from all over the world.

It is not surprising, in this regard, that foreign governments would attempt to influence policymakers, including incumbent presidents such as Bill Clinton. In fact, in **the case of China**, according to Judis, "increasingly, many of our most distinguished and, in theory, disinterested, experts on U.S. China policy are selling their reputations and knowledge to clients with very particular business interests in China. Almost every prominent former government official who speaks out on this subject, regardless of party affiliation, has direct or indirect financial ties to China." For example, "Kissinger, Vance and Eagleburger each have business ties to China. Kissinger is the founder of a firm, Kissinger Associates, which helps its corporate clients secure business in China; Vance is a corporate lawyer who chaperones clients seeking outlets in China; and Eagleburger, once the president of Kissinger Associates, now works for a Washington law firm where he has also helped businessmen secure contracts in China."[71]

Obviously, the close ties between interest groups and the U.S. government (and foreign officials) raise important questions concerning "personal" and "national" **conflicts of interest**, and ethical (and legal) behavior. These issues were illustrated clearly when **Michael Deaver**, deputy chief of staff and close friend to President Reagan, was convicted of perjury in federal court for lying about his lobbying activities in policy areas in which he was previously involved as a government official (an activity prohibited by law for just "one year"). Upon resigning from public office in 1985, Deaver immediately established his own consulting firm that represented domestic clients, such as Rockwell International, and foreign clients, such as the governments of Canada, South Korea, and Panama. In fact, a 1986 General Accounting Office study found seventy-six former high-level federal officials representing foreign interests from fifty-two countries after leaving office during the period from 1980 to 1985.[72]

Such revolving-door behavior is not uncommon within the Washington political community, as discussed earlier in this chapter, and the military establishment. **Clark Clifford**, former Truman adviser and Secretary of Defense under LBJ, is probably the most prominent political player to have fallen victim to charges of ethical and legal violations.[73] Such a result is actually the exception to the rule, given the weakness of lobbying and conflict of interest laws, and the normalcy of such political behavior (for example, review essay 15.1 on money, campaigning, and politics).

Kissinger Associates was, for example, also a part of **the U.S.-Iraq Business Forum** during the 1980s: a conglomeration of predominantly large American corporations—such as Amoco, Bell Helicopter, Caterpillar, General Motors, Mobil, Westinghouse, Xerox—responsible for increasing business and trade with the Iraqi regime, thus contributing to Saddam Hussein's buildup of his military into a regional threat. With its officers and staff based in Washington, D.C., the Iraqi-Business Forum pressured the Reagan and Bush administrations to continue to provide government credits and loan guarantees to Iraq and oppose congressional sanctions, despite Iraq's terrible human rights record. Nevertheless, when Iraq invaded Kuwait in 1990, Henry Kissinger, acting as former national security adviser and secretary of state, was a leading proponent to expel Iraq with the use of force.[74]

All of these conflicts of interest, most of which are not well known, raise all sorts of questions about "the practice" of American democracy.[75] What Judis concludes about all the linkages between China and former (and current) government officials may speak to a larger truth:

Perhaps more important, the new China hands could have a corrosive effect on American democracy. In foreign policy debates, average Americans, as well as many of their political representatives, often defer to prominent former officials whom they believe speak disinterestedly for the national interest. When the public becomes aware that they are also speaking for the interests of their business clients, the cynicism about how important policy decisions are made will deepen. This, together with revelations about the Clinton Commerce Department and presidential campaign, and a growing anxiety about the role of money, especially foreign money, in American politics, could precipitate a crisis of political confidence.[76]

At a minimum, it will feed the apathy and cynicism that is all too prevalent among much of the public already.

Beyond attempting to influence domestic politics and government policymaking, the **international activities of private groups** affect the conduct and making of U.S. foreign policy. As Michael Doyle has demonstrated in *Empires,* throughout world history settlers, missionaries, merchants, and commerical companies, in addition to diplomats, soldiers, and officials—each with their own interests and mode of operation—have acted as **"agents of foreign policy."**[77] Likewise, Emily Rosenberg has highlighted the important role such agents played during the expansion of United States foreign policy abroad from 1890 to World War II, especially those more economically and culturally oriented.[78] Such international activities by private groups are often quite pervasive and visible in foreign countries, especially smaller third-world countries, affecting how foreign elite and mass publics perceive and act toward the United States.

Most noticeable in this regard, as discussed above, have been the *missionary activities* of American religious organizations and the *business activities* of American multinational corporations (MNCs). The business activities of American corporations abroad, for example, represent about 20 percent of the total output of all American companies.[79] In fact, the gross sales of the largest American MNCs are greater than the gross national products (GNP) of most third-world countries (see **table 16.2** on this). Thus, the mere presence of American religious groups and, in particular, big business abroad affect the politics of U.S. foreign policy.

TABLE 16.2
REVENUES OF LARGEST U.S. CORPORATIONS RELATIVE TO VARIOUS COUNTRIES' GNP

CORPORATION (RANK) OR *COUNTRY*	REVENUES OR GNP (IN $BILLIONS)	CORPORATION (RANK) OR *COUNTRY*	REVENUES OR GNP (IN $BILLIONS)
United Kingdom	1,027	**Hewlett-Packard (20)**	32
Brazil	580	*Morocco*	30
India	287	**Pepsico (21)**	30
Taiwan	238	*Kuwait*	28
Poland	206	**Met Life Insurance (22)**	28
General Motors (1)	169	**Amoco (23)**	28
Indonesia	168	**Motorola (24)**	27
Ford (2)	137	*Bangladesh*	26
Iran	125	**American Int'l Group (25)**	26
Saudi Arabia	121	**Conagra (26)**	24
Exxon (3)	110	**Kroger (27)**	24
Wal-Mart Stores (4)	94	**Dayton Hudson (28)**	24
Czech Republic	81	**Lockheed Martin (29)**	23
AT&T (5)	80	**United Technologies (30)**	23
Greece	78	**Allstate (31)**	23
IBM (6)	72	**Fed Natl Mortgage Assn (32)**	22
General Electric (7)	70	*Cuba*	22
Malaysia	67	**Merrill Lynch (33)**	22
Mobil (8)	67	**J.C. Penney (34)**	21
Philippines	66	**United Parcel Service (35)**	21
Hungary	64	**Dow Chemical (36)**	21
Venezuela	58	*North Korea*	21
Chrylser (9)	53	**Bankamerica Corp. (37)**	20
Philip Morris (10)	53	**GTE (38)**	20
Pakistan	51	**International Paper (39)**	20
Peru	49	**Boeing (40)**	20
Egypt	42	**Xerox (41)**	19
Prudential Insurance (11)	41	**Cigna (42)**	19
Nigeria	41	**Johnson & Johnson (43)**	19
State Farm Group (12)	41	**Loews (44)**	19
Du Pont (13)	38	**American Stores (45)**	18
Texaco (14)	37	**Pricecostco (46)**	18
Bulgaria	37	**USX (47)**	18
Sears Roebuck (15)	35	*Sri Lanka*	12
Kmart (16)	35	*El Salvador*	9
Procter & Gamble (17)	33	*Kenya*	7
Chevron (18)	32	*Ethiopia*	5
Citicorp (19)	32	*Tanzania*	2

SOURCES: "500 Largest U.S. Corporations," *Fortune,* 29 April, 1996; *U.S. Statistical Abstract,* 1996.

But other types of private groups are active abroad as well. Many private consulting firms and individuals, for instance, sell their services to foreign governments to provide advice on domestic and foreign policies. Such activity has become particularly noticeable **in Eastern Europe** with the end of the cold war, a region in which many American firms and individuals currently are instructing Eastern Europeans on the operation of democracies and market economies.

The international activities of **private voluntary organizations (PVOs)**, such as CARE, Catholic Relief Services, and Lutheran World Relief, many religion affiliated, have proliferated since Vietnam as well. Although they originated primarily as relief organizations during and immediately after World War II and focused most of their attention on the war-torn countries of Europe, over the past thirty years these and newer PVOs have diversified their activities and geographical focus to emphasize emergency and developmental assistance to third-world countries. In 1981, over 125 U.S. PVOs received over $740 million from the United States Agency for International Development (AID) in support of their overseas work—a ten-fold increase since 1964.[80] Even "private individuals," such as former President **Jimmy Carter**, through the Carter Center in Atlanta, have pursued their own foreign policy agendas abroad (which has increased his public approval since he left the oval office). It is through such international activities that private groups and individuals affect the making and conduct of U.S. foreign policy.

In sum, the post–Vietnam War and post–cold war years have been accompanied by the proliferation of interest group and social movement activity in foreign policy. Older cold war-oriented groups have been joined by more liberal and conservative groups. Ideologically motivated groups have been joined by hundreds of other groups representing specialized interests, including business, ethnic, and foreign interests. Such *groups have flocked to Washington, D.C.,* which explains the explosion of lobbyists (365 officially registered in 1961, over 23,000 by 1987), lawyers (the District of Columbia Bar Association listed roughly 12,000 members in 1961 and

over 45,000 in 1987), and journalists (1,500 were accredited to congressional press galleries in 1961, over 5,200 in 1987).[81]

These social movements and interest groups *try to influence the political agenda and policymaking process in a variety of specific ways:* by gaining access to policymakers and participating in policymaking; having individuals appointed to governmental positions; providing information; contributing campaign funds and other money; actively campaigning; engaging in litigation; demonstrating; attracting media coverage; networking with other groups; and attempting to gain general public support. The decline of the Soviet threat and the collapse of communism in Eastern Europe in a post–cold war global environment has accentuated these patterns in group politics.

As political scientist Chung-in Moon makes clear, groups typically engage in four general **lobbying strategies** in American politics:[82]

1. The access to power approach;
2. The technocratic approach;
3. The coalition-building approach;
4. The grass-roots mobilization approach.

In the "access to power" approach, interest groups use high-powered power brokers, law firms, public relations firms, and consultants to gain direct access to top policymakers within the government. The "technocratic" approach is another form of direct lobbying, in which groups retain lawyers and technical consultants who use their expertise and contacts to influence mid-level decision makers in government, the media, and other relevant groups in society. The other two lobbying strategies used by groups and social movements attempt to affect the policymaking process more indirectly by targeting electoral politics and domestic politics in general. The "coalition-building" approach emphasizes the formation of group alliances based on mutual interests in order to politicize issues, get issues on the political agenda, and place pressure on the government's policymaking process. Finally, the "grass-roots mobilization" approach attempts to rally mass support in order to politicize issues, affect electoral and group politics, and increase public pressure on the policymaking process. As Hedrick Smith points out in *The Power Game,* the old game of **"inside" politics** within the Washington community has been supplemented by a new game of **"outside" politics** in the post–Vietnam War era.[83]

Social movements and groups are politically active because of their potential impact on domestic politics and, more specifically, on the government's policymaking process. With respect to Congress, for example, a study by the Congressional Research Service found that:

> Groups come to represent significant allies, or formidable opponents, when they are well organized; when they represent a sizable, well-educated, and middle- to upper-class constituency and when the positions they wish members of Congress to support are viewed as mainstream and respectable, entailing little or no political cost, and some political gains (e.g., support for Israel, Greece, Taiwan, Ireland, etc.); when the groups confront no significant internal counterlobbies in the private sector, or can count on the neutral stance of much of the public when an opinion is yet unformed.[84]

As Smith explains, "to politicians, lobbyists, lawyers, journalists, staff aides, and high-level policymakers, access is bread and butter. . . . Without it, your case doesn't get heard; you can't be a player in the power game. Obviously that's why corporations, unions, and lobbyists of all sorts pay enormous fees for prestigious Washington lawyers or pump millions into campaigning. They are buying access, if not more."[85]

Overall, the expansion of group politics allows one to better understand the making of U.S. foreign policy. One of the major implications of this, as stated by Thomas Mann in "Making Foreign Policy," is that "conflict between the President and Congress must be seen as a consequence of a broader set of developments affecting America's place in the world and domestic political interests and processes." The cold war consensus years in group politics have been replaced by group competi-

tion for public support and control of the government. Domestic politics have become more divisive, complex, and fluid. Therefore, Mann concludes, "it is no wonder that the President today occupies a less than dominant position in American foreign policy."[86]

Continuation of the Military-Industrial-Scientific Infrastructure. Although the foreign policy establishment collapsed while groups proliferated and became more diverse, a massive military-industrial-scientific infrastructure still pervades the government and American society. The military establishment continues to require weaponry and other services, private industry manufactures and supplies weapons and material, Congress approves the programs and appropriates the funds that provide jobs and votes back home, and members of the scientific community still offer national security expertise and advice.[87] The major difference is that, in the absence of the anticommunist consensus, the national security infrastructure no longer operates in a highly supportive domestic political environment. Instead, the institutions and activities of the military-industrial-scientific infrastructure are more likely to be challenged in the domestic politics of the contemporary era—this began following the Vietnam War and has intensified with the collapse of the Soviet Union and the end of the cold war.

While defense spending represents a smaller percentage of the federal government's budget and the domestic economy since Vietnam, the national security infrastructure remains huge and is embedded in American society. According to a *Los Angeles Times* analysis on the U.S. defense establishment during the 1970s and 1980s, "the jobs of one out of ten Americans depend directly or indirectly on defense spending. The Pentagon is the largest single purchaser of goods and services in the nation. Defense industries account for 10 percent of all U.S. manufacturing. In certain states, including California, defense-related employment is the largest single source of personal income. Defense employs more than 25 percent of all the nation's scientists and engineers."[88] Throughout the 1980s the federal government continued to devote the largest share of its budget to defense spending—roughly 30 percent. Defense products, such as arms, also accounted for over one-third of American exports abroad.

Many **local communities and economies** remain heavily dependent on defense spending. During the late 1980s, for example, the Pentagon spent over $5 billion in South Carolina, a state with roughly 3 million people and a gross domestic product of roughly $50 billion at the time. According to an article in *The State* newspaper entitled "Military Might: Military Installations Give Firepower to S.C. Economy," defense spending in the state primarily involved local defense firms, the Savannah River nuclear weapons plant, and military research and development (for example, at the major universities). Most importantly, defense spending supported the state's "eight" military bases through military and civilian payrolls, construction and related services, and materials equipment and supplies. According to the thinking of South Carolina state officials at the time, "military bases, in general, are relatively stable elements in South Carolina's economy, a virtually recession-proof 'industry' that provides steady employment and training in high-tech skills while bringing to their respective communities a civic-minded crew of service volunteers that often choose to retire in South Carolina."[89]

The **"pork barrel" politics** of defense spending also has become more sophisticated. For example, hundreds of private defense think tanks, lobbying offices, corporate government relations offices, and law firms specializing in military contracts have sprung up around Washington, D.C., in order to lobby for defense spending and support the military establishment; these groups are known as **"Beltway Bandits."** According to the Fairfax County Office of Economic Development, during the 1980s over 620 high-tech firms with 47,000 employees, more than 70 percent of whom work on defense-sponsored projects, were located in the four northern Virginia cities closest to Washington.[90]

And the "revolving door" system remains alive and well. As Gordon Adams documents in a definitive study of *The Iron Triangle*, "Our review of DOD data showed that 1,942 individuals (uniformed and civilian) moved between DOD/NASA and the eight [largest defense] companies between 1970 and 1979. Of these, 1,672 were hired by the companies, while 270 company employees went to work for DOD and NASA."[91] These types of developments have intensified the mutually supportive networks existing between members of the military establishment, Congress, and private industry at national and local levels.

As explained by David Wood in the *Los Angeles Times,* "the story of **the B-1** provides a casebook example of how the military-industrial complex works, how the personal, professional, political and economic interests of thousands of individuals and institutions in government and the defense industries intertwine to influence what America does in the name of national security."[92] The Air Force wanted a new bomber to replace the B-52 since the late 1950s. However, critics emphasized the B-1's cost, limited capabilities, and unclear mission. Not surprisingly, the bomber project was started and stopped half a dozen times during the 1960s and 1970s in response to the political dynamics of the times. Nevertheless, "the Air Force battled Presidents, Secretaries of Defense, and members of Congress for more than thirty years to build a new bomber."[93] For three years beginning in 1975, air force and Rockwell International officials planned, coordinated, and executed a major political campaign on behalf of the struggling B-1 bomber program, which was on the verge of cancellation. The company urged its 114,000 employees and holders of its 35 million shares of stock to write to their members of Congress. More than "three thousand" subcontractors and suppliers in forty-eight states were also asked to contact Congress concerning the economic impact B-1 production would have on their states and congressional districts.

Under President Reagan, Congress finally agreed to the full-scale production of one hundred B-1s at a cost of almost $500 million per plane. The air force and its supporters not only finally acquired the B-1 bomber, but, to their delight, the B-2 "Stealth" bomber as well (at a cost of over $1 billion per plane). In *Wild Blue Yonder: Money, Politics, and the B-1 Bomber,* Nick Kotz concluded that over the years "the Air Force and its allies in science, industry, labor, and politics have relentlessly pursued their goals—and other groups have opposed them. On both sides, the motives of patriotism, financial gain, career ambition, political aggrandizement, and loyalty to an institution or idea were often so mixed that it is hard to tell what was narrow self-interest and what was concern for the national good."[94]

Once approval is given for its production, the geography and politics of production virtually guarantees the future of a weapons system such as the B-1 bomber. Although Rockwell International was awarded the $40 billion-plus contract, as many as 5,200 subcontractors were involved in the forty-eight continental states. These subcontractors included most of the large defense contractors, such as Boeing, TRW, Westinghouse, General Electric, Goodyear, Singer, Sperry, Bendix, Martin Marietta, Northrop, Litton, Westinghouse, IBM, and others. Unions such as the United Auto Workers and the Machinists were also involved. "Contract spreading" involved as many as 400 of 435 congressional districts. For many Americans, this meant jobs—good-paying jobs. Thus, thousands of individuals and groups at the local and national level had a vested interest in providing support for B-1 production (see **figure 16.2** on the geographic contract spreading of the B-1 bomber).

The military-industrial-scientific infrastructure is so embedded in the U.S. government and American society that weapons systems and defense spending seem to acquire lives of their own. According to David Packard, deputy secretary of defense in the Nixon administration and chair of President Reagan's 1986 blue-ribbon commission on defense management, "There are strong perverse incentives for Congress, the military services, and defense contractors to play games with the budget to accommodate pet projects. Programs are kept alive to satisfy parochial, not national, interests and are introduced without realistic notions of future costs. In this environment, coherent long-range budget planning has become impossible."[95] Instead, the tendency is to

produce what James Kurth in "Why We Buy the Weapons We Do" has called **"follow-on" and "bail-out" imperatives** for weapons systems and major defense contractors in the weapons acquisition process.[96]

The threat of the Soviet Union and communism has been the major justification for over $10 trillion of defense spending from the fifties to the eighties. The collapse of the cold war consensus and the cold war, however, have made the operations of the military-industrial-scientific infrastructure more open to scrutiny, even with all its secrecy. As waste, corruption, and threats to human health have become common knowledge, national security infrastructure operations increasingly have been challenged (review, for example, essay 8.2 on the Pentagon scandal). In this respect, the supportive political environment that existed during the cold war years has been replaced by an environment in which groups increasingly fight over the legitimacy and consequences of the national security infrastructure.

From the perspective of those dependent on the national security infrastructure for their livelihood, the end of the cold war represents a bad omen. The defense budget has faced cuts and the military has been forced to downsize. This also has led to greater "concentration" of the defense industry. For example, in 1997 Boeing Company (with $20 billion in revenues—about one-third military oriented) acquired McDonnell Douglas Corporation (with $15 billion in revenues—about two-thirds military oriented) in a $14 billion deal, the tenth-largest merger in American history and the largest ever in the aerospace industry. Boeing Company replaced Lockheed Martin Corporation as the world's largest aerospace company and makes it the only manufacturer of commercial jets in the United States.[97]

Such concentration raises serious questions about the future of defense politics. According to Lawrence Korb, former Assistant Secretary of Defense in the Reagan administration, in the 1990s "after 22 mergers, there will be only two mega-companies—Lockheed Martin and Boeing McDonnell Douglas—and three "major" companies, Hughes,

FIGURE 16.2
THE GEOGRAPHY OF THE B–1 BOMBER

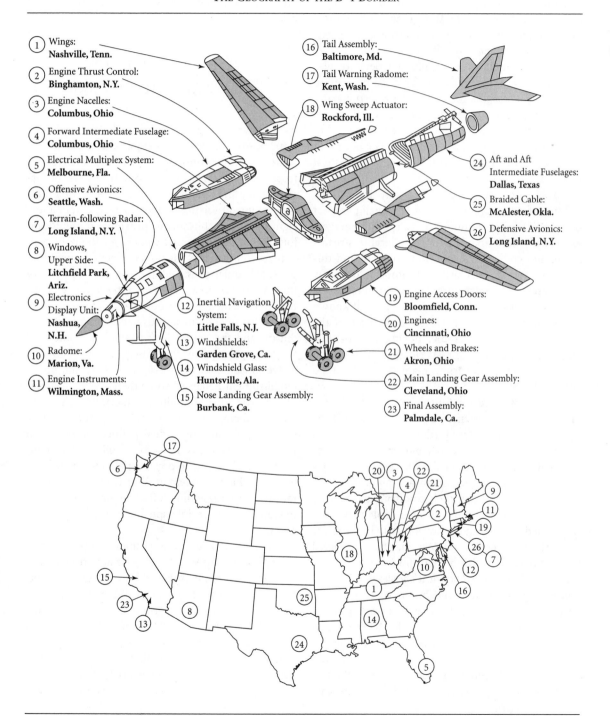

SOURCE: Mickie Garrett, *Los Angeles Times.*

Raytheon and Northrop." The likelihood of another mega-merger among the remaining major companies is pretty high in order to maintain competitiveness. And, unbeknownst to most taxpayers, the federal government has contributed to such mergers and concentration by interpreting federal regulations in a way that allows defense companies to charge the Pentagon for the cost of carrying out these mergers. The previous "Lockheed [Corporation] Martin [Marietta] merger alone is estimated to have cost the taxpayers $1.8 billion." The net result is a few mega-companies with "tremendous political clout."[98]

These defense mergers not only impact the politics of defense, they also have a major impact on people and communities. Corporate mergers are usually accompanied by considerable streamlining and cutbacks, to minimize overlap and duplication and to cut costs. The impact for many employees, subcontractors, and communities is likely to be quite profound, but often is not known for months, maybe even years. At the time of the recent merger, for example, Boeing had 145,000 employees and McDonnell Douglas had 64,000 employees located in various plants throughout the country.[99]

For the foreseeable future, some will argue in favor of "higher" defense cuts, while some will be opposed. To what extent further cuts are warranted and will occur will likely depend on the extent to which the military and civilian leadership successfully promote its two regional wars military strategy and Americans feel that their country's national security is threatened (and how large a role they think the United States should play abroad). The military triumph in the Persian Gulf War may have alleviated some of the calls for further cuts for a while.

Nevertheless, hard political choices are required concerning the amount and importance of defense spending. These choices have serious consequences, not only for the government, but for the economy, hundreds of local communities, and the livelihoods of thousands of individuals that have become dependent on the military-industrial-scientific infrastructure. These choices are not likely to get any eas-ier as the United States enters the twenty-first century (see **essay 16.4** on the politics and economics of base closures).[100]

GROUP POLITICS TOWARD THE FUTURE
....

As we have seen, group politics, like electoral politics, has experienced considerable change, as well as some important continuities, from the cold war era to present. Following World War II, the rise of foreign policy and cold war-oriented groups, of a military-industrial-scientific infrastructure, and of a foreign policy establishment provided a significant foundation and domestic context for the politics of anticommunism and the policy of containment that prevailed under presidential leadership. The rise of the civil rights, new Left, and antiwar movements, however, challenged the dominance of presidential power, the liberal-conservative anticommunist consensus, and the national security ethos of the cold war years. Along with the subsequent rise of conservative movements and the Right, the foreign policy establishment collapsed while there was a proliferation of new and old groups in American politics, increased ideological diversity and competition among groups, and more individual political participation in social movements and group politics. This contributed to a decline in presidential power in foreign policy in the post–Vietnam War era while the military-industrial-scientific infrastructure continued to operate in a more inhospitable domestic environment.

The patterns of group politics that prevailed in the post–Vietnam War era thus far have been accentuated with the end of the cold war. In order to better understand the historical evolution and future of political participation in group, as well as electoral, politics, we need to briefly examine the exercise of American civil rights and liberties over time. Doing so in the next chapter will allow for a stronger understanding of how the tensions between the demands of national security and democracy have

ESSAY 16.4
THE POLITICS AND ECONOMICS OF BASE CLOSURES

As the Cold War began to wane in the late 1980s, one could hear calls in Washington for a "peace dividend." In brief, this term described the expected budgetary windfalls from the closure and realignment of American military bases and facilities at home and abroad. Additionally, Pentagon planners asserted the need for such actions in order to utilize budget dollars for badly needed research and development, and the procurement of new weapons systems. The only drawback was the economic effect on those communities that depended on the targeted bases for their livelihood. Since 1988, ninety-seven bases have been shut down. In locations where there is nothing on which to fall back (such as tourism), communities have found themselves left out in the cold. These economic impacts and the associated political costs for the elected representatives of the affected communities have produced the current climate of indecision concerning future rounds of closures.

In order to deal with the "hard" political decisions involved over base closings, Congress created an independent commission—the Base Realignment and Closure (BRAC) Commission. The commission was empowered to examine America's basing needs and propose which bases should close—which would go before Congress for a simple "up" or "down" vote. This way all the pork barrel politics, and amendments to save (or enhance) bases in one's district—so much a part of the normal legislative process—would be avoided and overcome (similar to "fast track" legislative trade authority given to the president periodically).

The first round of base closures occurred in 1988. Aimed at reaping budgetary savings from lower maintenance costs, and in turn being able to use those savings in other areas, the BRAC Commission compiled a list of sixteen major bases for closure. These bases were scattered all over the country, from California (particularly hard-hit with four of the sixteen) to New Hampshire. In 1991 a second

BRAC Commission targeted twenty-six more major bases. In 1993 and 1995, twenty-eight and twenty-seven (respectively) more major bases were marked for closure for a total over the seven-year period of ninety-seven.

The pandemonium produced in the targeted communities was considerable. Populations which had relied for years upon the nearby bases for what in some instances was their employer or customer (for various goods and services), were now faced with the prospect of their economic livelihoods jeopardized. The location of the bases had direct bearing upon the potential survivability of the community after the closure. If the base was located in an area with other industry or commercial activity, then the impact of a base closure—though hard on the local economy—could still be weathered. However, if the base was the sole reason for there *being* a community, then the departure of the base and its associated jobs and customers would be devastating and turn the community into a virtual ghost town.

The example of the Charleston Naval Base and Shipyard is an interesting one in this respect. When it was announced in 1993 that the base would be closed, the 8,900 civilian and 29,000 military jobs were immediately in jeopardy. Although the city of **Charleston, South Carolina**, took in a fair amount of tourism dollars annually (and with a metropolitan population approaching half a million), the effect on the local economy of losing so many jobs and the residual income was still considerable. In fact, since 1993 there have been 23,000 jobs lost in the area due to the base closure. Charleston, however, has responded creatively. The naval yard is coming back to life, with more than fifty businesses and federal agencies leasing old buildings and docks. Large-scale development of the base awaits the Navy selling the property and cleaning up the environmental pollution of nearly a century of operation. Although the economic demography will never be the same, Charleston is slowly making progress.

In May 1997, the Pentagon issued as part of their Quadrennial Defense Review (QDR) plans for two more rounds of closures. Again, it was asserted that these new BRAC rounds were necessary in order to secure money for procurement and R&D. Again, the economic tremors were felt all around the country. In localities such as **Sumter, South Carolina**, home of Shaw Air Force Base, the threat to the area's economic livelihood was quite real. The base there accounts for $500 million annually, or fully one third of the community's economy. Shaw AFB is also Sumter's largest employer, providing jobs for 7,100 military and civilian personnel in a city of about 25,000 people.

It seems that after four rounds of base closings, however, the political costs for the elected represen-tatives of these communities is becoming too great. In July 1997, as reported in the *New York Times*, the Senate voted "overwhelmingly to delay the next two rounds of closings until the government can study the economic effect of past and future shutdowns."

Although Secretary of Defense William Cohen, the Joint Chiefs of Staff, and the White House continue to push for the new round of closures, the signal from Capitol Hill is a clear one. No new closures will be put forth until the effects on local economies will be further examined. Also, there appears to be some doubt as to the savings professed by the Pentagon from previous closures. Until such time as these new political-economic concerns are addressed, the economic futures of such places as Sumter, South Carolina, are secure at least for the short term.

SOURCES: Chris Burritt, "Charleston Still Struggling to Replace Old Economy," *The State* (June 1, 1997): A10; Lee Bandy, "Not Again: Sumter Steels Itself" *The State* (June 1, 1997): A1; U.S., Department of Defense, *Major Base Closure Summary* (1997 fact sheet); Jerry Gray, "Senate Delays Military Base Closings," *New York Times* (July 10, 1997): 1; Charles Pope, "2 Military Towns on Alert," *The State* (June 1, 1997): A1, A10.

evolved and how this has affected the politics of U.S. foreign policy.

BIBLIOGRAPHIC ESSAY

· · · · · · · · · · · · · ·

As with the study of political participation and electoral politics, most scholars of U.S. foreign policy traditionally have ignored and dismissed the role of group politics in the foreign policy process. However, changes in the foreign policy process during the post–Vietnam War era have led to serious reconsideration of the role of group politics. A good general overview is *Interest Group Politics*, edited by Allan J. Cigler and Burdett A. Loomis (Washington, D.C.: Congressional Quarterly Press, 1995). William A. Gamson provides an excellent general and conceptual analysis of the nature of group politics in the United States, focusing on the opportunities and outcomes of challenging groups, in *The Strategy of Social Protest* (Homewood, Ill.: Dorsey Press, 1975). I. M. Destler, Leslie H. Gelb, and Anthony Lake, in *Our Own Worst Enemy: The Unmaking of American Foreign Policy* (New York: Simon and Schuster, 1984), and Godfrey Hodgson, in *America in Our Time* (New York: Vintage, 1976), provide excellent overviews of the anticommunist consensus in group politics during the cold war years, the rise and collapse of the foreign policy establishment, and the expansion of group politics in the post–Vietnam War era.

Ross Y. Koen provides an informative account of *The China Lobby in American Politics* (New York: Harper & Row, 1974), while Lawrence P. Frank discusses the power of corporations and their relationship to government in foreign policy during the cold war era in "The First Oil Regime," *World Politics* (July 1985): 586–98. Nick Kotz, in *Wild Blue Yonder and the B-1 Bomber* (Princeton, N.J.: Princeton University Press, 1988), and Patrick Tyler, in *Running Critical: The Silent War, Rickover, and General Dynamics* (New York: Harper & Row, 1986), provide a strong understanding of the military-industrial-scientific infrastructure and the politics of defense spending. Fred Kaplan, in *The Wizards of Armageddon* (New York: Touchstone, 1983), discusses the vital role played by prominent scientists and academics in devising the U.S. government's strategic policy with respect to deterrence and the fighting of nuclear war. For a fascinating portrayal of the foreign policy establishment, see David Halberstam, in *The Best and the Brightest*

(New York: Random House, 1969), and Walter Isaacson and Evan Thomas, in *The Wise Men: Six Friends and the World They Made* (New York: Touchstone, 1986).

An excellent understanding of the rise, orientation, and evolution of the new Left and the counterculture can be found in Maurice Isserman, *If I Had a Hammer . . . The Death of the Old Left and the Birth of the New Left* (New York: Basic Books, 1987); James Miller, *Democracy Is in the Streets: From Port Huron to the Siege of Chicago* (New York: Simon and Schuster); and Keith Melville, *Communes in the Counterculture: Origins, Theories, Styles of Life* (New York: William Morrow, 1972). Insightful analyses of the rise of the conservative movement can be found in Sidney Blumenthal, in *The Rise of the Counter-establishment: From Conservative Ideology to Political Power* (New York: Times Books, 1986), Jerome L. Himmelstein, *The Right: The Transformation of American Conservatism* (Berkeley, Calif.: University of California Press, 1991), and George H. Nash, *The Conservative Intellectual Movement in America* (New York: Basic Books, 1976).

For a good discussion of contemporary group politics, including the role of consulting firms and foreign lobbies, see Joe Conason, "The Iraq Lobby," *The New Republic* (October 1, 1990): 14–17, as well as the work of John Judis such as "The Pressure Elite: Inside the Narrow World of Advocacy Group Politics," *The American Prospect* (Spring 1992): 15–29, "The Contract with K Street," *The New Republic* (December 4, 1995): 18–25, and "Chinatown," *The New Republic* (March 10, 1997): 17–21. A good conceptual discussion of general lobbying strategies can be found in the study by Chung-in Moon, "Complex Interdependence and Transnational Lobbying: South Korea in the United States," *International Studies Quarterly* 32 (March 1988): 67–89. A broad historical context for understanding the expansion of group politics and its implications for the workings of American democracy is addressed by David M. Ricci in *The Transformation of American Politics: The New Washington and the Rise of Think Tanks* (New Haven, Conn.: Yale University Press, 1993).

ENDNOTES

1. For an overview of social movements and interest groups see, for example, Jeffrey M. Berry, *The Interest Group Society* (Glenview, Ill.: Scott, Foresman, 1989); Allan J. Cigler and Burdett A. Loomis, eds., *Interest Group Politics* (Washington, D.C., Congressional Quarterly Press, 1995); Ronald J. Hrebenar and Ruth K. Scott, *Interest Group Politics in America* (Englewood Cliffs, N.J.: Prentice-Hall, 1982); Norman J. Ornstein and Shirley Elder, *Interest Groups, Lobbying and Policymaking* (Washington, D.C.: Congressional Quarterly Press, 1978); David B. Truman, *The Governmental Process: Political Interests and Public Opinion* (New York: Alfred A. Knopf, 1971); and James Q. Wilson, *Political Organizations* (New York: Basic Books, 1973). For a cross-national assessment of political oppositions on regimes and their effect on foreign policy, see Joe D. Hagan, "Regimes, Political Oppositions, and the Comparative Analysis of Foreign Policy," in Charles F. Hermann, Charles W. Kegley, Jr., and James N. Rosenau, eds., *New Directions in the Study of Foreign Policy* (Boston: Allen & Unwin, 1987), pp. 339–65.

2. Truman, *The Governmental Process*, p. xii.

3. James MacGregor Burns, *The Crosswinds of Freedom* (New York: Vintage, 1989), p. 656.

4. William A. Gamson, *The Strategy of Social Protest* (Homewood, Ill.: Dorsey Press, 1975), p. 140.

5. For a brief overview of group politics during this time, see Gabriel A. Almond, *The American People and Foreign Policy* (New York: Praeger, 1965), chapter 8.

6. See, for example, Colin S. Gray, "What RAND Hath Wrought," *Foreign Policy* 4 (Fall 1971): 111–29, and Jerry W. Sanders, *Peddlers of Crisis: The Committee on the Present Danger and the Politics of Containment* (Boston: South End Press, 1983).

7. See, for example, Walter LaFeber, *America, Russia, and the Cold War, 1945–1980* (New York: John Wiley, 1980), pp. 47–48.

8. William Appleman Williams, *The Tragedy of American Diplomacy* (New York: Delta, 1962) and *The Roots of the Modern American Empire* (New York: Random House, 1969). See also William I. Cohen, *Empire Without Tears: America's Foreign Relations, 1921–1933* (New York: Knopf, 1987); David A. Lake, *Power, Protection, and Free Trade: International Sources of U.S. Commercial Strategy, 1887–1939* (Ithaca, N.Y.: Cornell University Press, 1988).

9. U.S., Congress, Senate, *Nomination Hearings Before the Committee on Armed Services* (83rd Cong., 1st sess., 1953), p. 26.

10. Michael B. Stoff, *Oil, War and American Security: The Search for a National Policy on Foreign Oil,*

1941–1947 (New Haven, Conn.: Yale University Press, 1980), p. 208. See also Lawrence P. Frank, "The First Oil Regime," *World Politics* (July 1985): 586–98; G. John Ikenberry, *Reasons of State: Oil Politics and the Capacities of American Government* (Ithaca, N.Y.: Cornell University Press, 1988); and Anthony Sampson, *The Seven Sisters: The Great Oil Companies and the World They Shaped* (New York: Bantam, 1975); Daniel Yergin, *The Prize: The Epic Quest for Oil, Money and Power* (New York: Simon and Schuster, 1990).

11. See Richard J. Barnet, *Roots of War: The Men and Institutions Behind U.S. Foreign Policy* (Baltimore: Penguin, 1971), chapters 6 and 7; Ron Chernow, *The House of Morgan: An American Banking Dynasty and the Rise of Modern Finance* (New York: Atlantic Monthly Press, 1990); Joanne Gowa, "Subsidizing American Corporate Expansion Abroad: Pitfalls in the Analysis of Public and Private Power," *World Politics* 37 (January 1985): 180–203; David Horowitz, *Corporations and the Cold War* (New York: Bertrand Russell Peace Foundation, 1969). On the other hand, Raymond A. Bauer, Ithiel de Sola Pool, and Lewis Anthony Dexter found that business "pressure groups" had limited success in "directly" influencing the specifics of U.S. trade policy in *American Business and Public Policy: The Politics of Foreign Trade* (New York: Atherton Press, 1964).

12. See Steve Fraser and Gary Gerstle, eds., *The Rise and Decline of the New Deal Order, 1930–1980* (Princeton, N.J.: Princeton University Press, 1989); Rhodri Jeffreys-Jones, *The CIA and American Democracy* (New Haven, Conn.: Yale University Press, 1989); and Ronald Radosh, *American Labor and United States Foreign Policy: The Cold War in the Unions from Gompers to Lovestone* (New York: Vintage, 1970).

13. Garry Wills, *Under God: Religion and American Politics* (New York: Simon and Schuster, 1990), p. 25.

14. See James C. Thomson, Jr., Peter W. Stanley, and John Curtis Perry, *Sentimental Imperialists: The American Experience in East Asia* (New York: Harper & Row, 1981).

15. See A. James Reichley, *Religion in American Public Life* (Washington, D.C.: Brookings Institution, 1985); and Mark Silk, *Spiritual Politics: Religion and America Since World War II* (New York: Simon and Schuster, 1988).

16. U.S. Congress, House Commitee on Foreign Affairs, "Foreign Policy Interest Groups as Information Sources," *Executive-Legislative Consultation on Foreign Policy: Strengthening Foreign Policy Information Sources for Congress* (Washington, D.C.: U.S. Government Printing Office, February 1982), p. 45. See also Stanley D. Bachrack, *The Committee of One Million: "China Lobby" Politics, 1953–1971* (New York: Columbia University Press, 1976), and Ross Y. Koen, *The China Lobby in American Politics* (New York: Harper & Row, 1974). Ross Koen's book originally was intended for publication by Macmillan in 1960, but it was suppressed by the politics of the times and the opposition of the China lobby.

17. Peter Coleman, *The Liberal Conspiracy: The Congress for Cultural Freedom and the Struggle for the Mind of Postwar Europe* (New York: Free Press, 1989). See also Seymour Martin Lipset, *Political Man: The Social Bases of Politics* (Garden City, N.Y.: Anchor, 1963), chapter 10, and Richard H. Pells, *The Liberal Mind in a Conservative Age: American Intellectuals in the 1940s and 1950s* (New York: Harper & Row, 1985).

18. See, for example, Wayne Biddle, *Barons of the Sky: From Early Flight to Strategic Warfare, The Story of the American Aerospace Industry* (New York: Simon and Schuster, 1991); Geoffrey Perret, *A Country Made by War: From the Revolution to Vietnam–The Story of America's Rise to Power* (New York: Vintage, 1983); Ronald Schaffer, *American in the Great War: The Rise of the War Welfare State* (New York: Oxford University Press, 1991). For its development during and after World War II, see Daniel Yergin, *Shattered Peace: The Origins of the Cold War and the National Security State* (Boston: Houghton-Mifflin, 1978).

19. For an overview of the military-industrial-scientific infrastructure, see Adam Yarmolinsky, *The Military Establishment: Its Impacts on American Society* (New York: Harper & Row, 1971).

20. See also Seymour Melman, *Pentagon Capitalism* (New York: McGraw-Hill, 1970), and Richard J. Barnet, *The Permanent War Economy: American Capitalism in Decline* (New York: Touchstone, 1985).

21. See Richard Rhodes, *The Making of the Atomic Bomb* (New York: Simon and Schuster, 1986).

22. Stuart W. Leslie, *The Cold War and American Science* (New York: Columbia University Press, 1994), p. 1.

23. For a general overview of the relationship between the scientific community and government, see Bruce L. R. Smith, *American Science Policy Since World War II* (Washington, D.C.: Brookings Institution, 1990). For more specific discussions of the role of scientists and academia in national security affairs, see Noam

Chomsky, *American Power and the New Mandarins* (New York: Penguin, 1967); Gregg Herken, *Counsels of War* (New York: Oxford University Press, 1987); Fred Kaplan, *The Wizards of Armageddon* (New York: Touchstone, 1983); Robert A. Packenham, *Liberal America and the Third World: Political Development Ideas in Foreign Aid and Social Science* (Princeton, N.J.: Princeton University Press, 1973); Warner R. Schilling, "Scientists, Foreign Policy, and Politics," *American Political Science Review* (June 1962): 287–300; D. Michael Shafer, *Deadly Paradigms: The Failure of U.S. Counterinsurgency Policy* (Princeton, N.J.: Princeton University Press, 1988); Christopher Simpson, *Science of Coercion: Communication Research and Psychological Warfare, 1945–1960* (New York: Oxford University Press, 1994).

24. See Stanley Hoffmann, "An American Social Science: International Relations," *Daedalus* (1977): 41–60.

25. In James Miller, *Democracy Is in the Streets: From Port Huron to the Siege of Chicago* (New York: Simon and Schuster, 1987), p. 25.

26. J. William Fulbright, "The War and Its Effects: The Military-Industrial-Academic Complex," in Herbit I. Schiller, ed., *Super-State: Readings in the Military-Industrial Complex,* (Urbana: University of Illinois Press, 1970), pp. 177–78.

27. See, for example, U.S. Congress, General Accounting Office, *DOD Revolving Door* (September 1989).

28. Nick Kotz, *Wild Blue Yonder and the B-1 Bomber* (Princeton, N.J.: Princeton University Press, 1988), p. viii.

29. Godfrey Hodgson, "The Establishment," *Foreign Policy* 10 (Spring 1973): 3–40. See also Kai Bird, *The Chairman: John J. McCloy, the Making of the American Establishment* (New York: Simon and Schuster, 1992); Barnet, *Roots of War;* Peter Grose, *Gentleman Spy: The Life of Allen Dulles* (Houghton Mifflin, 1995); David Halbertstam, *The Best and the Brightest* (New York: Random House, 1969); James G. Hershberg, *James B. Conant: Harvard to Hiroshima and the Making of the Nuclear Age* (New York: Knopf, 1994); Max Holland, "Citizen McCloy," *The Wilson Quarterly* (Autumn 1991): 22–42; Walter Isaacson and Evan Thomas, *The Wise Men: Six Friends and the World They Made* (New York: Touchstone, 1986); John B. Judis, "Twilight of the Gods," *The Wilson Quarterly* (Autumn 1991): 43–55.

30. Hodgson, "The Establishment," p. 8.

31. Ibid., p. 9.

32. Ibid., pp. 6–7.

33. Ibid., p. 9.

34. See E. H. Carr, *The Twenty Years Crisis, 1919–1939* (New York: Harper & Row, 1964); Hans J. Morgenthau, *Politics Among Nations: The Struggle for Power Peace* (New York: Alfred A. Knopf, 1978); and A. F. K. Organski, *World Politics* (New York: Alfred A. Knopf, 1958).

35. Hodgson, "The Establishment," p. 11.

36. Halberstam, *The Best and the Brightest;* Isaacson and Thomas, *The Wise Men.*

37. Halberstam, *The Best and the Brightest,* pp. 100, 41.

38. J. William Fulbright, *The Arrogance of Power* (New York: Vintage, 1966).

39. Reinhold Niebuhr, "The Foreign Policy of American Conservatism and Liberalism," in *Christian Realism and Political Problems,* by Reinhold Neibuhr (New York, Scribner, 1953).

40. Hodgson, "The Establishment," p. 12.

41. Halberstam, *The Best and the Brightest,* p. 49. See also Godfrey Hodgson, *The Colonel: The Life and Wars of Henry Stimson, 1867–1959* (New York: Knopf, 1990); Edmund Morris, *The Rise of Theodore Roosevelt* (New York: Putnam, 1979).

42. Ibid., p. 13.

43. Ibid., pp. 16–17.

44. For an overview of the civil rights movement, see Taylor Branch, *Parting the Waters: America in the King Years, 1954–1963* (New York: Simon and Schuster, 1988), and David J. Garrow, *Bearing the Cross: Martin Luther King, Jr., and the Southern Christian Leadership Conference* (New York: Vintage, 1986).

45. See Charles De Benedetti, with Charles Chatfield, *An American Ordeal: The Antiwar Movement of the Vietnam Era* (Syracuse, N.Y.: Syracuse University Press, 1990); Thomas Powers, *The War at Home: Vietnam and the American People, 1964–1968* (New York: Grossman, 1973); "Protest in the Sixties," *The Annals of the American Academy of Political and Social Science* (March 1969); and Nancy Zaroulis and Gerald Sullivan, *Who Spoke Up? American Protest Against the War in Vietnam 1963–1975* (New York: Holt, Rinehart and Winston, 1984).

46. See John A. Vasquez, "A Learning Theory of the American Anti-Vietnam War Movement," *Journal of Peace Research* 13 (1976): 299–314.

47. Zaroulis and Sullivan, *Who Spoke Up?,* p. xi.

48. See, for example, Melvin Small, "Influencing the Decision Makers: The Vietnam Experience," *Journal of Peace Research* 24 (1987): 185–98.

49. See Burns, *The Crosswinds of Freedom;* Godfrey Hodgson, *America in Our Time* (New York: Vintage, 1976); and Ronald Inglehart, *Culture Shift in Advanced Industrial Society* (Princeton, N.J.: Princeton University Press, 1990). For a general discussion, see Russell J. Dalton and Manfred Kuechler, eds., *Challenging the Political Order: New Social and Political Movements in Western Democracies* (New York: Oxford University Press, 1990).

50. See Sara Evans, *Personal Politics: The Roots of Women's Liberation in the Civil Rights Movement and the New Left* (New York: Vintage, 1979); Jo Freeman, *The Origins of the Women's Liberation Movement* (New York: David McKay, 1975); and Laura Woliver, "Feminism at the Grass Roots: The Recall of Judge Archie Simonson," *Frontiers* 11 (1990): 111–19.

51. See Barbara Epstein, *Political Protest and Cultural Revolution: Nonviolent Direct Action in the 1970s and 1980s* (Berkeley: University of California Press, 1991); Paul Rogat Loeb, *Hope in Hard Times: America's Peace Movement and the Reagan Era* (Lexington, Mass.: Lexington Books, 1987); Steven Metz, "Anti-Apartheid Movement in American Politics," *Political Science Quarterly* 101 (1986): 379–96; David S. Meyer, *A "Winter of Discontent": The Nuclear Freeze and American Politics* (New York: Praeger, 1990); and Douglas C. Waller, *Congress and the Nuclear Freeze: An Inside Look at the Politics of a Mass Movement* (Amherst, Mass.: University of Massachusetts Press, 1987).

52. For an overview of the rise of conservatism and the political Right in American politics, see Sidney Blumenthal, *The Rise of the Counter-establishment: From Conservative Ideology to Political Power* (New York: Times Books, 1986); Alan Crawford, *Thunder on the Right: The "New Right" and the Politics of Resentment* (New York: Pantheon, 1980); Paul Gottfried and Thomas Fleming, *The Conservative Movement* (Boston: Twayne Publishers, 1988); Jerome L. Himmelstein, *The Right: The Transformation of American Conservatism* (Berkeley, Calif..: University of California Press, 1991); George H. Nash, *The Conservative Intellectual Movement in America* (New York: Basic Books, 1976); and Peter Steinfels, *The Neoconservatives: The Men Who Are Changing America's Politics* (New York: Simon and Schuster, 1979).

53. See, for example, Walter H. Capps, *The New Religious Right: Piety, Patriotism, and Politics* (Columbia, S.C.: University of South Carolina Press, 1990); James Coates, *Armed and Dangerous: The Rise of the Survivalist Right* (New York: Noonday Press, 1987); Carol Flake, *Redemptorama: Culture, Politics, and the New Evangelicalism* (New York: Penguin, 1984); Michael Lind, "Rev. Robertson's Grand International Conspiracy," *The New York Times Review of Books* (February 2, 1995): 21–25; Clyde Wilcox, *God's Warriors: The Christian Right in Twentieth-Century America* (Baltimore: Johns Hopkins University Press, 1991).

54. Truman, *The Governmental Process,* p. 52.

55. Hodgson, "The Establishment," pp. 23–24.

56. Ibid., p. 24.

57. For a more in-depth discussion of this process, see Daniel C. Hallin, *The Uncensored War: The Media and Vietnam* (Berkeley, Calif.: University of California Press, 1986).

58. See also I. M. Destler, Leslie H. Gelb, and Anthony Lake, *Our Own Worst Enemy: The Unmaking of American Foreign Policy* (New York: Simon and Schuster, 1984), chapter 2; Isaacson and Thomas, *The Wise Men;* Judis, "Twilight of the Gods".

59. See Cigler and Loomis, *Interest Group Politics;* John B. Judis, "The Pressure Elite: Inside the Narrow World of Advocacy Group Politics," *The American Prospect* (Spring 1992): 15–29.

60. David M. Ricci, *The Transformation of American Politics: The New Washington and the Rise of Think Tanks* (New Haven, Colo.: Yale University Press, 1993), p. 208.

61. See also Destler, Lake, and Gelb, *Our Own Worst Enemy,* chapter 2; William J. Lanouette, "The Private Foundations with a Very Public Role," *National Journal* (February 17, 1979): 256–61; James G. McGann, "Academic to Ideologues: A Brief History of the Public Policy Research Industry," *Political Science* (December 1992): 733–40; James Allen Smith, *The Idea Brokers: Think Tanks and the Rise of the New Policy Elite* (New York: Free Press, 1991); and R. Kent Weaver, "The Changing World of Think Tanks," *Political Science and Politics* (September 1989): 563–78. For a description of the linkage and dynamics between private foreign policy groups and government, see Roger A. Coate, *Unilateralism, Ideology, and U.S. Foreign Policy: The U.S. In and Out of UNESCO* (Boulder, Colo.: Lynne Rienner, 1988), and Sanders, *Peddlers of Crisis.*

62. See Richard J. Barnet and Ronald E. Muller, *Global Reach: The Power of Multinational Corporations* (New York: Simon and Schuster, 1974); Benjamin J. Cohen, *In Whose Interest? International Banking and American Foreign Policy* (New Haven, Conn.: Yale

University Press, 1986); Helen V. Milner, *Resisting Protectionism: Global Industries and the Politics of International Trade* (Princeton, N.J.: Princeton University Press, 1989); Robert A. Reich, *The Work of Nations: Preparing Ourselves for 21st Century Capitalism* (New York: Knopf, 1991).

63. John B. Judis, "K Street's Rise to Power of Special Interest to U.S.," *In These Times* (November 1–7, 1989): 7. See also his "The Contract with K Street," *The New Republic* (December 4, 1995): 18–25.

64. See Allen D. Hertzke, *Representing God in Washington: The Role of Religious Lobbies in the American Polity* (Knoxville, Tenn.: University of Tennessee Press, 1988).

65. See Mitchell Bard, "The Influence of Ethnic Interest Groups on American Middle East Policy," in Charles W. Kegley, Jr., and Eugene R. Wittkopf, ed., *The Domestic Sources of American Foreign Policy: Insights and Evidence* (New York: St. Martin's Press, 1988), pp. 57–69; Kenneth Longmyer, "Black American Demands," *Foreign Policy* 60 (Fall 1985): 3–17; Bill Richardson, "Hispanic American Concerns," *Foreign Policy* 60 (Fall 1985): 30–39; David J. Sadd and G. Neal Lendenmann, "Arab American Grievances," *Foreign Policy* 60 (Fall 1985): 17–30; Smith, *The Power Game*, chapter 9; and U.S. Congress, "Foreign Policy Interest Groups," pp. 38–58.

66. "The Kissinger Clique," *Newsweek* (March 27, 1989): 30–31; "Scowcroft, in Ethics Report, Tells of Consulting Ties to 70 Concerns," *New York Times* (March 15, 1989): 10; and Elaine Sciolino, "Eagleburger Won't Disclose Kissinger's Client List," *New York Times* (November 12, 1989): 17.

67. See Russell Warren Howe and Sarah Hays Trott, *The Power Peddlers: How Lobbyists Mold America's Foreign Policy* (New York: Doubleday, 1977).

68. Judis, "K Street's Rise to Power," p. 7. See also Pat Choate, *Agents of Influence: How Japan's Lobbyists in the United States Manipulate America's Political and Economic System* (New York: Knopf, 1991), Ronald J. Hrebenar and Clive S. Thomas, "The Japanese Lobby in Washington: How Different Is It?" *Interest Group Politics*, edited by Allan J. Cigler and Burdett A. Loomis (Washington, D.C., Congressional Quarterly Press, 1995), and John B. Judis, "The Japanese Megaphone," *The New Republic* (January 22, 1980): 20–25.

69. See Barbara Bradley, "Lobbying for Foreign Interests Is Booming Business in Washington," *Christian Science Monitor* (February 5, 1986): 6; Steven Emerson, "The American House of Saud" (three-part series),

New Republic (February 17, 1982: 18–25; May 19, 1982: 11–16; June 16, 1992: 18–23); Deborah M. Levy, "Advice for Sale," *Foreign Policy* 67 (Summer 1987): 64–86; and Norman J. Ornstein, "Lobbying for Fun and Policy," *Foreign Policy* 28 (Fall 1977): 156–65.

70. Judis, "K Street's Rise to Power," p. 7.

71. John B. Judis, "Chinatown," *The New Republic* (March 10, 1997): 17–18.

72. U.S., Congress, General Accounting Office, *Foreign Representation: Former High-Level Federal Officials Representing Foreign Interests* (July 1986). Lester W. Milbrath, on the other hand, in *The Washington Lobbyists* (Chicago: Rand McNally, 1963), emphasizes the limited amount of corruption and direct influence exercised by lobbyists on policymakers.

73. For his policymaking role from his perspective, see Clark Clifford with Richard Holbrooke, *Counsel to the President: A Memoir* (New York: Random House, 1991).

74. Joe Conason, "The Iraq Lobby," *The New Republic* (October 1, 1990): 14–17.

75. See Ricci, *The Transformation of American Politics.*

76. Judis, "Chinatown," p. 20.

77. Michael W. Doyle, *Empires* (Ithaca, N.Y.: Cornell University Press, 1986). See also Rosenberg.

78. Emily S. Rosenberg, *Spreading the American Dream: American Economic and Cultural Expansion, 1890–1945* (New York: Hill and Wang, 1992).

79. DeAnne Julius, "Foreign Investment and the Big Picture," *New York Times* (September 2, 1990): 13.

80. Bruce H. Smith, "U.S. and Canadian PVOs as Transnational Development Institutions," in Robert F. Gorman, ed., *Private Voluntary Organizations as Agents of Development* (London: Westview Press, 1984), p. 116. See also J. Bruce Nichols, *The Uneasy Alliance: Religion, Refugee Work, and U.S. Foreign Policy* (New York: Oxford University Press, 1988).

81. Smith, *The Power Game*, p. 29.

82. Chung-in Moon, "Complex Interdependence and Transnational Lobbying: South Korea in the United States," *International Studies Quarterly* 32 (March 1988): 67–89.

83. Smith, *The Power Game*, chapter 9.

84. U.S., Congress, "Foreign Policy Interest Groups," p. 38. See also, for example, Thomas M. Franck and Edward Weisband, *Foreign Policy by Congress* (New York: Oxford University Press, 1979), chapter 8.

85. Smith, *The Power Game*, p. 71.

86. Thomas E. Mann, "Making Foreign Policy: President and Congress," in Thomas E. Mann, ed., *A Question*

of Balance: The President, The Congress, and Foreign Policy (Washington, D.C.: Brookings Institution, 1990), p. 16.

87. For an overview of the contemporary nature of the military-industrial-scientific infrastructure and defense politics, see Gordon Adams, *The Politics of Defense Contracting: The Iron Triangle* (New Brunswick, N.J.: Transaction, 1982); Jacob Goodwin, *Brotherhood of Arms: General Dynamics and the Business of Defending America* (New York: Times Books, 1985); William H. Gregory, *The Defense Procurement Mess* (Lexington, Mass: Lexington Books, 1989); Kotz, *Wild Blue Yonder;* and Patrick Tyler, *Running Critical: The Silent War, Rickover, and General Dynamics* (New York: Harper & Row, 1986).

88. Rone Tempest, "U.S. Defense Establishment Wields a Pervasive Power," *Los Angeles Times* (July 10, 1983): part VI, p.: 1.

89. Jan Tuten, "Military Might: Military Installations Give Firepower to S.C. Economy," *The State,* Columbia, S.C. (September 11, 1989): Business Section, pp. 10–12.

90. Rone Tempest, "Beltway Bandits Ring Washington," *Los Angeles Times* (July 10, 1983): part VI, p. 14.

91. Gordon Adams, *The Iron Triangle: The Politics of Defense Contracting* (New York: Council on Economic Priorities, 1981).

92. David Wood, "B-1 Symbolizes Power of Military-Industrial Complex," *Los Angeles Times* (July 10, 1983): part VI, pp. 8–9.

93. Kotz, *Wild Blue Yonder,* p. 22.

94. Ibid., p. 8.

95. Ibid., p. 239.

96. James R. Kurth, "Why We Buy the Weapons We Do," *Foreign Policy* (Summer 1973), and James R. Kurth, "A Widening Gyre: The Logic of American Weapons Procurement," *Public Policy* 19 (Summer 1971).

97. Adam Bryant, "Boeing Offering $13 Billion to Buy McDonnell Douglas, Last U.S. Commercial Rival," *New York Times* (December 16, 1996): A1, D14.

98. Lawrence. J. Korb, "A Military Monopoly," *New York Times* December 21, 1996): 25.

99. Bryant, "Boeing Offering $13 Billion to Buy McDonnell Douglas," p. A1.

100. See Harry Anderson, "Bracing for the Build-Down," *Los Angeles Times* (December 24, 1989): D1, D6; Peter Southwood, *Disarming Military Industries: Turning an Outbreak of Peace into an Enduring Legacy* (New York: St. Martin's Press, 1990); Ralph Vartabedian, "How Defense Contractors Hope to Cope," *Los Angeles Times* (December 24, 1989): D1, D9; and Ralph Vartabedian, "The Crisis Ahead for Aerospace," *Los Angeles Times* (December 24, 1989): A1, A16.

CHAPTER 17

NATIONAL SECURITY, CIVIL RIGHTS, AND CIVIL LIBERTIES

What is the future of electoral and group politics in U.S. foreign policy? Much depends not only on global developments but also on the evolution of political participation and the exercise of democratic citizenship in American society. As we have seen in chapters 15 and 16, political participation in electoral politics has declined over the cold war years while participation in social movements and group politics has increased since the 1960s. Overall, only a minority of the public has been motivated to regularly participate in American politics, whether to promote change or maintain the status quo.

In order to better understand the evolution of electoral and group politics and their implications for the future we must briefly examine political participation and the exercise of civil liberties in American history, especially in relation to the ebb and flow of the politics of national security. Not only does the evolution of political participation and the exercise

of civil liberties provide a richer understanding of continuity and change in the politics of U.S. foreign policy and the president's ability to govern, it deepens an understanding of the significance of the historical contradictions between the demands of national security and democracy in the making of U.S. foreign policy.

HISTORICAL DEVELOPMENTS

Political participation is guaranteed, not under the Constitution of the United States as originally written, but within its first ten amendments. After delegates from the various states produced a "new" Constitution in Philadelphia in 1787, a controversial ratification process ensued. A Bill of Rights was promised to allay the fears widespread among Americans that the new Constitution would restrict personal freedoms in order to guarantee approval by the states, which happened in 1788. Ten amendments to the Constitution were eventually passed and took effect in 1791—three years after the Constitution was ratified. These ten amendments, which restrain the national government from limiting personal freedoms, have come to be known as the **Bill of Rights**.[1]

According to the **First Amendment** of the Bill of Rights, "Congress shall make no law . . . abridging the freedom of speech, or of the press; or the right of the people peaceably to assemble, and to petition the Government for a redress of grievances." Such civil rights and liberties were considered essential to prevent the majority from tyrannizing the minority and to prevent minority factions from controlling the majority. These rights and liberties allowed people to participate and speak out without fear of persecution or political repression—a necessary core requirement of democratic politics.[2]

The **Declaration of Independence**, written by Thomas Jefferson and signed by many of America's founding fathers in 1776, went so far as to argue "that whenever any form of government becomes destructive to these ends [life, liberty, and the pursuit of happiness], it is the right of the people to alter or to abolish it, and to institute new government." Hence, a democratic form of electoral and group politics requires the opportunity for its citizens to participate, engage in political dialogue and debate, and have the opportunity to criticize and change public policies.

Although citizen participation and a broad exercise of civil liberties represented an "ideal" of the American revolution and the United States Constitution, the historical record has varied over time. *Three contradictory patterns in civil rights and liberties have predominated:*

1. Historically, many individuals have been denied full citizenship rights and suffered from discrimination;
2. Civil rights and liberties have expanded steadily over time;
3. There have been times of contraction in the actual exercise of civil liberties, especially during and after war.

These patterns in civil rights and the exercise of civil liberties impact American politics and the making of U.S. foreign policy as will be discussed further below.

First, the right to participate and exercise civil liberties—that is, American **civil rights**—was "extremely limited" throughout much of American history. At the country's founding, for example, only white males with property enjoyed the rights of full citizenship, such as voting. To keep things in historical perspective, we must recognize that these rights represented a revolutionary development particularly given the despotic and aristocratic political systems prevailing throughout Europe. Nevertheless, most Americans—the non-propertied, women, ethnic minorities, Native Americans, and slaves—had few, if any, civil rights and liberties. Such legal disenfranchisement by federal and local governments, supported by the judiciary, has been encountered by many American citizens throughout the country's history.[3]

Second, civil rights and liberties have "expanded" throughout American history. Even though "women and minorities" were initially denied civil rights and liberties, they fought for them and were eventually successful. With the passage of the Nineteenth Amendment in 1920, for example, women finally won the right to vote. Blacks, on the other hand, had to go through a much greater ordeal before their rights, won through the Civil War and the passage of the Fourteenth Amendment, were finally guaranteed with passage of the Civil Rights Act of 1964 and Voting Rights Act of 1965. Today, all American citizens have the constitutional right to exercise the civil liberties stipulated in the First Amendment.[4]

Yet, it is important to understand that the expansion of civil rights was bitterly fought over and resisted by many forces. The extension of civil rights to some people and their denial to others was a function of the history of American politics. Most of the "haves" who enjoyed civil rights, such as white males, resisted granting those rights to others. The "have-nots," therefore, had to challenge the politics of the status quo by speaking out, demanding their civil rights and liberties, and influencing the policymaking process in order to change the law. The successful expansion of civil rights and liberties was accomplished at the price of considerable "blood, sweat, and tears."

Finally, while civil rights and liberties have expanded throughout history, there also have been "times of contraction" in the exercise of civil liberties. The freedom of Americans to exercise **civil liberties**, once they gained the "right" to do so, has varied over time. Historically, *people have experienced political discrimination* because of their race (particularly new immigrants and minority ethnic groups) and their political beliefs (especially those who challenge government policy, established groups, and the status quo).

Times of contraction in the exercise of civil liberties tend to occur particularly in response to events that generate political instability and fear. Examples of such destabilizing events include the rise of industrialization and efforts to unionize, economic depressions and downturns, large waves of immigration to the states (review essay 10.2 on demographics, immigration, and the INS), and, most importantly, periods of national emergency and war.[5]

The Preoccupation with National Security versus Democratic Liberties

. . . .

Under conditions of war, civil rights and liberties are often curtailed and violated in a systematic way by the government, usually with the active support of groups and people throughout society. This typically occurs because the demands of national security take precedence over the demands of democracy during war, where most segments of society tend to rally behind the president and the government in order to fight the enemy abroad. It is in the context of this political environment that the government's and, in particular, the president's ability to dominate the politics of U.S. foreign policy is maximized. This is because **wars and national emergencies**, in particular, tend to be times when little tolerance ex-

ists for individuals and groups that criticize or challenge the government's foreign policy or the status quo within society.

The general American tendency toward conformity, as stated by political scientist Seymour Martin Lipset in 1963, "has been noted as a major aspect of American culture from Tocqueville in the 1830s to [David] Riesman [in *The Lonely Crowd*] in the 1950s."[6] In fact, times of perceived threats to national security are often accompanied by what historian Richard Hofstadter has called **"the paranoid style in American politics."**[7] In other words, war often produces a preoccupation with internal threats to national security, and certain groups within society are targeted as security risks because of their ethnicity or political beliefs.

"No nation in history has ever managed permanent war and a permanent military Leviathan at its heart and been able to maintain a truly representative character." So states sociologist Robert Nisbet. Nisbet continues,

> Is the United States somehow the divinely created exception to this ubiquitous fact of world history? Not, assuredly, if instead of a foreign policy based upon national security and finite objectives associated with this security, we indulge ourselves in a foreign policy with an "itch to intervene," and a purpose flowing out of the preposterous fantasy of a world recreated in the image and likeness of that city on a hill known as the United States of America.[8]

The net result is that the ability to exercise civil liberties tends to be limited during periods of conflict because the government's war effort, combined with American nationalism, tolerates little dissent and encourages political repression, as was briefly discussed in chapter 14 on American political culture. This is the "underside" of American history, yet it has been part of American history and is important to know in order to understand the evolution of political participation and the politics of U.S. foreign policy.

There have been *three major periods in the twentieth century when the demands of national security have prevailed over the demands of democracy and the exercise of civil liberties in domestic politics has been severely curtailed.*[9] Contraction of American civil liberties has been evident during:

1. World War I;
2. World War II;
3. The cold war.

Each of these periods has been accompanied by the supremacy of the president in the making of U.S. foreign policy.

The years after the Vietnam War, however, have been characterized by a decline in the demands of national security throughout society, creating an uneasy tension between national security and democracy. This development has led to a corresponding rise in the liberty of Americans to fully exercise their civil rights in electoral and group politics in order to influence the future of U.S. foreign policy. The net result is that presidents have had to operate in a political environment where they have had greater difficulty exercising power in the politics of U.S. foreign policy.

WORLD WAR I

Civil liberties were heavily curtailed and circumscribed as a result of World War I developments. Strong antiwar sentiment existed as President Woodrow Wilson asked Congress to declare war on Germany. Convinced that he had done everything humanly possible to keep America out of the war, Woodrow Wilson demanded uncritical support. The government thus decided to clamp down on civil liberties, a move which was reinforced by intolerance and bigotry throughout much of the public. The administration instituted a vast "propaganda campaign" to convince Americans that the U.S. was fighting to make the world safe for democracy.

Most of the press accepted voluntary censorship and actively promoted the war effort. And with the fear of the Germanic "Hun" increasing, **German-Americans became the target** of political attacks and hostility. Popular prejudices equated most anything German—names, language, culture—with disloyalty.

Members of the Socialist party and the political Left also were targets of the narrowing and violation of civil liberties. This came at a time when **the Socialist party**, launched in 1901, was growing in popularity and making remarkable gains as a political force throughout American society. In 1912 Socialist party leader Eugene V. Debs received over nine hundred thousand votes for president, about 6 percent of the total. "No fewer than 1,200 municipal officials—including fifty-six socialist mayors and many more aldermen and city councilmen—were elected, and there were now socialist police chiefs as well as state legislators."[10] In 1917, socialist candidates received 21 percent of the vote in New York City, 25 percent in Buffalo, 34 percent in Chicago, and 44 percent in Dayton, Ohio.

But the Socialist party and the Left experienced rapid decline with the rise of political repression imposed by the government in the name of national security, which was reinforced by the rise of progressivism represented by Woodrow Wilson and Teddy Roosevelt as well as factional infighting among socialists and the Left.[11] In order to squash political dissent and opposition, the government ultimately passed the **Espionage Act in 1917,** forbidding any action that helped the enemy or interference with the draft. This move was followed shortly by the **Sedition Act of 1918,** which virtually eliminated free speech in the United States. The Sedition Act forbade Americans to "utter, print, or publish disloyal, profane, scurrilous, or abusive language about the form of government, the Constitution, soldiers and sailors, the flag, or uniform of the armed forces . . . or by word or act oppose the cause of the United States."[12]

By the end of the war, as many as two hundred thousand Americans were accused or indicted for remarks heard in public; those found guilty were fined heavily or imprisoned. Eugene Debs, the Socialist party leader, received a twenty-year sentence in a federal prison for speaking out publicly against American participation in the war (and in 1920, while still in jail, he polled nearly 1 million votes for president).

With the Bolshevik revolution in 1917, **a wave of anti-Bolshevism and antiradicalism** hit the country. The U.S. government, led by the Justice Department and the Federal Bureau of Investigation (FBI), initiated a "Red Scare" campaign that completely destroyed socialist and other left-wing organizations. Numerous radicals and hundreds of innocent immigrants were deported back to Russia, while thousands of U.S. citizens were incarcerated by the government without charges. By the early 1920s, the FBI had secretly labeled a half million Americans as dangerous.

These government actions violated civil rights and liberties of people, many of whom were American citizens. Nevertheless, the actions were supported by nativist and conservative groups that promoted "100 percent Americanism." They saw eastern and southern European immigrants, the Jewish and Catholic religions, and different cultures and views as threats to their image of small-town, Protestant America. These discriminatory actions were reinforced by big business, which welcomed the influx of immigrants as a cheap source of labor, but bitterly fought against the rise of unionization, liberal reform, and socialism. Thus, World War I was instrumental in the widespread violation and curtailment of civil rights and liberties that virtually destroyed the political Left—pacifists as well as socialists—who were the major challengers to the politics of the status quo (review essay 9.1 on "J. Edgar Hoover and the Pursuit of Security").

WORLD WAR II

During World War II, the government censored the press and the FBI became more active in investigating fascist and communist subversive activity at home. The "Smith Act" was passed in 1940, making it illegal to advocate the overthrow of the U.S. government by force or to organize or belong to a group with such a goal. The House of Representatives Un-American Activities Committee engaged in antiradical investigations that focused on the threat of communism. Yet, overall, the civil liberties of Americans were curtailed to a much less considerable degree during World War II in comparison to World War I.

Germans and the political Left were not severely targeted by discriminatory and repressive measures. This may be explained in part by the assimilation of most German-Americans, and other Europeans, within society (especially after World War I), the rise of liberalism under President Franklin Roosevelt, the fact that the Soviet Union was allied with the United States against fascism, and by the existence of only minimal dissent in the face of the clear national security threat posed by the Axis powers.

Nevertheless, many American citizens and immigrants of "European" descent who were associated with the fascist countries were victims of wartime fears. This was especially the case for **Italian immigrants and Italian-Americans**: over 600,000 Italian citizens who were "legal" immigrants within the United States were classified as "enemy aliens" during the war, and had to face travel restrictions and curfews; many Italians lost their jobs; about 1,600 Italian immigrants were "interned," which cost them their livelihoods, possessions, and freedom; and about 10,000 Italian-American "citizens" were forced to move from their houses in California coastal communities to inland homes. Italian cultural organizations, language schools, and newspapers were often closed. Italian-Americans represented the largest group of foreign-born residents—over 5 million, in which about 500,000 Italian-American "sons" served in the United States armed forces. At Fort Missoula in Montana—an old frontier Army post which served as one of the nation's largest internment camps—along with Italians, about 11,000 Germans and German-Americans as well as some Bulgarians, Czechs, Hungarians, and Romanians were interned as well during the war.[13]

A much more grave situation, however, faced those Americans who were "not" of European heritage. The fear of enemy sabotage and a Japanese attack on the West Coast led to such hysteria among Americans that the U.S. military collected "all" individuals of Japanese descent, most of whom were naturalized American citizens, and held them in concentration camps throughout the war. This was one of the most blatant examples of political repression in American history. It was such a sad episode, in fact, that the American government eventually apologized to **Japanese-Americans** and provided reparations to the (few) internees surviving forty years later. (See **essay 17.1** for more on the Japanese Internment and the process of dehumanization.)

THE COLD WAR

Even with the end of World War II, the civil liberties of Americans were again attacked with the onset of the cold war. The strong anticommunist legacy in American history and the growth of McCarthyism as a political force made communism an enemy to be feared and fought both abroad and at home. As discussed in earlier chapters, McCarthyism represented a broad political coalition of conservative and nativist groups throughout American society. Nothing was immune to their attack, for communists and un-Americanism seemed to be everywhere—within the Truman administration, the government, the Democratic party, in academia and local schools, in Hollywood and the media, and all other walks of life. The anticommunist hysteria became so intense, and the demands of national security overwhelmed the demands of democracy so thoroughly, that even defending the constitutional rights and liberties of Americans was considered evidence of disloyalty— of aiding and abetting the enemy (review essay 12.1 on Joseph McCarthy and McCarthyism). The domestic politics of anticommunism curtailed the exercise of civil liberties and contributed to the liberal-conservative consensus that provided the foundation for the president's ability to exercise "prerogative government" in the making of U.S. foreign policy.

Under these warlike conditions during the "cold war," many Americans became paranoid and preoccupied with the threat of communism. Criticizing the status quo exposed one to **charges of being "unpatriotic," "un-American" and "disloyal."** Given this environment, it is easy to see why most liberals moderated their beliefs and behavior to become part of the liberal-conservative consensus. Most Americans learned to go along and "shut up" in public even if they did not fully agree with the dominant beliefs and institutions. This resignation also helps to explain why the cold war years were a period of mass apathy. Clearly, it was a **time of great conformity and intolerance** in American politics,

and these sentiments were driven largely by McCarthyism and the cold war politics of anticommunism. Those who did not conform to the anticommunist norm were often silenced by political repression or lost their legitimacy and credibility throughout society for their beliefs.[14]

Government employees were compelled to take "loyalty" oaths, a "secrecy system" was erected to protect classified information, and personnel involved in national security affairs were given lie-detector tests and had their backgrounds investigated. It has been estimated that during the McCarthy era, of a total work force of 65 million, 13 million people were affected by loyalty and security programs.[15] In the name of national security, the government even restricted travel to communist countries by Americans. All these actions were originally intended to protect U.S. national security and respond to congressional investigations of communism in government. However, the "national security ethos" that arose was quickly abused in order to keep information from the public domain and to maximize support throughout society for the government's policies (review the discussion of the impact of intelligence activities on the practice of national security and democracy at the end of chapter 9).

Yet the real abuse during the cold war years involved attempts by the government and allied groups throughout society to weed out communists and stifle public dissent in the name of national security. Congressional committees engaged in one investigation after another in an effort to identify and destroy communist influence, and this directly affected people's lives and careers. The attorney general kept a list of hundreds of subversive organizations, making individuals vulnerable to charges of disloyalty if they were affiliated with any of these groups, even if their membership was before or during World War II. Even the courts ruled in favor of national security over individual civil liberties, as in the 1951 *Dennis v. United States* case in which the Supreme Court ruled that advocating or teaching revolutionary philosophy constituted a crime.[16]

David Caute, in *The Great Fear: The Anti-Communist Purge Under Truman and Eisenhower*, documents how thousands of government employees,

ESSAY 17.1
THE JAPANESE INTERNMENT AND THE PROCESS OF DEHUMANIZATION

On February 19, 1942, President Franklin Roosevelt signed Executive Order 9066, ordering that individuals of Japanese descent living within the continental United States be moved to concentration camps in an effort to ensure the internal security of the country. Those affected had only forty-eight hours to dispose of their homes and businesses, they had to forfeit all bank accounts and investments, and they were permitted to take only personal belongings that could be carried in hand luggage. Over 110,000 individuals of Japanese descent, including men, women, and children—mostly American citizens—were rounded up and spent the next three years of their lives in camps located in desolate locations throughout the western United States.

The Japanese were particularly suspect of being un-American and maintaining allegiance to Japan, especially on the West Coast where they generally resided. General John L. De Witt, commander of the Western Defense Command, expressed the popular sentiment of the times: "A Jap's a Jap! It makes no difference whether he's an American or not." Although the constitutional rights of Japanese-Americans were ruthlessly violated, the Supreme Court actually upheld the executive order in 1944 in *Korematsu v. U.S.*, thus reflecting the politics of the times and the preoccupation with national security over the demands of democracy.

Yet, American fears and paranoia proved to be completely unfounded. The Japanese proved to be very "patriotic" Americans. The executive order did not apply to the Hawaiian Islands, where over 150,000 Japanese-Americans remained free and where no charges of sabotage were ever reported. The Japanese were model citizens during their stay in the camps. In fact, over 17,000 Japanese-Americans volunteered in the U.S. military to fight in the war once they were allowed to join in 1944. No Japanese-American soldier ever deserted the U.S. military, even though they were kept in segregated units. Their wartime exploits became legendary. For example, the 442nd Infantry was composed of Japanese-Americans who fought in the Italian campaign, which became one of the most highly decorated units in the war. Members of the unit received 3,000 Purple Hearts with 500 oak leaf clusters, 810 Bronze Stars, 342 Silver Stars, 47 Distinguished Service Crosses, and 17 Legion of Merit Awards. After the war, Japanese-Americans were released from the camps and given only $25 and transportation to make their way back into American society.

The American Civil Liberties Union would call it "the worst single wholesale violation of civil rights of American citizens in our history." How and why did this occur? The Japanese internment case demonstrates that even people who share a strong democratic tradition and philosophical commitment to civil liberties are vulnerable to fear and stereotypical thinking. "The wave of antipathy toward Japanese Americans which engulfed the Pacific Coast in the opening months of World War II had its origin far back in the history of California and the West. It was generated in the climate of indiscriminate antiforeignism which characterized the gold-rush period, and took definite shape during half a century of anti-Chinese activity, during which a hostile image of the 'Oriental' emerged that was subsequently shifted to the Japanese," especially following the attack on Pearl Harbor.[A]

According to John Dower, in *War Without Mercy: Race and Power in the Pacific War,* periods of war usually lead to strong nationalist feelings of self-righteousness, fueled by prejudices of "racial pride, arrogance, and rage on many sides" in which the enemy is dehumanized.[B] Not only does this unify national support for the war effort, it also makes it easier for people to wreak destruction and death on others. On the home front, it leads to a hypervigilance

---

A. Jacobus TenBroek, Edward N. Barnhart, and Floyd W. Matson, *Prejudice, War and the Constitution* (Berkeley, Calif.: University of California Press, 1954), p. 11.
B. John W. Dower, *War Without Mercy: Race and Power in the Pacific War* (New York: Pantheon, 1986), p. 4.

for subversives and intolerance of dissent. The **process of dehumanization** typically results in simplistic black-and-white views in terms of both one's self-image—as innocent, righteous, superior—and the "image of the enemy" or "others"—as aggressive, evil, inferior (review essay 14.2 on the world of cognition and enemy images).

"The racist code words and imagery that accompanied the war in Asia were often exceedingly graphic and contemptuous" for all parties involved.[C] From the American perspective, the Japanese were portrayed as subhuman and cruel, repeatedly associated with images of apes and vermin in order to convey these traits. Milder images depicted the Japanese as inferior to Westerners and Caucasians, primitive and childish at best, and mentally and emotionally deficient. "Cartoonists, songwriters, film-makers, war correspondents, and the mass media in general all seized on these images—and so did the social scientists and Asia experts who ventured to analyze the Japanese 'national character' during the war." As Japanese wartime successes

mounted early in the war, another stereotype took hold: the Japanese superman, possessed of uncanny discipline and military ferocity. "Subhuman, inhuman, lesser human, superhuman—all that was lacking in the perception of the Japanese enemy was a human like oneself."[D]

Thus, Japanese-Americans became the major targets of fear and repression within the United States for they represented America's enemy, most Americans felt a need for vengeance for the attack on Pearl Harbor, and the Japanese were racially and culturally different. Hence, World War II heightened a process of dehumanization within the United States that bred intolerance and repression, with Japanese-Americans becoming the primary victims. Although most obvious during times of war when the demands for national security and national unity are at their height, the process of dehumanization resulting in stereotypical pictures of the enemy tends to occur throughout government and society whenever individual rights and liberties are restricted.

C. Ibid., p. 9.

D. Ibid.

SOURCES: John W. Dower, *War Without Mercy: Race and Power in the Pacific War* (New York: Pantheon, 1986); Audrie Girdner and Anne Loftis, *The Great Betrayal: The Evacuation of the Japanese-Americans During World War II* (New York: Macmillan, 1969); Peter Irons, *Justice at War: The Story of the Japanese-American Internment Cases* (New York: Oxford University Press, 1983);

William Manchester, *The Glory and the Dream: A Narrative History of America, 1932–1972* (New York: Bantam, 1975); Jacobus TenBroek, Edward N. Barnhart, and Floyd W. Matson, *Prejudice, War and the Constitution* (Berkeley, Calif.: University of California Press, 1954); and Michi Weglyn, *Years of Infamy: The Untold Story of America's Concentration Camps* (New York: Morrow, 1976).

---

teachers, labor leaders, journalists, librarians, scientists, writers, and entertainers at national, state and local levels—virtually all innocent of charges of "disloyalty"—lost jobs, careers and reputations as a result of wild accusations and guilt by association.[17] The most celebrated cases, for example, involved people in the movie business who were dismissed and "blacklisted" from working in major Hollywood studios.[18] Yet, "every segment of society was involved. From General Motors, General Electric, and CBS to the *New York Times*, the New York City Board of Education, and the United Auto Workers."[19]

Even academia, with its commitment to academic freedom, failed to fight McCarthyism. Nearly one-half of the social science professors teaching in universities at the time expressed medium or high apprehension about possible adverse repercussions to them as a result of their political beliefs and activities.[20] In fact, Ellen Schrecker, in *No Ivory Tower: McCarthyism and the Universities,* found that academia contributed to McCarthyism. "The dismissals, the blacklists, and above all the almost universal acceptance of the legitimacy of what the congressional committees and other official investigators were doing conferred respectability upon the most repressive elements of the anti-Communist crusade. In its collaboration with McCarthyism, the academic community behaved just like every other major institution in American life."[21]

As David Caute has shown, by 1949 twenty-two states required teachers to sign loyalty oaths as a condition of employment, twenty-one forbade "seditious" classroom instruction, and thirty-one considered membership in subversive organizations as defined by the Department of Justice a sufficient cause for dismissal. In California, twenty-eight public and private colleges, including Stanford University and the University of California at Berkeley, installed security officers—usually former FBI agents—to compile information on the political beliefs and affiliations of professors for state officials. Caute has calculated that as a consequence of these anticommunist laws and practices, more than six hundred public school teachers and professors lost their jobs. Throughout the University of California system alone, twenty-six professors were dismissed who refused to sign the loyalty oath, thirty-seven others resigned in protest, forty-seven professors from other institutions turned down offers of appointment in California, and fifty-five courses from the university curriculum were eliminated.[22] In *Compromised Campus: The Collaboration of Universities with the Intelligence Community*, Sigmund Desmond demonstrates that university officials, including the presidents of Yale and Harvard, secretly cooperated with the FBI while publicly portraying their institutions as bastions of academic freedom.[23]

Perhaps most important, McCarthyism had a "chilling" effect throughout society; millions of Americans were intimidated by these actions, for they sent clear messages to the public about what constituted proper political thought and behavior in American politics. As early as 1947 in response to the House Un-American Activities Committee's investigation of **the Hollywood Ten**, Martha Gellhorn, a former leftist and one-time wife of Ernest Hemingway, sarcastically referred to it as "a little terror, calculated to frighten little people." But "it works"; under such pressure "a man can be well and truly destroyed." Her comments were prophetic. Someone "with a family will think many times before

speaking his mind fearlessly and critically when there lies ahead the threat of an Un-Americans' investigation, a publicized branding, and his job gone." For if you could destroy the Hollywood Ten, "pretty soon you can ruin a painter and a teacher and a writer and a lawyer and an actor and a scientist; and presently you have made a silent place."[24]

During this time the FBI maintained a widespread network of informants to weed out subversives and covertly instituted Operation Cointelpro to target the Communist Party, USA. One of the "informants" was Ronald Reagan who, while serving as the president of the Screen Actors Guild, was secretly reporting to the FBI on suspect members of the union he was elected to represent.[25] Under Director J. Edgar Hoover this counterintelligence program soon broadened to include the civil rights movement and then the antiwar movement during the 1960s.[26]

The FBI ended up carrying out over five hundred thousand investigations of so-called subversives without a single court conviction and created files on over one million Americans. Hoover stated the goals of the activities of the "Disruption of the New Left" Internal Security Counter Intelligence Program to the FBI's Albany, New York, office in the following manner:

> The purpose of this program is to expose, disrupt, and otherwise neutralize the activities of the various new left organizations, their leadership and their adherents. It is imperative that activities of those groups be followed on a continuous basis so we may take advantage of all opportunities for counter intelligence and also inspire action where circumstances warrant. . . . We must frustrate every effort of these groups and individuals to consolidate their forces or to recruit new or youthful adherents. In every instance, consideration should be given to disrupting organized activity of these groups and no opportunity should be missed to capitalize on organizational or personal conflicts of their leadership. [underscoring in original][27]

These steps, which violated the ability of Americans to exercise their liberties in accordance with the Constitution, were legitimate in the "minds" of Hoover and many American conservatives, for they believed that the civil rights movement and the new Left, including people like Martin Luther King, Jr., and Students for a Democratic Society leader Tom Hayden, were too radical, too un-American, and too threatening to the status quo, if not downright communist directed.

More moderate political leaders, including cold war liberals such as Lyndon Johnson and Hubert Humphrey, tended to support these counterintelligence actions because they were unsure about the influence of communism, their governmental legitimacy and power were being challenged, and they were repulsed by such nonconformist political behavior—especially since they were accustomed to a "passive" population. As David Halberstam described LBJ's increasingly "bunker" mentality in the White House by 1966: "So instead of leading, he was immobilized, surrounded, seeing critics everywhere. Critics became enemies; enemies became traitors."[28]

Although most Americans remained unaware of these covert actions at home, American nationalism believed in anticommunism and tolerated little dissent from the norm. This was, after all, the height of presidential power in exercising prerogative government in support of foreign policy in the name of national security (see **essay 17.2** on the governmental drive for nuclear weaponry and its implications for public safety).

The politics of the cold war was serious business. Political instability was typically portrayed by supporters of the cold war and the Vietnam War as a function of communists or "outside agitators" who were trying to stir up trouble. Cold war proponents simply could not understand that growing numbers of Americans were sincerely speaking out against them and their policies. Therefore, as was discussed briefly in chapter 9 on the intelligence community, the FBI's programs were complemented by similar covert counterintelligence activities conducted throughout the national security bureaucracy. The Central Intelligence Agency opened the mail of American citizens, kept over 1.5 million names on

file, and infiltrated religious, media, and academic groups. The National Security Agency monitored every cable sent overseas or received by Americans from 1947 to 1975. Army Intelligence investigated over one hundred thousand American citizens during the Vietnam War era. The Internal Revenue Service allowed tax information to be misused by intelligence agencies for political purposes.

The U.S. government, moreover, worked closely with local leaders, relying on the police and the national guard, to prevent demonstrations and officially restore law and order.[29] The criminal justice system, for example, was used to arrest, try, and, in some cases, convict demonstrators as a means to prevent and deter the exercise of their civil liberties, thus producing "political prisoners." These efforts to repress dissent resulted in dozens of Americans being fatally shot by the police and the militia during the turbulent years of the 1960s, including four students at Kent State University in Ohio and two students at Jackson State University in Mississippi. Finally, President Nixon attempted to take things into his own hands by allowing the "plumbers," operating out of the White House, to destroy Nixon's enemies and guarantee the reelection of the president, leading to the Watergate crisis.

In almost every situation during the cold war years, the "political dynamics" were the same. Those who attempted to peacefully exercise their civil liberties through the political system and change the status quo from a liberal or Left perspective were resisted by the government and its conservative allies in virtually all levels of society. While the civil rights and antiwar movements were overwhelmingly involved in political acts of nonviolence and civil disobedience, among both leaders and followers, the government was engaged in a massive campaign to limit and stifle the exercise of civil rights and liberties. Acts by the police to disrupt demonstrations often resulted in violence, radicalization, increased repression, and more violence until society seemed to be at war with itself. Ultimately, these efforts to restrict and neutralize the civil rights and liberties of Americans failed to contain the growth of massive political dissent against the Vietnam War during the 1960s and early 1970s.

ESSAY 17.2
NUCLEAR TESTING, DOWNWINDERS, AND HUMAN SAFETY

The Soviet Union detonated an atomic device in 1949, years earlier than most American scientists and political leaders had predicted. This event, combined with the rise of the cold war and growing fears of communism, resulted in an effort of "maximum production and maximum secrecy" in the United States to develop the hydrogen bomb and expand America's nuclear weapons stockpile. As part of the research and development of nuclear weapons, an **above ground atomic testing program** was conducted by the Atomic Energy Commission from 1951 to 1958 at the Nevada Test Site, northwest of Las Vegas. Almost one hundred nuclear devices were tested above ground. Over 100,000 people who lived downwind from the Nevada Test Site felt the nuclear blasts and, more importantly, were exposed to the resulting radioactive fallout. These people were predominantly Mormons, very patriotic believers in God and country, who lived in small towns in Nevada and Utah.

When some of the "downwinders" began to express concern about the fallout, the U.S. government—with the support of local political, business, and religious leaders—initiated a campaign to educate the public. Local citizens were told by the U.S. government that there was no need to worry because radioactive fallout is harmless (no more dangerous than medical x-rays) and that the atomic tests were a crucial component of efforts to safeguard the security of the United States. In 1955, before a new series of nuclear tests was to begin, a message from the Nevada Test Site manager appeared in an Atomic Energy Commission pamphlet given to schoolchildren and their parents:

> You are in a very real sense active participants in the Nation's atomic test program. You have been close observers of tests which have contributed greatly to building the defenses of our country and of the free world. . . . Some of you have been inconvenienced by our test operations. At times, some of you have been exposed to potential risk from flash, blast, or

fallout. You have accepted the inconvenience or the risk without fuss, without alarm and without panic. Your cooperation has helped achieve an unusual record of safety. . . . I want you to know that each shot is justified by national or international security need and that none will be fired unless there is adequate assurance of public safety. We are grateful for your continued cooperation and your understanding.[A]

Most residents, especially in the early years of the program, believed their government and acted accordingly. The following incident, as recalled by one resident when she was 12 years old, was far from unusual:

> I remember playing under the oleander tree, which is a wide-leaf tree, and the fallout was so thick that it was like snow . . . [We] liked to play under the trees and shake this fallout onto our heads and our bodies, thinking that we were playing in the snow. I remember writing my name on the car because the fallout dust was so thick. Then I would go home and eat. If my mother caught me as a young child, I would wash my hands; if not, then I would eat with the fallout on my hands.[B]

By the late 1950s, many local citizens became increasingly skeptical of the U.S. government's bland assurances of their safety. Medical research, in fact, was indicating that radioactive fallout could be extremely harmful. The 1960s reinforced these concerns as an alarming increase in the number of leukemia patients was detected in the small communities that were downwind of the Nevada Test Site, particularly among the young (the most vulnerable). Feelings of great bitterness resulted. As expressed by

---

A. Howard Ball, *Justice Downwind: America's Atomic Testing Program in the 1950s* (New York: Oxford University Press, 1986), p. 73.
B. Ibid., p. 92.

one local citizen, "We trusted the government when they told us that it was safe and so we didn't take precautions that we might have otherwise done had they told us the methods to protect ourselves."[C]

The government's position didn't change: the nuclear tests were safe and there was no proof that they were responsible for the cancers that were increasingly evident. Some local residents formed groups to fight for justice, for they felt they were victims of the government's negligence. Little ground was gained over the next ten to fifteen years. In the late 1970s, however, the Atomic Energy Commission was forced to release classified information. The information demonstrated that members of the Atomic Energy Commission and the U.S. government had shown little interest in questions of safety during the nuclear testing program, knowingly lied about the harmlessness of radioactive fallout, and kept medical studies classified indicating the dangerous effects of low-level radiation in order to avoid adverse publicity.

This led to a lawsuit in 1979 by twenty-four downwinders against the U.S. government in U.S. District Court. Although the law was written so as to

favor the government, in 1984 the district judge found the government to have been negligent in the case of ten of the twenty-four plaintiffs and awarded $2.66 million to the survivors of the deceased. However, the victory was only temporary, for a federal court of appeals overturned the decision in favor of the U.S. government, and the U.S. Congress has failed to pass legislation compensating the victims of atomic testing from the Nevada Test Site. Other lawsuits by downwinders have suffered a similar fate.

The U.S. government's overwhelming preoccupation with national security while neglecting the safety and rights of its people was not confined to the Nevada Test case. In addition to the 100,000 civilians who lived downwind from the Nevada Test Site, islanders have been exposed to radioactive fallout from nuclear tests in the Pacific; military troops have been exposed to radioactive fallout while engaged in war exercises following nuclear tests in the Pacific and the Nevada Test Site; civilians have been exposed to dangerous bacteria as a result of the army's germ warfare tests over populated areas; civilians were injected with radioactive substances in experimental experiments to determine the effects of radiation; workers and local residents have been exposed to radiation from the government's nuclear

---

C. Ibid., p. 93.

THE POST–VIETNAM WAR RESURGENCE OF CIVIL LIBERTIES

. . . .

Two major patterns involving civil liberties have prevailed in the post-Vietnam years. On the one hand, the breakdown of the liberal-conservative and anticommunist consensus have allowed Americans to exercise their civil liberties as never before. The civil rights and anti-war movements that arose during the late fifties and sixties fundamentally challenged the conformity and passivity that prevailed during the height of the cold war, and were highly responsible for expanding the world of group and participatory politics by the late sixties and seventies. The

events surrounding civil rights and Vietnam produced greater ideological, electoral, and political diversity. Clearly, individuals and groups throughout American society have greater opportunities to exercise their civil liberties and participate in politics then previously. Furthermore, one of the offshoots of the social movements of the 1960s and 1970s is that, although participation in elections has decreased, more Americans actively participate in group politics than before.

On the other hand, some cold war patterns prevail where threats to national security still take precedence over the ability of Americans to exercise their democratic rights. This continues to be the case because a large intelligence community continues to exist and engage in counterintelligence activities, a national security ethos still pervades the government weapons production facilities (as was discussed in essay 8.1); miners and nearby residents have been exposed to radioactive material from uranium mines; Vietnam veterans (and countless local Vietnamese) have been exposed to dioxin in the chemical defoliant "Agent Orange"; and military personnel and civilians are exposed to military toxic wastes while they work and live near toxic waste dumps on military bases.

Overall, it is estimated that millions of Americans, military and civilian, have been exposed to radioactive and toxic substances used by the military in the name of national security. Since the Vietnam War, more information about threats to public health has come to light and efforts to redress these threats have grown. In each situation, the government response tends to be the same: the substances and facilities are claimed to be safe for humans, the release of relevant information is resisted, and any political or legal challenge that arises is fought. There have been some court settlements and the U.S. government, usually through the Veterans Administration, has been forced to be somewhat more responsive. Estimates for environmental cleanup of the toxic waste and pollution at the nuclear weapons production facilities alone are in the hundreds of billions of dollars over the next generation. Clearly, with the rise of the cold war, the military establishment, and the national security ethos, a preoccupation with national security has often prevailed over the safety and rights of American citizens. Such tension between the demands of national security and democracy has continued in the post–Vietnam War and post–cold war years.

SOURCES: Howard Ball, *Justice Downwind: America's Atomic Testing Program in the 1950s* (New York: Oxford University Press, 1986); Leonard A. Cole, *Clouds of Secrecy: The Army's Germ Warfare Tests Over Populated Areas* (Totowa, N.J.: Rowman & Littlefield, 1988); Michael D'Antonio, *Atomic Harvest: Hanford and the Lethal Toll of America's Nuclear Arsenal* (New York: Crown, 1993); Carole Gallagher, *American Ground Zero: The Secret Nuclear War* (Cambridge: MIT Press, 1993); Clifford T. Honicker, "America's Radiation Victims: The Hidden Files," *New York Times Magazine* (November 19, 1989): 38–41, 98–103, 120; Thomas H. Saffer and Orville E. Kelly, *Countdown Zero: GI Victims of U.S. Atomic Testing* (Middlesex, England: Penguin, 1982); U.S., Congress, General Accounting Office, *Nuclear Health and Safety: Summary of Major Problems at DOE's Rocky Flats Plant* (October 1988); and U.S., Congress, General Accounting Office, *Nuclear Waste: DOE's Program to Prepare High-Level Radioactive Waste for Final Disposal* (November 1989).

---

and the military-industrial-scientific support infrastructure, and many Americans have a more conservative internationalist view of the world. Therefore, presidents have experienced a paradox of power in the post–Vietnam War political environment.

The Iran-Contra affair demonstrates both of these patterns. Many of the Iran-Contra activities of the Reagan administration involved efforts to stifle legitimate dissent to its policies. According to Robert Parry and Pete Kornbluh, in "Iran-Contra's Untold Story": "The White House deployed secretly funded private-sector surrogates to attack anti-contra [congressional] lawmakers through television and newspaper advertisements and to promote the contra cause through organizations with hidden funding ties to the administration. The FBI mounted intrusive and intimidating investigations of groups opposed to Reagan's Central American policies. . . . administration officials sought to manipulate criminal probes to protect their operations from exposure."[30]

Activities of the FBI, as part of its international terrorism counterintelligence program, included the investigation of over 18,000 individuals and 1,300 groups opposed to President Reagan's Central American policies, including the National Council of Churches, the Maryknoll Sisters, the United Automobile Workers, and the National Education Association, even though no criminal activity was ever uncovered. Of these, the U.S. General Accounting Office found that the FBI investigated 6,985 U.S. citizens and permanent resident aliens, over two thousand cases were selected simply because the individuals were from foreign countries that sponsored terrorism, and that the FBI "monitored First Amendment-type activities" in more than two thousand other cases.[31]

Even though these efforts to silence the exercise of civil rights and liberties occurred throughout much of the 1980s, this cold war and national security orientation operated in a post–Vietnam War domestic political environment, where such views and activities were much more likely to be exposed and criticized. Although Congress, the media, and the public were very slow to initially respond to the Reagan administration's involvement in Iran-Contra, many of these activities, nevertheless, were eventually challenged, exposed and stopped when the Iran-Contra affair became the issue on the political agenda beginning in the fall of 1986 (as discussed in the previous chapter on group politics). Such a political and constitutional crisis for President Reagan and the nation could only have occurred in a post–Vietnam War environment following the decline of the cold war. This also helps to explain the greater toleration for dissent and opposition experienced during the Persian Gulf crisis and war, even though some individuals were harassed for their beliefs and Arab-Americans were placed under FBI surveillance.[32]

Thus, contradictory patterns of continuity and change have created a new and uneasy tension between the demands of national security and the demands of democracy. With increasing numbers of Americans exercising their civil liberties, constraints on the president's ability to govern and potential opposition to his policies have grown. At the same time, if a president tries to limit dissent by violating civil rights and liberties in the name of national security, he risks political scandal, constitutional crisis, and disaster. Such was the fate of Richard Nixon and Ronald Reagan with Watergate and Iran-Contra. Only in less intrusive ways can a president rely on the cold war patterns of the past in governing foreign policy, such as denying the public information through use of the secrecy system or involving the intelligence community in much more limited counterintelligence operations. By doing anything more, the president risks great political uncertainty, especially if the actions become

public knowledge and find their way onto the political agenda.

It also means that the foreign policy bureaucracy is also more likely to be challenged in such a political environment as well. For example, in the late eighties the government tried to build a Special Isotope Separation Project, a plutonium purifying plant, at the Idaho National Engineering Laboratory in eastern Idaho. An important reason this site was chosen was because it was thought the plan would face little resistance in rural Idaho. The Bush administration miscalculated, however, as a number of interest groups as well as local newspapers feverishly opposed the project. Despite the promise of jobs, the local population was swayed in opposition to the plutonium plant and the project was dropped, demonstrating that concern for public safety and civil liberties can prevail over the needs of national security, as least since Vietnam and the end of the cold war.[33]

THE POST–COLD WAR FUTURE

A type of dualism with respect to the exercise of civil liberties has existed in the practice of American politics. On the one hand, American civil rights and liberties have steadily expanded throughout American history. In the post–Vietnam War era, Americans on the whole have become freer and more tolerant than during any previous period. This tolerance and freedom is much more in accordance with the ideals set down by the Declaration of Independence and the Constitution of the United States. On the other hand, there also have been periods of contraction in the exercise of civil liberties within the United States. Americans have been vulnerable to streaks of intolerance and discriminatory practices usually accompanied by emotional appeals to Americanism and nationalism, especially during times of war. These contradictory patterns in the exercise of civil liberties are reflected in the beliefs among both the mass and elite publics.[34]

This **dualism in thought and practice** is important for understanding continuity and change in the politics of U.S. foreign policy over the years. It is not mere coincidence that the height of presidential power in foreign policy occurred during a time when the demands of national security took precedence over the exercise of civil rights and liberties demanded by democratic practice. Likewise, as Americans have come to enjoy a greater ability to exercise their constitutional rights and liberties since the Vietnam War, it should not be surprising that domestic politics has constrained the president's ability to govern foreign policy and for the bureaucracy to act with abandon.

What does the future entail? Throughout twentieth-century American history, *threats to the democratic exercise of civil rights and liberties have tended to come predominantly from the political Right.* This has been the case for two reasons. First, conservatives and the political Right have traditionally been most intolerant of civil liberties and concerned with combating the threat of "alien" ideas, such as communism and socialism. Second, conservatives and the political Right have been powerful forces in government and have successfully generated political support throughout society by using the strong symbolic appeals of nationalism and Americanism. Their success explains the red scares of World War I and the cold war years.[35]

It must be recognized, however, that the far Right has no monopoly on intolerance and repression. Elements of the far Left, such as Marxist-Leninist groups, are also quite dogmatic and authoritarian. However, the nondemocratic, authoritarian far Left has never had more than a minute following within American society and has never been influential within the government. Furthermore, liberals have been guilty of initiating violations of civil liberties, as with the internment of Japanese-Americans under California Governor Earl Warren and President Franklin Roosevelt, and of feeding and appeasing the political Right, such as the internal security measures instituted by the Truman administration following World War II that fanned the flames of anticommunism and McCarthyism during the cold war years.[36]

With the collapse of the Soviet Union and communism in Eastern Europe, *the end of the cold war has important implications for the exercise of civil liberties and the future of American politics.* First, Americans can rest assured that communism likely will have almost no appeal within the United States any longer. Therefore, Americans should have little reason to fear the threat of communism into the foreseeable future. Second, the decline of international communism means that anticommunism should fade as an important conservative issue, although the most extreme groups may continue to see the communist bogeyman on the march. In other words, where the threat of bolshevism and communism has been used throughout the twentieth century by conservatives and the political Right to resist change and promote their policies, it should no longer have the symbolic value for uniting conservatives and attracting the support of Americans it had in the past. Third, the threat of communism will no longer be the principal means of justifying the need for an immense national security bureaucracy and support infrastructure. This may result in the reduction, and possible reform, of the intelligence community, military-industrial-scientific support infrastructure, and prevalence of the national security ethos.

The collapse of communism, in other words, should further expand the ability of Americans to exercise their civil liberties in American politics. Americans can choose to participate in electoral and group politics with little fear for their civil liberties, personal standing, and livelihood, especially in comparison to the cold war years. This suggests that ideological diversity will continue to increase in electoral and group politics, while new foreign policy issues are likely to generate more political involvement in social movements and groups. Therefore, the tension between the requirements of national security and democracy is likely to intensify with less predictability.

An example of the changes and continuing tension between national security and democracy can be found in the evolution of the **McCarran-Walter Immigration Act**. The act was passed at the height of McCarthyism in 1952 over the veto of President Harry Truman in order to protect American citizens from subversive ideas, primarily communism. The McCarran-Walter Act established thirty-three categories of beliefs and activities for excluding visitors and those seeking to become American residents, ranging from espionage and drug trafficking to believing in polygamy and engaging in "deviant sexual practices." The law has been used over the years to deny entry to such figures as Pierre Trudeau, who later became prime minister of Canada, Graham Greene, British author of *The Quiet American*, and Yasser Arafat, chairman of the Palestine Liberation Organization. During the 1980s under the Reagan administration, State Department officials in Washington and in embassies and consulates around the world added the names of over 264,000 "political undesirables" to the list that already included 100,000 people cited for national security and foreign policy reasons. During the 1980s, for example, the Immigration and Naturalization Service estimated that as many as eight thousand people from ninety-eight countries were denied entry into the United States because of their beliefs or political affiliations.

With these revelations made public, Congress in 1990 finally repealed the provision of the McCarran-Walter Act that bars foreigners from visiting the United States because of their political beliefs—although the secretary of state has the discretion to exclude people for ideological reasons if he finds that a "compelling" foreign policy interest is involved. In June 1991 the Bush administration agreed to remove those on the secret list for their political beliefs, although the State Department estimated that it would take at least three years to purge the list of those cited for ideological reason. Such is how the McCarran-Walter Immigration Act today represents both continuity and change from the cold war years.[37]

It must be pointed out that, even with the decline of communism, international conflict and new issues—such as drugs—will continue to plague the world, bureaucratic institutions created to protect national security will continue to exist, and American nationalism will continue to promote conformity in response to crises. However, the cold war appears to be a historic artifact. Thus, Americans and foreigners alike should experience less repression and more civil liberties in the future politics of U.S. foreign policy—that is, unless the United States becomes involved in another war of global proportions.

BIBLIOGRAPHIC ESSAY

. . . .

The relationship between national security and the exercise of civil liberties has received considerable attention, although little of this work has been integrated in the traditional scholarship on U.S. foreign policy. A good overview of government efforts to limit the exercise of civil liberties by Americans with respect to U.S. foreign policy can be found in Frank J. Donner, *The Age of Surveillance: The Aims and Methods of America's Political Intelligence System* (New York: Vintage, 1981). Richard Hofstadter provides provocative insights into the vulnerability of American political culture to intolerance and repression in *The Paranoid Style in American Politics and Other Essays* (New York: Alfred A. Knopf, 1965). An excellent discussion concerning the dynamics of dehumanizing the enemy in the context of World War II is provided by John W. Dower in *War Without Mercy: Race and Power in the Pacific War* (New York: Pantheon, 1986).

David Caute exhaustively documents the consequences of the politics of anticommunism on civil liberties during the cold war years in *The Great Fear: The Anti-Communist Purge Under Truman and Eisenhower* (New York: Simon and Schuster, 1978). The impact within higher education is well told by Ellen W. Schrecker in *No Ivory Tower: McCarthyism and the Universities* (New York: Oxford University Press, 1986). The role of the Truman administration in contributing to the politics of anticommunism is told by Richard M. Freeland in *The Truman Doctrine and the Origins of McCarthyism: Foreign Policy, Domestic Politics, and Internal Security, 1946–1948* (New York: Alfred A. Knopf, 1972). McCarthyism as an elite-led phenomena is further demonstrated by James L. Gibson, in "Political Intolerance and Political Repression During the McCarthy Red Scare," *American Political Science Review* 82 (June 1988): 511–29, and Michael Paul Rogin, *The Intellectuals and McCarthy: The Radical Specter* (Cambridge, Mass.: MIT Press, 1967).

David H. Bennett provides the historical context for understanding the politics of anticommunism embedded in the political Right in *The Party of Fear: From Nativist Movements to the New Right in American*

History (Chapel Hill: University of North Carolina Press, 1988). Herbert McClosky and Alida Brill discuss public beliefs about civil liberties since the Vietnam War in *Dimensions of Tolerance: What Americans Believe About Civil Liberties* (New York: Russell Sage Foundation, 1983). The implications of the end of the cold war for the exercise of civil liberties relative to the demands of national security are discussed by Morton H. Halperin and Jeanne M. Woods in "Ending the Cold War at Home," *Foreign Policy* 81 (Winter 1990–1991): 128–43.

ENDNOTES

1. See Gordon S. Wood, *The Radicalism of the American Revolution* (New York: Knopf, 1992).
2. For some valuable context, see David Lowenthal, *Possessed by the Past; The Heritage Crusade and the Spoils of History* (New York: Free Press, 1996); Pauline Maier, *American Scripture: Making the Declaration of Independence* (New York: Knopf, 1997).
3. For an overview, see Sara M. Evans, *Born for Liberty: A History of Women in America* (New York: Free Press, 1989); Leonard Dinnerstein, Roger L. Nichols, and David M. Reimers, *Natives and Strangers: Ethnic Groups and the Building of America* (New York: Oxford University Press, 1979); Joel B. Grossman and Richard S. Wells, *Constitutional Law and Judicial Policy Making* (New York: Longman, 1988); Alphonso Pinkney, *Black Americans* (Englewood Cliffs, N.J.: Prentice-Hall, 1969); and Howard Zinn, *A People's History of the United States* (New York: Harper & Row, 1980).
4. See also James MacGregor Burns and Stewart Burns, *A People's Charter: The Pursuit of Rights in America* (New York: Knopf, 1991).
5. See, for example, John H. Broesamle, *Reform and Reaction in Twentieth Century American Politics* (Westport, Conn: Greenwood Press, 1990); James MacGregor Burns, *The Crosswinds of Freedom* (New York: Knopf, 1989); Arthur A. Stein and Bruce M. Russett, "Evaluating War: Outcomes and Consequences," in *Handbook of Political Conflict: Theory and Research,* edited by Ted R. Gurr (New York: Free Press, 1980), pp. 399–422.
6. Seymour Martin Lipset, *Political Man: The Social Bases of Politics* (Garden City, N.Y.: Anchor, 1968), p. 448. See also David Riesman, Nathan Glazer, and Reuel Denney, *The Lonely Crowd: A Study of the Changing American Character* (Garden City, N.Y.: Anchor, 1953).
7. Richard Hofstadter, *The Paranoid Style in American Politics and Other Essays* (New York: Alfred A. Knopf, 1965).
8. Robert Nisbet, *The Present Age: Progress and Anarchy in Modern America* (New York: Harper & Row, 1988), p. 39.
9. For an overview, see William H. Chafe, *The Unfinished Journey: America Since World War II* (New York: Oxford University Press, 1986); Frank J. Donner, *The Age of Surveillance* (New York: Vintage, 1981); Robert J. Goldstein, *Political Repression in Modern America: From 1870 to the Present* (Cambridge, Mass.: Schenkman, 1977); M. J. Heale, *American Anticommunism: Combating the Enemy Within, 1930–1970* (Baltimore: Johns Hopkins University Press, 1990); Michael Linfield, *Freedom Under Fire: U.S. Civil Liberties in Times of War* (Boston: South End Press, 1990); Richard Gid Powers, *Secrecy and Power: The Life of J. Edgar Hoover* (New York: Free Press, 1987); George Brown Tindall, *America: A Narrative History* (New York: W.W. Norton, 1988); and Zinn, *A People's History.*
10. Milton Cantor, *The Divided Left: American Radicalism, 1900–1975* (New York: Hill and Wang, 1978), p. 31.
11. James MacGregor Burns, *The Workshop of Democracy* (New York: Alfred A. Knopf, 1985), and Tindall, *America.*
12. In Paul Goodman and Frank Otto Gatell, *USA: An American Record,* vol. 2 (Hinsdale, Ill.: Dryden Press, 1972), p. 380.
13. James Brooke, "After Silence, Italians Recall the Internment," *New York Times* (August 13, 1997): A8.
14. See, for example, Stephen J. Whitfield, *The Culture of the Cold War* (Baltimore: Johns Hopkins University Press, 1991).
15. Ralph S. Brown, *Loyalty and Security* (New Haven, Conn.: Yale University Press, 1958).
16. See Stanley I. Kutler, *The American Inquisition: Justice and Injustice in the Cold War* (New York: Hill and Wang, 1982).
17. David Caute, *The Great Fear: The Anti-Communist Purge Under Truman and Eisenhower* (New York: Simon and Schuster, 1978).
18. See, for example, Victor S. Navasky, *Naming Names* (New York: Penguin, 1980).
19. Ellen W. Schrecker, *No Ivory Tower: McCarthyism and the Universities* (New York: Oxford University Press, 1986), pp. 10–11.

20. Paul Lazarsfeld and Wagner Thielens, Jr., *The Academic Mind* (Glencoe, Ill.: Free Press, 1958).

21. Schrecker, *No Ivory Tower*, p. 340. See also Lionel S. Lewis, *Cold War on Campus: A Study of the Politics of Organizational Control* (New Brunswick, N.J.: Transaction, 1988).

22. Caute, *The Great Fear*, pp. 406–24. See also David Caute, *The Fellow Travelers: A Postscript to the Enlightenment* (London: Weidenfeld and Nicolson, 1973).

23. Sigmund Desmond, *Compromised Campus: The Collaboration of Universities with the Intelligence Community, 1945–1955* (New York: Oxford University Press, 1992).

24. Martha Gellhorn, "Cry Shame ... !" *New Republic* (October 6, 1947): 21.

25. Gary Wills, *Reagan's America* (New York: Penguin, 1988), pp. 295–97.

26. See James Kirkpatrick Davis, *Spying on America: The FBI's Domestic Counterintelligence Program* (New York: Praeger, 1992).

27. Cited in Tom Hayden, *Reunion: A Memoir* (New York: Collier, 1988), p. 283.

28. David Halberstam, *The Best and the Brightest* (New York: Random House, 1969), p. 623.

29. See Frank J. Donner, *Protectors of Privilege: Red Squads and Police Repression in Urban America* (Berkeley: University of California Press, 1990).

30. Robert Parry and Peter Kornbluh, "Iran-Contra's Untold Story," *Foreign Policy* (Fall 1988): 5.

31. U.S., Congress, General Accounting Office, *International Terrorism: FBI Investigates Domestic Activities to Identify Terrorists* (September 1990). See also Richard O. Curry, ed., *Freedom at Risk: Secrecy, Censorship, and Repression in the 1980s* (Philadelphia: Temple University Press, 1988); "FBI Will Purge Files on Protesters," *New York Times* (November 5, 1989): 17; and "Going After Dissidents," *Newsweek* (February 8, 1988). p. 29.

32. See, for example, Lisa Belkin, "For Many Arab Americans, FBI Scrutiny Renews Fears," *New York Times* (January 12, 1991): 1A.

33. Keith Schneider, "Idaho Says No," *New York Times Magazine* (March 11, 1990): 57–61.

34. See, for example, James L. Gibson, "The Political Consequences of Intolerance: Cultural Conformity and Political Freedom," *American Political Science Review* (June 1992): 338–56; Herbert McClosky and Alida Brill, *Dimensions of Tolerance: What Americans Believe About Civil Liberties* (New York: Russell Sage Foundation, 1983).

35. See David H. Bennett, *The Party of Fear: From Nativist Movements to the New Right in American History* (Chapel Hill: University of North Carolina Press, 1988); Michael Paul Rogin, *The Intellectuals and McCarthy: The Radical Specter* (Cambridge, Mass.: MIT Press, 1967); and McCloskey and Brill, *Dimensions of Tolerance.*

36. See Richard M. Freeland, *The Truman Doctrine and the Origins of McCarthyism: Foreign Policy, Domestic Politics, and Internal Security, 1946–1948* (New York: Alfred A. Knopf, 1972); James L. Gibson, "Political Intolerance and Political Repression During the McCarthy Red Scare," *American Political Science Review* 82 (June 1988): 511–29; William Keller, *The Liberals and J. Edgar Hoover: Rise and Fall of a Domestic Intelligence State* (Princeton, N.J.: Princeton University Press, 1989); Coleman, *The Liberal Conspiracy;* and Richard H. Pells, *The Liberal Mind in a Conservative Age: American Intellectuals in the 1940s and 1950s* (New York: Harper & Row, 1965).

37. Philip J. Hilts, "Landmark Accord Promises to Ease Immigration Curbs," *New York Times* (October 26, 1990): A1, A14; Steven A. Holmes, "Congress Drops Barrier to Aliens Based on Beliefs," *New York Times* (February 2, 1990): A1, A4; and Martin Tolchin, "U.S. Will Remove 250,000 Aliens on List of Those Barred for Beliefs," *New York Times* (June 14, 1991): A1, A10. See also Sanford J. Ungar, "J. Edgar Hoover Leaves the State Department," *Foreign Policy* 28 (Fall 1977): 110–16.

CHAPTER 18

. . . .

THE MEDIA
AND THE COMMUNICATIONS PROCESS

he mass media and the communications process have become very significant elements in the politics of U.S. foreign policy. Two factors account for this. First, as society and the global environment have grown in complexity and in importance in affecting the lives of Americans, people have developed a greater need for information about national and international affairs. Second, throughout the twentieth century a communications revolution has occurred which makes it possible for the mass media to rapidly communicate information anywhere on the planet. The net result is that much of the information, knowledge and images that individuals have of the world come from the mass media.

This chapter examines the type of "mediated reality" that Americans tend to acquire through the American mass media and the communications process. This will shed light on many of the developments discussed previously throughout the book concerning the making of U.S. foreign policy, such as the existence of the paradox of presidential power, the importance of agenda setting on the policymaking process, the role of public beliefs and political participation, and the significance of symbolism in American politics. In this respect, examining the role of the mass media and the communications process allows one to better understand the patterns of continuity and change, presidential governance, and tension between national security and democracy that have evolved over time.

THE INFLUENCE OF THE MASS MEDIA AND THE NEWS

. . . .

Many people hold strong opinions about the role of the mass media and the news. No single conventional view predominates. Rather, *three competing views seem prevalent throughout American society.* Conservatives tend to argue that the media play a powerful role in American politics and that there is a liberal bias within the American news media. Liberals tend to agree that the media play a powerful role in American politics, but they believe that there is a conservative bias within the news media. Journalists, on the other hand, tend to argue that the power of the media has been overblown; the news media simply attempt to "mirror" reality, reporting events and the facts as they exist.

All three views tend to be overly stereotypical and self-serving. First, the news media are the major sources of information for Americans concerning national and international affairs; therefore, they occupy an important role in American politics. Second, because the news media are the major source of information, media coverage often affects the "political agenda," that is, which issues gain (and do not gain) the attention of the public and policymakers. Third, news media coverage often affects the **"climate of opinion"** as well. In other words, the news media not only determine what issues Americans consider important, but also how they think about those issues. Finally, because of the mass media's dominant role in the communication process, individuals and groups—government officials, national leaders, established groups, and challenging groups and social movements—compete for media attention and access in order to get their issues on the agenda and promote a favorable climate of opinion for their interests. In sum, as Shanto Iyengar and Donald R. Kinder demonstrate, the news media provide *News That Matters.*[1]

The news media and the communications process affect the politics of U.S. foreign policy in ways that journalists tend to downplay, but in a much more complex fashion than either conservatives or liberals argue. In order to understand the media's role in the politics of U.S. foreign policy, we need to examine closely the news media and the communications process.

CONTEMPORARY NEWS MEDIA COVERAGE
. . . .

The American public, both the mass and elite publics, have become dependent on the news media for information and understanding of national and international affairs. Clearly, a variety of different sources of information is available, as is obvious from a visit to any major urban newsstand or public library. However, most Americans get their information from the **mainstream media:** the major newspapers, radio stations, and television stations available in their communities. The mass public, being relatively uninterested and uninformed about national and international affairs, tends to be most receptive to "headline" news, such as lead stories on the front page in the newspaper and, in particular, on television. The elite public follows the media's coverage of the news more closely and is most likely to supplement its information beyond television and the local newspaper. In both cases, news coverage by the mainstream media directly affects the information and perceptions that Americans have of the world.

In many ways, overall news media coverage today is better than ever before. The mainstream media are more informative regarding national and international affairs. The quality of journalism has improved and become more professional. More public affairs programs are on television than in the past. Quality newspapers, such as the *New York Times* and the *Wall Street Journal,* are readily available in urban areas throughout the country. In sum, members of the public who rely on the mainstream media can gain considerable information about national and international affairs if they are interested, especially if they already possess a good base of information.

At the same time, the mainstream media do not provide a comprehensive and complete picture of reality. The news media are highly selective with respect to which events are reported and how they are presented. Many public affairs programs provide "soft" news. Television news coverage is usually brief and simplistic, appealing to a mass public and the least common denominator. Little real investigative reporting is conducted by the mainstream media, while sources of information from alternative media outlets are ignored. Finally, the public typically has a short attention span and demonstrates little interest in becoming truly informed. Therefore, the net result of reliance on the mainstream media is often a simplistic understanding of reality; members of the mass public are as much confused as enlightened, while members of the elite public usually lack the historical context to place the immediacy of the news in perspective.

These contradictory patterns in American news media coverage and their implications for the foreign policy process can be better understood if we take a closer look at coverage of contemporary affairs. What do we know about *media coverage of contemporary national and international affairs?* For one thing, we know that the news media display considerable **"selective attention"** to the world around them. Most of the American media focus on local and national news, with little attention given to international news. Most studies examining media coverage found that the percentage of news stories devoted to international affairs by major mainstream media organizations ranged from 10 to 40 percent, representing anywhere from five to fifteen international news stories daily.[2]

Media coverage of international affairs varies to a considerable extent depending on the **type of medium**. National news on television has a higher percentage of stories devoted to international affairs, but they are few in number. National news programs broadcast an average of five to seven international stories (representing a total of seven to eleven minutes) out of fifteen to seventeen stories broadcast daily. International coverage by major newspapers represents a smaller percentage of their total news coverage, but newspapers tend to cover more international stories overall. The *New York Times*—considered the best daily American source of international news—averages ten to fifteen international news stories per day. In order to receive media coverage on television or in print, it has been found that foreign news in general must be more consequential,

must involve people of higher status, and must entail more violence or disaster than national news. Overall, only a limited number of events and issues become news, especially in the media's coverage of the world beyond American shores.

Which international topics tend to be covered by the American media? According to *Deciding What's News*, a 1979 study of CBS, NBC, *Newsweek*, and *Time* by Herbert Gans, *the following international topics tended to receive the most attention:*

1. American activities abroad (especially official visits);
2. Foreign events directly affecting the United States (such as wars and inflation);
3. East-West governmental relations;
4. Changes in heads of state (with a special interest in European royalty);
5. Dramatic political conflicts (such as wars, coups, revolutions, terrorism);
6. Natural disasters;
7. Excesses of foreign dictators.[3]

Others have found similar results. Andrew Semmel, in "Foreign News in Four U.S. Elite Dailies," concluded that the American press "pays far greater attention to countries which are economically affluent, politically powerful and culturally similar to the United States."[4] Not only do issues throughout the developing world receive little attention; when they do get covered they often entail more sensational items (military coups, wars, natural disasters, accidents, and crime).[5]

News coverage of events abroad by the U.S. media, in other words, tends to be American- and Western-centric (as opposed to being globally oriented), focuses on government officials (as opposed to nongovernmental groups and publics), highlights political and national security issues (as opposed to economic or environmental issues), and emphasizes "negative" events such as conflict (as opposed to "positive" stories emphasizing cooperation). Therefore, the news media not only provide selective coverage, but they emphasize a particular picture of reality.

This selective attention is reinforced during times of crisis, whether domestic or international.

"Crisis coverage" is often so great that most other national and international news of consequence disappears entirely. Crisis coverage by the American news media also tends to be limited to events in which the United States is heavily involved or affected; little or no media coverage, for example, would be accorded a civil war in a small third-world country where the United States has little involvement, even though this may clearly be a crisis situation for the people involved.

INFLUENCES
ON THE NEWS MEDIA
. . . .

Why does the mainstream media in the United States present information and portray reality in a way that is incomplete, selective, and particularistic? *Three basic explanations account for the selectivity of news media coverage:*

1. The complexity of the world;
2. The characteristics of the news business;
3. The politics of the communications process.

THE COMPLEXITY AND
AMBIGUITY OF THE WORLD

The American news media have no monopoly in selectivity in reporting about the world around us.[6] This is inevitable, for the world is so complex that the media must be selective in determining which items of significance are to be covered and how. Also, while American journalism has become more professional, the world has grown in complexity. A world of over 160 governments, thousands of nongovernmental groups, and over five billion people in constant interaction concerning hundreds of issues produces much potential news. Hence, the *New York Times* slogan—"All the News That's Fit to Print"—implies not only coverage of the most significant news available, but that decisions were made by people in selecting and determining what was "fit to print."

The complexity and ambiguity of the world makes selectivity of media coverage inevitable because different people will see different realities. People possess different beliefs about the world around them due to unique backgrounds and varying life experiences. This is most obvious when people from different cultures and parts of the world are involved, but different perceptions of the same issue are also evident within the same culture. Therefore, decisions are made within the news media concerning which issues to cover and how these issues will be presented; and these decisions are consequential in affecting the kind of national and international reality readers, viewers, and listeners are likely to perceive.

The "type" of medium also is important, for it affects the space available for news coverage as well as how the news is presented.[7] The print media, especially newspapers, usually cover more news stories and devote more space to each story than the electronic media. At best, national news shown on a major television network, such as ABC, CBS, or NBC, provides only a brief digest of national and international events in less than twenty-five minutes—not much time to cover the world. Television news stories are also unique because they are accompanied by video images that provide the viewer with a greater sense of immediacy—of "being there"—further affecting viewers' perceptions.

The **power of television** is particularly noticeable during crisis reporting, a time when issues and stories that are part of the crisis are highlighted and most vulnerable to being sensationalized. "Television is driven to dramatize the news, to give it plot, theme, and continuity to make it comprehensive to a mass audience. Television needs action and drama. It needs to boil down complexities. It needs identifiable characters. Hence the focus on personality, preferably one personality."[8] And the "tendency to present (and understand) politics in terms of demons and friends, good guys and bad guys."[9] Overall, television news coverage tends to simplify reality the most for it tends to be more incomplete and provide less depth than the print media while, at the same time, its visual images make it more compelling and powerful. Television is, nevertheless, the major medium by which most Americans gain their information and understanding of national and international affairs.

Therefore, the media provide a **mediated reality.**[10] This was cleverly portrayed in a simple political cartoon concerning the news media in which a young boy asked his father, "Dad, if a tree falls in the forest, and the media aren't there to cover it, has the tree really fallen?"[11] The news media not only select but shape the way we see reality, oftentimes in storybook fashion. In other words, each news medium acts as a "filter" of reality for its audience—although some news sources do a better job than others. Conservative and liberal critics of the American media agree that the news media must select, simplify, and, consequently, distort reality. Most mainstream journalists, however, have difficulty acknowledging or admitting this, because it contradicts their belief that they are able to mirror reality. Maybe most importantly, this admission would damage the news media's credibility with the American public as providers of information and the "watchdog" of government. The news media, nevertheless, can only provide a mediated reality, yet a mediated reality that has an important impact on the politics of U.S. foreign policy.

CHARACTERISTICS OF THE NEWS BUSINESS

News media coverage is also affected by the history, functions, organization, and subculture of the mass media (as with any bureaucratic organization). In order to better understand the type of mediated reality the mainstream media tend to provide, we must examine *a number of important characteristics concerning the nature of the mass media and journalism in American society:*[12]

1. The media have become concentrated;
2. The media are big business;
3. The media are very competitive;
4. The media have become bureaucratic and professionalized.

The Concentrated Media. The first important characteristic involves the increasing concentration of the mass media throughout the course of American history. Although thousands of independent media organizations once existed in a very competitive environment—especially in the print media—a few large media conglomerates now dominate the national and local markets. Ben Bagdikian, in *The Media Monopoly,* notes that of the 1,600 daily newspapers that existed in 1989, 98 percent were local monopolies and fourteen corporations controlled most of the country's circulation.[13] Independently owned newspapers, once dominant, have been replaced by large media chains, such as Gannett, which operates *USA Today* and over ninety other dailies (representing 10 percent of total circulation in the country), Knight-Ridder, which runs the *Philadelphia Inquirer, Miami Herald* and over thirty other daily newspapers, and the *New York Times,* which operates the *New York Times,* the *Boston Globe,* and over thirty other dailies (as well as 20 magazines, five television and two radio stations).[14]

A handful of firms control most of the magazine business, with Time, Inc., alone accounting for nearly 40 percent of magazine revenues. And in mid-1989 Time merged with Warner to form Time Warner, the largest media firm in the world. The three broadcasting networks continue to enjoy more than two-thirds of the television audience, even with the rise of cable (which operates local monopolies and has become increasingly concentrated nationally). And five companies own over 300 radio stations throughout the country. Most book publishers are controlled by fewer than a dozen companies. Overall, Bagdikian found that concentration in the communications industry grew rapidly in the 1980s, especially given all the mergers. "In 1981, forty-six corporations controlled most of the business in daily newspapers, magazines, television, books, and motion pictures. Today, these media generate even larger amounts of money, but the number of giants that get most of the business has shrunk from forty-six to twenty-three."[15] Such concentration of the media has continued and resulted in a narrower, less diverse, mediated reality presented to the general public.[16]

In fact, the **national media**—sometimes referred to as the elite press—has developed and become the primary source of information on national and international affairs for the mainstream media in general and, consequently, for most Americans. The national media consist of the following organizations: ABC, NBC, CBS, CNN (Cable News Network), the *New York Times,* the *Washington Post,* the *Los Angeles Times,* Associated Press (AP), and United Press International (UPI); one could also include the *Wall Street Journal* for economic news as well as *Newsweek*—owned by the *Washington Post-Time,* and *U.S. News & World Report* for the attentive public. Other large urban media organizations, such as the *Boston Globe,* the *Chicago Tribune,* the *Miami Herald,* and the *Philadelphia Inquirer,* are junior partners of the national media for they lack national reach beyond their regional market.

The national media, in addition to being the direct source of information for many people, also operate **"wire services."** For example, The Associated Press, unknown to most Americans, is a significant part of the national media because it makes available a large number of news stories from its reporters throughout the world (at a cost) to other media organizations through its wire service. Not surprisingly, other major news media organizations have come to operate their own wire services, such as the *New York Times* wire service and the *Washington Post-Los Angeles Times* wire service. Through the wire services these national media organizations have become the basic source of national and international news for most television stations, radio stations, and newspapers in the country—the media through which most Americans acquire information about the world around them. Most local newspapers, for example, rely on the national media for the source of their stories on national and international affairs; only the major urban newspapers can afford their own national and foreign correspondents.

A key consequence of the growing concentration of the media industry is greater concentration in news media coverage. While the existence of a dozen or so major news sources provides the appearance of considerable diversity, choice is much more limited at the local level. More importantly, the national media tend to present **"homogeneous" news coverage** rather than a diverse picture of the news and the world. Regardless of which of the national television news programs or newspapers one watches or reads, all of these sources usually select the same lead news item, cover the same stories, and provide similar information and interpretations. Differences do exist, but they tend to be minor, concerning detail and nuance. Overall, the news and the basic pictures of reality presented by the national media tend to be amazingly similar.

The Media Business. One reason the news media have become concentrated and their coverage so homogenized is that the mass media have **increasingly become a big business**. Historically, the American press used to consist of small, independent operations that were usually quite partisan. Presses frequently were operated to make money and provide a living for those involved. In addition, many were financed by wealthy patrons who were more interested in providing news and political interpretation, even at a financial loss. With the rise of industrialization, urbanization, and mass society, however, the media have become a big business where the bottom line—financial worth and profit—predominates.[17] As economics has replaced politics as the basic source of motivation within the news business, "muckraking" journalism has declined and partisan viewpoints have been relegated to the editorial pages. Today, the major news media organizations are part of "large media corporations and conglomerates."[18]

NBC News, for example, is part of the National Broadcasting Corporation, and was once owned by RCA. General Electric, one of the ten largest U.S. corporations (and a major defense contractor) with total revenues of over $50 billion, purchased RCA during the 1980s at the cost of $6.3 billion and generated $3.64 billion in revenues from communications in 1988. CBS News, part of CBS, generated $2.8 billion in revenues during the same year; in 1995 it was purchased by Westinghouse. ABC News is part of the American Broadcasting Corporation, which was owned in 1988 by Capital Cities, Inc., with revenues from its communications business totaling $3.75 billion. In 1995 Walt Disney Pictures purchased Capital Cities/ABC for $19 billion. The news and communications process, in other words, has become big business.

The financial worth of these media organizations and their corporate ownership is a reminder that the media field has become an arena open only to giant corporations and extremely wealthy individuals, as when Rupert Murdoch purchased Walter Annenberg's Triangle Publications for $3 billion. The growing emphasis on the need to remain financially solvent and, preferably, expand profits affects the resources available to media organizations and choices concerning the breadth and depth of news coverage. Most importantly, growing concern with generating revenue and maintaining profitability has led to the mass media's preoccupation with "maximizing its appeal to a large and broad audience," reinforcing the tendency to provide a selective and homogenized picture of national and international politics.

The Competitive Media. The third characteristic is that the news media are also very competitive, but in a narrow sense that reflects their concentrated and big business orientation. The phrase used by one scholar to describe this situation is that the mass media are **"rivals in conformity" for audiences and advertisers.**[19] The news media, as in any business, attempt to increase their market share because their revenues are obtained through advertising (and sales of newspapers). Hence, a key concern of national media organizations is to present news in such a way that attracts, not alienates, audiences and advertisers—that, in other words, takes into consideration the beliefs of the mass and elite publics. This would include not alienating business since it is the source of most media advertising. Therefore, the news business has its competitive elements, many of which have little to do with improving the quality of media coverage and which actually contribute to the homogenization of the news.

Television is probably the most competitive because the national networks compete for the same viewing audience (and national advertisers). Although advertising rates are lower for news than for entertainment programs, it still costs advertisers as much as $300,000 a minute for a commercial on one of the nightly network news shows. Having a larger or smaller audience than one's network competitors means a difference of millions of dollars in what one can charge for advertising and millions of dollars in yearly revenues. As with any program on television, therefore, news programs are as heavily oriented toward maximizing a broad audience as they are toward informing the public.

This competitiveness, ironically, tends to promote a "risk-avoidance approach" within the mass media. Rather than taking risks, the fear of losing viewers and offending corporate sponsors makes the media act with great caution in their programming. They usually prefer to emulate the news organization currently enjoying the greatest amount of success. This is especially true of television, where, for example, news media executives have become increasingly attuned to the entertainment aspects of the news as a means of attracting the attention of the public. As depicted by David Halberstam about television in general in *The Powers That Be:*

> The impulse to take risks in quality programming, to serve the national interest in public affairs, became weaker all the time. And the enormity of the new profits did not make the company stronger or more confident of itself. Ironically, as it became greedier, it became more nervous, more insecure. The race was getting faster and faster and the ice was getting thinner and thinner. . . . Now broadcasting was obsessed with the ratings.[20]

"Soft" public affairs programs that emphasize entertainment and personalities, such as "Good Morning America" and "20/20," have proliferated. The television networks have also responded with "tabloid" shows such as "A Current Affair," which reflects the popularity of tabloid magazines such as the *National Enquirer* and the *Star,* as well as more "news magazines" that try to do a little bit of everything, such as "Dateline" and "Prime Time Live."

Even the nightly network news programs on television have tried numerous gimmicks, such as having the anchorperson report "live" from abroad or purchasing full-page ads in the *New York Times* to tell readers that they were first to predict who won the presidential election; such ploys are not designed to improve the quality of coverage, but to increase popular appeal and viewership.[21]

Such competitive attributes of the national media contribute to the selectivity and similarity of news coverage discussed above. This is further reinforced by the fact that American "journalism is also a competitive profession," especially among the national media. Journalists and the major media organizations are preoccupied with getting the story first and being the "number one" source of news. This concern with being the media leader tends to result in the phenomena of **pack journalism,** in which journalists from different media organizations chase the same "headline" stories. Pack journalism is most noticeable, for instance, during crisis coverage or with the media's effort to cover presidential election campaigns, as depicted by Timothy Crouse in *The Boys on the Bus.*[22] This tendency to congregate while in search of the same story is reinforced by the strong "esprit de corps" that develops among journalists. Thus, the competitiveness of the journalistic profession often results in pack journalism and great similarity in news coverage.[23]

At the same time, journalists are highly motivated, especially at the national level, to excel within their profession and to stand out from the pack. They compete for promotion and vie for more rewarding and prestigious assignments. Top journalists, in particular, are in great demand within the media business. Those most successful not only tend to become better journalists, they also command considerable fame, prestige, power, and fortune—strong factors motivating individual journalists. Television anchorpersons and journalists—such as Tom Brokaw, Peter Jennings, Ted Koppel, Dan Rather, Diane Sawyer, and Barbara Walters—have become well-known celebrities who enjoy annual salaries from $2 million to $10 million a year.[24] This success is typically accomplished as a result of operating within the routines and norms of the media business and journalistic profession.

The Media Bureaucracy and Professional Journalism. The fourth important characteristic of the national media, in addition to its concentration, big business orientation, and competitiveness, is that it has become extremely bureaucratic and professionalized in the production of the news. National media organizations are large, complex bureaucratic enterprises involving thousands of people organized in terms of hierarchy, specialization, and routines. They are also heavily influenced by a media subculture based on certain norms and standards of professional journalism. This affects how the news media portray contemporary national and international affairs in terms of which issues, places, and events get covered (or do not get covered), how things are reported, which stories are finally run, and how they are presented to the public.

Much of the news is a function of the **beat system,** in which reporters are given responsibility for covering a particular issue or institution. Although journalists like to talk about the age of investigative reporting following the Vietnam War and Watergate, there are very "few investigative reporters" per se who make a concerted effort to uncover as many relevant sources and pieces of information as possible in putting a story together. Instead, "beat reporters" are assigned by their media organizations to cover established institutions, such as government and business, and rely on the authorities available as their basic source of information. The national media, for example, regularly assign political correspondents to cover the major institutions and agencies of the federal government, such as the White House, Pentagon, State Department, Congress, and Supreme Court. Not surprisingly, much of the news is about what government officials from these institutions have said or done.

In the *New York Times* or *Washington Post,* for instance, Leon Sigal, in *Reporters and Officials,* found that stories from regularly covered beats outnumbered offbeat stories two to one, including front-page headlines.[25] Such routinized news coverage means that news stories are also affected by the timing of events, because media organizations have deadlines for going to press and are less active over the weekend. Because so many journalists cover the same institutions and issues while operating under the same time constraints, the beat system also sets the stage for pack journalism. For example, while the entire White House press corps consisted of 25 reporters in 1945, over 1,700 people had regular White House press passes by the late 1980s.[26]

International coverage, likewise, is heavily a function of the **location of foreign correspondents**, who tend to be stationed in countries that are allied with the U.S. government and in major cities. Of roughly 700 foreign correspondents, at least half are routinely stationed in Europe, while fewer than 10 percent are stationed in each of the three regions of Africa, Latin America, and the Middle East. For example, of *Newsweek's* twenty-two full-time foreign correspondents in 1989, eleven were located in bureaus throughout the major cities of Europe (in London, Paris, Bonn-Berlin, Rome, Moscow, and Warsaw), six in Asia (in Tokyo, Beijing, Hong Kong, and Bangkok), only two in the Middle East (in Cairo and Jerusalem), two in Africa (in Nairobi and Johannesburg), and one in Latin America (in Mexico City). A decade later and well into a post–Cold War world, "nothing" had changed—the same number and location of foreign correspondents and bureaus![27] Not surprisingly, given the distribution of the American news media, there is much more international news coverage of Europe than of the rest of the world.

Editors and officials at the top of the bureaucratic hierarchy also play an important role, for they supervise and oversee the news production process. They make crucial decisions concerning which journalists are hired, what gets covered and by whom, which stories are published, the length and location of the stories, and the final presentation and wording of the news stories. The importance of this is evident, for example, by studies that have found a much higher proportion of stories on the third world in the AP and UPI wire services than appear in the American press.[28] Journalists of major news organizations who work in the field recognize that editors have certain idiosyncrasies and beliefs that make them more receptive to certain kinds of information and new angles than others. In this sense, a type of "self-censorship" actually occurs within the news process, as it does in all professions, given the incentives and disincentives built into the media bureaucracy and the journalistic profession.

Sometimes, in fact, **"conflicts of interest"** exist in which the content of news may be directly affected by personal, rather than journalistic, concerns. Editors and executives, for example, may intervene in the news production process to prevent or sanitize stories for purely self-interested reasons. The roles of political activist and reporter were clearly in conflict in 1980 when ABC reporter George Will secretly coached candidate Ronald Reagan for a presidential debate with Jimmy Carter, yet Will continued to cover the campaign for ABC News and the *Washington Post* as a neutral party. Conflicts of interest also arise when individuals, in their role as policy experts, speak or are quoted by the news media on topics for which they also serve as private consultants to business firms or foreign countries involved in the issue at hand without any public acknowledgment (as discussed in the chapter on group politics). Naturally, these situations usually go unreported and remain hidden from the general public.

The mediated reality that most Americans see and read is not only affected by the bureaucratic nature of the beat system and the editorial process; much of news media coverage is heavily affected by the "subculture" of the journalistic profession that prevails throughout the media organizations as well. Journalists tend to be generalists, not specialists. As was briefly discussed in chapter 7 concerning foreign service officers, what a generalist gains in terms of breadth of information is offset by limited depth of knowledge and understanding relative to any particular issue or area. This is particularly a problem in international coverage because most foreign correspondents have limited language competency beyond English (or possibly Spanish and French for some) and face the additional constraint of government censorship in many countries.

Therefore, foreign correspondents are often dependent for their information on local elites who speak English, which often limits access to a range of information and views.

This generalist orientation is reinforced by the **professionalization of journalism**. While media coverage was once quite partisan, the contemporary mainstream media takes a nonpartisan approach in its news coverage, often referred to as **objective journalism** within the profession. Journalistic norms emphasize the importance of independence (acting free of "outside" political pressures), objectivity (presenting the facts without prejudice or distortion), and impartiality (avoiding partisanship and providing balance in representing without favor the views of contending parties.). On the one hand, this results in less personal bias affecting the selection and content of news coverage. On the other hand, such so-called objectivity in reporting usually results in a preoccupation with the immediacy of "news"—in other words, what is new and currently factual in a news story. Although informative, this allows others to influence the newsworthiness of stories, most stories tend to be accompanied by little historical background or context to better inform the reader, and news stories come and go based on their timeliness, with little follow-up, producing little continuity in coverage over time. Most importantly, as we will see in the next section, the concept of "objective journalism" is a misnomer for journalists do not operate in a political vacuum and they have political values that affect what they see and how they behave. Such "nonpartisan" journalism, in fact, is heavily affected by the political environment and plays a major role in the politics of U.S foreign policy.

THE POLITICAL ENVIRONMENT AND THE COMMUNICATIONS PROCESS

The third general explanation that accounts for the selectivity and content of news media coverage, in addition to the complexity of the world and the characteristics of the news business, is the impact of the political environment on the communications process. News coverage by the national media is heavily affected by the political environment in two fundamental ways. First, journalistic perceptions of the world are shaped by the dominant political ideology and culture of American society. Second, the media is perceived as so important in affecting American politics that individuals and groups in and out of government actively attempt to influence and manipulate news media coverage.[29] These factors not only reinforce the tendency of selective and homogenized news coverage, but they result in the national and mainstream media usually communicating a politically centrist understanding of reality to the American public.

Ideology, Culture, and the Centrist Media. Journalists of the mainstream media tend to downplay and dispute the ideological basis of American reporting. They point out, quite correctly, that while the news media historically have been partisan, modern journalism is much more nonpartisan and professional. Although nonpartisan, American journalists, nevertheless, are not "value-free." They hold cultural and ideological beliefs—as Americans they are socialized to see the world in terms of a liberal-conservative orientation. As Walter Lippmann, one of America's most prominent twentieth-century journalists, asserted in 1922, "We do not first see, and then define, we define first and then see."[30] This is inevitable and perfectly understandable because, as we discussed in chapter 14, liberalism and conservatism, or some blend of the two, are the basis of political thought for most Americans. Therefore, it would be more accurate to say that mainstream members of the mass media tend to operate from a nonpartisan tradition and cover the news from a centrist ideological perspective that ranges within a liberal-conservative understanding of the world.

This **centrist ideological orientation** obviously colors how journalists see the world, what issues they believe are of consequence, why this is the case, and how these issues will be communicated to others. No matter how hard American journalists try to be objective, they are influenced by the values of democracy and capitalism they tend to hold dear.

Viewpoints that are critical of this classical liberal orientation are rarely heard or communicated within the mainstream American media. The political consequences, as Doris Graber claims in *Mass Media and American Politics,* are that "the media usually support the political system and rarely question its fundamental tenets. They limit their criticism to what they perceive as perversions of fundamental social and political values."[31] The impact of culture and ideology is not unique to American journalism, but affects media coverage in all countries. Nevertheless, the role of American culture and ideology deserve close attention in order to fully understand American news coverage, especially within the mainstream media that operate under the guise of objective journalism.[32]

The cultural and ideological foundations of American journalism are "particularly noticeable during periods of crisis." During such times American journalism is extremely vulnerable to becoming consumed by patriotic and nationalistic fervor. Typically, journalists act as a medium for promoting the president's views and policies and, thus, contribute to the phenomena of "rallying around the flag." This was clearly evident, for example, in early coverage of the Iraqi invasion of Kuwait and the U.S. government's response under President George Bush, and it occurred again following the start of the Persian Gulf War. During such times, in fact, journalists often lose their nonpartisan nature and closely identify with the United States government and its policies; this is evidenced when journalists speak in terms of "we" and "they" as opposed to speaking in a more neutral language that distances them and their reporting from the parties and the events in accordance with the norms of objective journalism.

In sum, conservative groups who argue a liberal bias and liberal groups who argue a conservative bias both oversimplify the ideological nature of the news media. In fact, greater ideological diversity exists among journalists within the mainstream media than is suggested by either view. For example, whereas most reporters within the mainstream and national media tend to be moderate to liberal in orientation, editors and owners tend to be more conservative. Furthermore, one is more likely to find

journalists who are extremely conservative and right wing as opposed to extremely liberal or left wing. Nevertheless, their personal beliefs are often moderated by their professional journalistic roles, for they must operate within the constraints of a mainstream media that is concentrated, run as a business, competitive, and bureaucratic. The net result is a tendency for the national media to present a homogenized view of the news, with coverage reflecting a more centrist ideological orientation.

Within this centrist ideological orientation, *news media coverage sometimes may be more liberal and at other times may be more conservative*—it ultimately depends on the issue, the times, and the political environment. The particular ideological slant of the coverage for any issue will normally reflect political thought prevalent throughout the mass and, in particular, elite public in American society at that time. As Stephen Hess argues in *The Washington Reporters,* "Washington news gathering, in other words, is an interaction among elites. One elite reports on another elite."[33] More specifically, the content of national media coverage tends to reflect the beliefs of the individuals within institutions and groups, in and out of government, that prevail in American politics. The communication of the news reflecting such beliefs subsequently affects the politics of U.S. foreign policy. Therefore, the news media and the political environment are part of an interactive process where more centrist views and positions tend to set the political agenda and influence the climate of opinion in domestic politics and the policymaking process.

As Herbert Gans explains, "It would be incorrect to say that the news is about elites per se or a single elite; rather, the news deals with those who hold the power within various national or societal strata, with the most powerful officials in the most powerful agencies, with the coalition of upper-class and upper-middle class people which dominates the socioeconomic hierarchy."[34] For instance, a study of the guests on ABC's "Nightline" from 1985 to 1988 found that over 89 percent were men, over 92 percent were white, and over 80 percent were professionals, corporate representatives, or government officials.[35] In the area of foreign policy, the national media rely overwhelmingly on prominent government and ex-government officials as sources of information and for guests on public affairs programs, with the same faces—such as Henry Kissinger—appearing time and time again.[36]

The news media, in other words, tend to practice **source journalism** as opposed to "investigative journalism." "Very few newspaper stories are the result of reporters digging through files; poring over documents; or interviewing experts, dissenters, or ordinary people. The overwhelming majority of stories are based on official sources—on information provided by members of Congress, presidential aides, and other political insiders."[37] As Carl Bernstein has pointed out, this was the case during Watergate where:

> America's news organizations assigned only fourteen of those 2,000 men and women [reporters working in Washington, D.C.] to cover the Watergate story on a full-time basis. And of those fourteen, only six were assigned to the story on what might be called an "investigative" basis, that is , to go beyond recording the obvious daily statements and court proceedings, and try to find out exactly what had happened.[38]

And according to Bernstein, not much has changed in post-Watergate journalism.

As Daniel Hallin concluded in *The Uncensored War: The Media and Vietnam,* the national media reflect the views of prominent leaders and government officials: when they agree, the news media reflect the consensus view (the sphere of consensus); when they disagree, the media reflect their level of diversity (the sphere of legitimate controversy). Topics and viewpoints that do not reflect prominent leaders and the political mainstream tend to be ignored, and not covered, by the national media (the sphere of illegitimate sources and views).[39] In this respect, news media coverage of the world is heavily dependent and conditioned by the national politics that transpire at home (see **figure 18.1** on the political boundaries of national media coverage).

This symbiotic relationship between the national media and the political environment ensures centrist news coverage within an ideological spectrum occupied by most Americans, especially the most prominent opinion leaders. This produces coverage which sometimes is more liberal and other times more conservative. In the post–Vietnam War era, for example, the rise of liberalism has resulted in civil rights coverage that often represented a more liberal viewpoint. On the other hand, economic issues tend to be cov-

FIGURE 18.1

THE POLITICAL BOUNDARIES OF NATIONAL MEDIA COVERAGE

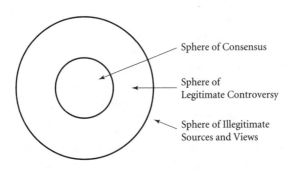

SOURCE: Daniel Hallin, *The Uncensored War: The Media and Vietnam* (Berkeley: University of California Press, 1986).

ered from a more conservative perspective, especially since the resurgence of conservatism. To illustrate the point further, economic news in the mainstream media is equated with the coverage of business and finance (as reflected in the title of that section of the newspaper); however, coverage of labor and unions tends to be nonexistent except during a major strike where it is usually portrayed, through the eyes of government and business leaders, unsympathetically as a threat to the economy and law and order.[40]

"Foreign policy coverage" is much less consistent, for it reflects the greater ideological diversity that grew out of the breakdown of the cold war consensus. Sometimes foreign policy coverage is more supportive of the president and other times more critical; sometimes it's more liberal and other times more conservative. During a foreign policy crisis, early coverage tends to be highly supportive of presidential policies, while late coverage tends to become diverse and critical. When the political forces of liberalism are on the rise throughout society, such as during the early and mid-1970s, news media coverage often leans to the liberal side. However, when the political forces of conservatism are ascendant, such as during the late 1970s and the early 1980s, news media coverage often becomes more conservative. Overall, news media coverage tends to reflect a centrist position operating with a liberal-conservative political orientation.

The Media and Politics. In addition to the underlying role of American political ideology (and culture) and the distribution of power among different ideological forces throughout society, the news media are also directly affected by the political dynamics of the policymaking process and domestic politics. In fact, government officials and societal groups attempt to "influence and manipulate" the media's coverage of domestic and international affairs because they are aware of the power of the media, through its ability to influence the political agenda and the climate of opinion, to affect domestic politics and the policymaking process. They understand that the images communicated by the media, especially television, are powerful symbols that affect the political beliefs and behavior of the public.

Politically active individuals and groups within government and throughout society compete with each other for "access" to the news media in an effort to promote their interests and causes. In other words, groups engage in **public relations and propaganda activities**, attempting to influence the media in order to promote a favorable image and response among the general public. According to David Truman in *The Governmental Process,* "one of the first results of the formal organization of any interest group is its embarking upon a program of propaganda, though rarely so labeled, designed to affect opinions concerning the interests and claims of the new group."[41]

Competing groups attempt to take advantage and manipulate the news business. For example, as Doris Graber observes, "Public relations managers know the deadlines of important publications, such as the *New York Times, Wall Street Journal, Time, Newsweek,* and network television news. They schedule events and news releases so that stories arrive in gatekeepers' offices precisely when needed. If their releases are attractively presented and meet newsworthiness criteria, journalists find it hard to resist using them. . . . If news sources want to stifle publicity, they can announce the news just past the deadlines, preferably on weekends when few newscasts are scheduled."[42] Thus, American politics is very much a competition between different individuals and groups in society and government for influence over ideas, images, and symbols throughout the mass communications process.

As discussed in the section above, established groups and institutions, such as government and business, tend to be successful more often in gaining access to the mainstream media and having their views communicated. David Truman maintains that "because propaganda must rest upon and use preexisting attitudes, certain groups at any time enjoy special propaganda advantages."[43] Established groups are typically seen as more significant, newsworthy, and credible sources of information. Challenging groups—more critical of the president, big business, and the status quo in general—have greater difficulty in gaining access to the media for they are treated as less mainstream, less credible, and less newsworthy sources of information. Although much depends on the politics of the times, the activities of challenging groups covered by the mainstream media are often depicted in a more negative light than the activities of more established groups and institutions.[44]

The institution most successful in gaining access to the news media and influencing its coverage is, in general, the government and, in particular, the presidency.[45] With the president considered the center of foreign policy activity, the national media, with their beat system and norms of objective journalism, have become heavily dependent on the government and especially the executive branch for much of its information concerning U.S. foreign policy and international affairs. As Bernard Cohen explained in his classic *The Press and Foreign Policy* written in 1963, "the more 'neutral' the press is . . . the more easily it lends itself to the uses of others, and particularly to public officials whom reporters have come to regard as prime sources of news merely by virtue of their positions in government. This is unquestionably the case at the Presidential level."[46] In other words, as Daniel Hallin discovered in his study of the Vietnam War, with the rise of so-called objective journalism, "journalists gave up the right to speak with a political voice of their own, and in turn they were granted a regular right of access to the inner councils of government, a right they had never enjoyed in the era of partisan journalism."[47]

Thus, **the president has a unique advantage** in gaining access to the news media and having them communicate his views and preferences to the American public, most visibly during the early stages of a foreign policy crisis. Whatever and whenever the president speaks or acts, it is newsworthy by definition. Also, with the rise of the paradox of presidential power since Vietnam, the president and government officials have become much more public relations conscious than ever before and strive to promote the kind of media coverage that strengthens their political position. It would not be an overstatement to say that all presidents are preoccupied with their public image. President Lyndon Johnson, for example, was legendary for viewing all three television news networks at the same time to see how he and his policies were portrayed. Not surprisingly, presidents have increasingly institutionalized and expanded their White House press and communications operations, beginning with Richard Nixon. This machinery allows presidents to maximize *a number of tools at their disposal to influence media coverage* of national and, in particular, international affairs. This would include taking advantage of the presidency's newsworthiness, credibility as a source of information, control of classified information, and contacts throughout the media.[48]

Realizing that presidential acts are newsworthy, presidential appearances in public are often "staged" to maximize positive news coverage and communicate the desired information and message. This reflects a growing preoccupation with the creation and communication of what historian Daniel Boorstin called "pseudo-events."[49] According to David Gergen, a member of the White House staff to Presidents Richard Nixon and Ronald Reagan and subsequent editor of *U.S. News & World Report*, "We had a rule in the Nixon operation that before any public event was put on his schedule, you had to know what the headline out of that event was going to be, what the picture was going to be, and what the lead paragraph would be. You had to think of it in those terms, and if you couldn't justify it, it didn't go on the [president's] schedule."[50] President Reagan's public appearances were also carefully staged and choreographed, down to where the president would stand and what he would say. The Reagan presidency—which has been referred to as the "Teflon" presidency—in fact, was probably the most adept at using the mass media, in particular television coverage, to promote its agenda and a positive climate of opinion.

Another important advantage is that the government is routinely "the source" of much of the media's information. Part of this is a function of journalists' reliance on the beat system and their coverage of such institutions as the White House, the State Department, and the Pentagon. Under the beat system, government officials are able to control the release of information through press releases, briefings, and public statements.[51] During foreign policy crises, the news media are almost exclusively dependent (or allow themselves to become almost exclusively dependent) on the executive branch for their information. For example, media reporting of the president's use of armed force in places such as Grenada, Panama, and the Persian Gulf was totally dependent on the executive branch for information, especially early on when the country rallied around the flag. Obviously, executive branch officials attempt to influence the political agenda and the climate of opinion by providing selective information to the news media that is intended to reinforce the government's policies and promote political support throughout the public and society.

Another way that the executive branch controls information is to "take advantage of the classification of information" by denying the news media and the public access to information for national security reasons. Covert actions are therefore often an attractive option for the president, for they maximize the possibility of keeping information "hidden" from the news media and the public eye. Another favorite technique that government officials use to control the information flow to the news media is to **"leak"** confidential and classified information to selective reporters. As Hedrick Smith points out in *The Power Game,* "On Wall Street, passing insider information to others is an indictable offense. In Washington, it is the regular stuff of the power game."[52] Classified information is regularly leaked by "proponents" of a policy to gain its approval as well as by "opponents" designed to discredit policy. Oliver North, who vilified Congress during the Iran-Contra hearings for leaking classified information, regularly leaked information in his efforts to win public support for Reagan's Central American policy. Although leaking is widespread throughout the Washington community, it tends to be more frequent within the executive branch, especially the closer one gets to the president.

Two of the more blatant governmental techniques used to manipulate the news media through information control have involved the use of systematic "propaganda campaigns" and censorship. The Pentagon, for example, spends millions of dollars each year for military bands and air shows throughout the country as part of a massive public relations campaign to promote strong public support for the military. More ominous illustrations, however, have been documented. Members of the Reagan administration, for instance, orchestrated public relations campaigns using propaganda (consciously distorting information and lying) and disinformation (knowingly manufacturing false information) to use the media and rally public support for their efforts to destabilize Colonel Moammar Gadhafi of Libya and overthrow the Sandinistas in Nicaragua.

Discussing the covert contra war in **"Iran-Contra's Untold Story,"** Robert Parry and Peter Kornbluh assert that "to win this war at home the White House created a sophisticated apparatus that mixed propaganda with intimidation, consciously misleading the American people and at times trampling on the right to dissent."[53] The administration's strategy was to distort the record by exaggerating the threat and abuses of the Sandinistas while hiding those of the contras. "To be sure, previous administrations have tried to impose their political wills on the news media, dissembling and lying when necessary to protect foreign-policy misadventures," argue Parry and Kornbluh. "But the Reagan White House appears to be the first to have institutionalized the process. Employing the scientific methods of modern public relations and the war-tested techniques of psychological operations, the administration built an unprecedented bureaucracy in the National Security Council and the State Department designed to keep the news media in line and to restrict conflicting information from reaching the American public."[54]

Censorship has also been used by the government and its use during a time of war has grown since the 1980s. One of the major "lessons of the Vietnam War" learned by many within the national security bureaucracy was the need to keep the news media under control. During the **invasion of Grenada**, for example, the Reagan administration censored the press by preventing journalists from accompanying soldiers on the ground. This made the media totally dependent on the Reagan administration's version of the invasion, which depicted it as a tremendous military success in support of a humanitarian cause while it ignored both the geopolitical reasons behind the invasion and the military foul-ups on the ground. (See essay 8.4 on the Grenada operation.)

Given news media resistance to outright censorship, the government and mainstream media organizations have informally agreed to allow a small "pool of reporters" to represent all of the news media and accompany the military under strict guidelines when it intervenes abroad. Although many within the national media initially protested, they have nonetheless gone along with the restrictions, as occurred during the invasion of Panama and the Persian Gulf War, thereby providing the facade of an independent news media. Such censorship by the executive branch, and the national media's willingness to accept it, has resulted in the administration's views and interpretations of events becoming accepted and shared by most members of American society—a powerful advantage in the politics of U.S. foreign policy. (See **essay 18.1** on government censorship and the Persian Gulf War.)

Finally, government officials often promote favorable news media coverage by building upon their many "contacts and personal relationships" within the media. **Henry Kissinger was a master** at wooing the media in order to promote his foreign policy purposes. He was a constant source of information, often classified, anonymously provided to the media in general or to selective journalists, which they would then attribute to a "senior government official." (See essay 6.2 on "t Kissinger's ability to control the policymaking process.) As Stanley Hoffmann pointed out long ago:

> The closeness to official Washington of the nation's leading columnists and reporters, writing for the main newspapers and television networks, is especially responsible for numbing the mass media's capacity to question and challenge. . . . Enjoying the confidence of the great usually kills the urge to investigate. Officials disarm these men by giving them the illusion of being admitted to the mysteries of

decision-making, and by making them sympathize with their ordeals.[55]

The news media are open to such use and manipulation because journalists and editors have become dependent on government officials for information, many are ideological "kindred spirits" of these officials and, being part of the Washington community discussed in chapter 13, they are often driven to gain access and socialize with the famous and the powerful. Presidents regularly invite journalists to White House functions and often engage in informal interaction as a means of promoting good relations and positive images.[56] And as journalist Walter Lippmann once wrote in his diary, "A writer on public affairs can't pretend to despise reputation, for reputation is not only flattering to the vanity, it is the only way of meeting the people you've got to know in order to understand the world."[57]

In sum, three major patterns exist in the politics of the media. First, government-media relations are very much a symbiotic process. The nature of the news business and the political environment in American society have made the news media more dependent on the government, especially the president and the executive branch, while, at the same time, the president and government have become more dependent on the media. Second, the president and the executive branch have considerable advantages in promoting positive news media coverage, especially early in an administration, over issues of foreign policy, and during crises, when presidential legitimacy and support are at their highest. Third, even with all its advantages, the president in the post–Vietnam War and post–cold war eras is unable to dominate and influence media coverage to the same extent that it was able to do during the cold war past, even in the area of foreign policy.

In the contemporary political environment the paradox of presidential power has required that the president exert greater effort and sophistication in public relations at a time of greater uncertainty and difficulty in dominating the media—clearly evident throughout the Clinton years. The collapse of the

ESSAY 18.1
GOVERNMENT CENSORSHIP AND THE PERSIAN GULF WAR

Although the American national media pride themselves on being an independent, nonpartisan, and objective source of news, government censorship and manipulation of the news media was almost complete during the war in the Persian Gulf. As reported in an article entitled "The Propaganda War" in *Newsweek* near the end of the war, "In theory, reporters in democratic societies work independent of propaganda. In practice they are treated during war as simply more pieces of military hardware to be deployed."[A] The result was that the government controlled the type of war that the American public saw in order to minimize dissent and maximize political support, which reinforces the old adage that "truth is the first casualty of war."

According to one assessment, "one casualty of the Gulf War appears to be the independent, itinerant war correspondent. The press pool system used in the Gulf encouraged the most docile sort of pack journalism" where members of the national media competed in tandem for whatever censored information and video images that the White House and the Pentagon allowed them to communicate.[B] The public relations and propaganda strategy was fairly straightforward: "provide a lot of military briefings and high-tech videos to keep the press supplied with images and reports, impose strict censorship on everything you don't want covered (including images of people returning home in 'human-remains pouches'), overemphasize your successes and tell nothing of your failures. Most of all, keep the human dimension to a minimum."[C]

The Pentagon communicated through the news media to the American public a picture of an American military machine that was flawless in action. Television, for example, replayed again and again successful hits by American smart bombs that never seemed to miss their targets. The war seemed to be fought so efficiently and cleanly that it seemed more like a "Nintendo" game than a war. As impressive as the air war was conducted by the United States and its allies, however, information released by the Department of Defense after completion of the war indicates that of the 88,000 tons of bombs dropped on Kuwait and Iraq only 7 percent were "precision-guided" munitions that approximated their targets 90 percent of the time, while over 90 percent were "dumb" conventional bombs that missed their target 75 percent of the time. This accurate portrait of the air war "contrasted sharply with the high-tech, never-miss image that the Pentagon carefully cultivated during the war."[D]

Although this was the most massive bombing and military campaign since the Vietnam War, Americans did not see any bloodshed during the war. American folks at home saw a "sanitized" war even though there were massive deaths, involving anywhere from 100,000 to 200,000 casualties suffered by Iraqi military and civilians (with thousands dying indirectly after hostilities ceased due to destruction of urban infrastructures). The Pentagon took the ultimate step to shield the American public from witnessing the costs of the Persian Gulf War: the honors ceremonies given to U.S. troops killed in action when their flag-draped coffins returned to the military's main East Coast mortuary at Dover Air Force Base in Delaware were, unlike previous wars, not open to the public and the press.[E]

Walter Cronkite, the granddaddy of television anchors for CBS News throughout the 1960s, concluded that "with an arrogance foreign to the democratic system, the U.S. military in Saudi Arabia is trampling on the American people's right to

A. "The Propaganda War," *Newsweek* (February 25, 1991): 38.
B. Peter Schmeisser, "Shooting Pool," *New Republic* (March 18, 1991): 21.
C. Susan J. Douglas, "Camouflaging Reality with Faux News, Clever Decoys," *In These Times* (February 13–19, 1991): 20.

D. Barton Gellman, "U.S. Bombs Missed 70% of Time," *Washington Post* (March 16, 1991): A18.
E. Mark Thompson, "Pentagon Dictating Coverage of Conflict," *The State*, Columbia, S.C. (January 20, 1991): 1A, 7A.

know."[F] Nevertheless, even though freedom of the press was heavily censored during the war and the government fed the public what has been referred to as "Iraq, the Movie," the American people seemed to like it that way. The public, typical of a national crisis and war, rallied around the troops and the president. Under these circumstances, the rise of American nationalism accepted government censorship while tolerating little dissent, such as treating the CNN broadcasts of Peter Arnett, the last American reporter in Iraq, as Iraqi propaganda.

Not surprisingly, given the political environment, members of the national media went along and allowed themselves to be managed completely by the government. According to *New York Times* writer Tom Wicker, the press and television "to their discredit" did not "protest as effectively as they should have, or always made it clear as they could have, that much of what they conveyed—like the can't miss version of Air Force bombings—was not only controlled by the military but prettified for home consumption."[G]

If the war had been prolonged and not gone well, dissent would have increased within the mass and elite publics, increasing news media resistance to government censorship. Ultimately, however, the war was quick and went extraordinarily well, thereby allowing government censorship of the media to work to perfection. The White House and the Pentagon proved to be quite successful in using the national media to communicate the information and symbols by which the American public saw and would remember the Persian Gulf War. According to Michael Deaver, President Reagan's deputy chief of staff and communications chief, "The Department of Defense has done an excellent job of managing the news in an almost classic way. There's plenty of access to some things and at least one visual a day. If you were going to hire a public relations firm to do the media relations for an international event, it couldn't be done any better than this is being done."[H] Such successful control and manipulation of the news media reinforced the lessons that the government learned from Vietnam, increasing the likelihood that it will revert to such censorship when war occurs in the future.

F. Walter Cronkite, "What Is There to Hide?" *Newsweek* (February 25, 1991): 43.
G. Tom Wicker, "First Amendment a Casualty of War," *The State*, Columbia, S.C. (March 21, 1991): 14.

H. Alex S. Jones, "Process of News Reporting on Display," *New York Times* (February 15, 1991): A9.

SOURCES: John J. Fialka, *Hotel Warriors: Covering the Gulf War* (Baltimore: Johns Hopkins University Press, 1992); Marie Gottschalk, "Operation Desert Cloud: The Media and the Gulf War," *World Policy Journal* (Summer 1992): 449–86; John R. MacArthur, *Second Front: Censorship and Propaganda in the Gulf* *War* (New York: Hill & Wang, 1992); Michah L. Sifry and Christopher Cerf, eds., *The Gulf War Reader: History, Documents* (New York: Random House, 1991); and U.S., Congress, Senate, Committee on Governmental Affairs, Hearings, *Pentagon Rules on Media Access to the Persian Gulf War* (February 20, 1991).

---

cold war consensus, the rise of Congress, and the proliferation of groups have increased and widened the pool of credible sources of information that the news media may draw upon, which is most likely to occur when government leaders are divided on issues. Ultimately, the politics of U.S. foreign policy since Vietnam involves different individuals and groups in competition for news media access and influence to affect domestic politics and the policymaking process.

IMPLICATIONS FOR THE POLITICS OF U.S. FOREIGN POLICY

· · · · · · · · · · · · · ·

At least six conclusions about news media coverage can be drawn from the discussion above. First, most Americans are dependent on the news media, especially the national media, for information and understanding of national and international affairs. Second, the national media provide a considerable amount of information regarding national and international affairs. Third, coverage tends to be selective and disjointed as stories come and go with little history or context provided. Fourth, the national media tend to provide a homogenized and centrist picture of national and international news consistent with mainstream American political ideology and culture. Fifth, media coverage is influenced by politics and, at the same time, influences domestic politics and the policymaking process. Finally, these patterns are magnified during times of crisis, when certain issues are often inflated and sensationalized. (See **essay 18.2** on crisis coverage.)

These patterns in news media coverage play an important role in the complex politics of U.S. foreign policy. In the words of Doris Graber in *Mass Media and American Politics*:

> The mass media are more than passive transmission agents for available information. Decisions made by media personnel determine what information becomes available to media audiences and what remains unavailable. By putting stories into perspective and interpreting them, media personnel assign meaning to the information and indicate the values by which it ought to be judged. News shaping is unavoidable because space is limited and because facts do not speak for themselves. Hence the media select and shape much of the raw material needed by political elites and the general public for thinking about the political world and planning political action.[58]

In this way the news media and the communications process affect continuity and change in the foreign policy process over time, the president's ability to govern U.S. foreign policy, and the tension between national security and democracy. The media's impact on these three themes can be seen by briefly examining its post–World War II coverage, its consequences for public knowledge, and its role

in the politics of symbolism that have come to pervade American society.

THE MEDIA AND U.S. FOREIGN POLICY SINCE WORLD WAR II

Since the beginning of World War II, there have been three broad patterns in news media coverage as it has related to the making of U.S. foreign policy:

1. During World War II, coverage by the American news media both reflected and reinforced the U.S. government's war effort;
2. During the cold war years, news media coverage reflected and reinforced the anticommunist consensus prevailing throughout society and the government;
3. Since the Vietnam War, news media coverage has had a greater tendency to reflect diverse views and, consequently, become less consistently supportive of the government's foreign policy.

These generalizations refer to general tendencies concerning coverage by the mainstream media most of the time.[59]

World War II Coverage. Once the U.S. government declared war on Japan and entered World War II, the American mass media quickly acted as a medium to rally mass support behind the cause. As we discussed in the previous chapter, times of war are also times of immense nationalism and narrowing of civil liberties, including free speech and free press. The U.S. government censored the media and conducted a domestic propaganda campaign of vast proportions in order to maximize public support and minimize dissent. Despite this censorship, most American journalists were repulsed by Japanese and German imperialism and saw it as their patriotic duty to defend and promote the American way of life.[60]

The media became the principal means by which pictures of the enemy were portrayed to the

---

ESSAY 18.2
CRISIS COVERAGE

Crisis coverage by the news media is extremely important in American politics because crises become major agenda items throughout the country, occupying the attention of policymakers and the general public alike. In order to fully understand the significance of crisis coverage, we must examine patterns in *news media coverage as they proceed through three general stages:* pre-crisis coverage, crisis coverage, and post-crisis coverage. During "crisis coverage," the resources of the media are heavily devoted to covering "the key issue or event" as the lead story. During "pre-crisis coverage" and "post-crisis coverage," however, the bureaucratic and routine nature of media politics prevails where any single issue typically receives little and uneven news coverage.

The **cycle in news media coverage** of an issue—from minimal coverage during routine times to maximum coverage during crisis and then back to minimal coverage after the crisis—deeply impacts the foreign policy process because it affects the understanding and images that people acquire of the issue involved. James Reston of the *New York Times* explained the reactive nature of media crisis coverage this way: "We are fascinated by events but not by the things that cause the events. We will send 500 correspondents to Vietnam after the war breaks out, and fill the front pages with their reports, meanwhile ignoring the rest of the world, but we will not send five reporters there when the danger of war is developing."[A] A study conducted for the State Department's Foreign Service Institute by A. Raphael, for example, found that the three television networks covered Iran an average of only five minutes each year from 1972 to 1977.[B] Yet, with the fall of the Shah of Iran and the taking of American diplomats, the Iran hostage crisis became the ultimate

media event throughout 1979 and 1980 for 444 days. Yet, once the international crisis is perceived to be over—whether Vietnam, Iran, Grenada, or Panama—there is little subsequent attention and follow-up by the media. It is the stark contrast between the media attention given to an issue during a crisis, in comparison to the little attention devoted both before and after, that allows crisis coverage to dramatically impact on people and the politics of U.S. foreign policy.

Unlike the pre- and post-crisis phases, the news media reassign personnel and focus their attention on covering the "lead" story during crisis coverage. Crisis coverage, in fact, often results in "media diplomacy," where television in particular is used as an instrument of communication and negotiation by world leaders. Yet, concentration on the lead story comes at the cost of curtailing coverage of most other national and international news. For example, American media coverage of the Persian Gulf conflict following Iraq's invasion of Kuwait in 1990 overshadowed all other news. Such major domestic and international issues as the savings and loan industry's insolvency and scandal, the government's growing federal debt, the collapse of communism in the Soviet Union and Eastern Europe, the reunification of Germany, and rapid developments in South Africa received little or no media attention throughout much of the crisis.

Most importantly, for all the information provided about a crisis, coverage is incomplete, inflated, and often "sensationalized," especially as a result of the immediacy and powerful images provided by television. Who can forget (for those who aren't too young) the image, for instance, of President Ronald Reagan being shot and pushed into the presidential limousine. Television stations began round-the-clock news coverage and, with little to report, repeatedly replayed tapes of Reagan being shot. In fact Frank Reynolds, ABC's news anchor, announced the death of Jim Brady, the White House press spokesman who was also shot—only to apologize

A. James Reston, *Sketches in the Sand* (New York: Alfred A. Knopf, 1967), p. 195.
B. A. Raphael, "Media Coverage of the Hostage Negotiations—From Fact to Fiction," *Executive Seminars in National and International Affairs* (U.S. Department of State, Foreign Service Institute, 1981–1982).

later when it was learned that Brady actually survived the attack after all. This news blunder is but an extreme example of incomplete and unreliable media coverage that frequently characterizes times of crisis; and with the rise of CNN as part of the national media, round-the-clock coverage has become a more permanent feature of news coverage.

Crises, by definition, are periods of considerable uncertainty and fluidity. Yet, crisis coverage is delivered as if it is comprehensive and accurate because of news media competition to get the story out first and gain the highest audience, especially in television. This is reinforced by the media's preoccupation with reporting new and current developments. Furthermore, crisis coverage is usually accompanied by pack journalism, with most journalists pursuing the same story virtually in unison. During such frenzied searches for news, the news media become even more dependent on a few external sources of information—such as government officials—and, thus, are more vulnerable to being used or manipulated for political ends.

One of the most blatant examples of the president's ability to dominate and manipulate the news media occurred under President Lyndon Johnson. During the **Tonkin Gulf crisis** in the spring of 1965, government officials charged that American destroyers sustained two unprovoked attacks by North Vietnamese warships in international waters. This led to congressional passage of the Tonkin Gulf resolution, with only two dissenting votes, which supported any presidential action taken in Vietnam and helped to legitimize the subsequent Americanization of the war. In fact, accounts now reveal that one of the two North Vietnamese attacks on American destroyers probably never took place and that the American ships were providing intelligence support for South Vietnamese covert military attacks of North Vietnam. Furthermore, the congressional resolution was actually prepared by the Johnson administration before both the Tonkin Gulf crisis and the 1964 presidential election. This suggests that President Johnson and his administration were able to use the Tonkin Gulf crisis to manipulate the media and maximize domestic political support in order to "get tough" and exercise greater force in

Vietnam. In other words, "because of the secrecy and covert nature of the operation, because of administration lies, both the Congress and the public were seriously misled."[C]

What are *the implications of crisis coverage for presidential governance?* First, crisis coverage usually strengthens presidential foreign policy power in the short term. This is primarily because the president becomes the focus of news media attention and the executive branch becomes the major source of information for the media, allowing the president's perspective to dominate the communications process. Such was the case, for example, with President Johnson's Vietnam actions discussed above, for President Reagan with the Grenada invasion, and for President George Bush in the Panama invasion and the conflict in the Persian Gulf. In fact, during the early phases of foreign policy crises, the American media are extremely responsive and vulnerable to becoming overwhelmed with patriotic and nationalistic fervor, typically acting as a medium that promotes the president's views and policies, and contributing to a rally-around-the-flag phenomena throughout the country.

A retired propagandist who spent much of his career with the United States Information Agency noted this nationalistic tendency with respect to media coverage of the Persian Gulf crisis and the initial movement of American troops to Saudi Arabia: "This is the old America we remember. Skipping Vietnam, this is the America our regular propaganda from the turn of the century was all about. It's very interesting to see these very up-to-date electronic media telling the old American story so successfully."[D] Kathleen Hall Jamieson of the Annenberg School of Communications at the University of Pennsylvania made the telling point about the Persian Gulf crisis that "in the early days, the coverage suggested to me that, if you didn't know our television wasn't state-owned, you would have thought it was."[E] At times, in fact, the fixation on communicating the latest tidbits

---

C. David Halberstam, *The Best and the Brightest* (New York: Random House, 1969), p. 412.
D. Gary Blonston, "In War of Words, Who Will Be on the Casualty List?" *The State,* Columbia, S.C. (August 27, 1990): 1A.
E. Ibid.: 7A.

of information provided by the U.S. government on American military troops and war battles by the media reflected a feeling of **journalistic jingoism** (similar to the so-called "yellow" journalism at the turn of the century).

Second, sometimes early crisis coverage may actually weaken presidential power. The most obvious examples involved Presidents Richard Nixon and Ronald Reagan, who each suffered significant political blows, one from Watergate and the other from Iran-Contra. In these cases the crises involved questions of presidential abuse of power and the president's credibility, forcing the news media to turn to other sources of information in covering the crisis. Such a crisis outcome is rare. The media is usually quite hesitant to report news that directly challenges a sitting president due to the rally-around-the-flag norm during a crisis, the public's positive identification with the office of the presidency, and the grave political stakes involved in being too critical of a president.

In this respect, it is important to point out that the national media were actually slow to cover Watergate and Iran-Contra, even though bits and pieces of information had been available and reported for some time. In fact, Watergate became a big story only due to the persistence of Carl Bernstein and Bob Woodward (and unusual risk-taking by certain executives and editors of the *Washington Post*), while Iran-Contra made headlines only after the story was broken by a small Lebanese newspaper.

Third, the longer the crisis endures, the more likely that news media coverage will weaken presidential power. Although Vietnam contributed to presidential power early on, it ended up being the principal cause of President Johnson's political fall. Likewise, the Iran hostage crisis initially boosted President Jimmy Carter's political fortunes, but eventually led to increasing public questioning of his leadership as the crisis dragged on. President Bush began to experience this with the Persian Gulf crisis during the last two months before war broke out. Very simply, the longer a crisis continues, the greater the likelihood that domestic dissent will surface and intensify, both in and out of government, and that the public will tire of policies that are not perceived as successful. Under these conditions, media coverage is likely to reflect the more critical aspects of the evolving political environment, thus constraining the president's power to persuade others to support him and his policies.

SOURCES: Peter Braestrup, *Big Story: How the American Press and Television Reported and Interpreted the Crisis of Tet 1968 in Vietnam and Washington* (New Haven, Conn.: Yale University Press, 1983); Joseph C. Goulden, *Truth is the First Casualty: The Gulf of Tonkin Affair—Illusion and Reality* (Chicago: Rand McNally, 1969); Doris A. Graber, *Mass Media and American Politics* (Washington, D.C.: Congressional Quarterly Press, 1989); Brigitte Lebens Nacos, *The Press, Presidents, and Crises* (New York: Columbia University Press, 1990); Tom Rosentiel, "The Myth of CNN," *New Republic* (August 22 & 29, 1994): 27–33.

American public and acted as an important source for unifying the country against the Axis powers. The media depicted the allied countries as righteous defenders of democracy and freedom against the aggression and evil represented by Germany and Japan. This contributed, among other things, to a West Coast hysteria concerning Japanese sabotage and the internment of Japanese-Americans in concentration camps during the war. (Review essay 17.1 on the World War II internment of Japanese.)

American leaders also used the media to preach the **value of Soviet-American friendship** and continued cooperation following the war. The media popularized the Soviet Union as the great ally of the United States, frequently referring to Joseph Stalin as "Uncle Joe." Stalin, in fact, became *Time* magazine's "Man of the Year" in 1943. Americans, furthermore, were regularly told that Russians were becoming more like them. For instance, *Life* magazine announced in March 1943 that the Russians were "one hell of a people" who "look like Americans, dress like Americans, and think like Americans." In April 1944, the *New York Times* went so far as to declare that it was not a misrepresentation "to say that Marxian thinking in Soviet Russia is out. The capitalist system, better described as the competitive system, is back."[61] Thus, not only did the media play a prominent role during World War II in reflecting the views of the U.S. government and promoting American nationalism, they also contributed to creating a set of unrealistic expectations about Soviet-American friendship that would haunt the postwar years.

Cold War Coverage. Immediately following World War II, the American news media began to reflect greater diversity of views, consistent with the great political debate raging over the future of U.S. foreign policy. However, with the rise of the cold war, media coverage again began to narrow and reflect the growing anticommunist political environment. The administrations of Harry Truman and Dwight Eisenhower communicated their fears of communism through the media to both educate the mass public and rally support for the containment policy. Such media coverage both reflected and contributed to the rise of the political Right and anticommunism, further narrowing public debate.

A prime example of the active influence of the news media in the politics of anticommunism can be seen in the **portrayal of American-Chinese relations** after 1949: Taiwan, or the Republic of China, was the "real" China and ally of the United States, while the People's Republic of China was an illegitimate and expansionist communist state in alliance with Soviet communism. "Substantial elements of the press helped to promote the China lobby's line: Henry Luce, whose family had China ties, and his forceful wife Claire then had more influence over some of their publications than most major news publishers have today—especially *Life.*" According to Russell Howe and Sarah Trott in *The Power Peddlers,* "pro-Chiang policy was imposed on the *Washington Times-Herald,* the *Chicago Tribune,* and the Hearst press—notably the *New York Journal-American,* the *Los Angeles Examiner,* and the *San Francisco Examiner.*" In addition, other publications put out the lobby line such as *Collier's, The Saturday Evening Post, Reader's Digest,* and *U.S. News & World Report.* Furthermore, "countless unsuspecting editors also printed China lobby copy, given free of charge to wire and feature services."[62]

As Edwin Bayley found in *Joe McCarthy and the Press,* charges of internal subversion were news and contributed to the rise of Senator Joseph McCarthy and McCarthyism.[63] Media coverage also eventually led to the downfall of Senator McCarthy. Nevertheless, by the mid-1950s an anticommunist consensus pervaded American society, including American journalism. There was no outright government censorship of the news media during the cold war (except for Korean War coverage)—there didn't need to be for a consensus of thought clearly existed throughout American society. In other words, during the 1950s and most of the 1960s, anti-Soviet communist and pro-American democratic-capitalist perceptions colored how the world and U.S. foreign policy were seen and interpreted by the media to the American public.

In fact, as Carl Bernstein has reported, over 400 American journalists occasionally worked closely for the CIA, and many carried out assignments (not always knowingly). This included major executives and reporters in the field from every major news organization in the country, as well as a few minor ones.[64] As pointed out by the Senate "Church" committee investigation in 1975, such "cozy" relationships between **the media and the CIA** (and the intelligence community) raise serious concerns: about the "potential, inherent in covert media operations, for manipulating or incidentally misleading the American public," and the "damage to the credibility and independence of a free press."[65] Such concerns about the integrity of a "free press" gets to the heart of the contradictions that are endemic between the demands of national security and democratic practice.

Although the media is credited with being critical of the Vietnam War, it is usually forgotten that during the late 1950s and early 1960s the media dutifully communicated the government's position and **promoted the Americanization of the Vietnam War.** As described by David Halberstam in *The Powers That Be,* "The great heads of the media were anxious to be good and loyal citizens, and the working reporters had almost without question accepted the word of the White House on foreign policy.... The press corps might be congenitally skeptical in assessing the intentions and ambitions of domestic politicians, but it brought no such toughness of mind to the politics of foreign policy."[66] Thus, the media contributed to the growth of presidential power in foreign affairs and the rise of a national security ethos in which the demands of national security often prevailed over the demands of democracy in response to the cold war.[67]

Given the national emergencies represented by World War II and the cold war, it is understandable that the views dominating the executive branch pervaded the news media and became the orthodoxy by which Americans understood international politics and U.S. foreign policy. As a popular saying goes, "winners write history." In other words, those individuals and groups most politically successful within government and throughout society are better able, through use of the media and the communications process, to **define the popular or orthodox interpretation** of the United States and the world—in this case, of the origins of the cold war in the postwar years. Therefore, most Americans, including journalists, came to believe that the cold war was caused by Soviet communist expansion throughout Europe and the world, necessitating an American response that emphasized containment and the use of force—which was consistent with the government's position during the cold war years.

Post–Vietnam War Coverage. Reflecting the breakdown of the anticommunist consensus, it was not until the mid- and late 1960s that the news media's coverage of the Vietnam War became more critical of the government. As Daniel Hallin found in *The Uncensored War,* media coverage of U.S. foreign policy in general and Vietnam policy in particular tended to reflect events occurring inside the government. As long as consensus prevailed within the government, media coverage reflected this consensus and supported government policy. It was only when dissent increased within the government—both in Congress and in the Johnson administration—that media coverage became more critical of the war and the government's policies.[68]

By the late 1960s and early 1970s, media coverage increasingly reflected the collapse of the anti-

communist consensus throughout the government and society. The Watergate crisis, in fact, represented the height of a "critical" and "cynical" media independent of the administration and engaged in investigative reporting. Still, the American failure in the Vietnam War was one of the few times that the popular interpretation—that Vietnam did not represent a vital interest and that the war was a mistake—was inconsistent with the presidential view that had prevailed under John Kennedy and Lyndon Johnson.

Today's news media retain some of the legacy of the Vietnam and Watergate experience. Clearly, since Vietnam the president no longer monopolizes media coverage as he did during World War II and the cold war. With the collapse of the anticommunist consensus, the media are more likely to represent a greater diversity of foreign policy thought, rely on more sources of information throughout society and in the policymaking process, and present news in a more critical and cynical fashion. This has contributed to the rise of Congress, the proliferation of group politics in the making of U.S. foreign policy, and the expansion of public affairs programs on television: public television aired "The MacNeil-Lehrer Report" in 1975, in 1980 ABC's "Nightline" went nightly and CNN was born, and a year later the Sunday morning news shows saw the addition of ABC's "This Week with David Brinkley."

At the same time, there remains a strong cold war and realpolitik legacy among American journalists in their coverage of foreign policy and international affairs. This tendency is evidenced by the media's continued reliance on governmental sources of information, particularly the White House and the national security bureaucracy, and preoccupation with international conflict, especially the use of force. These contradictory patterns of continuity and change are reflected, for example, in the media coverage of the Iran-Contra affair (see **essay 18.3**).

Iran-Contra coverage demonstrated both the strengths and limitations of news media coverage as a source of information and understanding, which have important implications for presidential governance in the post–Vietnam War era. Although the president continues to enjoy great media visibility

ESSAY 18.3
MEDIA COVERAGE OF THE IRAN-CONTRA AFFAIR

News media coverage of Iran-Contra and its political impact went through three general stages: sporadic coverage of Iran-Contra from 1981 to 1986 in which the Ronald Reagan administration was able to keep most of its covert activities hidden; crisis coverage in 1986 and 1987 in which much of the covert foreign policy came to light and damaged the Reagan presidency; and minimal coverage following 1987 when the issue and its political impact faded. Where news media coverage during the second stage was more reflective of the Vietnam legacy, coverage during the first and third stages was more reminiscent of the national security and realpolitik legacy in American journalism.

Throughout the 1980s, Central American policy was high on the foreign policy agenda for the Reagan administration and, consequently, for the news media. Most of the media coverage from 1981 to 1986, however, focused on the administration's "overt" foreign policy in Central America and legislative-executive battles over contra funding. There was some investigative reporting on the Reagan administration's "covert" contra war abroad and at home, but it was sporadic with little follow-up.

In "Iran-Contra: Was the Press Any Match for All the President's Men?," Scott Armstrong observes that "Exotic-sounding theories about an elaborate private arms network seemed to scare away the very papers—*The New York Times, The Wall Street Journal, The Washington Post*—that had earlier exposed the complicated exploits of CIA renegade Edwin Wilson, who had used some of the same personnel that would turn up in the Iran-Contra arms network."[A] Furthermore, the covert Iranian transactions remained almost totally hidden from the media. Overall, Armstrong concluded that the "press showed an ability to pick up pieces but less skill at putting them together. . . . There was no in-

stitutional memory. Breakthroughs by star reporters passed largely unnoticed by peers until months or years after they were first published or aired."[B]

This situation changed dramatically when a CIA proprietary airplane with Americans on board, attempting to resupply the contras, was shot down over Nicaragua on October, 5, 1986, clearly exposing the Reagan administration's effort to circumvent the congressional ban on assisting the contras. Shortly afterwards, on November 3, a small Lebanese newspaper, *al-Shiraa*—not the American news media—broke the story of the secret arms-for-hostage dealings between the U.S. and Iran in violation of the president's public proclamations against negotiating with terrorists. With these headline stories, the national media began "frenzied" coverage of President Reagan's denials, Attorney General Edwin Meese's announcement of the diversion of funds from Iranian arms sales to the contras, the Tower Commission report, and finally the congressional hearings during the summer of 1987.

Although considerable information was revealed, the news media ultimately "sensationalized and simplified" the Iran-Contra affair. In covering the congressional inquiry, discussed in chapter 12, efforts to acquire a full understanding of Iran-Contra were lost in the search for "good guys" and "bad guys." According to Armstrong, reporters began to concentrate "on who was scoring more public relations points on any given day—the witnesses or the committee members and their counsel."[C] Hence, while Colonel Oliver North was initially depicted as a villain by the news media, he was later portrayed as a hero as a result of his testimony. The same simplification of reality occurred with the growth in preoccupation about the question of what did the president know of the "diversion" of monies from the Iran arms deal to the contras? As described by Armstrong, "What had been an informed and effective

---

A. Scott Armstrong, "Iran-Contra: Was the Press Any Match for All the President's Men?", *Columbia Journalism Review* (May/June 1990): 28.

B. Ibid.: 28, 29.
C. Ibid.: 31.

corps of journalists, independently pursuing the story in the preceding months, mysteriously gravitated toward this one question."[D]

Following the congressional hearings and the publication of their report, news media coverage of Iran-Contra declined precipitously as the 1988 electoral race heated up, even though Vice President George Bush's role remained unclear. "While the North trial should have provided all the fuel that was necessary to keep the journalistic inquiry running, the press seemed to lose interest, perking up briefly only when some key Iran-Contra players were nominated for high-level posts in the new administration."[E] Hence, Iran-Contra became news media history.

Overall, much was revealed, much remained hidden, and the larger questions were ignored. Most Americans, therefore, came away from the Iran-Contra coverage with an interpretation consistent with either the more optimistic Tower Commission report, which emphasized the flawed policies of the Iran initiative, or the more pessimistic report published by the congressional inquiry, which emphasized a disregard for the law by a small group of administration officials. In both cases, however, the president was portrayed as having lost control of the

ship of state in which the covert operations were aberrations. Thus, the prime lesson was the need for competent and vigilant personnel in the White House and the executive branch.

Yet, neither Congress nor the news media sufficiently explored the full complexity and implications of Iran-Contra (see chapter 9 on intelligence activities). To what extent have such covert operations been an integral part of U.S. foreign policy since the start of the cold war? What was the full scope of the covert activities involving Iran and, in particular, the contras? How widespread was knowledge and involvement in Iran-Contra throughout the executive branch, the legislative branch, and beyond? To what extent did the national security demands of Iran-Contra contradict and circumvent the demands of democracy and the Constitution? In conclusion, Armstrong and the handful of other journalists who attempted to investigate the story and present a comprehensive picture expressed their frustration at the half-hearted congressional investigation, and stressed that "their strongest complaints were reserved for their peers—those editors and colleagues who treated the subject of constitutional violations as academic or, worse, as trivial, precisely because Congress had not responded with outrage."[F]

D. Ibid.: 30.
E. Ibid.: 34.

F. Ibid.

SOURCES: Scott Armstrong, "Iran-Contra: Was the Press Any Match for All the President's Men?" *Columbia Journalism Review* (May/June 1990): 27–35; Robert Parry and Peter Kornbluh, "Iran-Contra's Untold Story," *Foreign Policy* (Fall 1988): 3–30; and Bob Woodward, *Veil: The Secret Wars of the CIA, 1981–1987* (New York: Pocket Books, 1987).

and influence, his policies and views are much less likely to dominate the news for an extended period of time due to the decline of presidential power, rise of Congress, increase in ideological diversity, and proliferation of interest groups and social movements. Because the pattern of media coverage since Vietnam is much more complex than during World War II and the cold war years, we can expect much greater uncertainty as to whether media coverage will strengthen the president or act as a constraint on the exercise of his power.

Sometimes news media coverage ends up being more supportive of the president, sometimes it is more critical—much depends on the nature of the issue, the political environment, and the times. This was the case not only with media coverage of Iran-Contra but with "coverage of the Persian Gulf crisis" and war as well. Early in the crisis, the cold war legacy prevailed as the bulk of the country rallied around the flag and the media acted as the bullhorn of the Bush administration's Persian Gulf policy. By the middle of the crisis, when dissension began to spread among the mass and elite publics symbolized by the Senate Armed Services Committee hearings and divisions in Congress, media coverage became more independent and open to critical views of presidential policy reminiscent of the latter stages of the Vietnam War. But with the start of the war, the media communicated the White House and military perspective while acquiescing in its censorship by the government. This cyclical pattern in media coverage was similar to the evolution of public opinion during the Persian Gulf crisis (as depicted in essay 14.1). Therefore, the media act as a major source of both presidential power and the paradox of presidential power.

PUBLIC KNOWLEDGE AND DEMOCRATIC CITIZENSHIP

Because Americans are dependent on the media as their fundamental source of information concerning national and international affairs, the news media have a major impact on **public knowledge and democratic citizenship** in the politics of U.S. foreign policy. At best, "most Americans" acquire a simplistic awareness and familiarity of the world around them. This is because the mass public, as discussed in chapter 14, tends to be uninterested, inattentive, uninformed, and, therefore, most receptive to media headlines. This simplistic awareness also is due to the public's tendency to be "overnewsed" and "underinformed" by the media: issues appear one day and disappear the next, coverage jumps from one crisis to another, the emphasis is on the immediacy of news over history and context, the focus is on established institutions and government officials—especially the president—as opposed to the complexity of society and the world.

This problem is much more severe with respect to international news, for most Americans lack the context to make sense of the information and images being communicated to them about "foreign" places abroad. Not surprisingly, most members of the mass public often find events confusing and acquire only very simplistic images of the world.[69] The net result is a mass public that bears little resemblance to the "alert and knowledgeable citizenry" called for by President Eisenhower (see essay 14.3 on his farewell address). Instead, we see a mass public that is overwhelmingly uninterested and uninformed, yet heavily dependent on the media. As a consequence, the nature of media coverage contributes to wild fluctuations in public opinion and swings in public mood, which affect both domestic politics and the policymaking process.[70]

If Eisenhower's alert and knowledgeable citizenry is to be found anywhere, it would most likely be among the "elite public" within American society. Yet, most members of the elite public also tend to rely heavily on the national media for their basic sources of information. They become informed, but learn little history and acquire only a rather narrow range of ideological interpretations of national and international affairs. Furthermore, unless individuals are already knowledgeable about the world and make a concerted effort to use that knowledge when viewing or reading the media, media coverage, especially during crises, will likely determine not only what issues members of the elite public think about but how they go about examining those issues.[71]

The information and images communicated by the media, therefore, contributed to the rise of antifascism during World War II and anticommunism during the cold war among the mass and elite publics. This promoted a preoccupation with the demands of national security over the demands of democracy, and contributed to the political conformity and passivity of most Americans even though the civil liberties of many citizens were being violated (as discussed in the previous chapter). Although post–Vietnam War media coverage has broadened and reflects a greater concern for the demands of democracy, it nonetheless continues to affect public knowledge and political participation. Crisis coverage by the mainstream media, for example, exerts a powerful influence over both elite and mass publics in terms of how they see and react to the world.

News media **coverage of the Iran hostage crisis** in 1979 and 1980, for instance, contributed to an increase in American nationalism, accompanied by a fear of Islam and intense hatred of the Ayatollah

Khomeini and Iran. Yet, even with massive reporting of the Iran hostage crisis, rarely was it communicated to the American people that their government (along with the British) was responsible for covertly overthrowing the nationalist leader of Iran in 1953 and imposing the Shah on the Iranian people. Furthermore, continuous U.S. government support for the Shah's regime over the years, even though he increasingly governed as a ruthless dictator, was downplayed. Consequently, it is not surprising that most Americans, within the mass and elite public, had great difficulty understanding the predominant Iranian view of the U.S. government as the "Great Satan." Instead, they saw the United States as an innocent victim at the hands of the "crazed" Iranian government and people.[72] Not only did this affect the fate of President Jimmy Carter and his administration, this simple and intensely nationalistic view shared by most Americans was triggered once again when it became public that the Reagan administration was selling arms to Iran in exchange for American hostages years later.

News media **coverage of the electoral process** provides another illustration of the powerful role played by the media in affecting public knowledge, democratic citizenship, and the outcomes of elections. On the one hand, interested and knowledgeable members of the public have access to a considerable amount of information concerning the candidates, the parties, and their policy positions. On the other hand, studies have demonstrated that the media emphasize "personal rather than professional qualities of the candidates and campaign events rather than substantive issues. Stories are chosen for their newsworthiness, not their educational value."[73] Overall, the media is overwhelmingly preoccupied with the "horse race" aspects of elections, that is, who is up, who is down, and why. This is especially true with respect to the presidency—the "superbowl" of news media coverage. This not only fails to promote a knowledgeable citizenry, but the television networks have demonstrated a disregard for the "right to vote" by their competitiveness to predict winners even before the polls closed.[74]

In addition to the "lack of depth" of election coverage, the "narrow breadth" of news media coverage also impacts on public knowledge of candidates and participation in electoral politics. Most Americans believe, for example, that only two candidates compete for the presidency. True, only two "major" candidates from the Democratic and Republican parties actually have a viable chance to win election. However, sixteen official candidates and parties competed for the presidency in 1984; in 1980, there were twenty-one candidates and parties; and in 1976 fifteen candidates and parties entered the fray (see **table 18.1** for an example of the presidential candidates in the 1980 election). Although third parties have little chance of winning, their efforts nonetheless have the potential to influence the major parties and American politics—as evidenced by the recent presidential campaigns of Ross Perot, thus indirectly impacting public policy and U.S. foreign policy.

The numbers of candidates actually have grown over time: from 1920 to 1948, there were an average of seven to eight presidential candidates entered in each election; from 1956 to 1972, the average was eleven; and since 1976, the average has been seventeen presidential candidates. Most Americans, however, are unaware of this because the media only cover the campaigns of the two major parties. Rather than informing the public about the various candidates and parties running for office, thus allowing the public to choose in accordance with democratic practice, concentrated media coverage of the two major parties "de-legitimizes" and "marginalizes" the other parties, reducing their potential political influence and, ultimately, narrowing the choice of presidential candidates for Americans down to two.

The best illustration of the power of the media in this respect is the independent presidential "candidacy" of John B. Anderson. In 1980, when Anderson broke from the Republican party and ran as an independent, he received considerable media coverage and over 5,720,000 votes. In the 1984 campaign, he was totally ignored by the media and received only 1,486 votes.[75] Ross Perot also received much less media attention the second time he ran; not surprisingly his popular vote dropped from 1992 to 1996 by almost half. Such media selectivity of the

TABLE 18.1
1980 PRESIDENTIAL ELECTION RESULTS

Ronald Reagan and George Bush, *Republican*	43,904,153
Jimmy Carter and Walter F. Mondale, *Democratic*	35,483,883
John B. Anderson and Patrick J. Lucey, *Independent*	5,720,060
Edward B. Clark and David Koch, *Libertarian*	921,299
Barry Commoner and LaDonna Davis, *Citizens*	234,294
Gus Hall and Angela Davis, *Communist*	45,023
John R. Rarick and Eileen M. Shearer, *American Independent*	41.268
Clifton DeBerry and Matilde Zimmermann, *Socialist Workers*	38,737
Ellen McCormack and Carroll Driscoll, *Right to Life*	32,327
Maureen Smith and Elizabeth Barron, *Peace and Freedom*	18, 116
Dierdre Griswold and Larry Holmes, *Workers World*	13,300
Benjamin C. Bubar and Earl F. Dodge, *Statesman*	7,212
David McReynolds and Diane Drufenbrock, *Socialist*	6,898
Percy L. Greaves and Frank L. Varnum, *American*	6,647
Andrew Pulley and Matilde Zimmermann, *Socialist Workers*	6,272
Richard Congress and Matilde Zimmermann, *Socialist Workers*	4,029
Kurt Lynen and Harry Kieve, *Middle Class*	3,694
Bill Gahres and J. F. Laughlin, *Down With Lawyers*	1,718
Frank W. Shelton and George E. Jackson, *American*	1,555
Martin E. Wendelken with no vice-presidential candidate, *Independent*	923
Harley McLain, and Jewelie Goeller, *Natural Peoples*	296

NOTE: The candidates listed above are those who appeared on ballots in at least one state.

SOURCE: Richard M. Scammon and Alice V. McGillivray, eds., *America at the Polls: The Vote for President, 1968–1984* (Washington, DC: Congressional Quarterly Press, 1988).

electoral process serves to reinforce the status quo in American politics and the making of U.S. foreign policy.

Therefore, while most Americans rely on the mainstream and national media for their information and understanding of the world around them, they should be sensitive, and somewhat cynical, to the limits inherent in mainstream media coverage. In fact, much of the public probably realizes this at times, contributing to a certain "need-hate" relationship with the news media.[76] Such tension between the public in general and the media may simply be unavoidable in today's world.

Nevertheless, as Jerome Barron argues in *Freedom of the Press for Whom? The Right of Access to the Mass Media,* the mainstream media have fought for broad rights of free expression for themselves while, at the same time, they have denied much of the public access to media coverage.[77] Timothy Cook, in *Making Laws and Making News,* concludes that the democratization of political news requires perspectives besides those provided by members of the

Washington political community. In other words, a "multiperspectival" news is needed—"news that would include opinions of the public as well as those of officials, news about programs as they actually operate rather than as they are intended to work, and news that reflects a much greater variety of sources."[78]

THE PREVALENCE OF SYMBOLIC POLITICS

Public knowledge and political participation are affected not only by the information communicated by the media, but also by the **politics of symbolism** that pervades the political system and the mass media. Symbolism has been important in politics throughout history, especially given the role of American political culture as discussed in chapter 14. However, its presence today may be even more pervasive due to the rise of mass communications, particularly television.[79]

Symbolism is a powerful force in American politics because of the interaction of the media—which affects the information and images acquired by Americans, the political agenda, and the climate of opinion—and an overwhelmingly inattentive and uninformed public. Therefore, individuals and groups involved in American politics have increasingly attempted to use the media, especially television, to make symbolic appeals to the people in an attempt to gain their attention and support. Ultimately, the politics of symbolism seriously affects the **political legitimacy** of political actors and institutions, including the president and his ability to govern the country and make foreign policy.[80]

Power, for the president or any political actor, depends heavily on the illusion of power and the politics of symbolism. This was one of the key elements used by the Reagan presidency in overcoming the paradox of presidential power. In *The Power Game*, Hedrick Smith referred to the Reagan administration as the **"Television Presidency."** As he explained it, "Reagan is so natural onstage that, unlike most politicians, he creates the illusion of not being onstage."[81] Furthermore, "Reagan has a political genius for selling his message—like the genius of Franklin Roosevelt. His secret is his mastery of political shorthand. He knows how to make ideas accessible and popular."[82] Since Vietnam, Reagan and his administration have been the masters of the "soundbite" and the politics of symbolism:

Politicians and voters depend on labels, slogans, quick-stick, fast-fix clichés immediately recognizable to millions (though vaguely understood): Communists, welfare cheats, bureaucrats, New Right, New Deal, Star Wars, deficit spenders, supply-side, tax reform, evil empire. Reagan has a knack for coining phrases that tap into reservoirs of popular feeling—like his refrain to "get government off your back"—without having to explain what he means in policy terms, what his ideas will cost, or whom they will hurt. He is a master at using symbols that convey broad intention and leave him free to interpret their meaning.[83]

The **Bush administration's depiction of General Manuel Noriega** is a classic example of the politics of symbolism as it used the news media to rally the American public in support of the invasion of Panama in December of 1989. According to an article in the *Los Angeles Times*, "American military officials, from General Thurman on down, in a procession of news conferences, guided tours and press releases, released unsavory material—much of which has been accepted by American reporters on the scene—to emphasize that Noriega was too base ever to have merited legitimate leadership and too evil to be allowed to go on unbridled." Through this public relations campaign, Americans learned that Noriega was a narco-terrorist who "wore red underwear to ward off the evil eye, practiced voodoo with vats of blood and animal entrails, kept a witch's diary in the same room with his favorite pornography and a portrait of Adolf Hitler, cavorted with his mistress in the mirror-walled bedroom of a luxurious yacht, and loutishly ignored the well-being of his wife while warning only his mistress that the American invasion was on its way."[84]

As the authors of this article observe, these official actions resemble "classic war propaganda" in which an enemy country is personified as the devil. (See essay 17.1 on pictures of the enemy.) Who was the target of the public relations campaign? The American people, since their support is crucial to the president's ability to govern. Therefore, administration officials utilized powerful symbols that would elicit a negative emotional reaction at the mere thought of Noriega. However, as we saw in chapter 9, U.S. relations with Noriega had a more complex and longer history than most Americans realize: Noriega had been on the Central Intelligence Agency (CIA) payroll since 1960, providing intelligence information and cooperation. Even though Noriega was involved in drug trafficking since 1971, he continued on the CIA payroll and was reportedly paid over $100,000 a year in 1976 when Bush was director of Central Intelligence and $200,000 when William Casey became the DCI under President Reagan. He also had helped the Reagan administration support the contras with guns, money, and training in its covert war against the Sandinistas. Obviously, these facts were not shared with the American people by administration officials—it would not have been "smart" politics—and they were correspondingly downplayed or ignored by the mainstream media. Ultimately this strategy worked—the politics of symbolism orchestrated by the Bush administration were successful in manipulating the media and rallying public support behind the invasion, making an ally into an enemy.

This pattern of using the art of persuasion and the politics of symbolism to mobilize the support of the public is not unique to the Panama invasion but *occurs whenever the U.S. government has relied on the "use of force" abroad.* Throughout the cold war, military intervention abroad was sold as essential in order to eradicate the threat of communism. Daniel Hallin, in The *Uncensored War,* found that:

Television coverage of Vietnam dehumanized the enemy, drained him of all recog-

nizable emotions and motives and thus banished him not only from the political sphere, but from human society itself. The North Vietnamese and Vietcong were "fanatical," "suicidal," "savage," "halfcrazed." They were lower than mere criminals (there is usually some "human interest" angle in crime reporting): they were vermin. Television reports routinely referred to areas controlled by the NLF [National Liberation Front] as "Communist infested" or "Vietcong infested."[85]

In the post–cold war global environment new pictures of the enemy have to be highlighted and sold to the public. Hence, Saddam Hussein of Iraq ultimately was not portrayed as a communist threat (or a threat to cheap oil or American geopolitical interests in the Middle East) by the Bush administration following his invasion of Kuwait, but as an aggressor in the vein of Adolf Hitler and Nazi Germany. Such politics of symbolism are more important to the president in the post–Vietnam War era than ever before because of the uncertainty of presidential control of the media and the need to overcome the paradox of presidential power.

The politics of symbolism pervades American politics because perceptions of reality are as important as reality itself, especially given the limited interest of most Americans for national and international affairs. For example, the rise of the crisis of governance since the Vietnam War and the decline in public trust of government officials and the policymaking process have resulted in what Hedrick Smith calls the rise of **blame game politics.**[86] In other words, when the policymaking process becomes gridlocked, when policies fail, or when they are poorly received by the public, all government and private parties involved rush to disclaim any responsibility and blame others: the president blames Congress, members of Congress blame the president, Republicans blame Democrats, and Democrats blame Republicans. Given this atmosphere, it has become fashionable for politicians to "run against Washington."

Elections are, in fact, the ultimate manifestation of media and symbolic politics. As Joe McGinniss demonstrated in 1968, the successful presidential campaign of Richard Nixon represented *The Selling of the President.*[87] Although the marketing of candidates, the use of symbolic appeals, and negative campaigning have been the hallmarks of election campaigns throughout American history, such efforts have become more systematic and pervasive with time. Today, as discussed in chapter 16, candidates rely heavily on marketing firms, political consultants, advertising and public relations campaigns, and, most importantly, the power of television to attract voter attention and support—or, at least, turn voters against opposition candidates.[88]

This emphasis on marketing and symbolism has been reinforced by the media's coverage of elections, including presidential elections. For example, "an analysis of all week day evening network newscasts from Labor Day to Election Day in 1968 and 1988 reveals that the average 'sound bite' [on television] fell from 42 seconds in 1968 to only 9 seconds in 1988. Meanwhile the time the networks devoted to visuals of the candidates, unaccompanied by their words, increased by more than 300 percent."[89] Not much has changed as the U.S. approaches the twenty-first century.

While the politics of symbolism have become more pervasive with time, everybody involved nonetheless makes a concerted effort to **appear "above politics."** This is because politicians want to appear principled and statesmanlike, journalists are steeped in a culture of objective reporting, and the public expects politics in the United States, in comparison to politics in other countries and domains, to be more consistent with American political culture and, thus, "less political"—that is, more moral and clean. As Timothy Wirth, a Democratic congressman from Colorado, commented while preparing a video news release for the local media back home, "You have to get over the embarrassment of doing [public relations] and feeling it's hokey."[90] After all, as Hedrick Smith would say, it's all part of *The Power Game.* Thus, the gap between the symbolic politics seen by most Americans and the day-to-day practice of politics and the making of U.S. foreign policy continues, and may be growing.

THE ENTERTAINMENT MEDIA

While attention has focused on the influence of the news media on American politics, the role of the **entertainment media** must also be considered. The news, after all, is only a small part of mass media offerings. The mass media's basic orientation is to entertain people: through television, radio, movies, novels, and more. Americans respond voraciously; most Americans are much more interested in being entertained than in being informed about public affairs and, thus, devote a considerable amount of attention to the entertainment media, especially television. Given the importance of entertainment programming—accompanied by a considerable amount of advertising—for the mass media and the general public, the entertainment media may have an indirect and subtle effect on American political beliefs and behavior. If anything, *the entertainment media appear to reinforce the consequences of the news media on American politics and U.S. foreign policy discussed above.*[91]

First, the entertainment media reinforce the pattern of public knowledge and democratic citizenship that prevails for most Americans. For example, watching and listening to entertainment shows (with an occasional newsbreak) on the television on a daily basis contributes to a public that is uninterested and uninformed concerning national and international affairs. Not only does a preference for entertainment lower the priority for information about the world, the contents of the programs themselves often promote simplistic and stereotypical images of the world. As Todd Gitlin observes in *Inside Prime Time*, "what comes across the small screen amounts to an entertaining version of the world."[92] Therefore, it should not be surprising that entertainment often is substituted for information.

A study by George Gerbner and the Annenberg School of Communications, for example, found that perceptions of reality concerning American sex roles, age, race, work, health, and crime by "heavy viewers" of television (those who watch more than four hours a day, representing about one-third of the population) closely reflected the misrepresentations and biases of the world found on entertainment television.[93] If entertainment viewing affects Americans' perceptions of their own country, imagine the effect it may have on the image that Americans acquire of the rest of the world. According to Gerbner, "no other medium reaches into every home or has a comparable, cradle-to-grave influence over what a society learns about itself."[94]

Second, the content and images of the entertainment media reflect the political environment of the times, reinforcing the evolution of news coverage. During World War II, for example, **Hollywood movies**—one of the major forms of mass entertainment—were overwhelmingly patriotic in nature, depicting the United States as the "land of the free and the home of the brave."[95] In war movies, Americans tended to be portrayed as innocent victims of aggression by ruthless and evil heathens, such as the Nazis and the Japanese. Some of this was a function of an industry that allowed itself to be censored in the name of national security. As explained by Clayton Koppes and Gregory Black in *Hollywood Goes to War:*

> During the war the government, convinced that movies had extraordinary power to mobilize public opinion for war, carried out an intensive, unprecedented effort to mold the content of Hollywood feature films. Officials of the Office of War Information, the government's propaganda agency, issued a constantly updated manual instructing the studios in how to assist the war effort, sat in on story conferences with Hollywood's top brass, reviewed the screenplays of every major studio (except the recalcitrant Paramount), pressured the movie makers to change scripts and even scrap pictures when they found objectionable material, and sometimes wrote dialogue for key speeches.[96]

This pattern continued into the cold war years. Although government censorship was lifted, its legacy remained with the rise of McCarthyism, the "blacklists," and the anticommunist consensus throughout society. "Enemies changed, with wrenching suddenness," observed John Dower in *War Without Mercy,* "but the concept of 'the enemy' remained impressively impervious to drastic alteration, and in its peculiar way provided psychological continuity and stability from the world war to the cold war."[97] Hence, as J. Fred MacDonald describes in *Television and the Red Menace: The Video Road to Vietnam,* the entertainment media during the cold war years became filled with dehumanized images of the communist bogeyman and the totalitarian threat to the United States and the "free" world.[98]

Such images reinforced and contributed to the anticommunist consensus throughout American society. It was not until the 1960s that this cold war image of America was finally challenged within the entertainment media, most noticeably by the youth culture and, in part, through the growing popularity of **rock music**—another form of entertainment media (see **essay 18.4** on the politics of rock 'n' roll). With the eventual collapse of the anticommunist and ideological consensus following the Vietnam War, the topics and images in the entertainment media pertaining to national and international affairs began to reflect the greater diversity of the times.

John Wayne's *Green Berets,* reflecting the classic cold warrior view of an overconfident America (inevitably) containing the threat of communism in Vietnam, for example, has given way to interpretations and impressions of the Vietnam War ranging from *Rambo* to *Apocalypse Now* to *Platoon* to *Born on the Fourth of July* (as well as to television's "China Beach" and "Tour of Duty," as well as the movie and television show "M*A*S*H," despite its Korean War context).[99] Greater ideological diversity is reflected in the entertainment industry in general, including situation comedies, dramatic series, and docudramas on television. However, these shows remain entertainment oriented. Therefore, given the levels of public interest and information, the entertainment

ESSAY 18.4
THE POLITICS OF ROCK MUSIC

Rock music first became popular with American youth during the 1950s. The roots of what initially became known as **"rock 'n' roll"** are found in country music, gospel, and, most importantly, the blues, which was quite prevalent throughout the black community. Most American adults were initially repulsed by the growing popularity of rock 'n' roll among youths in mainstream, middle America. The electricity and sensuality of the music, symbolized by Elvis Presley shaking his hips in the 1950s and the long-haired Beatles (at the time) singing "I Want to Hold Your Hand" to screaming fans in the early 1960s, was scandalous for many Americans, resulting in efforts to censor the music.

Although most rock 'n' roll was relatively innocent "top 40," critics at the time felt rock 'n' roll was a major source of juvenile delinquency, as depicted in the movie *Rebel Without a Cause.* What was happening, as Tom Wolfe pointed out in *The Kandy Kolored Tangerine Flake Streamline Baby,* was that "increasing American affluence" provided adolescent youth with the means to develop their own popular culture for the first time in the history of the world. One of the places to which American youth turned was rock 'n' roll.

Changes in technology, culture, and politics during the 1960s affected the development of rock music. Rock 'n' roll became more sophisticated and refined due to technological improvements such as the development of full-length albums, FM radio, and stereo. Rock 'n' roll also became more experimental and eclectic with time, as indicated by the development of different genres, such as the "Motown sound" of the Supremes and the Temptations; the "folk rock" of Bob Dylan, Simon and Garfunkel, and Joan Baez; the "British rock" of the Beatles and the Rolling Stones; and the "hard rock" of Jefferson Airplane and Jimi Hendrix.

By the mid-1960s, rock 'n' roll had become increasingly popular, particularly due to the incredible popularity of the "Fab Four"—John, Paul, George, and Ringo. Thus, the so-called "golden age of rock music" was born, representing a wide diversity of music and artists. Most importantly, given our interest in the politics of U.S. foreign policy, rock music became increasingly political in both content and style.

With the rise of the civil rights and antiwar movements, rock music began to reflect the values and beliefs of the new Left and, in particular, the counterculture. The *lyrics of songs* increasingly dealt with American injustices at home and abroad and argued for the need to replace war and hatred with peace and love. This was symbolized, for example, by such songs as Bob Dylan's "Blowin' in the Wind," Neil Young's "Southern Man," Graham Nash's "Chicago," Peter, Paul & Mary's "If I Had a Hammer" (written by Pete Seeger), and John Lennon's "Imagine." American exceptionalism during the cold war years and the Vietnam War were commonly caricatured by such songs as "With God on Our Side" by Dylan, "Back in the U.S.S.R." by the Beatles, and "I Feel Like I'm Fixin to Die" by Country Joe and the Fish.

In "The Music of Protest," Robert Rosenstone asserts that in addition to the traditional concerns of war and injustice, the music of youth "worried about such things as the impact of technology on man, the confused state of American sexual practices, and the repressive nature of supposedly democratic institutions."[A] These cultural concerns with the quality of life and personal freedom were popularized, for instance, by such songs as "For What It's Worth" by Buffalo Springfield, the "Sounds of Silence" by Simon and Garfunkel, "Stairway to Heaven" by Led Zeppelin, and Crosby, Stills & Nash's "Teach Your Children." Stylistically, rock concerts—the sound, clothes, hair, drugs, and camaraderie—came to represent an alternative approach to mainstream culture.

A. Robert A. Rosenstone, " 'The Times They Are A-Changin': The Music of Protest," *The Annals* (March 1969), p. 131.

Bob Dylan's "The Times They Are A-Changin'," written in 1963, in many ways became the anthem for the growing generation gap:

Come mothers and fathers throughout the land
And don't criticize what you can't understand
Your sons and daughters are beyond your command.
There's a battle outside and it's ragin'
It'll soon shake your windows and rattle your
  walls . . .
For the times they are a-changin'.

At the same time, the Rolling Stones' "Street Fighting Man," the Doors' "Five to One," the Beatles' "Revolution," and the Youngbloods' "Get Together" were indicative of growing internal differences within the 1960s movements over goals and strategies of change. Differences notwithstanding, the rock music of the time represented a consensus in protest against the status quo. Moreover, it symbolized hope for a rejuvenated America that was best illustrated by Jimi Hendrix's eerie guitar solo of the "American national anthem" at the Woodstock concert in 1969.

The politics of rock music not only reflected the growth of the new Left and the counterculture, but increasingly pervaded all of American society, especially the country's youth. The culture of American youth increasingly revolved around peer interaction and the popularity of rock music. Thus, **youth culture** acted as a major socializing force in the development of political beliefs and individual lifestyles, and rock music became one of the major means of communicating the values and beliefs of the new Left and the counterculture. As described by Godfrey Hodgson, in *America in Our Time,* "the promise that intoxicated initiates was that of a wider revolution of consciousness and culture, of which political revolution would come as a by-product."[B] According to one of the political bibles of the counterculture at the time, written by Charles Reich, rock music was part of a progress that would lead to the *Greening of America.*[C]

Rock music and the youth culture clearly helped to shatter the liberal-conservative ideological consensus that prevailed throughout the cold war years and promoted other post–Vietnam War changes. However, reliance on rock music to "raise consciousness" and "change the world" also represented the height of political naiveté, such as ignoring more politically oriented activism and group politics as well as rock music's increasing commercialization by the entertainment business, that guaranteed only limited success at best. With the decline of the movements of the 1960s and the end of the Vietnam War, the golden age of rock came to a close. What was once an "alternative" music form became the dominant mainstream music—and the classic rock—of American society in general.

Today, rock includes many different forms of music that span a forty-year period. While rock is less politically oriented than during the Vietnam War era, it has become more popular (as symbolized by *MTV*) and politically diverse than ever before. Some of the music continues to represent a liberal-Left orientation, such as the songs of Bruce Springsteen and Tracy Chapman, "Live Aid" concerts, and rap music; on the other hand, some of the music represents a more conservative-Right orientation. Most of all, rock music has become primarily big business—another story in the lives of the rich and famous—and increasingly commercialized—best epitomized by the advertising of "Nike" tennis shoes to the sound of the Beatles' "Revolution." Ultimately, rock music has become another form of mass entertainment and consumption, rocking 'n' rolling much of the American public into the 1990s.

B. Godfrey Hodgson, *America in Our Time* (New York: Vintage, 1976), p. 336.

C. Charles A. Reich, *The Greening of America* (New York: Random House, 1970).

SOURCES: Simon Frith, *Sound Effects: Youth, Leisure, and the Politics of Rock 'n' Roll* (New York: Pantheon, 1981); Charlie Gillett, *The Sound of the City: The Rise of Rock and Roll* (New York: Pantheon, 1983); Don J. Hibbard with Carol Kaleialoha, *The Role of Rock* (Englewood Cliffs, N.J.: Prentice-Hall, 1983); Godfrey Hodgson, *America in Our Time* (New York: Vintage, 1976); Robert A. Rosenstone, " 'The Times They Are A-Changin': The Music of Protest," *The Annals* (March 1969): 131–44; and Tom Wolfe, *The Kandy Kolored Tangerine Flake Streamline Baby* (New York: Pocket Books, 1965).

media in the post–Vietnam War era are likely to reflect and reinforce the beliefs, stereotypical views, and simplistic images of national and international affairs held by most Americans.[100]

Finally, the prevalence of the entertainment media in the lives of most Americans reinforces the politics of symbolism. As Daniel Boorstin argued over thirty years ago, "The making of the illusions which flood our experience has become the business of America."[101] Much of the entertainment media, especially on television, deals with the world of symbols and make-believe. Although Paddy Chayefsky overstates the nature of the entertainment industry in his 1976 screenplay *Network,* he nonetheless provides some important insights when he has the protagonist—a former news anchorman—shout out through the television:

> Television is not the truth! Television is a goddamned amusement park, that's what television is! Television is a circus, a carnival, a traveling troupe of acrobats and storytellers, singers and dancers, jugglers, sideshow freaks, lion-tamers and football players! We are in the boredom-killing business. . . . We'll tell you Kojak always gets the killer. . . . No matter how much trouble the hero is in, don't worry: just look at your watch—at the end of the hour he's going to win. We'll tell you any shit you want to hear! We deal in illusion, man![102]

Not only is interest in the news and knowledge of the world overwhelmed by the growth of mass entertainment, **constant advertising and mass marketing** has inculcated a consumption and materialistic ethic in most Americans. One study found that an average U.S. family is exposed to as many as 1,600 ads a day.[103] Nowhere is advertising more noticeable than through the power of television where, on the average, Americans spend one and one-half years of their lives watching television commercials alone. In the words of J. Fred MacDonald in *One Nation Under Television,* "TV has operated as a commercial billboard, rudely invading the privacy of every American with its pitches for dog food, cloth-

ing, Buicks, fast-food chains, and even candidates for the presidency of the United States. Still, the audience has never ceased to remain fascinated with the splashy spectacle."[104]

As Ernest Calkins explained as far back as 1930 in his classic book on advertising, *Modern Publicity,* "The purpose is to make the customer discontented with his old type of fountain pen, kitchen utensil, bathroom, or motor car, because it is old-fashioned, out-of-date. The technical term for this idea is obsoletism. We no longer wait for things to wear out. We displace them with others that are not more effective but more attractive."[105] Not only does this create insecurity and impatience for a new product that individuals believe will fulfill their needs, it contributes to a public opinion that has a short attention span, is impatient with history and failure, and is very receptive to the politics of symbolism. Therefore, it naturally follows that candidates are marketed and sold to the public as an AT&T commercial or a box of Tide. And it becomes more understandable why Ronald Reagan's Hollywood and acting experience served him so well as governor and president, for he excelled in symbolic appeals and made Americans feel good about themselves and their country.

THE ALTERNATIVE MEDIA

Although most Americans rely on the mainstream media for information about the world, alternative sources of information are available. The **alternative media** simply refers to those media outlets—such as television and radio programs, books, and magazines—that tend to address more various issues, provide additional information, and offer interpretations beyond those available in the mainstream media. According to Lauren Kessler in *The Dissident Press: Alternative Journalism in American History,* "If we look only at the popular press, we will get little feeling for the richness, complexity, and conflict that have always been a part of American society. For historically the conventional press has spoken to and for the homogeneous middle."[106]

Throughout American history, an alternative media has always existed. In fact, the alternative media may have had greater visibility and influence for more Americans before the rise of the mass media and mass society during the twentieth century. Nevertheless, a large and diverse alternative media has proliferated since Vietnam, although Americans are generally so dependent on the national media that the alternative media remains invisible and unknown.[107]

There are *alternative sources on television.* Some of the public affairs programs, such as "Frontline" on the Public Broadcasting System (PBS), tend to provide information from a more liberal orientation. Another basically liberal program, "60 Minutes," can also be considered an alternative news source because its stories, although broadcast on CBS, tend to be ignored by other journalists within the national news media. However, most alternative public affairs programs on television are not on the network stations and tend to be more conservative in orientation. For example, PBS airs weekly programs hosted by editors of the extremely conservative *National Review* magazine, such as "Firing Line," "The McLaughlin Group," and "One on One." PBS also broadcasts economic public affairs programs that reflect business interests such as "Wall Street Week," "Adam Smith's Money World," and the "Nightly Business Report." The tendency of PBS to favor more conservative public affairs programs is mirrored throughout cable television as well. In fact, conservative fundamentalism is not only regularly aired Sunday morning on many television stations, but Pat Robertson and the 700 Club run their own national television station known as the Family Channel.

Radio has become an increasing alternative source of programming and information for more Americans over the last few decades (in part because broadcasting costs and infrastructure are relatively low). This would include the rise of public radio, such as National Public Radio (NPR), university radio stations, progressive and community radio, and Christian broadcasting. Probably of greatest visibility since the 1980s has been the rise of "talk shows," best symbolized by Rush Limbaugh. Overall, hundreds of radio stations representing considerable diversity exist throughout the country, although choice and diversity fluctuates dramatically depending on one's particular location.[108]

It is in the print media where diversity most proliferates. An *alternative and underground print press* has always existed, especially in large urban cities. During the 1960s and 1970s, for example, the rise of the Left was accompanied by the development of a "free press," with the *Village Voice* the most prominent remnant of that movement today. *The Washington Times,* on the other hand, reflects the rise of the Right. Small publishing houses and large publishing firms also produce thousands of "books" a year, ranging from the far Right to the far Left. Hundreds of "newsletters" also are produced by a variety of private individuals and groups, each with a topic or cause to promote (as discussed in the chapter on group politics). Such diversity is reflected in the variety of journals and magazines that compete for political influence and the attention of the elite public, from the *American Spectator, Commentary, Human Events, National Review, New American, Policy Review,* and *Public Interest* on the Right, to the centrist *New Republic,* to the *American Prospect, Dissent, In These Time, Mother Jones, Nation, New York Review of Books, Progressive,* and *Utne Reader* on the Left.[109]

The alternative media have four important functions in American politics. First, the alternative media are often a major source of information for the most intellectually and politically active individuals throughout society. Second, information and interpretations arising within the alternative media occasionally affect news coverage by the mainstream media. Third, the variety of alternative media available reflects the ideological diversity and complexity of life that exists throughout American society. Finally, the alternative media also serve as valuable sources of information and interpretations for improving one's understanding, thus supplementing the selective attention of the mainstream media's news coverage of the world.

While the national media, for instance, tend to rally around the flag early in a crisis and communicate the presidential view to the American public, the alternative media often provide information and interpretations that furnish valuable insights. Initial "mainstream coverage of the Persian Gulf crisis" in 1990, for example, reflected the presidential view that Iraqi President Saddam Hussein was a threat to American vital interests, thus justifying an immediate and tough American response involving thousands of armed troops in the region. Hussein was portrayed by Bush administration officials and the American media as a ruthless tyrant, comparable to "Hitler," who gassed his own people and has the ability to engage in chemical, biological, and possibly nuclear warfare. As has been the case throughout the history of U.S. foreign policy, events behind the Persian Gulf crisis were much more complex than the simple picture portrayed through the inflated rhetoric communicated by the Bush administration through the national media. It is to the alternative media that one must often turn to obtain a fuller picture, especially while it is an ongoing issue.

What the Bush administration and the media ignored in their **Persian Gulf crisis coverage** was the history and origins of the crisis. A one-hour special "Frontline" (aired in early September just before President Bush addressed the country before a joint session of Congress concerning the crisis), entitled "The Arming of Iraq," demonstrated the close relationship that had developed between the United States and Iraq during the 1980s.[110] Not only had the Reagan administration actively supported President Hussein during the Iran-Iraq war, Western corporations—in particular, German, French, British, and American—had received their governments' approval to provide the equipment and personnel which allowed Hussein to build chemical, biological, and nuclear weapons capabilities. Much of the equipment, although officially provided for civilian use, was essential for weapons production as well. According to an unclassified government document, from 1985 to the invasion of August 2, 1990, the Commerce Department, State Department, Department of Energy, and the Defense Department approved 771 licenses by American companies to export $1.5 billion worth of high-technological goods to Iraq; of 1,133 license applications only 39 (3 percent) were rejected by the government.[111]

According to an October 1990 article in the *New Republic,* "Before the current crisis erupted,

dozens of major U.S. and multinational corporations—nearly all of them members of a little-known trade association called the U.S.-Iraq Business Forum—eagerly supplied the Hussein regime with everything from rice to computers to helicopters, and anticipated that Hussein would spend billions more."[112] Annual sales to Iraq grew from about $400 million in 1985 to $1.5 billion in 1989. The Forum's membership, as discussed in chapter 16, included more than fifty companies, including Amoco, Mobil, Occidental Petroleum, Westinghouse, Xerox, Bell Helicopter, Caterpillar, General Motors, and the First City Bancorporation of Texas. In some cases, "the companies seeking Iraq's petrodollars arranged for U.S. taxpayers to assume the risk of doing business with Hussein through commodity credits and loan guarantees underwritten by the federal government," such as through the Department of Agriculture's Commodity Credit Corporation and the U.S. Export-Import Bank.[113] In addition, consulting firms were involved, such as Kissinger Associates, which represented several corporations, domestic and foreign, that had won large contracts from Iraq in the past few years, such as Coca-Cola, Volvo (Swedish), and the Yugoslav construction giant Energoprojekt. Yet, once American policymakers decided to respond massively after the invasion and portray Hussein as the Hitler of the Middle East, this history was avoided by the Bush administration and all but ignored by the mainstream media.[114]

Furthermore, one of the biggest stories of the 1980s involving the Iran hostage crisis was completely ignored by the national and mainstream media. The story involved fear among the Reagan campaign team during the presidential elections that the Carter administration's efforts to negotiate with the Iranian government to release the American hostages would result in an **"October surprise"** and reelection victory for President Carter in what was a close and uncertain presidential race to the end. Under the direction of campaign manager William Casey, Reagan's soon-to-be director of central intelligence and architect of the Iran-Contra covert actions, Reagan campaign personnel secretly opened up channels and negotiated with Iranian leaders to *prevent* the release of the American hostages until after the election in return for shipment of American spare parts and arms to Iran that they badly needed in their war with Iraq. The evidence is quite strong that negotiations were pursued; whether an actual "deal" was struck between the Reagan team and the Iranians is much more uncertain. It is interesting to point out that the American hostages, in fact, were not released by Iran until minutes after Ronald Reagan took the presidential oath of office and Israeli's first arms shipments to Iran with the Reagan administration's approval began in February 1981.

The key point, however, is that the national media did not report or even investigate a potentially significant story about the presidential election, U.S. foreign policy, and the origins of Iran-Contra that had circulated since the election. The normal inclination of people, supported by governmental denials, was to dismiss the notion of an October surprise as rumor and a fanciful conspiracy theory. Investigation and reporting of the October surprise since the election, however, was conducted by the alternative media, such as *In These Times* and *The Nation,* who were heavily responsible for uncovering much of the story.[115] Yet, it was not until eleven years later that the October surprise story was reported in the national media, and then only in the editorial section of the *New York Times* by Gary Sick, an established member of President Carter's NSC responsible for the Middle East, and in a "Frontline" show on the "Election Held Hostage."[116]

As these illustrations demonstrate, one must acquire information from a variety of sources in order to obtain a comprehensive understanding of reality. Clearly, considerable information on national and international affairs is provided by the mainstream news media. However, given the media coverage patterns discussed in this chapter, it is important that mainstream media be supplemented by additional information and interpretations available only in the alternative news media. While difficult, it is possible for individuals to become "alert and knowledgeable" citizens, by relying on a variety of mainstream and alternative sources of information.

An alternative medium: the Internet. One medium that has made it possible for people to access a mul-titude of mainstream and alternative sources is through the **Internet** (or the world wide web). The popularity, affordability, and increasing technological capabilities of the personal computer (pc) has been "revolutionary" in the last two decades, especially for the world of communications. Through the Internet people can be in direct contact with an amazing number and assortment of information sources and views (with varying degrees of reliability and credibility). **Table 18.2** provides a listing of a number of valuable sources—mainstream and alternative—on the politics of United States foreign policy, and their Internet addresses. To what extent such a new and alternative medium will impact the communications process and American politics remains a speculative but fascinating question as the United States enters the next millenium.

THE SPECIALIZED FOREIGN POLICY MEDIA

There is one other important source of U.S. foreign policy information: the **specialized media.** All professions—whether medicine, law, business, or international affairs—have spawned a specialized literature that communicates information to members of the professional community. With respect to U.S. foreign policy and international relations, various **foreign policy journals** are published containing articles that revolve around contemporary issues and policy recommendations written and read by government officials, journalists, policy analysts, and academics. As with the historical patterns discussed throughout this chapter (and on group politics), the foreign policy specialized media have expanded and become more diverse over time (see **table 18.3**).

During the cold war years, there were only two foreign policy journals to speak of: *Foreign Affairs,* a publication of the Council on Foreign Relations, and *Orbis.* These journals were influential, especially *Foreign Affairs,* for they were read by individuals in and out of government who were involved in the policy-making process. They were important because the contents of the articles reflected and promoted the

TABLE 18.2
WEB SITES FOR VARIOUS GOVERNMENTAL, POLITICAL, AND MEDIA SOURCES

TYPE	SOURCE	WEB ADDRESS
GOVERNMENTAL	White House	http://www.whitehouse.gov
	Secretary of State	http://www.state.gov
	Secretary of Defense	http://www.defenselink.mil
	Central Intelligence Agency	http://www.odci.gov/cia
	National Security Agency	http://www.nsa.gov
	Secretary of Treasury	http://www.ustreas.gov
	Secretary of Commerce	http://www.doc.gov
	US Agency for International Development	http://www.info.usaid.gov
	US Information Agency	http://www/usia.gov
	US Senate	http://www.senate.gov
	US House of Representatives	http://www.house.gov
	Library of Congress	http://www.loc.gov
	Supreme Court	http://www.usscplus.com
	Congressional Quarterly	http://www.cq.com
	Democratic National Committee	http://www.democrats.org
	Republican National Committee	http://www.rnc.org
TELEVISION	ABC	http://www.abc.com
	CBS	http://www.cbs.com
	NBC	http://www.nbc.com
	CNN Interactive	http://cnn.com
	C-SPAN Networks	http://www.c-span.org
	PBS	http://www.pbs.org
RADIO	NPR	http://www.npr.org
NEWSPAPERS	New York Times	http://www.nytimes.com
	Washington Post	http://www.washingtonpost.com
	Wall Street Journal	http://www.wsj.com
	AP Online	http://wire.ap.org
NEWSWEEKLIES	In These Times	http://www.inthesetimes.com
	Newsweek	http://www/aol.com (keyword:NEWSWEEK)
	Time	http://pathfinder.com/time/magazine
	US News & World Report	http://www.usnews.com
MAGAZINES	American Prospect	http://epn.org/prospect.html
	American Spectator	http://www.spectator.org

TABLE 18.2 *(continued)*
WEB SITES FOR VARIOUS GOVERNMENTAL, POLITICAL, AND MEDIA SOURCES

TYPE	SOURCE	WEB ADDRESS
	Commentary	http://www.commentarymagazine.com
	Dissent	http://www.igc.apc.org/dissent
	Mother Jones	http://www.motherjones.com
	National Review	http://www.nationalreview.com
	New Republic	http://www.enews.com/magazines/tnr
	New York Times Review of Books	http://www.nybooks.com:6900/nyrev/index.html
	Policy Review	http://www.heritage.org/heritage/p_review
	Utne Reader	http://www.utne.com/reader/magazine.html

TABLE 18.3
MAJOR CONTEMPORARY FOREIGN POLICY JOURNALS

NAME	YEAR BEGAN	AFFILIATION	FOREIGN POLICY ORIENTATION*	WEB ADDRESS
ORBIS	1957	Foreign Policy Research Institute	Conservative	http://www.fpri.org/
THE NATIONAL INTEREST	1985	(unaffiliated)	Conservative/ Centrist	http://csf.colorado.edu/isa/ press/nationalinterest.edu/
FOREIGN AFFAIRS	1922	Council on Foreign Relations	Centrist	http://www.foreignaffairs.org/
FOREIGN POLICY	1970	Carnegie Endowment	Liberal/Centrist	http://www.foreignpolicy.com/
INTERNATIONAL SECURITY	1976	Harvard University	Centrist	http://mitpress.mit.edu/ journals.tcl/
WASHINGTON QUARTERLY	1978	Ctr for Strategic & International Studies	Conservative	http://mitpress.mit.edu/ journals.tcl/
WORLD POLICY JOURNAL	1983	World Policy Institute	Liberal	http://worldpolicy.org/wpj.html/

*Most of the journals publish more diverse viewpoints today beyond their predominant orientation.

thinking of the foreign policy establishment and the realpolitik/anticommunist consensus dominating American government and society. With the shattering of the foreign policy establishment and the anticommunist consensus after the Vietnam War, however, new journals appeared that reflected greater ideological diversity of foreign policy thought. In 1970, when *Foreign Affairs* was reluctant to criticize the U.S. government's Vietnam policy, a group of regular contributors created a new, and more liberal, journal, *Foreign Policy*. Soon, other foreign policy journals appeared: *International Security* reflecting a more centrist perspective, the *National Interest* and *Global Affairs* emphasizing a more conservative perspective, and *World Policy Journal* reflecting a more liberal perspective. Since Vietnam, therefore, there is a more diverse foreign policy specialized media that affects the communications process and the politics of U.S. foreign policy. A similar pattern has characterized the academic and scholarly journals, which emphasize a more theoretical, analytic, and systematic study of international relations.[117]

INFORMATION, IDEAS, SYMBOLS, AND POLITICS

As we have found, the mainstream news media do not simply mirror reality, nor are they consistently biased in one ideological orientation as both liberals and conservatives contend. Instead, the mediated reality of national and international affairs that is communicated to most Americans tends to provide selective information and a particular understanding of reality because of the complexity of the world, the nature of the media business, and the role of politics in the communications process. Therefore, the national media's foreign affairs coverage is both informative and narrow: it tends to present homogenized news and a centrist ideological understanding that reflects the prevailing political environment in government and society. These patterns in news media coverage, reinforced by the entertainment media, have heavily affected the foreign policy process throughout history, influenced public knowledge and democratic citizenship, and contributed to the politics of symbolism. The alternative media and the specialized media have also played a role, especially among those more active in politics and foreign policy. These sources serve as valuable supplements to the mainstream media, enabling individuals to acquire a greater breadth and depth of understanding about national and international affairs.

In a democratic society it is through the media and the communications process that the political competition over ideas and symbols are played out to a great extent. In this respect, *the media and communications process are consequential throughout society and the politics of U.S. foreign policy for they fulfill three very important functions:* they are the basic source of information for people about world events, they interpret the meaning of those events for people, and they socialize individuals into their dominant cultural settings.[118] Therefore, the media affect the political agenda and the climate of opinion around the policymaking process for they act as the eyes through which people see and define the world. This explains why the media and the communications process have become a political battleground for access and influence between competing groups and interests within government and throughout society. Together, the mainstream, alternative, and specialized media occupy a critical role in the communication of information, ideas, and symbols to the mass and elite publics, affecting continuity and change, the president's ability to govern, and the tension between national security and democracy in the politics of U.S. foreign policy. If anything, the communications process and the role of information, ideas, and symbols will grow in importance in domestic and world politics as we enter the twenty-first century.

BIBLIOGRAPHIC ESSAY

Throughout the 1960s and 1970s, the study of the media in American politics was largely ignored by social scientists, especially in political science. Since this time, the situation has changed dramatically, demonstrating a renewed interest in the role of the media in American society and U.S. foreign policy. The best general overviews of the news media are supplied by Doris Graber in *Mass Media and American Politics* (Washington, D.C.: Congressional Quarterly Press, 1992), and Gary Woodward in *Perspectives on American Political Media* (Boston: Allyn and Bacon, 1997).

Shanto Iyengar and Donald R. Kinder demonstrate the influence of the news media on politics in *News That Matters: Television and American Opinion* (Chicago: University of Chicago Press, 1987). Daniel C. Hallin provides an excellent discussion of major patterns of foreign affairs media coverage and media-governmental relations in *The Uncensored War: The Media and Vietnam* (Berkeley, Calif.: University of California Press, 1986). Informative descriptions of the Reagan administration's efforts to dominate the communications process and the politics of symbolism are provided by Robert Parry and Peter Kornbluh, "Iran-Contra's Untold Story," *Foreign Policy* (Fall 1988): 3–30, and Hedrick Smith, *The Power Game: How Washington Works* (New York: Ballantine, 1988), chapter 12. Marie Gottschalk provides a disturbing picture of media coverage of the Persian Gulf War that was submissive to the Pentagon and the Bush administration in "Operation Desert Cloud: The Media and the Gulf War," *World Policy Journal* (Summer 1992): 449–86.

David Halberstam, in *The Powers That Be* (New York: Alfred A. Knopf, 1979), gives a very informative narrative history of the growth and power of the national media. Ronald Steel provides an excellent history of one of America's most prominent twentieth century journalists in *Walter Lippmann and the American Century* (New York: Vintage, 1980). Joe McGinniss's *The Selling of the President 1968* (New York: Pocket Books, 1969) remains a classic statement on presidential campaigning and the use of the mass media, as does Timothy Crouse's *The Boys on the Bus* (New York: Ballantine, 1972)—a fascinating look at pack journalism and political reporting during the 1972 presidential election.

For an excellent analysis of the role of the entertainment industry and film in American politics during time of war, see *Hollywood Goes to War: How Politics, Profits, and Propaganda Shaped World War II Movies* by Clayton Koppes and Gregory Black (New York: Free Press, 1987), as well as Noral Sayre on the cold war years in "Assaulting Hollywood," *World Policy Journal* (Winter 1995–96): 51–60. Walter Hixson discusses the role of popular fiction in "Red Storm Rising: Tom Clancy Novels and the Cult of National Security," *Diplomatic History* (Fall 1993): 599–613. A penetrating and lively look behind the scenes of the three television networks and the entertainment business can be found in *Inside Prime Time* (New York: Pantheon, 1983) by Todd Gitlin.

RECOMMENDED MEDIA SOURCES

. . . .

The following are among the most significant and useful American "mainstream" sources for becoming "knowledgeable and alert" with regard to national and international affairs. The *New York Times* is probably the single best daily source of news on national and international affairs. The *Washington Post* also provides strong political coverage, especially of the U.S. government, and is read religiously throughout the Washington political community. [The *International Herald Tribune*—consisting of both *New York Times* and *Washington Post* articles—has been available outside of the United States for years, but can now be found in the United States.] The *Wall Street Journal* is the best source of national and international economic news. On television, in addition to the nightly national news programs on ABC, CBS, NBC, and CNN, the "NewsHour with Jim Lehrer" (PBS), "Nightline" (ABC), "Meet the Press" (NBC), and "This Week" (ABC) are three of the more interesting public affairs news and talk shows. Although not well known, National Public Radio (NPR) provides excellent news coverage with "Morning Edition" (weekday mornings), "Weekend Edition" (weekend mornings), and "All Things Considered" (evenings). These mainstream sources of news not only provide valuable information about national and international affairs, they are also important because they indicate what government officials and national leaders are thinking.

There are also many good "alternative" sources of information and knowledge, from varying perspectives, to supplement the mainstream media. On television, "60 Minutes" on CBS and "Frontline" on PBS are excellent sources of information based on investigative reporting. Most of the alternative media, however, is located in the print media. From a liberal-Left perspective, the *American Prospect* and *Dissent* are quarterly intellectual journals of articles and book reviews; *Mother Jones* is an investigative monthly; the *New York Review of Books* provides a wide-ranging biweekly source of book review essays and intellectual commentary; *In These Times* is an excellent weekly source of news and analysis of politics and culture; and the *Utne Reader* (subtitled *The Best of the Alternative Press*) is a good bimonthly collection of news and general articles from diverse sources. From a conservative-Right perspective, the *American Spectator* is a monthly intellectual journal of articles and book reviews; *Commentary* is a good monthly source of commentary and articles; the *National Review* is a biweekly source of information and opinion; and *Policy Review* is a quarterly journal of intellectual thought. The *New Republic* is a weekly opinion magazine of short articles and book reviews representing an ideological hodgepodge of liberalism and conservatism.

Clearly, this is only a selective overview of sources for acquiring information and knowledge (table 18.2 lists their Internet addresses). Other television, radio, and print sources (such as the foreign policy journals listed in table 18.3) are available, including fictional accounts, such as novels and movies, that provide valuable information and interpretations.

ENDNOTES

1. Shanto Iyengar and Donald R. Kinder, *News That Matters: Television and American Opinion* (Chicago: University of Chicago Press, 1987). See also Richard A. Brody, *Assessing the President: The Media, Elite Opinion, and Public Support* (Stanford: Stanford University Press, 1991); Shanto Iyengar, *Is Anyone Responsible? How Television Frames Political Issues* (Chicago: University of Chicago Press, 1991); W. Russell Neuman, Marion R. Just, and Ann N. Crigler, *Common Knowledge: News and the Construction of Political Meaning* (Chicago: University of Chicago Press, 1992); Michael J. Robinson, "Public Affairs Television and the Growth of Political Malaise: The Case of 'The Selling of the Pentagon,'" *American Political Science Review* (1976): 409–32; Donald L. Shaw and Maxwell E. McCombs, *The Emergence of American Political Issues: The Agenda-Setting Function of the Press* (St. Paul, Minn.: West, 1978).

2. See William C. Adams, ed., *Television Coverage of International Affairs* (Norwood, N.J.: Ablex, 1982); George Gerbner and George Marvanyi, "The Many Worlds of the World's Press," *Journal of Communications* 27 (Winter 1971): 52–66; James F. Larson, *Television's Window on the World* (Norwood, N.J.: Ablex, 1984); Hamid Mowlana, "World's Best-Informed Public?" *SAIS Review* 6 (Winter-Spring 1986): 177–88; Sophia Peterson, "International News Selection by the Elite Press: A Case Study," *Public Opinion Quarterly* 45 (Summer 1981): 143–63; Gary C. Woodward, *Perspectives on American Political Media* (Boston: Allyn and Bacon, 1997).

3. Herbert J. Gans, *Deciding What's News: A Study of CBS Evening News, NBC Nightly News, Newsweek and Time* (New York: Pantheon, 1979), pp. 31–38.

4. Andrew K. Semmel, "Foreign News in Four U.S. Elite Dailies: Some Comparisons," *Journalism Quarterly* 53 (1976): 736.

5. See, for example, Mohamed Kirat and David Weaver, "Foreign News Coverage in Three Wire Services: A Study of AP, UPI, and the Nonaligned News Agencies Pool," *Gazritte* 35 (Spring 1985): 31–47; W. James Potter, "News From Three Worlds in Prestige U.S. Newspapers," *Journalism Quarterly* 64 (Spring 1987): 73–79, 276; and G. Cleveland Wilhoit and David Weaver, "Foreign News Coverage in Two U.S. Wire Services: An Update," *Journal of Communications* 33 (Spring 1983): 132–48.

6. See, for example, J. Herbert Altschull, *Agents of Power: The Role of the News Media in Human Affairs* (New York: Longman, 1984).

7. See, for example, Lloyd N. Cutler, "Foreign Policy by Deadline," *Foreign Policy* (Fall 1984): 113–28.

8. Hedrick Smith, *The Power Game: How Washington Works* (New York: Ballantine, 1988), p. 395.

9. Stanley Hoffmann, *Gulliver's Troubles or the Setting of American Foreign Policy* (New York: McGraw-Hill, 1968), p. 311.

10. See, for example, Dan Nimmo and James E. Combs, *Mediated Political Realities* (New York: Longman, 1983).

11. In Martin P. Wattenberg, *The Decline of American Political Parties* (Cambridge, Mass.: Harvard University Press, 1984), p. 110.

12. For an overview of the nature and operations of the American media, see Robert M. Batscha, *Foreign Affairs News and the Broadcast Journalist* (New York: Praeger, 1975); Bernard C. Cohen, *The Press and Foreign Policy* (Princeton, N.J.: Princeton University Press, 1963); Edward Jay Epstein, *News From Nowhere: Television and the News* (New York: Vintage, 1973); Gans, *Deciding What's News;* Doris A. Graber, *Mass Media and American Politics* (Washington, D.C.: Congressional Quarterly Press, 1989); Stephen Hess, *The Washington Reporters* (Washington, D.C.: Brookings, 1981); Leon V. Sigal, *Reporters and Officials: The Organization and Politics of Newsmaking* (Lexington, Mass.: D.C. Heath, 1973); Woodward, *Perspectives on American Political Media.*

13. Ben Bagdikian, *The Media Monopoly* (Boston: Beacon, 1989). See also Phillip H. Ault, "Mass Ownership Takes Over the Media," In Warren K. Agee, Phillip H. Ault, and Edwin Emery, eds., *Main Currents in Mass Communications* (New York: Harper & Row, 1986), pp. 168–73; John C. Busterna, "Trends

in Daily Newspaper Ownership," *Journalism Quarterly* (Winter 1988): 831–38; Richard Turner, "An Ear for the CBS Eye," *Newsweek* (December 16, 1996): 58–59.

14. William Glaberson, "Times Co. Acquiring Boston Globe for $1.1 billion," *New York Times* (June 11, 1993): A1, A4.

15. Bagdikian, *The Media Monopoly*, p. 21.

16. See Ben H. Bagdikian, "Journalism," *Mother Jones* (May/June 1992): 48–51. See also Anthony Smith, *The Age of Behemoths: The Globalization of Mass Media Firms* (New York: Priority Press, 1991).

17. See, for example, Bernard Roshco, *Newsmaking* (Chicago: University of Chicago Press, 1975).

18. See Bagdikian, *Media Monopoly*, and "Fifth Estate Fortunes: The Top 100 Top $38 Billion," *Broadcasting* (June 5, 1989): 54–56.

19. Stanley K. Bigman, "Rivals in Conformity: A Study of Two Competing Dailies," *Journalism Quarterly* 25 (Autumn 1949): 127–31.

20. David Halberstam, *The Powers That Be* (New York: Alfred A. Knopf, 1979), p. 415.

21. See, for example, Joshua Gamson, "Incredible News," *American Prospect* (Fall 1994): 28–35; Larry Reibstein, "The Battle of the TV News Magazine Shows," *Newsweek* (April 11, 1994): 61–65; William Powers, "Getting Kathie Lee," *The New Republic* (June 9, 1997): 11–12.

22. Timothy Crouse, *The Boys on the Bus* (New York: Ballantine, 1972).

23. See also Larry Sabato, *Feeding Frenzy: How Attack Journalism Has Transformed American Politics* (New York: Free Press, 1991).

24. "A Star Is Rehired, Fabulously," *Newsweek* (February 28, 1994): 56.

25. Leon V. Sigal, *Reporters and Officials: The Organization and Politics of Newsmaking* (Lexington, Mass.: Heath, 1973):, pp. 119–30. See also Leon V. Sigal, "Sources Make the News," in Robert Karl Manoff and Michael Schudson, eds., *Reading the News* (New York: Pantheon, 1987), pp. 9–37.

26. Smith, *The Power Game*, p. 29.

27. *Newsweek* (October 15, 1989; November 17, 1997). See also John A. Lent, "Foreign News in American Media," *Journal of Communications* 27 (Winter 1977).

28. See Gerbner and Marvanyi, "The Many Worlds of the World's Press"; Kirat and Weaver, "Foreign News Coverage in Three Wire Services"; Semmel, "Foreign News in Four U.S. Dailies"; and Wilhoit

and Weaver, "Foreign News Coverage in Two U.S. Wire Services."

29. For an overview of the relationship between the political environment and the media, see Timothy E. Cook, *Making Laws and Making News: Media Strategies in the U.S. House of Representatives* (Washington, D.C.: Brookings, 1989); Epstein, *News From Nowhere;* Gans, *Deciding What's News;* Graber, *Mass Media and American Politics;* Halberstam, *The Powers That Be;* Michael Parenti, *Inventing Reality: The Politics of the Mass Media* (New York: St. Martin's Press, 1977); and Sigal, *Reporters and Officials.*

30. In Ronald Steel, *Walter Lippmann and the American Century* (New York: Vintage, 1980), p. 181.

31. Graber, *Mass Media and American Politics*, p. 24.

32. See, for example, Marie Gottschalk, "Operation Desert Cloud: The Media and the Gulf War," *World Policy Journal* (Summer 1992): 449–86.

33. Hess, *The Washington Reporters*, p. 118.

34. Gans, *Deciding What's News*, p. 62.

35. "Are You on the Nightline Guestlist?" *Fairness and Accuracy in Reporting, Extra!* (January/February 1989): 1–15.

36. See Marc Cooper and Lawrence C. Soley, "All the Right Sources," *Mother Jones* (February/March 1990): 20–27, 45–48; and Lawrence C. Soley, *The News Shapers: The Individuals Who Explain the News* (Minneapolis: School of Journalism and Mass Communication, University of Minnesota, 1989).

37. Walter Karp, "Who Decides What is News? (Hint: It's Not Journalists)," *Utne Reader* (November/December 1989): 61.

38. Carl Bernstein, "The Idiot Culture: Reflections of Post-Watergate Journalism," *New Republic* (June 8, 1992): 22.

39. Daniel C. Hallin, *The Uncensored War: The Media and Vietnam* (Berkeley, Calif.: University of California Press, 1986). See also Nicholas O. Berry, *Foreign Policy and the Press: An Analysis of The New York Times' Coverage of U.S. Foreign Policy* (Westport, Conn.: Greenwood Press, 1990).

40. See, for example, Jonathan Tasini, *Lost in the Margins: Labor and the Media,* (New York: Fairness and Accuracy in Reporting, 1990).

41. David Truman, *The Governmental Process: Political Interests and Public Opinion* (New York: Alfred A. Knopf, 1971), p. 213.

42. Graber, *Mass Media and American Politics*, p. 92.

43. Ibid., p. 260.

44. See, for example, Todd Gitlin, *The Whole World Is Watching: Mass Media in the Making and Unmaking of the New Left* (Berkeley, Calif.: University of California Press, 1981).

45. For an overview of governmental and presidential access to the media, see Gans, *Deciding What's News;* Michael Baruch Grossman and Martha Joynt Kumar, *Portraying the President: The White House and the News Media* (Baltimore: Johns Hopkins University Press, 1981); Charles Press and Kenneth Verburg, *American Politicians and Journalists* (Glenview, Ill.: Scott, Foresman, 1988); and Sigal, *Reporters and Officials.*

46. Cohen, *The Press and Foreign Policy*, p. 28.

47. Hallin, *The Uncensored War*, p. 8. See also Daniel Hallin, "The Media, the War in Vietnam, and Political Support: A Critique of the Thesis of an Oppositional Media," *Journal of Politics* 46 (1984): 13.

48. See John Anthony Maltese, *Spin Control: The White House Office of Communications and the Management of Presidential News* (Chapel Hill: University of North Carolina Press, 1992).

49. Daniel J. Boorstin, *The Image: A Guide to Pseudo-Events in America* (New York: Atheneum, 1961).

50. Smith, *The Power Game*, p. 401.

51. See, for example, Juergen A. Heise, *Minimum Disclosure: How the Pentagon Manipulates the News* (New York: W.W. Norton, 1979).

52. Smith, *The Power Game*, p. 80. See also Morton H. Halperin, *Bureaucratic Politics and Foreign Policy.* (Washington, D.C.: Brookings Institution, 1974), chapter 10.

53. Robert Parry and Peter Kornbluh, "Iran-Contra's Untold Story," *Foreign Policy* (Fall 1988): 3.

54. Ibid.: 16.

55. Hoffmann, *Gulliver's Troubles*, pp. 308–09.

56. See, for example, Maureen Dowd, "President and the Press: A Clash of Two Obsessions," *New York Times* (February 21, 1990): A12.

57. Steel, *Walter Lippmann and the American Century*, p. 67.

58. Graber, *Mass Media and American Politics*, p. 29.

59. See, for example, Godfrey Hodgson, *America in Our Time* (New York: Vintage, 1976), chapter 7.

60. See George H. Roeder, Jr., *The Censored War: American Visual Experience During World War Two* (New Haven: Yale University Press, 1993).

61. Robert Dallek, *The American Style of Foreign Policy: Cultural Politics and Foreign Affairs* (New York: Alfred A. Knopf, 1983), p. 139.

62. Russell Warren Howe and Sarah Hays Trott, *The Power Peddlers: How Lobbyists Mold America's Foreign Policy* (Garden City, N.Y.: Doubleday, 1977), p. 30. James L. Baughman, *Henry R. Luce and the Rise of the American News Media* (New York: Macmillan, 1990).

63. Edwin R. Bayley, *Joe McCarthy and the Press* (Madison, Wis.: University of Wisconsin Press, 1981).

64. Carl Bernstein, "The CIA and the Media," *Rolling Stone* (October 1977).

65. U.S., Congress, Senate, *Final Report of the Select Committee to Study Governmental Operations with Respect to Intelligence Activities, Book 1* Congressional Report (94th Cong., 2nd sess., April 14, 1976), pp. 197–98.

66. Halberstam, *The Powers That Be*, pp. 446–47.

67. See, for example, James Aronson, *The Press and the Cold War* (Indianapolis: Bobbs-Merrill, 1970), and J. Fred MacDonald, *Television and the Red Menace: The Video Road to Vietnam* (New York: Praeger, 1985).

68. Hallin, *The Uncensored War.*

69. See Doris A. Graber, *Processing the News: How People Tame the Information Tide* (New York: Longman, 1988); Neuman, Just, and Crigler, *Common Knowledge.*

70. See, for example, William C. Adams, "Mass Media and Public Opinion about Foreign Affairs: A Typology of News Dynamics," *Political Communication and Persuasion* 4 (1987): 263–78.

71. See, for example, Iyengar and Kinder, *News That Matters.*

72. See, for example, William A. Dorman and Mansour Farhang, *The U.S. Press and Iran: Foreign Policy and the Journalism of Deference* (Berkeley, Calif.: University of California Press, 1987).

73. Graber, *Mass Media and American Politics*, p. 227. See also Thomas E. Patterson, *The Mass Media Election: How Americans Choose Their President* (New York: Praeger, 1980).

74. Beginning in 1990, the networks informally agreed to wait at least until after the polls closed to predict winning candidates.

75. Richard M. Scammon and Alice V. McGillivray, eds., *America at the Polls: The Vote for President, 1968–1984* (Washington, D.C.: Congressional Quarterly Press, 1988), pp. 2, 3.

76. See James Fallows, "Why Americans Hate the Media," *Atlantic Monthly* (February 1996): 45–64; and Judith Valente, "Do You Believe What Newspeople Tell You?" *Parade Magazine* (March 2, 1997): 4–6.

77. Jerome Barron, *Freedom of the Press for Whom? The Right of Access to the Mass Media* (Bloomington, Ind.: Indiana University Press, 1973).

78. Cook, *Making Laws and Making News,* pp. 177–78. See also W. Lance Bennett, *News: The Politics of Illusion* (New York: Longman, 1988); Robert M. Entman, *Democracy Without Citizens: Media and the Decay of American Politics* (New York: Oxford University Press, 1989); and Gans, *Deciding What's News,* chapter 10.

79. See Denise M. Bostdorff, *The Presidency and the Rhetoric of Foreign Crisis* (Columbia, S.C.: University of South Carolina Press, 1993); Murray Edelman, *The Symbolic Uses of Politics* (Urbana, Ill.: University of Illinois Press, 1964); Michael Kazin, *The Populist Persuasion: An American History* (New York: Basic Books, 1995).

80. See B. Thomas Trout, "Rhetoric Revisited: Political Legitimation and the Cold War," *International Studies Quarterly* 19 (September 1975): 251–84.

81. Smith, *The Power Game,* p. 418.

82. Ibid., pp. 345–46.

83. Ibid., p. 346.

84. Stanley Meisler and Thomas B. Rosensteil, "Epithets, Voodoo Reports Help U.S. Demean Noriega," *Los Angeles Times* (December 31, 1989): A1, A12. See also George Klay Kieh, Jr., "Propaganda and United States Foreign Policy: The Case of Panama," *Political Communication* 7 (April–June 1990): 61–72.

85. Hallin, *The Uncensored War,* p. 158.

86. Smith, *The Power Game,* chapter 17. See also R. Kent Weaver, "The Politics of Blame Avoidance," *Journal of Public Policy* 6 (October–December 1986): 371–98.

87. Joe McGinniss, *The Selling of the President 1968* (New York: Pocket Books, 1970).

88. See also Kathleen Hall Jamieson, *Dirty Politics: Deception, Distraction, and Democracy* (New York: Oxford University Press, 1992); and Darrell M. West, *Air Wars: Television Advertising in Election Campaigns, 1952–1992* (Washington, D.C.: Congressional Quarterly Press, 1993).

89. Kiku Adatto, "The Incredible Shrinking Sound Bite," *New Republic* (May 28, 1990), p. 20; Daniel C. Hallin, "Sound Bite News: Television Coverage of Elections, 1968–1988," *Journal of Communication* (Spring 1992): 5–24.

90. In Smith, *The Power Game,* pp. 129–30.

91. For an overview of the entertainment media, see Todd Gitlin, *Inside Prime Time* (New York: Pantheon, 1985); Walter L. Hixson, "Red Storm Rising: Tom Clancy Novels and the Cult of National Security," *Diplomatic History* (Fall 1993): 599–613; J. Fred MacDonald, *One Nation Under Television: The Rise and Decline of Network TV* (New York: Pantheon, 1990); Michael Parenti, *Make-Believe Media: The Politics of Entertainment* (New York: St. Martin's Press, 1992); Sally Bedell Smith, *In All His Glory, The Life of William S. Paley: The Legendary Tycoon and His Brilliant Circle* (New York: Simon and Schuster, 1990); and Woodward, *Perspectives on American Political Media.*

92. Gitlin, *Inside Prime Time,* p. 203.

93. George Gerbner, Larry Gross, Michael Morgan, and Nancy Signorielli, "Charting the Mainstream: Television's Contributions to Political Orientations," *Journal of Communication* 32 (1982): 100–27, and "Life According to TV," *Newsweek* (December 6, 1982): 136–40.

94. "Life According to TV," p. 140.

95. See, for example, Richard Slotkin, *Gunfighter Nation: The Myth of the Frontier in Twentieth-Century America* (New York: Atheneum, 1992).

96. Clayton R. Koppes and Gregory D. Black, *Hollywood Goes to War: How Politics, Profits, and Propaganda Shaped World War II Movies* (New York: Free Press, 1987), p. vii.

97. John W. Dower, *War Without Mercy: Race and Power in the Pacific War* (New York: Pantheon, 1986), p. 309.

98. MacDonald, *Television and the Red Menace.* See also Nora Sayre, *Running Time: Films of the Cold War* (New York: Dial Press, 1982); Stephen J. Whitfield, *The Culture of the Cold War* (Baltimore: Johns Hopkins University Press, 1991).

99. See, for example, Martha Bayles, "The Road to *Rambo III*: Hollywood's Visions of Vietnam," *New Republic* (July 18 and 25, 1988): 30–35.

100. For a particularly critical review, see Richard Grenier, "Oliver Stone's JFK," *National Interest* (Spring 1992): 76–84.

101. Boorstin, *The Image,* p. 5.

102. Paddy Chayefsky, *Network* (New York: Pocket Books, 1976), p. 98.

103. Robert L. Heibroner, "Advertising as Agitprop," *Harper's* (January 1985): 72.

104. MacDonald, *One Nation Under Television,* p. ix.

105. Stuart Ewen, "Waste a Lot, Want a Lot: Our All-consuming Quest for Style," *Utne Reader* (September/October 1989): 84. See also Vance Packard, *The Hidden Persuaders* (New York: McKay, 1957).

106. Lauren Kessler, *The Dissident Press: Alternative Journalism in American History* (Beverley Hills, Calif.: Sage, 1984), p. 14.

107. For an overview of the alternative media, see, for example, David Armstrong, *A Trumpet to Arms: Alternative Media in America* (Los Angeles: J. P. Tarcher, 1981), and Kessler, *The Dissident Press.*

108. See Thomas Byrne Edsall, America's Sweetheart," *New York Review of Books* (October 6, 1994): 6–10; Monika Bauerlein, "Radio Activity," *Utne Reader* (September/October 1992): 110–12.

109. There are also a rash of alternative publications that are politically oriented and that reflect women, blacks, Hispanics, labor, environmental groups, and other more specialized audiences and interests. See B. Katz and L.S. Katz, *Magazines for Libraries* (New York: R.R. Bowker, 1986); Lynette Lamb, "Parallel Worlds: Newsletters Provide Varied and Vital Alternative Information," *Utne Reader* (November/December 1992): 111–14; J. Wanniski, *1992 Media Guide: A Critical Review of the Media* (Morristown, N.J.: Polyeconomics, 1992).

110. "The Arming of Iraq," *Frontline* (September 11, 1990). See also Judith Miller and Laurie Mylroie, *Saddam Hussein and the Crisis in the Gulf* (New York: Times Books, 1990); Kenneth R. Timmerman, *The Death Lobby: How the West Armed Iraq* (Boston: Houghton Mifflin, 1991).

111. Three hundred twenty-three (29 percent) applications were returned to the companies without action (without explanation in the report). United States, Department of Commerce, *Fact Sheet on Export Licensing for Iraq* (undated).

112. Joe Conason, "The Iraq Lobby," *New Republic* (October 1, 1990): 14.

113. Ibid.: 15.

114. Some of this information eventually seeped into the mainstream press, such as *Newsweek,* but it was two months after the invasion and limited to a brief article in the business section. More importantly, *Newsweek* failed to integrate this information into a larger article on the Gulf crisis in the international section within the same issue. See "Should Iran Be a Lesson?" *Newsweek* (October 15, 1990): 58, and "Under the Boot," *Newsweek* (October 15, 1990) pp. 36–37. It needs to be pointed out that most members of Congress from both parties went along with the administration's policies and many members, in fact, actively promoted increased ties with Iraq so as to lead to greater exports from their states and districts. See Pamela Fessler, "Congress' Record on Saddam: Decade of Talk, Not Action," *Congressional Quarterly* (April 27, 1991): 1068–77.

115. See, for example, Leslie Cockburn, *Out of Control: The Story of the Reagan Administration's Secret War in Nicaragua, the Illegal Arms Pipeline, and the Contra Drug Connection* (New York: Atlantic Monthly Press, 1987), and Barbara Honegger with Jim Naureckas, "Did Reagan Steal the 1980 Election?" *In These Times* (June 24–July 7, 1987): 12–13.

116. "Election Held Hostage," *Frontline* (April 16, 1991), and Gary Sick, "The Election Story of the Decade," *New York Times* (April 15, 1991): 17.

117. During the cold war period, there were only two major international relations journals–*International Organization* and *World Politics*—and two general political science journals—*Political Science Quarterly* and *American Political Science Review.* However, beginning in the 1960s, new political science and, more importantly, international relations journals were born, such as *Journal of Conflict Resolution, International Studies Quarterly,* and *International Interactions.* During the cold war years, these journals represented primarily conventional and *realpolitik* perspectives on international relations (which became increasingly quantitative). Over the past decade, however, the scholarly journals have become receptive to a greater diversity of theoretical and systematic perspectives. Foreign policy practitioners and analysts generally find little of value in these more academic journals, limiting their immediate impact. Still, they often play a prominent role in the graduate education of individuals in political science and international studies programs throughout the country, many of whom go on to play relevant foreign policy roles in government and society. As John Maynard Keynes once observed, practical men are usually unconscious captives of conceptions created by "some academic scribbler of a few years back." See John Maynard Keynes, *The General Theory of Employment, Interest and Money* (London: Macmillan, 1957), p. 383.

118. Harold D. Lasswell, "The Structure and Function of Communication in Society," in Wilbur Schramm, ed., *Mass Communications* (Urbana, Ill.: University of Illinois Press, 1969), p. 103.

PART
*F*IVE

· · · · · · · · · · · · · ·

CONCLUSION

*Part V provides an overall synthesis and conclusion about the politics of
U.S. foreign policy. Chapter 19 discusses different models of state-societal
relations, summarizes how U.S. foreign policy has been made, and
discusses the dynamics of foreign policy change; chapter 20 examines some
of the major trends into the twenty-first century and its implication for the
future politics of U.S. foreign policy.*

CHAPTER
19
. . . .

STATE-SOCIETY RELATIONS,
MAKING FOREIGN POLICY,
AND FOREIGN POLICY CHANGE

This chapter provides a summary of the major patterns discussed throughout the book and the conceptual tools necessary for making sense of the overall politics of U.S. foreign policy. In part I, we examined the historical and global context of U.S. foreign policy. In part II, we looked at the government and the policymaking process by focusing on the president, the National Security Council (NSC), the foreign policy bureaucracy, decision-making within the executive branch, and Congress. In part III, we examined the role of society and domestic politics: concentrating on the public and their beliefs, electoral politics, group politics, the exercise of civil liberties, and the mass media and communications process. Here, we integrate these differing perspectives and separate elements to afford a better understanding of how the foreign policy process operates in its entirety.

We first describe the evolution of three conceptual models for making sense of the relationship between government and society. This is followed by a summary of the basic patterns discussed throughout the book in order to determine which of the models best fits and explain the politics of U.S. foreign policy since World War II. This **synthesis** allows us to understand more fully the dominant themes, or questions, raised at the beginning of the book (and discussed throughout) concerning continuity and change, the president's ability to govern, and the tension between the demands of national security and democracy in the making of U.S. foreign policy. The chapter concludes with a discussion of the dynamics of foreign policy change as a result of the interplay of all three perspectives: the context, the state, and society.

Competing Theoretical Models
. . . .

Most students of United States politics agree that a **"republican model" of democracy** does not accurately reflect the workings of the American political system. In a republican polity, power is exercised on a daily basis by government officials who are elected and held accountable by a "sovereign" public: that is, the public exercises the ultimate power of majority rule. By the twentieth century, most scholars realized that this understanding of American politics was much too simplistic.[1]

Instead, *three competing interpretations or conceptual models have been developed to explain how the overall political process operates throughout society and the government (or state):*

1. Pluralism;
2. Elitism; and,
3. Hyperpluralism.

Each model provides a different understanding of the distribution of power and beliefs that exist throughout society and the government.[2]

Although each model should be considered an "ideal type," intellectual battles have raged over which of the models best captures the basic workings of American politics. When applied to the making of U.S. foreign policy, each model provides a unique understanding of the foreign policy process. Therefore, each model provides a different interpretation of the nature of American governance and democracy (see **table 19.1** for an overview).[3]

Pluralism

Beginning in the 1940s, many American scholars and analysts saw a country in which democratic practice bore little resemblance to the republican ideal. Instead, they perceived a situation where power was dispersed among numerous groups throughout society, with each competing for control of the government. According to Arnold Rose, in *The Power Structure,* pluralism "conceives of a society consisting of many elites, each relatively small numerically and operating in different spheres of life, and of the bulk of the population classifiable into organized groups and publics as well as masses."[4] Under this conception, power is dispersed among different groups throughout society and the government. **Pluralism,** therefore, is a type of competing group politics, in which various groups (and elites) representing different goals and beliefs compete for influence throughout society and the government.

Robert Dahl was one of the most popular proponents of pluralism in American politics. In *Pluralist Democracy in America,* he stipulated that "the fundamental axiom in the theory and practice of American pluralism is this: instead of a single center of sovereign power there must be multiple centers of power, none of which is or can be wholly sovereign."[5] Pluralism did not argue for the existence of a republican form of democratic politics. However, pluralists did argue that the decentralization of power among groups with competing goals represented a different form of democratic practice. Virtually all Americans were part of this democratic practice because of their membership in different groups. Moreover, even if they did not participate, their beliefs were represented by different organized interests throughout society. Therefore, as Dahl stated, pluralist politics "will help to tame power, to secure the consent of all, and to settle conflicts peacefully."[6] Thus, pluralists maintained that "pluralist democracy" existed within the United States.

The "empirical" argument underlying pluralism also contained a "normative" or partisan element. Pluralists tended to see a world in which democratic practice had been challenged by the rise of totalitarianism throughout the twentieth century. They feared that the economic and social changes confronting people in modern societies contributed to the rise of fascism on the Right and communism on the Left—best exemplified at the time by the fall of the Weimar Republic in Germany and the rise to power of Adolf Hitler and the Third Reich. Therefore, pluralism was seen as a means to prevent the collapse of democracy stimulated by the rise of

TABLE 19.1
MODELS OF THE STATE AND SOCIETY

THE MODEL	POWER	VIEWS	IMPLICATIONS FOR POLITICAL CHANGE
PLURALISM	Diffused	Diverse	Incrementalism
ELITISM	Concentrated	Shared	Status quo-oriented
HYPERPLURALISM	Decentralized overall Concentrated networks for each issue	Diverse overall Shared for each issue	Status quo-oriented

mass society, mass communications, and charismatic leadership.[7]

William Kornhauser laid out the argument in *The Politics of Mass Society.* "The central argument of this study is that insofar as a society is a 'mass society' it will be vulnerable to political movements destructive of liberal-democratic institutions; while insofar as a society is 'pluralist' the institutions will be strong."[8] Hence, the mass or "atomized society invites the totalitarian movement."[9] Likewise, Robert Nisbet in *The Quest for Community* argued that "there must be in any stable culture, in any civilization that prizes its integrity, functionally significant and psychologically meaningful groups and associations lying intermediate to the individual and the larger values and purposes of his society."[10]

A pluralistic political system, it was argued, based on the prevalence of competing groups (and elites) representing diverse views decreased the likelihood of major change. As Robert Dahl stated, pluralism "encourages incremental change, it discourages comprehensive change."[11] This was important to most pluralists, because the rise of mass society promoted too much freedom and too much potential for change with too little order. "Consequently," stated Dahl, "no part of the people, such as a majority, ought to be absolutely sovereign."[12] Competing groups representing diverse interests created the barriers between national leaders and the mass public that pluralists believed were essential to prevent the rise of authoritarianism. Therefore, proponents of pluralist democracy argued that it provided a balance between the demands of freedom and order.

ELITISM

Disputing the pluralist interpretation, some scholars and intellectuals began to seriously question the democratic nature of American society. They did not see a republican system characterized by dispersal of power among a public that elected and held the key leaders accountable. Nor did they see the essence of American politics in a pluralistic light. Instead, they saw a policymaking process in terms of **elitism**: one in which power was concentrated among elites who represented a small segment of the society, shared similar values and beliefs, and dominated the political and policymaking process.

Actually, *two somewhat different versions or proponents of elitism* existed: 1) those who saw class elitism, and 2) those who saw institutional elitism.[13] The "class elitist" perspective emphasized class differences and the disproportionate amount of power that resided with the upper class throughout American society and government. The "institutional elitist" perspective emphasized how elites, not necessarily from the upper class, occupied and dominated key institutional positions of power within society and government. Regardless of whether the focus was on the prevailing class or the prevailing institutions, the general public exercised little real influence within a governmental-societal political system which was essentially elitist in nature. As E. E. Schattschneider wrote in *The Semi-Sovereign People* in 1960, "The flaw in the pluralist heaven is that the heavenly chorus sings with a strong upper-class accent. Probably about 90 percent of the people cannot get into the pressure [group] system."[14] Instead of pluralist democracy, therefore, many concluded that elitism actually prevailed throughout American society.

In the mid-1950s, an elitist interpretation was popularized by C. Wright Mills in *The Power Elite*.[15] He argued that behind the facade of pluralistic politics a disproportionate amount of power lay with *the leaders of three key sets of institutions:* business, the military establishment, and the federal bureaucracy. Furthermore, these national leaders shared the same general beliefs as a result of common socioeconomic backgrounds, similar socialization experiences, and professional interaction. Not only did the general public exercise little influence over these institutions, but the institutions tended to respond to the wishes of national leaders.

Therefore, for Mills *American politics consisted of a three-tiered system of power:* a large, apathetic mass society at the bottom, a limited pluralist politics involving organized interests active in government and society at the middle levels of power (such as within the legislative process), and an elitist politics dominated by top government officials, military leaders, and corporate executives operating within the confines of a narrow ideological consensus at the highest levels of power. Hence, his response to pluralist claims was:

> That on the bottom level there has come into being a mass-like society which has little resemblance to the image of a society in which voluntary associations and class publics hold the keys to power. The top of the American system of power is much more unified and much more powerful, the bottom is much more fragmented, and in truth, impotent, than is generally supposed by those who are distracted by the middling units of power which neither express such will as exists at the bottom nor determine the decisions at the top.[16]

In effect, pluralist politics actually operated within a narrow set of parameters determined by the elitist structure of society. Power, in other words, was ultimately exercised from the "top-down" with only a small cross-section of elites dominating do-

mestic politics and policymaking for the most "significant" issues, especially at the "national" level, throughout society and the government.

In addition to describing the nature of American politics, elitism also contained a "normative" or partisan dimension. Most proponents of elitist interpretations of American politics believed in democracy and the principles embodied in the American Constitution. However, they also believed that with the rise of big business, big government, and mass (urban) society since the Civil War, American democracy had slowly been transformed into an elitist system. As Mills put it, "The history of modern society may readily be understood as the story of the enlargement and the centralization of the means of power—in economic, in political, and in military institutions."[17]

Therefore, elitists argued that "major change" had to occur in the elitist system that arose before American democracy could be restored. They tended to emphasize the development of countervailing power as a prerequisite for such change and to stress that members of the public had to become more interested and active in politics if they were to begin exercising the influence predicated by democratic practice. Despite their hopes, it was realized that it would be very difficult to change a system that was fundamentally elitist and status quo-oriented.

THE GREAT DEBATE

During the late 1950s and early 1960s, elitists and pluralists fought intellectual and scholarly battles over the nature of politics in American society. Studies were done by elitists demonstrating that American politics was elitist at both the local and national levels. Similarly, contrasting studies performed by pluralists supported the existence of pluralist politics at the local and national levels as well.[18]

Ultimately, however, the great debate between elitists and pluralists was not resolved on the basis of evidence, for reasonable people could differ. Instead, it was determined by the evolution of American politics. Very simply, the pluralist interpretation prevailed by the early 1960s because most members of the elite public, including American academics and intellectuals, believed that the United States was, in fact, democratic in nature. Pluralism clearly became the most popular and powerful interpretation of American politics at the time.[19]

The **rise of pluralist thought** is understandable if one recalls the evolution of American ideology during the cold war era discussed throughout the book, for it reflected the formation of the liberal-conservative consensus throughout American society. People not included in the liberal-conservative consensus, whether on the Right or the Left, were more likely to conclude that American politics was basically elitist. However, this elitist interpretation was limited to certain circles that remained largely outside the political mainstream and, therefore, invisible to most Americans.

HYPERPLURALISM

During the late 1960s and 1970s, pluralism was again openly challenged. The collapse of the liberal-conservative consensus, along with the rise of the Left and the Right, renewed the pluralist-elitist debate to some extent.[20] During this time a third interpretation of American democracy also gained popularity, sometimes referred to as **hyperpluralism** by students of American politics. Pluralists emphasize the diffusion of power and diversity of thought characterizing the competition between groups in society and government on any single issue. Elitists emphasize the concentration of power and shared beliefs among a small segment of society which dominate politics with respect to the most important issues. Hyperpluralism blends the two models together, making it both similar to and distinct from pluralism and elitism.[21]

Hyperpluralists emphasize the rise of bureaucratic institutions and groups throughout government and society, and the close ties established between them over issues of public policy. Therefore, a particular issue tends to produce a distinct **networks** of interactive and mutually supportive ties between specific individuals (or elites) and groups throughout society and government that dominate the politics of that issue. The existence of a military-industrial-scientific infrastructure in defense policy is often cited as a classic example of hyperpluralist politics. This hyperpluralist view of American politics was popularized by Grant McConnell's *Private Power and American Democracy* and Theodore Lowi's *The End of Liberalism*.[22] Scholars have subsequently referred to the development of hyperpluralist networks of interaction throughout society and government as "iron triangles," "subgovernments," "issue networks" and "policy networks."[23]

Hyperpluralism borrows elements from both pluralism and elitism. Looking at American politics from a distance (or macro perspective), the existence of hundreds of different issue networks dominating hundreds of different issues appears pluralist. Rather than competing for political access and influence, however, groups tend to establish networks of mutually reinforcing relationships that dominate access and influence in their particular area of interest. Issue networks develop among established governmental and private groups which, through their political access and influence, are able to keep challenging groups outside the power loop. Taking a close look (or micro perspective) at any single issue, therefore, the dominance of an issue network leads to concentration of power and is, in fact, quite elitist for that issue. Overall, however, *different policy issues result in the dominance of different subgovernments or issue networks*—the same coalition of individuals (or elites) and groups do not always dominate, in contrast to the elitist interpretation above.

Hyperpluralism, in other words, is an exaggerated or perverted form of pluralism in which American politics are not merely decentralized and pluralistic; rather, the system is so decentralized around single issues that little room is left for the exercise of democratic practice and the prospects of change are slim.[24] This is because the individuals and groups comprising the issue networks that dominate society and government have both vested interests and the power to protect and promote the status quo. In other words, the federal government, including the executive branch, is not only weak but ineffective in responding to change. Yet, as hyperpluralists point out, change in the politics of hyperpluralism can occur. However, it is infrequent and usually results from outside efforts to open up the informal networks that control the placement of issues on the public agenda.

THE MAKING OF FOREIGN POLICY SINCE WORLD WAR II
. . . .

To what extent do these competing conceptual models reflect the foreign policy process since World War II? Since that war, *two sets of conventional wisdom have prevailed during different periods about the making of U.S. foreign policy:*

1. During the cold war era, the prevailing interpretation of the foreign policy process has approximated the pluralist interpretation.
2. Since the end of the Vietnam War, the dominant interpretation has been that the foreign policy process tended to be more elitist during the cold war years, but has become more pluralist since Vietnam.

After briefly reviewing these two leading interpretations of the nature of the foreign policy process, we will discuss some important facets which have not been sufficiently explored by either conventional wisdom, such as the role of hyperpluralist politics. Overall, a summary analysis through use of the conceptual models will allow for a better understanding of continuity and change, presidential governance, and the tension between national security and democracy which has characterized the foreign policy process since World War II.

PLURALISM AND THE COLD WAR YEARS

During the cold war years, the prevalent interpretation viewed the making of U.S. foreign policy as rather pluralist in nature. This was reflected in the work of foreign policy scholars and analysts such as Gabriel Almond, Paul Hammond, Samuel Huntington, Warner Schilling, and Glenn Snyder.[25] The most popular and powerful statement of this interpretation was Roger Hilsman's *To Move A Nation: The Politics of Foreign Policy in the Administration of John F. Kennedy.*[26]

"In its broadest meaning," states Hilsman, "politics concerns the activities and relationships of groups of people as groups."[27] *The group process shares three characteristics.* First, the political process includes the presence of competing groups or factions. Second, "politics implies a diversity of goals and values that must be reconciled."[28] Third, the relative power of the different groups prevents the same groups from dominating the policymaking process time and time again. Hence, the politics of U.S. foreign policy is essentially pluralist in nature. "The fact that policy is made through a political process of conflict and consensus-building accounts for much of the untidiness and turmoil on the Washington scene. The issues are important; there are rival policies for dealing with them; and the rival policies are sponsored by different groups of advocates competing for the approval or support of a variety of different constituencies."[29]

Therefore, policymaking for Hilsman involves a political process of conflict, compromise, and incrementalism due to the multiplicity of actors attempting to reconcile competing goals. A nation, hence, is moved as a result of "the interaction of the President, the Congress, the press, and special interests" and "the rivalries of the great Executive departments, State, Defense, and the Central Intelligence Agency, as they clash in the actual making of policy."[30]

The implications of such a political and messy policymaking process is that "over some of this at certain times, the President may merely preside—if it is a matter of slight interest to him and has little impact on his position. But if *he* is an advocate or if the outcome affects *his* position and power, then the President, too, must engage in the politics of policymaking. In the field of foreign affairs, the President's power is immense. . . . But he, too, must build a consensus for his policy if it is to succeed." This means that "he must bring along enough of the different factions in Congress to forestall revolt, and he must contend for the support of wider constituencies, the press, interest groups, and 'attentive publics'. Even within the Executive Branch itself, his policy will not succeed merely at his command, and he must build co-operation and support, obtain approval from some, acquiescence from others, and enthusiasm from enough to carry it to completion."[31] Hence, for Hilsman the making of U.S. foreign policy during the cold war years was basically in accordance with pluralist politics.

Although Hilsman portrays the politics of U.S. foreign policy in pluralist terms, *upon close examination it is a very restricted or limited form of pluralism for three basic reasons.* First, competing groups are not found throughout society, but predominantly within the government. Second, in most cases, members of the executive branch have a disproportionate amount of influence within the policymaking process. Third, the mass public plays virtually no role in the policymaking process at all. Each of these points is briefly considered below.

As Hilsman sees it, the policymaking process consists of a *series of "three concentric circles"*: an innermost circle of the president, his chief advisers, and his major appointments throughout the executive branch; a middle circle of the other departments, agencies, and layers of personnel within the executive branch; and an outermost circle consisting of "Congress, the press, interest groups, and—inevitably—the 'attentive publics'."[32] The first two of these concentric circles involve policymaking solely within the executive branch. Hilsman maintains that some matters never go beyond the innermost circle, "but even here the process is political—the 'closed politics' of highly secret decision-making." However, "the longer a policy debate goes on, no matter how delicate the issue is, the more people will become involved until eventually the debate spills over into the public arena."[33]

While this may represent pluralist politics, it is a type of pluralism which is often limited to only a narrow range of government officials and groups located predominantly within the executive branch. According to this interpretation, Congress, the press, interest groups, and the attentive publics play a peripheral role, becoming involved only when issues become politicized beyond the executive branch. Even when this occurs, the influence of

Congress tends to be "indirect or limit-setting rather than direct or initiative-taking. In domestic policy, Congress occasionally can take the initiative and force a new policy according to its tastes, but rarely in foreign policy. In foreign policy, the Executive calls the tune … it is the Executive who sets the framework in which policies are discussed, who defines the problems we will essay as a government and the alternatives from which we choose the courses of action to meet them."[34] Hence, for Hilsman pluralist foreign policymaking is largely a function of executive branch activity, with only a peripheral role for the outermost circle.

The outermost circle also seems to exclude any role for the mass public—the bulk of the American people. Hilsman never discusses the mass public—only attentive publics—in terms of the influence or constraints that they place on domestic politics and the policymaking process. Instead, the public is indirectly referred to solely as a political target for different groups in their efforts to gain widespread support. For Hilsman, this leads to an inevitable oversimplification of foreign policy debates and the overselling of policies. As he explains, "If the debate is taking place in front of a variety of audiences whose attention is easily diverted, then the alternatives must be very clear-cut, simple, and dramatic and the arguments painted in colors that are both bold and bright."[35] Thus, a foreign policy process that virtually excludes most Americans raises serious questions concerning the extent to which the political system is democratic and pluralist.

In sum, the pluralist interpretation of U.S. foreign policymaking presented in Hilsman's work prevailed during the cold war era. However, it was a pluralistic political process largely dominated by executive branch politics; Congress, the press, interest groups, and attentive publics were on the periphery and only occasionally involved when issues became politicized; and there was little role for the mass public. Therefore, the president and the executive branch tended to dominate a political process in which the demands of national security took precedence over the demands of democracy. This general interpretation described such a limited form of pluralism in practice that the growth in popularity of a different overall interpretation of the foreign policy process during the post–Vietnam War era is hardly surprising.

THE POST–VIETNAM WAR ERA, FROM ELITISM TO PLURALISM

Beginning in the 1970s, scholars and analysts of U.S. foreign policy developed a new interpretation concerning the making of U.S. foreign policy: during the cold war era, the political process tended to be elitist; with the post–Vietnam War era, it became increasingly pluralist. This growing consensus concerning the politics of U.S. foreign policy is represented by such works as Richard Barnet's *Roots of War*, Destler, Gelb and Lake's *Our Own Worst Enemy*, John Donovan's *The Cold-Warriors*, Gelb and Bett's *The Irony of Vietnam*, David Halberstam's *The Best and the Brightest*, Godfrey Hodgson's *America in Our Time*, Isaacson and Thomas' *The Wise Men*, and Hedrick Smith's *The Power Game*.[36] This interpretation is also consistent with the basic understanding of the post–World War II foreign policy process provided by this book.

It is not really a case of disagreement over the particulars of Hilsman's analysis of the foreign policymaking process during the cold war years. In fact, there is a great deal of shared understanding concerning the power of the president and the executive branch in a political process where national security requirements took precedence over the demands of democracy. *The key dispute involves a different interpretation and conclusion concerning the overall political process:* that the foreign policy process during the cold war years was, in fact, more elitist in nature, as opposed to pluralist. In other words, the argument is that while close inspection of the politics of any particular decision appears to resemble a pluralistic process, the overall general political process was in fact relatively elitist in nature.

An elitist interpretation of the cold war years tends to place great weight on the concentration of power and thought that existed throughout society and government in the making of U.S. foreign policy. The focus is not only on the "immediate" politics of U.S. foreign policy, but the general "setting" and domestic context that molds and constrains the making of U.S. foreign policy. In other words, where Hilsman emphasizes the **direct (and immediate) influence** of the innermost and middle circles—the executive branch—beyond all other concerns, a more elitist interpretation is concerned with both the direct influence enjoyed by the innermost and middle circles on day-to-day policy as well as the **indirect (and underlying and contextual) influence** that the outermost circle has in terms of the constraints on policy and the limits it sets on the political process.[37] In this respect, the pluralist interpretation completely underemphasizes the crucial development and impact of the foreign policy establishment and the ideological consensus on the communications process, electoral and group politics, and the governmental policymaking process.

Very simply, during the cold war years power became increasingly concentrated within the executive branch—especially in the White House and the national security bureaucracy—and in its linkages to key private groups, especially more prominent corporations, foreign policy groups such as the Council on Foreign Relations, and academic institutions. Furthermore, the politics that permeated society and government operated within a strong liberal-conservative ideological consensus, resulting in considerable bipartisanship among the most politically active supported by a largely apathetic and compliant mass public. Thus, in order to understand the foreign policy process during the cold war era, it is important to recognize that power was relatively concentrated and that a consensus of thought reigned supreme throughout society and the government.

The position that the foreign policy process tended to be elitist during the cold war years is consistent with the major patterns discussed in this book. *To briefly summarize, the dominant patterns that prevailed during the cold war years were the following:*

Growth of American power;

Growth of presidential power;

Ascent of the NSC system;

Expansion of the national security bureaucracy;

Rise of the national security ethos;

Development of an acquiescent Congress;

Existence of a Washington political community;

Rise of a liberal-conservative and anticommunist consensus;

Development of bipartisanship in electoral politics;

Prevalence of cold war-oriented groups and movements;

Growth of a foreign policy establishment;

Development of a military-industrial-scientific infrastructure;

Existence of mass apathy and a decline in the exercise of civil liberties; and,

Development of a nonpartisan and centrist mass media.

The cold war years, hence, represented a period when the presidency and the executive branch dominated the foreign policy process at the height of American power, with the involvement and support of mainstream groups and institutions throughout society and government, held together by a foreign policy consensus that pervaded the elite and mass public.

One can debate *the extent of presidential and executive branch power* as a result of these patterns in the making of U.S. foreign policy. However, the cold war years were clearly the height of presidential power in U.S. foreign policy when the president faced the fewest constraints within government and throughout society. The development of the foreign policy bureaucracy, military-industrial-scientific infrastructure, cold war-oriented groups, and foreign policy establishment further provided the support and means by which to pursue and implement a cold war policy. The rise of the foreign policy establishment and the military-industrial-scientific infrastructure, in particular, were consequential in the formation of significant ties and networks that developed between society and government in support of a cold war foreign policy. All of these developments were held together by the rise of a cold war

consensus in which most Americans—throughout the mass and elite publics—came to believe that a national emergency existed due to the threat posed by Soviet communism. This promoted an acquiescent Congress, supportive mass media, and responsive public. Altogether, these elitist patterns produced the phenomenon of the "two presidencies," allowing the president and the national security bureaucracy to exercise "prerogative government" in foreign policy abroad and at home in the name of national security.

One can also debate *how much, or how little, democratic practice existed* in the politics of U.S. foreign policy during the cold war. Yet, widespread fear of the Soviet Union and communism, symbolized by McCarthyism at its height, clearly meant that the demands of national security took precedence over the demands of democracy in the two decades following the end of the Second World War. Consequently, the development of a national security ethos limited the availability of information to the public; Democratic and Republican candidates for national office were cold warriors and offered voters little political choice; political participation declined with little room allowed for the exercise of political dissent; and the rise of bureaucracy—in the executive branch and the private sector—minimized political accountability. Therefore, the existence of powerful groups in the government and throughout society operating under a cold war consensus considerably narrowed democratic practice within mainstream American politics.

To what extent, for example, was the mass public manipulated or educated? *Was the public responsive to national leaders or were they a constraint on foreign policy leadership?* Answers to these questions are consequential in determining the extent of elitism within the politics of U.S. foreign policy during the cold war era. Contradictory patterns are evident, depending on different publics and the times. Whereas the public for the most part may have been manipulated and responsive to national leaders, especially during the late 1940s and early 1950s when cold war policies were devised and sold, the belief in anticommunism once acquired by the public served as a future constraint on domestic politics and the policymaking process. Therefore, it is with some irony that the more elitist interpretation, in comparison to the so-called pluralist interpretation discussed above, actually allows for a greater role for the mass public in the politics of U.S. foreign policy.

Such an elitist interpretation suggests the following. First, that the height of presidential power was reached during the cold war years, especially from the mid-1950s to the mid-1960s. Second, that the demands of national security took precedence over the demands of democracy. Finally, elitism notwithstanding, the politics of U.S. foreign policy was quite complex, as this book has attempted to demonstrate throughout. Together, the politics of U.S. foreign policy were mutually reinforcing and provided political support in government and throughout society for American cold war policy abroad and decisions which led, for example, to the Americanization of the war in Vietnam. That war contributed to the political turbulence of the late 1960s and early 1970s that produced important changes in the complex politics of U.S. foreign policy. American intervention in the Vietnam War, therefore, represented the height and decline of elitism in the making of U.S. foreign policy.

The argument that the foreign policy process became more pluralist since Vietnam is also consistent with the major patterns discussed within the book. *To briefly summarize, the dominant patterns that have prevailed since the Vietnam War have been the following:*

(Relative) decline of American power;

Decline of presidential power;

Rise of the foreign economic bureaucracy and "low" policy;

Reassertion of Congress;

Greater involvement of the judiciary and state and local governments;

Opening up of the Washington political community;

Shattering of the liberal-conservative cold war consensus and its replacement by greater ideological diversity;

Collapse of bipartisan electoral politics and the rise of divided government;

Collapse of the foreign policy establishment;

Proliferation of diverse social movements and groups;

Expansion in the exercise of civil liberties; and,

Rise of a more diverse and independent mass media.

Ultimately, the rise of pluralism has led to a decline in the president's ability to govern foreign policy and an increase in democratic practice relative to the demands of national security.

Since the late 1960s, *presidents face greater obstacles and constraints* than during the cold war years. The two presidencies scenario—weak in domestic policy, strong in foreign policy—has been replaced by the paradox of presidential power that requires the exercise of strong presidential leadership to govern, even in the making of U.S. foreign policy. The crisis of governance facing most post–Vietnam War presidents, however, is so severe that a president has great difficulty fulfilling the high expectations created among the public and, consequently, is prone to experience failure. Most importantly, a president can no longer exercise prerogative government with virtual impunity, as occurred during the cold war years. To do so is to risk "overshoot and collapse" or "political backlash"—as President Richard Nixon experienced with the Watergate affair and President Ronald Reagan suffered with Iran-Contra.

Presidents have greater difficulty governing U.S. foreign policy because *the political process has become more democratic* since the 1960s. In this respect, it is important to understand that the demands of national security and democracy are contradictory and have different implications for the ability of the president to govern foreign policy. While the demands of national security took precedence during the cold war era, the political process in the post–Vietnam War era has become more responsive to the demands of democracy. The public has greater access to information, a choice between more liberal and conservative presidential candidates, and increased opportunities to actively participate. Furthermore, the separation of powers has been renewed, diversity in ideological and foreign policy thought has grown, and group politics have diversified and proliferated.

This is not to say that no elitist elements remain. The president and the executive branch retain significant advantages in the politics of U.S. foreign policy due to the legacy of the cold war and the cloak of the national security ethos, especially during times of crises. Furthermore, political competition among members of the elite public is heavily circumscribed by ideological thought that reflects the liberal-conservative political spectrum. Nevertheless, the politics of U.S. foreign policy has evolved from a more elitist form of politics during the cold war years to a more pluralist form of politics during the post–Vietnam War era.

Therefore, presidents have less support and face considerably stronger constraints in exercising prerogative government in the name of national security in the post–Vietnam War era. During the 1950s, for example, the effort to fight a covert war to overthrow communism in Central America would not have led to the constitutional and political crisis which President Reagan faced with the Iran-Contra scandal; instead, the president would have been able to secretly pursue such a policy with widespread support and little opposition, as President Dwight Eisenhower did in Guatemala in 1954. In other words, where elitist politics considerably strengthened presidential power during the cold war era, the rise of pluralist politics has weakened the president's ability to govern foreign policy since the Vietnam War (see **essay 19.1** for the implications of the role of democracy and the actual conduct of foreign policy).

CONTINUITY IN HYPERPLURALIST POLITICS AND AN APOLITICAL MASS PUBLIC

The complex politics of U.S. foreign policy have not only experienced change but also have been characterized by continuity since the 1960s. *Continuity has occurred relative to two very important facets of the foreign policy process:*

The hyperpluralist politics of national security policy; and,

The continuing withdrawal of much of the mass public from politics.

These are two very important dimensions that are often ignored or downplayed by those who conclude that the political process has become more pluralist since the Vietnam War.

Since World War II and the cold war years, foreign policy has become increasingly bureaucratic, which has led to the development of extensive networks between individuals and groups within the executive branch, Congress, and the private sector. Hyperpluralist politics are most visible in the development of defense politics during the cold war and their continuation in the post–Vietnam War era. Therefore, *an important element of hyperpluralism within the foreign policy process continues to exist to this day,* as discussed throughout the book:

The national security bureaucracy;

The national security ethos;

The Washington political community;

The military-industrial-scientific infrastructure;

The existence of cold war-oriented groups; and,

The existence of conservative internationalism among a segment of the public.

It is important to point out, however, that hyperpluralism is not limited to national security politics. In fact, wherever established groups and bureaucracies have arisen throughout society and government, issue networks have formed and, subsequently, resisted changes to the status quo.

Such hyperpluralist politics *both strengthen and weaken presidential power.* For example, the existence of a large national security bureaucracy and military-industrial-scientific support infrastructure strengthens the power of a president who wants to pursue a cold war-oriented foreign policy. At the same time, however, presidential policies remain heavily affected by what the bureaucracy is able and

ESSAY 19.1
ARE DEMOCRACIES AND THE UNITED STATES PACIFIC?

What is the likelihood of war breaking out between the United States and one of the other industrialized democracies, such as France, Great Britain, or Japan? Or the likelihood of war along the U.S.-Canadian border—the longest, unmilitarized border in the world? Today, wars among such countries seem inconceivable. And yet, each of these countries participated in the Persian Gulf War against Iraq. Not surprisingly, scholars have begun to theorize that a "zone of peace" develops among liberal, democratic states: that although democracies may be as likely to wage war toward other kinds of states, democracies "do not fight other democracies."

The existence of a democratic peace was first espoused by the German philosopher Immanuel Kant in 1795. Kant's *Perpetual Peace* predicted expanding pacification in international politics as more and more states developed into liberal democracies. Perpetual peace would be established when states accepted three "definitive articles": 1) the adoption of a constitutional republic; 2) the making of agreements among liberal democracies creating a pacific union; and 3) the creation of cosmopolitan law forming norms of "universal hospitality" allowing for high levels of international trade. On the other hand, Kant realized that democratic states were prone to conflict and war relative to nonliberal states.

Many of Kant's ideas were reflected in Woodrow Wilson's hopes for the world after World War I as espoused in his "Fourteen Points," especially the formation of a League of Nations and a liberal international political economic order. Although the world was once again swept up in international war, the liberal democracies allied together against fascism during World War II and communism during the Cold War years. Recently, this pattern of democracies not waging war against other democracies has been increasingly noticed by students of international affairs and labeled the **"democratic peace."**

Although there may be much truth to the existence of a democratic peace, the *"causes"* are very much open to debate. One major line of thought is that policymakers are "constrained" by the limits on executive power found in democratic political systems. Policymakers depend on domestic support and are reluctant to embark on unpopular foreign policies because it could quickly cost them political support and, ultimately, their jobs. This may also make it difficult for democratic states to quickly launch surprise attacks. Maintaining domestic support may also be more difficult to sustain if a conflict lasts longer than expected, if the goals are not clear or important, or if the numbers of casualties mount—witness Korea and Vietnam, versus the Persian Gulf War, in U.S. foreign policy. Another hallmark of democratic societies is the peaceful succession of political leaders, a problem that continues to plague non-democratic states. A more cultural argument is that stable democracies develop established norms and expectations on resolving disputes with each other—norms in which violence is not an acceptable option.

As convincing as the democratic peace seems, there are plenty of *critics*. "Realists," in particular, claim that democracies act no differently than other states in an anarchical, self-help, international system—that democracies are just as prone to conflict and war as any state. After all, it is the pursuit of national power and national interests, not regime type, that determines war or peace. The United States, for example, has had a long history of supporting authoritarian regimes in the name of national security and political stability. Other critics emphasize the role of political stability, economic growth and wealth, alliances, nuclear weapons, and international institutions for furthering the goal of international peace, especially among democracies.

In fact, many students of foreign policy have traditionally argued that the constraints on democratic leaders actually make democratic states more "unpredictable and dangerous" in the international arena, because not only may democracies be slow to react to aggression, but once engaged in war they often overreact and embark on moral crusades to unrealistically "fight wars to end all wars." This has been a common criticism of United States foreign policy throughout much of the twentieth century.

To what extent has United States foreign policy been pacific towards other democratic states? In the twentieth century, the empirical record appears to be quite strong in support of the democratic peace. The United States has been engaged in a number of wars and has relied on the (threat and) use of force extensively, but not towards other democratic states. The focus, however, has been on **overt war**; not much attention has been devoted to analyzing the role of **"covert war"** as well. As was discussed in some depth in chapter 6 on intelligence, while the U.S. government attempted to deter Soviet expansion through the threat of nuclear war and conventional war, it relied "heavily" on covert political and paramilitary intervention to fight communism throughout the globe.

The record relative to covert war is not as clear-cut as with overt war. *Two cases, in particular, stand out* where the United States engaged in a "covert war" against democratic states: Guatemala and Chile. In 1954 in Guatemala, the U.S. government overthrew an "uncooperative" democratically elected president of a country which was in the "formative" stages of democracy in favor of a "friendly" military dictator. Chile, which had a much longer democratic tradition since its independence in the early nineteenth century (although periodically interrupted by authoritarian rule), had been operating as an "established" democracy since the early 1960s. However, with the election of Salvador Allende in 1970, the Nixon administration led a covert campaign to destabilize the Chilean economy and persuade the Chilean military to stage a coup, which came in 1973 and installed Augusto Pinochet as the dictator of Chile for the next 16 years. It may be that covert war and action may be a way for liberal democracies to overcome many of the democratic constraints and obstacles to the use of force discussed above.

And what about *war "turned inward"* towards one's own democratic citizens? With the rise of the cold war, a preoccupation with national security and secrecy also bred distrust of democracy and constitutional rights within the United States. As discussed in chapter 6 on intelligence and chapter 17 on civil liberties, the fear of communism was so great that the president and the intelligence community saw domestic dissent as an internal threat and acted to repress it. Domestic covert operations included the CIA's Operation Chaos, the FBI's Operation Cointelpro, and large spying operations by the NSA and army intelligence. In other words, a wide-ranging set of domestic covert operations were performed that broke the law and violated the civil rights and liberties of American citizens in the name of the protection of American democracy. The cold war clearly was a time when the demands of national security took precedence over the demands of democracy, when the president was able to exercise prerogative government, and elitist politics dominated the making of U.S. foreign policy—suggesting that the United States became somewhat of a *"garrison state."* Ultimately, this type of unconstitutional and undemocratic behavior by the early 1970s led to the tragedy of Watergate and the resignation of President Nixon. Clearly, the existence and nature of democratic states is not a simple open and shut case.

Despite the criticisms, many Americans and American policymakers believe and act as if democracies are more pacific and that expanding liberal democracy is not only important to the spread of American values, but also to the enhancement of international peace and stability. Such an approach to U.S. foreign policy, popularized under Woodrow Wilson, has played a role under most presidents to the present day, certainly at the rhetorical level but also for actual policy. President Clinton's "policy of enlargement" is very consistent with the twentieth century tradition in U.S. foreign policy to promote political and economic development in a liberal democratic direction (review, for example, essay 10.1 on foreign assistance, nation-building, and AID). To what extent liberal enlargement may (and should) become the guiding principle of U.S. foreign policy in a post–cold war world is a question that only time will tell.

SOURCES: Michael E. Brown, Sean M. Lynn-Jones, and Steven E. Miller, editors, *Debating the Democratic Peace* (Cambridge, Mass.: MIT Press, 1997); Michael Doyle, "Liberalism and World Politics," *American Political Science Review* 80 (December 1986): 1151–1169; David P. Forsythe, "Democracy, War, and Covert Action," *Journal of Peace Research* 29 (November 1992): 385–95; Joe D. Hagan, "Domestic Political Systems and War Proneness," *Mershon International Studies Review* 38 (October 1994): 183–207; Harold Lasswell, *The Garrison State,* edited by Jay Stanley (New Brunswick, N.J.: Transaction Books, 1996).

willing to implement. Should a president want to pursue a post–cold war foreign policy, hyperpluralist politics act as a major constraint on new policy initiatives. The need to manage and circumvent the bureaucracy is one of the main reasons why most presidents have increasingly come to rely on a closed policymaking process revolving around a small circle of advisers and the NSC staff.

Hyperpluralist politics also has *implications for the tension between national security and democracy* that exists in American politics. The existence of a huge national security bureaucracy and support infrastructure means that a strong constituency continues to exist throughout society and the government that remains sympathetic to the demands of national security. In other words, a national security ethos of independence, secrecy, and realpolitik continues to affect domestic politics and, in particular, pervade the governmental policymaking process. Therefore, the rise of pluralism and the continuation of hyperpluralism in the post–Vietnam War era have increased the political contradictions and tensions between the demands of national security and democracy.

One other important trend of continuity concerns the role of the mass public in the politics of U.S. foreign policy. *The patterns of continuity prevalent among the mass public that we have discussed throughout the book are as follows:*

An uninformed, uninterested, and erratic public opinion;

A strong sense of political culture and nationalism;

Decline in political participation, especially in electoral politics; and,

The prevalence of the politics of symbolism.

These patterns indicate that there has been a continual process in which a large segment of the public has basically withdrawn from American politics. Such mass apathy has added considerable uncertainty to the president's ability to govern and the contradictions between national security and democracy in the post–Vietnam War era.

This continuity in the role of the mass public during a time when there is no consensus throughout society and government *adds considerable uncertainty to the president's ability to govern* foreign policy. On the one hand, the opinions and cultural beliefs of the mass public, reflecting the split in elite beliefs, reinforces the dominant patterns that prevail in the post–Vietnam War era. At the same time, because most of the public tends to be tuned out of politics, there is a likelihood of greater mood swings—which can strengthen or weaken the president depending on their direction. Therefore, the political withdrawal of much of the mass public at a time of great foreign policy disagreement and competition is a source of great uncertainty and potential instability in the future politics of U.S. foreign policy.

This has important *implications for the practice of democracy* in American politics. Although the rise of pluralism has resulted in greater democracy and a more responsive political system, the prevalence of a predominantly apolitical mass public is a poor omen for the future of democratic politics. It is shocking how little information many Americans possess concerning national and international affairs. Furthermore, public cynicism toward politics appears to have grown. The political result has been a continual decline in mass participation in the electoral process, for example, and a mass public that has become increasingly vulnerable to the politics of symbolism. All of this is a far cry from the "knowledgeable and alert" citizenry that President Eisenhower called for and democratic practice demands. In other words, the increase in democratic politics since the Vietnam War has been paradoxically accompanied by the bulk of the American public "tuning out" of politics altogether. Not surprisingly, some contemporary political analysts have resurrected fears commonly espoused by pluralists during the 1950s concerning the decline of democracy and the rise of authoritarianism in American society.

COMPLEXITY IN THE CONTEMPORARY POLITICS OF U.S. FOREIGN POLICY

. . . .

In sum, the politics of U.S. foreign policy are too complex for any single model of the political process to cap-

ture for much depends on the time and the issues of concern. Overall, the complex politics of U.S. foreign policy has experienced continuity and change since World War II: a more elitist form of politics dominated the cold war years; during the post–Vietnam War years, elitism was replaced by a more pluralist form of politics; politics during the cold war years was also characterized by the rise of hyperpluralism in defense politics and a mass public that remained beyond politics altogether, which continued into the post-Vietnam era. With the collapse of the Soviet Union and the cold war, these post-Vietnam patterns have continued and intensified. Therefore, the cold war years represented the height of the president's ability to govern foreign policy where the demands of national security prevailed over the demands of democracy. In contrast, the years since Vietnam represented a decline in presidential power due to growing contradictions between the growth of democracy and the persistence of national security demands.

Conceptually, it is interesting to note that more and more scholars have come to recognize the **growing "convergence"** between elitist and pluralist interpretations of American politics that have evolved during the post–Vietnam War era. Whereas the competing conceptual models of government-society relations in American politics that were developed during the cold war era were often incomplete and simplistic—and therefore divergent, each of these models has become much more sophisticated with time, thus capturing a greater amount of the complexity and dynamics of American politics— producing greater overlap. Therefore, even though like-minded scholars and analysts tend to communicate among themselves in their own language, often being insensitive to work developed from competing perspectives, pluralist and elitist studies of American politics have become much less incompatible and much more complementary in the post–Vietnam War era.

Much depends, as Pat McGowan and Steve Walker point out in "Radical and Conventional Models of U.S. Foreign Economic Policy Making," on the question and the level of generality that one is addressing: "On the one hand, if one is interested in delineating the outer parameters of change in American policy, an [elitist] perspective identifies the constraints that limit the range of variation and provides insights into the deeper structural changes that appear to be required in order to reshape U.S. foreign economic policy. If, on the other hand, the analyst is interested in short-run, incremental changes in U.S. foreign economic policy, then the [pluralist] perspective sensitizes him to the immediate surface causes of these fluctuations."[38]

The rise of pluralism, accompanied by the continuity of hyperpluralist politics and an apolitical mass public, that has come to dominate the politics of U.S. foreign policy was quite **evident during the Persian Gulf crisis of 1990–1991**. Following Iraq's invasion of Kuwait on August 2, 1990, President Bush was able to exercise prerogative government by sending a massive force of American troops to the Persian Gulf to defend Saudi Arabia. The political response throughout the rest of the government and most of society—Congress, the public, and the media—was to rally around the flag. With President George Bush's announcement in early November, however, that American forces would increase from two hundred thousand to over four hundred thousand personnel and take a new "offensive" military posture to force Iraq out of Kuwait, the domestic political climate changed dramatically, reflecting its more pluralist form. Dissent began to appear in Congress, among former government officials, in group politics, and in public opinion, increasingly communicated by the mass media. Within a three-month period, in other words, the president went from exercising extraordinary power during a foreign policy crisis to experiencing a crisis of governance that would determine the political fate of his presidency. Such contrasting political patterns occurred once again when the country rallied around the flag following President Bush's decision to go to war on January 16, 1991.

The Persian Gulf crisis also illustrates the contradictions in the making of U.S. foreign policy between the demands for national security—emphasized by President Bush—and the demands of democracy—emphasized by those who dissented from the president's policy. At the same time, the outcome of the crisis has also strengthened the networks of individuals and groups in government and throughout society who have been resisting cutting the military establishment in light of the collapse of communism in the Soviet Union and Eastern Europe. Such effects directly reflect the complexity and contradictions of the contemporary nature of the foreign policy process within the United States. It is important to understand that the foreign policy process is actually more complex and messy than this summary analysis suggests because the *role of chance or "fortune"* in the unfolding of politics has been ignored, often leading to a false sense of clarity about the making of U.S. foreign policy due to the benefit of hindsight.[39]

FOREIGN POLICY CHANGE

. . . .

What will the future entail? Why do some patterns remain the same over time? When does **foreign policy change** occur? This is an area which has only received sporadic attention despite its importance, especially with the United States about to enter the twenty-first century.[40] Nevertheless, tentative generalizations can be derived from the work that has been done on the study of political change.

Although political systems can proceed down different historical paths, certain patterns of continuity and change tend to prevail in the politics of U.S. foreign policy. Very simply, American politics normally tends to resist change but is interrupted occasionally by political crises which stimulate change. **"Incremental change,"** that is, little change over a period of time, tends to be the prevailing norm during times of high political legitimacy and stability—a period of equilibrium in the political system. **"Major change"** tends to be infrequent and often abrupt, usually triggered by major crises indicative of failed policies and the rise of political instability—a time of disequilibrium in the political system.

As described by David Truman in *The Governmental Process,* "The moving pattern of a complex society such as the one in which we live is one of changes and disturbances in the habitual subpatterns of interaction, followed by a return to the pre-

vious state of equilibrium or, if the disturbances are intense or prolonged, by the emergence of new groups" which establish "a new balance, a new adjustment in the habitual interactions of individuals."[41] In other words, American politics tends to evolve from periods of political stability in which continuity (and incrementalism) prevails to periods of political instability and transition in which change is most likely. These **cyclical patterns of continuity and change** are consistent with those found in this book on the politics of U.S. foreign policy and have been described by scholars such as Samuel Huntington, Charles Hermann, and Jerel Rosati (see **figure 19.1**).[42]

Why does *"status quo politics"* tend to prevail? Very simply, all political systems, whether pluralist, elitist, or hyperpluralist in nature, tend to resist change. This situation prevails because established groups and institutions throughout government and society engage in politics to promote their interests and protect the status quo from challenging groups and ideas. This influence is usually reinforced by the support of the mass public. Although predominantly apolitical, they support mainstream institutions and beliefs, ultimately providing the political system with its legitimacy and political stability. According to V. O. Key, Jr., in *Politics, Parties, and Pressure Groups,*

> The system—the established way of doing things—constitutes a powerful brake on political change. Those who agitate for a new order invariably encounter the resistance of the old order which exists, in considerable degree at least, in the revered values more or less firmly anchored in group life. These patterns of behavior, traditional modes of action, group norms, or social equilibria—the concept employed in their description may not matter—possess a powerful capacity for their own perpetuation and resist movements that would disturb them.[43]

In other words, all political systems with an established set of institutions and beliefs in place throughout the society and government resist

FIGURE 19.1
CYCLES OF FOREIGN POLICY CONTINUITY AND CHANGE

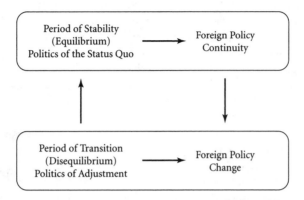

SOURCE: Jerel A. Rosati, "Cylces in Foreign Policy Restructuring: The Politics of Continuity and Change in U.S. Foreign Policy," in Jerel A. Rosati, Joe D. Hagan, and Martin W. Sampson, eds., *Foreign Policy Restructuring: How Governments Respond to Global Change* (Columbia, SC: University of South Carolina Press, 1994), p. 227.

change, although with varying degrees of rigidity and success. The implication is that change, if it occurs at all, tends to be incremental in nature.

Although continuity and incrementalism tend to be the norm, major change periodically occurs throughout society and the government. The *"politics of change and adjustment"* is most likely to prevail over the politics of the status quo during times of crisis and political instability, when the legitimacy of the political system is most likely to be questioned by members of society. This eventually occurs because of the growing gap that develops between the incrementalist policies of the government and the inevitable change experienced throughout the global environment and society. As the politics of the status quo continues to prevail and governmental policies fail to adjust to new developments in the international and domestic environment, the contradictions grow, increasing the likelihood of policy failure abroad and the growth of internal opposition at home. As stated by Stanley Hoffmann, "When rigidity leads to failure—but only then—the policy becomes unstuck and sudden reversals become possible."[44] Should these contradictory developments

continue and intensify with time, governmental policy becomes increasingly maladaptive. Eventually, this may lead to major political crises at home that politicize members of society to challenge the legitimacy of the policies and the beliefs held by the individuals and groups that dominate society and the state.

The key to understanding the dynamics of foreign policy, in other words, is the interaction of the state, the society and the global environment (or context) which produces a political process that usually reinforces governmental resistance to change and the maintenance of foreign policy continuity; sometimes, however, it produces contradictions to the status quo that contribute to foreign policy change. Whatever the causes, public policies that were once considered to be successful are now increasingly seen as failures and counterproductive. During such periods of political instability, greater numbers of people are likely to question and criticize the status quo, new and more issues are placed on the political agenda, challenging groups and ideas gain strength, and the dominant groups and beliefs throughout society and government have less success dominating politics. Therefore, times of major crises and political instability are often transitional periods which "may" produce major political change (see **figure 19.2** for an overview).

The making of U.S. foreign policy has followed this evolutionary pattern in which the politics of the status quo tends to be superseded by the politics of transition, producing change and a new politics of the status quo. The political crises faced by the United States in association with World War II, the rise of American power, and the development of the cold war triggered a number of significant changes in government and society, resulting in the more elitist political patterns of U.S. foreign policy during the cold war years that we have identified in this book. These patterns in the foreign policy process prevailed throughout the 1950s and early 1960s until the political crises and instability of the late 1960s and early 1970s, especially over U.S. foreign policy in the Viet-

nam War, triggered additional political changes in government and society in a more pluralist direction which have prevailed since Vietnam. At the same time, the hyperpluralism of defense politics and the political apathy among the mass public are continuing legacies of the cold war years. Thus, the politics of U.S. foreign policy has experienced continuity and change over time, with significant implications for both the president's ability to govern and for the contradictory tension between the demands of national security and democracy as the United States approaches the next century, to which we now turn.

BIBLIOGRAPHIC ESSAY
· · · · · · · · · · · · · ·

There is a rich literature involved in the study of pluralism, elitism, and hyperpluralism, although not much of it has been directly applied to the making of U.S.

FIGURE 19.2
THE DYNAMICS OF FOREIGN POLICY CHANGE

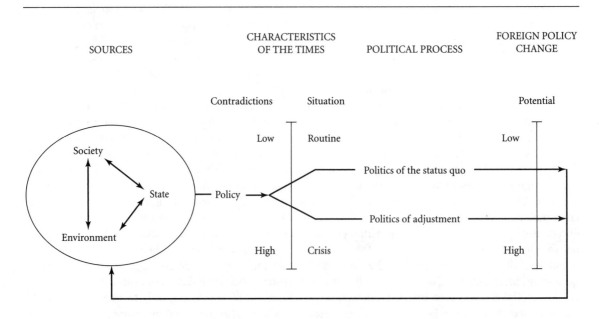

SOURCE: Jerel A. Rosati, "Cycles in Foreign Policy Restructuring: The Politics of Continuity and Change in U.S. Foreign Policy," in Jerel A. Rosati, Joe D. Hagan, and Martin W. Sampson, eds., *Foreign Policy Restructuring: How Governments Respond to Global Change* (Columbia, S.C.: University of South Carolina Press, 1994), p. 237.

foreign policy. For a general discussion of pluralism and its significance for democratic practice, classic statements can be found in William Kornhauser, *The Politics of Mass Society* (New York: Free Press, 1956), and Robert A. Nisbet, *The Quest for Community* (New York: Oxford University Press, 1953). Roger Hilsman, in *To Move a Nation: The Politics of Foreign Policy in the Administration of John F. Kennedy* (New York: Delta, 1964), especially chapters 1 and 35, provides the best example of the pluralist perspective applied to the making of U.S. foreign policy for the cold war years.

For a general discussion of elitism, the classic statement is provided by C. Wright Mills in *The Power Elite* (London: Oxford University Press, 1956). A more contemporary account with a greater emphasis on the concept of class can be found in Ralph Miliband, *The State in Capitalist Society: The Analysis of the Western System of Power* (London: Quartet Books, 1969). For an elitist perspective on the politics of U.S. foreign policy during the cold war era, excellent accounts are provided by Richard Barnet in *Roots of War: Men and Institutions Behind U.S. Foreign Policy* (New York: Penguin, 1972); Leslie H. Gelb with Richard K. Betts, *The Irony of Vietnam: The System Worked* (Washington, DC: Brookings, 1979); David Halberstam in *The Best and the Brightest* (New York: Random House, 1972); and Walter Isaacson and Evan Thomas in *The Wise Men: Six Friends and the World They Made* (New York: Touchstone, 1986).

Godfrey Hodgson, in *America in Our Time* (New York: Vintage, 1976), provides an impressive overview of the evolution of American politics since World War II in terms of movement from elitism to pluralism. Likewise, I. M. Destler, Leslie H. Gelb, and Anthony Lake, in *Our Own Worst Enemy: The Unmaking of American Foreign Policy* (Simon and Schuster, 1984), and Hedrick Smith, in *The Power Game* (New York: Ballantine, 1988), emphasize the rise of pluralist politics during the post–Vietnam War era. The classic statements on hyperpluralism remain Grant McConnell, *Private Power and American Democracy* (New York: Vintage, 1966), Theodore J. Lowi, *The End of Liberalism: Ideology, Policy, and the Crisis of Public Authority* (New York: W.W. Norton, 1969), and Hugh Heclo, "Issue Networks and the Executive Establishment," in Anthony King, ed., *The New American Political System* (Washington, DC: American Enterprise Institute, 1978): 87–124.

An informative and provocative analysis of the dynamics of continuity and change in American politics can be found in Samuel P. Huntington, *American Politics: The Politics of Disharmony* (Cambridge, Mass.: Harvard University Press, 1981). More theoretical discussions that specifically address the dynamics of foreign policy change are provided by Charles F. Hermann in "Changing Course: When Governments Choose to Redirect Foreign Policy," *International Studies Quarterly* 34 (March 1990): 3–21, and Jerel A. Rosati, in "Cycles in Foreign Policy Restructuring: The Politics of Continuity and Change in U.S. Foreign Policy," in Jerel A. Rosati, Joe D. Hagan, and Martin W. Sampson, eds., *Foreign Policy Restructuring: How Governments Respond to Global Change* (Columbia, S.C.: University of South Carolina Press, 1994): 221–61.

ENDNOTES

1. This was probably communicated most forcefully by the writings of journalist Walter Lippmann. See, in particular, *Public Opinion* (New York: Harcourt, Brace, 1922) and *The Phantom Public* (New York: Macmillan, 1927).

2. For an overview of state-societal relations and different theoretical approaches, see Douglas M. Fox, ed., *The Politics of U.S. Foreign Policy Making* (Pacific Palisades, Calif.: Goodyear Pub., 1971); G. David Garson, *Group Theories of Politics* (Beverly Hills: Sage, 1978); Martin N. Marger, *Elites and Masses: An Introduction to Political Sociology* (Belmont, Calif.; Wadsworth, 1987); Joel S. Migdal, *Strong Societies and Weak States: State-Society Relations and State Capabilities in the Third World* (Princeton, N.J.: Princeton University Press, 1988); David Skidmore and Valerie M. Hudson, *The Limits of State Autonomy: Societal Groups and Foreign Policy Formulation* (Boulder, Colo.: Westview Press, 1993); Alfred Stepan, *The State and Society: Peru in Comparative Perspective* (Princeton, N.J.: Princeton University Press, 1978).

3. The elitist, pluralist and hyperpluralist models tend to assume the existence of a so-called "weak state," in American politics—that is, of a permeable or symbiotic government relative to society—as opposed to a "strong state" that is relatively independent of domestic politics and societal forces. Although the strong-state perspective used to dominate the (realist) study of international relations, it has become increasingly

questioned, especially in the making of U.S. foreign policy. The terms "strong" and "weak" states, actually, are somewhat simplistic: an elitist perspective, for example, allows for a very powerful state to prevail in the area of foreign policy, despite its societal interconnections and structural constraints. For a more traditional realist perspective to the making of U.S. foreign policy, see Stephen D. Krasner, *Defending the National Interest: Raw Materials Investments and U.S. Foreign Policy* (Princeton, N.J.: Princeton University Press, 1978). For a more complex "neo-realist" understanding, see G. John Ikenberry, *Reasons of State: Oil Politics and the Capacities of American Government* (Ithaca, N.Y.: Cornell University Press, 1988); Peter J. Katzenstein, ed., *Between Power and Plenty: Foreign Economic Policies of Advanced Industrial States* (Madison, Wis.: University of Wisconsin Press, 1978); David A. Lake, *Power, Protection, and Free Trade: International Sources of U.S. Commercial Strategy, 1887–1939* (Ithaca, N.Y.: Cornell University Press, 1988); Richard Rosecrance and Arthur A. Stein, eds., *The Domestic Bases of Grand Strategy* (Ithaca, N.Y.: Cornell University Press, 1993); Jack Snyder, *Myths of Empire: Domestic Politics and International Ambition* (Ithaca, N.Y.: Cornell University Press, 1991). This more complex understanding is more consistent with the early theorists of U.S. foreign policy—such as Gabriel Almond, Roger Hilsman, Stanley Hoffmann, Charles Lindblom, Richard Neustadt, and Richard Snyder—and those who followed in their paths, as discussed in chapter 1 and throughout this book, although this has rarely been acknowledged by neo-realist authors.

4. Arnold H. Rose, *The Power Structure: Political Process in American Society* (New York: Oxford University Press, 1967), p. 5.

5. Robert A. Dahl, *Pluralist Democracy in the United States: Conflict and Consent* (Chicago: Rand McNally, 1967), p. 24.

6. Ibid.

7. For some intellectual background, see Neil McInnes, "Ortega and the Myth of the Mass," *National Interest* (Summer 1996): 78–88.

8. William Kornhauser, *The Politics of Mass Society* (New York: Free Press, 1956), p. 5.

9. Ibid., p. 16.

10. Robert A. Nisbet, *The Quest for Community: A Study in the Ethics of Order and Freedom* (New York: Oxford University Press, 1953).

11. Dahl, *Pluralist Democracy in America*, p. 298.

12. Ibid., p. 24.

13. For an overview and background, see T. B. Bottomore, *Elites and Society* (Penguin, 1966).

14. E. E. Schattschneider, *The Semi-Sovereign People: A Realist's View of Democracy in America* (New York: Holt, Rinehart and Winston, 1960), p. 35.

15. C. Wright Mills, *The Power Elite* (London: Oxford University Press, 1956).

16. Ibid.: 28–29.

17. C. Wright Mills, "The Structure of Power in American Society," in Pietro S. Nivola and David H. Rosenbloom, eds., *Classic Readings in American Politics* (New York: St. Martin's Press, 1986), p. 131.

18. For pluralist and elitist studies of American politics and an overview of the debate, see Peter Bachrach, ed., *Political Elites in a Democracy* (New York: Atherton Press, 1971); Robert A. Dahl, *Who Governs? Democracy and Power in an American City* (New Haven, Conn.: Yale University Press, 1961); G. William Domhoff and Hoyt B. Ballard, eds., *C. Wright Mills and the Power Elite* (Boston: Beacon Press, 1968); Floyd Hunter, *Top Leadership U.S.A.* (Chapel Hill: University of North Carolina Press, 1959); Seymour Martin Lipset, *Political Man: The Social Bases of Politics* (New York: Doubleday, 1960); Nelson W. Polsby, *Community Power and Political Theory* (New Haven, CT: Yale University Press, 1963).

19. For an overview of such intellectual thought during the cold war years, see Richard H. Pells, *The Liberal Mind in a Conservative Age: American Intellectuals in the 1940s and 1950s* (New York: Harper & Row, 1985).

20. See, for example, Robert A. Dahl, "Pluralism Revisited," *Comparative Politics* (1978): 191–203; Thomas R. Dye, *Who's Running America* (Englewood Cliffs, N.J.: Prentice-Hall, 1976); Kenneth Prewitt and Alan Stone, *The Ruling Elites: Elite Theory, Power, and American Democracy* (New York: Harper & Row, 1973); and David M. Ricci, *The Tragedy of Political Science: Politics, Scholarship, and Democracy* (New Haven, Conn.: Yale University Press, 1984), chapter 8. This also led to the rise of neo-Marxist and class analysis of American politics. See G. William Domhoff, *The Higher Circles: Governing Class in America* (New York: Vintage, 1970); G. William Domhoff, *The Powers That Be: Processes of Ruling Class Domination in America* (New York: Vintage, 1978); and Ralph Miliband, *The State in Capitalist Society: The Analysis of the Western System of Power* (London: Quartet Books, 1969). For a discussion of the more simplistic elitist interpretations of the far Left and far Right, see Gary Allen, *None Dare Call It Conspiracy* (Rossmoor, Calif.: Concord Press,

1976), and Ole R. Holsti, "The Study of International Politics Makes Strange Bedfellows: Theories of the Radical Right and the Radical Left," *American Political Science Review* 68 (1974): 217–41. For a good overview of more sophisticated interpretations that have developed, see Clyde W. Barrow, *Critical Theories of the State: Marxist, Neo-Marxist, Post-Marxist* (Madison, Wis.: University of Wisconsin Press, 1993).

21. Unlike the labels pluralism and elitism, there is no common label for this third interpretation or model of American politics. During the late 1960s and 1970s, hyperpluralism probably was more commonly used than any other single term in the study of American politics.

22. Theodore J. Lowi, *The End of Liberalism: Ideology, Policy, and the Crisis of Public Authority* (New York: W.W. Norton, 1969), and Grant McConnell, *Private Power and American Democracy* (New York: Vintage, 1966). See also Marc Pilisuk and Tom Hayden, "Is There a Military-Industrial Complex Which Prevents Peace?" in William C. Vocke, ed., *American Foreign Policy: An Analytical Approach* (New York: Free Press, 1976): 215–28.

23. See, for example, Douglass Cater, *Power in Washington* (New York: Vintage, 1964); and Hugh Heclo, "Issue Networks and the Executive Establishment," in Anthony King, ed., *The New American Political System* (Washington, D.C.: American Enterprise Institute, 1978): 87–124. For more contemporary overviews, see Michael M. Atkinson and William D. Coleman, "Policy Networks, Policy Communities and the Problems of Governance," *Governance: An International Journal of Policy and Administration* (April 1992): 154–80; Jeffrey M. Berry, *The Interest Group Society* (Glenview, Ill.: Scott, Foresman, 1989); David Knoke, *Political Networks: The Structural Perspective* (Cambridge: Cambridge University Press, 1990); and Barry Wellman and S. D. Berkowitz, eds., *Social Structures: A Network Approach* (New York: Cambridge University Press, 1988).

24. This is an interpretation with which Robert Dahl, for example, became increasingly sympathetic with time. See Robert A. Dahl, *Dilemmas of Pluralist Democracy: Autonomy vs. Control* (New Haven, Conn.: Yale University Press, 1982), and John F. Manley, "Neo-Pluralism: A Class Analysis of Pluralism I and Pluralism II," *American Political Science Review* 77 (June 1983): 368–83.

25. Gabriel A. Almond, *The American People and Foreign Policy* (New York: Praeger, 1960); Samuel P. Hunting-

ton, *The Common Defense: Strategic Programs in National Politics* (New York: Columbia University Press, 1961); and Warner R. Schilling, Paul T. Hammond, and Glenn H. Snyder, *Strategy, Politics and Defense Budgets* (New York: Columbia University Press, 1962). See also Graham T. Allison, *Essence of Decision: Explaining the Cuban Missile Crisis* (Boston: Little, Brown, 1971), chapter 5; Stanley Hoffmann, *Gulliver's Troubles or the Setting of American Foreign Policy* (New York: McGraw-Hill, 1968); Theodore J. Lowi, "Making Democracy Safe for the World: National Politics and Foreign Policy," in *Domestic Sources of Foreign Policy,* edited by James N. Rosenau (New York: Free Press, 1967): 295–331; Richard A. Neusdadt, *Presidential Power: The Politics of Leadership* (New York: John Wiley, 1960); and Burton M. Sapin, *The Making of United States Foreign Policy* (New York: Praeger, 1966).

26. Roger Hilsman, *To Move A Nation: The Politics of Foreign Policy in the Administration of John F. Kennedy* (New York: Delta, 1964).

27. Ibid., p. 552.

28. Ibid., p. 553.

29. Ibid., p. 544.

30. Ibid., p. 13.

31. Ibid.: 561–62.

32. Ibid., p. 543.

33. Ibid.: 542, 543.

34. Ibid., p. 557.

35. Ibid., p. 546.

36. Richard Barnet, *Roots of War: Men and Institutions Behind U.S. Foreign Policy* (New York: Penguin, 1972); I. M. Destler, Leslie H. Gelb, and Anthony Lake, *Our Own Worst Enemy: The Unmaking of American Foreign Policy* (Simon and Schuster, 1984); John C. Donovan, *The Cold-Warriors: A Policy-Making Elite* (Lexington, Mass.: D.C. Heath, 1974); Leslie H. Gelb with Richard K. Betts, *The Irony of Vietnam: The System Worked* (Washington, D.C.: Brookings, 1979); David Halberstam, *The Best and the Brightest* (New York: Random House, 1972); Godfrey Hodgson, *America in Our Time* (New York: Vintage, 1976); Walter Isaacson and Evan Thomas, *The Wise Men: Six Friends and the World They Made* (New York: Touchstone, 1986); and Hedrick Smith, *The Power Game* (New York: Ballantine, 1988). Hedrick Smith provides a more general overview of the changes that have occurred throughout American politics, along with Anthony King, ed., *The New American Political System* (Washington, D.C.: AEI Press, 1990). For a somewhat different but

complementary perspective, see Mark Edward Rupert, "Producing Hegemony: State/Society Relations and the Politics of Productivity in the United States," *International Studies Quarterly* 34 (1990): 427–56.

37. For a general discussion of direct and indirect influence, see, for example, Peter Bachrach and Morton Baratz, "Two Faces of Power," *American Political Science Review* 56 (December 1962): 947–52.

38. Pat McGowan and Stephen G. Walker, "Radical and Conventional Models of U.S. Foreign Economic Policy Making" *World Politics* 33 (April 1981): 378.

39. See Niccolo Machiavelli in *The Prince and The Discourses* (New York: Modern Library, 1950) on "fortune," and Carl Von Clausewitz in *On War* (New York: Penguin, 1832) on the concept of "friction."

40. See Jerel A. Rosati, Joe D. Hagan, and Martin W. Sampson, eds., *Foreign Policy Restructuring: How Governments Respond to Global Change* (Columbia, S.C.: University of South Carolina Press, 1994), especially chapter 1 on "The Study of Change in Foreign Policy."

41. David B. Truman, *The Governmental Process: Political Interests and Public Opinion* (New York: Alfred A. Knopf, 1951), p. 44.

42. See Charles F. Hermann, "Changing Course: When Governments Choose to Redirect Foreign Policy." *International Studies Quarterly* 34 (March 1990): 3–21; Samuel P. Huntington, *American Politics: The Politics of Disharmony* (Cambridge, Mass.: Harvard University Press, 1981); and Jerel A. Rosati, "Cycles in Foreign Policy Restructuring: The Politics of Continuity and Change in U.S. Foreign Policy," in Jerel A. Rosati, Joe D. Hagan, and Martin W. Sampson, eds., *Foreign Policy Restructuring: How Governments Respond to Global Change* (Columbia, S.C.: University of South Carolina Press, 1994): 221–61. See also John H. Broesamle, *Reform and Reaction in Twentieth Century American Politics* (Westport, Conn: Greenwood Press, 1990); Frank R. Baumgartner and Bryan D. Jones, *Agendas and Instability in American Politics* (Chicago: University of Chicago Press, 1993); James MacGregor Burns, *The Deadlock of Democracy: Four-Party Politics in America* (Englewood Cliffs, N.J.: Prentice-Hall, 1963); Steve Fraser and Gary Gerstle, editors, *The Rise and Fall of the New Deal Order, 1930–1980* (Princeton: Princeton University Press, 1989); Theodore J. Lowi, *The Politics of Disorder* (New York: Basic Books, 1971); Arthur M. Schlesinger, Jr., *Cycles of American History* (Boston: Houghton Mifflin, 1986); Schattschneider, *The Semisovereign People;* and James L. Sundquist, *Politics and Policy* (Washington, D.C.: Brookings, 1968).

43. V.O. Key, Jr., *Politics, Parties, and Pressure Groups* (New York: Thomas W. Crowell, 1964), p. 70.

44. Hoffmann, *Gulliver's Troubles,* p. 277.

$\mathcal{C}$HAPTER 20

. . . .

INTO THE TWENTY-FIRST CENTURY

$\mathcal{W}$hat is the future of the politics of United States foreign policy? How will the interaction of context, government, and society affect continuity and change, presidential governance, and the tension between national security and democracy in the making of U.S. foreign policy? Obviously, no one really knows or can predict with any degree of certainty. Nevertheless, we can point to some key trends and discuss their possible implications.

The future implications of developments throughout the context, government, and society for the foreign policy process appear to be contradictory. Some developments seem to reinforce continuity while others appear to promote change in the politics of U.S. foreign policy. Thus far, *two countervailing trends appear to be most important for the future politics of U.S. foreign policy:*

1. The collapse of the cold war abroad and at home; and

2. The maintenance of American power, involvement, and interests in the world.

The most significant long-term development is the collapse of the Soviet empire, which appears to have reinforced and intensified the changes that have occurred in the politics of U.S. foreign policy since the Vietnam War. The decline of America's major adversary has ended the cold war and, consequently, has reduced the demands of national security and further weakened the power of the presidency. On the other hand, the United States continues to exercise a powerful presence in pursuit of a variety of interests throughout a world of greater complexity and turbulence. The most significant short-term development in this regard has been the Persian Gulf War, which has reinforced concern with national security and the elements supporting strong presidential power in the foreign policy process. Ultimately, the politics of U.S. foreign policy is likely to experience continuity and change in the future as developments throughout government, society, and the global context interact over time.[1]

THE COLLAPSE OF THE COLD WAR ABROAD AND AT HOME

. . . .

The most significant recent global development has been the collapse of communism in Eastern Europe and the Soviet Union. The collapse of the Soviet empire is a momentous event in the twentieth century and world history, and it occurred so suddenly and unpredictably. Such global developments mean the end of the cold war and a world of greater complexity. However, such a world also has contradictory implications for the future of American power and the politics of U.S. foreign policy.

The collapse of communism and the Soviet Union is consequential for the future politics of U.S. foreign policy for a very simple, but fundamental, reason. The rise of Soviet communism and the cold war following World War II was the principal justification for development of the institutions and beliefs throughout American society and government that led to the policy of global containment and intervention, the preeminence of presidential power, and the demands of national security over the demands of democracy in the making of U.S. foreign policy. Although foreign policy changes occurred following the Vietnam War, much continuity prevailed in the national security process, especially in light of the growing Soviet buildup during the 1970s.

Therefore, given the impact of the threat of the Soviet Union and communism on the politics of U.S. foreign policy from the late 1940s through the 1980s, the collapse of communism and the decline of the Soviet threat *should further reduce the demands of national security and presidential power.* The end of the cold war should place national security-oriented institutions and beliefs throughout society and government in greater jeopardy, raising serious questions concerning the extent to which they

have become anachronistic and counterproductive as the United States enters the twenty-first century.

United States foreign policy during the cold war years was based predominantly on the threat and use of coercion, especially force, and revolved around the strategy of containing Soviet communist expansion throughout the world. Therefore, a huge military establishment developed and expanded during peacetime to prevent the cold war from turning into a hot war and, if deterrence failed, to actually fight the Soviet Union and its "proxies" that were believed to be acting in its name. The Central Intelligence Agency and the intelligence community expanded, and covert paramilitary operations became the major instrument for actually fighting the Soviet Union and communism throughout the world. Although the national security bureaucracy and national security ethos have had to operate in a largely inhospitable domestic and global environment since the Vietnam War, they persisted and continued to play a significant role in U.S. foreign policy.

With the end of the cold war, the major adversaries—the Soviet Union and communism—have declined or disappeared as a potent force in global affairs. Therefore, *obvious questions arise:* What national security threats does the United States face in the 1990s and into the next century? How large must the military be in order to protect American national security in the future? What should be the function of the intelligence community, and to what extent are covert paramilitary operations necessary? With the end of the cold war, it logically follows that the United States could afford a smaller and more efficient military establishment, a smaller and redirected intelligence community, and a covert paramilitary capability that could be scaled back considerably.[2]

Other changes in government and throughout society would logically follow from the end of the cold war as well. With a more streamlined national security bureaucracy, the country could operate with a smaller and more efficient military-industrial-scientific infrastructure. The end of the cold war also seems to suggest that the cold war (and conservative) internationalist beliefs, which formed the basis of the consensus during the cold war years and have persisted during the post–Vietnam War era, are likely to decline in a post–cold war era, reinforcing the expansion in group and electoral politics. It would also follow that there is less need for foreign policy institutions in the government and society based on a national security ethos of independence and secrecy. In other words, a global environment that is less threatening to the United States suggests that the demands of democracy should prevail over the demands of national security.

The end of the cold war would also seem to imply that developments divorced from national security issues should gain in prominence in the politics of U.S. foreign policy. *Issues once "low" on the foreign policy agenda should become increasingly "high" policy.* This is most obvious with respect to the growing importance of the economic aspects of U.S. foreign policy, but is also likely to be the case concerning North-South, immigration and refugee, public health, and environmental issues among others. In this respect, the collapse of communism and the decline of the Soviet Union are reinforced by other significant global developments, such as the reunification of Germany, the growing integration of Western Europe, the expansion and intensification of the marketplace throughout the world, the growth of third world debt, the global spread of the AIDS disease, and the growth of environmental destruction throughout the world.

The growing prominence of these so-called "low" policy issues does not mean that they will be easy to address, only that they are more likely to make it on the international political agenda and receive attention in the politics of U.S. foreign policy. In fact, many of these issues are very problematic and increasingly beyond the control of national governments in a world of growing complexity, which may further exacerbate the difficulty the U.S. government and society have in adjusting to global change and arresting America's relative decline.

The rise of economics and other issues in U.S. foreign policy is *likely to intensify the crisis of governance that exists in American politics.* This will further weaken the president's ability to govern foreign policy, for the key to presidential power has involved national security issues, especially when they

have necessitated the use of force. In the economic arena, for example, constraints on presidential power should increase due to the rise of the foreign economic bureaucracy, growing congressional influence, and an increasingly active role of the courts and state and local governments—all of which operate in a more diverse and pluralistic domestic and global environment. This political situation is the case as well for other issues divorced from traditional national security concerns. Therefore, the logical portents for the future politics of U.S. foreign policy in a post–cold war world include the relative decline in the overwhelming importance of national security issues, an increasing paradox of presidential power, and a political process in which the demands of democracy prevail over the demands of national security.

No matter how logical and sound this scenario might seem given the end of the cold war, it "ignores the role of politics" in accounting for continuity and change. As we have continually stressed, it is very difficult to change the status quo throughout society and the government: private and public institutions establish vested interests and become increasingly bureaucratic, networks develop between people and groups throughout society and the government that have access and influence over particular areas of policy, people's beliefs are resistant to change, and much of the public remains apolitical and cynical, feeling powerless concerning the complexity and rigidity of the system.

Furthermore, American policymakers have often been guided by a *realpolitik* and power politics vision of the world where the demands of national security and an active American presence abroad remain a high priority in the politics of U.S. foreign policy. The decline of the Soviet Union as the major adversary also has provided the United States with new opportunities to exercise global leadership and intervene. This is reinforced by the fact that much of the elite public is "internationalist" oriented (unlike the mass public).

In other words, the collapse of communism in Eastern Europe and the Soviet Union has not changed the fact that there are powerful political forces at work throughout American government and society that will resist change and promote continuity in the politics of U.S. foreign policy. The containment strategy of the cold war years, after all, was ultimately successful and policy failure is usually necessary to help trigger substantial change.

In sum, the collapse of communism and the end of the cold war have provided unique opportunities for major changes in the politics of U.S. foreign policy. These global changes are so dramatic and momentous that they will likely spur changes in the political agenda and the politics of foreign policy throughout society and in government; however, how much, where, and in what direction these changes proceed will be a function of how American politics is played out over time. Ultimately, the overall political system tends to be so resistant to change and operate with so much momentum that a crisis is frequently necessary to have a great impact on the politics of U.S. foreign policy, and the crisis that has had the most immediate impact since the end of the cold war remains, thus far, the Persian Gulf conflict.

THE CONTINUATION OF AMERICAN POWER, INVOLVEMENT, AND INTERESTS
. . . .

The end of the cold war does not mean the end of American interests and involvement abroad. The United States continues to exercise a powerful presence in pursuit of a variety of interests throughout a world of greater complexity and turbulence. Over the course of its history, the United States has had an active foreign policy which has increased in scope throughout the continent and eventually throughout the world. Today, with the collapse of the Soviet Union, the United States has become the preeminent power in a world of increasing complexity, interdependence, and turbulence. This reinforces the need for an infrastructure, institutions, and personnel throughout government and society in support of America's global orientation into the twenty-first century.

In fact, it could be argued that the collapse of communism and the end of the cold war have given the United States *greater opportunity to exercise leadership and force abroad.* Now that the Soviet Union is no longer the major adversary of the United States, a major constraint has been eliminated with respect to U.S. ability to use political influence and, in particular, exercise force abroad. During the cold war, American policymakers had to be extremely cautious in actually using overt military force for fear that it could trigger a direct confrontation with the Soviet Union and, ultimately, a nuclear war. This explains why covert paramilitary action became the principal coercive instrument of U.S. foreign policy. With the end of the cold war, American policymakers have much greater flexibility in using force as demonstrated in the Persian Gulf. In fact, some people have argued that recent changes in the global environment have not only allowed for the restoration of American power, but the potential to develop a "Pax Americana" if American leaders and U.S. foreign policy would seize "the unipolar moment."[3]

At the same time, the end of the cold war and the preeminence of the United States does not signal the end of conflict throughout the world, nor does it mean "peace is at hand." Numerous issues occupy the global agenda and have implications for the United States, if for no other reason because of its pervasive global presence—not only traditional security and diplomatic issues, but issues involving international economic and financial transactions, migration and refugees, drugs, human rights and humanitarian concerns, the global environment, communications, and so on. In fact, the end of the cold war may produce more conflict in a world of greater complexity where global issues proliferate and power is diffused. Although not on the scale of a U.S.-Soviet conflict, such conflicts have the potential to result in American involvement and trigger a crisis in American politics, thus dominating the political agenda.

This is exactly what happened in the aftermath of Iraq's invasion of Kuwait on August 2, 1990. While the end of the cold war appeared to reinforce the decline of the cold war patterns in the politics of

U.S. foreign policy that began following the Vietnam War, the Persian Gulf conflict has clearly given them a new lease on life for a while. This may be equally true of other conflicts in the world if American policymakers and the politics of U.S. foreign policy define them as threats to American national security and American national interests.

Iraq's invasion of Kuwait and the strong American response, emphasizing the threat and use of force to contain Iraq from further expansion and compel its withdrawal from Kuwait, brought concern with national security to the forefront of American politics once again. American action, furthermore, was legitimized by the support it received by other countries on the ground in the Persian Gulf and from the United Nations. The successful military outcome of the Persian Gulf War reinforced the cold war patterns that operated throughout the post–Vietnam War era, such as the need for strong presidential power during periods of crisis and national emergency, a large military establishment and national security bureaucracy, a military-industrial-scientific infrastructure to support the national security mission abroad, and a national security ethos for maintaining vital secrets and a more efficient policymaking process. Hence, the outcome of the Persian Gulf crisis and war has reinforced the power of political forces in American society and government that are resistant to changes which may seem warranted by the collapse of communism and the end of the cold war.

Although the post–cold war global environment and the Persian Gulf conflict have increased the opportunities of the United States to exercise leadership and force abroad in the "short term," going to war and relying on force in the "long run" may contribute to a further weakening of American power at home and abroad. As the world has grown in complexity, military success requires the use of greater force and more flexible strategies than in the past, with "no guarantees" of rapid and relatively painless success. Although easily defeated militarily, it is important to remember that the victory over Iraq required the use of over half a million American troops—a massive military intervention on the scale

of the Korean War and the Vietnam War. In this respect the military victory over Iraq was not a simple repeat of "Grenada" and "Panama."

It also has been argued that the Bush administration's strategy of brinkmanship not only accelerated the pace of war, but squandered a unique opportunity to punish Iraq for its invasion and coerce it to withdraw through the patient use of economic sanctions and an embargo that enjoyed unprecedented international and United Nations support. War often fails to address important issues and triggers new political instabilities and animosities in world politics, and these are likely to further constrain the exercise of American power. For example, not only were the intractable problems of the Middle East little closer to solution, new conflicts, such as the Kurdish situation, were heightened after the Persian Gulf War. Most importantly, the economic costs of war tend to be exorbitant, and are likely to further damage America's economic and financial health. Finally, it is important to recall that the country was divided as it entered the war, reinforcing a domestic political environment that has been much less receptive to the presidential use of force in the post–Vietnam War era. In other words, it appears likely that the costs of the Persian Gulf War and the exercise of force resulting in future wars may exacerbate the symptoms Paul Kennedy has associated with "imperial overstretch" (review essay 3.1).

In sum, the Persian Gulf War and emerging conflicts in a post–cold war global environment have contradictory implications for American power, involvement, and interests abroad. In the short run, they increase the opportunities the United States has to exercise force abroad while reinforcing presidential power and the demands of national security in the making of U.S. foreign policy. This has counteracted the effect that the collapse of the Soviet Union and the communist threat to America had in prompting changes to the politics of U.S. foreign policy in a post–cold war world. In the long run, however, this may further weaken American power and the role of the United States in the global environment for it has not addressed the myriad issues that impact the world and the United States in a post–cold war world of ever-greater complexity. Such issues, especially the importance and difficulty of operating in an increasingly interdependent and complex international political economy, guarantees the active involvement of the United States in global affairs for the foreseeable future.

THE FUTURE POLITICS OF U.S. FOREIGN POLICY

. . . .

Clearly, the end of the cold war and the evolving post–cold war global environment *have contradictory implications for the future politics of U.S. foreign policy*. The end of the cold war has created increasing global complexity, posing both greater opportunities and constraints for the evolution and exercise of American power. The collapse of communism, the decline of the Soviet Union, and the rise of new issues on the political agenda suggest the likelihood of more foreign policy change heading away from cold war-era policies of the past, further weakening the president's ability to govern foreign policy and increasing the demands of democracy. Yet, the continued existence of instability and conflict throughout the world, although on a smaller scale than a potential U.S.-Soviet war, reinforces the likelihood of an active United States presence in the world and the continued exercise of presidential power in the name of national security.

It was the sense of national emergency associated with the cold war during the fifties and sixties, after all, that was the ultimate source of presidential power and American global leadership following World War II. Clearly, such a sense of national emergency no longer exists in the post–cold war era—the perception of a "cold war" has been replaced with the perception of a time of "relative peace" abroad in the minds of most Americans. This means that the fragmented and pluralist political environment that has prevailed since Vietnam—resulting in a paradox of presidential power and a strong tension between national security and democracy—will likely continue into the twenty-

first century, posing greater foreign policy opportunities and political risks for presidents and American leadership abroad. Such continuity in the politics of U.S. foreign policy is most open to change and adjustment in response to new global and internal developments that prevail in the post–cold war era, especially if they are accompanied by political crises.

There is no doubt that the United States will continue to have a powerful international presence given its relative power and its legacy of global leadership since World War II. There is also little doubt that the future leadership role of the United States in the world will be influenced by who emerges as president as a result of the dynamics of American politics. Presidents can affect the general direction of U.S. foreign policy within the legitimate parameters of foreign policy orientations and constraints that prevail throughout American society. But much will depend on the image that Americans have of a president's policies and of their relative success, at home and abroad—a function of the fate of events and the strength of presidential leadership. And much will depend on the president's ability to manage and harness the huge bureaucracy that has developed over the years.

Although the boundaries or parameters of the future politics of U.S. foreign policy have been suggested, one cannot specify how politics will actually play out and affect U.S. foreign policy. One must honestly acknowledge "considerable uncertainty and ignorance" about more specific dynamics and their long-term impact in the formulation and conduct of U.S. foreign policy into the twenty-first century. Therefore, *answers to the questions below concerning the future of American foreign policy remain open to the workings of history:*

> What opportunities and constraints will the United States face as it enters the twenty-first century?
>
> Will American power experience relative decline or renewal in world politics?
>
> Will American politics continue to operate in a more pluralist fashion or will it undergo significant change?
>
> What is the future of the paradox of presidential power in foreign policy?

How will the tension between the demands of national security and democracy evolve?

Will a new consensus in foreign policy beliefs emerge throughout society and government or will fragmentation in foreign policy thought continue to prevail?

What is the future of a more conservative internationalist orientation that emphasizes the significance of more traditional national security issues of global conflict and order, and a power politics approach to foreign affairs?

What is the future of a more liberal internationalist orientation that emphasizes the importance of democracy and capitalism abroad, and the need to address a wide variety of issues in a world of great complexity (where it is argued that the utility of force has become more costly)?

Or, what is the future of a non-internationalist orientation that highlights the need for U.S. political and military disengagement from much of the world and a turning inward to focus on domestic issues?

Will the free trade ethos continue to prevail or will the American response to changes in the international political economy result in movement toward multilateral managerialism, economic revitalization, or economic nationalism?

To what extent will "new" beliefs in the foreign policy orientations of Americans and America's cultural approach to the world arise in prominence?

How will the actual institutions and mechanisms that have arisen for making and implementing foreign policy be effected?

Clearly, although much continuity may prevail, the future may also be accompanied by considerable foreign policy change. Much will depend on the forces that underlie the politics of the status quo relative to forces in support of change over time. Ultimately, it is the dynamic interaction of the government, the society, and the environment that will determine the complexity and direction of the future politics of United States foreign policy as the country enters the twenty-first century.

BIBLIOGRAPHIC ESSAY

There is a considerable amount of material that discusses the future of the world and of United States foreign policy. Much of this can be found in chapter 3 on global context and in the variety of foreign policy journals and magazines of opinion that were highlighted in chapter 18 on media sources (see table 18.2 and table 18.3, as well as recommended media sources at the end of the chapter). A spirited dialogue and debate has been occurring since the collapse of the Soviet Union and communism. Most of this material focuses on developments in the global environment and their implications for U.S. foreign policy, where the authors usually offer "policy recommendations" for the future—much of which is quite thoughtful and provocative.

Much more difficult to find are works that provide an in-depth analysis of developments within American government and society, and their implications for the future of U.S. foreign policy. Good overviews can be found in Randall B. Ripley and James M. Lindsay, editors, *U.S. Foreign Policy After the Cold War* (Pittsburgh: University of Pittsburgh Press, 1997), and James M. Scott, editor, *After the End: Making U.S. Foreign Policy in the Post–Cold War Environment* (Durham, N.C.: Duke University Press, 1998). Jerel Rosati also addresses the political implications of the end of the cold war on presidential power and U.S. leadership abroad in "United States Leadership into the Next Millennium: A Question of Politics," *International Journal* (Spring 1997): 297–315.

ENDNOTES

1. For an overview of future global prospects and its implications for U.S. foreign policy, see Daniel Bell, "The Future World Disorder," *Foreign Policy* 27 (Summer 1977): 109–35; Seyom Brown, *New Forces, Old Forces and the Future of World Politics* (Glenview, Ill.: Scott, Foresman, 1988); James M. Goldgeier and Michael McFaul, "A Tale of Two Worlds: Core and Periphery in the Post–Cold War Era," *International Organization* 46 (Spring 1992): 467–91; Paul Kennedy, *Preparing for the*

Twenty-first Century (New York: Random House, 1993); Robert Kuttner, *The End of Laissez-Faire: National Purpose and the Global Economy After the Cold War* (New York: Alfred A. Knopf, 1991); Michael Howard, "Cold War, Chill Peace," *World Policy Journal* (Winter 1993/94): 27–34; William Pfaff, "Redefining World Power," *Foreign Affairs* 70 (America and the World 1990/91): 34–48; John J. Mearsheimer, "Why We Will Soon Miss the Cold War," *The Atlantic Monthly* (August 1990): 35–50; John Mueller, *Retreat from Doomsday: The Obsolescence of Major War* (New York: Basic Books, 1989); Nicholas X. Rizopoulos, ed., *Sea-Changes: American Foreign Policy in a World Transformed* (New York: Council on Foreign Relations Press, 1990), Richard Rosecrance, "The Rise of the Virtual State," *Foreign Affairs* (July/August 1996): 45–61.

2. See, for example, Morton H. Halperin and Jeanne M. Woods, "Ending the Cold War at Home," *Foreign Policy* 81 (Winter 1990–1991): 128–43, and James Traub, "Daniel Patrick Moynihan: Liberal? Conservative? Or Just Pat?" *New York Times Magazine* (September 16, 1990): 38, 78–81. For other interesting views, see also Charles William Maynes, "America Without the Cold War," *Foreign Policy* 78 (Spring 1990): 3–25, and George A. Carver, Jr., "Intelligence in the Age of Glasnost," *Foreign Affairs* (Summer 1990): 147–66.

3. See, for example, Charles Krauthammer, "The Unipolar Moment," *Foreign Affairs* 70 (America and the World 1990–91): 23–33, and Joshua Muravchik, "At Last, Pax Americana," *New York Times* (January 24, 1991): 23A. To place this in a broader historical context, see Donald J. Puchala, "The History of the Future of International Relations," *Ethics & International Affairs* 8 (1994): 177–202, and "International Encounters of Another Kind," *Global Society* 11 (1997): 5–29.

Author Index

C

H

I

J

K

N

S

SUBJECT INDEX

A

Academia. *See also* Education
    and defense politics, 455, 457–458
    and international studies, 455
    and McCarthyism, 494–496
    and presidential appointments, 119
    and the CIA, 231
    militarization research, 455–456
    and the foreign policy establishment, 458
Advertising
    and elections, 536
    and the entertainment media, 540
    and the news media, 511
Afghanistan, Soviet invasion of, 137, 233
African Development Foundation, 272
Agency for International Development (AID), 260–261
Agenda-setting
    and the president, 98, 114–115
    and the Washington political community, 371
    and legislative-executive relations, 69, 322
    and the media, 506
    and the policymaking process, 278, 291, 294
Agents of foreign policy, 23, 471
Agriculture, Department of, 257
Air Force Intelligence, 215
Air-Land Battle Doctrine, 204
Albright, Madeline, 167, 169–170
Allende, Salvador, overthrow of, 230
Alternative media, 540–548
Ambassadors, 156–158, 160, 161
America in Our Time, 390, 391, 401, 539, 562
America's Economic Resurgence, 55
American century, the, 413. *See also* American Power
American exceptionalism, 408. *See also* Political Culture
American Federation of Labor-Congress of Industrial
        Organizations (AFL-CIO), 268, 452, 467
American Israel Public Affairs Committee (AIPAC), 471
American Leadership in World Affairs, 390, 433
American power. *See also* Global Context
    and the State Department, 151
    arrogance of, 34–35, 459
    as hegemonic power, 48
    paradox of, 51

relative decline of, 51–56
rise of, 46–49, 570–573
the future of, 57, 62, 580–583
American Presidency, The, 99
American Prospect, 544, 547
American Spectator, 544, 547
Americans for Democratic Action (ADA), 449
Ames Spy Scandal, 246
Anderson, John, 533
Angleton, James J., 245–246
Angola civil war, 233, 336
Anti-apartheid movement, 361
Anticommunism
    See also Containment; Ideology; national security
    and civil liberties, 490–499
    and elections, 428–429
    and J. Edgar Hoover, 218–220
    and group politics, 448–450
    and legislative-executive relations, 307–313
    and presidential power, 34–35, 107–108
    and state and local governments, 362–364
    and the media, 527–529, 537
    and the State Department, 164–165
    collapse of, 398–399, 460–462
    rise of, 391–397
Antiwar movement, 379–380, 398, 420–421
Appointments. *See also* Presidential management;
        Recruitment
    Ambassadorial, 156–158, 160
    and discrimination, 162, 163
    and presidential power, 69, 115–122
    criteria and background, 119–121, 162
    director of central intelligence, 225
    insiders v. in-outers, 160
    judicial, 29, 70, 337
    resignations, 137, 146
    Senate approval, 121–122, 331–333
    State Department, 159–161
Appropriations process, 338
Arms control. *See* Strategic Arms Limitation Talks
Arms Control and Disarmament Agency (ACDA), 176
Army and Vietnam, The, 203
Army Intelligence (G-2), 215, 240
Army Special Forces (Green Berets), 189–190

O

Q

R